Roy and Lesley Adkins are husband-and-wife historians and archaeologists, the bestselling authors of eighteen acclaimed books on social history, naval history, archaeology, ancient Rome, ancient Greece and Egyptology, so far translated into seventeen languages. Their books include *Jack Tar*, *Trafalgar*, *The War for All the Oceans*, *Empires of the Plain* and *The Keys of Egypt*. They are Fellows of the Society of Antiquaries of London and Members of the Institute of Archaeologists. For further information, see their website www.adkinshistory.com.

'A comprehensive survey of daily life in the time of Jane Austen ... It is full of nuggets of surprising information ... This is a fine book for browsing' Peter Lewis, *Daily Mail*

'A lively and impressionistic guide to the age, enjoyable for those entirely new to the subject, but also for the better informed' Rosemary Goring, *Sunday Herald*

'This is an admirable work for general readers, building on an acquaintance with the novels to recreate the world in which Austen lived. It will keep anyone happy for several days ... and will bear being taken up and read again and again' Professor Nicholas Orme, *Church Times*

'It's a dense and scholarly work but full of fascinating and intimate details, especially about the quality of life' Susan Kurosawa, *Australian*

'A rich, fascinating, accessible and entertaining history of the ordinary people of Georgian England ... Georgian England comes to life, sounds and smells, warts and all' Anna Creer, *Sydney Morning Herald*

'An incisive flavour of Regency England in every hue emerges' *Good Book Guide*

'An excellent read, with each chapter offering a treasury of insights into the lives of Austen's contemporaries, both rich and poor' Carmela Ciuraru, *USA Today*

'A richly detailed portrait ... immensely useful and informative book' Jonathan Yardley, *Washington Post*

'Fascinating reading for any classical fiction or history enthusiast. And for Janeites? It's an essential guide to getting your Austenian life accurate to the last detail' Kate Hutchings, *Huffington Post*

'An excellent resource for Austen devotees interested in rich details of the late 18th- and early 19th-century English life' Kathryn Bartelt, *Library Journal*

'Here, we are at the heart of what drives Austen's characters, what preoccupies their minds and what must have preoccupied the mind of Austen and her sister Cassandra' Katie Baker, *Daily Beast*

'This is a fantastic holiday gift for an Austen fan or history buff' Gabrielle Pantera, *British Weekly*

'This encyclopedic and entertaining volume will suit readers who daydream about going back in time to walk alongside literary figures such as Austen ... readers will appreciate its exciting sweep' *Publishers Weekly*

'For fans of Austen and English history, a deeply informative picture of Regency life' *Kirkus Reviews*

'Very readable new book ... sending you back to read Jane Austen's novels with the ability to see so much more' Christopher Catling, *Salon*

Eavesdropping on Jane Austen's England

How Our Ancestors Lived
Two Centuries Ago

ROY and LESLEY ADKINS

ABACUS

First published in Great Britain in 2013 by Little, Brown
This paperback edition published in 2014 by Abacus
Reprinted 2014

Maps by John Gilkes

A CIP catalogue record for this book
is available from the British Library.

ISBN 978-0-349-13860-2

Typeset in Caslon by M Rules
Printed and bound in Great Britain by
Clays Ltd, St Ives plc

Papers used by Abacus are from well-managed forests
and other responsible sources.

MIX
Paper from
responsible sources
FSC® C104740

Abacus
An imprint of
Little, Brown Book Group
100 Victoria Embankment
London EC4Y 0DY

An Hachette UK Company
www.hachette.co.uk

www.littlebrown.co.uk

To Anne and David Barclay
For their friendship, support and encouragement

CONTENTS

———◆———

England with the main place-names mentioned

Jane Austen Territory

N
W   E
S

Kingsclere •

Basingstoke
Fleet •   Farnborough •
Ashe • Deane •   Odiham •   Aldershot •
Andover •   Steventon •
Whitchurch •

    Alton •
• Stockbridge   Chawton •
    Alresford •   Selborne •
• Winchester

Romsey •   Petersfield •

• Eastleigh
Fordingbridge •   • Bishops Waltham
Cadnam •   Southampton •   Horndean •
   Wickham •
• Lyndhurst   Fareham •   Havant •
Ringwood •
• Brockenhurst
   Gosport •
Lymington •   *The Solent*   Portsmouth

ISLE OF WIGHT

English Channel

| 0 | 5 | 10 | 15 miles |
| 0 | 5 | 10 | 15   20 kms |

Map showing the main places in Hampshire, where Jane Austen lived

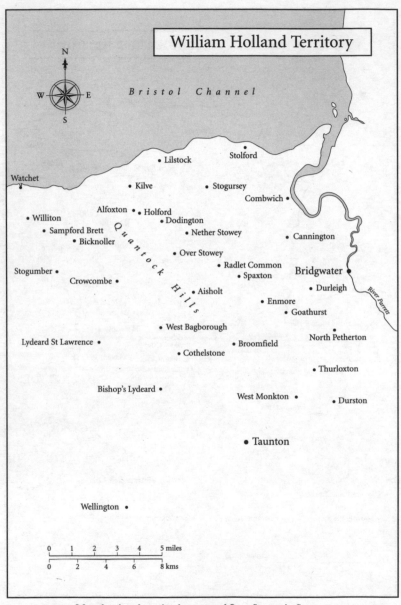

Map showing the main places around Over Stowey in Somerset,
where William Holland lived

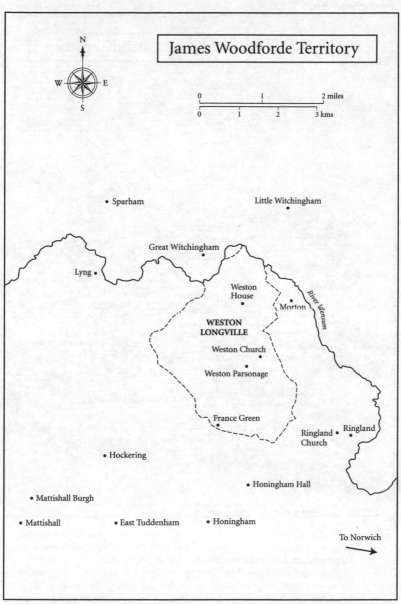

Map showing the main places around Weston Longville in Norfolk, where James Woodforde lived for many years. The parish boundary is shown as a dashed line

The counties of England and Wales in 1809, with major place-names and mail coach routes.
The English counties (as spelled on the map) are: 1. Northumberland; 2. Cumberland;
3. Durham; 4. Yorkshire; 5. Westmoreland; 6. Lancashire; 7. Cheshire; 8. Shropshire;
9. Herefordshire; 10. Monmouthshire; 11. Nottinghamshire; 12. Derbyshire; 13. Staffordshire;
14. Leicestershire; 15. Rutlandshire; 16. Northamptonshire; 17. Warwickshire;
18. Worcestershire; 19 Glocestershire; 20. Oxfordshire; 21. Buckinghamshire; 22. Bedfordshire;
23. Lincolnshire; 24. Huntingdonshire; 25. Cambridgeshire; 26. Norfolk; 27. Suffolk;
28. Essex; 29. Hertfordshire; 30. Middlesex; 31. Surrey; 32. Kent; 33. Sussex; 34. Berkshire; 35.
Wiltshire; 36. Hampshire; 37. Dorsetshire; 38. Somersetshire; 39. Devonshire; 40. Cornwall

A 1797 map of London showing Covent Garden, the British Museum and the Foundling Hospital on the west side, extending to Whitechapel Road and Mile End on the east. Southwark lies to the south of the River Thames

Detail from a 1797 map of London, with Holborn running from east to west, St Giles on the left and Fleet Street, Strand and Covent Garden at the bottom

Detail from a 1797 map of London, with (from left to right) Blackfriars Bridge, Ludgate Hill, St Paul's cathedral, Bethlem Hospital and the Royal Exchange (the Bank of England is adjacent)

INTRODUCTION

---·◆·---

KNOW YOUR PLACE

> One does not love a place the less for having suffered in it,
> unless it has been all suffering, nothing but suffering.
>
> *Persuasion*, by Jane Austen

The *place* is an austere, wartime England. In the north Hampshire village of Steventon, Jane Austen was born in December 1775, and just 12 miles away in the cathedral city of Winchester, she died in July 1817. Such a short distance separates her birth and death, yet during her lifetime of forty-one years she travelled more than most women of this era, westwards as far as Dawlish in Devon, eastwards to Ramsgate in Kent, southwards to Portsmouth and probably as far north as Hamstall Ridware in Staffordshire.[1] England was the only country she knew, and for most of her adult life, that country was at war. In fact, England was at peace for only twelve years and eight months of her entire life – a decade of peace was enjoyed from the end of the American Revolutionary War in 1783, with another brief interlude of peace between the ending of the Revolutionary Wars with France in 1801 and the start of the Napoleonic Wars from 1803, and then more permanent peace when the wars with France and America ended in 1815.[2]

Yet wartime England makes only a low-key appearance in Jane Austen's novels. George Wickham, the villain of *Pride and Prejudice*, is a lieutenant in the militia who is bought off with a commission in the regular army, while Fanny Price in *Mansfield Park* has a brother in the Royal Navy and a father who is a retired marine lieutenant. War forms a backdrop to the novels, but no fighting took place on English soil – men sailed away to war at sea or in other lands. Even so, military men, preparations for war and foreign prisoners-of-war were encountered everywhere, and the threat of invasion by the French generated immense unease and, at times, panic. With a strong and efficient British navy, the danger of invasion was in fact small, but public perception was different. Invasion scares helped to make the population tolerate relentless rises in taxes, much of which went on the wars and on the extravagant royal family. This was a time of glaring disparity between the immensely rich minority and the poor majority, who suffered from steep rises in the price of food and from falling wages. It is hardly surprising that a good deal of support was shown for the French Revolution when it began in 1789.

The ruling class and the Church of England dreaded such an uprising in which they might be stripped of power and even put to death if the country became a truly democratic state. The Reverend William Holland, a Somerset clergyman whose background and status were similar to that of Jane Austen's father, was forthright in his views about some of the lower classes: 'They expect to be kept in idleness or supported in extravagance and drunkenness. They do not trust to their own industry for support. They grow insolent, subordination is lost and [they] make their demands on other people's purses as if they were their own.'[3] Even so, he was broadly sympathetic towards the plight of the poor: 'I wish I could prevail on the farmers to sell their wheat to the parish at the rate of ten shillings per bushel and then keep the poor to their usual standard of allowance.'[4]

This was a period of drastic, sweeping changes that affected almost everyone and everything in England. The upper classes became fearful that the class structure was under threat, while the oppressed lower classes had to endure constant hardships. Although the poor were increasingly assisted by charities, such as the provision of free education and hospitals, they continued to be treated as an inferior part of society and were expected to know their place and show absolute deference towards their betters.

Despite some political protests and anti-royalist affrays, a French-style revolution never materialised. Instead, England experienced a revolution within industry and agriculture, with more efficient, often more scientific, production of food and manufactured goods. The people who did the hard work were at best regarded as just another factor in the economy, alongside raw materials, capital and land – those who had the least often lost the most, while the wealthy literally capitalised on the improvements. In both wartime and peacetime, Jane Austen's England was not a tranquil place. Hundreds of disturbances and riots were ignited by protests against industrial change, the enclosure of common land and, above all else, high food prices. One desperate mob at Brandon in Suffolk in 1816 gathered under the banner 'Bread or Blood' and threatened to march on London.[5]

Throughout Jane Austen's lifetime, King George III was on the throne. Only her last few years fall within the Regency period, when Prince George ruled as regent on behalf of his father, who was declared insane in 1811. When he died in 1820, the prince became King George IV, but immediately after his own death a decade later, historians, satirists and political commentators began to write about the evils of his regency and his reign as king. By the mid-nineteenth century the Regency period was recognised as an episode that had impoverished the nation at a time of war and damaged the influence of royalty through the lazy, self-indulgent and profligate life led by the Prince Regent. One saving grace was his patronage of art and architecture, creating a climate where all kinds of art, writing and music flourished. It was a world inhabited by poets such as John Keats, Samuel Taylor Coleridge and William Wordsworth, painters including John Constable, J.M.W. Turner and David Wilkie, and novelists like Jane Austen, Fanny Burney and Walter Scott.

Novels were in fact a fairly new art form in England that were able to develop from around 1700 once government controls over publishing had been relaxed. Being part of a family of avid readers, Jane Austen was well acquainted with the books being published, and for the first half of her life she had access to her father's extensive library.[6] One trend was for Gothic novels of horror, suspense and the supernatural, which flourished after the publication in 1764 of Horace Walpole's *The Castle of Otranto*. Subsequent successful writers of this genre included Ann Radcliffe, William Beckford and Matthew Lewis, while other novelists were drawn towards the dilemma of young women finding suitable marriage partners, as in Fanny Burney's first novel *Evelina*, published in 1778, which she followed by *Cecilia* (1782) and *Camilla* (1796). Maria Edgeworth also wrote popular novels about English society, manners and marriage, most famously *Belinda* in 1801. Such novels were treated with suspicion by many, an attitude that Jane Austen described with amusement in her own works. In *Northanger Abbey* the narrator criticises those who are embarrassed by novels: "'I am no novel-reader – I seldom look into novels – Do not imagine that I often read novels – It is really very well for a novel.' Such is the common cant. 'And what are you reading, Miss – ?' 'Oh! It is only a novel!' replies the young lady, while she lays down her book with affected indifference, or momentary shame. 'It is only *Cecilia*, or *Camilla*, or *Belinda*".'

Having moved to Ireland with her father in 1782, Maria Edgeworth was better known for her four Irish novels, in particular *Castle Rackrent* (1800). Other writers also ignored England and chose the more romantic backdrops of Ireland, Wales, Scotland or the Continent, such as the Spanish setting of Matthew Lewis's *The Monk* (1796) and the French location for Ann Radcliffe's *The Romance of the Forest* (1791), while her *Mysteries of Udolpho* (1794) took place in sixteenth-century southern France and Italy. It was Sir Walter Scott who raised the status of historical fiction with his immensely popular Scottish tales, the first of which was *Waverley*, dealing with the Jacobite uprising of 1745, an event still remembered by many when Jane Austen was born. As she remarked to her niece Anna a few weeks after its publication in 1814, 'Walter Scott has no business to write novels, especially good ones. It is not fair. He has fame and profit enough as a poet, and should not be taking the bread out of other people's mouths. I do not like him, and do not mean to like

Waverley if I can help it, but I fear I must ... I have made up my mind to like no novels really but Miss Edgeworth's, yours, and my own.'[7] Anna was currently immersed in writing a novel, some of which she had recently shown to her aunt.

An article in the *Edinburgh Magazine* in January 1799 examined why novels were so popular:

> we fly for relief from the sameness of real life to the composition called Novels. In them we find common things related in an uncommon way, which is precisely the remedy we have been seeking to vary our amusements ... It is this art of making much out of little that reconciles us to a course of novel-reading. We find how tame and insipid real life is; we awake in the morning, dress ourselves, go out shopping or visiting, and return in perfect safety to the same employment or amusements this day that we returned to yesterday, and which will probably engage our time to-morrow. It is not remarkable, therefore, if young and active spirits become tired of a routine so dull and unvarying, and are desirous of adventures which may distinguish them from the common herd of neighbours ... Such are to be found in novels.[8]

In short, novels were considered as cheap escapism, the pulp fiction of their time, and not to be regarded as in any way realistic.

Jane Austen took a different direction, writing about what she observed of contemporary English society. She advocated authenticity and so advised Anna to steer clear of Ireland in writing her own novel: 'you had better not leave England. Let the Portmans go to Ireland; but as you know nothing of the manners there, you had better not go with them. You will be in danger of giving false representations. Stick to Bath and the Foresters. There you will be quite at home.'[9] Her meticulous attention to detail is highlighted by another comment to her niece: 'Lyme will not do. Lyme is towards forty miles' distance from Dawlish and would not be talked of there. I have put Starcross indeed. If you prefer Exeter that must be always safe. I have also scratched out the introduction between Lord Portman and his brother, and Mr. Griffin. A country surgeon ... would not be introduced to men of their rank.'[10] Other errors in

Anna's novel were also pointed out, such as the amount of time consumed by travelling: 'They must be two days going from Dawlish to Bath. They are nearly 100 miles apart.'[11]

The novels and letters of Jane Austen provide realistic glimpses into the way of life in England, even if the world she depicts is largely the privileged end of society. But in order to understand the context of her novels, the rest of the nation needs to be considered. England was highly stratified, and everyone knew their place or 'rank'. In 1709 Daniel Defoe roughly summarised the social strata as 'The great, who live profusely; the rich, who live plentifully; the middle sort, who live well; the working trades, who labour hard, but feel no want; the country people, farmers, etc. who fare indifferently; the poor that fare hard; the miserable, that really pinch and suffer want.'[12]

In the ensuing decades little had changed to alter his sketch of society. The bulk of the population comprised skilled and unskilled labourers, craftsmen, servants, apprentices, the unemployed, vagrants and criminals. Even these lower ranks had subtle gradations, and social mobility was rare. Anyone's hopes of bettering themselves might well be frowned upon by the ranks above, and William Holland certainly took a sceptical view of his servant's aspirations: 'Robert borrowed my horse to go to his brother's wedding. He is [to be] married to a farmer's daughter which has turned poor Robert's head and he begins to think that both he and his family in a short time must rank with the principal men in the kingdom.'[13]

Apart from this strict social ranking, a person's place in society was frequently influenced by their wealth. An increase in wealth could improve status, but would not erase memories of humble beginnings, as Holland revealed in a comment about a local man, Andrew Guy, 'alias squire Guy, a rich old widower ... the son of a grazier [who reared cattle] lifted up to the rank of gentleman, but ignorant and illiterate'.[14] Nor could money alone bridge the gap between the elite and the working majority, as many newly prosperous merchants and manufacturers discovered. They would never be fully accepted, and the best hope was for their children to marry 'above their station', something that nevertheless carried a stigma. In the novels of Jane Austen, wealth and income often form part of a character's description, and in *Persuasion* a rich bride is described as a 'very low woman' because, despite her wealth, 'her father was a grazier, her grandfather a butcher'.

England itself measures roughly 360 miles north to south and 330 miles east to west at its widest extent. Jane Austen's England was not an overcrowded country – in 1801 the entire population was approximately that of London today. Even though London was the largest city in Europe, most people at that time still lived and worked on the land. To the residents of London, the city seemed vast, prompting the politician George Canning to lament that it was possible to lose close acquaintances for days on end.[15]

There were pronounced regional differences and much variety in the way people lived – more so for the poorer classes who relied on local resources than for wealthier people who could afford to do or buy whatever they wanted. In the closing years of the eighteenth century, the insurance businessman Sir Frederick Morton Eden carried out a remarkable survey, which was published as *The State of the Poor*. In it he included a wide range of prices for common items across the country, such as potatoes selling at 1 shilling the bushel in Petersfield, Hampshire, 2 shillings and 8 pence in Winslow, Buckinghamshire, and 3 shillings in Brixworth, Northamptonshire.[16]

Fundamental changes were taking place in the very appearance of the countryside, as hedges, walls and fences sprang up to mark the boundaries of newly enclosed fields, while new turnpike roads and canals carved fresh lines across the land. The open landscape that had existed since before medieval times was fast evolving into the chequered pattern of fields still seen in some places today, or else was being devoured by rapidly expanding industrial towns such as Birmingham and Manchester. As William Blake saw it, 'England's green and pleasant land' was in grave danger from 'dark Satanic mills'.[17]

This place of radical change is the real England of Jane Austen and the subject of this book. We wanted to show how the mass of ordinary people, our ancestors, lived and fitted into her England. It used to be fashionable to trace your ancestry back to royalty, even if on the wrong side of the sheets, but the most humble or nefarious ancestors are just as interesting. They all had a part to play in shaping events and influencing history. Without them, history is nothing.

We used a similar approach for *Jack Tar: The Extraordinary Lives of Ordinary Seamen in Nelson's Navy*, in which we charted the everyday details of what it was like to be a seaman rather than a high-ranking officer. The period we chose for *Jack Tar* was roughly 1771 to 1815, from when Horatio Nelson first joined the navy as a captain's servant to a decade after his death, when peace finally came. This coincided with Jane Austen's lifetime, and so we hope that *Eavesdropping on Jane Austen's England* will provide a fascinating contrast and give a flavour of life on land two centuries ago.

When encountering a remote era of history, such as Roman or medieval times, it is not surprising to find an alien world, but life in Georgian England was also very different to the world of the twenty-first century. The basic amenities that we take for granted, like electricity, a water supply and sewerage, were non-existent or just being introduced, so that simply keeping warm, clean and free from hunger entailed laborious, time-consuming and inefficient tasks. Steam engines were transforming some industries, but travel relied on horsepower, manpower or windpower. If someone went away for several years, perhaps serving in the Royal Navy, they might not be recognised on their return, because there were no photographs to refresh memories.

Even walking the streets in bad weather was a different experience, since few buildings had guttering. Instead, roofs overhung the walls so as to throw rainwater away from the foundations. Naturally, people kept close to the walls for shelter, under the overhang – the eaves – and caught snatches of conversation from within as they passed. In a similar way to this eavesdropping, we have caught snatches of the lives of Jane Austen's contemporaries from the writings they left behind. Our book is a snapshot of her era, reflecting the variety of life at that time. It is not a narrative of events, but of people's daily lives. We have opted for a loose chronological thread, running from marriage (the main theme of Jane Austen's novels) to the birth of babies, progressing through childhood, domestic work, religion, occupations, entertainment, travel, illnesses and finally death and burial.

We have relied upon the words of people who lived at that time, recorded in documents such as letters, diaries, travelogues, accounts of criminal trials and newspapers. The spelling in these eyewitness accounts has occasionally been corrected and the punctuation and style sometimes modernised, particularly the tendency to use dashes instead of full-stops, ampersands (&) instead of 'and', and upper-case letters for the start of many words. Most quotations have been only slightly altered, if at all, and the words and meaning have not been changed.

Personal letters and diaries were rarely intended to be published, but were written for the information and enjoyment of one or two people, or at most a family and their descendants, as William Holland revealed in January 1801: 'I began reading my diary to my family from its commencement and shall continue to do so as far as the last year goes.'[18] His extensive diaries allow us to become acquainted not just with him and his family in the Somerset parish of Over Stowey and beyond, but also with his overworked servants and the local people including various paupers, labourers and tradesmen. Only an abridged selection of these diaries has ever been published,[19] and so the full, original manuscript diaries provide a fresh window on English life, rather like the diaries of the Reverend James Woodforde. Six years younger than Holland, he was an unmarried clergyman from Ansford in Somerset who spent much of his working life on the other side of England, in his Norfolk parish of Weston Longville. Although classically educated, Woodforde turned his back on such learning after leaving Oxford university, and instead filled his diaries with extraordinary details about everyday life. We have made use of the complete text of his extensive diaries that have been so ably transcribed over the years by the Parson Woodforde Society, superseding the edited extracts published decades ago.

In northern England, from Wigan to Liverpool, through the Lake District and Yorkshire, Nelly Weeton provides another perspective on life at that time. She was clearly very intelligent, but her potential was stifled by poverty and by her low-class status as a governess. Nelly's letters and diaries are filled with comments that were often as satirical and perceptive as those of Jane Austen herself. Numerous other voices are heard in this book, including Sarah and William Wilkinson, whose mundane letters to each other (while he was at sea) convey valuable insights into daily life, while the writings of foreign visitors such as the American Benjamin Silliman and the German Carl Moritz provide an outsider's viewpoint. Such documents take us right to the heart of Jane Austen's England, allowing us to eavesdrop on what people thought and discussed among themselves – the very words of those who lived two centuries ago.

In her novels Jane Austen brilliantly portrayed the lives of the middle and upper classes, but barely mentioned the cast of characters who constituted the bulk of the population. *Mansfield Park* was started in 1811 and published in 1814, and her account of how the Price family lived at Portsmouth is the closest she came to portraying the lower classes. It would be left to the genius of the next generation, Charles Dickens, to write novels about the poor, the workers and the lower middle classes. Born in Portsmouth in 1812, before most of Jane Austen's books had even been published, Dickens was sent to work in a factory in London at the age of twelve and came to rely on writing to earn money. Looking back to the time of the French Revolution, his novel *A Tale of Two Cities* starts with the celebrated words: 'It was the best of times, it was the worst of times, it was the age of wisdom, it was the age of foolishness, it was the epoch of belief, it was the epoch of incredulity, it was the season of Light, it was the season of Darkness, it was the spring of hope, it was the winter of despair.' This is a succinct summary of Jane Austen's England, on which we are about to eavesdrop.

A chronological overview of the main historical events is given on p. 347, including some key events of Jane Austen's lifetime. For more about this book, see our website www.adkinshistory.com.

ONE

———◆———

WEDDING BELLS

It is a truth universally acknowledged, that a single man in possession of a good fortune, must be in want of a wife.

Pride and Prejudice, by Jane Austen

On a bitterly cold Norfolk morning in January 1787, Parson James Woodforde left the comfort of his rectory at Weston Longville and rode on horseback over a mile and a half along a muddy lane until he reached the imposing church of St Peter in the village of Ringland.[1] Because its vicar was away, he had been asked by the parish officers to perform an urgent marriage ceremony – for the customary fee of 10 shillings and 6 pence. Inside this medieval church, the spectacular nave roof enhanced the impressive setting for the wedding, but it was not a day for joy and celebration, as Woodforde noted in his diary: 'Rode to Ringland this morning and married one Robert Astick and Elizabeth Howlett by licence ... the man being in custody, the woman being with child by him. The man was a long time before he could be prevailed on to marry her when in the church yard; and at the altar behaved very unbecoming.'[2]

Standing in the numbing cold before the altar, poor Elizabeth surely dreaded the prospect of being saddled with this man. Although his only alternative was to return to gaol, Robert proved highly reluctant to marry and almost needed to be dragged to the altar. His crime was not premarital sex, but causing a penniless woman and baby to be a burden on the parish, and as a result he was forced into marriage. Under the Bastardy Act of 1733, unmarried pregnant women were taken before the magistrate by the parish overseers of the poor and forced on oath to name the father – or alleged father. The named man then had the dubious choice of paying the parish for the upkeep of the child, marrying the woman (unless he was already married) or a spell in prison. If he ran away, a reward might be offered for his recapture. Nine days after Robert and Elizabeth's forced marriage, John Hammonway in Northumberland escaped from prison, and the *Newcastle Courant* carried a detailed description of the offender:

COUNTY OF NORTHUMBERLAND

Made his Escape over a wall, in a yard joining to the House of Correction, at Morpeth, on the 3rd of Feb. instant [1787], JOHN HAMMONWAY, late of the town and county of Newcastle upon Tyne, nailer, was committed for bastardy.– The said John Hammonway is about 23 years of age, five feet five inches high, slender made, swarthy complexion, short black hair, dark-brown sully eyes; had on, when he escaped, a dark-blue coat, flowered cotton waistcoat, leather breeches, with metal buttons.

Whoever will secure the said John Hammonway, and give notice to John Doxford, Keeper of the said House of Correction, shall receive a reward of TWO GUINEAS, to be paid by JOHN DOXFORD.[3]

Forced marriages were commonplace, but the unmarried Parson Woodforde disliked them intensely: 'It is a cruel thing that any person should be compelled by law to marry ... It is very disagreeable to me to marry such persons.'[4] He himself conducted several such weddings at his own church in Weston Longville. 'I walked to church this morning between 10 and 11 o'clock,' he recorded some years later, 'and married by licence, one Daniel Tabble of Ling [Lyng] and Anne Dunnel of Weston, a forced match, she being very near her time, and he under custody of the parish officers ever since yesterday morning. I recd. of the officers for marrying them 0.10.6, being the usual fee for marrying by licence here.'[5] Anne gave birth two months later.[6] These weddings were a far cry from the romantic notion of courtship, love and marriage that form the essence of Jane Austen's fiction.

Marriage based on love and on freedom of choice was becoming more common, and from the later eighteenth century romantic novels such as *Evelina* by Fanny Burney and *Belinda* by Maria Edgeworth confronted such issues, to be followed a few years later by the novels of Jane Austen. For many, though, particularly if accustomed to wealth, such an approach to marriage was totally impractical. A husband with a respectable income or a wife with a generous dowry was still extremely desirable, if not an absolute necessity, and the conflict between marrying for love and marrying for money and social advantage is a common element in Jane Austen's writing. In *Northanger Abbey* she parodied novels such as Ann Radcliffe's Gothic romance *The Mysteries of Udolpho*,[7] and when Isabella's impecunious brother John wants to marry her friend Catherine, she is pleased that Catherine is not interested, 'for what were you both to live upon, supposing you came together? You have both of you something [some income] to be sure, but it is not a trifle that will support a family nowadays; and after all that romancers may say, there is no doing without money.'

A good number of parents arranged marriages to ensure that their children were securely established in life, and girls from wealthy families were provided with dowries, or 'portions', to make them attractive to male suitors. In Jane Austen's novel *Sense and Sensibility*, Edward Ferrars is to marry the wealthy Miss Morton, and on learning that his older brother Robert is also contemplating her, Elinor Dashwood says: 'The lady, I suppose, has no choice in the affair.' Elinor's own brother is puzzled by her reaction: 'Choice! – how do you mean?'

Wealth was the key factor. Happiness was of secondary importance. For the upper classes, marriage was essential for the provision of legitimate heirs and for the survival of estates, fortunes and families, but for women of all classes marriage was crucial, because ways of supporting themselves were severely limited, resulting in the obsession with pairing off daughters with suitable men. For Mrs Bennet in *Pride and Prejudice*, 'The business of her life was to get her daughters married.'

It was customary to marry within the same social class – because of hypocrisy and snobbery, marrying into a different class was problematic. It was frequently acceptable for a wealthy man to maintain a mistress of low rank, but he was despised and even shunned if he had the temerity to marry her. In 1810 Nelly Weeton was working as a governess at Dove Nest, a house near Ambleside in the Lake District. The previous year her wealthy employer, Edward Pedder, had married his dairymaid, as Nelly told her unmarried friend Bessy Winkley: 'if you knew the sorrow that person must undergo who marries above herself, you would never be ambitious to marry out of your own rank; people call it doing well; they are most egregiously mistaken. Let the husband be ever so kind, it cannot compensate for the numberless mortifications a woman so raised must endure. Those married people have the greatest chance of being happy whose original rank was most nearly equal.'[8]

Nelly's parents, who came from Lancashire, were both dead, and her younger brother Tom was a lawyer. She was forced to work because she had little money and at the age of thirty-three was still unmarried. A few months later, she elaborated on the former servant girl's family:

> Mrs. P. [Pedder] has a brother and sister ... the sister keeps her father's house, working in the fields, on the peat moss, or her father's house, as occasion serves. What a difference in the situation of the two sisters! The one with her father wishes much to emerge from her present obscurity; but her father, an honest, warm-hearted, affectionate parent, sensibly says 'there is more happiness in his humble situation, than where there is more bustle, show, and finery'; he thinks his eldest daughter might do just as well, or better, in marrying a farmer, as the youngest has done in marrying a gentleman. 'People,' he says, 'do not always do well that marry so much above them, for they only get despised and abused by their fine new relations.'[9]

Finding a suitable marriage partner could prove stressful, since there were insufficient numbers of eligible men to go round, particularly with so many fatalities and injuries in the wars. Accurate figures are impossible to calculate, but throughout the Napoleonic Wars the combined casualties in the army and navy were on average about twenty thousand a year, and many thousands more were engaged in fighting overseas. Some eligible bachelors inevitably preferred the freedom of the single life, and countless young working men were prevented from marrying by restrictions such as apprenticeship contracts. Matchmaking and courtship therefore provided admirable material for Jane Austen's fiction.

The most effective way for the middle and upper classes to meet prospective partners was at the various balls that were so frequently held in both public and private venues, but courting couples were expected to behave formally, even when greeting each other in public. In *Sense and Sensibility*, Elinor hears Willoughby using Marianne's first name and so assumes they are to be married: 'in his addressing her sister by her Christian name alone, she instantly saw an intimacy so decided, a meaning so direct, as marked a perfect agreement between them. From that moment she doubted not of their being engaged to each other.'

When a woman married she passed from the control of her father, who 'gave her away' at the wedding to the control of her husband. Her property became her husband's, despite his promise in the marriage ceremony, 'with all my worldly goods I thee endow'. As a wife, she could not legally own land or have a separate source of income, unless set out in a specific contract – the marriage settlement. Such a settlement might entitle her to receive the interest from her dowry in her lifetime and to bequeath the dowry to her children or use it as income if her husband died. Otherwise, she effectively had no legal status, and any children belonged to her husband.

The law governing marriage was Lord Hardwicke's Marriage Act of 1753, which decreed that after 25 March 1754 marriages were valid in law only if they had been advertised by banns or sanctioned by a special licence and were conducted by an Anglican clergyman in a church. Marriages also had to be recorded in a register. A marriage conducted in any other way was not legal, and the person performing it was guilty of a felony and liable to transportation. The Act also advised that the ceremony should take place in the church of the parish where the bride or groom resided, but this was not essential for the marriage to be valid. The main intention of the Act was to prevent clandestine or irregular marriages and to prevent minors from marrying without parental consent – something that was of considerable consequence to the upper classes, who feared wealthy heiresses marrying impoverished husbands.

This Act was the first statutory law to require a formal marriage ceremony. Before 1753 all such matters were in the sole control of the Church of England, with the single requirement that the marriage should be conducted by an Anglican clergyman. Other requirements such as banns were not then essential, so all kinds of rapid and irregular marriages had been valid in law, and various places became notorious for the availability of pliable clergymen willing to perform clandestine marriages. Many churches in London conducted such weddings, mainly of Londoners, but some accepted outsiders as well. Weddings also took place at the Fleet prison, which claimed to be outside the jurisdiction of the Church. It was a prison for debtors whose inmates invariably included some clergy, and marriages performed there were called 'Fleet marriages'. Most nonconformists, or dissenters, believed that marriage was not a religious ceremony, but for purposes of legality their marriages before and after the 1753 Act tended to be in parish churches, whereas Jews and Quakers, exempt from the Act, were allowed to marry according to their own customs. Not until 1837 could couples legally marry in register offices, or in their own chapels if a civil registrar was present.

After 1754 it was still possible to have a discreet wedding in a parish where neither bride nor groom was known, and for rapid marriages couples fled across the border to Scotland where the laws were much less restrictive. For those complying with the law, banns were called in the parish church of both parties on three consecutive Sundays or holy days in order to publicly proclaim the intended marriage. This allowed anyone to raise objections – something that happened in January 1791 at Weston Longville, as Parson Woodforde noted: 'One Bush of this parish (whose daughter's banns were published last Sunday) came to my house this evening to forbid the banns, the man being found out to be a very infamous character.'[10] Five days later, he added: 'Brown (whose banns were forbid last week by the girl whose name is Bush) called on me this morning and I returned him the half crown that I recd. last Sunday sennight [seven nights ago] by my clerk for publishing the banns that day.'[11]

For anyone with an urgent need to marry or who did not wish banns to be proclaimed in public, the more expensive option was to obtain a licence, for which an 'allegation' had to be sworn, usually by the groom, giving details of the couple and assurances of no impediments to the marriage. Normally, common licences were issued by archbishops, bishops and some archdeacons, or by clergy in certain parishes and officials acting on their behalf. A marriage was then permitted to take place within the jurisdiction of the person issuing the licence, in one of the parishes named on the licence, but the requirement to be married in a named parish was often ignored. The wedding could take place later that day, but usually happened the day after. In August 1788 Woodforde conducted such a ceremony: 'About 11 o'clock this morning I took a walk to Weston Church and there married by Licence Jas. [James] Herring of Norwich to Miss [Elizabeth Ann] Peachman of this parish, for which I recd. of Mr. Herring 2.2.0 which I think very handsome of him.'[12]

Parental consent was required for anyone under the age of twenty-one marrying by licence, but minors could marry by publication of the banns, though parents were at liberty to object. The age of consent was fourteen for boys and twelve for girls, but most did not marry until their early twenties, even if they were betrothed at an earlier age. Apprentices were not permitted to marry, so many young men married late, in their mid- to late twenties. Richard Cureton, on becoming an apprentice in London in 1783, had to sign an indenture stating that during the seven years of apprenticeship he would 'not commit fornication, nor contract matrimony'.[13]

For rich and poor alike, a church was the venue for weddings. By today's standards most were low-key affairs, with few guests and moderate expenditure on wedding clothes and celebrations. 'Smock weddings' were a peculiar type of ceremony at which the bride was married naked – although usually she was barefoot and *en chemise*, wearing only a shift ('chemise'), smock or sheet for propriety. The point was that if she brought no clothes or property to the union, the husband-to-be was thought not liable for any debts she might have. Such weddings, randomly reported, occurred mainly in the eighteenth century, particularly for widowed women whose deceased husbands had left debts.

One Derby newspaper in September 1775 chose to run a story about a marriage that had taken place over a hundred miles to the south: 'Thursday se'nnight was married by licence, at Bishop's Waltham, Winchester, Mr. Richard Elcock, bricklayer, to Mrs. Judith Redding, who, to exempt her future husband from the payment of any debts she might have contracted, went into one of the pews in the church, and stript herself of all her cloaths except her shift, in which only she went to the altar, and was married, much to the astonishment of the parson, clerk, &c.'[14] A few years earlier, a similar wedding took place at St Michael's church at Ashton-under-Lyne in Lancashire: 'On Thursday last, was married, at Ashton-under-Lyne, Nathaniel Eller to the widow Hibbert, both upwards of fifty years of age; the widow had only her shift on, with her hair tied behind with horse hair, as a means to free them both from any obligation of paying her former husband's debts.'[15]

It was sometimes wrongly supposed that a smock wedding enabled a bride to retain her own wealth if her husband-to-be had debts. In December 1797 such a wedding was held at St Philip's parish church (now the cathedral) in Birmingham, with several newspapers reporting that the bride wore nothing (possibly not even a chemise) so that the creditors of her debt-ridden new husband could not seize her property:

There is an opinion generally prevalent in Staffordshire, that if a woman should marry a man in distressed circumstances, none of his creditors can touch her property, if she should be *in puris naturalibus* [stark naked] while the ceremony is performed. In consequence of this prejudice, a woman of some property lately came with her intended husband into the vestry of the great church of Birmingham, and the moment she understood that the

Priest was ready at the altar, she threw off a large cloak, and in the exact state of Eve in Paradise, walked deliberately to the spot, and remained in that state till the ceremony ended.[16]

For the wealthier classes, a wedding was an opportunity to flaunt status and the latest fashions, as happens in *Sense and Sensibility*. With the marriage of Miss Grey to Willoughby being imminent, Elinor 'could soon tell at what coachmaker's the new carriage was building, by what painter Mr Willoughby's portrait was drawn, and at what warehouse Miss Grey's clothes might be seen'. The wealthy wore fine clothes for weddings, with white chosen for the bride and sometimes for the bridesmaids as well. Most people, including the brides, simply wore their Sunday best or something that could be subsequently used for that purpose. The bride's wedding clothes were secondary to her trousseau, for which she might be given household linen, items of clothing and other articles for her new life. In *Mansfield Park*, Jane Austen wryly says of the wedding between Maria Bertram and Mr Rushworth: 'It was a very proper wedding. The bride was elegantly dressed; the two bridesmaids were duly inferior; her father gave her away; her mother stood with salts in her hand, expecting to be agitated; her aunt tried to cry; and the service was impressively read by Dr Grant.'

At the wedding that he conducted by licence in August 1788 between James Herring and Elizabeth Peachman, Woodforde was impressed by everything:

It was a smart genteel marriage, 2 close carriages with smart liveries attended. Sheriff Buckle of Norwich and Mr. John Herring who was Sheriff of Norwich the last year and his son, old Mr. Peachman, Mrs. John Herring, Mrs. Forster of this Parish, and a very pretty young lady very neatly dressed, and attended as a bride maid and whose name was Miss Wingfield were at the ceremony. The bells rang merry after. Mr. Buckle, Mr. Herring and son and old Mr. Peachman returned with me on foot from Church to my house and eat some cake and drank some cyder &c. Mr. Peachman pressed me much to dine with them but I was not well enough to go into company.[17]

Rather than riding in a carriage, most people walked to church, and it was customary for flowers, herbs and rushes to be strewn along the route or at the church porch. A poem published in 1796 by Henry Rowe, rector of Ringshall in Suffolk, alludes to this practice:

> The wheaten ear was scatter'd near the porch.
> The green broom blossom'd strew'd the way to church.[18]

For the lower classes, wedding ceremonies were simple. In November 1810 the Reverend William Holland of Over Stowey in Somerset described the marriage of two of his servants:

> I went to church and married my servants Robert Dyer and Phebe [Phoebe Symons], and I trust they will be happy in each other and I gave them and their friends a dinner on the occasion and they are to continue with me as servants till Lady [Day] next ... Dyer desired me to publish the banns now and they were to be married about Christmas. I answer'd if the banns be publish'd, 'tis best marrying immediately, and they took my advice. My wife [Mary] is to take Phebe with her to Bath where we mean to go if it please God after Christmas and Dyer will stay in the house to take care of things here.[19]

All weddings were morning events, since canon law decreed that they could be solemnised only between 8 a.m. and noon – a rule that held until 1886. Particular times of the year (especially Lent) were traditionally avoided, and Sundays could be a nuisance. Holland certainly grumbled in October 1800: 'Had a wedding, but the clerk did not give me notice of the same the day before which made me very angry. Indeed Sunday is a bad day for these things, as it hurries me and I can scarce get myself ready for prayers.'[20]

The oldest customs, survivals from antiquity, were the wedding cake and the ring that was given to the bride during the ceremony. 'The Wedding Ring is worn on the fourth finger of the left hand,' according to the antiquary and clergyman John Brand, 'because it was antiently believed ... that a small artery ran from this finger to the heart.'[21] Because the dissection of human bodies had disproved this fact, he added: 'though the opinion has been justly exploded by the

Anatomists of modern times'.[22] He also mentioned that some wives never removed their wedding ring: 'Many married women are so rigid, not to say superstitious, in their notions concerning their wedding rings, that neither when they wash their hands, nor at any other time, will they take it off from their finger, extending, it should seem, the expression of "till Death us do part" even to this golden circlet, the token and pledge of matrimony.'[23]

Brand was fascinated by old customs and folklore, and when conducting weddings in London and in Newcastle, he had observed the tradition of saluting the bride: 'It is still customary among persons of middling rank as well as the Vulgar, in most parts of England, for the young men at the marriage ceremony to salute the Bride, one by one, the moment it is concluded. This, after officiating in the ceremony myself, I have seen frequently done.'[24] For those who could afford to pay the ringers, a wedding was often marked by a peal of bells, and in the church of the Holy Trinity at Kendal, Westmorland, one bell bore the inscription:

In wedlock bands,
All ye who join with hands,
Your hearts unite;
So shall our tuneful tongues combine
To laud the nuptial rite.[25]

After the event, a meal might be laid on, and being a morning ceremony, a wedding breakfast was most common. More elaborate celebrations could continue the whole day, perhaps with a dinner and a supper, along with music, dancing, games and sports. Then as now, the wedding cake was an important element of the ceremony and was subsequently distributed to family and friends, something Jane Austen mentioned when writing to her sister Cassandra in 1808: 'Do you recollect whether the Manydown family send about their wedding cake? Mrs Dundas has set her heart upon having a piece from her friend Catherine, and Martha, who knows what importance she attaches to this sort of thing, is anxious for the sake of both, that there should not be a disappointment.'[26]

Customs varied across the country, and in northern England the cake was broken up over the bride's and groom's heads or scattered into the crowd. Elsewhere, the traditions relating to the ring and the cake were linked when pieces of cake were passed through the ring and thrown over the heads of the newly-weds, or placed beneath the pillows of young people to induce prophetic dreams of lovers and marriage. Henry Rowe wrote that after the bells rang out for the married couple, the cake was passed through the ring:

> The wedding cake now thro' the ring was led,
> The stocking thrown across the nuptial bed.[27]

There were many local variations of the old custom of throwing the bride's stocking. In one, the married couple sat up in bed and the bridesmaids sat at the end of the bed, with their backs to the couple. They then threw the stockings over their shoulders, and whoever managed to hit the bride would soon be married themselves.

The next day, most married couples began their everyday life together. No modern concept of a 'honeymoon' then existed – the term still referred to the month after the wedding. Rich newly-weds might make an extended tour, usually in Britain as the country was so often at war. The couple rarely went away alone, but were accompanied by friends, relatives and, of course, servants. The less well-off settled for whatever they could afford, perhaps staying with relatives for a week or two, while the lower classes had little or nothing in the way of a holiday, most returning to work the next day. Unless it was a royal or aristocratic wedding, in which case the newspapers would report the event at length, a modest notice might appear in a local newspaper. One from the *Derby Mercury* in June 1802 is typical: 'Married ... Sunday se'nnight, Mr. James York, chymist and druggist, to Miss Weston, both of Nottingham.'[28] These notices were more common after 1800, though still confined to the middle and upper classes.

Less welcome to the families involved were sensational newspaper accounts of elopements, as in February 1815 when the *Western Luminary* reported:

ELOPEMENT.– Another fashionable couple have eloped, it is supposed from the neighbourhood of Bristol. They arrived at Stourbridge about half-past six o'clock on the morning of Saturday se'nnight, in a post-chaise and four, and stopped at the Talbot hotel, where they changed horses. The Lady must have emerged in great haste from her bed-chamber, having no covering but a flannel petticoat and a great coat. They wished to purchase a bonnet in that town; but did not procure any other covering for the damsel until they reached Penkridge. They gave the different post-boys a 1*l*. [£1] note each, and proceeded northward from Stafford, for that celebrated spot, Gretna Green. The parties were unknown.[29]

In novels such as Jane Austen's, the heroines are invariably concerned with relationships and about overcoming impediments to those relationships. Had she been writing some decades earlier, clandestine marriages might well have featured, but as they were now illegal, elopement was the solution where a couple was desperate to marry without parental consent. The Bennet family in *Pride and Prejudice* is dismayed to discover that young Lydia has run off with Wickham. In a letter, Lydia describes her happiness: 'I am going to Gretna Green ... for there is but one man in the world I love, and he is an angel ... I can hardly write for laughing.' Wickham actually has no intention of marrying, and they are eventually tracked down in London.

Villages just over the Scottish border were favoured locations for couples fleeing from England to be married, and the best known was Gretna Green, some 10 miles from Carlisle. In a letter to Bessy Winkley written at Dove Nest in the final days of 1809, Nelly Weeton described how her employer had eloped: 'Mrs. Pedder was a dairy maid at Darwen-Bank, Mr. P's house near Preston [Lancashire], when he fell in love with her. Her father heard of the connexion and fearing his daughter might be seduced, sent for her home. He lives near-by here. Mr. P. followed her, took her off to Gretna Green and married her ... She is not eighteen yet ... Mr. P. is a little man of about 34.'[30]

Scottish marriage law required only a declaration before witnesses, a role performed by various Gretna Green inhabitants, including

Joseph Paisley, who was a farmer, fisherman and smuggler. For sixty years from 1753 he officiated as Gretna Green's parson. He was known as a blacksmith, though according to his successor Robert Elliott, he 'only acquired that name from his quickness in uniting eloping parties, for the common saying there was, "strike the iron when it is hot, Joseph".'[31] Robert had become acquainted with Paisley in 1810 and took over his business three years later. He left his version of the marriage ceremony:

It is very simple. The parties are first asked their names and places of abode; they are then asked to stand up, and enquired of if they are both single persons; if the answer be in the affirmative, the ceremony proceeds.

Each is next asked:—'Did you come here of your own free will and accord?' Upon receiving an affirmative answer the priest commences filling in the printed form of the certificate.

The man is then asked, 'Do you take this woman to be your lawful wedded wife, forsaking all other, [and] keep to her as long as you both shall live?' He answers 'I will.' The woman is asked the same question, which being answered the same, the woman then produces a ring which she gives to the man, who hands it to the priest; the priest then returns it to the man, and orders him to put it on the fourth finger of the woman's left hand, repeat these words, with this ring I thee wed, with my body I thee worship, with all my worldly goods I thee endow in the name of the Father, Son, and Holy Ghost, Amen. They then take hold of each other's right hands, and the woman says 'what God joins together let no man put asunder.' The priest says 'forasmuch as this man and this woman have consented to go together by giving and receiving a ring, I, therefore, declare them to be man and wife before God and these witnesses in the name of the Father, Son, and Holy Ghost, Amen.'[32]

The upper classes set great store by the legalities of marriage, but the lower classes were rarely worried by such niceties, and many couples simply lived together rather than pay fees to marry in church, particularly after the 1753 Act made the less costly clandestine marriages illegal. Some only married once the woman was pregnant. There were alternative, cheaper methods of marrying, mainly comprising informal declarations, but although acceptable by custom they were not actually legal. Few poor people could afford to elope to Gretna Green unless they were marrying someone wealthy, but the clergy could make life difficult for those living together without marrying.

William Holland kept a close eye on what was happening in his Somerset parish of Over Stowey, and in October 1800 one couple felt obliged to marry: 'It seems the persons were but lately come into the Parish and they had lived together before and they brought a bouncing child to be christened the very day of their wedding. I gave them a good jubation [severe rebuke], and told them that had I known there were such people in my Parish I would not have suffered them to have remained long in that situation. This they were aware of, so came to be married.'[33]

While unmarried couples were censured, single unmarried women like Nelly Weeton were pitied, because with their limited options in life they most likely faced penury unless they had a private income. They had long been referred to as 'old maids', a disparaging term for spinsters not destined ever to marry.[34] The poet and biographer William Hayley wrote a substantial work on old maids. For an unmarried woman from a good family, he said,

> it is probable, that after having passed the sprightly years of youth in the comfortable mansion of an opulent father, she is reduced to the shelter of some contracted lodging in a country town, attended by a single female servant, and with difficulty living on the interest of two or three thousand pounds, reluctantly, and perhaps irregularly, paid to her by an avaricious or extravagant brother, who considers such payment as a heavy incumbrance on his paternal estate. Such is the condition in which the unmarried daughters of English gentlemen are too frequently found.[35]

After her father died in 1805 such was the condition of Jane Austen herself, and she would remain single for the rest of her life. In her novel *Emma*, published a decade later, she has Harriet express her horror that her friend Emma might never marry:

'But still, you will be an old maid! And that's so dreadful!'

'Never mind, Harriet, I shall not be a poor old maid; and it is poverty only which makes celibacy contemptible to a generous public! A single woman, with a very narrow income, must be a ridiculous, disagreeable old maid! The proper sport of boys and girls; but a single woman, of good fortune, is always respectable.'

This was fiction, but Jane Austen said something similar when writing to her niece Fanny Knight in March 1817: 'Single women have a dreadful propensity for being poor, which is one very strong argument in favour of matrimony.'[36]

The same point was made by Nelly Weeton to her brother Tom a few years earlier, in 1809, after he accused her of having the ideas of an old maid. She hinted that she might soon be married, but only 'to avoid the finger of contempt, the smile of ridicule. If it were not for that, I am too happy to wish for any change.'[37] She added: 'An old maid is a stock for everyone to laugh at. Every article of dress, every word, every movement is satirized. Boys play tricks upon them, and are applauded. Girls sneer at them, and are unreproved. Upon my word, I think I will write an essay upon the pitiable state of old maids for some Magazine or Paper.'[38] Her hints at marriage were not then realised, but in 1814 she wed the Wigan widower Aaron Stock, a cotton manufacturer. The following year a daughter Mary was born, but it turned out to be a desperately unhappy and violent marriage that ended in a deed of separation in 1822.[39]

It was not easy to end unhappy marriages – and just about impossible for women, short of deserting the husband, murdering him or waiting for him to die. There was no divorce law before 1857. Instead, couples could obtain an annulment or separation through the ecclesiastical courts, which was costly. A divorce could then be sought by private Act of Parliament, which ensured that inheritance and legal heirs were safeguarded. Such a process was prohibitively expensive, and between 1700 and 1857 only around three hundred such Acts were passed, almost always undertaken by the husband, virtually never by the wife, who usually had no wealth to bequeath and no funds to secure an Act of Parliament. It was customary that the mother lost custody of (and usually all contact with) her children.[40]

General William Dyott's wife, when an invalid in Bath in 1814, asked him for a separation, having fallen in love with someone else. Two years later, when he was fifty-five, his bill was passed, as he described:

> The second reading of the bill for the divorce in Parliament was fixed for the 7th of the month, when it was necessary for me to attend. Nothing was more kind than the exertion of Lord Lauderdale in carrying the bill through the House of Lords; the third reading having taken place in the House of Commons on the 2nd July and was passed in the House of Lords the next day previous to Parliament being prorogued. Thus ended the most melancholy event, which deprived my children of a mother and me of a wife.[41]

Dyott never remarried, and he and his children never saw or heard of his wife again until she died in 1841, six years before his own death.[42] Most people could not afford to involve lawyers, and so many suffered terrible marriages instead. Women could not even divorce on the grounds of cruelty, since a man was allowed to beat his wife and ill-treat her, unless his behaviour was judged as life-threatening. Because this was difficult to prove, the law usually sided with the husband, sometimes showing a surprising leniency towards the guilty party. At Winchester in 1796 William Gamon received a mild sentence after being found guilty 'for ill-treating, and threatening to murder Hannah Gamon, his wife, and for refusing to ... appear at the next General Quarter Sessions'.[43] As punishment, he was bound over to keep the peace for three years. Many, probably most, cases of husbands abusing their wives never even came before the courts.

One way of ending a wretched marriage was for a husband to sell his wife – regarded as the poor man's divorce. Some sales were by consent of the wife, but at other times they were carried out against her will. Leading a wife to a public place with a rope tied round her neck and then selling her, like an animal at a market, was thought – wrongly – to be a legal and binding transaction, transferring the marriage to somebody else. Commentators considered wife-selling a barbaric practice, but it persisted to the late nineteenth century, and John Brand noted: 'A remarkable superstition still prevails among the lowest of our Vulgar, that a man may lawfully sell his wife to another, provided he deliver her over with a halter about her neck. It is painful to observe, that instances of this occur frequently in our newspapers.'[44]

Many such sales were to pre-arranged buyers, but they still needed to be carried out in a public place, as one newspaper reported in January 1790: '*Another Bargain and Sale of a Wife.*—A Man in the Neighbourhood of Thame, in Oxfordshire, two or three Years ago, sold his Wife for *Half a Guinea*; and his Neighbours telling him that the Bargain would not stand good, as she was not sold in public Market, he last Tuesday led her seven Miles in a String to Thame Market, and there sold her for Two Shillings and Six-pence, and paid *Four-Pence Toll*.'[45]

The *Morning Post* newspaper described another incident in January 1815 at Maidstone in Kent, after one man, John Osborne, realised it was not market day:

> the auction was removed to the sign of the coal-barge, in Earl street, where she was actually sold to a man named William Serjeant, with her child for the sum of one pound: the business was transacted in a very regular manner, a deed and covenant being given by the seller, of which the following is a literal copy:—
>
> 'I, John Osborne, doth agree to part with my wife, Mary Osborne, and child, to William Sergeant, for the sum of one pound, in consideration of giving up all claim whatever: wherunto I have made my mark as an acknowledgement.
>
> 'Maidstone, Jan. 3, 1815. X'
>
> This document was witnessed in due form, and the woman and child turned over to the buyer, to the apparent satisfaction of all parties; the husband expressing his willingness to take his spouse again at any future period.[46]

A woman being widowed could result in her sinking into poverty, because property and wealth usually passed to male descendants or relatives. Remarriage was therefore desirable, and in December 1808 Jane Austen wrote to Cassandra from Southampton: 'Lady Sondes' match surprises me, but does not offend me; had her first marriage been of affection, or had there been a grown-up single daughter, I should not have forgiven her; but I consider everybody as having a right to marry <u>once</u> in their lives for love, if they can, and provided she will now leave off having bad headaches and being pathetic, I can allow her, I can <u>wish</u> her to be happy.'[47] Mary Elizabeth Milles had entered into an arranged marriage in 1785, becoming Lady Sondes, but Lord Sondes died in 1806, and she was now remarrying for love.

In 1805, forty-nine-year-old Welshman William Jones was vicar at Broxbourne in Hertfordshire, then a peaceful country village a few miles north of London. He noted in his diary: 'Many mothers have I heard warn their dear daughters against "hateful matrimony," yet few, very few daughters have I known inclined to listen to the warning.'[48] He believed that daughters were in part encouraged by widows who remarried time and again: 'They will ... try the experiment for themselves!—&, with the less apprehension, when they observe widows, (even their own Mothers ...) adventure a *second*, & perhaps a *third*, time.'[49]

For many, whether in happy or unhappy relationships, marriage was an end to childhood and the start of adulthood and running a household. For young women it most likely meant years of childbearing, which was considered to be the very purpose of a Christian marriage. Jane Austen, in almost her last letter to her niece Fanny, warned her not to worry about getting married too soon, because 'by not beginning the business of Mothering quite so early in life, you will be young in Constitution, spirits, figure and countenance'.[50] Given the prospect of at least one partner succumbing to an early death through disease, accident or childbirth, many marriages did not survive for long.

TWO

———◆———

BREEDING

If tenderness could ever be supposed wanting, good sense and good breeding supplied its place.

Mansfield Park, by Jane Austen

Some years before her daughter Jane was born, Mrs Cassandra Austen wrote to her sister-in-law: 'My sister Cooper has made us a visit . . . Her boy and girl are well, the youngest almost two years old, and she has not been breeding since, so perhaps she has done.'[1] The word 'breeding' had two meanings – on the one hand, education, manners and respectability; on the other, the reproduction of children, which may sound strange today when applied to humans rather than birds or animals. In an era without effective contraception, breeding could be never-ending. In February 1798 the newspapers announced one mother's latest birth: 'On the 21st ult. Mrs Banting, of Little-Rissington, near Stow-on-the Wold, Gloucestershire, was safely delivered of a daughter, being the thirty-second child by the same husband.'[2]

A few months later, Jane Austen wrote to her sister Cassandra: 'I believe I never told you that Mrs. Coulthard and Anne, late of Manydown, are both dead, and both died in childbed. We have not regaled Mary with this news.'[3] Mary, the wife of their brother James, was due to give birth, but the family shielded her from these tragedies, a reminder of the dangers of childbirth. The next day Jane had pleasing news: 'I have just received a note from James to say that Mary was brought to bed last night, at eleven o'clock, of a fine little boy, and that everything is going on very well.'[4]

A good marriage was measured by a couple's ability to produce children, which for many women meant a succession of pregnancies unless they were unfortunate enough to die in the process. Maybe this influenced Jane Austen to remain single, preferring not to face the constant possibility of death and referring instead to at least one of her books as 'my own darling child'.[5] For the upper classes and royalty a male heir (or more than one, as a spare, in case of death) was essential, given that property and the family name descended via the male line. In 1809, on a visit to her former home village of Upholland in Lancashire, Nelly Weeton heard about the scale of preparations for the birth of the first child of Mr and Mrs Bankes at nearby Winstanley Hall,[6] a Tudor mansion on the edge of Wigan:

> She [Mrs Bankes] had been married eleven or twelve years, I think, and had never been in the family way before ... When her pregnancy was announced, it occasioned great joy at Winstanley, and great preparations were made. It was determined upon that the child should positively be a son. Malt was procured for brewing ale, to be drank when he came of age. The caps and other garments were all ordered, and made in the boyish forms; not so much as a *single one* for a girl. For the child and for Mrs. B. upon the occasion, between 5 and £600 worth of linen were purchased, £400 worth of which came from London. Alterations were made in the house, partitions taken down, and rebuilt for the accommodation of a couple of nurses ... She had scarcely been allowed to stir during the whole time of her pregnancy, not so much as to reach a chair nor shut a door; nor to remove from one room to another without one or two assistants, for fear of a miscarriage.[7]

During pregnancy, there was a superstitious dread of omens that might affect the fate of the baby. The physician Hugh Smith was scathing about such beliefs and related the story of when one pregnant woman, 'a lady of quality', suffered convulsions:

When her ladyship came a little to herself, she cried out, 'The black cat! the black cat!' . . . the servants diligently searched for the object; when in a tub, placed to receive the rain water, near her ladyship's dressing-room window, poor puss was discovered. This sight so terribly affected the lady, that her fears were ever uppermost, and she was miserable until the time of her delivery . . . she was fully persuaded that her child's face would be like this black cat's.[8]

Her fears were unfounded, and she was 'brought to bed of a lovely boy without either mark or blemish'.[9]

Women due to give birth were treated like invalids and confined to the house. During this period of 'confinement' or 'lying-in', they were expected to stay indoors, preferably in bed, for up to six weeks after the birth. The same terms were also used for the entire pregnancy, as was the expression 'in for it', which Jane Austen put in a letter to Cassandra in January 1801: 'So Lady Bridges, in the delicate language of Coulson Wallop [MP for Andover], is in for it!'[10] This was her first child, a son born five months later, called Brook-William Bridges.

In readiness for the birth, one tradition required the husband to provide a cake and a large cheese, which John Brand described:

It is customary at Oxford to cut the cheese (called in the North of England, in allusion to the mother's complaints at her delivery, 'the Groaning Cheese') in the middle when the child is born, and so by degrees form it into a large kind of ring, through which the child must be passed on the day of the christening. In other places the first cut of the sick Wife's cheese (so also they call the Groaning Cheese) is to be divided into little pieces, and tossed in the midwife's smock, to cause young women to dream of their lovers. Slices of the first cut of the Groaning Cheese are in the North of England laid under the pillows of young persons for the above purpose.[11]

Most women gave birth at home; only the poorest went to a hospital or the workhouse. Poor married women in London had access to charitable lying-in hospitals that had been established from the mid-eighteenth century. Other towns and cities were slow to follow, though at Newcastle-upon-Tyne one was founded in 1760, while at Manchester a lying-in charity was established in 1790 by Charles White.[12] Working-class women rarely had the luxury of preparing for a birth, but worked as long as possible. Those with access to a hospital were admitted during the last month of pregnancy and remained there for a while after the birth.

Around 5–7 per cent of children were illegitimate, a figure that had been rising steadily since the early eighteenth century and would reach a peak of about 7 per cent by the early Victorian period, before falling again in the late nineteenth century. However, the numbers of illegitimate children were probably under-reported, and so the percentage may be a little higher. Describing Upholland during her visit in 1809, Nelly Weeton complained: '[it] is, if possible, more licentious and more scandalous than when I lived in it; such numbers of unmarried women have children, many of whom one would have thought had years, discretion, sense, and virtue to have guarded them'.[13]

Unmarried mothers-to-be were not well treated. In Norfolk in November 1794 Parson Woodforde was unhappy to learn about his servant: 'My maid Molly has declared herself with child, more than half gone. Molly is with child by one Sam. Cudble, a carpenter of the parish of Coulton, and he says that he will marry her. The man bears a fair character. However, in her situation, it is necessary for me to part with her as soon as possible. To morrow therefore I intend at present to dismiss her. She is a very poor, weak girl, but I believe honest.'[14] Being unmarried himself, Woodforde was obliged to dismiss Molly to avoid scandal and so sent her away the next day:

> After breakfast, I talked with Molly, paid her three quarters of a year and one months wages, which amounted in the whole to 4.7.0 and after packing up her things, about one o'clock she left my house, and walked off for Coulton [Colton] where she is to be at Cudble's father's, till such time that they are married. She says that Cudble made not the least objection to marrying her, she foolishly denied being with child till the middle of last week, and then obliged to, the work becoming too much for her present situation. I don't think that she is far from lying-in by her appearance. For my own part, I have long thought her breeding.[15]

Molly, who was actually called Mary Woods, did marry Samuel Cudble, and their daughter Elizabeth was born on Christmas Eve 1794. Sadly, Elizabeth died on Christmas Day 1810, just sixteen years old.

Stillbirths and premature births were feared by all classes, and in October 1798 Jane Austen wrote to Cassandra from Steventon: 'Mrs. Hall, of Sherbourn, was brought to bed yesterday of a dead child, some weeks before she expected, owing to a fright. I suppose she happened unawares to look at her husband.'[16] Parson Woodforde noted when the squire's wife went unexpectedly into labour one summer afternoon in 1783:

> Nancy [his niece] and myself dined and spent part of the afternoon at Weston House with Mr and Mrs Custance ... Whilst we were at dinner Mrs Custance was obliged to go from table about 4 o'clock, labour pains coming on fast upon her. We went home soon after dinner on the occasion ... After supper we went up to Mr. Custances to enquire after Mrs Custance who was brought to bed of a fine girl about 7 o'clock and as well as could be expected.[17]

The next day Woodforde baptised the baby at Weston House: 'I walked up to Mr Custance's this morning soon after, named the little girl by name Frances Ann[e], and a very pretty infant she is.'[18] Since the baby had arrived earlier than anticipated, this was a precautionary measure in case she did not survive to be christened in church, though Frances actually lived to beyond her ninetieth birthday.

Two years later, in July 1785, Woodforde recorded another premature birth: 'I was sent for to go to Weston House to name a child of Mrs. Custance's who was brought to bed this afternoon about 2 o'clock. I therefore walked up directly to Weston House and named the child by name Mary Anne, the smallest infant I think I ever had in my arms. The child came 10 weeks before its time, therefore afraid that it would not live.'[19] Mary Anne survived just seventeen weeks.

Childbirth traditionally involved only female friends and family to assist in the birth and possibly a paid midwife – someone possessing experience, though no formal qualifications. When educated surgeons became involved in obstetrics, as 'man-midwives' or 'accoucheurs', they replaced some of the female midwives. In London the radical Francis Place, by trade a breeches maker, related: 'After the birth of our first child [in 1792] ... we employed a medical man in good practice, he had two guineas for his first attendance and a guinea for each of the succeeding two. The guinea was always carefully saved and immediately paid.'[20]

Man-midwives transformed childbirth, making use of the recently invented forceps and scientifically researching, debating and publishing on aspects of pregnancy. The most famous man-midwife was the Scottish anatomist William Hunter, at whose anatomy school in London deceased women in various stages of pregnancy were dissected. After years of work, he published *The Anatomy of the Human Gravid Uterus Exhibited in Figures* in 1774, containing for the first time life-sized images of the developing foetus.

In this era before anaesthetics, antibiotics or any understanding of infection, giving birth was hazardous and painful. Most mothers suffered at least one miscarriage or stillbirth, and many died of complications during labour or afterwards from sepsis (usually called 'puerperal fever').[21] Those in the lying-in hospitals were at particular risk of bacterial infection, which could spread rapidly. Jane Austen in *Northanger Abbey* made Catherine Morland's mother more robust: 'She had three sons before Catherine was born; and instead of dying in bringing the latter into the world, as anybody might expect, she still lived on – lived to have six children more – to see them growing up around her, and to enjoy excellent health herself.'

For women who experienced complications in childbirth, the only option was a caesarean section, but surgeons were reluctant to attempt this procedure. The first operation in which the baby survived, though not the mother, was performed in London in 1774 on Elizabeth Foster. When twenty-four-year-old Elizabeth Sedgley had married Joseph Foster at St Andrew's church, Holborn, in April 1759, she was 'perfectly strait, very thin, and measured five feet four inches'.[22] A succession of children and deteriorating health followed. 'When in labour of her eighth child,' the physician William Cooper related, 'she was a patient of the lying-in charity, for delivering poor married women at their own habitations, to which I am one of the physicians. The attending midwife, therefore, after waiting a proper time, sent for me on December 18, 1770.'[23] Elizabeth was in such a bad state that Cooper removed the foetus by an embryotomy.

For the next two and a half years she was helpless, with severe curvature of the spine, 'scarce ever able, without assistance, even to turn herself in bed'.[24] Yet in this state her husband impregnated her twice more, the first time leading to a miscarriage. By the next pregnancy, 'she measured only four feet four inches; and she generally stooped so very much, especially lately, as to appear to be little more than three feet high'.[25] In mid-August 1774 Elizabeth was ready to give birth and in such severe pain that Cooper persuaded John Hunter (brother of William Hunter) to come to her home in Robinhood Court, close to St Andrew's church, and perform a caesarean. 'During the whole of the operation,' Cooper recorded, 'the poor woman behaved with remarkable patience and fortitude.'[26] Without anaesthetics she was, of course, fully conscious. The next day she died and two days later was buried in St Andrew's churchyard.[27] Incredibly, the baby girl, Sarah, survived and was baptised at the same church in July the following year.

It was the surgeon James Barlow from Blackburn in Lancashire who performed the first caesarean in England where the mother survived. She was forty-year-old Mrs Jane Foster, a mother of several children from the village of Blackrod near Wigan. Some months earlier, she had been attended by Charles White of Manchester and Mr Hawarden from Wigan after falling beneath a cart and fracturing her pelvis.[28] Not long afterwards, she became pregnant again, and when she went into labour in late November 1793, it was realised that the pelvic injury made giving birth impossible. Barlow was consulted, and he recommended a caesarean, even though 'of the nine or ten instances then on record, in which that operation had been performed in this country, not one had furnished a voucher for its success'.[29] Mrs Foster refused to give consent, but relented on the fifth day of labour. The baby was pulled out dead, but the woman survived and lived another three decades.[30]

Barlow later discussed the case with Charles White, the celebrated man-midwife and former pupil of William Hunter in London. In 1773 White had advanced the understanding of caesareans and other aspects of childbirth when he published *A Treatise on the Management of Pregnant and Lying-In Women*. With old traditions difficult to eradicate, he warned: 'The nurses in London are a numerous and powerful body, and an attempt to reform their ancient customs might be looked upon as an open attack upon them, and an actual declaration of war.'[31]

Meanwhile, their practices were killing women, and White advocated that mothers-to-be should give birth naturally, with minimal interference from midwives or instruments, and that they should be clean and not remain stationary in bed. In his opinion, 'The thick fustian waistcoats and petticoats usually worn during the lying-in, are much too warm.'[32] He disagreed with the old customs that were intended to prevent women from catching cold:

> As soon as she is delivered, if she is a person in affluent circumstances, she is covered up close in bed with additional cloaths, the curtains are drawn round the bed, and pinned together, every crevice in the windows and door is stopped close, not excepting even the key hole, the windows are guarded not only with shutters and curtains, but even with blankets, the more effectually to exclude the fresh air, and the good woman is not suffered to put her arm, or even her nose out of bed, for fear of catching cold.[33]

One of White's recommendations was for increased ventilation, so that the 'lying-in chamber should in every respect be as sweet, as clean, and as free from any disagreeable smell, as any other part of the house'.[34] In most cases the bedroom where the birth occurred was anything but sweet and clean. Women traditionally recovered in overheated, airless rooms, which was no doubt true for Mrs Austen when her daughter Jane was born on 16 December 1775, at the start of a severe winter.

Before 1800 around 1.5 per cent of mothers died in childbirth, but where White worked, in Manchester, the situation was much improved, with a mortality rate of less than 1 per cent. The details he gave of one woman who became ill after giving birth must have been typical of paupers across the country:

> MARY LORD of Manchester, a poor woman aged 31, was delivered on the 25th of May 1772, in the morning, by a midwife in the neighbourhood. She had an easy labor ... her third lying-in ... [but] she gradually grew worse till I first saw her, which was on the fourth day in the evening ... The whole family lived in the same room in which she lay, being the only one they had; it was very warm, having a large fire in it, and smelt very disagreeably. I desired the fire might be lessened, and more air let into the room, accordingly the window was set open and remained open all night. She had scarcely sitten up in bed since her delivery, but had lain in a horizontal position all the time. I advised her to sit up frequently in bed, and to get out of it once every day, to put on clean linen ... On the fifth day the room was much cooler, and did not smell so disagreeably ... On the sixth day all her complaints were vanished.[35]

The wealthy were not immune from death in childbirth. Despite the lavish arrangements for the birth of the first child of Mr and Mrs Bankes at Winstanley Hall, both mother and baby died, even though the renowned Charles White attended. Nelly Weeton described what happened: 'Dr. White from Manchester resided in the house upwards of three weeks before Mrs. B's confinement ... After suffering a most severely painful time, a *son was born*, but heir only to the grave, for it was dead. The mother survived little more than a week – and died too; few more beloved or more lamented, she was so kind to her servants, so charitable to the poor.'[36]

Another eminent man-midwife was Edward Rigby of Norwich, and he and his wife Anne had twelve children. Two were twins, a girl and a boy born on 1 August 1804, and four were quadruplets, three boys and a girl, born on 15 August 1817. This remarkable event was reported in the newspapers: 'BIRTHS EXTRAORDINARY – The Lady of Edward Rigby, Esq. M.D. of Norwich, was safely delivered of three sons and a daughter. Mrs. R. is as well as usual so soon after childbirth; and the children are all alive and hearty. Before the birth of these little ones Dr. R. was the father, by his present wife, of eight most lovely and healthy children, the two eldest of whom are twins.'[37] Tragically, all the quadruplets died, the girl surviving the longest, for almost three months.[38]

Multiple births were rare, and such babies stood little chance of surviving. For the village of Selborne in Hampshire, close to the Austens, the curate Gilbert White compiled a statistical analysis of its population. The period 1720 to 1780, he said, saw just under a thousand baptisms, including 'Twins thirteen times, many ... dying young'.[39] Any exceptional birth was worthy of comment, as in January 1789 when the *New Exeter Journal* mentioned the arrival of triplets: 'Tuesday the 6th instant the wife of Richard Hannaford, of South-Brent, in the county of Devon, was delivered of three fine girls, all of whom are likely to do well.'[40] The more mundane births of prominent citizens were also announced in the local newspapers. As with all such news, the name of the mother was traditionally ignored, as in the *Hull Packet* in October 1801, which reported: 'BIRTH. Lately, at Everingham, near Pocklington, the lady of M. Constable, Esq. was safely delivered of a daughter.'[41]

It was not unusual for fathers to be absent from home when their children were born, and it took some time for the news to reach William Wilkinson, at sea in the navy, that he was a father. Finally he held the letter that his sister-in-law Fanny Platt had excitedly written from their lodgings at Kensington in London, a few hours after his daughter's birth. 'Heartily do I wish you were now here,' she said, 'that we might congratulate with each other on the happy arrival of your little daughter. It was born at 17 minutes past 9 o'clock this 9th day of Nov[br] [1807].'[42] Fanny next gave William an affectionate description: 'the precious Babe, it is, I think, the loveliest little creature I ever saw. Its eyes are dark and beautifully bright, its nose and chin we all agree in our opinion as to their being exactly like your own. It has a pretty little head with a good bit of hair, which is very dark. It is in good health and so plump you cannot think.'[43] Fanny's use of 'it', not 'she', was commonplace when speaking of infants and would not have appeared uncaring. William was extremely happy, and early the next year he wrote to his wife: 'in my Prayer Book (which I keep in my desk) I have your hair, Baby's and a piece of my own. I cut mine off the other day to see the contrast. They are all in a small piece of fine India paper ... and they do look very pretty, yours light, mine dark, and Baby's between both.'[44]

For those who could afford it, a wet-nurse might be hired, a centuries-old tradition but an alien concept today and one that could be detrimental, even fatal, to the health of the newborn infant. Wet-nurses were usually married working-class women, capable of producing milk, perhaps having just lost a baby or recently weaned their own child. Some worked continuously for years. They took over the care and feeding of newborn babies, primarily from middle- and upper-class families. All too often, babies did not stay with their mothers, but were transferred to the homes of wet-nurses, especially if those women lived in the countryside rather than the less healthy town.[45] There is no conclusive evidence about Sarah Wilkinson's newborn daughter, but Fanny told William that 'We have a nurse who thoroughly understands her business',[46] implying that a wet-nurse was employed.

Various taboos deterred mothers from breastfeeding, such as the belief that they should be churched first as they were unclean from having given birth; that their first milk, the colostrum, was harmful; or that babies should be purged for a few days after birth with liquids such as wine, sugared water, or butter and honey. However, physicians and midwives were gradually realising the benefits of breastfeeding right from birth. In the late eighteenth century the employment of wet-nurses began to decline, and the increase in breastfeeding led to a drop in the mortality rate of newborn infants. Georgiana, Duchess of Devonshire, decided to breastfeed her daughter 'Little G' because the wet-nurse was a drunk, but she was criticised by the family as they believed it would prevent another pregnancy, and Georgiana's duty was to produce a male heir.[47]

Some women did not breastfeed for other reasons, such as husbands forbidding the practice, or because of physical problems and illness. The Exeter physician Hugh Downman was a pioneer in understanding how infants should be nursed, unfortunately setting down his recommendations in a lengthy, albeit well-received, piece of blank verse, *Infancy*, published in six books from 1774. For mothers unable to breastfeed, he advised choosing a wet-nurse in the countryside:

> Far from the bounds
> Of the rank city, let some trusty mind
> Explore the straw-rooft cott; there, firm of nerve
> Her blood from every grosser particle,
> By hardy labour, and abstemious fare,
> Sublimed; the honest peasant's mate shall ope
> Her hospitable arms, receive with joy
> The infant stranger, and profusely yield
> Her pure balsamic nurture to his lip.[48]

Tight clothing, especially stays, hindered breastfeeding, according to Charles White: 'This dress by constantly pressing upon the breast and nipple reduces it to a flat form ... and the nipple is buried in the breast. By being constantly kept in this position, it contracts adhesions; it is prevented from coming out ... The tightness of the stays is alone sufficient to do much harm, but they are also, often made hard and unpliable by packthread and whalebone, which must greatly increase the mischief.'[49] Working-class women, he observed, were better at breastfeeding, because many did not wear stays: 'Hence it will appear evident why women of rank, and those in the middle stations of life meet with difficulty in giving suck to children ... why hard working, labouring women, who are obliged to go very loose about their breasts generally make good nurses, and that too with very little trouble.'[50]

Distress in weaning, it was recommended, could be lessened by administering laudanum or alcohol. Once babies were weaned, they were fed with a semi-liquid pap, which, as the man-midwife and surgeon William Moss explained, 'is composed of bread and water boiled and sweetened with brown sugar; to which is, sometimes, added a small quantity of milk: or; oatmeal and water, in the form of thin water gruel, with the same additions'.[51] From the late eighteenth century various types of feeding vessels were used, including animal horns, spoons, boat-shaped sucking bottles and upright pots with spouts, but sterilisation was unheard-of.

Some children were breastfed by their mothers and then handed to foster-parents after weaning. This is how Jane Austen and her siblings were brought up, fostered for several months (possibly by a woman called Bessy Littleworth) until deemed old enough to return home. In November 1772 Mrs Austen told her sister-in-law Mrs Walter: 'My little boy [Henry, born in June 1771] is come home from nurse, and a fine stout little fellow he is, and can run anywhere, so now I have all four at home, and some time in January I expect a fifth.'[52] This fifth one would be Cassandra.

In June 1773 Mrs Austen wrote: 'I suckled my little girl thro' the first quarter; she has been weaned and settled at a good woman's at Deane just eight weeks; she is very healthy and lively.'[53] Deane village was 2 miles from their parsonage at Steventon, and years later James Austen-Leigh, the nephew of Jane and Cassandra, mentioned this peculiar start to their lives:

> Her [Jane's] mother followed a custom, not unusual in those days, though it seems strange to us, of putting out her babies to be nursed in a cottage in the village. The infant was daily visited by one or both of its parents, and frequently brought to them at the parsonage, but the cottage was its home, and must have remained so till it was old enough to run about and talk ... It may be that the contrast between the parsonage house and the best class of cottage was not quite so extreme then as it would be now, that the one was somewhat less luxurious, and the other less squalid.[54]

Writing in the Victorian era, he was perplexed by the concept of babies from the middle class or above being raised by their social inferiors.

Another custom that now seems strange or superstitious was that of 'churching'. A woman who gave birth was considered by many to be spiritually unclean and was supposed to be confined until her churching ceremony a few weeks later, when she left home for the first time to go straight to church and be ritually cleansed. Although sanctioned by a passage in the Old Testament,[55] this was a contentious issue within the Church, variously condemned as a relic of the Jewish religion or as a Catholic rite. It remained a widespread practice, probably bolstered by superstitions about women being dangerous and bringers of bad luck after childbirth until such ritual cleansing had taken place. The Church explained the ceremony as one of purification or of thanksgiving for the birth.

Both Parson Woodforde and William Holland regularly churched women. On one occasion, Holland recorded a conversation with a Mr Hurley: 'A civil man but an odd spoken one and an Anabaptist. His wife desired to be churched by me. Yes returned I, if you bring your child to be christened, otherwise not, for why should a person be indulged with the offices of the Church in one case who despises them in all other cases?'[56] The actual ceremony varied from place to place, but was primarily a blessing. While in Lincolnshire in 1791, the traveller John Byng witnessed such a service: 'In the church, this evening, were two women church'd by the clergyman ... in the space of two minutes: which office I did not know could be thus huddled over, privately, in a church?'[57]

Inevitably, the parson charged a fee, but Woodforde frequently returned the money to poor women, particularly ones with large families. He routinely performed this rite, as in March 1787 when 'I read prayers, preached and churched a woman this morning at Weston Church – gave the woman her ᵈ6 [sixpence] ... very soon after I mounted my horse and went to Witchingham, and there read prayers, churched one woman ... Recd. for churching the woman at Witchingham o: o: 6.'[58] And a week later: 'I read prayers and preached this afternoon at Weston C[hurch]. Also churched 2 poor women ... I gave the two poor women the churching fee.'[59]

Most children were baptised in church soon after birth, and so mothers waiting to be churched could not attend. The baptism ceremony, the sacramental rite admitting an individual to the Christian Church, included naming the child, as it still does today. Although births were not registered, baptisms had to be recorded in parish registers.[60] Private baptisms at home also took place, particularly where the baby was too ill to be brought to church. Having privately baptised baby Frances in June 1783, Woodforde performed a church baptism for her three months later: 'I walked to church this morning between 11 and 12, and publickly baptised Mr Custance's little maid by name Frances Anne. Lady Bacon and Lady Beauchamp stood Godmothers, and Mr Custance stood proxy.'[61] He also baptised illegitimate ('spurious') children privately, as in December 1786: 'I privately named a spurious child of one Mary Parkers this morning by name John. The fathers name I could not get intelligence of.'[62]

William Holland lamented the plight of one destitute pregnant girl who had been forcibly returned to her home parish of Over Stowey: 'A worthless girl in the poor house is in a sad state. She has begun to be in labour but when it will end is a melancholy consideration. She was brought home to the parish by an order with every kind of disease about her, the child they say is already dead. She at times suffers a great deal and has neither comfort nor a word of pity from any one around but indeed medical assistance she has.'[63] The next morning he was taken aback:

> While I was at breakfast this day the sad young woman whom I spoke of the day before was brought to bed of a fine girl to the astonishment of everyone for it was supposed that the child was dead. It was brought to me while I was at breakfast to be baptised and so I left breakfast and went to the kitchen, and poured water on its face and baptised the child but the mother had the itch and many other bad disorders [so] that I did not care to handle it much.[64]

The baby did not survive, and Holland was called on to bury her one week later.[65]

It was rare to give babies more than one name, and so Jane Austen and most of her contemporaries had no middle name. William Wilkinson's new baby had two names – Sarah Frances, after her mother Sally and her aunt Fanny, the popular pet-names for Sarah and Frances. In *Northanger Abbey* Isabella and Catherine become such good friends that 'They called each other by their Christian name, were always arm in arm when they walked.' Unless they were very close, it was customary to address most people by their title and surname, and because of such formality Jane Austen was frustrated at being ignorant of the Christian name of a woman she knew only as Miss Wapshire from Salisbury, who was soon to be married. 'I wish

I could be certain that her name were Emma,' she told Cassandra; 'but her being the eldest daughter leaves that circumstance doubtful.'[66] In upper-class families, it was usual to call the eldest unmarried daughter 'Miss', so those who did not know the family well might be unaware of her Christian name, which was the case here. In fact, she was Mary Wapshare, and on 12 December 1800 she married the widowed naval captain Sir Thomas Williams in Salisbury Cathedral.

Names were chosen for being traditional, for their biblical associations, for being names of royalty or perhaps those of dead siblings. They tended to perpetuate long-established family names ranging from the plain Jane to the uncommon Cassandra. In June 1783 Woodforde recorded: 'I privately named a child this morning of Dinah Bushell's by name Keziah, one of Job's daughters names ... I privately named a child of Brands of East Tuddenham, by name John this afternoon.'[67] For boys, common names included John, James, George, Joseph, Richard, Thomas and William, while Anne (or Ann), Sarah, Susan, Jane, Elizabeth, Mary and Hannah were popular names for girls. When commenting on a novel written by her niece Anna, Jane Austen said: 'I like the scene itself, the Miss Lesleys, Lady Anne, & the music, very much. Lesley is a noble name.'[68]

In January 1807 Jane Austen wrote to Cassandra from Southampton: 'I cannot yet satisfy Fanny as to Mrs. Foote's baby's name, and I must not encourage her to expect a good one, as Captain Foote is a professed adversary to all but the plainest; he likes only Mary, Elizabeth, Anne, &c. Our best chance is of "Caroline", which in compliment to a sister seems the only exception.'[69] This was Captain Foote's second marriage, to Mary Patton, having divorced his first wife. Shortly afterwards, at Southampton, the baby was in fact baptised as Elizabeth.

Babies, both male and female, were traditionally immobilised from birth in tight swaddling bands of cloth, in the mistaken belief that this prevented crooked limbs, a condition that was actually rickets caused by vitamin D deficiency. In order to minimise soiling by urine and faeces, the baby might not be completely swaddled, and periodically the cloths were removed for drying or washing. In a treatise on caring for babies, published in 1781, William Moss advised against tight swaddling: 'In dressing a new-born child ... great care ought to be

taken that no part of the body or limbs be tight bound, or closely confined by rollers or any part of the dress ... children thrive much better
without it, and are much more likely to be free from deformity.'[70]

By the 1790s the practice of swaddling was on the decline. Instead,
babies were dressed in gowns or tunics, and all wore bonnets or caps,
so that in *Emma*, 'Mrs Weston, with her baby on her knee ... was one
of the happiest women in the world. If any thing could increase her
delight, it was perceiving that the baby would soon have outgrown its
first set of caps.' Moss recommended 'foundling dresses':

> The number of PINS used in the dress of a child is sometimes very great;
> but when *tapes* or *strings* can be substituted for them, they are much
> preferable. The *foundling dresses*, so called from being first invented at the
> *foundling* hospital, for the sake, no doubt, of convenience and dispatch,
> are come much into use. They draw and tye with strings, and are other-
> wise so contrived, that very few pins become needful in putting them
> on ... the risque of pricking and wounding the tender bodies of children
> is avoided.[71]

Mass-produced safety-pins were as yet unknown, so these garments developed by London's Foundling Hospital were the best
option. When babies were ready to crawl they progressed from long
gowns to short clothes, and so when Cassandra was almost six
months old in 1773, Mrs Austen noted that 'she ... puts on her short
petticoats to-day'.[72] Some babies may have had clouts or diapers
(strips or squares of linen cloth) wrapped round them – the word
'nappy' was not then used – also fastened with pins or ties.
Impoverished families might have used rags, but the amount of laundry needed would have made this burdensome.

Neither toilet training nor diapers figured in childcare and mid-
wifery manuals, suggesting that most babies soiled their bedding or
gowns. All Moss says is that babies 'ought to be dry and clean; for
which purpose it will be necessary to renew and change them very
frequently'.[73] Had they worn diapers, babies would probably have
suffered much more than the occasional soreness mentioned by him:
'A child will sometimes have his backside red, inflamed, and sore, by

the frequency and sharpness of his stools ... Take of, *extract of lead*, and *brandy*, each thirty drops; put them into a small vial with four ounces (or eight tablespoonful) of water. With a little of this, aired by the fire in a teacup, let the parts be bathed, once or twice a day, with a soft linen rag.'[74]

There was no tradition of babies being given soft toys and other playthings apart from rattles. Instead, they were sedated with proprietary soothers, especially Dr Godfrey's Cordial. Such concoctions contained opium, morphine and a mercury compound like calomel and were widely advertised, as in the *Derby Mercury* for March 1775:

> The Original GODFREY'S GENERAL CORDIAL, is a Medicine which answers to its Name, having a general Tendency to the curing [of] Diseases ... This CORDIAL is of the greatest help to weakly Women, when they are with Child, to prevent Miscarriages ... Also it's of excellent Use for young Children that are weakly and restless, and breed their Teeth hardly; and for those that are inclined to the Rickets, &c.[75]

Moss was especially critical of such medication:

> There are a number of quack medicines imposed upon the public under various titles, as Godfrey's cordial, &c. &c. ... but as their compositions are as mysterious and difficult to discover as their good qualities, nothing more can be said in their favour ... There is a *drug* however upon which, it is well known, their chief efficacy depends; and that is, *opium*; hence it happens they all have a stilling or sedative power ... I have known Godfrey's cordial given to children, successively for months, with no other design ... than keeping them quiet in the nights ... The abuse of spiritous liquors, and quack medicines of the opiate or composing kind, may be observed to happen most frequently ... with children who are nursed [away] from home.[76]

Child mortality was high, and particularly with the scant knowledge of hygiene, young babies were especially vulnerable to gastro-intestinal disorders as well as untold infectious diseases. In London, the baby Sally Wilkinson initially thrived and was doted on by her parents, but at the age of ten months she fell sick. William learned from his wife that after showing signs of recovery, his daughter was again unwell: 'she has not kept her food so well on her stomach. Last night I was told to get some sago powder and give her some port wine in it which I did and gave her some of the wine in the same arrowroot ... and once or twice today I gave her a little savoury biscuit rather too soon after taking the stuff with the wine in it that it made her so sick which with the little fever the wine occasioned alarmed me a little.'[77] This medical advice came from Mr Thomson, the doctor who had delivered the baby, but his remedies were proving harmful. A few days later her mother Sarah wrote:

> She has taken two or three doses of physic ... for Mr T said her bowels were in a bad state and must be thoroughly cleansed before she would get better. Which of course must be the case. Last night she got into a nice perspiration which I hoped would do her a wonderful deal of good. She is, dear creature, very weak this morning ... Mr T has ordered her asses milk and today he said she was to take some gravy that ran out of roast beef or mutton which she has done and sucked some beef.[78]

One week later, on 25 September 1808, their brother-in-law James Brothers broke tragic news to William:

> It is with much pain I am obliged to acquaint you with the little baby's death. She died this morning between 10 and 11 ... There was one comfort, if in such a case such a thing is possible, that she did not any of the time appear to suffer from pain, but her death seemed to be occasioned by gradual weakness. Sally and Fanny are as you may well suppose in great affliction, but yet I am happy in telling you, they bear it, considering how much their distress must be heightened by your absence, better than I could have supposed.[79]

It was rare for any family not to suffer the death of at least one child. In his commonplace book, Matthew Buckle recorded intricate details of his family tree, in which we see that his relatives and ancestors experienced numerous tragedies. At the age of forty-two in

February 1803, Buckle married his wife Hannah, who would give birth to seven children in the space of thirteen years. Their first, an unnamed daughter, was born on Christmas Eve 1803 and died 'one week and five days' later. The next child was Louisa, born in 1804, followed by Emma in 1807, Frances in 1809, Eleanor in 1811, Mary in 1814 and finally a boy, Christopher, born in 1816.[80] Keeping track of families was important. In 1782 Carl Philipp Moritz, a twenty-six-year-old German pastor, teacher and prolific writer, was travelling for seven weeks through England, mainly on foot. At Nettlebed in Oxfordshire he attended a church service: 'The prayer-book, which my landlord lent me, was quite a family piece; for all his children's births, and names, and also his own wedding-day, were very carefully set down in it.'[81]

Lack of proper information made it impossible to be certain about the size of England's population, and commentators gave opinions based on imprecise figures obtained from records such as local surveys, assessments of houses for the window tax and on the Bills of Mortality – tallies of the number of burials and causes of death compiled by parish clerks in London and elsewhere, originally to monitor the spread of plague. Records of baptisms and burials did not give a true picture, and some were convinced the population was getting smaller, even though places like London were expanding. In 1783 Dr Richard Price calculated that the population of England and Wales was five million maximum: 'Let ... the number of houses in England and Wales be called a million, and the number of people will be four millions and a half, or five millions at most.'[82] London's expansion, Price believed, was due to mass immigration from the surrounding countryside: 'The more London increases, the more the rest of the kingdom must be deserted; the fewer hands must be left for agriculture.'[83] He was partially correct, because there was massive movement into cities and towns, especially of families seeking work in the new factories, boys bound as apprentices and girls looking for positions as servants.

The first proper national census of Great Britain took place on 10 March 1801, though the information requested was limited – mainly the number of people, including children, in each household, their occupations and the number of inhabited and uninhabited houses. In the town of Falmouth in Cornwall, 465 houses were occupied by 947 families, and the population comprised 3684 people – 1466 males and 2218 females. Cornwall was an agricultural and mining county, but because Falmouth was a port, only 25 were employed in agriculture, with 626 in trade, manufacture or handicraft and 3053 in the general category of 'All other persons not comprized in the two preceding classes'.[84]

The 1801 census demonstrated that England's population was actually expanding rapidly and exceeded 8,300,000 – far more than previously reckoned.[85] In the 2011 census London alone had nearly 8,200,000 people, but in 1801 it was the largest city in Europe with barely a million inhabitants. The next largest places in England in 1801 were Manchester (still a town, not a city) and Liverpool. Both were expanding rapidly. Manchester's population had risen to nearly 95,000 from just over 27,000 in 1773, and Liverpool had nearly 83,000, having risen from 34,000 in 1770.[86] By 1801 one in seven of the population lived in large towns, which meant that the vast majority of people were still in rural areas.

In 1811 the census revealed that the population of England had increased by more than a million, to almost 9,500,000, and by then London had over a million inhabitants.[87] In May of that year, forty-four-year-old Louis Simond, a Frenchman who had gone to America before the Revolution and was now a successful New York merchant, commented on London's expansion:

> We have spent a few days with some of our friends in Hertfordshire, 20 miles north of London. For half that distance you travel between two rows of houses, to which new ones are added every day ... London extends its great polypus-arms over the country around. The population is not increased by any means in proportion to these appearances, only transferred from the centre to the extremities. This centre is become a mere counting-house, or place of business.[88]

What is not apparent in census information is the origins of people, such as that of the black population, which in some places was so small that their presence was noteworthy. In 1808 Silvester Treleaven related how the people of Moretonhampstead in Devon reacted joyfully to the wedding of a black servant: 'Married with licence Peter the black servant to General Rochambeau to Susanna Parker. The bells rang merrily all day. From the novelty of this wedding being the first negro ever married in Moreton a great number assembled in the church yard, and paraded down the street with them.'[89] Some prejudice certainly existed on a personal level, such as that revealed by William Holland, who wrote in his diary in January 1805:

> I met young [Brian] Mackey, who is come to see his father … This young man is his son by a negro woman, and has had from the father an excellent education, and is in [holy] orders and has two livings, and is in good circumstances. Pity that he should suffer his father to feel distress in his latter days. But he is so far from assisting him that in all his visits he is drawing money from him and plundering him and I fear now poor Mrs. Mackey [his stepmother] will be left without a shilling. I am not very partial to West Indians, especially to your negro half-blood people.[90]

The fact that 'young Mackey' had received an Oxford education and was parish priest of Coates in Gloucestershire is some indication that black people from a wealthy background were not necessarily handicapped by their colour.[91]

Holland's dislike of Mackey was possibly influenced by his conviction that this ungrateful son was treating his father badly, although he did hold strong opinions about anyone he perceived as different. A Welshman himself, from Llanelian in Denbighshire, Holland described the Somerset people he lived among as 'of a large size and strong, but in my opinion very slow and lazy and discontented … and very much given to eating and drinking'.[92] He was repeatedly dissatisfied with the work done by his servants, referring to one of them in his diary as a 'strange nog-headed blockhead' – 'nog-headed' was Anglo-Welsh dialect for 'wooden-headed'.[93]

Prejudice and suspicion towards foreigners were widespread, though people were also wary of anyone from different parts of

England. The Irish and the Jews were generally more reviled than enemy nations like France. There was an ever-growing Irish population, who were flocking to places like Manchester to work in the textile industries or migrating to London to work mainly as unskilled labourers. By 1780 there may have been as many as 23,000 Irish in the capital,[94] and the main Irish quarter was the parish of St Giles, a desperately overcrowded area known as the Rookery. When being questioned in 1816 about the inhabitants, one Irish teacher, Thomas Augustine Finnegan of the St Giles's Irish Free School in George Street, was not complimentary about his fellow countrymen. He reckoned that the children were 'most depraved; they are exposed to every species of vice with which the streets abound; they generally associate with gangs of pickpockets', and as for the parents, they were 'very dissolute, generally; on Sundays particularly they take their children with them to public-houses, and the children witness the scenes of riot and sanguinary conflict that happen among the parents in the streets.'[95]

Hostility was likewise suffered by the Jews. In 1796 the magistrate Patrick Colquhoun wrote: 'It is estimated that there are about twenty thousand Jews in the city of London, besides, perhaps, about five or six thousand more in the great provincial and sea-port towns ... Educated in idleness, from their earliest infancy, they acquire every debauched and vicious principle which can fit them for the most complicated arts of fraud and deception.'[96] According to Francis Place, such prejudice was rife: 'It was thought good sport to maltreat a Jew, and they were often most barbarously used, even in the principal streets ... I have seen many Jews hooted, hunted, cuffed, pulled by the beard, spit up [upon], and so barbarously assaulted in the streets, without any protection from the passers-by or the police, as seems ... almost impossible.'[97]

Prejudice against gypsies was universal, even though for the middle and upper classes the idea of a gypsy lifestyle often seemed romantic, and gypsy characters figured in popular plays, while gypsy dress was adopted for fancy-dress balls and sometimes influenced high fashion. However, gypsies themselves were regarded as thieves and swindlers. They, and anyone consorting with them, often fell foul of the vagrancy laws, which carried penalties of whipping, imprisonment and transportation.

Gypsies were also frequently blamed for the abduction of children. In June 1802 the *Morning Post and Gazetteer* carried a story about a young girl 'in most wretched attire', who had been found near Lewisham in Kent. She said that 'she was the daughter of a Captain Kellen, of the Marines, at Plymouth; that about seven months ago, being sent a small distance out of the town, on some business for her parents, she was met by a gang of gypsies, consisting of five men and six women who seized her, and forcibly carried her away'.[98] A band of gypsies was arrested, and the continuing story made good copy, but a week later the same newspaper admitted they were innocent:

> This tale of wonder, at length, proves to be a gross imposition, on the part of the girl, almost in every respect, and that the account given by the gypsey, of meeting her on Kennington Common, is true ... Andrew Dew, a serjeant of marines belonging to the Plymouth Division, stated, that he well knew the girl ... he remembered her in January last at Stonehouse Barracks near Plymouth, selling apples and nuts for her mother; that he had lately seen her father, who informed him the girl had absconded from them soon after January.[99]

The gypsies were released, and the girl 'was sent to the House of Correction, until her place of legal settlement can be ascertained. She is very little, and plain in person, and cannot be above eleven or twelve years of age, though she says she is seventeen.'[100]

Unwanted children, usually of paupers or unmarried mothers, might be abandoned in public places like a market square or church porch, making them the responsibility of the parish, which had to care for infants born or abandoned within their boundary whose relatives were unknown. Some of these foundlings were looked after in the workhouse, while others were boarded out to poor women or widows who were paid, but the mortality rate was exceptionally high. This was one reason why in 1741 Thomas Coram had opened the London Foundling Hospital, England's first home for abandoned children and, from 1801, for illegitimate children as well.

Some unmarried mothers were so desperate and ashamed that they murdered their children or left them to die. Others tried to abort the foetus, such as by inserting a wire or knife into the uterus or by ingesting some potion that was poisonous to the foetus in order to induce a miscarriage. Midwives were well aware of the best abortifacients, recommending ergot, rue, penny royal, tansy and savin. When living in Upholland, Nelly Weeton wrote of one attempted abortion: 'Mary Downall is in a poor state of health … I am afraid she took something when pregnant of her little girl intended to fall on the child, and it has light on herself. She has looked a bad colour ever since.'[101]

For those women who needed to hide their pregnancy and who could afford to pay, discreet services were available. One London business advertised on the front page of a West Country newspaper in 1803:

PREGNANT LADIES, whose situation requires a temporary retirement, may be accommodated with an Apartment, in an airy situation, to Lye-in, agreeably to their circumstances, their infants put out to nurse, and taken care of. Tenderness, honour, and secrecy, have been the basis of this concern for many years.—Those regardless of reputation will not be treated with.

Apply to SYMONS, late Dr. WHITE, No. 4, London-House-yard, St. Paul's Church-yard.[102]

There was no contraception for married women apart from sexual abstinence or breastfeeding, and on average they had six to seven live babies. After Sophia Deedes gave birth to her eighteenth child, Marianne, Jane Austen wrote to her niece Fanny: 'I wd recommend to her and Mr. D. the simple regimen of separate rooms.'[103] In fact, Mrs Deedes would give birth to yet another child. It was deemed morally unacceptable for married women to use artificial contraception, though some undoubtedly tried methods like inserting a natural sponge soaked in lemon juice or vinegar. There was a thriving market for condoms (also called 'cundums', 'armour' or 'preservatives'), which were primarily for prophylactic purposes, worn by men using prostitutes to guard against disease or with mistresses to guard against pregnancy. Made from animal intestines, condoms had a hand-sewn seam at one end and were secured by a silk ribbon. They could be washed out and reused. The term 'armour' was defined in a contemporary dictionary of slang as 'to make use of Mrs. Philips's ware. See C—D—M', and 'cundum' was defined as:

> The dried gut of a sheep, worn by men in the act of coition, to prevent venereal infection ... These machines were long prepared and sold by a matron of the name of Philips, at the Green Canister, in Half-moon-street, in the Strand. That good lady having acquired a fortune, retired from business, but learning that the town was not well served by her successors, she, out of a patriotic zeal for the public welfare, returned to her occupation; of which she gave notice by divers hand-bills, in circulation in the year 1776.[104]

Mistresses were kept mainly by married and unmarried men of the upper class and gentry, who could afford the costs. Parson Woodforde met one such mistress in mid-May 1777: 'Mr. Custance [Press Custance, the squire's brother] called on me this morning to go a fishing. We rode down to the river [Wensum]. Mr. Custances mistress a Miss Sherman and one Sandall an oldish man a broken gentleman and who keeps a mistress also tho' he has a wife living, went with us on horseback.'[105] Despite being a clergyman, he made no comment in his diary about the Christian morality of gentlemen keeping mistresses.

Two years earlier Woodforde had seen a play at Covent Garden in London and afterwards noted: 'I met many fine women (common prostitutes) in my return home [to his inn] and very impudent indeed.'[106] Men of all classes resorted to prostitutes, of which there was no shortage, particularly in London and in seaports like Portsmouth and Plymouth. A directory to Covent Garden prostitutes, *Harris's List*, was published annually from 1757 until 1795 when the publisher was jailed for a year for indecency. Appearing around Christmastime, it reputedly sold up to eight thousand copies annually in brothels, taverns and even reputable bookstores.[107] Its entries gave clues as to why the women were prostitutes – some had escaped from abusive husbands, while others were abandoned mistresses. Their rates ranged from a few shillings to a few guineas, and one of the cheaper prostitutes in Harris's 1789 directory, charging one guinea, was Miss Pheby Cambell from Norfolk, evidently seeking a better life in the city:

Miss Pheby C—mb—ll, No. 9, Holland Street, near Wardour Street ... About the month of May or June, this young lass arrived in town from Norfolk, unhackneyed in the Cyprian Game [prostitution], she now treads the common path ... Her age is now only twenty one, and she is both good tempered and able to sing an excellent song, no one can imagine so many shillings badly spent in her company.[108]

Young women flocked to the cities to find work as servants and to seek their fortune, but very often turned to prostitution, especially if they were abused by their employer and then thrown out when pregnant. 'Mr. Meyrick ... is said to have seduced the servant girl of the house where he lives,' Nelly Weeton wrote from Liverpool in 1809. 'He is so much disliked in many respects, that whether the report be true or false, people seem determined to believe it.'[109] The Newcastle seaman George Watson certainly believed the prostitutes at Portsmouth to be seduced and abandoned women:

This is always a stirring place, and particularly so in war time, owing to its being such a rendezvous for his Majesty's ships, and transports, for the same reason it is a place notoriously wicked young women flock here from all corners of our island, and some from Ireland, and live by prostitution, I mean women that are previously seduced, and cast upon the world, abandoned by the villains that caused their ruin: it would be absurd to suppose any truly modest girl, though brought to the greatest extremity of penury and want, would deliberately come hither to join herself to such an unblushing set of wretches as pervade the Point at Portsmouth, where a modest woman would be as hard to find as a Mermaid.[110]

Prostitution was not illegal, but when visiting Bath in the summer of 1779, Woodforde was concerned about the plight of two young women: 'After tea this evening I took a walk in the fields and met in my walk two girls, the eldest about 17, the other about 15, both common prostitutes even at that early age. I gave them some good advice to consider the end of things. I gave them o.1.o.'[111] In London a few years later, he went to a service at the Magdalen Hospital for Penitent Prostitutes: 'we took coach and went to Magdalen Chapel in St. Georges Fields being Sunday and heard prayers read and a sermon. Very excellent singing at Magdalen Chapel. The women had a thin green curtain before them all the time, one of them played the organ.'[112] The Magdalen Hospital had been established in 1758, and its chapel was a fashionable place to be seen on Sundays.

The preface to the 1789 edition of *Harris's List* claimed that prostitution prevented crime: 'What villainies do they not prevent? What plots, what combinations, do they not dissolve? Clasped in the arms of beauty, the factious malcontent forgets the black workings of his soul.'[113] Furthermore, it was stated, their earnings were beneficial to the community: 'The toyman, the mercer, the milener, the play, and opera, nay even the parish church (sometimes) is gladdened with the chink of their gold.'[114] This was special pleading to keep pimps and brothels in business. Life was wretched for women who ended up like those witnessed by Francis Place near his house at Charing Cross in London: 'Along the front of Privy Gardens [now Whitehall near Downing Street] . . . there was an old wall . . . At night there were a set of prostitutes along this wall, so horridly ragged, dirty and disgusting that I doubt much there are now any such in any part of London. These miserable wretches used to take any customer who would pay them twopence, behind the wall.'[115]

Too often young prostitutes were servants abandoned by men like Charles Fothergill, a younger son of a successful Yorkshire family involved in farming, the law, medicine and manufacturing. His father manufactured ivory products such as combs and toothbrushes, but Charles had literary ambitions. Having already squandered a legacy and fallen into debt, in 1805 he was in Yorkshire collecting material and subscribers for a proposed natural and antiquarian history of the county that he had decided to undertake. His private diary reveals that during his excursions, he preyed on several young women, with little thought for the consequences. He stayed several times at the White Swan inn at Middleham in the Yorkshire Dales, where that August he was drawn to a servant girl 'J . . .' – probably Jane – whose 'temperament was very warm and easily worked upon: I succeeded quite as far as I wished this evening'.[116]

The next evening he tried his luck once more: 'It was dark when I got to the inn again: successful with my nymph; partly make her promise to admit me. In the middle of the night I rise and grope my way to her room; find another girl sleeping with her . . . I stay about two hours and spend the time in great part as I had wished.'[117] Fothergill related similar incidents, as in October: 'From my going to bed 'till 4 o'clock in the morning I enjoyed my nymph tho' my pleasure was not a little damped by occasional qualms of conscience on her account.'[118] Without reliable contraceptives, what was for Fothergill a bit of fun with an unmarried servant girl may well have ended in pregnancy for her, with its devastating consequences.

Although prostitutes and mistresses were tolerated by much of society, homosexuality and bestiality were feared, abhorred and illegal. In the summer of 1810, William Holland was utterly shocked to learn that his manservant George had committed bestiality, which was a capital crime. He spoke to George, telling him that he had to leave: 'he cried most bitterly and it indeed affected me very much. I then told him that I hoped what had passed would sink deep into his heart and that he would fall down on his knees and pray to his God (whom he had most grievously offended) that he might repent of his great wickedness . . . I paid him his wages and he left me overwhelmed with tears.'[119] A few days later, Holland met his friend the Reverend John Mathew of nearby Kilve and apologised for cancelling an invitation. The reason, he explained, was having to dismiss his servant. When he told him the details, Mathew was sympathetic:

> He approved of all I had done yet was in doubt (he said) on account of the effect it might have on society, whether I should have him go off

without prosecuting him. I answer'd that as soon as I came to the knowledge of the business I discharged him, but (wretch as he was) and horrid as the deed was, I felt a disinclination to hang him. Well (he returned), you have got rid of him. Perhaps it is as well.[120]

THREE

———◆———

TODDLER TO
TEENAGER

... she was moreover noisy and wild, hated confinement and cleanliness, and loved nothing so well in the world as rolling down the green slope at the back of the house. Such was Catherine Morland at ten. At fifteen appearances were mending ... Her love of dirt gave way to an inclination for finery.

Northanger Abbey, by Jane Austen

Walking was one early challenge for a toddler, but the initial steps may well have been a bruising experience without the protection of fitted carpets that are commonplace in today's homes. Various devices to help young children walk included harnesses for support and trolleys they could grasp, the ancestors of modern babywalkers, but by the early nineteenth century medical opinion was turning against such aids. 'Before infants attempt to walk alone,' one writer recommended,

they should first learn to crawl: by feeling the want of their legs, they will gradually try to use them. With this intention they might be placed on a large carpet, and surrounded by toys: here they will busily employ themselves, move and extend their limbs, or roll about to reach their playthings ... While in the nursery, they may be taught to rise from the floor, by laying hold of chairs; and, if occasionally supported under the arms, they will easily learn to stand erect; but they should never be raised up by one arm only.[1]

This was good advice for families who could afford carpets, nurseries and toys, but irrelevant to those poorer families who, through lack of resources, allowed their children to fend for themselves.

Babies who had wet-nurses learned their first words with these women and were influenced by their way of speech. Likewise, live-in servants contributed to a melting-pot of language, with people of contrasting levels of education and manners of speech in the same household for toddlers to copy. Regional accents and dialect were very distinctive two centuries ago, and even dialects of adjoining counties were noticeably different. When Elizabeth Ham's family was living in Weymouth, Dorset, where her father ran a brewery, one brother stayed with relatives in neighbouring Somerset, causing her to comment: 'My brother William ... spoke broad Somerset.'[2]

Accents from other regions were not encountered every day. When men from all parts of the country were brought together on board naval or merchant ships, the diversity of dialect was striking. Going to sea for the first time, the young seaman Robert Hay was amazed by 'all the provincial dialects which prevail between Landsend and John O'Groats'.[3] During his travels through England each summer, John Byng was irritated rather than charmed by the different ways of speaking. 'I enquired if the river was navigable to this place,' he noted at Ringwood, Hampshire, in 1782, 'but could not explain myself, till a man told me I certainly meant *navigal* and that it was not.'[4] He was impatient not just with regional accents, but with the manner of speaking, as in the Midlands (near Castle Donington) seven years later: 'The slowness of answer in this county is very irritable; when I stop to ask the plainest question, as the name of our road to, any village, they being [begin] with "Why as to that" "Let me consider" "You seem to be out of your way" "And so I was saying". Here I ride off; for life were not long enough to hear them out.'[5]

In 1805 the twenty-five-year-old American Benjamin Silliman arrived in England to further his studies in science. He had initially read law at Yale College and then studied chemistry and natural philosophy – in time he would become a foremost figure in science. On his return to America in 1806, he published detailed observations and impressions of his travels, including his thoughts on language. In May 1805 he had been at Tideswell in Derbyshire, virtually the centre of England. 'They speak the language with many peculiarities of pronunciation,' he noted, 'and with a considerable number of words which we never hear in America.'[6]

A few months later, he visited Cambridge university, where he was informed that as he spoke the English language so perfectly, he could not possibly have been educated in America. He thought this was an inexcusable error on the part of supposedly educated people: 'They ... know that the Anglo-Americans speak the English language; but they imagine that it is a colonial dialect, with a corrupt and barbarous pronunciation, and a vocabulary, interspersed with strange and unknown terms of transatlantic manufacture.'[7]

Silliman reckoned that Americans had the advantage, as everyone there could understand each other, whereas the 'provincial dialects ... render the language of the common people of one county in England in a considerable degree unintelligible to those of another, even of the country gentlemen'.[8] He himself was usually taken for a Londoner: 'a well-educated American may travel from London to John a Groat's house [Scotland], and thence to the Land's-end [Cornwall], and every where pass for a Londoner; this is the universal presumption concerning him'.[9]

Adam Walker, a travelling lecturer and writer, described the dialect of his home county:

A speciment of the Westmoreland Dialect I shall give in one of that Country's Riddles:

> I went toth' wood an I gat it,
> I sat me doon en I leakt at it;
> En when e saa I cudn't git't,
> I teakt heam we ma.

Made in English thus:

I went to the wood, and I got it,
I sat me down and I look'd at it;
And when I saw I could not get it,
I took it home with me.

It is perhaps unnecessary to say, that the solution is, 'a thorn in the foot.'[10]

The accents of boys sent away to boarding schools or perhaps to sea would have become diluted, though even as an adult Nelson was said to have retained his 'true Norfolk drawl'.[11] Jane Austen and her siblings must have learned to speak with a north Hampshire accent, but through education, travel and socialising, they most likely dropped the use of dialect words. Adam Walker was of the opinion that dialects were becoming less distinctive, something he blamed on the influence of increasing numbers of people travelling round England. In 1791 he described the situation in northern England: 'I could once have traced the exact extent of the various dialects of England, and had them coloured in a map. I traced the limits of the Saxon burr (or what is called the Newcastle burr) from Haddington in Scotland to Chester-Le-Street in the County of Durham, and made its western boundary the mountains that divide Northumberland from Cumberland. This singular croak is produced by pronouncing the r with the middle of the tongue instead of the tip.'[12]

Also in 1791 John Walker brought out a dictionary, partly in an effort to improve pronunciation. It became influential, particularly with the middle classes – what Beau Brummell was to high fashion, Walker was to spoken English. The dictionary included a section on the pronunciation faults of Londoners, such as 'Not sounding h where it ought to be sounded, and inversely' and 'Pronouncing w for v, and inversely'.[13] His examples highlight how language has changed over two centuries, since he advised that h should be silent in words like 'humour' ('umour) and 'hospital' ('ospital), whereas h, he said, should be clearly pronounced in a word like 'whet' to distinguish it from 'wet'. In his advice not to confuse w and v, he pointed out that many Londoners pronounced words like 'veal' and 'vinegar' as 'weal' and 'winegar' and conversely pronounced words like 'wine' and 'wind' as 'vine' and 'vind'. Despite his efforts, wide variations persisted in the way English was spoken.

George III was in fact the first Hanoverian monarch to speak English as his main language, declaring to Parliament after ascending to the throne in 1760: 'Born and educated in this country, I glory in the name of Briton.'[14] The upper classes adopted affected forms of talking, which was mocked by Jane Austen in *Northanger Abbey*, where the heroine, Catherine Morland, says, 'I cannot speak well enough to be unintelligible', to which the well-read young clergyman, Henry Tilney, replies, 'Bravo! – an excellent satire on modern language.'

Having learned to walk and talk, children would have learned games and played with different toys, which all too often meant improvising with available materials; anything from words to water. In October 1808 Jane Austen's nephews George and Edward were staying with her at Southampton, while in mourning for their recently deceased mother. 'George is almost a new acquaintance to me,' Jane wrote to Cassandra, 'and I find him in a different way as engaging as Edward. We do not want amusement; bilbocatch, at which George is indefatigable, spillikins, paper ships, riddles, conundrums, and cards, with watching the flow and ebb of the river, and now and then a stroll out, keep us well employed.'[15] Those traditional games, now regarded with nostalgia, included seeing whose handmade paper ships sailed furthest before sinking. In bilbocatch, or 'cup and ball', a ball was caught in a cup of wood or ivory, while in spillikins, a bundle of thin sticks was spilled on to a table, and players tried to pick up a stick without disturbing the rest.

Other toys included marbles and the spinning top or whipping top: 'Boys have different kinds of tops, some which are kept up by whipping, some made to spin by winding string round them . . . It is curious, too, to observe the humming top, the sound occasioned by the wind rushing into the hole, which there always is on one side of these tops.'[16] The Reverend Holland remarked on his convalescent son playing with such a toy: 'Little William whipping his top in the passage for he must not stir out as he has taken physick.'[17] On another occasion he noted: 'Mr. Blake call'd here about his son Johnny, but he permitted him to continue with William till the evening and they have been playing and jumping, and flying a kite and at marbles and various things.'[18] Holland doted on his young son, born when he was fifty-one and his wife forty-seven, and left a vivid account of him in his diary.

More and more toys were available for wealthier parents to purchase, some of which served moral or educational purposes, such as geographical jigsaw puzzles. There were also increasing numbers of books for children, some to entertain and others evangelical in tone. Newspapers carried advertisements for such books, and one in the *Northampton Mercury* in April 1772 announced: 'Books for the Instruction and Amusement of Children, Printed for T. CARNAN and F. NEWBERRY, junior, at No. 65, in St. Paul's Church-Yard, London.'[19] The long list included *Tom Thumb's Folio*, *The London Cries* and *Nurse Truelove's Christmas Box*, all priced at one penny, while for sixpence *The History of Little Goody Two-shoes* and *Fables in Verse, by Abraham Aesop, Esq.* were offered. Collections of nursery rhymes were also sold cheaply in little books. Children often learned nursery rhymes from their parents, but new rhymes such as 'There was an old woman who lived in a shoe' and 'The Queen of Hearts' were composed throughout the eighteenth and into the nineteenth centuries.

Young girls were expected to play with suitable toys like dolls, and Elizabeth Ham remembered once being left alone with a friend: 'We were so absorbed in our interesting occupation, making a frock for the doll from a piece of *real India* gingham, that we took no note of the fire.'[20] The fire dwindled to nothing, their candle was accidentally extinguished, and they were left terrified in the darkness until the adults returned. Often, though, girls preferred boys' toys and games, and as a five-year-old in rural Somerset in the 1780s, Elizabeth had freedom to play:

> When not in school I ran wild with my playmate. The unoccupied saw-pit made a delightful house; then in the summer we could play under the bridge on the turnpike road. The little clear stream was then so shallow as

to leave a gravelly strand by which we could pass from one flowery meadow to the other without being seen from the road. There was one field where in haymaking time we had a delightful hidden bower round the bole of a large tree that grew out of a double hedge. We always ran home after the load of hay that we might ride back to the field on the empty wagon.[21]

Some girls may have yearned for boyish pursuits, but to modern eyes the young boys of the time resemble girls in contemporary illustrations, because they wore dresses or tunics, making it difficult to deduce a child's sex. In an Old Bailey trial in 1811, relating to the abduction of a three-year-old boy, his clothes and those of his five-year-old sister were described: 'The boy had a white frock, black skirt, a blue pinafore, and black half boots; the little girl, she had a light buff-coloured frock on, a black skirt, a dark coloured pinafore, and half boots.'[22] Boys' hair could be shorter, but in this case it was 'turned up on the right side; his hair rather wanted cutting'.[23]

When they were about four or five years of age, in what was sometimes a formal ceremony to mark the transition from babyhood into boyhood, boys were breeched. They gave up dresses and instead wore breeches and short jackets. Girls likewise lost their freedom. Their skirts became longer, more like women's clothing, and they were fitted with whalebone stays to ensure a good figure, though this practice was waning. When Elizabeth Ham was nine or ten years old, her wild childhood days ended:

> I was at this time a little rustic, uncouth child ... The first reformation made in my appearance was effected by a staymaker. I was stood on the window-seat, whilst a man measured me for the machine [stays], which, in consideration of my youth, was to be only what was called half-boned, that is, instead of having the bones placed as close as they could lie, an interval the breadth of one was left vacant between each. Notwithstanding, the first day of wearing them was very nearly purgatory.[24]

If their clothing was at times akin to purgatory, some of the punishments meted out to children for wrongdoing seem brutal. In May

1803 Holland noted his six-year-old son's misbehaviour: 'William saying his lesson to his Mama but he has been very unruly and I have been obliged to strap him.'[25] Four months later he pilfered nectarines and peaches from trees in the garden. 'I gave my boy two or three straps,' his father recorded, 'but as he told the truth and promised never to do the like again I did not chastise him any further.'[26]

Cases of extreme cruelty to children were not tolerated, though. In 1814 one couple from the Yorkshire village of Cottingham were prosecuted for such an offence:

> At the late Quarter Sessions at Beverley, the following case of cruelty came before the court:— *George Clarke*, and *Elizabeth*, his wife, were indicted for an assault on their servant, a boy of eight or nine years age. The parties were chimney sweepers at Cottingham, and had bought the child of a travelling tinker for 6s. and a pair of shoes ... Several witnesses deposed to seeing the boy tied up in a stable by both his wrists, and there suffered to hang for a long time ... Another mode of treatment ... consisted in tying his leg to a horse's leg – by this means preventing both from making their escape. As the horse moved for the sake of pasture, he dragged his companion after him; and by these and other means his back was dreadfully bruised and lacerated. Both defendants were convicted; the husband was sentenced to imprisonment and hard labour for one year, and the wife for one month.[27]

This abused boy may not have been the tinker's son, but a stolen child, because when babies and young children were seized, they were almost impossible to locate. *The Times* mentioned one such kidnap: 'This being the first day of May [1799], Mrs MONTAGUE will give her annual entertainment of roast meat and plum-pudding to the Chimney-sweepers of the Metropolis, in the court-yard of her house in Portman-square, in commemoration of discovering her child among them long after it had been trepanned [stolen] away.'[28] Elizabeth Montagu was a wealthy widow who gave annual feasts for the chimney boys, but the kidnap tale was a myth – her only son had died at the age of sixteen months.[29]

Children were stolen for various reasons, such as by couples desperate for a family, to be used as cheap labour on land or at sea or even for selling into slavery. In June 1789 *The Times* described an abduction in Lambeth:

> A fine little boy, the son of an eminent tradesman, was taken from the gate of the garden, to which he had walked, and which unfortunately happened to be open. He was about three years of age. The woman who committed this theft was seen by several persons on the Black Friars Road, with the Child on her back crying bitterly, and being better dressed than it could be supposed she was able to afford, she was questioned by several people whose it was.[30]

The woman had a convincing story, claiming the boy was 'a Mr Smith's in the Temple [London], who with his wife were gone on faster than she could walk, on account of the rain'.[31] Thirty minutes later, the boy was missed: 'the usual enquiries were made in the neighbourhood—but without success, and the Child is probably lost for ever ... What makes this peculiarly distressing, is, that the poor little boy was an only son, and at the death of his Grandfather will become entitled to an Estate of *fourteen hundred pounds* per annum, in Yorkshire.'[32]

Such crimes were so heinous, *The Times* suggested, that the pillory was insufficient punishment – the death penalty was needed. Gypsies and other itinerant people were the prime suspects: 'Persons have been dispatched to all places where it is probable these thieves dwell, and hand bills distributed among the Gypsies in the vicinity of London; and an application made to the King of those gangs, offering a large reward for the Child.'[33] It was the newspaper's belief that a market for stolen children existed, especially babies, who were intended for slavery or prostitution: 'The general opinion is, that those Children are sent down into a cheap part of the Country, and reared to about nine years of age, when they are shipped off, and sold to the Barbary States, who are excellent customers for the females in particular, if there be any signs of growing beauty.'[34]

Another London abduction was that of Thomas Dillone, the three-year-old son of a warehouseman in Thames Street. On 18

November 1811 his mother left Thomas and his sister Rebecca with Mary Cox, a fruiterer in St Martin's Lane. While Mary was busy with other customers, a woman purchased some apples and then enticed both children away. 'I ran to the door, and the children was not there,' Mary reported. 'I ran half-way up St. Martin's-lane; I called Beckey, Beckey, they did not answer; I returned down to No. 11, to the yard, and called, Beckey. I did not find them there. I did not think of their being stolen away; I ran down to the wharf, and as I was crossing of Swan-lane, I saw the little girl returning with a penny plumb cake in her hand, and an apple.'[35]

The woman who had taken Thomas was a Mrs Magnes, and that same night 'she left town [London] for Gosport [Hampshire], with the boy, having *rigged* him out according to the taste of her husband, with a new dress, and a black hat and feather'.[36] Her husband Richard had recently returned home after a long period of absence while serving as a gunner in the Royal Navy. He was desperate to meet his son Richard for the first time – a son that his wife had invented to please him. He was overjoyed to see Thomas Dillone, believing him to be his son, but back in London the parish churchwardens distributed notices offering a hundred-guinea reward for the child's return, which led to the deception being uncovered in late December.

In rural Somerset, William Holland was struck by the idea that 'In London tis the practice to teach children to mention their names and the street they live in, which is a good method lest by some accident or other they should run out or be lost in the croud that pass along constantly.'[37] He was therefore pleased that his young son William could state where he lived in the local dialect: 'tis to Overstowey near Bridgewater Somersetshire'.[38] William was using the common West Country construction 'it is to' rather than 'it is at'.

A few days afterwards Holland noted: 'My little boy [is] saying his lesson to his Mama in the study by my elbow, he spells well and will read very soon, not much above three years old, he is a quick child.'[39] When he was abducted, Thomas Dillone had been the same age and was wearing a frock, as he was too young to be breeched. Once they were breeched, boys of the middle class and above started their education. Most began with reading and were then taught writing, and by the time he was six years old Holland's son was learning both skills: 'After breakfast I had William up to write and his Mama heard him read.'[40] Education, particularly the ability to read and write, was a prized asset that was passed on to other family members – parents taught their children, who in turn helped each other.

Either at school or at home, children were taught to write on slates with soft slate pencils or else they made their first letters in sand, progressing when older to paper, pencils and pen and ink. Slates and pencils were also used for rough notes and drawing, something that William Jones kept to hand: 'I frequently have a slate and pencil by my bed-side, and when I wake, at perhaps far too early an hour to rise, I scribble down any thoughts or reflexions which present themselves to my mind.'[41] Black lead pencil production was initially a cottage industry, based around Keswick in the Lake District, the only place in Europe with deposits of solid graphite. The graphite core of pencils used on paper is still called 'lead', because it was originally thought to be a type of lead. In the late eighteenth century a Frenchman, Nicolas Conté, invented a pencil with a lead made from a mixture of crushed graphite and clay. Pencils were relatively expensive, usually sixpence each, and they were bought singly, as in December 1800 when Holland wrote in his diary: 'I walked to [Nether] Stowey, bought a pencil and returned.'[42]

Pen and ink had been used for centuries, and for children and adults alike the technology had hardly changed. Quill pens, usually made from goose or similar feathers, were the norm, although pens with metal nibs were making an appearance. Whatever the kind of pen, it needed constant dipping into an inkwell, and after writing about a dozen lines, nibs of quill pens needed trimming with a small knife – giving us the term 'penknife'. Writing to his wife Sarah from HMS *Minotaur* when moored in Yarmouth Roads, William Wilkinson commented: 'I am obliged to borrow this ink and paper, and am writing with the back of the pen.'[43] This was one way of prolonging the use of a quill pen rather than trimming it.

Because quill pens wore out, there was a perpetual market for goose feathers. Many came from a traditional production area in the Lincolnshire Fens, which one visitor there described:

The geese are plucked five times in the year; the first plucking is at *Lady-Day*, for feathers and quills, and the same is renewed, for feathers only, four times more between that and *Michaelmas*. The old geese submit quietly to the operation, but the young ones are very noisy and unruly. I once saw this performed, and observed that goslings of six weeks old were not spared; for their tails were plucked ... to habituate them early to what they were to come to. If the season proves cold, numbers of geese die by this barbarous custom.[44]

Ink could be bought in shops, but many households made their own. In 1805 a mineral agent called William Jenkin wrote down his recipe:

¾ lb. of Alleppo Galls – bruised (but not small)
4 oz. of Clean Coperas – 4 oz. of Gum Arabick
1 oz. of Roche Allum –
Put the above in 3 quarts of rain water; shake it often for about 6 or 7 days.[45]

Aleppo galls were good-quality oak galls that formed a substance which etched the ink into the paper, while the other ingredients provided extra colour and diluted the mixture. To stop the ink from smudging, it could be dried quickly with blotting paper.

While parchment or vellum was preferred for some official documents, paper was used for most other purposes. It was manufactured by hand, largely using finely shredded rags. This produced a paper that was much more durable than modern types made from wood pulp. Paper was sold in several grades from very fine to coarse, and it varied in colour (the whiter the better) and price. Hot-pressed paper was finished by being rolled between heated rollers, resulting in a higher-quality paper with a smoother surface. In 1775 Parson Woodforde noted: 'For a quire of paper of a man at the door, pd. o.1.o',[46] and over a decade later he paid the same in a shop for 'a quire of black edg'd letter paper'.[47] A quire was a bundle of twenty-four sheets, and two quires cost roughly a week's wages for a housemaid, far more expensive than paper today.

Well-to-do young boys might start their education at home,

taught by their parents, as with young William Holland, or tutored by a governess, alongside any sisters. Next, they might attend a small private school or academy. In 1782, when Carl Moritz was travelling through England, he visited one such establishment:

> I found means to see the regulation of one seminary of learning, here called an academy. Of these places of education, there is a prodigious number in London and its vicinity; though, notwithstanding their pompous names, they are, in reality, nothing more than small schools, set up by private persons, for children and young people ... From forty to fifty pounds [per annum] is the most that is generally paid in these academies ... It is, in general, the clergy, who have small incomes, who set up these schools both in town and country.[48]

This is precisely what Jane Austen's father George did for several years at the Steventon parsonage, where he taught reading, writing and the classics to his own sons (but not his daughters) alongside a handful of fee-paying pupils, some of them boarders.

Older boys could next attend a local grammar school, most of which had been set up after the dissolution of the monasteries as charitable endowments by wealthy benefactors, teaching Latin grammar to the virtual exclusion of anything else so as to enable pupils to enter Oxford or Cambridge University where Latin was also predominant. By the late eighteenth century many of these schools also taught ancient Greek and subjects like mathematics and literature, as well as oratory and team sports such as cricket. Some grammar schools were founded even earlier, in the medieval period, including Winchester College (1382) and Eton College (1440), which was granted a monopoly 10 miles around Eton 'so it may excel all other grammar schools ... and be called the lady mother and mistress of all other grammar schools'.[49]

Almost every English town had an endowed grammar school. They were open to the public with a public management, unlike privately run schools. However, the landed elite in particular chose to send their sons as boarders to a select number of these public grammar schools, notably Eton, Harrow, Winchester, Westminster, Rugby,

Charterhouse and Shrewsbury, and in England the term 'public school' came to describe, bizarrely, such exclusive, private, fee-paying boarding schools for the privileged minority. When on his walking tour of England, Moritz found himself at Eton:

I passed Eton College, one of the first public schools in England ... I suppose it was during the hour of recreation, or in playtime, when I got to Eton; for I saw the boys in the yard before the college, which was inclosed by a low wall, in great numbers, walking and running up and down. Their dress struck me particularly: from the biggest to the least, they all wore black cloaks, or gowns, over coloured clothes; through which there was an aperture for their arms. They also wore, besides, a square hat, or cap, that seemed to be covered with velvet ... They were differently employed: some talking together, some playing, and some had their books in their hands, and were reading; but I was soon obliged to get out of their sight, they stared at me so, as I came along, all over dust, with my stick in my hand.[50]

Connections with influential people were needed to get children into these public schools, and William Holland was thrilled when, in 1808, his ten-year-old son William was accepted by Charterhouse in London: 'He was nominated by Mr Windham [an Eton-educated politician] by the application of my good friend Mrs Benwell and Mrs Windham both which ladies I was well acquainted with in my younger days ... It is a Glorious Act and deserves to be recorded, this has settled the education of my son William for the time to come and [I] hope it will be the foundation of his future advancement in this life.'[51] As well as admitting fee-paying scholars, Charterhouse accepted poor boys, primarily the sons of impecunious gentlemen. That same year his friend Mrs Penelope Benwell (née Loveday) became Mrs Hind when she married John Hind, vicar of Findon in Sussex – her previous husband was the Reverend William Benwell, who had died in 1796.

A few years later, in 1813, Holland was even happier on hearing from the Dean of Christ Church, Oxford, who promised

a studentship ... for my son as soon as he can arrange matters for that purpose ... so this is an important thing indeed. He is sure of patronage of the Dean, and studentships are in fact fellowships, they succeed to [church] livings ... and all this I have gained through my very valuable and zealous friend Mrs. Hind and not only this but his appointment to the Charter House was through the same channel. Mrs. Hind was the first mover, and her cousin Mrs. Wyndham [Windham] took it up.[52]

While boys might be sent to school, girls were generally taught at home – if at all – by governesses or by their mothers, who might themselves have received minimal education. In the summer of 1812, Nelly Weeton moved to High Royd in Yorkshire as a governess for the Armitage family. In a letter to a friend, she described her status:

> A *governess* is almost shut out of society; not choosing to associate with servants, and not being treated as an equal by the heads of the house or their visitors, she must possess some fortitude and strength of mind to render herself tranquil or happy; but indeed, the master or mistress of a house, if they have any goodness of heart, would take pains to prevent her feeling her inferiority. For my own part, I have no cause of just complaint; but I know some that are treated in a most mortifying manner.[53]

As a child, Nelly's own desire to learn had been stifled, even though her widowed mother was running a school in Upholland:

> my mother continually checked any propensity I shewed to writing or composing; representing to me what a useless being I should prove if I were allowed to give up my time to writing or reading, when domestic duties were likely to have so frequent a call upon me. 'It is very likely, my dear girl,' she would often say, 'that you will have to earn your livelihood, at least in great measure; and a wretched subsistence do they obtain who have it to earn by their literary abilities! Or should you become a wife, think in what a ragged, neglected state your family would be if you gave up much of your time to books.'[54]

In Somerset, Holland grumbled about one educated girl, Elizabeth Poole: 'This little girl is very clever and learns surprizingly and writes Latin letters but I should not like any woman the better for understanding Latin and Greek. All pedantick learning of this kind makes them conceited. I do not approve of the manner of boys in petticoats.'[55] The same age as his son William, the two children enjoyed playing together whenever she was visiting her uncle Tom Poole at nearby Nether Stowey. A few years later, when she was fourteen, Holland elaborated: 'She has a thirst after knowledge of every kind to the greatest degree. She has made great proficiency in Latin and Greek and is making the same advance in French and Italian ... It is a pity she was not a boy for then such studies would turn to better account ... I know not where this will end but is not a likely mode to get her well married.'[56]

Holland's own daughter Margaret was given a basic education at home, with private tutors for music and French, but she never married. In spite of her education, Elizabeth did marry in 1825, at the age of twenty-eight, becoming the wife of John Sandford, Archdeacon at Wells in Somerset.[57] In Nelly Weeton's view, women deserved equal opportunities: 'Why are not females permitted to study physic, divinity, astronomy, &c., &c., with their attendants, chemistry, botany, logic, mathematics, &c. To be sure the mere study is not prohibited, but the practise is in great measure. Who would employ a female physician? who would listen to a female divine, except to ridicule? I could myself almost laugh at the idea.'[58]

Young ladies were expected to become accomplished with practical skills. Education for girls was viewed as a luxury, though by Jane Austen's childhood there was an increasing number of fee-paying 'dame schools' for young girls and boys. The standard of such establishments varied hugely. Many were run by older women like Nelly's mother, who lacked qualifications and could not earn a living any other way. The term 'dame' was a respectful way of addressing these women, who might have no claim to rank other than schoolmistress.

At the age of seven Jane Austen was sent away to Oxford with her sister Cassandra and her cousin Jane Cooper to be taught by a private tutor.[59] In the summer of 1783, after the tutor and her pupils moved to Southampton, all three girls fell ill with typhus, and Jane Austen nearly died. She and her sister recuperated at home and then joined their cousin in 1785 at the Reading Ladies' Boarding School, but were removed at the end of the following year, putting a stop to their tuition. By the time Jane Austen was eleven years old, her formal education was over.[60]

If educating females was considered pointless, educating the poorest in society, both boys and girls, generated real fear that it might encourage bloody revolution, as in France, or, at the very least, a lack of deference to the elite. This opinion was not universal, and many charity schools for the poor had long been established by the Society for the Promotion of Christian Knowledge. With the rapid population growth and movement into towns, increased worries about the lack of schooling for poor and destitute children led to the formation of many more charity schools and Sunday schools. Some were free of charge, others charged a penny or twopence weekly.

In the early years of the nineteenth century nonconformist churches actively set up Sunday schools and charity schools. The main group of nonconformist schools were the British Schools, established by the British and Foreign School Society, in which Joseph Lancaster was especially prominent with his Lancasterian system of schools. Following this nonconformist lead, the Church of England – through the National Society for Promoting Religious Education – began to found schools of its own for the poor that became known as National Schools and in which the clergyman Andrew Bell played a leading role.[61]

While touring the Midlands in 1790, John Byng expressed his prejudice against schools for the lower classes: 'I have met some of the newly-adopted Sunday-schools today, and seen others in their schools; I am point blank against these institutions; the poor shou'd not read, and of writing I never heard, for them, the use.'[62] In July 1802 William Holland took an opposite view, in support of the local Sunday school at Over Stowey, convinced that it could teach the poor to be good Christians and know their place:

We had some talk about Sunday schools yesterday. Mr King [a wealthy physician] thought that they did harm, that plowmen were better without learning. I answered that I could not think that the teaching them of their duty could do any harm; obliging children to go to Church, teaching them to read and say their Catechism, to give them some sense of Religion and a due subordination to their superiors must be of some service in these times.[63]

Five years later the Cornishman Davies Giddy, Member of Parliament for Bodmin in Cornwall, spoke during a House of Commons debate about the Parochial Schools Bill, which attempted (but failed) to make all parishes provide free education for the labouring poor. A renowned scientist, Giddy had himself received a privileged education, but he was unconvinced about mass education:

it would ... be found to be prejudicial to their morals and happiness; it would teach them to despise their lot in life, instead of making them good servants in agriculture, and other laborious employments to which their rank in society had destined them; instead of teaching them subordination, it would render them factious and refractory ... it would enable them to read seditious pamphlets, vicious books, and publications against Christianity; it would render them insolent to their superiors.[64]

Despite such opposition, goodwill increased towards charity schools, and in Cornwall in 1811 contributions were sought for a Sunday school at Wheal Alfred, which the mineral agent William Jenkin outlined:

Captains [of mines] John Davey and Samuel Grose (the two principal agents in Wheal Alfred Mine) having observed the profligacy [lack of decency] of the Children of many of the Labourers in that Mine, – and particularly of those who cannot read – have begun a Sundays School and have from 250 to 300 Boys and Girls under their care. But finding the expense of Books and rewards for the meritorious to be too heavy for them, they are under the necessity of soliciting the aid of those Gentlemen who are interested in the Mine, and of others who may feel disposed to assist such a praiseworthy undertaking ... W. H. Hore [Hoare], a banker in London, is amongst the list of subscribers with a £5 donation. The number of Men, Boys and Girls employed in the Mine is about 1000.[65]

Most charity schools were obsessed with religious teaching and moral improvement, though children did acquire elementary literacy skills. James Lackington was born in Wellington, Somerset, in 1746, the eldest of a family of eleven children. He was apprenticed to a shoemaker in Taunton at the age of fourteen, later moving to Bristol and in 1773 to London. Taught to read by the Methodists, he became obsessed with books, and with a legacy of £10 from his grandfather and a loan of £5 from the Methodists, he established what became a thriving bookselling business. His was a rare success story. Most lower-class children never realised their potential, as was the case with Thomas Carter, who worked as a tailor in often wretched circumstances. His autobiography, published in 1845, reveals a highly intelligent man, trapped by poverty.[66]

In 1816 witnesses before a Parliamentary Select Committee testified that education was improving the general behaviour of 'the lower orders' in London. Henry Althens described the East London Auxiliary Sunday School Union Society, which had ten Sunday schools teaching nearly 1300 children: 'First, they are taught to read, and our main object is to teach them to read the Bible, and we exhort them to attend to all the moral duties of life. Our chief object is to convey religious instruction to the children, believing that to be the foundation of all moral good.'[67] Writing was taught only in the evenings, as a reward, more often to boys than to girls, who were considered better suited to needlework.

It was reckoned that about half of all children in England received no education at all, not even at Sunday schools which gave children an opportunity for education on their one day off work. The concept of teenagers, a time of adolescence, did not exist until the twentieth century. Females of teenage years were either working, seeking husbands, or both, but rarely being educated. Charity schools taught boys until they were fourteen, the usual age to start an apprenticeship, though many went to work before then: the poorer the family, the shorter the childhood. By thirteen or fourteen, if not sooner, childhood for the majority was over. Only a privileged few, like William Holland's son, remained in education.

For boys of the upper and middle classes who did not prolong their education, joining the Royal Navy was a popular next step. Nelson joined as a captain's servant in 1771 at the age of twelve, but some boys were even younger. Jane Austen had two brothers, Francis (Frank) and Charles, who joined the navy. Francis attended the Royal Naval Academy at Portsmouth from the age of twelve and joined his first ship two years later, while Charles went to the same Academy in 1791 at the same age and joined his first ship three years later. Jane had four other brothers. The oldest, James, went to Oxford University and then became a clergyman. George, a sickly child who suffered from fits, was looked after by foster-parents, funded by the Austens. Edward was adopted by distant cousins, Thomas Knight and his wife, and inherited a fortune, while Henry, Jane's favourite brother, had a varied career. After Oxford University, he joined the militia and later became an army agent and a banker, but after his bank failed, he too went into the Church and spent the rest of his life as a clergyman.

Most poor children needed to start earning money as early as possible, because their meagre wages were essential to their family's survival. In 1816 Frederick Augustus Earle, a clerk in London's parish of St Giles, reckoned that countless young girls were prostitutes. The previous week about thirty had been arrested, and 'several of them were very young, two or three of them not above thirteen or fourteen years of age'.[68] Even younger children were put to work in various manufacturing trades and as labourers, while others were apprenticed, bound by indenture, usually for seven years, which meant that the parents, the parish or a charity had to pay for them to learn a trade.

Rules governing apprentices were strict. When fourteen-year-old Richard Cureton of Bow Lane off Cheapside in London became apprenticed on 5 August 1783, he was bound for seven years to William Wakelin, a girdler (who made ceremonial girdles). The official indenture, written on parchment, gave a list of rules to which the apprentice had to agree, including:

> He shall do no damage to his said Master nor see to be done of others, but that to his power shall let, or forthwith give warning to his said Master of the same. He shall not wast the goods of his said Master nor

lend them unlawfully to any. He shall not commit Fornication, nor contract Matrimony within the said Term. He shall not play at Cards, Dice,
Tables, or any other unlawful Games whereby his said Master may have
any loss with his own goods or others during the said Term, Without
License of his said Master; he shall neither buy nor sell. He shall not
haunt Taverns or Playhouses nor absent himself from his said Master's
service day nor night unlawfully: But in all things, as a faithful apprentice
he shall behave himself towards his said Master and all his during the said
Term.[69]

Richard's fee of £10 was paid to Wakelin by a charity administered
by the Merchant Taylors' Company that gave money for apprenticing
poor children.[70] In return, Wakelin was expected to ensure that the
apprentice was 'taught and instructed the best way and manner that
he can, finding & allowing unto the said Apprentice sufficiant Meat
Drink Apparel Lodging and all other Necessaries according to the
Custom of the City of London, during the said Term'.[71] Five years
after finishing his apprenticeship, Richard was married to Frances
Carter, but died in 1804 at the early age of thirty-five, a year after his
only child Joseph was born. In 1817 Joseph was apprenticed at the age
of fourteen to a fishing-rod and tackle maker. He himself had nine
children, and direct descendants today live in Canada and the USA.

Innumerable apprentices, bound to a skilled master, learned a valuable trade, but others suffered seven years of virtual servitude.
Children of destitute families were compulsorily apprenticed by the
parish as allowed by the Poor Law, usually in lower-status positions
like servants or agricultural labourers. If they could be apprenticed
outside the parish, so much the better, because responsibility for
them was then transferred to their new parish. Any child living in the
workhouse or whose parents received poor relief could be apprenticed
in this way. Mines regularly took children from local workhouses,
while countless children from London's workhouses ended up in
northern textile mills. Until 1814, when compulsory apprenticeships
were abolished, it was an offence to run away, and notices in the
newspapers warned about such culprits. Two apprentices in a cotton
spinning mill fled in May 1793:

TWO RUNAWAY APPRENTICES

ABSCONDED from LITTON MILL, near *Tideswell*, in the County of *Derby*, on Tuesday morning the 14th of May Instant.

DAVID POWELL, about 13 Years of Age, fair Complexion, and light Hair; had on a light Cloth Coat and Breeches, or else a Fustian Coat and Breeches.

Also, MARY BEDINGFIELD, about 14 Years of Age, dark Complexion, and dark Hair, and has remarkably thick Lips; had on a blue Gown, green stuff Petticoat and black Hat.

Whoever will apprehend the said Apprentices and give information thereof to Messrs. Needham, Frith, and Co at Litton Mill aforesaid, shall receive ONE GUINEA Reward, and be paid all reasonable Expences.[72]

A few years later, around August 1799, an orphan called Robert Blincoe was sent to Litton Mill from London's St Pancras workhouse. Believed to have reached the age of seven, he was bound as an apprentice for fourteen years. He survived the ordeal, though he lost a finger and was left with crooked legs. As he explained, 'I got deformed there; my knees began to bend in when I was fifteen ... a very little makes me sweat in walking; I have not the strength of those who are straight.'[73] In 1833 he gave evidence to the Select Committee on the employment of children in factories. When asked if he would send his own children to such a mill, he replied:

No; I would rather have them transported. In the first place, they are standing upon one leg, lifting up one knee, a great part of the day, keeping the ends up from the spindle; I consider that that employment makes many cripples; then there is the heat and the dust; then there are so many different forms of cruelty used upon them; then they are so liable to have their fingers catched and to suffer other accidents from the machinery; then the hours is so long, that I have seen them tumble down asleep among the straps and machinery, and so get cruelly hurt.[74]

Questioned about this cruelty, he said:

I have seen the time when two hand-vices of a pound weight each, more or less, have been screwed to my ears, at Lytton mill in Derbyshire. Here are the scars still remaining behind my ears. Then three or four of us have been hung at once on a cross beam above the machinery, hanging by our hands, without shirts or stockings. Mind, we were apprentices, without father or mother to take care of us ... we used to stand up, in a skip, without our shirts, and be beat with straps or sticks; the skip was to prevent us from running away from the strap.[75]

Litton Mill was far from exceptional. Throughout England the textile industry relied on unskilled child workers. Four different threads were manufactured that could be made into fabrics – these were silk, wool, linen (from flax) and cotton threads. Silk, the finest of threads and used for sewing and weaving, depended on the labour of children because their small and dexterous fingers could handle the threads more efficiently. In 1800 the antiquary Richard Warner, who was a curate at Bath, visited a silk-spinning factory in a nearby Somerset village:

A little silk manufactory enlivens Maiden-Bradley, established by Mr. Ward of Bruton, about nine miles from this village. Fifty-three children great and small, are employed in spinning two of the fine filaments, as produced by the worm, together; this work is carried to Bruton, when, with the assistance of ingenious machinery, the silk thread for use is made ... The children employed (who begin working before they are six years of age) earn wages proportioned to their expedition and ability; the youngest make about three half-pence or two-pence per day, and the most experienced half-a-crown or three shilling per week; but for this they are expected to work from five o'clock in the morning till six at night![76]

Warner was obviously concerned about the long working hours, and in 1816 during a parliamentary debate on children working in cotton factories, Sir Robert Peel stated that 'little children of very tender age were employed with grown persons at the machinery, and those poor little creatures, torn from their beds, were compelled to work even at the age of six years, from early morn till late at night—a space of perhaps 15 to 16 hours!'[77]

Children in agriculture also worked excessively long hours. Some were hired as farm servants, usually on a yearly basis, for indoor and outdoor labour, while others were apprentices, bound to the farm for several years as unpaid hired hands, receiving board and lodging in return. Mrs Mary Rendalls described being apprenticed at the age of eight or nine, in about 1811, to Thomas Nicholls, a small farmer at Lower Woodrow near Brampford Speke in Devon:

> When I was an apprentice, I got up as early as half-past two, three, four, or five, to get cows in, feed them, milk them, and look after the pigs. I then had breakfast, and afterwards went into the fields. In the fields I used to drive the plough, pick stones, weed, pull turnips, when snow was lying about, sow corn, dig potatoes, hoe turnips, and reap. I did everything that boys did. Master made me do everything ... My mistress was a very bad temper; when bad tempered she treated me very ill; she beats me very much; she would throw me on the ground, hold me by the ears, kneel upon me, and use me very ill; I used to scream. This has happened several times a week ... My master beat me, and I went to my father's house. My father was afraid to let me stop, as he might be summoned, as I was an apprentice.[78]

Some of the most physically exhausting work of all was in the mines, both underground and on the surface. In 1841 shocking evidence was collected for a parliamentary commission on the conditions then being suffered by children, though older miners reckoned it had actually been far worse several decades earlier. When they were children, many had started work at six or seven years of age, some even younger. Their first job would be to open and close the heavy wooden tunnel doors. In Cumberland in 1813, the traveller and writer Richard Ayton went down the William Pit near Whitehaven, a coal mine that extended under the sea. He was horrified at what he saw:

> a number of children ... attend at the doors to open them when the horses pass through, and ... in this duty are compelled to linger their

lives, in silence, solitude, and darkness, for sixpence a day. When I first came to one of these doors, I saw it open without perceiving by what means, till, looking behind it, I beheld a miserable little wretch standing without a light, silent and motionless ... On speaking to it I was touched with the patience and uncomplaining meekness with which it submitted to its horrible imprisonment, and the little sense it had of the barbarity of its unnatural parents. Few of the children thus inhumanly sacrificed were more than eight years old, and several were considerably less, and had barely strength sufficient to perform the office that was required from them. On their first introduction into the mine the poor little victims struggle and scream with terror at the darkness, but there are found people brutal enough to force them to compliance, and after a few trials they become tame and spiritless, and yield themselves up at last without noise and resistance to any cruel slavery that it pleases their masters to impose upon them. In the winter-time they never see day-light except on a Sunday, for it has been discovered that they can serve for thirteen hours a day without perishing ... As soon as they rise from their beds they descend down the pit, and they are not relieved from their prison till, exhausted with watching and fatigue, they return to their beds again.[79]

Ayton described what else he and his companion witnessed:

We traced our way through passage after passage in the blackest darkness ... Occasionally a light appeared in the distance before us, which did not dispel the darkness ... but advanced like a meteor through the gloom, accompanied by a loud rumbling noise, the cause of which was not explained to the eye till we were called upon to make way for a horse, which passed by with its long line of baskets, and driven by a young girl, covered with filth, debased and profligate [indecent], and uttering some low obscenity as she hurried by us. We were frequently interrupted in our march by the horses proceeding in this manner with their cargoes to the shaft, and always driven by girls, all of the same description, ragged and beastly in their appearance, and with a shameless indecency in their behaviour.[80]

At least there was standing room in this Whitehaven pit, because in many mines the coal was dragged or pushed along low passageways by 'hurriers', or 'drawers', crawling along on their hands and knees. This barbaric work was done by girls, boys and women (even when they were pregnant), wearing round their waist a belt from which a chain passed between their legs and was attached to the huge baskets or tubs. Years later Joseph Gledhill related his first experiences down a coal mine in Yorkshire, in about 1798:

> I began life as a hurrier when I was between five and six years of age; I was a hurrier till I was 16 . . . there was no such thing as rails upon the roads; we used to hurry then upon 'sleds', with a belt and chain, and with a pair of short crutches we held in our hands to enable us to hurry on our hands and feet; I remember at that time such things as crooked legs, but whether that resulted from the employment I cannot tell; they [the boys] worked then about 12 hours.[81]

Even before the steam engines and furnaces of the accelerating industrial revolution began to devour vast quantities of coal, a constant supply was required for open fires for cooking, as well as for heating water and keeping rooms warm. With so many domestic fires kept constantly alight or relit each day, smoke hung in the air summer and winter. All houses and many other buildings needed chimneys to allow the smoke from fireplaces and cooking ranges to be channelled outside, and an accumulation of soot caused chimney fires that could spread rapidly through buildings. To remove this danger, chimneys were cleaned about four times a year, but adults were too big for this job. It had to be done by boys and girls who would climb up the narrow flues, sweeping with a handbrush and using a scraper to dislodge compacted soot. The youngest climbing boys were made to seek work by 'calling of the streets', and the soot itself was a valuable commodity, sold to farmers as fertiliser.

Sweeping chimneys was hard, dangerous and claustrophobic. The choking black dust harmed the children's eyes and lungs, and like those employed down mines, climbing boys rarely washed, though some masters ensured they washed on Sundays. The chimney sweep David Porter, it was reported to Parliament in 1788, 'knows many instances of boys who have served four or five years without being at all washed'.[82] Because soot is a carcinogen, chimney sweeps were particularly prone to 'Sooty Warts',[83] which was cancer of the scrotum.

In 1802 the writer Samuel Pratt commented on the awful plight of these children: 'Where a chimney sweeper's boy is not regularly cleansed once a week, and is kept in filth and nastiness, he is often afflicted by violent itchings, which break out in small pimples, and soon become an ulcer, and ultimately end in an incurable cancer, the consequence of obstructed perspiration.'[84] He was saddened by three pitiful boys he encountered in London's St Martin's Lane:

> The three poor creatures immediately under my eyes, were melancholy both to see and to hear ... They were in their boyhood; the youngest six, the next seven, and the third told me he was 'past nine a little bit, and going on for ten.' They were all brothers, and apprenticed to a huge grim being, who soon after came up with them, damned the elder apprentice for leaving one of his brushes, with which he struck him on the shoulders.[85]

An Act of Parliament in 1788 had made it illegal to employ children under eight years of age, but this law was constantly ignored, particularly by sweeps using their own children. The three boys observed by Pratt were barely clothed, and the youngest was limping so badly that he begged his master to let him rest on the church steps:

> Rest, said the black man, that's a fine story indeed; I have two chimneys to sweep now before half past eight, in Covent Garden, and don't you hear St. Martin's is now striking seven, and there is one of the chimneys as crooked as a cork screw, that none but such a shrimp as you can crawl up. While he was growling out these words, he took up the child and slung him over his shoulder, just as he would have slung one of his sacks.[86]

A tradesman suddenly called out for a sweep, so he went inside to examine the chimneys, and Pratt seized the opportunity to question the boys:

> the elder apprentice who appeared to be in extreme ill health, told me in a fearful whisper, on my asking concerning his mode of living and labour,

that ... if he lived would rather be a shoe black or a galley slave than a chimney sweeper, especially to the brute who is gone into that house, for he not only almost starves but beats me and my brothers to death, though I have gone all weathers through my morning work for many years. I have nothing to sleep on but some of these sacks in a soot cellar, and what's worse, my master won't allow us to wash and tight ourselves up [free from rags] not once a month: so that I am quite sore with the clogged stuff that has almost eat into my flesh – only look, Sir, at these sore places and these great lumps.[97]

Effective alternative methods of sweeping chimneys, using long rods and brushes, without the need to climb chimneys, were being developed, but a reluctance to use them prevailed. Children were preferred, not just for sweeping but for ascending flues to extinguish fires. Some chimneys were so narrow that even a small child could become stuck. Before a parliamentary committee in 1788, James Dunn described what happened to him during one chimney fire:

he himself had been very ill-treated by his Master, having been bound Apprentice at 5 Years of Age, for 7 Years ... when he was about 10 Years old, he was sent up a Chimney which had been on Fire for 48 Hours ... during the Time he was up the Chimney, his Master came, and found Fault with him, in so angry a Manner, as to occasion a Fright, by which Means he fell down into the Fire [having reached the fire by ascending an interconnecting flue], and was much burnt, and crippled by it for Life.[88]

In early 1806, in what was then the western edge of London, one chimney of a well-to-do house leased by Richard Creed of Marsh and Creed navy agents was in need of cleaning:

a boy was sent up a chimney in the house of Mr. Creed, Navy Agent, No. 23 Hans Place, Knightsbridge. Being unable to extricate himself, he remained there for about half an hour, while a person went to fetch assistance. A hole was made through the brick-work, and the boy, at length, released. It appeared that, in consequence of the unusual construction of the flue in one part, a vast quantity of soot had accumulated there, into which the boy had plunged, and was not able, probably from partial suffocation, to get back again.[89]

James Dunn was by now a master sweep, working in the same part of London, but he was unwilling to deal with this particular chimney: 'So dangerous was the sweeping of this chimney considered, that James Dunn, chimney sweeper, No. 46, Hans Town, refused to let his apprentice ascend the flue'.[90] A few years later, in 1814, this same house at 23 Hans Place became the home of Jane Austen's brother Henry. 'It is a delightful place – more than answers my expectation,' Jane wrote that August, apparently oblivious of the wretched chimney boy's plight.[91]

The boy was lucky to be pulled out alive. An inquest in London in November 1810 heard that Lewis Realy, about eight years old, had suffocated in a similar accident. He 'was sent up a chimney in the house of Susanna Whitfield, in Little Shire Lane, Temple Bar. After ascending the first part of the flue, he came down, and objected to attempt climbing it a second time.'[92] Despite his terror, he was forced back up:

> He remained in the chimney a considerable time, and then a boy (William Best) went up, and tried to pull him down by the legs; this not succeeding ... [he] ascended another flue, which communicated, but could not extricate Realy, though he received from him his cap and scraper. At a quarter past one, William Herring, a bricklayer, was sent for, who broke an opening into the flue, through which the body of Realy, then dead, was taken. The body, when extricated, was naked, and completely jammed in the chimney.[93]

The writer of this report was indignant: 'When we assure our readers this is only one of many authenticated accounts equally dreadful, we leave it to them to reflect how much they are called on to mitigate, by every means in their power, the sufferings of these wretched children, by encouraging the use of mechanical means of sweeping chimneys.'[94]

Chimneys were of course swept all over England, not just in the great smoky cities. In rural Norfolk on 12 August 1797, James Woodforde had several chimneys cleaned: 'Holland the chimney sweeper swept my study chimney, parlour ditto – and the chamber chimneys, with kitchen and back-kitchen ditto – in all six. He had a new boy with him who had likely to have lost his life this morning at Weston House in sticking in one [of] their chimnies. I gave the poor boy a shilling.'[95] Campaigners had long tried to ban the use of climbing boys, and finally in June 1817 a Bill was passed, only to be thrown out in the House of Lords the following year. It was not until 1875 that the practice of employing climbing boys was banned.

◆

FOUR

HOME AND HEARTH

She was then taken into a parlour, so small that her first conviction was of its being only a passage-room to something better.

Mansfield Park, by Jane Austen

William Pitt the Elder, who died in 1778, once declared: 'The poorest man may in his cottage bid defiance to all the forces of the Crown. It may be frail – its roof may shake – the wind may blow through it – the storm may enter – the rain may enter – but the King of England cannot enter! – all his force dares not cross the threshold of the ruined tenement!'[1]

While this centuries-old sentiment is normally expressed as 'an Englishman's home is his castle', the upper classes did live in country mansions and even occasionally real castles, with an army of servants to run the house and tend the grounds. By the time of the 1801 census, England had a population of just over 8 million living in a country of some 32 million acres – and about 80 to 90 per cent of this land was owned by the aristocracy or landed gentry.[2] Some of them had estates of thousands of acres, including large kitchen gardens, lawns, shrubberies and other landscape features, as well as orchards for fruit, woodlands for fuel, rivers and lakes for fishing, and huge swathes of land for farming and shooting wild animals and birds.[3] They received ever-increasing income from their tenant farmers, mines and other industrial concerns, as well as from urban developments.

It was accepted that respectable individuals could ask to view these lavish homes, and usually a small sum of money was handed to the gardener or housekeeper for their trouble. In Oxfordshire in July 1785, though, John Byng, the younger son of George Byng, 3rd Viscount Torrington, who would himself succeed to the title, was annoyed to be refused entry to the fourteenth-century Shirburn Castle:

> Our ride was to Wheatley, and, leaving the high road, to the village of Gt Milton ... thence over an openish country to Aisley ... cross'd many pasture grounds and much nasty country to Sherborne Castle, Ld Macclesfields seat, the object of our ride; but were refused admission, as his L'dship was at home. This is the second rebuff we have lately experienc'd, and which, after a tedious sultry ride of 16 miles, fretted us not a little: let people proclaim that their great houses are not to be view'd, and then travellers will not ride out of their way with false hopes.[4]

In *Pride and Prejudice*, when Elizabeth Bennet and her aunt and uncle are touring round Derbyshire, they visit Mr Darcy's house on his Pemberley estate: 'It was a large, handsome, stone building, standing well on rising ground, and backed by a ridge of high woody hills; and in front, a stream of some natural importance ... Elizabeth was delighted.' If the fictional Pemberley existed, it would now be considered a 'stately home', a term coined by Felicia Hemans in 1827 in a poem that begins 'The stately Homes of England, How beautiful they stand!'[5] While travelling from Slough to Bath in 1805, the American Benjamin Silliman noticed many such houses: 'Throughout our whole ride, at intervals of a mile or two, beautiful country seats adorned the road, and with their forests, their parks, their sloping fields, and their herds of deer, presented a most interesting succession of objects.'[6]

Many grand country homes and smaller houses were being constructed or rebuilt in what we today call the 'Georgian' style, such as Dodington House near Bath, a sixteenth-century manor house that was completely rebuilt over many years from 1796. Other older buildings were remodelled so that, certainly from the front, they appeared to conform to fashion. At Althorp in Northamptonshire, the original sixteenth-century house was greatly in need of repair by the 1780s, and so Lord Spencer brought in the architect Henry Holland. He transformed the external appearance of the house and went on to remodel some of the interior as well. The Georgian style of architecture, which evolved over a hundred years, was at its most developed form in Jane Austen's lifetime, influenced by classical Greek and Roman architecture and less heavily ornamented than earlier in the century. While the term Regency is now applied to architecture dating from about 1800 until about 1837, at the time it was of course regarded as modern.

Along with their servants, wealthy families moved 'up to' London from their country establishments, renting a house or staying in their own property for 'the Season', which coincided with parliamentary sittings. Benjamin Silliman explained that 'in England, *down* means *from* London, and *up, to* London: they speak of going down into the country, no matter in what direction. The Londoners talk of going down to Scotland. Is this a figure of speech unconsciously adopted because London is the great fountain supplying all the kingdom with streams of wealth and knowledge. Perhaps the country might dispute the claim.'[7]

For want of money, John Byng reluctantly worked in London from 1782 as a commissioner of stamps and was relieved to leave his employment each summer and travel round rural England, which he so loved. In August 1790, as he headed northwards to Biggleswade, Byng witnessed the annual desertion of the city: 'The roads are now crowded as London empties in August, and fills in February.'[8] In a guide to London published that same year, advice was given on renting houses: 'The dearest season is from Christmas to June, when families are in town and the parliament sitting; the cheapest, when families are out of town, and the parliament prorogued.'[9]

Even though the poor had to stay put, London did become visibly depleted, particularly during the summer when anyone who could afford to do so would abandon the stinking city. However, in August 1811 Louis Simond, on a tour of Britain, was actually surprised that 'London is less empty than we expected, and the wheels of numerous carriages are still rattling over the pavement of Portman Square, near which we occupy the house of an absent friend, obligingly lent to us.'[10]

Towns and cities across England were expanding rapidly, leading Horace Walpole in 1791 to comment: 'There will soon be one street from London to Brentford, ay, and from London to every village ten miles round! ... Bath shoots out into new crescents, circuses, and squares every year: Birmingham, Manchester, Hull, and Liverpool would serve any King in Europe for a capital.'[11] The previous summer Miss Mary Heber of Weston Hall in Northamptonshire received a letter from a friend: 'We intend going to spend the day at Bath some day this week ... imagine I shall scarcely know the place, there are so many new Buildings erected since I had the pleasure of meeting you there.'[12]

In places like London and Bath, many new houses were appearing, including grand terraces or squares with their mews buildings behind for carriages and horses. In June 1797 George MacAulay, a merchant and insurer, remarked on London's expansion: 'In the evening I walked sev'ral times round Finsbury Square, a place which now approaches nearly to the elegance of the Squares in the West. I remember it a place for rubbish, and not a House built!'[13] This square was where James Lackington had just established London's largest bookstore.

The fashionable Georgian architectural style was also adopted for the more humble terraced houses of the middle classes and even those of the better-off skilled workers, but the rapid expansion of towns resulted in poorly constructed houses. On the outskirts of London Simond watched brick terraces being built: 'their walls are frightfully thin, a single brick of eight inches, – and, instead of beams, mere planks lying on edge. I am informed, it is made an express condition in the leases of these ... houses, that there shall be no dances given in them.'[14] Even so, he said, 'People live in the out-skirts of the town in better air, – larger houses, – and at a smaller rent, – and stages [stagecoaches] passing every half hour facilitate communications.'[15]

Although England's population was a fraction of today's, living conditions were overcrowded by modern standards. Privacy was not valued so highly, and even families with modest incomes had live-in servants who needed basic accommodation. Simond gave a vivid description of a typical rented London terraced house 'of the middling or low kind':

> Each family occupy a whole house, unless very poor ... These narrow houses, three or four stories high,—one for eating, one for sleeping, a third for company, a fourth under ground for the kitchen, a fifth perhaps at top for the servants ... The plan of these houses is very simple, two rooms on each story; one in the front with two or three windows looking on the street, the other on a yard behind, often very small; the stairs generally taken out of the breadth of the back-room. The ground-floor is usually elevated a few feet above the level of the street, and separated from it by an area, a sort of ditch, a few feet wide ... and six or eight feet deep, inclosed by an iron railing; the windows of the kitchen are in this area. A bridge of stone or brick leads to the door of the house. The front of these houses is about twenty or twenty-five feet wide; they certainly have rather a paltry appearance,—but you cannot pass the threshold without being struck with the look of order and neatness of the interior.[16]

Filled with large families and several servants, such houses could be crowded, but nothing like the dwellings of the poor, who might not have servants but had numerous children who were squeezed into homes that often served as their workplace as well. Noisy, cramped conditions were the lot of most town dwellers, about which Jane Austen was sensitive in *Mansfield Park* when Fanny Price is back home in the tiny terraced house in Portsmouth: 'The living in incessant noise was ... the greatest misery of all ... Here, everybody was noisy, every voice was loud ... Whatever was wanted was halloo'd for, and the servants halloo'd out their excuses from the kitchen. The doors were in constant banging, the stairs were never at rest, nothing was done without a clatter, nobody sat still, and nobody could command attention when they spoke.'

In spite of his aristocratic background, John Byng was aware of

problems faced by the lower classes. To him it made sense for every
poor person to be housed in a cottage with some land attached. He
outlined his vision of an ideal place to live:

> As for poverty, rags and misery they should not exist in my village; for the
> cottages should not be only comfortable and low-rented, but attached to
> each should be, at least, 2 acres of ground, which on first possession the
> hirers should find well cropped with potatoes, and planted with fruit
> trees;– teach them how to proceed, redeem the poor from misery, make a
> large public enclosure at the end of the village, for their cows, &c., and
> then poverty would soon quit your neighbourhood.[17]

This was Byng's dream, but the clergyman William Jones in 1802
made comments in his diary that were closer to reality: 'In most
towns and villages the poor and indigent class, I fear, have very
wretched accommodations. They are generally crowded together in
dark courts and narrow alleys, in cellars, or in garrets; where damps,
stagnated air, and accumulated filthiness, injure their health, and
facilitate the progress of contagious diseases.'[18]

In 1816 a parliamentary committee heard evidence about the state
of houses in streets close to Covent Garden, including Short's
Gardens, 'occupied by poor room-keepers, generally with families,
living in apparent wretchedness, unhealthy, filthy in their persons,
their rooms, and their bedding; the staircases of the houses of course
common to the numerous families which occupied them, and being
common to all, appeared to be cleaned by none; the rooms in want of
ventilation and white-washing.'[19] London was notorious for its war-
rens of alleyways and courts, the haunt of beggars and criminals,
with squalid houses only a few streets from fashionable squares and
their fine town-houses. Louis Simond was struck by the proximity of
low and high life:

> We have in our neighbourhood one of those no-thoroughfare lanes or
> courts ... This one is inhabited by a colony of Irish labourers, who fill
> every cellar and every garret,–a family in each room; very poor, very
> uncleanly, and very turbulent. They give each other battle every Saturday

night ... We should never have known that there were such wretches as these in London, if we had not happened to reside in Orchard Street, Portman Square, which is one of the finest parts of the town.[20]

Renting a home was far more common than owning one. In April 1808 Nelly Weeton decided to let out the house that she had inherited from her mother at Upholland in Lancashire: 'On Wednesday, I let my house to a Mr. Winstanley, a watch-maker, who I am told is very likely to pay his rent regularly. His wife and children are above the common order and not likely to injure the house. I mean to draw up a little agreement for him to sign; to leave the house in as good repair as he finds it; to pay half a year's rent on entering it &c. He is to pay eight guineas a year'.[21] The plan was to close her late mother's dame school that generated a modest income, move to cheaper rented lodgings and live off her small amount of capital and Mr Winstanley's rent, but first of all she needed to 'dispose of my furniture, pack up what I shall want, and whitewash the house'.[22]

Whitewash, a solution of lime and chalk mixed with other additives, was brushed on interior and exterior walls like paint. It took several days to set, forming a white surface that could be coloured with other substances; in some areas animal blood or vegetable dye was added to give exterior walls a pink colour. Whitewash was a cheap way of decorating rooms. More expensive options included textile hangings, wallpaper, painting and wainscoting. In 1817 William Holland was decorating parts of the vicarage at Over Stowey. His daughter's bedroom had wallpaper, but he hired a painter for some of the woodwork, inside and out: 'The painter from Stowey has been here and painted the outward gate green and the skirting boards along the passage and stairs a chocolate colour.'[23]

Wallpaper became especially popular with the middle classes from the late eighteenth century, and businesses based primarily in London would send out samples to customers far beyond the capital.[24] Local upholsterers usually sold wallpaper and advertised their wares in newspapers. In April 1789 the *Ipswich Journal* announced: 'John Sparrow, Upholsterer, Cabinet-maker, Appraiser, and Auctioneer, Buttermarket, Ipswich ... has just laid in a fresh assortment of every article in the upholstery branch, particularly ... a great variety of elegant paper hangings, from 2½d. to 2s. 6d. per yard; every pattern sold at the London prices, and hung at a very low rate. Patterns sent to any distance.'[25]

The customer would select a wallpaper pattern and place an order for a number of rolls, just as James Woodforde did in 1785. He visited an upholsterer in Norwich to choose what to order for the Weston Longville parsonage, and when the paper arrived he and his niece did the work themselves: 'Nancy and self very busy most of the morning and evening in papering the attic chamber over my bedchamber.'[26] Whether one or two rooms were papered is unclear, but the job took them four days. The reason for middle-class people taking on such a task rather than hiring workmen or using their servants may have been the high cost of even the cheapest papers and the fear that a bungled job would waste a great deal of money.

In the summer of 1808, having let out her Upholland property, Nelly Weeton stayed with acquaintances in Liverpool until she found lodgings in an isolated house on the banks of the River Mersey, close to what is now the Wellington Dock:

> I came here on the 18th of October, to a small, white, shabby-looking house, close to the sea shore, called Beacon's Gutter ... Edward Smith, his wife, and little boy (about 8 years old), compose the whole of the family, besides myself. Edward is in a tobacconist's warehouse, as a jour-neyman; his wife does nothing but take care of the house. In the summer they take in lodgers. They have, in general, very respectable families.[27]

Even a middle-class clergyman like William Jones could not pro-vide for a growing family without sharing his home with lodgers, which he lamented: 'Though my wife often reminds me that I could not have *this* & *that*, without foreigners, and, now & then, threatens to put me on coarse fare and short allowance, when we have none of these inmates;– yet I cannot help thinking that I shall never truly enjoy my dear cottage, till it is clear of all but my own dear family ... If the taking of boarders enlarges my *income*, it most certainly curtails my *comforts*.'[28]

After one year, Nelly Weeton returned to Liverpool and then moved to the Lake District as governess at Dove Nest, a house overlooking Lake Windermere that was originally built for John Benson (who also owned Dove Cottage which he rented to William Wordsworth). Nelly's employer, Edward Pedder, was now renting Dove Nest, as she told her brother Tom: 'Mr. P. gives a hundred a year for the house and land. Estates here let and sell amazingly high.'[29] Two decades later the poet Felicia Hemans rented Dove Nest, which she described as 'a lonely but beautifully situated cottage on the banks of Windermere'.[30]

A familiar theme in Jane Austen's novels and letters is lack of security and tenure – something she experienced when her father died. Wives often had to vacate the marital home on their husband's death, and the families of deceased clergymen were particularly vulnerable. In June 1798 William Jones expressed sympathy for the plight of a fellow cleric's family: 'Poor Mr. Fowler is gone – he died about 11 o'clock last night ... His poor wife and three unestablished daughters, (the youngest of them not very young), are, I fear, left in distressed circumstances. How must their hearts droop at exchanging their present large, convenient, beautiful house for a cottage! A rectory, or a vicarage house, is certainly but a caravanseray; for it frequently exchanges its inmates.'[31]

Because rents varied enormously, finding somewhere reasonable could be difficult. Sarah Wilkinson considered all kinds of accommodation in London in 1809 while her husband was away, serving in the navy: 'I was looking at some lodgings that were to let in Knightsbridge the other evening,' she told him. 'For a first floor 3 rooms and a kitchen thirty pounds; without the kitchen twenty five pounds, and another place with only two rooms on the floor twenty pounds per year.'[32] To consider a place without a kitchen might seem strange, but the urban poor were lucky even to share a kitchen, relying instead on street vendors and inns for cooked food if they had no fireplace. Two months later, William Wilkinson decided that they should rent a terraced house in east London. 'I think I see us now living in our house in Poplar Row,' he wrote, 'and sitting in the parlour in a winter evening, you and Fanny at your needle and myself reading ... We would let the first floor and one of the rooms upstairs.'[33] Not even a naval warrant officer could afford to rent a London house without subletting.

Finding a place to live was only the start, since many houses were let unfurnished. Ready-made furniture, both new and secondhand, could be bought, and in November 1789 Parson Woodforde purchased items from one of the cabinet makers on Hog Hill in Norwich: 'Bought this day of Willm Hart, Cabinet Maker on Hog Hill Norwich, 2 large second hand double-flapped mohogany tables, also one second hand mohogany dressing table with drawers, also one new mohogany washing-stand, for all which paid 4.14.6, that is, for the 2 tables 2.12.6, dressing table 1.11.6, mohogany wash-stand 0.10.6. I think the whole of it to be very cheap.'[34]

Furniture was also built to order. Designs would be agreed with the cabinet-maker, often with reference to one of the design books issued by fashionable London craftsmen. Thomas Chippendale was the first to publish such a book (*The Gentleman and Cabinet Maker's Directory*) in 1754, but by the end of the century George Hepplewhite's designs (published in 1788 as *The Cabinet-Maker and Upholsterer's Guide*) and Thomas Sheraton's four volumes of *The Cabinet Maker's and Upholsterer's Drawing Book* (published from 1791) were more in vogue. Less famous designers also issued catalogues. Cabinet makers could remodel furniture, making a piece more fashionable or turning it into something entirely different. This is what the Austens chose to do at Southampton. 'Our dressing table is constructing on the spot,' Jane told Cassandra in February 1807, 'out of a large kitchen table.'[35]

Most families owned very few items of furniture and could not afford to buy anything new. Travelling from Taunton to Bristol in 1810, soon after arriving in England, Louis Simond glimpsed inside several rural cottages which were modestly furnished: 'The villages along the road are in general not beautiful,—the houses very poor; the walls old and rough ... Peeping in, as we pass along, the floors appear to be a pavement of round stones like the streets,—a few seats, in the form of short benches,—a table or two,—a spinning wheel,—a few shelves.'[36]

The more expensive the house, the larger the rooms, the higher the ceilings and the more windows they possessed. Every house incurred a window tax, in two parts: a relatively low flat-rate tax (which in 1778 became a variable tax related to the value of the house) and a higher variable rate depending on the number of windows. The tax on windows was constantly changing, and the introduction of further taxes in 1784 may have prompted Woodforde to take action: 'Mr Hardy and boy fastened up 3 windows with brick for me.'[37] Blocking up windows was a common way of avoiding the tax – widely regarded as a tax on light and air. Woodforde, who ran a modest establishment, frequently noted what he paid, as in May 1788 when the taxes ranged from windows to servants:

To Jⁱ. Pegg [tax collector] this morning – Qrs. Land Tax	3.0.0
To Dᵒ. ½ years window tax	2.13.3
To Dᵒ. ditto house ditto	0.1.9
To Dᵒ. ditto male servant tax	1.5.0
To Dᵒ. ditto female Do	0.10.0
To Dᵒ. ditto horse tax	0.10.0
To Dᵒ. ditto cart Do	0.1.0[38]

Upper- and middle-class people such as Woodforde had leisure time because their household chores were done by servants. Without servants their lives would have been so very different. The lower classes had less time and energy because they had no servants – they *were* the servants. Jane Austen was accustomed to having servants, often mentioning them in her letters. In October 1798 she wrote to Cassandra from Steventon when one of them left: 'We do not seem likely to have any other maidservant at present, but Dame Staples will supply the place of one. Mary has hired a young girl from Ashe who has never been out to service to be her scrub, but James fears her not being strong enough for the place.'[39] She added: 'Earle [Harwood] and his wife live in the most private manner imaginable at Portsmouth, without keeping a servant of any kind. What a prodigious innate love of virtue she must have, to marry under such circumstances!'[40] Her tone is ironic, but in an era without electricity or labour-saving appliances, domestic chores were hard and time-consuming.

When a family's income was reduced, servants had to go. In *Sense and Sensibility* Miss Elinor Dashwood persuades her widowed mother to economise: 'Her wisdom ... limited the number of their servants to three; two maids and a man, with whom they were speedily provided from amongst those who had formed their establishment at Norland.'

By contrast, Nelly Weeton was not brought up with servants, but spent her time looking after her mother and their house. In her new role as governess at Dove Nest she took time to adjust to the wealthy household. 'At supper we had two servants in livery attending,' she confided to a friend, 'and some display of plate, silver nutcrackers, &c., and some things of which poor ignorant I knew not the use. I felt a little awkward, but as you may suppose, strove not to let it appear.'[41] In respectable households, manservants were expected to wear livery, usually a recognisable jacket and breeches. Because the lifestyle at Dove Nest was so different to what she had previously known, Nelly described the household to another friend: 'I found on my arrival here, an establishment of five servants (two men and three maids), a curricle, four or five horses, five or six dogs, two pigs, and a whole host of rats, too many to be counted.'[42]

Servants often found employment at hiring fairs, or were recommended by friends and family.[43] Many were hired for one year only and were at the mercy of their employers, who could dismiss them with bad character references or no references at all and abuse them without fear of reprisals. In 1777 a tax was imposed on manservants, which affected the numbers employed, and in 1785 a tax was also imposed on female servants but repealed six years later. It was customary to pay servants a sum of money on taking up their post, with the rest of their wages paid in arrears. In mid-January 1798 Woodforde was late paying his servants:

After breakfast I paid my servants their year's wages due Janry 5th 1798 as follows.

To Benj. Leggatt, my farming man	pd.	10.0.0
To Bretingham Scurl, my footman	pd.	8.0.0
To Betty Dade, my house-maid	pd.	5.5.0
To Sally Gunton, my cook & dairy maid	pd.	5.5.0
To Barnabas Woodcock, my yard-boy	pd.	2.2.0[44]

Apart from these live-in servants, Woodforde also relied on his unmarried niece Anna Maria Woodforde, usually called Nancy or Miss Woodforde. Born at Ansford in Somerset in 1757, she went to live at the Weston Longville parsonage in Norfolk in 1779 and remained there for the rest of her uncle's life, becoming his house-keeper.[45] The wages of his servants were lower than those of agricultural workers, who usually earned £12 a year or more, or those of industrial workers, who almost always earned more than that, while wages of skilled craftsmen might be in the region of £20 or £30. Live-in servants did have board and lodging and received other extras, such as cast-off clothes and sometimes lengths of cloth for making their garments.

Nothing like a career structure existed, but a good servant might aspire to grander households, higher wages and perhaps a better position. In 1784 Woodforde lost one maid and immediately hired another:

After dinner I paid Lizzy half a years wages due this day, and then dismissed her from my service, as she is going on my recommendation to Weston House. I gave her extraordinary 0.2.6. I paid her for wages 1.6.6. In the evening sent Ben with a market cart for my new maid who lives at Mattishall and she came here about 8 at night and she supped and slept here. Her name is Molly Dade about 17 years of age – a very smart girl and pretty I think. Her friends bear great characters of industry &c.[46]

This was a rise in status for Lizzy, because Weston House was the residence of Squire Custance, though this did not mean that conditions would necessarily be better. A few years later Woodforde noted: 'Great complainings at Weston-House. Servants complaining to their Master that they had not victuals enough owing to the house-keeper,

Hetty Yallop, keeping them very short.'[47]

Servants worked long hours and could be called upon at any time of the day or night. William Holland was extremely intolerant of anything resembling idleness and expected his servants to labour tirelessly. His diary is littered with complaints about his manservant Robert Coles, as in November 1799: 'Tis a difficult thing to get a servant that is worth any thing. He has some good qualities, but the bad ones outweigh them. His slowness and laziness and want of method puts me out of patience. When the year is out he must go.'[48] He obviously changed his mind, as Robert was kept on, though the circumstances of his eventual parting are unknown because the relevant volume of Holland's diary is missing.

Someone with only one or two small, sparsely furnished rooms to call their home might have no servants at all. Nelly Weeton remembered her old room at Upholland: 'A fire in my room on a cold winter's evening, was one of the greatest comforts I had during that long, dreary, solitary season; and many a snug sit have I had there, shut up in a box 7 feet by 9, with a bed, a chest of drawers, two chairs, and a wash-stand in it, (don't peep under the bed now!) with just spare room for myself and the fire, and a tea-tray put over the washstand to serve for a table.'[49]

Descriptions of the everyday contents of rooms, such as chamberpots hidden beneath the bed as Nelly alludes to here, are uncommon in letters and diaries because they were considered unexceptional, but the observations of travellers like Carl Moritz can provide fascinating glimpses of how people lived. He was struck by the bedding in England that was so different to his native Germany: 'The custom of sleeping without a feather-bed for a covering, particularly pleased me. You here lie between two sheets, and are covered with blankets, which, without oppressing you, keep you sufficiently warm.'[50] Feather beds in England meant mattresses to lie on, not quilts or duvets, and when travelling through Hampshire in 1782, John Byng criticised the Crown Inn at Ringwood: 'Of all the beds I ever lay in, that of last night was the very worst, for there could not be more than fifty feathers in the bolster, and pillow, or double that number in the feather-bed; so there I lay tossing, and tumbling all night, without any sleep, or place to lay my head upon, tho' I rowl'd [rolled] all the bolster into one heap.'[51]

Warm bedding was essential because houses were so cold and draughty, at the mercy of the weather, with ill-fitting doors and windows. All too often they were in some state of disrepair, especially with poorly maintained roofs. Following the Great Fire of 1666, thatched roofs were banned in London – tiles and slates had to be used instead. Elsewhere in England, roofing and other construction materials reflected local geology and the resources available, creating a distinctive character in each region. Many buildings outside London had thatched roofs of reed or straw, and in January 1784 Woodforde noted: 'I rejoiced much this morning on shooting an old wood-pecker, which had teised [teased] me a long time in pulling out the reed from my house. He had been often shot at by me and others ... For this last 3 years in very cold weather did he use to come here and destroy my thatch. Many holes he has made this year in the roof, and as many before.'[52]

Unlike modern heating that can be switched on or off, rooms were heated by inefficient open fires. In the summer of 1808, Jane Austen complained to Cassandra: 'What cold, disagreeable weather, ever since Sunday! I dare say you have fires every day. My kerseymere Spencer [woollen jacket] is quite the comfort of our evening walks.'[53] The winter cold could be dreadful, something that Woodforde described in January 1789 in Norfolk: 'I never felt the cold so much in my life before. It froze the whole day long within doors and very sharp ... The air very clear and very piercing.'[54]

It is difficult to imagine the temperature *indoors* being below freezing, but the 1790s saw particularly harsh winters, as Woodforde described in 1792: 'The most severe frost last night and this morning as I ever felt. The milk in the dairy in the pans was one piece of ice and the water above stairs in the basons [ceramic wash basins] froze in a few minutes after being put there this morn.'[55] Two years later the winter was even worse: 'Very severe frost indeed, freezes sharp within doors and bitter cold it is now. Two women froze to death Saturday last going from Norwich Market to their home.'[56] The next year, January 1795, was also bad: 'The frost ... froze last night the chamber pots above stairs . . . The ice in the pond in the yard which is broke every morning for the horses, froze two inches in thickness last night, when broke this morning.'[57]

At the end of the decade, harsh winters were causing widespread problems, and Woodforde reported heavy snowfalls in February 1799:

> The weather more severe than ever with continued snow all last night and continued snowing all this whole day, with a good deal of wind which have drifted the snow in some places so very deep as to make almost every road impassable – in many roads 15 feet deep . . . Such weather with so much snow I never knew before, not able to go to Jericho [the outside toilet]. Dreadful weather for the poor people and likewise for all kinds of cattle &c. &c. It is dangerous almost for any person to be out.[58]

Coal was the predominant fuel for households wherever it could be supplied cheaply by sea, rivers and canals. The growing canal network made coal increasingly available inland, as Frederick Eden recorded in 1795 in Louth, Lincolnshire, as part of his survey of the poor: 'Coal is now brought by a canal from the Humber to within ½ a mile of this town, which has considerably lessened the prices of fuel. It is hoped, that the introduction of coal will induce the inhabitants to desist from their ancient practice . . . of using the dung of their cattle for fuel.'[59] Peat and turf were cut in some areas, something Eden observed at Orton in Westmorland: 'The fuel is principally turf, procured from the commons: coal must be brought 30 miles by land carriage.'[60]

Where coal was too expensive, wood was frequently burned, though gathering firewood was a constant struggle for the poor, especially when the common land was enclosed. Eden described how the children of poor agricultural labourers obtained their firewood at the village of Seend in Wiltshire: 'If the labourer is employed in hedging and ditching, he is allowed to take home a faggot every evening, while that work lasts: but this is by no means sufficient for his consumption: his children, therefore, are sent into the fields, to collect wood where they can; and neither hedges nor trees are spared by the young marauders, who are thus . . . educated in the art of thieving.'[61]

In Over Stowey, Holland complained about some village children who 'have committed great depradations on my new hedges by drawing off the laid sticks. I must call them to account for this. There is wood sufficient on the hills [Quantocks], and yet these wretches prefer damaging the hedges of their neighbours to fetching it.'[62] In 1798 Dorothy and William Wordsworth were living at nearby Alfoxton House, while Samuel Taylor Coleridge ('a democratic libertine', according to Holland)[63] was at Nether Stowey – writing some of his best poetry. They often took walks together over the Quantock hills, gathering firewood as they went, as on one occasion when Dorothy recorded: 'Walked with Coleridge over the hills ... Gathered sticks in the wood.'[64]

In winter the fire was the focal point of any room – usually the kitchen in poorer households. With open fires used for cooking, smoke actually poured from the chimneys all year round. The black fallout from soot in the air and the pervading smell of coal smoke might diminish in towns in the summer, but it never disappeared. While in London in the summer of 1802, Dorothy Wordsworth was therefore surprised by the unusual distance they could see: 'The city ... made a most beautiful sight as we crossed Westminster Bridge. The houses were not overhung by their cloud of smoke, and they were spread out endlessly.'[65] In March 1810 Louis Simond gave a vivid description of the more normal winter smog:

It is difficult to form an idea of the kind of winter days in London; the smoke of fossil coals forms an atmosphere, perceivable for many miles, like a great round cloud attached to the earth. In the town itself, when the weather is cloudy and foggy, which is frequently the case in winter, this smoke increases the general dingy hue, and terminates the length of every street with a fixed grey mist, receding as you advance. But when some rays of sun happens to fall on this artificial atmosphere, its impure mass assumes immediately a pale orange tint ... loaded with small flakes of soot ... so light as to float without falling. This black snow sticks to your clothes and linen, or lights on your face. You just feel something on your nose, or your cheek,—the finger is applied mechanically, and fixes it into a black patch![66]

Smoke from open fires was also a nuisance indoors, and at Alfoxton Dorothy noted: 'The room smoked so that we were obliged to quit it'.[67] Woodforde had similar trouble: 'Very windy all the day, obliged to be in the parlour as our study smoaked so very much. Wind W.N.W.'[68] He had a running battle with this particular fire-place, commenting four years later: 'Had my study chimney-piece altered to day by Mr Hardy and to prevent its smoking, but am still afraid of it. This is, I believe the 4th time of altering it.'[69] Smoking chimneys were so common that specialist workmen, 'chimney doctors', offered to remedy such problems.

On cold, dark evenings better-off families would sit together in the parlour or drawing room with its comforting fire. The temptation to get close to the hearth meant that long garments easily caught alight, and newspapers were full of reports of women being burnt to death. This was a hazard that had no class boundaries, with rich women as much at risk as poor ones. Nelly Weeton was horrified to witness her ten-year-old pupil Mary Gertrude (Mr Pedder's daughter by his previous marriage) die at Dove Nest in February 1810:

I heard a scream. I ran instantly. I heard her scream again, and, opening the parlour door, met her running towards it, the flames higher than her head – What a sight it was! Without the loss of a moment, I flew into the servants' hall for the ironing blanket – it was washing week and I recollected seeing it there ... I threw the blanket to the nurse, who was trying to extinguish the flames with her apron. While she was rolling her in the blanket, I ran again into the butler's pantry and servants' hall, to find some water to throw upon her, and cool the burning flesh. I could find no liquid of any kind.[70]

There was no water to hand because Dove Nest, like most houses, had no piped supply. When a house caught fire, little could be done, as on Easter morning in 1793 at Weston Longville, while Woodforde was conducting a service:

Before I got out of Church ... heard that one of the widow's cottages on Greensgate, where poor old John Peachman and his wife lived, was burnt to the ground whilst we were at Church. The poor woman was at Church, and her husband gone to Lyng. It almost distracted the poor woman, having lost almost all that she had. The house was burnt down to the ground in about an hour. Poor John Heaver's house [adjacent] caught fire once or twice, and if it had not been for the kind assistance of neighbours, it must have been burnt.[71]

The need for efficient fire fighting and insurance against losses was made clear by the Great Fire of London and led to the formation of fire insurance companies such as the Sun Fire Office and the Royal Exchange. These companies operated their own fire brigades, and insured properties were identified by the fire marks of the companies on the front wall of the property – a lead or copper plaque with a readily recognisable design.[72] These fire brigades operated primarily in towns, where industrial and domestic buildings crowded together, increasing the risk of fire spreading. While a fire brigade's primary concern was dealing with insured buildings, it was in their interests to assist with nearby fires, and by the early nineteenth century the brigades from different insurance companies frequently cooperated.

Unattended candles were a common cause of fires, something that agitated Woodforde:

> Ben [his manservant] went to help Stephen Andrews's men at harvest, came home in the evening in liquor ... I saw a light burning in Ben's room, upon that I walked up into his room, and there saw him laying flat upon his back on the bed asleep with his cloaths on and the candle burning on the table. I waked him, made him put out the candle and talked with him a little on it, but not much as he was not in a capacity of answering but little. I was very uneasy to see matters go on so badly.[73]

Although experiments were taking place with gas street lighting, it would be many years before homes had gas lamps. As with heating, no instant lighting system existed. Instead, candles could be lit with spills ignited from the hearth or from another burning candle, or else tinderboxes were employed. These metal or wooden containers held a flint, a firesteel and some combustible material (the 'tinder'), such as very dry cloth fibres, lichen or thin bark. The flint from the tinderbox would be struck against the firesteel to create a spark that ignited the tinder. It was then convenient to use matches, which were little pieces of card, rope or wood dipped in sulphur that caught fire easily.[74] A match would be lit from the glowing tinder to produce a flame that lit the candle. Lighted candles were carried in holders to avoid spilling the hot wax, but walking too fast with the candle or walking through a draught could easily extinguish the flame. Outdoors, candles were put into protective metal lanterns (or 'lanthorns') with pierced sides or panels of thin translucent horn or sometimes of glass.

Candles, made and sold by licensed chandlers, were heavily taxed, which encouraged their clandestine manufacture.[75] The best-quality ones were of beeswax – some were made from thin sheets of beeswax wrapped round a flax or cotton wick and others were laboriously manufactured as solid candles.[76] Such candles were favoured by the wealthy and the Church, and they were better for chandeliers (often called 'lustres') in public buildings like theatres, where the light would be reflected and magnified by the numerous pieces of glass ('drops'). Beeswax candles might also be mounted in candelabra or candle-sticks, or fixed on wall brackets. Also of high quality were candles of spermaceti, a waxy oil from the head of sperm whales. Unlike beeswax candles, these could be made in moulds. Both beeswax and spermaceti candles burned slowly and brightly, producing little smoke or smell.

Louis Simond found the inns in southern England superior to those elsewhere in the country, but was annoyed to discover that 'wax-candles are forced upon the travellers, whether they choose or not this piece of luxury, for which 2s. 6d. a-night is added to the bill'.[77] He expected cheaper, everyday tallow candles, which were manufac-tured by repeatedly dipping a cotton or flax wick into hot animal fat, which hardened on cooling. These candles ('dips') yielded a poor flickering light and an unpleasant smell.

Tallow candles were also formed in metal moulds using superior mutton tallow rather than beef or pig, with some of their wicks dipped in wax, as seen in one London advertisement in 1807:

TALLOW CANDLES with WAXED WICKS –
In consequence of the Wicks of these Candles being coated with Wax,
These Candles have the following advantages:– 1st, They are seldom, if
ever, subject to what is called a thief in the candle:– 2ndly, They will not
gutter, except from bad snuffing, or carrying about:– and 3dly, They burn
longer and give a brighter light than the usual mould candles. Sold only
at the Candle and Soap Company's Warehouse, No. 182, Fleet-street, two
doors from Fetter-lane.[78]

Tallow candles burned at a lower temperature and produced a large
amount of hot fat, which could run down the sides, a process called
guttering. They needed thicker wicks, which tended to smoke and
could cause guttering when they became too long – something
described as a 'thief in the candle' because so much of the candle was
wasted. The wick was therefore trimmed or 'snuffed' with snuffers (a
type of scissors) while in use, without snuffing out the flame.

Poorer families could not even afford tallow candles, but might
make rushlights, which were not taxed. Writing at Selborne in 1775,
where he was curate, Gilbert White explained that after obtaining
rushes for the wicks, their outer coating was peeled off except for one
strip supporting the inner pith. After drying, the rushes were drawn
through waste cooking grease and fat:

A pound of common grease may be procured for four pence; and about six
pounds of grease will dip a pound of rushes; and one pound of rushes may
be bought for one shilling: so that a pound of rushes, medicated and
ready for use, will cost three shillings. If men that keep bees will mix a
little wax with the grease, it will give it a consistency, and render it more
cleanly; and make the rushes burn longer ... A good rush, which measured in length two feet four inches and an half ... burnt only three
minutes short of an hour: and a rush still of greater length has been
known to burn one hour and a quarter. These rushes give a good clear
light.[79]

White estimated that a farthing's worth of rushlights provided over
five hours of illumination. Because rushlights burned best at an angle

of about 45 degrees, they were placed in basic metal or wooden holders.[80]

Another simple centuries-old method of lighting was the open
lamp – a shallow metal or ceramic container filled with oil in which
a wick floated. Such lamps were practical in coastal areas where cheap
fish oil was available, such as train oil from pilchards, but they generated more smoke and foul smells than candles. Towards the end of
the eighteenth century the Argand lamp with a glass chimney was
introduced, which used whale or vegetable oil as fuel. Visiting
London in 1786, Sophie von La Roche was impressed by the new
lamps: 'We finished the evening at tea investigating Argand lamps of
all descriptions. Their advantage lies in a wick which burns around a
tube fixed inside a glass funnel higher than the flame, with an air current beneath to prevent flickering and smoke. There is a paper screen
on top.'[81]

Candles or lamps illuminated only small parts of rooms, but open
fires were brighter, so that everyone congregated around the hearth
for light as well as for warmth. In poorer households this was the
kitchen fire. In all types of home, from the poorest to the aristocratic,
cooking was done over open fires, and the Frenchman Louis Simond
observed that 'an English cook only boils and roasts'.[82] At the most
basic level, food was boiled in pots suspended over a fire, but wealthier families had an open range for cooking.[83]

Early open ranges had a freestanding grate – a container raised
above the hearth, so that the ashes fell through and enabled the coal
to burn efficiently. These ranges became more sophisticated, acquiring sides and backs, and any oven was built to one side with its own
grate and flue. By the late eighteenth century ironfounders were
developing integral ovens that took their heat from the open fire. As
well as adjustable hooks for suspending pots over the flames, other
accessories might be fitted to the grate, such as hotplates over part of
the fire. Years later, Victorian cast-iron ranges had an integral oven,
water heater with tap and hotplates, and the fire was fully enclosed.

The roasting of meat was not done in an oven. Instead, horizontal spits were placed in front of (not above) the open fire, and the
juices and fat were collected in a pan underneath. These horizontal

spits were turned by hand or by mechanical contrivances such as weight-driven jacks and smoke jacks (fitted inside a chimney so that they rotated by the hot smoke rising from the fire). Alternatively, clockwork bottle jacks might be suspended over the open range – the meat was hung from a hook, and the clockwork mechanism kept the meat turning while it roasted. The *Morning Chronicle* in 1807 advertised these cooking aids:

IMPROVED OECONOMICAL KITCHEN RANGES, &c.– At the London Patent Register Stove Manufactory, the corner of Brooke-street, Holborn, are finished and ready for the inspection of the Public, KITCHEN RANGES, from the latest improved principle, combining oeconomy with utility. Likewise, Smoke Jacks, which may be oiled by any servant, without going up the chimney.[84]

Such machines needed maintenance and repair, as Woodforde found with his weight-driven jack: 'Mr Symonds came here this afternoon and cleaned my jack and took away the compass wheel, as it required so large a weight to it and was always breaking the line. I hope now it will go better and with a less weight.'[85]

In better-off homes, cookbooks were increasingly used in the kitchen. Many were published during the eighteenth century, and the most popular ones remained in print for years, such as *The Art of Cookery Made Plain and Easy*, first published by Hannah Glasse in 1747. Aimed at households with servants, it was designed both for the servants and for the mistress of the house (so that she could direct them). Because Glasse was writing a book to be read by servants, she apologised to her lady readers for the use of simple language: 'my intention is to instruct the lower sort, and therefore [I] must treat them in their own way'.[86]

Glasse's cookbook contained a variety of household information, including all kinds of recipes, such as how to 'roast a pig' and 'make a currey the indian way', handy tips on how to 'keep venison or hares sweet, or to make them fresh when they stink' and 'how to keep clear from bugs'.[87] The latter process advised sealing the draught holes in the affected room and then fumigating it by burning brimstone on a charcoal fire, but after six hours, 'If you find great swarms about the room, and some not dead, do this over again, and you will be clear.'[88]

This and other popular cookbooks were reprinted, copied and plagiarised over many years, but they would have been of little use to working-class people, who subsisted mainly on bread, potatoes and cheese, with some vegetables, fruit and meat. The type of food varied across the regions of England, so that in Kendal in Westmorland in March 1795, Frederick Eden recorded: 'Oat-cake is the principal bread used by the labouring classes: the men generally eat hasty-pudding, or boiled milk, twice a day: the women live much on tea, but have, of late, discontinued the use of sugar. Potatoes are a general article for dinner: they are sometimes eaten with a little butter, and sometimes with meat.'[89] The poor were accustomed to buying grain in small quantities and having it ground at the local mill, or else they purchased flour direct from the millers. Mills, particularly windmills, were to be seen everywhere. When he arrived at Liverpool in 1805, Benjamin Silliman remarked: 'The city is surrounded by lofty windmills, which are among the first objects that strike a stranger coming in from the sea.'[90] They were so commonplace in the landscape that after one violent gale in Norfolk, Woodforde simply noted: 'Many windmills blown down.'[91]

The increase in population, bad harvests in the 1790s and the lengthy wars with France led to food shortages. Farmers made more profits by selling in bulk to the millers and by holding back their crops until prices rose. This withholding was made possible by the banks lending farmers money as a low-risk investment. Similarly, the millers increased their income by selling flour directly to the bakers. Inevitably, bread prices rose, and in November 1795 Eden noted at Hereford: 'The labouring classes, who usually bake their own bread, say, it is extremely difficult to procure a small quantity of corn from the farmer; and that the millers and mealmen buy it in large quantities, and exact a large profit from the consumer.'[92]

A few months before, the caricaturist James Gillray had lampooned William Pitt, the Prime Minister, for having advised people to eat meat rather than bread, a remark worthy of Marie Antoinette, demonstrating how little the politician knew about England's poor. Gillray's cartoon, 'The British butcher, supplying John Bull with a substitute for bread', depicted Pitt as a butcher, accompanied by a verse:

BILLY the BUTCHER'S advice to JOHN BULL.

Since bread is so dear, (and you say you must Eat,)
For to save the expence, you must live upon Meat;
And as Twelve Pence the Quartern you can't pay for Bread
Get a Crown's worth of Meat, – it will serve in its stead.[93]

Sporadic food riots were breaking out across England, but rather than loot, the mob used the threat of violence to force profiteers to sell their goods more cheaply. The tailor Thomas Carter recalled these wretched times of his childhood in Colchester, Essex:

The first [memory] is the great scarcity of wheat and other bread-corn during the year 1800. This to poor people was the source of much distress. My father's wages were but ten shillings and sixpence per week, and my mother's little [dame] school brought from two to three shillings more. With very little besides this scanty income, they had to provide for the wants of themselves and four children, while bread was sold at the enormous price of one shilling and tenpence for the quartern loaf. We were consequently forced to put up with very insufficient fare, and sometimes with that which was rather hurtful than nutritious.[94]

Unscrupulous bakers concealed cheaper, often harmful, additives in brown bread. Consumers therefore preferred white bread, but bakers could also adulterate this bread with chalk, alum or even bone-meal. Another ploy was selling undersize loaves, though authorities did try to prevent such abuses. News of the arrest and prosecution of bakers was always popular, as in London in October 1807: 'MARL-BOROUGH-STREET.– A Baker, of the name of Dix, who resides in High-street, Mary-le-Bonne, was charged by the Parish Inspectors with exposing a quantity of bread deficient by weight. A quantity of light bread was produced by the Officers, and there appeared in the whole a deficiency of 29 ounces, for which the Defendant was fined 7l. 10s.'[95]

Underhand tricks were likewise done with milk. In a survey of agriculture in 1806, John Middleton, a land surveyor, reckoned that over 8500 cows were kept for milk near London.[96] Farmers were paid for milking the herds by dairy retailers who, as he explained, diluted the milk:

> Every cow-house is provided with a milk room ... mostly furnished with a pump, to which the retailers apply in rotation; not secretly but openly, before any person that may be standing by; from which they pump water into the milk vessels at their discretion. The pump is placed there expressly for that purpose, and it is seldom used for any other. A considerable cow-keeper in Surrey has a pump of this kind, which goes by the name of the *black cow* (from the circumstance of its being painted with that colour); it is said to yield more than all the rest put together.[97]

Matters were worse where no pump was provided,

> for in that case the retailers are not even careful to use clean water. Some of them have been seen to dip their pails in a common horse-trough. And, what is still more disgusting, though equally true, one cow-house happens to stand close to the edge of a stream, into which runs much of the dung, and most of the urine, of the cows; and even in this stream, so foully impregnated, they have been observed to dip their milk-pails.[98]

The milk was next taken to the retailers' homes and left for a day, so that the cream rose to the surface to be skimmed off. The deteriorating milk was then sold as fresh, while the cream was sold separately or made into butter, particularly when the upper classes were in town: 'When the families of fashion are in London for the winter season, the consumption, and consequent deterioration, of milk, are at the highest. During the summer months, when such families are for the most part in the country, the milk may probably be of a better quality.'[99] Middleton rightly thought that the situation was scandalous: 'A cow-keeper informs me, that the retail milk-dealers are, for the most part, the refuse of other employments;

possessing neither character, decency of manners, nor cleanliness. No delicate person could possibly drink the milk, were they fully acquainted with the filthy manners of these dealers.'[100]

All kinds of other foods were adulterated, either by adding cheaper substances to increase profits, or else by freshening unfit food, such as sprinkling fresh blood over putrid meat. For the lower classes, the best meat they might eat was ham or bacon, but more likely the less popular parts of pigs or else rabbits and hares, sometimes obtained by poaching. Birds of all sizes were eaten by all classes, from larks and pigeons to pheasants, chickens and occasionally swans. In June 1808 Nelly Weeton received a gift from her brother Tom: 'My uncle is obliged to you for your present of rooks. As my uncle is so very fond of those little nick-nacks ... I took the liberty of presenting the two you intended for me, to him, so that the whole five composed a handsome pie for his dinner, and my Aunt's too.'[101] Rooks were a nuisance, but at least they were edible.

Other birds were often considered a delicacy. In 1788, when John Byng and a friend were exploring the Sussex downland around Hastings, they gathered ingredients for their dinner:

After walking the beach, we ascended the steep hill ... searching many turf-traps set for wheat-ears [which nest in holes in the ground], when the custom is to leave a penny for every caught bird you take away. Within the castle, we seated ourselves for some time, delighted with the weather, the freshness of the sea-breeze and the cheerfulness of the scenery; till the shepherd came to survey his traps, when we paid him sevenpence for his capture of seven birds, whom we sat instantly to pluck in preparation of our dinner spit; and it wou'd have made others laugh to have seen us at our poulterers work; which, being finish'd, we hasten'd back to the inn [to have them cooked].[102]

Some cookbooks included recipes for preserving these birds: '*To pot wheatears*. Pick them very clean, season them with pepper and salt, put them in a pot, cover them with butter, and bake them one hour; take them and put them in a colander to drain the liquor away; then cover them with clarified butter, and they will keep.'[103]

Parson Woodforde enjoyed his meals and recorded numerous details about food in his diary. In January 1780 he ate some swan at a dinner with the squire:

> We had for dinner a calfs head, boiled fowl and tongue, a saddle of mutton rosted on the side table, and a fine swan rosted with currant jelly sauce for the first course. The second course a couple of wild fowl called dun fowls, larks, blamange, tarts &c. &c. and a good desert of fruit after amongst which was a damson cheese. I never eat a bit of swan before, and I think it good eating with sweet sauce. The swan was killed 2 weeks before it was eat and yet not the least bad taste in it.[104]

Beef roasted on spits was so popular that the French nickname for the English was 'le rosbif' (roast beef), though mutton, lamb, pork and venison were likewise favoured. Most of the carcass was cooked, with nothing allowed to go to waste, as seen in cookbooks which had recipes for dishes like 'Ox cheeks, baked', 'Neat's feet, fried', 'Pigs feet and ears, to pickle', 'Lamb stones, fried' and 'Calves heads, in ragout'.[105] Various kinds of fish were consumed, and being cheap and plentiful, oysters were widely eaten by the lower classes.

Vegetables were frequently referred to as 'garden stuff', which most people with gardens grew. Virtually nothing was imported, but wealthy estates had hothouses (greenhouses) for delicate produce like grapes. William Holland with his manservant was constantly growing vegetables. 'Busy in my garden this day with Robert,' he noted in mid-March 1800, 'preparing ground for early potatoes.'[106] Four days later: 'Very busy with Robert in the garden, we sowed some onions and carrots',[107] then 'Five rows of peas put in this morning, and I myself raked the asparagus bed and howed the cabbage.'[108] Later that week he recorded: 'Robert ... sowed some turnap [turnip] seeds among the currant and gooseberry bushes.'[109] Salads largely comprised lettuce and cucumbers, with Holland commenting later in June: 'Robert busy in the garden. He manages a cucumber bed for me but brings it on very slow, and late, like himself, yet the plants look healthy. As to myself I regard cucumbers little, and only eat them stewed, and the dung of the bed serves afterwards for the garden.'[110]

Holland never mentioned tomatoes. Few people grew them, and like most vegetables including cucumbers they were cooked, a fortunate precaution considering that cesspit contents were spread as manure.

He also took pride in the rest of his garden, with its lawns, shrubs and flower borders, and Louis Simond certainly found English lawns attractive, as he noted in June 1810:

> The ground, ploughed and harrowed carefully, is either sown or sodded; rolling and mowing, and a moist climate do the rest, for there is nothing at all peculiar in the grass itself. The rolling is principally done in the spring ... The mowing, or rather shaving of this smooth surface, is done once a week ... The grass must be wet with dew or rain, and the scythe very sharp; the blade is wide, and set so obliquely on the handle, as to lye very flat on the sod. The rollers are generally of cast iron, 18 or 20 inches in diameter, and two and a half or three feet long, hollow, and weigh about 500 pounds, moved about by one man; those drawn by a horse are, of course, three or four times heavier.[111]

In Norfolk Woodforde was also obsessed with his garden, and in June 1794 he bought a new roller for £4: 'Sent Ben early this morning to Norwich with my great cart, after my new garden roller of cast-iron. He returned home with it before two o'clock ... It is a very clever roller and is called the ballance roller, as the handle never goes to the ground. It is certainly very expensive, but certainly also very handy.'[112]

Most fruit that was grown in people's gardens was cooked rather than eaten raw, and sweet boiled puddings were so popular with all classes that they were another characteristic of the English. Along with roast beef, plum (or 'plumb') pudding was a national dish, frequently appearing in satirical prints – 'plums' in these puddings meant dried raisins:

A good plum pudding.
    TAKE a pound and a quarter of beef sewet [suet], when skinned, and shred it very fine; then stone three quarters of a pound of raisins, and mix with it; add a grated nutmeg, a quarter of a pound of sugar, a little salt, a little sack, four eggs, four spoonsful of cream, and about half a pound of

fine flour, mixing them well together, pretty stiff; tie it in a cloth, and let it boil four hours. Melt butter thick for sauce.[113]

Food was difficult to keep fresh. In order to survive the winter, fruit and vegetables were stored, but vermin, mildew and freezing weather were constant hazards. Caught by an unusually hard frost in December 1784, Gilbert White in Selborne recorded: 'We were much obliged to the thermometers for the early information they gave us; and hurried our apples, pears, onions, potatoes, &c. into the cellar, and warm closets; while those who had not, or neglected such warnings, lost all their store of roots and fruits, and had their very bread and cheese frozen.'[114] The dreadful winter of 1798–9 prompted Woodforde to despair: 'Scarce ever known such distressed times ... no vegetation, every thing almost dead in the gardens ... All kind of garden-stuff, except potatoes that have been well covered and in ground, are almost all gone dead; potatoes that have been dug up, tho' kept in house are allmost all froze and useless.'[115]

Meat and dairy produce could be kept cool in pantries and cellars, but in hot weather everything deteriorated rapidly, as White observed in the summer of 1783: 'from *June* 23 to *July* 20 inclusive ... the heat was so intense that butchers' meat could hardly be eaten on the day after it was killed'.[116] Even during normal summers meat did not remain fresh for long, and so animals were slaughtered close to markets in the heart of towns and cities, especially in London. Cattle were driven to fairs across England from as far afield as Ireland, Wales and Scotland, their hooves fitted by blacksmiths with iron shoes specifically for the lengthy journey. Such was the huge number seen at Wetherby in Yorkshire in the autumn of 1789 that the local newspaper commented: 'A greater quantity of Scotch and Irish cattle have passed through Wetherby turnpike-bar, this season, than the oldest person ever remembers to have seen – most of which were for the South-country markets. One drover in particular had near 1000 beasts, all Irish ones.'[117]

A lot of food could be preserved by smoking, pickling or salting, while fruit might be made into jams and meat potted to keep it longer. Ice helped to chill food and drinks and enabled iced dishes to be made, including ice creams and sorbets. When she was staying at Lyme Regis in September 1804, Jane Austen wrote satirically to Cassandra: 'Your account of Weymouth contains nothing which strikes me so forcibly as there being no ice in the town. For every other vexation I was in some measure prepared, and particularly for your disappointment in not seeing the Royal Family go on board ... but for there being no ice what could prepare me? Weymouth is altogether a shocking place.'[118]

The wealthy had ice-houses in their gardens, in which ice could be kept successfully for much of the year. In severe winters, servants and labourers obtained ice from frozen lakes, canals and rivers, piling it on sledges or carts and then taking it to these ice-houses. During mild winters, ice may have been obtained instead from whaling vessels.[119] Most ice-houses were brick-built, domed or arched structures, partly underground, and the ice was loaded through the roof or a doorway. Bundles of straw or reeds were placed on the floor and sides as further insulation, enabling the ice to remain frozen for months. One story amused the *Morning Post* newspaper in 1811: 'A well-known miser not having given an entertainment during a summer, and his ice-house remaining still quite full in the month of January, his steward asked him what he should do with all the ice? "Why!" replied Mr. B. "let it *be given to the poor!*"'[120]

Ice-houses were even constructed beneath London's streets, sometimes with disastrous consequences, such as in 1802 by St Mary le Strand church: 'A Confectioner, who rents a house directly opposite ... on the northern side of the Strand, some time ago formed a plan of making an ice-house directly in front, under the street ... The workmen then proceeded to excavate ... digging below the cellars of the neighbouring houses.'[121] The whole lot caved in and 'the three houses next to it were placed in the most imminent danger, the flagway and cellars having fallen into the excavation'.[122]

The wealthy might have had ice, but water itself was not widely drunk because palatable supplies were not readily available. Elizabeth Ham recalled that for supper at her boarding school at Tiverton in Devon, 'we had a little bit of bread with a little bit of cheese on it, and a little cider in a little mug. No one in these days ever dreamt of

drinking water.'[123] Devon was a county that made prodigious quantities of cider, but the main drink in England was 'small beer', also
referred to as 'small ale' or 'common beer'. Woodforde called it 'table
beer', while strong ales were just 'beer' or 'strong beer'. Small beer was
safer than water, and because of its low alcohol content, it was not
intoxicating.

As well as making his own table beer, Woodforde also made mead:
'Busy most part of the afternoon in making some mead wine, to
fourteen pound of honey, I put four gallons of water, boiled it more
than an hour with ginger and two handfulls of dried elder-flowers in
it, and skimmed it well. Then I put it into a small tub to cool, and
when almost cold I put in a large gravey-spoon full of fresh yeast,
keeping it in a warm place, the kitchen during night.'[124] The honey for
the mead came from the beehives that both he and his niece Nancy
kept. In January 1798 Nancy received a new swarm: 'Mr. Stoughton of
Sparham sent Miss Woodforde to day a skep of bees by his farming
man Jon. Springle who brought them all the way on foot and upon
his head tyed up in a cloth. He was 4 hours almost coming from
Sparham [about 4 miles away]. I gave the man a good dinner, some
strong beer, and made him a present besides of half a guinea in gold
10.6.'[125]

Alcohol was popular and drunk to excess by many, but a class
divide existed, because the poorest drank beer and spirits – but rarely
wine. The tax known as excise duty, payable on all alcoholic drinks,
was frequently increased to help fund the ongoing wars. This was a
highly unpopular move with most consumers, such as the clergyman
William Jones: 'Most men know when they have had too little wine,
especially since Mr. Pitt has *poisoned – alias* – highly taxed – wine.'[126]
Apart from home brewing, one way of avoiding tax was buying liquor
from smugglers. Smuggling formed a nationwide industry operated
by numerous gangs, such as those encountered by John Byng in
August 1782 when travelling through the New Forest: 'I cross'd a
black heath where I met two gangs of smugglers, whom I wonder'd
not to have seen oftener in my ride.'[127]

Parson Woodforde constantly bought gin, brandy and rum, as on
one occasion the previous year when 'Clerk Hewitt of Mattishall

Burgh called on me this even' by desire of Mrs. Davy to taste some smuggled gin which I tasted and he is to bring me a tub this week.'[128] With much else heavily taxed, smugglers supplied a range of goods, including tea, which Woodforde also purchased: 'Andrews the Smuggler brought me this night about 11 o'clock a bagg of hyson tea 6 Pd weight. He frightned us a little by whistling under the parlour window just as we were going to bed. I . . . paid him for the tea at 10s/6d per Pd.'[129] He regularly recorded illicit purchases, as in his diary entry for 17 May 1780: 'I did not go to bed till after 12 at night, as I expected Richd. Andrews the honest smuggler with some gin.'[130] Ten days later he paid Andrews £2 10s for two casks, so avoiding around £3 in duty – at a time when his senior maid earned £5 11s 6d a year and his highest-paid manservant £10.[131] In September 1809 William Wilkinson, serving in the Royal Navy, warned his wife: 'Don't buy any more tea or sugar. I expect some from Guernsey, but say nothing about it for fear that it should be seized.'[132]

Better-off families kept their tea in special lockable tea-caddies to prevent it being pilfered by the servants. It tended to be used sparingly, so that it was made as a fairly weak drink, to which milk and sugar were added. Temperance campaigners advocated tea instead of beer, but others insisted that beer was more nutritious for working people on poor diets, as well as better value for money. While tea had filtered down to the working classes, coffee remained the preserve of the coffee house and the middle and upper classes. It was drunk at home less frequently than tea, and the quality was extremely variable, often being criticised for being too dark and burnt, though Carl Moritz found the opposite: 'I would always advise those who wish to drink coffee in England, to mention before hand how many cups are to be made with half an ounce, or else the people will probably bring them a prodigious quantity of brown water; which (notwithstanding all my admonitions) I have not yet been able wholly to avoid.'[133]

For those who could afford to eat well, breakfast was the first meal of the day, though a minimal affair, rarely more than toast with tea or coffee, while poorer households drank small beer. Often the toast was made during the meal by holding slices of bread in front of the fire on toasting forks. 'A breakfast is a comfortable meal when our little family assemble around the breakfast table in good spirits with a strong blazing fire,' William Holland wrote in February 1800.[134] His daughter Margaret usually prepared the family's breakfast, which they had in the study or the arbour outdoors when fine, and a few months later he noted: 'Margaret made breakfast in the study. My wife did not join us, tho Little William [did] and tho he had breakfasted before, [he] eat up a great quantity of toast, whey and curds and sugar.'[135]

On another morning, Holland grumbled: 'We did not breakfast before ten this morning... I do not like this,'[136] and when Woodforde rose late after a rather long night, he observed: 'We breakfasted quite at a fashionable hour 11-o' clock.'[137] Holland preferred having breakfast fairly early, but the lower classes worked for several hours before they had anything to eat.

In Georgian times lunch hardly existed, although for those who breakfasted early, a small snack might be eaten. In towns many shops sold pies and pastries, while street sellers offered shellfish and other ready-to-eat items. Dinner was the main meal, eaten at any time in the afternoon between two and five o'clock. The timing of dinner was related to the hours of daylight, since the cooks needed to work in daylight, especially for formal dinners with guests where preparations could take hours. Dinnertime for the elite became later and later, and in contrast to the meagre breakfast, a formal dinner could be a dazzling array of food. The first course, served on the table all at once, had numerous dishes, and was followed by a second course with a smaller selection of meats and fish, along with savoury and sweet items. Finally, a selection of nuts, sweetmeats and occasionally fruit constituted the dessert course, at which point the servants withdrew.

When Woodforde entertained Squire Custance and other guests, he did his best to provide a suitable feast: 'I gave them for dinner, a couple of chicken boiled and a tongue, a leg of mutton boiled and capers, and batter pudding for the first course. Second, a couple of ducks rosted and green peas, some artichokes, tarts and blamange. After dinner, almonds and raisins, oranges and strawberries. Mountain and port wines.'[138] Even in more modest households, the hostess rose after the dessert course when guests were present and led the ladies to the drawing room, leaving the men to their own conversation for a while before they rejoined the ladies for tea or coffee.

An everyday family dinner was more restrained, and Woodforde routinely recorded meals such as 'Dinner calfs feet stewed, hash mutton &c'[139] or 'Dinner to day hashed calfs head and a loin of lamb rosted with stewed gooseberrries'.[140] For better-off people like Woodforde, even mundane dinners could be lengthy affairs, but most working people had no more than an hour's break for dinner, before continuing with their labours. Supper was the day's final meal and was usually something insubstantial.

Table manners were of importance to the higher classes, although the poorest were more concerned with survival than etiquette. In a book on manners, the Reverend John Trusler warned how to avoid appearing low class or impolite: 'Eating quick, or very slow, at meals, is characteristic of the vulgar; the first infers poverty, that you have not had a good meal for some time; the last, if abroad [dining out], that you dislike your entertainment: if at home [and eating slowly], that you are rude enough to set before your friends what you cannot eat yourself.'[141]

Some hosts did offer food that we would now discard, and just before Christmas 1778 Woodforde unashamedly set before his guests a dinner that included 'part of a ham, the major part of which ham was entirely eaten out by the flies getting into it'.[142] Even so, his guests also stayed for supper, and 'We were exceeding merry indeed all the night.'[143]

FIVE

FASHIONS AND FILTH

I hope you saw her petticoat, six inches deep in mud, I am
absolutely certain; and the gown which had been let down to
hide it not doing its office.

Pride and Prejudice, by Jane Austen

Clothing for men and women changed markedly, in both styles and
fabrics, over Jane Austen's lifetime. Following the French Revolution
grotesquely elaborate fashions gave way to naturalistic styles, imitat-
ing the Classical world. Ladies wore simple gowns based on Greek
and Roman styles that were copied from the many archaeological
finds then being unearthed at places like Pompeii and Herculaneum.
Men's fashions were influenced by more practical military dress,
which resulted in sober clothing, more suitable for country life than
the extravagance of the urban fashions of the preceding period.
Advances in technology also saw the textile industry shifting into factories, so that many more clothes were made from new cotton fabrics
(using imported cotton-wool)[1] rather than the traditional woollen,
linen and silk fabrics.

In order to appear a gentleman, it was necessary to wear breeches
and stockings. Breeches ('culottes') were made of wool, linen, silk or
buckskin (a very soft leather), secured at the knee by ties, buckles or
buttons. They had a front opening covered by a flap, and could look
baggy, though buckskin ones fitted more snugly. Breeches were held

up not by belts but by leather braces or gallowses. The more comfortable pantaloons became fashionable, particularly with the influence of George 'Beau' Brummell; these pantaloons were longer than breeches and were tied or buttoned at the calf – the forerunner of full-length trousers. They were worn with shoes and stockings or else were tucked into boots.[2]

Stockings (hose) were secured beneath the knee by a ribbon or cord garter. For a muscular look, some men put artificial calves under their stockings, but this trend disappeared when pantaloons took over. Stockings were hand knitted from wool or woven in wool, cotton or silk. 'You have said nothing about how you pass your time or amuse yourself,' William Wilkinson wrote to his wife Sarah in December 1809. 'I should think you must be at a loss at times for something to do, tho' I suppose you nit [knit] a great deal now, and must have improved much. I never expect to have to buy any more worsted [woven wool] stockings.'[3] Prone to holes or to runs forming, stockings required constant mending, which made them uncomfortable, as Nelly Weeton warned her brother: 'I would advise you, my dear Tom, that you have the feet of your silk stockings lined with something soft when you put them on, or the darning will hurt your feet.'[4]

To prevent clothes being lost or muddled, they were sewn with identification marks, and at Northampton in April 1778 one thief made off with the clothing of an unnamed aristocrat:

STOLEN, out of the George Inn Yard ... between Eight and Nine o'Clock on Saturday Evening ... A PORTMANTEAU, containing six Shirts, marked S. and a Coronet; six Pair of Silk Stockings, marked S. and a Coronet; Six Stocks, marked S. six Handkerchiefs, marked S. and a Coronet; three Shirts, marked I.H. three Stocks, marked H. two Pair of Silk Stockings, marked I.H. one Sky-blue Coat with gilt Buttons; and divers other Articles.[5]

Some breeches had a lining, known as drawers, that could be washed separately, with longer versions for pantaloons. Shirts and drawers were the male underwear of the day, though drawers were not universally worn. Shirts were longer at the back than at the front, with voluminous sleeves and an ornate cuff that had no holes for cufflinks. 'I would have completed the repair of your shirt,' Nelly told Tom, 'but had no cloth fine enough to make a new neck; and I did not know what to do with the ruffles, so I left them as they were. I have sent some wrist-bands which I stitched a few years ago for your old shirts. I fear they will be too strait; if not, they may be useful perhaps.'[6]

Shirts tended to be white in colour, shorter than nightshirts but similar in style. They were pulled on over the head and fastened with ties or buttons. The fastenings were concealed by a frill, often detach-able, known then as a jabot or chitterlon. Above the jabot, a stiff stock covered the neck, or else a cravat was wound round and tied at the front.[7] In June 1810, when William Holland was sixty-four years old, he was lucky to escape severe injury or worse, as he explained:

A bad accident had nearly happened to me last night as I was moving about the house with a candle in my hand to see all safe just before I went up stairs to bed. The point of my cravat caught fire and blazed immedi-ately up to my chin and was going round my neck and to my shirt like wild fire. I holloed out and George [his servant] stood stupidly by me. Providentially however I seised the blazing cravat and all with both my hands and squeeze [squeezed] them hard and stifled the blaze almost instantaneously or I know not what might have been the consequence.[8]

Such ornate shirts were a sign of a gentleman, but instead of put-ting on a clean shirt, it was useful to have a false shirt front or dickey – defined in a dictionary of 1811 as 'a sham shirt'.[9] Two years earlier Nelly Weeton had noted that 'Mr. Chorley is quite a buck, and dashes away in his silk stockings, his Dickey and his quizzing glass [a single-lens glass held in the hand].'[10] Waistcoats were worn by men over their shirts, but when it became fashionable to have them fully buttoned up, frilly shirts were barely visible and so became less pop-ular for daytime use.[11] In *Sense and Sensibility* Marianne Dashwood despises Colonel Brandon because 'he talked of flannel waistcoats; and with me a flannel waistcoat is invariably connected with aches, cramps, rheumatisms, and every species of ailment that can afflict the old and the feeble'. Flannel was a type of woollen fabric associated with keeping warm and protecting the infirm.

Gentlemen had their breeches and jackets made to measure by tailors. There was no concept of buying good-quality, ready-made clothes. Long jackets or coats, often dark blue, were worn over waistcoats and by 1800 they were 'cut-away' – short at the front with long tails at the back – while greatcoats provided even more protection against the weather. Short jackets known as spencers (after the 2nd Earl Spencer who started the trend)[12] became popular from the 1790s. This type of double-breasted jacket had no tails, though they were often put on over a traditional jacket with tails.

The poor wore whatever was affordable, either purchased second-hand or from slop-shops supplying new, cheap, ready-made clothes. Labourers preferred comfortable, hard-wearing garb, and in London the writer Samuel Pratt described one coal heaver who was wearing a 'coarse and heavy doublet [waistcoat] of many different coloured patches, formed of pieces of carpeting of brown sacking, and of yellow plush, all brought into the same sable [blackened with coal] uniform – his hose ungartered, his breeches knees unbuttoned, his shirt opened almost to the waist'.[13] Loose full-length trousers were the preserve of labourers and seamen.

When women got dressed, they first of all donned a shift or chemise,[14] which was a simple sleeved linen undergarment that reached just below the knees. It was put on over the head and secured at the neck with a drawstring or buttons. A similar longer garment was worn at night, with a cap. Over the shift went stays or a corset – a shaped garment with strips of pliable whalebone (baleen) or cane sewn into the fabric. Stays were wrapped round the upper torso and tightly laced at the back. They were lower at the front and usually had shoulder straps. Worn from childhood, stays kept the figure shapely and the waist tiny.

In May 1780 Parson Woodforde recorded that his niece Nancy 'had a new pr. of stays brought home this morn' by one Mottram a staymaker at Norwich. She paid him for the same 1.11.6. For his journey from Norwich to measure her she pd. 2.6.'[15] The style of stays

A possible portrait of Jane Austen (though disputed), published by William and Richard A. Austen-Leigh in *Jane Austen: Her Life and Letters. A Family Record* (1913). The girl wears a muslin gown and flimsy shoes, and carries a parasol.

The cottage in Chawton, Hampshire, where Jane Austen lived from 1809 to 1817. It overlooked the main road from London to Gosport (Portsmouth) as well as another road leading to Winchester. The cottage is now a popular museum.

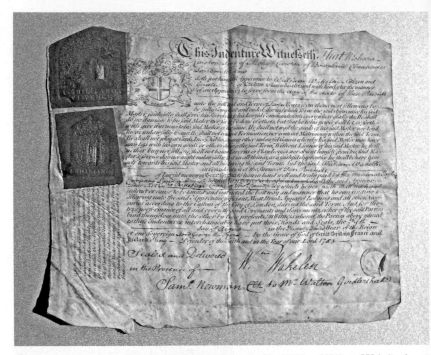

Parchment indenture of Richard Cureton, apprenticed in 1783 to William Wakelin (or Wakelen), girdler.

A view of London and the River Thames in 1814 from Blackfriars Bridge, with St Paul's cathedral on the left and Southwark on the far right. Before its embankment, the river was much wider than today.

A woman using water from a pump near cottages in
Wenlock, Shropshire, in 1815.

A 1794 halfpenny token of John Fowler,
a London whale oil merchant, depicting
four men in a boat about to hurl a
harpoon at a whale spouting water.

Building new terraced houses, with a
bricklayer standing on wooden scaffolding
while a labourer mixes mortar.

A fashion plate of 1800 called 'Afternoon dress', which was the formal 'half dress' worn by wealthier women for attending afternoon functions like dinners. The women are carrying fans and wearing simple muslin gowns and fashionable caps.

A weaver making worsted stockings on a stocking loom.

A hairdresser cutting and dressing the long hair of a male customer. Both men are wearing knee-length breeches and stockings.

St Peter and St Paul church in Over Stowey, Somerset, where William Holland was vicar from 1798 until his death in 1819. He lived in the vicarage on the opposite side of the lane

A copper penny token issued at Bath in 1811 depicting the city arms with clasped hands above. The reverse says 'a pound note for 240 tokens given by S. Whitchurch and W. Dore'. Whitchurch was an ironmonger and Dore a hatter and draper.

Reverse of a copper 'cartwheel' twopence of George III, so-called because of its large size (41mm diameter, 5mm thickness and weighing 2 ounces). Such coins were made from 1797 at Matthew Boulton's Soho mint in Birmingham using the new steam-powered machinery.

A copper halfpenny of 1791 (obverse and reverse) issued by the copper works of Charles Roe at Macclesfield. The year before John Byng received Macclesfield halfpennies as change at a turnpike.

The obverse and reverse of a halfpenny copper token of the industrialist John Wilkinson. The reverse shows a drop hammer suspended above a piece of iron on an anvil. Around the edge the place-names Willey, Snedshill, Bersham and Bradley showed where the tokens were redeemable.

A man viewed from the rear seated at a loom, depicted on a 1791 copper halfpenny token. It was payable at the warehouse of John Kershaw, a Rochdale mercer and draper.

By 1792 the design changed, as seen on this halfpenny token, also payable at the warehouse of John Kershaw, a Rochdale mercer and draper.

Advertisements requesting employment as a mantua maker and a cook in the *Morning Chronicle* newspaper for 29 October 1807.

A workhouse depicted on a copper penny token issued by the Overseers of the Poor at Sheffield. This workhouse was located at Workhouse Croft (now Paradise Street), West Bar. Such workhouse tokens were given as poor relief and were accepted by local retailers.

Joseph Johnson, a crippled black beggar and former merchant seaman, travelled round London and nearby villages and market towns, performing nautical songs and wearing on his head a model of the warship *Nelson*.

A boy selling matches in a London street.

"POTATOES, FULL WEIGHT!"

A child street hawker selling potatoes from a wooden wheelbarrow. This romanticised view dating to 1812 shows an unlikely well-nourished child.

The River Tyne in 1789 with shallow-draught keels for transporting coal, looking towards Newcastle-upon-Tyne, with the castle keep and cathedral on the right.

changed with the fashion, but the physician Hugh Smith praised those women who stopped wearing stays, so 'giving themselves room in the waist'.[16] Young girls, he reckoned, 'were greatly injured by the stiffness of their stays, and by being laced so exceedingly close'.[17] By 1785 their popularity was declining, prompting him to add: 'We now rarely see ladies fainting in public places.'[18]

Also worn over the shift was an ankle-length waist petticoat, with a gown over the petticoat. Gowns had a bodice and a full-length skirt that was wide open at the front, revealing the often-matching petticoat – these petticoats were not underwear intended to be concealed. Since 1710 immensely wide, cumbersome hoop petticoats had been fashionable, supported on a framework of whalebone or lighter cane rods and wire.[19] The gown's skirt was sometimes bunched up at the rear, accompanied by a false rump called a bustle, which was a padded roll filled with cork or other stuffing. With artificial contrivances like the hoop and bustle, one poem in 1777 issued a mock warning to husbands of fashionable women:

> Let her gown be tuck'd up to the hip on each side;
> Shoes too high for to walk, or to jump;
> And, to deck the sweet creature complete for a bride,
> Let the cork-cutter make her a rump.
> Thus finish'd in taste, while on Chloe you gaze,
> You may take the dear charmer for life;
> But never undress her—for, out of her stays,
> You'll find you have lost half your wife.[20]

Hoop petticoats fell out of favour in the 1780s, though they persisted as court dress until the 1820s. In 1805 the young American Benjamin Silliman was amused at the sight of the nobility parading near St James's Palace for the king's birthday: 'The ladies wore hoop petticoats; the hoop was not a circle, but a large oval ... the ladies, as they passed through the crowd contrived to twist the whole machinery round, so as to bring the shortest diameter across the path ... it was no small achievement to deposit one of the ladies safely in her coach'.[21]

The new fashion was for round gowns, which had skirts completely encircling the body, so that petticoats were now more of an undergarment. By the 1790s the style of gowns was further transformed, with a slimmer, more naturalistic, classical shape, white or pale in colour. Sashes were tied round the waist or under the bust, and trains became fashionable, though mainly for evening wear. By about 1800 gowns had short sleeves and a short bodice – a low neckline and high waistline. With the constantly changing fashions, long and short sleeves went in and out of favour.

Fabrics such as fine muslins were initially imported from India, but the invention by James Hargreaves around 1767 of the spinning jenny enabled the production of greater quantities of cotton yarn for weaving into cloth, initially by workers in their homes, while Richard Arkwright's spinning frame, powered by water, produced stronger cotton yarn for the warp threads. From 1779 Samuel Crompton's spinning mule, driven by water and later steam, combined features from both inventions, enabling fine cotton thread to be spun in factories on a massive scale. These developments led to cheaper muslins and calicoes becoming widely available, and cotton surpassed silk, linen and woollen fabrics in popularity. By 1793 it was said that 'every shop offers British muslins for sale equal in appearance, and of more elegant patterns than those of India, for one-fourth, or perhaps more than one-third, less in price'.[22]

With these fine fabrics, gowns could be virtually transparent, and modesty was forsaken. At the end of 1799 *The Times* ridiculed such women's dress and the fashion for false bosoms:

> If the present fashion of nudity continues its career, the Milliners must give way to the carvers, and the most elegant *fig-leaves* will be all the mode. The fashion of false bosoms has at least this utility, that it compels our fashionable fair to wear *something*. The stuffed bosoms of our females are at least *oeconomical* – they are made out of the old *Jean Debry* coats [no longer in fashion] of their husbands.[23]

William Holland was appalled by one woman's dress when he was dining at South Molton in Devon in September 1803: 'Captain and

Mrs Law, the gentleman handsome and of pleasing manners, the lady diminutive, affected and almost naked in her dress. It disgusts me much to see such conduct.'[24]

Undergarments were kept to a minimum beneath these thin gowns, and a shorter corset had replaced the restrictive stays. In mid-September 1813, when Jane Austen was in London, she wrote to Cassandra: 'I learnt from Mrs Tickar's young lady, to my high amusement, that the stays now are not made to force the bosom up at all; that was a very unbecoming, unnatural fashion. I was really glad to hear that they are not to be so much off the shoulders as they were.'[25] These new fashions proved rather chilly to wear, and invisible stockinette petticoats manufactured on a stocking loom were one solution, as advertised in the *Morning Chronicle* in 1807:

> INVISIBLE PETTICOATS.– Mrs. ROBERT-SHAW informs the Ladies, that her Patent, Elastic, Spanish Lamb's-wool INVISIBLE PETTICOATS, Drawers, Waistcoats, and Dresses, all in one, are now ready for their inspection – articles much approved of by every lady that has made trial of them, for their pleasant elasticity, softness and warmth; are found very convenient to ladies who ride on horseback.[26]

Because stockings were only knee high, women's thighs were bare beneath their gowns. They did not wear drawers until the early nineteenth century, when they apparently became acceptable after Princess Charlotte was seen wearing them. Previously, they were considered masculine and therefore immodest. Similar to men's drawers, the legs were fastened just below the knee.

Gloves were commonly worn in all weathers, not just for keeping warm, but thin gowns led to the fashion for enormous fur muffs and shawls. Men's coats, such as riding coats and spencers, were adapted for female use, and in his diary in June 1799 Woodforde wrote: 'Very cold indeed again to day, so cold that Mrs Custance came walking in her Spenser with a bosom-friend.'[27] He meant that she had a large handkerchief or scarf at her throat to keep her warm, a fashion that arose because of the low necklines and acquired the name 'bosom-friend'.

Pockets were sewn into the breeches, jackets and waistcoats worn by men. For women, large detached pockets, held in place by ties, could be worn under more substantial skirts and were used for items like coins, pocket watches and pocket books. Such pockets were impossible to wear with flimsy muslin gowns, and instead women carried small decorative bags or purses, frequently handmade, that came to be known as ridicules, reticules or indispensables.[28] These were the first handbags. In *Emma*, Emma herself 'saw her [Mrs Elton] ... fold up a letter ... and return it into the purple and gold reticule by her side'. These pockets and bags were vulnerable to theft, as a pickpocket or cut-purse might steal the entire pocket or purse, not just some of the contents. Folding fans were another essential fashion accessory, particularly in overcrowded, overheated environments like balls or theatres, and after one ball Jane Austen told Cassandra: 'I wore my green shoes last night, and took my <u>white fan</u> with me.'[29]

In fashionable circles, the term 'undress' referred to the more practical gowns worn at home in the morning, 'half dress' described smarter clothes worn during afternoon and evening visits, while 'full dress' involved more elaborate, formal garments worn to balls and other evening events. The upper classes followed fashions avidly, while the middle classes did the best they could, but rarely owned many outfits. At home most women wore an apron to protect their clothes, which were expected to last many years.

In his analysis of the poor in the 1790s, Frederick Eden noted the prices of ready-made clothes in slop-shops around London and how long they should last. For women, they included: 'A hat, the cheapest sort; (will last two years,) 1s. 8d ... Cheapest kind of cloak, (will last two years,) 4s. 6d.; Pair of stays, (will last six years), 6s. od.'[30] At Shrewsbury in Shropshire in November 1795 he listed the basic clothing doled out in the workhouse: 'A woman's dress, consisting of a bed-gown, 2 petticoats, linsey apron, shoes, 2 shifts, 2 pair of stockings, and a handkerchief, costs £1 7s. od. ... The women's cloaths are manufactured in the house, at 1s. 6d. a yard; except the flannel petticoats, which cost about 10d. a yard.'[31]

From what Carl Moritz observed during his travels, even the poorest strived to be modern: 'Fashion is so generally attended to among the English women, that the poorest maid servant is careful to be in fashion.'[32] Despite the death of her pupil, Nelly Weeton was kept on as companion to Mrs Pedder, but being in the remote Lake District it was difficult to keep up-to-date, as she admitted to a friend in August 1810: 'I am almost out of the world here, so far as regards fashion, seeing and hearing less than I used to do at Holland [Upholland]; for Mrs. P. and I have no female acquaintance except a village surgeon's wife, and an acquaintance of hers, both of them as plain in their dress, and knowing as little about fashion as can be.'[33]

Jane Austen displayed considerable interest in fashion. On Christmas Day 1798 she wrote to Cassandra: 'I cannot determine what to do about my new gown; I wish such things were to be bought ready-made.'[34] Many women had their clothes such as gowns and jackets made to measure by professional dressmakers, commonly called mantua makers (from the French *manteau*, a 'coat'). When she was living near Liverpool in 1808, Nelly lamented her lack of decent clothes: 'This week I am going to be busy with the mantua maker for two or three days, that I may have something fit to appear in when I get to Mr. C's; for Miss Chorley told me the other day that she could not for shame take me to Christ-Church, I had nothing fit to go in.'[35] Jane confessed similar embarrassment at her outfits to Cassandra: 'I am determined to buy a handsome one [muslin gown] whenever I can, and I am so tired and ashamed of half my present stock, that I even blush at the sight of the wardrobe which contains them.'[36]

Customers either went to the mantua maker's house or were visited by them at home. Woodforde recorded his niece's gowns being altered at home: 'Nancy's mantua-maker, Betty Burroughs of Mattishall-Burgh [4 miles away], came this morning early to our house, to alter some mourning for her. She appears to be a steady, clever young woman. She breakfasted, dined, supped, and slept here. She worked in the parlour and had a good fire &c.'[37] The work lasted three days: 'Betty Burroughs left our house this morning before breakfast, to go to her mother at Mattishall Burgh, having work to do at home ... Nancy paid her for her 3 days work 0.2.0 which I think very reasonable tho' boarded here.'[38] Mantua makers often refurbished old garments: 'Nancy had a brown silk gown trimmed with furr brought home by Cary from the mantua maker Miss Bell. It was a very good rich silk that I gave her that formerly belonged to my poor Aunt Parr, whose effects came to me.'[39]

Whatever their class, most girls learned crafts like needlework, embroidery and knitting, which were vital accomplishments for everyday life, because women spent much of their time mending, altering and embellishing garments and bonnets, turning something old into something new, either for themselves, for younger family members or for charitable gifts. Smaller items of clothing, such as nightwear and undergarments (including men's shirts), were commonly made at home from new fabrics or by reusing old garments and linen. Dorothy Wordsworth was frequently sewing and mending, as in August 1800: 'I sate on the wall making my shifts till I could see no longer.'[40] Jane Austen was likewise proficient at needlework. In one letter to Cassandra she mentioned her plans for a gown that was unfit to wear: 'I will not be much longer libelled by the possession of my coarse spot; I shall turn it into a petticoat very soon.'[41] Jane also sewed shirts for her brothers: 'We are very busy making Edward's shirts, and I am proud to say that I am the neatest worker of the party.'[42]

When women talked of buying new gowns, they meant lengths of cloth for their mantua maker to form into garments. Numerous shops, market stalls and salesmen travelling on foot or by cart sold everything needed for needlework. In mid-April 1782 Woodforde purchased a quantity of fabrics, ribbon and lace from one Norwich salesman:

One Mr [William] Aldridge who carries about cottons, linens, muslins, lace, holland, &c. in a cart and comes round regularly this way once in ten weeks, called at my house this morning, and I bought of him a piece of holland (alias Irish cloth) for shirts, 25 yards at 3s/od per yard, for which I pd him 3.15.0. For half of yard of cambrich for chitterlons 0.5.0. For 7 yards of lace edging for Nancy pd 0.5.0. For 4 yards of ribband for my 2 maids pd 0.2.0.[43]

Beautiful lace for embellishing garments was also sold by travelling 'lacemen' (rarely women) and in shops, but it was frequently made in deplorable conditions by women and children. A letter to the *Gentleman's Magazine* in 1785 about lacemaking in Buckinghamshire and Northamptonshire revealed that 'many of the *workers of lace* are deformed, occasioned by their uneasy posture, and many more are diseased, seemingly owing, in a great measure, to their inclined posture while working'.[44] The duty on foreign lace made it expensive to import, so it was smuggled in by ingenious methods. One seaman near Custom House Quay in London was spotted walking from his ship with a loaf of bread:

> the guardian of public revenue therefore demanded of the man what he embraced so closely; '*Only a stale loaf,*' was the answer. The Officer then took hold of the loaf, which immediately came asunder, and discovered a quantity of valuable prohibited foreign lace. After seizing the lace, the officer returned the loaf to the unfortunate smuggler, and coolly observed, 'this is indeed a very stale loaf, and you may keep it for your breakfast.'[45]

Sometimes smaller items were hawked by salesmen travelling on foot, and in March 1784 Woodforde obtained ribbon and sewing thread from one such packman who periodically called at his village: 'Of one Bagshaw a Derbyshire man and who carries a pack with divers things in it to sell, bought a whole piece of black ribbon 18 yards of it at 3¼d per yard worth 5d, pd. 0.3.3. Nancy bought some coloured ribbon at 5d worth 8d ... To a qr of a pound of 4d thread very good, pd. 0.1.4. To 2 oz: of 4d thread and 2 oz: of 3d thread pd. 0.1.0.'[46] Most sewing thread was of silk, but cotton thread was becoming available.

When in London the Woodfordes visited the better drapery stores with their greater range of goods. Jane Austen did likewise, her favourite stores being Bedford House in Covent Garden and Grafton House in New Bond Street. 'We ... must have reached Grafton House by half-past 11,' she told Cassandra on one visit, 'but when we entered the shop, the whole counter was thronged, and we waited full half an hour before we could be attended to. When we were served, however, I was very well satisfied with my purchases.'[47] Benjamin Silliman praised how the merchandise was displayed in such stores:

You will see a shop at the corner of two streets, completely glazed on both sides, that is, forming one continued window from top to bottom, and from the sides to the corner. This is filled with goods, unrolled and displayed in the most advantageous manner, and cards are usually pinned to the articles, informing the reader how good and how cheap they are. For instance;—'this beautiful piece of muslin at so much, two shillings in a yard cheaper than any other shop in London.'[48]

In northern England in the 1790s, according to Frederick Eden, most families made their own clothes, but there were 'many labourers so poor, that they cannot even afford to purchase the raw material necessary to spin thread or yarn at home'.[49] In London, he said, 'working-people seldom buy new cloaths: they content themselves with a cast-off coat, which may be usually purchased for about 5s. and second-hand waistcoats and breeches. Their wives seldom make up any article of dress, except making and mending cloaths for the children.'[50]

Unwanted garments might be sold as rags for papermaking, for making into items such as rag carpets or for the thriving second-hand clothing market (giving rise to the term 'rag trade' for the entire garment industry). In her native Lake District Dorothy Wordsworth was collecting mosses one morning near Grasmere when she noticed 'sitting in the open field upon his sack of rags the old Ragman that I know. His coat is of scarlet in a thousand patches.'[51] To Silliman, the spectacle of worn-out clothes being sold in London was surprising:

June 24 [1805].—As I was going to the London Dock, this evening, with some companions, we passed through a great crowd of dirty ragged people, to the number of some hundreds. They appeared to be very busy in displaying and examining old clothes which they were pulling out from bags ... This, I was informed, is *rag fair*. It is held here every evening for the sale of old clothes which are collected all over London, principally by Jews, who go about with bags on their shoulders, crying, with a peculiarly harsh guttural sound, *clothes, clothes, old clothes*. You will meet them in every street and alley in London, and at evening they repair to Wapping, where a grand display is made of every species of apparel in every stage of decay. Sometimes they are in tatters, and at other times merely soiled. Here people of the lower ranks may make a selection which is to them really useful.[52]

Old footwear was also recycled, and shortly after meeting the ragman Dorothy Wordsworth encountered 'a woman with two little girls, one in her arms, the other, about four years old, walking by her side, a pretty little thing, but half-starved. She had on a pair of slippers that had belonged to some gentleman's child, down at the heels ... it was not easy to keep them on, but, poor thing! young as she was, she walked carefully with them.'[53] Some retailers offered ready-made footwear, and one shop in London's Fleet Street advertised 'a large assortment of fashionable BOOTS and SHOES, warranted of the best materials and workmanship, equal to bespoke, where Gentlemen may be fitted as well as when measured, without the trouble of waiting'.[54] Silliman also saw much poor-quality footwear on sale in the city: 'there are hundreds of boot and shoe stores, where these articles are sold of such rude workmanship and of such inferior materials that there are few who cannot buy, at least among those articles which are second hand'.[55]

Those with money had their shoes made to measure by cobblers. Men's footwear mainly comprised conservative black leather shoes with a small heel and a large buckle. As styles changed according to fashions, they sometimes sported square toes, sometimes pointed. When dining with friends in June 1784 James Woodforde was astonished to note that 'Mr Micklethwaite had in his shoes a pair of silver buckles which cost between 7 and 8 pounds. Miles Branthwaite had a pair that cost 5 guineas.'[56] Men's shoes were not sufficiently robust to cope with poor weather, and in the Lake District in February 1802 Dorothy Wordsworth recorded: 'We stopped at Park's to get some straw in William's shoes'[57] – the age-old custom of stuffing footwear with anything that might keep feet warm and dry.

That same month, February 1802, James Woodforde wrote in his diary: 'Mrs. Custance with her two daughters called on us this morning, they came walking and very wet and dirty walk they had. Nancy let them have a change of shoes for each of them.'[58] Fashions in women's shoes moved from pointed styles and high stubby heels to lower heels and by 1800 to flat, pointed shoes made from fabric and secured by ribbons. Most were unsuitable for poor weather, as they resembled slippers rather than outdoor shoes. Laced boots provided more robust female footwear, as seen in *Emma* when Harriet is out walking with Emma, who stops 'under pretence of having some alteration to make in the lacing of her half-boot'.

Men increasingly wore leather riding boots, of calf or knee length, which were influenced by boots worn by army officers. In January 1806 William Holland commented on how he and his wife Mary walked home: 'Tho the road was wet yet as my wife had pattens and I boots we got on very well.'[59] In wet conditions boots were the usual footwear for men, while pattens were worn by women. These were a kind of overshoe resembling a wooden-soled sandal to the bottom of which was fastened an iron ring. When women slipped their shoes into pattens, they gained several inches in height and so raised their dress hems above the worst of the wet and the mud. In *Persuasion* Lady Russell enters Bath on a wet afternoon amidst 'the ceaseless clink of pattens'.

Labourers, male and female, were more likely to wear wooden clogs, and at Cumwhitton near Carlisle in April 1796 Frederick Eden noted their prices: 'The common expence of clogs, for a year, in this country (supposing no shoes to be worn), is 4s. 4d. for a man that works out of doors; and about 3s. 8d. for a man within doors; for a woman, 3s. 6d.; and for a boy, about 12 years old, 3s. &c.'[60] Almost a decade later, Charles Fothergill was fascinated to see the lead miners at Reeth in North Yorkshire:

On their feet they wear very formidable clogs, so large, loose and ponderous that they give their wearers a peculiarly ... awkward gait in walking; they must be worn large and loose because the soles, being made of thick wood and shod with iron cannot spring or be in any degree elastic: there is more iron put round the soles of these clogs than is used in the shoes or plates of race horses; indeed it is nailed on and formed in a similar manner.[61]

Heads were usually covered outdoors, and on the Isle of Wight in 1811 Louis Simond was gratified when 'Children and grown people took off their hats, or gave us a nod, as we passed along,'[62] but he felt disappointment with London: 'People do not pull off their hats when ... addressing anybody ... a slight inclination of the head, or motion of the hand, is thought sufficient.'[63] Carl Moritz found he could distinguish army and navy officers by their hats: 'Officers rarely wear their uniforms, but dress like other people, and are to be known to be officers only by a cockade in their hats.'[64] These cockades were ribbon decorations, like rosettes.[65]

For men, the most common waterproof hats were of felted beaver fur, for which many thousands of pelts were imported annually from Europe and North America. Three-cornered hats (known now as tricornes) gave way to flat-crowned, broad-brimmed hats (which later evolved into top-hats). By the early nineteenth century silk hats were fashionable, which were made from hatters' plush, a fine silk weave. Hats were the only item of clothing to be taxed (apart from gloves, for a brief period), and from 1784 hat retailers had to possess an annual licence and charge duty on each hat sold. This tax was repealed in 1811.

The less well-off wore whatever hats they could obtain or make themselves, including ones of oiled cloth, felted wool or the fur of rabbits and other animals. The town of Moretonhampstead in Devon was accustomed to constant military activity, but a month after the 2nd Surrey Militia arrived in July 1799, the townspeople were complaining, as Silvester Treleaven noted in his diary: 'Several cats stolen from different people, supposed to be [by] the soldiers for the skins to make caps. Mr Geo. Gray offered (by public cry) a reward of 5s/- to any person that would bring his cat alive, or if killed one Guinea to the person discovering the same.'[66]

For everyday use as well as special occasions, women would wear fabric caps indoors, and in January 1799 Jane Austen told Cassandra: 'I am not to wear my white satin cap to-night after all; I am to wear a mamalone [Mameluke] cap instead, which Charles Fowle sent to Mary, and which she lends me. It is all the fashion now; worn at the opera, and by Lady Mildmays at Hackwood balls. I hate describing

such things, and I dare say you will be able to guess what it is like.'[67]
Military and naval victories often influenced fashions, and as Nelson
had won a stunning victory at the Battle of the Nile a few months
earlier, these Egyptian-style Mameluke[68] turban-like caps were in
vogue. Women's caps were mostly made at home, but they could be
bought from milliners, who also made and sold items like bonnets,
ribbons, handkerchiefs and aprons. At Canterbury in May 1804, a
Mrs Jones advertised that 'she has *A large and fashionable selection of
Millinery*, prepared for the summer season; a great variety of Straw
Hats and Bonnets; white and coloured Chips [bonnets made from
strips of shaved wood]; Muslin Pelices and Spencers; Fancy Cloaks;
black and white Lace of the best quality, and at very reasonable
prices'.[69]

Ladies wore hats or bonnets outdoors, and they also carried para-
sols for sunshades. These were similar to umbrellas but made from
lighter silk fabrics, because they did not need to be waterproofed.
Umbrellas were heavy to carry, with ribs of whalebone or split cane
mounted on a sturdy stick and covered with a heavy oiled fabric.
They were sold in all colours, though green was especially popular.[70]
Walking along the streets during rainstorms was hazardous, as the
drains or 'kennels' forced pedestrians to keep close to buildings, yet
rain poured off roofs as few gutters or downpipes existed. In
Northanger Abbey Catherine Morland is longing to go out with
friends at Bath, but rain starts to fall. 'There are four umbrellas up
already. How I hate the sight of an umbrella!' she says to Mrs Allen,
who replies: 'They are disagreeable things to carry. I would much
rather take a chair at any time.' Coachmen and the chairmen who
operated sedan chairs objected to umbrellas, because they competed
with their own businesses.

The philanthropist Jonas Hanway died in 1786, and the following
year his biographer wrote: 'He was the first man to walk the streets of
London with an umbrella over his head: After carrying one near
thirty years, he saw them come into general use.'[71] The Scotsman
John Macdonald also claimed to have set the trend for carrying
umbrellas in the capital. He was a well-dressed gentleman's manservant, who had often served abroad, and in January 1778, after

spending more than a year in France, Spain and Portugal, he was back in London:

> If it rained, I wore my fine silk umbrella, then the people would call after me, What, Frenchman, why do you not get a coach? In particular the hackney coachmen and hackney chairmen would call after me; but I ... went straight on, and took no notice. At this time there was no umbrellas worn in London, except in noblemen and gentlemen's houses; where, there was a large one hung in the hall, to hold over a lady or gentleman if it rained, between the door and their carriage. I was going to dine in Norfolk Street, one Sunday. It rained, my sister had hold of my arm, and I had the umbrella over our heads. In Tavistock-street, we met so many young men, calling after us *Frenchman!* take care of your umbrella. *Frenchman*, why do you not get a coach, Monsieur?' My sister was so much ashamed, that she quitted my arm, and ran on before, but I still took no notice but answered in French or Spanish that I did not understand what they said. I went on so for three months, till they took no further notice of me, only *How do you do Frenchman?* After this, the foreigners seeing me with my umbrella, one after another used theirs, then the English. Now it is become a great trade in London, and a very useful branch of business.[72]

By the 1780s umbrellas were more commonly seen, and in January 1787 a blizzard at Weston Longville forced Parson Woodforde to use one in the churchyard when officiating at a funeral: 'I buried a daughter of Harrisons, an infant aged only 5 weeks. I think I never felt the cold more severe than when I was burying the above infant. The wind blowed very strong and snow falling all the time, and the wind almost directly in my face, that it almost stopped my breath in reading the funeral service at the grave, tho' I had an umbrella held over my head during the time.'[73]

As a respectable man, Woodforde would also have worn a wig, made of human or animal hair. In order to wear wigs comfortably, gentlemen had their own hair cropped short or shaved. To display their higher status, professional men like clergy, lawyers and physicians had formerly worn voluminous, full-bottomed wigs – the big wigs of society – but by the late 1770s most gentlemen preferred smaller wigs, sometimes with pigtails or queues. Wigs were kept fresh with hair-powder made from starch, giving them a white or off-white appearance, and so wig wearers invariably had powder over their shoulders and backs. Younger men especially started to give up wigs and instead had their own hair styled and powdered to resemble a wig. In 1786 hair-powder was taxed, which precipitated the abandonment of wigs altogether, and while staying at Cole in Somerset three years later, Woodforde wrote: 'Old Mr. Dalton and son John called on me this morning, stayed half an hour with us. I did not know old Mr. Dalton at first as he now wears his hair.'[74]

Two years later John Byng was at Winchelsea in Sussex. 'I walk'd early to a barbers shop,' he said, 'bought a pound of powder, had my razor set, and did hope for some intelligence from him; but he was deaf!'[75] Barbers, also called hairdressers, 'dressed' men's hair and wigs and shaved them with cut-throat razors, which was a necessary service for those without access to a mirror. The following summer Byng was staying at the Tontine Inn at Sheffield, and as ever he preferred to shave himself: 'My first direction was to the hair-dressers room, where he dress'd my hair, and where I shaved myself; receiving many compliments (for the first time) on my adroitness: "Never did he see a gentleman shave so well!"'[76]

Woodforde often visited barbers to be shaved, at times accompanied by his niece for her hair to be styled, as in London in June 1786: 'Nancy walked with me to one Smiths in Surry Street, Strand, a Barber, and there had her hair full dressed ... I was shaved and had my wig dressed there. I gave him for shaving and dressing 0.1.6.'[77] In 1795 a tax of one guinea on hair-powder was made payable by the head of each household, and this triggered a radical change in men's hairstyles. Instead of paying the tax, the Whigs cut their hair short, in a style called *à la guillotine*, after those forced to have their hair cropped before being executed during the French Revolution. Those Tories who paid the tax were called guinea-pigs. The *Chester Chronicle* printed a short poem on the unwelcome tax:

On Mr. Pitt's Tax of a *Guinea* a-year, for wearing Hair-powder:

> By bob that's black, or brown, and greasy,
> You may distinguish very easy
> One of the common herd of *swine*—
> This is a never-failing sign;
> But by the powder'd hair, or wig,
> You recognize the *Guinea*-pig.[78]

Woodforde was conservative in his ways, even wearing an old wig while in the garden: 'Mr. Charles Townshend of Honingham [Hall] called on me this morning about 11 o'clock and walked round my gardens with me ... He caught me on the hop, being in my garden and dressed in my cotton morning gown, old wigg and hat.'[79] He therefore duly complied with the tax, which he noted in mid-April 1796: 'Paid Mr. Corbould £3. 3s. 0d to day to get three receipts for the powder tax from Norwich on Saturday next, as he goes to Norwich that day.'[80]

Dispensing with wigs markedly changed people's appearance, and their hair was now visible in its natural state. Grey or red hair was considered undesirable, but hair dyes were available, as one newspaper advertised:

ATKINSON'S VEGETABLE DYE

for changing grey or red hair to an auburn or black. This article is presumed to merit the attention of all who have the misfortune to have grey hair early in life, a defect which always makes a person look old, the Vegetable Dye changes it whether red or grey, to a beautiful and permanent auburn or black by so simple a mode of application that a Lady or Gentleman may change the colour of their own hair with ease and secrecy. Price 5s. 7s. 6d. 10s. 6d. and one guinea. CAUTION.–Ask for Atkinson's Fluid, or Atkinson's Dye, and observe the signature, as there are counterfeits.[81]

For women, caps were almost the equivalent of wigs, as they could hide their hair beneath them,[82] something Jane Austen described to Cassandra in December 1798: 'I have made myself two or three caps to wear of evenings since I came home, and they save me a world of torment as to hair-dressing, which at present gives me no trouble beyond washing and brushing, for my long hair is always plaited up out of sight, and my short hair curls well enough to want not papering. I have had it cut lately by Mr. Butler.'[83] Women curled their hair by twisting it in curling paper and allowing it to dry, or better still by applying heated iron tongs to the paper, taking care not to singe the hair. 'Mr. Howes made us a morning visit,' Woodforde remarked in 1781, 'and brought Nancy a Pr of tongs to pinch her hair with from Mrs. Davy, as a present to her.'[84] A decade later his niece was suffering from hair loss: 'Nancy made use of some rum, honey and oil, equal quantity of each, this evening, on her head to prevent the hair falling off, which it has done very much of late, it rather makes her uneasy.'[85]

Until the end of the eighteenth century, female hair fashions became increasingly high on the head, with added feathers and other decorations, sometimes making it difficult for women to move. From the 1790s, as a protest against the French Revolution, fashionable women cut their hair short in sympathetic imitation of victims' hair before they were guillotined. Writing from her lodgings near Liverpool in 1809, Nelly Weeton asked a friend: 'I am considering whether to continue my hair a crop, or let it grow again. What says Miss C. Scott? She hears more of fashion than I do. I like it best as it is, but if out of fashion, I must conform.'[86] Washing of hair must have been infrequent, and lice infestation was a nuisance for all classes. In the 1780s Francis Place associated with poor prostitutes in London: 'their hair among the generality was straight and "hung in rat tails" over their eyes, and was filled with lice, [or] at least was inhabited by considerable colonies of those insects'.[87]

Hair washing was not a simple task, because water was not readily available, and obtaining it for everyday household purposes was a constant chore. One of the greatest uses of water was for laundry – the arduous tasks of washing, drying and ironing of clothing and linen. Where feasible, houses collected rainwater from their roofs in wooden barrels, something that the surgeon Lionel Gillespie noticed on the bleak Isle of Sheppey in December 1787: 'I believe there is not a stream on the island and ... most of the inhabitants supply themselves with water by spouts from their houses.'[88]

Elsewhere, water was fetched in heavy iron-bound wooden buckets from streams or communal wells and pumps, which was a time-consuming and laborious process considering that an imperial gallon of water weighs 10 pounds.[89] Particularly in towns, water was obtained from pumps in the streets, which were enclosed in protective wooden cases. Below ground was a shaft or bore with a wood or lead pipe containing a wooden plunger that was attached above ground to an iron handle. The pump handle was worked up and down to lift the water and force it through a spout protruding from the wooden case.

In rural areas fortunate households had a well in their garden, with winding gear to raise the water in a bucket, and when staying at Bath William Holland satirised his brother-in-law Arthur Dodwell roaming about their rented house as 'moving up and down stairs like a bucket in a well'.[90] Buckets in wells were not always reliable, and in September 1801 at his Norfolk parsonage Woodforde recorded: 'Our well-bucket fell into [the] well this morning as our folks were drawing water, the chain breaking in drawing it up. We tryed all the whole day to get it up, but in vain.'[91] The next day brought success: 'About noon we got up our well-bucket out of the well, by some large iron-creepers which we borrowed of Mr. Michael Andrews. We had some small creepers, but they did not do.'[92]

Even in towns and cities piped water supplies were uncommon and in any case were only for those who could afford to pay. William Darter recalled memories of piped water in his home town of Reading in 1814:

> a large lead reservoir stood in the centre of Broad Street opposite the Wool Pack Inn, which was supplied with water by means of a three-action pump fixed in Mill Lane; its distribution being through wooden pipes. The only other means of obtaining water was from wells and pumps, but ... some wells were 30 to 90 feet in depth ... The wooden pipes to which I refer were simply elm trees, selected for straightness.[93]

These elm trunks were formed into pipes by boring, and then much smaller ¾-inch lead pipes distributed the water to individual properties, but not without problems, as there were constant complaints about an insufficient supply and obstructions from fish and eels. Some of London's better houses had a piped supply, but as in Reading the water was impure. In 1811 Louis Simond saw the old wooden pipes being replaced there:

> The water with which London is supplied, was ... conveyed by means of wooden pipes or logs, perforated, lying under ground, from which small leaden pipes branched out to each house. Workmen are now employed in taking up these logs, which appear mostly decayed, and substituting cast-iron pipes. Those in the main streets, such as Oxford Street and Holborn, are enormously large; upwards of two feet diameter, branching out, down into the side streets, into pipes of the diameter of six inches.[94]

In times of drought, water supplies would run perilously low. In a letter to Mary Heber in the summer of 1785, her friend Miss Iremonger described a visit to Uppark in West Sussex: 'I suppose the dry summer has incommoded the country where you have been, as well as elsewhere. I never saw so little appearance of verdure, and almost all the wells and reservoirs in Sussex were exhausted ... The near wells were guarded, and the poor people obliged to go to a distance for supply.'[95] Some years later, in October 1803, William Holland in Somerset showed more compassion for the poor in another drought when he noted: 'Most of the village coming to my well for water, never was such a scarcity before.'[96]

Water was heated for many household purposes. Some homes had a copper in a scullery, where crockery and cooking utensils were cleaned, or perhaps in a separate wash-house. A copper was like a large cauldron, used for heating water and for boiling linen such as sheets. It was supported within an encircling wall, so that its top was at waist height, and a fire was lit underneath to heat the water. In November 1795 Woodforde took delivery of an improved copper: 'A new substantial washing copper from my brazier, Manning, from Norwich, 26 inches and ¾ wide, 19 inches ½ deep, weight 45 lb ½.'[97]

The poor had no such facilities, but cleaned their clothes and linen as best they could. All classes changed their clothing infrequently, and the laundry was done only every few weeks. Many households hired washerwomen to assist their own servants or else sent everything to a washerwoman. The whole operation was so labour intensive and expensive that it might last a week or more in larger households, where people regularly referred to the 'washing week'. William Wilkinson worried about the costs. 'I hope you will find a cheap method of getting our things washed,' he warned his wife Sarah in August 1809, 'as otherwise it will be a great expense. You had better endeavour to iron them yourself, and get a woman to wash them at home.'[98]

Woodforde certainly hired washerwomen, as in June 1799: 'Washing week with us this week. We wash every five weeks. Our present washerwomen are Anne Downing and Anne Richmond. Washing and ironing generally take us four days. The washerwomen breakfast and dine the Monday and Tuesday, and have each one shilling on their going away in the evening of Tuesday.'[99] His washerwomen therefore worked for two days, and his own servants dried and ironed everything for two more. The Austens also employed a washerwoman, and with her customary wit Jane wrote to Cassandra about a new one: 'Dame Bushell washes for us only one week more. John Stevens' wife [then] undertakes our purification. She does not look as if anything she touched would ever be clean, but who knows?'[100]

Much was never washed at all, and Francis Place recollected his London childhood of the 1770s and 1780s being full of dirty people:

> I can remember the wives and daughters of journeymen tradesmen and shopkeepers, [who] either wore leather stays or what some called full boned stays, and these latter sort were worn by women of all ranks. These were never washed although worn day by day for years. The wives and grown daughters of tradesmen and gentlemen even wore petticoats of camblet, lined with dyed linen, stuffed with wool or horse hair and quilted. These were also worn day by day until they were rotten, and never were washed.[101]

It was not just clothing that was infrequently washed, but linen such as sheets and towels. One physician, Robert Willan, commented in 1801: 'It will scarcely appear credible ... that persons of the lowest class do not put clean sheets on their beds three times a year; that ... they never wash or scour their blankets and coverlets, nor renew them till they are no longer tenable; that curtains, if unfortunately there should be any, are never cleaned, but suffered to continue in the same state till they drop to pieces.'[102]

Some landladies provided a washing service, as Nelly Weeton told her aunt when she was lodging at Beacon's Gutter in 1808:

> Since I came here I have had my cloathes washed by the woman of the house, who does them a great deal cheaper than Ellen [Oaks] did, or the other washer-woman I employed before Ellen came. They both charged me after the same rate – 8d. for a gown, 4d. for a petticoat, and 3d. for a shift, which made my bill for washing near 8 shillings a fortnight. Here I have them done at a shilling a dozen for large things, and sixpence small when I iron them myself; and 1s. 6d., and 8d., when I don't, which makes a very great difference.[103]

Placed in hot or cold water, the laundry was pounded or beaten with wooden bats or dollies, but washing machines constructed of wooden drums rotated by a handle were appearing. One was invented in 1782 by Henry Sidgier in London and is now a symbol on the shield of the Coat of Arms of the Worshipful Company of Launderers.[104] Other machines followed, such as those advertised in the *Hampshire Chronicle* in 1791: 'S. BIRD, original Maker and Inventor of WASHING MACHINES ... The Prices are as follow, with a Wringing Machine to each Size included: A Machine to wash 8 Shirts, three Guineas–ditto to wash 14 Shirts, three Guineas and a Half–ditto to wash 18 Shirts, four Guineas ... Carriage paid to any Part of England.'[105] Most households, though, preferred hired help and servants rather than strange machines.

Cleaning agents could be added to the water to loosen grease and dirt, such as wood ash and stale urine. Soap was better, but it was a highly taxed commodity and needed hot water to be most effective. The stench of manufacturing both soft and hard soap was terrible, using wood ash or vegetable ashes (potash) boiled with whale oil, tallow (animal fat) or olive oil (for finer soap).

The next stage in the laundry process was rinsing in cleaner water and then wringing out excess moisture, either by hand or mangled between wooden bats or rollers, which were sometimes incorporated into mechanical devices fitted with handles. Wet laundry was dried by being suspended from lines, spread over hedges or on the ground, or draped over wooden drying racks. Describing an attempted theft in March 1801, Woodforde revealed that his stockings were dried on flat wooden stocking stretchers: 'A pair of stockings that happened to be out just by the back door upon some wooden legs to dry were attempted to be taken off by some person or another, but being wet they could not pull them off.'[106]

Dorothy Wordsworth often mentioned doing the laundry, as on 16 October 1800 at Grasmere: 'A very fine morning–starched and hung out linen . . . Ironed till six.'[107] Ironing was strenuous, using heavy one-piece cast-iron smoothing irons ('flat irons'), with iron handles, which were heated by an open fire and so were liable to get dirty. The correct temperature of the iron was gauged by spitting on the flat surface, and because the handle became so hot, a cloth pad was necessary for protection. Irons cooled down rapidly, so while one was in use, another was heating by the fire. Those with no access to irons used implements like wooden rollers, pebbles and glass linen smoothers – or did not bother.

Apart from the laundry, the rest of the house needed to be kept clean, and methods remained much the same until the advent of electricity. Sweeping was the most obvious form of cleaning, using handmade besoms or brooms. Carpets were taken outside where they were placed over a line or a hedge and then beaten. William Holland, out riding, 'was stopp'd by some young bullocks who stood across the road affrighted at a carpet which hung over the hedge into the road'.[108] Damp and mildew caused a big problem in houses, as well as vermin and all sorts of bugs.

Personal hygiene, or lack of it, would undoubtedly shock us today, with the overpowering body odours and the stink of clothing, stale with sweat and often musty from damp houses. Some people smelled rather worse than others, particularly if employed in a noisome industry. This was an era before anti-perspirants, before the widespread use of soap, before a time when people washed their bodies and changed their clothing on a regular basis, and when virtually nobody immersed themselves in baths or showers. Everyone would have smelled, even genteel women like Jane Austen, who in mid-September 1796 admitted to Cassandra: 'What dreadful hot weather we have! It keeps one in a continual state of inelegance.'[109]

In the Houses of Parliament the stench could be unbearable, as Elizabeth Fremantle found during a visit in May 1806: 'Mr. Campbell and John Poulett breakfasted with us, and accompanied us to Westminster Hall. We had Peers' tickets and being rather late could only get bad places in a crowded high Gallery behind the Throne. We could see and hear but little, the heat and smell were insufferable, we therefore got away by two o'clock.'[110]

As with laundry, soap was a luxury when washing bodies. Some fine soaps were imported, and in London in 1789 Andrew Pears started manufacturing a fine, transparent soap. The washing of bodies, or more likely parts of bodies, was done with water poured from a jug into a basin, usually at a washstand within a bedroom. Bath-tubs and showers were rare, as were public baths. Manual workers such as miners and agricultural labourers were easily spotted from their stained, chapped hands and swarthy, suntanned or even blackened skin. Many never washed or washed only on Sundays. Rivers and streams provided one means of washing for those who could swim, but Robert Willan advocated public baths: 'all ranks of society would be greatly benefited by the establishment of cold and tepid baths, accessible at a moderate expense; for, by a strange thoughtlessness, most men resident in London, and very many ladies, though accustomed to wash their hands and face daily, neglect washing their bodies from year to year.'[111]

Cosmetics were used as much to hide blemishes such as smallpox scars as to add beauty. Similarly, perfumes were probably used more for hiding smells than creating a pleasing impression. Some body odours were overpowering and difficult to tolerate, as Jane Austen found in November 1800: 'Miss Debary, Susan and Sally all in black ... made their appearance, and I was as civil to them as their bad breath would allow me.'[112] Toothpicks were the most effective means of dental hygiene, commonly made from pointed pieces of wood or quill, which the wealthy kept in ornate silver or gold cases. One housewives' manual suggested: 'For a stinking breath. GET two handfuls of cummin, stamp it to powder, and boil it in wine; and drink the sirup morning and evening, for fifteen days.'[113]

Toothpowder comprised abrasive materials such as bicarbonate of soda that whitened the teeth. 'The Amboyna Mouth Powder is prepared from a DRUG the Produce of a far foreign Country, and imported by a GENTLEMAN of FORTUNE,' one advertisement claimed, '... It fastens, whitens, and preserves the Teeth, makes the Gums and Lips of a beautiful red, instantly sweetens the breath ... It removes all foulness the Mouth is subject to from Diet or a disordered Stomach.'[114] Some toothpowders were so abrasive that another advertisement warned: 'Enamel becomes thinner and thinner, and at last, being quite eaten away, and clean gone, a once beautiful Set of teeth are changed into so many unsightly fibrous and rotten Stumps.'[115]

Mr James Rymer of Reigate in Surrey advocated the use of his own toothpowder, priced at 2s. 9d. per box, which 'is used in the common Way with a Tooth-Brush, or the Teeth may be rubbed with a little of it upon the Corner of a Towel by those who dislike a Brush'.[116] Bone and ivory toothbrushes had bored holes filled with coarse animal bristle, held in place by thin wire. Rymer called his toothpowder the Cinchona Dentifrice, and its main ingredient was Peruvian bark, which was also used in treating malaria and from which quinine is derived.

Menstruation is an aspect of women's personal hygiene about which little was written, except occasionally by medical men, who also advised Peruvian bark to treat period pain. An early form of hot-water bottle was also recommended by the physician Alexander Hamilton: 'If ... the pain become violent ... a bladder, two-thirds filled with hot water, should be kept applied to the lower part of the belly.'[117] It is uncertain whether girls and women wore any sanitary protection, especially as most of them wore no underwear. They may have fixed strips of linen between their legs, which would have been rinsed in water and reused, and some women possibly made disposable pads from absorbent material like cotton-wool or sheep's wool, though such materials were too expensive for most. It is also likely that women, especially outdoor manual workers, did nothing. Certainly Hamilton observed that 'Women in the higher ranks of life, and those of a delicate nervous constitution, are subject to sickness, headache, and pains in the back and loins, during the periodical evaccuation. Those of the lower rank, inured to exercise and labour, and strangers to those refinements which debilitate the system, and interrupt the functions essential to the preservation of health, are seldom observed to suffer at these times.'[118] How those women of 'the higher ranks of life' coped is difficult to comprehend, especially when thin gowns became fashionable.

How people relieved themselves while out and about is another area shrouded in uncertainty. When at their clubs or out to dinner, men urinated into ceramic chamberpots (also called 'jordans' or 'piss pots') that were hidden behind curtains, screens or in cupboards, though Louis Simond found that at dinners he attended, there was no attempt by men to be discreet: 'Drinking much and long leads to unavoidable consequences. Will it be credited, that, in a corner of the very dining-room, there is a certain convenient piece of furniture, to be used by any body who wants it. The operation is performed very deliberately and undisguisedly, as a matter of course, and occasions no interruption of the conversation.'[119] He could not understand why chamberpots were 'not placed out of the room, in some adjoining closet'.[120]

Outdoors, women and men were known to urinate and defecate in streets and side alleys. At his trial for theft Samuel Duck claimed: 'I had been to Knightsbridge [London]; coming home about a quarter after eleven, I had occasion to go up this alley to ease myself.'[121] In a letter published in the *Bath Chronicle* in July 1777, one citizen appealed for cleaner streets: 'By a proper attention to regulations, some plan might be, doubtless, formed for restraining, not only the nasty practice of easing nature on the pavement in almost every corner, but also the equally disagreeable one, of throwing urine and other foul water, &c. from the windows into the streets, (where it is very common for passengers to be greatly incommoded and injured).'[122]

Indoors at home, especially at night, ceramic chamberpots or wooden buckets were used, and chamberpots were sometimes built into a piece of wooden furniture known as a 'close stool' or 'commode'. Confusingly, some leading furniture designers began calling any piece of furniture fitted with drawers a commode, and so the term 'night commode' was adopted to distinguish those with chamberpots.[123] Servants were responsible for emptying the chamberpots into slop-pails for collection by the nightsoil men, or else the contents were poured into the outside cesspit, on a dunghill in the garden and sometimes even into the street.

Toilets for daytime use were generally in small outhouses in a corner of the garden or a yard, with a half-door for ventilation and light. The terminology is confusing, but usually the primitive toilet comprised one or more wooden seats over a cesspit or cesspool and was called an earth or ash closet. The outhouse building containing the toilet was the privy, necessary, necessary house, house of office or jericho. The Weston Longville parsonage garden had separate facilities for the servants, as Woodforde's diary entry for 13 July 1780 revealed: 'The old Jericho (alias servants necessary house) pulled down to day and a new one going to be built elsewhere.'[124] At Over Stowey in the terrible winter of 1814, William Holland referred obliquely to his building: 'It freezes hard ... The path made through the snow to a Certain House in the garden is as slippery as glass and I more than once had nearly fallen in passing along notwithstanding the caution I took.'[125] Houses and taverns without gardens or yards might have necessaries in their cellars, and communal necessaries with several seats for men and women were to be found at public attractions like pleasure gardens.[126]

The stench was minimised by sprinkling soil or ashes into the pit now and again, and while some cesspits might drain to a nearby watercourse, most had to be emptied when full. Accidents did occur, as in the summer of 1808: 'The body of a child, belonging to Sarah Lord, of Rochdale, which had been missing three weeks, was, on Tuesday se'nnight, found in a necessary, into which it is supposed to have accidentally fallen, and was smothered in the soil.'[127] In London in December 1814, another accident occurred when Catherine Tewner dropped her newborn baby into the cesspool of her necessary house. At her trial for murder, one man testified that 'we tore up the privy to get the child out; I gave all the assistance to find the child; we did not find the child; we sent for a nightman.'[128] The nightman was George Nicholls, and he also gave evidence: 'I immediately stripped, and went down; I dragged seven times, and the eighth time I brought a female child up ... A child that fell from its mother could not have gone down so low, without it had been poked down with a pole it could not.'[129] Despite his damning words, Catherine was acquitted.

Toilet paper was not then manufactured, and people cleaned themselves with whatever cheap or free materials were to hand, like leaves and moss. Necessaries might be provided with scrap paper, especially torn-up newspapers and letters, and in October 1814 Patrick Smith was found guilty of robbing David Weit, recently discharged from the militia, at Chelsea. 'This is the piece of paper that was dropped in the necessary,' one witness declared. 'The prisoner took part of this paper to wipe his backside with ... here is Weit, drummer, upon it; it is part of his discharge.'[130] In the Lake District Nelly Weeton was puzzled why human excrement was not utilised to improve the farmland, considering that 'The people in this house have, most of them, very great natural abilities that way, as the devastation amongst Mr. Pedder's newspapers can daily testify.'[131]

From the 1770s public health began to be taken more seriously. Streets were widened and paved, open drains covered over and new ones constructed, though drains were not intended for sewage, as flushing toilets – water-closets – were still rare. These water-closets had wooden seating placed over lead or glazed ceramic bowls, and in order to remove the waste, they were flushed with water from a piped supply or water stored in a cistern tank. Decent drainage was needed, and experiments were done with handles and plunger mechanisms to empty the waste into pipes, but as these pipes were unventilated, noxious gases filled the rooms. The first patent taken out to resolve the problem of the closet's inefficient valve was by the London watchmaker Alexander Cumming, and a patent for an improved version was taken out three years later in 1778 by Joseph Bramah. By 1797 nearly six thousand of Bramah's water-closets had been made, and it remained the standard model for decades. Even so, the old-style water-closets with their terrible smells continued to be built, while most people kept their cesspits and chamberpots.

In towns and cities, the contents of chamberpots were taken away in carts by nightsoil men (the 'nightmen'), who also cleared cesspits by climbing into the shafts and digging out the contents, which is what George Nicholls did when looking for the newborn child. There was no organised system of removing detritus, not just for nightsoil but everything from butchery waste to cinders from open fires. The unscrupulous dumped their waste in streets and streams, and at Cowley in Gloucestershire Samuel Rudder observed that 'the poor labouring people are so abandoned to nastiness, that they throw everything within a yard or two of their doors, where the filth makes a putrid stench, to the injury of their own health, and the annoyance of travellers, if any come among them'.[132]

Animal carcasses were disposed of in various ways, and thousands of worn-out horses died each year and were fed to dogs or passed to knackers' yards, where every part was used, such as for tallow, glue and horsehair. Some authorities employed scavengers to keep the streets clean, especially of horse dung. Much of the detritus including night-soil was sold to farmers for manuring their fields. A survey of agriculture around London in 1794 showed how much farmers paid:

> The price of night-soil, horse-bones raw, bones boiled, bones burnt, and coal-ashes, six shillings a load; soot eight pence a bushel; horn-shavings from six to seven shillings a sack . . . and hogs hair, if wet, fifteen shillings a cart-load . . . The barges on the river Thames, supply from the different dung-wharfs, those cultivators of land who reside near the banks of the river, at a much cheaper rate. This manure is composed of horse-dung and the sweepings of the streets mixed together.[133]

Jane Austen sometimes stayed with her brother Henry at his London apartment in Henrietta Street. This was a fashionable part of Covent Garden, but it was only a short distance from scenes of squalor. The state of one street just a few minutes' walk away was brought to the attention of a parliamentary committee in 1816:

I cannot pass by the filthy state of the street, and the alleys and yards in Short's-gardens, which is of a fair width, and requires nothing but the attendance of the scavenger, to be as clean as any other part of the town; on the 10th of September at the ends towards Drury-lane there was a quantity of human ordure floating down the kennel, apparently the emptying of many privies, and causing a stench sufficient to breed a pestilence.[134]

SIX

·•·

SERMONS AND SUPERSTITIONS

> The rector of a parish has much to do ... he must make such
> an agreement for tithes as may be beneficial to himself and
> not offensive to his patron. He must write his own sermons;
> and the time that remains will not be too much for his parish
> duties, and the care and improvement of his dwelling.
>
> *Pride and Prejudice*, by Jane Austen

The Anglican version of Protestant Christianity practised by the Church of England was the official religion, upheld by the law and financed by the people. Within a list of Church of England livings printed in the *Hampshire Pocket Companion* of 1787, the rectories for the deanery of Basingstoke included 'Dean—George Austin; Steventon—ditto'.[1] This was Jane Austen's father, who was rector of the parish of Deane and of nearby Steventon. When he retired to Bath in 1801, his son James took over as his curate at Steventon. Jane wrote to Cassandra about how they were let down in their attempts to find a curate for Deane: 'Mr. Peter Debary has declined Deane curacy; he wishes to be settled near London. A foolish reason! as if Deane were not near London in comparison of Exeter or York.'[2]

Lords, landowners and clergy were intertwined, both socially and financially, and the appointment of clergy was generally due to friends, family, influence and attending the right university college, something that the Frenchman Louis Simond had observed: 'You meet in the best society a number of young clergymen, brought up in the expectancy of some good living, of which their friends or family have the presentation.'[3] Men might be selected who anticipated marrying into a particular family – the kind of social manoeuvring that occurs in Jane Austen's novels and also affected her own family. 'Yesterday came a letter to my mother from Edward Cooper to announce, not the birth of a child, but of a living,' she told her sister in 1799; 'for Mrs. Leigh has begged his acceptance of the Rectory of Hamstall-Ridware in Staffordshire, vacant by Mr. Johnson's death.'[4]

Entering the Church was for most clergymen not a religious calling but a traditional career choice for the middle classes, and also for the younger sons of the gentry and upper classes who were not in line to inherit the family's estates. Most were graduates of Oxford or Cambridge universities, such as George Austen (St John's College, Oxford) and William Holland (Jesus College, Oxford). A class divide therefore existed between clergymen and most of their parishioners, and that was exacerbated by resentment at paying tithes as well as fees for baptisms, burials and other services.

James Woodforde, also an Oxford graduate, became rector at Weston Longville in December 1774 when the living was presented to him by his college, as *Jackson's Oxford Journal* reported: 'A few days ago the Reverend James Woodford, Fellow of New College, was presented by the Warden and Scholars of that Society, to the Living of Weston-Longville, in the county of Norfolk, worth 300l. per annum.'[5] Nowadays he is usually referred to as Parson Woodforde.[6] 'Parson' is a title normally reserved for those clergy – rectors and vicars – who received tithes, but in popular usage any parish clergyman was called the parson.

Rectors and vicars were beneficed clergy who held the living of one or more parishes. If they had more than one living, a curate was employed to perform their duties. Charles Sturges was vicar at St Mary's Church in Reading and also rector at St Luke's in Chelsea. William Holland was his curate at Reading until 1779 when he became vicar for Over Stowey in Somerset. In 1786 Holland also became rector of Monkton Farleigh near Bath, but returned permanently to Over

Stowey in 1798, leaving a curate in charge at Monkton. These multiple livings (referred to as 'pluralism') were subject to criticism. In July 1790 John Byng was staying at Holbeach, Lincolnshire, in an inn opposite All Saints Church: 'The waiter ... did not advise me to stay the service of tomorrow [Sunday], as their poor curate ... had but a bad delivery ... as for the rector of this rich living, he never was here but when presented to it. Think of that ye bishops: and yet this living was given to him by the Bishop of Lincoln!'[7] Byng was constantly irritated by non-resident clergy, as at Knaresborough in Yorkshire: 'I enquired of the Clerk if the preaching was good? "Aye", said he, "from our Curate". "But where is your Rector"? "He never comes but once't a year, at election of the Parish officers ... He was put in by Ld. Loughborough".'[8]

The higher classes and the clergy were also bound together by Freemasonry. Woodforde summarised his introduction to the Order at Oxford on 21 April 1774:

> I went with Holmes to day to the Free-Masons Lodge held this day at
> the New Inn, was there admitted as a Member of the same and dined and
> spent the afternoon with them. The form and ceremony on the occasion
> I must beg leave to omit putting down. Paid on admission for fees etc.
> £3.5.0. It is a very honourable as well as charitable institution and much
> more than I could conceive it was. Am very glad in being a Member of it.[9]

There was nothing clandestine about the closeness of Freemasonry and the Church, and on a day of thanksgiving for the recovery of George III from his latest bout of insanity in 1789, one West Country newspaper covered the Freemasons' procession to St Andrew's Church at Stoke in Plymouth:

> Thursday morning, at ten o'clock ... between two and three hundred of
> Free and Accepted Masons, of this neighbourhood, assembled at Brother
> Lockyer's, at the King's Arms, properly clothed, with standards flying,
> wearing sashes and cockades, embroidered on white sattin, with 'Long
> Live the King', preceded by a band of music; they marched in procession
> to Stoke church, attended by thousands of spectators; they were received
> at the church door with an Anthem suitable to the occasion.[10]

Louis Simond was 'struck with the smart appearance of the English clergy ... A well-brushed suit of black forms the essential of their establishment.'[11] By contrast, William Holland, who despised Methodists, criticised the appearance of his neighbour William Poole: 'he looked like a Methodist parson, thin, pallid, tall, dressed in black with a curled yellow wig, walking very demurely, gravely and sententiously, and with a broad rimm'd hat, and every now and then turning up his head sideways as if he defied all the owls in the neighbourhood to compare with him for solemnity and wisdom'.[12] This description of wig and clothing could equally have applied to many Anglican clergymen, who often wore black with a white cravat (there was no distinctive clerical collar), as well as a wig.

For church services clergymen put on cassocks and surplices, and for more important occasions their university gowns. In March 1805 Holland was at Chelsea in London and attended Sunday service at the old riverside parish church: 'A fine morning but cold and keen. Went to church and Mr Sturges in his gown and cassock but he did not do duty. His curate Mr Rush did the whole, a pleasing young man whose father I knew very well formerly at Heckfield near Reading. The church is old and too small for the congregation.'[13] Sturges, who was sixty-six years old, died the following month. Holland also wore a gown for services, as on Christmas Day 1806: 'I had a new gown from Oxford which I put on to day, prince's stuff [a type of fabric], and it cost me a fine sum almost eight pounds.'[14] He refused to wear it at one funeral in September 1810: 'in the afternoon we had the funeral of Molly Selleck, where there was a great concourse of well dress'd, respectable people. But as they neither sent me a hatband or gloves I did not think I had occasion to show much respect to them and did not wear my gown.'[15]

The rector (literally, 'governor') was the incumbent of a parish church, eligible to receive all tithes and responsible for the upkeep of the chancel, while the parishioners were responsible for the nave. In the medieval period monasteries had controlled numerous parish churches and took their tithe rights. In place of rectors at those churches, the monasteries appointed vicars (from *vicarius*, a 'substitute'). After the dissolution of the monasteries during Henry VIII's reign, many of these monastic tithe rights were bought by local lords and gentry, putting approximately one-third of church income in secular hands. These lay rectors had the same responsibilities as clerical rectors and installed vicars in their churches to provide the services. How vicars were financed varied, but the layman owning the tithe rights generally took the great tithes such as those on cereal crops, hay and wood, leaving the small tithes for the vicar. Rectors therefore tended to be wealthier than vicars. Originally, all tithes were collected in kind, when the produce was stored in huge tithe barns, but by the end of the eighteenth century most tithes were paid in money after negotiations between the farmers and rector or between the lay rector and his vicar.

The way church organisation and finance evolved, with lay landowners and sometimes clerical rectors appointing vicars, produced anomalies. In some cases the right to collect tithes was leased to the highest bidder, as seen in the *Sussex Advertiser* in 1795:

TITHES.

To be Lett by private Contract, the Great and Small Tithes of the Rectory of Isfield, near Uckfield, in the county of Sussex. Proposals to be made to the Rector of the said Parish on or before the 14th February, 1795, and the lease to operate from Michaelmas preceding.[16]

Leasing of tithes was not straightforward, as demonstrated by Woodforde's comments when he was a curate in his native Somerset in 1772: 'Mr. Thos. and Seth Burge talked with Mr. Wickham about the tithe of Cary [Castle Cary in Somerset]. And Mr. Wickham agreed that if one Chaffin who has contracted for the tithe, will be of[f] from his agreement, Mr. Wickham will let it to them for 3 years for £130 per annum. N.B. If hay is proved to be a vicarial tithe to be excepted out of the agreement, the present tithe being only contracted for in the agreement.'[17]

A parson who held several livings could enjoy a good income from tithes, provided he could collect them, and Nelly Weeton described one clergyman she encountered as having 'that wolf-like keenness in his eyes, as if he knew which was the best method of taking tithe'.[18] Both clergymen and parishioners invariably saw the annual payment of tithes as a battleground. In 1803 William Jones, vicar of Broxbourne in Hertfordshire, gave his opinion: 'I am confident that I am *defrauded* by many of my parishioners of various vicarial dues and rights, to which the laws of Heaven and earth entitle me ... for the very word "tithe" has ever been as unpleasing and odious, to farmers especially, as "cuckoo" to the married ear. Those who pay them, pay them very partially, and I may add— "grudgingly and of necessity."'[19] Clergymen like him clearly felt they were owed a living by God-given right.

In Somerset William Holland was no less determined to receive everything owing to him. When trying to persuade a farmer to pay him a tithe of his apple crop, he pointed out that 'a tithe is but an acknowledgement of the providence of God over you and your affairs, a tribute offered in support of his worship to whom you owe everything'.[20] He encountered similar resistance on another occasion: 'I met old Ragged Ware [Thomas Ware] this day. "Well Ware," said I, "how is it not an apple have you brought me though you had many? Some acknowledgement I expect by way of paying respect to your Minister." "Sir, my wife talked of bringing some." "Talked – but that is not enough." "She shall sartainly come." "Only some acknowledgement, some mark of respect like touching your hat." "She shall sartainly come." And so we parted.'[21]

The parishioners remained reluctant to pay for the high standard of living many clergy enjoyed and resented losing one-tenth of their income on top of all the other taxes. Woodforde eased any discontent of the Weston Longville farmers by inviting them to what were evidently enjoyable 'frolics', as on one occasion in December 1776:

My frolic for my people to pay Tithe to me was this day and I gave them a good dinner, surloin of Beef rosted, a leg of mutton boiled and plumb puddings in plenty. Recd. to-day only for Tithe and Glebe of them 236.2.0. Mr. Browne called on me this morning and he and myself agreed and he paid me for Tithe only 55.0.0 included in the above, he could not stay to dinner. They all broke up about 10 at night. Dinner at 2. Every person well pleased, and were very happy indeed. They had to drink wine, punch, and ale as much as they pleased; they drank of wine 6 bottles, of rum 1 gallon and half, and I know not what ale. Old Harry Andrews, my clerk, Harry Dunnell and Harry Andrews at the Heart all dined etc. in kitchen. Some dined in the parlour, and some in the kitchen. 17 dined etc that paid me Tithe ... There was no supper at all provided for them. We had many droll songs from some of them.[22]

The most noticeable duty of a parson was conducting the church services on Sundays, and Woodforde frequently recorded his clerical duties. Nearly two weeks earlier he was well satisfied with the service:

I read prayers, preached, churched a woman, and christned two children by name Christopher and John this afternoon at Weston Church. A large congregation at church, Mr. and Mrs. Carr there. All people well pleased with the alterations at the church. This afternoon was the first time of my using the reading desk and pulpit, since its being removed, and also of a new Common Prayer Book in my desk. I can be heard much better than where it was, and easier.[23]

The main church service comprised prayers, singing of psalms and hymns, reading from the Bible and a sermon preached by the parson. When he was at Nettlebed in Oxfordshire in 1782, Carl Moritz attended a service at St Bartholomew's church:

I resolved to stop ... for the day, and attend divine service. For this purpose I borrowed a prayer-book ... It being called a prayer-book, rather than, like ours [in Germany], a hymn-book, arises from the nature of the English service, which is composed very little of singing; and almost entirely of praying. The Psalms of David, however, are here translated into English verse, and are generally printed at the end of English prayer-books ... At half past nine the service began. Directly opposite to the inn, the boys of the village were all drawn up ... to wait the arrival of the clergyman. At length came the parson on horseback. The boys pulled off their hats, and all made him very low bows. He appeared to be rather an elderly man, and wore his own hair, round and decently dressed.[24]

It was time to enter the church:

> The bell now rung in, and so I too, with a sort of secret proud sensation,
> as if I also had been an Englishman, went with my prayer-book under my
> arm to church, along with the rest of the congregation; and when I got
> into the church, the clerk very civilly seated me close to the pulpit ...
> Under the pulpit, near the steps that led up to it, was a desk, from which
> the clergyman read the liturgy. The responses were all regularly made by
> the clerk, the whole congregation joining occasionally, though but in a
> low voice.[25]

Moritz endured the entire service, but considered it exhausting for
the parson: 'The English service must needs be exceedingly fatiguing
to the officiating minister, inasmuch as, besides a sermon, the greatest
part of the liturgy falls to his share to read, besides the psalms and two
lessons. The joining of the whole congregation in prayer has something exceedingly solemn and affecting in it.'[26] He was impressed by
the singing, which a church band accompanied:

> The clergyman now stopped, and the clerk then said in a loud voice, 'Let
> us sing to the praise and glory of God, the forty-seventh psalm.' I cannot
> well express how affecting and edifying it seemed to me, to hear this
> whole, orderly, and decent congregation, in this small, country church,
> joining together, with vocal and instrumental music, in the praise of their
> Maker. It was the more grateful, as having been performed, not by mer-
> cenary musicians, but by the peaceful and pious inhabitants of this sweet
> village ... The congregation sang and prayed alternately several times; and
> the tunes of the psalms were particularly lively and cheerful, though, at
> the same time, sufficiently grave and uncommonly interesting. I am a
> warm admirer of all sacred music; and I cannot but add, that that of the
> church of England is particularly calculated to raise the heart to devotion.
> I own it often affected me even to tears.[27]

The musicians and singers were usually located in the gallery or
loft, and their standard of performance must have varied considerably.
Like Moritz, John Byng was an admirer of good church music but

also critical of bad, such as when he attended a service at Folkingham in Lincolnshire in June 1791: 'Here were a numerous, and decent congregation, with a singing loft crouded ... but the bassoons, and hautboys, were too loud and shreiking ... Much singing before the service; likewise the Magnificat, and two psalms.'[28] While visiting Knutsford in Cheshire the previous summer, he decided to stay for the Sunday service because the church was relatively new and dry – it had been consecrated in 1744. The church, he said, was 'a neat, well pew'd building; and was well fill'd with well dress'd company, many of whom came in their coaches; and there was one sedan chair.—The service open'd with a psalm, accompany'd by an organ [installed in 1773], and the Te Deum, and—were chaunted; so these with two other psalms, gave me singing enough: as for the sermon, it had the merit of being short. The bells are very tuneable, and they practise ringing.'[29]

On entering Aisholt church in Somerset, William Holland was met by the unpleasant noise of one musician: 'A disagreeable fellow was playing his fiddle in church when I came in, without tune or harmony intending I presume to accompany the psalm singers. I however ordered him to stop his noise, which he hardly would do and then he began trying his discordant hautboy. I had a good mind to order him to be turned out.'[30]

Apart from the services, the parson was required to perform any baptisms, burials and other duties, for which he charged fees. Often, the clergyman was given a gift of money as well, but in 1783 a stamp duty tax was also imposed on the registration of marriages, christenings and burials, as Woodforde noted in his diary in October: 'I rode down to Mr. Howletts this morning and christned a child of his, born last night, by name William – and it being the first child that I have christned since the Act took place concerning the duty to be raised on christnings burials and marriages, and therefore recd the duty of 0.0.3.'[31] Such a tax discouraged the poor from marrying in church or christening their children, and the law was repealed the following year on the grounds that it adversely affected public morals.

Some clergymen spent considerable time visiting the poor and sick in their parish and frequently made charitable donations.

Woodforde regularly gave a shilling to passing beggars who appeared deserving, as in February 1797: 'To a poor French emigrant woman, very short, who came to my house this morning to ask charity, being in great distress, gave 0.1.0 and also a mince pye and some beer. She told me as far as I understood her (as she talked but little English) that her husband with 2 or 3 children were killed in the late bloody commotions in France.'[32] At certain times of the year he favoured specific elements of his congregation, giving money to the poor housekeepers and single people of the parish on St Thomas's Day (21 December), and on Christmas Day he liked to invite the poor for a meal:

> This being Christmas Day, I went to Church this morn' and then read prayers and administered the Holy Sacrament. Mr. and Mrs. Custance [the squire and his wife] both at Church and both received the Sacrament from my hands. The following poor old men dined at my house to day, as usual, Js. Smith, Clerk; Richd. Bates, Richd. Buck; Thos. Cary; Thos. Dicker; Thos. Cushing; Thos. Carr – to each besides gave 1/0 – in all 0.7.0. I gave them for dinner a surloin of beef rosted and plenty of plumb-pudding. We had mince pies for the first time to-day.[33]

Of the thousands of parish churches across England, many were centuries old, built from the medieval period onwards and often orig-inally for the Catholic religion. High on the Quantocks, Holland encountered a parishioner, Jack Hunt, working in his garden and asked him why he did not cut down one hedge for a better view: 'Ah that is Mr Buller's hedge,' came the reply, 'but I can see twelve parish churches from my door.'[34] John Byng also admired seeing numerous churches in Lincolnshire:

> Within view, at short distance, are several churches ... I am of a very superstitious turn; and must think that the same Providence which urged great and pious people formerly, to build these houses of God still guards and preserves them. Who would, or could build them now? The expence would be enormous ... How beautiful does our land now look, from the spires and steeples; and what useful land and sea marks they are; numbers

are gone to ruin, and yearly suffered to fall down: how happens this? Have we no bishops, or do they not visit their dioceses?[35]

By the late eighteenth century few new churches were being constructed, even though there was a pressing need in the expanding towns. Elsewhere, churches were all too often in some state of disrepair, as well as being damp and cold (they had no heating), and their congregations were dwindling, particularly with the rise of Methodism.[36] Most churches were not intended as places of private prayer and were kept locked, so the first task of an interested visitor like Byng was to locate a key or find the clerk so as to gain entrance. Very often these buildings were in a sorry state, such as All Saints Church at Dodington in Somerset, where Holland officiated on a general fast day in February 1809:

> The weather dark and full of snow at last Mr. Huggins appear'd, and so I begun the service and two or three more came, finish'd the service and made some strong observations to Mr. Huggins on the state of the church, a torrent of rain pour'd in on one side so as to make one side quite black, one window half gone, and pains of glass in abundance wanting and the roof full of holes that the sky was visible in many places. I told Huggins that I could not do duty in the church in this state.
>
> Why sir replied he if next Sunday should be bad you need not come.
>
> You know the wind blows on from all quarters, answered I.
>
> Cant get a glazier and mason, return'd he not immediately.
>
> Church work said I, shaking my head, must be done without delay.[37]

Those attending church services in winter must have felt the biting cold, as is evident by Holland's remarks the following year, yet again at Dodington:

> The most foggy, frosty, dark morning I ever knew, the ground is glazed over and the twigs everywhere cover'd completely with a white hoar frost . . . I could not ride. It was so slippery and so walked to Dodington and with difficulty made up a congregation. Yet three of the Miss Hugginses came and Mrs. Farthing, but the great Mr. Farthing himself was not there, the churchwarden. Neither did I see my old friend John

Mogg's red nose there which I lament the more as it might have warm'd the church on so very cold a morning.[38]

During the eighteenth century the medieval bench pews were often replaced by enclosed box pews, which provided some privacy and protection against draughts. Inside the church, differences in social class were reflected by the size and quality of a family's pew and its position in the nave. Wealthy families could rent a pew or build their own, while the poor shared the common pews provided by the church at the back, or sat in a gallery. Pews were built to whatever shape and size their owners desired, and the curate Gilbert White at Selborne wrote that 'nothing can be more irregular than the pews of this church, which are of all dimensions and heights, being patched up according to the fancy of the owners'.[39] One newspaper in 1789 advertised a desirable pew for sale: 'To be SOLD, A PEW, in the West Gallery of the Parish Church, at Leeds, well situated for both Hearing and Seeing, and containing Sittings for Five People.'[40]

Where a person sat in church was so important for social status that Woodforde was forced to cancel permission for the use of a particular chancel seat:

After breakfast this morning I sent my maid Betty to Mr. Press Custance's mistress (Miss Sherman) to desire her not to make use of my seat in the chancel any more, as some reflections had been thrown on me for giving her leave. I likewise sent Will to Mr. Kerr's on the same account ... Miss Sherman sent word back by Betty that she was much obliged to me for the use she had already made of it, and did not take it at all amiss in me, she knew from whence it came – and that she would get a new seat made. Mr. Kerr sent me word that he was not the least angry with me, and he expected it.[41]

Nelly Weeton, keenly aware of class distinction, complained in a letter about her local church at Liverpool:

Christ's Church nowadays is not what the Church of Christ was formerly. He used to say, 'to the poor the Gospel is preached,' but now the age is grown more liberal, so that they pay their teachers. Of course, it is chiefly to the rich that the Gospel is preached. 'The rich and poor' do not 'meet together'. The poor go to pray – nobody knows where, and any scrubby fellow may instruct them. To be 'clothed in rags' was once a recommendation to the Church of Christ, but now the surest way of being denied entrance into it . . . the present age are so little scrupulous, that Fashion, whatever garb she wears, is permitted; indeed, every pains taken to allure her to take her seat in Christ-Church.[42]

Even if they were not concerned about such class distinction, parishioners frequently resented their duty to attend church on Sundays. Although the labouring classes worked six days a week, they were still expected to spend part of the Sabbath – their one day off – at church. Benjamin Silliman, though, was surprised how all classes in London treated Sundays:

I attended public worship to-day in a great church where there were only a few people. This I have very often seen before in London. Indeed a very great proportion of the people consider the Sabbath as a day of mere rest, of relaxation, of amusement, or of dissipation, according to their employments, and rank in society. A person, while walking the streets on the Sabbath, will meet numbers of the gentry with their splendid equipages, going out into the country for an airing, or perhaps to join a party at some village in the vicinity. It is also a favourite day with them to begin a journey, as it is every where with sailors to begin a journey.[43]

There was even greater reluctance to attend church services on weekdays, such as official 'fast days' or on the king's birthday, when sermons were sent to the parishes to be read out. 'This is the general fast and a disagreeable day it is,' remarked Holland in February 1809, 'very cold and piercing and windy . . . I could scarce get any to church but I went in at last but had a very small congregation for a fast. However I went through the intricate service, and gave them a sermon.'[44] Later that year, on Wednesday 25 October, he recorded:

This is the King's accession into the fiftieth year of his reign and the bells are ringing and we are to have prayers. Few assembled. Farmer Morle after promising fairly last Sunday and to provide cyder, disappointed us all, a mean shabby fellow and Farmer Landsey tho as rich as a Jew contributed nothing tho he was at church but the other was not. However we had some few ... I believe I gave them as good a sermon and as well deliver'd as any they will hear this day in these parts though I say it myself ... and moreover it was my own composition which will not be the case in general I presume.[45]

On the king's birthday a few years later, in 1816, Holland remarked: 'I had prayers to day, but we could collect no congregation besides our own family. Indeed in country places it is in vain to expect the common people on week days.'[46] A few months after, attendance had not improved: 'I have resolved to go with my wife to every person or house in the parish to remonstrate with the inhabitants about their neglect of the public worship of the church, and so we went off this day and had conversation with many of them and made them sensible of their duty and they promised fairly.'[47]

Byng blamed the deteriorating church attendance and the decline of the clergy on countless good families deserting the countryside:

For whilst decent, and pious families therein resided, the minister attended to his double Sunday duties, and to the weekly prayers on Wednesdays, and Fridays, besides the keeping of holidays; to which the aged, and virtuous poor were urged to attend, by good example.—But the families being gone, no longer are these duties continued; and the divine, himself, from lack of company, pays a pitiful stipend to a hackney curate (who rides over half the country on a Sunday) and retires to London, or to Bath.[48]

Byng himself was no model churchgoer, attending services but often more interested in antiquarian matters, as at Folkingham in June 1791: 'the bells rang for church, to which I repair'd with my landlord, and landlady [of the Greyhound Inn]; (this I may call my religious tour, tho' I sadly fear that curiosity oft'ner than devotion leads me to church) ... during the sermon mine host slept, and I slumber'd.'[49]

In many areas nonconformist sects ('dissenters') such as the Baptists, Unitarians, Methodists and Quakers were gaining ground. Their ministers, largely drawn from the middle and lower classes, were more in touch with their congregations and tended to ask only for voluntary contributions. The 1689 Toleration Act had given limited concessions to nonconformists and granted some freedom of worship, allowing them to hold meetings in unlocked, licensed meeting places. Although no longer obliged to attend parish churches, they remained barred from Cambridge and Oxford universities and from holding political or municipal office.

Attacks flared up sporadically against Catholics and nonconformists, as in the Birmingham (or 'Priestley') Riots of July 1791, when rioters attacked many chapels and homes of dissenters. Byng learned about this unrest on his Lincolnshire travels: 'I read, in the newspapers, the accounts of the riots at Birmingham: one party inflames, and then accuse the other of warmth!'[50] One of the casualties was the house of sixty-seven-year-old William Hutton, a dissenter, bookseller and historian. His daughter Catherine Hutton wrote to a friend how the mob was convinced that unless they destroyed the meeting houses, the dissenters would destroy the Church: 'Such was the belief of the *best* part of the mob, and such belief must have been occasioned by the insinuations of their superiors, but the motive of the *greatest* part was plunder ... Dr. Priestley ... unintentionally, and himself the first sufferer, he was, I think, one of the primary causes of the riots in Birmingham, by rousing the spirit of bigotry and all incharitableness in others.'[51] Joseph Priestley was a dissenting minister and vigorous supporter of liberal reform of government, education and theology, making him unpopular with the establishment, which was suspected of inciting the riots.[52]

In the 1730s John Wesley and George Whitefield had embarked on preaching a different, evangelical type of Christianity that became known as Methodism. Wesley's preaching was hugely influential with the middle and working classes. Although his followers were Anglican, they also attended Methodist services and were encouraged to build chapels or preaching houses. Wesley hoped to transform the Church of England, but at the end of the eighteenth century, after his death, groups of Methodists split from the Anglican church, and Methodism became a serious rival. According to Simond, 'The sect of the Methodists, who preach hell and damnation, and place faith before works, has made astonishing progress.'[53] Charles Fothergill thought they were a force for good. When passing through Wilberfoss in Yorkshire in 1805, he 'observed a Methodist meeting in a very small thatched cottage which was crammed full almost to suffocation: they were singing psalms. These meetings are common to almost every village, and this sect, though in general confined to the lowest and consequently to the most ignorant orders of the people, has certainly been productive of great good whatever may have been urged against it.'[54]

Holland particularly disapproved of Methodists when they neglected to attend his Sunday services:

> I saw a great number of people passing by about dusk, I suppose it was from a Methodist meeting at Hodges. These men do a great deal of harm, they pretend to great sanctity but it is ostentation not reality. They draw people from the established church, infuse prejudices in them against their legal pastors and of late they are all democratic [revolutionary] and favourers of French principles, and I suspect that some of the philosophers get among them under the character of celebrated preachers and so poison their minds against the established government.[55]

A few months later he was ranting again: 'Met the Methodist William Hill. He squinted at me under his hat as he passed. How now, said I, at neither church this day? I have been elsewhere replied he. So much the worse, returned I, the proper place is your own parish church.'[56] Over a decade later, he was still unhappy: 'These Methodistical people tho they talk much of their piety yet have very little of the true principle of religion in them. Their chief religion consists in censuring others but giving themselves what latitude they please. We have some in this parish ... who esteem themselves great saints yet indulge themselves in every kind of sensuality and moral turpitude.'[57]

Frequently critical of Anglican clergymen, Byng lamented that the rise of Methodism was due solely to their negligence:

> about religion I have made some enquiry, (having been in so many churches) and find it to be lodged in the hands of the Methodists; as the greater clergy do not attend their duty, and the lesser neglect it; that where the old psalm singing is abolish'd none is establish'd in its place; as the organ is inconvenient, and not understood; at most places the curates never attend regularly, or to any effect, or comfort, so no wonder that the people are gone over to Methodism.[58]

While Holland felt threatened by Methodists, he tolerated the Quakers but disliked Catholics and Jews, even though they formed only a small part of the population. By 1800 there were around 100,000 Catholics in England and Wales, and many of these were Irish immigrants.[59] Substantial numbers of Jews had moved to England from Europe in the early eighteenth century, adding to the established Jewish community, mostly poor refugees from the ghettos of Germany and eastern Europe. Many of them became pedlars and dealers in secondhand clothes, forming settlements in towns such as Birmingham and Canterbury from where they travelled into the surrounding countryside offering their wares. Others traded with sailors in ports like Liverpool, London, Plymouth, Bristol and Portsmouth. The main community of Jews at Portsmouth was clustered near the dockyard gate, and the only two synagogues recorded for Hampshire in a 1787 directory were at Portsmouth, one at White's Rowe and the other at Daniel's Row.[60] Some of the pedlars did so well in the seaports that they were able to found prosperous businesses, while the Jewish banker Nathan Mayer Rothschild became a major financier to the Government, helping to fund the Napoleonic Wars. Rothschild had originally been a textile merchant in Manchester, but moved to London and established his banking business there in 1805.

Another threat to the authority of the Church was superstition – despite the 'enlightenment' of the eighteenth century, superstitions were rife. In 1787 the antiquary Francis Grose published what he called a *Provincial Glossary*, and his section on popular superstitions in this book began:

It will scarcely be conceived how great a number of superstitious notions and practices are still remaining and prevalent in different parts of these kingdoms, many of which are still used and alluded to even in and about the metropolis [London]; and every person, however carefully educated, will, upon examination, find that he has some how or other imbibed and stored up in his memory a much greater number of these rules and maxims than he could at first have imagined.[61]

Gilbert White was conscious of the tenacity of superstitions:

It is the hardest thing in the world to shake off superstitious prejudices: they ... become so interwoven into our very constitutions, that the strongest good sense is required to disengage ourselves from them. No wonder therefore that the lower people retain them their whole lives through, since their minds are not invigorated by a liberal education, and therefore not enabled to make any efforts adequate to the occasion.[62]

As a clergyman preoccupied with studying natural history, he was probably more rational than most.

Belief in ghosts was certainly widespread, something that Nelly Weeton noted with amusement at Upholland in Lancashire in 1807: 'Scarcely a field, gate or stile is without its attendant spirit; and in some of the houses the noises these beings, or shadows, or sprites or whatever they are, are *said* to make, are terrible beyond anything.'[63] She estimated that more than 10 per cent of buildings around Upholland were haunted, and one ghost was especially troublesome:

the Mill-house below Mr. Dannett's, is the terror of the whole neighbourhood. I was the other evening at Mr. D's when a subject of this kind occupied two or three hours. Miss D. is superstitious in the *extreme* ... and she will repeat such a long string of the strangest apparitions, horrid yells, looking glasses falling, furniture moving, tongs, shovel and poker dancing, raps at the door or the window, windows being broken without hands or any living creature near, noises as if someone were spinning, churning, dancing, or a mill going; and many other appalling things not worth writing.[64]

Scornful of most superstitions, Nelly nevertheless admitted she was 'not entirely free from some little fears of this kind, but there are few, perhaps none, who in my situation would feel so little fear as I do'.[65]

Ghosts were feared as being the restless spirits of the dead, and in April 1810 the *Morning Post* reported on the superstitious rites behind one suicide's burial:

> The officers appointed to execute the ceremony of driving a stake through the dead body of *James Cowling*, a deserter from the London Militia, who deprived himself of existence, by cutting his throat, at a public-house in Gilbert Street, Clare Market, in consequence of which, the Coroner's Jury found a verdict of self-murder, very properly delayed the business until twelve o'clock on Wednesday night, when the deceased was buried in the cross roads at the end of Blackmoor Street, Clare Market.[66]

Suicides were routinely punished by denying their bodies a Christian burial, but the remaining ritual was to prevent the ghost haunting the living. Burial at night at the crossroads was intended to confuse the ghost if it tried to wander, and the stake was to stop it rising up to walk. Substantial stakes sometimes protruded above ground for years afterwards.

Many common beliefs concerned events that were interpreted as omens, usually bad omens. A howling dog signified a death in the family, while a coal spitting out of a fire and landing at someone's feet in the shape of a coffin foretold their imminent demise. 'Any person fasting on Midsummer eve, and sitting in the church porch,' Grose recorded, 'will at midnight see the spirits of the persons of that parish, who will die that year, come and knock at the church door, in the order and succession in which they will die.'[67] Tallow rising up the wick of a candle was sometimes called a 'winding-sheet' and foretold a death in the family. Even clergymen like Woodforde were not immune to such omens, and he noted several in his diary, including a similar one concerning a candle: 'There was a very large and long handle of a coffin in one of our candles this evening, as many people call it, and lasted a very long time indeed.'[68]

Another portent of death appeared when he was brewing beer: 'In the boiling of the beer this morn' I saw a great number of thick brownish kind of bubbles swimming on the surface of it, very much like ratafee-cakes, and they are called in Norfolk, burying-cakes, and the common people say here that is a sure sign of some of the family or their friends dying very soon. I never saw them before.'[69] Woodforde was frequently unnerved by such omens, and on another occasion he recorded: 'I dreamt very much last night of my losing my hat. It is said to be a sign of losing a very near friend.'[70]

Particularly popular were charms and rituals for assessing future marriage prospects, and Grose detailed one example: 'On St. Agnes night, 21st of January, take a row of pins, and pull out every one, one after another, saying a Pater-noster on sticking a pin in your sleeve, and you will dream of him or her you shall marry.'[71] He also mentioned superstitions relating to luck, many involving chance events: 'It is lucky to put on a stocking the wrong side outwards: changing it alters the luck. When a person goes out to transact any important business, it is lucky to throw an old shoe after him.'[72] Certain things were to be avoided: 'To kill a magpie, will certainly be punished with some terrible misfortune ... It is held unlucky to kill a cricket, a lady-bug, a swallow, martin, robin red-breast, or wren.'[73] To ward off bad luck or evil, amulets were valued, like the caul advertised at London in the *Morning Post* in August 1779, widely believed to be the most effective talisman against drowning:

> To the Gentlemen of the Navy, and others going long voyages to sea.
> To be disposed of a CHILD's CAWL. Enquire at the
> Bartlet Buildings Coffee-house, in Holborn.
> N.B. To avoid unnecessary trouble the price is Twenty Guineas.[74]

Grose recorded other strange amulets: 'The chips or cuttings of a gibbet or gallows, on which one or more persons have been executed or exposed, if worn next the skin, or round the neck, in a bag, will cure the ague, or prevent it.'[75] Witchcraft was behind some beliefs: 'A stone with a hole in it, hung at the bed's head, will prevent the nightmare: it is therefore called a hag-stone, from that disorder which is therefore occasioned by a hag, or witch, sitting on the stomach of the party afflicted. It also prevents witches riding horses; for which purpose it is often tied to a stable key.'[76] A horseshoe nailed over a doorway was a common talisman against witches, as well as against bad luck and evil.

Belief in witches was ridiculed by the more educated, but after explaining how witchcraft was nonsense, Grose did give some precautionary advice:

> Some hair, the parings of the nails, and urine, of any person bewitched – or as the term is, labouring under an evil tongue – being put into a stone bottle, with crooked nails, corked close and tied down with wire, and hung up the chimney, will cause the Witch to suffer the most acute torments imaginable, till the bottle is uncorked and the mixture dispersed; insomuch that they will even risk a detection, by coming to the house, and attempting to pull down the bottle.[77]

Such 'witch bottles' were also bricked up in walls of houses or placed under the hearth or eaves. They have occasionally been discovered while renovating old buildings, including one dating to the late eighteenth or early nineteenth century found beneath the hearth of Clapper Farm at Staplehurst in Kent.[78] Witches were widely feared, particularly in rural areas, and when meeting a suspected witch, Grose suggested: 'it is advisable to take the wall [side] of her in a town or street, and the right hand of her in a lane or field; and, whilst passing her, to clench both hands, doubling the thumbs beneath the fingers; this will prevent her having a power to injure the person so doing at that time. It is well to salute a Witch with civil words, on meeting her, before she speaks.'[79]

The law generally regarded anyone claiming to be a witch as a charlatan, but they could be prosecuted for fraud or for any specific crime that had been committed, as was the case with Mary Bateman.

She had made a good living in Leeds as a fortune teller for over twenty years, but was found guilty of poisoning a client, Rebecca Perigo. Having been tried and found guilty at York, she was executed there in March 1809, aged forty-one. Part of the sentence was for her body to be dissected, but such was the notoriety of the case that the corpse was publicly displayed first. Afterwards, it was sent to Leeds: 'when the cart with her body approached the town, it was met by a number of people. The following day it was exhibited in the Surgeons' Room at the Infirmary, at three-pence each person, and an immense number of people were admitted, some of whom evinced predominant superstition by touching the body before they left the room, to prevent her terrific [terrifying] interference with their nocturnal dreams.'[80] The dissection of the body was a public affair, and the local newspaper reported that 'Mr. Hey [the surgeon] is now delivering a course of twelve lectures on the body, for the benefit of the institution, and has diffused much edifying information to a crowded auditory.'[81] The remains of her skeleton are now displayed at the Thackray Museum in Leeds.[82]

Although witches were popularly regarded as malign, another kind of magic practitioner, the 'cunning man' or 'wise woman', was considered benevolent. They were approached for cures for illness in people or animals, or for resolving problems such as lost or stolen property. Very often their success was achieved by being skilled herbalists or through the suggestibility of clients. James Murrell worked with a chemist in London, but moved to Hadleigh in Essex around 1810 and carried on a dual trade of shoemaker and cunning man. It was said that he 'pretended to have the power of counteracting the designs of witches, discovering thieves, and where stolen property was secreted. He was a herbalist, and administered potions and drugs.'[83] On his death in 1860 numerous letters relating to his occult business were destroyed, but it was later said that 'enough remain to prove that an amount of ignorance, credulity, and superstition exists, which appears incredible'.[84]

Other ways of making money from superstition and foretelling the future included almanacs (or 'almanacks') that carried astrological predictions. Originally, almanacs were compiled by astrologers who were often practising astrological physicians, but with the development of science, astrology had fallen out of favour. From the early eighteenth century onwards almanacs provided more information and entertainment than astrological predictions. Of those still carrying predictions, the most popular was *Old Moore's Almanack*, first produced by the astrologer Francis Moore in 1699 under the title *Vox Stellarum* ('voice of the stars'). Moore's *Vox Stellarum* for 1803 contained optimistic prophecies, such as that for April: 'It now looks as if the Genius of the British Nation would triumph over all its adverse Fortune. Some eminent and weighty Affairs are now transacted, and brought to a final Determination, for the good of the Public and Increase of Trade.'[85] Other prophecies are almost too convoluted to understand, such as one for June: 'Heavens defend the English Nation from future War, and visible Actions and Commotions, and may *London* be as insensible of Sickness, Piratical Damages, and sudden Insurrections, as she is insensible of a Lunar Eclipse happening in her Horizon this Year.'[86]

Almanacs of all kinds were popular on account of their range of information, since they focused on astronomical rather than astrological events, including dates and times of eclipses, tide tables and, crucially, dates of the phases of the moon and the times when the moon would rise and set each day. Moonlight was so important for night-time travelling that this feature alone sold countless copies, and many evolved into local pocket books or diaries. Almanacs also contained calendars marked with Christian festivals and holy days.

Although Christmas was observed, it was not the major holiday that it is today. Houses were decorated with greenery, usually holly or laurel. 'This being Christmas Eve,' noted Woodforde in 1791, 'had my windows as usual ornamented with small branches of Hulver (alias Holley) properly seeded [with berries].'[87] Christmas Day was marked by a church service and then a dinner with plum pudding and mince pies. The custom of giving servants and tradesmen small gifts of money – 'Christmas boxes' – was growing, but most other rituals that we now associate with Christmas were imported in the later nineteenth century from America and the Continent. New Year was more often the time for celebration and the exchange of gifts, and many still clung to the Old Christmas Day of 6 January (from where the calendar was changed in 1752, causing eleven days to be lost).[88] On one occasion, Holland grumbled: 'The Clerk was here today carrying out dung tho not yesterday it being old Christmas day as he calls it and therefore a holiday; that is after he had kept a week of holidays for new Christmas day.'[89]

Traditional customs associated with particular days of the year were often excuses for the poor, especially children, to go begging. On 14 February 1788 Woodforde gave away thirty-seven pennies: 'This being Valentines Day, I had a good many children of my parish called on me, to each of whom, gave (as usual) one penny, in all 0.3.1.'[90] It was customary for children to 'earn' their money by reciting a verse that started with words like 'Morrow, Morrow, Valentine' or 'Good Morrow Valentine', and Woodforde usually made his young visitors recite at least the first line.

Easter was a festival frequently associated with more traditions than Christmas, though these varied from place to place. In April 1789 the *New Exeter Journal* was struck by events further north:

> It is still the custom in the North of England, at this season of Easter, to present paste (or pasche) eggs to young women; they are covered with gold leaf, and stained. This is a relic of antient superstition, an egg being in former times considered as a type of our Saviour's resurrection. Chandler, in his account of Asia Minor says, 'They presented us with coloured eggs at Easter.' Originally women used to beat their husbands on Easter-Tuesday; and on the Wednesday following the husbands beat their wives. Of the great number of customs and ceremonies which prevailed in times of old, very few now remain.[91]

This notion of old ceremonies fast disappearing was probably overstated, though a decline in observing rituals was partly due to changes in working practices. Someone working shifts in a factory was much less able to celebrate the old customs than someone doing piecework at home.

Other more practical traditions also declined, such as the perambulation of the parish boundaries – usually called 'beating the boundaries' (or 'bounds'). The purpose of this ancient custom was to mark the boundaries each year, because few maps existed and there were few indications of the position of boundaries in the open landscapes. However, enclosures by private Act of Parliament – Enclosure (or Inclosure) Acts – increasingly divided the countryside into small units bounded by hedges, walls and fences. From 1750 such enclosures affected around a quarter of the total area of England and Wales.[92] Because some of these new field boundaries followed the parish boundaries, the practical need for beating the bounds was disappearing.

Wherever the custom continued, it usually took place in Rogation Week, and the rituals involved beating boundary stones and other markers with sticks, which were often carried by young boys to ensure that the boundaries were learned by the younger generation. At Ripon in Yorkshire, the *Gentleman's Magazine* mentioned, 'the day before Holy Thursday [Ascension Day], all the clergy, attended by the singing men and boys of the choir, perambulate the town in their canonicals, singing hymns; and the blue-coat charity boys follow, singing, with green boughs in their hands'.[93] On Wednesday 3 May 1780, which was also the day before Ascension Day, Woodforde recorded the more down-to-earth ceremonies in his Norfolk parish of Weston Longville:

> About ½ past nine o'clock this morning my Squire called on me, and I took my mare and went with him to the Hart [inn] just by the Church where most of the parish were assembled to go the bounds of the parish, and at 10 we all set of[f] for the same about 30 in number. Went towards Ringland first, then to the breaks near Mr. Townsends clumps, from thence to Attertons on France Green, where the people had some liquor, and which I paid, being usual for the Rector – 0.4.6.[94]

Farmers along the route often provided sustenance, but on this occasion Woodforde was responsible.

The procession then continued: 'From France Green we went away to Mr. Dades, from thence towards Risings, from thence down to Mr. Gallands, then to the old Hall of my Squire's, thence to the old Bridge at Lenewade, then close to the River till we came near

Morton, then by Mr. Le Grisse's Clumps, then by Bakers and so back till we came to the place where we first set off.'[95] The complete circuit of the parish was quite a journey: 'Our bounds are supposed to be about 12 miles round. We were going of them full 5 hours. We set of[f] at 10 in the morning and got back a little after 3 in the afternoon ... Where there was no tree to mark, holes were made and stones cast in.'[96]

Some old customs could be seen in the church itself. When an unmarried woman died, a garland of flowers, usually called a 'maiden garland', might accompany the coffin. After the funeral it was hung up in the church above the seat she had used. This ritual was disappearing towards the close of the eighteenth century. In June 1790 John Byng, who was conscious of such fading traditions, noted it in the church of St John the Baptist at Tideswell in Derbyshire:

After dinner, I enter'd the church, which, without, is beautiful; (quite a model); and within, of excellent architecture: it has at one corner, a noble stone pulpit, now disused, and there are two fine old tombs, (one of the Meverils,) and several figures in stone; but the chancel, belonging to the deanery of Litchfield, is in disgraceful waste; and the church wants new benching, most grievously. They here continue to hang up maiden garlands, which, however laudable, as of tendency to virtue, will soon be laugh'd out of practice.'[97]

His melancholy thoughts led him to predict a dismal future: 'and as I now visit decay'd monasteries, so will my grandchildren ... view the ruins of churches, when they and religion altogether shall be o'erthrown'.[98]

——— •◆• ———

SEVEN

WEALTH AND WORK

'I am afraid,' replied Elinor, 'that the pleasantness of an
employment does not always evince its propriety.'

Sense and Sensibility, by Jane Austen

Most people needed to work for a living – from clergymen, merchants and lawyers down to the lowliest labourers and servants. The
professional classes were almost exclusively male, but amongst the
working class countless women and children toiled equally long hours
alongside the men. By contrast Sir John and Lady Middleton in
Sense and Sensibility lead somewhat empty lives: 'Sir John was a
sportsman, Lady Middleton a mother. He hunted and shot, and she
humoured her children; and these were their only resources. Lady
Middleton had the advantage of being able to spoil her children,
while Sir John's independent employments were in existence only
half the time.' The fictional Middletons represented the tiny minority who controlled the bulk of the wealth and disdained those in
trade.

While the basic inequalities of the class system were tolerated,
the necessity to finance the wars and the royal family through taxation caused resentment. The lower and middle classes struggled with
increased taxes and prices, and at the same time the wages of manual
workers were frequently being reduced. The tax burden fell dispro-
portionately on the lower ranks, widening the gulf between rich and

poor. The idea that the Government should be more equitable was expressed in 1795 by William Jenkin, a Quaker:

> I fear some of those great folks look more to their great salaries, Pensions and Synecures than to the real good of the state. If they wish to convince the public that the latter is their chief concern let them in these perilous times make a voluntary sacrifice of a part of their enormous income to the public good; or at least by acts of benevolence lighten the burdens of the lower orders of the people, many of whom now groan under the pressure of the high price of most of the necessaries of life.[1]

In his memoirs William Darter voiced a similar opinion: 'I have related these events, of which I have perfect recollection, to shew the straits to which the country was driven at this time. Everything almost was taxed, even light and air.'[2]

Although the Reverend James Woodforde was a loyal supporter of George III, in December 1797 his irritation surfaced:

> Great uneasiness in almost every part of the Kingdom respecting the new taxes to be raised for the next year. London very much against them and will not pay them. The times at present are ... very alarming. The King going in State next week, to St. Pauls, to return thanks to Almighty God, for the late signal victories, is much talked of, with regard to the great expence to the Nation must be put to. It is certainly a very good intention of his Majesty but he should come forward in it, by advancing money to pay the expences of the same out of his own purse, he being so exceedingly rich and at so critical a time.[3]

On top of more and more taxes, an income tax was introduced in 1799, which was particularly resented by the middle and upper classes. A few years later William Holland complained because deductions were made from the dividend on his shares for Maidenhead Bridge across the River Thames: 'We cannot have our dividends from Maidenhead Bridge this fortnight on account of the Income Tax. This is rather hard to detain 25 pound because thirty shillings are demanded by government.'[4]

The idle rich were truly idle, as epitomised by Edward Ferrars in *Sense and Sensibility*. He is in line to inherit a fortune, but Mrs Dashwood suggests adopting a profession to fill his time. 'I do assure you', he replies,

> that I have long thought on this point ... But unfortunately my own nicety, and the nicety of my friends, have made me what I am, an idle, helpless being. We never could agree in our choice of profession. I always preferred the church, as I still do. But that was not smart enough for my family. They recommended the army. That was a great deal too smart for me. The law was allowed to be genteel enough ... But I had no inclination for the law ... As for the navy, it had fashion in its side, but I was too old when the subject was first started to enter it – and, at length, as there was no necessity for my having any profession at all ... I was therefore entered at Oxford and have been properly idle since then.

In his travels round England, the American scientist Benjamin Silliman, a young man who was actively immersed in research and education, was dismayed by such empty lives: 'Bath ... is probably the most dissipated place in the kingdom. It is resorted to by many real invalids, but by far the greater number belong to that class who wear away life in a round of fashionable frivolities, without moral aim or intellectual dignity.'[5]

Wealth might be tied up in property, land and other investments, but cash was hoarded at home or deposited in banks. 'Very busy in settling Bathursts accounts,' Woodforde noted in mid-November 1782, 'as I intend going to Norwich on Monday next on his account.'[6] The clergyman Henry Bathurst held the livings of nearby Great and Little Witchingham, but his friend Woodforde collected the tithes for him because he was non-resident. Three days later Woodforde went to Norwich, calling at 'Kerrisons Bank and changed 100 pounds in cash for a note of the same value and sent it to Dr Bathurst and put the letter myself into the Post-Office'.[7] This local bank failed in 1808 with substantial debts, as did many others over the years – including the bank of Jane Austen's brother Henry.[8]

Banking was in a state of flux, and innumerable country banks were set up to meet local needs. Other businesses also conducted banking, such as a silversmiths at Oxford where Woodforde changed money in 1793: 'Called on my friend Locke the silversmith this morning who behaved very obligingly and knew me at first sight. I changed a ten pound note with him, he keeps a bank and does great business.'⁹ Banknotes were technically redeemable only at the issuing banks – standardised banknotes that were legal tender, accepted by all banks, would not be fully established until 1833.

The monetary system was based on gold and silver. Twenty shillings (20s.) were worth one pound sterling (£1 or 1l.), and twelve pennies (12d.) equalled one shilling. There were no one-pound coins. The guinea (worth £1 and 1 shilling, or 21 shillings, abbreviated to £1 1s.) was a gold coin, and other gold coins included a five guinea (£5 5s.), half a guinea (10s. 6d.), quarter of a guinea (5s. 3d.) and one-third of a guinea (7s.). Silver coins included one crown (5s.), half-a-crown (2s. 6d.), one shilling (1s.), sixpence (6d.), fourpence (4d.), twopence (2d.) and some earlier pennies. As the coinage devalued over time, pennies were instead minted of copper alloy, as were the halfpenny (½d.) and farthing (¼d.).¹⁰

Most people were paid in coins, and they would buy whatever they needed with coins. Anyone contracted for a year, such as servants and agricultural workers, were usually paid just once or twice over that period, but large quantities of coins were needed for day-labourers and for factory workers who were paid weekly or monthly. When he was at Reeth in Yorkshire, Charles Fothergill learned about problems paying the lead miners: 'The wages of this class of labourer are good and are generally paid monthly … this is occasioned by the scarcity of small change which must be obtained if the men are paid weekly. The men in consequence with their families are obliged weekly to go in debt to the shops for their necessary provisions.'¹¹

The official mint could not meet the demand for lower-value coins because of obsolete machinery and methods, and so private companies began to issue farthing, halfpenny and penny tokens as small change. From 1787 the Anglesey Copper Mines Company issued copper tokens – around three hundred tons over the next three decades. Other companies followed, and as these tokens proliferated, shopkeepers and traders used sorting boxes to arrange them by the names of the different issuing companies. Businesses were quick to realise the potential of tokens for advertising and propaganda, which resulted in numerous designs and inscriptions, and sets of tokens bearing portraits of famous people, buildings and other features were aimed at collectors. Tokens from various sources were encountered every day, as the traveller John Byng found in Derbyshire: 'at the turnpike, I was surprised to receive in change the Anglesea, and Macclesfield half-pence; a better coinage, and of more beauty than that of the mint, and not so likely to be counterfeited'.[12] These tokens had been issued by the Anglesey company and by Roe and Company, which was a Macclesfield copper company. In 1817 the Government prohibited the manufacture of tokens and ordered issuing companies to redeem them, the only exceptions being tokens of the Sheffield and Birmingham workhouses.

The wars were a continual drain on England's gold reserves, threatening the stability of the economy and hindering commerce. Fears of invasion also caused the hoarding of gold and a run on banks, and by February 1797 the situation was so serious that the Bank of England stopped redeeming its promissory banknotes in coin. This worrying news reached Woodforde in Norfolk on 1 March: 'Mr. Custance with his son Willm. made us a morning visit, informed us, that a proclamation from the Privy Council had been issued, to stop paying in cash at the Bank of England for some time, fearing that if not stopped, there would not be ... enough to transact necessary and urgent business. On that account, all country banks have done the same, and are at present shut up.'[13]

There was immediate opposition in Parliament, and the playwright and MP Richard Brinsley Sheridan derided the Bank of England as 'an elderly lady in the city'. James Gillray made use of this idea in a cartoon termed 'The Old Lady of Threadneedle Street', a nickname for the Bank that has persisted. The shortage of coins brought some industries to a standstill, and the radical writer and historian John Blackner related what happened in Nottingham where he was living: 'In 1797, the refusal of the Bank of England to pay its notes in cash [coins] in February was attended with the most serious consequences to Nottingham and its vicinity, by causing an immediate stoppage of a great number of [knitting] frames for want of cash to go on with, nor could the ordinary business of the town be carried on, until one or both of the then banking-houses had issued out a quantity of seven shilling tickets.'[14] In mid-March that year, Woodforde wrote anxiously: 'There being little or no cash stirring and the country bank notes being refused to be taken, create great uneasiness in almost all people, fearful what consequences may follow. Excise officers refuse taking country notes for the payment of the several duties. Many do not know what to do on the present occasion having but very little cash by them.'[15]

The Bank of England did have sufficient reserves and was now authorised to issue banknotes for £1 and £2, where previously it could not issue them below £5. Once the new paper currency was found to be convenient, the panic subsided. The drain on gold reserves was abated, and although banknotes were not officially legal tender, they effectively became token money.[16] Problems did recur, as William Holland discovered in July 1810: 'I walked to [Nether] Stowey to change a bank bill [banknote] for cash but no cash to be had and I would not take any country bills, there being a run on the banks at this time, and I would not part with what is good for what is doubtful.'[17] In case they proved to have no value, he had refused to accept smaller banknotes.

What did ease the coin shortage was the capture in naval battles of Spanish silver dollars, which were circulated as legal currency after being overstamped. Woodforde, who liked to collect unusual coins, commented in late March 1797: 'Went up to Betty Carys [his local shop] this evening and got of her two Spanish dollars, having our Kings Head in miniature stamped on the neck of the King of Spain, alluding to the great victory over the Spanish fleet [Battle of St Vincent], lately, by Sr. Jon. Jervis. They are made current now in England and go for 4s/9d. I gave Betty for the two 0.9.6.'[18]

It was not long before counterfeit dollars were being produced, and the increase in paper money also made banknotes a prime target for forgers. Many forgeries were the work of foreign prisoners-of-war, as one newspaper reported in 1810:

A great number of Bank of England forged notes and counterfeit seven
shilling-pieces are now in circulation in Plymouth and its neighbourhood:
several persons detected in uttering them were taken into custody on
Saturday night. They are supposed to be the manufacture of French prisoners, whose ingenuity this way is very astonishing. Several of the
one-pound notes had been sold at one shilling each.[19]

The main method of putting counterfeit coins and notes into circulation was through the retail trade, and the magistrate Patrick
Colquhoun said that many criminals, gamblers, hawkers and pedlars
left London in the spring, 'carrying with them considerable quantities of counterfeit silver and copper coin, by which they are
enabled ... to extend the circulation by cheating and defrauding
ignorant country people'.[20] London with its many shops also suffered. In 1815 James Hill appeared before a magistrate 'charged with
having passed several counterfeit sixpences, knowing them to be so.
It appeared that the prisoner had gone into many shops in the neigh
bourhood of Kentish-town, and purchased trivial articles, in payment
of which he tendered the sixpences.'[21]

A popular way of sending one-guinea gold coins in the post was to
hide them beneath the wax seal of a letter, while banknotes could be
slipped inside. Because the mail contained cash and banknotes, robbing unarmed post-boys proved lucrative, and so in 1782 the Post
Office advised sending banknotes in two separate halves. This led to
serial numbers being duplicated on banknotes, one at each end, so
that the two halves could be matched and presented to a bank. The
practice of duplicate numbers continues today.[22] As a precaution,
Holland sent his banknote halves on separate days to the surgeon
who had treated his wife's leg at Bath: 'I called at [Nether] Stowey
and deliver'd a letter to Mr Paddock directed to Mr Baynton with
banknotes in it for the cure of my wife's leg which (by the by) is not
perfectly cured, and the sum required is large, no less than thirty
pound and a multiplicity of expences besides.'[23] Then a week later: 'I
have been very busy in writing letters and inclosing halves of notes
for Mr Baynton for the cure of my wife's leg, if it may be call'd so, for
I do not think it is quite well.'[24]

Most people obtained goods and services locally and paid in cash. Living close to the busy city of Norwich, just 8 miles from Weston Longville, Woodforde had accounts with many tradesmen and merchants there. Norwich was a sizeable place, with a population of some 36,000 in 1801, and on special trips Woodforde settled outstanding bills and bought or ordered anything else that was needed, as in June 1780:

To my barber Mileham gave	0: 1: 0
To his boy for bringing down my wig, gave	0: 0: 2
I went to Freemans shop and bespoke some furniture	
To 4 Pappa-marche [papier-mâché] decanter stands	
of Baker pd.	0: 7: 6
To snuffer stand of ditto paid	0: 1: 6
To a small burning glass of do pd	0: 1: 0
To 2 small combs and cases of do pd	0: 1: 2
To Miss Bell, mantua maker, for Nancy, pd.	1: 4: 6.[25]

Those with money could purchase goods in London, and even Jane Austen's household had tea supplied direct from the city to Chawton.[26] In 1782 Carl Moritz was amazed by London's huge range of shops:

It has a strange appearance, especially in the Strand, where there is a constant succession of shop after shop, and where, not infrequently, people of different trades inhabit the same house, to see their doors, or the tops of their windows, or boards expressly for the purpose, all written over from top to bottom, with large painted letters ... there is hardly a cobbler, whose name and profession may not be read in large golden characters by every one that passes. It is here not at all uncommon to see on doors, in one continuous succession, 'Children educated here', 'Shoes mended here', 'Foreign spiritous liquors sold here', and 'Funerals furnished here'.[27]

Outside the major towns and cities, temporary market stalls were far more common than shops, and most towns and even large villages had weekly markets for fresh produce. Woodforde was fortunate to have Betty Cary's shop nearby, but for such retailers there was no modern system of distribution and supply. 'As posterity may be ignorant what a bag-man is,' John Byng explained, 'let them learn that he is a rider, who travells, with saddle bags, to receive of shop keepers a list of what goods are wanting from manufactories, and wholesale dealers; and to collect the debts.'[28]

In London and elsewhere, pedlars sold all kinds of goods in the streets, from fruit and vegetables to cooked food, milk, shellfish and flowers. Really poor street traders might be part-time beggars, selling the lowest-value items such as matches. Woodforde found it convenient to buy from pedlars who obtained their merchandise in small quantities from manufacturers and sold door-to-door. In May 1780 he noted his recent purchases: 'To a man (whose name was Pedralio an Italian and who is the manager of the fire works at Bunns Gardens at Norwich) and who makes thermometers and barometers and carries them about the country, called at my house this morning with some of them and I bought one each for which I paid him 1.16.0.'[29]

One of the most awkward household purchases was firewood and coal. William Holland in Somerset had an account with a local coal merchant: 'Hawkins brought in his bill for coal this day, which I paid,' he wrote in January 1802. 'I believe he has not charged one load, which I shall inquire into. He is a very civil, honest man.'[30] This was praise indeed from Holland, as he was normally highly critical of most people. Households and the steam-driven industries were ever hungry for coal – literally the power behind the Industrial Revolution. The conversion from manual labour to steam-driven machines led to increased coal production, which in turn led to a demand from the coal industry for steam engines for pumps and winding gear. The improved steam engines were also used for manufacturing, which brought about the factory system of working that replaced many cottage industries. Although coal was mined elsewhere in England, the predominant source was 'sea coal', an old term for coal mined in north-east England, while 'coal' tended to mean charcoal.

The export hub for sea coal was Newcastle-upon-Tyne, a large port surrounded by countless mines and associated industries. A traditional folk song from there begins:

> As I cam thro' Sandgate, thro' Sandgate, thro' Sandgate,
> As I cam thro' Sandgate, I heard a lassie sing,
> Weel may the keel row, the keel row, the keel row,
> Weel may the keel row, that my laddie's in.[31]

The Sandgate, taking its name from the Sand Gate in the city walls, was a street in Newcastle forming the heart of the community of keelmen, and the 'lassie' was very likely to sing 'well may the keel row that my laddie's in', because their income depended on it. A 'keel' was a small boat that carried a load of around 20 tons of coal from the mines down the River Tyne and then transferred it to the seagoing ships known as 'colliers'. During a visit to Newcastle in November 1787, the surgeon Lionel Gillespie was impressed by the industry's scale:

> The coals are brought down the river in flat vessels called keels and the number of those employed is immense, each of them carries three men and a boy or old man. These vessels are sail'd, row'd, dragged or poled along the river, and sometimes two or three of these means are put in practice at one and the same time, for as the keelmen are pay'd by the trip, the incentive to industry is strong.[32]

Thousands of keelmen were employed on the Tyne river, who Frederick Eden described a few years later: 'Keelmen, (of whom 6000 or 7000 are constantly employed in navigating keels with coal, from the collieries on the Tyne to Shields,) are paid from 15s. to 20s. a week. Sailors, in time of war, are paid, from 6 to 11 guineas, for a voyage to London, which is often performed in a month, or less.'[33] As the mines were clustered close to the port, land transport costs were minimised, giving Newcastle its supremacy and resulting in the phrase 'taking coals to Newcastle', meaning a pointless exercise.

When Louis Simond was at Newcastle in 1811, he was surprised that the coal was exported: 'The continent of Europe draws from

England, notwithstanding the war, a quantity of coals ... said to amount to £500,000 or £600,000 a year. Some are exported to the West India islands, and the inhabitants of the larger seaport towns of the United States warm themselves almost entirely with English coals, cheaper than the wood of their forests.'[34]

At all stages, the transportation of coal involved gruelling manual labour, sometimes coupled with considerable danger. Frequent accidents occurred in the loading and unloading of the coal, and the sea passage down the east coast saw numerous shipwrecks. The mines themselves held the greatest risks, and newspapers carried countless depressing reports of pit disasters. Even without explosions, though, coal mining was hazardous, with many miners killed or injured in accidents and roof falls. Simond chanced going down one mine:

> The mode is rather alarming. The extremity of the rope which works up and down the shaft being formed into a loop, you pass one leg through it, so as to sit, or to be almost astride on the rope; then, hugging it with both arms, you are turned off from the platform over a dark abyss, where you would hardly venture if the depth was seen. This was 63 fathoms (378 feet). One of the workmen bestrode the loop by the side of me, and down we went with considerable rapidity. The wall of rock seemed to rush upwards, the darkness increased, the mouth above appeared a mere speck of light. I shut my eyes for fear of growing giddy, the motion soon diminished, and we touched the ground ... Each of us had a flannel dress and a candle, and thus proceeded through a long passage, rock above, rock below, and a shining black wall of coal on each side.[35]

Conditions were more brutal down the mines than those endured in most other occupations, particularly as the amount of wages depended on the amount of coal produced. Simond observed how it was cut: 'The ceiling of [the main road is] ... high enough for a man to stand upright, while the side streets are no higher than the stratum of coals (4½ feet), therefore you must walk stooping. The whole extent of the mine is worked in streets intersecting each other at right angles, 24 feet wide and 36 feet asunder, leaving solid blocks 36 feet every way.'[36] This was the 'pillar and stall' method, which extracted about half the available coal. It was so-called because the coal was mined from areas called 'stalls', leaving large rectangular pillars of coal to support the roof. The other common method of mining was the 'long wall'. First, a shaft was dug following the coal seam. Then one side of the shaft was cut away by the miners who dumped the waste rock on the other side of the shaft. This helped to support the roof as the 'long wall' of the shaft moved sideways through the coal seam.

There were frequent roof falls, as happened to young Josh Gibson, who in about 1796 started working 'in a pit at Shipley [Yorkshire] when seven years old; drove a pony until he was above nine, when he then went behind, and was hooked to the waggon with a belt. He found it hurt him much ... when about 12 years old he was crushed bad by the roof falling.'[37] For the men, women and children who worked down the mines, there was often little alternative employment. In Scotland the miners were virtually slaves until an Act of Parliament came into force in 1775.[38] South of the border, in the northern counties of England, a similar situation prevailed, with the miners commonly hired on a yearly basis. They signed a bond agreeing to work without strikes or absences, and in return were paid a premium that could be relatively high. In 1795 Frederick Eden thought that the wages of the miners around Newcastle were generous:

> Pit men earn from 1s. 6d. to 3s. 6d. a day; on an average, about 16s. a week; besides which, they are allowed rye from their masters, at 4s. the bushel. Notwithstanding these high wages, they are seldom richer than their neighbours. They use a great deal of butcher's meat, during the three or four first days of the week; but, towards the close of it, as their earnings of the preceding week become nearly exhausted, they are generally obliged to live more frugally and abstemiously.[39]

Miners did break their bond from time to time, and mine owners would advertise for their capture, as in the *Newcastle Journal* in 1777:

PITMEN ABSCONDED.

Whereas Thomas Norton, aged about 35 years or thereabouts, and Thomas Green, aged 46 years or thereabouts, colliers, lawfully bound and hired to work at Byker-hill colliery from the 9th day of October 1776, to the 9th day of October 1777, have unlawfully absented themselves from the said colliery:– Notice is hereby given, to all Coal-owners, their agents, or others, not to employ the said persons, or they will be prosecuted as the law in that case directs; and any person giving information where they may be apprehended, to Mr Joseph Hunter, at Byker-hill, shall be well rewarded.[40]

The expansion of coal production depended on cheap transport. Once the coal reached the sea ports, it was taken inland by river and canal craft via a network of waterways, though the final few miles might need to be by horse and cart or by packhorse. From the early eighteenth century canals were built to join rivers, and rivers themselves were canalised to make them navigable. Canals were increasingly regarded as the solution to the problem of transporting heavy and bulky goods, including coal, though one canal between Stourbridge and Dudley, designed to carry cheaper coal to the Stourbridge-based industries, was not universally welcome:

an act [of Parliament] was obtained for carrying the plan into execution, though not without great opposition from the coal-owners upon the Birmingham canal, and the owners of the mills upon the river Stour: the first because this canal would enable the coal-owners upon it to under-sell the others at the market, and the latter upon account of the supposed loss of water to their mills, for which they had very little reason, for nearly all the water ... must be raised out of the mines.[41]

First proposed in 1775, this canal was given parliamentary assent the following year and was operational by the end of 1779.

The success of canals saw an explosion in canal building and speculation in the 1790s – such that it became known as 'canal mania'. There were no mechanical excavators because steam engines were not easily moved about, and so canals were formed by hundreds of labourers digging with hand tools and shifting the spoil in wheelbarrows. These workmen were drawn from all over the country, some through advertisements, such as one that appeared in an Exeter newspaper in 1810:

To CANAL CUTTERS &c.

WANTED, TWO or THREE HUNDRED good WORKMEN on the WORCESTER and BIRMINGHAM CANAL, where liberal Prices will be given to Agg Masters [subcontractors]; and good Wages to Workmen that are ready and deserving encouragement, by applying to Mr. Charles Holland, at Tibberton, near Worcester.[42]

With increasing numbers of canals being cut, gangs of labourers moved from job to job, setting up camp wherever they went. They were originally called 'canal cutters' or simply 'workmen', but because canals were known as 'inland navigations' and the engineers who oversaw the projects were called 'navigators', this term was eventually extended to the labourers and then abbreviated to 'navvies'. The better-known gangs of Victorian railway navvies evolved from these bands of Georgian canal navvies.

Relentless effort and skill were needed to wield tools like picks, mattocks, shovels and loaded wheelbarrows, and not all labourers could work sufficiently fast to earn a living, because it was piecework – a set price for digging a certain distance of canal or tunnel, such as the £7 per yard paid to the subcontractors cutting the Sapperton tunnel in Gloucestershire on the Thames and Severn Canal. When the Basingstoke Canal began to be constructed in 1788, this problem was witnessed by the Reverend Stebbing Shaw at the Greywell tunnel, some 13 miles from Steventon where Jane Austen was then living:

I ... saw above 100 men at work, preparing a wide passage for the approach to the mouth, but they had not entered the hill ... The contractor, agreeable to the request of the company of proprietors, gives the preference to all the natives who are desirous of this work, but such is the power of use over nature, that while these industrious poor are by all their efforts incapable of earning a sustenance, those who are brought from similar works, cheerfully obtain a comfortable support.[43]

The absence of safety measures was especially evident to John Byng during an uncomfortable visit to the tunnel being constructed at Sapperton:

Nothing cou'd be more gloomy than ... being dragg'd [by sledge cart] into the bowels of the earth, rumbling and jumbling thro mud, over stones, with a small lighted candle in my hand, giving me a sight of the last horse ... When the last peep of day light vanish'd, I was enveloped in thick smoke arising from the gunpowder of the miners, at whom, after passing by many labourers who work by small candles, I did at last arrive: they come from the Derbyshire and Cornish mines, are in eternal danger and frequently perish by the falls of earth. My cart being reladen with stone, I was hoisted thereon ... and had a worse journey back, as I cou'd scarcely keep my seat ... I understand that they have made an equal progress (½ mile) at the other end, and hope to meet in 3 years; when the first passage thro', in a barge, must be glorious, and horrid.[44]

When it opened in 1789, the Sapperton Tunnel was the longest in England at over 2 miles, and the canal running through it linked the Thames and Severn rivers.

Travelling near Bath over a decade later, Richard Warner commented on the growing canal network:

At a short distance from hence [South Stoke], in the bottom below, we meet with the *canal*, a recent undertaking, intended to convey the coals of the Timsbury, Paulton, Camerton, and Dunkerton pits to Bath. The course of this cut, which is not yet compleated, will embrace in its various windings, to its junction with the Radstock cut, a distance of ten miles, and pass through a country as highly picturesque as any in the kingdom.[45]

New canals provided an increasing amount of work for the many thousands who ran boats, but with real wages falling, it made sense for a boatman's family to live on board rather than pay rent for lodgings. In 1815–16 one Christian organisation undertook a survey of the Grand Junction Canal's floating population:

> It appeared upon inquiry, that the number of boats was between four and five hundred; that the number of men on the line of the Grand Junction Canal, the collateral branches, with the engine and lock houses, might be estimated at six thousand; and that, including their wives and children, the number of persons to be taken into consideration was probably not less than twenty thousand. These may be said almost to live upon the water, and, by the peculiar nature of their occupation, are precluded from all opportunity of attending public worship on the Sabbath-day.[46]

Once it became cheaper and easier to transport coal inland, there was a greater incentive to develop steam engines to power machinery of all kinds, from which the woollen and cotton textile industries in particular benefited. Since the Middle Ages textile manufacture based on wool was a major element of England's economy, organised and funded by businessmen dealing in finished cloth. Each process needed to transform raw sheep's wool into a saleable product was carried out by thousands of scattered individual workers, usually paid on a piecework basis. Middlemen bought and supplied the materials, such as spun yarn to the weavers or woven cloth to the fullers, afterwards collecting the finished work. They might even lend or lease looms and other equipment. Spinning was done by hand, mostly by the women of farming families or those who worked in the textile trade, and by the end of the seventeenth century the term 'spinster', originally meaning a female spinner, had become the term for an unmarried woman. Weaving was a task more often done by men. By the late eighteenth century none of the textile processes was particularly well paid, but being piecework with such a loose organisational basis, families could live and work together at home, taking off as much time as they wanted.

The introduction of machines made some workers redundant

and forced many more into the factories, which were considerably more efficient and yielded higher profits for their owners. However, the factory hands found that not only did they need to work more hours for the same money, but they lost the old freedom to choose when to work and when to rest. They even had to arrive punctually or lose wages. Although some factories installed a bell or whistle to signal shift changes, it was the individual's responsibility to get to work on time, and so a new job sprang up – that of the 'knocker-up', who for a small fee went round and roused workers for their shift.

Some workers owned pocket watches, and wealthier households might possess one or more clocks. William Holland had a seven-day clock, which he wound every Saturday evening, as he noted in October 1800: 'The evening by ourselves, and spent as we usually do the Saturday evenings, poring over sermons, winding the clock and to bed.'[47] The chiming of the church clock was also an important indicator of time, but most people estimated time by the level of daylight. In towns, night watchmen often called out the hour, and William Darter in Reading praised one watchman who was always helpful: 'I remember well Norcroft's features, and the sound of his voice "Past two o'clock and a cloudy morning," &c.'[48]

Another great change for the new factory workers was the necessity to travel to work, which could add significantly to the length and effort of an arduous day. Some began to view the recent past as a golden age, cruelly stolen from them, and a contemporary song lamented the changes:

> So come all you cotton-weavers, you must rise up very soon,
> For you must work in factories from morning until noon;
> You mustn't walk in your garden for two or three hours a day,
> And you must stand at their command and keep your shuttles in play.[49]

The textile industry thrived and remained the second largest employer in the country after agriculture, despite the job losses due to mechanisation. In 1800 Warner described the changing woollen cloth production in Somerset:

Frome has for many years been famous for working Spanish and English wool into broad-cloths and kerseymeres ... The quantity of wool manufactured here is since considerably increased, but the number of people employed is diminished, the introduction of machines having lessened, in a prodigious proportion, the call for manual labour. At present there are in the town of Frome twenty-seven manufacturers of cloth, who make ... about one hundred and sixty miles of cloth, in length, every year.[50]

The cotton industry was also on the rise, rapidly adopting the new ways of working, although it would not dominate British manufacturing as 'King Cotton' for many decades to come. In June 1790 at Cromford in Derbyshire, John Byng observed Arkwright's water-powered spinning mill: 'These cotton mills, seven stories high, and fill'd with inhabitants, remind me of a first rate man of war; and when they are lighted up, on a dark night, look most luminously beautiful.'[51] On a tour from Oxford to the Lake District a few years later, Johnson Grant stopped at nearby Bakewell, where he was concerned about the effects of such factories on the health of workers:

[I] passed a cotton manufactory; the people all coming out to dinner, for it was already one o'clock. From the glance I had of their appearance, the observations I made were these: They were pale, and their hats were covered with shreds of cotton. Exclusive of want of exercise, the general bane of all manufactures, the light particles of cotton must be inhaled with their breath, and occasion pulmonary affections. Owners of factories should consider this ... Let every such person, then, order his work-people to bathe every morning, and let him have a piece of playground for them, wherein some athletic and innocent exercise might be enjoyed for an hour or two, each day. In cottonworks, let them drink much water.[52]

Grant was a clergyman, traveller and prolific writer, and he was afraid that the factory workers might question the class system and therefore the established order. Wages, he argued, should not be exorbitant, though limited education was desirable: 'establish a

Sunday-school, where they might be instructed orally, without being taught to read. This I deem a necessary precaution, as they would have all the advantages of improvement of mind and morals, without their common banes – low political club-rooms, with their idleness, their liquors, and neglect of families.'[53] In his opinion, too much education might encourage the realisation that there was no natural or God-given basis to the inequalities in society, and this might be a road to revolution. He feared that factory hands already went unwillingly to work, 'discontented, and cursing all laws, human and divine, which have so arranged matters, that yon stately house [nearby Chatsworth], and the gilded coach in which its owner rides, should belong to what the Corresponding Society, the illuminati and illuminantes of this country, have deluded him … is an individual with no better title to it than himself.'[54] This particular individual was the immensely wealthy Duke of Devonshire.

Many workers were already pushed to the brink of destitution and starvation and were increasingly aware of injustices in society. The song known as 'The Hand-Loom Weavers' Lament' was written sometime between 1807 and 1815 and was about those made unemployed by the advent of the factories. Two verses in particular addressed their so-called superiors:

> When we look on our poor children, it grieves our hearts full sore,
> Their clothing it is worn to rags, while we can get no more,
> With little in their bellies, they to their work must go,
> Whilst yours do dress as manky as monkeys in a show.
>
> You go to church on Sundays, I'm sure it's nought but pride,
> There can be no religion where humanity's thrown aside;
> If there be a place in heaven, as there is in the Exchange,
> Our poor souls must not come near there; like lost sheep they
>   must range.[55]

The 'Exchange' was the Royal Exchange in London, equivalent to the modern shorthand of 'the City', meaning the financial establishment. If these verses caused discomfort, the chorus caused alarm:

> You tyrants of England, your race may soon be run,
> You may be brought unto account for what you've sorely done.[56]

Popular at the time, and intermittently popular ever since, this has been labelled a Luddite song, and it certainly arose at a time and place where the Luddites were active.

'Luddite' was the name given to a shadowy group of workers who reacted to the new practices within factories by destroying the machines. Their initial target was the wide knitting frames that were introduced to cut costs. These machines produced large pieces of cloth from which stockings were cut and then sewn into shape. Previously they were knitted into shape and the woven edges joined in a seam. The new process was faster and needed less skilled labour, but the resulting stockings were inferior, tending to lose their shape and unravel where the seams were formed from the cut edges. The drop in quality gave the whole trade a bad name and affected prices.

Several stories arose that tried to account for the Luddite name, and according to John Blackner in Nottingham, the Luddites 'assumed this appellation from the circumstance of an ignorant youth, in Leicestershire, of the name of Ludlam, who, when ordered by his father, a framework-knitter, to square his needles [adjust the machine because his knitting was too loose], took a hammer and beat them into a heap.'[57] Those factory owners and middlemen who did not produce the substandard stockings tacitly approved of the machine-breaking. Blackner recorded how Luddites operated in Nottinghamshire: 'The practice of these men was to assemble in parties of from six to sixty, according as circumstance required, under a supposed leader, that was stiled *General Ludd*, who had the absolute command of them, and directed their operations; placing the guards, who were armed with swords, firelocks, &c. in their proper places, while those armed with hammers, axes, &c. were ordered to enter the house and demolish the frames.'[58] Blackner also described the Government's frantic response:

> In consequence of these outrages being continued, a considerable military force was brought into the neighbourhood; two of the London police

magistrates, with some other officers, came down with a view of assisting the civil power in discovering the ringleaders; a considerable sum of money was also placed at the disposal of a secret committee, for the purpose of obtaining private information; but ... these deluded men [the Luddites] continued their course of devastation for several months, and at the end of February, 1812, it was found that no less than six hundred and twenty-four frames had been destroyed.[59]

More concerned with crushing dissension than promoting justice, the Government passed an Act in March 1812 making machine-breaking a capital offence, but the Luddites then attacked machines in other areas. In July that year Nelly Weeton moved from the Pedders in the Lake District to take another post as governess in Yorkshire. Her new employer was Joseph Armitage, a wool manufacturer, and she confided in a friend about the fear of reprisals there from machine-breakers:

> Mr. A is engaged in the woollen trade, has a handsome fortune of his own, and had another with his wife, though their parents are all living; at whose death, I suppose, they will have considerably more. They have no carriage, no in-door man-servant; there are four women servants. They kept a man till lately, but as Mr. Armitage's house at Lockwood was one of the first that was attacked by the Luddites a few months ago, he has not ventured to keep a man in his house, as many gentlemen have been betrayed by their servants, who have been discovered to be of the Luddite party.[60]

Very few men were arrested and tried for being Luddites. A few were hanged, more were transported, but the Government was unsuccessful in its attempts to crush the movement. It gradually faded away, having gained little more than a temporary halt to mechanisation. Rather than meaning someone who resists oppression, the word 'Luddite' nowadays refers to a person who holds back progress.

Improved machines had not yet made much impact on agricultural work, which was still labour-intensive. Over one-third of the population worked in farming, which remained England's largest employer.

The work was long and hard.[61] In a single day a ploughman might walk upwards of 11 miles behind a horse-drawn plough just to plough one acre. In October 1784 Woodforde's servant hoped to join their ranks: 'Jack [Wharton, about nineteen years old] told me this morning that he is advised to get another place, being too old for a Skip-Jack [servant boy] any longer. He wants to be a Plow Boy to some farmer to learn the farming business as he likes that best. I told him that he was very right to try to better himself, and at Lady Day next he is to leave my house for that purpose.'[62]

There was always a need for workers capable of handling horses. One enduring English folk song about ploughing, which has several titles, is most commonly known by its chorus line 'We're all jolly fellows who follow the plough'. A cheerful song, it was in circulation by at least 1794[63] and relates how the ploughmen rose around four in the morning to get the horses ready. After breakfast they each go out to plough an acre of ground, returning by two in the afternoon. The farmer then suggests that they have not finished their work:

> I stepped up to him, and I made this reply,
> 'We have all ploughed an acre, so you tell a lie,'
> Our master turned to us and laughed at the joke:
> 'It's past two o'clock boys, it's time to unyoke.'[64]

The horses then had to be cared for and settled down for the night before the men could go home after the long day's work.

Farming was not yet in any real sense mechanised, but improvements in stock breeding were resulting in healthier, hardier animals that provided more meat and milk, while the introduction of some machinery and experimentation with plants and seeds were improving crop yields. Emphasis was placed on improving the fertility of the soil, which had traditionally been maintained by rotating crops to allow fallow periods and by the penning of animals so that land could benefit from their manure. New methods of manuring included the spreading of chalk or lime, though old ways persisted, as a survey of agriculture in Dorset in 1812 noted:

Chamber-lye.– In the Isle of Portland, they have a practice of long standing, of preserving all the urine that is made in winter, carrying it out in
casks, and distributing it over the wheat crops, in a manner somewhat
similar to that used in watering the streets of large towns. This kind of
manure has been found to answer well, as may be believed, from the
average produce of the Isle being 18 bushels of wheat per acre.[65]

Many clergymen did some farming, either of church lands or
their own land, which supplemented their income. Jane Austen's
parents farmed land near her father's rectory at Steventon in
Hampshire, and farming activities are mentioned in her letters, as in
November 1798 when she asked Cassandra, who was staying at
Godmersham in Kent, to 'tell Edward that my father gives 25s. a
piece to Seward for his last lot of sheep, and, in return for this
news, my father wishes to receive some [news] of Edward's pigs'.[66]
Woodforde also farmed, generally employing a man and a boy for
much of the work and hiring extra labour when needed, particularly
for harvesting, as in September 1776: 'Very busy all day with my
barley, did not dine till near 5 in the afternoon, my harvest men
dined here to day, gave them some beef and some plumb pudding
and as much liquor as they would drink. This evening finished my
harvest and all carried into the barn – 8 acres. I had Mrs. Dunnell's
cart and horses, and 2 men, yesterday and to day. The men were her
son Thos. and Robin Buck.'[67]

Unlike today, farming activities were forced to follow the cycle of
the seasons, with the most intense work during the long days of
summer. Harvest time was the highlight, and the writer and com-
poser William Gardiner had fond memories of helping out at
Rothley near Leicester as a seven-year-old boy in 1778:

With what glee did I mount the harvest waggon for the fun of jolting
over the rugged roads, to the wheat field. From shock to shock it slowly
moved to gather the rustling sheaves. In the rear of the reapers were a
flock of gleaners – some pretty village girls ... The day's toil over, we
hastened home for the harvest supper. At the head of the board sat the
worthy host, by whose side I was placed. Then came Will, Ralph, Joe, and

Jim, with their wives and helpers. Presently a shoulder of mutton, scorching hot, as the day had been, a plum pudding, and a roasted goose were put on the table, when they soon fell to, each playing his part in good earnest ... The gingered ale went merrily round. Joe, who was a good singer, was called upon to entertain the company.[68]

Samuel Pratt gave an equally romantic picture, this time of when the work had subsided during the early winter months:

The fields are no longer populated, and labour is not so enlivened by the song, and the converse of the labourer ... Every store-house is full, and in every cottage, so benign has been the past season, there are the means of comfort and content. The alterations have increased, the beauty of the autumnal foliage has lost its last charm of variegation – and if the naked boughs remind us of the decline of nature, a few leaves only remain, and these tremble at every breath of wind, as if they were conscious of their defenceless situation.[69]

Yet he knew that after helping with the harvest, the poor could starve whenever the farmers withheld their crops to obtain better prices:

famine must enter the cottage of the peasant, whose industry has led smiling plenty into the houses of his employer – and multitudes of the most useful members of the community must cry aloud for bread, while those nefarious robbers of the public, known by the names of Forestallers and Monopolizers – which, I fear, are but other words to cover a certain class of the ENGLISH FARMERS – are permitted to hoard up the stores, which the indulgent God of nature gives to supply the wants of all his creatures.[70]

In the later eighteenth century, with grain prices rising and rents for farmland soaring, particularly for enclosed land, it became economic for large landowners to pay to have even more land enclosed. In old-fashioned open fields, small farmers in a community worked their own strips of land, an inefficient system dating back to the Middle Ages. Some claimed that enclosure was vital to improve these open fields, as well as the commons and waste land, so that more food could be produced. But others believed that enclosure was evil, because rents were forced upwards and the poor were deprived of their land, their common rights and the means to be self-sufficient.

Land was the most acceptable way for gentlemen to earn a living, and they relied on their agents and stewards to maximise the income from their estates. The largest landowners often had no legal right to all of the land they wished to enclose, but as enclosure of specific areas was by individual Act of Parliament, the rights of the poor were not considered, and the smaller landowners were squeezed out. The writer and educationalist William Fordyce Mavor commented on the pitfalls of the enclosure system: 'Various are the instances, within my own knowledge, of twelve farms, which once supported as many families in credit, having been thrown into three or four upon an inclosure.'[71]

In his lengthy poem *The Deserted Village*, published in 1770, Oliver Goldsmith expressed his sadness at the effects of enclosure. He imagines a deserted landscape, where all the old sounds of the former village have disappeared. Just one old woman remains:

> But now the sounds of population fail,
> No chearful murmurs fluctuate in the gale,
> No busy steps the grass-grown foot-way tread,
> But all the bloomy flush of life is fled.
> All but yon widowed solitary thing
> That feebly bends beside the plashy spring;
> She, wretched matron, forced, in age, for bread,
> To strip the brook with mantling cresses spread,
> To pick her wintry faggot from the thorn,
> To seek her nightly shed, and weep till morn;
> She only left of all the harmless train,
> The sad historian of the pensive plain.[72]

According to Mavor, the greed of large landowners created unemployment and hardship:

If three men monopolize the land which maintained and employed twelve before, nine of course and their families must turn day-labourers, or manufacturers [factory workers], and eventually become chargeable to the parish ... Will three farmers raise as much marketable produce as twelve would do? Was it not formerly owing to the small occupiers of land, that many of the necessaries and comforts of life were to be procured in such abundance, and sold at such a moderate rate?[73]

In many parts of England John Byng witnessed the changes caused by enclosures, which he prophesied would lead to the countryside's devastation:

How wisely did the fost'ring hand of ancestry provide for the poor, by an allotment of a cottage right of common in the open fields; the village green before their door; the orchard adjoining their house; and the long close behind it! These two latter being seiz'd by the greedy farmer, and the two former being forced from them by the hand of power (upon some inadequate infamous bargain) has driven away the poor; has levell'd the cottage; has impoverish'd the country; and must, finally, ruin it.[74]

He felt that Parliament was too focused on the problems of slavery in the British colonies and was deliberately ignoring the virtual slavery suffered by the working classes: 'I would that Mr Wilberforce, and Mr Burke were obliged to survey, and report upon Hamerton [in Lincolnshire], to a select committee of the House of Commons; and no more to think and prate of East, and West Indian miseries, and depopulations.'[75] William Wilberforce, now better known for his role in abolishing the slave trade, had a parliamentary record of enthusiastically supporting measures such as anti-trades union legislation that severely repressed the working class.

The position of black people in England was different to that in the British colonies. In a test case in 1772, brought by campaigners for the abolition of slavery, Lord Mansfield, the Lord Chief Justice, ruled that a black man purchased abroad as a slave and brought to England by his owner could not be forced to leave the country.[76] The basis of the judgment was that since slavery had no legal foundation in England, any coercion of the man was unlawful. But if he did return to America, he would revert to the status of a slave under that colony's laws. This was unacceptable to some owners, who considered these people were still their slaves in England.

Benjamin Silliman recorded that while he was at Liverpool in 1805, he descended into the hold of a slave ship 'and examined the cells where human beings are confined, under circumstances which equally disgust decency and shock humanity ... Liverpool is *deep, very deep* in the guilt of the slave-trade.'[77] Although black people formed a minority of England's population, they were present at all levels of society, mostly in urban areas. Silliman particularly noticed that many worked as servants in rich households:

> A black footman is considered as a great acquisition, and consequently negro servants are sought for and caressed. An ill dressed or starving negro is never seen in England, and in some instances even alliances are formed between them and white girls of the lower orders of society ... As there are no slaves in England, perhaps the English have not learned to regard negroes as a degraded class of men, as we do in the United States, where we have never seen them in any other condition.[78]

The plight of children forced down mines, up chimneys and into factories was perhaps the closest to the misery endured by slaves taken across the Atlantic from Africa, but other features of English society were compared with slavery, including impressment into the Royal Navy. Because press-gangs were permitted to force men and boys into the navy, seizing them from the streets or even their homes, impressment was said to be legalised slavery. One naval captain, Thomas Pasley, commented in 1780: 'Poor Sailors – you are the only class of beings in our famed Country of Liberty really *Slaves*, devoted and hardly [harshly] used, tho' the very being of the Country depends on you.'[79] The smuggler Jack Rattenbury from Beer in Devon was often targeted by the press-gangs. 'Our country is called the land of liberty', he complained; 'we possess a just and invincible aversion to slavery at home and in our foreign colonies, and it is triumphantly said that a slave cannot breathe in England. Yet how is this to be reconciled with the practice of tearing men from their weeping and afflicted families ... and chaining them to a situation which is alike repugnant to their feelings and principles?'[80]

Press-gangs caused much fear and anxiety in London and other ports and coastal settlements, as William Darter in Reading recalled:

> During the protracted war [with France and America] ... no young man could safely go to London. I remember a young fellow of the name of Chandler living in Mount Pleasant, who with another ... went to town for the purpose of working at their business as carpenters and joiners. They had not been there more than a few weeks, when on their way back to their shop after dinner they stopped to look into a shop window. A Press Gang came up and forcibly took them down to the water where they were put into an armed boat and taken down to the Nore. These men fought in several battles on board His Majesty's ships, and after many years Chandler returned home, but his comrade was killed in action.[81]

Unlike the navy, the army was not allowed to seize anyone it pleased, but had to tempt young men with cash bonuses or trick them into joining. The militias also needed men to defend Britain against invasion from abroad or revolution from within. They were organised on a local basis, and eligible men were put into a lottery. Those drawn had to serve or find someone else to take their place. In September 1779 Woodforde nearly lost a servant to the militia: 'Lent my man Ben my little mare to go to Norwich this morning to try to get a substitute to serve for him in the militia as he is drawn ... Ben Legate [Leggett] returned home in the evening from Norwich having got a substitute and seen him sworn in immediately as well as accepted. He is obliged to give the substitute 9.9.0. I gave him, in part of it, this evening 1.1.0.'[82] Woodforde's contribution appears less than generous considering that Ben was his valued farming man.

Plenty of unemployed people were available to replace men lost to the armed forces, but in rural areas the unemployed were trapped, unable to travel beyond their parish to the Midlands and northern England where expanding industries had jobs. This lack of mobility also hindered mill owners, who could not find enough workers. It was actually easier for the Irish to cross the sea and find work in Lancashire or Yorkshire than for destitute people from southern counties. The only options for the unemployed were to apply for poor relief or go into the workhouse or poorhouse. Such assistance was financed at parish level by the poor rates. At Castle Carrock in Cumberland in December 1794, Frederick Eden listed those receiving parish relief, including:

> J.G. aged 30; was incapacitated from working by a kick from a horse: he is allowed 2s. a week.
> J.D. aged 70; gained his settlement here by service: old age, and poverty, threw him on the parish: his weekly allowance is 1s. 6d. ...
> A child, 8 years old, whose parents are dead, costs the parish 1s. a week.
> A male bastard, of the same age, costs the parish 1s. a week.[83]

One woman receiving aid at nearby Cumwhitton was 'A.S. 60 years of age, a farmer's widow, receives a weekly allowance of 1s: she resided in another parish, but, upon becoming burthensome, was removed hither.'[84] A parish was responsible for anyone born within their jurisdiction, though on marriage a woman came under her husband's parish. If someone did manage to settle in another parish for a year, that parish was responsible for them if they became destitute. Wealthier households paid the poor rates, and because this was an increasing and often resented burden, every effort was made to repatriate paupers to their home parish. As Louis Simond put it: 'The poor of England are under certain regulations, called poor-laws, forming one of the distinctive features of this government. Their object is half police, and half charity; but their utility very questionable ... Parishes being bound to provide each for their own poor, it becomes a matter of importance to prevent new comers from acquiring a *settlement*, by removal to a new parish.'[85] John Byng considered the welfare system terrible:

'why, in God's name, is this country to be swallowed up by poor rates? And the oppress'd, miserable inhabitants to be hunted about from village, and village; and at last to be starved to death in a work house!!!'[86]

Some paupers were maintained in parish workhouses or poor-houses, while others were privatised or 'farmed' – given to private contractors for an agreed price. The clergyman William Jones described the facilities at Broxbourne, Hertfordshire: 'The poor house, as it is called, in this parish, is a wretched hovel, considerably below the level of the adjoining road. The workhouse of [nearby] Hoddesdon is not badly situated, but its almshouses are in a miserable, confined alley.'[87] In 1795 Eden noted how paupers at St Albans, a few miles west of Broxbourne, were farmed out for £400 a year: 'The Poor of this parish have generally been farmed ... The contractor finds food, cloaths, fuel, &c.; and the parish provides the house and furniture, which the farmer is bound to leave in good condition. He has 39 poor people at present in the house, 10 of which are old women, 7 men, and the rest children.'[88]

In Norfolk, Woodforde had few illusions about the workhouses. In March 1781 he and a companion visited one: 'we took a ride to the House of Industry about 2 miles west of Dereham, a very large building at present tho' there wants another wing. About 380 poor in it now, but they don't look either healthy or cheerful, a great number die there – 27 have died since Christmas last.'[89] The situation for the destitute was no better eleven years on, and Woodforde took pity on a man who had fled from a workhouse. He was heading for London but was so poor that he could have been arrested as a vagrant at any time and returned:

To a man of Bargewell (by name Brighton whose father and mother lately kept the Bell Inn at Billingford) who escaped this morning out of Bargewell's Poor House being hardly kept alive there, the allowance so very short, the house being farmed out at 1s/6d, per week for each poor person. I gave him as he appeared to be a very civil spoken man and as one that once knew better days 0.1.0. He was going for London he said to his wife who is a housekeeper to some person in town.[90]

Illegal ways of obtaining money, such as begging and stealing, might be resorted to by those unable or unwilling to work, especially if they were not eligible to receive assistance. Louis Simond was surprised that 'at the entrance of most towns or villages, you see written a notice, "To vagrants, and other idle and disorderly persons;—that such as may be found in it will be proceeded against with the utmost rigour of the law;" that is to say, of the poor-laws.'[91] Within their own parishes, clergymen often dispensed charitable gifts both on a casual basis and to meet specific needs. In the harsh winter of 1789 Woodforde made his servant distribute money among the poor: 'Bitter cold day again with high wind, it froze in all parts of the house. Sent Ben round my parish with some money to the poor people this severe weather, chiefly those that cannot work at this time, some 1 shilling apiece – some at 1s/6d apiece. In all, Ben gave for me this day 1.14.6.'[92]

While the war dragged on, changes in agriculture and industry threw increasing numbers of people out of work, so that by 1811 John Blackner in Nottingham despaired of the situation: 'Such was the reduced state of trade of this town, that half-famished workmen, belonging to almost every branch of its principal manufacture, were constrained to sweep the streets for a paltry support. They were employed by the overseers of St. Mary's parish, because the workhouse was too full to receive their families, and other employment could not be found.'[93]

Many were drawn to London in the hopes of improving their fortune, so that the city had increasing numbers of paupers and beggars on the streets – some literally scraped a living like the 'grubbers':

[They] procure a livelihood by whatever they find in grubbing out the dirt from between the stones with a crooked bit of iron, in search of nails that fall from horse-shoes, which are allowed to be the best iron that can be made use of for gun-barrels: and though the streets are constantly looked over at the dawn of the day by a set of men in search of sticks, handkerchiefs, shawls &c. that may have been dropt during the night, yet these grubbers now and then find rings that have been drawn off with the gloves, or small money that has been washed by the showers between the stones. These men are frequently employed to clear gully-holes and common sewers, the stench of which is so great that their breath becomes pestilential.[94]

Everyone pinned their hopes on the wars ending, but, as William Darter noted, improvements did not actually materialise for everyone: 'Cheap bread we did not get, and John Bull had to pay the piper ... At this time the working classes were suffering great privations, as there was very little call for their services, and provisions of all kinds were very dear.'[95] From 1814 when Napoleon was exiled and again in 1815 after Waterloo, thousands of soldiers and sailors were laid off. Unemployment rose sharply, and attempts to drive down wages caused unrest, as *The Times* reported in August 1816:

What is denominated a strike has ... taken place amongst the wool-sorters, who at the present rate of wages can earn from 3l. to three guineas a week. The masters wished to reduce the rate of wages one-third, on account of the reduction which has taken place in their prices, and to enable them to meet the foreign market. This proposition the men refused to accede to; and the masters, not being able to give more, many of them standing still, whilst the men, in consequence of their own obstinacy, are many hundreds of them become burdensome to their respective parishes, together with their families. Would it not be well, whilst so many thousands are out of employ and starving, or burdensome to their parishes from absolute want of employment, that parish officers should make inquiry and refuse to relieve all such as might have work and refuse to do it.[96]

The hardships of the labouring classes and the destitute poor are well documented in the works of Charles Dickens and other Victorian writers. Caused by wars, industrialisation and enclosure of the countryside, these hardships were approaching their worst by the end of Jane Austen's lifetime, with people literally starving in the streets:

Saturday last, a poor fellow, about thirty years of age, was going through Stoke Newington in search of employment, and being weak through hunger and want, sat down at the gate of Mr. Hugh's house, where he was found by the porter in an expiring state. On being questioned he was unable to answer anything, but that he was dying. He was taken inside the gate and some victuals offered to him, but he was too far gone to use any; he took half a glass of water and expired.[97]

EIGHT

LEISURE AND PLEASURE

One half of the world cannot understand the pleasures of the other.

Emma, by Jane Austen

Leisure was a luxury available only to those with time and money. Most working people had little opportunity for entertainment, and although his wages with a tailor were good, Thomas Carter thought the cost was high:

> I would gladly have taken three shillings per week less in wages, if thereby I could have escaped from the pressure of that incessant, and to me exhausting toil ... especially in so hot and otherwise unhealthy a place as is a tailor's workshop, in which I was confined for full twelve hours per day, the hours of working being from six o'clock in the morning until seven o'clock in the evening, one hour only being subtracted for dinner.[1]

For servants, apprentices, manual workers and many others, long hours were normal. The concept of the two-day weekend did not exist; the weekend was simply 'the end of the working week', usually just Sunday. Similarly, there were no long holidays, only 'holy days', the original meaning of the word. The poet Robert Southey, when writing in the guise of a foreign traveller, said that the English 'reproach the Catholic religion with the number of its holidays, never considering how the want of holidays breaks down and brutalizes the labouring classes'.[2]

Skilled workers, notably those on piecework, were accustomed to more generous free time. Many did only as much work as necessary, and according to the historian William Hutton in 1795, 'if a man can support his family with three days labour, he will not work six'.[3] These workers added Monday to their 'weekend' (and sometimes Tuesday and Wednesday too), a state of affairs so widespread that it was known as 'Saint Monday'. A satirical definition appeared in Francis Grose's dictionary of slang: 'SAINT MONDAY. A holiday most religiously observed by journeymen shoemakers, and other inferior mechanics. A profanation of that day, by working, is punishable by a fine, particularly among the gentle craft.'[4] Such chaotic working practices were condemned, not least by religious campaigners against alcohol consumption who believed that workers spent all this free time drinking to excess.

But not everyone considered the concept of Saint Monday harmful. Francis Spilsbury, a London chemist who wrote about illnesses such as gout and scurvy, was of the opinion that exercise and fresh air were beneficial to health, while bad air and working indoors were detrimental:

> In this view it may be doubted whether there is so much room for censure of a celebrated saint, so often idolized by the labouring mechanic ... for through an attention to sacrifice at his shrine on his festival day, many of the workmen are enabled to hold out much longer than they otherwise would do (particularly in some manufactories which are very inimical to health) provided they could abstain from partaking so freely of the libations generally poured out at their revels on SAINT MONDAY.[5]

The 'lower orders' were expected to work inordinately long hours, and live-in servants were given minimal freedom. In September 1805 one maidservant in William Holland's household was allowed to attend the fair at nearby Nether Stowey, but failed to return on time:

Kitty did not come till nine o'clock which her mistress [his wife Mary] resented much as she had ordered her to be back from the fair by six. John came a little after nine which was very well for him, being a man. Kitty was at the Globe in very good company as she says. However her mistress did not think a Publick House so proper for her and was angry and the girl inclined to be saucy, but my wife does not mean to give way to her.[6]

In the face of ongoing changes in industry and agriculture, many fairs were losing their original function, such as the hiring fairs where the labour exchange element was disappearing. Instead, fairs concentrated much more on entertainment, though some retained their cattle and produce markets. Nelly Weeton described the anticipation before Wigan's fair in 1816:

The town is going to be in a great bustle this week; for the fair commences tomorrow [23 May], on which occasion, it is usual for everybody to clean their houses thoroughly, to white-wash, paint, &c.; the confectioners begin of baking for the fair a week beforehand; and the shop-keepers to polish, and set their wares, in the neatest order; large caravans enter the town with wild beasts, monsters, and jugglers; likewise wooden horses, whirligigs, gambling tables, barrel organs, fiddlers, and hordes of beggars.[7]

Some two decades earlier, Johnson Grant was less enthusiastic about a fair he encountered: 'We set out for Leeds, where we found a fair in the market-place; a horrible scene of tygers roaring, organs grinding, trumpets sounding, blackguards bellowing and thronging, together with the effluvia of fish from the market, and every combination of attack upon the senses.'[8] Urban fairs like Wigan and Leeds were more sophisticated than rural ones, which perpetuated simple, traditional and sometimes barbaric entertainments. The *Reading Mercury* in June 1789 carried an advertisement for the annual country fair known as the Yattendon Revel:

THIS is to give notice, that Yattendon Revel will be kept as usual, on Friday the 10th of July next, and, for the encouragement of gentlemen gamesters, and others, there will be given a good Gold-Lac'd Hat, of 27s. value, to be played for at Cudgels; the man that breaks most heads to have the prize; 2s. will be given to each man that positively breaks a head, for the first ten heads that are broke; and 1s. to the man that has his head broke; but the man is not to receive the 2s. unless he gets up and plays the ties off; the blood to run an inch or be deemed no head.[9]

The revel's second day also featured long-established pastimes:

July the 11th, Will be given, Half-a-guinea to be run for by Jack Asses; the best of three heats. No less than three will be allowed to start. Also will be given, a fine Holland Smock to be run for by women; the best of three heats. No less than three will be allowed to start. Also, a Gold-Lac'd Hat, of 27s. value, to be played at Cudgels for . . . Likewise, Tobacco to be Grinn'd for, by old women, through a horse collar, as usual.[10]

The austere times were having an effect on some celebrations, and in Oxfordshire four years earlier, in the summer of 1785, John Byng lamented the decline of familiar traditions: 'A book of antient customs says – "That at Burford was a yearly procession of great jollity on midsummer eve; when a painted dragon, and a painted giant were carried about the town in commemoration of a battle won by the Saxons near this place":– But all such exhibitions are lost in the poverty and distress of the lower people; and a fair is now no more than a larger market.'[11]

Other customs were dying out for different reasons. Royal Oak Day on 29 May, later known as Oak Apple Day, marked the restoration in 1660 of Charles II after the Civil War. Now that the Hanoverian dynasty had superseded that of the Stuarts, this day of festivity was largely confined to Jacobite sympathisers, who regarded the Hanoverians as usurpers. Byng was therefore surprised to find Derby preparing a large celebration in 1790: 'Here every house was adorn'd with oaken boughs in honor of the old 29th of May; and the boys preparing and begging for their bonfires.'[12]

Apart from regular fairs and revels, special events such as the frost fairs were an excuse for merriment. In the bitterly cold winters the

River Thames in London would freeze over so hard that it was safe to walk on, as happened in January the previous year:

> No sooner had the Thames acquired a sufficient consistency than booths, turn-abouts, &c. &c. were erected; the puppet-shews, wild beasts, &c. were transported from every adjacent village; while the watermen, that they might draw their usual resources from the water, broke the ice close to the shore, and erected bridges, with toll-bars, to make every passenger pay a halfpenny for getting to the ice. One of the suttling booths has for its sign, 'Beer, Wine, and Spiritous Liquors, *without a License.*' A man who sells hot-gingerbread has a board, on which is written, 'No Shop Tax nor Window Duty' ... the Thames is generally crowded.[13]

The very last frost fair took place in February 1814. Never again would the Thames freeze so solidly once the old London Bridge was removed in 1831, after which the flow of the river improved.

Other celebrations were inspired by pleasing news about royal events or military victories, although sometimes the expressions of jubilation were hardly spontaneous, as William Darter saw in his home town of Reading:

> This year [1811] brought us intelligence of a victory, gained by Wellington over Soult in the Peninsula, and in consequence another illumination occurred of greater splendour than the last, as the inhabitants had by this time become accustomed to these demonstrations, and had provided themselves with appliances for lighting up, which they had not before. I may also mention that many of them had their sense of loyalty somewhat quickened by having their windows broken when they were not illuminated.[14]

Darter also enjoyed the start of each new year in Reading, when the military forces joined in:

> It was customary on New Year's Eve for the ringers of St. Lawrence's parish to ring a few peals of changes and leave the bells up on their stays, and some time before midnight to return. At the same time the

Militia Band assembled at the upper part of London Street, and all was still, until the moment St. Lawrence's clock began to strike twelve, when off went the merry peal of eight bells, and at the same moment three loud strokes of the big drum led off the Berkshire Band down London Street to the Market Place, and from thence through a portion of the town.[15]

The ringing of church bells was the dominant sound in towns and countryside, with few other noises able to compete. Even in Darter's old age, the bells at new year remained a happy childhood memory: 'Seventy-one years have elapsed since I first experienced the magic effect of this music of the band and the merry peal of St. Lawrence's bells breaking out in the stillness of midnight, suggesting that the old year had passed away, and welcoming the dawn of its successor. After a short interval, the old watchman, Norcroft, went up London Street, calling out "Past twelve and a starlight mornin'."'[16]

Blood sports were regularly enjoyed by all classes. The baiting of dogs, badgers, bulls, cockerels and other animals was legal, though bear-baiting had died out because the wars with the Continent had stopped the supply of bears. Cock-fighting was often carried on at public houses throughout England, and some had purpose-built cock-pits. In March 1772, when living at Ansford in Somerset, James Woodforde noted: 'Brother John came to the Parsonage this evening merry ... He had been to Evercreech, cock-fighting and won there six or seven guineas by betting.'[17]

Bull-baiting provided a more impressive spectacle, and Darter detailed one occasion at Wokingham in Berkshire:

It was St. Thomas' Day [21 December], which was dark, damp and foggy ... Very soon a stir occurred amongst the people, and they ran in all directions out of the way of a fine young bull, which was on his way to the Market Place. When the animal arrived he was fixed to a ring which was attached to an oak post level with the ground. The bull had about five yards of chain, and at first dashed about and tried to get his liberty; this had the effect of making the people rush against each other, and many of them tumbled down in the mud.[18]

Dogs were then set upon the tethered bull, along with active participation from the crowd:

> Soon arose a cry of 'A lane, a lane'; this was for the people to form a
> narrow avenue leading up to the bull, which was quickly done ... and
> then a man holding a bull-dog between his knees would let him slip and
> run up the 'lane' to catch hold of the bull's nose, which, if he succeeded,
> would pin his head down, and this would be called 'pinning the bull'. In
> this case, the dog, which I heard was brought from Staines, ran at the
> animal who instantly caught him on his horns and threw him high in the
> air. The people immediately closed together to catch him, or probably his
> neck would have been broken.[19]

The bull continued to be tormented until it was finally taken to
the slaughterhouse and killed, only to be replaced by another bull.
Darter found the whole event depressing: 'Then the men, most of
whom had been quarrelling, took to fighting ... Taking the affair
altogether, a more brutalising scene could not well be conceived.'[20] By
1802 the baiting of animals had fallen so far from favour with the
ruling classes that a bill for abolishing bull-baiting was presented to
Parliament. Despite vigorous support it was defeated, largely for fear
of public opposition at a time when the threat of revolution loomed.
It was not until 1835 that the baiting of animals for entertainment was
outlawed.

Wealthier sportsmen concentrated on hunting, shooting and fishing (with nets as well as rods). The abundant wildlife, far more
prolific than today, posed a real threat to crops, so there was a practical side to these sports, and only the hunting of foxes failed to
produce something edible. Jane Austen wrote of one of her brothers:
'Edward is no enthusiast in the beauties of nature. His enthusiasm is
for the sports of the field only ... He and George [Knight] are out
every morning either shooting or with the harriers. They are good
shots.'[21] Few people were bothered about the preservation of wildlife,
though occasionally some concerns were raised, like Holland's observation during deep snow in Somerset in early January 1802: 'What
terrible weather this is for all kind of birds, no food to be found, any

where. And man, cruel man adding to their calamity but hunting after their lives in every quarter, the whole region resound with pops and explosions.'[22]

Woodforde was an enthusiastic supporter of shooting, fishing and hare-coursing. On a visit to his native Somerset in the summer of 1789 he fished several times in the River Brue at Cole where he was staying, catching numerous trout and eels, which were eaten for dinner. On one successful day, he recorded: 'I spent most of the day a fishing, caught a brace of trout and three eels.'[23] Other days were less productive: 'Was out fishing almost the whole day but had no sport whatever – never caught a fish.'[24] Hare-coursing might be undertaken almost casually if a hare was spotted, but usually men set out deliberately to hunt for them. Woodforde frequently recorded his hare-coursing activities in Norfolk:

> After breakfast I walked out a coursing and took Ben, Briton and my boy
> Downing with me. I took my three greyhounds, Fly, Snip and Spring, and
> two spaniels, Spring and Carlo with me. We stayed out till two o'clock
> and coursed only one hare which we killed. We saw no people out either
> shooting or coursing, but heard some guns at a distance. Dinner to day,
> giblet-soup, fryed beef and potatoes, and a fine young hare rosted.[25]

Hares and other animals and birds killed in hunting would be given away to friends and neighbours if there were too many to use before they became inedible, and sharing and exchanging food in this way helped to bind country communities together.

Brutal sports did not just involve animals. Boxing was legal, but the newspapers routinely reported vicious prize fights (boxing for a cash prize), such as one near London in March 1812: 'A pugilist contest took place at Harford, near Hounslow, for twenty guineas a side, between William Swallow, a youth of promise, aged nineteen, from Suffolk, and a farmer of the name of Coulthard. The combatants fought fifty-seven hard rounds in one hour and forty-eight minutes, when Coulthard was declared the victor. It was what was termed a good stand up fight.'[26] These matches were fought for money and were subject to heavy gambling by the spectators. Prize fighting was in a dubious position legally, and magistrates often broke up fights or tried to prevent them, as in November 1805: 'The celebrated pugilist the *Chicken* arrived in town [London] on Saturday last from Somersetshire, where he had been several days in durance vile [prison], by order of the Magistrates of the District charged with attempting to disturb the public peace by the introduction of a prize fight intended to have been fought in the neighbourhood of Bath. Chicken was to have been second to the favourite.'[27] Generally, all the magistrates achieved was to postpone the fight for a few weeks or move it elsewhere. To avoid even this much interference, most prize-fight venues were kept secret until the last minute.

In Yorkshire in 1805, Charles Fothergill learned that the lead miners at Arkendale pursued various rough sports: 'Amusement amongst the miners: Fives, football, cricket, wrestling and leaping. Wrestling and leaping generally practised at public times, particularly at Whitsuntide and Easter when belts are wrestled for and gloves are leaped for.'[28] A few miles north, he chatted with the parish clerk at the public house at Fremington, who told him about the sports there:

Athletic exercises among the lower of the people are seldom practised now ... they have given place to pitchhalfpenny ... criket [cricket] and such like ... I am glad however to hear that wrestling is still in vogue amongst the miners on certain public occasions, festivals and merry-meetings: they have two modes of setting to; one by taking hold of each others hand and directing their efforts at the feet and legs, the other the old fashioned way round the waste [waist] where more strength is required.[29]

Fothergill was also told about a ferocious form of football that used to be played:

Football was amongst the former athletic games but it seems to have been dropped in consequence of accidents happening not unfrequently, particularly broken legs in consequence of the players wearing such terrible thick shoes armed with iron. The men of Arkendale were particularly famous at this game and they frequently challenged to play 13 of their men against 13 from any other quarter.[30]

Born in Derby, William Hutton had come across several football matches there. The best players, he said, were treated like celebrities:

> I have seen this coarse sport carried to the barbarous height of an election contest; nay, I have known a foot-ball hero chaired through the streets like a successful member [of parliament], although his utmost elevation of character was no more than that of a butcher's apprentice. Black eyes, bruised arms, and broken shins, are equally the marks of victory and defeat. I need not say this is the delight of the lower ranks, and is attained at an early period; the very infant learns to *kick*, and then to walk.[31]

Although cricket was played by miners and other labourers, the major matches were the preserve of the gentry. In 1787 Thomas Lord established a cricket ground in London, which became the home of Marylebone Cricket Club. John Blackner in Nottingham acknowledged that the club had the best players:

> 1791, during the summer, was played, what is called, *the great cricket match*, which was thus occasioned. A Colonel Churchill happening to be quartered here with his regiment, was struck with the superior activity of the Nottingham cricketplayers; added to which, their fame was already up by having won several matches. The colonel sent a challenge to the Mary-le-bonne club to play for a considerable sum; which challenge being accepted, eleven noblemen and gentlemen, with the Earl of Winchelsea at their head, came to Nottingham to play. But, notwithstanding the Nottingham players excited the admiration and applause of their opponents, they had no chance of success.[32]

Lord's Cricket Ground moved to its present-day site in St John's Wood in 1814, and the first match played there, with the usual gambling on the outcome, was between Marylebone Cricket Club and Hertfordshire on 22 June. The *Morning Post* carried a brief account: 'CRICKET.– The grand Cricket Match at Lord's Ground, between

the Marylebone Club against the County of Hertford, with HAM-
MOND, was decided on Saturday ... Marylebone won by 27 runs in
one Innings.– Bets 5 to 4 at starting in favour of Marylebone.'[33]

All kinds of races – on foot, horseback and in boats – provided
popular sport. Many events included races for women, and in
September 1772 Woodforde watched the sports at Castle Cary in
Somerset: 'There was running this morning in Cary Park between
two women for half a guinea, and which was run by Peg Francis; also
boys running. There was a great multitude to see it in the Park.'[34] Not
all events went to plan, as revealed by Silvester Treleaven's description
of the Whitsun revel at Mardon Down in Devon in May 1801:

> Being Tuesday in Whitsunweek a revel on Mardown, wrestling, skittle
> playing, and females racing for 2 yards of Holland [linen], three started
> but unfortunately for the girl who depended on getting the prize, after
> running a few land yards, triped [tripped] on a stone and fell with such
> violence that she exposed herself to vast numbers of spectators who gave
> such shouts at the unfortunate young woman's accident that she got off
> the course and was not seen on the ground afterwards.[35]

For ladies especially, the horse races were a fashionable place at
which to be seen, and in October 1809 the writer Mary Berry, a
prominent literary figure, went to a race meeting at Newmarket in
Suffolk:

> The inn is almost opposite what are called the rooms, where men only
> meet, and which have rather a handsome entrance of three arcades from
> the street; and in this street Tattersall was selling horses by auction, and
> all the young men, whose faces one knows in London, were walking
> about, as well as all the fathers of the turf, such as Sir Frank Standish, Sir
> Charles Bunbury, &c. &c. It had the oddest effect possible to see so
> many figures one hardly ever sees out of London, walking about in a sort
> of village-town, for Newmarket is no more [than that], with the exception
> of some good houses.[36]

They next moved to the Heath to follow the horses:

About one o'clock all these men mounted their horses, and proceeded towards the Heath, half a mile from the town. We followed them in the carriage, with many other carriages, and Lord Hardwicke[37] on horse-back ... When they got upon the Heath, it is so vast that they seemed only like small groups upon it ... But the style in which all this is managed here, the rapidity with which one race follows another, though on different courses – that is, on different parts of the Heath – the scene at the betting post, one of which belongs to each course, and is the only permanent thing upon it, for the ropes are immediately moved, and the winning post (a little machine upon wheels) is moved from one to the other, – all this was new and entertaining to me.[38]

As with so many sports, gambling was the prime attraction, and Mary observed that 'between each race all the men and all the carriages are collected at the betting-posts'.[39] The winning horses that day were Hymen, Yellow-hammer, Vexation and Morel, all somewhat conservative names, but there was a huge variety of names, from the patriotic Heart of Oak or Briton Strike Home to the whimsical – such as Blue Ruin, Shake My Rags and Bumtrap – and the down-to-earth Sod. Racecourses were to be found all over England, and in 1795, on another trip to his Somerset relatives, Woodforde joined a party heading for the local races:

About four o'clock this afternoon, my sister Pounsett and daughter, Mrs. Clarke, my brothers wife, and Mrs. Willm. Woodforde, and myself, all got into the coach, and drove to Bruton Races, to a field called Burrow-field where the races are kept, about half a mile from Bruton, and there we stayed till after 7 o'clock, and then returned home to Cole. The races were very indifferent, but a vast concourse of people attended, both gentle and simple ... We stayed in the coach all the time and very hot we were.[40]

Races also took place on the water, and one regatta held on Lake Windermere in July 1810 was described in the *Lancaster Gazette*:

The two fine sailing boats, the *Victory*, belonging to Mr. Bolton of Storrs, and *Endeavour*, the property of Mr. Wilson of Elleray, started a little after eleven o'clock, with a good breeze, and afforded the best entertainment to an immense crowd of spectators . . . This was the best boat-race that was ever seen on the lake [the *Victory* won a close contest]. There were many other races of inferior note, some of them well contested.[41]

Edward Pedder, Nelly Weeton's employer at nearby Dove Nest, was involved with staging this regatta, but another event in August fell below expectations. Nelly told her aunt what happened:

The second Regatta was expected to have been more splendid still, in consequence of which, Mr. Pedder invited a number of friends. We were sadly disappointed; it was one of the most blackguard things ever conducted. After a rowing match or two, which began the entertainment, there followed a footrace by four men. Two of them ran without shirts; one had breeches on, the other only drawers, very thin calico, without gallaces [braces]. Expecting they would burst or come off, the ladies durst not view the race, and turned away from the sight. And well it was they did.[42]

Nelly had no qualms in watching and gave an eyewitness description: 'during the race, and with the exertion of running, the drawers did actually burst, and the man cried out as he run – "Oh Lord! O Lord! I cannot keep my tackle in, G–d d–n it! I cannot keep my tackle in."'[43] The ladies were disgusted and left, she reported, and 'there were many of fashion and of rank; amongst other, Lady Diana Fleming, and her daughter Lady Fleming, and the Bishop of Landaff's daughters; several carriages, barouches, curricles; but all trooped off. Wrestling and leaping occupied the remainder of the day, we were told.'[44]

Seaside resorts also staged regattas, and John Byng witnessed one at Weymouth in Dorset in 1782, before the town became fashionable, but he was unimpressed:

To-day is a day of gala at Weymouth, and has been long announced for a regatta, and sailing-race, for the purpose of drawing company to the place; and of engaging seamen for the Orestes frigate, who lays in the road [safe anchorage] . . . the beach was crouded by horse, foot and phaetons, and the windows throng'd with beauties, to view this famous regatta, that consisted of a number of ill-looking luggers, sailing round the bay for two hours and an half; but of which the company understood not the skill, and so seem'd heartily tired; and of having raised their expectations to such little effect.[45]

Regattas were only one of the attractions of the seaside. Bathing in seawater (and even drinking it) became a popular health remedy that encouraged the rise of places like Brighton (then called Brighthelmstone) and Weymouth. As with inland spas such as Bath, seaside resorts became places where the higher ranks would spend their time socialising, dancing, gambling and gossiping. Jane Austen's final, unfinished novel *Sanditon* is set in the fictitious village of Sanditon, which is being remodelled into a resort, like so many on the south coast. One character, Mr Heywood, argues the case against resorts: 'Every five years, one hears of some new place or other starting up by the sea, and growing the fashion. – How they can half of them be filled, is the wonder! Where people can be found with money or time to go to them! – Bad things for a country; – sure to raise the price of provisions and make the poor good for nothing.' In fact, Jane Austen liked seaside places, and in September 1804 she was staying at Lyme Regis, where she wrote to Cassandra, who was further along the coast at Weymouth: 'I continue quite well; in proof of which I have bathed again this morning. It was absolutely necessary that I should have the little fever and indisposition which I had: it has been all the fashion this week in Lyme ... The Ball last night was pleasant, but not full for Thursday.'[46]

Dancing was enjoyed primarily by the better-off. Some balls were public occasions, but more often private entertainments held in someone's house. Jane Austen loved dancing and going to balls, and her letters gave critical comments about the latest ones attended, as in October in 1800 at Deane in Hampshire: 'It was a pleasant ball, and still more good than pleasant, for there were nearly sixty people, and sometimes we had seventeen couple ... I danced nine dances out of ten.'[47] This was a country ball that attracted nowhere near the numbers of the London events. Upper-class balls in wealthy London mansions were grand affairs, and a decade later Mary Berry arrived at one given by Lady Shaftesbury in Portland Place:

> The dancing began immediately: first, an English dance; then two quadrilles, admirably well danced; high benches round the room, upon which everybody mounted. Then another English dance; and then Miss Montgomery danced a Bolero, and Lady Barbara immediately afterwards the Tambourine dance, which was really admirable. The ball, upon the whole, both with respect to numbers, lighting, company, dress and dancing, one of the most brilliant I ever saw in London.[48]

Apart from occasional spontaneous dancing in inns, the working classes tended to dance mainly at festivals and celebrations such as those held after the harvest. For labourers and servants, such events were rare treats, and as in most households Woodforde's servants needed permission to attend: 'Our servant maid, Sally Gunton, had leave to go to Mr. Salisbury's harvest frolic this evening and to stay out all night. Our servant man, Bretingham Scurl, had also had leave to be at Mr. Bidewell's harvest frolic this evening and to stay out all night.'[49]

News of Nelson's victory at the Battle of the Nile in 1798 prompted displays of thanksgiving, and in a letter to her friend Mary Heber, Lady Banks described what they did in rural Isleworth, west of London:

> as we wish'd to have a little festivity to celebrate this famous victory, we had a treat in the evening. Besides all our own domesticks, we invited the labourers we usually employ, and their wives, and gave them some beef and plum pudding and punch in the servants' hall, and they had a dance in the barn. We went to visit them and sang *God Save the King* and *Rule, Britannia*, in which they all most heartily join'd in chorus.[50]

She explained how they deterred gatecrashers: 'by a little care in keeping our gate shut, we had no more *Company* than we chose, which is liable to happen so near London'.[51] Harriet Wynne mentioned a dance given on Lady Buckingham's birthday for the tenants on the Stowe estate: 'In the evening we all danced with the ten-ants ... I laughed a great deal to see the different mixture of people. We could hardly breathe it was so hot and the smell was beyond any-thing. We danced Sir Roger de Coverly, attended their supper &c. Delighted were we to go to bed.'[52]

Some balls were fancy-dress affairs, such as one enjoyed by Woodforde's niece:

> Nancy did not return till after 9 o'clock this evening as the young folks at Weston House had something of a Masquerade-Ball this evening. Dramatis Personae, Miss Custance in the character of an old woman, Emily Custance a flower girl, Devonshire Miss Bacon a fortune-teller alias gipsy, Miss Bacon in the character of a fool, Miss Maria Bacon, a ghost – none of the young gentlemen acted at all or were dressed.[53]

Amateur theatricals were also in fashion, something reflected in Jane Austen's novels, and as a teenager she herself had taken part in family plays. For those who could afford the price of tickets, going to the theatre was also popular, and in London and larger towns and cities, several theatres offered plays and sometimes concerts. London was a special case in that only three theatres, each called the 'Theatre Royal', were licensed for 'serious drama', usually defined as 'spoken drama'. They were often referred to simply by their location – Drury Lane, Covent Garden and Haymarket. Covent Garden put on operas as well as plays and later specialised in opera – it is now the Royal Opera House.

Other theatres in London were not supposed to allow plays to be performed, but avoided this ban by providing a mixture of entertain-ment, often musical, which might include part of a play. When visiting relatives in the capital, Jane Austen enjoyed the theatre and in September 1813 she wrote to her brother Frank: 'Of our three evenings in town, one was spent at the Lyceum and another at Covent Garden. "The Clandestine Marriage" was the most respectable of the per-formances, the rest were sing-song and trumpery ... I wanted better acting. There was no actor worth naming. I believe the theatres are thought at a low ebb at present.'[54] *The Clandestine Marriage* was a comedy by George Colman the Elder and David Garrick, first performed in 1766. Nelly Weeton sometimes saw famous performers at the theatre in Liverpool, as she told her brother Tom in July 1809:

> I wish you could have been here this week to have seen Mrs. Siddons ... Henry Latham [Nelly's cousin] has been with me a fortnight, and one day last week he and I went to see her as Lady Macbeth. We got a very comfortable front seat in the gallery, and I was highly gratified. I have seen her before at Lancaster as Belvidera, but had almost forgot her, it is so long ago. Much as I expected, my expectations were exceeded; particularly in that scene where Lady Macbeth is represented as walking in her sleep. The whole audience seemed wonder struck.[55]

In Nelly's view the stage was far too bright for Shakespeare's *Macbeth*, though by modern standards theatre lighting was wretched, relying on oil lamps and chandeliers of candles. Even so, she had trouble adjusting to the pitch-black streets and had 'a dismally dark walk home. It was eleven when we left the theatre. The glare of the house, with its lights, had so affected my eyes, that it was with difficulty I could distinguish my way. Luckily Henry could see better than me, and we got home very safely. We were a full hour in walking two miles and a half.'[56]

Theatres were not places of respectful, quiet calm, as Carl Moritz discovered at the Haymarket in 1782:

> For a seat in the boxes you pay five shillings, in the pit three, in the first gallery two, and in the second, or upper gallery, one shilling. And it is the tenants in this upper gallery who, for their shilling, make all that noise and uproar, for which the English playhouses are so famous. I was in the pit, which gradually rises, amphitheatre wise, from the orchestra, and is furnished with benches, one above another, from the top to the bottom. Often and often, whilst I sat here, did a rotten orange, or the peel of an orange, fly past me, or past some of my neighbours; and one of them actually hit my hat, without my daring to look round, for fear another might come plump in my face. Besides this perpetual pelting from the gallery, which renders an English playhouse so uncomfortable, there is no end to

their calling out, and knocking with their sticks, till the curtain is drawn up ... In the boxes, quite in a corner, sat several servants, who were said to be placed there, to keep the seats for the families they served, till they should arrive.[57]

Outside London, travelling players went from town to town putting on performances, something that Silvester Treleaven recorded at Moretonhampstead in Devon in May 1802: 'A company of comedians came here from Crediton, and are going to act a few nights in Mr. Hancock's Barn, in Pound Street, which is fitting up for said purpose. A Mr. Smith manager.'[58] Three days later, their makeshift theatre was ready: 'Last night the comedians acted for the first time in Mr. Hancock's Barn, in Pound Street, which is fitted up for the purpose in a very decent manner. The play was "The Farm House", after which an interlude called "The Village Barber". To which was added the farce of "The Spoil'd Child".'[59]

Rather than the theatre, Woodforde was more partial to music, but even for him the tickets were expensive – the equivalent of two weeks' wages for one servant:

The tickets to the miscellaneous concert to night [at Norwich] were 7 shillings and 6 pence each. Mrs Custance being a subscriber and having a transferable ticket, was so kind as to lend my niece hers for this evening ... A great deal of company indeed at the Hall and full dressed – 911 supposed to be present. The concert was very fine indeed, and Madame Mara, the famous singer, sung delightfully. I never heard so fine a voice – her notes so high. The kettle drums from Westminster Abbey sounded charmingly, beat by a Mr. Ashbridge. Near 100 performers in the orchestra.[60]

Especially with the attraction of celebrity performers, musical concerts were increasingly attended by the wealthier classes. Composers such as Haydn, Mozart and Beethoven were writing new works and exploring new musical forms that were becoming ever more popular. Music was no longer just an accompaniment to dancing, eating or singing, but an entertainment in its own right.

Whatever anyone's class or wealth, leisure occupations were largely active rather than passive. Songs and music were mostly learned from printed sheets. More formal music was sold in shops, while street sellers sold broadside song sheets, also called broadsheets, which were printed on one side of sheets of coarse paper. Moritz noticed the ballad sellers: 'The [English people's] love of their country, and its unparalleled feats in war, are in general the subject of their ballads and popular songs, which are sung about the streets by women, who sell them for a few farthings.'[61] Over two decades later, Benjamin Silliman also heard the ballad singers and saw them selling the words on printed sheets. Crowds gathered to hear and learn the tunes, since these song sheets had the words, but no music:

> Returning home, about 10 o'clock at night, I observed one of those little circles which are very common in the streets of London; I allude to the audiences which gather around the ballad singers. They are usually poor women, or little girls, with every appearance of extreme poverty, who collect a few pence by singing ballads at the corners of the streets, under the bow-windows of shops, and the porticoes of public buildings. Although their voices are harsh from being so often exerted, and their performances, in every respect indifferent, they immediately draw a circle around and detain them a long time.[62]

Contrary to the observations of Moritz and Silliman, ballad selling was not restricted to women, and in March 1780 Woodforde paid sixpence 'to a poor old man for some ballads'.[63] Three years earlier, George Williams appeared before a justice of the peace in Somerset, accused of being a 'rogue and vagabond'. He swore on oath that he was a former soldier, aged about sixty, and had worked as a day labourer and ballad seller for the last two decades.[64]

Most people created their own entertainment at home with friends and family, and diarists like Woodforde noted such everyday events, as in August 1788: 'Mr. Walker and Betsy Davy came over on single horses this morning from Foulsham and they breakfasted, dined and spent the afternoon with us. We had a good deal of singing to day from my niece and Mr. Walker – the latter sung many new songs. We spent a very agreeable day together.'⁶⁵ They may well have been singing new ballads bought from a street seller.

An afternoon spent with guests over dinner and in various forms of entertainment was something the idle rich could enjoy. The labouring classes could relax only in the evening, after their work, when the tavern provided a welcome refuge with its candles and a fire, where customers could drink beer, smoke a pipe and perhaps play cards or join in the singing. Francis Place recalled the taverns of the late 1770s: 'It was the custom at this time as it had long been for almost every man who had the means to spend his evenings at some public house or tavern, or other place of entertainment. Almost every public house had a parlour . . . for the better sort of customers. In this room which was large and well lighted with tallow candles the company drank and smoked and spent their evenings.'⁶⁶

Tobacco was used by all classes. It was sometimes chewed, but was more likely to be smoked in white clay pipes that were made locally and sold in shops or by the pipe makers themselves. Taverns were the biggest outlet, where pipes could be reburned in an iron rack in the fireplace. Some clay pipes were 12–15 inches long, though shorter ones were preferred by workers since pipes were easily broken – fragments of clay pipe stems are common finds on archaeological sites and in gardens of old houses. Smoking was more popular with the working classes, women and children included, and in July 1809 a woman's pipe set off an explosion at Portsmouth, killing many people. According to the local newspaper, 'The cause of this calamity is attributed to the wife of one of the soldiers, who relates, that she was washing near where the baggage lay, on the beach, when another soldier's wife, who was smoking, asked her if she would take a whiff? She did; but finding the tobacco would not burn, she struck the bowl of the pipe against the pebbles.'⁶⁷ The smouldering tobacco fell out, causing a fire that spread to several barrels of gunpowder.

Having given up smoking several years earlier, the clergyman William Jones decided to stop taking snuff as well: 'Left off snuff, & hope I shall never return to the *filthy*, worse than *beastly*, practice! Gave Mrs. Jones [his wife] my whole stock – four ½ lb canisters full of No 37, & Strasburgh – 1 lb. 37 in lead, ¾ lb. of Strasburgh in lead,

& my common box full.'[68] With a stock of around 4lb of snuff, Jones must have been a heavy user. Snuff was a fine tobacco that was inhaled, a habit largely confined to the upper classes. Woodforde noted purchases of both tobacco and snuff, as in 1790: 'at Mr. Carys shop for ½ lb. tobacco, pd. 0: 1: 4. At Ditto – for 2 oz: of Scotch snuff 0: 0: 2.'[69] After giving away his snuff, Jones said of his wife: 'O that my *deary* would give up *snuff* & *novels*!!'[70]

Woodforde also indulged in drinking a fair amount of alcohol and was particularly fond of card games and of gambling for moderate stakes with friends and family. He recorded his failures and successes in his diary and was triumphant in April 1783: 'At quadrille this evening won 0.4.0. I played the finest Sans Prendre Vole to night, that I ever had – not a loosing card in hand – it was Mattadores, 9 black trumps in spades and the King of Hearts – I was the last player; after the first card was played, I declared the Vole. I did not get home to Weston till 10 at night.'[71] Quadrille, a popular game for four players, originated in France, but its complicated rules and special vocabulary were later simplified to make it more like whist. It was eclipsed by other card games in the Victorian period. Lydia Bennet in *Pride and Prejudice* is obsessed by gambling and by card games, and 'talked incessantly of lottery tickets, of the fish she had lost and the fish she had won'. The lottery she was playing was a simple card game of chance, in which counters were amassed. Frequently in gaming, the bone or ivory counters were made in the shape of fish.[72]

A State Lottery was run by the Government to raise revenue, for which an Act of Parliament was passed each year. Licensed brokers sold tickets, which were expensive, as well as cheaper shares in tickets, frequently sixteenths, and the winning tickets were drawn by lot over several days. Prizes were substantial – half a million pounds in the years 1796 to 1798 and even more in subsequent years. For many, the lottery was their only chance of acquiring wealth, and lottery clubs sprang up, such as one at Moretonhampstead. In February 1800, Treleaven described the hysteria that gripped its members: 'Last night members of the Lottery Club met at the Red Lion. In the midst of their business a great confusion ensued, owing to many of the members being overheated with liquor, and almost in a state of insanity under an idea of gaining a 30,000 £ prize! Several battles fought ... the no. [number] of members now amount to 245, and consists of a few Christians, some Jews, and a number of heathens. Their meetings are every Monday fortnight.'[73] A few days later he wrote: 'Last night the members of the Lottery Club met at the Red Lion, and closed their books. No. of members were 241, each of which subscribed £1.5.0 (viz) £1.2.0 to the fund and 3/- spent in ale: amount to purchase lottery tickets £265.2.0, spent in ale £44.3.8.'[74]

In November 1807 William Holland went to Bridgwater to see his lawyer: 'Ruscombe Poole informed me that Mr Stone his father in law had got a prize in the Lottery of twenty thousand pound, a great thing indeed and will be chiefly for Ruscombe Poole's benefit, for Mr. Stone cannot want it and he has but two daughters and one of them is Ruscombe's wife. The Poole family are rising fast.'[75] Many poor people were ruined by such gambling, pawning their possessions in the expectation of winning. Frederick Eden described how they were addicted to gambling, especially the lottery: '[a]maidservant who has saved a guinea is sensible that if she attempts to be her own banker it will melt away piecemeal. Upon principles of prudence she purchases the sixteenth of a ticket, and concludes that her honesty and frugality will find their reward in a fortunate number.'[76]

For the wealthy, travelling abroad – particularly doing the Grand Tour of Europe – was once fashionable, but the continued wars had halted this trend. As Elizabeth Ham witnessed, 'the Continent was quite shut to the British idler, and Weymouth was all the fashion'.[77] She herself lived at this seaside resort, but such attractions were not to everyone's taste. Some travellers began to explore the more sparsely populated areas of Britain that were formerly regarded as barren and dangerous waste land. Accounts of these travels were increasingly published, many illustrated with topographical prints. What emerged from this new appreciation of the wilder parts of Britain was the Romantic Movement that developed in the arts, with poets such as Wordsworth in the Lake District who went on tours, taking inspiration from nature, and artists such as Constable and Turner painting scenes and landscapes.

Those inclined to scholarly study, but who were prevented from exploring the classical ruins of the Continent, turned their attention to the more prosaic sites and ruins at home. This happened to coincide with the adoption of the new farming methods, the improvement of roads and the digging of canals, all of which were damaging and destroying prehistoric and historic monuments and unearthing a great number of strange artefacts. Many of the well-to-do, and particularly clergymen who were classically educated and had time on their hands, became 'barrow diggers'. The architect John Repton, son of the landscape designer Humphry Repton, was one such barrow digger, and in 1808 he 'opened' a Bronze Age barrow near Aylsham in Norfolk: 'Having ordered a hole to be opened [by workmen] in the middle, about four yards wide, and two yards deep, we came to the sand, the natural soil of the whole heath, but continued digging through the sand, about two yards deeper, without finding anything; but on shoving down the side to fill up the cavity ... a curious Urn was discovered, which was cut through in the middle by the spade.'[78] After this unfortunate accident, all Repton could do was make a quick sketch before the rest of the urn 'was quite destroyed, it being too soft a substance to be taken up in large fragments'.[79]

From such clumsy beginnings, the modern science of archaeology was born and it ran in parallel with a growing curiosity about the history of the country, to the point where it was considered 'that without a competent fund of antiquarian learning, no one will ever make a respectable figure, either as a Divine, a Lawyer, Statesman, Soldier, or even a private Gentleman'.[80] In November 1805, Benjamin Silliman was in London: 'through the introduction of a friend, I attended a meeting of the Antiquarian Society, which holds its sittings in a spacious room in Somerset-House ... Lord Leicester, a nobleman, of a grave and plain appearance, was in the chair. The antiquities are still far from being exhausted, and this society is usefully employed in bringing them to light.'[81] This was the illustrious Society of Antiquaries of London, and Lord Leicester would be its president until his death in 1811.[82] The discovery and recording of antiquities had in fact barely started.

For those seeking an impression of places abroad, panorama displays provided the solution. These were models or large paintings (or a mixture of both), depicting views of foreign cities and battles as well as topics closer to home such as the British fleet at Spithead and the state funeral of Admiral Lord Nelson. In London in July 1809 Mary Berry visited the Panorama in Leicester Square, run by Henry Barker:

> Went in the morning with Mr. Playfair to see the two panoramas of Cairo and of Dublin. That of Cairo admirable. The sandy arid look of the country so well given, and contrasting so remarkably with the green fringe of land on each side of the course of the Nile. The near buildings – many of them picturesque and well painted. The interior of the city of Dublin is an ugly subject, but extremely well done, and giving a perfect idea of a meaner dirty-looking London.[83]

The purpose-built Panorama still survives, having been converted in 1868 to the Church of Notre Dame de France. Louis Simond saw new exhibits there two years after Mary Berry:

> There are new panoramas this year at Mr Barker's . . . We have just seen Malta. The gairish light of day, white and dazzling;—the strong and per-pendicular shadows;—the dusty land;—the calm and glassy sea . . . The inhabitants overcome, lie about in the shade of narrow streets;—a cen-tinel alone is seen pacing his watch before the gate of the arsenal. The smallest details are characteristic . . . We learned, with much regret, that the panorama of Dover, which we admired so much last year, was painted on this identical cloth. Malta is laid over Dover, and Dover covers half-a-dozen more *chefs-d'oeuvre!* . . . The circumference of the panorama is about 270 feet, the height 30 feet, the surface about 900 square yards.[84]

London possessed more leisure attractions than anywhere else, and the rival pleasure gardens of Vauxhall and Ranelagh were famous. In 1782 Moritz visited Vauxhall gardens:

> Vauxhall is, properly speaking, the name of a little village, in which the garden, now almost exclusively bearing the same name, is situated. You

pay a shilling on entrance ... As you enter the garden, you immediately hear the sound of vocal and instrumental music. There are several female singers constantly hired to sing here. On each side of the orchestra are small boxes, with tables and benches, in which you sup. The walks before these, as well as to every other part of the garden, are crowded with people of all ranks ... The rotunda, a magnificent circular building, in the garden, particularly engaged my attention. By means of beautiful chandeliers and large mirrors, it was illuminated in the most superb manner; and every where decorated with delightful paintings and statues, in the contemplation of which you may spend several hours very agreeably, when you are tired of the crowd and the bustle in the walks of the garden.[85]

Despite its attractive appearance, Moritz found Vauxhall to be a haunt of prostitutes: 'what most astonished me, was the boldness of the women of the town, who often rushed in upon us by half dozens, and in the most shameless manner importuned us for wine'.[86] Criminals also frequented the place, and at one point 'there arose all at once a loud cry of, "Take care of your pockets." This informed us, but too clearly, that there were some pickpockets among the crowd, who had already made some fortunate strokes.'[87]

Moritz was more impressed with Ranelagh:

coming out of the gloom of the garden, I suddenly entered a round building, illuminated by many hundred lamps, the splendour and beauty of which surpassed every thing of the kind I had ever seen before ... above, there was a gallery divided into boxes; and in one part of it an organ with a beautiful choir, from which issued both instrumental and vocal music. All around, under this gallery, are handsome painted boxes for those who wish to take refreshments ...

I sat down in one of the boxes, in order to take some refreshment ... when a waiter very civilly asked me what refreshment I wished to have, and in a few moments returned with what I asked for. To my astonishment, he would accept no money for these refreshments; which I could not comprehend, till he told me that every thing was included in the half-crown I had paid at the door.[88]

Such noisy and public entertainment contrasted sharply with the London coffee-houses he also visited:

In these coffee-houses there generally prevails a very decorous stillness and silence. Every one speaks softly to those only who sit next to him. The greater part read the newspapers, and no one ever disturbs another. The room is commonly on the ground floor, and the seats are divided by wooden wainscot partitions. Many letters and projects are here written and planned, and many of those that are inserted in the papers are dated from some of these coffee-houses.[89]

Newspapers were taxed with a stamp duty and were relatively expensive, and so men frequented coffee-houses in order to read them there rather than buy their own. Newspapers provided the only regular source of news, but they looked very different to those of today, because they had no illustrations, were printed in black ink only, and the front page was traditionally reserved for columns of advertisements rather than big headlines and leading news items. Despite their cost, annual sales were riding high both locally and nationally. This was partly because after the Franking Act of 1764, Members of Parliament were allowed to purchase newspapers in bulk and send them through the post free-of-charge,[90] greatly increasing the circulation of London newspapers and helping to keep down their price.

Literacy levels were improving, though the numbers of people who were literate varied according to class. Statistics on the subject are little more than guesswork, but it has been estimated that two out of three working men could read to some extent, though rather fewer had writing skills, and not nearly as many working women could read. If they did not read themselves, most people knew someone who would read to them. Moritz was surprised to meet so many people who could read:

My landlady, who was only a taylor's widow, reads her Milton; and told me, that her late husband fell first in love with her on this very account, because she read Milton with such proper emphasis. This single instance, perhaps, would prove but little; but I have conversed with several people of the lower class, who all knew their national authors, and who all have read many, if not all of them. This elevates the lower ranks, and brings them nearer to the higher.[91]

He attributed this apparently increasing spread of education to the availability of classical authors in 'cheap and convenient editions ... At stalls, and in the streets, you every now and then meet with a sort of bibliopolists [booksellers], who sell single or odd volumes; sometimes as low as a penny; nay even sometimes for a half-penny a-piece. Of one of these I bought the two volumes of the Vicar of Wakefield for sixpence.'[92] Street sellers who offered cheap song sheets and sensational stories would also sell chapbooks, which were flimsy booklets containing stories about ghosts, mermaids, recent crimes and executions, fables or anything else thought likely to titillate a mass market. One chapbook from 1772 began on an optimistic note – a fantastic tale perhaps purchased by those desperately hoping for better times:

Good News for England being A strange and remarkable ACCOUNT how a stranger in bright Raiment appeared to one Farmer Edwards near Lancaster, on the 12th of last Month, at night; containing the discourse that past [passed] between the said Farmer and the Stranger, who foretold what a wonderful Year of Plenty this will be, and how wheat will be sold for four shillings a bushel, and barley for two shillings this Year; all which was confirmed to the Farmer by four wonderful signs.[93]

There was an exciting boom in the publishing of books – not just novels, but an impressive range of volumes on history, travel, biography and science. The number of novels to choose from was large, and they were advertised in national and regional newspapers across the country, with many names of publishers still familiar today. On Christmas Day 1815 the front page of the *Morning Chronicle* – as usual – consisted of nothing but advertisements. Under 'Books published this day' was an extremely modest notice:

In 3 vols. 12mo price of 1l. 1s.
EMMA: a Novel. — By the Author of Pride and Prejudice.
Printed for John Murray, Albemarle-street.[94]

Traditionally, novels were published in several volumes, usually three. As in the book itself, the advertisement did not reveal Jane Austen's name. The same publisher placed larger notices for two other books, *An Account of the Kingdom of Nepaul* by Colonel Kirkpatrick and *Oriental Memoirs* by James Forbes, perhaps reflecting the publisher's slender expectations for *Emma*. Today, few people have heard of those two books, while *Emma* is known and loved worldwide.

The best places in London to buy books were Ludgate Hill, Paternoster Row and St Paul's Churchyard (not the burial ground but the adjacent street lined with small shops). Booksellers and printers were often one and the same, selling the books that they published, and most bookstores were small, but James Lackington's bookshop was huge. His first shop had been in Chiswell Street, but in 1794 he opened larger premises in Finsbury Square, a celebrated bookstore that became known as the 'Temple of the Muses'. This was one of the wonders of London until it burned down in 1841. Lackington accepted only cash, not credit, and claimed to sell the cheapest books in England.

Other places in London had bookshops clustered together, as Samuel Pratt observed:

On one side of a long narrow passage called Middle-row [in Holborn], I observed a few literary loungers inspecting the old book-shops, for which this part of the town has long been famous. Pausing a little at the different stalls, I noted several persons enquiring for odd volumes to compleat broken sets, which had been lost by the commerce of lending or borrowing; for you must know, that detention of books, is amongst the negligences, or petty larcenies in friendship ... The same spot is also frequented by authors, who are on the hunt for such of their writings, as are, what we technically call, 'out of print' – that is, not to be heard of either at the original publisher's, or amongst the regular trade.[95]

Books and newspapers tended to be a luxury because of their high price, but private subscription lending libraries existed, even if of varying quality – Jane Austen thought the library at Dawlish in

Devon 'pitiful and wretched'.[96] Most towns and many villages had a reading room or book club, something that Simond noticed:

> There are almost everywhere book societies or clubs, variously consti-
> tuted. They are generally composed of ten or twelve persons, contributing
> annually a certain sum for the purchase of books. Any of them may pro-
> pose a book, which, when read by all the associates who choose, is put up
> for sale among them. The person who recommended the purchase is
> obliged to take it at half price, if no one bids higher. The annual contri-
> bution is commonly from one to four guineas.[97]

William Holland belonged to a book club, and in May 1804 he wrote in his diary: 'we went to the Globe [Inn at Nether Stowey], where we all dined, being members of the Book Society ... We spent a very agreeable evening together, had a good dinner and sold our books and entered into fresh subscriptions.'[98]

Reading was not necessarily a solitary occupation. Books and newspapers were read aloud, as part of the tradition of shared entertainment. It was too expensive for everyone to read their own book on dark winter evenings, because each person would need a candle. Throughout her life, Jane Austen read books aloud or listened to others. Such a pastime was relatively cheap and always available, and on a day in October 1805 when it rained heavily for many hours, Holland recorded: 'My wife read the novel of Camilla to us all the whole day with little intermission so that we were all much entertained with that very affecting narration.'[99] Fanny Burney's *Camilla* – her third novel, an immensely long work in five volumes – had been published nearly a decade earlier, in 1796.

Books were also a fashion item, and most wealthy households had a library, although in some cases the books were there to be admired, not read, as Nelly Weeton lamented of her employer's library at Dove Nest: 'Mr. P[edder], like many of the wealthy, possesses a library of little real use. He himself reads little, so that the shelves make a dis-play of knowledge he possesses not; many a volume, I dare say, has never been opened. The collection is numerous, valuable, and well selected. How rich I should be in books if I had all in Mr. P's library that have never been read.'[100]

Letters also provided entertainment when read aloud among family and friends. Writing was essential for long-distance communication, and those who had the time corresponded on a daily basis with friends and family. Jane Austen was a prolific letter writer, but the greater part of her letters were destroyed by her sister Cassandra and other family members. One surviving letter to Cassandra, written in June 1808, gives a glimpse of the constant communication: 'I assure you I am as tired of writing long letters as you can be. What a pity that one should be so fond of receiving them!'[101]

The cost of sending a letter was relatively high, charged according to the distance travelled and the number of 'enclosures', such as if more than one sheet of paper was used. Most letters comprised a single sheet folded in on itself. A rectangle in the middle of the outer side of the sheet was left blank to carry the address, and the last fold was tucked in and sealed with red-coloured beeswax (black for funerary correspondence) or a piece of glued paper called a 'wafer'. Woodforde often recorded his purchases of wax, as in July 1788: 'at a bookseller's shop at Bungay for a large stick of red sealing wax, paid 0: 1: 0'.[102]

To minimise postal costs, writers needed to plan the length of a letter carefully, which did not always happen, as Nelly Weeton admitted to her brother Tom: 'I feel myself in a writing humour, and as I have entirely filled one large half sheet, I will, for once, put thee to the expence of a double letter; had I thought, when I begun, that I should have scribbled so much, I would not have cut the sheet, and then I might, with a safe conscience, have informed the Post-master that it was only a "single sheet".'[103] The cost of postage was paid by the recipient of the letter, not the sender, so a failure to economise might be unwelcome. Within London, a Penny Post pre-paid system operated, increased to twopence in 1801.[104]

One way of keeping to a single sheet of paper was by cross-writing. Once a sheet was covered with writing, it was turned 90 degrees and the writing was continued at right-angles over what was already written. This allowed double the number of lines of writing, but the resulting letter was difficult to read, as Nelly warned a friend: 'I am afraid you will scarcely be able to read this cross writing – a little more and I will have done.'[105] Envelopes only began to be manufactured and sold in large quantities when uniform (and lower) postal charges, irrespective of the number of enclosures, were introduced in 1840.

No mailboxes existed like the ones seen today, and letters had to be posted at a Post Office to be delivered to the Post Office closest to the recipient's address. Letters were collected in person, or arrangements were made for a servant or friend to collect and pay for them. The postal service was generally reliable, but over long distances, letters might be in transit for several days. It was well known that Members of Parliament would put their frank on letters written by their family, friends and even distant acquaintances, because they had the privilege of franking their own letters, which were delivered free-of-charge. Such a frank might merely consist of a sheet of paper with a legible and authentic signature. This sheet was used as part of the letter, folded so that the signature was visible on the outside.

The upper classes frequently resorted to such franks, and Jane Austen used them whenever the opportunity arose. In April 1811 she wrote to her sister: 'I had sent off my letter yesterday before yours came, which I was sorry for; but as Eliza has been so good as to get me a frank, your questions shall be answered without much further expense to you.'[106] Simond was not impressed by the stinginess of the wealthy and the business of franking: 'Nobody thinks of writing to a friend without a frank, and letters are received with a perceivable expression of surprise, at least, when there is postage to pay. You may pay the postage of your own letters; and I had availed myself of that expedient, as infinitely preferable to that of begging a frank, but I found it was considered as a great impropriety.'[107]

Most of Jane Austen's letters were to family members, but when her books began to be published, she also had business correspondence with her publishers, and a few of these letters have survived. In 1815 she commented on one letter from her publisher: 'Mr Murray's letter is come; he is a rogue of course, but a civil one. He offers £450 but wants to have the copyright of M.P. [*Mansfield Park*] & S.&S. [*Sense and Sensibility*] included. It will end in my publishing for myself I daresay. He sends more praise however than I expected. It is an amusing letter.'[108]

— ◆ —

NINE

ON THE MOVE

Open carriages are nasty things. A clean gown is not five minutes' wear in them. You are splashed getting in and getting out; and the wind takes your hair and your bonnet in every direction. I hate an open carriage myself.

Northanger Abbey, by Jane Austen

Some people never saw new places, never travelled any distance in their entire lives. Elizabeth Ham remembered her Uncle Thomas of Haselbury in Somerset, who lived to the age of ninety and 'died in the house in which he was born, and from which he was never absent but once in his life, when, in his youth, he went to Bristol for a week'.[1] His journey to Bristol, 30 miles away, was the furthest he ever travelled. Others did travel a great deal to see friends and family and on business, but nothing moved faster than a galloping horse. Horses were the main source of power, and engines are still measured in 'horsepower', a unit originally based on the number of horses needed to do the same work as a steam engine.

Walking was the most common means of transport, often over considerable distances and in miserable conditions. Thick, squelching mud was the bane of all travel, exhausting to walk through and a hazard for horses and wheeled vehicles alike. At Steventon in Hampshire, Jane Austen and Cassandra would certainly walk 'when the roads were dirty',[2] wearing pattens to raise their shoes above the mud. When conditions outside were bad, most middle- and upper-class ladies avoided travelling on foot altogether, and Jane wrote in one letter: 'Anna ... is quite equal to walking to Chawton, and comes over to us when she can, but the rain and dirt divide us a good deal.'[3] In Norfolk, Parson James Woodforde constantly noted in his diary that church attendances were low because of poor weather, as in late January 1790: 'None from Weston House at church, none of my gentry [family guests] at church being wet and dirty.'[4]

Even those who owned horses often walked a great deal. In the summer of 1794 Woodforde was visiting friends in the neighbourhood with his niece, but being concerned about her painful knee, he calculated the distance they covered: 'Nancy had a good deal of walking to day, near seven miles has she walked this day and very well.'[5] Few people chose to undertake long excursions on foot, but Carl Moritz was an exception, as he deliberately spent some seven weeks in 1782 walking through England. On one occasion, when leaving Oxford, he used a stagecoach and asked a fellow passenger why Englishmen avoided travelling on foot: 'O! said he, we are too rich, too lazy, and too proud. And most true it is, that the poorest Englishman one sees, is prouder and better pleased to expose himself to the danger of having his neck broken, on the outside of a stage [coach], than to walk any considerable distance, though it might be done ever so much at his ease.'[6]

Paupers could not travel long distances at all, not even on foot, because under the poor laws anyone found outside their own parish without sufficient money and reason to be there was liable to be arrested and returned. When he arrived at inns without horses, Moritz was invariably treated with contempt, as happened at Eton: 'I entered the inn and desired to have something to eat ... the waiter soon gave me to understand, that I should there find no very friendly reception. Whatever I got, they seemed to give me with such an air, as shewed too plainly how little they thought of me; and as if they considered me but as a beggar.'[7] Even so, he added, 'they suffered me to pay like a gentleman'.[8]

Elsewhere, he found various obstacles in his path and began to realise why pedestrians kept to the well-worn routes and avoided short-cuts. One morning he set out on foot from Windsor:

I rose very early ... in order to climb the two hills, which presented me with so inviting a prospect; and in particular that one of them, on the summit of which a high, white house, appeared among the dark green trees. I found no regular path leading to these hills; and therefore went straightforward, without minding roads; only keeping in view the object of my aim. This certainly created me some trouble: I had sometimes a hedge, and sometimes a bog to walk round; but at length I attained the foot of the so earnestly-wished-for hill, with the high, white house on its summit, when, just as I was going to ascend it ... behold I read these words on a board: 'Take care; there are steel traps and spring guns here.' All my labour was lost, and I now went round to the other hill; but here were also 'steel traps and spring guns'.[9]

These traps were mantraps that had two strong steel jaws, often with serrated edges, which snapped shut by means of powerful springs when someone stepped on the pressure plate between the jaws. Hidden in grass and undergrowth, they were designed to trap and detain intruders, but frequently resulted in a badly cut or broken leg. Spring guns were mounted with a trip wire to the trigger, and the gun was fired when the trip wire was pulled.

Wherever traps and spring guns were laid, being on horseback was no better than walking, but riding could be hazardous on the open road as well. In late January 1773, after spending a convivial afternoon with friends at Cole in Somerset, Woodforde and his brother returned to Ansford Parsonage:

Brother John got quite merry and coming home was thrown from his horse, but blessed be God received no great hurt. His horse run away home ... I walked with him home and led my horse in my hand. I was most miserably terrified by his fall, he riding in so disagreeable a manner as to frighten me every step till he was thrown. It was a great mercy of thine O God that he was not killed, as there was a waggon not twenty yards before him when he fell and the horse full stretch almost ... My man Willm. also met with an accident this evening at my door in his return from Cole. Soon as the chaise stopped, the horse which he rode fell down and bruised his leg much. The horses breath was stopped by the harness.[10]

Because so many men and some women rode horses and donkeys, alighting stones (mounting blocks) were common in public places, such as by churches or in market squares, and at Moretonhampstead in Devon in 1800, Silvester Treleaven noted: 'A new alighting stone erected at the lower end of the Shambles by subscription.'[11] Gentlemen wore spurs when riding, but the Reverend William Holland was annoyed to discover his manservant using them: 'Mr Robert among his other excellencies has been in the habit of wearing my spurs. I have once or twice had a hint of his riding hard and now I have found out the method he takes to get his horse on.'[12] Servants were not always reliable riders, as Woodforde also found: 'Ben went yesterday in the afternoon with a Mr. Watson steward to Sr. John Woodhouse to Kimberly Hall, where having made too free with the Baronets strong beer, fell of[f] his horse coming home and lost her, so that he walked about all the night after her and did not find her till about noon, she was found at Kimberly in a stable of Mr. Hares, a boy happening to see and put her in there.'[13]

Like modern vehicles, horses required much maintenance, as did carts and carriages. Apart from food, water, grooming, stabling, harness and veterinary care, horses needed to be properly shod. This was not a problem near home, close to familiar blacksmiths, but a cross-country traveller might have to make 'running repairs', like John Byng soon after leaving Basingstoke:

> In a miles riding I overtook a conversable farmer, and we jogged on together being both bound for Reading; but soon, oh grief of griefs! my horse went miserably lame as if he had wrenched his foot; the farmer said it would walk off but the poor beast being unable to move, I dismounted to examine his foot, into the frog of which a great horse-nail had enter'd so deeply that with difficulty we extracted it. As soon as possible we stop'd at a blacksmith's, who burnt in some turpentine, which, secured by tow, enabled my horse to go on tolerably.[14]

Horses and other pack animals were the only option for haulage in some parts of England, because wheeled vehicles were impossible on narrow, winding and steep roads. In counties such as Devon and

Cornwall, the roads tended to be simply packhorse trackways. In the summer of 1795, John Manners travelled westwards from Devon into Cornwall: 'To-day we for the first time observed the husbandmen bringing in their barley and oats ... The manner in which they carry their harvest in Cornwall is very curious. Having no carts on account of their hills, they make use only of little ponies, and carry their loads in a kind of pannier, placed like a saddle on the horse.'[15]

Coal was carried from the north Somerset mines into Bath using donkeys, and in September 1800 Richard Warner saw one of these animals at work, delivering to the grand houses, a 'little, wasted, panting wretch, staggering under its unconscionable burthen, and labouring up the steep streets of Bath; now dropping with fatigue, and again urged to exertion by reiterated blows'.[16] The animals, he explained, were kept overnight at nearby Holloway:

> Wearied and panting with the labour of the day, here the wretched beasts are driven ... as the evening closes, into yards hired for the purpose, not so much for the sake of rewarding their services with rest, as to prevent their escape from the toil of tomorrow. As they pick a scanty pittance from the ditches and hedges during the day, the inhuman master thinks himself exempted from the necessity of giving them food at night; and what is still more barbarous, never removes from their backs the heavy and incumbering wooden saddle on which the coals are packed, but suffers it to continue girded on for weeks together, inflaming and increasing those galls which its pressure originally occasioned.[17]

Normally, goods were conveyed in carriers' carts and waggons. Long-distance carriers made cross-country trips using large waggons pulled by six or eight horses, and some operated in the same way as stagecoaches, changing horses at wayside stops and claiming to be a fast service with names like 'Flying Waggon', even though their speed was slower than walking pace. Although these waggons primarily carried freight, they could also accommodate passengers. Other than walking, this was the cheapest means of travel and gave some shelter from the weather. A household might own horses and a small cart for transporting passengers and for haulage, and on one occasion Holland noted: 'My daughter [Margaret] is to return with the two Miss Lewis's and (because they cannot procure a better conveyance) to go in my cart. Robert is to drive.'[18] At other times this cart was involved in tasks like moving dung, hay, timber and coal.

Wealthy gentry and the aristocracy would own at least one carriage that was solely for passengers, but their horses might be used for riding and farm work as well. Small carriages that were open to the elements were not suited to winter conditions, as with the donkey carriage used at Chawton by Jane Austen: 'this is not a time of year [January] for donkey-carriages, and our donkeys are necessarily having so long a run of luxurious idleness that I suppose we shall find they have forgotten much of their education when we use them again. We do not use two [donkeys] at once however; don't imagine such excesses.'[19] Only the very rich could afford the cost of keeping large, enclosed carriages, emblazoned with their coats-of-arms, along with teams of horses and liveried servants.

There was a trade in secondhand carriages, and in London in May 1806 Ralph Heathcote accompanied a friend who was looking for something suitable to buy: 'We went out to look at carriages, T. [Colonel Taylor] meaning to buy a chaise ... We went to all the principal coachmakers. The average price for a second-hand chaise still in fashion (about two years ago) and good order, newly painted, etc., is £150.'[20] Then, as now, sellers emphasised the vehicle's good condition, and the following year this 'one careful lady owner' advertisement appeared in the *Morning Chronicle*:

COACH to be DISPOSED of, late the property of a lady, deceased; has been built but a few months, in the present stile, compass sides and projecting elbows, the lining and every part in the nicest condition, and scarce inferior to new, painted yellow and black, built by Hatchett and Co. at a considerable expence, and to be disposed of for about one-third of the original cost, at Turner's, coach-maker, opposite Shoreditch Church.[21]

With no restrictions on who could drive a vehicle, carriage drivers varied enormously in their abilities. Young aristocratic men had a reputation for driving fast and often irresponsibly, but elderly drivers could equally pose a hazard, as Woodforde observed:

> Mr. Du Quesne returned to his own home to dinner, though we asked him to dine with us ... He complained much of being terribly shook about in his chaise by the badness of the roads ... Mr. Du Quesne is very far advanced in years but he will not own it. He is by no means fit to drive a single horse chaise. His servant man that came on horseback with him, was afraid that he would overturn coming along, he cannot see the ruts distinctly, he will not however wear spectacles at all. He cannot bear to appear old.[22]

This was the Reverend Thomas Roger du Quesne, who died four months later at the age of seventy-five.

For long journeys across England, people resorted to public transport, of which the stagecoach was the most popular. These were roofed four-wheeled vehicles, driven by coachmen at speeds of 6–7 miles per hour and running to a schedule on established routes. The term 'stage' referred to each stage of the journey between the points where the horses were changed. To Moritz, stagecoaches seemed strange: 'Persons, to whom it is not convenient to pay a full price, instead of the inside, sit on the top of the coach, without any seats, or even a rail. By what means passengers thus fasten themselves securely on the roof of these vehicles, I know not; but you constantly see numbers seated there, apparently at their ease.'[23]

When he first arrived at Liverpool from America in May 1805, stagecoaches were also a novelty to Benjamin Silliman: 'people ride on the roofs of the English stage coaches. This situation affords fine views of the country, and is often a convenient refuge when the inside places are all taken. I mounted the roof, and although the situation was so giddy, that at first I grasped the iron railing with great care, I soon learned to hold my arms in security, trusting to the balance of position.'[24]

The horses slowed or stopped these vehicles – there were no brakes. In hilly areas Silliman noted that wheels would be chained: 'They took the wise precaution of chaining a wheel at the top of every steep hill, a practice which is common in England, and which is rendered doubly necessary by the great weight of people and luggage which an English stage coach carries on its roof. I have been one of a party of eighteen, twelve of whom were on the top.'[25] Unsurprisingly, the stagecoach was not always a safe means of transport, especially when coachmen drove their overloaded vehicles recklessly over potholed and rutted roads. In 1816 the *European Magazine* reported attempts at improvements:

The country magistrates are exerting themselves to bring to punishment all drivers of stage coaches within their jurisdiction, who shall be found furiously driving, or shall carry more passengers than allowed by law. The following are among the various penalties to which the offending parties are liable:– Coachmen driving furiously, or permitting others to drive, forfeit 10l [£10].

TEN passengers allowed on the outside of a carriage, drawn by *four* horses, besides the coachman: ONE only to sit on the BOX, THREE on the FRONT of the roof, and SIX BEHIND; a penalty of 10l. for each passenger beyond that number and DOUBLE that sum if the coachman is owner or part owner.

LUGGAGE not to EXCEED TWO FEET in HEIGHT ON THE ROOF; penalty 5l/ [£5] for every inch above two feet. No passenger to SIT on the LUGGAGE; penalty 50s. to be paid by the passenger.[26]

Travelling inside a stagecoach was more costly, but it was safer and gave shelter from the weather. The lurching motion could cause nausea, and being inside also meant suffering other passengers. In 1802 Henry Hole was on his way to India, and he wrote to his father about the stagecoach journey from Exeter to Plymouth:

We had scarcely got through the City when the coach suddenly stopp'd, the door opened and an overgrown female of the Wapping breed made her appearance, puffing and panting as if she had not half an hour to live. A considerable difficulty then arose how she was to get in. I look'd at her and the door alternately, and really conceived it impossible; however, by a little squeezing and a great deal of shoving in the rear by the coachman [the driver] and guard assisted by half a dozen by-standers she contrived to effect her purpose in something less than a quarter of an hour. We screw'd ourselves up in each corner and allowed her to take the middle, when she sat or rather fell down with the grunt of a rhinoceros and remained a complete fixture for the whole journey. Not so her tongue; for the moment she recovered a sufficiency of breath, she attack'd me in a most barbarous dialect.[27]

In addition to the driver, there was also a guard, as Silliman explained: 'Most of the English stage coaches travel with a guard. He is armed with a blunderbuss, or more commonly with pistols ... To the duty of defending the coach he is rarely called for; for ... the stage coaches are seldom attacked. Besides guarding the coach, he is expected to open and shut the door, and aid in case of accident, so that the coachman is never called upon to leave his seat.'[28]

In the event of a stagecoach overturning, the outside passengers were flung off and would undoubtedly suffer injuries, while those inside could be trapped, crushed or even drowned. Newspapers were full of coaching incidents, as in *The Times* in December 1807:

As the Salisbury coach was coming to town [London], on Tuesday night, it met with a shocking accident. The fog was so thick that the coachman could not see his way, and at the entrance of Belfont [now Bedfont, near Hounslow], the horses went off the road into a pond called the King's Water, dragging the coach along with them. A young man of the name of Williams was killed on the spot. He belonged to a regiment of dragoons ... In the inside of the coach were four females: the wife of the deceased, her maid, a Swiss governess who lived in the family of a gentleman in Davies Street, Berkeley Square, and another female. They all narrowly escaped drowning.[29]

Given such disaster stories, it is no wonder that Woodforde wrote in his diary on 6 July 1778: 'My poor dear sister shook like an aspin leave [aspen leaf] going away, she never went in a stage coach before in her life.'[30]

For faster journeys or ones not on stagecoach routes, post-chaises could be hired at post-houses, which were usually inns. 'Post' was equivalent to 'stage'. These chaises (literally, 'chairs') were roofed four-wheeled vehicles, yellow in colour. Their speed was maintained by frequent changes of horses, and like stagecoaches, they had no brake. The drivers rode on the horses, not on the chaises, and were called postillions or post-boys, even though they were usually men. In early June 1782, Moritz took a chaise from Dartford to London:

> these carriages are very neat, and lightly built, so that you hardly perceive their motion, as they roll along these firm, smooth roads; they have windows in front, and on both sides. The horses are generally good, and the postillions particularly smart and active, and always ride on a full trot. A thousand charming spots and beautiful landscapes, on which my eye would long have dwelt with rapture, ere now rapidly passed with the speed of an arrow.[31]

He may not have noticed some of the faults that the experienced horseman and carriage driver John Byng railed against two years later:

> My nerves are either so weak or my fears so overpowering, that I never (but from necessity) ride in an hackney post-chaise; jolted, winded; harness that don't fit, horses that won't draw; and left at the mercy of an ignorant, drunken post-boy, who cannot drive, and is everlastingly brutal to the poor beasts under his lash. Young gentlemen are ever in violent haste to hurry to nothing; and laugh when I desire a post-boy not to gallop; not to hurry down hill; or to abstain from cutting at the horses eyes![32]

In Somerset William Holland occasionally hired a chaise for local journeys, as in January 1807 when he and his wife were driven home from Enmore to Over Stowey along narrow lanes:

> We ... got on very well till we came past Radlet Common when we met a loaded waggon in a narrow part of the road. The waggoner did all he could to close the waggon up to the hedge but when we drove on a little

the chaise driver began to doubt our being able to pass, especially as there was an ugly ditch on our side. I call'd and told him it would be best to get out. You cannot, returned he, get out in this dirty place. Oh cannot we, answered I, I'll warrant you, for I deemed it far better to dirty our shoes and get wet than to be overturned and get our limbs broke, so out we got, but it was with some trouble and danger that they were able to pass afterwards. After this we got to Overstowey safe without further obstructions.[33]

From the 1790s onwards horse-drawn omnibuses were operating in London, from which modern buses developed, but the most common form of public transport in towns was the hackney coach, the forerunner of the hackney cab or taxi. The word 'hackney' meant a horse, or a horse for hire.[34] Hackney coaches tended not to be purpose-built vehicles until around 1814, when the 'chariot' was introduced, which carried two passengers inside and one outside. Before that, hackney coaches were usually old or worn-out private carriages, and their comfort varied considerably, as did the fares charged, which led to constant disputes. A succession of regulations tried – in vain – to control the exploitation of passengers by cabmen.

Particularly for elderly or invalid passengers, sedan chairs (also called hackney chairs if they were for hire) were an option. The sedan chair had a seat for a single passenger set inside a structure resembling a small sentry-box. A stout pole on either side provided the carrying handles for two chairmen, one in front and one behind. Chairmen waited at stands to catch passing trade, and a 1790 manual of advice for those staying in London said that the fares were a shilling for the first mile and sixpence for every subsequent mile. In cases of grievance, the customer should 'take the number of the chair, which is fixed just under the top, near the hinge, and complain at the hackney-coach office'.[35]

John Byng was not impressed by this form of transport at Cheltenham: 'their fare is very exorbitant; and as the master of ceremonies [at the spa pump rooms] dares not, and the company care not to make alterations, many such exactions and abuses continue here unrectified.'[36] Even this sedate method of travel carried risks, as revealed in a letter from William Jenkin to a friend: 'Thy mother met with an accident this week – as two men were carrying her in her chair, she slid out of it and fell to the ground, by which she received some hurt, one of her legs is bruised and she is likely to be confined to her room for some time.'[37]

For those who could afford the fare, sedan chairs were invaluable in towns in bad weather to avoid having to walk through filthy streets. Urban authorities were making some effort to install paved walkways or pavements for pedestrians, at least in the main thoroughfares, and London was sometimes hailed as the best paved city in Europe. Certainly Moritz was impressed by the capital's streets:

> The footway, paved with large stones, on both sides of the street, appears to a foreigner exceedingly convenient and pleasant; as one may there walk in perfect safety from the prodigious crowd of carts and coaches that fill the centre. However, politeness requires you to let a lady, or any one to whom you wish to show respect, pass, not as we do [in Germany], always to the right, but on the side next the houses or the wall, whether that happens to be on the right or on the left. People seldom walk in the middle of the streets in London, excepting when they cross over; which at Charing-Cross, and other places, where several streets meet, is sometimes really dangerous.[38]

The surfaces of the actual streets might be laid with cobbles, though they would still become filthy, while minor streets and lanes were more likely to remain unsurfaced, dusty in dry weather and a quagmire when wet. Paupers who could get hold of a broom appointed themselves crossing-sweepers, clearing a path for anyone wanting to cross the street, in the hope of a tip. This method of begging continued long into the Victorian era. With so many horses, huge quantities of manure filled the streets, made worse by the herds of animals that were driven to market, and so houses had boot scrapers outside for scraping footwear clean of detritus. In April 1809 Sarah Wilkinson was living in Church Street, Kensington, awaiting the return of her husband William from the navy: 'This morning while at breakfast, hearing the bell ring and somebody scrape their shoes as you used to do, I told Fanny it was you, and I ran down like a wild thing. Then think what I felt on seeing the washer woman stand at the door.'[39]

In towns and cities, the numerous wheeled vehicles led to congested streets and accidents, and there was endless noise from the iron tyres and the hooves of the horses, added to which was the sound of horns, animals being herded, the hubbub arising from traffic jams and the cries of pedlars and hawkers trying to sell their wares. In May 1805 Silliman arrived for the first time in London: 'We drove [on top of the stagecoach] through Piccadilly, and were instantly involved in the noise and tumult of London. We were obliged to hold fast as we were driven furiously over rough pavements [the street surfaces], while the clattering of wheels, the sounding of the coachman's horn, and the sharp reverberations of his whip, had there been no other noises, would have drowned conversation.'[40]

Only heavy snowfall could silence the city, as Gilbert White experienced in January 1776: 'the metropolis itself exhibited a still more singular appearance than the country; for being bedded deep in snow, the pavement of the streets could not be touched by the wheels or the horses' feet, so that the carriages ran about without the least noise. Such an exemption from din and clatter was strange, but not pleasant; it seemed to convey an uncomfortable idea of desolation.'[41]

In the countryside, the condition of roads varied greatly. The problem was that there was no central fund or taxation to pay for their upkeep. Instead, everyone was supposed to spend several days each year repairing the roads near where they lived, but the organisation of such labour was inefficient and haphazard. 'Mrs Poole's cart busy in doing statute labour,' William Holland noted with pleasure in June 1800. 'I hope we shall have the road a little better. A great many stones I see have been carried and laid down in the middle of the road. The Somersetshire Boobies have strangely mended the road.'[42] It was not feasible to bring in good-quality materials to those areas that had no stone, and so many roads in England remained pitted and rutted in dry conditions and deep in mud once it rained.

Such was the bad state of roads that John Byng preferred travelling on horseback during his annual summer excursions: 'Whoever speaks of touring in chaises or phaetons, (as many ignorants will,) let him attempt to travel thro' these ... rough roads; and then he will recant, and say with me, – there is no touring, but on horseback.'[43] He deplored the short-cut practices of the roadmenders in obtaining materials: 'how barbarous to pull down old ruins, as is commonly done; to fill up cart-ruts!'[44] Charles Fothergill in Yorkshire likewise opposed the destruction of ancient monuments for repairing roads: 'What will the lovers of antiquity and all wise and good men say to this when they are told ... that this is a co[u]ntry abounding with stones and every necessary material for the making and mending of roads.'[45]

On main cross-country routes, the solution to poor roads was privatisation, and from the mid-eighteenth century turnpike trusts had been established on a piecemeal basis, each one authorised by Act of Parliament. These private companies were licensed to maintain and operate turnpike roads as toll roads, and in return for collecting tolls, they took responsibility for their maintenance. Turnpike roads were so-called because of their barriers, often gates, that were set across the road where tolls were collected. The term 'turnpike' had been used from at least the early fifteenth century for a spiked barrier of pikes (a long-handled spear) that was rapidly placed as a makeshift obstacle, especially against attackers on horseback. By the mid-eighteenth century 'turnpike' was used generally for barriers, even for the locks and barriers on navigable waterways.

Turnpike trusts usually gained their initial capital by publishing a prospectus and inviting investors to lend them money, offering interest in the region of 4 or 5 per cent. This money covered initial repairs to the road, the establishment of gates and tollhouses at regular intervals and the wages of the toll collectors who were paid to live in the tollhouses and collect tolls at all hours, every day of the year. Once established, the trusts often farmed out the collection of tolls and repairs of the road to a contractor, in return for a guaranteed fixed sum, leaving the contractor to squeeze as much profit from travellers as possible. Understandably, toll collectors were unpopular, and 'turnpike man' became a derogatory term for a clergyman, on the grounds that his fees for baptisms and burials were tolls on passing in and out of the world of the living.

Many travellers tried to avoid the toll gates, but some trusts forced people to use them by blocking up alternative routes. Gangs occasionally broke down the gates, destroyed tollhouses and assaulted toll collectors. Turnpike roads did greatly improve many cross-country routes and opened up the country by making it easier to travel long distances, but not all were of high quality, as Byng found near Gloucester: 'No turnpike road is so bad as the last six miles to Gloster, narrow, wet, and stoney; and only mended with black iron ore, dangerous to man, and horse.'[46] Less than 20 per cent of the road network was run by the trusts; the majority of minor routes and side roads remained as bad as ever.

Along turnpike roads travellers had relatively little trouble finding their way, because there were milestones or mileposts at every mile, which appealed to Moritz: 'The English mile-stones gave me much pleasure, and they certainly are a great convenience to travellers. For, besides the distance from London, every mile-stone informs you, that to the next place is so many miles; and where there are cross-roads, there are direction-posts, so that it is hardly possible to lose one's self in walking.'[47] Each turnpike had an individual style of milestone, and a guidebook to Norfolk published in 1803 was impressed by the local design: 'The mile stones from Thetford to Norwich are well adapted for travelling in carriages, having two sides towards the road, not square, but slanted so that the number may be seen at a great distance.'[48] The turnpike trusts erected these milestones and mileposts, and they are still shown on modern Ordnance Survey maps, marked as MS or MP, revealing the old arterial roads.

Away from the turnpikes, following the correct route was not so easy, with no road names and little to guide the traveller. In August 1781, William Dyott was travelling by night in a post-chaise to Chester: 'I was awakened by the chaise stopping, when the post-boy did me the satisfaction of telling me he was lost, for which I made him a low bow and then kicked him. It was in the middle of an immense forest, and not near light.'[49] Even close to home it was easy to go astray, as Woodforde discovered: 'I went to Brand this morning for Mr. Bodham and there read prayers and administered the H.

Sacrament for him, as he served Mr. Hall's church at Garveston. Brand is about 7 mile from my house and very difficult road to find.'[50]

Most people had scant geographical knowledge beyond their own locality, something Byng noticed at Buxton in Derbyshire in June 1790: 'I travell by map, for none can inform you [of the way]; the only people who become acquainted with counties, are tourists, or a canvasser at a general election.'[51] Three weeks later he was exasperated with one hostler: 'enquiring the road to Grantchester, only 3 miles distant, he answer'd, (after a long stammer) "Were you ever there, sir?" "No, or I wou'd not have ask'd you the way".'[52] Maps were little better than sketches, which experienced travellers like him found wholly inadequate:

> I have often thought that maps, merely for tourists might be made. And have wish'd that some intelligent traveller (for instance Mr [Francis] Grose) wou'd mark on such touring maps, all the castles, Roman stations, views, canals, parks, &c &c. which accompanied by other common maps, wou'd lead the researching tourist to every proper point & object; and not subject him (as at present) to ask questions of ignorant innkeepers, or to hunt in books, for what is not to be found; for till lately we had no inquisitive travellers and but few views of remarkable places.[53]

The threat of invasion during the wars with France made an accurate survey of England essential. It was begun in 1790, and its primary purpose was to enable the best positions to be chosen for defensive gun (ordnance) emplacements. They were therefore called Ordnance Survey maps, the name by which they are still known. Surveying started in the southern counties, where invasion was most likely, and the first map, of Kent, was produced in 1801. These maps were not available to the public until years later.

Long-distance travel was so slow that overnight stops were unavoidable. While Moritz was shunned at inns whenever he was on foot, Silliman noticed the difference between the treatment shown towards those passengers arriving by post-chaise and those by stagecoach: 'the strangers in the post-chaise were expected to pay well ... while the men on top of the coach might possibly have money, but, in all probability, rode there to save it. Thus it is, that ... the attentions which a traveller receives at the inns are proportioned very exactly to the style in which he arrives.'[54] He also found that everyone expected to be tipped: 'The guard and coachman as well as the servants at hotels expect their regular douceur ... This tax is inevitable, and Americans, from ignorance of the country, and fear of being thought mean, usually pay more liberally than the natives.'[55]

When Silliman first arrived in London, 'We were driven through the Strand, Temple Row ... and Fleet-street. The coach stopped at the Belle Savage on Ludgate Hill. The coachman, by a short turn, drove us, with astonishing swiftness, through a narrow opening, where the least deviation would have overturned the coach, and we were set down in a large back yard, full of coaches, horses, servants, and baggage.'[56] Surviving inns of this period usually retain the telltale arched entranceway for horse-drawn vehicles, and some still have the yard at the rear as well.

Whenever he travelled to London, Woodforde always stayed at the same historic coaching inn as Silliman, the Belle Sauvage, despite its bedbugs. In June 1786 he wrote: 'I was bit so terribly with buggs again this night, that I got up at 4 o'clock this morning and took a long walk by myself about the City till breakfast time.'[57] The next night he tried a different tactic: 'I did not pull off my cloaths last night but sat up in a great chair all night with my feet on the bed and slept very well considering and not pestered with buggs.'[58]

In *Emma* Mrs Elton says of Selina, her sister, that if staying at an inn, 'She always travels with her own sheets; an excellent precaution.' Byng regularly took his own sheets, but failed to do so when he was at the Black Bear Inn at Rugby in July 1789: 'My sheets were so damp, and the blankets so dirty and stinking, and the room so smelling of putridity, that I slept very little; tho' I took off the sheets, and employed all the brandy, near a pint, in purifying the room, and sprinkling the quilt, and blankets.'[59] The following year, the Black Bull Inn in Trumpington Street in Cambridge provoked his anger even more:

I never was in a worse or a dirtier inn; for ALL Cambridge is in comparison of Oxford ... about 100 years behind hand: the best Cambridge inn wou'd form but a bad Oxford alehouse! – Dirty glasses; bad wine; vile cookery; but I answer to any question of hope, 'Oh, it is excellent'; and why should I not? ... I, resolv'd never to come again, don't like to vex myself; and so I say 'It is all very good'. Tho here it went much against the grain ... This wretched inn, with most of this wretched town, ought to be burnt down![60]

Cambridge was not burnt down, but the inn was rebuilt in 1828 and renamed 'The Bull'.

Rather than stay at inns, some people travelled all night, and Byng complained that inns wanted to do business only in horses, not hospitality: 'Most inns, now, are kept by, and for, a change of post horses, as fine gentleman never step out of their chaises in the longest journies; and all others travell in the mail, or post coaches: so that the tourist who wants only a supper and a bed, is consider'd as a troublesome unprofitable intruder.'[61] This kind of non-stop travel, with the horses being changed at intervals, was relatively fast but bitterly cold in winter. In November 1805 Silliman had left London and was journeying from Newark to York by stagecoach: 'The night had been one of the coldest that I have experienced in England; we were obliged to close the windows of the coach entirely; but still my feet suffered considerably ... The coachman and guard, who had been all night in the open air, were completely encrusted [with frost].'[62]

Night journeys were hazardous because of the absence of lighting. It was much easier if a full moon lit the way, which Woodforde and his niece Nancy found when travelling from Bath to London in 1795: 'I thank God we had fine weather and a good moon all last night, and about 10 o'clock this morning we got safe and well to London ... We were not much fatigued with our journey or otherwise indisposed, tho' travelling all night.'[63] In Weston Longville on another occasion Woodforde had an unpleasant night-time walk from a neighbouring house: 'As there was no moon to come home by, it was very disagreeable to come home thro' the wood that I did, but I thank God I got safe and well back tho' very dark. When there is no moon for the future will get back before it is dark.'[64] Moonlight was desirable for going to evening entertainments, and in

Sense and Sensibility Sir John Middleton is hoping to organise a small social gathering at the last minute, 'but it was moonlight and every body was full of engagements'.

Only in the main urban streets was there any street lighting, and London's was praised by Moritz in 1782: 'I was astonished at the admirable manner in which the streets are lighted up; compared to which our streets in Berlin make a most miserable show. The lamps are lighted whilst it is still day-light; and are so near each other, that even on the most ordinary and common nights, the city has the appearance of a festive illumination.'[65] An improved type of lighting was tried in May 1803, which *The Times* reported:

> A satisfactory experiment was first made on Friday evening last, at the Upper end of New Bond Street, to dissipate the great darkness that has long prevailed in the streets of this metropolis. It consisted in the adaption of twelve newly invented lamps with reflectors, in place of more than double that number of common ones; and notwithstanding the wetness of the evening ... that part of the street [was] illuminated with at least twice the quantity of light usually seen.[66]

Although this experimental lighting still comprised oil lamps, they were so effective that 'the faces of persons walking, the carriages passing &c. could be clearly seen',[67] an indication that the old lamps were very inadequate. Shops began to be lit by gas in 1805, and gas street lighting was demonstrated in Pall Mall in 1807, which gradually replaced oil lamps from 1812, making a significant improvement.

Lamps were useless during the dense fogs caused by adverse weather conditions and coal smoke, and Lady Bessborough described one terrifying journey she made in London on the night of 5 November 1805:

> The fog, which was bad when I set out, grew thicker and thicker, but when I got into the park was so complete it was impossible to find the way out. My footman got down to *feel* for the road, and the holloing of the drivers and screams of people on foot were dreadful. I was one hour driving thro' the park; Queen St it was impossible to find, and as ... it was

as dangerous to try to go home, I set out with two men walking before the horses with flambeaux [flaming torches], of which we could with difficulty perceive the flame – the men not at all. Every ten or twenty yards they *felt* for the door of a house to ask where we were – it was frightful beyond measure; in three hours' time I reached Chelsea.[68]

That very night Lieutenant Laponetiere was groping his way towards the Admiralty through the same fog, bringing news of the naval victory at Trafalgar and the death of Nelson.[69]

Bad weather regularly disrupted travel, particularly as winters in England were more severe than today. Heavy snowfall at times persisted into spring when the thaw would lead to severe floods. In Norfolk in early February 1799, during one bitter winter, Woodforde described the roads still blocked with snow:

Most of the poor people employed in clearing the public road from the late great fall of snow. Never known such a depth of snow for the last 40 yrs. People obliged to walk over hedges &c. In almost every place the roads impassable. The snow near our great gate in the yard almost as high as the gate, above the pales in some places. Dreadful weather indeed for the poor people now ... All travelling is almost at a stand, the drifting of the snow making almost every place impassable.[70]

Two weeks later, conditions had not changed:

Very dismal accounts on the papers respecting the last severe weather – many, many people having lost their lives thro' the inclemency of the same. Mail coaches &c unable to travel. The roads in very, very many places impassable. The long continuance of so severe cold weather having scarce been ever known for the last century. It has lasted now (with scarce any intermission) from the 17th of December last past and [more] still likely.[71]

In November 1800 an early winter snowstorm hit Exmoor, followed two days later by a violent rainstorm, which caused unprecedented flooding in St Thomas, a low-lying suburb of Exeter:

The inundation became violent on Sunday about noon, at which time the water began to flow over the streets of St. Thomas, and continued to increase with great rapidity until about five o'clock in the afternoon, when it had arisen in every street of that parish, and in the Exe Island, to the height of about six feet. At this period the appearance was dreadful, all the inhabitants were obliged to betake themselves to their upper rooms, whilst some, whose houses were built with mud (cobb) walls, were under the most serious alarm that they should be buried in the ruins. The current of the river [Exe] was then astonishingly strong, hurrying ... large pieces of wood, hayricks, and other matters which had been swept by its force from the neighbouring grounds, insomuch that serious apprehensions were entertained for the safety even of the New Exe Bridge.[72]

That same day two post-chaises set off from Okehampton to make their return journey to London, and on coming down the hill into St Thomas they suddenly encountered the floodwater:

here the water was so high, that it flowed over the backs of the horses, and reached nearly to the windows of the [first] carriage. One horse having dropped dead, it was necessary immediately to cut the traces, so as to extricate the others from the carriage, and prevent, if possible, the whole from being carried off by the violence of the current. As the waves continued rising it was judged impossible to preserve the lives of the persons in the carriage, unless a boat could be procured from the quay.[73]

In a dangerous operation, a boat was brought up close, 'just in time, for the persons were still sitting in the carriage, immersed above their middles, and so rapid did the water rise, that they had scarcely been extricated ... and the carriage lashed to prevent its being washed away, when the stream flowed over the roof'.[74] The travellers were the architect Henry Holland, his family and servants, who were all saved, along with the remaining horses.

Attempts at scientific weather forecasting were not published in newspapers until later in the nineteenth century, although most newspapers and magazines gave some weather details for preceding weeks or months. Many country gentlemen used barometers and thermometers to compile records, but forecasting relied heavily on observation and experience. Woodforde keenly observed the weather and had great faith in folklore. On 30 January 1794, after an intensely cold period, he wrote:

> A frost again but not so sharp as yesterday. It did not freeze within doors last night ... It froze ... in the afternoon, and the barometer still rising, but in the evening it thawed and some rain fell. I was saying before dinner that there would be alteration of weather soon as I a long time observed one of our cats wash over both her ears – an old observation and now I must believe it to be a pretty true one.[75]

Faced with poor weather and poor roads, it was cheaper and easier in coastal areas for freight and even passengers to be conveyed by sea. Small ships did not need proper ports, but could be loaded and unloaded by boat while anchored offshore. Alternatively, ships were beached, as on the north Norfolk coast at Cromer where in 1798 Samuel Pratt witnessed coal being offloaded from ships into carts: 'There is now no harbour at Cromer, yet corn is exported, and coals, deals, &c. received in return ... at high water they [the ships] are laid upon the beach, and, as soon as the water is sufficiently ebbed, carts are drawn to the side of the ship, and the coals shot into them, as they are into lighters in other places.'[76] The carts, he said, only carried a small load because of the steep road up the cliff: 'In this manner the carts continue working, till the water flows so high as to wash the sides of the horses, and just to float the carts ... When the vessel is empty it floats on a high tide, and continues at a little distance from the shore, and is then loaded with corn by boats.'[77]

With canals making substantial improvements in the carriage of goods by water to inland areas, the condition of roads consequently benefited, because heavy waggons were no longer using them. William Hutton who lived in Birmingham said that before the canal was constructed from there to the Wednesbury coalfields, 'It was common to see a train of carriages for miles, to the great destruction of the road, and the annoyance of travellers.'[78] Canals were also used for passenger transport, and as early as 1774 a letter to the *Annual Register* reported:

> The Duke of Bridgewater has just built two packet-boats, which are every day towed [by horses] from Manchester to Warrington; one carries six score passengers, the other eighty: each boat has a coffee-room at the head, from whence wines, &c. are sold out by the captain's wife. Next to this is the first cabin, which is 2s. 6d., the second cabin is 1s. 6d. and the third cabin 1s. for the passage or voyage upon the canal.[79]

A few years later Nelly Weeton travelled from Wigan to Liverpool in a similar packet-boat, on a branch of the same canal network, and because of the canal's winding route and the stops to pick up passengers, the journey took most of the day:

> I arrived again at my lodgings after a very pleasant sail down the canal, perfectly safe and sound both in body and mind, with a little less fat perhaps in the evening than I had set out with in the morning; for, whether inside or outside, I was almost half baked. The cook generally begins her operations by ten o'clock in the morning, frying bacon, eggs, beef steaks, potatoes, and mutton chops; roasting meat, warming meat pies, &c., and seldom finishes before 3 or 4 o'clock in the afternoon; for most people who go in the tail end of the packet seem to think that eating and drinking is the most delightful amusement of travelling.[80]

It was also convenient to transport troops by canal boats, as *The Times* showed in 1806:

> The first division of the troops that are to proceed by the Paddington canal [London end of the Grand Junction Canal] for Liverpool, and thence by transports for Dublin, will leave Paddington today, and will be followed by others tomorrow and Sunday. By this mode of conveyance the men will be only seven days in reaching Liverpool, and with comparatively little fatigue, as it would take them above fourteen days to march that distance. Relays of fresh horses for the canal boats have been ordered to be in readiness at all stages.[81]

Canal boats did not yet have engines, but were pulled by horses, and Hutton was appalled by the cruelty he witnessed on the Birmingham to Wednesbury canal: 'The boats are nearly alike, constructed to fit the locks ... and are each drawn by something like the skeleton of a horse, covered with skin; whether he subsists upon the scent of the water, is a doubt; but whether his life is a scene of affliction is not; for the unfeeling driver has no employment but to whip him from one end of the canal to the other.'[82]

Steam engines, already transforming manufacturing industries, would soon do the same for transport. The Cornish engineer Richard Trevithick began working on models and prototypes of a portable steam engine, and in London in 1808 he demonstrated a self-propelled engine running on a rail track. Other engineers were making similar experiments, and although steam engines began to be used for the haulage of coal on rail tracks from mines, it would not be until 1825 that the Stockton and Darlington railway provided the first steam train for passengers.

Steamboats were also making an appearance, and a passenger service between Yarmouth and Norwich was started in 1813, but it was balloons that caught people's imagination. Balloon flights had already taken place on the Continent, and the first man to ascend in a balloon in England was an Italian, Vincenzo Lunardi. After some problems with the hydrogen balloon, Lunardi successfully took off from the grounds of the Honourable Artillery Company in City Road, London, on 15 September 1784. Once the mooring ropes were cast off, 'For a moment, the globe hung suspended, as if inclined to fall, but Mr. Lunardi instantly kicking out a considerable portion of his ... ballast, ascended triumphantly, standing erect in the gallery, and waving his flag as a return to the incessant acclamations that were paid him at his departure.'[83]

The crowd watching the balloon flight numbered over a hundred thousand and included the Prince of Wales. They had never seen anything like it, as the newspapers reported: 'The fine spectacle presented to the public, produced curious effects upon John Bull – while Lunardi ascended, some held up their hands in admiration, while others burst into tears, very expressive of sensibility and pleasure ...

Old persons ... declared they had lived till now to see the greatest Wonder of their Age.'[84] It was reported that 'Mr Sheldon, who followed Mr. Lunardi from London, on a fine hunter, changed his horse three times, and kept so well up with him, as to be enabled to dine in his company at Ware [in Hertfordshire]'.[85] For now the horse could still keep pace, but its days as the fastest form of travel were drawing to an end.

TEN

————◆◆————

DARK DEEDS

Let other pens dwell on guilt and misery.

Mansfield Park, by Jane Austen

The novels and surviving letters of Jane Austen give an impression of a world barely touched by crime or warfare. Yet for much of her life Britain was at war and threatened by invasion, there was widespread fear of crime, and criminals were treated harshly. By the early Victorian era, the laws of England in the late eighteenth and early nineteenth centuries were being referred to as the 'Bloody Code', because of the number of offences that carried the death penalty. Indeed, the phrase 'You might as well be hung for a sheep as a lamb'[1] arose when stealing a sheep was added to that list. There was more meat on a sheep, but stealing either a lamb or a sheep could mean execution.

A major part of the Bloody Code was the Black Act, an Act of Parliament that came into law in 1723 in response to two gangs of poachers in Hampshire and Berkshire who were known as 'blacks' because they blackened their faces. This Act made many offences punishable by death, including activities not previously treated as crimes, such as entering a forest in disguise or with a blackened face. The modern equivalent might be a mandatory death sentence for wearing a mask or hooded jacket. This draconian law was deliberately designed to protect the interests of the elite, particularly those with large estates, and it remained the backbone of the Bloody Code for a century.

It was the lower ranks who felt the brunt of the Bloody Code. The rich and powerful could, and did, bribe their way out of almost anything. Most laws were designed to protect people's possessions, and as the gap between rich and poor widened, more and more property-related offences were made punishable by hanging. In reality, though, the death penalty was only routinely carried out for murder, violent crimes or those involving valuable property. Before the 1770s nearly 150 crimes were capital offences, increasing to over 220 during Jane Austen's lifetime. Many capital crimes were by modern standards no more than misdemeanours.[2] John Byng expressed his dismay at the justice system: 'Go on my poor deluded country ... Transport felons by thousands: fill the globe with your convicts. Hang by hundreds: and when reason is almost lost, and laws multiplied beyond comprehension, may some surviving few of the nation who do not thrive by politics and stratagem, endeavour at a reform.'[3]

Depending on the nature of the crime, including the type of goods stolen and where the offence took place, such as inside a shop or in the street, criminals could be executed for stealing goods valued at more than a shilling. This was a period when the lowliest labourers earned less than £25 a year and often as little as £12, while the upper classes enjoyed incomes of £10,000 or more, sometimes as much as £50,000,[4] and the annual Civil List payment – from taxes – to support the royal family exceeded £1,000,000.[5] With such great disparities of wealth and living conditions, when one person's pocket watch cost as much as another's yearly wage, the temptation to steal was strong. The number of crimes against property rose and fell in line with bad and good harvests, and famine could drive normally law-abiding but desperate people to steal rather than starve.

Such vicious penalties were intended as a deterrent, but proved woefully ineffective. A better deterrent would have been effective policing, but this was resisted because of fears of a repressive police state as witnessed in France before the Revolution and under Napoleon. Even county police forces would not be introduced for decades to come because of the dread of introducing networks of informers and secret police. While London had its Bow Street Runners, outside the capital reliance was placed on parish constables.

There were rarely more than one or two constables in any parish, but these officers could swear in temporary constables to help when needed, as William Darter explained for his home town of Reading: 'We had no police, but a head constable was chosen from the ratepayers on the election of Mayor, and he selected a number of others to serve under him, the names being submitted to the Chief Magistrate before being sworn.'[6]

Towns also paid night watchmen, literally to watch out for wrong-doers, but the provision of watchmen could be poor, and John Blackner outlined how Nottingham's citizens made their system work:

> about 35,000 inhabitants are scattered through upwards of 400 streets, lanes &c. and ... nine or ten men, four of whom watch the market-place, are employed to walk *almost* twenty streets. In 1815, in consequence of the numerous depredations committed in several streets, *where no watch was kept*, the housekeepers therein obtained permission to be sworn in the capacity of special constables, and by taking their turns as watchmen of the night, have preserved the neighbourhood in security.[7]

If a public disturbance could not be contained by the constables, magistrates could call for troops, but they might take some time to arrive. Magistrates, also known as Justices of the Peace, were the mainstay of the law. Appointed from among the large landowners of an area, they were unpaid and performed relatively mundane duties such as the regulation of markets, fairs and alehouses, as well as judging and punishing minor offenders, without a jury, in petty sessions (later known as 'magistrates' courts'). Those accused of more serious offences were tried at the Quarter Sessions, held in towns and cities four times a year, where the Justices of the Peace presided in courts with a jury. The main criminal courts were the Assizes (literally, 'sittings'), and judges moved from town to town within their circuit to hear serious cases like murder and counterfeiting. The Assizes were usually held two or three times a year, so that prisoners could wait months for their trial. In London serious crimes were tried at the Old Bailey.

The Assizes were also an excuse for social gatherings, and in March 1811 Louis Simond saw the ceremonial first day at York: 'On Sunday the judges, just arrived for the assizes, came to church *en grand costume*, with their huge powdered wigs, and black robes ... The mayor and corporation swelled the train, and in the rear footmen and white liveries, and large nosegays at the button-hole; the whole town was in motion. The assizes in a country town are an event.'[8] The following day provided an even better spectacle:

> we met the judges going to open the sessions, with the same wigs and the same train as yesterday. The whole town was in motion,—the streets full of misses in white muslin,—citizens in dark-blue coats, carefully brushed, glossy hats, and shining boots,—and military people in red. It seemed a day of rejoicing; and, in fact, the whole of the sessions is a period of amusement; yet we learn that the prisons here are unusually full. There are eight cases of murder, and among them a young couple for beating their own child, an infant, to death.[9]

The Assizes covered their surrounding area and on this occasion at York cases were about to be heard from as far away as Halifax and Hunslet near Leeds.[10]

Crime rates were lower outside the main towns and cities, as Byng observed: 'When I was at Knutsford [Cheshire], I remark'd the purity of the country, at seeing young women riding alone: why, within 50 miles of the devilish metropolis, they would have been all robb'd, and r—.'[11] Crime was indeed an urban plague, and London as the capital city was also the capital of crime. To try to reduce its high levels of crime, the Bow Street Runners had been established by the novelist and magistrate Henry Fielding in 1749.[12] In 1792 seven more 'police stations', besides the magistrates' office in Bow Street, were set up, and the runners were even called on to tackle crimes outside the capital.[13] William Darter spotted them at the horse races at Ascot in Berkshire in 1814: 'I arrived at Ascot some time before the races were to commence ... where I saw [John] Townsend, at the time a well-known Bow Street officer, giving instructions to his men, who were usually called Bow Street Runners.'[14]

Large gatherings, as at racecourses, were the haunt of pickpockets, the cream of criminals according to Carl Moritz: 'The highest order of thieves are the pick-pockets or cutpurses, whom you find every where; and sometimes even in the best companies. They are generally well and handsomely dressed, so that you take them to be persons of condition.'[15] Benjamin Silliman gave useful tips on how to elude pickpockets:

If you are going, by night, into crowds, or any where on foot, leave your money at home, except what you want for immediate use; either leave your watch, or drop the chain into the fob [small pocket]; if you have valuable papers or a pocket book, carry it in a pocket in the breast of your coat; button your coat; if in a crowd and danger be apprehended, fold your arms, and let one hand rest on the pocket book. The pocket handkerchief may be in danger, but the loss of this is not serious, and even this may be prevented by wearing it in a pocket opening within the skirt of the coat ... By observing these precautions, I have never lost any thing in London.[16]

In the streets, pickpocketing was often committed by young boys in gangs, and if one was caught, he might be beaten and released, rather than handed to the law, as happened on one occasion in London during the summer of 1784:

A gentleman gazing at a print-shop in the Strand, had his pocket picked of his purse, in which were bank notes to the amount of 700l. A poor woman that stood by observed the transaction, gave notice, and the fellow was pursued and taken, and the purse recovered. The fellow, after being rolled in the kennel [drain], and had undergone the discipline of the mob, was permitted to escape, and the woman who had discovered the theft rewarded with five guineas.[17]

This pickpocket may not have realised what he was stealing, but had he been prosecuted, such a substantial theft would have warranted the death sentence.

For lesser amounts, the judge might reduce the sentence to

transportation, as in the case of thirty-five-year-old Sarah Smith. At her trial for 'pocketpicking' in April 1793, John Harrison testified:

> I am a breeches maker in Fleet-street, and I keep the Crown, Clement's Inn-passage. I was coming from that house to my house in Fleet-street, this woman accosted me with, my dear, will you go home with me? I said, good woman is that your home, pointing to the Hole in the Wall [a tavern], the next door but one to mine, she said it was, and ran after me down to my own door; I said, good woman I am at home, you had better go home yourself and I rung the bell to go into my own house; she hung about me, my breeches pocket being open, and she took the money out of my breeches, and I never perceived it.[18]

On being asked 'Where did she rob you?' Harrison replied, 'In the street; it was at my own door ... I pushed her from me, and she went away easy enough, I did not miss the money till after I had rung the bell ... and I put my hand into my breeches pocket as I was standing by the door, and I found my money gone.'[19] Harrison said that he immediately cried out for the night watchman, before pursuing the woman, who was arrested and his money recovered.

Sarah Smith was accused of stealing nine guineas and three half-crowns, a total of 196s. 6d. (£9 16s. 6d.). Before the law was changed in 1808, the theft of property worth more than forty shillings by picking a pocket would incur a death sentence, but the jury found her guilty of a lesser charge, valuing the guineas and half-crowns well below the amount she had actually taken. This legal fiction was regularly used by juries to allow a judge to avoid a mandatory death penalty. Sarah Smith was sentenced to seven years' transportation, and she sailed on board the *Surprise* in February 1794, landing in New South Wales in October after a voyage of 176 days.[20]

Next to pickpockets in the hierarchy of criminals, according to Moritz,

> come the highwaymen, who rob on horseback; and often, they say, even with unloaded pistols, they terrify travellers, in order to put themselves in possession of their purses. Among these persons, however, there are

instances of true greatness of soul; there are numberless instances of their returning a part of their booty, where the party robbed has appeared to be particularly distressed; and they are seldom guilty of murder.[21]

Highwaymen haunted roads (highways) on the outskirts of towns and cities, preying on travellers. Many were ex-soldiers – officers and cavalrymen – who were excellent horsemen and could make a rapid escape. They had some reputation for gallantry, even chivalry, and a few tried to portray themselves as latter-day Robin Hoods. Most were not particularly violent or brutal and might even be deferential towards their victims.

Dick Turpin, the highwayman best known today, belonged to an earlier era. He was executed in 1739, but his legend lived on, and Francis Place noted that 'Oh Rare Turpin Hero' was a popular ballad sung in the streets.[22] It was first published as a broadside ballad around the time of Turpin's execution under the title 'Turpin's Rant: A New Song',[23] but over the years the song changed and expanded as it circulated by word-of-mouth.[24] Only the central theme remained constant, that of Turpin fooling the better-off, which three verses common to most versions related:

On Hounslow Heath, as I rid o'er,
I spy'd a Lawyer just before,
I asked him if he was not afraid,
Of TURPIN, that mischievous blade?
Sing, O rare Turpin, O rare Turpin, O.

Says Turpin, I have been most cute,
For my Money is hid within my Boot,
Says the Lawyer, there is none can find
For mine lies in my Cape behind.

They rid till they came to the Powder Mill,
When Turpin bid the Lawyer to stand still,
Stand, Sir, your Cape I must cut off,
For my Horse does want a saddle cloth.
Sing, &c.[25]

Whether the victim was a lawyer, exciseman, judge or wealthy farmer, what made the song popular was the notion of an establishment figure being brought low. Turpin may not have been a true Robin Hood, as he did not bestow money on the poor, but widespread satisfaction was felt from his robbing the rich.

Highwaymen could be violent, and a common tactic of theirs was to shatter the glass windows of vehicles and then fire at passengers, though some resisted, as in one incident reported by the *Oxford Journal* in January 1797:

> Tuesday night, as the Earl of Strathmore was returning to town [London] from Wimbledon, he was attacked by a highwayman, who, without ceremony, broke the glass, and fired into the carriage, but luckily missed his aim; on which the Earl, who had a loaded blunderbuss between his knees, fired, and immediately killed the assailant on the spot, who appears to be one Lancaster, liberated out of prison for want of evidence only a few days since. He had an accomplice, who escaped.[26]

The dead highwayman was the notorious criminal William Lancaster, who had until recently been detained on a charge of robbing Lord Boringdon.[27] The death penalty seemed little deterrent to highwaymen, and the unpredictability of their behaviour and the number of robberies made travellers nervous. In 1805 a Horse Patrol of mainly ex-cavalrymen was established as an offshoot of the Bow Street Runners, which led to a decline in the number of highwaymen.

Footpads (highway robbers on foot) were another source of anxiety for travellers, and Moritz considered them worst of all because they 'often murder in the most inhuman manner, for the sake of only a few shillings, any unfortunate people who happen to fall in their way. Of this several mournful instances may be occasionally read in the English papers. Probably they murder, because they cannot, like the highwaymen, aided by their horses, make a rapid flight.'[28] Footpads often operated in gangs, and they would even ambush coaches at bridges and other constricted places where horses were reined in: 'On Wednesday [13 June 1792] night as JAMES FRY, Esq. of Wimpole-street, in company with five young Ladies, were returning home from the Richmond Theatre, they were stopped in a coach by six footpads, who robbed Mr. FRY of four guineas and some silver. Previous to the robbery the villains fired a pistol at the window, the bullet of which shot away one of the young Ladies earrings.'[29]

In 1796 the magistrate Patrick Colquhoun published a treatise on crime in London,[30] demonstrating that it went far beyond the obvious street offences and burglary. In his view, there were worse crimes, such as counterfeiting, metal theft and the vast amount of pilfering from warehouses and ships along the Thames. As a result, the Marine Police Force was set up in 1798 at Wapping, and when William Holland was in London in 1805, he visited the Wapping police office as a guest of his friend William Kinnaird, one of the justices there. Holland was impressed by the office and amazed at the river traffic it policed: 'We padded through many dirty narrow streets and got at last to the water side. There we took boat, and pass'd through groves of shipping. There seem'd to be no end of 'em; it was a gloriously awful [awesome] sight and gave a lively idea of the greatness of this nation. Boats were passing and repassing continuously.'[31]

Most people were understandably terrified of being robbed at home, and stories were constantly circulating about all manner of thefts from houses. In the summer of 1775 the *Bath Chronicle* reported: 'Monday morning [31 July], at two o'clock, three fellows got into Copt-hall [Copped Hall], the seat of John Conyers, Esq., near Epping, and bound the butler neck and heels and took away [silver] plate to the value of near 2000l. They carried it off in a post-chaise which waited for them at the Park-gate.'[32] This weekly newspaper was published far from the scene of the robbery, but such unsettling crimes were newsworthy right across England.

The *Bath Chronicle*'s account had actually been overtaken by events, because the ringleader was already in custody – Lambert Reading, a former coachman at Copped Hall. In the ensuing one-day trial, the butler testified as to how he had been threatened: 'three men entered his chamber [around 3.00 a.m.], one of whom, with a drawn sword and dark lanthorn, came to his bedside, and swore in a most violent manner, that, if he spoke or made any resistance, he would cut his throat; after which he threw the bed-cloaths over his head, and stood as a guard over him, whilst the others collected a large quantity of plate'.[33] This was an ambitious robbery: 'from the conversation that passed between them, he apprehended they filled four sacks with the house-plate'.[34] Their downfall was locking the butler in his room rather than killing him, and while the rest of the gang was not apprehended for some weeks, Lambert Reading was executed just five days afterwards.

Such a deliberately planned theft from a large country house was exceptional. It was easier to attack less wealthy establishments, which generated a universal dread of burglary, and in January 1808 Fanny Platt wrote from Kensington to her sister Sarah Wilkinson: 'The robbing trade is so brisk here you cannot think, scarce a night but one or more houses are broken into and robbed. James has hitherto escaped but I believe he quakes thinking he shall not much longer, as they last night were robbing on each side of him.'[35]

Thefts were often little more than opportunistic crimes, but the penalties could still be severe. In August 1814 the *Morning Chronicle* reported:

> an old man, who makes a living by picking up bones in the street, was yesterday charged by Mrs. Hill, of Tottenham-court-road, with stealing a silver spoon, her property, which she gave a child at the door to play with, who having dropped it, the prisoner picked it up and went off with it ... he denied any knowledge of it, but being searched by a constable the spoon was found in his possession. He was committed to Newgate for trial.[36]

The accused man was Thomas Norman, a street scavenger. The charge was grand larceny, stealing property with a value of more than one shilling with no aggravating circumstances. Because the spoon was valued at fifteen pence (1s. 3d.), he was facing a possible death sentence if found guilty. As was customary, the victim or any interested party was the prosecutor, not the state. The husband William Hill actually owned the spoon, but he failed to attend the court case three weeks later, and so the old man was acquitted.[37]

Servants were often accused of stealing from their employers, and one such theft at a London public house was featured by the *Morning Chronicle* in August 1806 in its regular 'Police' column:

> On Sunday se'night a female servant of Mr. Jaggers, of the Hand and Racket, in Whitcomb-street, very unexpectedly left her place. In a short time after she was gone, Mrs. Jaggers discovered that she had been robbed of cash, several articles of plate, and wearing apparel.— Application was made to Donaldson, a constable, to apprehend her; the officer learnt, from her connection in St. Giles's, that she was gone to Bristol, whither he pursued her.[38]

St Giles was the overcrowded warren of narrow streets, courts and alleys centred around Seven Dials, a refuge for beggars, poor street traders and criminals, with a substantial Irish population. For George Donaldson, a Bow Street Runner, it was the obvious place to start pursuing the servant Eleanor Russel, because it was not many streets away from the Hand and Racquet public house. He finally caught up with her in Bristol, just before she sailed to Ireland, as he testified at her trial for 'theft from a specified place': 'GEORGE DONALDSON sworn. I am an officer; I went to Bristol after this woman, I . . . took [arrested] her there; I found the gown, the shirt, the pinafore, and the gold pin, in her box, and two guineas and a half in gold, and three shillings and six pence in silver.'[39]

Despite the value of the recovered items exceeding seventy shillings, the jury merely found her guilty of 'stealing to the value of thirty-nine shillings',[40] a shilling short of a capital punishment for this crime. She was sentenced to seven years' transportation and sailed for New South Wales on board the *Sydney Cove* in January 1807. The transportation register describes her as 'Eleanor ux [*uxor* — Latin for 'spouse'] William Russell',[41] though soon after arriving in Australia she married another convict, Simon McGuigin.[42]

It was rare for any member of the gentry and upper classes to be tried for theft. They were much more likely to buy off the prosecutor before their case came to trial, and if that failed, they had a much greater chance of being acquitted since they could afford to pay for lawyers or resort to bribery. When Mrs Jane Leigh-Perrot was arrested in August 1799 for stealing lace worth twenty shillings from Elizabeth Gregory's shop in Bath, she was refused bail, but instead of being held in the County Gaol at Ilchester, she was allowed to live with her husband in the adjacent prison-keeper's house. For people of their rank, even this situation was intolerable, as a letter written a few months later to Mrs Leigh-Perrot from a cousin reveals: 'You tell me that your good sister Austen has offered you one, or both, of her daughters to continue with you during your stay at that vile place, but you decline the kind offer, as you canot procure them accommodation in the house with you, and you cannot let these elegant young women be your inmates in a prison nor be subject to the inconveniences which you are obliged to put up with.'[43] The two elegant young women were Jane Austen and her sister Cassandra, and Mrs Leigh-Perrot was their aunt.

The trial took place at the next Assizes at Taunton Castle, at the end of March 1800, when Mrs Leigh-Perrot was accused of grand larceny. Whether or not she was guilty of shoplifting (and many believed the shopkeeper had deliberately set out to extort money), the stakes were high because such a high-value theft from a shop was a capital offence. On 22 March, a few days before her trial, William Holland was in Nether Stowey, some 10 miles from Taunton, and he was told about rumours that the prosecutor (the shopkeeper Elizabeth Gregory) had been bribed:

Met Mr Symes the lawyer at Stowey. He told me that Mrs Parrot [Perrot] had bought off her prosecutor. Alas, Alas! that money should be able to screen a person from justice in this kingdom so remarkable for good laws and uncorrupted judges. She was accused of stealing lace out of a shop in Bath, is a person of considerable fortune and has a poor Jerry Sneak of a husband, who adheres to her through all difficulties.[44]

Mrs Leigh-Perrot was acquitted by the jury, but her expenses were considerable. The case was still being gossiped about a month later when Holland was in Bath and went to a different shop from the one that had accused her of theft: 'Went to Brookman's the milliner, a clever woman, sensible and well behaved ... Miss Brookman was present at a detection of Mrs Lee Perrot [in another crime] many years ago, confirmed the fact, everything clear against her.'[45]

Penelope Hind, the long-time friend of Holland, learned in November 1804 that she was once again being accused of theft in Bath, this time of a plant, but no prosecution followed.[46] Five months later, the extremely wealthy Mrs Leigh-Perrot appeared in one of Jane Austen's letters, none too favourably: 'My aunt is in a great hurry to pay me for my cap, but cannot find it in her heart to give me good money.'[47] Instead, Jane was invited to accompany her to 'the Grand Sydney-Garden Breakfast'. Polite society in Bath was already avoiding her aunt, and possibly for this reason Jane declared: 'such an offer I shall of course decline'.[48] Two days later, she added to her letter: 'My Uncle and Aunt drank tea with us last night, and in spite of my resolution to the contrary, I could not help putting forward to invite them again this Evening. I thought it was of the first conse-quence to avoid anything that might seem a slight to them. I shall be glad when it is over.'[49]

Other prisoners on trial at the same Assizes at Taunton in March 1800 were not so lucky as Mrs Leigh-Perrot. Those found guilty included 'John Branch, aged 14, for burglary ... Robert Phillips, for sheep-stealing; Thomas Coles, and William Hartland, for burglary at Langport'.[50] They were all sentenced to death – a real demonstration of the Bloody Code in action – while three more were sentenced to seven years' transportation: 'Wm. Spratt, for stealing wheat from an out-house; Thomas Broadhurst for stealing sundry pieces of muslin from his master, Mr. Slack, of this city [Bath]; and Joseph Jones, for stealing a trunk'.[51]

While it was very rare for any of the elite to be sentenced to death or transportation, even for killing someone, most convicted murder-ers faced execution. Sensational crimes generated lengthy accounts far beyond their locality, and murders were avidly covered by the news-papers. In Somerset on 25 October 1807, Holland wrote in his diary: 'No material news in the paper but a shocking account of a murder committed in Hertfordshire.'[52] The murder scene was a house in the High Street of Hoddesdon village, in the parish of the Reverend William Jones, who wrote in his diary:

Poor, wretched mortals! what horrible consequences follow their being given up into the power of Satan, & their own mad, unbridled passions, for ever so short a season! I know not how even to glance at two most horrid murders, which were last night committed in my parish [Hoddesdon], at old Mr. Borham, the farmer's house. Mrs. Warner, B— m's daughter, who was within 5 or 6 weeks of her delivery, & Mrs. Hummerstone, Batty's housekeeper, were the poor sufferers. The villain's name is Simmons, not more than 20 years of age! To describe the shocking circumstances would be too painful![53]

The newspapers were not so sensitive, and the *Hampshire Chronicle* revelled in the gory detail:

Elizabeth Harris, on seeing his approach, retired within the scullery, and shut the door against him. He demanded admittance, which she refused: high words accordingly arose and he plunged his hand, armed with a knife, through a window-lattice at her, but missed his aim. The noise alarmed the company in the parlour ... Mrs Hummerstone was the first to come forth, in hope of being able to intimidate and send away the disturber, but just as she had reached the back-door, leading from the parlour to the stone-yard, Simmons, who was proceeding to enter the house that way, met her.[54]

Thomas Simmons was a former servant of the house and had been courting Elizabeth, but he had an uncontrollable temper and was judged unstable. She was persuaded to break off the relationship, and Simmons was dismissed. Now he was seeking revenge and attacking anyone in his path:

with his knife he stabbed her [Mrs. Hummerstone] in the jugular artery, and pulling the knife forward, laid open her throat on the left side. She ran forward ... but fell, and rose no more. The murderer pursued his sanguinary purpose, and rushing into the parlour, raised and brandished his bloody knife, swearing a dreadful oath, that 'he would give it to them all'. Mrs. Warner was the person next to him, and without giving her time to rise from the chair, he gave her so many stabs about her neck and breast that she fell from her chair, covered with streams of blood, and expired.[55]

Several others were injured in the confusion, and Elizabeth was again targeted: 'she struggled with him, caught at the knife, and was severely wounded in the hand and arm. The knife fell in the struggle. She, however, got out at the back door, and made her way into the street, where, by her screams of murder, she alarmed the neighbourhood.'[56] Simmons fled and tried to hide, but was arrested, covered in blood.

When the trial took place at Hertford Assizes, the counsel for the prosecution 'intreated them [the jury] to dismiss from their minds all they had heard elsewhere, and attend only to the evidence'.[57] The jury found Simmons guilty, and the young man was hanged three days later, on Monday 7 March 1808. It was suggested that he suffered from hallucinations.

In this instance, murder had definitely been committed, but the circumstances of death were not always so clear, as little forensic investigation of sudden deaths was carried out. Some murders certainly went undetected, and in April 1808 Nelly Weeton told a friend about a suicide case at Upholland in Lancashire that seemed more like murder:

an old woman ... quite a cripple, was found hung in about two hours after her husband (who was a good deal younger) had left her to go to his work. She was suspended from the tester [canopy over a bed] at the foot of the bed. From her being such a cripple, the neighbours say she could not possibly have done it herself, and her husband, who has been known to have used her ill, is strongly suspected to have done it. But no proof can be brought.[58]

Suicide or 'self-murder' was a crime because it was considered blasphemy by the Church and it robbed the king of a subject. The archaic legal term was *felo de se* (Latin for 'felon of oneself'). Although insanity was technically no defence, coroners' juries often found that a suicide was 'not of a sound mind', because if a suicide was judged sane, his property was forfeited. Anyone assisting a suicide was tried for murder, but one problem for the law was how to punish the corpse for the crime. All that could be done was to deny burial in consecrated ground. In 1790, the year before his own death, the Methodist preacher John Wesley expressed his thoughts:

> there is no country in Europe, or perhaps in the habitable world, where the horrid crime of self-murder is so common as it is in England! ... we have laws against it, and officers with juries are appointed to inquire into every fact of the kind. And these are to give their verdict upon oath, whether the self-murderer was sane or insane. If he is brought in insane, he is excused, and the law does not affect him. By this means it is totally eluded, for the juries constantly bring him in insane ... let a law be made and rigorously executed, that the body of every self-murderer, lord or peasant, shall be hanged in chains, and the English fury [the high suicide rate] will cease at once.[59]

Few agreed with Wesley, and some thought that eradicating the gloomy preaching of the Methodists would be more effective in decreasing the number of suicides.

Spending money on criminals was unpopular, which ruled out imprisonment as the main method of punishment. Prisons were largely for those awaiting trial, transportation or execution, but debt could lead to people ending up in prison (gaol) for a long time, because usually the only way a creditor had of recovering money was to have the debtor imprisoned until he paid up. Since many individuals had no money to pay debts, they might be confined for lengthy periods, and being held in a debtors' prison was itself costly.

The stupidity of such punishment was obvious to Benjamin Silliman: 'There is a great number of debtors confined in Newgate and the adjoining prisons, and most of them are immured for small sums, and have little hope of escaping, because they are miserably poor.'[60] Such was the case with the Devon County debtors' prison, called Sheriff's Ward, in the St Thomas suburb of Exeter, which the penal reformer John Howard visited: 'In 1779 one debtor, on attachment from the court of chancery, had continued here from May

KING's THEATRE.

TO-MORROW will be performed the favourite Comic Opera, called, IL FORBO CONTRO IL FORBO. In which Madame Catalani will perform the principal Character.

End of the Opera (2d time), a new grand Indian Ballet, called CONSTANCE ET ALMOZOR, composed by Mr. D'Egville, with entire new Sceneryy, Dresses and Decorations; the Music by F. Venna.

On Tuesday, May 31, will be produced a New Comic Opera, called, Le Virtuose in Pugtiglio; in which Signior Miartini will make his first appearance on this stage, and in which Madame Catalani will perform the principal character.

Mr. JOHNSTONE's NIGHT.
THEATRE-ROYAL, DRURY-LANE.

THIS EVENING, FALSE ALARMS; in which will be introduced the following Songs: 'Should e'er I brave the foaming Seas.' 'A Smile and a Tear;' and 'Smiling Kate.' End of the Play, the favourite Comic Interlude of SYLVESTER DAGGERWOOD; Sylvester Daggerwood, Mr. Bannister, with a new Comic Song, called 'The Tragedy of Othello, or fine Fleecy Hosiery.' To which will be added (first time), compressed into two Acts, a Musical Comedy, which will open with a Grand Masquerade, in which will be introduced a Shawl Dance, by Miss Gayton; and a new Allemande and Waltz, by Mr. D'Egville's pupils, called the IRISH-MAN IN ITALY. O'Rafarty, by Mr. Johnstone, who will introduce the following Songs: 'O'Rafarty's Christening,' 'A Chapter on Pockets,' 'The Bold Dragoon,' and 'Paddy Shannon's Court-ship, or the Cruel Widow Wilkins.'

Performances at theatres in London advertised in *The Times* newspaper for 23 May 1808.

A state lottery ticket sold in 1808, a one-sixteenth share. The lottery was drawn from 20 October 1809.

LACKINGTON'S CATALOGUE.

This Day is published, Price 1s. 6d.

THE FIRST PART of a VERY EXTENSIVE and VALUABLE COLLECTION OF BOOKS; Containing the Classes—Books of Prints, and other costly Works —Atlasses, Maps and Plans—English History, Biography and Topography—Books relating to Scotland and Ireland—Foreign and General History, Antiquities, Voyages, Travels, Biography, &c. —Miscellanies, Moral Philosophy, Criticism, Education, Political Science, Law, Periodical Writings, Romances, and other Works of Fiction, &c. &c. which are now on Sale, at very low Prices, for ready Money, by LACKINGTON, HUGHES, HARDING, MAVOR, and JONES, Finsbury-square, London.

The Second Part of this Catalogue will be published in the ensuing Month, and the remaining Portions as early as they can be passed through the Press.

Libraries purchased or exchanged on the most liberal Terms.

The latest catalogue of Lackington's bookseller in London being advertised in the *St James Chronicle* newspaper on 19 June 1817.

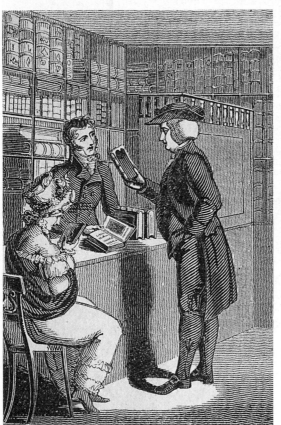

A bookseller with two customers choosing books.

Obverse and reverse of a halfpenny token issued in 1795 by Lackington's bookseller in Finsbury Square, London. The obverse had a portrait of James Lackington while the reverse claimed to be the 'Cheapest Booksellers in the World'. Lackington's issued vast quantities of tokens (about 700,000) in 1794–5, during the first two years of moving to their larger premises.

A view of Hotwells spa, near Bristol, in 1801. The spa was at the foot of the cliffs overlooking the River Avon, where hot springs were located.

Front page of the *Morning Chronicle* newspaper for 24 October 1807, with numerous advertisements, typical of newspapers at that time.

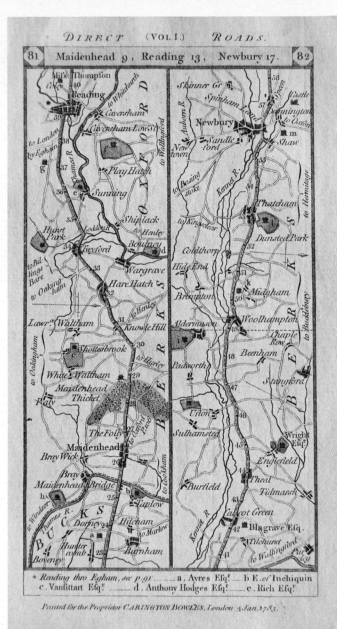

A road map of January 1785 showing the route from Newbury eastwards to Woolhampton, Theale, Reading, Hare Hatch (where the Leigh-Perrots lived) and Maidenhead, along the Bath road from London.

William Tomlins, a crossing sweeper and beggar. His stand was on Piccadilly in London, between Albemarle and St James's Streets.

A coachmaker constructing a post-chaise.

A woman being burned at the stake, used to illustrate the chapbook recounting the execution of Christian Bowman in March 1789 for counterfeiting coins.

An apothecary (or druggist) making his own medicines.

Ching's Worm Lozenges advertised in the *St James Chronicle* newspaper for 19 June 1817, claiming to cure and prevent intestinal worms.

A beggar with a wooden leg and crutches, then a common sight in England, especially with injured soldiers and sailors returning from the wars.

Newcastle's charitable infirmary depicted in 1789. It was constructed in 1751 on Forth Banks and was extended in 1803. The building was demolished in the 1950s.

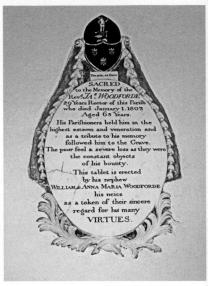

No. 8 College Street in Winchester, Hampshire, where Jane Austen died on 18 July 1817.

The memorial tablet to the Reverend ('Parson') James Woodforde inside All Saints church, Weston Longville, Norfolk. It was erected by his nephew Bill and niece Nancy.

The cathedral at Winchester in 1809, where Jane Austen was buried in 1817 beneath the floor of the north aisle of the nave.

1758 ... but at my last visit he was dead. Here is still an older prisoner, *Grace Hooper*, whose warrant of commitment is dated 30th of November 1741.'[61] Grace had been a prisoner there for over forty years. Howard noted Exeter's table of charges:

A TABLE of the RATES and FEES allowed to be taken
by the Keeper of the Sheriff's Ward for the County of *Devon.* £. s. d.

For the commitment fee of every prisoner for debt, damages,
and contempts though it be on several actions or processes only   0 13 4

To the turnkey   0 1 0

For every *liberate*   0 2 0

For the use of a bed in a single room for one person by the
week   0 3 0

The use of a room where there are two or more beds and
two lodge in a bed each person   0 1 3

The use of the common room if the keeper finds bedding
each person by the week   0 1 0

If the prisoner finds bedding   nothing[62]

A debtor could usually pay for extras by arrangement with the prison-keeper. Charges varied between prisons, but there were always some compulsory fees, such as for beds, because many prisons were privately run businesses.

Houses of correction, or 'bridewells', were for punishing minor offenders who had been given short sentences of imprisonment by Justices of the Peace. Most were put to hard labour during their sentence. The original Bridewell was a combined prison and poor-house converted from one of Henry VIII's London palaces. By the eighteenth century the term was used loosely for a local prison for minor offenders, for a workhouse or for a combination of both. During his penal reform work, Howard inspected England's county gaols, but was unimpressed by the County Bridewell at Winchester in Hampshire:

The four rooms are too close, and the court (which is not paved, 37 feet 5 inches, by 13 feet 10) is too small for the prisoners, who are commonly

numerous; especially at quarter sessions, when they are brought hither
from the other bridewells. There is only *one* day-room (26 feet by 20 feet
4 inches) for *men* and *women* ... At my visit in 1779, there were four *young
women*, and in 1782 five, among the prisoners ... This prison has been
fatal to vast numbers.[63]

Many houses of correction kept inmates crammed together, provided
poor food and dire sanitation and often had no source of water within
the building. Disease always threatened, and typhus, often called
'gaol fever', was a frequent killer. It was probably the cause of so
many deaths at Winchester.

In this period when England was often at war, another Winchester
prison housed foreign prisoners-of-war, one of many such prisons for
those men (mainly ordinary soldiers and sailors) who were considered
unlikely to honour their word not to escape.[64] From time to time Jane
Austen must have witnessed them being marched from ports to their
place of imprisonment, especially as prisoners-of-war were at
Southampton where she lived from 1806 to 1809. William Darter
described some he saw in Reading: 'One day, about the year 1813, I
saw a long line of French prisoners escorted down London Street to
the "Saracen's Head" stables, where they were put with clean straw to
lie down upon; they were formed three or four deep, and presented a
very miserable appearance, their clothes being in rags, and shoes
nearly worn out.'[65]

In numerous 'parole towns', captured officers who gave their word
of honour (*parole d'honneur*) not to try to escape were allowed freedom within the limits of the town. One parole town was Odiham in
Hampshire, 10 miles north of Chawton where Jane Austen later
lived, and another was Alresford, about 9 miles to the south-west.
She almost certainly saw and may even have met foreign officers on
parole in such places. They tried to live as normal lives as possible,
were often accepted by the gentry and sometimes married and settled
in England.

Hundreds of prisoners-of-war of lower rank were confined
aboard prison hulks – redundant naval ships with their masts
removed, which were converted into floating prisons and moored

in rivers and creeks. These hulks had initially been sanctioned for housing convicted criminals ('convicts') by a law passed in 1776 when the American War of Independence stopped the transportation of convicts to the former colonies. When convicts began being sent to Australia, the hulks were also used to hold prisoners-of-war.

Transportation to America had begun in the seventeenth century. This was the punishment given to Alice Walker when she was tried at the Old Bailey on 9 September 1772 for stealing from Thomas Atkins two days earlier. She was accused of taking a canvas bag and some money, worth more than £24 in all. 'I did not rob him at all;' she said in her defence, 'he took me to Bartholomew fair, and asked me to drink; he asked me to go to the Inn, I went with him; then he asked me to go down into the country with him, and gave me the money to buy some wearing apparel. I did not confess I took the money, he gave it me.'[66] The jury found Alice guilty of theft (grand larceny). She was sentenced to transportation and sailed for America in the *Justitia*, landing at Rappahannock, Virginia, in March 1773.[67] Like her fellow convicts, she was sold as an indentured servant – effectively a slave – to plantation owners looking for labour. The local newspaper, the *Virginia Gazette*, carried advertisements of such sales:

JUST ARRIVED *in RAPPAHANNOCK, The* GOOD INTENT, *Captain* CLODD, With FORTY HEALTHY INDENTED SERVANTS, among whom are many TRADESMEN, particularly shoemakers, a cooper, a tailor, a carpenter and joiner, a blacksmith and farrier, some good clerks, a surgeon, several country labourers, some fine boys, many good sempstresses, mantuamakers, house women &c. &c. The sale will commence at Leedstown on Tuesday the 3rd of August; and, if required, a reasonable credit will be allowed, on giving bond and approved security.[68]

Alice was purchased by two prominent members of the colony, Sampson and George Matthews, but after only a few weeks she made a bid for freedom. The same newspaper carried a notice of the reward offered for her recapture:

TEN POUNDS REWARD. RUN away, last night [May 1773] ...
English convict servants, viz. JOHN EATON, by trade a shipcarpenter,
about 23 years of age, and 5 feet 3 or 4 inches high; had on, and took with
him, a blue broadcloth coat and breeches, a Damascus waistcoat, a pair of
ticken trousers, worsted stockings, three striped cotton shirts, one
oznabrig [coarse linen] over shirt, a felt hat, and a pair of old shoes.
ALICE EATON, alias WALKER (who goes for the said John Eaton's
wife) a low, well set woman, about 20 years of age, and has sandy coloured
hair; had on a brown stuff gown, a red stuff petticoat, and four red silk
handkerchiefs ... Whoever secures the above servants in any gaol, so
that we may get them, shall receive FIVE POUNDS, and if brought to
Mr. Sampson Matthews, in Richmond, the above reward. SAMPSON &
GEORGE MATTHEWS. All masters of vessels are hereby forwarned
from carrying either of the said servants out of the colony.[69]

Despite this warning, Alice did manage to sail back to England, but
was then recognised and rearrested. This time the offence was returning from transportation before the end of her sentence. She was found
guilty and sentenced to death, but the jury recommended mercy. In July
1774 her sentence was changed to fourteen years' transportation.[70]

People could be punished with transportation for extremely minor
crimes, such as Robert Jones, a pickpocket who was sentenced in
May 1774 to seven years' transportation for stealing a linen handkerchief.[71] The following January, Elizabeth Smith received the same
sentence, this time for stealing twelve pounds of sugar valued at four
shillings.[72] After the American War of Independence started, over ten
years elapsed before convicts began to be transported to Australia,
and the first fleet of ships sailed for Botany Bay on 13 May 1787.
Between then and 1810 over twelve thousand convicts were sent to
Australia. Several ships, often carrying over a thousand convicts
between them, sailed every year until 1868.[73] Transportation was considered a deterrent to crime and usefully removed many criminals
from England, but it was not without expense. To reduce costs the
Government passed the responsibility for transportation to private
contractors, and it was their cost-cutting that caused many of the
hardships suffered by the convicts during their voyage to Australia.

Because of the reluctance to use imprisonment as punishment, anyone convicted of crimes not sufficiently serious to warrant the death sentence or transportation might well receive corporal punishment such as the pillory or whipping. The pillory was intended to expose offenders to public shame and ridicule. It had a wooden frame, usually on a raised platform or scaffolding, and the culprit stood with head and hands placed through openings in a tightly secured, two-part hinged wooden board. If offenders were lucky, they were pelted with soft missiles such as eggs, something Darter witnessed:

> About the year 1811 or 1812 I was standing with my father near the *Mercury* Office [in Reading], when a man was placed in the pillory, which stood in a central part of the Market Place, for some offence; and the people threw eggs at him, many missing. I saw Mr. Moody, the coach proprietor, bring two baskets of eggs ... and he threw so well that the poor fellow, whose head and arms were fixed, was literally covered with yolks of eggs and other matter, and to complete the affair he was bespattered with refuse from Hiscock's slaughter house. I don't know what his offence was.[74]

If the crowd was particularly hostile, they would throw all manner of missiles, including stones, causing serious injury or even death. It was this unpredictable nature of the pillory as a form of punishment that led to it being used only for minor offences or as an additional penalty for a serious crime.

For other crimes culprits might be publicly whipped, sometimes from where the crime had been committed to where they lived, or over some other specified distance. They were tied to the back of a cart and made to walk, as Darter described:

> A man of the labouring class, living on the west side of Silver Street [in Reading], in one of those old houses which have overhanging eaves ... had been out of work for some time and in want of food. In passing up Castle Street he stole a loaf of bread from the shop of a baker of the name of Turner. He was apprehended, tried and sentenced ... to be publicly

whipped at the cart's tail from the Grey Friars Prison to his cottage in Silver Street. He was stripped to his waist, and he had to walk behind a horse and cart with his hands so tied that he could not alter his position.[75]

Darter was so appalled that the memory of the scene never faded:

When the crowd arrived opposite our house, I ran to see the cause of it. I then witnessed a shocking sight ... There was not a portion of this poor fellow's back that was not literally cut into shreds; his sufferings were dreadful, and with the blood running down, it presented a dreadful and sickening sight. I merely followed at a distance to see where they took him ... In point of fact, the poor fellow, for merely stealing a loaf, was whipped to death, for he never left his room alive; therefore, for this trifling offence, this man was punished to a greater extent than would have happened had he committed murder.[76]

Desperation drove many to crime, anything from stealing a loaf of bread to murder. In December 1775, the same month Jane Austen was born, her local newspaper reported the execution of an unmarried mother who had killed her newborn son in London:

Sarah Reynolds was executed at Tyburn ... for the murder of her bastard child. The unhappy convict wept bitterly, and was very intent on her devotions. The fate of this unhappy woman naturally gives rise to the following reflections: What a false pride is that which can induce a woman to murder her own infant, rather than submit to a temporary disgrace? What punishment is due to a man who willfully debauches a poor girl, and then refuses to make her the only reparation in his power by marriage?[77]

Sarah had given birth to a healthy boy, strangled him with a handkerchief and dumped his body in 'a ditch or gully-hole by Broad Street, Mary-le-bon',[78] a watercourse probably located north of Oxford Street.[79] She was tried for infanticide, found guilty and ordered 'to be executed ... and her body to be afterwards dissected and anatomized'.[80] With the death penalty intended as a deterrent, executions were performed in public, usually by hanging. A noose was put around the condemned person's neck, and the rope was either hauled up or, more often, the cart or other support was removed to leave the victim hanging. Strangulation was usually the cause of death, but some fell so violently that they broke their necks.

Sarah was hanged at Tyburn, which was London's public place of execution, but because the final journey of prisoners from Newgate prison to Tyburn became such a carnival, not the sober warning the authorities desired, executions were later moved to Newgate. The first ones took place there on 9 December 1783, when nine men and one woman were executed on a temporary scaffold.[81] A different method of execution was introduced as well – a noose was placed round the neck of each prisoner, and they were then dropped through a trapdoor. One Oxford newspaper, in a lengthy account of the new location, commented:

> The unhappy Criminals themselves acknowledged the Propriety of the Change, and professed themselves happy in not being, as usual, dragged through the Streets from Newgate to Tyburn. A Bell tolled all the Time of the Ceremony, and produced a wonderful Effect upon the Prisoners [in Newgate] who survived their more unfortunate Fellows. The Spectators who attended appeared much impressed by the solemnity of the Ceremony.[82]

Nearly all urban centres had their own gallows, usually erected for a particular execution and dismantled afterwards, and occasionally criminals were hanged at the scene of their crime. Following execution, the body might be 'hung in chains' in a public place as a warning to others – this involved the corpse being bound by iron chains or fitted into a cage of iron bands to hold it together while it rotted. Sometimes the corpse was coated with tar to delay putrefaction. In March 1785 Woodforde remarked on the trials at Thetford in Norfolk:

> At the Assizes at Thetford in this county 8 Prisoners were condemned, three of the above were reprieved. The other five left for execution. One J⁵ Cliffen a most daring fellow was hanged ... on Thursday last at Norwich on Castle-Hill and behaved most daringly audacious. His crime

was robbing 2 old men, brothers, by names Seaman on the Yaxham Road, knocked them both down first of which blows one of them died soon after; the other recovered. Cliffen's body was this day carried to Badley Moor and there hung in chains at one corner of the said moor.[83]

Over a week later Woodforde and a manservant 'took a ride ... thro' Hockering, North-Tuddenham to Baddeley Moor where Cliffen stands in chains, most shocking road all around where he stands ... thought we should have been mired'.[84]

Gibbets with corpses suspended from them were such features of the landscape that they were landmarks for travellers, and Johnson Grant described the Sheffield neighbourhood '*adorned* with men hanging in chains'.[85] Gibbets were commonly set up on waste ground within sight of thoroughfares, but one anonymous author of the poem 'On The New Gibbet On Hounslow Heath' considered some were too close to the highway, causing a foul stench:

> In former times, whene'er in chains
> Judges hung rogues up, like Jack Hains,
> Whose Gibbets, Hounslow-heath adorning,
> To their old fellow-rogues gave warning,
> 'Twas thought the Gibbets did their duty
> If they stood near enough to shew t'ye
> Their tenants in a distant ken,
> Far from the highway path of men.
> So distant stood they, no offence
> Was giv'n to any other sense.
> But K_ _, or some Judge as wise,
> Not satisfied to strike our eyes,
> Now sets his gibbet at our noses;
> And, forasmuch as he supposes
> That folks may turn their head or wink,
> He makes examples by the stink.[86]

Whatever remained of the corpse was eventually taken down and buried in unconsecrated ground. In Reading in the early 1800s Darter saw one that was discovered 'in sinking a grave at the north-west corner of the church-yard (as you enter to the Butts); it seemed perfect, but it had on the legs and wrists, rings with a chain which were attached to a ring in the centre; on inquiry I was informed that this man must have been hung in chains, as the ground where the body lay was for many years appropriated to the burial of those who were executed at Gallows Tree Common.'[87]

In the eyes of the law, criminals found guilty of treason deserved the harshest penalties of all. Women were burned at the stake, while men were hung, drawn and quartered. In 1782 David Tyrie was put on trial at Winchester Assizes for

> falsely, wickedly, and traitorously, (being a subject of Great Britain) compassing, imagining and intending, the king of and from the royal state, crown, title, power, and government of Great Britain, to depose and wholly deprive; and the king to kill, and bring and put to death, and to fulfil, perfect, and bring to effect, his treason, compassings and imaginations, as such a false traitor, falsely, wickedly and traitorously composing and writing, and causing to be composed and wrote, divers letters.[88]

The indictment goes on at length in this overblown legal language, but basically Tyrie had been caught sending letters to the French giving sensitive strategic information about the Royal Navy. As a clerk in a naval office at Portsmouth, he was well placed to obtain such information.

There was little doubt that Tyrie was guilty of spying, and he was sentenced to be hung, drawn and quartered at Portsmouth on 24 August 1782:

> The Crowd of People of all Ranks assembled by Four o'Clock this Morning at the Gates of the Gaol to see Tyrie set off for the Place of Execution, was very great. About Five o'Clock he was put into a Coach with six Horses, attended by the Ordinary, Under Sheriff, Gaoler, &c. and conveyed to Portsmouth, where being delivered up to the Mayor and Police of the Town, he was drawn on a Sledge to the Place of Execution. After praying a little Time he was turned off, and hanged till

almost dead; was then cut down, his head severed from his Body, his Bowels taken out, and his Heart shewed to the surrounding Multitude, and then thrown into a Fire made for that Purpose; the Body was then quartered, and put into a Coffin. The Concourse of People was immense, and such was the singular Avarice of many who were near the Body, that happy was he who could procure a Finger, or some Vestige of the Criminal.[89]

Tyrie was the last man to be executed in this way. Although men in later trials were given the same sentence, they were simply hanged or else hanged and their corpse beheaded.

Other treasonable offences included counterfeiting, and in 1789 husband and wife 'Hugh and Christian Bowman were convicted of counterfeiting divers pieces of base metal so as to resemble shillings and sixpences.'[90] Christian was taken from Newgate and 'chained to the stake, placed a few yards nearer Newgate-street than the scaffold, and a stool being taken from beneath her feet, she was suspended by the neck for near half an hour, when the faggots surrounding her were set on fire, and her body was consumed to ashes'.[91] Because this kind of execution was unusual, her story was quickly written and printed as a chapbook, described as 'The Life and Death of Christian Bowman, Alias Murphy; Who was burnt at a Stake, in the Old Bailey, on Wednesday the 18th of March 1789 for High Treason in feloniously and traitorously counterfeiting the Silver Coin of the Realm. Containing her Birth and Parentage, youthful Adventures, Love Amours, fatal Marriage, unhappy Connections, and untimely Death.'[92]

The law changed the following year, 1790, and the sentence for such crimes for both men and women was reduced to hanging or transportation. Those convicted of capital crimes were being increasingly sentenced to transportation, and many people condemned to death were reprieved and transported. It was not until the 1820s–30s that the death penalty was abolished for numerous lesser offences – the last person hanged for stealing a sheep was executed in 1831.[93]

Surprisingly, riots were not generally punished by death or transportation, unless the rioters were guilty of other crimes, and people

were certainly not deterred from protesting against personal hardships like lack of work and food. Some riots were more sinister,
verging on revolution, and summoning the troops was often the only
way of quelling them. On 29 October 1795 Woodforde and his niece
Nancy witnessed an assassination attempt on George III during a riot
in London:

> As we heard when we got to London that the Sessions of Parliament was
> to be opened this day, at one o'clock I walked with Nancy to St. James's
> Park about half a mile, where at two o'clock or rather after we saw the
> King go in his State Coach drawn with eight fine cream-coloured horses
> in red morrocco-leather harness, to the House of Lords. The Park was
> uncommonly crouded indeed, never was known a greater concourse of
> people before, and I am very [sorry] to insert that his Majesty was very
> grossly insulted by some of the Mob, and had a very narrow escape of
> being killed going to the House, a ball [bullet] passing thro' the windows
> as he went thro' old Palace-Yard, supposed to be discharged from an air
> gun, but very fortunately did not strike the King or Lords.[94]

The jeers of the crowd that day were mingled with shouts of 'Give us
peace and bread!', 'No war!', and 'No King!'[95] – as ever, the king and
his government were blamed for prices having risen to famine levels,
causing widespread hardship. It was with some difficulty that a strong
force of Guards enabled the royal coach to reach Parliament.

The crowd did not disperse, and Woodforde watched as the king
departed:

> On his return from the House to James's Palace he was very much hissed
> and hooted at, and on his going from St. James's to the Queen's Palace in
> his private coach, he had another very lucky escape, as the mob sur-
> rounded his coach and one of them was going to open the door but the
> Horse Guards coming up very providentially at the time, prevented any
> further danger. The state-coach windows going from St. James's to the
> Mews were broke all to pieces by the Mob, but no other damage done to
> the coach ... The Mob was composed of the most violent and lowest
> Democrats. Thank God the King received no injury whatever, neither did

we as it happened . . . It was said that there were near two hundred thousand people in St. James Park about 3 o'clock. I never was in such a croud in all my Life.[96]

This was by no means the largest riot of the era. Serious disturbances had taken place four years earlier in Birmingham against dissenters, and before that anti-Catholic riots had terrified London in early June 1780, incited by Lord George Gordon. For several days, the mob effectively had a free hand, despite being confronted by troops.[97] Many buildings were set ablaze and several prisons destroyed, including Newgate and the Fleet. It was the worst riot in London's history and was brought under control only when large numbers of troops were ordered into the capital with instructions to shoot to kill.

Riots on a smaller scale were endemic, and Woodforde's diaries are littered with incidents. At the beginning of 1801, another year of shortages, successive entries show the growing unrest, as in early April: 'A great many mobs or risings of the poor in many parts of the country, said to be owing to the enormous price that wheat is at, risings in Somersetshire particularly named. Pray God! preserve our friends we have there.'[98] Only five days later he noted: 'Mobs in the West of England, Plymouth, Wellington and other places on account of the dearness of corn and other provisions – some lives lost.'[99] Many disturbances were not true riots but the actions of desperate crowds, often of angry women, whose purpose was to force a farmer, miller or baker to sell at the old uninflated prices. Although such actions were illegal, many sympathetic magistrates ignored them, particularly if no violence was used.

People were trying to survive in difficult circumstances, and one way was through the crimes of smuggling and buying goods from smugglers, something that people of all classes did. Because taxes on imported goods were particularly resented, there was no stigma in purchasing smuggled goods. Even clergymen happily bought from smugglers, though people with status were fearful of informers. In October 1792 Woodforde recorded: 'John Buck, the blacksmith, who was lately informed against for having a tub of gin found in his house that was smuggled, by two excise officers, was pretty easy fined'[100] –

something of an understatement, since Buck was a key smuggler in that part of Norfolk. Smugglers were shielded because few people would testify against them, and even magistrates were their customers. Some of the elite actually financed smuggling ventures and were powerful enough to influence or bribe the authorities to protect their associates.

So many people were involved in smuggling that it was only a partially covert trade. Smugglers were often surprisingly open about their activities, and it was not unusual to come across caravans of smuggled goods comprising more than a hundred packhorses or a long string of carts. One day in September 1790 John Byng stopped at an inn at Aylesford in Kent and gazed enviously at some fine horses: 'We saw, whilst at dinner, a gang of well-mounted smugglers pass by. How often have I wish'd to be able to purchase a horse from their excellent stables.'[101]

Such gangs often outnumbered the excisemen, who dared not tackle them or were easily bribed to stay away. Occasionally, excisemen were keen to publicise significant captures, as in June 1792 when *The Times* reported: 'A gang of near 100 smugglers, a few nights since, were overtaken by the Supervisor of Yarmouth, and three other officers, near Helmsley Beech, and, with very little resistance, had seven carts and eight horses taken from them, containing 1012 gallons of gin, and 200 wt. [2 cwt] of tobacco, the largest seizure ever remembered by so small a number of persons.'[102]

The biggest single market was London, where smuggled merchandise was openly peddled in the streets, something that Benjamin Silliman noticed:

as I was returning home from the strand, a short fat man, in a scarlet waistcoat, addressed me in this style; 'young gentleman–sir–your honour!' So many titles, in such rapid succession, made me stop short, when he put his mouth to my ear, and said in a low voice; 'I have got some nice French cambric, will you buy?' ... To-day, while I was passing rapidly along Holborn, a fellow singled me out with his eye, and after following me a few paces through the crowd, said with a low, cautious voice, 'sir, sir, will you buy a little French cambric? I have some very fine' ... They were undoubtedly smugglers of that article, and had either evaded or defied the laws of the country.[103]

With London expanding at a rapid rate, there was a growing market for both legal and illicit goods, and all kinds of criminals besides smugglers were attracted to the city. It was effectively a boom town, seen as a place of boundless opportunities. In the popular comedy *The Heir-at-Law* by George Colman the Younger, first performed in 1797, one character sings a few lines conveying that message:

> Oh, London is a fine town,
> A very famous city,
> Where all the streets are paved with gold,
> And all the maidens pretty.[104]

Not everyone took such a rose-tinted view, and visitors from the countryside rightly saw the city as the crime capital of England. William Jones in 1803 summed up the views of many: 'Returned from Town last night, where I had been since Wedny., & I never came home with more pleasure. Nothing, I think, could tempt me to live in London; indeed, its bustle, & dissipation, (without taking its fog & variety of stench into account), would soon destroy me.'[105]

ELEVEN

MEDICINE MEN

Nobody is healthy in London, nobody can be.

Emma, by Jane Austen

Illness or accident could happen to anyone, irrespective of their rank in society, but how they were treated depended on what they could afford to pay. In October 1815 Jane Austen's brother Henry was seriously ill in London. 'Henry is an excellent patient, lies quietly in bed and is ready to swallow anything,' she told Cassandra. 'He lives upon medicine, tea and barley water.'[1] It is unlikely that his medicine was proving beneficial, because so little was understood of the nature of illnesses, infection and treatment. Even minor medical complaints generated fear, and unexplained deaths were especially unnerving.

Letters and diaries of the time are littered with obsessive details of daily evacuations and putrid discharges, all trying to make sense of the body's behaviour. 'I have had an attack of my old complaint,' Nelly Weeton confided in a letter to her brother Tom in 1809,

a pain at my stomach, brought on by eating sallad with a little vinegar, and drinking milk to it. The milk turned sour, and came up again as black as ink; and from that time till within these two days I have scarcely been able to crawl. My appetite was quite gone. Last Saturday I ventured to get an emetic at a Druggist's. I took it that afternoon, and got up an amazing quantity of yellow stuff, since which time I have recovered rapidly.[2]

While medical knowledge advanced slowly, deep ignorance prevailed. The world of superstition merged imperceptibly into that of folk wisdom, and much was blamed on the weather or the moon. Before going to the expense of calling on a professional medical man, it was customary to try remedies known to the family or possibly a local healer. Alternatively, information was obtained from the growing number of medical books or herbalist manuals such as *Culpeper's Complete Herbal*. James Woodforde habitually tried such cures. In his diary for 23 March 1779 he described a method of first aid: 'in shaving my face this morning I happened to cut one of my moles which bled much, and happening also to kill a small moth that was flying about, I applied it to my mole and it instantaneously stopped the bleeding'.[3] On another occasion he had a painful sty:

> The stiony on my right eye-lid still swelled and inflamed very much. As it is commonly said that the eye-lid being rubbed by the tail of a black cat would do it much good if not entirely cure it, and having a black cat, a little before dinner I made a trial of it, and very soon after dinner I found my eye-lid much abated of the swelling and almost free from pain. I cannot therefore but conclude it to be of the greatest service to a stiony on the eye-lid. Any other cats tail may have the above effect in all probability – but I did my eye-lid with my own black tom cat's tail.[4]

After putting his faith in a feline cure, his eye worsened: 'My right eye again, that is, its eye-lid much inflamed again and rather painful. I put on a plaistor to it this morning, but in the aft[ernoon] took it of[f] again, as I perceived no good from it.'[5] The following day brought mixed results: 'My eye-lid is I think rather better than it was, I bathed it with warm milk and water last night. I took a little rhubarb going to bed to night. My eye-lid about noon rather worse owing perhaps to the warm milk and water, therefore just before dinner I washed it well with cold water and in the evening appeared much better for it.'[6]

The root of rhubarb, dried and powdered for medicinal purposes, was a popular cure-all, and in February 1807 William Holland wrote down a description of how it was used:

[I] mounted my horse and rode to farmer Morle. He seemed poorly and feverish and had a bad cough. I told him he should take something. He answer'd that he did not like doctor's stuff. I asked him whether he had got any rhubarb. He believ'd there was some so they brought sad stuff. However I called for a grater, put my hand in my pocket and took out a lump of rhubarb and grated it and then some ginger and mixed all together and then had some brandy and water and made him presently a draught and off it went and they all seemed wonderfully pleased.[7]

A few days later, he was convinced that his remedy had worked: 'He is got pure and well since I gave him a dose of rhubarb.'[8]

Woodforde also habitually used rhubarb for all manner of ailments: 'I was taken very ill this afternoon with a violent pain in my right ear and it continued so till I went to bed. I took a good dose of rhubarb.'[9] The next day he felt unwell:

I got up very ill this morning about 8 o'clock, having had very little sleep all the night, owing to the pain in my ear which was much worse in the night and broke and a good deal of blood only came away. The pain continued still very bad all the morning, tho' not quite so bad as before. It made me very uneasy abt it. A throbbing pain in my ear continued till I went to bed. I put a rosted onion in my ear going to bed to night.[10]

An onion roasted in embers was an old herbal remedy, one recommended by *Culpeper's Complete Herbal*: 'The juice of Onions . . . takes away all blemishes, spots and marks in the skin: and dropped in the ears eases the pains and noise of them.'[11] Woodforde also tested various cures on his niece Nancy and on his servants. One servant was probably suffering from malaria, which was then common in England: 'My boy Jack [Wharton] had another touch of the ague about noon. I gave him a dram of gin at the beginning of the fit and pushed him headlong into one of my ponds and ordered him to bed immediately and he was better after it – and had nothing of the cold fit after, but was very hot.'[12]

If all else failed, an apothecary, a surgeon or a physician might be consulted. Apothecaries (druggists) were allowed to prescribe, prepare and sell substances for medicinal purposes, but many of these were little better than the strange concoctions sold by itinerant quacks. Such professional treatment often cost a great deal and may even have caused more harm than the folklore remedies. Many in the medical profession were not highly regarded, and as he set out on an excursion from London in 1781, John Byng was hoping to remain healthy so that he could avoid the country doctors: 'We are tolerably well accompany'd with touring, road books, maps &c., and I am also stock'd with James's powder; so shou'd a fever overtake me, I will hope that by taking some of his doses and being well wrap't up in blankets I shall chase away sickness, without consulting the medical country blockheads, who kill, or cure, by chance.'[13] In a diary entry in January 1800, Holland was of a similar opinion, saying of his local surgeon from Nether Stowey: 'met Mr. Forbes on foot going to kill a few patients'.[14]

Most surgeons were reasonably educated, and in their early to mid-teens they were apprenticed from three to seven years to surgeons or surgeon-apothecaries. At the end of their apprenticeship some continued practising without formal qualifications, while others were examined in London so that they could become members of the Company of Surgeons, a professional body formed when surgeons broke away from barber-surgeons in 1745.[15] Many surgeons had medical degrees from universities such as Edinburgh, Glasgow and Leiden. London had no university, but it was an important medical centre where students were taught in private anatomy schools and by walking the wards at the leading charitable hospitals, practising their art on the poor.

Holland's acquaintance Penelope Benwell (later Hind) was distressed by the situation of the poor: 'In sickness they must labour on till they sink into their beds; when there they have often neither medicine or food to assist them.'[16] Catherine Hutton was equally concerned about the plight of the poor, and when staying at Blackpool in August 1788, she heard about the 'Whitworth Doctors', James and John Taylor, from the village of Whitworth near Rochdale: 'Surgery is practised in a curious manner by some individuals [two brothers] of the name of Taylor ... They were originally farriers [treating horse ailments], and, by a transition easy in the country, they became bonesetters and surgeons.'[17]

Although untrained, the Taylors were highly successful and widely consulted by poor and royalty alike, and their business was passed down through the family.[18] 'No patient is visited at his lodgings,' Catherine learned, 'if he is able to attend at the house of his doctors; and there, no attention is paid to rank or circumstances, the first comer being first served.'[19] The most famous of the two brothers was John Taylor, and Catherine related that the eminent Manchester physician Charles White 'said to Dr. John ... "Well, how many patients have you killed this year?" "It matters not how many," replied John; "I kill them cheaper than you."'[20] Catherine added: 'Cheap, indeed, does this doctor kill or cure; his terms to those who attend at his house being only two shillings a week, including operations, applications, and medicines.'[21]

Even though surgery was developing into a skilled profession, physicians were higher in status because they did not undertake manual work. Instead, they examined patients and prescribed appropriate treatments and medication, largely for internal ailments. In order to become a fellow of the Royal College of Physicians, it was necessary to belong to the Church of England and to be a graduate of Cambridge or Oxford university (where practical training was of no consequence). Graduates of other universities were admitted only as licentiates. For medical training, physicians went to universities like Leiden or Edinburgh or into hospitals and the private anatomy schools.

The Royal Navy employed surgeons, not physicians, on board their warships, because they needed medical men with practical skills. These surgeons were also expected to act as apothecaries and physicians. The medical men employed in the army varied, with some highly trained and experienced surgeons and physicians, while others had a limited education. There was no government regulation of medicine, and especially outside London, a medical man would often practise as a combined apothecary, surgeon and physician, rather like the Whitworth Doctors. The Apothecaries Act of 1815 introduced some regulation, after which such general practitioners were obliged to be qualified apothecaries.[22]

Some effective medical treatments were beginning to be developed, the most notable of which was a method of preventing smallpox – a frightening, virulent disease that affected all classes. It had a high mortality rate (up to 60 per cent) and left survivors with disfiguring scars and sometimes even blindness. Inoculation (or variolation) had begun in Britain from 1721, using the technique of cutting a patient's arm or leg and introducing infected pus from someone already ill with smallpox. Around 2 per cent of those inoculated died. Parson Woodforde made several references to smallpox and inoculation in his diary, as in November 1776:

> Dr. Thorne of Mattishall came to my house and inoculated my servants, Ben Legate and little Jack Warton ... Ben is about 25 years old, Jack about 9. The Dr. took out of his pocket a small [container] where the matter was ... They then each stripped, and the Dr. taking a small bit of the cotton thread saturated with matter between his left hand finger and thumb, with the launcet in his other hand, he then dipt the point of the launcet in the cotton thread, and with the point of the launcet made two dotts ... about two inches apart in each of their arms, dipping now and then his launcet in water and then with the cotton thread, scarce to be felt or to draw blood, they then stood with their arms exposed to the cold air for about 3 minutes, till almost dried up. The matter took effect almost instantaneously ... No plaister or any thing else whatever to be put to their arms afterwards.[23]

Inoculation was too expensive for the poor, but Woodforde paid for these servants because smallpox was ravaging the parish at the time. Five days later, he settled Dr Thorne's bill:

> My inoculating folks brave [well]. Ben complained of a pain under his arms to day. Jack complained of nothing at all ... Dr. Thorne who inoculated my servants dined and spent the afternoon with us ... I paid the Dr. for inoculating our people 0.10.6. I gave him also towards inoculating a poor family 0.10.6 ... The Doctor's price for inoculating a single person is only 0.5.3 ... Ben's arms look much inflamed, much forwarder than the boy's, Jack complained of a pain under his arms to night.[24]

Smallpox remained a killer despite inoculation, but the situation was transformed when Edward Jenner developed vaccination. After serving an apprenticeship to a surgeon in Gloucestershire, Jenner had studied at St George's Hospital in London and then returned home in 1772, where he made the first scientific investigation into cowpox (vaccinia). He experimented by inoculating patients with cowpox to offer some protection against smallpox, calling this procedure vaccination. By 1800 vaccination was increasingly employed, making smallpox the first infectious disease to be curbed in this manner. Even so, medical men could be backward, and in 1809 Holland was unhappy that Jenner's vaccination was not being used:

I went to Dodington in the morning very few at church as there is an innoculation for the small pox which shuts up Mr. Farthing and one or two families more. But now the cow pox [vaccination] is so much approved of and so much safer I do not think it right in Mr. Bennet recommending innoculation for the small pox, which is infectious and if one family begins it obliges others to adopt the same measure whether they approve of it or not.[25]

Despite new medical discoveries, there was much to dread from other viral and bacterial diseases and assorted afflictions, including consumption (tuberculosis), gonorrhoea, syphilis, malaria, cholera, typhus, scarlet fever, measles, rabies from dog bites, cancer and influenza. 'Very sickly in London in the influenza. Very few escape,' Woodforde remarked during a visit to the capital in June 1782.[26] Luckily, he kept healthy, since an influenza pandemic had recently spread across Europe from Asia, and deaths in London reached a peak during his visit.[27] In November 1807 Nelly Weeton expressed concern in a letter to her brother about another killer, whooping cough (also then called 'chincough'): 'How are your little ones? Do they escape the hooping cough? Great numbers have it here, and it is very fatal. Many die of it; several children have gone blind with it, and some thrown into fits. My cousin Latham's two youngest boys have it; the youngest is very ill.'[28]

In an age of poor food, scant hygiene and no refrigeration, other commonplace disorders included intestinal worms and food poisoning. Gout was a problem that often afflicted the better-off who consumed too much alcohol and meat, causing a crippling inflammation of the joints of the extremities, especially the big toe. Holland wryly recorded that 'Old Weymouth our neighbour I called upon to see his foot which is much swelled. I think it is the gout. I congratulated him on becoming a gentleman, as the gout never attacked any but gentlemen. He shook his head and said that he could not be a gentleman without money.'[29]

Woodforde was first aware that he himself had gout in April 1790: 'When I got up this morning, perceived a violent pain in my right great toe on my foot about the middle joint and swelled a great deal indeed, could scarce get on my slipper, and then could not keep him on long, but get into a pair of shoes. I should think it must be the gout. This is the first attack I ever met with before now.'[30] Gout becomes a recurring topic of his subsequent diary entries, as in mid-January 1795: 'Got up this morning very bad indeed in the gout in my right foot, could scarce bare to put him on the ground, and so it continued the whole day and night, not free one minute from violent pain ... I had my bed warmed to night and a fire in my bed-room. I never was attacked so severe before in my life. Obliged to put on my great shoe, lined with flannel.'[31] Like many at the time, he thought gout floated around the body: 'The gout, tho' not very painful, but continually flying about my constitution makes me very weak both in body and mind &c.'[32] His constant dosing with rhubarb would actually have exacerbated his condition.

For those with money, it was fashionable to take the waters at spas, to maintain good health or to cure disease, sometimes as a last resort. Spas were situated where a good supply of mineral water could be exploited, such as at Bath, Cheltenham, Leamington, Hotwells in Bristol, Buxton and Harrogate. The water was not simply drunk. Communal baths, filled with warm or hot water from the springs, were considered especially effective for those with skin diseases and running sores. Such collective bathing was a novelty for most people, who otherwise never bathed in their lives, in the same way that sea bathing became popular for reasons of health.

It was still widely believed that health problems were caused by an imbalance of the four humours of the body – blood, phlegm, black bile (melancholy) and yellow bile (choler). Dr Radcliffe's Elixir claimed to cure this problem: 'FOR a general alterative Medicine this Elixir has stood unrivalled for more than Eighty Years, and the Public cannot have recourse to a more efficacious Remedy, as a Purifier of the Blood from all Humours, whether contracted by too free Living, or from Surfeits, Jaundice, Scurvy, or Humours after the Measles, or Small-Pox, &c.'[33] For good measure, the advertisement added: 'For all Obstructions in the Bowels and for the Cure of Worms in Children or Adults, it will be found equally serviceable.'[34]

Medical treatments to ensure the proper balance of these humours concentrated on purging and bleeding, and such treatments mainly comprised bloodletting, cupping (blistering), the application of leeches, emetics to cause vomiting and clysters (enemas). When his maid Nanny was ill, Woodforde 'gave her a vomit [emetic] about noon and it kept down near an hour and then it operated very briskly indeed, brought off a great quantity of nasty green thick stuff from her stomach. She was soon after better ... in the evening gave her a small dose of rhubarb with a little ginger.'[35]

Bloodletting was the staple work of surgeons, though it was more likely to weaken sick patients and give them blood poisoning. Cupping involved applying a warmed glass to the skin, which created a vacuum as it cooled and caused a blister, or else it could be used to extract pus from a boil. The skin might be incised or scarified beforehand so that blood was drawn. Woodforde certainly believed in blistering: 'This morning taken very ill, could scarce get down stairs. Sent for Mr. Thorne, who ordered me immediately to bed ... In the night had a blister put between my shoulders which discharged very much indeed in the night and which made me soon better.'[36]

Cupping was a treatment to which Jane Austen's father at Bath was subjected, as she described in a letter to her brother Francis: 'Our dear Father ... was taken ill on Saturday morning, exactly in the same way as heretofore, an oppression in the head, with fever, violent tremulousness, and the greatest degree of feebleness. The same remedy of cupping, which had before been so successful, was immediately applied to, but without such happy effects. The attack was more violent, and at first he seemed scarcely at all relieved by the operation. Towards the evening however he got better.'[37] Two days later, on 21 January 1805, he died.

The most common method of taking blood was to cut the vein of an arm with a lancet or fleam, and Catherine Hutton was told that the Whitworth Doctors undertook bloodletting in a workshop which patients visited: 'on Sundays, the days they bleed gratuitously, the patients are arranged around the room; one operator opens the veins, another holds the basins, and a third follows and binds the arms'.[38] Applying live bloodsucking leeches, obtained from ponds and streams, did a similar job. When walking in the Lake District in October 1800, Dorothy Wordsworth and her brother William encountered an elderly man, bent almost double. 'His trade was to gather leeches,' she remarked, 'but now leeches were scarce, and he had not strength for it. He lived by begging, and was making his way to Carlisle ... He said leeches were very scarce ... He supposed it owing to their being much sought after, that they did not breed fast, and were of slow growth. Leeches were formerly 2s 6d per 100; they are now 30s.'[39] Based on this chance meeting, William wrote a poem, 'The Leech-Gatherer', with the lines:

> He with a smile did then his words repeat;
> And said that, gathering leeches, far and wide
> He travelled; stirring thus about his feet
> The waters of the pools where they abide.
> 'Once I could meet with them on every side;
> But they have dwindled long by slow decay;
> Yet still I persevere, and find them where I may.'[40]

When Holland was at the hamlet of Rose Ash in Devon in September 1803, he suffered such severe pain in his face that he requested Mr Bryan from nearby South Molton to call: 'He soon perceived what was the matter with me, a perfectly nervous case he said ... Said that he would send over Mr Ling [his assistant] with leeches and give me Dover's powders.'[41] Mr Ling called later that evening, but Holland found the treatment with leeches distasteful: 'He did come at last, we dined and after dinner I had leeches put to my cheek, or rather lip under the nose. It is a tedious, unpleasant operation and I hope it will do me good. It is over after two or three hours.'[42]

Similar notions of medicine were applied to animals, and blood-letting was commonly carried out with the aim of curing and preventing illness. In mid-May 1779, Woodforde noted: 'Bled my three horses this morning – 2 quarts each.'[43] Treatises were published to help farmers and others keep animals healthy, but Woodforde's methods were contrary to the advice of a manual published five years earlier: 'It is safer to take a gallon at five or six bleedings, than two quarts at once, for it robs him of two [too] much animal spirits. Always bleed a horse in a pint or quart pot, for when you bleed at random upon the ground, you never can know what quantity you take, nor what quality his blood is. From such violent methods used with ignorance, proceed the death of a great number of horses.'[44]

On a post-chaise trip in Sussex in July 1811, Louis Simond encountered similar ignorance:

> we perceived that one of the horses was streaming with blood about the neck; he had been put in harness too soon after a bleeding. The post-boy stopped on the road, and wept through the operation of fresh twisting the skin, tying, and pinning,—very clumsy and painful,—but unavoidable: he agreed with me that it was very wrong to work the horses too soon after bleeding, *for*, said he, this is the third time we have had in this situation, and the others died of a mortification, and *they cost L.37 [£37] a-piece!*[45]

Although animals were so often treated cruelly, there were instances of kindness: 'Mr. Willm Custance also called here but did not come in,' Woodforde recorded in November 1799, 'a favourite spaniel of his by name, Dash, having his leg broke by another dog in pursuit of a hare near us. My nephew assisted him in binding up the leg, with a bandage and splices of wood, and bathing it with vinegar.'[46] When all else failed, injured animals were killed. Like most country people, Woodforde allowed his dogs to wander: 'In the afternoon my dog Pompey came home shot terribly so bad that I had her hanged directly out of her misery. My greyhound Minx who was with her did not come and we suppose she has met with the same fate.'[47] The next day Minx returned, 'very much shot in one side, but I hope not mortally. They were both shot by black Jack [a gamekeeper].'[48] Stray dogs were a common sight and could pose a real hazard as rabies was prevalent. John Byng also loathed their constant barking, as on one occasion in Lincolnshire: 'This morning I was awaken'd by the barkings and fightings of dogs, upon the market place; such nuisance, and noise is intolerable: one dog can disturb a whole town.'[49]

For dog bites and other serious injuries to people, a surgeon might need to be called in. The Whitworth Doctors boiled up salves in their workshop for treating wounds: 'In the shop stand two jars containing four gallons each; the one filled with a green digestive ointment, the other with a white cerate; and from one of these every patient, who is able, spreads his own plaister, on paper, if he has not brought his own lint or rag. On an average, the doctors dress one hundred and forty persons daily.'[50] What they were dispensing was a form of healing sticking plaster, and recipes abounded for making such plaster at home. For superficial wounds court-plaister wrapped in paper was sold, made from silk or cotton coated with adhesive isinglass (a form of gelatine) – 'ladies' court-plaister' cost sixpence, and other types of plaister sold by apothecaries included 'corn plaister' for feet and 'family plaister'.[51] Woodforde kept this sort at home: 'My servant Will has a bad leg owing to its being scalded two days ago ... I put to it some family plaister and a poultice over it.'[52]

Broken bones could heal if there were no complications, and farriers were usually willing to help. The Whitworth Doctors were renowned as bonesetters, but in hospitals the incidence of infection meant that amputation was often the best solution. Any complicated breaks that could not be set or dealt with by amputation were effectively untreatable. In February 1796 Woodforde heard news of the death of a relative: 'Nancy had a letter this evening from Miss Pounsett brought from Norwich ... The death of my Uncle Thos. Woodfordes wife occasioned by a late fall she met with, wch. broke one of her thigh bones, and being at an advanced age, above 84, could not be set.'[53]

Because manual labour was so physically demanding, working-class people often suffered from hernias, usually referred to as ruptures. Hernias occurred where an organ protruded into another part of the body, generally part of the intestine through the abdominal wall. The army and navy, although constantly short of men, refused to accept new recruits with hernias. Little could be done for this distressing condition except to wear a supporting truss. Different models were devised, and in 1805 George Barwick, a gunmaker at Norwich, advertised: 'Elastic Steel Trusses and Bandages, OF EVERY DESCRIPTION, For Ruptures in Men, Women, & Children ... Hundreds have been made by him, and many entirely cured ... These Trusses, Bandages, &c. for Groin, Navel, and other Ruptures, are made on a superior plan, and worn without any inconvenience whatever.'[54]

That same year saw the founding of the New Rupture Society, whose aim was to provide the poor with effective trusses. One report stated: 'at least one person in fifteen is ruptured: but among those classes of the community which are much exposed to laborious employment, the average may be fixed at one in eight or nine [and] ... in some particular parishes, the proportion may be computed at even a *fourth of the labouring population!*'[55] At least a quarter of a million people (perhaps many more) suffered from a rupture at any one time.

The Whitworth Doctors, Catherine Hutton said, also helped patients with constipation, for which 'Glauber salts were bought by the hogshead'[56] – naturally occurring salts that were used as a laxative. This was an age when many people's diet was poor, not helped by the state of their teeth. There were no trained dentists, but from the 1770s dentistry was becoming a respectable profession, and surgeons such as John Hunter were undertaking research and publishing their results on the subject. Cavities in teeth could be filled with lead, silver or gold, but most sufferers had their painful teeth extracted. In London and large towns surgeons were available to pull out teeth, but elsewhere apothecaries, quack tooth-drawers and even blacksmiths might oblige. At Weston Longville in June 1776 Woodforde had a tooth removed by the farrier:

> My tooth pained me all night, got up a little after 5 this morning and sent for one Reeves, a man who draws teeth in this parish, and about 7 he came and drew my tooth but shockingly bad indeed, he broke away a great piece of my gum and broke one of the fangs of the tooth, it gave me exquisite pain all the day after and my face was swelled prodigiously in the evening and much pain. Very bad and in much pain the whole day long. Gave the old man that drew it however 0.2.6. He is too old, I think, to draw teeth, can't see very well.[57]

Years later Jane Austen accompanied three of her nieces to a more reputable dentist in London, as she related to Cassandra:

> The poor Girls and their Teeth! ... we were a whole hour at Spence's, and Lizzy's were filed and lamented over again and poor Marianne had two taken out after all, the two just beyond the eye teeth, to make room for those in front. When her doom was fixed, Fanny, Lizzy and I walked into the next room, where we heard each of the two sharp hasty screams. Fanny's teeth were cleaned too – and pretty as they are, Spence found something to do to them, putting in gold and talking gravely ... I would not have had him look at mine for a shilling a tooth and double it.[58]

When living near Liverpool in 1808, Nelly Weeton had four teeth removed, as she told a friend:

> I might have been Boreas [god of the north wind] himself, with one cheek, it was so puffed, and had you met me, you would have seen that cheek almost half a mile before you saw the other ... However, as I am a great advocate of equality, I sent for Mr. Aranson, who extracted four teeth, and the operation soon reduced the great cheek to the level of its neighbour. Since that time, I have been in perfect good health, equally good spirits, and, (if you will believe me) in a good humour.[59]

Mr Pascoe Aranson was a surgeon-dentist who practised at Liverpool but also offered his services elsewhere for short periods. Two weeks after Nelly's extractions, he was advertising in the *Leeds Mercury* that 'he Purposes spending a few Weeks in Leeds, and any Lady or Gentleman who may favour him with their Commands, will please to address him at his Lodgings, at Mr. Hodgson's, Tea-Dealer, No. 2 Boar-Lane.'[60] Aranson claimed to provide a range of services 'without the least pain or Injury to the enamel ... Mr. A. is also noted for Drawing Teeth, with the greatest Ease, and extracts stumps, even if covered with the Gum.'[61]

When most people smiled, they displayed rotten teeth and gaps where teeth were missing. Holland complained that one man, by the name of Briffet, had 'a mouth as wide as a barn door and lips as thick and projecting they look like two rollers of raw beef bolstered up to guard as it were the approach to his nasty rotten ragged teeth. However he is a good pig killer.'[62] For many afflicted with toothache, it must have been a blessing when they lost all their teeth. Dorothy Wordsworth noted in May 1802: 'My tooth broke today. They will soon be gone.'[63] Already at the age of thirty, she was facing the prospect of no teeth.

Some chose to have a rogue tooth rammed back into place, and Colonel Peter Hawker in March 1812 wrote of this brutal experience: 'After being tortured for three days and three nights with the toothache, I had a tooth drawn and driven in again, by which severe operation you effectually remove all pain (by destroying the nerve), and at the same time restore the tooth for mastication.'[64] An alternative solution for front teeth was to insert a dead person's tooth. 'I would recommend to every dentist to have some dead teeth at hand,' wrote the surgeon John Hunter, 'that he may have a chance to fit the socket. I have known these sometimes last for years, especially when well supported by the neighbouring teeth.'[65]

Another possibility was a live tooth transplant, which was fashionable for a few decades from the 1770s. As a desperate way of earning money, a pauper might allow a sound front tooth to be extracted, which was then implanted in a wealthy patient. Transplanted teeth could transmit diseases like syphilis, but Hunter did not understand this risk: 'the new teeth should always be perfectly sound, and taken from a mouth which has the appearance of that of a person sound and healthy; not that I believe it possible to transplant an infection'.[66] In order to avoid filing the tooth to the correct shape, he said, the 'best remedy is to have several people ready, whose teeth in appearance are fit; for if the first will not answer, the second may'.[67]

A few women practised medicine, usually alongside their husband as apothecaries, surgeons, oculists, opticians or dentists, or perhaps continuing a business on his death. In the 1770s and 1780s Mrs de St Raymond was a dentist in York and London, and on occasions she went to Winchester for short periods, as in January 1782:

MRS. DE ST. RAYMOND, DENTIST, at Mr. SHEPPARD's, fronting the White Lion, High-street ... She takes judiciously away from the teeth all *Tartarous Concretions*, destructive to them and the gums: draws and transplants teeth, and extracts stumps, be they ever so difficult, even when the skills of others proves ineffectual. She fills up and fastens teeth ... fits in either *human* or *artificial Teeth*, from one to an entire set; and executes her newly invented *Obturators* for the loss of the *Palate*.[68]

Artificial teeth or dentures were crafted from a single piece of bone, ivory or porcelain, but none was satisfactory, as bone and ivory had no enamel coating and so became discoloured and decayed rapidly, and porcelain was noisy, lost its glaze and tended to shatter. The best dentures were constructed from human teeth taken from corpses and set on an ivory or animal-bone base, but these were expensive to manufacture. Lower dentures were more commonly made than upper ones because they could be securely fitted.

The battles of the Napoleonic Wars provided many opportunities for obtaining human teeth and satisfying a great demand amongst the wealthy for dentures. In 1814, during the Peninsular Wars, the London surgeon Astley Cooper sent a man by the name of Butler to his nephew Bransby Cooper in Spain in order to obtain teeth. When Bransby asked him how this was to be achieved, Butler replied: 'Oh, Sir, only let there be a battle, and there'll be no want of teeth. I'll draw them as fast as the men are knocked down.'[69] Bransby noted that some of the legitimate sutlers were also bodysnatchers who followed the army to strip teeth and other valuables from the dead:

> They generally obtained the teeth on the night succeeding the battle, only drawing them from those soldiers whose youth and health rendered them peculiarly fitted for the purposes to which they were to be employed. Nothing but the large sums of money derived from the depradations could have prompted them to encounter the risk ... for I do not believe a soldier in the whole army would have hesitated one moment to blow out the brains of a person whom he found robbing the corpse of a comrade in this manner.[70]

At the Battle of Waterloo in June 1815, over eighteen thousand men died on the battlefield itself,[71] and they were ruthlessly plundered. Clients back in England were happy to wear dentures made from the teeth of fit young men killed in battle, which became known as 'Waterloo teeth' or, more coyly, 'Waterloo ivory'. They would have been less happy to learn that many dentures were actually made from teeth plundered from English graveyards.

Bodysnatchers mainly sold bodies to anatomists for dissection, but they also sold teeth to dentists or surgeon-dentists. Even if a body was putrefying and no good for the anatomists, its teeth could still be taken. Joseph Naples, a former able seaman in the Royal Navy, recorded in a diary his gang's activities in London, which included sales of 'canines' (sets of teeth). After obtaining some corpses in November 1812, Naples noted that Jack, one of his gang, 'sold the canines to Mr. Thomson for 5 Guineas'.[72] According to Bransby Cooper, 'Every dentist in London would at that time purchase teeth from these men and the public can have but little idea of the immense sums of money which persons thus occupied could earn.'[73]

False teeth and trusses were not the only aids and accessories available. With amputations being the remedy for some injuries, wooden legs used with wooden crutches provided some mobility. Invalids, particularly at Bath, were carried about in sedan chairs, as well as in three- or four-wheeled 'Bath chairs' with folding hoods. Constructed by coachmakers, they could be manoeuvred by one person, rather than the two chairmen needed for sedan chairs. Benjamin Silliman noticed these chairs in Bath and described how 'infirm people are drawn about by servants, in little hand carriages, with three wheels; a pair of wheels is placed behind, in the usual manner, and the third beneath the middle of the carriage before [in front]; connected with this last there is a lever, passing to the hand of the invalid, who is thus enabled to steer the vehicle.'[74]

For those who were partially deaf, hearing trumpets could offer an effective solution, consisting of a flaring end and a long narrow tube that channelled sound when inserted into the ear. Problems with vision such as myopia could be corrected with spectacles, which had convex or concave glass lenses that were round in shape, though by the early 1800s an oval shape was preferred. The lenses were set in frames that were lodged on the nose or held in front of the eyes by means of a short handle (which might fold up and serve as a protective case). Other frames resembled the form of modern spectacles, with sides or arms that gripped the head. These were made from materials such as steel, silver, brass, whalebone, leather, horn and tortoiseshell.

Opticians stocked a range of lenses with different focal lengths, and clients picked the most suitable, at times choosing split lenses or 'double spectacles', an early form of bifocals.[75] A quizzing glass (or 'quizzer') was a single lens in a frame that was held in the hand by a handle. Magnifying glasses that folded into a case were similar, but were for close work such as reading. Opticians also made mirrors and anything else that needed glass, from tooth mirrors for dentists to linen smoothers for laundry. Some even offered framing services for prints. Like dentists, a few opticians moved between towns, such as G. Lyons who advertised in the *Hampshire Chronicle* in 1802:

G. LYONS, OPTICIAN

RESPECTFULLY informs his numerous Friends he is arrived in Winchester with a large Assortment of SPECTACLES, to suit any Age or Sight; READING and OPERA GLASSES, TELESCOPES, MICROSCOPES, &c. &c. and being regularly Bred to the Science of

Optics, will, he trusts, be enabled to give entire Satisfaction. N.B.– G.L. will stay about a Fortnight, and will attend any Lady or Gentleman, being applied to at the Three Tuns Inn, Gaol-Street.[76]

The poor would not have been able to afford spectacles and so had to live with eye defects, while somebody like William Holland owned more than one pair. On New Year's Day 1809 he had to conduct an afternoon church service at Over Stowey, but found it too dark and gloomy to see clearly: 'I begun the service so late and the evenings now so short and the fogg so thick and dark, that I knew not how to make out my sermon. I had two spectacles with me and one magnified more than the other, so I very deliberately put up one and took out the other and then went on, and by that means got through.'[77]

People of all classes wore hats and therefore had some protection against the sun, but sunglasses with green or blue tinted lenses were available. Chronic contagious conjunctivitis of the eyes known as 'Egyptian ophthalmia' afflicted soldiers fighting the French in Egypt after Napoleon's invasion of 1798. It was brought back to England and transmitted to the civilian population, and William Darter recalled that in Reading and elsewhere in Berkshire 'we had many ... who were partially or wholly blind from opthalmia caught in the earlier war in Egypt. Some of these invalids from the East could be easily distinguished from others on account of their wearing green shades or coloured glasses.'[78] If left untreated, cataracts in the eye could also cause blindness, but some surgeons (oculists) carried out procedures to dislodge ('couch') or extract the affected lens.

With an inadequate understanding of the body, all surgery was risky. There were also no modern aids like blood transfusions and anaesthetics, although in the late 1790s the physician Thomas Beddoes and his assistant Humphry Davy tried out various gases on tuberculosis patients at the Pneumatic Institution in Hotwells, Bristol.[79] Nitrous oxide ('laughing gas') was found to relieve pain and cause sedation. 'As nitrous oxide in its extensive operation appears capable of destroying physical pain,' Davy wrote in 1800, 'it may probably be used with advantage during surgical operations in which no great effusion of blood takes place.'[80] Despite these findings, more than four decades would elapse before nitrous oxide was used in anaesthetics for surgery and dentistry.[81] Instead, patients were given alcohol or laudanum, their hands were tied together, and they were held down while the surgery was carried out. One of the keys to a successful operation was speed, otherwise the patient might die of shock or bleed to death.

Most types of surgery undertaken today were simply not attempted then, because infection could not be prevented, and survival rates were appallingly low. Surgery was limited mainly to the amputation of limbs, along with operations that were not too invasive, such as on cysts, some cancers, cataracts, strangulated hernias and bladder stones (by lithotomy). Although surgeons might strive after cleanliness, they did not realise that they were transmitting lethal bacteria from sources such as their instruments and dissected corpses. Surgery on private patients was done in their homes, a far safer environment than any hospital – wealthy people did not attend hospitals for any treatment whatsoever.

As well as seeing private patients, some surgeons held positions in hospitals. Many of these had been established as charities in towns and cities from the early eighteenth century and were funded through public subscriptions to provide free medical care for the deserving poor with injuries and ailments.[82] However, any hospital patient too ill to be cured was released, as were those with infectious diseases. When John Byng was in Northampton in 1793, he saw the town's brand-new hospital for the poor: 'Their new County Infirmary looks magnificently, let a foreigner travell England, and he must suppose it the land of disease and roguery; "What great building is that? That is an infirmary. What magnificent house is this? This is the county jail." Every poor man must wish himself in one, or the other.'[83]

Surgical operations in hospitals were undertaken either on the wards alongside other patients or in theatres, which were literally places of spectacle for students and visitors.[84] In 1771 the surgeon John Aikin wrote about the perils of hospitals and recommended amputation for complicated fractures: 'Every Surgeon attending a large and crowded hospital, knows the very great difficulty of curing a compound fracture in them. This is so universally acknowledged, that the most humane and judicious of them have been obliged to comply with that dreadful rule of practice, immediate amputation in every compound fracture.'[85] Because he had no idea of infection, Aikin thought that the 'malignancy of hospital air' was to blame, because he knew that such fractures could heal successfully at home and in rural hospitals.

Dr John Percival of Manchester gave some advice to Aikin on how to control 'the noxious effluvia which arise from so many distempered bodies, afflicted perhaps with mortifications, carious bones, malignant ulcers, or putrid fevers'.[86] His suggestions included washing hospital wards with vinegar and tar water, fumigating with the steam from boiling vinegar and tar, ventilating the bedclothes of patients who could sit up or walk about, and 'obliging the sick to conform strictly to the rules of nicety and cleanliness'.[87] He also recommended that patients should smoke tobacco:

> If any of them have been accustomed to smoaking, they should be allowed pipes and tobacco, when such an indulgence will not be injurious to them. The patients should have their linen very frequently renewed, and their shirts and sheets should be fumigated with frankincense, before they are used. The dressings of foul ulcers, &c. as soon as they are removed, should be thrown into vessels of vinegar, and carried out of the wards with all convenient expedition.[88]

For the poor, there were also charitable hospitals that provided specialist care, such as the lying-in hospitals for pregnant women and a few lock hospitals for venereal disease.[89] Eye hospitals were established as a direct result of the contagious ophthalmia brought back from Egypt, and the first one opened in 1805 in London (which is now the Moorfields Eye Hospital). Other specialist institutions included the lunatic asylum and madhouse, which imprisoned those regarded as insane, including sufferers from conditions like epilepsy, post-natal depression and dementia. Whatever their illness, they were often locked away as nobody knew what else to do. As Aikin said in 1771, 'besides their own sufferings, they are rendered a nuisance and terror to others; and are not only themselves lost to society, but take up the whole time and attention of others'.[90]

Private madhouses, some very small, were intended for patients whose families could afford to pay. Pauper lunatics might also be put in these private madhouses if their fees were paid by the parish, but more likely they were confined in poorhouses or workhouses, as described by Holland in Over Stowey:

> The man in the workhouse is chained and lies upon straw, shocking situation – Alas! poor human nature. How many afflictions art thou liable to ... Went to the messrs Riches this evening about the madman in the workhouse, both determined to join in sending him to the madhouse in Bristol, be the expense what it will. Eh, says James [Rich], Master Holland I reckon it be a bad business. He is a very bad fellow there is something in it more than madness I count. In short, James thinks ... that he is possessed by the Devil or bewitched.[91]

It was commonly believed that lunacy was due to evil or to an imbalance in the body's humours, for which William Ricketts, a surgeon who had run a madhouse at Droitwich in Worcestershire for twenty years, undertook purging:

> When a patient is brought ... I generally found depletion necessary, if the Lunatic is violent; I afterwards have him cupped; and the first thing I do is to empty the stomach and bowels by small doses of emetic tartar, or to purge them briskly with calomel ... I believe the disease to proceed most frequently from a derangement of the digestive organs ... In the majority of females between the ages of fourteen and forty, I think, it arises from a sexual cause.[92]

He was also convinced that too much hair was harmful: 'I conceive in all cases of excessive mania, there is too great a determination of blood to the head, and that the head ought to be kept as cool as possible, the head being loaded with hair, that must increase the heat.'[93]

Conditions in madhouses and asylums were often no better than those of prisons, though humane treatment and good intentions were evident, with a gradual shift from confinement towards cure and care. Even so, lunatics were commonly shackled or kept in straitjackets. Some charitable asylums existed, and the most famous institution was Bethlem ('Bedlam') Hospital at Moorfields, which accepted lunatics from the entire country. At Newcastle-upon-Tyne a charitable hospital for pauper lunatics was opened in 1767, but the 'chains, iron bars, and dungeon-like cells, presented to the unhappy inmates all the irritating and melancholy characteristics of a prison ... Many of the cells were close, dark, cold holes (less comfortable than cow-houses)'.[94] Its physician was Dr John Hall, and he also ran a private madhouse that claimed to offer humane treatment. One advertisement appeared in the *Newcastle Courant* in May 1774:

> Dr Hall's Private House for Lunatics, Known by the Name of St LUKE's HOUSE. DIET, WASHING, and LODGING, for lunatics, at 20l. a year, or 8s. per week, or less where the circumstances of the patient require the expence to be made still more moderate. This house has been universally admired for its healthy, pleasant situation; as also its conveniences for the accommodation of boarders ... The greatest care will be taken of all Patients intrusted to him.[95]

In 1774 an Act for regulating private madhouses was passed, requiring them to hold a licence and for two doctors to sign a certificate, so as to stop wrongful confinement. In 1808 the County Asylum Act also allowed Justices of the Peace to levy a rate for the establishment of publicly funded asylums for pauper and criminal lunatics, in order to remove them from the workhouses.[96] After the General Lunatic Asylum opened in Nottingham in 1812, John Blackner congratulated those responsible, who 'very early saw the necessity of an asylum for the wandering, half lost, and sometimes wholly neglected maniacs ... These humane and praise-worthy gentlemen could not see their fellow creatures, clothed in rags, or half naked, when deprived of their reason, parading the streets, the sport of coxcombs and thoughtless boys, without being painfully struck with the sight.'[97] However, few new county lunatic asylums were built over the following decades.

A House of Commons Select Committee in 1816 revealed the dreadful conditions in licensed madhouses in England. William Ricketts of the Droitwich madhouse gave evidence of the gulf that existed between the rich and the poor, even in lunacy:

> I think about one half [of about eighty-five inmates] are paupers ... I have accommodations according to the different classes; according to their pay; patients of a superior class pay, some four guineas a week, some three, some two and a half, some two, some a guinea, and fourteen shillings a week pauper Lunatics, except the town of Birmingham, they pay only ten shillings, and the major part of the pauper Lunatics are from the town of Birmingham ... we have different sitting rooms for the different classes ... the pauper Lunatics are taken out by my men-servants and work in the garden ... Patients of the superior orders amuse themselves at cards; some of them are musical; they have a piano-forte; one lady plays and sings most admirably.[98]

The previous year, 1815, a new Bethlem Hospital (now home to the Imperial War Museum) had opened at St George's Fields. Conditions were not ideal at this new building, and because Ricketts had seen this new hospital only the month before, the Select Committee cross-examined him: 'Do you remember that in the old gallery in Bethlem [at Moorfields] many of the patients were chained round a table on the left-hand side, almost in a state of nudity?—Yes, I do. There is nothing of that kind now?—No, they are better covered now. There are several patients in what is called the dirty room.'[99] Mrs Elizabeth Forbes, the matron in charge of female patients, was also questioned by the committee:

> Do you consider the patients in the basement story to have suffered from the damp?—They have had bad colds, and have been rather unhealthy this winter.
>
> Have you lost any patients in that story this winter?—Yes, Four ...
>
> What were the circumstances of the four deaths which have taken place?—It was from cold.

What were their ages?—None of them were under forty; one was eighty years of age, the other three between forty and fifty.[100]

Many elderly people who were treated as lunatics probably had dementia, but most old people were obliged to work for as long as they could, rather than being rewarded with retirement: 'I met old John French on the road hard at work, tho' 83,' William Holland noted in his diary in April 1813.[101] State aid for the elderly consisted of relief given by the parish, which all too often meant going to live in the workhouse. In 1795 at Petersfield in Hampshire, Frederick Eden reported: '22 persons, (mostly old women and children,) are at present in the work-house: they are, principally, employed in cleansing the streets.'[102] Apart from the Chelsea Hospital, which supported some old soldiers ('Chelsea Pensioners'), and a similar Greenwich Hospital for old naval seamen, the workhouses and some charitable almshouses were the only institutions providing for the elderly.

Most workhouses were inadequate and badly run, and the poet George Crabbe bitterly condemned them in 'The Parish Workhouse' (part of his long poem *The Village*, published in 1783). He pointed out that people who were comfortably off had no idea of the deprivation and loss of pride, dignity and hope suffered by workhouse inmates. John Byng set down his own compassionate vision of an ideal place for the elderly to live:

> As for the very aged, and helpless, I should revert to that good, old (now neglected,) Custom of Alms Houses ... therein I should place 12 of the most pitiable and deserving aged poor, with each their several slips of garden ground; where such as were able might employ themselves: before their doors, a shady walk of trees fronting the south, with some benches, would tempt forth the, not unhappy, lodgers, to bask in a summer's sun, or to endeavour at a winter's walk. Is not this a reasonable, a cheap, an heartfelt satisfaction?[103]

For elderly paupers, Crabbe wrote, their only escape from the work-house was death:

Up yonder hill, behold how sadly slow
The bier moves winding from the vale below;
There lie the happy dead, from trouble free,
And the glad parish pays the frugal [burial] fee.[104]

Whatever the cause of death – perhaps illness, childbirth, accident, old age or execution – it was not necessarily a case of resting in peace, particularly for the poor. In some parts of the country, especially those within convenient distance of a medical school, bodies were in danger of being stolen immediately after burial. Anatomists (who were usually surgeons) in the private medical schools and teaching hospitals were always desperate for corpses to dissect in front of students and for their own research. Not enough corpses could be acquired through legitimate means (only a few bodies of executed criminals), and the Government was reluctant to draw up a Bill for the proper provision of bodies, as happened on the Continent. Cadavers were therefore bought from bodysnatchers, and surgeons knew exactly what was happening. It was an abhorrent trade, but one without which medical advances would not have happened.

Some corpses were stolen from their coffins before burial, but most were robbed from graveyards soon after a funeral when the soil was loose and the body relatively fresh. Graverobbers, or bodysnatchers, chose dark nights, without the light of the moon, and their work was so skilled that graves would look undisturbed. Even where thefts were noticed, records of such crimes seldom survive. Pauper bodies were preferred, as their graves were more shallow. Because of decomposition and the overpowering stench, corpses were useless for the anatomists after a few days.

Bodies were sometimes shipped in casks to the capital from elsewhere in the country or else were sold to anatomists in places like Bristol and Manchester, but the heart of the trade was London – from October to May, when the private anatomy school classes were running. A satirical piece, published in the *Morning Post* newspaper at the start of the classes in October 1811, claimed to be the minutes of a general meeting of the guild of bodysnatchers who were worried about their profession:

ADVERTISEMENT EXTRAORDINARY.

At a general meeting of the Gentlemen in the *resurrection* line, vulgarly called '*body snatchers*,' '*dead carcase stealers*,' &c. held at their hall the *Bonehouse, Rotten-row*, in the parish of *St. Sepulchre, Gravesend*.

Dick Drybones in the chair,—it was resolved unanimously

1. That as anatomy is the end of *physic*, all those who contribute to the study and improvement of that noble science, are entitled to public support and the most liberal remuneration.
2. That of late certain persons not regularly brought up to the profession, have tried to introduce the practice of seizing dead bodies previous to their interment, to the great injury of the industrious members of this right worshipful fraternity.
3. That this assembly can view such conduct in no other light than as being illegal, and as a scandalous outrage of the rights and privileges of this community.
4. That persons concerned in such practices be forthwith scouted [scorned], unless they chuse to become regular members, paying the usual introductory gallon of gin, as also a forfeit of five shillings, to be spent in bread, cheese, and porter.
5. That in consequence of the effect of the Comet on the weather, they have been unable to commence their season in the present year, till the close of October.
6. That through the circumstances above stated, they are in such distress, they scarcely know how to keep *soul* and *body* together, and consequently feel it incumbent upon them to charge an extra guinea for every subject.[105]

The imaginary meeting also urged physicians not to increase the price of physic, or medicines. The logic of this statement was that knowing the harm caused by most medicines, if the amount taken by patients decreased, then the number of deaths would be fewer and the graverobbing business would suffer. These so-called minutes concluded: '(Signed) DICK DRYBONES, PAUL PUTRID, MAT MARROWLESS, KIT COFFIN, TOM TOMBSTONE,

VALENTINE VAULT, KICKUP RESURGAM, Secretary to the Meeting.'[106]

The graverobbing business was actually thriving. In his diary for the years 1811 and 1812, Joseph Naples recorded details of his gang's activities – taking orders from surgeons, raiding graveyards, delivering corpses and collecting payment. On 7 December 1811, a few weeks after the satirical piece in the *Morning Post*, Naples noted: 'At night went out & got 3 at Bunhill Row. 1 S^t· Thomas's, 2 Brookes'[107] – this meant that he had stolen three bodies from the dissenters' burial ground at Bunhill Fields or possibly the nearby Quaker burial ground, one of which was taken to St Thomas's Hospital for dissection, and two were sold to Joshua Brookes.

A month later, Naples wrote: 'At 2 A.M. got up, the Party went to Harps, got 4 adults and 1 small [child], took 4 to S^t· Thomas's. Came home, went to Mr. Wilson & Brookes. Danl· [Daniel] got paid £8 8 0 from Mr. Wilson, I recd. 9 9 0 from Mr. Brookes. Came over to the borough [Southwark], sold small for £1 10 0, Rec^d· £4 4 0 for adult. At home all night.'[108] James Wilson taught anatomy at the Great Windmill Street Anatomy School, which he had founded, and Joshua Brookes ran another anatomy school on Great Marlborough Street, which he advertised in newspapers across England, as in the *Leicester Journal* in January 1812:

THEATRE OF ANATOMY.
BLENHEIM-STREET, GREAT MARLBOROUGH-STREET.

The Spring course of Lectures on Anatomy,
Physiology, and Surgery, will be commenced on
Monday, the 20th of January, at 2 o'clock,

By Mr. BROOKES ... Spacious apartments thoroughly ventilated,
and replete with every convenience, are open all the morning, for the
purposes of dissecting and injecting, where Mr. Brookes attends to
direct the students, and demonstrates the various parts as they appear
on dissection ... Gentlemen established in practice desirous of
renewing their anatomical knowledge, may be accommodated
with an apartment to dissect in privately.[109]

Some of the London corpses were even packed up and sent to Edinburgh for dissection in the medical schools there, and on 5 December that same year Naples recorded: 'packing up for Edinboro, sent 12 to the wharf for the above place, at home all night'.[110] This was more than a decade before the infamous Burke and Hare murders would supply the anatomists in Edinburgh with bodies. It was only in 1832 that the Anatomy Act was passed to provide an adequate, legal source of cadavers for dissection.

TWELVE

LAST WORDS

Everybody had a degree of gravity and sorrow; tenderness towards the departed, solicitude for the surviving friends; and, in a reasonable time, curiosity to know where she would be buried.

Emma, by Jane Austen

The service for the burial of the dead in the Church of England prayer book contains the line 'In the midst of life we are in death',[1] and this was the everyday experience of Jane Austen's contemporaries, especially when sudden, unexplained deaths occurred. In May 1793 Parson Woodforde was shocked to hear bad news from a friend:

Recd. a note this morning from Mr. Wright of Mattishall informing us of the death of his wife and requesting my attendance at her funeral ... It much surprised us as we did not hear that she had been ill at all – it was indeed very suddenly on Monday night last after eating a very hearty supper and apparently very well – but going to bed about 10. o'clock, after she got into her chamber and sitting down on a chair, her maid Judith perceived her mistress suddenly to change in her countenance and immediately fall into a fit ... in less than half an hour after she was dead, and great was the uneasiness and distress of the family on the occasion and at such a time of night. Mr. and Mrs. Bodham immediately on notice went thither – but found their sister dead. It shocked them much.[2]

Most deaths that did not result from a recognisable illness were assumed to be the natural close of 'old age'. For those who survived childhood and for women who survived childbirth, there was every chance of living to beyond seventy years of age, and William Holland was perplexed by the distraught behaviour of one of his parishioners: 'Old Kibby who was buried this day was 83 and yet his sister cried and seem'd half distracted. I could not forbear observing that she could not expect him to live for ever and therefore she might moderate her grief.'[3] The question of life expectancy interested John Byng, and at Towcester in Northamptonshire in 1789 he was pleased to learn about one elderly man from a nearby village:

In all my walks and of all the clerks, who have shewn me churches, (and I have seen some few) I have allways asked, from hope and curiosity, 'Have you any person of remarkable old age in your town?' The answer being, for ever, no, has terrify'd me. but tonight, reading this in the county paper, had rather comforted me:–

'April 27th, 1789, Mr James French, of Fritwell, 90 years of age, walked from thence through Aynho to Banbury before breakfast, being about nine miles. He appears remarkably healthy for his age, has a fine bloom on his countenance, enjoys a good appetite, and seems likely to live many years. He ... was for a good part of his life a servant in the Mr Child's family ... by whom his faithful service is rewarded with an annuity of 20£ during life. Not long since he walked to London in three days, and there, amidst the multitude observed, that he could not find an old man. He eats but two meals a day, and never drinks any strong liquors, nor very often ale, but generally mixed beer.'[4]

Byng was an impoverished aristocrat who well understood that life expectancy depended on a person's wealth and way of life. At Sibsey in Lincolnshire two years later, he commented: 'walking about the churchyard, and reading the grave stone epitaphs, made me to remark that poor people died early, for they must work when ill; ... it is the rich man who lives longest, who has every comfort, a nice bed, and physicians at hand: look into the mausoleums of the great, and you'll find that they outlive the parish.'[5]

This was of course a generalisation, because although Jane Austen was moderately well-off, like so many others she succumbed to an illness that could not be cured or even accurately identified.[6] She was only forty-one years old when she died in the arms of her sister Cassandra – at Winchester on 18 July 1817. A few days later Cassandra was able to write to friends and relatives about Jane's final moments:

> She felt herself to be dying about half-an-hour before she became tranquil and apparently unconscious. During that half-hour was her struggle, poor soul! She said she could not tell us what she suffered, though she complained of little fixed pain. When I asked her if there was anything she wanted, her answer was she wanted nothing but death, and some of her words were: 'God grant me patience, pray for me, oh pray for me!' Her voice was affected, but as long as she spoke she was intelligible.[7]

Most people, like Jane Austen, firmly believed in an afterlife, but the quality of that afterlife was thought to depend on how well someone had adhered to religion and how moral they had been during their lifetime. The duties of Church of England clergymen included trying to convert those who had no religion, as well as visiting the sick. A few weeks before Jane's death, William Holland visited one of his poor Somerset parishioners:

> under the Quantock hill I found old ... [Thomas] Ware and his wife. He dying, he is past four score and has been a hard working man, this is his second wife, they formerly lived in the poor house. He scarce knows what religion means yet I have brought him to church at times. He lead in his younger days a reprobate kind of life, a mixture of immorality, irreligion and oddity there. He lay in his bed in a most miserable cottage or hut near the fire with pieces of linen wrapt round his head and much flushed in the face as if in a fever.[8]

Ware asked, 'Have you seen my flowers?', and Holland promised to look at them, later commenting: 'He was always fond of gardening and what he pursued all his life time continued till death for he died the next day. A few polyanthus he had but not worth much anxiety of mind during his last moments.'[9]

Parson Woodforde frequently recorded deaths in his own diary and added wishes for their afterlife, such as 'I hope he is happy' for a boy who had drowned in a clay pit.[10] Holland shared this attitude, as shown by his description of one funeral: 'After the service I walked up to the grave to view the coffin and saw his age [on the coffin plate] 72. Poor Ben said I, and turning round to the people, This man has been a good and pious man. Let us endeavour to imitate him, for he is now in a state of happiness. Yes answered someone, I hope he is now happy. No doubt of it returned I, for he was a pious inoffensive man.'[11]

This was the professional stance of the clergyman, but clerics could be just as much affected by deaths within their own family. William Holland had suffered his own terrible tragedy, with four of his five young children dying of scarlet fever in the space of two weeks in 1795.[12] Only his daughter Margaret was spared, and another son, William, was born later on, in 1797.

The lives of the lower classes were generally so wretched that clergymen felt a person's death was to be welcomed as a gateway to a better afterlife, although sometimes their own faith was shaken. The prolonged suffering of a young girl with tuberculosis led Holland to observe: 'we do not in general (whatever their wickedness may have been) find always that the misery and sufferings of this world bears a proportion to the magnitude of man's sins ... On the whole there is so much suffering in this world that I trust the next will be a world of happiness.'[13] He clearly recognised society's evils, yet was firmly against change and often railed against 'democrats' who wanted to improve society.[14] To him, justice would only come in the afterlife.

When someone died, the burial took place shortly afterwards, usually within three or four days, because it was difficult to slow down the decomposition of a corpse, particularly in warm summer months, though not everybody appreciated this necessity. In the summer of 1810, seven years before Thomas Ware died, he and his wife lost a child, and Holland had noted: 'Mrs Ware ... came here about burying her child on Sunday next. She has kept the child already above a week, this very sultry weather. I told her that I insisted on bringing the child immediately. She answered she would bring it tomorrow. I told her she had no right to keep the child so long, to keep the dead to destroy the living.'[15]

For this reason, and because of the expense of transporting a corpse, most people were buried in the parish in which they died. If they died far from where they lived, the possibility of being buried in their own parish was not even considered, though when Woodforde was in Somerset in 1772, he recorded the unusual circumstance of a funeral for a boy who died outside the parish: 'I ... buried a child of Giles Francis by the name J. Francis – aged 5 years. The child died at Bath owing to a kick in the groin by another lad. Giles works at Bath and he and his son brought the child in a coffin upon their heads from Bath, they set out from Bath last night at 12.'[16]

The very wealthy proved the exception, because they could afford to transport their dead relatives to be buried in the family vault or burial plot, even if they had died abroad. In November 1810 Holland recorded that the body of one of the Acland family had come back to England: 'He is brought I understand in a pipe of Madeira [wine] to preserve him through the voyage, the usual mode they tell me there being no lead coffin to be obtained.'[17] This was a son of John Acland, the main landowner in the area, of whom Holland was not overly fond. 'Mr. Acland has now lost six children,' he commented, 'and one only remains to preserve the family name if God preserve his life too. Their wealth is immense but what is wealth alone, it cannot keep them from the grave.'[18]

People were informed about a death as fast as possible in case they wanted to attend the funeral, and letters were sent to distant relatives. The etiquette was to use black wax instead of the usual red for the seal, so that people were warned of bad news before even opening the letter. On Christmas Eve 1792 Woodforde received two letters: 'One letter was for me from my niece Pounsett sealed with black, which at first alarmed me but on my opening the letter found it was owing to the late death of Mrs. Donne of Bath, who had left a legacy of 100 pound to her.'[19]

The usual reason for delaying a burial was that there were suspicions about the cause of death. Such cases were referred to the coroner, who might decide to hold an inquest, with a jury. 'A burial this morning, but the Coroner first is to have sight of the corpse,' Holland noted in December 1799. 'How this comes about or what suspicions there are I cannot tell.'[20] A few months earlier, Silvester Treleaven in Devon had noted: 'A young woman of Bridford [a village 8 miles south-west of Exeter] called Potter apprehended on suspicion of her having had child and destroyed it.'[21] She revealed where the baby boy was buried, in a wood 3 miles away, and the next day a coroner's inquest was held at Bridford: 'Coroner – Hugo Gent. Mr Ponsford Surgeon attended and dissected the body, from whose deposition, and from a chain of circumstances, it evidently appeared that the child was strangled. The jury returned a verdict of murder by the hand of the mother.'[22]

Woodforde also encountered suspicious or sudden deaths, recording one instance in September 1790:

The young woman Spincks (who lately had a bastard child by one Garthon of Norwich) called on me this morning to acquaint me that her child is dead, died last night, owing it is supposed to her [having] given him a sleeping pill which she had of her neighbour Nobbs whose husband is very ill and had some composing pills ... one of which Nobbs wife advised her to give her child to put him to sleep whilst she was out. The child slept for about 5 hours, then he waked and fell into convulsion fits which continued for 4 hours and half and then died in great agonies.[23]

Two days later he wrote: 'few farmers at Church this afternoon on account of an inquest being taken by a Coroner from Norwich on the body of Eliz. Spincks boy. They were from 1 till near 5 on the above business. The jury brought in their verdict – not intentionally given by the mother to her child. This evening between 6 and 7, I buried the child (by name Garthon Spincks) in the churchyard.'[24]

If the coroner was a physician, he might conduct the post-mortem examination himself, but otherwise a medical practitioner could be called in to examine or even dissect the body. When the Prime

Minister, the Marquis of Rockingham, died suddenly in 1782, his body was dissected by the eminent surgeon John Hunter, not because murder was suspected, but through a desire to know the cause of death. Subsequently, thorough post-mortem examinations were gradually accepted by the upper classes, but not yet by the masses.

Usually, the corpse was kept at home in an open coffin until the funeral, so that relatives could say farewell to the deceased, and in October 1808 when Jane Austen was informed of the sudden death of Elizabeth, wife of her brother Edward, she wrote to Cassandra: 'I suppose you see the corpse? How does it appear?'[25] When Neast Grevile Prideaux, an articled law clerk at Ilchester in Somerset, learned that his aunt had died, he hurriedly travelled to Bristol, but was too late: 'I had pleased myself, with the hope that, ere my departed relative was conveyed to the tomb, I should have had a last look at her in her coffin. But this melancholy pleasure I could not enjoy for in such a putrid state was the body, that ... it was closed up before my arrival a day or two.'[26]

It was customary for someone to sit with the corpse day and night, something that was not just a spiritual vigil, but might be of practical benefit, as Nelly Weeton discovered at Dove Nest when the body of her pupil, who had died in a fire, was awaiting burial: 'The house is so remarkably infested with rats, that whilst the body remained in it, people were obliged to sit constantly in the room, night and day, lest the body should be injured by them.'[27] The preservation of bodies by embalming started to become popular during the eighteenth century, something that was brought to wider public attention when ancient Egyptian mummies began to be shipped to western Europe, but the expense of the process ruled it out for most people.

Nonconformists such as Quakers and Baptists might choose to be buried in one of the growing number of dissenters' burial grounds, but most people were buried in churchyards. *Everyone* was buried – there was no cremation in England at this time. The only bodies that might not be buried were those of executed criminals, which could be dissected by anatomists or hung on a gibbet as a warning. Sometimes they were buried in unconsecrated ground, but unlike the bodies of suicides, there was rarely any ritual to stop their ghosts from haunting the living.

While the wealthy had ostentatious funerals and elaborate tomb monuments, paupers were buried in unmarked graves, and the parish authorities paid the cost of burial – and sometimes the cost of a priest to lead a service over the corpse. In the Lake District a pauper burial was witnessed by Dorothy Wordsworth in September 1800:

> About 10 men and 4 women. Bread, cheese and ale [for the mourners]. They talked sensibly and cheerfully about common things. The dead person, 56 years of age, buried by the parish. The coffin was neatly lettered and painted black and covered with a decent cloth. They set the corpse down at the door and, while we stood within the threshold, the men with their hats off, sang, with decent and solemn countenances a verse of a funeral psalm. The corpse was then born down the hill, and they sang till they had passed the Town-End. I was affected to tears while we stood in the house, the coffin lying before me. There were no near kindred, no children ... When we came to the bridge they began to sing again and stopped ... before they entered the churchyard.[28]

Holland reflected on one pauper's funeral that was paid for by a relative: 'They brought a corps from Spaxton a pauper and yet it is astonishing what a number of people attended, the brother ... was at the expence, which indeed was generous, the coffin was very handsome indeed.'[29] For working-class people who could afford regular contributions, many places had burial clubs that operated as friendly societies. Contributions to the club were used to fund the funeral costs of any members who died, and the club provided a group of similarly minded people who could support each other in difficult times. Poor people were starting to imitate the more costly and ostentatious funerals of the upper classes, and Frederick Eden commented on Anne Hurst of Witley in Surrey, a poor farm labourer's wife, who wanted to give her husband a respectable burial:

> people in affluence thought her haughty; and the Paupers of the parish, seeing, as they could not help seeing, that her life was a reproach to

theirs, aggravated [exaggerated] all her little failings. Yet, the worst thing they had to say of her was, that she was proud; which, they said, was manifested by the manner in which she buried her husband. Resolute, as she owned she was, to have the funeral, and everything that related to it, what she called decent, nothing could dissuade her from having handles to his coffin, and a plate on it, mentioning his age.[30]

Even for poor people funerals in rural communities were solemn, respectful ceremonies, but they might be more rushed in towns and cities, especially London, as Carl Moritz observed in 1782:

A few dirty-looking men, who bear the coffin, endeavour to make their way through the crowd as well as they can, and some mourners follow. The people seem to pay as little serious attention to such a procession as if a hay cart were driving past. The funerals of people of distinction are, however, differently regarded. These funerals always appear to me the more indecent in a populous city, from the total indifference of the beholders, and the perfect unconcern with which they are beheld. The body of a fellow-creature is carried to his long home, as though it had been utterly unconnected with the rest of mankind. Whereas, in a small town or village, every one knows every one, and no one can be so insignificant as not to be missed when he is taken away.[31]

Particularly in the countryside, local funeral customs might seem strange to outsiders. In parts of northern England, according to William Wordsworth, 'a bason full of Sprigs of Box-wood is placed at the door of the house from which the Coffin is taken up, and each person who attends the funeral ordinarily takes a Sprig of this Box-wood, and throws it into the grave of the deceased'.[32] At Porlock in Somerset, the traveller and writer Richard Ayton witnessed a quite different custom:

Before the procession moved to the church all the mourners met before the house of the deceased, and there chanted a hymn, assisted by a most incongruous accompaniment from the belfry, in which a merry and vigorous peal was ringing the whole time. The sobs and cries and singing of

the people, heard only at intervals, and indistinctly, through the deafen-
ing clangor of the bells, had a strange and most mournful effect.[33]

Ayton initially assumed this was a special kind of funeral, but was
informed that it 'was and had always been considered as a simple part
of the ceremony'.[34]

For the middle classes funerals could be quite elaborate events,
already showing signs of being the displays of status and wealth that
would be common in the later nineteenth century. When Catherine
Howes (wife of the Reverend George Howes) died in February 1782,
Parson Woodforde was impressed by her funeral at Hockering in
Norfolk: 'Before we went to Church there was chocolate and toast
and cake with red wine and white. At half past 11 o'clock we went to
Church with the corpse in the following procession – The corpse first
in an hearse and pair of horses, then followed the chaises'.[35] There
were six chaises in all, carrying family, fellow clergymen, the under-
taker and 'Mrs Howes two servant maid[s] in deep mourning'.[36] At
the rear, on foot, 'servants all in hatbands black closed the procession
and a handsome appearance the whole procession made'.[37]
Woodforde had himself conducted many funerals, and in his view
this 'was as decent, neat, handsome funeral as I ever saw and every
thing conducted in the best manner ... After our return from Church
we had cake and wine and chocolate and dried toast carried round.'[38]

Whatever the status of the dead person, funerals largely conformed
to a basic pattern. The coffin was carried from the deceased's home to
the churchyard – in a carriage, on the shoulders of pall bearers or on
a special wooden frame called a bier, sometimes supported on wheels.
Moritz noticed that the coffins were different from those in his native
Germany: 'The English coffins are made very economically, according to the exact form of the body; they are flat and broad at top,
tapering gradually from the middle, and drawing to a point at the
feet, not very unlike the case of a violin.'[39]

Funerals were usually heralded by tolling a bell, which was often
regarded as an integral part of the ceremony. When asked if a bell
could be sounded for the burial of an unbaptised child, Woodforde
refused, saying that 'as the funeral service could not be read over it,

the tolling of the bell at any time [was] to be inadmissible'.[40] Being unbaptised, the baby was denied a Christian funeral, and its burial could not even be marked by a funeral bell. Before lightning conductors were properly understood, bell ringing, a seemingly mundane occupation, could actually be dangerous. One particular stormy day in June 1782, Woodforde was shocked to hear that 'there were 3 men struck down in Pilton Church [in Somerset] by the lightning this morning – one of them killed instantly, but the others like to recover. The man that was struck dead was tolling a bell for a person lately dead, the other two were near him.'[41]

When the coffin arrived at the churchyard, it was customary for the priest to meet the funeral procession at the entrance. Many churchyards had a lich-gate where mourners could wait until the clergyman arrived. These lich-gates (or lych-gates, literally 'corpse-gates' from 'lych' or 'lich', an Old English word for 'corpse') often had some means of resting the coffin and sometimes seats for the pall bearers and a roof to shelter them from the weather. After a service inside the church, the burial service was carried out at the side of the grave, which had been dug earlier, but the ceremony did not always proceed smoothly. On one occasion Woodforde was irritated by the carelessness of his clerk: 'I buried poor Miss Rose this evening at Weston aged 20 years. It was a very pretty, decent funeral. But Js. Smith the Clerk made me wait in performing the office at the grave near a qr of an hour, the grave not being long enough a good deal. It was a very great interruption. I gave it to Js. afterwards.'[42] At another funeral, this time of a young man, a different problem occurred: 'as they were about to let the corpse into the grave one of the leathern straps gave way by the thread with which it was joined being quite decayed, but luckily it slipped before the corpse was moved far from the ground. A rope was then sent for to a neighbouring House with which it was safely deposited in the ground.'[43]

After the funeral, one widely observed custom was the distribution of mourning mementos, or 'favours', to the main people involved. When Woodforde attended the funeral of an old friend, 'We each of us had a rich black silk scarf [usually tied on as an armband] and hatband, and a pr. of beaver gloves.'[44] The servant accompanying him was also given a silk hatband and a pair of gloves – servants were expected to observe the same mourning as their employers.

These favours were a diplomatic part of the etiquette, and when a friend who died was buried in a neighbouring parish, the Reverend William Holland was initially offended. But the next day the family of the deceased made amends by sending him 'a very handsome sattin hatband and scarf, white and two pair of white gloves, one for my wife as well as one for myself. I expected a hatband, but not a scarf, and it is not the value of it either I regard so much as the intimation of respect it conveys.'[45] The following Sunday Holland conducted a service at a distant church and then officiated at his own church in Over Stowey, 'which was tolerably full and a great appearance there was of hatbands, and all white, and my own sattin scarf white also ... looked quite conspicuous'.[46] He particularly mentioned that the funeral favours were white, because this was unusual. Black was always the traditional mourning colour, but white could be used for people thought to be innocent in the sight of God, usually children and young unmarried women. In this instance it was a young man who had been buried, and Holland stressed that 'He was a well disposed young man ... of great moral integrity, and uprightness and sincerity of heart.'[47]

The actual place of burial depended on social status, and the most sought-after place was inside the church, either in the ground under the floor or sometimes in a family vault. If it was not possible to have a vault inside the church, a wealthy family might have one built close by in the churchyard. Doors or hatchways provided access to some vaults, and at his aunt's funeral in Bristol, Neast Prideaux remarked: 'When the coffin was put into the vault, I looked in, and saw my late sister's coffin, which was perfectly entire.'[48]

In Woodforde's parish of Weston Longville, the privilege of burial inside the church was assumed by the local squire Mr Custance and his family, and in November 1780 Woodforde buried their infant Edward Custance, just fifty-two days old: 'Neither Mr. nor Mrs. Custance there. The coffin was lead with a copper breast plate on it and on that was engraved the age and name of the child. The breast-plate was plain and made thus ◊. The child was buried in the chancel in the north aile.'[49]

These gradations of status were satirised on a gravestone set by the door to the chancel of St Edmund's Church at Kingsbridge in Devon, which carries the inscription:

UNDERNEATH
Lieth the Body of ROBERT
Comonly called BONE PHILLIP,
who died July 27th, 1793,
Aged 63 years,
At whose request the following lines are here inserted.
Here lie I at the Chancel door;
Here lie I because I'm poor;
The forther in the more you'll pay;
Here lie I as warm as they.[50]

It was not just a simple matter of being buried inside or outside the church, since different parts of the churchyard were more desirable than others. On a gravestone dated 1807 at the Church of St Andrews at Epworth in Lincolnshire, the inscription included the lines:

And that I might longer undisturbed abide,
I choosed to be laid on this Northern side.[51]

There was a reluctance to be buried on the north side of the church, which many people considered was for strangers, unbaptised infants, the poor and those suspected of suicide. In some places, there was also a superstitious dread of being buried on the north side, probably made worse by the fact that such graves were in the shadow of the church and away from the main paths leading to the west and south doors. At the Church of St Mary in Selborne, Hampshire, the curate Gilbert White expressed his concern:

all wish to be buried on the south side, which is becoming such a mass of mortality that no person can be interred there without disturbing or dis-placing the bones of his ancestors ... At the east end are a few graves; yet none till very lately on the north-side but, as two or three families of best

repute have begun to bury in that quarter, prejudice may wear out by
degrees, and their example be followed by the rest of the neighbourhood.[52]

White himself was buried in 1793 on the north side of the church at
Selborne, with a simple headstone giving his initials and date of
death.

In large cities and towns with growing populations, and particularly in London, entire churchyards were becoming crammed full
with burials. However, the situation had not yet reached the level of
dire overcrowding that would lead to large new cemeteries being
established in the mid-nineteenth century.

Burials were recorded in parish registers, and often the entry simply
consisted of the name of the deceased, some indication of where they
were living when they died and the burial date (not the date of death).
Ever since the Burial in Woollen Acts of 1666–80, registers were also
supposed to record whether a sworn affidavit had confirmed that the
dead person was buried in a woollen shroud. In November 1783 Parson
Woodforde recorded that he had received a shilling fee for providing
'a Certificate of Persons being buried in Woolen at Hockering according to the Act'.[53] Such a certificate ensured that the person responsible
for the burial was not liable to pay the £5 fine for not burying a person
in wool. The law had been designed to promote the English woollen
industry, but by Woodforde's time it was already widely ignored, and
the law was repealed in 1814.

After a funeral, the period of mourning continued, but the social
code was not so rigid as it would become in the Victorian era. As in
later decades, the time that women, particularly widows, spent in
mourning was longer than for men, and their mourning dress was
more conspicuous. Although there were variations between different
places, between social classes and even within families, it was
common for widows and close female relatives to stay in mourning
for at least a year. If someone died suddenly, people might be unpre-
pared and have no suitable clothes. Some black clothes might be
quickly obtained for the funeral, but the weeks and months of
mourning afterwards required a full wardrobe.

Having had to go into mourning with the family employing her at Dove Nest, Nelly Weeton asked a friend to forward her some clothes: 'Little expecting to wear black so soon after I left you, I brought nothing of the kind with me; and there are several things which might be worn to save better [ones]. What I have now is too good for every day.'[54] She asked for a parcel of her old clothes to be sent, including 'a black Chambray gown, a silk petticoat, a cambric muslin petticoat ... some black lace net, wrapped in a piece of black mode, and a black silk work bag with some crape'.[55]

When Cassandra Austen was with her brother Edward in October 1808, she found herself in a similar predicament on the sudden death of his wife Elizabeth. Jane therefore wrote to her:

> Your parcel shall set off on Monday, and I hope the shoes will fit; Martha and I both tried them on. I shall send you such of your mourning as I think most likely to be useful, reserving for myself your stockings and half the velvet, in which selfish arrangement I know I am doing what you wish. *I* am to be in bombazeen and crape, according to what we are told is universal *here*, and which agrees with Martha's previous observation. My mourning, however, will not impoverish me, for by having my velvet pelisse fresh lined and made up, I am sure I shall have no occasion *this winter* for anything new of that sort.[56]

The fact that Jane and Martha had discussed the correct mourning dress demonstrates how variable social etiquette was at this time. After being in full black mourning for a year or more, a woman might go into half-mourning, with less sombre clothes or a mixture of white and black. Men seldom went to such extremes. They generally wore dark-coloured clothes anyway, to which a black hatband and armband could be added. They also wore their mourning for shorter periods and were less likely to be censured for flouting such social conventions. In any case, mourning etiquette was largely for those who could afford to follow fashion – and fashion was set by the wealthy. The middle classes tried to follow their example, while the working classes made do with armbands, hatbands and whatever else they could afford. Servants might have mourning clothes provided for a bereavement in their employer's family, but not for a death in their own family.

When members of the royal family died, a time of national mourning was announced and the whole nation (being subjects of the monarch, rather than citizens of a state) was expected to respond. Because of the sudden overwhelming demand for black fabrics and the corresponding slump in the sale of most other colours, periods of national mourning frequently disrupted the textile industry. Sometimes, though, the response was less than zealous, and when the Duke of Gloucester died in 1805, Jane Austen wrote to Cassandra: 'I suppose everybody will be black for the D. of G. Must we buy lace, or will ribbon do?'[57] Yet when the popular Princess Charlotte died in childbirth in November 1817, a few months after Jane's death, genuine public grief was evident as William Darter recalled:

> the lamented death of the Princess Charlotte occurred at the age of 22, leaving a husband (Prince Leopold) and the whole nation in deep sorrow. No public event in my time ever produced such a universal union of spontaneous sympathy. All business was suspended and shops closed; blinds were drawn down to the windows of private houses, and even the poorest of the poor wore some humble token of sympathy.[58]

Before the period of mourning was well under way, but usually after the funeral, the will of the dead person was read, proven and executed. For anyone with any wealth to bequeath, however small, a will was essential. Jane Austen left a simple will, bequeathing to her sister most of her estate:

> I JANE AUSTEN of the Parish of Chawton do by this my last Will and testament give and bequeath to my dearest sister Cassandra Eliz'th every thing of which I may die possessed or which may hereafter be due to me subject to the payment of my funeral expenses and to a legacy of £50 to my brother Henry and £50 to Mde Bijion which I request may be paid as soon as convenient and I appoint my said dear sister EXECUTRIX of this my last Will and testament JANE AUSTEN April 27; 1817.[59]

As executrix, Cassandra distributed a few personal items among relatives and close friends, including some of her sister's hair. It was common to cut hair from a dead person as a memento, which was often put into a locket or incorporated into mourning jewellery such as a ring or a brooch.

Wills were crucial in ensuring that wealth was kept within the family and that the estate passed intact to the eldest son or another male relative. This situation is a frequent feature of Jane Austen's novels and drives the plot in *Pride and Prejudice* – although Mr Bennet owns a modest estate and has enough to keep his family comfortably, he has five daughters and no son. The terms under which he himself inherited the estate ensure that without a male heir, it will pass to his next male relative – the unpleasant Mr Collins. Mr Bennet's family could therefore be left destitute. Mrs Bennet and her daughters would never be able to find occupations to support themselves and so would be dependent on charity from relatives.

All this unspoken anxiety, resulting from middle-class attempts to maintain their position in society, is behind Mrs Bennet's hysterical outbursts. On hearing that Mr Collins is engaged to Charlotte Lucas, Mrs Bennet is immediately convinced that they will be uncharitable towards her family: 'Indeed, Mr Bennet, it is very hard to think that Charlotte Lucas should ever be mistress of this house, that *I* should be forced to make way for *her*, and live to see her take my place in it!' This complaint brings forth a typically ironic reply from her husband: 'My dear, do not give way to such gloomy thoughts. Let us hope for better things. Let us flatter ourselves that *I* may be the survivor.' The humour masks the gravity of the underlying situation, but as Jane Austen's contemporaries might have personally known people in similar situations, or be in such a position themselves, the humour was obviously pointed.

While the relatives argued over the will, the body of the dead person was left to rest in peace – except where bodysnatchers were at work. People visiting graveyards today to discover where their ancestors lie may be unaware that the body occupied the grave for only a few hours. Various measures were taken to stop bodysnatchers where they were particularly active, the simplest being to bury the coffin deeper in the ground, making it more difficult to reach. Strong, well-made coffins, especially those lined with lead, provided some deterrent, and coffins designed to foil bodysnatchers were advertised in newspapers such as the *Morning Post*:

> INFORMATION to the PUBLIC.—The FRAUD of ROBBING GRAVES and VAULTS, in and near London, is constantly practised, and the bodies missing bearing a small proportion to the numbers dissected, it is presumed a security for the dead from such depredations, must prove a great consolation to the living. This security is the PATENT COFFIN, which not only protects the body, but prevents the lead being stolen; nor is lead necessary where the Patent Coffin is used, but in particular cases. The Patent Coffin may be had, at a few hours notice, of Jarvis, Son, and Co. Undertakers, 15, Piccadilly.[60]

More bodies were dissected than were reported stolen, and so the advertisement was playing on the fear of readers that they might be weeping over an empty grave. Jarvis's Patent Coffins were supposedly impossible to open, but ordinary coffin lids could also be reinforced and various obstructions, such as branches and stones, placed on top, while the grave itself could be covered with heavy stone slabs. Unfortunately, most of these precautions were circumvented by bodysnatchers digging alongside the coffin rather than directly over it and breaking into the grave from the side. In some churchyards traps were set with spring guns fired by tripwires, but they could be disarmed in advance by an accomplice. Watchmen were hired to guard churchyards at night, but they could be bribed, and the only way to be certain that a corpse remained undisturbed was for trusted family and friends to keep a vigil until the body was no longer fresh enough to be a valuable commodity.

For poor people, the possibility of mustering enough friends and family to guard the grave was severely limited by their own need to keep working to survive. Nor could working-class people afford patent coffins, or indeed anything but the cheapest coffins, so it is hardly surprising that bodysnatchers preyed mainly on the graves of the poor – and there were so many more of them. In death, as in life, the wealthy enjoyed distinct advantages. This situation was summarised in a verse that is found, with minor variations, on many gravestones of the eighteenth and nineteenth centuries:

> This world's a City full of Crooked streets,
> And death the Market place where all men Meets,
> If life was Merchandise that men could buy,
> The rich would live and none but poor would die.[61]

Quite often poorer people could not afford gravemarkers, while many simply put up wooden markers, such as a cross. Alternatively, a wooden post might be placed at each end of the grave, supporting a plank on which an inscription was carved or painted. Commemorative monuments inside the church were a mark of privilege, and so those with money but insufficient influence opted for monuments in the churchyard. This fashion was gradually copied by the middle and lower classes, so that it became desirable to set up a headstone, however humble, to mark a relative's grave. More elaborate gravemarkers evolved, and from the end of the eighteenth century those churchyards with large numbers of burials had a variety of shapes, sizes and designs of tombstone.

The expansion of the canal system helped to reduce the cost of gravestones, since suitable blocks of stone were transported more cheaply by barge than by road. Although many areas had local quarries that supplied stone at a reasonable price, not all stone was well suited to gravestones, as John Byng sadly noted at Leicester in 1789: 'Much black slate, cut thick, is used here for hearths, chimney pieces, &c, looking very black and shining; but the coarser sort, used for tombstones, is very bad for us travellers, as the letters thereon are soon unintelligible.'[62]

It was already becoming popular with travellers like him to read and record the gravestones. After the service one Sunday morning in 1782, at Nettlebed in Oxfordshire, Carl Moritz wandered round the churchyard and wrote down the inscription on the gravestone of blacksmith William Strange, who had died on 6 June 1746:

I ... went out of the church with the congregation, and amused myself with reading the inscriptions on the tomb-stones, in the church yard; which in general, are simpler, more pathetic, and better written than ours [in Germany]. There are some of them which, to be sure, were ludicrous and laughable enough. Among these is one on the tomb of a smith, which, on account of its singularity, I copied.

> My sledge and anvil lie declined,
> My bellows too have lost their wind;
> My fire's extinct, my forge decay'd,
> And in the dust my vice is laid;
> My coals are spent, my iron's gone,
> My nails are drove, my work is done.[63]

Another foreign visitor, Louis Simond from the United States, was impressed by the way the living remembered the dead, marking the graves with

> an urn, an iron railing, a stone, a simple board, all bearing inscriptions, where something more than mere name and date is recorded. Rank and titles stand first, and require nothing else; these wanting, virtues are told of, and some ambitious quotation from the poets is made to vouch for them; the deceased was either great or good. I have noticed, however, inscriptions boasting of obscurity, as if it had been a matter of choice.[64]

Even sailors on shore leave would occasionally shun the dockside taverns and explore further afield, like Robert Hay in 1809. When his ship was moored at Plymouth, he and a companion travelled across Dartmoor to the village of Sourton, near Okehampton:

> After washing down a comfortable supper with a glass of first-rate cyder, we strolled out for an hour to examine the village. I had lately been reading in Pope[65] an account of the partiality of the English peasantry for poetical epitaphs. This complete master of the art of rhyming quotes the following lines which he says are to be found in almost every country church yard in England:

'Afflictions sore, long time I bore
Physicians tried in vain,
Till God it pleased that death me seized
To terminate my pain.'

As an antique church and burrying ground adjoined the village, we repaired thither to see whither the above motto could be found, and to indulge in the perusal of other memento moris, which always reminds us of our favourite amusement – a half hour's lounge in a bookseller's shop. The first poetical epitaph that met our eye consisted of these identical lines.[66]

Reading memorials in churchyards and browsing in bookshops are still – of course – popular pastimes.

The trend towards stone gravemarkers and the desire for a permanent memorial have provided a huge resource for investigating the lives and deaths of our ancestors from two centuries ago. The epitaphs and other inscriptions often go beyond the plain record of who is buried to tell us something of their lives and characters. Memorial stones, records, buildings and artefacts from Jane Austen's time ensure that the dead – the ancestors – are not forgotten. The memorial stone to Jane herself is inside Winchester Cathedral. She was probably buried there because it was the nearest burial place to the house in College Street where she died, and some of her family, particularly her brother Henry, had influence with the Dean of the Cathedral. Her grave slab in the floor of the north aisle carries the inscription:

In Memory of
JANE AUSTEN,
youngest daughter of the late
Revd GEORGE AUSTEN,
formerly Rector of Steventon in this County,
she departed this Life on the 18th of July 1817,
aged 41, after a long illness supported with
the patience and the hopes of a Christian.
The benevolence of her heart,

the sweetness of her temper, and
the extraordinary endowments of her mind
obtained the regard of all who knew her and
the warmest love of her intimate connections.
Their grief is in proportion to their affection,
they know their loss to be irreparable,
but in their deepest affliction they are consoled
by a firm though humble hope that her charity,
devotion, faith and purity have rendered
her soul acceptable in the sight of her
REDEEMER.

The mention of the 'extraordinary endowments of her mind' is the only hint of her career as a novelist, because this was essentially a family epitaph. Only later were other memorials set up in the cathedral to acknowledge her literary achievement. But in reality Jane Austen needs no such memorial. Her books live on as classics of the art of the novelist and as a constant reminder of herself, her contemporaries and an England that has passed.

WEIGHTS AND MEASURES

Some units of measurement that are used today had different values two centuries ago, and there were also many local variations, even between neighbouring counties and towns. Attempts to make weights and measures consistent were not entirely successful, and people still talked of a 'country mile', meaning a distance much longer than a 'standard' mile. An Act of Parliament standardising weights and measures came into force in 1826, but it was not very effective, and further changes of the law were necessary in 1834 and 1835 before any real uniformity was achieved.

In Jane Austen's time even common measures such as the stone and the bushel varied from place to place – a serious hindrance to merchants trading across the country. After the French Revolution metric measurements were adopted in France, but in England these were used only by a few, largely for scientific purposes.

Nominal weights and measures in Jane Austen's time are given below, taken from contemporary sources (Branch 1801 and Mortimer 1810).

Length

3 barley-corns	1 inch (in.)
4 inches	1 hand
12 inches	1 foot (ft)
3 feet	1 yard (yd)
6 feet	1 fathom
5½ yards	1 rod, pole or perch
40 rods	1 furlong
8 furlongs (1760 yards)	1 mile

Area

144 square inches	1 square foot
9 square feet	1 square yard
4 roods (4840 square yards)	10 square chains or 1 acre

Volume

2 pints	1 quart
4 quarts	1 gallon
2 gallons	1 peck
4 pecks	1 bushel
3 bushels	1 sack

Weight

16 ounces (oz)	1 pound (lb.)
14 pounds	1 stone
28 pounds	1 quarter
8 stone or 4 quarters	1 hundredweight (cwt)
20 hundredweight	1 ton

Metric equivalents

1 centimetre	0.3937 inches
1 metre	1.09364 yards
1 square metre	1.1960 square yards
1 litre	1.7313 ale pints or 2.1135 wine pints
1 kilogram	2 pounds, 3 ounces and 5 drams (avoirdupois)

1 inch	2.54 centimetres
1 foot	30.48 centimetres
1 yard	0.9144 metres
1 mile	1609.344 metres (1.609 kilometres)

CHRONOLOGICAL OVERVIEW

Some key events relating to Jane Austen's life and episodes in Britain's history are given below. For a detailed Jane Austen chronology, see Le Faye 2006.

1760	25 October	George III became king.
1770	7 April	William Wordsworth, poet, was born.
1771	March	Nelson joined the Royal Navy.
	15 August	Walter Scott, novelist, was born.
1772	22 June	British case law established that a slave landing in England was a free person.
	21 October	Samuel Taylor Coleridge, poet, was born.
1773	16 December	Boston Tea Party, when American colonists protested against the unjust taxation of tea imports.
1774	10 May	Accession of Louis XVI as king of France.
	12 August	Robert Southey, poet, was born.
1775	19 April	War of American Independence (American Revolutionary War) began, with the British defeat at Lexington.
	23 August	J.M.W. Turner, painter, was born.
	16 December	Jane Austen was born.
1776	11 June	John Constable, painter, was born.
	4 July	American Declaration of Independence.
1778	6 February	The French became allies of America.
	17 March	Britain declared war on France.
	11 May	William Pitt the Elder died.
	17 December	Humphry Davy, engineer and chemist, was born.

1779	16 June	Spain declared war on Britain.
1780	1 January	The first iron bridge, across the River Severn at Coalbrookdale, was officially opened.
	2–9 June	Gordon Riots in London.
	20 November	Britain declared war on the Netherlands.
1781	9 June	George Stephenson, engineer, was born.
1782	24 August	David Tyrie was the last man in England to be hung, drawn and quartered.
1783	3 September	Peace of Versailles between Britain, France, Spain and America. Britain, France and Spain each recovered some of the territories they had lost. Britain recognised American independence.
1784	20 May	Peace treaty between Britain and Holland.
	15 September	Lunardi was the first man in England to ascend in a balloon.
	13 December	Samuel Johnson died.
1787	May	The first convoy of convicts ('First Fleet') sailed from Britain to begin the European colonisation of Australia.
1788	1 January	John Walter founded *The Times* newspaper.
	22 January	Lord Byron, poet, was born.
	15 April	Alliance between Britain and Netherlands.
	2 August	Thomas Gainsborough, painter, died.
	13 August	Triple Alliance between Britain, Netherlands and Prussia.
1789	18 March	Christian Bowman was the last woman in England to be burned at the stake.
	30 April	George Washington became first President of the USA.
	14 July	The storming of the Bastille in Paris, and the beginning of the French Revolution.
1790	17 April	Benjamin Franklin died.
1791	July	Priestley riots in Birmingham.
1792	20 April	France began the Revolutionary War by declaring war against Austria.
	4 August	Percy Bysshe Shelley, poet, was born.

1793	21 January	Execution of Louis XVI.
	1 February	France declared war on Britain and Holland.
	26 June	Gilbert White of Selborne died.
	16 October	Execution of Marie Antoinette.
1794	1 June	The British defeated the French at the Battle of 'Glorious First of June'.
1795	29 October	Assassination attempt on George III in London.
	31 October	John Keats, poet, was born.
1796	5 October	Spain declared war on Britain.
1797	14 February	The British defeated the Spanish at the Battle of St Vincent.
	May–June	Mutinies aboard British warships at Spithead and the Nore.
	11 October	The British defeated the Dutch at the Battle of Camperdown.
1798	1 August	The French fleet was destroyed by Nelson at the Battle of the Nile.
1799	14 December	George Washington died.
1800	5 September	Britain captured Malta from France.
1801	1 January	Act of Union, uniting Great Britain and Ireland.
	10 March	First census of Great Britain.
	1 October	Peace treaty (of Amiens) between France and Britain.
1802	27 March	The Peace of Amiens between France and Britain was ratified.
1803	1 January	Parson James Woodforde died.
	30 April	The Louisiana territories were sold by Napoleon to America.
	18 May	Start of the Napoleonic Wars between Britain and France.
1804	2 December	Napoleon was crowned Napoleon I.
	12 December	Spain declared war on Britain.
1805	21 January	George Austen died at Bath.
	21 October	Battle of Trafalgar, when the French and Spanish were defeated by the British and Nelson was killed.

1806	9 January	Funeral of Nelson.
	23 January	Death of Prime Minister William Pitt (the Younger).
1807	28 January	Gas street lighting was demonstrated in Pall Mall.
	25 March	The British slave trade (but not slavery) was abolished.
1811	5 February	George III was declared insane and the Prince of Wales became Prince Regent.
	27 May	Census in Great Britain.
	30 October	Jane Austen's first novel, *Sense and Sensibility*, was published.
1812	7 February	Charles Dickens was born.
	19 June	United States declared war on Britain (the so-called '1812 war').
1813	28 January	*Pride and Prejudice* was published.
1814	February	Last frost fair on the River Thames.
	11 April	Napoleon abdicated and went into exile on Elba.
	9 May	*Mansfield Park* was published.
	24 December	A peace treaty was signed at Ghent, ending the 1812 war between Britain and America.
1815	8 January	Battle of New Orleans in America.
	15 January	Emma Hamilton died.
	February	End of the war between Britain and America.
	1 March	Napoleon escaped from Elba and landed in France.
	18 June	Battle of Waterloo.
	23 December	*Emma* was published.
1816	21 April	Charlotte Brontë was born.
	17 July	Richard Brinsley Sheridan died.
1817	18 July	Jane Austen died at Winchester.
	20 December	*Northanger Abbey* was published.
	20 December	*Persuasion* was published.

| 1871 | June | Jane Austen's novel *Lady Susan* and the unfinished fragment of *The Watsons* were published. |
| 1925 | | The unfinished fragment of Jane Austen's novel *Sanditon* was published. |

NOTES

INTRODUCTION: KNOW YOUR PLACE

1 In 1806 the Austen family journeyed north to visit relatives, and in August they stayed at Stoneleigh Abbey. On 13 August Mrs Austen wrote to Mary, wife of her son James, that they would travel to Hamstall Ridware the next day (Austen-Leigh 1942, p. 247). It is not certain if they actually made this journey, or even if they travelled further north. Letters destroyed after Jane Austen's death may have revealed other places she visited.

2 See the Chronological Overview on p. 347.

3 October 1800. Somerset Archives and Local Studies, A\BTL/2/10.

4 13 October 1800. Somerset Archives and Local Studies, A\BTL/2/10.

5 *The Annual Register or a View of the History, Politics, and Literature for the Year 1816* (1817), p. 67.

6 George Austen's library contained some 500 volumes, which were sold off when he retired to Bath.

7 28 September 1814. Austen-Leigh and Austen-Leigh 1913, pp. 359–60. Her niece was Anna Austen, who became Anna Lefroy on her marriage to Ben Lefroy in November 1814. Anna's novel was never published.

8 *Edinburgh Magazine or Literary Miscellany* January 1799, 'On the Cause of the Popularity of Novels', pp. 33–6. First published in the *Universal Magazine* of 1798.

9 Austen-Leigh and Austen-Leigh 1913, p. 356.

10 August 1814. Austen-Leigh and Austen-Leigh 1913, p. 355.

11 Austen-Leigh and Austen-Leigh 1913, p. 356.

12 *A Review of the State of the British Nation* 25 June 1709 (vol. 6, p. 26).

13 4 December 1800. Somerset Archives and Local Studies, A\BTL/2/12.

14 29 January 1810. Somerset Archives and Local Studies, A\BTL/2/31. Andrew Guy lived at Barford near Bridgwater in Somerset.

15 Diary entry for 10 February 1795; Jupp 1991, p. 204.

16 Eden 1797b, pp. 30, 223, 528. Sir Frederick Morton Eden was born in 1766, became a baronet in 1784 and died in 1809. The three volumes of *The State of the Poor* were published under his name Frederic, but elsewhere he is spelled as Frederick. Many thanks to Professor Donald Winch for discussing this problem with us. Eden founded the Globe Insurance Company.

17 From Blake's untitled poem, written around 1804, in his Preface to *Milton, a Poem*.

18 25 January 1801. Somerset Archives and Local Studies, A\BTL/2/13. Born in 1746, Holland is known to have kept a diary from 1799 until 1818, the year before he died.

19 Ayres 1984. The diaries are now in the Somerset Archives and Local Studies, A\BTL/2.

1: WEDDING BELLS

1   The Reverend James Woodforde is traditionally referred to as Parson Woodforde, because abridged diary extracts were first published in 1923 using this title, decades before the Parson Woodforde Society embarked on full publication (Winstanley 1996).

2   The marriage took place on 25 January 1787. Winstanley and Jameson 1999, p. 205. The absent vicar of St Peter's was the Reverend Carter.

3   *Newcastle Courant* 10 February 1787.

4   Winstanley and Jameson 1999, p. 205.

5   The wedding was on 23 September 1794. Jameson 2004, p. 73. Anne's surname was actually Dunnell.

6   Brayne 1998, pp. 13–14.

7   *The Mysteries of Udolpho* was first published in 1794.

8   25 February 1810. Hall 1936, p. 239. She is referred to as Ellen in her biography, but was actually called Nelly after her father's merchant ship. Bessy Winkley did later marry, becoming Bessy Price.

9   Hall 1936, pp. 310–11. Letter to Miss Bessy Winkley dated 18 October 1810.

10 27 January 1791. Original copy of the diary for this date is missing. Jameson 2003, p. 4.

11 31 January 1791. Original copy of the diary for this date is missing. Jameson 2003, p. 4.

12 Jameson 2001, p. 66.

13 Apprenticeship indenture in authors' collection. See Chapter 3 for further details.

14 *Drewry's Derby Mercury* 29 September 1775.

15 Andrews 1891, p. 187, quoting *Harrop's Manchester Mercury* 12 March 1771.

16 *Derby Mercury* 28 December 1797. The wedding took place before 23 December.

17 28 August 1788. Jameson 2001, p. 66; Beresford 1927, p. 45. Many thanks to Martin Brayne and Peter Jameson for clarifying this quote.

18 Rowe 1796, p. 113.

19 12 November 1810. Somerset Archives and Local Studies A\BTL/2/34.

20 19 October 1800. Somerset Archives and Local Studies A\BTL/2/11.

21 Brand 1813, p. 33. John Brand lived from 1744 to 1806.

22 Brand 1813, p. 33.

23 Brand 1813, p. 35.

24 Brand 1813, p. 67.

25 Nicholson and Burn 1776, p. 620. In 1816 this bell cracked, and when it was recast, the inscription was reinstated on the new bell, with minor changes.

26 Brabourne 1884b, p. 16.

27 Rowe 1796, p. 112.

28 *Derby Mercury* 10 June 1802.

29 *Western Luminary* 21 February 1815.

30 28 December 1809. Hall 1936, p. 218.

31 Elliott 1842, p. 2.

32 Elliott 1842, pp. 18–19.

33 19 October 1800. Somerset Archives and Local Studies A\BTL/2/11.

34 The *Oxford English Dictionary* dates the first use of 'old maid' ('oulde mayde') to 1530.

35 Hayley 1786, p. 7.

36 Brabourne 1884b, p. 296.

37 17 July 1809. Hall 1936, p. 178.

38 Hall 1936, p. 178.

39 Information from Ruth A. Symes in *Oxford Dictionary of National Biography* online. Her daughter Mary was removed from her care at the separation.

40 See Vickery 2003, pp. 72–83; Moore 2009, pp. 297–303.

41 Jeffery 1907, p. 314.

42 Jeffery 1907, p. xxii.

43 *Hampshire Chronicle and Portsmouth and Chichester Journal* 9 April 1796.

44 Brand 1813, p. 37.

45 *Northampton Mercury* 7 January 1790.

46 *Morning Post* 13 January 1815. The sale took place ten days earlier.

47 27 December 1808. Brabourne 1884b, pp. 46–7.

48 Christie 1929, p. 179. William Jones had been vicar from 1801 and a curate before then.

49 Christie 1929, pp. 179–80. This was June 1805.

50 13 March 1817. Chapman 1932b, p. 483.

2: BREEDING

1 Austen-Leigh 1942, p. 29. Letter of 6 June 1773 to Mrs Walter, wife of the half-brother of George Austen (Jane Austen's father).

2 For example, *Derby Mercury* 8 February 1798.

3 Brabourne 1884a, p. 166. Letter written on Saturday 17 November 1798.

4 Brabourne 1884a, p. 167. The boy grew up to become the Reverend James Edward Austen-Leigh (1798–1874).

5 Chapman 1932b, p. 76. Letter to Cassandra of 29 January 1813.

6 Winstanley Hall is a Grade II* listed building but has become derelict in a planning dispute. Winstanley Park and the buildings are bordered today by the M6 motorway.

7 Hall 1936, pp. 166–7. Letter to Miss Whitehead, 23 May 1809. Despite their preparations, Mrs Bankes died in childbirth and the infant soon after. Nelly Weeton used the spelling 'Banks' in her letters.

8 Smith 1785, pp. 19–20.

9 Smith 1785, p. 20.

10 Brabourne 1884a, p. 253. Letter written at Steventon on 3 January 1801. Coulson Wallop MP died as a prisoner-of-war in France in 1807.

11 Brand 1813, pp. 6–7.

12 Later lying-in hospitals included Liverpool in 1841 and Sheffield in 1863. Most were for married women, but the New Westminster Lying-in Hospital (later the General Lying-in Hospital) admitted unmarried women. The first lying-in wards (within hospitals) were opened in London in 1747, and several lying-in hospitals were established there during the next five years.

13 Letter written at Beacon's Gutter, near Liverpool, on 23 May 1809. Hall 1936, p. 167.

14 2 November 1794. Jameson 2004, p. 91.

15 3 November 1794. Jameson 2004, p. 92.

16 Brabourne 1884a, p. 159. Letter written on 27 October 1798.

17 25 June 1783. Winstanley 1998, pp. 146–7.

18 26 June 1783. Winstanley 1998, p. 147. Frances Anne married Robert Marsham around 1804 and died in January 1874.

19 13 July 1785. Winstanley and Jameson 1999, pp. 53–4.

20 British Library Add MS 35143, fol. 71.

21 See Vickery 2003, pp. 97–8.

22 Cooper 1776, p. 231.

23 Cooper 1776, p. 221.

24 Cooper 1776, p. 222.

25 Cooper 1776, p. 231.

26 Cooper 1776, p. 227.

27 She was buried on 16 August 1774, two days after the caesarean. The churchyard was later sold to construct the Holborn Viaduct, and some bodies were placed in the church crypt (since reinterred in the City of London Cemetery).

28 She had been travelling on top of a loaded cart, had fallen off and been crushed beneath one of the cartwheels.

29 Barlow 1834, p. 569.

30 The operation was performed on 27 November 1793. Jane Foster died about 1826; her age at death is given as sixty-eight or seventy-two.

31 White 1773, p. 157.

32 White 1773, p. 115.

33 White 1773, p. 6.

34 White 1773, p. 130.

35 White 1773, pp. 283–5.

36 23 May 1809. Hall 1936, pp. 166–7.

37 *Cheltenham Chronicle and Gloucestershire Advertiser* 28 August 1817. They were John, Charles, Robert and Caroline.

38 *Norfolk Chronicle* 8 November 1817. She died on 5 November 1817.

39 White 1789, p. 13.

40 *New Exeter Journal* 22 January 1789.

41 *Hull Packet* 27 October 1801. The Constable family of Everingham Park in East Yorkshire were gentry, a branch of the large Constable-Maxwell family.

42 Upton-Wilkinson archive (071109fpwwo1).

43 Upton-Wilkinson archive (071109fpwwo1).

44 Upton-Wilkinson archive (080105wwsp).

45 This provided the perfect setting for stories about changelings.

46 Upton-Wilkinson archive (071109wwwspo1). A wet-nurse is far more likely than a nursemaid, because the family was so short of money for such a luxury.

47 Foreman 1998, pp. 122–3.

48 Downman 1803, p. 19. *Infancy* was later published as a single volume.

49 White 1773, pp. 58–9.

50 White 1773, p. 63.

51 Moss 1781, p. 60.

52 Austen-Leigh 1942, p. 28. Letter of 8 November 1772, written at Steventon.

53 Austen-Leigh 1942, p. 29. Letter to Mrs Walter of 6 June 1773, written at Steventon.

54 Austen Leigh 1871, p. 41.

55 Leviticus 12.2–8.

56 6 December 1800. Somerset Archives and Local Studies A\BTL/2/12.

57 Andrews 1935, p. 370.

58 11 March 1787. Winstanley and Jameson 1999, p. 222.

59 18 March 1787. Winstanley and Jameson 1999, p. 224.

60 More detailed pre-printed forms were required from 1812 as part of the Rose's Act of 1812.

61 10 September 1783. Winstanley 1998, p. 170.

62 11 December 1786. Winstanley and Jameson 1999, p. 192.

63 17 February 1810. Somerset Archives and Local Studies A\BTL/2/31.

64 18 February 1810. Somerset Archives and Local Studies A\BTL/2/31.

65 Sunday 25 February 1810.

66 Chapman 1932a, p. 97.

67 30 June 1783. Winstanley 1998, p. 148.

68 September 1814. Chapman 1932b, p. 400.

69 Brabourne 1884a, p. 315. Written at Southampton on 7 January 1807. Captain Edward James Foote divorced his first wife by Act of Parliament in July 1803, and one of the children of that earlier marriage was called Caroline. He married Mary Patton in August 1803 and had four daughters, including Elizabeth.

70 Moss 1781, p. 41.

71 Moss 1781, p. 44.

72 Austen-Leigh 1942, p. 29. Letter to Mrs Walter 6 June 1773, written at Steventon.

73 Moss 1781, pp. 43–4.

74 Moss 1781, pp. 159–60.

75 *Derby Mercury* 24 March 1775.

76 Moss 1781, pp. 164–6.

77 16 September 1808. Upton-Wilkinson archive (080916spww).

78 18 September 1808. Upton-Wilkinson archive (080918spww). He was either Mr Thomson or Thompson, possibly Frederick Thompson who had been a Royal Navy surgeon and was resident in Kensington from at least 1790.

79 Upton-Wilkinson archive (080925jbww).

80 Buckle commonplace book, courtesy of Trustees of the National Museum of the Royal Navy NMRN, P2002 73, f.23.

81 Moritz 1809, p. 10. Carl is also spelled Karl and at times written as Charles in English translations. Born in Hameln in 1756, Carl Moritz struggled with poverty for much of his life. He died in 1793, barely a decade after his visit to England (Winstanley 2012).

82 Price 1783, p. 253.

83 Price 1783, p. 281.

84 'Abstract of the Answers and Returns made pursuant to an act, passed in the forty-first year of His Majesty King George III, Parish Registers, ordered to be printed 21st December 1801. Abstract of the answers and returns to the population act, 42 Geo III, 1800 County of Cornwall'.

85 Perhaps as many as 8,658,265, allowing for uncounted children and those in the armed forces (Wrigley and Schofield 1989, p. 595).

86   Percival 1774, p. 55.

87   In 1811 England had a population of 9,476,700, including 1,009,546 living in London (Wrigley and Schofield 1989, p. 66).

88   Simond 1817, pp. 259–60.

89   17 October 1808. Moretonhampstead History Society manuscript of Treleaven's diary (box 2 of the Society's archives). Silvester Treleaven seems to have been the son of the first postmaster of Moretonhampstead, John Treleaven (information from the Moretonhampstead History Society website).

90   25 January 1805. Somerset Archives and Local Studies A\BTL/2/20.

91   See Chater 2009, p. 238.

92   29 October 1799. Somerset Archives and Local Studies A\BTL/2/1.

93   9 October 1800. Somerset Archives and Local Studies A\BTL/2/10. See Penhallurick 1991, p. 290.

94   White 2012, pp. 156–7.

95   *Report from Select Committee on the Education of the Lower Orders in the Metropolis* (London, 1816), p. 1.

96   Colquhoun 1796, pp. 167–8. The overall Jewish population in England certainly exceeded twenty thousand. London did have the largest Jewish community, but Colquhoun probably overestimated the numbers.

97   British Library Add MS 27827, fols 145–6. Place was writing especially of the 1770s.

98   *Morning Post and Gazetteer* 7 June 1802.

99   *Morning Post and Gazetteer* 14 June 1802.

100 *Morning Post and Gazetteer* 14 June 1802.

101 Hall 1936, p. 60. This was mid-December 1807.

102 *Western Flying Post* 7 November 1803.

103 Chapman 1932b, p. 480. Sophia Deedes was the sister-in-law of Edward, Jane Austen's brother.

104 Grose 1811. Such handbills were distributed in the streets to likely customers. Mrs Phillips had long since died by 1776, but her name continued to be used.

105 15 May 1777. Winstanley 1981, p. 130.

106 18 May 1775. Winstanley 1989, p. 141.

107 Rubenhold 2005.

108 Cyprus was home to the ancient Greek goddess of love and prostitutes, Aphrodite, hence the use of 'Cyprian' relating to prostitutes. *Harris's List of Covent-Garden Ladies: or, Man of Pleasure's Kalendar, for the year 1789* (London), p. 39.

109 Hall 1936, p. 167.

110 Watson 1827, pp. 22–3.

111 12 August 1779. Winstanley 1983, p. 164.

112 8 October 1786. Winstanley and Jameson 1999, p. 173.

113 *Harris's List of Covent-Garden Ladies: or, Man of Pleasure's Kalendar, for the year 1789* (London), p. iii.

114 *Harris's List of Covent-Garden Ladies: or, Man of Pleasure's Kalendar, for the year 1789* (London), p. viii. The 'toyman' dealt in small metal goods, of which children's toys formed only a small part. The hub of the toy trade was Birmingham.

115 British Library Add MS 35143, fol. 143.

116 Romney 1984, pp. 94–5. The White Swan is still a hotel. Fothergill went to

Canada in 1816 and became involved in politics. He died in 1840. His life was
marked by profligacy and failure.

117 Romney 1984, p. 94.
118 Romney 1984, p. 171.
119 3 July 1810. Somerset Archives and Local Studies A\BTL/2/33.
120 9 July 1810. Somerset Archives and Local Studies A\BTL/2/33.

3: TODDLER TO TEENAGER

1 Struve 1802, p. 328.
2 Gillett 1945, p. 27. Elizabeth Ham was born on 30 November 1783 at North
   Perrott, Somerset.
3 Hay 1953, p. 44. This was August 1803.
4 Andrews 1934, p. 83.
5 Andrews 1935, p. 72.
6 15 May 1805. Silliman 1810, p. 86.
7 Silliman 1820b, p. 132. This was in November 1805.
8 Silliman 1820b, p. 133.
9 Silliman 1820b, p. 132.
10 Walker 1792, p. 84. He was largely self-taught and was especially accomplished in
   mechanics. Describing dialects as far south as Worcestershire, he commented:
   'Dialects more south and east have run too much into one another to admit of
   definition; and ere long that will be the case with the whole kingdom.' (1792,
   p. 84).
11 Millard 1895, p. 44.
12 Walker 1792, p. 83. Adam Walker was no relation of John Walker.
13 *Walker's Critical Pronouncing Dictionary, and Expositor of the English Language*
   (1819).
14 Belsham 1795, p. 1. Briton is often misquoted as Britain. George III was
   deliberately identifying himself with his subjects and distancing himself from his
   forebears, who were often despised as German interlopers. This realignment of
   the monarchy mirrored a fashion for elocution. Thomas Sheridan, father of the
   politician-playwright Richard Brinsley Sheridan, ran extremely popular and
   lucrative courses of elocution lessons and published in 1762 *A Course of Lectures on
   Elocution*, followed by a pronunciation dictionary that ran to several editions, the
   precursor of Walker's dictionary.
15 24 October 1808. Brabourne 1884b, p. 26.
16 *The Mother's Remarks on a Set of Three Hundred and Thirty Six Cuts for Children*
   1802 (London), p. 22, quoted in *Journal of the British Archaeological Association* 30
   (1874), p. 40.
17 17 July 1802. Somerset Archives and Local Studies A\BTL/2/15.
18 10 January 1806. Somerset Archives and Local Studies A\BTL/2/25.
19 *Northampton Mercury* 27 April 1772.
20 Gillett 1945, p. 24.
21 Gillett 1945, p. 19.
22 Old Bailey Proceedings online, December 1811 (t18111204-3). This trial was of a
   woman wrongly acused of stealing the boy's clothes, before his real abductor had
   been found.

23 Old Bailey Proceedings online, December 1811 (t18111204-3). The two children
    were Thomas Dillone and his sister Rebecca. Thomas's abduction is described
    later in this chapter (pp. 58–9).
24 Gillett 1945, p. 27.
25 10 May 1803. Somerset Archives and Local Studies A\BTL/2/16.
26 10 September 1803. Somerset Archives and Local Studies A\BTL/2/17.
27 *Bell's Weekly Messenger* 6 November 1814.
28 *The Times* 1 May 1799.
29 This was probably a confusion with Edward Wortley Montagu, son of Lady
    Mary Wortley Montagu, who periodically ran away from home, and in 1726
    became a climbing boy for a short while (Cullingford 2000).
30 *The Times* 12 June 1789.
31 *The Times* 12 June 1789.
32 *The Times* 12 June 1789.
33 *The Times* 12 June 1789.
34 *The Times* 12 June 1789.
35 Old Bailey Proceedings online, December 1811 (t18111204-3).
36 *Hampshire Telegraph and Sussex Chronicle* 6 January 1812. Mr Richard Magnes was
    a gunner on board HMS *Lightning*. The surname of Thomas was stated variously
    as Dillone, Deloe and Dellow in the newspapers.
37 13 June 1800. Somerset Archives and Local Studies A\BTL/2/7.
38 13 June 1800. Somerset Archives and Local Studies A\BTL/2/7.
39 19 June 1800. Somerset Archives and Local Studies A\BTL/2/7.
40 26 September 1803. Somerset Archives and Local Studies A\BTL/2/17.
41 Christie 1929, p. 128.
42 4 December 1800. Somerset Archives and Local Studies A\BTL/2/12. A pencil
    factory was later established at Worsley in Lancashire. In a pocket diary of 1799,
    fifteen-year-old Mary Filliter of Wareham in Dorset recorded purchases of a
    pencil costing sixpence and a slate pencil costing twopence (Dorset History
    Centre D/FIL/F53).
43 6 April 1807. Upton-Wilkinson archive (070406wwsp).
44 The traveller was Thomas Pennant in 1769. Pennant 1776, pp. 10–11.
45 Jenkin 1951, p. 120.
46 27 September 1775. Winstanley 1989, p. 172.
47 2 April 1789. Jameson 2001, p. 132.
48 Moritz 1809, pp. 37–9.
49 Leach 1911, p. 413. The purpose of the original medieval grammar schools, which
    were attached to cathedrals and monasteries, was to teach Latin to future priests
    and monks. Some like Winchester and Eton were independent of the Church.
    From 1944 the term 'grammar school' was applied to state-funded schools that
    required pupils to pass the 11-plus examination.
50 Moritz 1809, p. 59. The term 'public school' was officially used in England from
    1860 for Eton and others. They took in pupils from all over the country.
51 11 January 1808. Somerset Archives and Local Studies A\BTL/2/28.
    Charterhouse was founded in London in 1611, but the school is now situated near
    Godalming in Surrey.
52 4 September 1813. Somerset Archives and Local Studies A\BTL/2/39. Mrs

Cecilia Windham had been widowed in 1810 on the death of her husband William (1750–1810).

53   Hall 1939, p. 62. Letter to Mrs Dodson written on 18 August 1812.

54   14 June 1809. Hall 1936, p. 173.

55   19 October 1812. Somerset Archives and Local Studies A\BTL/2/37.

56   19 and 20 October 1812. Somerset Archives and Local Studies A\BTL/2/37. Elizabeth Poole (1798–1853) was also gifted at music and algebra. Tom Poole was a patron of Coleridge.

57   Information from David Worthy and from Sandford 1888.

58   Hall 1936, p. 197. Letter written at Liverpool, 15 November 1809.

59   Corley 2005, p. 14.

60   The school was in the Abbey gatehouse at Reading in Berkshire.

61   Joseph Lancaster established his first free school around 1801 in Southwark, in which older boys, called monitors, taught the younger children.

62   Andrews 1935, p. 178.

63   18 July 1802. Somerset Archives and Local Studies A\BTL/2/15.

64   *The Parliamentary Debates* vol. 9 for 1807 (London, 1812), p. 798. Such attempts were made in 1796, 1797, 1807, 1820 and 1833, finally succeeding in 1870. Giddy later changed his surname to Gilbert so that he could inherit substantial estates from his wife's uncle (*Oxford Dictionary of National Biography* online).

65   Jenkin 1951, p. 161. Letter of 17 September 1811 to George Wilbraham of Delamere House near Northwich in Cheshire.

66   Carter 1845.

67   *Report from Select Committee on the Education of the Lower Orders in the Metropolis: with the minutes of evidence taken before the committee* (London, 1816), p. 54.

68   *Report from Select Committee on the Education of the Lower Orders in the Metropolis: with the minutes of evidence taken before the committee* (London, 1816), p. 10.

69   Manuscript in authors' possession.

70   This was Coventry's Charity, established by Thomas Coventry and Hugh Dashfield in 1636. Farm rents were paid into the charity.

71   Manuscript in authors' possession.

72   *Derby Mercury* 16 May 1793.

73   Evidence of Robert Blincoe, sworn and examined by Dr Hawkins at Manchester on 18 May 1833, in *Factories Inquiry Commission* 1833, section D3, p. 17.

74   Evidence of Robert Blincoe, sworn and examined by Dr Hawkins at Manchester on 18 May 1833, in *Factories Inquiry Commission* 1833, section D3, p. 18.

75   Evidence of Robert Blincoe, sworn and examined by Dr Hawkins at Manchester on 18 May 1833, in *Factories Inquiry Commission* 1833, section D3, p. 18.

76   Warner 1801, pp. 90–1. Maiden Bradley is now in Wiltshire.

77   *Parliamentary Debates from the year 1803 to the present time* vol. 33 (London, 1816), p. 884.

78   *Reports of special assistant poor law commissioners on the employment of women and children in agriculture* (London, 1843), pp. 112–13.

79   Ayton 1815, pp. 155–6.

80   Ayton 1815, p. 155.

81 *Children's Employment Commission. Appendix to First Report of Commissioners. Mines. Part II. Reports and Evidence from Sub-Commissioners. Presented to both Houses of Parliament by Command of Her Majesty* (London, 1842), p. 122.

82 *Journal of the House of Commons* 43 (1788), pp. 436–7.

83 *Journal of the House of Commons* 43 (1788), evidence of James Dunn, p. 436.

84 Pratt 1803, p. 434.

85 Pratt 1803, pp. 428, 431–2.

86 Pratt 1803, pp. 432–3.

87 Pratt 1803, pp. 433–4.

88 *Journal of the House of Commons* 43 (1788), p. 436.

89 *Christian Observer* 9 (1811), p. 614. The same evidence was later given to the parliamentary committee *Report from the Committee on Employment of Boys in Sweeping Chimnies: together with the minutes of the evidence taken before the committee and an appendix* (London, 1817), p. 35.

90 *Christian Observer* 9 (1811), p. 614.

91 Brabourne 1884b, p. 241. The house has since been largely rebuilt, but a blue plaque records Jane Austen's residence there.

92 *Christian Observer* 9 (1811), p. 182.

93 *Christian Observer* 9 (1811), p. 182. The inquest was 24 November 1810.

94 *Christian Observer* 9 (1811), p. 182.

95 Jameson 2005, p. 169.

4: HOME AND HEARTH

1   Brougham 1840, pp. 41–2 (speech to Parliament).

2   The situation has not improved since then. With increased landholding by institutions such as the Forestry Commission and the National Trust and also by commercial companies, the percentage of land owned by lower- and middle-class individuals has dwindled even further. See Cahill 2001.

3   Henry 2002, p. 313; Mingay 2002, p. 143.

4   11 July 1785. Andrews 1934, pp. 236–7. The Grade I listed castle is currently empty and visitors barred, so history repeats itself here. Born in 1743, John Byng was nephew of Admiral John Byng who was executed.

5   In the poem, 'The Homes of England', written in 1827. Usually known simply as 'Mrs Hemans', she was born in Liverpool in 1793, a brilliant linguist and scholar who was an extremely popular poet in Victorian times.

6   Silliman 1820a, p. 12.

7   Silliman 1820b, p. 145 footnote.

8   Andrews 1935, p. 275.

9   Trusler 1790, p. 2.

10 Simond 1817, p. 337.

11 Cunningham 1859, p. 324. Walpole (1717–97) was the 4th Earl of Orford, author, politician, antiquarian and patron of the arts.

12 6 July 1790. Bamford 1936, p. 71. Letter from Arabella Pennant. Weston Hall became the home of Sir Sacheverell Sitwell. Little is known of Mary Heber (1758–1809).

13 Mackenzie 1916, p. 179. George MacAulay (1750–1803) was originally from the Outer Hebrides but had come to London at the age of fifteen, in 1774. He

became an alderman in 1786. The construction of Finsbury Square began in 1777. The square was severely damaged in the Second World War.

14 Simond 1817, p. 259.

15 Simond 1817, p. 260.

16 Simond 1815, pp. 50–1.

17 Andrews 1935, pp. 9–10.

18 19 April 1802. Christie 1929, pp. 138–9.

19 *Report from Select Committee on the Education of the Lower Orders in the Metropolis* (1816, London), p. 40.

20 Simond 1817, pp. 338–9. He puts this in his diary as 1811.

21 Letter dated 'Good Friday 1808'. Hall 1936, p. 82.

22 Hall 1936, p. 82.

23 7 May 1817. Somerset Archives and Local Studies A\BTL/2/43.

24 See Vickery 2009, chapter 6. The first known English patterned wallpaper dates to around 1509. By the late eighteenth century London was the centre of the wallpaper industry.

25 *Ipswich Journal* 18 April 1789.

26 30 June 1785. Winstanley and Jameson 1999, p. 50.

27 Hall 1936, p. 140.

28 1 September 1809. Christie 1929, p. 230.

29 13 April 1810. Hall 1936, p. 251 (with an image of Dove Nest opp. p. 225). Nelly Weeton called the house Dove's Nest, but Dove Nest is the more usual form (Green 1819, p. 165).

30 Chorley 1836, p. 118. Mrs Hemans paid visits to Wordsworth from Dove Nest. It is today a luxury hotel, much altered.

31 10 June 1798. Christie 1929, pp. 105–6.

32 21 August 1809. Upton-Wilkinson archive (091082ispww).

33 13 November 1809. National Maritime Museum WIL/1/38.

34 13 November 1789. Jameson 2001, p. 206.

35 8 February 1807. Brabourne 1884a, p. 324.

36 Simond 1815, pp. 12–13.

37 1 September 1784. Winstanley 1998, p. 273. Buildings still exist with such bricked-up windows.

38 15 May 1788. Jameson 2001, p. 36 (where the horse tax is omitted, though it is in Beresford 1927, p. 24).

39 27 October 1798. Brabourne 1884a, pp. 160–1.

40 Brabourne 1884a, p. 161.

41 28 December 1809. Hall 1936, p. 217.

42 18 January 1810. Hall 1936, p. 221.

43 For the problems of finding and keeping servants in northern England, see Vickery 2003, chapter 4 and appendix 5.

44 15 January 1798. Jameson 2006, p. 3.

45 On her uncle's death, Nancy Woodforde returned in 1805 to Castle Cary, which is adjacent to Ansford, in Somerset, and remained there until her death in 1830. She never married.

46 5 July 1784. Winstanley 1998, p. 256.

47 8 December 1801. Jameson 2007, pp. 90–1.

48   9 November 1799. Somerset Archives and Local Studies A\BTL/2/1.

49   Hall 1936, p. 126. Nelly was writing at Beacon's Gutter, near Liverpool, 14 November 1808.

50   Moritz 1809, pp. 12–13.

51   26 August 1782. Andrews 1934, p. 85. Byng stayed in many inns during his excursions and was very critical of poor ones.

52   26 January 1784. Winstanley 1998, p. 209.

53   30 June 1808. Brabourne 1884a, p. 367 (who cites the wrong date). Jane Austen was staying at Godmersham in Kent.

54   4 January 1789. Jameson 2001, p. 108.

55   14 January 1792. Jameson 2003, p. 103.

56   28 January 1794. Jameson 2004, p. 7.

57   25 January 1795. Jameson 2004, p. 118.

58   3 February 1799. Jameson 2006, p. 86.

59   A report from 1795. Eden 1797b, p. 397.

60   Writing in April 1795. Eden 1797c, pp. 776–7.

61   Eden 1797c, p. 797.

62   24 March 1800. Somerset Archives and Local Studies A\BTL/2/4. The 'sticks' were from where the hedge had been laid.

63   23 October 1799, Somerset Archives and Local Studies A\BTL/2/1.

64   February 1798. Knight 1904, p. 7.

65   31 July 1802. Knight 1904, p. 144.

66   Simond 1815, pp. 37–8.

67   At Alfoxton in Somerset on 2 February 1798. Knight 1904, p. 7.

68   17 December 1797. Jameson 2005, p. 198.

69   28 December 1781. Winstanley 1984, p. 192.

70   25 February 1810. Hall 1936, p. 232. Mary Gertrude Pedder died on 17 February 1810. Her mother, of the same name, had died on 18 December 1807 at the age of thirty-two.

71   31 March 1793. Jameson 2003, pp. 231–2.

72   Fire marks are still seen on some houses today.

73   25 August 1778. Winstanley 1983, p. 66.

74   Matches had to be set alight with a flame from a tinderbox, candle or fire. They could not be ignited by 'striking' them on a rough surface like modern matches. They could only be used for transferring, not originating, a flame.

75   Beeswax candles were taxed at eight pence a pound, which was reduced to threepence in 1784, the same as spermaceti candles. Tallow was taxed at one penny a pound, increased by a halfpenny in 1784 but reduced back to a penny in 1792 (Dowell 1888, pp. 306–10).

76   Beeswax candles could not be made in a mould because they contracted on cooling and stuck to the mould. Instead, the hot beeswax was ladled over the wick, layer by layer, and the soft, warm candles were rolled to shape on a moistened surface, which was an expensive process (Eveleigh 2003).

77   Simond 1817, p. 150.

78   *Morning Chronicle* 24 October 1807.

79   White 1789, p. 198.

80   A rushlight holder was a simple clamp, commonly of wood or metal, that was set

on a base that stood upright or was made to be fixed to a wall. All that was needed was a stable form of clamp to hold the rushlight at a 45-degree angle while it burned.

81 Williams 1933, p. 173.

82 Simond 1815, pp. 3–4.

83 The term 'range' was used from the seventeenth century for kitchen grates for cooking, while for fireplaces in rooms such as the parlour and bedroom, the word 'grate' was retained (Eveleigh 1983).

84 *Morning Chronicle* 24 October 1807. Spits were horizontal, but when the open fireplaces of the ranges became more narrow, with the inclusion of ovens and boilers either side, vertical spits were developed.

85 23 October 1782. Winstanley 1998, p. 71.

86 Glasse 1774, p. i.

87 Glasse 1774, pp. 3, 10, 101, 329.

88 Glasse 1774, p. 330.

89 Eden 1797c, p. 753.

90 Silliman 1810, p. 50.

91 6 November 1795. Jameson 2004, p. 220.

92 Eden 1797b, p. 267.

93 Published by Hannah Humphrey on 6 July 1795. Wright 1867, p. 496. Twelvepence was one shilling, and a crown was five shillings.

94 Carter 1845, p. 42. He was born on 5 July 1792.

95 *Morning Chronicle* 28 October 1807.

96 Middleton 1807, p. 419. This survey, done in 1806, updated a 1793 survey for the Board of Agriculture.

97 Middleton 1807, p. 423.

98 Middleton 1807, p. 424.

99 Middleton 1807, p. 422.

100 Middleton 1807, p. 424.

101 Letter written at Upholland 9 June 1808. Hall 1936, p. 91.

102 Andrews 1934, p. 359.

103 Montague 1785, p. 112.

104 28 January 1780. Winstanley 1984, p. 12.

105 From the contents list of Montague 1785, pp. 1–7.

106 13 March 1800. Somerset Archives and Local Studies A\BTL/2/4.

107 17 March 1800. Somerset Archives and Local Studies A\BTL/2/4.

108 19 March 1800. Somerset Archives and Local Studies A\BTL/2/4.

109 21 March 1800. Somerset Archives and Local Studies A\BTL/2/4.

110 18 June 1800. Somerset Archives and Local Studies A\BTL/2/4.

111 Simond 1815, pp. 154–5. Lawnmowers were not yet invented. Rollers were also used on paths and yards.

112 11 June 1794. Jameson 2004, p. 42.

113 Montague 1785, p. 139. Sack was then 'a kind of sweet wine, now brought chiefly from the Canaries'.

114 White 1789, p. 298.

115 Diary entries for 2 and 4 April 1799. Jameson 2006, pp. 105–6.

116 White 1789, pp. 301–2. This was a freak heatwave caused by volcanic activity.

117 *Leeds Intelligencer* 20 October 1789.

118 Chapman 1932a, pp. 138–9. Letter of 14 September 1804.

119 David 1994, pp. 325–7.

120 *Morning Post* 7 October 1811.

121 *Morning Post* 7 September 1802.

122 *Morning Post* 7 September 1802. The houses no longer exist.

123 Gillett 1945, pp. 39–40.

124 20 October 1794. Jameson 2004, p. 86.

125 4 January 1798. Jameson 2006, p. 1.

126 Christie 1929, pp. 208–9.

127 25 August 1782. Andrews 1934, p. 82.

128 29 October 1781. Winstanley 1984, p. 175.

129 29 March 1777. Winstanley 1981, p. 119.

130 17 May 1780. Winstanley 1984, p. 42.

131 5 January 1781. Winstanley 1984, p. 102.

132 4 September 1809. Upton-Wilkinson archive (090904wwsp).

133 Moritz 1809, p. 12.

134 11 February 1800. Somerset Archives and Local Studies A\BTL/2/3.

135 29 May 1800. Somerset Archives and Local Studies A\BTL/2/6.

136 7 February 1806. Somerset Archives and Local Studies A\BTL/2/25.

137 1 December 1790. Jameson 2001, p. 271.

138 8 June 1781. Winstanley 1984, p. 140.

139 28 May 1792. Jameson 2003, p. 141.

140 25 June 1792. Jameson 2003, p. 149.

141 Trusler 1784, p. 83. This was an updated, effectively plagiarised, version of the advice given in letters to his son by Lord Chesterfield.

142 23 December 1778. Winstanley 1983, p. 98.

143 Winstanley 1983, p. 98. Woodforde was a very sociable man, and such gatherings were undoubtedly enjoyable occasions.

5: FASHIONS AND FILTH

1 Raw cotton-wool was imported from many places, including South and North America, the West Indies, the Mediterranean, the Levant and India.

2 Pantaloons were based on the full-length version worn by the military, with instep stirrups, which Beau Brummell (1778–1840) made fashionable. See Kelly 2005.

3 28 December 1809. Upton-Wilkinson archive (091223wwsp).

4 14 January 1808. Hall 1936, p. 664.

5 *Northampton Mercury* 20 April 1778. The theft was on 11 April. A surviving pair of Admiral Lord Nelson's stockings are marked with II, N and a coronet.

6 Letter written at Upholland, Lancashire, 14 January 1808. Hall 1936, p. 64.

7 Some men wore a coloured cravat over a white one, which later evolved into a white collar and bowtie.

8 9 June 1810. Somerset Archives and Local Studies A\BTL/2/33.

9 Grose 1811 no pagination.

10 Written at Beacon's Gutter, near Liverpool, 17 March 1809. Hall 1936, p. 159.

11 They persist today in dress or formal shirts for evening events.

12 George Spencer, 2nd Earl Spencer, allegedly burnt his tails in an accident before the fire and ordered his tailor to cut them off.

13 Pratt 1803, pp. 632–3.

14 We might today call this a full-length petticoat or slip.

15 21 May 1780.Winstanley 1984, p. 43.

16 Smith 1785, p. 54.

17 Smith 1785, p. 55.

18 Smith 1785, p. 55.

19 The term coat, skirt and petticoat were interchangeable.

20 *The Universal Magazine* 60, 1777, p. 379.

21 4 June 1805. Silliman 1810, p. 173.

22 *Report of the Select Committee of the Court of Directors of the East India Company, upon the subject of the cotton manufacture of this country*, 1793, quoted in Baines 1835, p. 334.

23 *The Times* 11 December 1799. These coats were named after the Frenchman Jean de Bry and had padded shoulders and narrow waists.

24 21 September 1803. Somerset Archives and Local Studies A\BTL/2/17.

25 15 September 1813. Brabourne 1884b, p. 150.

26 *Morning Chronicle* 30 October 1807.

27 19 June 1799. Jameson 2006, p. 128. The term 'bosom-friend' was already in use for an intimate friend.

28 The term 'ridicule' was from the French and 'reticule' from the Latin meaning 'net' (as many of these bags were made by knotting).

29 9 January 1799. Brabourne 1884a, p. 195. Letter written at Steventon.

30 Eden 1797a, p. 558.

31 Eden 1797b, p. 639. This was the House of Industry at Shrewsbury.

32 Moritz 1809, p. 85.

33 13 August 1810. Letter written to Miss Bessy Winkley at Dove Nest. Hall 1936, p. 285.

34 Brabourne 1884a, p. 187.

35 7 November 1808. She was living at Beacon's Gutter, near Liverpool. Hall 1936, p. 122.

36 Brabourne 1884a, p. 186. Letter written at Steventon on Christmas Day 1798.

37 27 March 1799. Jameson 2006, p. 102.

38 30 March 1799. Jameson 2006, p. 104.

39 30 November 1782. Winstanley 1998, p. 82.

40 5 August 1800. Darbishire 1958, p. 46.

41 Brabourne 1884a, p. 186. Letter of Christmas Day 1798, written at Steventon.

42 Brabourne 1884a, p. 138. Letter of 1 September 1796, written at Rowling in Kent.

43 16 April 1782.This was William Aldridge of Norwich. Winstanley 1998, p. 31.

44 *Gentleman's Magazine* 55, December 1785, p. 938.

45 *Lancaster Gazette* 20 August 1808.

46 31 March 1784. Winstanley 1998, p. 226.

47 18 April 1811. Brabourne 1884b, pp. 84–5.

48 Silliman 1810, p. 283. This was in London in 1805.

49 Eden 1797a, p. 555.

50 Eden 1797a, p. 554.

51 5 March 1802. Darbishire 1958, p. 127.
52 Silliman 1810, p. 215.
53 4 May 1802, about 2 miles north of Grasmere. Darbishire 1958, p. 156.
54 *Morning Post* 8 December 1804.
55 Silliman 1810, pp. 215–16.
56 10 June 1784. Winstanley 1998, p. 249.
57 8 February 1802, in the Lake District. Darbishire 1958, p. 112.
58 10 February 1802. Jameson 2007, p. 107.
59 9 January 1806. Somerset Archives and Local Studies A\BTL/2/25. In a pocket diary for 1799, fifteen-year-old Mary Filliter recorded the purchase of 'pattens 1s 10d' (Dorset History Centre D/FIL/F53).
60 Eden 1797b, p. 76.
61 9 November 1805. Romney 1984, p. 219.
62 This was in 1811. Simond 1817, p. 307.
63 This was in 1810. Simond 1815, p. 21.
64 Moritz 1809, p. 41.
65 Military cockades with colours other than black signified rebels or enemy troops. A plume of a different colour might be worn above a black cockade. Political cockades, worn mostly at election times, were of various colours.
66 6 August 1799. Moretonhampstead History Society manuscript of Treleaven's diary.
67 Brabourne 1884a, p. 192.
68 The Mamelukes were Egyptian cavalry who had fought Napoleon's troops in Egypt.
69 *Kentish Gazette* 15 May 1804.
70 It is often said that umbrellas were usually black in colour to disguise the filthy rain, which was heavily polluted with soot from coal fires, but there is no evidence that black umbrellas were popular at this date.
71 Pugh 1787, p. 221.
72 Macdonald 1790, pp. 382–3.
73 28 January 1787. Winstanley and Jameson 1999, p. 207.
74 29 June 1789. Jameson 2001, p. 160.
75 18 August 1788. Andrews 1934, p. 355.
76 This was June 1789. Andrews 1935, p. 24. The Tontine Inn was the main coaching inn at Sheffield, near today's Dixon Lane. It was demolished in 1850.
77 28 June 1786. Winstanley and Jameson 1999, p. 145.
78 *Chester Chronicle* 20 March 1795.
79 5 October 1781. Winstanley 1984, p. 168.
80 14 April 1796. Jameson 2005, p. 28.
81 *Sussex Advertiser* 30 May 1814.
82 Women did not wear wigs, but at times their hair was styled and powdered to resemble wigs.
83 Brabourne 1884a, p. 174. Letter of 1 December 1798 written at Steventon.
84 17 February 1781. Winstanley 1984, p. 112.
85 15 October 1792. Jameson 2003, p. 182.
86 Nelly Weeton was writing from Beacon's Gutter, near Liverpool, on 6 February 1809. Hall 1936, p. 149.
87 British Library Add MS 27828 fol. 119.
88 The National Archives ADM 101/102/3.

89 A US gallon is just over 8 pounds.
90 25 April 1800. Somerset Archives and Local Studies A\BTL/2/5.
91 3 September 1801. Jameson 2007, p. 65.
92 4 September 1801. Jameson 2007, p. 65.
93 Darter 1888, pp. 58–9.
94 Simond 1817, pp. 363–4.
95 Bamford 1936, p. 18.
96 24 October 1804. Somerset Archives and Local Studies A\BTL/2/17.
97 21 November 1795. Jameson 2004, p. 224.
98 27 August 1809. Upton-Wilkinson archive (090827wwsp).
99 10 June 1799. Jameson 2006, p. 125.
100 27 October 1798. Brabourne 1884a, pp. 160–1.
101 British Library Add MS 27827, fols 50–1. Francis Place was born in 1771.
102 Willan 1801, p 255.
103 15 October 1808. Hall 1936, pp. 115–16.
104 The Worshipful Company of Launderers website is www.launderers.co.uk.
105 *Hampshire Chronicle* 12 December 1791.
106 11 March 1801. Jameson 2007, p. 19.
107 The Wordsworths were then living at Dove Cottage. Darbishire 1958, p. 61.
108 25 March 1814. Somerset Archives and Local Studies A\BTL/2/40.
109 Brabourne 1884a, p. 147. This was 18 September 1796, when staying at Rowling in Kent.
110 3 May 1806. Fremantle 1940, p. 258. This was during the trial of Henry Dundas (Lord Melville, 1742–1811). He had been impeached in Parliament on grounds of corruption in 1805. He had served as Treasurer of the Navy and First Lord of the Admiralty. This was of interest to Elizabeth Fremantle, who was married to a naval captain. She is also known by her maiden name Elizabeth (Betsey) Wynne, author of one of the Wynne diaries.
111 Willan 1801, p. 304.
112 20 November 1800. Chapman 1932a, p. 92. Letter to Cassandra, written at Steventon.
113 Montague 1785, p. 187.
114 *Northampton Mercury* 5 March 1803.
115 *Northampton Mercury* 10 June 1809.
116 *Northampton Mercury* 10 June 1809.
117 Hamilton 1813, p. 29.
118 Hamilton 1813, p. 24.
119 Simond 1815, p. 49. He was writing about London in 1810.
120 Simond 1815, p. 49.
121 Trial of Catherine Mason and Samuel Duck, April 1770, Old Bailey Proceedings online (t17700425-1).
122 *Bath Chronicle* 17 July 1777.
123 Wright 1960, p. 118.
124 Winstanley 1984, p. 57.
125 21 January 1814. Somerset Archives and Local Studies A\BTL/2/40.
126 See the satirical print of the ladies' communal facilities at Vauxhall Gardens in Gatrell 2006, p. 377.

127 *Lancaster Gazette* 20 August 1808.

128 Trial of Catherine Tewner, Old Bailey Proceedings Online, January 1815, t18150111-44. The incident occurred at Robinson's Buildings, London.

129 Trial of Catherine Tewner, Old Bailey Proceedings Online, January 1815, t18150111-44.

130 Trial of Patrick Smith, Old Bailey Proceedings Online, October 1814, t18141026-3.

131 13 April 1810. Hall 1936, p. 252.

132 Rudder 1779, p. 395.

133 Foot 1794, p. 26.

134 *Report from Select Committee on the Education of the Lower Orders in the Metropolis* (London, 1816), p. 40. The evidence was given by Edward Wakefield, a philanthropist.

6: SERMONS AND SUPERSTITIONS

1 Note the incorrect spelling of the Austen surname. Somerset Archives and Local Studies DD/HY 7/2/5.

2 9 January 1801. Brabourne 1884a p. 256.

3 This was 1811. Simond 1817, p. 175.

4 Letter to Cassandra Austen dated 21 January 1799. Brabourne 1884a p. 200. Cooper did take the living.

5 *Jackson's Oxford Journal* 31 December 1774.

6 Woodforde is called 'Parson' because the publication of abridged diaries in the 1920s used that term. For an explanation of the different publications of his diaries, see Winstanley 1996, pp. 3–8.

7 Andrews 1935, p. 228. Byng was staying at the Chequers Inn, which is still in the High Street. The vicar was Jacob Mountain, who also held the living of St Andrew in Norwich and in 1793 became the first Anglican bishop of Quebec.

8 6 June 1792. Andrews 1936, p. 43.

9 21 April 1774. Winstanley 1989, pp. 37–8.

10 *New Exeter Journal or General Advertiser for Devon, Cornwall, Dorset and Somerset* 30 April 1789. Stoke was also known as Stoke Damerel. The church was enlarged in 1751 to cater for the dockland population.

11 Simond 1815, pp. 174–5.

12 23 October 1804. Somerset Archives and Local Studies A\BTL/2/19.

13 March 1805. Somerset Archives and Local Studies A\BTL/2/21. When Sturges died, the new rector was a brother of the Duke of Wellington. A new St Luke's Church was consecrated in 1824, and the old one became a chapel of ease, now known as the Old Church Chelsea. Sturges had been vicar of St Mary's Church in Reading for over four decades.

14 25 December 1806. Somerset Archives and Local Studies A\BTL/2/26. Holland refers to payment for the gown in mid-January 1807, calling it a Master of Arts gown.

15 15 September 1810. Somerset Archives and Local Studies A\BTL/2/33.

16 *Sussex Advertiser* 19 January 1795.

17 31 March 1772. Winstanley 1988, p. 25.

18 Hall 1936, pp. 165–6. Written at Beacon's Gutter, near Liverpool, 19 May 1809.

19 Christie 1929, p. 147.

20 2 December 1799. Somerset Archives and Local Studies A\BTL/2/3.

21 November 1799. Somerset Archives and Local Studies A\BTL/2/1.

22 3 December 1776. Winstanley 1981, p. 94.

23 Sunday 10 November 1776. Winstanley 1981, p. 87.

24 Moritz 1809, p. 70.

25 Moritz 1809, p. 71. The church was largely rebuilt in 1846.

26 Moritz 1809, p. 71.

27 Moritz 1809, pp. 71–2.

28 26 June 1791. Andrews 1935, p. 338.

29 13 June 1790. Andrews 1935, p. 175.

30 15 April 1804. Somerset Archives and Local Studies A\BTL/2/18.

31 6 October 1783. Winstanley 1998, p. 176.

32 3 February 1797. Jameson 2005, p. 118. For all his years of learning Classical languages, Woodforde was unable to converse in French.

33 25 December 1782. Winstanley 1998, p. 91.

34 21 February 1816. Somerset Archives and Local Studies A\BTL/2/41. Jack (John) Hunt's cottage was near Over Stowey between the Crowcombe Road and Friarn Farm (information from David Worthy).

35 27 June 1791. Andrews 1935, p. 342.

36 Simon Jenkins (1999, p. *xxx*) says that 'There are roughly 8,000 extant pre-Reformation churches in England and about the same number of Anglican churches.'

37 8 February 1809. Somerset Archives and Local Studies A\BTL/2/29. The church was restored some decades later.

38 28 January 1810. Somerset Archives and Local Studies A\BTL/2/31.

39 White 1789, p. 316.

40 *Leeds Intelligencer* 20 October 1789. This was the church of St Peter, demolished in 1838 and replaced by a huge Victorian structure.

41 23 June 1780. Winstanley 1984, p. 53.

42 7 November 1808. Nelly Weeton was living at Beacon's Gutter, near Liverpool. Hall 1936, pp. 122–3.

43 Silliman 1810, p. 315.

44 8 February 1809. Somerset Archives and Local Studies A\BTL/2/29.

45 25 October 1809. Somerset Archives and Local Studies A\BTL/2/30.

46 3 June 1816. Somerset Archives and Local Studies A\BTL/2/42. The king's birthday was usually celebrated on 4 June.

47 24 March 1817. Somerset Archives and Local Studies A\BTL/2/43.

48 Andrews 1935, p. 238.

49 26 June 1791. Andrews 1935, pp. 337–8.

50 Andrews 1935, p. 411.

51 Beale 1891, pp. 87–9. A letter to Mrs André in August 1791. William Hutton (1723–1815) was born in Derby, worked in the textile trade and was later a bookseller and printer, being largely self-educated.

52 Joseph Priestley (1733–1804) is better known today for his scientific achievements.

53 Simond 1817, p. 178.

54 Romney 1984, p. 24.

55 11 May 1800. Somerset Archives and Local Studies A\BTL/2/5.

56   13 July 1800. Somerset Archives and Local Studies A\BTL/2/8.

57   3 June 1816. Somerset Archives and Local Studies A\BTL/2/42.

58   Andrews 1935, p. 130. Byng expressed his views while touring the Midlands in 1789.

59   Haydon 2002.

60   *Hampshire Pocket Companion* 1787, Somerset Archives and Local Studies DD/HY 7/2/5.

61   Grose 1787, p. 1 of 'Superstitions' (the pagination is duplicated within this volume for different sections). Grose was born in London and lived from 1731 to 1790.

62   White 1789, p. 202.

63   Hall 1936, p. 46.

64   Hall 1936, p. 46.

65   Hall 1936, pp. 45–6.

66   *Morning Post* 27 April 1810, quoted in Ashton 1906, p. 452. This took place close to the London School of Economics which stands on the site of Clare Market.

67   Grose 1787, p. 52 of 'Superstitions'.

68   18 November 1793. Jameson 2003, p. 309.

69   5 January 1796. Jameson 2005, p. 2.

70   24 February 1795. Jameson 2004, p. 127.

71   Grose 1787, p. 53 of 'Superstitions'.

72   Grose 1787, p. 62 of 'Superstitions'.

73   Grose 1787, pp. 62, 64 of 'Superstitions'.

74   *Morning Post* 21 August 1779. A caul is a membrane found over the head of some babies at birth.

75   Grose 1787, p. 57 of 'Superstitions'.

76   Grose 1787, pp. 57–8 of 'Superstitions'.

77   Grose 1787, p. 29 of 'Superstitions'.

78   *Archaeologia Cantiana* 80, 1965, p. 255.

79   Grose 1787, pp. 29–30.

80   *Leeds Intelligencer* 27 March 1809.

81   *Leeds Intelligencer* 27 March 1809.

82   In the second-floor gallery. Personal communication, Liz Egan of the Thackray Museum.

83   Benton 1867, p. 254.

84   He was born around 1780. Benton 1867, p. 254.

85   F. Moore 1803 *Vox Stellarum: or, A Loyal Almanack For the Year of Human Redemption* 1803, p. 9.

86   F. Moore 1803 *Vox Stellarum: or, A Loyal Almanack For the Year of Human Redemption* 1803, p. 13.

87   Jameson 2003, p. 94.

88   Traditionally, Old Christmas Day fell on 6 January and was observed widely on this date, but there are several instances in William Holland's diary of servants asking for time off to celebrate Old Christmas Day on 5 January, and at other times 6 January, so it seems that in this part of Somerset the actual date was imprecise.

89   6 January 1807. Somerset Heritage Centre A\BTL/2/26.

90   Jameson 2001, p. 12.

91 *The New Exeter Journal or General Advertiser for Devon, Cornwall, Dorset and Somerset* 23 April 1789.

92 Mingay 2002.

93 *Gentleman's Magazine* 68 (1790), p. 719.

94 Winstanley 1984, p. 38.

95 Winstanley 1984, p. 38.

96 Winstanley 1984, pp. 38–9.

97 11 June 1790. Andrews 1935, pp. 168–70.

98 Andrews 1935, p. 170.

7: WEALTH AND WORK

1 Letter to George Hunt of 24 January 1795. Jenkin 1951, p. 30.

2 Darter 1888, p. 35.

3 13 December 1797. Jameson 2005, p. 196.

4 28 March 1804. Somerset Archives and Local Studies A\BTL/2/18. The road bridge was built in the 1770s.

5 28 August 1805. Silliman 1820a, p. 142.

6 15 November 1782. Winstanley 1998, p. 77.

7 18 November 1782. Winstanley 1998, p. 77. Like Woodforde, Bathurst held the livings through New College, Oxford.

8 In 1801 Henry Austen had gone into partnership with two other men as an army agent and banker in London, which turned into a banking business (Austen and Co.) with country branches at Alton and Petersfield in Hampshire and at Hythe in Kent. The end of the war in Europe in 1815 brought a sharp deflation, and his bank crashed with huge debts in 1816 because it did not keep sufficient reserves to cover its loans. See Caplan 2004 and Ellis 2011.

9 17 October 1793. Jameson 2003, p. 299.

10 The approximate equivalents of money in Jane Austen's time to UK decimal coinage are one guinea = £1.05; one pound = £1; one crown = 25p; and one shilling = 5p. In terms of purchasing power, a shilling at that time would be about £1.60 today and a guinea about £34 (using The National Archives currency converter which translates prices in 1800 to values in 2005). However, wages were low. Woodforde paid his housemaid 3½d (47p) per day plus board and lodging and gave occasional presents such as a length of cloth to make a garment.

11 9 November 1805. Romney 1984, p. 219.

12 Andrews 1935, p. 167.

13 1 March 1797. Jameson 2005, p. 125.

14 Blackner 1815, p. 392. John Blackner (about 1770 to 1816) was originally apprenticed to a stocking maker in Derbyshire.

15 16 March 1797. Jameson 2005, p. 130.

16 This continued until 1821, and in 1833 they became legal tender for amounts over £5.

17 21 July 1810. Somerset Archives and Local Studies A\BTL/2/33. People usually preferred local banknotes, as the people running the bank would be known and trusted. Outside London, Bank of England notes were likely to be discounted (Ellis 2011).

18 24 March 1797. Jameson 2005, p. 132.

19 *Alfred and Westminster Evening Gazette* 26 April 1810.

20 Colquhoun 1796, p. 124. He was a founder of the Thames Police.

21 *The Times* 13 February 1815.

22 Campbell-Smith 2011, pp. 87–8.

23 19 June 1811. Somerset Archives and Local Studies A\BTL/2/35.

24 26 June 1811. Somerset Archives and Local Studies A\BTL/2/35.

25 21 June 1780. Winstanley 1984, p. 53.

26 The Austens lived at Chawton in Hampshire from 1809, in a cottage on the extensive estate of Jane's brother Edward.

27 In London in 1782. Moritz 1809, p. 10.

28 Andrews 1935, p. 372.

29 9 May 1780. Winstanley 1984, p. 40.

30 8 January 1802. Somerset Archives and Local Studies A\BTL/2/14.

31 Bell 1812, p. 5.

32 18 November 1787. Surgeon Lionel Gillespie's journal, The National Archives ADM 101/102/3.

33 May 1795. Eden 1797b, p. 551.

34 Simond 1817, p. 79.

35 March 1811. Simond 1817, p. 76. He does not specify the precise coal pit.

36 Simond 1817, p. 77.

37 *Children's Employment Commission. Appendix to First Report of Commissioners. Mines. Part II. Reports and Evidence from Sub-Commissioners. Presented to both Houses of Parliament by Command of Her Majesty* (London, 1842), p. 288.

38 This only became properly effective with an amendment in 1799.

39 Eden 1797b, p. 552.

40 *Newcastle Journal* 24 June 1777.

41 'An Account of the Navigable Canal now making from the several Coal-Mines in the Neighbourhood of *Stourbridge* and *Dudley*, to communicate with the Great Canal from the *Trent to the Severn*, near *Stourton*, in the County of *Stafford*', *Gentleman's Magazine*, 1777, p. 313.

42 *Trewman's Exeter Flying Post* 30 August 1810.

43 Shaw 1808, p. 318. The tunnel is east of Basingstoke, while Steventon lies to the west. Many of the investors in the Basingstoke Canal Navigation Company were known to Jane Austen and her family (Horsfall 2005).

44 Andrews 1934, pp. 259–60.

45 Warner 1801, p. 16. September 1800. This same canal may have been visited by Jane Austen a few months later, in May 1801 (Le Faye 2011, pp. 592–3).

46 'Grand Junction Canal Association' in *The Christian Observer* 17, 1818, pp. 556–7. This canal extended from Braunston in Northamptonshire to the River Thames at Brentford.

47 11 October 1800. Somerset Archives and Local Studies A\BTL/2/10.

48 Darter 1888, p. 33.

49 Known to have been sung and probably written by 'Common' John Grimshaw of Gorton near Manchester within this period. Harland 1865, p. 253.

50 Warner 1801, pp. 39–40

51 18 June 1790. Andrews 1935, p. 196. The mill was built in 1771.

52 This was in 1797. Grant 1809, p. 243.

53 Grant 1809, pp. 243–4.

54 Grant 1809, p. 244.
55 Harland 1865, pp. 259–60.
56 Harland 1865, p. 259.
57 Blackner 1815, p. 402.
58 Blackner 1815, pp. 402–3. Many proclamations and anonymous threatening letters referred to or were signed by a 'General Ludd' or 'Ned Ludd'.
59 Blackner 1815, p. 403.
60 Hall 1939, p. 57.
61 Mingay 2002, p. 141.
62 7 October 1784. Winstanley 1998, p. 282.
63 The earliest known published version was printed in London in 1794 (Roud and Bishop 2012, p. 456).
64 From the version sung by Mr Alfred Lockey, of Bedwyn, Wiltshire, published in *The Wiltshire Magazine* 50, no. 179, December 1943, pp. 283–4.
65 Stevenson 1812, p. 350.
66 Brabourne 1884a, p. 170.
67 14 September 1776. Winstanley 1981, p. 72.
68 Gardiner 1853, pp. 46–7 .
69 Pratt 1803, pp. 316–17.
70 Pratt 1801, pp. 276–7.
71 Pratt 1801, p. 287. Mavor lived from 1758 to 1837. These were Enclosure (or Inclosure) Acts.
72 Goldsmith 1770, p. 8.
73 Pratt 1801, pp. 287–8.
74 Andrews 1935, p. 324.
75 Andrews 1935, pp. 322–4.
76 This case effectively abolished slavery in England, although the slave trade was not abolished until 1807.
77 Silliman 1810, p. 47.
78 24 June 1805. Silliman 1810, pp. 216–17.
79 12 February 1780. Pasley 1931, p. 61.
80 Rattenbury 1837, pp. 15–16.
81 Darter 1888, p. 35. The Nore was the naval anchorage in the Thames estuary near Sheerness.
82 30 September 1779. Winstanley 1983, pp. 180–1.
83 Eden 1797b, p. 66.
84 April 1796. Eden 1797b, p. 73.
85 Simond 1815, pp. 222, 225.
86 Andrews 1935, p. 10.
87 Christie 1929, p. 139.
88 Eden 1797b, pp. 272–3.
89 20 March 1781. Winstanley 1984, p. 120.
90 27 October 1792. Jameson 2003, p. 186. 'Bargewell' was the nearby village of Bawdeswell.
91 Simond 1817, p. 94. Written in March 1811.
92 6 January 1789. Jameson 2001, p. 109.
93 Blackner 1815, p. 401.

94 Smith 1874, p. 30.
95 Darter 1888, p. 68.
96 *The Times* 28 August 1816.
97 *St. James's Chronicle and London Evening Post* 19 June 1817.

8: LEISURE AND PLEASURE

 1 Carter 1845, p. 124. He was working in London in 1810.
 2 Southey 1814, p. 190.
 3 Hutton 1795, p. 97. He had originally worked in the textile trade.
 4 Grose 1811, no pagination.
 5 Spilsbury 1791, p. 64.
 6 18 September 1805. Somerset Archives and Local Studies A\BTL/2/23.
 7 Hall 1939, p. 145.
 8 Grant 1809, p. 252.
 9 *Reading Mercury* 29 June 1789.
10 *Reading Mercury* 29 June 1789.
11 Andrews 1934, p. 217.
12 Andrews 1935, p. 163. Byng was in Derby on 9 June – the inhabitants were
    celebrating Oak Apple Day according to the old calendar. After the reform of the
    calendar in 1752, eleven days had been lost, so that the old 29 May became 9 June.
13 *Oxford Journal* 17 January 1789.
14 Darter 1888, p. 31.
15 Darter 1888, pp. 82–3.
16 Darter 1888, p. 83.
17 16 March 1772. Winstanley 1988, p. 21.
18 Darter 1888, pp. 36–7.
19 Darter 1888, p. 37.
20 Darter 1888, p. 37.
21 25 September 1813. Hubback and Hubback 1906, pp. 246–7.
22 6 January 1802. Somerset Archives and Local Studies A\BTL/2/14.
23 6 July 1789. Jameson 2001, p. 162.
24 1 July 1789. Jameson 2001, p. 161.
25 13 September 1791. Jameson 2003, p. 62.
26 *Morning Chronicle* 27 March 1812.
27 *Morning Post* 5 November 1805.
28 14 November 1805. Romney 1984, p. 224.
29 4 October 1805. Romney 1984, p. 161.
30 4 October 1805. Romney 1984, p. 163.
31 Hutton 1791, pp. 218–19.
32 Blackner 1815, p. 385.
33 *Morning Post* 27 June 1814.
34 18 September 1772. Winstanley 1988, p. 73.
35 Moretonhampstead History Society manuscript of Treleaven's diary.
36 Lewis 1866, p. 398.
37 3rd Earl of Hardwicke, grandson of the Lord Hardwicke who gave his name to
    the 1753 Marriage Act.
38 Lewis 1866, pp. 398–9.

39 Lewis 1866, p. 399.

40 23 September 1795. Jameson 2004, pp. 201–2.

41 *Lancaster Gazette* 11 August 1810.

42 5 September 1810. Hall 1936, p. 294.

43 Hall 1936, p. 294.

44 Hall 1936, p. 294.

45 Andrews 1934, p. 100.

46 Austen Leigh 1871, p. 69.

47 Brabourne 1884a, p. 238. The ball took place on 30 October 1800.

48 Lewis 1866, p. 418. The ball was on 17 May 1810.

49 27 August 1801. Jameson 2007, p. 63.

50 Bamford 1936, pp. 183–4. Letter of 4 October 1798 to Miss Heber. Lady Banks was wife of Sir Joseph Banks.

51 Bamford 1936, p. 186.

52 19 December 1804. Fremantle 1940, p. 147. The stately home of Stowe is now the independent Stowe School, just north of Buckingham.

53 24 March 1800. Jameson 2006, p. 196.

54 Hubback and Hubback 1906, p. 246. The Lyceum was unlicensed except for the period when the Drury Lane theatre moved there while being rebuilt after a devastating fire.

55 17 July 1809. Hall 1936, p. 175. Sarah Siddons (1755–1831) was a famous actor known for playing in tragedies.

56 Hall 1936, pp. 175–6.

57 Moritz 1809, pp. 33–4.

58 25 May 1802. Moretonhampstead History Society manuscript of Treleaven's diary.

59 Moretonhampstead History Society manuscript of Treleaven's diary.

60 25 September 1788. Jameson 2001, p. 73.

61 Moritz 1809, p. 31.

62 This was June 1805. Silliman 1810, p. 171.

63 22 March 1780 at Weston Longville. Winstanley 1984, p. 26.

64 6 January 1777. Somerset Archives and Local Studies Q/SR/345/1, quarter session rolls. Williams could presumably read, even though he was unable to write.

65 11 August 1788. Jameson 2001, p. 62.

66 British Library Add MS 35142, fols 57–8.

67 *Hampshire Chronicle* 3 July 1809. Many thanks to Dr David Higgins for information about how clay pipes were sold.

68 Christie 1929, pp. 130–1.

69 5 March 1790. Jameson 2001, p. 246.

70 Christie 1929, p. 131.

71 30 April 1783. Winstanley 1998, pp. 128–9.

72 Bone fish counters are on display at Castle Cary Museum in Somerset, along with contemporary playing cards that were found during the renovation of Ansford Parsonage and were very likely used by the Woodforde family there.

73 Moretonhampstead History Society manuscript of Treleaven's diary.

74 Moretonhampstead History Society manuscript of Treleaven's diary.

75 6 November 1807. Somerset Archives and Local Studies A\BTL/2/58. Joseph Ruscombe Poole was a lawyer and his wife was Elizabeth Stone.

76 George 1930, p. 317, quoting F. Eden 1801 *Observations on Friendly Societies* p. 29.
77 Gillett 1945, p. 44.
78 Repton 1812.
79 Repton 1812. An illustration of the urn shows it to be Bronze Age.
80 Grose et al 1780, p. iii.
81 7 November 1805. Silliman 1820b, p. 75.
82 Evans 2009, pp. 350–3. The Society is now based at Burlington House, London.
83 10 July 1809. Lewis 1866, p. 385.
84 16 May 1811. Simond 1817, pp. 252–3.
85 Moritz 1809, pp. 15–17.
86 Moritz 1809, p. 16.
87 Moritz 1809, pp. 15.
88 Moritz 1809, pp. 19–22.
89 Moritz 1809, p. 10.
90 Campbell-Smith 2011, p. 82.
91 Moritz 1809, p. 18.
92 Moritz 1809, p. 18. This was Oliver Goldsmith's *The Vicar of Wakefield*, published in 1766.
93 Ashton 1882, p. 458.
94 *Morning Chronicle* 25 December 1815.
95 Pratt 1803, pp. 444–5.
96 Brabourne 1884b, p. 306 (writing in August 1814 that Dawlish was wretched twelve years previously).
97 This is June 1810. Simond 1815, p. 187.
98 9 May 1804. Somerset Archives and Local Studies A\BTL/2/18.
99 28 October 1805. Somerset Archives and Local Studies A\BTL/2/24. This was the same storm that hit the fleet at Trafalgar.
100 18 April 1810. Hall 1936, p. 255.
101 Brabourne 1884a, p. 369.
102 31 July 1788. Jameson 2001, p. 59.
103 Letter written 11–15 November 1810. Hall 1936, p. 315.
104 The Penny Post was originally set up in 1680 by William Dockwra, but was taken over by the General Post Office (Campbell-Smith 2011, pp. 59–61).
105 25 May 1810. Hall 1936, p. 264.
106 30 April 1811. Brabourne 1884b, p. 97.
107 7 May 1811. Simond 1817, p. 200.
108 Chapman 1932b, p. 425.

9: ON THE MOVE

1 Gillett 1945, p. 16.
2 Austen Leigh 1871, p. 38.
3 Chapman 1932b, p. 475. Letter of 24 January 1817 to Alethea Bigg.
4 31 January 1790. Jameson 2001, p. 233.
5 1 August 1794. Jameson 2004, p. 57.
6 Moritz 1809, p. 87.
7 Moritz 1809, pp. 59–60.
8 Moritz 1809, p. 60.

9 Moritz 1809, p. 64.

10 21 January 1773. Winstanley 1988, p. 103.

11 14 March 1800. Moretonhampstead History Society manuscript of Treleaven's diary. The Shambles was where the butchers plied their trade.

12 9 November 1799. Somerset Archives and Local Studies A\BTL/2/1.

13 13 December 1790. Jameson 2001, p. 272.

14 8 September 1782. Andrews 1934, p. 108.

15 14 August 1795. Manners 1805, pp. 137–8. John Henry Manners was the Fifth Duke of Rutland.

16 September 1800. Warner 1801, p. 10.

17 Warner 1801, pp. 9–10.

18 26 November 1799. Somerset Archives and Local Studies A\BTL/2/3.

19 Austen Leigh 1871, p. 159. Letter of January 1817 to Alethea Bigg.

20 Gröben 1907, p. 87. Colonel Taylor was the brother of Sir Brook Taylor, and Ralph Heathcote was a diplomat in Germany (born in 1782).

21 *Morning Chronicle* 26 October 1807.

22 2 May 1793. Jameson 2003, p. 242.

23 Moritz 1809, p. 52.

24 11 May 1805. Silliman 1810, p. 67.

25 18 May 1805, while travelling in Warwickshire. Silliman 1810, p. 123.

26 *European Magazine* February 1816, p. 129.

27 May 1802. Courtesy of Trustees of the National Museum of the Royal Navy (NMRN), P 1985/323.

28 15 May 1805. Silliman 1810, p. 82.

29 *The Times* 25 December 1807.

30 6 July 1778. Winstanley 1983, p. 55.

31 Moritz 1809, p. 3.

32 August 1790. Andrews 1935, p. 275.

33 31 January 1807. Somerset Archives and Local Studies A\BTL/2/26.

34 'Hackney' derives from an Old French word meaning a horse and had passed into Middle English by the fourteenth century. Because many hackneys were hired out, this gave rise to the word 'hack' for an ordinary horse (or for poor writers who hire out their services).

35 Trusler 1790, p. 97.

36 Andrews 1934, p. 32.

37 Jenkin 1951, p. 18. Letter of 15 September 1792. As a Quaker, Jenkin is using the archaic form 'thy' rather than 'your'.

38 Moritz 1809, pp. 9–10.

39 26 April 1809. Upton-Wilkinson archive (090426spwwo1).

40 20 May 1805. Silliman 1810, p. 122.

41 22 January 1776. White 1837, pp. 389–90.

42 27 June 1800. Somerset Archives and Local Studies A\BTL/2/7. William Holland had a low opinion of Somerset workmen, which is why he referred to them as 'Somersetshire Boobies' among other things.

43 Andrews 1934, pp. 211–12. Byng made these comments in an Oxfordshire tour in 1785.

44 Andrews 1935, p. 64.

45 25 August 1805. Romney 1984, p. 93.

46 Andrews 1934, p. 261.

47 Moritz 1809, p. 66.

48 Cooke 1803, p. 102.

49 5 August 1781. Jeffery 1907, pp. 2–3. Dyott had recently joined the army and was on his way to Dublin.

50 26 March 1780. Winstanley 1984, p. 27.

51 12 June 1790. Andrews 1935, pp. 170–1.

52 6 July 1790. Andrews 1935, p. 236. This was at the Black Bull Inn in Cambridge.

53 July 1787. Andrews 1934, p. 249.

54 Silliman 1820a, p. 148. This was August 1805.

55 15 May 1805. Silliman 1810, p. 83.

56 20 May 1805. Silliman 1810, pp. 129–30.

57 26 June 1786. Winstanley and Jameson 1999, p. 144. The fifteenth-century Belle Sauvage inn was more frequently referred to as the 'Belle Savage'. It was demolished in 1873.

58 27 June 1786. Winstanley and Jameson 1999, p. 145.

59 30 June 1789. Andrews 1935, p. 116.

60 5 July 1790. Andrews 1935, p. 235. This fifteenth-century inn was rebuilt in 1828, and the replacement building, called 'The Bull' not 'The Black Bull', is grade II listed and has become part of St Catherine's College, at 68 Trumpington Street.

61 Andrews 1935, p. 151.

62 18 November 1805. Silliman 1820b, p. 145.

63 29 October 1795. Jameson 2004, p. 215.

64 13 January 1777. Winstanley 1981, pp. 103–4.

65 Moritz 1809, p. 13.

66 *The Times* 23 May 1803.

67 *The Times* 23 May 1803.

68 Granville 1916, p. 131. Lady Bessborough was sister of Georgiana, Duchess of Devonshire.

69 Adkins 2004, pp. 266–8.

70 4 February 1799. Jameson 2006, pp. 86–7.

71 17 February 1799. Jameson 2006, p. 91.

72 *Exeter Flying Post* 13 November 1800. St Thomas is on the west side of the River Exe, whereas most of Exeter is on an eminence on the east side.

73 *Exeter Flying Post* 13 November 1800. The post-chaises took the old ridgeway route into Exeter, which has since been named the Trafalgar Way. Henry Holland was a prominent architect and worked on Brighton Pavilion for the Prince Regent, as well as several notable buildings in London, including Hans Place, home of Henry Austen. He had estates at Okehampton.

74 *Exeter Flying Post* 13 November 1800.

75 30 January 1794. Jameson 2004, p. 8.

76 Pratt 1804, pp. 353–4.

77 Pratt 1804, p. 354.

78 Hutton 1795, p. 402.

79 'Extract of a Letter from Warrington, September 1' in *The Annual Register, or a View of the History, Politics, and Literature for the Year 1774* (London, 1778), p. 145.

80 Hall 1936, p. 164. Letter written at Beacon's Gutter, 19 May 1809. The direct distance was about 14 miles, but it was cheaper and more comfortable by canal than by stagecoach.

81 *The Times* 19 December 1806.

82 Hutton 1795, p. 404. This is now the Wednesbury Old Canal.

83 *Salisbury and Winchester Journal & Hampshire Chronicle* 20 September 1784.

84 *Northampton Mercury* 20 September 1784.

85 *Salisbury and Winchester Journal & Hampshire Chronicle* 27 September 1784.

10: DARK DEEDS

1 *Cobbetts Weekly Political Register* vol. 30, January–June 1816, col. 397.

2 McLynn 1989, pp. xi–xii.

3 June 1790. Andrews 1935, p. 209.

4 Wilson 2002, p. 161.

5 Porter 1851, p. 509.

6 Darter 1888, p. 33.

7 Blackner 1815, p. 280.

8 Sunday 10 March 1811. Simond 1817, p. 87.

9 11 March 1811. Simond 1817, pp. 94–5.

10 *York Herald* 16 March 1811.

11 Andrews 1935, p. 178.

12 McLynn 1989, p. 32.

13 McLynn 1989, p. 35.

14 Darter 1888, p. 65.

15 Moritz 1809, p. 51.

16 November 1805. Silliman 1820b, p. 101.

17 *Gentleman's Magazine* 54, 1784, p. 635. The report in its 'Historical Chronicle' was dated 14 August.

18 Trial of Sarah Smith, Old Bailey Proceedings online, April 1793, t17930410-95.

19 Trial of Sarah Smith, Old Bailey Proceedings online, April 1793, t17930410-95.

20 The National Archives manuscript HO 11/1; Bateson 1969, pp. 147–8.

21 Moritz 1809, p. 51.

22 British Library Add MS 27825 (Francis Place unpublished manuscript, vol. 1.B, p. 147).

23 An example is in the Bodleian Library, Harding B22 (304).

24 Since 1739, the song has had a number of titles, including 'The Dunghill Cock, or Turpin's Valiant Exploits', 'Turpin's Valour', 'Oh, Rare Turpin Hero' and 'Turpin Hero'. It is still performed today.

25 Broadside ballad 1739 'Turpin's Rant: A New Song', Bodleian Library, Harding B22 (304).

26 *Oxford Journal* 14 January 1797.

27 *Norfolk Chronicle or the Norwich Gazette* 4 February 1797.

28 Moritz 1809, pp. 51–2.

29 *The Times* 22 June 1792.

30 *A Treatise on the Police of the Metropolis* (1796).

31 14 March 1805. Somerset Archives and Local Studies A\BTL/2/21.

32 *Bath Chronicle and Weekly Gazette* 3 August 1775.

33 *Northampton Mercury* 7 August 1775.

34 *Northampton Mercury* 7 August 1775.

35 27 January 1808, letter to Sarah Wilkinson. Upton-Wilkinson archive (080127fpsp02).

36 *Morning Chronicle* 25 August 1814. This newspaper muddles Thomas Norman's name.

37 Trial of Thomas Norman, Old Bailey Proceedings online, September 1814, t18140914-167. The court case was 14 September.

38 *Morning Chronicle* 2 September 1806. The theft was on 24 August.

39 Trial of Eleanor Russel, Old Bailey Proceedings online, September 1806, t18060917-43. She was tried for 'theft from a specified place'.

40 Trial of Eleanor Russel, Old Bailey Proceedings online, September 1806, t18060917-43.

41 The National Archives manuscript HO 11/1.

42 The National Archives manuscript HO 10/2.

43 Austen-Leigh 1942, pp. 197–8. Letter of Mountague Cholmeley Junior to Jane Leigh-Perrot on 11 January 1800. Mrs Leigh-Perrot was Mrs Austen's sister-in-law (her husband being Mrs Austen's brother).

44 22 March 1800. Somerset Archives and Local Studies A\BTL/2/4. Mrs Leigh-Perrot's trial was on 29 March 1800. Her crime was grand larceny, a capital offence for the theft of goods worth more than one shilling.

45 30 April 1800. Somerset Archives and Local Studies A\BTL/2/5.

46 Markham 1997.

47 Chapman 1932a, pp. 154–5. Written from Bath on 21 April 1805.

48 Chapman 1932a, p. 155.

49 Chapman 1932a, p. 159. Addition to letter of 23 April 1805.

50 *Bath Chronicle* 3 April 1800.

51 *Bath Chronicle* 3 April 1800.

52 25 October 1807. Somerset Archives and Local Studies A\BTL/2/28.

53 Christie 1929, pp. 216–17. Hoddesdon was then in the parish of Broxbourne.

54 *Hampshire Chronicle* 26 October 1807.

55 *Hampshire Chronicle* 26 October 1807. The house in the High Street was later called Borham House and was close to the present Lowewood Museum. It has since been demolished.

56 *Hampshire Chronicle* 26 October 1807.

57 Anon. 1808, p. 11.

58 Hall 1936, p. 84. Letter to Miss Chorley of 15 April 1808.

59 Wesley 1831, pp. 462–3, paragraph 'Thoughts on Suicide', dated Liverpool April 8 1790.

60 13 July 1805. Silliman 1820a, p. 27.

61 Howard 1784, p. 384. Even though John Howard was a dissenter, he became high sheriff of Bedfordshire. He was appalled at the treatment of prisoners, leading to his involvement with penal reform. He died in 1790.

62 A liberate was a writ issued to a gaoler for the release of a prisoner on bail. Howard 1784, p. 385.

63 Howard 1784, p. 371.

64 For POW prisons and parole towns, see Adkins and Adkins 2006.

65 Darter 1888, p. 34.
66 Trial of Alice Walker, Old Bailey Proceedings online, 9 September 1772, t17720909-46.
67 *Virginia Gazette* (printer: Purdie and Dixon) 12 August 1773.
68 *Virginia Gazette* (printer: Rind) 12 August 1773.
69 *Virginia Gazette* (printer: Rind) 27 May 1773.
70 At this point she disappears from the records.
71 Trial of Robert Jones and Thomas Cliff, Old Bailey Proceedings online, 18 May 1774, t17740518-61.
72 Trial of Elizabeth Smith, Old Bailey Proceedings online, 11 January 1775, t17750111-33.
73 Bateson 1969.
74 Darter 1888, pp. 20–1.
75 Darter 1888, pp. 51–2.
76 Darter 1888, p. 52.
77 *Hampshire Chronicle* 18 December 1775.
78 Trial of Sarah Reynolds and Elizabeth Vale, Old Bailey Proceedings online, December 1775, t17751206-82.
79 It is difficult to tell exactly where the body was found, since the two people who searched for it got out of the coach at 'the top of Broad Street' and walked an unknown distance before they came to the ditch 'with a great current of water', where they paid a passer-by to go down the slope and retrieve the bundle.
80 Trial of Sarah Reynolds and Elizabeth Vale, Old Bailey Proceedings online, December 1775, t17751206-82.
81 They were George Morley and John Burke for highway robbery; William Munro for forgery; Samuel Wilson for counterfeiting coins; William Busby and Francis Burke for returning from transportation before their seven years had expired; and John Wallis, Richard Martin, John Lawler and the woman Frances Warren for burglary. They were all tried and convicted at the Old Bailey on 29 October 1783. Information on the individuals is in Old Bailey Proceedings online, and a full report on the execution is in *Jackson's Oxford Journal* 13 December 1783.
82 *Jackson's Oxford Journal* 13 December 1783.
83 26 March 1785. Winstanley and Jameson 1999, p. 23.
84 4 April 1785. Winstanley and Jameson 1999, p. 23.
85 Grant 1809, pp. 243–4.
86 Huddesford 1804, p. 153. 'Jack Hains' was probably the highwayman John Haines, executed in 1799, whose body was gibbeted on Hounslow Heath.
87 Darter 1888, pp. 24–5. Gallows Tree Common was on the borders of Earley and Shinfield in Berkshire, near Elm Lane. Until 1793 it was the place of execution for Reading. An elm tree was used as gallows and gibbet, but it was struck by Dutch Elm Disease in the 1970s.
88 Howell 1816, p. 816.
89 *Jackson's Oxford Journal* 31 August 1782.
90 *Ipswich Journal* 21 March 1789.
91 *Ipswich Journal* 21 March 1789.
92 Ashton 1882, p. 453.
93 Halliday 2009, p. 204.

94   29 October 1795. Jameson 2004, p. 215.
95   Wright 1867, p. 497.
96   29 October 1795. Jameson 2004, pp. 215–16.
97   The Gordon Riots took place 2 to 9 June 1780 after Lord George Gordon
     (1751–93), leader of the Protestant Association, had failed in his attempt to get
     parts of the Catholic Relief Act of 1778 repealed.
98   4 April 1801. Jameson 2007, p. 25.
99   9 April 1801. Jameson 2007, p. 26.
100 12 October 1792. Jameson 2003, p. 181.
101 Andrews 1938, p. 153.
102 *The Times* 14 June 1792.
103 Silliman 1810, p. 239.
104 *The Heir-at-Law* was first performed at the Haymarket theatre in London.
105 13 November 1803. Christie 1929, p. 161.

11: MEDICINE MEN

1   Chapman 1932b, p. 426.
2   Hall 1936, p. 172. Letter written at Beacon's Gutter, near Liverpool, 14 June 1809.
3   23 March 1779. Winstanley 1983, p. 122.
4   11 March 1791. Jameson 2003, p. 7.
5   15 March 1791. Jameson 2003, p. 8.
6   16 March 1791. Jameson 2003, p. 8.
7   16 February 1807. Somerset Archives and Local Studies A\BTL/2/26. Simon
    Morle of Plainsfield Court died in 1811 and his wife in 1812 (information from
    David Worthy).
8   18 February 1807. Somerset Archives and Local Studies A\BTL/2/26.
9   13 April 1781. Winstanley 1984, p. 125.
10 14 April 1781. Winstanley 1984, pp. 125–6.
11 *Culpeper's Complete Herbal*, enlarged edn (London), 1814, p. 130.
12 22 May 1779. Winstanley 1983, p. 139.
13 Andrews 1934, p. 8.
14 29 January 1800. Somerset Archives and Local Studies A\BTL/2/3. This was Dr
    Alyster Forbes of Nether Stowey (information from David Worthy).
15 In 1800 this became the Royal Company of Surgeons of London (later 'of
    England'). The barber-surgeons developed from barbers, who added bloodletting
    to their hair-cutting and shaving services.
16 Markham 1990, p. 55. Penelope Benwell would in 1808 marry the Reverend John
    Hind. Her diary entry is 1 January 1805.
17 Beale 1891, p. 57.
18 West 1977.
19 Beale 1891, p. 58.
20 Beale 1891, p. 58.
21 Beale 1891, p. 58.
22 In Britain physicians are nowadays referred to as 'doctors' or 'GPs' (general
    practitioners).
23 3 November 1776. Winstanley 1981, p. 83. He was Jack Wharton.
24 8 November 1776. Winstanley 1981, pp. 86–7.

25 8 April 1809. Somerset Archives and Local Studies A\BTL/2/32.

26 20 June 1782. Winstanley 1998, p. 52.

27 The surge in influenza deaths came in the second and third weeks of June 1782.

28 Hall 1936, p. 51. Letter of 18 November 1807 written at Upholland.

29 27 March 1800. Somerset Archives and Local Studies A\BTL/2/4. William Weymouth was the sexton (information from David Worthy).

30 6 April 1790. Jameson 2001, p. 248.

31 15 January 1795. Jameson 2004, p. 115.

32 14 December 1800. Jameson 2006, p. 261.

33 *Hereford Journal* 18 October 1815.

34 *Hereford Journal* 18 October 1815.

35 7 June 1791. Jameson 2003, p. 33.

36 13 May 1797. Jameson 2005, p. 149.

37 Chapman 1932a, p. 144. Letter dated 21 January 1805.

38 Beale 1891, p. 58. This was in August 1788.

39 Knight 1904, p. 51.

40 Johnston 1857, pp. 284–5. This poem was first published in 1807 as 'Resolution and Independence'.

41 18 September 1803. Somerset Archives and Local Studies A\BTL/2/17.

42 18 September 1803. Somerset Archives and Local Studies A\BTL/2/17. Holland's problems continued and were most likely dental in origin.

43 15 May 1779. Winstanley 1983, p. 137.

44 Ringsted 1774, pp. 11–12.

45 Simond 1817, pp. 329–30.

46 2 November 1799. Jameson 2006, p. 161.

47 21 September 1777. Winstanley 1981, 165.

48 22 September 1777. Winstanley 1981, 166.

49 7 July 1791, in Lincolnshire. Andrews 1935, p. 371.

50 Beale 1891, p. 58.

51 Some court-plaister was black, and it was so-called after the black patches formerly used by ladies at court to cover facial blemishes such as smallpox scars. It was priced at sixpence in various advertisements.

52 1 October 1777. Winstanley 1981, p. 168.

53 17 February 1796. Jameson 2005, p. 13.

54 *Norfolk Chronicle* 21 September 1805. Barwick was author of *An essay on shooting*.

55 *The Literary Panorama* 2 (1807), p. 989. A Rupture Society was founded in 1796, but was later disbanded. The New Rupture Society was founded either on 4 July 1804 or 15 May 1805 (see UCL Bloomsbury Project) and was active until 1950.

56 Beale 1891, p. 58.

57 4 June 1776. Winstanley 1981, p. 51

58 16 September 1813. Chapman 1932b, pp. 327–8. Fanny was twenty years old, Lizzy thirteen and Marianne twelve (her birthday was the previous day).

59 November 1808. Hall 1936, p. 122.

60 *Leeds Mercury* 19 November 1808.

61 *Leeds Mercury* 19 November 1808.

62 11 November 1799. Somerset Archives and Local Studies A\BTL/2/1.

63 31 May 1802. Darbishire 1958, p. 167.

64 1 March 1812. Hawker 1893, p. 36. It is unclear where the dental surgery took place, but probably in London.

65 Hunter 1778, p. 219.

66 Hunter 1778, p. 221.

67 Hunter 1778, p. 223.

68 *Hampshire Chronicle* 21 January 1782.

69 Cooper 1843, p. 401. When Butler returned to England, he set up as a dentist in Liverpool under an assumed name.

70 Cooper 1843, pp. 414–15.

71 The number of overall dead and wounded was 50,000, a figure sometimes said to be the number who died on the battlefield.

72 Bailey 1896, p. 174. Tuesday 24 November 1812. Naples served under Collingwood at the Battle of St Vincent on board the *Excellent*.

73 Cooper 1843, p. 399.

74 Silliman 1820a, p. 143.

75 Benjamin Franklin wore bifocals but probably did not invent them, as is sometimes claimed.

76 *Hampshire Chronicle* 1 February 1802.

77 1 January 1809. Somerset Archives and Local Studies A\BTL/2/29.

78 Darter 1888, p. 68.

79 Davy was not the apprentice of Beddoes, as is sometimes stated.

80 Davy 1800, p. 556. Nitrous oxide was first discovered in 1772 by Joseph Priestley.

81 The first operation under anaesthesia in England was in 1846.

82 This was a belated response to the dissolution of the monasteries in the sixteenth century, which had destroyed healthcare for the poor.

83 20 August 1793. Andrews 1936, p. 315. A hospital had been established in Northampton in 1744, but this new one was built by subscription. It still survives, in Billing Road.

84 The oldest operating theatre in England of 1822 can be visited. It was once part of St Thomas's Hospital in London but became hidden and was rediscovered in 1956.

85 Aikin 1771, p. 25. Aikin later became a physician, and as a dissenter was a bitter opponent of injustice and an early supporter of the French Revolution.

86 Letter of 1 October 1771. Aikin 1771, p. 89.

87 Letter of 1 October 1771. Aikin 1771, p. 89.

88 Letter of 1 October 1771. Aikin 1771, p. 90.

89 The name 'lock hospital' was derived from the earlier leprosy hospitals.

90 Aikin 1771, p. 65.

91 5 and 7 December 1799. Somerset Archives and Local Studies A\BTL/2/3. The small Over Stowey workhouse is also referred to as the poorhouse.

92 *First Report: Minutes of Evidence taken before the Select Committee appointed to consider of provision being made for the better regulation of madhouses in England* 1816 (London), p. 51.

93 *First Report: Minutes of Evidence taken before the Select Committee appointed to consider of provision being made for the better regulation of madhouses in England* 1816 (London), p. 53.

94 Mackenzie 1827, p. 525.

95 *Newcastle Courant* 14 May 1774.

96 The provision of county lunatic asylums was not a legal requirement until 1845.

97 Blackner 1815, p. 180.

98 *First Report: Minutes of Evidence taken before the Select Committee appointed to consider of provision being made for the better regulation of madhouses in England* 1816 (London), pp. 51–2.

99 *First Report: Minutes of Evidence taken before the Select Committee appointed to consider of provision being made for the better regulation of madhouses in England* 1816 (London), p. 53.

100 *First Report: Minutes of Evidence taken before the Select Committee appointed to consider of provision being made for the better regulation of madhouses in England* 1816 (London), p. 56.

101 15 April 1813. Somerset Archives and Local Studies A\BTL/2/38.

102 Eden 1797b, p. 223.

103 Andrews 1935, p. 10.

104 Extract published in *Annual Register* (1783), p. 186.

105 *Morning Post* 29 October 1811.

106 *Morning Post* 29 October 1811.

107 Bailey 1896, p. 141.

108 8 January 1812. Bailey 1896, p. 147. 'Harps' was probably Harper, keeper of a burial ground (Bailey 1896, p. 139). The surname of Daniel is unknown.

109 *Leicester Journal* 10 January 1812.

110 Bailey 1896, p. 176.

12: LAST WORDS

1 From 'The Order for the Burial of the Dead' in *The Book of Common Prayer, and Administration of the Sacraments, and Other Rites and Ceremonies of the Church, According to the Use of the Church of England: Together with the Psalter or Psalms of David, Pointed as they are to be Sung or Said in Churches* (Oxford, 1784).

2 1 May 1793. Jameson 2003, p. 241.

3 9 February 1806. Somerset Archives and Local Studies A\BTL/2/25.

4 1 July 1789. Andrews 1935, p. 120. Fritwell is about 16 miles from Towcester.

5 6 July 1791. Andrews 1935, pp. 368–9.

6 Jane Austen probably had Hodgkin's disease (a form of lymphoma) or possibly Addison's disease.

7 Brabourne 1884b, pp. 334–5.

8 24 March 1817. Somerset Archives and Local Studies A\BTL/2/43.

9 24 March 1817. Somerset Archives and Local Studies A\BTL/2/43.

10 6 June 1780. Winstanley 1984, p. 48.

11 5 February 1806. Somerset Archives and Local Studies A\BTL/2/26.

12 Holland was then rector at Monkton Farleigh in Somerset. The children's names were William, Thomas, John and Mary (information from David Worthy).

13 6 August 1805. Somerset Archives and Local Studies A\BTL/2/23.

14 For example, in the entry for Sunday 18 May 1800 (Somerset Archives and Local Studies A\BTL/2/5), he says 'These democrats are dreadful creatures', when he was talking about the people who attempted to assassinate the king.

15 7 June 1810. Somerset Archives and Local Studies A\BTL/2/33.

16   7 June 1772. Winstanley 1988, p. 42.

17   30 November 1810. Somerset Archives and Local Studies A\BTL/2/34.

18   30 November 1810. Somerset Archives and Local Studies A\BTL/2/34. The dead man was Hugh Acland, and he died at Madeira (information from David Worthy).

19   24 December 1792. Jameson 2003, p. 204.

20   8 December 1799. Somerset Archives and Local Studies A\BTL/2/3.

21   28 August 1799. Moretonhampstead History Society manuscript of Treleaven's diary.

22   Moretonhampstead History Society manuscript of Treleaven's diary.

23   17 September 1790. Jameson 2001, p. 263. The original manuscript of Woodforde's diary has been lost since it was published in Beresford 1927, p. 214.

24   19 September 1790. Jameson 2001, p. 264. The original manuscript of Woodforde's diary has been lost since it was published in Beresford 1927, p. 216.

25   15 October 1808. Brabourne 1884b, p. 21.

26   15 December 1802. Somerset Archives and Local Studies DD\SAS/C795/FA/185.

27   February 1810. Hall 1936, p. 236. Her pupil was Mary Gertrude Pedder.

28   Knight 1904, pp. 48–9.

29   9 June 1811. Somerset Archives and Local Studies A\BTL/2/35.

30   Eden 1797a, p. 579.

31   Moritz 1809, p. 11.

32   Wordsworth 1815, p. 163.

33   Ayton 1814, p. 55. The funeral took place in the summer of 1813, probably in July. This is the same man who went down William Pit at Whitehaven.

34   Ayton 1814, p. 55.

35   12 February 1782. Winstanley 1998, p. 14.

36   Winstanley 1998, p. 14.

37   Winstanley 1998, p. 14.

38   Winstanley 1998, p. 15.

39   Moritz 1809, p. 11. This was in 1782.

40   1 February 1788. Jameson 2001, p. 9.

41   18 June 1782.Winstanley 1998, p. 51.

42   18 August 1778. Winstanley 1983, p. 64.

43   23 March 1791. Jameson 2003, p. 10.

44   25 June 1796. Jameson 2005, p. 53.

45   14 November 1799. Somerset Archives and Local Studies A\BTL/2/1.

46   17 November 1799. Somerset Archives and Local Studies A\BTL/2/1.

47   6 November 1799. Somerset Archives and Local Studies A\BTL/2/1.

48   16 December 1802. Somerset Archives and Local Studies DD\SAS/C795/FA/185.

49   15 November 1780. Winstanley 1984, p. 87.

50   The stone is now fixed to the chancel wall. Robert Phillips was a cooper by profession and made it well known what verse he wanted on his gravestone. See Hawkins 1819, pp. 19–20, which has a slightly different inscription.

51   Andrews 1895, p. 137.

52   White 1789, p. 322.

53   5 November 1783.Winstanley 1998, p. 185.

54   11 May 1810. Hall, 1936, p. 260. Letter to Miss Bessy Winkley from Dove Nest.

55 11 May 1810. Hall, 1936, p. 261. Letter to Miss Bessy Winkley from Dove Nest. Crape was a thin, loosely woven fabric.

56 Brabourne 1884b, pp. 21–2. Letter from Southampton dated Saturday 15 October 1808. Bombazeen was a thin silken material used especially for mourning clothes.

57 Brabourne 1884a, p. 311. Letter dated Friday 30 August 1805.

58 Darter 1888, p. 97.

59 Chapman 1932b, p. 509. Madame Bijion (or Bigeon) was an old family retainer.

60 *Morning Post* 1 May 1804.

61 The full text of the inscription is: 'In MEMORY OF ANTHONY CURTIS who died April 11th 1787. Aged 77 Years. This world's a City full of Crooked streets, And death the Market Place where all men Meets, If life was Merchandise that men could buy, The rich would live and none but poor would die.' From a gravestone said to be in Basingstoke Cemetery, Hampshire, and recorded in Maiben 1870, p. 38.

62 Andrews 1935, p. 91.

63 Moritz 1809, p. 72.

64 5 September 1811. Simond 1817, pp. 358–9.

65 The account does not appear to have been by Pope, but is more likely to have come from *Essays Moral and Literary* vol. 2 by the Reverend Vicesimus Knox (London, 1779), where Pope and part of this epitaph are mentioned in the same paragraph.

66 Hay 1953, p. 174.

BIBLIOGRAPHY

Adkins, R. 2004 *Trafalgar: The Biography of a Battle* (London)

Adkins, R. and Adkins, L. 2006 *The War for All the Oceans. From Nelson at the Nile to Napoleon at Waterloo* (London)

Adkins, R. and Adkins, L. 2008 *Jack Tar: Life in Nelson's Navy* (London)

Aikin J. 1771 *Thoughts on Hospitals* (London)

Andrews, C.B. (ed.) 1934 *The Torrington Diaries containing the tours through England and Wales of the Hon. John Byng (later fifth Viscount Torrington) between the years 1781 and 1794* vol. 1 (London)

Andrews, C.B. (ed.) 1935 *The Torrington Diaries containing the tours through England and Wales of the Hon. John Byng (later fifth Viscount Torrington) between the years 1781 and 1794* vol. 2 (London)

Andrews, C.B. (ed.) 1936 *The Torrington Diaries containing the tours through England and Wales of the Hon. John Byng (later fifth Viscount Torrington) between the years 1781 and 1794* vol. 3 (London)

Andrews, C.B. (ed.) 1938 *The Torrington Diaries containing the tours through England and Wales of the Hon. John Byng (later fifth Viscount Torrington) between the years 1781 and 1794* vol. 4 (New York)

Andrews, W. 1891 *Old Church Lore* (Hull and London)

Andrews, W. 1895 *Curious Church Customs and Cognate Subjects* (Hull and London)

Anon. 1808 *The Trial of Thomas Simmons, for the Wilful Murder of Mrs. Hummerstone and Mrs Warner, at Hoddesdon, in Hertfordshire, Who was found Guilty at the Assizes Held at Hertford, Friday, March 4, 1808* (London)

Ashton, J. 1882 *Chap-Books of the Eighteenth Century with Facsimiles, Notes, and Introduction* (London)

Ashton, J. 1906 *The Dawn of the XIXth Century in England* (London)

Austen Leigh, J.E. 1871 *A Memoir of Jane Austen* (London)

Austen-Leigh, R.A. 1942 *Austen Papers 1704–1856* (privately printed)

Austen-Leigh, W. and Austen-Leigh, R.A. 1913 *Jane Austen. Her Life and Letters. A Family Record* (New York)

Ayres, J. (ed.) 1984 *Paupers & Pig Killers. The Diary of William Holland, A Somerset Parson, 1799–1818* (Stroud)

Ayton, R. 1814 *A Voyage round Great Britain undertaken in the summer of the year 1813, and commencing from the Lands-End, Cornwall* (London)

Ayton, R. 1815 *A Voyage round Great Britain undertaken in the summer of the year 1813, and commencing from the Lands-End, Cornwall* vol. 2 (London)

Bailey, J.B. 1896 *The Diary of a Resurrectionist 1811–1812* (London)

Baines, E. 1835 *History of the Cotton Manufacture in Great Britain* (London)

Bamford, F. (ed.) 1936 *Dear Miss Heber. An Eighteenth Century Correspondence* (London)

Barlow, J. 1834 'Cases of Caesarean Operations' *London Medical and Surgical Journal* 4, pp. 564–70

Bateson, C. 1969 *The Convict Ships 1787–1868* (Glasgow)

Beale, C.H. 1891 (ed.) *Reminiscences of a Gentlewoman of the Last Century: Letters of Catherine Hutton* (Birmingham)

Bell, J. (ed.) 1812 *Rhymes of the Northern Bards: Being a curious collection of old and new songs and poems, Peculiar to the counties of Newcastle Upon Tyne, Northumberland, and Durham* (Newcastle upon Tyne)

Belsham, W. 1795 *Memoirs of the Reign of George III to the Session of Parliament Ending A.D. 1793* vol. 1 (London)

Benton, P. 1867 *The History of Rochford Hundred* (Rochford)

Beresford, J. (ed.) 1927 *The Diary of a Country Parson: The Reverend James Woodforde. Vol. III 1788–1792* (Oxford)

Blackner, J. 1815 *The History of Nottingham Embracing its Antiquities, Trade, and Manufactures, from the Earliest Authentic Records to The Present Period* (Nottingham)

Brabourne, E. (ed.) 1884a *Letters of Jane Austen* vol. 1 (London)

Brabourne, E. (ed.) 1884b *Letters of Jane Austen* vol. 2 (London)

Branch, J. 1801 *Tables Comprizing a Complete Ready Reckoner* (Manchester)

Brand, J. 1813 *Observations on Popular Antiquities: chiefly illustrating the origin of our vulgar customs, ceremonies, and superstitions* vol. 2 (rev. edn by H. Ellis) (London)

Brayne, M. 1998 'Weston weddings' *Parson Woodforde Society Quarterly Journal* 31, pp. 12–20

Brougham, H. 1840 *Historical Sketches of Statesmen who flourished in the time of George III to which is added remarks on party, and an appendix*, 1st series, vol. 1 (London)

Cahill, K. 2001 *Who Owns Britain* (Edinburgh)

Campbell-Smith, D. 2011 *Masters of the Post: The Authorized History of the Royal Mail* (London)

Caplan, C. 2004 'Henry Austen's Buxton Bank' *Jane Austen Society Report for 2004*, pp. 46–8

Carter, T. 1845 *Memoirs of a Working Man* (London)

Chapman, R.W. (ed.) 1932a *Jane Austen's Letters to her sister Cassandra and others, Volume I 1796–1809* (Oxford)

Chapman, R.W. (ed.) 1932b *Jane Austen's Letters to her sister Cassandra and others, Volume II 1811–1817* (Oxford)

Chater, K. 2009 *Untold Histories. Black people in England and Wales during the period of the British slave trade, c. 1660–1807* (Manchester)

Chorley, H.F. 1836 *Memorials of Mrs. Hemans with illustrations of her literary character from her private correspondence* vol. 2 (New York, London)

Christie, O.F. (ed.) 1929 *The Diary of the Revd. William Jones 1777–1821* (New York, London, Paris)

Colquhoun, P. 1796 *A Treatise on the Police of the Metropolis* (by a magistrate) (London)

Cooke, G.A. 1803 *Topographical and Statistical Description of the County of Norfolk* (London)

Cooper, B.B. 1843 *The Life of Sir Astley Cooper, Bart.* vol. 1 (London)

Cooper, W. 1776 'An Account of the Caesarean Operation, communicated in a letter to William Hunter, M.D. F.R.S.' *Medical Observations and Inquiries* 5, pp. 217–32

Corley, T.A.B. 2005 'Jane Austen's School Days' *Jane Austen Society Collected Reports 1996–2000*, pp. 14–24

Cullingford, B. 2000 *British Chimney Sweeps. Five Centuries of Chimney Sweeping* (London)

Cunningham, P. (ed.) 1859 *The Letters of Horace Walpole, Earl of Orford* vol. 9 (London)

Darbishire, H. (ed.) 1958 *Journals of Dorothy Wordsworth* (London)

Darter, W.S. 1888 *Reminiscences of Reading* (Reading)

David, E. 1994 (ed. J. Norman) *Harvest of the Cold Months. The Social History of Ice and Ices* (London)

Davy, H. 1800 *Researches, Chemical and Philosophical; chiefly concerning nitrous oxide or dephlogisticated nitrous air and its respiration* (London)

Dowell, S. 1888 (2nd edn) *A History of Taxation and Taxes in England. Vol. IV Taxes on Articles of Consumption* (London, New York)

Downman, H. 1803 *Infancy, or, The management of children: a didactic poem, in six books* (Exeter)

Eden, F.M. 1797a *The State of the Poor: or, an history of the labouring classes in England vol. I* (London)

Eden, F.M. 1797b *The State of the Poor: or, an history of the labouring classes in England vol. II* (London)

Eden, F.M. 1797c *The State of the Poor: or, an history of the labouring classes in England vol. III* (London)

Elliott, R. 1842 *The Gretna Green Memoirs* (London)

Ellis, M. 2011 'Jane Austen and the credit crunch of 1816' *Jane Austen Society Report for 2011*, pp. 42–53

Evans, D.M. 2009 'Banks is the Villain?' *Antiquaries Journal* 89, pp. 337–63

Eveleigh, D.J. 1983 *Firegrates and Kitchen Hearths* (Princes Risborough)

Eveleigh, D.J. 2003 *Candle Lighting* (Princes Risborough)

Factories Inquiry Commission 1833 *Second Report of the Central Board of His Majesty's Commissioners appointed to collect information in the manufacturing districts, as to the Employment of Children in Factories, and as to the Propriety and Means of Curtailing the Hours of their Labour* (London)

Foot, P. 1794 *General view of the agriculture of the county of Middlesex: with observations on the means of their improvement* (London)

Foreman, A. 1998 *Georgiana Duchess of Devonshire* (London)

Fremantle, A. (ed.) 1940 *The Wynne Diaries Volume III 1798–1820* (Oxford)

Gardiner, W. 1853 *Music and Friends; or, Pleasant Recollections of A Dilettante* vol. 3 (London)

Gatrell, V. 2006 *City of Laughter: Sex and Satire in Eighteenth-Century London* (London)

George, D. 1930 *London Life in the Eighteenth Century* (London)

Gillett, E. (ed.) 1945 *Elizabeth Ham by Herself 1783–1820* (London)

Glasse, H. 1774 *The Art of Cookery Made Plain and Easy* (actually by 'a Lady' but attributed to Glasse) (London)

Goldsmith, O. 1770 *The Deserted Village, A Poem* (London)

Grant, J. 1809 'Journal of a Three Weeks Tour in 1797, Through Derbyshire to the Lakes', pp. 219–92 in W. Mavor 1809 *The British Tourist's, or Traveller's, Pocket Companion* vol. 4 (London)

Granville, C. (ed.) 1916 *Lord Granville Leveson Gower (First Earl Granville), Private Correspondence 1781 to 1821* vol. 2 (London)

Green, W. 1819 *The Tourist's New Guide, containing a description of the lakes, mountains, and scenery* vol. 1 (Kendal)

Gröben, L. 1907 *Ralph Heathcote: Letters of a Young Diplomatist and soldier during the time of Napoleon giving an account of the dispute between the emperor and the elector of Hesse* (London)

Grose, F. et al. 1780 (2nd edn) *The Antiquarian Repertory* vol. 1 (London)

Grose, F. 1787 *A Provincial Glossary, with A Collection of Local Proverbs and Popular Superstitions* (London)

Grose, F. 1811 *Lexicon Balatronicum. A Dictionary of Buckish Slang, University Wit, and Pickpocket Eloquence* (London)

Hall, E. (ed.) 1936 *Miss Weeton: Journal of a Governess 1807–1811* (London)

Hall, E. (ed.) 1939 *Miss Weeton. Journal of a Governess 1811–1825* (London)

Halliday, S. 2009 *Newgate: London's Prototype of Hell* (Stroud)

Hamilton, A. 1813 (7th edn) *A Treatise on the Management of Female Complaints* (Edinburgh)

Harland, J. (ed.) 1865 *Ballads & Songs of Lancashire Chiefly Older than the 19th century* (London)

Hawker, P. 1893 *The Diary of Colonel Peter Hawker* vol. 1 (London)

Hawkins, A. 1819 *Kingsbridge and Salcombe with the Intermediate Estuary* (anonymous, but attributed to Abraham Hawkins) (Kingsbridge)

Hay, M.D. (ed.) 1953 *Landsman Hay: The Memoirs of Robert Hay 1789–1847* (London)

Haydon, C. 2002 'Religious Minorities in England', pp. 241–51 in H.T. Dickinson (ed.) 2002 *A Companion to Eighteenth-Century Britain* (Oxford)

Hayley, W. 1786 (2nd edn) *A Philosophical, Historical, and Moral Essay on Old Maids by a friend to the sisterhood* vol. 1 (London)

Henry, M.A. 2002 'The Making of Elite Culture', pp. 311–28 in H.T. Dickinson (ed.) 2002 *A Companion to Eighteenth-Century Britain* (Oxford)

Horsfall, P. 2005 'The Austen Family and Friends and the Construction of the Basingstoke Canal 1788–94 or, How the Austen Friends Sank Their Money' *Jane Austen Society Report for 2005*, pp. 66–9

Howard, J. 1784 (3rd edn) *The State of the Prisons in England and Wales with Preliminary Observations and an Account of Some Foreign Prisons and Hospitals* (Warrington)

Howell, T.B. (ed.) 1816 *A Complete Collection of State Trials and Proceedings for High Treason and Other Crimes and Misdemeanors from the Earliest Period to the Year 1783* vol. 21 (London)

Hubback, J.H. and Hubback, E.C. 1906 *Jane Austen's Sailor Brothers* (London, New York)

Huddesford, G. (ed.) 1804 *The Wiccamical Chaplet, A Selection of Original Poetry* (London)

Hunter, J. 1778 *The Natural History of the Human Teeth, part 2: A Practical Treatise on the Diseases of the Teeth* (London)

Hutton, W. 1791 *The History of Derby from the remote ages of antiquity to the year MDCCXCI* (London)

Hutton, W. 1795 *An History of Birmingham* (Birmingham)

Jameson, P. 2001 *The Diary of James Woodforde. Volume 12 1788–1790* (Castle Cary)

Jameson, P. 2003 *The Diary of James Woodforde. Volume 13 1791–1793* (Castle Cary)

Jameson, P. 2004 *The Diary of James Woodforde. Volume 14 1794–1795* (Castle Cary)

Jameson, P. 2005 *The Diary of James Woodforde. Volume 15 1796–1797* (Castle Cary)

Jameson, P. 2006 *The Diary of James Woodforde. Volume 16 1798–1800* (Castle Cary)

Jameson, P. 2007 *The Diary of James Woodforde. Volume 17 1801–1802* (Castle Cary)

Jeffery, R.W. (ed.) 1907 *Dyott's Diary 1781–1845. A Selection from the Journal of William Dyott, sometime general in the British Army and aide-de-camp to his Majesty King George III* vol. 1 (London)

Jenkin, A.K.H. 1951 *News from Cornwall with a memoir of William Jenkin* (London)

Jenkins, S. 1999 *England's Thousand Best Churches* (London)

Johnston, W. (ed.) 1857 *The Earlier Poems of William Wordsworth Corrected as in the Latest Editions* (London)

Jupp, P. (ed.) 1991 *The Letter-Journal of George Canning, 1793–1795* (London)

Kelly, I. 2005 *Beau Brummell: The Ultimate Dandy* (London)

Knight, W. (ed.) 1904 *Journals of Dorothy Wordsworth* vol. 1 (London)

Leach, A.F. 1911 *Educational Charters and Documents 598 to 1909* (Cambridge)

Le Faye, D. 2006 *A Chronology of Jane Austen and her Family* (Cambridge, New York)

Le Faye, D. (ed.) 2011 (4th edn) *Jane Austen's Letters* (Oxford)

Lewis, T. (ed.) 1866 *Extracts from the Journals and Correspondence of Miss Berry from the Year 1783 to 1852* vol. 2 (London)

Macdonald, J. 1790 *Travels in various parts of Europe, Asia, and Africa during a series of thirty years and upwards* (London)

Mackenzie, E. 1827 *A Descriptive and Historical Account of the Town and County of Newcastle upon Tyne including the borough of Gateshead* (Newcastle upon Tyne)

Mackenzie, W.C. 1916 *The War Diary of a London Scot (Alderman G.M. MacAulay) 1796–7 with a review of the year* (Paisley)

McLynn, F. 1989 *Crime and Punishment in Eighteenth-century England* (London)

Maiben, F. 1870 *An Original Collection of Extant Epitaphs Gathered by a Commercial in Spare Moments* (London, published anonymously)

Manners, J.H. 1805 *Journal of a Tour round the southern Coasts of England* (London, published anonymously)

Markham, S. 1990 *A Testimony of Her Times. Based on Penelope Hind's Diaries and Correspondence 1787–1838* (London)

Markham, S. 1997 'A gardener's question for Mrs Leigh Perrot' *Jane Austen Society Collected Reports 1986–1995*, pp. 213–14

Middleton, J. 1807 *View of the Agriculture of Middlesex* (London)

Millard, W.S. 1895 'The Battle of Copenhagen' *Macmillan's Magazine* 72, pp. 81–93

Mingay, G. 2002 'Agriculture and rural life', pp. 141–57 in H.T. Dickinson (ed.) 2002 *A Companion to Eighteenth-Century Britain* (Oxford)

Montague, L. 1785 *The Housewife. Being a Most Useful Assistant in all Domestic Concerns, Whether In a Town or Country Situation* (London)

Moore, W. 2009 *Wedlock: How Georgian Britain's Worst Husband Met His Match* (London)

Moritz, C.P. 1809 'Travels Through Various Parts of England in 1782', pp. 1–120 in W. Mavor 1809 *The British Tourist's, or Traveller's, Pocket Companion* vol. 4 (London)

Mortimer, T. 1810 *A General Dictionary of Commerce, Trade, and Manufactures* (London)

Moss, W. 1781 *An Essay on the Management and Nursing of Children in the earlier periods of infancy* (London)

Nicholson, J. and Burn, R. 1776 *The History and Antiquities of the Counties of Westmorland and Cumberland* vol. 1 (London)

Pasley, T. 1931 (ed. R.M.S. Pasley) *Private Sea Journals 1778–1782* (London, Toronto)

Penhallurick, R.J. 1991 *The Anglo-Welsh Dialects of North Wales* (Frankfurt, Bern, New York, Paris)

Pennant, T. 1776 (4th edn) *A Tour in Scotland* (London)

Percival, R. 1774 'Observations on the State of Population in *Manchester*, and other adjacent Places' *Philosophical Transactions of the Royal Society of London* vol. 64, pp. 54–66

Porter, G.R. 1851 *The Progress of The Nation in its Various Social and Economical Relations from the Beginning of the Nineteenth Century* (London)

Pratt, S.J. 1801 *Gleanings in England* vol. 2 (London)

Pratt, S.J. 1803 *Gleanings in England* vol. 3 (London)

Pratt, S.J. 1804 (3rd edn) *Gleanings in England* vol. 1 (London)

Price, R. 1783 (4th edn) *Observations on Reversionary Payments on schemes for providing annuities for widows, and for persons in old age* vol. 1 (London)

Pugh, J. 1787 *Remarkable Occurrences in the Life of Jonas Hanway, Esq.* (London)

Rattenbury, J. 1837 *Memoirs of a Smuggler, compiled from his diary and journal* (Sidmouth)

Repton, J.A. 1812 'An Account of the Opening of the Great Barrow at Stow-Heath, near Aylsham, in Norfolk, in July 1808. Communicated by John Adey Repton, Esq., F.A.S. in a letter to Craven Ord, Esq. F.R.S. and F.A.S., V.P.' *Archaeologia* vol. 16, pp. 354–5

Ringsted, J. 1774 *The Cattle Keeper's Assistant, or genuine directions for country-gentlemen, sportsmen, farmers, grasiers, farriers, &c.* (London)

Romney, P. 1984 *The Diary of Charles Fothergill 1805. An Itinerary to York, Flamborough and the North-Western Dales of Yorkshire* (Leeds)

Roud, S. and Bishop, J. (eds) 2012 *The New Penguin Book of English Folk Songs* (London)

Rowe, H. 1796 *Poems* vol. 1 (London)

Rubenhold, H. 2005 *The Covent Garden Ladies: Pimp General Jack & The Extraordinary Story of Harris's List* (Stroud)

Rudder, S. 1779 *A New History of Gloucestershire* (Cirencester)

Sandford, H. 1888 *Thomas Poole and his Friends* vol. 2 (London)

Shaw, S. 1808 'A Tour to the West of England, in 1788', pp. 172–335 in J.A. Pinkerton *General Collection of the Best and Most Interesting Voyages and Travels in All Parts of the World* (London)

Sheridan, T. 1762 *A Course of Lectures on Elocution* (London)

Silliman, B. 1810 *A Journal of Travels in England, Holland and Scotland, and of two passages over the Atlantic, in the years 1805 and 1806* vol 1 (New York)

Silliman, B. 1820a (3rd edn) *A Journal of Travels in England, Holland and Scotland, and of two passages over the Atlantic, in the years 1805 and 1806* vol 2 (New Haven)

Silliman, B. 1820b (3rd edn) *A Journal of Travels in England, Holland and Scotland, and of two passages over the Atlantic, in the years 1805 and 1806* vol 3 (New Haven)

Simond, L. 1815 *Journal of a tour and residence in Great Britain, during the years 1810 and 1811, by a French Traveller* vol. 1 (Edinburgh)

Simond, L. 1817 (2nd edn) *Journal of a tour and residence in Great Britain during the years 1810 and 1811* vol. 2 (Edinburgh, London)

Smith, H. 1785 (4th edn) *Letters to Married Women* (London)

Smith, J.T. 1874 *Vagabondiana or, Anecdotes of Mendicant Wanderers Through the Streets of London* (London)

Southey, R. 1814 *Letters from England by Don Manuel Alvarez Espriella* vol. 3 (London)

Spilsbury, F. 1791 *Free Observations on the Scurvy, Gout, Diet and Remedy* (Norwich)

Stevenson, W. 1812 *General View of the Agriculture of the County of Dorset* (London)

Struve, C.A. 1802 *A Familiar View of the Domestic Education of Children* (trans. from the German, with three letters by A.F.M. Willich) (London)

Trusler, J. 1784 *Principles of Politeness and of Knowing the World* (Berlin)

Trusler, J. 1790 (2nd edn) *The London Adviser and Guide* (London)

Vickery, A. 2003 *The Gentleman's Daughter: Women's Lives in Georgian England* (New Haven and London)

Vickery, A. 2009 *Behind Closed Doors: At Home in Georgian England* (New Haven and London)

Walker, A. 1792 *Remarks made in a Tour from London to the Lakes of Westmoreland and Cumberland, in the summer of M,DCC,XCI* (London)

Walker, J. 1791 *A critical pronouncing dictionary and expositor of the English language* (London)

Warner, R. 1801 *Excursions from Bath* (Bath)

Watson, G. 1827 *A Narrative of the Adventures of a Greenwich Pensioner written by himself* (Newcastle)

Wesley, J. 1831 *The Works of the Reverend John Wesley, A.M.* vol. 7 (New York)

West, J.L. 1977 *The Taylors of Lancashire: Bonesetters and Doctors 1750–1890* (Worsley)

White, C. 1773 *A Treatise on the Management of Pregnant and Lying-In Women* (London)

White, G. 1789 *The Natural History and Antiquities of Selborne, in the County of Southampton: with Engravings, and an Appendix* (London)

White, G. 1837 (new edn) *The Natural History and Antiquities of Selborne, in the County of Southampton.* (London)

White, J. 2012 *London in the Eighteenth Century. A Great and Monstrous Thing* (London)

Willan, R. 1801 *Reports on the Diseases in London during the years 1796, 97, 98, 99 and 1800* (London)

Williams, C. (trans.) 1933 *Sophie in London 1786 being the Diary of Sophie v. la Roche* (London)

Wilson, R.G. 2002 'The Landed Elite', pp. 158–71 in H.T. Dickinson (ed.) 2002 *A Companion to Eighteenth-Century Britain* (Oxford)

Winstanley, R.L. 1981 *The Diary of James Woodforde (The first six Norfolk years 1776–1781). Volume 1 1776–1781* (Parson Woodforde Society)

Winstanley, R.L. 1983 *The Diary of James Woodforde (The first six Norfolk years 1776–1781). Volume 2 1778–1779* (Parson Woodforde Society)

Winstanley, R.L. 1984 *The Diary of James Woodforde (The first six Norfolk years 1776–1781). Volume 3 1780–1781* (Parson Woodforde Society)

Winstanley, R.L. 1988 *The Ansford Diary of James Woodforde. Volume 5: 1772–1773* (Parson Woodforde Society)

Winstanley, R.L. 1989 *The Oxford & Somerset Diary of James Woodforde 1774–1775* (Parson Woodforde Society)

Winstanley, R.L. 1996 *Parson Woodforde – The Life & Times of a Country Diarist* (Bungay)

Winstanley, R.L. 1998 *The Diary of James Woodforde. Volume 10 1782–1784* (Castle Cary)

Winstanley, R.L. 2012 'Carl Philipp Moritz – A German Traveller in Georgian England' *Parson Woodforde Society Quarterly Journal* 45, pp. 35–48

Winstanley, R. and Jameson, P. (eds) 1999 *The Diary of James Woodforde. Volume 11 1785–1787* (Castle Cary)

Wordsworth, W. 1815 *Poems by William Wordsworth Including Lyrical Ballads, and the Miscellaneous Pieces of the Author* vol. 1 (London)

Wright, L. 1960 *Clean and Decent. The History of the Bathroom and the W.C.* (London, Boston)

Wright, T. 1867 *Caricature History of the Georges* (London)

Wrigley, E.A. and Schofield, R.S. 1989 *The Population History of England 1541–1871: A Reconstruction* (Cambridge)

LIST OF MAPS

LIST OF ILLUSTRATIONS

Joseph Johnson, a crippled black beggar and former merchant seaman. The print, dated December 1815, is from Smith, J. T. 1874 (first published 1817) *Vagabondiana; or, Anecdotes of Mendicant Wanderers Through the Streets of London* (London)

A workhouse depicted on a copper penny token issued by the Overseers of the Poor at Sheffield (Authors' collection)

A boy selling matches in a London street. The print, dated December 1815, is from Smith, J. T. 1874 (first published 1817) *Vagabondiana; or, Anecdotes of Mendicant Wanderers Through the Streets of London* (London)

A child street hawker selling potatoes from a wooden wheelbarrow. Printed by S. & J. Fuller at the Temple of Fancy, Rathbone Place, London (Authors' collection)

The River Tyne in 1789. From Brand, J. 1789 *The history and antiquities of the town and county of the town of Newcastle upon Tyne vol. 2* (London)

SECTION TWO

Performances at theatres in London advertised in *The Times* newspaper for 23 May 1808 (Authors' collection)

A state lottery ticket sold in 1808 (Authors' collection)

The latest catalogue of Lackington's bookseller in London advertised in the *St James Chronicle* on 19 June 1817 (Authors' collection)

A bookseller with two customers choosing books. From *The Book of English Trades and Library of the Useful Arts* 1808 (new edn) (London)

Obverse and reverse of a halfpenny token issued in 1795 by Lackington's bookseller (Authors' collection)

A view of Hotwells spa, near Bristol, in 1801. Artist G. Holmes. Engraved by J. Walker, 44 Paternoster Row, London, published 1 June 1801 (Authors' collection)

Front page of the *Morning Chronicle* for 24 October 1807 (Authors' collection)

A road map of January 1785 showing the route from Newbury eastwards along the Bath road from London. From *A New and General view of the direct roads of England & Wales as described in Paterson's British Itinerary* 1785 (London)

William Tomlins, a crossing sweeper and beggar. The print, dated May 1816, is from Smith, J.T. 1874 (first published 1817) *Vagabondiana; or, Anecdotes of Mendicant Wanderers Through the Streets of London* (London)

A coachmaker constructing a post-chaise. The print, dated August 1804, is from *The Book of English Trades and Library of the Useful Arts* 1818 (new edn) (London)

A woman being burned at the stake, illustrating the execution of Christian Bowman in 1789. From Ashton, J. 1882 *Chap-Books of the Eighteenth Century with Facsimiles, Notes, and Introduction* (London), p. 452

An apothecary (or druggist) making his own medicines. From *The Book of English Trades and Library of the Useful Arts* 1818 (new edn) (London)

Ching's Worm Lozenges advertised in the *St James Chronicle* for 19 June 1817 (Authors' collection)

A beggar with a wooden leg and crutches. The print, dated April 1816, is from Smith, J. T. 1874 (first published 1817) *Vagabondiana; or, Anecdotes of Mendicant Wanderers Through the Streets of London* (London)

Newcastle's charitable infirmary, depicted in 1789. From Brand, J. 1789 *The history and antiquities of the town and county of the town of Newcastle upon Tyne vol. 2* (London)

ACKNOWLEDGEMENTS

During our research, we have been assisted by several libraries and archives, as well as by various individuals and institutions who have kindly given permission to reproduce quotations or have helped in other ways. We are very grateful to the London Library, especially the Trustees of the London Library Trust for the Carlyle Membership. Thanks are also due to Exeter University's Library, the Devon and Exeter Institution (notably Roger Brien, James Turner and Su Conniff) and the British Library (especially Manuscripts and the Document Supply Service).

As ever, special mention must be made of everyone at the St Thomas branch of the Devon Library Services, including Karen Lee, Judith Prescott and Lee Rawlings, who dealt brilliantly with our constant requests, despite having to operate from temporary premises. Karen's car was written off (though thankfully she was unhurt) while in pursuit of our Jane Austen requests, which was way beyond the call of duty. We are also indebted to Lesley Wiltshire for all her work in the Devon Library Services interlibrary loans department.

We enjoyed working at the Somerset Heritage Centre, where we greatly appreciated the friendly and helpful staff. This archive holds the original copies of the extensive diaries of William Holland, which have yet to be published in their entirety. David Worthy has been incredibly generous in sharing information about the Holland diaries, and his help has been invaluable. We would also like to thank John Upton for kindly allowing us to quote from the Upton-Wilkinson archive; the Trustees of the National Museum of the Royal Navy (NMRN) for the use of their archives; Moretonhampstead History Society for giving permission to use their Treleaven's diary archive; the Yorkshire Archaeological Society for permission to use *The Diary of Charles Fothergill 1805*; and the Thomas Fisher Rare Book Library of the University of Toronto, which holds the original manuscript of the Fothergill Papers.

The Parson Woodforde Society very generously gave us permission to use their wonderful editions of the complete Woodforde diaries. We are also grateful to Jenny Alderson from the society for her help, while Martin Brayne kindly provided much valuable information, as did Peter Jameson. Since Parson Woodforde is usually regarded as a Norfolk man, we were pleased to find that he had deep roots in Ansford and nearby Castle Cary in Somerset. We visit Castle Cary at least twice a year, and everyone at Max Foote Associates there deserves a special mention.

Stephen Lysch (of Palgrave, Ontario, Canada) freely shared information on the Cureton family, which was much appreciated. Many thanks as well to Jane Wickenden, Historic Collections Librarian at the Institute of Naval Medicine for her generous help, as well as to Robin Agnew, Andrew Butcher, Dr Tony Corley, Dr Ian Mortimer, Deirdre Le Faye, Keith Gregson, Dr David Higgins of the Society for Clay Pipe Research, David Warner, Chris Mortimer of Blacksnow Web Design for his constant expertise and support, the Dorset History Centre, Matthew Sheldon of the National Museum of the Royal Navy, Richard Walker of the British Library, Simon Foote of Exeter University library, Professor David Watkin, Liz Egan and Lauren Ryall-Stockton of the Thackray Museum in Leeds and Joan Livesey of Wigan Archives Service. As ever, we have neglected friends and family while writing this book, and we are grateful for their understanding.

Finally, we owe a big vote of thanks to Richard Beswick at Little, Brown (UK) and to Rick Kot at Viking Penguin (US) for taking on this book, and to all those involved in the various publishing processes including Zoe Gullen (indomitable desk editor), Victoria Pepe, Anniina Vuori, Nathalie Morse, John Gilkes (for his maps), Sue Phillpott (copy-editing), Alison Tulett (proofreading), Sarah Ereira (indexing) and Naomi Doerge (publicity).

INDEX

abortion 44

accents 51–4; *see also* dialects

Acland, Hugh 388

Acland, John 326

afterlife 324, 325

agriculture 39, 40, 193–8; child workers 70, 73; dairy 105–6; improvements/changes xix, 194, 203, 208; servants/workers 67, 92, 95, 140, 176, 189, 193–4; *see also* cattle, enclosures, harvests, manure, milk, ploughmen, wheat

Aikin, John 312–13, 386

alcohol 31, 111–12, 207, 210, 226, 300, 312; *see also* beer, gin, wine

alighting stones 241

Allen, Mrs (*Northanger Abbey*) 130

almanacs 168–9

almshouses 202, 317

Althens, Henry 68

America: beaver imports 129; language 52; *see also* Silliman, Simond, slaves, transportation, wars

American Revolutionary War (War of Independence) xvii, 281, 282

amputation 304, 309, 312–13

amulets 166

anaesthetics 25, 26, 311–12

anatomists/anatomy schools 11, 25, 296, 297, 309, 318, 319–21, 328; *see also* dissection

Andrews, Harry 153

Andrews, Michael 135

Andrews, Richard 112

animals *see* birds, cats, cattle dogs, farriers, horses

Ansford, Somerset xxv, 92, 211

apothecaries (druggists) 12, 293, 295–6, 297, 304, 305, 308

apples 43, 59, 109, 152

apprentices xxii, 5, 7, 39, 68, 69–73, 76, 77, 78, 206, 215, 296, 299

Aranson, Pascoe 306–7

archaeology 115, 228

architecture xix, 81–2, 83, 172

Arkwright, Richard 120, 190

Armitage, Joseph 193

army: agents 69, 373; boots 128; career 175; casualties 5, 309; hats 129; JA's brother's career 69; in JA's work xvii–xviii; medical men 297; recruitment 200, 305, 380; *see also* militias, wars

ashes 101, 143, 145; potash 138

Ashton-under-Lyne, Lancs 8

Assizes 265–6, 274, 275, 277, 285, 287

Astick, Robert 1–2

Atkins, Thomas 281

Austen, Anna (niece of JA) xx–xxii, 35, 239, 353

Austen, Cassandra (mother of JA) 20, 27, 32, 36, 353, 382

Austen, Cassandra (sister of JA): as a baby 32, 36; birth 32; death of sister-in-law 336; destroyed JA's letters 235; education 65; executrix of JA's will 337–8; at Gomersham 195; at JA's death 324; niece of Mrs Leigh-Perrot 274; walking 238; in Weymouth 110, 219

Austen, Charles (brother of JA) 69

Austen, Edward (brother of JA) *see* Knight

Austen, Edward (nephew of JA) 54

Austen, Francis (Frank, brother of JA) 69

Austen, George (nephew of JA) 54

Austen, George (brother of JA) 69

Austen, George (father of JA) 62, 147, 148, 195, 301

Austen, Henry (brother of JA): banker 69, 175, 373; career 69, 175, 373; childhood 32; homes 78, 145, 380; illness 293; JA's memorial 342; in JA's will 337; Oxford university 69

Austen, James (brother of JA) 20–1, 69, 90, 147

Austen, Jane: accent 53; aunt charged with theft 274, 275; on ball at Deane 219; birth 27; on brother's health 293; on brother's house 78, 145–6; clothes 122, 123, 129–30, 133–4; on cousin's career 148; on curate for Deane 147; death 324; on deaths 20, 88, 302, 328; on dentistry 306; on donkey

Applied Statistics for Economists

Applied Statistics for Economists

FOURTH EDITION

P H Karmel
Chairman, Tertiary Education Commission

M Polasek
Senior Lecturer in Economics, The Flinders University of South Australia

Pitman Australia

First published in Australia 1957
Reprinted 1959
Second edition 1963
Reprinted 1963, 1965, 1967
Third edition 1970
Reprinted 1971, 1975
Fourth edition 1978

Pitman Publishing Pty Ltd
158 Bouverie Street
Carlton
Victoria 3053

© P H Karmel, M Polasek 1977

National Library of Australia
Cataloguing in Publication data

Karmel, Peter Henry, 1922–.
    Applied statistics for economists.

    Index.
    Bibliography.
    ISBN 0 85896 579 8.

    1. Mathematical statistics. 2. Economics,
Mathematical. I. Polasek, Metodey, joint
author. II. Title.

519.5′024′33

Associated companies

Pitman Publishing Ltd
London

Copp Clark Ltd
Toronto

Fearon-Pitman Publishers Inc
Belmont, California

Pitman Publishing New Zealand Ltd
Wellington

Text set in Monophoto Times Mathematics by
Asco Trade Typesetting Ltd, Hong Kong

Printed and bound by
South China Printing Co Ltd, Hong Kong

PREFACE
To the Fourth Edition

The revisions in the present edition of *Applied Statistics for Economists* are the most extensive of the three revisions that have been made since the original text was first published in 1957. Although the general format of the book remains much as before, several of the chapters have been rearranged and rewritten while others, dealing with statistical techniques of special interest to economists, have been modified in varying degrees to accord more with current statistical practice. Chapters 2 to 4 of the previous editions dealing with collection and presentation of statistical data have been condensed and amalgamated into a single chapter. The revised chapter on probability and probability distributions contains a much expanded treatment of basic probability and attempts a greater fusion of the theories of probability and inference. In addition, there are new sections on Bayes' formula, on elementary combinatorial probability, on the multinomial, hypergeometric and Poisson distributions, on continuous random variables, on normal approximations, and on joint probability distributions; the latter section may be read in conjunction with Chapter 8 on regression and correlation. Chapter 5 on sampling and significance gives fuller treatment to the t- and χ^2-distributions and to the procedures for hypothesis testing and estimation, as well as introducing new material which includes, *inter alia*, new sections on estimators and on certain χ^2 tests which are not found in the earlier editions. The chapter on regression and correlation has been enlarged by the addition of new material on the F-distribution and F-tests, partial correlation, multicollinearity and autocorrelation. Apart from these changes, the treatment of regression has been modernised by the inclusion of computerised calculations. Throughout the book all examples based on actual data have been brought up to date as far as practicable, and numerous new examples illustrating the text have been added in the revised sections. As in the previous editions, Appendix B has been thoroughly revised to include up-to-date information on the sources of Australian statistics.

I should like to express the authors' appreciation and indebtedness to Professor E S Pearson and the Biometrika Trustees for permission to include in this edition statistical tables reproduced from *Biometrika* and *Biometrika Tables for Statisticians*, Vol I, 1962; these tables appear as Tables 4A, 4B and 5 in Appendix A. The authors' thanks are due also to the Australian Statistician and to members of the Central Office of the Australian Bureau of Statistics for their help in updating Appendix

B; and to the Deputy Commonwealth Statistician in Adelaide and to members of his staff for their assistance with some of the statistical material contained in Chapters 12 and 13. Dr John McDonald of the Flinders University of South Australia has read certain sections of the text and has made a number of critical comments and helpful suggestions; however, the usual disclaimer applies. Finally, I wish to thank Mrs Sue Dolman for typing major portions of the revised text.

Adelaide, 1977   MP

PREFACE
To the First Edition

This book, which is based on a course of about fifty lectures which I have been giving annually in the University of Adelaide, is designed to cater for the needs of economics and commerce students. It contains a treatment both of basic statistical methods and of those aspects of statistics which are of special interest to economists. The basic statistical methods are treated in quite general terms, but where possible their relevance to economic problems has been indicated. Methods which do not find much application in the field of economics have been omitted. The examples and illustrations are drawn from Australian data.

The text provides the framework for a full one-year course at second- or third-year undergraduate level and covers those topics which in my view ought to be included as minimum requirements for economics and commerce graduates. In this respect the book can be regarded as complete in itself. However, for students intending to undertake work in econometrics the text provides an appropriate preliminary course, in which the earlier chapters can be covered fairly rapidly. The general emphasis of the text is on the understanding of the reasoning lying behind the various techniques, rather than on the techniques themselves. The danger of using the techniques without such an understanding is stressed.

Although mathematical formulations are used freely, they are for the most part of an elementary character, and verbal explanations are given throughout. Mathematics has been used wherever I have considered it helpful for an understanding of the methods given, but I have not attempted to provide a rigorous mathematical presentation, which would indeed be beyond the capacity of the student for whom the text is intended. In the few places where the mathematics is difficult, it can be omitted by students without the necessary mathematical equipment; my personal experience is that the course set out in this book can be handled quite well by students with little mathematics. Statistical methods cannot be taught satisfactorily by presenting them as if they were not of a mathematical nature, although they can be taught without placing too much reliance on any but the most elementary algebraic processes. Some facility in working in terms of symbols and in handling formulae is quite essential, and the non-mathematical student is likely to make better progress once he has recognised this.

I am indebted to Professor Sir Ronald A Fisher, Cambridge, to Dr Frank Yates, Rothamsted, and to Messrs Oliver and Boyd Ltd, Edinburgh, for permission to reproduce material from their book *Statistical Tables for Biological, Agricultural, and Medical Research*; this appears in my text as Table 7.1 and Tables II and III in Appendix A. I am indebted also to the Imperial Chemical Industries, Ltd, and to Messrs Oliver and Boyd, Ltd, for permission to base my Chapter VIII on Chapter X of their book *Statistical Methods in Research and Production*. My thanks are due also to the Houghton Mifflin Company of Boston, USA, for permission to use in my Table I of Appendix A material from Rugg's *Statistical Methods Applied to Education*.

I wish to thank Dr F G Jarrett of the University of Adelaide who has helped me considerably in the preparation of the text with comment and criticism, and Mr H P Brown of the Australian National University and Mr R R Hirst and Mr R L Mathews of the University of Adelaide who have read and commented on certain sections of the text. The Acting Commonwealth Statistician and members of the staff of the Commonwealth Bureau of Census and Statistics have been most co-operative in providing me with information on the activities and publications of the Bureau. I am much in the debt of Associate-Professor Jean Polglaze, MBE, of the University of Melbourne, not only for her helpful criticisms of the text, but also for first introducing me to statistical methods in the field of economics during a course of lectures at the University of Melbourne which in many respects has been the foundation upon which I have built. Finally, my thanks are due to Miss L M Sutton who has assisted me greatly in the preparation of the manuscript and who drew the diagrams, and to Miss J Hanson who typed the manuscript.

Adelaide, 1957   PHK

CONTENTS

CHAPTER 5

SAMPLING AND SIGNIFICANCE

CHAPTER 6

SAMPLE SURVEYS

CHAPTER 7

QUALITY CONTROL

CHAPTER 8

REGRESSION AND CORRELATION

CHAPTER 9

TIME SERIES

CHAPTER 10

SOCIAL ACCOUNTS AND THE MEASUREMENT OF NATIONAL INCOME

CHAPTER 11

PRICE INDEX NUMBERS

CHAPTER 1

INTRODUCTION

1.1 The Nature of Statistics

The subject 'statistics' is concerned with the *collection, presentation, description* and *analysis* of data which are measurable in numerical terms. The word 'statistics' is used sometimes to refer to the data themselves, as when we speak of 'statistics of national income' or 'vital statistics', but it is also used to refer to the whole field of study of which statistics in the narrower sense of statistical data are the subject-matter. The subject 'statistics' has a very wide application; and the basic principles and practice are the same irrespective of the field of application. This text is concerned with the use of 'statistics' in the field of economics.

When data are obtained as a result of an experiment, as occurs in the physical or biological sciences, the collection of the data is part and parcel of the experiment itself. The experiment must be designed to produce data from which meaningful results can be derived; and the main problems associated with the collection of data are the problems of the design of the experiment. However, in the social sciences, and particularly in economics, experimentation is seldom possible, and data must for the most part be collected by requiring people to fill in questionnaires. First, the design of questionnaires is itself a matter raising considerable statistical problems. Secondly, it is often impossible or impracticable to make a survey of all the data in which one is interested. There then arises the question of how a fraction of the field can be surveyed in a way which will provide meaningful results about the whole. These are the two major problems which occur in the collection of economic data. Thus, if we wish to collect data on peoples' spending habits, we have to decide not only the sort of information we want, including precise definitions of the facts we wish to record and hence the sort of questions we must ask people, but also how we shall select particular people to answer our questions.

Once collected, data must be assembled into a useful form. This process is the statistical presentation of data. Data are usually presented in tabular form and are frequently made more readily comprehensible by being presented pictorially in charts and graphs. But presentation involves much more than this. The raw data must be classified into forms appropriate to the purpose in hand. Classification cannot proceed in a vacuum and must depend upon theoretical categories which determine whether one or another classification is meaningful. Thus, if one had a great list of all the economic transactions which took place in an economy over a year, one would have to know the purpose for which the classification was to be used before classifying them. If this purpose were an investigation into the levels of consumption, investment, savings, etc, in the economy, the classification would have to be designed to take into account the theoretical meaning of these concepts and their relationships.

The description of statistical data involves the computation of measures to summarise the data. There are a host of such measures of wide application, of which the commonest perhaps is the average. However, in certain fields highly-specialised and complicated measures are required, as, for example, when we are concerned with measuring the rate of mortality of a human population. Moreover, it is sometimes impossible to fabricate a measure which will measure precisely what we are after, as, for example, when we want to measure changes in the cost of living.

The methods by which statistical data are analysed are called *statistical methods*, although the term is sometimes used more loosely to cover the subject 'statistics' as a whole. The mathematical theory which is the basis of these methods is called the *theory of statistics* or *mathematical statistics*. Statistical methods have a very wide application and have had perhaps their greatest development in the biological and agricultural sciences. They are specially appropriate for handling data which are subject to variations that cannot be fully controlled by experimental method and for which we can observe only a fraction of the totality of observations which may exist. Thus, if a particular phenomenon were quite uniform, a single observation on it could be used to discover its nature, but when the phenomenon exhibits variability which cannot be controlled experimentally, techniques must be devised by which we can make inferences about the nature of the totality and by which we can test hypotheses about it from the particular observations we have. One of the main concerns of statistical methods is with such techniques, so that, for example, by observing a fraction of all rents in a particular city we can make inferences about the level of rents or test hypotheses about the nature of rents in the city as a whole.

The situation becomes more complex when instead of being interested in the characteristics of one particular phenomenon, like rent, we are concerned with relationships between phenomena. Suppose we wished to ascertain the numerical effect of a percentage change in the price of tea on the quantity of tea demanded, other things being equal.

If we could conduct a controlled experiment we should hold all relevant factors constant, vary the price of tea and observe the resulting changes in the quantity demanded. But this is impossible, and all we are likely to have is a series of varying tea prices observed over a period of time with the corresponding amounts of tea bought. Over this period many factors which affect the demand for tea will have varied, for example the level of income or the price of coffee, and it will be necessary to isolate the effect of the changes in the price of tea from the effects of these other factors. This can be attempted only by means of statistical methods. Even so it will not be possible to take into account the whole multiplicity of factors which may have affected the price of tea.

1.2 Economics and Statistics

As far as the economist is concerned, he needs a knowledge of the relevant statistical material and of how to handle it. This requires an understanding of statistical methods as such, although some methods are more appropriate than others to the field in which he works. Broadly speaking, the first half of this book is concerned with methods which have very general application, although naturally the emphasis is on their application in the field of economics. The second half is concerned with techniques which are more specialised. For example, the problems which arise in measuring growth of population or movements in price levels call for the development of special sorts of methods.

There is little doubt that a facility with statistics and statistical methods is an essential qualification for the student of economics. This does not mean that he has to have any intimate acquaintance with the mathematical theory of statistics, however desirable that may be. But he ought to know how to handle numerical data within his field —how to collect it, present it, describe it and analyse it. Above all he should be able to discriminate between valid and invalid inferences from such data.

Statistical methods make possible the development of the empirical side of economics. Their use is necessary to give real content to theoretical formulations. Many concepts which are commonplace in economic theory present major problems when we come to measure them in numerical terms. One of the major tasks of economic statisticians is that of measurement. The difficulty in measuring movements in 'real income' or in the 'general level of prices' is well known, but even such a deceptively simple concept as 'number unemployed' conceals intricate problems of statistical measurement.

Empirical investigations involving statistical data are needed to test the hypotheses of pure economic theory and the conclusions drawn from these hypotheses. Thus the proposition that consumers' expenditure depends on persons' disposable income can be tested in the sense of whether observed data are or are not consistent with it; and the nature of the dependence and whether any variables other than income influence consumers' expenditure can be examined. At the same time empirical investigations may suggest new hypotheses for theoretical speculation—for example, the apparent stability in labour's share of national income evident in some economies has led to a number of important contributions to economic theory.

1.3 Need for Care in Statistical Work

Statistical data are a powerful aid in economic analysis, but they must be used with care. You cannot 'prove' an hypothesis with statistics; you can show only that the hypothesis is not inconsistent with the known facts. Indeed it is nearly always possible by a careful selection of data to bolster up an argument, and this makes it essential that in considering any problem *all* the relevant material should be examined. Thus, in comparing the current level of production in Australia with the pre-war one, it would be possible to use some figures (say gold, lead, clay bricks) to indicate stagnation and to use others (say electricity, refrigerators, brown coal) to indicate rapid growth. But what we require, of course, is the picture as a whole. Furthermore, since much of the data used by economists is published material which they have not collected themselves, it is important to find out the exact nature of the data, and whether or not there have been any changes in definition. To interpret a particular body of data without some knowledge of the background to it is a dangerous procedure. Thus it would be foolish to use the published budget surpluses or deficits of a government as an indication of the extent to which the government was becoming indebted to the rest of the economy, without first inquiring whether there are any funds through which the government operates which are not included in the published figures.

The points made in the preceding paragraph are obvious. What is not so obvious is the need for a careful examination of all statistical material to ensure that inappropriate measures are not used and invalid inferences are not drawn. An example of the careless use of statistics occurred in a press report which stated that 'more working-class than middle-class homes have television sets in the United Kingdom', the inference being that the tendency to possess television sets was greater in working-class than in middle-class homes. The facts may be correct, but the inference is invalid. To test the inference we should compare the proportion of all working-class homes which possess television sets with the proportion of middle-class homes which have them.

A more complex example may be worth quoting. In South Australia there were 9·01 and 8·06 deaths per 1000 of the population in 1954 and 1961 respectively. In Queensland the corresponding rates were 8·63 and 8·42. This might lead one to conclude that whereas Queensland was the healthier state in 1954, the situation had been reversed by 1961. But the rate at which a group of persons die varies directly with their age (apart from the very young); and the age distribution of the two states differed (and in different ways) in the two years under consideration. South Australia contained relatively more old people in 1954, but, through a higher rate of population growth over the period 1954 to 1961, contained relatively more young people in 1961. In fact in both years the rate at which people died was lower at almost every age in South Australia. Had the two states possessed the same age distributions, the death rates in South Australia would have been 4 per cent and 6 per cent lower than in Queensland for 1954 or 1961 respectively—results quite different from those obtained by observing the crude death rates per 1000 of the population.

In this case the measures used in making the comparison were inappropriate. More complicated measures are needed. One such measure is the average age to which people could expect to live if they were subject to the mortality conditions under consideration. If such a measure were calculated for the two states, South Australia would be shown to have a higher average expectation of life than Queensland.

The need to look beneath the surface appearance of statistics can be further illustrated. The 1971 Census in Australia, for example, revealed that the average issue of married women was 2·31 in major urban areas, 2·67 in other urban areas, and 2·95 in rural areas. *Prima facie*, this suggests that where people live affects family size. But it would be dangerous to infer this without further examination. For example, it might be the case that family size and educational attainment are inversely related and that city dwellers on the average enjoy higher educational attainments than country dwellers. In this case an apparent relationship between place of residence and family size would occur, even though place of residence has no direct influence whatsoever on family size. To discover whether this was so, it would be necessary to compare family size of people of the same educational attainments living in urban and rural areas. Place of residence might indeed influence family size, but that cannot be concluded from the three figures given above without examining carefully the influence of factors such as educational attainment, income, occupation and perhaps many others.

Attention should also be drawn to the danger of inferring a relationship between two phenomena because they happen to vary together. Thus over the past two decades the number of television sets in use and the number of criminal convictions have both increased in Australia. On the basis of this covariation it might be suggested that the spread of television has encouraged crime, ie that there is a causal relationship between television and crime. However, the increase in the number of television sets could be accounted for by the increase in the population and by the spread of the television habit, and the increase in the number of criminal convictions by the increase in the population also and perhaps by the increased efficiency of the police force. Consequently television sets and criminal convictions would exhibit a high degree of covariation without there being any direct relationship between them. Thus, although such a relationship as the one postulated above might obtain, the existence of covariation itself could not be taken as evidence of it. Further analysis would be required.

CHAPTER 2

COLLECTION AND PRESENTATION OF DATA

Although it would be logical to discuss the collection of data first, it is convenient to start with a brief discussion of statistical tables. Data when collected are summarised and set out in tabular form. The problems of collection are more readily appreciated when one has some idea of how the data have to be organised in tables.

2.1 Drawing up a Table

A table summarises the data by using columns and rows and entering figures in the body of the table. An example is given below.

Table 2.1

CARGO LOADED IN AUSTRALIA FOR DISCHARGE OVERSEAS ACCORDING TO TYPE OF SERVICE BY MAJOR TRADE AREA, YEAR ENDED JUNE 1975 ('000 tonnes)

Major Trade Area	Type of Service		
	Liner Services (a)	Tramps, Bulkships, Tankers	All Vessels
North America and Hawaii	718	5 547	6 265
South America	35	839	874
Europe (including USSR)	1 119	34 267	35 386
Africa	100	1 530	1 630
Asia	1 784	116 381	118 165
Papua, New Guinea, New Zealand and Pacific islands	887	1 647	2 534
Indian Ocean islands and Antarctic area	..	12	12
Total	4 643	160 223	164 866

(a) Includes cargo and passenger liners
Source: Australian Bureau of Statistics: *Quarterly Summary of Australian Statistics*, No. 299, 1976, p 50

In drawing up statistical tables the following points should be noted:

1. The table as a whole includes its title and all explanatory notes. As such it should be *self-explanatory*.

2. The title should state what is being classified, the nature of the classification and the place and time concerned. See, for example, the title of Table 2.1.

3. Units of measurement should always be given.

4. Terms should be defined, in footnotes if necessary.

5. If the table is quoted or derived from other tables, the source must be given at the foot of the table.

6. Figures may be rounded to avoid unnecessary detail in the table. But, if necessary, a footnote should be added to the effect that figures do not necessarily add to totals because of rounding.

Classification

All tables involve the classification of the subject-matter in some way or another. The classification may be through a characteristic of the subject-matter which varies *qualitatively* or *quantitatively*. If the variation is qualitative we speak of the characteristic as an *attribute*, if quantitative as a *variable*. A variable may be *discrete* or *continuous*. A discrete variable is one which can vary only by finite 'jumps', eg number of factories. A continuous variable can vary continuously in the sense that, if *a* and *b* are two values of the variable, a third value *c* can be located between *a* and *b*, no matter how close *a* and *b* are, eg age.

When we make a classification, we break up the subject-matter into a number of classes. It is important that the classification should be *exhaustive* and *mutually exclusive*. A classification is exhaustive if there is no item which cannot find a class. For example, a classification of persons by conjugal condition is not exhaustive if only the two classes 'married' and 'single' are included, since there are no classes in which widowed, divorced or separated persons can be placed. An exhaustive classification would require 'never married', 'widowed', 'divorced', 'separated' and 'married' categories.

For a classification to be mutually exclusive there must be no item which can find its way into more than one class. For example, a classification of persons according to weekly earnings is not mutually exclusive if it contains the classes '$160 to $170', '$170 to $180', etc, since a person with weekly earnings of $170 can be placed into two classes. A mutually exclusive classification would require classes '$160 and under $170', '$170 and under $180', etc.

Types of Table

Tables are broadly of two types:

1. Frequency Type

The subject-matter is classified according to some characteristic, and the frequencies of occurrence of the subject-matter in the various classes are recorded. The classification may be single or multiple. For instance, in Table 2.1 above, the two sets of marginal totals each give a single classification, and the body of the table gives a double classification.

When the characteristic concerned is a variable we have what we call a *frequency distribution*. For example:

Table 2.2

NUMBER OF MINING ESTABLISHMENTS OF FOREIGN CONTROLLED ENTERPRISES BY EXTENT OF DIRECT FOREIGN OWNERSHIP AUSTRALIA, 1972–73

Extent of Direct Foreign Ownership	Number of Establishments
Less than 50 per cent	23
50 per cent and less than 75 per cent	51
75 per cent and over	52
Total	126

Source: Australian Bureau of Statistics, *Year Book*, No. 60, 1974, p 970

2. Aggregative Type

The subject-matter is some aggregate or average, eg national income, value of exports, production of steel, average price of wheat. When the aggregate or average is shown to vary over *time* we have what is called a *time series*. For example:

Table 2.3

EXPORTS AND IMPORTS, AUSTRALIA, 1969–70 TO 1974–75 (f.o.b. Port of Shipment)

Monthly Average	Value of Exports $A million	Value of Imports $A million
1969–70 (a)	344	323
1970–71	364	346
1971–72	408	334
1972–73	518	344
1973–74	574	507
1974–75	723	674

(a) Australian financial years are 1 July to 30 June
Source: Australian Bureau of Statistics: *Monthly Review of Business Statistics*, No. 453, 1976, pp 19, 20

Comparisons in Tables

Frequently tables are drawn up in order to make comparisons. In these cases it is often convenient to include figures *derived* from the basic statistics, such as *ratios* or *percentages*.

1. Relatives

The movements in a time series are often made easier to comprehend by selecting one year as base and converting the other years to ratios to that base. In relative form, Table 2.3 appears as Table 2.4.

Table 2.4

EXPORTS AND IMPORTS, AUSTRALIA, 1969–70 TO 1974–75
(Base: 1969–70 = 100)

	Value of Exports	Value of Imports
1969–70	100	100
1970–71	106	107
1971–72	119	103
1972–73	151	107
1973–74	167	157
1974–75	210	209

From this table we can see that in 1974–75 exports had increased, in value terms, by 110 per cent and imports by 109 per cent on their 1969–70 levels. The absolute values of the relatives depend on the year which has been selected as base. If 1974–75 were used as the base instead of 1969–70, Table 2.4 would appear as shown in Table 2.5.

Table 2.5

EXPORTS AND IMPORTS, AUSTRALIA, 1969–70 TO 1974–75
(Base: 1974–75 = 100)

	Value of Exports	Value of Imports
1969–70	48	48
1970–71	50	51
1971–72	56	50
1972–73	72	51
1973–74	79	75
1974–75	100	100

Relatives show relative movements, not absolute levels. Thus, the relative figure of 48 for 1969–70 in the above table should not be taken to mean that exports and imports in that year were about the same but that they were the same percentage of their respective levels in the base year 1974–75. Naturally the base is selected with a view to the purpose of the comparison.

2. Percentage Distributions

The percentage rather than the absolute distribution of a classification is often very useful. For example:

Table 2.6

UNIVERSITY STUDENTS ACCORDING TO SEX BY LEVEL OF COURSE AUSTRALIA, 1975

Level of Course	Number of Students		Percentage Distribution	
	Males	Females	Males	Females
Higher Degree	13 044	3 632	13·87	6·69
Bachelor Degree	74 793	45 326	79·50	83·54
Other	6 241	5 302	6·63	9·77
Total	94 078	54 260	100·00	100·00

Source: Australian Bureau of Statistics: *Social Indicators*, No. 1, 1976 p 37

2.2 Collection of Data

Economic and social statistics are collected *incidentally* or *intentionally*. A considerable body of data is available as a result of administrative acts and is collected only incidentally to them, eg statistics of crime, car accidents, numbers of wage- and salary-earners incidental to payroll tax collections, details of imports incidental to collection of customs duties. These statistics are not collected primarily for research purposes, although they may be very useful in the field of research. Since they are not collected primarily for research, they may not be in a form completely appropriate to research. On the other hand, some statistics are collected *for their own sake*, ie to give general information and/or for use by research workers. It is these intentionally collected statistics with which we shall be mainly concerned, eg the census, statistics of prices, production, etc. Frequently statistics are collected incidentally to some administrative act but are also used for general information purposes. But whatever happens, it should be clear that when there is some intention of using the data collected for some purpose or other, then much more attention can and will be paid to the method of collection and to the precise nature of the statistics collected.

The collection of economic and social statistics generally requires the *filling in of forms*. These forms are called *questionnaires*. The questionnaire asks for certain information and has spaces on it for the answers. The answers may be filled in either by the *respondent*, ie the person or institution to whom the questionnaire is addressed, or by an *enumerator*, ie by a person, employed by the organisation running the inquiry, who interviews the respondent and notes his answers to the questions. The enumerator must make personal contact with the respondent and, since his work carries him out into the field of inquiry itself, he is often called a *field-worker*.

A questionnaire is the operational instrument of any inquiry and inquiries can be of two broad types. They may be *general purpose* or *special purpose*. A general-purpose inquiry attempts to obtain data which may be useful for many purposes, and it does not try necessarily to obtain data to answer specific problems. The best example of a general-purpose inquiry is a population census. A special-purpose inquiry tries to obtain information in a form suitable for analysing a specific problem or problems, eg an inquiry into rents of tenanted dwellings, an inquiry to discover whether there is any difference between the intelligence of children from large and small families. An example of a questionnaire is given on p 13.

Questionnaires

We now consider the drawing up of questionnaires. Several factors require careful consideration.

1. *The Object of the Inquiry*

Specification of the general object of an inquiry is not enough in framing the questions which are to enter into the questionnaire. We must know the uses to which the answers are subsequently going to be put, in order to get the questions (and hence the answers) into the right form. It is for this very reason that administrative statistics are often not as useful for research workers as they would be had they been collected intentionally. It is also for this reason that a general-purpose survey is not likely to be as useful for research into specific problems as a survey undertaken for a specific purpose, since the object of a general-purpose survey is to provide information *in general*.

Let us suppose that we are concerned with drawing up a questionnaire for a specific-purpose inquiry into the level of rents in a certain city. That is the subject-matter of the inquiry, but we cannot attempt to draw up the questionnaire unless we know the questions which the results of our inquiry are supposed to answer. Suppose one of these questions is: 'What are the factors governing the rent of a particular house?' We must now ask: 'What are the ideal data necessary for answering that question?' These data might include the locality of the house, its construction, its age, the size of the block, etc. Given the ideal data, we can then set about framing the questions to obtain them. Alternatively, if another question is: 'What are the

SOUTH AUSTRALIA
BIRTHS, DEATHS AND MARRIAGES REGISTRATION ACT, 1966
Seventh Schedule
INFORMATION STATEMENT FOR DEATH REGISTRATION

PARTICULARS OF DECEASED

1. Name—(a) Surname.....
   (b) Christian names.....
2. Date of death .....
3. Place where death occurred .....
4. Date of burial or cremation .....
5. Place of burial or cremation .....
6. Sex.....
   Date of birth.....
   Age last birthday.....
7. Usual profession or occupation .....
8. Usual residence .....
9. Birthplace.....
10. Length of residence in Australia.....
11. To be completed where deceased is under 21 years at date of death—
    (a) Father of deceased—
       Name and surname.....
       Profession or occupation .....
    (b) Mother of deceased—
       Name and surname.....
       Maiden surname.....
12. State whether deceased was bachelor, spinster,.....
    married, widowed or divorced.....

PARTICULARS OF MARRIAGE AND ISSUE

(This part is to be completed if the deceased has been married at any time, whether or not the deceased was married at date of death.)

| | First Marriage | Each subsequent marriage | |
| | | Second | Third, etc. |

13. Date of or age at first marriage.....
14. To whom married.....
    Note: In the case of a deceased male, please quote the former surname of his wife.
15. Issue living at death of deceased (insert names and date of birth)—

    (a) Issue of first marriage—

MALES		FEMALES	
Name	Date of Birth	Name	Date of Birth

    (b) Issue of subsequent marriages. Specify second, third, etc.—

16. Issue not living (dates of birth are not necessary—insert names only)—

OTHER PARTICULARS

17. (a) Name and address of Medical Practitioner .....
    or
    (b) Name and address of Coroner .....
18. Name and address of Funeral Director.....

CERTIFICATION OF INFORMANT

I certify that I have read the foregoing particulars and that the information is, to the best of my knowledge and belief, correct for the purpose of being inserted in the register of deaths.
Signed by me this.....day of.....19.....
Signature of informant.....
Description (occupier of building where death occurred, relationship to deceased, etc.).....
Address of informant .....

factors governing the rent which a particular breadwinner pays for his house?' our ideal data might include his income, age, conjugal condition, number of dependants, occupation, etc.

We may generalise from the above. Before attempting to draw up the questionnaire, *we should set out in detail the ideal data* which we desire from the answers to the questionnaire. It might be wise to go even a stage further and actually construct the sorts of tables which we should like to emerge from our inquiry. Of course, it is not always possible to set out all the ideal data we should like in advance, since we may learn things in the course of the inquiry itself and may find that what we believed to be ideal does not quite meet the bill. Furthermore, it may be impossible to obtain all the ideal data from the inquiry. But detailed consideration of the ideal data is essential before drawing up the questionnaire. For this reason those who will be concerned with analysing the results of the inquiry should be called in at the very earliest stage. For example, it would be foolish for a government statistician to collect some data on, say, retail trade and then hand them over to an economist to analyse. The economist should have first been consulted on what data were desirable. This point cannot be overstressed. But it should be noted that with a general purpose inquiry like a population census, it is impossible to anticipate in detail all the problems to the solution of which the results of the census may be put.

2. *The Practicability of the Questions*

Having determined our ideal data, we have in effect determined our ideal questionnaire, although we have not considered the precise form of the questions. Before doing this, we must consider whether certain information can or cannot be obtained. It may not be practicable to ask questions to ascertain some of the ideal data required. It may well be that the answers to some questions are not likely to be accurate enough to make them worth asking. Questions may be inaccurately answered either because the answers are deliberately falsified by the respondents or because the respondents do not really know the answers accurately enough themselves. In the former category fall, for example, questions about income and wealth. There is always reluctance to reveal one's private financial situation. It is probably better not to ask a question about income at all than to ask one which you feel sure will be falsely answered. We can often infer the approximate level of a person's income from other sources, eg the rent he pays for his house or the car he drives, so that it may be better to ask such questions rather than a question on income directly.

Questions which require a recollection are frequently inaccurately answered, eg 'How old were your grandparents when they died?'; 'How much did you spend on holidays in the past three years?'; 'How many pairs of socks do you buy in a year?'; and so on. This does not mean that such questions should never be asked, only that the resulting data be treated with great caution.

To some questions we will never get the right answer, not because people deliberately falsify the answers or their answers are inaccurate in the everyday sense, but because subconscious factors, of which the respondents are not aware or are only vaguely aware, enter into the matter. Questions concerned with people's *motives* or *opinions* are of this nature. If we ask women the main reason for the limitation of their families, the economic factor will inevitably be stressed. But we cannot be certain that this is the real factor; it is quite likely that other motives are the fundamental ones and that women rationalise these into the rather neutral economic motive, eg the main motive may be fear of pain or dislike of children. Or if we ask people their opinions, we can never be quite certain what we are getting. Many people feel that there are certain opinions which they 'ought' to hold, and they may give these opinions rather than the ones they really hold, eg if we ask people how they will vote at an election, they may say 'Party A' because they expect most other people to say 'Party A' or because they expect most other people will in fact vote for Party A or because it is considered respectable to vote for Party A.

This latter discussion leads to a division of questions into two types: those the answers to which are *refutable*, and those the answers to which are *non-refutable*. With the non-refutable type of question we can never be certain that the answers are correct, because we can never prove that they are wrong. This type includes questions about motives and opinions. These questions may be well worth asking, but the answers do *not* tell us people's motives and opinions, only what they *say* are their motives and opinions. With the refutable type of question, the answers may be inaccurate, but we can theoretically check up on them, eg a person's age or income. Some questions may be likely to result in more inaccurate answers than others. But usually we have a fairly good idea of the accuracy of the answers *a priori*, and we should avoid asking any question the answers to which are likely to be too inaccurate.

3. The Form of the Questions

Having decided on what questions to include, one must now decide on the form which the questions are to take. This is by no means easy. To some extent the form of the questions depends on whether they are to be answered by the respondent or by an enumerator. If the questionnaire is to be filled in by an enumerator in a personal interview, the questions need not be quite as carefully worded, since the enumerator can be given instructions as to how they are to be answered. But in general the following considerations apply to all types of questionnaires:

(i) The questions should be *clear, unambiguous* and *precise*. They should be capable of being answered in only a limited number of ways. For example, 'What is the size of your house?' This is an unsatisfactory question, since it may be answered in terms of the dimensions of the house or the number of rooms. 'Do you like living in a brick house or would you prefer to live in a wooden one?' This may be answered ambiguously by stating *yes* or *no*.

(ii) Most questions ask the respondent to place himself in a category. When the categories are few in number, the best method is to have a square for each category and for the respondent to place a cross in the appropriate square. When this is done, it is essential that the listed categories should be *exhaustive* and *mutually exclusive*.

NOT   Are you married?   □ ⎫
      never married?   □ ⎬ not exhaustive

BUT   Are you married?   □
      widowed?   □
      divorced?   □
      separated?   □
      never married?   □

NOT   Do you own your farm?   □ ⎫
      rent your farm?   □ ⎬ not mutually exclusive

BUT   Do you own your farm?   □
      rent your farm?   □
      part own and part
      rent your farm?   □

When categories are large in number and cannot be listed, it should be made clear to the respondent what sort of answer is required. For example:

State present age .... years .... months.

Occupation ....
(eg carpenter, labourer, school-teacher, etc)

The categories into which the answers to a question are to be placed should be carefully selected, bearing in mind the nature of the data and the purpose for which they will be used. The person framing the question needs a detailed knowledge of the field of inquiry. Thus the question on farm-tenure quoted above may be quite unsatisfactory if, unknown to the framer of the question, other forms of tenure than those provided for exist, eg share cropping.

(iii) The question should be framed to get the desired information. Suppose it is desired to obtain information about the age distribution of the respondents, if we ask 'present age?' or 'age last birthday?' we shall get the age distribution at the date of the inquiry. But if we ask 'year of birth?' we shall not be able to get an age distribution at all, although for some purposes a distribution by year of birth may be more useful than one by age.

(iv) Avoid leading questions, ie questions which suggest the answers. For example, in a depression year do not ask 'By how much has your income fallen?' but 'Has your income fallen? $\frac{\text{YES}}{\text{NO}}$. If yes, by how much?'

(v) Questions should be capable of objective answers, ie avoid questions of opinion and keep to questions of fact. For example, instead of asking a worker 'whether he is content with his present job', ask him 'if he desires to change his job and, if so, to what sort of job would he like to shift?'

(vi) Questions should be arranged in some logical order. For example, in an inquiry into the size of families, do not ask women the size of their family before you ask them whether they are married or single. Start with the simplest questions first.

(vii) Give precise and definite instructions and (if necessary) examples of how to fill in the questionnaire. It is better to include the instructions in the body of the questionnaire than to make them footnotes or put them all together on the other side of the page. But if instructions are very lengthy, this may not be possible. It is always necessary to define carefully all terms. For example, in the question 'Do you own your own house?' does 'house ownership' include purchasing by instalments or owning a share of a house? Precise definition is essential. Instructions should be simple and not too legalistic.

(viii) Some care should be taken in the actual setting out of the questionnaire. It should be made to look as attractive as possible. Plenty of room should be given for answers.

(ix) Having drawn up the actual questions and arranged them on a form, it is wise to try out the questionnaire by filling it in oneself and getting acquaintances to fill it in or, better still, by using it in a pilot (trial) survey. This will reveal weaknesses in the questions and layout. In all this work no precepts can replace practical experience.

4. The Field of the Inquiry

Before the questionnaire itself has been finally drafted, it is necessary to decide the respondents to whom it is to be addressed, ie the field of the inquiry. For example, if the inquiry is on rents, will you send the questionnaires to house-owners or house-occupiers? If it is on juvenile employment, will you send it to households, to the juveniles themselves or to employers? This will largely depend on which form of contact you expect to lead to the best results. It will also be necessary to decide whether the questionnaire is to be addressed to all possible respondents or only to a sample of them. This matter is discussed in Chapter 6 below.

Sources of Economic and Social Statistics

Economic and social statistics are collected both by government and private agencies. For the most part they are collected by the former, although banks, stock exchanges, trade associations, etc, do make some collections, and research organisations sometimes make special-purpose collections.

Most statistical collections are continuous, ie they cover, say, all months or all years without gaps, eg vital statistics, employment statistics. Some, however, are made only every so often. Of these the most important is the *population census*. The population census aims at making a complete count of the whole population and ascertaining information about how the population is distributed according to sex, age, conjugal condition, family size, occupation, industry, employment status, racial origin, birthplace, housing accommodation, etc. Some of the information derived from the census can be obtained nowhere else, but some is also obtained through continuous collection and the census is used as a periodic check on it. In addition to the population census, periodic censuses of production, retail trade, etc, may also be undertaken.

In most countries there is a government department charged with the collection and publication of statistics. In addition to the statistical publications of this department, other governmentally collected statistics are to be found in the reports of various government departments, such as the Taxation Department, in the budget papers and public accounts, in the reports of nationally operated business undertakings, etc. There are also usually some private statistical publications sponsored by banks and other financial institutions. Useful international summaries of statistics, containing a great deal of comparative material, are issued by the various agencies of the *United Nations*.

2.3 Graphs and Charts

A graph is a simple and effective way of illustrating and comprehending a table. It gives pictorial effect to what would otherwise be just a mass of figures. Drawing charts and graphs requires the observance of a few simple rules, the adoption of which lends to the effectiveness of graphs. It is important to avoid drawing misleading diagrams, and one must always be on one's guard against graphs which are drawn to bring an unwarranted conclusion out of the figures on which they are based.

Bar Charts

The most elementary type of graph is the bar chart. When a bar chart illustrates movements or comparisons in one variable only, as in

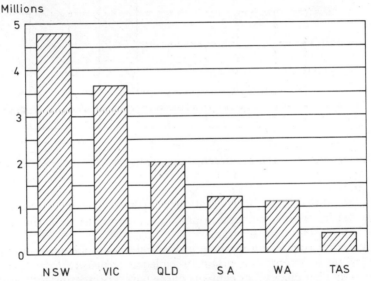

Fig 2.1 Estimated population of Australian states, 30 June 1975
Source: Australian Bureau of Statistics: *Quarterly Summary of Australian Statistics*, No. 299, 1976, p 2

Fig 2.1, it is referred to as a *simple bar chart*. The following procedure should be followed in drawing bar charts.

1. Examine the data carefully, and then select the scales. The appearance of the graph depends entirely on the scale. The graph must not be allowed to distort the data. Dimensions in the ratio of about 7 to 10 are found in practice to be most satisfactory.

2. Having decided on the scale, draw in the frame and print in the scale. The vertical scale should start from zero, otherwise the graph can be very misleading. Thus suppose the values 200, 190, 220, 230

are to be compared graphically. If the scale were to start at, say, 150, the graph would give an impression of greater variability in the data than is in fact the case. Sometimes, however, the range of the variable is so great as to make a full scale from zero impracticable. In that case the graph should be broken as illustrated by Fig 2.2.

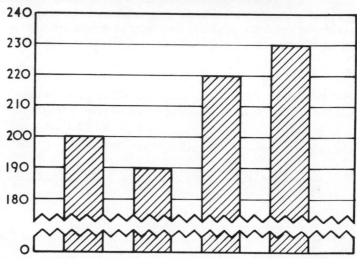

Fig 2.2

3. Draw in the bars.

4. Draw in horizontal reference lines. The grid on the graph should be regarded as invisible. The most effective graphs are not drawn on graph paper.

5. Head the graph clearly and unambiguously, observing the same rules as for tabular presentation. The source of the data should be printed at the foot of the graph.

A bar chart showing the bars broken into components, eg imports according to country of origin, is called a *composite bar chart*. In composite bar charts the segments of the bars representing the various components must be hatched differently, with the darkest hatching at the bottom.

Bar charts which enable comparisons of more than one variable to be made at the same time are called *multiple bar charts*. The bars referring to each variable are placed next to each other, and are distinguished by being hatched differently. In doing this, it is good practice not to use simply black and white, and to avoid those diagonal hatchings that result in optical illusions. In drawing multiple and composite bar charts it is important not to overload the diagram with too many comparisons. A key to indicate what is being represented by each hatching must always be included.

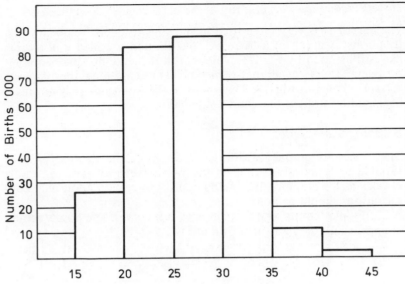

Fig 2.3 Live births by age of mother—Australia, 1974
Source: Australian Bureau of Statistics, *Births*, 1974, (Ref 4.4), p 24

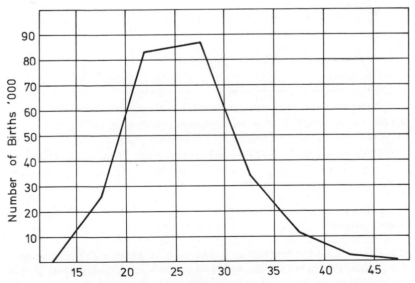

Fig 2.4 Live births by age of mother—Australia, 1974
Source: Australian Bureau of Statistics, *Births*, 1974 (Ref 4.4), p 24

Histograms

The bar chart is very often used in statistics to depict frequency distributions. A graph of a frequency distribution is called a *histogram* and is illustrated by Fig 2.3. Note that in this case no spaces are left between the bars. An alternative method of presentation is the *frequency polygon*, shown in Fig 2.4. The points in the frequency polygon must be joined by straight lines and not by curves.

Graphing Time Series

Time series are graphed with time on the X-axis (horizontal) and the variable under consideration on the Y-axis (vertical). The same sort of rules as for graphing bar charts apply, but certain additional considerations should be noted:

1. Join plot points with straight lines, not curves. The points should disappear into the lines, as shown in Fig 2.5.

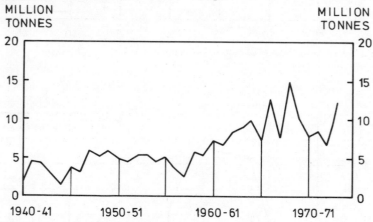

Fig 2.5 Production of wheat for grain—Australia 1940–41 to 1973–74
Source: Australian Bureau of Statistics, *Year Book*, No. 60, 1974, p 758

2. The time scale should be fixed very carefully. Time is a continuous variable, so the following type of scale should be used as far as possible.

The variable under consideration can then be plotted at the appropriate places. For example, the value of exports in calendar years would be plotted at 30 June, the value of exports in financial years would be plotted at 31 December, the average price of wheat for quarters would be plotted at the middle of quarters, population as at 30 June would be plotted at 30 June.

3. The unit of time in which the variable under consideration is measured should be clearly stated in the title, eg an indication should be given as to whether the years are calendar or financial, or whether the variable is measured as at a date.

2.4 Semi-Logarithmic (or Ratio) Charts

In graphing time series in the preceding section we plotted time on the horizontal axis and the values of the related variable against the vertical axis. When the scale on the Y-axis is proportionate to the absolute values of the variable, it is said to be an *arithmetic* scale. On an arithmetic scale, equal absolute amounts are represented by equal distances. Consequently, a graph drawn on an arithmetic scale, as well as showing us how the variable has changed, enables us to make comparisons of the *amounts* by which it has changed from time to time. If a time series exhibited a constant amount of change per period, it would appear on the graph as a straight line.

Frequently, however, the absolute amount of change in a variable is not of great interest to us, but rather the rate at which the variable is increasing or decreasing is of significance. For instance, in comparing the Australian and the United States populations over time, the significant thing is the comparative rates at which the two populations have grown and not the fact that the United States population is so many times larger than the Australian one. In an arithmetic scale, equal amounts of change are shown by equal vertical distances (or equal slopes). It would be very useful for some purposes if we could draw a graph in which equal vertical distances (or equal slopes) indicated equal *relative rates* of change, ie equal percentage changes.

Suppose that, instead of plotting the variable under consideration itself, we plot the logarithms of the variable. If three successive values of the variable are Y_1, Y_2 and Y_3, we shall be plotting log Y_1, log Y_2 and log Y_3. The movement from Y_1 to Y_2 will now be shown on the graph as a movement from log Y_1 to log Y_2. The amount of this movement will equal log Y_2 − log Y_1, ie $\log\dfrac{Y_2}{Y_1}$. Hence, if it happens that

log Y_2 − log Y_1 = log Y_3 − log Y_2, this will mean that $\log\dfrac{Y_2}{Y_1} =$

$\log\dfrac{Y_3}{Y_2}$, ie $\dfrac{Y_2}{Y_1} = \dfrac{Y_3}{Y_2}$. In other words vertical distances now refer to relative rates of changes and not to amounts of change. Equal vertical distances (or equal slopes) mean equal relative rates of change (ie equal percentage changes). When we graph the logarithms of a variable rather than the original data themselves, we are plotting on a *logarithmic scale*. When we plot a time series in this way we have what is called a *semi-logarithmic* (or *ratio*) *chart*. It is called 'semi-' because, although the variable under consideration is plotted logarithmically, time is still plotted arithmetically.

If a time series turns out to be a straight line on a semi-logarithmic scale, this means that the series exhibits a constant percentage rate of growth, eg 2 per cent per annum. Such a time series plotted arithmetically will result in a curve which is concave upwards, indicating an increasing *amount* of growth per period. Thus:

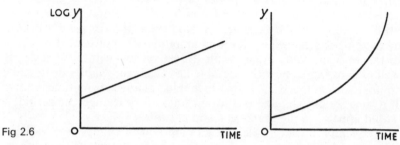

Fig 2.6

On the other hand, a time series which is a straight line when plotted arithmetically, indicating a constant amount of growth per period, will yield a curve which is concave downwards when plotted logarithmically. Thus:

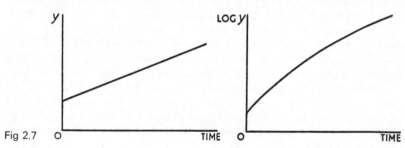

Fig 2.7

As a numerical illustration, consider the series Y and Z given by the table:

t	Y_t	$\log Y_t$	Z_t	$\log Z_t$
1	100	2·0000	100	2·0000
2	110	2·0414	110	2·0414
3	120	2·0792	121	2·0828
4	130	2·1139	133·1	2·1242
5	140	2·1461	146·41	2·1656

When plotted against time (t) the values Y_t trace out a straight line, but the logarithms of these values will give a curve concave downwards. The percentage rate of growth is falling, the rates of change being 10 per cent, 9·1 per cent, 8·3 per cent, and 7·7 per cent respectively for the four spans. On the other hand, the amount of growth per period shown by the series Z is increasing, so that graphed arithmetically the curve will be concave upwards. But the logarithms of the values of Z plot a straight line, indicating a constant percentage rate of growth. As can be seen from the original figures, this rate is 10 per cent per period. To summarise: equal vertical distances or equal slopes mean equal amounts of change on an arithmetic chart, but mean equal relative rates of change on a semi-logarithmic chart.

The procedure for drawing a semi-logarithmic chart is as follows:

1. Convert the variable to logarithms.

2. Select the scales to be used. It should be noted that, since we are interested here in relative changes, there is no need to start the scale at zero. In any case there is no finite number corresponding to log 0. It is not possible to plot zero or negative numbers on a logarithmic scale. The logarithmic scale should start at the logarithm corresponding to a convenient natural number.

3. Complete the drawing of the graph.

4. Although the logarithms of the variable have been plotted, there is little value in attaching to the vertical scale these logarithmic values, since in themselves they do not convey very much. It would be preferable to include a scale of natural numbers so that the graph will portray absolute values as well as relative rates of growth. The logarithmic scale can readily be translated back into natural numbers.

Consider the natural numbers 1 to 10. We have:

Natural Number	Logarithm
1	0·00
2	0·30
3	0·48
4	0·60
5	0·70
6	0·78
7	0·85
8	0·90
9	0·95
10	1·00

If we draw up a scale of the logarithms and write in the corresponding natural numbers, the result is as shown in Fig 2.8 overleaf.

This gives us what is known as a complete *deck* or *cycle* in a logarithmic grid. We note that equally spaced natural numbers have diminishing spaces on the grid, and that the distance between, say, 1 and 2 is the same as that between 2 and 4 or 3 and 6 or 5 and 10, etc, because the *relative* relation between these pairs of numbers is the same. If we go on to draw up a scale of the numbers 10 to 100, it will simply duplicate the scale from 1 to 10 giving a second deck. Similarly the numbers 100 to 1000 will give a third deck. The size of a deck is always a multiple of 10. We could have decks rising from 3 to 30, 30 to 300, etc.

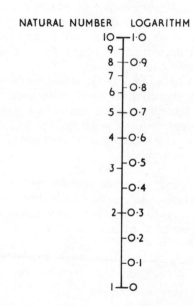

NATURAL NUMBER   LOGARITHM

Fig 2.8

Returning now to the marking-in of a vertical scale on our graph, we take convenient natural numbers, locate them on the scale and write them in. We then draw in a grid corresponding to these values. Suppose, for example, we have values of the variable under consideration ranging from 73 900 to 3 022 000. We can conveniently start our scale at the logarithm corresponding to 50 000. Reference lines can then be drawn at 50 000; 100 000; 150 000; 200 000 etc. As the figures get closer to the top of each deck rather less detail will be needed.

5. The graph is completed by writing in title, scales, source, etc. An indication should be given that the scale is semi-logarithmic.

The diagrams below show the number of television viewers' licences in force at 30 June in Australia for the years 1957 to 1974. Fig 2.9 is arithmetic, Fig 2.10 is semi-logarithmic. Whereas the arithmetic graph gives the impression that the upward movement in the series has only

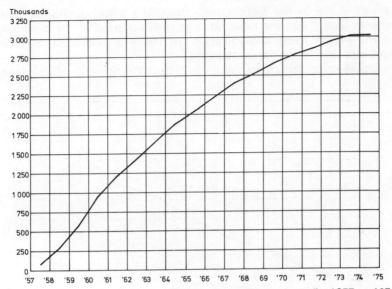

Fig 2.9 Television viewers' licences in force at 30 June—Australia, 1957 to 1974
(arithmetic scale)

Source: Australian Bureau of Statistics, *Year Book*, No. 53, 1967, p 485, No. 56, 1970, p 561 and *Quarterly Summary of Australian Statistics*, No. 294, 1974, p 63

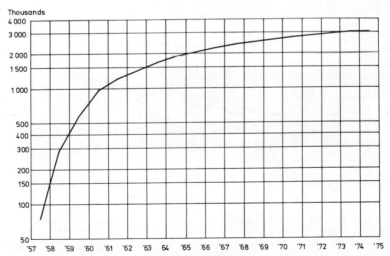

Fig 2.10 Television viewers' licences in force at 30 June—Australia, 1957 to 1974
(semi-logarithmic scale)

Source: Australian Bureau of Statistics, *Year Book*, No. 53, 1967, p 485; No. 56, 1970; p 561 and *Quarterly Summary of Australian Statistics*, No. 294, 1974, p 63

slowed down in the more recent years, the semi-logarithmic chart reveals clearly that the most rapid growth occurred at the beginning of the period under consideration. In many respects the semi-logarithmic chart is the more interesting.

Semi-logarithmic charts are a useful device for plotting data of very

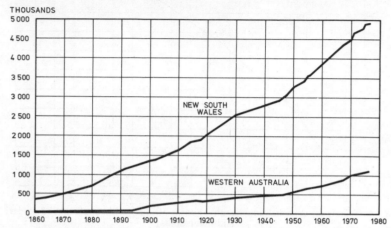

Fig 2.11 Population of New South Wales and Western Australia, as at 31 December 1860 to 1975
(arithmetic scale)

Source: Commonwealth Bureau of Census and Statistics, Australia: *Demography Bulletin*, No. 67, 1949, pp 154–55; No. 77, 1959, p 174; No. 82, 1964, p 119; *Australian Demographic Review*, No. 248, 1968, p 4, and *Quarterly Summary of Australian Statistics*, No. 299, 1976, p 2

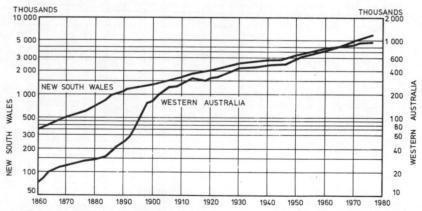

Fig 2.12 Population of New South Wales and Western Australia, as at 31 December 1860 to 1975
(semi-logarithmic scale)

Source: Commonwealth Bureau of Census and Statistics, Australia: *Demography Bulletin*, No. 67, 1949, pp 154–55; No. 77, 1959, p 174; No. 82, 1964, p 119; *Australian Demographic Review*, No. 248, 1968, p 4; and *Quarterly Summary of Australian Statistics*, No. 299, 1976, p 2

Table 27

DISTRIBUTION OF TAXABLE INCOME, AUSTRALIA, 1973–74

Grade of Taxable Income	Number of Taxpayers	Taxable Income	Percentage in Income Grade		Accumulated Percentage	
			Number	Amount	Number	Amount
(1)	(2)	(3)	(4)	(5)	(6)	(7)
$		$'000	%	%	%	%
Under 1 200	119 312	130 725	2·13	0·50	2·13	0·50
1 200–1 599	282 294	395 513	5·03	1·51	7·16	2·01
1 600–1 999	301 201	543 977	5·38	2·06	12·54	4·07
2 000–2 399	351 705	773 007	6·28	2·93	18·82	7·00
2 400–2 799	352 297	916 492	6·29	3·47	25·11	10·47
2 800–3 199	380 032	1 141 392	6·78	4·33	31·89	14·80
3 200–3 599	416 597	1 417 721	7·43	5·37	39·32	20·17
3 600–3 999	444 625	1 690 622	7·93	6·41	47·25	26·58
4 000–4 799	837 870	3 677 720	14·95	13·94	62·20	40·52
4 800–5 599	665 649	3 448 365	11·88	13·07	74·08	53·59
5 600–6 399	466 233	2 785 529	8·32	10·56	82·40	64·15
6 400–7 199	304 771	2 063 612	5·44	7·82	87·84	71·97
7 200–7 999	195 514	1 480 255	3·49	5·61	91·33	77·58
8 000–8 799	125 740	1 052 749	2·24	3·99	93·57	81·57
8 800–9 999	115 155	1 076 144	2·05	4·08	95·62	85·65
10 000–11 999	98 546	1 071 370	1·76	4·06	97·38	89·71
12 000–15 999	79 826	1 090 369	1·43	4·13	98·81	93·84
16 000–19 999	31 477	557 818	0·56	2·11	99·37	95·95
20 000–39 999	31 079	802 948	0·55	3·04	99·92	98·99
40 000 and over	4 564	265 910	0·08	1·01	100·00	100·00
Total	5 604 487	26 382 238	100·00	100·00		

Source: The Parliament of the Commonwealth of Australia, *Fifty-Fourth Report of the Commissioner of Taxation*, Parliamentary Paper No. 162, 1974/75, pp 101 and 103

different magnitudes on the same chart, and for making comparisons between the rates of growth of two or more series. Thus, consider a graph of the movement of the Australian population from 1788 to date. The variable ranges from about 700 to 13·5 million. If this were drawn arithmetically on a scale of, say, $\frac{1}{2}$ million: 1 cm, it would be almost impossible to graph the population at all in the earlier years. However, semi-logarithmically the same distance is given to the range 700 to 7000 as to 700 000 to 7 000 000, and hence the same relative detail can be included for earlier and later years.

By the same token, when two series, one of which is very large in magnitude compared with the other, have to be compared, a semi-logarithmic chart can be used to advantage. This is illustrated in the comparison of the growth of population in New South Wales and Western Australia shown in Figs 2.11 and 2.12. With an arithmetic scale it is only just possible to represent Western Australia on the same chart as New South Wales. However, the two states can be readily graphed on a semi-logarithmic chart by attaching different scales to the two sides of the grid and graphing New South Wales in relation to the left-hand scale and Western Australia to the right-hand scale. Once the left-hand scale has been determined, the right-hand one can be written in as any given multiple or fraction of it. Thus in Fig 2.12 the Western Australia scale is one-fifth of the New South Wales scale. The former scale runs 10, 20, 40, 60, etc, and the latter 50, 100, 200, 300, etc. The scales are the same relatively and accordingly are represented by the same absolute distances on a semi-logarithmic grid. It will be noted that on the arithmetic chart (Fig 2.11) Western Australia appears to have grown little and much less rapidly than New South Wales. This is of course true in absolute terms. However, by plotting the data on a semi-logarithmic chart (Fig 2.12), it can be seen that in the latter half of the period Western Australia has had a relative rate of growth comparable with that of New South Wales and that for certain periods, including the past few years, it had a relative rate of growth which was in fact greater than that of New South Wales.

2.5 Lorenz Curves

Economists are very often interested in the distribution of something by size, eg incomes, factories, etc. It is often important to know how far such a distribution departs from one of equality, or whether one distribution is more, or less, unequal than another. Table 2.7 gives details of the distribution of taxable income for Australia, 1973–74.

Columns (1) and (2) taken together are a simple frequency distribution of taxable income. In column (3) is given the amount of the taxable income earned by the individuals in the various income grades, and columns (4) and (5) give the percentage distributions of columns (2) and (3). Columns (6) and (7) give columns (4) and (5) accumulated downwards. From these last two columns we can learn that the 2·13 per cent lowest income-earners earned between them 0·50 per cent of total taxable income, whereas the 95·62 per cent lowest income earners earned 85·65 per cent of total taxable income. This latter implies, of course, that the 4·38 per cent highest income-earners earned 14·35 per cent of total taxable income. When columns (6) and (7) are graphed, one against the other, as in Fig 2.13, we have what is called a *Lorenz curve*. If income were exactly equally distributed so that every individual had the same income, the first 10 per cent

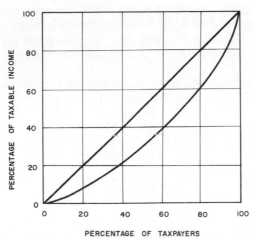

Fig 2.13 Distribution of taxable income of individual taxpayers, Australia, 1973–74
(Lorenz curve)

Source: The Parliament of the Commonwealth of Australia, *Fifty-Fourth Report of the Commissioner of Taxation*, Parliamentary Paper No. 162, 1974/75, pp 101 and 103

of income-earners would receive 10 per cent of total income, the first 20 per cent would receive 20 per cent, and so on. Strictly speaking, there would be only one grade of income and only two points on the diagram—0 per cent of income-earners would receive 0 per cent total income, and 100 per cent of income-earners would receive 100 per cent of total income. Consequently, in this situation the Lorenz curve would become a straight line drawn diagonally across the graph. The extent to which the actual curve diverges from the diagonal line is, therefore, illustrative of the degree of inequality of income. Naturally, Lorenz curves are most useful in making comparisons between different income distributions.

CHAPTER 3

THE FREQUENCY DISTRIBUTION AND ITS DESCRIPTION

3.1 Forming a Frequency Distribution

Having considered the collection of data and their presentation in both tabular and graphical forms, we now proceed to the *description* of data. We shall consider in some detail the way in which we can describe statistical data when they consist of a large number of observations of a particular variable, eg rents of houses. The number of observations is designated by N, the variable observed (in this case, rent) by X.

Below are set out the rents of 200 houses of a particular type, eg unfurnished. The example is a hypothetical one.

Table 3.1

WEEKLY RENTS OF 200 TENANTED HOUSES (QUOTED TO THE LAST COMPLETE HALF-DOLLAR)

30,	25,	25,	39,	11·5,	24,	34,	39,	16,	10,
25,	22·5,	8,	23,	36,	19·5,	26,	10,	35,	17·5,
29·5,	30,	25,	26,	27,	33,	19,	30,	21,	10,
25,	20,	9,	12,	25,	33,	14·5,	27·5,	12,	21,
37,	11,	12·5,	32,	15,	22·5,	34,	44,	27,	24,
40,	25,	33,	14,	25,	29·5,	12·5,	26,	24·5,	26,
16,	32,	15,	35,	29,	19,	25,	32,	40,	17·5,
17,	26·5,	20,	23·5,	25,	45,	29·5,	10,	15,	24·5,
22,	26,	28,	9·5,	28,	18,	31,	19,	24,	15,
20,	26,	15,	25,	14·5,	26,	30,	28,	19·5,	22,
31,	20,	35,	28,	24,	25,	19·5,	25,	30,	40,
29,	24,	30,	14,	19·5,	32,	24·5,	8,	22·5,	30,
26,	13,	30,	22,	15,	18,	20,	20·5,	24,	32,
23,	26,	24·5,	22,	29,	24,	14,	22,	24,	32,
25,	24,	25,	16,	18,	16,	23,	20,	27,	35,
34·5,	20,	19,	27·5,	31,	27,	24,	20,	24,	26,
29,	28,	25,	15,	28,	25,	21,	26,	19·5,	18,
19,	30,	19·5,	24,	20,	35,	17,	25,	25,	29·5,
20,	16,	20,	14,	21,	13,	20,	18,	23,	14,
22,	30,	22,	30,	20,	18·5,	25,	31,	19,	13.

From this unorganised data it is difficult to draw any conclusions at all about the distribution of rents in the given area. It would be somewhat more informative if we were to arrange the data into what is called an *array*, ie in their order of magnitude, but even so this would only indicate the range of the data and the way in which the individual items find their places within the range.

The most satisfactory procedure is to arrange the data into a *frequency distribution*, showing the frequency with which rents occur in certain specified intervals. The purpose of drawing up frequency distributions is to bring out the essential features in the data and to permit the use of analytical techniques in their description. One possible way of organising the given raw data is shown in Table 3.2.

Table 3.2

WEEKLY RENT OF 200 TENANTED HOUSES

Weekly Rent (dollars) X	Number of Houses f
7·5 and under 12·5	12
12·5 " 17·5	26
17·5 " 22·5	45
22·5 " 27·5	60
27·5 " 32·5	37
32·5 " 37·5	13
37·5 " 42·5	5
42·5 " 47·5	2
All rents	200

The left-hand column shows the *classes*, the right-hand column the *frequencies of occurrence*. Thus in the first class $7·5 is the *lower class limit*, $12·5 the *upper class limit* and the *class interval* is $5. The frequency distribution immediately gives us a picture of the form of the distri-

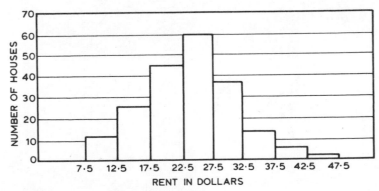

Fig 3.1 Weekly rent of 200 tenanted houses

bution when the results in Table 3.2 are plotted as a histogram or frequency polygon. (See Figs 3.1 and 3.2.)

Several important considerations enter into the construction of frequency distributions. The first of these concerns the determination

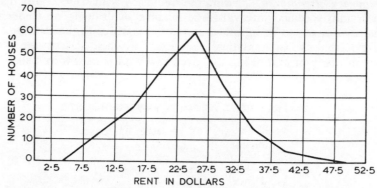

Fig 3.2 Weekly rent of 200 tenanted houses

Table 3.3

WEEKLY RENT OF 200 TENANTED HOUSES

Weekly Rent (dollars) X		Number of Houses f	Weekly Rent (dollars) X		Number of Houses f
7·5 and under	8·5	2	27·5 and under	28·5	8
8·5 "	9·5	1	28·5 "	29·5	4
9·5 "	10·5	5	29·5 "	30·5	15
10·5 "	11·5	1	30·5 "	31·5	4
11·5 "	12·5	3	31·5 "	32·5	6
12·5 "	13·5	5	32·5 "	33·5	3
13·5 "	14·5	5	33·5 "	34·5	2
14·5 "	15·5	9	34·5 "	35·5	6
15·5 "	16·5	5	35·5 "	36·5	1
16·5 "	17·5	2	36·5 "	37·5	1
17·5 "	18·5	7	37·5 "	38·5	0
18·5 "	19·5	7	38·5 "	39·5	2
19·5 "	20·5	19	39·5 "	40.5	3
20·5 "	21·5	5	40·5 "	41·5	0
21·5 "	22·5	7	41·5 "	42·5	0
22·5 "	23·5	7	42·5 "	43·5	0
23·5 "	24·5	13	43·5 "	44·5	1
24·5 "	25·5	24	44·5 "	45·5	1
25·5 "	26·5	11	45·5 "	46·5	0
26·5 "	27·5	5	46·5 "	47·5	0
			All Rents		200

of an appropriate number of classes. Though formulae are available for this purpose, generally no hard and fast rules can be given and the ultimate decision will depend partly on personal judgment. The smaller the number of classes the more likely it is that important characteristics of the distribution will be concealed. On the other hand, too many classes will bring out more detail but summarise the distribution less well. Furthermore, the more classes the less the regularity of the frequency distribution. This can be easily seen by forming the given data into a frequency distribution with classes of, say, one dollar. The results are shown in Table 3.3 and Fig 3.3.

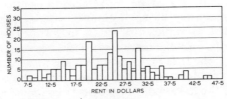

Fig 3.3 Weekly rent of 200 tenanted houses

Although the frequencies display a pattern similar to the results obtained with wider class intervals, they show great irregularity with a number of classes showing zero frequency. A compromise must be struck between too much detail and too little. In general, few distributions require more than sixteen to twenty or less than eight to ten classes. Unless the frequency distribution is very highly skewed, all classes should have *equal intervals*.[1]

The second important consideration in drawing up frequency distributions lies in the choice of *class mid-points*. While the choice of class intervals is governed by convenience (eg in terms of multiples of 5 and 10), the classes must be correctly centred. The class mid-point is then regarded as representative of the cases occurring in the class, and should be half-way between the true upper and lower limits of each class. If there is a tendency in the original data for concentrations at particular values, the class limits should be so arranged that these values fall in the centre of the class or are evenly spaced throughout the class. This has in fact been the case in the present example. The data show strong concentrations at multiples of 5 dollars (ie at 10, 15, 20, etc, dollars), and if class intervals of 5 dollars are chosen, the classes should be $7·5 and under $12·5, $12·5 and under $17·5, etc, to ensure that each class is correctly centred.[2]

[1] For discussion of skewness in frequency distributions, see section 3.6 below.
[2] See p 45 below.

For the purpose of selecting class limits, it is important to determine whether the variable under observation can be regarded as a *continuous* or *discrete* variable. The class limits can be stated in terms of either '*this* amount to *that* amount', or '*this* amount and *under that* amount'. The latter form must be used in the case of continuous variables, where the upper class limit of one class and the lower limit of the next class should coincide in order to ensure an exhaustive classification.[1] Thus the variable age, being inherently a continuous variable, should be stated as, for example, '10 years and under 20', '20 years and under 30', etc. The other form should in general be used for discrete variables, although in the case of a variable expressed in a unit which moves by very small jumps, it may be convenient to use the '*this* and under *that*' form. In recording money amounts, discrete jumps of one cent may be regarded as sufficiently small to justify the latter form of stating class limits. Thus the rent of, say, $12·5 belongs to the class '$12·5 and under $17·5' the true limits of which are $12·5 and $17·49. When we use the discrete form of stating class limits, the upper class limit of one class and the lower limit of the next class must be appropriately differentiated in order to ensure mutually exclusive classification. Thus in classifying factories according to size, the limits should be stated as, for example, 100–199 employees, 200–299 employees, and not 100–200, 200–300, etc.

In selecting class limits, it is essential that the stated class limits clearly indicate the range of values falling within each class. When the variable is capable of being measured exactly, this requirement poses little difficulty. Thus, in classifying houses by number of rooms, we might have classes 1 to 2 rooms, 3 to 4 rooms, and these are clearly the true limits of the chosen classes; the mid-points are simply the averages of the true class limits, ie $1\frac{1}{2}$ rooms and $3\frac{1}{2}$ rooms. On the other hand, the true class limits of a money variable stated in the '*this* and under *that*' form have implicit class limits which differ by one cent between the adjacent classes, and strictly speaking the mid-point should be calculated by computing the averages of the true class limits and not of the stated limits. Thus, for instance, the mid-point of the class '$7·5 and under $12·5' should be (7·5 + 12·49) ÷ 2 and not (7·5 + 12·50) ÷ 2 which is the mean of the stated class limits. However, little accuracy will be lost by performing the latter calculation in computing class mid-points which then become $10, $15, $20, etc.

If a discrete variable is recorded only approximately, special care must be taken. Thus, for instance, if rents were quoted not exactly but to the *nearest half-dollar* (ie only in jumps of 50 cents), the true classes

[1] See p 8 above.

would be '$7·25 to $12·24', '$12·25 to $17·24', etc, reflecting the general principle that the points lying to the left of the mid-point of the new unit of measurement (ie half-dollars) would be rounded downwards with the remaining points being rounded upwards. The mid-points for each class would be computed by averaging the true limits, ie (7·25 + 12·24) ÷ 2 = 9 dollars 74·5 cents, which would be rounded to $9·75. It should be noted that the class mid-point is not 10 dollars, ie that the effect of rounding each recorded amount to the nearest half-dollar, compared with exact measurement, is to lower all class mid-points by 25 cents.

On the other hand, rents may be quoted to the *last complete half-dollar*. If 5-dollar class intervals were required, the true class limits would be '$7·50 to $12·49', '$12·50 to $17·49', etc, with class mid-points $10, $15, etc. It was in fact on this principle that the frequency distribution in Table 3.2 was constructed.

In the case of a continuous variable (like age or weight) the observed data are always approximations and are usually quoted to the nearest ten or unit, or first or second decimal place, etc. Thus the variable age may be quoted to one decimal place, eg 51·3 years. This implies that the third digit is significant and we may assume that the correct value does not lie beyond the limits 51·3 ± 0·05. Accordingly, if we set up class limits, say 50 years and under 60, this really means 49·95 and under 59·95, and hence the true mid-point of that class is 54·95 and not 55. If age were quoted to the last full year, the class limits of 50 years and under 60 would be correct, and the mid-point of that class would lie at 55 years. The most important consideration in calculating class mid-points is that they lie halfway between the lowest true value and the highest true value which can occur in each class. This does not necessarily coincide with the halfway point between lower and upper class limits as stated. Thus, if factories are classified according to the number of their employees, a class '100 employees and under 200' has a mid-point of 149·5 and not 150.

The final point to remember is that the width of a class interval must be measured by the difference between the lower (or upper) class limits of two adjacent classes and not by the difference between the lower and upper class limit of a given class. The use of the latter measure may easily lead to error in the case of a discrete variable. Thus, if, in a distribution of houses by number of rooms, the classes are 1 to 2 rooms, 3 to 4 rooms, etc, the class interval is 2 rooms and not 1 room.

The actual mechanics of drawing up a frequency distribution are simple. The best plan is to select class intervals rather narrower than those which will be finally used and then go through the data allocating them as follows:

Weekly Rent (dollars)	Cases	Frequency
7·5 and under 8·5	8, 8	2
8·5 „ 9·5	9	1
9·5 „ 10·5	10, 10, 10, 9·5, 10	5
etc	etc	etc

The narrow classes can then easily be rearranged and combined to form a frequency distribution which will combine sufficient smoothness with sufficient detail.

The frequency distribution can also be written down to show relative (percentage) frequencies rather than absolute frequencies. The relative frequencies column must add up to 100 per cent. This procedure is very useful for purposes of making comparisons. Table 3.4 expresses the frequency distribution of rents derived earlier on a relative basis.

Table 3.4

RELATIVE FREQUENCY DISTRIBUTION OF WEEKLY RENTS OF 200 TENANTED HOUSES

Weekly Rent (dollars)	Relative Frequency (per cent)
7·5 and under 12·5	6·0
12·5 „ 17·5	13·0
17·5 „ 22·5	22·5
22·5 „ 27·5	30·0
27·5 „ 32·5	18·5
32·5 „ 37·5	6·5
37·5 „ 42·5	2·5
42·5 „ 47·5	1·0
All Rents	100·0

3.2 Cumulative Frequency Distributions

For some purposes it is useful to show cumulative frequencies rather than frequencies of occurrence in any particular class. Thus, in our previous example we may wish to know what number (or proportion) of houses were rented at less than various amounts of rent. For quick reference we construct a cumulative frequency curve, or *ogive*.

The first step is to determine whether lower or upper class limits should serve as dividing points. In the case of a continuous variable, or a variable which can vary in small discrete jumps, this is a relatively simple matter. Thus the number of houses with rents smaller than, say, $22·5 will include all houses having rents ranging from $7·5 to $22·49.

Similarly we can construct an ogive showing the number of houses with rents 'equal to or more than' specified amounts. To distinguish between these two types of cumulative frequency curves, the first is often referred to as a 'less than', and the second as an 'or more' cumulative frequency curve.

In Table 3.5 the data on rents are shown on a cumulative basis. The table enables us to read off directly the aggregate frequencies of houses with rents lower than any particular value (middle column),

Table 3.5

CUMULATIVE FREQUENCY DISTRIBUTION OF 200 TENANTED HOUSES

Weekly Rent (dollars) X	Number of Houses with Rents *less than* X	Number of Houses with Rents *equal to or greater than X*
7·5	0	200
12·5	12	188
17·5	38	162
22·5	83	117
27·5	143	57
32·5	180	20
37·5	193	7
42·5	198	2
47·5	200	0

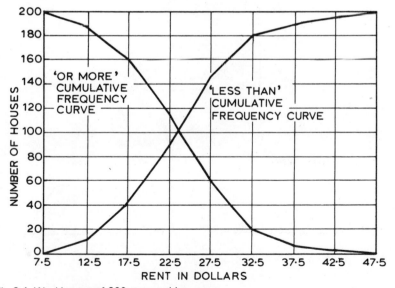

Fig 3.4 Weekly rent of 200 tenanted houses

or the number of houses whose rents are equal to or exceed a given value (last column). In Fig 3.4 this information is shown graphically.

If we translate frequency distributions into relative (percentage) frequency distributions, we may use the same principle to construct percentage ogives. These can then be used for comparing different sets of data. It may be noted here that Lorenz curves are an example of cumulative percentage frequency distributions constructed so as to bring out equality or inequality of distribution of two sets of data.[1]

3.3 Types of Frequency Distribution

Two tendencies are frequently observed in economic and business data, and indeed in most quantifiable data. One is a general tendency towards great diversity in observable phenomena. In our example, rents vary over a wide range depending on the age, location, size, etc, of the selected houses. Despite this diversity, however, most economic and business data have a tendency for clustering around particular values. Both tendencies are summarised by the shape of frequency distributions. As the variable under observation increases, frequency of occurrence increases to a maximum and then decreases. Graphed, the distributions most commonly found will be more or less bell-shaped, but they may be *symmetrical* or *skewed*. As seen in Fig 3.5, the skewness may be *positive* (to the right) or *negative* (to the left).

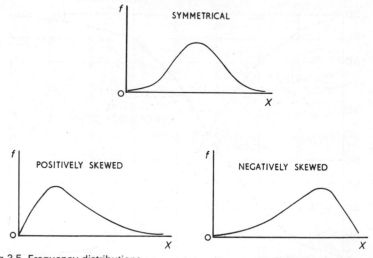

Fig 3.5 Frequency distributions

[1] See section 2.5 above.

Frequency distributions with only one peak are called *unimodal*. Two-peaked or *bimodal* distributions also occur, but their bimodality may often be caused by lack of homogeneity in the underlying data; when properly classified, such data often yield distributions with unimodal characteristics. Less commonly found distributions in the case of economic data are J- and U-shaped.

3.4 Measures of Central Value

Graphical representations of frequency distributions give us a good general picture of the 'shape' of the original data. What we need now, however, are summary measures to describe frequency distributions. The characteristics we seek are those relating to:
(a) their central value,
(b) the degree of dispersion around the central value,
(c) their degree of skewness, if any.
The present section is concerned with measures of central value. Such measures may be looked upon as representative values about which a given distribution is centred. They will furthermore indicate the general level of magnitude of the distribution. Before developing such measures, we should first discuss the use of the summation sign in statistical work.

The Summation Sign

The symbol Σ (Greek capital sigma) means the 'sum of'. Thus if X consists of three values, eg 4, 7, and 9, ΣX instructs us to sum all the values of X:

$$\Sigma X = 4 + 7 + 9 = 20$$

For clarity, we sometimes attach subscripts to the individual values of the variable X, ie $X_1 = 4$, $X_2 = 7$, $X_3 = 9$. Then we write

$$\sum_{i=1}^{3} X_i = X_1 + X_2 + X_3 = 20$$

This method of using Σ specifies the number of values of X which are being added. In general

$$\sum_{i=1}^{n} X_i = X_1 + X_2 + \ldots X_n$$

But the choice of the first subscript is entirely arbitrary and we may equally well attach the subscript 0, or any other number, to the first value of X, eg

$$\sum_{i=0}^{n-1} X_i = X_0 + X_1 + \ldots X_{n-1}$$

The following rules apply to operations with summation signs.

Rule 1: If X is a variable with n observations, and A a constant

$$\Sigma AX = A\Sigma X$$

Rule 2: If A is a constant number

$$\sum^{n} A = nA$$

ie the constant A is added n times.

Combining these two rules, if

$$Z = A + BX,$$

$$\Sigma Z = nA + B\Sigma X$$

Rule 3: The sum of squares of a variable X is not equal to the square of its sum.

Suppose that there are n positive observations of X. Then

$$\Sigma X^2 = X_1{}^2 + X_2{}^2 + \ldots X_n{}^2$$

But $\quad (\Sigma X)^2 = (X_1 + X_2 + \ldots X_n)(X_1 + X_2 + \ldots X_n)$

$$= (X_1{}^2 + X_1 X_2 + X_1 X_3 + \ldots X_1 X_n)$$

$$+ (X_2 X_1 + X_2{}^2 + X_2 X_3 + \ldots X_2 X_n)$$

$$\cdot$$
$$\cdot$$
$$\cdot$$

$$+ (X_n X_1 + X_n X_2 + X_n X_3 + \ldots X_n{}^2)$$

Clearly $\quad (\Sigma X)^2 > \Sigma X^2$

Rule 4: The sum of products of n pairs of observations of variables X and Y is not equal to the product of their sums. For n such pairs of positive observations

$$\Sigma XY = X_1 Y_1 + X_2 Y_2 + \ldots X_n Y_n$$

But $\quad \Sigma X \Sigma Y = (X_1 + X_2 + \ldots X_n)(Y_1 + Y_2 + \ldots Y_n)$

$$= (X_1 Y_1 + X_1 Y_2 + \ldots X_1 Y_n)$$

$$+ (X_2 Y_1 + X_2 Y_2 + \ldots X_2 Y_n)$$

$$\cdot$$
$$\cdot$$
$$\cdot$$

$$+ (X_n Y_1 + X_n Y_2 + \ldots X_n Y_n)$$

Thus
$$\Sigma X \Sigma Y > \Sigma XY$$

Rule 5: $\Sigma(X + Y) = \Sigma X + \Sigma Y$. This rule merely states that the order of addition is immaterial, ie addition of numbers is commutative.

Arithmetic Mean

The simplest representative value of an array of numbers is the ordinary *average* or the *arithmetic mean*. For ungrouped data the mean is defined as

$$\bar{X} = \frac{X_1 + X_2 + \ldots X_N}{N} = \frac{\Sigma X}{N}$$

where N represents the number of observations of the variable X.

Example 3.1

Given the following ten rents, calculate their mean.

X
Rent
(dollars)
10·0
10·5
12·0
14·5
15·0
18·0
21·0
24·5
26·0
30·0

$$\bar{X} = \frac{\Sigma X}{N} = \frac{181·5}{10} = 18·15 \text{ dollars}$$

The arithmetic mean has two important properties. The first is that the sum of the deviations of values from their mean is zero.

Writing $x = X - \bar{X}$ as the deviation of a value from the mean in the above example, we have

X	x
10·0	−8·15
10·5	−7·65
12·0	−6·15
14·5	−3·65
15·0	−3·15
18·0	−0·15
21·0	2·85
24·5	6·35
26·0	7·85
30·0	11·85
$\Sigma X = 181·5$	$\Sigma x = 0$

Algebraically,

$$x = X - \bar{X},$$

$$\Sigma x = \Sigma X - N\bar{X}$$

$$= \Sigma X - N \cdot \frac{\Sigma X}{N}$$

$$= 0$$

This property of the mean can be used to facilitate computation. If we choose a value A such that $A \neq \bar{X}$, the sum of deviations will no longer be zero. Dividing this sum by N we obtain a correction factor by which A will need to be adjusted to yield the correct value of $\bar{X}$. Since A can be selected arbitrarily, it is known as *arbitrary origin*. Writing

$$x' = X - A$$

$$X = A + x'$$

$$\Sigma X = NA + \Sigma x'$$

and
$$\bar{X} = A + \frac{\Sigma x'}{N} \quad \text{(or } \bar{X} = A + \bar{x}')$$

where $\bar{x}'$ is the correction factor.

A second important property of the mean is that the sum of the squares of the deviations of values from any origin is a minimum when that origin is their mean. Using the above notation we shall require

$$\Sigma x'^2 = \Sigma(X - A)^2 \text{ to be a minimum.}$$

Since the values of X are given, the sum $\Sigma x'^2$ will depend only on the value of A as A is varied by small steps. This sum will be a minimum when its first derivative with respect to A is zero, ie when

$$-2\Sigma(X - A) = 0$$

ie when
$$-\Sigma X + NA = 0$$

ie when
$$A = \frac{\Sigma X}{N} = \bar{X}$$

Example 3.2

Calculate the mean rent in the above example, by using an arbitrary origin. Choosing a convenient A, eg $A = 20$, we have:

Rent (dollars) X	Arbitrary Deviations $A = 20$ x'
10·0	−10·0
10·5	−9·5
12·0	−8·0
14·5	−5·5
15·0	−5·0
18·0	−2·0
21·0	1·0
24·5	4·5
26·0	6·0
30·0	10·0
	$\Sigma x' = -18\cdot5$

$$\bar{X} = A + \frac{\Sigma x'}{N} = 20 + \left(\frac{-18\cdot5}{10}\right) = 18\cdot15 \text{ dollars}$$

This method will prove very convenient in calculating the mean of a frequency distribution.

Computing the Mean from Grouped Data

The main point to remember is that we regard the class mid-point as representative of the observations in the class. For instance, if there are 12 rents in the class '$7·5 and under $12·5', we essentially treat these rents as though they were each 10 dollars. Evidently, the mean of a number of observations calculated from a frequency distribution of the observations will generally be only an approximation to the mean calculated from the original data. It is for this reason that it is of paramount importance to centre the classes at points which are typical of the whole classes. Consider our example of 200 rents. If instead of choosing intervals '$7·5 and under $12·5', etc, we were to define our class limits as '$5 and under $10', '$10 and under $15', etc, the mid-points would fall on $7·5, $12·5, etc. Since the rents tend to be concentrated on the '5s', the mean rent computed on this basis would be quite substantially out as compared with the mean computed directly from the original ungrouped data. So long then as the class mid-points are representative of the observations within classes, in the sense that they lie fairly close to the mean for each class, the arithmetic mean computed from grouped data will be a close approximation to the true mean, provided that the distribution is not too badly skewed. With a great mass of data, working with grouped observations is the only practicable way. In any case the nature of the data can best be appreciated when it is in the frequency distribution form.

Writing X for class mid-points and f for the frequencies in the classes, the mean for grouped data is defined as

$$\bar{X} = \frac{\Sigma fX}{\Sigma f} = \frac{\Sigma fX}{N}, \text{ where } N = \Sigma f$$

In calculating the mean for a frequency distribution, the work can be reduced by using an arbitrary origin located at the mid-point of a class. We shall have

$$\bar{X} = A + \frac{\Sigma fx'}{N}$$

where x' is the deviation of a class mid-point from an arbitrary origin. But the x's in this formula are all multiples of the class interval. For instance, in the frequency distribution in Table 3.2, the class mid-points are 10, 15, 20, 25, 30, 35, 40, 45. If 20 is selected as arbitrary origin, the deviations of the mid-points will be -10, -5, 0, 5, 10, 15, 20, 25, respectively. These are all multiples of the class interval of 5 dollars and, in terms of the class interval, can be written -2, -1, 0, 1, 2, 3, 4, 5. When we express the arbitrary deviations in class interval units, the expression $\frac{\Sigma fx'}{N}$ will be in units of the width of the class interval, so that it must be multiplied by the width of the class interval to transform it into the original units. The formula then becomes

$$\bar{X} = A + \left(\frac{\Sigma fx'}{N} \times h \right)$$

where x' is in class-interval units and h is the width of the class interval. Use of this formula simplifies the arithmetic considerably.

Example 3.3

Calculate the mean rent of the frequency distribution set out in Table 3.2.

Rent (dollars)		Class Mid-point X	Frequency f	fX
7·5 and under	12·5	10	12	120
12·5 "	17·5	15	26	390
17·5 "	22·5	20	45	900
22·5 "	27·5	25	60	1 500
27·5 "	32·5	30	37	1 110
32·5 "	37·5	35	13	455
37·5 "	42·5	40	5	200
42·5 "	47·5	45	2	90
Total			200	4 765

$$\bar{X} = \frac{\Sigma fX}{N} = \frac{4\,765}{200} = 23\!\cdot\!825, \text{ ie } 23\!\cdot\!8 \text{ dollars (to one decimal place).}$$

However, we can reduce the work in our calculations by using an arbitrary origin and by working in terms of class interval units. Select as arbitrary origin the class mid-point, which from inspection appears to be near the mean. In this case we may choose $A = \$20$. As the width of the class interval we have $h = \$5$.

Rent (dollars)	Class Mid-point X	Arbitrary Deviations in C.I. Units $(A = 20)$ x'	Frequency f	fx'
7·5 and under 12·5	10	−2	12	−24
12·5 " 17·5	15	−1	26	−26
17·5 " 22·5	20	0	45	0
22·5 " 27·5	25	1	60	60
27·5 " 32·5	30	2	37	74
32·5 " 37·5	35	3	13	39
37·5 " 42·5	40	4	5	20
42·5 " 47·5	45	5	2	10
Total			200	153

$$\bar{X} = A + \left(\frac{\Sigma fx'}{N} \times h \right) = 20 + \left(\frac{153}{200} \times 5 \right) = 23\cdot8 \text{ dollars}$$

Weighted Arithmetic Mean

The mean for a frequency distribution, $\bar{X} = \dfrac{\Sigma fX}{\Sigma f}$, is in fact a mean of the Xs (class mid-points), where each X is weighted by its importance. This is only a special case of the more general notion of a weighted mean $\bar{X} = \dfrac{\Sigma WX}{\Sigma W}$, where the Ws are weights.

The concept of a weighted mean can be simplified by expressing the given weights W as relative weights $V = \dfrac{W}{\Sigma W}$ so that $\Sigma V = 1$. Then

$$\bar{X} = \Sigma VX$$

Example 3.4
Suppose that bread is sold at three prices: 17 cents, 19 cents and 22 cents a loaf. The simple mean price is 19·3 cents, but a more useful measure is the mean which results from attaching to each price the quantity of bread sold at that price, ie a weighted mean. If the sales per week of the three types of bread are 50 thousand, 30 thousand and 20 thousand loaves respectively, we should have

$$\bar{X} = \frac{17 \times 50\,000 + 19 \times 30\,000 + 22 \times 20\,000}{100\,000}$$
$$= 18\cdot6 \text{ cents}$$

Using relative weights this reduces to
$$\bar{X} = (17 \times 0\cdot5) + (19 \times 0\cdot3) + (22 \times 0\cdot2) = 18\cdot6 \text{ cents}$$

Median

The mean is not the only measure of central value. Indeed, a simpler one is the *median*. The *median* is that value which exceeds, in magnitude, half the values and is exceeded by half the values. In the case of un-grouped data all we have to do is to arrange the data in order of magnitude and locate the median by inspection. If we have N items, the median will have to be located so that it exceeds $\dfrac{N}{2}$ items and is exceeded by $\dfrac{N}{2}$ items. By convention, when N is odd the median is located as the middle item, and when N is even the median is located as half-way between the two middle items.

Example 3.5

What is the median of the following rents?

(a) 12, 12·5, 14, 15, 16, 18, 19·5
     $Md = 15$ dollars.
(b) 12, 12·5, 14, 15, 16, 18
     $Md = 14·5$ dollars.

In the case of grouped data we have the frequencies in the various classes and not the detailed observations. Consequently the median cannot be located as a particular observation or midway between two observations. What we do is to find the value which will divide the total number of frequencies into halves. This can best be understood in terms of the histogram corresponding to the frequency distribution. We fix the median at a point on the X-axis such that a vertical line drawn at that point will divide the area of the histogram exactly in half. The area to the left of the median will then represent the lower half of the frequencies and the area to the right the upper half.

If the total number of the frequencies is N, the median will have to be such that $\dfrac{N}{2}$ values lie below it and $\dfrac{N}{2}$ above it. First, locate the median class by inspection, ie the class in which the median will lie. Let f_b be the number of frequencies in the classes below the median class, f_m the number in that class, and f_a the number above that class, so that $f_b + f_m + f_a = N$. If we assume that the distribution of observations in the median class is uniform over the class interval, then, by travelling a fraction $\left(\dfrac{N}{2} - f_b\right) \Big/ f_m$ along the class interval from the lower class limit, we shall reach a point below which $f_b + \left(\dfrac{N}{2} - f_b\right)$ $= \dfrac{N}{2}$ observations lie. This point will be the median, and it is given by the formula

$$Md = l_m + \left(\frac{\frac{N}{2} - f_b}{f_m} \times h \right)$$

where l_m is the lower limit of the median class and h is the class interval. The same result is reached by travelling in the opposite direction. For, travelling a fraction $\left(\frac{N}{2} - f_a \right) \Big/ f_m$ along the median class interval from the lower class limit of the class immediately above the median class, we shall reach a point above which $f_a + \left(\frac{N}{2} - f_a \right) = \frac{N}{2}$ observations lie, and which is the same point as that derived from the above formula. This method holds irrespective of whether N is even or odd, because under the assumption of a uniform distribution within the median class no point other than the one given by the above method will divide the frequencies into halves.

Example 3.6
Calculate the median rent of the frequency distribution set out in Table 3.2

Rent (dollars)			f
7·5 and under	12·5		12
12·5	„	17·5	26
17·5	„	22·5	45
22·5	„	27·5	60
27·5	„	32·5	37
32·5	„	37·5	13
37·5	„	42·5	5
42·5	„	47·5	2
All Rents			200

The median lies in the class $22·5 and under $27·5, for this class must contain the value which divides the frequencies into two parts containing 100 each. Since there are 83 items below this class, we shall have to travel another 17 items along this class to locate the median. We have

$$Md = l_m + \left(\frac{\frac{N}{2} - f_b}{f_m} \times h \right)$$

$$= 22·5 + \left(\frac{100 - 83}{60} \times 5 \right)$$

$$= 23·9 \text{ dollars}$$

Quartiles

A knowledge of the median helps to characterise a frequency distribution by virtue of its central position. The quartiles are analogous measures. The first quartile (Q_1) is the value which exceeds, in magnitude, one-quarter of the values and is exceeded by three-quarters of the values. The second quartile is the median. The third quartile (Q_3) is the value which exceeds, in magnitude, three-quarters of the values and is exceeded by one-quarter of the values. The quartiles are calculated in a similar fashion to the median.

Example 3.7

Calculate the first and third quartiles of the frequency distribution set out in Table 3.2.

$$Q_1 = 17 \cdot 5 + \left(\frac{50 - 38}{45} \times 5 \right)$$

$$= 18 \cdot 8 \text{ dollars}$$

$$Q_3 = 27 \cdot 5 + \left(\frac{150 - 143}{37} \times 5 \right)$$

$$= 28 \cdot 4 \text{ dollars}$$

Quintiles, deciles and percentiles can be defined and calculated similarly.

Mode

If we were to increase our number of observations very greatly and at the same time narrow the class interval, the histogram of our frequency distribution would approach a smooth curve. Such a smooth curve is shown in the diagram below.

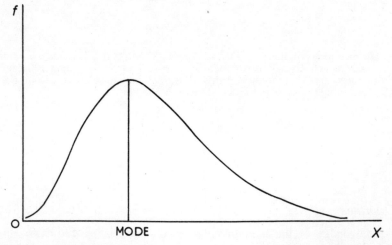

Fig 3.6

The value of the variable at which the frequency curve reaches a maximum is called the *mode*. It is the value around which the items tend to be most heavily concentrated.

In a frequency distribution it is quite easy to locate the modal class, ie the class in which the mode lies. It is the most populous class and in Table 3.2 above is $22·5 and under $27·5. The location of an estimate of the mode itself is more difficult, for it is in a sense a hypothetical measure relating to the smooth curve underlying the observed frequency distribution. One procedure is to pass a smooth curve through the three central frequencies (a parabola) and to locate the mode in that fashion. This has the effect of locating the mode at a point away from the centre of the modal class towards the one of the two adjoining classes which has the greater frequency. Thus, if the class below the modal class contains more cases than the one above, the mode will be less than the mid-point of the modal class. This accords with common sense, as it is reasonable to suppose that, in these circumstances, the point of concentration lies to the left of the centre of the modal class. The method is illustrated in the diagram below.

This method yields the following formula:

$$Mo = l + \left(\frac{f_0 - f_{-1}}{(f_0 - f_{-1}) + (f_0 - f_1)} \times h \right)$$

where l is the lower limit of the modal class,

f_0 is the frequency of modal class,

f_{-1} is the frequency of next lower class,

f_1 is the frequency of next higher class.

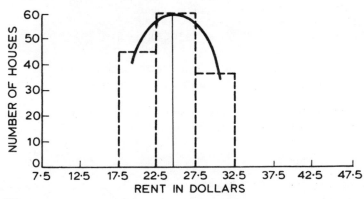

Fig 3.7

Example 3.8

Estimate the mode of the frequency distribution in Table 3.2.

$$Mo = l + \left(\frac{(f_0 - f_{-1})}{(f_0 - f_{-1}) + (f_0 - f_1)} \times h \right)$$

$$= 22{\cdot}5 + \left(\frac{60 - 45}{60 - 45 + 60 - 37} \times 5 \right)$$

$$= 24{\cdot}4 \text{ dollars}$$

Geometric Mean

The geometric mean is defined as

$$\text{G.M.} = \sqrt[N]{X_1 . X_2 \ldots X_N}$$

ie as the Nth root of the product of N observations of a variable X. Its meaning can perhaps be best understood with the aid of simple algebra.

It will be remembered that an arithmetic progression is a sequence of numbers each of which differs from the one which precedes it by a constant amount called the common difference. A geometric progression is a sequence of numbers such that any term after the first is obtained from the preceding term by multiplying it by a fixed number called the common ratio. Consider two sequences 2, 4, 6 ... and 2, 4, 8 ... which from our definitions form an arithmetic progression and a geometric progression, respectively. We may now define the term of a progression, which lies between any two given terms, as the mean of those two terms. The middle term in the first sequence is equal to its arithmetic mean; the middle term of the second sequence, however, coincides with its geometric mean, ie

$$\text{G.M.} = \sqrt[3]{(2)(4)(8)} = 4$$

The arithmetic mean of any sequence of positive numbers will be greater than the geometric mean so long as the items averaged are not all of the same value.

In practice, the computation of the geometric mean is greatly facilitated by logarithms. Thus for ungrouped data

$$\log \text{G.M.} = \frac{1}{N}(\log X_1 + \log X_2 + \ldots \log X_N)$$

$$= \frac{\Sigma \log X}{N}$$

For grouped data

$$\log \text{G.M.} = \frac{1}{N}(f_1 \log X_1 + f_2 \log X_2 + \ldots f_n \log X_N)$$

$$= \frac{\Sigma f \log X}{N}$$

where f represents class frequencies and X the mid-point of each class. The logarithm of the geometric mean is the arithmetic mean (or, where appropriate, the weighted arithmetic mean) of the logarithms of the variable.

The most important property of the geometric mean is that the product of the ratio deviations of the observed values below and above the mean equals unity. This property makes the geometric mean a particularly suitable measure for averaging ratios and for computing average rates of change. In averaging ratios, the use of the arithmetic mean sometimes leads to inconsistent results, for instance in index-number construction.[1] Such inconsistencies may be overcome by averaging relatives geometrically rather than arithmetically.

Harmonic Mean

The harmonic mean is not used a great deal, but it does occur in index-number formulae and should be mentioned here. It is defined as

$$\text{H.M.} = \frac{1}{\frac{1}{N}\Sigma\frac{1}{X}} = \frac{N}{\Sigma\frac{1}{X}}$$

ie the harmonic mean is the reciprocal of the arithmetic mean of the reciprocals of the variable. Thus, given the values 2, 4, 8 in the previous example

$$\text{H.M.} = \frac{3}{\frac{1}{2} + \frac{1}{4} + \frac{1}{8}} = 3 \cdot 4.$$

This is less than 4·7 and 4 which were the values of the arithmetic mean and the geometric mean, respectively. In general,

$$\text{H.M.} < \text{G.M.} < \bar{X}$$

unless the values being averaged are all of the same positive magnitude, in which case H.M. = G.M. = $\bar{X}$.

---

[1] See Ch. 11, p 448.

Relations between the Mean, Median and Mode

The most commonly applied measures of central tendency in statistical data are the arithmetic mean, the median and the mode, and we now discuss further their characteristics and their respective advantages and disadvantages in description of statistical data.

If we interpret these three measures in terms of the smooth frequency curve which we should get if we had a very large number of observations, we can say that the mean is the value of the variable which is the point of balance or centre of gravity of the distribution, the median is the value which divides the distribution exactly in half, and the mode is the value at which the peak of the distribution occurs. In a symmetrical distribution all three measures coincide; but skewness pushes the measures apart. This can be seen by starting with a symmetrical distribution and then adding some high values at the upper end of the distribution. Positive skewness will result. The mode will remain unchanged, but the median will increase as the mode will now be exceeded by more than half the values. The mean will tend to increase even more. The reason for this can be appreciated when it is realised that the sum of the negative deviations, from the mean, of the values below the mean must equal in magnitude that of the positive deviations of the values above the mean, since the algebraic sum of the deviations from the mean must be zero. If the values are deviated from the new median, the sum will tend to be positive because that half of the values above the median will contain more extreme values than that half below the median. Hence the new mean will tend to be higher than the new median.

In practice, in moderately skewed distributions it is found that the median is usually one-third along the distance between the mean and the mode, the order being mode, median, mean in positively skewed distributions and mean, median, mode in negatively skewed distributions. This empirical relation can be expressed as

$$\bar{X} - Mo = 3(\bar{X} - Md)$$

This is illustrated in Fig 3.8.

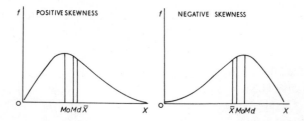

Fig 3.8

When a distribution is perfectly symmetrical, the three measures coincide and in cases of near symmetry they will be very close. However, in general, the mean possesses important advantages over the other two measures and is to be preferred in such cases as a measure of central value.

The first advantage is that the mean is defined algebraically, and is therefore capable of algebraic treatment. For example, if we have the means of several separate distributions of the same variable, we can combine them to obtain the mean of the combined distribution. This can be done by weighting the means of the separate distributions by their respective total frequencies, so that we have

$$\bar{X} = \frac{N_1\bar{X}_1 + N_2\bar{X}_2 + N_3\bar{X}_3 + \cdots}{N_1 + N_2 + N_3 \cdots}$$

where the subscripts refer to the separate distributions and $\bar{X}$ is the average of the means for the combined distribution. This cannot be done for the median or the mode. Similarly, if we have N values of a variable and we know the aggregate of the values (ΣX), we can calculate the mean even though we do not know the distribution in detail and hence cannot calculate the median or the mode. The mean is a key measure in statistical methods. Its two important properties, namely that the sum of the deviations of values from their mean is zero and that the sum of the squares of the deviations of values from an origin is a minimum when the origin is the mean, should be recalled at this point.

Secondly, when an attempt is made to estimate from sample data the central value of a totality of observations, the distribution of which is symmetrical, the mean will give a more reliable estimate in the sense that the means of repeated samples will show less dispersion than either the modes or medians. This is tantamount to saying that the sampling error of the mean is less than that of the median or mode. Sampling error is discussed in detail in Chapters 5 and 6.

On the other hand, the median and mode must be used when the mean cannot be satisfactorily calculated. This is the case when the distribution has open-end classes, ie when the lower limit of the bottom class and the upper limit of the top class are not defined, and to a lesser extent when the class intervals are unequal. Evidently, one can still compute the mode, as well as the median, since the latter is not affected by the values of the variable but merely by their frequencies of occurrence.

When, however, the distribution is skewed, the mean, median and mode differ in their significance. They are no longer measures of *the* central value, and each has its use. The use of the median can be best illustrated by reference to distributions of income. These are usually positively skewed. This results in less than half of the income-earners receiving the mean income or more. Consequently the median income may, for some purposes, be regarded as a more representative figure, for half the income-earners must be receiving at least the median income. One can say that as many receive at least the median income as do not. Whether the median or the mean should be used in analysis of income data often depends on the purpose of the exercise. Thus suppose that in a certain district there are five farmers with annual incomes of $3000, $4000, $6000, $8000 and $14 000. The mean is $7000 and the median $6000. If the last farmer's income were to increase substantially, eg to $29 000, the mean would increase to $10 000 whereas the median would be unaffected. The fact that the median is unaffected by extreme values, while the mean is, makes the mean a useful measure for some purposes, ie for measuring the overall level of income in the district, and the median for others, ie for inferring something about the division of incomes within the district.

The usefulness of the mode can be best illustrated by reference to certain types of distributions of discrete variables. Consider, for example, family size, which invariably is positively skewed. The mode will be the most common sized family and may for some purposes be regarded as more representative than the mean. It certainly is the 'typical' family, in the everyday sense of the word. Mean family size may be, say, 2·8 children whereas the modal family is a two-child one. In the extreme case of reversed J-shaped distributions, the mean or median are in no sense 'representative' values, whereas the mode may still be regarded as a representative or typical value, although it is clearly not a central value. Thus the distribution of number of cars owned by one household would be of this kind, with a modal value of one, and a mean higher than one.

Irrespective of whether or not the mean or the median can in certain cases be used as 'representative' values, they always indicate important characteristics of the distribution. The mean gives a measure of the general level of magnitude of the variable under consideration in the sense that, if we multiply the mean by the total number of observations, we get their aggregate value (ie $N\bar{X} = \Sigma X$, by definition). Likewise the chances are even that any one observation in the distribution under consideration will be at least as large as the median.

3.5 Measures of Dispersion

The central value of a frequency distribution tells us something about the general level of magnitude of the distribution and, in the case of the usual bell-shaped distribution, indicates the point about which the observations tend to concentrate. This concentration can be more or less dispersed, however, as is illustrated in Fig 3.9. Some measure of the dispersion about the central value is, therefore, required.

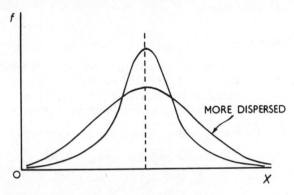

Fig 3.9

Range

One elementary measure is the *range*, ie the highest minus the lowest value. This is clearly unsatisfactory, since it depends on only the two extreme values and will, in general, get larger the larger the number of observations made.

Quartile Deviation

A more useful measure is the *quartile deviation*, defined as

$$Q.D. = \frac{Q_3 - Q_1}{2}$$

In a symmetrical distribution, $Md \pm Q.D.$ will contain 50 per cent of the cases, and in an asymmetrical distribution this will be approximately true. It clearly measures concentration of the observations around the median. The greater the quartile deviation the more the dispersion.

Example 3.9
Calculate the quartile deviation of the frequency distribution set out in Table 3.2 above.

$$Q.D. = \frac{Q_3 - Q_1}{2}$$

$$= \frac{28\cdot4 - 18\cdot8}{2}$$

$$= 4\cdot8 \text{ dollars}$$

In general the quartile deviation is not very satisfactory, because it is not based on all the values in the distribution and it is not capable of mathematical manipulation.

Standard Deviation

Ideally a measure of dispersion should take into account the deviations of all the observations from their central value. The obvious suggestion is to calculate the mean of the deviations of all the items from their mean, ie if the deviation of an observation from the mean is written $x = X - \bar{X}$, calculate $\dfrac{\Sigma x}{N}$. But this always equals zero. If we ignore the minus signs in the deviations, we shall get a measure called the *mean deviation*:

$$\text{M.D.} = \frac{\Sigma|x|}{N}$$

where $|x|$ means the magnitude of x, irrespective of sign, ie the absolute value of a deviation. The mean deviation, however, is very awkward to calculate for grouped data, and it is not capable of mathematical manipulation, so it is used as infrequently as the quartile deviation.

If, instead of ignoring the signs of the xs, we square them, the result will be a series of positive squared deviations. The mean of these, ie the quantity $\dfrac{\Sigma x^2}{N}$, gives us what is called the *variance*. However, when we calculate the variance for a group of N observations, the group usually comes from a still larger group which is the totality of all possible observations of X. Generally we require the variance of our group as an estimate of the variance of the totality from which our observations have come. It can be shown[1] that the variance of a set of observations $X_1, X_2, \ldots, X_N$, denoted by s^2, should then be defined as

$$s^2 = \frac{\Sigma(X - \bar{X})^2}{N - 1} = \frac{\Sigma x^2}{N - 1}$$

in order for it to be a good estimate of the variance of all X.

Consequently we shall use $N - 1$ rather than N as the divisor. The reason for doing this will be elaborated in a later chapter. Some texts on statistical methods use N as the divisor and make adjustments for the resulting bias at a later stage. So long as N is large, it is immaterial whether N or $N - 1$ is used, but the matter is of some importance in small groups of observations of X.

[1] See pp 225–6 below.

The variance measures the variation or dispersion of the observations about their mean. It is a most important concept. The units in which the variance is expressed will be the original units squared and, to make the units of our measure of dispersion comparable with our original units, we take the square root. The result is known as the *standard deviation* and is defined by

$$s = \sqrt{\frac{\Sigma x^2}{N - 1}}$$

Like the mean, the standard deviation is expressed in the same units as the original data. Both the standard deviation (s) and its square the variance (s^2) are used as measures of dispersion. For some purposes, it is convenient to use the one, for other purposes the other.

Example 3.10
Calculate the standard deviation of the following seven rents: $12, $12·5, $14, $15, $16, $18, $19·5.
The mean must first be calculated so that the deviations of the observations from their mean can be computed. If we require our standard deviation correct to, say, one decimal place, we shall have to work with three decimal places.

Rent (dollars) X	Deviation from Mean x	x^2
12·0	−3·286	10·798
12·5	−2·786	7·762
14·0	−1·286	1·654
15·0	−0·286	0·082
16·0	0·714	0·510
18·0	2·714	7·366
19·5	4·214	17·758
107·0		45·930

$$\bar{X} = \frac{\Sigma X}{N} = \frac{107}{7} = 15·286, \text{ ie } 15·3 \text{ dollars to one decimal place.}$$

$$s = \sqrt{\frac{\Sigma x^2}{N - 1}} = \sqrt{\frac{45·930}{6}} = 2·8 \text{ dollars to one decimal place.}$$

It will be readily seen that the calculations in the above example are onerous and would be even more so if greater accuracy were desired. Fortunately a method is available which combines as high a degree of accuracy as one pleases with less arduous arithmetic. This 'short method' makes use of an arbitrary origin. If we put

$$x' = X - A, \text{ where } A \text{ is an arbitrary origin,}$$

then $\quad \bar{X} = A + \bar{x}'$

From this we have

$$X - \bar{X} = x' - \bar{x}'$$

ie $\qquad\qquad x = x' - \bar{x}'$

$$x^2 = x'^2 - 2x'\bar{x}' + \bar{x}'^2$$

and $\qquad \Sigma x^2 = \Sigma x'^2 - 2\bar{x}'\Sigma x' + N\bar{x}'^2$

$$= \Sigma x'^2 - 2N\bar{x}'^2 + N\bar{x}'^2$$

$$= \Sigma x'^2 - N\bar{x}'^2$$

Hence $\qquad s = \sqrt{\dfrac{\Sigma x^2}{N-1}} = \sqrt{\dfrac{\Sigma x'^2 - N\bar{x}'^2}{N-1}}$

For machine computation it is most convenient to work with the arbitrary origin of zero. Then

$$\Sigma x^2 = \Sigma X^2 - N\bar{X}^2$$

and $\qquad\qquad s = \sqrt{\dfrac{\Sigma X^2 - N\bar{X}^2}{N-1}}$

Example 3.11

Calculate the standard deviation in the above example, using an arbitrary origin. Setting $A = 0$, we can work directly with the original observations.

Rent (dollars) X	X^2
12·0	144·00
12·5	156·25
14·0	196·00
15·0	225·00
16·0	256·00
18·0	324·00
19·5	380·25
	1 681·50

$$s = \sqrt{\frac{\Sigma X^2 - N\bar{X}^2}{N-1}} = \sqrt{\frac{1681\cdot5 - 7(15\cdot286)^2}{6}}$$

$$= 2\cdot765, \text{ ie } 2\cdot8 \text{ dollars to one decimal place.}$$

It should be noted that the same result would be achieved if we chose, say, $15 as our arbitrary origin:

Rent (dollars) X	Arbitrary Deviation $(A = 15)$ x'	x'^2
12·0	−3·0	9·00
12·5	−2·5	6·25
14·0	−1·0	1·00
15·0	0	0
16·0	1·0	1·00
18·0	3·0	9·00
19·5	4·5	20·25
	2·0	46·50

$$\bar{x}' = \frac{\Sigma x'}{N} = \frac{2}{7} = 0.286$$

$$s = \sqrt{\frac{\Sigma x'^2 - N\bar{x}'^2}{N - 1}} = \sqrt{\frac{46·50 - 7(0·286)^2}{6}}$$

$$= 2·8 \text{ dollars.}$$

Note also that $\bar{X}$ can be readily calculated at the same time as s. Here

$$\bar{X} = A + \bar{x}' = 15 + 0·286 = 15·286, \text{ ie } 15·3 \text{ to one decimal place.}$$

This method is simpler and more accurate than the original one, even though the formulae are somewhat more complicated. When we come to the case of grouped data, the deviations are deviations of class mid-points, and we have to weight these by their respective class frequencies. The formula becomes

$$s = \sqrt{\frac{\Sigma f(X - \bar{X})^2}{N - 1}} = \sqrt{\frac{\Sigma fx^2}{N - 1}} = \sqrt{\frac{\Sigma fx'^2 - N\bar{x}'^2}{N - 1}}$$

where the Xs refer to class mid-points and the fs to the corresponding frequencies. If we express the deviations in class interval units, we have

$$s = \sqrt{\frac{\Sigma fx'^2 - N\bar{x}'^2}{N - 1}} \times h$$

Example 3.12

Calculate the standard deviation of the frequency distribution set out in Table 3.2 above.

We first perform the calculation by using the original formula

$$s = \sqrt{\frac{\Sigma fx^2}{N - 1}}$$

From example 3.3 above we know that the mean is 23·825 dollars. We then have

$$s = \sqrt{\frac{\Sigma fx^2}{N-1}} = \sqrt{\frac{10\,298\cdot849}{199}} = 7\cdot194, \text{ ie } 7\cdot2 \text{ dollars to one decimal place.}$$

The computations are too burdensome, and once again by working from an arbitrary origin, the arithmetic can be greatly reduced. Thus we have

$$\bar{x}' = \frac{\Sigma fx'}{N} = -\frac{47}{200} = -0\cdot235$$

$$s = \sqrt{\frac{\Sigma fx'^2 - N\bar{x}'^2}{N-1}} \times h = \sqrt{\frac{423 - 200(-0\cdot235)^2}{199}} \times 5$$

$$= 7\cdot2 \text{ dollars to one decimal place.}$$

Note that $\bar{X}$ can be readily calculated at the same time as s. Here

$$\bar{X} = A + (\bar{x}' \times h) = 25 + (-0\cdot235 \times 5) = 23\cdot8$$

Rent (dollars)	Class Mid-point X	x	Frequency f	x^2	fx^2
7·5 and under 12·5	10	−13·825	12	191·131	2 293·572
12·5 ,, 17·5	15	−8·825	26	77·880	2 024·880
17·5 ,, 22·5	20	−3·825	45	14·631	658·395
22·5 ,, 27·5	25	1·175	60	1·380	82·800
27·5 ,, 32·5	30	6·175	37	38·131	1 410·847
32·5 ,, 37·5	35	11·175	13	124·880	1 623·440
37·5 ,, 42·5	40	16·175	5	261·631	1 308·155
42·5 ,, 47·5	45	21·175	2	448·380	896·760
Total			200		10 298·849

Rent (dollars)	Class Mid-point X	Arbitrary Deviations in C.I. Units $(A = 25)$ x'	Frequency f	fx'	fx'^2
7·5 and under 12·5	10	−3	12	−36	108
12·5 ,, 17·5	15	−2	26	−52	104
17·5 ,, 22·5	20	−1	45	−45	45
22·5 ,, 27·5	25	0	60	0	0
27·5 ,, 32·5	30	1	37	37	37
32·5 ,, 37·5	35	2	13	26	52
37·5 ,, 42·5	40	3	5	15	45
42·5 ,, 47·5	45	4	2	8	32
Total			200	−47	423

Characteristics of the Standard Deviation

The mean and the standard deviation are fundamental measures in statistical theory. They play a key part in a special distribution of great importance known as the *normal distribution*. The normal distribution is a symmetrical bell-shaped distribution, and is completely determined by its mean and standard deviation. It will be discussed in detail in the following chapter.

Many actual distributions closely approximate the normal one. If we have a frequency distribution which is normally distributed and we lay off a distance equal to one standard deviation on both sides of the mean, the resulting range will contain 68·27 per cent of the items of the distribution, ie 68·27 per cent of the items will have values lying between the mean ± one standard deviation. Similarly, the range given by two standard deviations on both sides of the mean will contain 95·45 per cent of the items, and one given by three standard deviations will contain 99·73 per cent of the items. Although the above holds exactly only for normal distributions, it holds approximately for distributions which are moderately skewed away from the normal. Incidentally, in the normal distribution the quartile deviation is always 0·6745 of the standard deviation, and the mean deviation is 0·7979 of the standard deviation.

The standard deviation measures the absolute dispersion or variability of a distribution in terms of the original units, ie in the case of rents, in dollars. Thus in example 3.12 the absolute dispersion is 7·2 dollars, and approximately two-thirds of the rents will be included within the range $23·8 ± $7·2. The greater the amount of dispersion or variability in a frequency distribution, the greater the standard deviation, and the greater the absolute magnitude of the deviations of the values from their mean. This can be clearly seen from the properties of the standard deviation referred to in the preceding paragraph. The range given by one standard deviation marked off on both sides of the mean contains about two-thirds of the items. Hence the greater the standard deviation the greater will be the range required to include the middle two-thirds of the items.

Relative Dispersion

The standard deviation, being a measure of absolute dispersion, is expressed in the units in which the observations concerned have been made. This limits its use for comparative purposes in cases where we wish to compare the dispersion of two series of values, whose means are very different or which are expressed in different units. Suppose we are told that the weekly wages of males and females have the following properties:

$$\text{Male:} \quad \bar{X} = \$50 \qquad s = \$5$$

$$\text{Female:} \quad \bar{X} = \$40 \qquad s = \$4 \cdot 8$$

Male wages show greater dispersion or variability than female, but the general level of male wages is higher. In this case we may measure relative dispersion, by what is known as the *coefficient of variation*. It is defined by

$$V = \frac{s}{\bar{X}}$$

In our example,

$$\text{Male:} \quad V = \frac{5 \cdot 0}{50} = 0 \cdot 10, \text{ or } 10 \text{ per cent}$$

and

$$\text{Female:} \quad V = \frac{4 \cdot 8}{40} = 0 \cdot 12, \text{ or } 12 \text{ per cent.}$$

Accordingly, female wages show greater relative dispersion or variability than male. Similarly we may have two series expressed in different units. For example, the weights and heights of a group of persons:

$$\text{Weight:} \quad \bar{X} = 70 \text{ kg} \qquad s = 6 \text{ kg}$$

$$\text{Height:} \quad \bar{X} = 174 \text{ cm} \qquad s = 5 \text{ cm}$$

Is the variability in weight or height greater? This could only be answered by calculating V, which here is $8 \cdot 6$ per cent for weight and $2 \cdot 9$ per cent for height.

Standard Deviation Units

Sometimes we are interested in measuring how much above or below average a particular observation is. Suppose that a man's weight is 76 kg and his height is 181 cm. Is he relatively more above average in weight or height? If the data in the previous example apply, we can calculate for weight,

$$\frac{X - \bar{X}}{s} = \frac{76 - 70}{6} = 1 \text{ standard deviation above average}$$

for height,

$$\frac{X - \bar{X}}{s} = \frac{181 - 174}{5} = 1 \cdot 4 \text{ standard deviations above average.}$$

Clearly he is relatively taller. The formula $\dfrac{X - \bar{X}}{s}$, known as *standard measure* or *standardised value,* expresses the deviation of an observation from the mean in terms of standard deviation units, ie the extent to which X is above (or below) average in terms of the mean variability of the data. Standardised values play an important role in statistical analysis and will be again referred to later.

3.6 Measures of Skewness

We have already discussed the nature of skewness, and it was shown that positive skewness results in the mean being greater than the mode and negative skewness in the mean being less than the mode. Pearson has suggested a measure of skewness, known as the *Pearsonian measure of skewness:*

$$Sk_P = \frac{\bar{X} - Mo}{s}$$

or
$$Sk_P = \frac{3(\bar{X} - Med)}{s}$$

The standard deviation is included as the denominator, so that the degree of skewness is measured relative to the dispersion of the distribution. This measure, being a ratio, is a pure number and it varies between the limits ± 3. Values as large as ± 1 are quite unusual. It is positive for positive skewness, negative for negative skewness, and zero when the distribution is symmetrical.

Another measure of skewness is based on the quartiles. In a symmetrical distribution the third quartile is the same distance above the median as the first quartile is below it, ie

$$Q_3 - Md = Md - Q_1$$

If the distribution is positively skewed, the top 25 per cent of the values will tend to be further from the median than the bottom 25 per cent, ie Q_3 will be further from Md than Q_1 is from Md, and the reverse for negative skewness. Hence a possible measure is

$$Sk_Q = \frac{(Q_3 - Md) - (Md - Q_1)}{Q_3 - Q_1}$$

The denominator is in fact twice the quartile deviation, so that the degree of skewness is again measured relative to the dispersion of the distribution. This measure is called the *quartile measure of skewness,* and it varies between the limits of ± 1.

There is no relation between the magnitudes of Sk_P and Sk_Q. Sk_Q suffers from the defect that only the middle 50 per cent of the distribution is taken into account. It is possible to have Sk_P positive and Sk_Q negative. Both Sk_P and Sk_Q are empirical measures and are useful only for comparative purposes. More complicated analytical measures are available, but these will not be discussed here.

Example 3.13

Calculate a measure of skewness for the frequency distribution in Table 3.2 above.

$$Sk_P = \frac{\bar{X} - Mo}{s}$$

$$= \frac{23\cdot8 - 24\cdot4}{7\cdot2} = -\frac{0\cdot6}{7\cdot2}$$

$$= -0\cdot08$$

and

$$Sk_Q = \frac{(Q_3 - Md) - (Md - Q_1)}{Q_3 - Q_1}$$

$$= \frac{(28\cdot4 - 23\cdot9) - (23\cdot9 - 18\cdot8)}{28\cdot4 - 18\cdot8}$$

$$= -0\cdot06$$

Both measures indicate a very slight degree of negative skewness. Our distribution of 200 rents is very nearly symmetrical, as already indicated by the mean, median and mode which are $23·8, $23·9 and $24·4 (to one decimal point), respectively.

3.7 Description of Frequency Distributions

We have now discussed the methods by which we can describe an unorganised mass of data. First, we form it into a frequency distribution. We can then draw a histogram which will give us a clear picture of the general shape of the distribution. Secondly, we calculate measures of central value, dispersion and skewness, which will characterise the distribution.

If we have two distributions to compare, it is useful to draw frequency polygons of the relative frequencies on the same scale and superimpose them. This immediately enables us to pick out the salient similarities and differences between the two distributions. We can then compute the various characteristic measures of the two distributions. Given the mean, the standard deviation and a measure of skewness, we shall be able to describe the main features of the distributions. A more detailed description can be made with the aid of the mode, median and quartiles.

Example 3.14

We are given a frequency distribution of metropolitan rents as set out in Table 3.2 above, and another distribution of 100 tenanted houses in a rural urban area, as set out in the third column of the table below. Compare and discuss the two distributions.

Rent (dollars)	Number of Houses		Percentage Distribution	
	Metropolitan	Rural Urban	Metropolitan	Rural Urban
2·5 and under 7·5	0	11	0	11·0
7·5 ,, 12·5	12	30	6·0	30·0
12·5 ,, 17·5	26	32	13·0	32·0
17·5 ,, 22·5	45	19	22·5	19·0
22·5 ,, 27·5	60	5	30·0	5·0
27·5 ,, 32·5	37	2	18·5	2·0
32·5 ,, 37·5	13	1	6·5	1·0
37·5 ,, 42·5	5	0	2·5	0
42·5 ,, 47·5	2	0	1·0	0
Total	200	100	100·0	100·0

The relative distributions of the rents are shown in the right-hand side of the above table and the corresponding frequency polygons are shown in Fig 3.10.

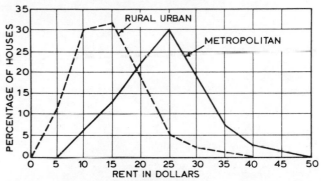

Fig 3.10 Weekly rent of tenanted houses in a metropolitan area and a rural urban area (percentage distribution)

Below are set out various characteristic measures of the two distributions:

Measure	Metropolitan	Rural Urban
$\bar{X}$	$23·8	$14·4
Md	$23·9	$13·9
Mo	$24·4	$13·2
Q_1	$18·8	$ 9·8
Q_3	$28·4	$18·0
s	$ 7·2	$ 6·1
V	30·2%	42·4%
Sk_P	−0·08	0·20
Sk_Q	−0·06	0

In comparison with metropolitan rents the distribution of which is very nearly symmetrical the distribution of rural urban rents appears slightly skewed to the right. The Pearsonian measure of skewness indicates a small degree of positive skewness, whereas the quartile measure suggests a symmetrical distribution. This apparent contradiction is due to the fact that the former measure takes the whole distribution into account; the latter concentrates on the middle of the distribution and ignores the tails, the influence of the positive tail with a small number of high rents thus being left out. The general level of rents in the urban centre is markedly lower than in the metropolitan area, as indicated clearly by all three measures of central tendency. Finally, although the metropolitan rents have a greater absolute dispersion, the variability relative to the general level of rents is greater in the rural urban district.

CHAPTER 4

PROBABILITY AND PROBABILITY DISTRIBUTIONS

4.1 Statistical Methods and Probability

So far we have dealt with the various techniques and measures by which a collection of data can be described and summarised. The next step is to introduce some elementary techniques of statistical analysis which will enable us to make valid inferences from the particular to the general. Thus, often we have a group of observations of a particular variable which covers only a fraction of all possible cases, and on the basis of this information we wish to infer something about the characteristics of the larger group from which our sample of data had been drawn. The theory of statistics provides a scientific basis for making such judgments, and enables us to test hypotheses about the nature of the larger groups from which a particular set of data had presumably been obtained. The techniques employed in such analysis will be dealt with in subsequent chapters.

Before embarking on this task, however, we need to introduce some basic ideas relating to probability and its measurement. Such ideas derive from a special branch of statistical methods known as the *theory of probability*. In general, the theory of probability provides a foundation for the scientific analysis of problems involving uncertainty, and its applications enable us to obtain a degree of predictability from uncertain states of nature. It has many specialised applications in economics and commerce, but these will not be considered here.

Although the term 'probability' has a broad meaning with which we are all familiar, its definition and interpretation raise some difficulties when the term is to be defined strictly. As we shall see below, probability statements can be derived both on an objective and subjective basis, experimentally as well as by *a priori* reasoning. Here we shall approach the problem by first introducing some basic probability concepts, and then by defining the relations between these concepts by means of statements known as the axioms of the theory of probability; these axioms provide the mathematical foundations of probability. With the use of these axioms we then discuss the basic rules for the algebraic manipulation of probabilities and show their applications. In the remaining sections of this chapter, the concepts and theorems of probability theory are used to develop the notion of a probability distribution which lies at the basis of the theory of statistical inference.

4.2 Sample Spaces and Events

Uncertainty arises when any given situation has more than one possible outcome. Thus it may, or may not, rain later today and we shall never be completely certain whether to take an umbrella or not. Nevertheless, we may wish to study uncertain events with a view to predicting which of the outcomes appears to be the most likely. The basis for such predictions stems from the empirical fact that when observations of seemingly haphazard phenomena are repeated a very large number of times it is possible to discern a regularity in the occurrence of particular outcomes. Empirical phenomena which display such regularity are often referred to as *random* phenomena.

In studying the behaviour of random phenomena, statisticians often perform experiments, real or conceptual. Thus the toss of a coin, whether actually performed or not, is a statistical or random experiment in so far as it gives rise to two possible outcomes 'heads' and 'tails', and the toss may be regarded as the first in a long sequence of repetitions of the experiment; each such repetition is called a *trial* of the experiment. Thus, if the basic experiment of flipping a coin is repeated, say, twice, we speak of the two tosses as two repeated trials.

Sample Spaces

Consider an experiment in which an ordinary six-sided die is rolled once. If we are interested in the face value of any single toss, then there are six possible outcomes, of which one must occur. In general, if we have a collection of distinct objects, whether such objects are concrete or abstract objects (such as numbers and letters) we call such a collection a *set*. Henceforth, we shall symbolize a set by { }. Evidently, the outcomes of our die experiment form a set of all possible outcomes. Indicating this by the symbol S, we may write

$$S = \{1, 2, 3, 4, 5, 6\}$$

As can be seen, there are six *elements* or *members* of this set, each corresponding exactly to one possible outcome. A set consisting of elements representing all possible outcomes of an experiment is called a *sample space*. Elements of sets which are sample spaces are referred to as *sample points*. If the number of sample points in a sample space S is finite, then S is a *finite sample space*. For the present, we confine our attention to finite sample spaces.

If we perform a particular random experiment, it is frequently possible to describe the sample space associated with the experiment in more than one way. To illustrate this, suppose that a die with face values 1 to 6 has three sides painted black and three sides painted red. As long as we are interested in the number of spots that may appear on a single trial, the sample space is described by the set $S = \{1, 2, 3, 4, 5, 6\}$. But if we are only interested in the occurrence of 'black' (B) or 'red' (R), the appropriate sample space may be described as $S = \{B, R\}$. Suppose further that in yet another trial of the experiment our concern is with the occurrence or non-occurrence of 'red'. It is then natural to assign the value of 1 to the occurrence of 'red' and the value of 0 to occurrence of 'not-red' ie, 'black'. The sample space describing the experiment may thus be written as $S = \{0, 1\}$. We observe that in each case the definition of a sample space is satisfied, since to each sample point there corresponds only one identifiable possible outcome. Although in many instances sample spaces may be described either by letters or by numbers, we shall see below that numerical descriptions of sample spaces offer some very important advantages.

Consider next an experiment consisting of two repeated trials, eg two successive rolls of the 'black and red' die. In this case, the joint outcomes of the two trials form the sample space

$$S = \{(B, B), (B, R), (R, B), (R, R)\}$$

We note that each of the four possible sample points consists of the outcomes of the first and the second roll of our two-colour die. Hence, the order of the letters B and R is of importance in distinguishing between the two middle elements (B, R) and (R, B). The round brackets ( ) in this case indicate *ordered pairs*, ie pairs of objects whose ordering within the brackets is of importance. Ordered arrays of n objects are called *n-tuples*, and are likewise indicated by round brackets. On the other hand, we should note that the order in which the four elements of the above set are listed within the braces { } is of no importance, ie the order of listing the elements of a set is immaterial. Also, in all our examples each element is listed only once.

A comment may now be in order about the term 'sample space'. In a mathematical sense, any set consisting of a well-defined range of objects, such as the possible outcomes of a specified experiment, may be called a space. The significance of the word 'sample' may become clearer further below; here it suffices to note that a sample space lists all the possible observations, or 'samples', that may be obtained in a given experiment. For some purposes, and in relatively simple cases, it is helpful to visualise sample spaces geometrically. For instance, the possible outcomes generated by the experiment of rolling a six-sided die once may be plotted as points on a line representing a one-dimensional space. Similarly, the set $S = \{(B, B), (B, R), (R, B), (R, R)\}$ may be represented as a two-dimensional sample space, as shown in Fig 4.1(b):

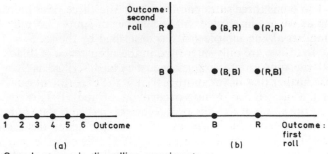

Fig 4.1 Sample spaces in die-rolling experiments

Events

We have seen that a set of all possible outcomes of an experiment is called a sample space. In general, however, we are only interested in those outcomes that satisfy some specified property, eg that the number rolled on an ordinary die is a 6, or that it is an even number. Given a sample space S, the outcomes so specified are referred to as *events*.

Events may be classified as *simple events* and *compound events*. A simple event is an event corresponding to a single sample point in a given sample space S. Suppose, for instance, that we define event A as the event of rolling a 6 on an ordinary die. This may be written as $A = \{6\}$. Since A is a set consisting of an element which is also an element of another set $S = \{1, 2, 3, 4, 5, 6\}$, A is said to be a *subset* of S. In general, every event defined in the sample space S will be a subset of S.

Less formally, a simple event may be defined as an event which cannot be decomposed any further. Suppose, for example, that the 'black and red' die in our earlier example is rolled twice and event D is defined as the event 'red occurs on the first and on the second roll', ie $D = \{(R, R)\}$. Clearly, since the outcomes of the first and second roll must be considered jointly, D is an event which cannot be subdivided further into other events, and it is therefore a simple event.

Compound events are events which can be formed as a combination of simple events. Let C be the event that the number rolled on an ordinary die is an even number. Then $C = \{2, 4, 6\}$, and C is a compound event in the sample space $S = \{1, 2, 3, 4, 5, 6\}$. The event C is said to occur if a 2, or a 4, or a 6 is obtained on any single roll of the die.

If an event is so defined that it must occur on every trial, it is called the *certain event*, eg obtaining a number between 1 and 6 inclusive in tossing an ordinary die. Evidently, the statement 'event E occurs on every trial' can only be true if E is the sample space S itself; hence, the certain event is generally denoted by the letter S. If we make the statement 'event E cannot occur on any trial', the statement implies that E cannot be defined in terms of any of the elements of the sample space S. In this case, event E contains no sample points. An event which is the null or empty set is called the *impossible event*, and is usually denoted by the symbol ϕ.

Suppose an event E is defined in the sample space S. Then the sample points included in S fall into two groups: those belonging to E and those not belonging to E. The latter form a set corresponding to an event which is called the *complement* of the event E in the sample space S. The complement of E is often written as $\bar{E}$, or $\tilde{E}$, or 'not-E'; here we shall write $\bar{E}$. A convenient way of showing complementary events graphically is with the use of an expository device known as a Venn diagram, which later we shall find useful in discussing relations between two or more events. The main advantage of Venn diagrams is that we may represent more or less complex events as areas. Thus, in Fig 4.2, all the sample points in S may be thought of as being included in the rectangular area S. Those belonging to E are enclosed within the circular area E, and those not belonging to E form the complement of E, ie $\bar{E}$. As an illustration of the notion of the complement, if C is the event of obtaining an even number on a single roll of a die, then the complement of C is the event that an even number does not occur, ie $\bar{C} = \{1, 3, 5\}$.

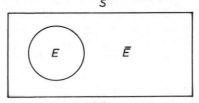

Fig 4.2 Venn diagram of complement of E

Example 4.1

Consider an experiment consisting of rolling a six-sided die and then tossing a coin. Let H (heads) $= 0$ and T (tails) $= 1$. List the possible outcomes of the experiment.

The possible outcomes can be conveniently enumerated with the aid of a graphical device known as a *tree diagram*:

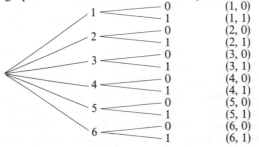

Following the uppermost branch of the diagram, we obtain the sample point (1, 0), and similarly for the remaining branches. There are thus twelve sample points (simple events) in the sample space associated with the experiment.

Let now E be the event 'even number of spots and heads'. This may be written as

$$E = \{(2, 0), (4, 0), 6, 0)\}$$

and E is therefore a compound event.

4.3 Probability of an Event

We may introduce the concept of probability by the general statement that probabilities are assignments of numerical values to possible outcomes of random experiments. For the present we shall consider only random experiments with a finite number of possible outcomes, or experiments consisting of an unending sequence of outcomes, eg repeated tosses of a coin. Sample spaces having these characteristics are said to be *discrete*. Given a discrete sample space, the numerical values assigned as probabilities must satisfy two mathematical requirements. First, to every event E in the sample space S there corresponds exactly one real number which is called the probability of the event E, and may be written as $P(E)$. A relation which pairs each element of a set of objects, in our case events, with exactly one real number is called a function. Thus, the symbol P in $P(E)$ denotes a function rule according to which probability values are assigned to each and every event in S. The second requirement is that probability assignments satisfy three *axioms*, or *postulates*, of the theory of probability:

Axiom 1 $0 \leqslant P(E) \leqslant 1$ for every event E

Axiom 2 $P(S) = 1$ for the certain event S

Axiom 3 $P(E_1 \text{ or } E_2) = P(E_1) + P(E_2)$ for any mutually exclusive events E_1 and E_2

A mathematical relation which satisfies these requirements is often referred to as a *probability function*. In this section we discuss the probability function by reference to the various ways of interpreting probabilities. Axiom 3, and the theorems that may be deduced from it, will be further considered in the following section.

The first axiom states that numerical values assigned as probabilities are real, non-negative numbers not exceeding unity. The second axiom requires that the certain event, ie an event whose occurrence is inevitable on any single trial, is assigned a probability value of one. If an event cannot occur on any trial, it is called the impossible event; with the use of the axioms of probability a theorem can be established which states that the probability associated with the impossible event is zero, ie $P(\phi) = 0$. Axiom 3 gives the basic rule of addition of probabilities: if the events E_1 and E_2 are so defined that the occurrence of one precludes the occurrence of the other on any single trial, then the probability of either E_1 or E_2 occurring is given by the sum of their respective probabilities.

The axioms of probability define the properties of probabilities in abstract mathematical terms. However, the axioms themselves do not tell us how probabilities might be assigned in particular applications of probability theory to the study of real-world phenomena. As we have already remarked, several different conceptual approaches to probability measurement are possible, and we now discuss the *a priori*, the *relative frequency*, and the *subjective* interpretations of probability. The usefulness of the axiomatic approach derives from the fact that it provides us with a set of operational rules applicable to all methods of probability measurement.

A Priori Probability

In the study of certain types of random phenomena, it is often possible to agree on the possible outcomes, ie sample spaces of particular experiments, and the experiments themselves can be assumed to take place under postulated conditions. Thus, often we find it helpful to illustrate the principles of probability theory by considering examples of experiments involving perfectly balanced coins or dice, ie coins or dice whose physical properties are assumed to be such that no particular side is favoured to occur more often than the others. In other instances, it may be of interest to study the various ways in which different combinations of objects can be selected at random from larger groups of objects. In such cases, it is possible to determine probabilities associated with various events on the basis of logical reasoning and without reference to experimental data. Probabilities assigned in this manner are referred to as *a priori* probabilities.

The *a priori* concept of probability is based on the notion of an *equiprobable event*. Suppose a given sample space consists of n sample points (simple events), and it may reasonably be supposed that one simple event is just as likely to occur as any other simple event. It is then natural to assign the ratio $1/n$ as a measure of probability associated with each simple event. Suppose event E is a compound event defined in terms of the elements of the sample space S. Let $n(E)$ represent the number of elements in event E, and $n(S)$ the number of elements in the entire sample space S. Then, if the possible outcomes of the experiment are equiprobable events, the ratio

$$P(E) = \frac{n(E)}{n(S)}$$

measures the probability of the event E, since each of the $n(E)$ simple events can be assigned an equal probability weight $1/n(S)$. Thus, suppose that a six-sided die is rolled. If it is a balanced die, each of the six possible outcomes can be regarded as an equiprobable event, and we have

$$P(\{1\}) = P(\{2\}) = \ldots P(\{6\}) = \frac{1}{6}$$

If an event F is defined as 'obtaining a number of spots greater than 4', we have $n(F) = 2$, $n(S) = 6$, and hence $P(F) = \frac{2}{6}$, ie the probability associated with the event F is $2/6$ since there are two possible ways of obtaining a number greater than 4, and each of these can be assigned an equal measure of probability. We note that if an event, say, G is certain to occur, $n(G) = n(S)$, and $P(G) = 1$. Hence, probability values assigned by the *a priori* method are non-negative numbers not exceeding unity, and the ratio $n(E)/n(S)$ has the required properties of a probability function.

Example 4.2

In example 4.1, what is the probability of the event 'even number of spots and heads'?

There are twelve simple events in the experiment, each equally likely to occur with unbiased die and coin; thus $n(S) = 12$. There are three simple events in the compound event E 'even number of spots and heads', and so $n(E) = 3$. Hence, the required probability is $3/12$.

As another illustration, suppose an urn contains ten numbered balls, of which three are white and seven are black. If a ball is drawn at random from the urn, what is the probability that it is white?

Because the balls are distinguishable by number as well as by colour, the sample space consists of ten distinct sample points. These are equally likely, and hence $1/n(S) = 1/10$. Denoting by G the event of selecting a white ball, we have $n(G) = 3$. Thus

$$P(G) = \frac{3}{10}$$

Relative Frequency Approach

In the *a priori* definition of probability, equiprobable events are assigned equal probabilities. But this is nothing more than a tautological, or circular, definition of probability: one probability concept is defined in terms of another probability concept. More important, in many practical situations it is not feasible to establish an exhaustive set of possible outcomes, nor is it possible to assume that the outcomes of an experiment are all equally likely. In these circumstances we have little choice but to estimate probabilities by reference to empirical data. The general method for obtaining such estimates is the relative frequency method of measuring probabilities.

Consider a situation in which an experimental outcome can be observed over an indefinitely long sequence of repeated trials performed under uniform experimental conditions, eg tosses of a coin. Let N represent the number of trials observed, and let the symbol N_E denote the number of occurrences of an experimental outcome, eg heads, in the N trials. The ratio $\frac{N_E}{N}$ is called the *relative frequency* of the event E. Suppose that as the number of trials N is increased indefinitely, the observed frequency ratio $\frac{N_E}{N}$ fluctuates around or approaches some fixed value. This value is the mathematical limit of the relative frequency ratio, and measures the proportion of times the event E can be expected to occur 'in the long run'. The probability of occurrence of the event E may then be defined as the limit of its relative frequency as the number of trials N tends to infinity. The applicability of this definition, however, is limited, since observations of most random phenomena can only be made for a finite number of trials, and the limit of relative frequency cannot be established even if we could be assured that it exists. It would then seem reasonable that we accept the ratio $\frac{N_E}{N}$ as the probability of E occuring, provided that the number of trials N is large enough. Thus, accepting $\frac{N_E}{N}$ as an *estimate* of the unknown true probability of E, we may write

$$P(E) = \frac{N_E}{N}$$

We observe that in this definition of probability if the event E cannot occur, its frequency of occurrence must be zero. If it occurs on every trial, then $N_E = N$, and the probabilities assigned by this method must therefore fall within the range 0 to 1 inclusive.

The experimental or frequency concept of probability rests on a fundamental principle of the theory of probability known as the *law of large numbers*. Briefly, this principle states that if the number of repeated trials N is large enough we can be virtually certain that the observed relative frequency of an experimental outcome E will not differ from its theoretical long-run frequency, which we accept as the true probability of E occurring, by more than some arbitrarily chosen small amount. In other words, the principle of large numbers tells us that even though probabilities derived by the frequency method are only approximations of the true probabilities, these approximations will be the more accurate the larger the number of trials N. Thus, while we would not have much faith in any estimates of probabilities based on, say, 10 tosses of a coin, an experiment consisting of 1000 such tosses would greatly increase our confidence that the result provides a reasonable approximation of the underlying probabilities.

Example 4.3

A manufacturer of tiles produces a certain standard type of tile in three colours: blue, pink and white. An examination of his records shows that of 800 orders received over the past six months, 203 were orders of blue tiles, 40 of pink tiles, and 557 of white tiles. What probability might be assigned to the event that a randomly received order will be an order of white tiles?

If we can regard the receipt of orders as a repetitive process consisting of 800 independent trials, we may reasonably assign the respective frequencies of occurrence as probabilities. Hence, we estimate the required probability as $557/800 \simeq 0.7$.

Subjective Probabilities

We have now dealt with the *a priori* and relative frequency concepts of probability. In the course of this discussion, we have noted that if certain experimental conditions can be assumed to hold, probability assignments can be made on the basis of prior logical reasoning. When no logical basis for assigning probabilities exists, we may attempt to estimate probabilities from observed frequencies of occurrence. Although at first sight these two approaches may appear to be rather different, they have one essential feature in common: in both cases probabilities are determined by reference to possible outcomes of statistical experiments, ie sequences of trials which are repeated, or can be regarded as being repeatable, under uniform conditions. In some instances we can infer the results of the repetitive process from prior knowledge of the conditions under which actual experiments would take place, eg when we are drawing lottery tickets from an urn containing, say, 5000 tickets, tossing perfectly balanced coins or dice, etc. In other instances, repeated observations are an indispensable part of the process by which relevant probability values are established, as in the experiments of tossing biased coins, recording births and deaths in a population, or taking measurements of various phenomena, such as rainfall, temperatures, or industrial accidents.

In many practical applications, particularly those relating to economic and business decision-making under uncertainty, the repetitive process which characterises the so called 'objective' approach to probability is absent. The events of interest to the decision-maker are often events which can occur only once or which can only be repeated under conditions so dissimilar that they should be regarded as single episodic events. If the theory of probability is to play a useful role in such applications, the definition of probability needs to be widened so as to permit assignments of *subjective* probabilities for which frequency data are not available. By subjective probabilities we mean probabilities which are determined, to varying degrees, by personal judgment. In interpreting subjective probabilities, two main points need to be borne in mind. First, since subjective-probability statements cannot be independent of the observer, different persons may attach different probabilities to the same event. This does not mean, however, that in the subjective approach probability values can be assigned arbitrarily. We would expect that two rational decision-makers equipped with the same body of data and having similar experience would form similar judgments, and assign roughly the same probabilities. Second, being based on personal judgment, subjective-probability assignments are not independent of the body of evidence that may be available to the decision-maker at any one time. Thus we would expect a rational individual to alter his probability assignment if more complete information had come to light in the course of the decision-making process.

With these points in mind, we may simply view subjective probabilities as assignments of numerical values measuring an individual's degree of confidence in the occurrence of particular events, or in the truth of particular propositions, after full account had been taken of all the relevant information. Thus, in a typical example, an entrepreneur may contemplate undertaking some new risky venture whose chances of being successful or unsuccessful he rates equally: he may then assign an equal probability of one-half to each of the possible outcomes. We may suppose next that additional information has become available so that success of the venture now appears twice as likely as failure. The event 'success' may then be allotted a probability weight of 2/3, and the event 'failure' a weight of 1/3, the assignment of the new weights reflecting the entrepreneur's increased confidence in the viability of the project.

The concept of subjective probability enables us to formulate more or less complex criteria for rational action in the face of uncertainty, and lends itself to many applications in the fields of business and economics. We shall not deal with such specialised applications here, although we shall have occasion to refer to subjective probabilities again when in a later section we discuss the so-called Bayes' rule of probability.

Example 4.4

In a television interview, an economist states that he regards 'no change' and 'improvement' in economic conditions over the next quarter as being equally likely; however, he also rates 'improvement' as being twice as likely as 'deterioration'. What sample space is implied by his statement? What probability is associated with each of the sample points?

The statement suggests that the sample space is the set

$$S = \{\text{no change, improvement, deterioration}\}$$

We observe that the occurrence of any one of these three simple events precludes the occurrence of the remaining two; as we shall see in the following section, the probabilities must in this case sum to unity. Since

$$P(\{\text{no change}\}) = P(\{\text{improvement}\}) = 2P(\{\text{deterioration}\})$$

we can readily see that this condition is satisfied when

$$P(\{\text{no change}\}) = P(\{\text{improvement}\}) = 2/5$$

and $$P(\{\text{deterioration}\}) = 1/5$$

The probabilities assigned in this case represent measures of the confidence of the economist that each of the conditions predicted will occur, and must therefore be interpreted as subjective probabilities.

4.4 Addition of Probabilities

Most events of interest in practical situations are compound events requiring enumeration of a large number of sample points. It is often more convenient, and mathematically simpler, to define such more-complex events in terms of other simpler events, and then evaluate the required probabilities by means of simple algebraic operations. In this and in the following section we discuss the basic operations of addition and multiplication of probabilities.

Suppose E_1 and E_2 are any two events in a sample space S. The *union* of the events E_1 and E_2 is defined as the event which consists of those elements of S that belong either to E_1, or to E_2, or to both E_1 and E_2. In set-theoretic notation, this is written as $E_1 \cup E_2$, but here we shall adopt a convention followed in elementary treatment of probability and write the union of two events E_1 and E_2 as 'E_1 or E_2'. For the union of more than two events, we have 'E_1 or E_2 or ... or E_n'.

An *intersection* or *product* of two events E_1 and E_2 (written in set theory as $E_1 \cap E_2$) is the event which consists of elements belonging to *both* E_1 and E_2. Here we shall indicate the intersection of two events E_1 and E_2 by the multiplicative notation $E_1 E_2$. For more than two events, we shall write $E_1 E_2 \ldots E_n$.

As an illustration, let the sample space be $S = \{1, 2, 3, 4, 5, 6\}$, and let $E_1 = \{2, 4, 6\}$ (even number), and $E_2 = \{5, 6\}$ (number greater than 4). Then the union of E_1 and E_2 is written as E_1 or $E_2 = \{2, 4, 5, 6\}$, and the intersection is $E_1 E_2 = \{6\}$.

As mentioned in the previous section, two events are said to be *mutually exclusive* or *disjoint* if the occurrence of one precludes the occurrence of the other. More formally, the events E_1 and E_2 are mutually exclusive if

$$E_1 E_2 = \phi$$

ie if their intersection contains no elements (is the empty set ϕ). In a Venn diagram, two mutually exclusive events may be represented as two non-intersecting circles, as shown in Fig 4.3(a). If two events E_1 and E_2 are not mutually exclusive, then E_1 and E_2 overlap, having in common the sample points included in $E_1 E_2$; this is illustrated in Fig 4.3(b). In the general case of n events, the n events are mutually exclusive if no two events have any points in common. For example, consider the three events $E = \{2, 4, 6\}$, $F = \{5, 6\}$, and $G = \{1, 3, 5\}$ in the sample space $S = \{1, 2, 3, 4, 5, 6\}$. Here the events E and G are mutually exclusive, since there are no points that belong to both E and G. However, we also have $EF = \{6\}$ and $FG = \{5\}$, and hence the three events E, F and G are not mutually exclusive.

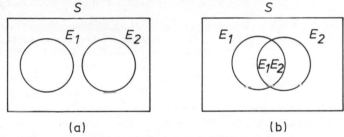

(a)   (b)

Fig 4.3 Venn diagrams of disjoint and non-disjoint events

With this background, let us now consider the question of evaluating probabilities associated with the union of two or more events. By the additive property of probability postulated by the third axiom of probability, if E_1 and E_2 are mutually exclusive events, then

$$P(E_1 \text{ or } E_2) = P(E_1) + P(E_2)$$

This additive law holds generally for any number of events. Thus, given n mutually exclusive events $E_1, E_2, \ldots, E_n$,

$$P(E_1 \text{ or } E_2 \text{ or } \ldots \text{ or } E_n) = P(E_1) + P(E_2) + \ldots + P(E_n)$$

We interpret this by saying that the probability of any one of n mutually exclusive events occurring is equal to the sum of their separate probabilities. Suppose further that events $E_1, E_2 \ldots, E_n$ constitute a set of mutually exclusive events which is also an exhaustive set, ie it covers the entire sample space. Then the events $E_1, E_2, \ldots, E_n$ are said to form a *partition* of the sample space S. By definition, the union of events which are mutually exclusive and exhaustive is the certain event S. Hence, for any partition of S,

$$P(E_1) + P(E_2) + \ldots + P(E_n) = P(S) = 1$$

This result is frequently used in practice to check that the probabilities assigned to an exhaustive set of mutually exclusive events correctly sum to unity. A special case of this rule arises when a sample space is partitioned into an event E and its complement $\bar{E}$ (see p 73 above). Then

$$P(E) + P(\bar{E}) = 1$$

and
$$P(\bar{E}) = 1 - P(E)$$

ie the probability that the event E does *not* occur is equal to one minus the probability that E occurs. Frequent use will be made of these rules in our subsequent discussion.

Example 4.5

If an unbiased coin is tossed twice, what is the probability of obtaining exactly one head?

The event 'exactly one head' occurs if 'heads' is obtained on the first toss and 'tails' on the second, or 'tails' is obtained on the first toss and 'heads' on the second. Hence the required event is the union of the simple events {HT} and {TH} and

$$P(\text{HT or TH}) = P(\text{HT}) + P(\text{TH}) = 1/4 + 1/4 = 1/2$$

To derive the addition rule for two events which are not mutually exclusive, consider the Venn diagram of Fig 4.4. In the diagram, the event that E_1 and E_2 both occur is represented by the sample points lying within the intersection $E_1 E_2$; let there be $n(E_1 E_2)$ such points. Similarly, we may write the event 'E_1 but not E_2' as $E_1 \bar{E}_2$, and the event 'E_2 but not E_1' as $\bar{E}_1 E_2$; let the events $E_1 \bar{E}_2$ and $\bar{E}_1 E_2$ contain $n(E_1 \bar{E}_2)$ and $n(\bar{E}_1 E_2)$ sample points, respectively. In the diagram, these three cross-partitions of the events E_1 and E_2 are represented by the areas labelled a, b and c, respectively. Consider now the union of the events E_1 and E_2, ie the event 'E_1 or E_2'. In this case, the word 'or' must be interpreted in the *inclusive* sense: either E_1, or E_2, or both.

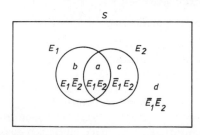

Fig 4.4 Venn diagram of two intersecting sets

It is fairly apparent from the diagram that the number of sample points representing the event 'E_1 or E_2' is given by the relation

$$n(E_1 \text{ or } E_2) = n(E_1 \bar{E}_2) + n(E_1 E_2) + n(\bar{E}_1 E_2)$$

Dividing through by $n(S)$, the number of sample points in the entire sample space S, we obtain

$$\frac{n(E_1 \text{ or } E_2)}{n(S)} = \frac{n(E_1 \bar{E}_2)}{n(S)} + \frac{n(E_1 E_2)}{n(S)} + \frac{n(\bar{E}_1 E_2)}{n(S)}$$

and identifying the resulting ratios as probabilities, we may write

$$P(E_1 \text{ or } E_2) = P(E_1 \bar{E}_2) + P(E_1 E_2) + P(\bar{E}_1 E_2)$$

From inspection of Fig 4.4 it can also be readily seen that

$$P(E_1) = P(E_1 \bar{E}_2) + P(E_1 E_2)$$

and
$$P(E_2) = P(\bar{E}_1 E_2) + P(E_1 E_2)$$

Adding these two equations together and arranging the terms gives

$$P(E_1 \bar{E}_2) + P(E_1 E_2) + P(\bar{E}_1 E_2) = P(E_1) + P(E_2) - P(E_1 E_2)$$

from which it follows directly that

$$P(E_1 \text{ or } E_2) = P(E_1) + P(E_2) - P(E_1 E_2)$$

The last equation gives the *general addition rule* for any two events which are not mutually exclusive. In this formula, the probability element $P(E_1 E_2)$ is included in the term $P(E_1)$ and then once again in the term $P(E_2)$, and hence must be subtracted to avoid double counting.

In Fig 4.4, the union of E_1 and E_2 may be looked upon as being represented by the combined arca a, b and c. The residual area, marked in the diagram as d, then represents the event 'neither E_1 nor E_2' (or 'not-E_1 and not-E_2') which may be written as $\bar{E}_1 \bar{E}_2$. By the theorem of complementary events

$$P(\bar{E}_1 \bar{E}_2) = 1 - P(E_1 \text{ or } E_2)$$

Example 4.6

Of every 100 persons entering a newsagency, 30 persons buy newspaper A, 50 persons buy newspaper B, and 20 persons buy both, on the average. What is the probability of a randomly selected person buying
(a) newspaper A, but not newspaper B;
(b) at least one of the two newspapers;
(c) neither of the two newspapers?

(a) Denote by A the event of buying newspaper A, and by B the event of buying newspaper B. From given information,

$$n(A) = 30, n(B) = 50, \text{ and } n(AB) = 20$$

Referring to Fig 4.4, we find the number of sample points in the event $A\bar{B}$ (A but not B) as

$$n(A\bar{B}) = n(A) - n(AB) = 30 - 20 = 10$$

Hence, the probability of buying newspaper A, but not newspaper B, is

$$P(A\bar{B}) = 10/100 = 1/10$$

(b) The event 'at least one of the two newspapers' is the event 'either A, or B, or both', ie the union of the events A and B. By the addition rule

$$P(A \text{ or } B) = P(A) + P(B) - P(AB)$$
$$= 30/100 + 50/100 - 20/100$$
$$= 3/5$$

Alternatively, let us first compute the probability of the event 'newspaper B, but not newspaper A'. We have

$$n(\bar{A}B) = n(B) - n(AB) = 50 - 20 = 30,$$

and hence $\quad P(\bar{A}B) = 3/10$

Then $\qquad P(A \text{ or } B) = P(A\bar{B}) + P(AB) + P(\bar{A}B)$
$$= 1/10 + 2/10 + 3/10$$
$$= 3/5$$

which agrees with the result obtained by the addition rule.

(c) Writing the required event as $\bar{A}\bar{B}$, we have

$$P(\bar{A}\bar{B}) = 1 - P(A \text{ or } B)$$
$$= 2/5$$

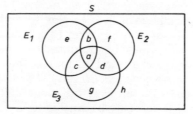

Fig 4.5 Venn diagram of three intersecting sets

As an illustration of how the addition rule can be extended to more than two events, let us consider the three events E_1, E_2 and E_3 depicted in the Venn diagram of Fig 4.5. The sample space S is now subdivided into eight non-overlapping regions a to h. The area marked a corresponds to the event $E_1 E_2 E_3$, ie the event that E_1, E_2 and E_3 occur jointly, the area b to the event $E_1 E_2 \bar{E}_3$, ie that E_1 and E_2 both occur, but not E_3, etc. By applying a method analogous to that for two events, we may derive the addition formula

$$P(E_1 \text{ or } E_2 \text{ or } E_3) = P(E_1) + P(E_2) + P(E_3)$$
$$- P(E_1 E_2) - P(E_1 E_3) - P(E_2 E_3)$$
$$+ P(E_1 E_2 E_3)$$

The validity of this formula can be readily checked by reference to Fig 4.5. As there are now three possible two-way intersections E_1E_2, E_1E_3 and E_2E_3, their respective probabilities must be subtracted from the sum of the first three terms in the addition formula to avoid double counting. Because the probability element $P(E_1E_2E_3)$ is first counted three times, and then subtracted three times, it must be included as a separate term.

Example 4.7

A potential home purchaser estimates that 70 per cent of houses currently offered for sale are of the desired size, 30 per cent are in preferred locations, and 20 per cent are in a price range which he can afford. He also estimates that 25 per cent of the houses are suitable with respect to size and location, 15 per cent are suitable with respect to size and price, and 5 per cent are suitable with respect to location and price. Only 1 per cent of the houses meet all the three desired characteristics. How should be estimate the probability of finding a house which meets *at least one* of the desired characteristics?

Let us use the following notation to represent the relevant events:

C_1: size suitable C_2: location suitable C_3: price suitable

Then, from the information given, we may write:

$$P(C_1) = 0.70 \qquad P(C_2) = 0.30 \qquad P(C_3) = 0.20$$

$$P(C_1C_2) = 0.25 \qquad P(C_1C_3) = 0.15 \qquad P(C_2C_3) = 0.05$$

$$P(C_1C_2C_3) = 0.01$$

The statement 'at least one of the desired characteristics' must be interpreted as meaning that exactly one, or exactly two, or exactly three of the purchaser's requirements with respect to size, location and price are met. In Fig 4.5 above, this compound event is shown as the combined area a to g, which represents the union of the events C_1, C_2 and C_3. The probability which we are seeking, therefore, is $P(C_1$ or C_2 or $C)$. Evaluating this probability by the addition rule, we find

$$P(C_1 \text{ or } C_2 \text{ or } C_3) = 0.70 + 0.30 + 0.20$$
$$- 0.25 - 0.15 - 0.05$$
$$+ 0.01$$
$$= 0.76$$

4.5 Multiplication of Probabilities

In probability problems, it is frequently necessary to consider probabilities associated with the joint occurrence of two or more specified outcomes. For instance, in game-of-chance experiments, we may be concerned with calculating the probability of observing a particular sequence of outcomes in n trials of the experiment, eg obtaining a sequence of five heads in five tosses of a coin, or getting two aces and a king in three successive draws of a card from a well-shuffled deck. The probability of the joint occurrence (intersection) of a number of events is referred to as the *joint probability*. Before explaining how the probability of the intersection of two or more events can be ascertained from information relating to the probabilities of the constituent events, we need to introduce an important new concept, the concept of *conditional probability*.

Conditional Probability

In many probability situations in which the possible experimental outcomes are known it is often the case that additional information becomes available to the investigator after the experiment had begun. If this new information restricts the possible outcomes of the experiment to some segment of the original sample space S, we refer to the probabilities defined in the reduced sample space as conditional probabilities.

Let us illustrate with a simple example. Suppose we are concerned with the probability of obtaining a number greater than 3 in a single roll of a balanced die. By the *a priori* principle of probability, the probability value assigned to this event is 1/2. Suppose, however, that a balanced die has actually been rolled by someone else, and we are told that the outcome is an even number. How should we revise the probability that a number greater than 3 has been rolled? Evidently, the effect of the new information is that the sample space to be considered is now restricted to the set of even numbers $\{2, 4, 6\}$. In this reduced sample space the event 'number greater than 3' can occur in two out of three possible ways, ie if either a 4 or a 6 is rolled. Hence, given the additional experimental information, we revise our assessment of the probability from 1/2 to 2/3.

More generally, if we have two events E_1 and E_2, of which E_1 is known to have occurred, we define the conditional probability $P(E_2|E_1)$, ie the probability of E_2, given E_1, by the equation

$$P(E_2|E_1) = \frac{P(E_1 E_2)}{P(E_1)} \quad \text{for } P(E_1) \neq 0$$

To clarify the meaning of this equation, let us consider again the Venn diagram shown in Fig 4.3(b) on p 81 above. Because E_1 is known to have occurred, the outcome of the experiment must correspond to one of the $n(E_1)$ sample points included in the circular area E_1. But event E_2 clearly cannot occur unless the outcome is also one of the $n(E_1 E_2)$ sample points included in the overlapping region $E_1 E_2$. Hence, from our earlier definition of probability, we may calculate the probability of E_2 occurring, given that E_1 has occurred, as the ratio $n(E_1 E_2)/n(E_1)$. If we next divide the numerator and denominator of this ratio by $n(S)$, the total number of sample points in S, we obtain the result $P(E_1E_2)/P(E_1)$. By similar reasoning, the probability of E_1, given E_2, is defined as

$$P(E_1|E_2) = \frac{P(E_1E_2)}{P(E_2)} \quad \text{for } P(E_2) \neq 0$$

If E_1 and E_2 are so defined that they are equal or equivalent events, ie E_2 contains exactly the same elements as E_1, and conversely, then $n(E_1E_2) = n(E_1) = n(E_2)$, and hence $P(E_2|E_1) = P(E_1|E_2) = 1$. If E_1 and E_2 are mutually exclusive, as illustrated in Fig 4.3(a) above, then $P(E_1E_2) = 0$, and so $P(E_2|E_1) = P(E_1|E_2) = 0$. Thus conditional probabilities obey the axioms of probability, and cannot lie beyond the limits of zero and one.

Example 4.8
An ordinary deck of 52 cards consists of 4 suits of 13 cards each: hearts and diamonds (red) and spades and clubs (black). The jack, queen and king of each suit are called 'face cards'. Suppose a card is drawn from a well-shuffled deck. If the card drawn is known to be a face card, what is the probability that
(a) it will be a black king;
(b) it will be a card other than a black king?

(a) Let K be the event 'black king' and F the event 'face card'. In the pack there are two black kings which are also face cards; hence $P(KF) = 2/52$. Twelve of the cards are face cards; hence $P(F) = 12/52$.

We have
$$P(K|F) = \frac{P(KF)}{P(F)} = \frac{1}{6}$$

(b) If $n(F) = 12$, and $n(KF) = 2$, then $n(\bar{K}F) = 10$. Therefore

$$P(\bar{K}|F) = \frac{P(\bar{K}F)}{P(F)} = \frac{5}{6}$$

Making use of the fact that the events KF and $\bar{K}F$ are complements in the reduced sample space F, we may also compute the required probability as

$$P(\bar{K}|F) = 1 - P(K|F) = 5/6.$$

Multiplication Rule

From the definition of conditional probability it follows directly that

$$P(E_1E_2) = P(E_1)P(E_2|E_1) = P(E_2)P(E_1|E_2)$$

This result is known as the basic rule of probability multiplication. The theorem states that the probability of any two events E_1 and E_2 occurring jointly is found by multiplying the probability of one of the events by the probability of the other, given the condition that the first event has occurred or will occur. When the occurrence of one event is conditional upon the occurrence of another event, the events are said to be *dependent events*. The multiplication rule stated above is thus applicable in computing probabilities of two dependent events occurring jointly when the respective conditional and unconditional probabilities are known or can be ascertained from available data.

Example 4.9

Assume that there are equal numbers of male and female students in a university. Of all male students, 10 per cent major in economics; and of all female students, 5 per cent major in economics. What is the probability that

(a) a student selected at random will be a male economics student?
(b) a student selected at random will be an economics student?
Let

$$M: \text{male student} \qquad \bar{M}: \text{female student} \qquad E: \text{economics student}$$

From the information given, the probability of a student specialising in economics, if the student is male, is 0.10; hence $P(E|M) = 0.10$, and similarly $P(E|\bar{M}) = 0.05$. Also, there are equal numbers of male and female students; hence $P(M) = P(\bar{M}) = 0.5$

(a) The event 'male economics student' is the event ME. Applying the multiplication formula, we have

$$P(ME) = P(M)P(E|M) = (0.5)(0.1)$$
$$= 0.05.$$

(b) The event 'economics student' (E) consists of the events 'male economics student' (ME) and 'female economics student' $(\bar{M}E)$. These are mutually exclusive, and hence

$$P(E) = P(ME) + P(\bar{M}E)$$

where

$$P(\bar{M}E) = P(\bar{M})P(E|\bar{M}) = (0.5)(0.05) = 0.025$$

Thus

$$P(E) = 0.05 + 0.025$$
$$= 0.075$$

As already mentioned earlier in this section, in many types of situations we are concerned with computing probabilities associated with the results of several repetitions of some basic experiment, eg of tossing a coin, or of drawing an object from a well-defined group of objects. When in the latter case the objects drawn are not replaced, the sample space of the experiment is altered after each draw, and the events representing the outcomes of the successive drawings are dependent events. The probability of the joint occurrence of n dependent events $E_1, E_2, \ldots, E_n$ is given by the general multiplication formula

$$P(E_1 E_2 \ldots E_n) = P(E_1)P(E_2|E_1)P(E_3|E_2 E_1) \ldots P(E_n|E_{n-1}E_{n-2} \ldots E_1)$$

where $P(E_3|E_2 E_1)$ is the probability of E_3 occurring, given that both E_1 and E_2 have occurred, ... and the last term $P(E_n|E_{n-1}E_{n-2} \ldots E_1)$

is the probability of E_n occurring, given that all the remaining $n - 1$ events have occurred.

Example 4.10

A box contains ten numbered marbles, of which three are white and seven are black. A marble is drawn at random from the box, and then another marble is drawn also at random, without the first marble being replaced in the box. What is the probability that

(a) (i) the first marble is white and the second is black;
(ii) exactly one of the marbles is white?

(b) If three marbles are drawn from the box without replacement, what is the probability that
(i) all three are white;
(ii) the first two are white and the third is black;
(iii) exactly two of the marbles are white?

(a) (i) Let $W_1 B_2$ be the event that the first marble is white and the second is black. Now, the probability of drawing a white marble first is 3/10. If the outcome of the first draw is indeed 'white', then there are 9 marbles left in the box of which 7 are black. Thus $P(B_2|W_1) = 7/9$, and by the multiplication rule for two dependent events

$$P(W_1 B_2) = P(W_1)P(B_2|W_1) = \frac{3}{10} \cdot \frac{7}{9}$$

$$= \frac{7}{30}$$

(ii) The event 'exactly one white' can occur in one of two possible ways: 'white' first, then 'black' ($W_1 B_2$) or 'black' first, then 'white' ($B_1 W_2$). These are mutually exclusive; hence

$$P(\text{exactly one white}) = P(W_1 B_2) + P(B_1 W_2)$$

$$= \frac{3}{10} \cdot \frac{7}{9} + \frac{7}{10} \cdot \frac{3}{9}$$

$$= \frac{7}{15}$$

(b) (i) Let the symbols W_1, W_2 and W_3 indicate the occurrence of white marble on the first, second and third draw, respectively. We have

$$P(W_1) = 3/10$$
$$P(W_2|W_1) = 2/9$$
$$P(W_3|W_2 W_1) = 1/8$$

Multiplying these three quantities, we obtain

$$P(W_1 W_2 W_3) = \frac{1}{120}$$

(ii) Similarly, $$P(W_1 W_2 B_3) = \frac{3}{10} \cdot \frac{2}{9} \cdot \frac{7}{8}$$

$$= \frac{7}{120}$$

(iii) The event of obtaining exactly two white marbles in three successive drawings is a compound event consisting of the simple events $W_1 W_2 B_3$, $W_1 B_2 W_3$ and $B_1 W_2 W_3$, each of which is equally likely. Thus,

$$P(\text{exactly two white}) = (3)\left(\frac{7}{120}\right)$$

$$= \frac{7}{40}$$

Independent Events

A concept which plays an important role in many common applications of probability theory is the concept of *statistical independence* of two or more events. Generally speaking, two events will be statistically independent if the occurrence of one of the events does not affect our assessment of the probability of the other. Thus, if we toss a coin twice, the probability which we assign to the event heads (or tails) is completely unaffected by the outcome of the first toss.

To state the conditions of statistical independence somewhat more formally, let us consider again the multiplication formulae for two dependent events

$$P(E_1 E_2) = P(E_1)P(E_2|E_1)$$

$$P(E_1 E_2) = P(E_2)P(E_1|E_2)$$

If E_2 is independent of E_1, ie if the probability that E_2 occurs is unaffected by the occurrence or non-occurrence of E_1, then $P(E_2|E_1) = P(E_2)$, and the first equation may be written as $P(E_1 E_2) = P(E_1)P(E_2)$. Substituting this into the second equation, we have $P(E_1)P(E_2) = P(E_2)P(E_1|E_2)$, and hence, for $P(E_2) \neq 0$, $P(E_1|E_2) = P(E_1)$. Thus, if we make the statement 'E_2 is independent of E_1', the statement implies that E_1 is independent of E_2, ie events E_1 and E_2 are mutually independent. Because of this mutual independence, the property of statistical independence of two events may also be defined as follows: two events E_1 and E_2 are independent if and only if

$$P(E_1 E_2) = P(E_1)P(E_2),$$

ie if the joint probability of E_1 and E_2 is equal to the product of their separate probabilities. Conversely, if events E_1 and E_2 are known or can be assumed to be independent, then the above result can be used to calculate their joint probability; hence, the above formula is frequently referred to as the multiplication rule for independent events.

As a further consequence of statistical independence, if E_1 and E_2 are independent events defined in the sample space S, then the events E_1 and $\bar{E}_2$, $\bar{E}_1$ and E_2, and $\bar{E}_1$ and $\bar{E}_2$ will likewise be independent.[1] Also, it is important to note that the terms 'mutual exclusiveness' and

[1] For E_1 and $\bar{E}_2$, this may be shown as follows. Using the general multiplication theorem, we may write

$$P(E_1 \bar{E}_2) = P(E_1)P(\bar{E}_2|E_1)$$

'mutual independence' are not synonymous. Thus, suppose that E_1 and E_2 are defined as mutually exclusive events; then $P(E_1 E_2) = 0$. Because $P(E_1)$ and $P(E_2)$ are positive quantities, so must be their product $P(E_1)P(E_2)$. It follows that $P(E_1 E_2) \neq P(E_1)P(E_2)$, and the condition of statistical independence is not met. Thus we conclude that two mutually exclusive events cannot be independent.

Example 4.11
Suppose a fair coin is tossed twice. If A is the event 'head on the first toss' and B the event 'exactly one tail', are A and B independent events?

Here we have

$$P(A) = P(\text{HH or HT}) = 1/4 + 1/4 = \tfrac{1}{2}$$
$$P(B) = P(\text{HT or TH}) = 1/4 + 1/4 = \tfrac{1}{2}$$

Since the joint event AB consists of a single sample point $\{HT\}$, we also have

$$P(AB) = 1/4$$

Hence

$$P(AB) = P(A)P(B) = 1/4$$

and A and B are shown to be independent events.

Example 4.12
An oil exploration company intends to drill an exploratory well in each of two geologically unrelated regions A and B. If the probability of finding oil in significant quantities is assessed as 1/8 for area A and 1/10 for area B, what is the probability that at least one of the wells will be successful?

Let

$$P(A) = 1/8 \text{ (the probability of a successful well in area A)}$$
$$P(B) = 1/10 \text{ (the probability of a successful well in area B)}$$

The probability which we are seeking is

$$P(A \text{ or } B) = P(A) + P(B) - P(AB)$$

From given information, we may assume statistical independence of the events A and B. Hence, by the multiplication formula for two independent events

---

In the reduced sample space E_1, the events $\bar{E}_2|E_1$ and $E_2|E_1$ are complements. Hence

$$P(\bar{E}_2|E_1) = 1 - P(E_2|E_1)$$

But by assumption E_1 and E_2 are independent. Therefore,

$$P(E_2|E_1) = P(E_2)$$

and

$$P(E_1\bar{E}_2) = P(E_1)[1 - P(E_2)]$$
$$= P(E_1)P(\bar{E}_2)$$

Thus, if E_1 and E_2 are independent, E_1 and $\bar{E}_2$ are also independent.

$$P(AB) = P(A)P(B) = \frac{1}{8} \cdot \frac{1}{10} = \frac{1}{80}$$

and

$$P(A \text{ or } B) = 1/8 + 1/10 - 1/80$$

$$= \frac{17}{80}$$

Alternatively, we recall that

$$P(A \text{ or } B) = 1 - P(\bar{A}\bar{B})$$

Since A and B are independent, $\bar{A}$ and $\bar{B}$ are also independent. We then have

$$P(\bar{A}\bar{B}) = P(\bar{A})P(\bar{B}) = \frac{7}{8} \cdot \frac{9}{10} = \frac{63}{80}$$

and

$$1 - P(\bar{A}\bar{B}) = \frac{17}{80}$$

The notion of statistical independence may be extended to the general case of n events. Events $E_1, E_2, \ldots, E_n$ are said to be mutually independent if the conditions for the multiplication of probabilities are satisfied for all the combinations of two or more events, ie if for *all* such combinations the constituent events are independent. If these conditions hold, the joint probability of n statistically independent events is given by the formula

$$P(E_1 E_2 \ldots E_n) = P(E_1)P(E_2) \ldots P(E_n).$$

Example 4.13
A sample poll of 100 voters reveals the following information about candidates A, B and C, who were nominated for three different offices:

        20 are in favour of candidate A,
        50 are in favour of candidate B,
        50 are in favour of candidate C,
        10 favour both candidates A and B,
        10 favour both candidates A and C,
        25 favour both candidates B and C,
        10 favour all three candidates.

Denote by A, B and C the events that a selected voter favours candidate A, candidate B and candidate C, respectively. Are the three events statistically independent?

Here we have $P(A) = 1/5$ $P(B) = 1/2$ $P(C) = 1/2$

                     $P(AB) = 1/10$ $P(AC) = 1/10$ $P(BC) = 1/4$

                               $P(ABC) = 1/10$

Three events A, B and C will be mutually independent if and only if

(a) $P(AB) = P(A)P(B), P(AC) = P(A)P(C), P(BC) = P(B)P(C),$ *and*

(b) $P(ABC) = P(A)P(B)P(C)$

In the present case, we have

$$P(AB) = \frac{1}{10} \quad \text{and } P(A)P(B) = \frac{1}{5} \cdot \frac{1}{2} = \frac{1}{10}$$

$$P(AC) = \frac{1}{10} \quad \text{and } P(A)P(C) = \frac{1}{5} \cdot \frac{1}{2} = \frac{1}{10}$$

$$P(BC) = \frac{1}{4} \quad \text{and } P(B)P(C) = \frac{1}{2} \cdot \frac{1}{2} = \frac{1}{4}$$

Hence, the events A, B and C satisfy the condition of pairwise independence. However, we also have

$$P(ABC) = \frac{1}{10} \quad \text{and} \quad P(A)P(B)P(C) = \frac{1}{5} \cdot \frac{1}{2} \cdot \frac{1}{2} = \frac{1}{20}$$

The condition of three-way independence is not met, and the events A, B and C are not statistically independent.

It should be mentioned that when the condition of three-way independence is met, while any one of the conditions for pairwise independence is not, the three events are *not* statistically independent. Thus, to show independence, we must verify that both conditions (a) and (b) are met.

Independent Trials

Some of the examples given so far have dealt with experiments consisting of the repetition, under uniform conditions, of some specified basic experiment. When an experiment is conducted in this way and the probability of observing a particular outcome on a given trial of the experiment is unaffected by the outcomes of previous trials, we refer to the trials as *independent trials*. Thus, let us suppose that an experiment gives rise to n possible outcomes $D_1, D_2 \ldots D_n$. If two trials of the experiment are independent, then the probability of observing outcome D_i on one trial and outcome D_j on another trial is

$$P(D_i D_j) = P(D_i)P(D_j)$$

In general, if two or more trials are independent, then any possible outcome of a sequence of such trials can be assigned a probability which is equal to the product of the probabilities of a single trial. To illustrate, let us refer again to our earlier example of rolling a 'black and red' die (ie a die with three black sides and three red sides). In any single trial of this experiment, the sample space is $S = \{B, R\}$, where B denotes the occurrence of a black side, and R the occurrence of a red side. Let us write the probabilities associated with these two events as P_B and P_R, respectively. These probabilities must be such that $P_B \geqslant 0$, $P_R \geqslant 0$, and $P_B + P_R = 1$. If the experiment of rolling the die is repeated, the two rolls clearly constitute two independent trials with the sample space $S = \{(B, B), (B, R), (R, B), (R, R)\}$; this was shown graphically in Fig 4.1 on p 72 above. Let us now denote by

B_1 the event that in two repeated trials 'black' occurs on the first trial, and by B_2 the event that 'black' occurs on the second trial, and similarly for the outcome 'red'. Evidently, the probability of getting 'black' or 'red' on the second trial in no way depends on the outcome of the first trial. Thus, $P(B_1) = P(B_2) = P_B$, and $P(R_1) = P(R_2) = P_R$, and the following relations can be seen to hold:

$$P((B, B)) = P(B_1 B_2) = (P_B)(P_B)$$

$$P((B, R)) = P(B_1 R_2) = (P_B)(P_R)$$

$$P((R, B)) = P(R_1 B_2) = (P_R)(P_B)$$

$$P((R, R)) = P(R_1 R_2) = (P_R)(P_R)$$

Each of these relations assigns a probability to one of the simple events in the sample space S in such a way that the first axiom of probability is satisfied. Summing the probabilities thus assigned, we get

$$P_B{}^2 + 2P_B P_R + P_R{}^2 = (P_B + P_R)^2 = 1^2 = 1$$

as required by the second axiom of probability. We conclude that the multiplication rule correctly assigns probabilities to sample spaces formed by a sequence of two independent trials. These results hold generally for n independent trials.

Example 4.14

What is the probability of rolling either a 5 or a 6 on each of six successive tosses of an unbiased die?

Denote by D the event of getting a 5 or a 6 on a single roll, and by E the event of getting a 5 or 6 on six successive rolls of the die. The event E is one of the possible outcomes of a sequence of six independent trials with known and constant probability $P(D) = 2/6 = 1/3$ for each single trial. Consequently, we have

$$P(E) = [P(D)]^6 = \left(\frac{1}{3}\right)^6$$

$$= \frac{1}{729}$$

4.6 Bayes' Rule

In practical applications of probability, we sometimes encounter situations in which an event can occur only as a consequence of the occurrence of one of several mutually exclusive and exhaustive outcomes at some intermediate stage of the experiment. To illustrate this type of problem, suppose we have two urns each containing six balls; urn 1 contains two black and four white balls, and urn 2 holds three black and three white balls. We then conduct the following two-stage experiment: we chose an urn at random, and from the urn chosen we draw a single ball. What is the probability that the ball drawn will be a black ball?

Let us describe the possible outcomes at each stage as follows:

U_1 : the urn selected is urn 1

U_2 : the urn selected is urn 2

B : the ball drawn is black

W : the ball drawn is white

The four possible ways in which a ball can be drawn in our two-stage experiment can be displayed by the tree diagram

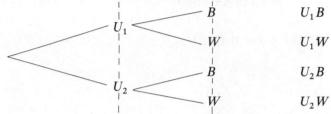

		$U_1 B$
		$U_1 W$
		$U_2 B$
		$U_2 W$

By the principle of probability multiplication, the joint probabilities along each path are

$$P(U_1 B) = P(U_1)P(B|U_1)$$

$$P(U_1 W) = P(U_1)P(W|U_1)$$

$$P(U_2 B) = P(U_2)P(B|U_2)$$

$$P(U_2 W) = P(U_2)P(W|U_2)$$

The event 'black ball is drawn' occurs if either the event $U_1 B$ occurs, or the event $U_2 B$ occurs, but not both. Hence, by the addition rule for mutually exclusive events

$$P(B) = P(U_1)P(B|U_1) + P(U_2)P(B|U_2)$$

By assumption, the urn from which a ball is drawn is chosen at random; hence, we may set $P(U_1) = P(U_2) = \frac{1}{2}$. Also, from given information, the probability of drawing a black ball, given that urn 1 is chosen, is $2/6$; if urn 2 is chosen, the probability of a black ball is $3/6$. Symbolically, $P(B|U_1) = \frac{2}{6} = \frac{1}{3}$, and $P(B|U_2) = \frac{3}{6} = \frac{1}{2}$. Substituting these probability values into the above formula, we compute the probability of drawing a black ball as

$$P(B) = \frac{1}{2}\cdot\frac{1}{3} + \frac{1}{2}\cdot\frac{1}{2}$$

$$= \frac{5}{12}$$

Similarly, the probability of drawing a white ball is

$$P(W) = \frac{1}{2}\cdot\frac{2}{3} + \frac{1}{2}\cdot\frac{1}{2}$$

$$= \frac{7}{12}$$

Since the events B and W are mutually exclusive, we have $P(B) + P(W) = 1$.

In general, if events $E_1, E_2, \ldots, E_n$ constitute a set of mutually exclusive and exhaustive events (or alternatives) and F is an event known to occur as a result of the occurrence of one of the events E_i, then

$$P(F) = P(E_1)P(F|E_1) + P(E_2)P(F|E_2) + \ldots + P(E_n)P(F|E_n)$$

$$= \sum_{i=1}^{n} P(E_i)P(F|E_i)$$

This formula is often found useful in evaluating probabilities when we have information about the probabilities of the alternatives E_i, and the conditional probabilities of given events relative to these alternatives can be computed from available data.

Example 4.15

A manufacturing firm purchases a certain component for its manufacturing process from three sub-contractors A, B and C. These supply 60 per cent, 30 per cent and 10 per cent of the firm's requirements, respectively. It is known that 2 per cent, 5 per cent and 8 per cent of the items supplied by the respective suppliers are defective items. On a particular day, a normal shipment arrives from each of the three suppliers and the contents get mixed up together. If a component is chosen at random from the day's shipment, what is the probability that it is defective?

Let A be the event that a component originates from supplier A, B that it originates from supplier B, and C that it originates from supplier C. Let also D be the event 'defective item'. The probabilities of the alternatives are given as

$$P(A) = 0\cdot6 \qquad P(B) = 0\cdot3 \qquad P(C) = 0\cdot1$$

These probabilities sum to unity, as required. Now, if a component has been supplied by A, then the probability of its being defective is $0\cdot02$. Thus, $P(D|A) = 0\cdot02$, and similarly $P(D|B) = 0\cdot05$ and $P(D|C) = 0\cdot08$. The probability of a defective item is

$$P(D) = (0\cdot6)(0\cdot02) + (0\cdot3)(0\cdot05) + (0\cdot1)(0\cdot08)$$

$$= 0\cdot035$$

It will be noticed that in applying the above probability formula we must have some basis on which to assign probabilities to the alternative events E_i. Since, before the actual experiment takes place, we do not know which of the alternatives will occur, we often refer to these events as *hypotheses*. Thus, in our example of two urns, we may refer to the event 'urn 1 will be chosen' as 'hypothesis U_1' and to the event 'urn 2 will be chosen' as 'hypothesis U_2'. If, before the commencement of the experiment, we have no ground for believing that one hypothesis is more likely to be correct than another, it is natural that each hypothesis should be assigned an equal probability; in our example, this is tantamount to assuming that one of the urns will be chosen at random. Probabilities which are assigned to hypotheses are called *prior probabilities*.

Let us now suppose that a trial of a given experiment is performed, and we are informed of the outcome. Can we utilise this experimental information to revise the prior probabilities associated with the hypotheses? For instance, we may know that the ball drawn from one of the urns U_1 and U_2 is a black ball. The identity of the urn from which the ball has been drawn still remaining unknown, it would seem reasonable to say that since the proportion of black balls in urn 2 is known to be higher than the proportion in urn 1, the probability that urn 2 had in fact been selected, given the result 'black ball', should be higher than the probability for urn 1. Conditional probabilities assigned to hypotheses on the basis of experimental evidence are called *posterior probabilities*.

Let $P(U_2|B)$ be the posterior probability of selecting urn 2, given the experimental result 'black ball'. From the definition of conditional probability

$$P(U_2|B) = \frac{P(U_2B)}{P(B)}$$

where $P(U_2B) = P(U_2)P(B|U_2)$ and $P(B) = P(U_1)P(B|U_1) + P(U_2)P(B|U_2)$, as shown above. Therefore, the posterior probability $P(U_2|B)$ is computed as

$$P(U_2|B) = \frac{P(U_2)P(B|U_2)}{P(U_1)P(B|U_1) + P(U_2)P(B|U_2)}$$

In our case the prior probabilities $P(U_1)$ and $P(U_2)$ are equal, and hence may be cancelled out. Thus

$$P(U_2|B) = \frac{\dfrac{1}{2}}{\dfrac{1}{3} + \dfrac{1}{2}} = \frac{3}{5}$$

and similarly

$$P(U_1|B) = \frac{\frac{1}{3}}{\frac{1}{3} + \frac{1}{2}} = \frac{2}{5}$$

As a general principle, if E_1, E_2, ..., E_n are mutually exclusive events such that $P(E_1) + P(E_2) + \ldots + P(E_n) = 1$, and F is an event which can occur as a result of the occurrence of one of the events E_i ($i = 1, 2, \ldots n$), then

$$P(E_i|F) = \frac{P(E_i)P(F|E_i)}{P(F)}$$

where $P(F) = \sum_{i=1}^{n} P(E_i)P(F|E_i)$. This theorem is known as *Bayes'* *formula.*

It is important to note that in applying Bayes' formula to practical problems it is not sufficient that we know the conditional probabilities $P(F|E_i)$. We must also be able to assign prior probabilities to the events E_i in advance of any experimental information becoming available. When prior information about the distribution of these events is obtainable, this requirement presents no problem, and the application of Bayes' rule is quite straightforward. What has been a matter of considerable controversy, however, is the meaning of Bayes' theorem when prior probabilities cannot be assessed objectively. In section 4.3 above we saw that probabilities which are expressions of personal belief or confidence in the validity of particular statements are called subjective probabilities. Modern statistical decision theory, in contrast with the classical approach, admits the use of subjective probabilities as prior probabilities in Bayesian applications. In the modern view, therefore, we may regard subjectively assigned prior probabilities as measures of the observer's degree of confidence in the correctness of particular hypotheses. The Bayes' rule for computing posterior probabilities then provides a method of revising these measures in the light of supplementary experimental information.

Example 4.16

In example 4.15, suppose a component has been picked at random and is found to be defective. What is the probability that it comes from supplier C?

The probability of the joint event C and D, ie the probability that a component selected at random was supplied by C and is defective is

$$P(CD) = P(C)P(D|C)$$
$$= (0 \cdot 1)(0 \cdot 08)$$
$$= 0 \cdot 008$$

Using our previous result

$$P(D) = P(A)P(D|A) + P(B)P(D|B) + P(C)P(D|C) = 0.035$$

we have, by Bayes' formula,

$$P(C|D) = \frac{P(C)P(D|C)}{P(D)} = \frac{0.008}{0.035} \simeq 0.23$$

Thus, given a defective item, the probability that it originates from supplier C is 0.23.

Example 4.17

From current economic indicators, an economic forecaster expects an upturn in economic activity over the next four quarters with probability 0.4. Subsequently, a survey of business intentions to expand plant and equipment is undertaken, and an improvement in economic conditions over the next twelve months is indicated by the results. Similar surveys undertaken in the past predicted a recovery, when a recovery did actually occur, eight times out of ten; in two cases out of ten, a recovery was predicted, but did not occur. In the light of this additional information, how might the forecaster revise his assessment of the probability that a recovery will occur?

The probabilities associated with the forecaster's hypotheses are

$$P(R) = 0.4 \text{ (recovery will occur)}$$

$$P(\bar{R}) = 0.6 \text{ (recovery will not occur)}$$

These probabilities are based on the forecaster's own assessment of economic conditions, and should therefore be interpreted as subjective probabilities. Let S represent 'the survey of business intentions predicts recovery'. The conditional probabilities relating to the survey's past accuracy of prediction are given as

$$P(S|R) = 0.8$$

and

$$P(S|\bar{R}) = 0.2$$

By Bayes' formula, the revised probabilities associated with R and $\bar{R}$ are computed as

$$P(R|S) = \frac{P(R)P(S|R)}{P(R)P(S|R) + P(\bar{R})P(S|\bar{R})} = \frac{0.32}{0.44} \simeq 0.73$$

and

$$P(\bar{R}|S) = \frac{P(\bar{R})P(S|\bar{R})}{P(R)P(S|R) + P(\bar{R})P(S|\bar{R})} = \frac{0.12}{0.44} \simeq 0.27$$

The events $R|S$ and $\bar{R}|S$ represent two mutually exclusive possibilities, and their probabilities therefore sum to one.

We note that in the present case the posterior probability $P(R|S)$ exceeds the prior probability $P(R) = 0.4$. Thus, as a result of additional information becoming available, the hypothesis R is strengthened. Should further empirical evidence come to light, the computed posterior probabilities can be treated as prior probabilities, and the process of re-estimating the probabilities of the hypotheses R and $\bar{R}$ repeated. As this process continues, the importance of the initial subjective probabilities assigned as prior probabilities is progressively diminished.

4.7 Rules of Counting and Elements of Combinatorial Probability

As we have seen in many of our examples, the problem of defining probabilities in finite sample spaces often becomes one of counting the number of sample points belonging to an event E relative to the number of sample points in the entire sample space S. If the sample spaces with which we are dealing are very large, a complete enumeration of possible outcomes becomes an impracticable task, and we need to resort to algebraic methods for counting the sample points. While many counting rules of considerable complexity have been evolved by a branch of mathematics known as *combinatorial analysis*, here we shall only be concerned with those most commonly used in elementary applications.

The Multiplication Rule of Counting

A basic rule of combinatorial analysis is the following: if some process or experiment consists of several sequential operations, such that the first operation can be performed in n_1 distinct ways, the second in n_2 distinct ways, . . . , and the kth operation in n_k distinct ways, then the entire process or experiment can be performed in

$$(n_1)(n_2) \ldots (n_k) \text{ distinct ways.}$$

This principle is sometimes referred to as the *principle of sequential counting*.

Example 4.18
An automobile dealer offers six different models each of which is available in seven different colours and with or without a radio. How many different selections of a car are possible?

The first choice (model) can be made in six different ways. For each of these, the second choice (colour) can be made in seven different ways, and for each of these the third choice (with or without a radio) can be made in two ways. Hence, there are

$$(6)(7)(2) = 84$$

different choices.

Permutations

Often the multiplication principle of counting is applied to the following situation. We have a group of n distinct objects and we wish to know how many different ordered arrangements can be made of the n objects. An ordered arrangement of a set of objects is called a *permutation*. To find the total number of permutations of n objects taken n at a time, which we shall write here as $P(n;n)$, we first count the number of ways in which an object can be assigned to the first position in the arrangement; this can be done in n different ways. Once the first position has been filled, there are $n - 1$ objects to be placed in the second position, $n - 2$ objects to be placed in the third position, and so on until there remains only one object which is placed in the last, ie nth position. By the principle of multiplication, the total number of permutations that can thus be formed is

$$P(n;n) = n! = (n)(n - 1)(n - 2) \ldots (2)(1)$$

In this formula, the symbol $n!$ indicates the product of a descending sequence of whole numbers, from n to 1, and is called n *factorial*. For $n = 3$, we have $n! = 3! = (3)(2)(1)$; also $2! = (2)(1) = 2$, and $1! = 1$. Zero factorial is defined as being equal to one, ie $0! = 1$.

As an illustration, consider the set $S = \{A, B, C\}$. There are

$$P(3;3) = 3! = 6$$

permutations of the three letters. These may be listed as

ABC	BAC	CAB
ACB	BCA	CBA

We observe that each of the six groupings is made up of the same letters. The order of arrangement being different, each grouping is a distinct permutation.

Let us consider next the number of permutations of n distinct objects taken r at a time, where r is a number smaller than n. As before, the first position in the arrangement can be filled in n ways, the second position in $(n - 1)$ ways, $\ldots$, and the rth position in $(n - r + 1)$ ways. Therefore

$$P(n;r) = (n)(n - 1)(n - 2) \ldots (n - r + 1)$$

where $P(n;r)$ denotes that r of the n elements are being arranged at a time. If we multiply and divide the right-hand side of this expression by $(n - r)!$ we obtain

$$P(n;r) = \frac{n!}{(n - r)!}$$

When $n = r$, we have $(n - r)! = 0! = 1$, and the above result reduces to $P(n;n)$; hence the formula holds for $r \leqslant n$.

For the set $S = \{A, B, C\}$, if $r = 2$, there are

$$P(3;2) = \frac{3!}{(3 - 2)!} = (3)(2)(1) = 6$$

permutations of the three letters taken two at a time:

AB	BA
AC	CA
BC	CB

Example 4.19

Suppose that there are five different tasks to be allocated among seven persons. If only one person is to be assigned to each task, how many different possible assignments can be made?

In this case there are seven ways of assigning the first task, and for each of these there are six ways of assigning the second task, and so on. Hence, the total number of possible assignments (permutations) is

$$P(7;5) = \frac{7!}{(7 - 5)!}$$

$$= (7)(6)(5)(4)(3)$$

$$= 2520$$

Up until now we have been assuming that the objects being arranged are in some way distinguishable from one another. In some instances, however, we shall not be able to distinguish among some of the elements of a set of objects, or it may simply not be convenient to do so. Thus, consider a group of n objects of which r are classified as being alike with respect to one characteristic, and the remaining $(n - r)$ objects are classified as being alike with respect to another characteristic. If all the n objects were distinct, there would be $n!$ permutations. However, there are now $r!$ orderings of the r objects of the first kind; for each of these, there are $(n - r)!$ orderings of the $(n - r)$ objects of the second kind. Hence, to count the total number of distinguishable arrangements of the n objects, we must divide $n!$ by $r!(n - r)!$ Writing $P(n;r,n - r)$ as the number of permutations that can be formed from two groups of indistinguishable elements, we have

$$P(n;r,n - r) = \frac{n!}{r!(n - r)!}$$

Example 4.20

Let an experiment consist of three successive tosses of a coin, and let E represent the event 'exactly two heads'. How many distinct sequences of outcomes correspond to the event E?

We are interested in all the sequences which consist of two elements of one type (heads) and one element of another type (tails). Therefore, the number of sequences is

$$P(3;2,1) = \frac{3!}{2!1!} = 3$$

Listing these, we have

$$E = \{HHT, HTH, THH\}$$

The principle stated so far applies in the general case of more than two classifications. If there are n objects, of which n_1 are classified as being alike, n_2 others are classified as being alike, ..., and n_k are classified as being alike, the number of distinguishable arrangements (permutations) of the n objects is given by

$$\frac{n!}{n_1!\,n_2!\ldots n_k!}$$

where $n_1 + n_2 + \ldots + n_k = n$.

Example 4.21

Suppose we have a balanced six-sided die, with three sides painted black (B), two sides painted red (R), and one side painted white (W). If the die is rolled four times in succession, what is the total number of sequences in which 'black' appears twice, and 'red' and 'white' appear once?

This is an application of the permutation formula given above, with $n = 4$, $n_1 = 2$, $n_2 = 1$ and $n_3 = 1$. We have

$$P(4;2,1,1) = \frac{4!}{2!1!1!}$$

$$= 12$$

Thus, there are 12 distinguishable sequences, which may be listed as follows:

BBRW	RBBW
BBWR	RBWB
BRBW	RWBB
BRWB	WBBR
BWBR	WBRB
BWRB	WRBB

Combinations

We have seen that when r objects are selected from n distinct objects, and the order of selection is of consequence, the arrangements are called permutations. Arrangements of objects which differ from one another only in the composition of the elements, and not in the order in which the elements appear, are called *combinations*. The number of combinations of n distinct objects taken r at a time is denoted by the symbol $\binom{n}{r}$. Since any r elements selected from a set of n elements can be ordered in $r!$ different ways, from the multiplication principle of counting it follows that the quantities $P(n;r)$ and $\binom{n}{r}$ are linked by the relation

$$P(n;r) = \binom{n}{r}r!$$

Using this relation, we find

$$\binom{n}{r} = \frac{P(n;r)}{r!} = \frac{n!}{(n-r)!} \div r!$$

$$= \frac{n!}{r!(n-r)!}$$

Example 4.22

Consider a set of four letters $S = \{A, B, C, D\}$. How many combinations can be formed from the four letters when three letters are taken at a time? The number of combinations is

$$\binom{4}{3} = \frac{4!}{3!1!} = 4$$

These four combinations are

$$\{A, B, C\}, \{A, B, D\}, \{A, C, D\}, \{B, C, D\}$$

We observe that each of these combinations is a set consisting of the elements of $S = \{A, B, C, D\}$. Hence each combination is a distinct subset of S.

Binomial Coefficients

Thus far we have introduced the symbol $\binom{n}{r}$ to denote the number of combinations of r objects taken from a set of n distinct objects. We further recall from our earlier discussion that the number of permutations or distinguishable sequences that can be formed from r elements of one type and $(n - r)$ elements of another type is also equal to $\binom{n}{r} = \dfrac{n!}{r!(n - r)!}$. For these reasons, the quantity $\binom{n}{r}$ plays an important role in elementary combinatorial analysis, and we now consider briefly its main mathematical properties.

Consider again the set of four letters $S = \{A, B, C, D\}$, as in example 4.22 above. From the elements of this set we can form $\binom{4}{1} = 4$ combinations of *one* element, $\binom{4}{2} = 6$ combinations of *two* elements, $\binom{4}{3} = 4$ combinations of *three* elements, and $\binom{4}{4} = 1$ combination of *four* elements. By definition, we also have $\binom{4}{0} = 1$. An important property of these numbers is that they form the coefficients obtained by expanding the expression $(x + y)^n$, where $n = 4$ and x and y are any real numbers. Thus, by actual multiplication, we have

$$(x + y)^4 = x^4 + 4x^3y + 6x^2y^2 + 4xy^3 + y^4$$

A generalisation of this result is known as the *binomial theorem*. For any non-negative integer (whole number) n

$$(x + y)^n = \binom{n}{0}x^n + \binom{n}{1}x^{n-1}y + \binom{n}{2}x^{n-2}y^2 + \ldots \binom{n}{r}x^{n-r}y^r + \ldots \binom{n}{n}y^n$$

or, in summation form,

$$(x + y)^n = \sum_{r=0}^{n} \binom{n}{r}x^{n-r}y^r$$

Because the numbers $\binom{n}{r}$ appear as coefficients in the binomial theorem, they are referred to as *binomial coefficients*.

A convenient method for finding binomial coefficients when n is not very large is by constructing an array of numbers known as *Pascal's triangle*:

n	Binomial coefficients $\binom{n}{r}$
0	1
1	1 1
2	1 2 1
3	1 3 3 1
4	1 4 6 4 1
5	1 5 10 10 5 1
	. . . .

We observe that the number at the beginning and end of each row is equal to 1, since $\binom{n}{0} = \binom{n}{n} = 1$. The apex of the triangle is also 1, since, for example, if $x = y = 1, (1 + 1)^0 = 1$. To obtain any other number within the triangle, we sum the two numbers appearing immediately above it, eg for $n = 6$, we have $\binom{6}{1} = 1 + 5 = 6, \binom{6}{2} = 5 + 10 = 15,$ $\binom{6}{3} = 10 + 10 = 20$, etc. An important feature of the triangle is its symmetry with respect to the middle entry (when n is even) or entries (when n is odd). This implies that for any positive value of n and $r = 0, 1, \ldots, n$

$$\binom{n}{n - r} = \binom{n}{r}$$

For instance, had we found $\binom{6}{1} = 6$ and $\binom{6}{2} = 15$, then, by the symmetry property, $\binom{6}{5} = \binom{6}{1} = 6, \binom{6}{4} = \binom{6}{2} = 15$, etc.

Earlier we saw that if we have n objects, of which n_1 can be treated as being alike, n_2 others can be treated as being alike, $\ldots$, and n_k can be treated as being alike, the rule for counting the possible distinguishable arrangements becomes

$$\binom{n}{n_1, n_2, \ldots, n_k} = \frac{n!}{n_1! \, n_2! \ldots n_k!}$$

for $n_1 + n_2 + \ldots + n_k = n$. By analogy with the binomial coefficients, these quantities are known as *multinomial coefficients*, since they form the successive coefficients in the expansion $(x_1 + x_2 + \ldots + x_k)^n$. Further reference to the binomial and multinomial coefficients will be made when later we discuss the binomial and multinomial probability distributions.

Applications to Sampling

A basic random process which is of fundamental importance for all our future work is that of a *sampling experiment*. In general, whenever we draw a group of objects or observations of some phenomenon from a still larger group, we perform a sampling experiment. We then refer to the former group as a *sample* and to the latter as the *population* from which the sample has been drawn. For example, suppose that we have an urn containing ten balls, which are numbered 1 to 10, and from this urn we wish to select, say, two balls at random. The ten balls in the urn may be considered as constituting the population in the sampling experiment, and the two drawings may be regarded as a sample of size 2 drawn from this population. For the present we shall use the letter M to denote the number of elements in a population, and the letter N to indicate sample size.

An important application of the counting techniques we have discussed thus far arises in choosing a sample from all possible samples. Thus, if we have a population of M items, we may wish to know how many possible samples of size N can be selected from its elements and what probabilities are associated with each of the possible samples. If a sample is drawn in such a way that it has the same probability of being selected as any other sample of the same size N, then the sample is said to be a *random sample*. As will be further explained in Chapters 5 and 6 below, the essential reason for taking random samples is that such samples are more likely to reflect the characteristics of the population from which they are drawn than any other method of selection. However, before we can determine the probability of a random sample drawn from a given population, we must specify the exact nature of the sampling procedure to be followed. In particular, we must specify whether the sampling is to be with or without replacement. Second, we shall need to consider whether the order of selection of the sampled units is of consequence or not.

A sample is said to be *with replacement* if the process of sampling is such that each sampled unit is returned to the population so that it can recur in subsequent draws. A sample is said to be *without replacement* if the unit drawn is not returned and the size and composition of the population are altered after each successive draw. Before considering what is meant by ordered and unordered sampling, it is important to stress that in sampling experiments we always need to establish the identity of the individual units in the population; if there are M such units, this may be accomplished by numbering them 1 to M. If in a sample attention must be paid to the order in which the population units are drawn, the sample is said to be an *ordered* sample. If we only pay attention to the identity of the elements, and not to the order of their selection, the sample is said to be *unordered*. With this background, let us now investigate how many different samples of size N can be drawn from a population of M items under the following three basic sampling procedures:

1. successive selection with replacement;
2. selection without replacement, the samples being ordered;
3. selection without replacement, the samples being unordered.

1. *Successive selection with replacement*

Suppose we have a group of M objects, which are numbered 1 to M, and from this group we draw N items in succession, replacing each item after it had been drawn. How many sample points are generated by the experiment?

The N drawings can be regarded as a sample of size N drawn from the given population of M items. Since the sampling is with replacement, each of the N elements in the sample can be selected in M different ways. Hence, by the principle of multiplication, there are M^N possible sequences of observations (possible samples). If the successive selections of items from the population are random, in the sense that every element in the population has the same probability of being selected on each draw, then each of the M^N possible samples is equally likely to occur in an actual experiment and may therefore be assigned an equal probability $\frac{1}{M^N}$.

Example 4.23

Suppose that a population consists of the nine digits $1, 2, \ldots, 9$. If three digits are selected at random and with replacement, how many different samples can be selected?

In this case every succession of three digits represents a sample of size $N = 3$ drawn from a population of size $M = 9$. Hence, there are $9^3 = 729$ possible samples.

Let us next denote by A the event of observing a sample in which all three consecutive digits are the same. Evidently, the event A occurs if the digits drawn are all 1s, or 2s, or 3s, etc. We therefore have $n(A) = 9$ and

$$P(A) = \frac{n(A)}{M^N} = \frac{9}{729}$$

$$= \frac{1}{81}$$

As another illustration, consider the sample space generated by an experiment of rolling an ordinary die four times in succession. The experiment is conceptually equivalent to sampling with replacement, where the number of repeated tosses corresponds to the size of the random sample and M corresponds to the number of faces on the die. Thus, the experiment generates

$$6^4 = 1296 \text{ sample points}$$

2. *Selection without replacement, the samples being ordered*

Consider again a group of numbered objects from which we now select an item at random, record its identity, and then draw another item without replacing the first. How many sample points shall we have?

We observe first that by noting the identity of the first item drawn we regard the order of selection as being relevant to the selection process. If ordered samples of size 2 are to be drawn from a population of M items, then the first element in the sample can be selected in M ways, and, for each of these, the second element can be selected in $M - 1$ ways. More generally, ordered samples of size N can be drawn in $M(M - 1)(M - 2) \ldots (M - N - 1)$ ways. Recalling that this is the number of permutations of M objects taken N at a time, we count the number of sample points (possible samples) generated by the experiment as

$$P(M;N) = \frac{M!}{(M - N)!}$$

For greater simplicity of notation, let us write $M!/(M - N)! = (M)_N$. If the sampling is random, in the sense that each unit in the population not yet included in the sample has an equal chance of being drawn, each of the $(M)_N$ sample points may be assigned an equal probability $\frac{1}{(M)_N}$.

Example 4.24

A raffle is to be run for which thirty tickets, which are numbered 1 to 30, have been sold. In how many ways can two tickets be drawn for the first and second prizes?

If we assume that each ticket can win only one prize, ie the first ticket drawn is not replaced, we have

$$(M)_N = \frac{30!}{(30 - 2)!} = \frac{(30)(29)(28)(27) \ldots (2)(1)}{(28)(27) \ldots (2)(1)}$$
$$= (30)(29)$$
$$= 870$$

possible selections. Hence, the probability, for example, of ticket No. 13 winning the first prize and ticket No. 7 winning the second prize is 1/870.

3. Selection without replacement, the samples being unordered

If in the previous sampling scheme the order in which N elements are taken from a larger group of M elements is disregarded, the total number of possible arrangements will be the number of combinations of M things taken N at a time. Hence, if the population is of size M and the sample is of size N, the total number of different samples is $\binom{M}{N}$

$$= \frac{M!}{N!(M-N)!}.$$ If the sampling is random, each of these has an equal probability $\dfrac{1}{\binom{M}{N}}$.

Example 4.25

Suppose that a random sample of four families is to be selected from the thirteen families living in a certain area. How many different samples are possible?

If, as in most empirical sampling problems, the sampling is to be made without replacement and without regard to the order of selection, there are

$$\binom{13}{4} = \frac{13!}{4!\,9!} = \frac{(13)(12)(11)(10)\,9!}{4!\,9!}$$
$$= 715$$

possible samples.

Suppose further that of the thirteen families eight are families with children and five are families without children. What is the probability that the sample drawn will include two families with children and two families without children?

Two families with children can be selected from eight in $\binom{8}{2}$ different ways; and for each of these, there are $\binom{5}{2}$ ways of selecting two families without children. By the rule of multiplication, there are

$$\binom{8}{2}\binom{5}{2} = (28)(10) = 280$$

different samples consisting of two families with children and two families without children, and the required probability is

$$\frac{\binom{8}{2}\binom{5}{2}}{715} = \frac{280}{715}$$
$$= 0\cdot392$$

4.8 Probability Distributions of Random Variables

In applications of probability to practical situations, interest usually centres not on the detailed outcomes of a random experiment but rather on some numerical characteristic associated with these outcomes. For example, in drawing samples of size 3 from an urn containing three white and seven black marbles we may only be interested in the number of white marbles occurring in each sample. In some instances, numerical descriptions of sample spaces are the natural ones to use, as, for instance, in experiments with ordinary six-sided dice. In others, we can translate physical descriptions of experimental outcomes into numerical descriptions by means of some specified rule. A variable whose value is defined by a mathematical rule or function for every possible outcome of a random experiment is called a *random variable*.

To develop this concept further, suppose that a fair coin is tossed three times and we are interested in the random variable 'number of heads'. The sample space of this experiment, the number of heads corresponding to each point, and the associated probabilities are shown in Table 4.1.

Table 4.1

RANDOM VARIABLE FOR A COIN EXPERIMENT

Outcome	Number of Heads	Probability
T T T	0	1/8
H T T	1	1/8
T H T	1	1/8
T T H	1	1/8
H H T	2	1/8
H T H	2	1/8
T H H	2	1/8
H H H	3	1/8

As can be seen, to each sample point there corresponds one and only one value of the random variable 'number of heads'. A mathematical relationship which has this property is called a function. Hence, a random variable may be said to be a function which associates a real number with each and every sample point in the sample space S. It is customary to indicate random variables by capital letters, such as X, Y etc. It is, of course, possible to have more than one random variable defined on the sample space of a given experiment. Thus, in our case, another random variable may be the number of tails occurring in the three tosses of the coin.

If X represents the random variable 'number of heads', it can be readily seen from Table 4.1 that in an actual experiment X can assume one of the four possible values: 0, 1, 2, 3. One advantage of our new numerical description of the sample space becomes immediately apparent: we now have a simpler sample space consisting of four, instead of eight, points. A further advantage is that the events defined in this new sample space can be described in a more compact way. Thus, if we let the symbol x represent one of the possible values of X, then the event 'x heads occur' may be written as $(X = x)$. For instance, if a trial of the experiment results in the outcome TTT, we say that X has 'assumed' the value of 0, and we may write the probability of this event as

$$P(\text{TTT}) = P(X = 0) = 1/8$$

Similarly, for the event of exactly one head occurring on the three tosses, we have

$$P(\text{HTT or THT or TTH}) = P(X = 1) = 3/8$$

Often, for convenience, we write this more simply as $P(1) = 3/8$. In general, we shall write the probability that X assumes a value x as $P(x)$. An alternative way of stating this is to use the general function notation and write $P(X = x) = f(x)$

We may now state the following important definition: a mathematical relation which to each value x_i that can be assumed by a random variable X assigns a real number such that

$$0 \leqslant P(x_i) \leqslant 1$$

and $$\sum_i P(x_i) = 1$$

is called the *probability function* or the *probability distribution* of the random variable X. The reader will recognise these two conditions as the first and second axioms of probability: the real numbers assigned as probabilities to the possible values of X must lie in the interval 0 to 1 inclusive, and the sum of the probabilities thus assigned must equal unity.

A probability distribution may be represented in tabular form, as a graph, or in the form of a mathematical equation. In our example:

Table 4.2

**PROBABILITY DISTRIBUTION OF NUMBER OF HEADS:
THREE TOSSES OF A COIN**

Number of Heads x	Probability $P(x)$
0	1/8
1	3/8
2	3/8
3	1/8
Total	1

Graphically, this distribution may be drawn either as a line chart (Fig 4.6 (a)) or as a probability histogram (Fig 4.6 (b)). In either diagram, the probabilities corresponding to the various values of X can be read off the vertical axis. However, in the histogram, we may also think of each probability value as being equal to the proportionate area of each bar. Since the numerical outcomes plotted on the horizontal axis are mutually exclusive and exhaustive, the area of the histogram will correspond to unity.

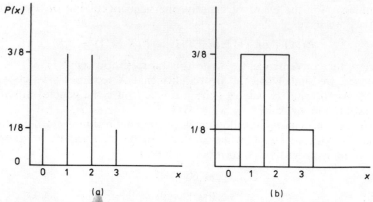

Fig 4.6 Probability distribution of number of heads: three tosses of a coin

When a random variable can vary only by finite 'jumps', it is referred to as a *discrete random* variable, and its probability distribution is referred to as a *discrete probability distribution*. In this section, we restrict our attention to discrete distributions.

By analogy with ogives constructed from frequency data (see section 3.2) we often wish to know the probability that X is equal to or less than some specified value x. Let us write this probability as $P(X \leqslant x)$. By cumulating the probabilities $P(x)$ as x varies over the given range, we obtain the *cumulative* probability distribution of X, as shown in Fig 4.7. We observe that this function is discontinuous for each successive value of x. Reading off the cumulative probabilities from the vertical scale, we find $P(X \leqslant 0) = 1/8, P(X \leqslant 1) = 4/8$, etc. The 'step' function depicted by Fig 4.7 reaches the maximum value of 1 when $x = 3$; hence, in the given experiment, the event that X assumes a value equal to or less than 3 is certain to occur.

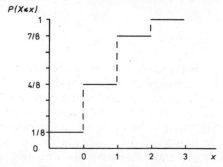

Fig 4.7 Cumulative probability distribution: three tosses of a coin

Example 4.26

Suppose that a fair six-sided die and a balanced coin are tossed together. Let X_1 be a random variable 'number of spots on the die' and let X_2 be a random variable 'number of heads'; evidently, X_2 can only take on two possible values: 0 and 1. Define next the random variable Y as the sum of values that may turn up in tossing the die and the coin together; thus $Y = X_1 + X_2$. What is the probability distribution of Y?

Let us derive the probability distribution of Y by constructing the following table:

Sample points	Value of Y y	Probability $P(y)$
$\{1,0\}$	1	1/12
$\{1,1\}, \{2,0\}$	2	2/12
$\{2,1\}, \{3,0\}$	3	2/12
$\{3,1\}, \{4,0\}$	4	2/12
$\{4,1\}, \{5,0\}$	5	2/12
$\{5,1\}, \{6,0\}$	6	2/12
$\{6,1\}$	7	1/12
Total		1

The first column lists all the possible outcomes of the experiment (see also example 4.1). Now if $X_1 = 1$ and $X_2 = 0$, we have $Y = 1$; if $X_1 = 1$ and $X_2 = 1$ or $X_1 = 2$ and $X_2 = 0$, we have $Y = 2$, etc. The possible values of the random variable Y and the respective probabilities are listed in the last two columns of the table. This listing gives the probability distribution of Y. In graphical form, the distribution of Y may be shown as follows:

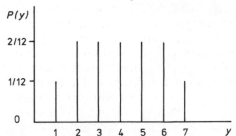

Fig 4.8

4.9 The Mean and Variance of a Random Variable

In interpreting the concept of a probability distribution introduced in the preceding section it is important to bear in mind the fundamental distinction between *populations* and *samples*.[1] In statistics, the term 'population' always refers to the universe or totality of observations of a variable. The word 'sample' then refers to any group of observations drawn from this universe. Many empirical populations whose characteristics we study with the aid of statistical methods are *finite*, eg a population of family sizes, or a population of rents. Others, those

[1] See also section 4.7, p 106 above.

containing an unlimited number of elements, are *infinite*. Sometimes, the sampled population is so large that for practical purposes it may be treated as being infinite.

A special class of infinite populations are theoretical populations generated by a hypothetically infinite number of repetitions of the same experiment. For the purpose of illustrating this, let us consider the following simple sampling experiment. We have an urn containing four tags numbered 1, 2, 3 and 4. Let a random variable X be defined as the number that may be observed by drawing a single tag at random from the urn. Then X can assume one of the possible four values 1, 2, 3, 4, each of which is equally likely to occur in an actual experiment. When equal probabilities can be assigned to all the possible values that a random variable may take, the resulting distribution is referred to as a *uniform distribution*. Thus, in the present case, we can postulate that X has the uniform distribution

$$P(x) = \frac{1}{4}, \qquad x = 1, 2, 3, 4$$

This distribution is shown graphically in Fig 4.9.

If the experiment of drawing a tag at random from the urn were repeated a very large number of times, with the tag drawn being replaced each time, we would expect the relative frequency distribution of the four possible outcomes to approach the probability distribution of the random variable X; in the limit, this relative frequency distribution and the theoretical probability distribution $P(x) = 1/4$ would be the same. We may then regard the uniform probability distribution of the variable X as being the distribution of the theoretical population generated by an unlimited number of observations of the variable X. If the number of trials, ie repeated drawings with replacement, were large, we would still expect the empirical frequency distribution to be a good approximation to the probability distribution of X. In general, we may interpret probability distributions as theoretical frequency distributions based on very many repeated observations of the same experiment.

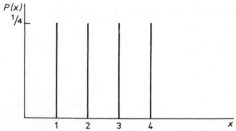

Fig 4.9 Probability distribution for an experiment of drawing one tag at random with replacement

Although a probability distribution provides a complete description of a random variable, or of the population over which the random variable is defined, it is often necessary to characterise the distribution by a few summary measures. We have already dealt with the question of how a sample of data may be arranged into a frequency distribution and summarised by measures such as the arithmetic mean and standard deviation (or variance). The corresponding population measures are the *mean* or *expected* value of a random variable, and its *variance*.

If X is a discrete random variable with n possible values x_i and with a probability distribution $P(x_i)$, the expected value of X, written as $E(X)$, is defined as

$$E(X) = x_1 P(x_1) + x_2 P(x_2) + \ldots + x_n P(x_n)$$
$$= \Sigma x_i P(x_i)$$

Thus, expected value, or mathematical expectation, is seen to be a weighted mean of the possible values of a random variable with probabilities as weights.

To clarify the meaning of this important concept, suppose that we play a simple game of tossing one coin in which we receive \$3 when 'heads' turns up and lose \$2 when 'tails' turns up. If the coin is an unbiased coin

$$E(X) = x_1 P(x_1) + x_2 P(x_2) = (3)(\tfrac{1}{2}) + (-2)(\tfrac{1}{2}) = \$0\cdot5$$

Evidently, it is not possible to win that amount in any *single* game since in order to participate we must contract to pay \$2 if 'tails' occurs and receive \$3 if 'heads' occurs, and this exhausts all possibilities. However, if we interpret the probabilities of heads and tails occurring as the limits of relative frequencies in a long sequence of repeated trials, then, in a large number of games, we can expect to win in 50 per cent of the cases and lose in 50 per cent of the cases. Thus, the net winnings per game can be expected to be $0 \cdot 5$ dollar. In general, mathematical expectation can be interpreted as the 'average' value obtained in a long sequence of repeated experiments.

In our example, the game is evidently favourable to us since the expected value is positive. If the expected value were zero, the game would be a 'fair' game, and we would expect to break even in the long run. In life, we very frequently play games unfavourable to us, for instance, in taking out various insurance policies protecting us against contingencies such as fire, accident, etc. The word 'unfavourable' should, however, not be interpreted that such games are in some ethical sense 'unfair', but merely that they result in negative expected values; in any event, most people consider the unfavourable expectations to be outweighed by other advantages.

Example 4.27

A man wishes to insure his house against fire. The value of the house is assessed to be $30 000. The annual premium which he must pay to insure this house is $20. If the probability that a fire will destroy his house is 1/10 000, is his insurance contract a 'fair' game?

$$E(X) = (30\,000)(1/10\,000) + (-20)(9999/10\,000)$$
$$\simeq -\$17$$

The game must be considered 'unfavourable'.

Expected value is an important measure in statistical analysis. It represents the arithmetic mean of a theoretical probability distribution and of its underlying population. In practice, the population mean is also denoted by the Greek symbol μ (read 'mu') and we shall use this symbol synonymously with $E(X)$ in our subsequent discussion.

The variance of a probability distribution and of its associated population is derived analogously with the variance computed from a sample frequency distribution by weighting the squared deviations of the values of the random variable from its mean by their respective probabilities. The variance so derived, however, differs from the sample variance in that it is a measure of dispersion of the values that a random variable can take *over a long sequence of experiments*, eg tosses of three coins. Accordingly, if X is a random variable with a probability distribution $P(x_i)$ and expected value $E(X)$, its variance is defined as the expectation

$$\text{Var}(X) = E[X - E(X)]^2 = \Sigma[x_i - E(X)]^2 P(x_i)$$

When referring to the population of observations of X, we often denote the variance of X by the symbol σ^2, and its square root, the standard deviation, by σ (Greek sigma). The measure σ is analogous to the standard deviation of a sample, and is commonly used to measure dispersion of values in the population.

Example 4.28

Consider again the experiment of drawing a tag at random with replacement from an urn containing four numbered tags 1, 2, 3 and 4. If X represents the number of the tag drawn, what is the variance of X?

We first find

$$E(X) = (1)(1/4) + 2(1/4) + 3(1/4) + 4(1/4)$$
$$= 2\cdot5$$

In computing $\text{Var}(X)$, it is convenient to set out the calculations as below:

x	$[x - E(X)]$	$[x - E(X)]^2$	$P(x)$	$[x - E(X)]^2 P(x)$
1	−1·5	2·25	1/4	0·5625
2	−0·5	0·25	1/4	0·0625
3	0·5	0·25	1/4	0·0625
4	1·5	2·25	1/4	0·5625

Summing the entries in the last column, we get

$$\text{Var}(X) = 1\cdot25$$

Thus far we have derived simple probability distributions from first principles by applying the axioms and theorems of probability. As the next step, we shall examine several discrete probability distributions which serve as useful probability models in a wide variety of practical situations. A theoretical distribution of special importance in elementary applications is the *binomial distribution*.

4.10 The Binomial Distribution

The binomial distribution is a theoretical probability distribution applicable to situations with the following characteristics:

1. An experiment consists of a finite number of repeated trials each of which has only two possible outcomes which we denote as 'success' and 'failure'.

2. The repeated trials are statistically independent in the sense that the outcome of any one trial has no effect on the outcomes of the successive trials.

3. The probabilities associated with 'success' and 'failure' are known and remain unchanged throughout the experiment. Repeated independent trials with constant probabilities of success and failure are known as *Bernoulli* or *binomial* trials.

Let there be n binomial trials and let the probability of a success and a failure on any single trial be p and q, respectively. Since for any given trial the events 'success' and 'failure' are mutually exclusive, we must have $p + q = 1$. The question we now wish to answer may be stated as follows: if there are n binomial trials of an experiment, can we determine the probability with which exactly x successes will occur in the n trials?

To develop a general formula which would enable us to compute this probability for any given values of n and x, we recall first that if the n trials of the experiment are independent, then the probability of observing any particular sequence of x successes and $(n - x)$ failures in the n trials is equal to the product of the x probabilities of success (p) and the $(n - x)$ probabilities of failure (q) (see section 4.5); hence, the probability of any such sequence is $p^x q^{n-x}$. Next, we must count how many sequences consisting of exactly x successes and $(n - x)$ failures are possible. To find this number is equivalent to finding the number of distinguishable arrangements of n elements, of which x are alike (successes) and another $(n - x)$ are alike (failures). By the formula given on p 102 of section 4.7, this number is

$$\binom{n}{x} = \frac{n!}{x!\,(n - x)!}$$

Hence, there are $\binom{n}{x}$ possible sequences of x successes and $(n - x)$ failures, each occurring with probability $p^x q^{n-x}$. Summing these $\binom{n}{x}$ equal probabilities gives the result

$$P(\text{exactly } x \text{ successes}) = \binom{n}{x} p^x q^{n-x}$$

We observe next that the random variable 'number of successes in n trials' X, often referred to as the *binomial variable* X, can assume one of the possible values $x = 0, 1, 2, \ldots, n$. The event that X assumes any one of these values is the certain event S. By the addition law of probability, we have

$$\sum_{x=0}^{n} \binom{n}{x} p^x q^{n-x} = P(S)$$

But by the binomial theorem (see section 4.7 above) we also have

$$\sum_{x=0}^{n} \binom{n}{x} p^x q^{n-x} = (p + q)^n = 1^n = 1$$

since $(p + q) = 1$. Hence, the sum of values assigned as probabilities to the binomial variable X is unity, as required by the axiomatic definition of probability.

Summarising these results, if an experiment consists of n binomial trials, then the probability of observing exactly x successes in the n trials is given by the formula

$$P(X = x) = \binom{n}{x} p^x q^{n-x} \qquad x = 0, 1, 2, \ldots, n$$

where p and q represent the probabilities of success and failure at each trial. Since it is based on the binomial theorem, the probability distribution given by the above formula is known as the *binomial distribution*.

As a numerical example of this distribution, let us consider again the random variable 'number of heads' in three successive tosses of a coin. For the sake of illustration, let us suppose that the coin is not balanced, and we have $p = 0.4$ (probability of heads) and $q = 0.6$ (probability of tails). To calculate $P(X = 0)$ we observe that a sequence of outcomes that contains no heads can occur only in $\binom{3}{0} = 1$ way; this is the sequence TTT. Corresponding to the event $(X = 1)$, there are $\binom{3}{1} = 3$ distinct sequences of heads and tails, ie HTT, THT and TTH, and similarly for the event $(X = 2)$. Substituting the values $n = 3$, $p = 0.4$ and $q = 0.6$ into the binomial formula, we obtain the following probability table:

Table 4.3

BINOMIAL PROBABILITY DISTRIBUTION OF NUMBER OF HEADS THREE TOSSES OF UNBALANCED COIN

$(p = 0.4; q = 0.6)$

No. of Heads x	Binomial Coefficient $\binom{n}{x}$	$p^x q^{n-x}$	$P(x)$
0	1	0.216	0.216
1	3	0.144	0.432
2	3	0.096	0.288
3	1	0.064	0.064
			1.000

To facilitate the use of the binomial formula in practical applications, binomial probabilities have been extensively tabulated. An excerpt of a binomial table, for specified values of n and p, is given as Table VI in Appendix A.

When the probabilities of 'success' and 'failure' are equal, the binomial distribution formula reduces to

$$P(x) = \binom{n}{x} p^n$$

It can be readily verified that by applying this formula we obtain the probability distribution for our earlier example of tossing three balanced coins, as shown in Table 4.2. Fig 4.6 shows this distribution to be symmetrical. When $p < q$, the binomial distribution is positively skewed, as seen from Table 4.3, and when $p > q$, it is negatively skewed.

In applying the binomial probability model we are often interested in the probability of obtaining at least x successes in n trials. In other instances, we wish to know the probability that a number of successes *equal to or less* than a given number will occur. These probabilities are referred to as *cumulative binomial probabilities*, and may be written symbolically as $P(X \geqslant x)$ and $P(X \leqslant x)$. A cumulative probability distribution of either type may be constructed by simply adding the probabilities across the range of X. For our coin-tossing example, this is illustrated in Table 4.4. Reading the entries in this table for, say, $X = 1$, we find the probability of *exactly* one head occurring to

Table 4.4

BINOMIAL DISTRIBUTION WITH CUMULATIVE PROBABILITIES: THREE TOSSES OF AN UNBALANCED COIN

$(p = 0.4)$

No. of Heads x	$P(X = x)$	$P(X \geqslant x)$	$P(X \leqslant x)$
0	0·216	1·000	0·216
1	0·432	0·784	0·648
2	0·288	0·352	0·936
3	0·064	0·064	1·000

be 0·432; the probability of *at least* one head is 0·784, and the probability of *at most* one head, ie of one head or less, is 0·648.

The assumptions underlying the binomial distribution are quite general, and the distribution can be applied as a probability model for any experiment consisting of n independent observations of some random phenomenon which can occur in one of two possible ways. Thus, consider an experiment of drawing a sample of N items from a population of M elements, of which M_1 elements have characteristic A and $M_2 = M - M_1$ elements have characteristic B. If the sampling is random and *with replacement*, then the probability of observing an element with characteristic A (success) will be equal to $p = \dfrac{M_1}{M}$ and will remain constant throughout the sampling experiment; and similarly, the probability of observing an element with characteristic B (failure) will be given by the ratio $q = \dfrac{M_2}{M}$. In this case, the sample is a sequence of N independent observations of the two population characteristics A and B, and the probability of obtaining a sample containing exactly x elements of type A and $(N - x)$ elements of type B is given by the binomial formula

$$P(x) = \binom{N}{x} p^x q^{N-x}$$

where N is the size of the sample and $x = 0, 1, \ldots N$.

If a sample of size N is drawn from a finite population with M items, and the items drawn are not replaced, then, strictly speaking, the condition of independence of successive observations will not be met. However, the extent to which this condition is violated will depend also on the *relative* sample size, as measured by the ratio N/M. If this ratio is very small, ie if the sample constitutes only a very small fraction of the population, it will evidently make little practical difference whether the items drawn are replaced or not, and the probabilities p and q may be assumed to remain unchanged throughout the experiment. We conclude that the binomial distribution provides an appropriate probability model when sampling is with replacement from a finite population or when samples are drawn from an infinite population with or without replacement. When small samples are drawn without replacement from large populations, we may still regard the binomial distribution as being sufficiently accurate for most practical purposes.

We now illustrate the uses of the binomial distribution with several examples.

Example 4.29

A sample of size $N = 3$ is drawn with replacement from a box containing three white and seven black marbles. If X is a random variable denoting the number of white marbles that may be observed in the sample, what is the probability distribution of X?

Let M_1 and M_2 represent the number of white and black marbles in the box respectively, and p the probability of observing a white marble on a single draw. We have

$$M_1 = 3 \qquad M_2 = 7 \qquad M = 10$$

and

$$p = \frac{M_1}{M} = 0.3 \qquad \text{and} \qquad q = \frac{M_2}{M} = 0.7$$

Since the sampling is with replacement, the probability distribution of X is the binomial distribution with $N = 3$, $p = 0.3$ and $q = 0.7$. Substituting these values into the binomial formula, we obtain the following probability table:

x	$\binom{N}{x}$	$p^x q^{N-x}$	$P(x)$
0	1	0.343	0.343
1	3	0.147	0.441
2	3	0.063	0.189
3	1	0.027	0.027

We interpret this result by saying that if the sampling experiment of drawing three marbles from the box with replacement were repeated a very large number of times, we would expect to draw samples containing 0, 1, 2 and 3 white marbles in approximately 34·3 per cent, 44·1 per cent, 18·9 per cent and 2·7 per cent of all such samples.

Example 4.30

A book-store proprietor estimates that only one of every four persons entering his shop will actually make a purchase. If six persons enter his store at a particular time, what is the probability that (a) exactly three of the persons will make a purchase (b) at least three of them will make a purchase.

Assuming that the six persons act independently, we may regard the situation as a binomial experiment with $n = 6$ and $p = 0.25$.

(a) Let $(X = 3)$ represent the event that three of the six persons will make a purchase. We have

$$P(3) = \binom{6}{3}(0.25)^3(0.75)^3 = 0.1318$$

(b) For $X \geqslant 3$ we have

$$P(X \geqslant 3) = P(3) + P(4) + P(5) + P(6)$$

where

$$P(4) = \binom{6}{4}(0.25)^4(0.75)^2 = 0.0330$$
$$P(5) = \binom{6}{5}(0.25)^5(0.75) = 0.0044$$
$$P(6) = \binom{6}{6}(0.25)^6 = 0.0002$$

The required probability is 0·1694.

Example 4.31

Of 920 families living in a certain area, 20 per cent are known to have an annual family income of over $8000. If a random sample of ten families is selected without replacement, what is the probability that no more than two families included in the sample will have a family income exceeding $8000?

Let $p = 0.2$ denote the probability that a randomly selected family has an income of over $8000. Although the sampling is without replacement, the sample selected is small relative to population size, and we may approximate the required probability by the binomial distribution. In Table VI, Appendix A, binomial probabilities are listed for several selected values of n. The entries in the body of the table give the binomial probabilities for the values of p indicated in the top row and the values of x shown in the first column. Referring to the portion of the table for $n = 10$, we find

$$P(0) = 0.1074$$
$$P(1) = 0.2684$$
$$P(2) = 0.3020$$

and hence $P(X \leqslant 2) = 0.6778$. The probability that at most two of the households in the sample earn an income of over $8000 is 0·6778.

The Mean and Variance of the Binomial Distribution

Before discussing further the characteristics of the binomial distribution, we need to draw a distinction between *parameters* and *statistics*. By the term 'statistic' is meant a numerical measure which describes some characteristic of a sample. Thus the sample mean, the sample standard deviation, or the sample number of successes obtained in

n trials of a binomial experiment, are all examples of measures generically referred to as statistics. In contrast to statistics, measures which describe some characteristic of the population and its probability distribution are known as parameters. In order to specify a particular probability distribution, generally we shall need to know the equation by which such a distribution is defined. This requirement can be split up into two parts (i) the general form of the equation, (ii) the particular member of the family of the general form. Thus $y = a + bx + cx^2$ is the general form known as the parabola, but a particular parabola depends on the actual values of the coefficients a, b and c. These coefficients are known as parameters. Similarly for probability distributions, given the general form of the distribution, a particular distribution is determined by the values of the parameters. In statistical work, parameters are usually expressed in terms of the arithmetic mean and standard deviation of the population values. Thus we have *parameters* in populations and *statistics* in samples. As we shall see below, the statistics are often used as estimates of parameters. To distinguish between parameters and statistics, it is common to denote the former by Greek and the latter by Roman letters. Thus, whereas $\bar{X}$ and s indicate the mean and standard deviation of a sample, we use μ and σ for the mean and standard deviation of the population.

Returning now to the binomial distribution, we can readily see from inspection of the binomial formula that the probabilities $P(x)$ can be computed only if we know the values of n and p. To each pair of values for n and p there corresponds a different member of the family of binomial distributions. Thus, the binomial distribution is completely determined by two quantities: the probability of success on a single trial p, and the number of trials n; these are the parameters of the distribution. We now consider the mean and variance of binomial distributions with given parameters.

The mean or expected value of a binomially distributed variable is defined as the average number of successes we can expect in a long sequence of repetitions of a binomial experiment. Considered in somewhat more abstract terms, each sequence of n trials may be regarded as a sample of size N drawn from a hypothetical population of all such samples; then $E(X)$, or μ, is the mean of this hypothetical population. Using the definition of expected value $E(X)$, we may compute the expected value of a binomial variable as

$$E(X) = \mu = \Sigma x_i P(x_i)$$

where x_i are the possible values of X and $P(x_i)$ are their respective binomial probabilities. Fortunately, this rather tedious method may be considerably simplified by making use of the fact that all the characteristics of the binomial distribution are determined by its two parameters, n and p. It can then be shown[1] that the mean value of a binomially distributed variable reduces to

$$\mu = np$$

By an algebraic manipulation similar to that for the mean μ it may be shown that the variance of a binomially distributed variable is

$$\sigma^2 = npq$$

and hence the standard deviation is

$$\sigma = \sqrt{npq}$$

Example 4.32

A train arrives late at a commuting station with probability 0·2. If X is a random variable denoting the number of late arrivals in any given week of five working days, what is $E(X)$? What is $\text{Var}(X)$?

Setting $p = 0·2$ and $n = 5$, we have

$$E(X) = \mu = np = 1$$

and $$\text{Var}(X) = \sigma^2 = npq = 0·8$$

In the long run, we should expect the train to be late, on average, once a week.

4.11 Other Discrete Probability Distributions

We now continue our discussion of the discrete random variable by briefly examining several probability distributions commonly found

---

[1] This may be seen as follows:
By definition

$$\mu = E(X) = \sum_{x=0}^{n} x\binom{n}{x} p^x q^{n-x}$$

In this summation, the first term vanishes since $x_0 = 0$, and we may write

$$\mu = \sum_{x=1}^{n} x\binom{n}{x} p^x q^{n-x}$$

Simplifying

$$x\binom{n}{x} = \frac{n!}{(x-1)!(n-x)!}$$

and factoring out n and one of the factors of p, we get

$$\mu = np \sum_{x=1}^{n} \frac{(n-1)!}{(x-1)!(n-x)!} p^{x-1} q^{n-x}$$

Letting $m = n - 1$ and $y = x - 1$

$$\mu = np \sum_{y=0}^{m} \binom{m}{y} p^y q^{m-y}$$

where the summation term relates to a binomial distribution $P(y)$ for $y = 0, 1, 2, \ldots m$, and is thus equal to unity (see p 118 above). Hence

$$\mu = np$$

in practice: the *multinomial*, the *negative binomial*, the *hypergeometric*, and the *Poisson* distributions. For our purpose it will suffice to describe the salient features of each distribution and to indicate the general nature of the problem to which it may be applied; a detailed treatment of the mathematical properties of these distributions may be found in some of the references listed in Appendix C.

The Multinomial Distribution

The binomial distribution applies in the special case when the sample space of each trial consists of only two possible outcomes, 'success' and 'failure'. When there are more than two outcomes, and the assumption of independence of the successive observations is met, the process of n repeated trials may be described by a theoretical distribution known as the *multinomial probability distribution*.

Let us suppose that a trial of a multinomial experiment gives rise to k mutually exclusive and exhaustive outcomes D_1, D_2, ..., D_k. Let the probabilities associated with these outcome be p_1, p_2, ..., p_k, respectively. If there are n trials, and the trials are independent, these probabilities will remain constant throughout the experiment. Given these conditions, the probability that in a sequence of n trials the outcome D_1 will be observed exactly x_1 times, the outcome D_2 exactly x_2 times, ..., and the outcome D_k exactly x_k times is given by the multinomial formula

$$P(x_1, x_2, \ldots, x_k) = \frac{n!}{x_1! x_2! \ldots x_k!} p_1^{x_1} p_2^{x_2} \ldots p^{x_k}$$

where $x_1 + x_2 + \ldots + x_k = n$ and $p_1 + p_2 + \ldots p_k = 1$

Example 4.33

Suppose that a balanced die with three black sides, two red sides and one white side is rolled four times in succession. What is the probability that in the four rolls 'black' will appear twice, and 'red' and 'white' will each appear once?

Let us denote by p_1 the probability that in a single roll of the die 'black' appears, by p_2 the probability that 'red' appears, and by p_3 the probability that 'white' appears. Since the die is fair, we have

$$p_1 = \tfrac{1}{2} \qquad p_2 = \tfrac{1}{3} \qquad p_3 = \tfrac{1}{6}$$

and $p_1 + p_2 + p_3 = 1$

If we denote by X_1, X_2 and X_3 the random variables

X_1: number of occurrences of 'black'
X_2: number of occurrences of 'red'
X_3: number of occurrences of 'white'

we also have

$$x_1 = 2 \qquad x_2 = 1 \qquad x_3 = 1$$

and

$$x_1 + x_2 + x_3 = n = 4$$

Because in the present case the four trials of the experiment are clearly independent, the probability of observing any particular sequence of outcomes in which 'black' appears exactly twice and both 'red' and 'white' appear exactly once is given by the probability product

$$p_1^{x_1} p_2^{x_2} p_3^{x_3} = \left(\frac{1}{2}\right)^2 \left(\frac{1}{3}\right)\left(\frac{1}{6}\right)$$

$$= \frac{1}{72}$$

$$= 0 \cdot 0139$$

Next we must count the possible sequences in which each of the colours appears exactly the required number of times. The number of such sequences is given by the multinomial coefficient (see section 4.7, p 105)

$$\binom{n}{x_1, x_2, x_3} = \frac{n!}{x_1! x_2! x_3!}$$

In the present case we have

$$\frac{4!}{2! 1! 1!} = 12$$

possible sequences (see also example 4.21 on p 103 above). Hence the required probability is calculated as

$$P(2, 1, 1) = (12)(0 \cdot 0139)$$

$$= 0 \cdot 1668$$

The Negative Binomial Distribution

In the applications of probability theory, we sometimes meet situations in which a binomial experiment is repeated until a given number of successes is scored. This situation differs from the earlier binomial model in that we now wish to determine the probability of obtaining a *fixed* number of successes, say k, in a variable number of trials x. The random variable X, denoting the number of trials needed to achieve exactly k successes, follows a variant of the binomial distribution known as the *negative binomial distribution*.

To derive this distribution, suppose that $(x - 1)$ trials of a binomial experiment have been performed and $(k - 1)$ successes have been scored. If the kth success occurs on the xth trial, the experiment ends. By the binomial formula, the probability of obtaining $(k - 1)$ successes and $[x - 1 - (k - 1)] = (x - k)$ failures in $(x - 1)$ trials is

$$\binom{x - 1}{k - 1} p^{k-1} q^{x-k}$$

Since the probability of a success being scored on the last, ie xth, trial is p, then, if the trials are independent, the probability of observing exactly k successes in x trials is given by[1]

$$P^*(x) = \binom{x - 1}{k - 1} p^{k-1} q^{x-k} p$$

$$= \binom{x - 1}{k - 1} p^k q^{x-k}$$

where $x = k, k + 1, k + 2, \ldots,$ and

$$\binom{x - 1}{k - 1} = \frac{(x - 1)!}{(k - 1)!(x - k)!}$$

We observe that in this case the number of trials, x, may be equal to or greater than the desired number of successes k. As with the binomial distribution, a particular negative binomial distribution is determined by two parameters: the number of successes, k, and the probability of success at each trial, p. When the values of these parameters are specified, the mean and variance of the negative binomial distribution may be computed as

$$E(X) = \mu = \frac{k}{p}$$

and

$$\mathrm{Var}(X) = \sigma^2 = \frac{k(1 - p)}{p^2}$$

Example 4.34

A manufacturer orders his production materials from several independent suppliers. From experience he knows that only 60 per cent of his orders are delivered on time. What is the probability that no more than five orders will be required to obtain exactly three deliveries on time?

Since statistical independence of orders may be assumed, we apply the negative binomial distribution formula with $p = 0.6$, $k = 3$, and $x = 3, 4, 5$.

For $x = 3$, we have

$$P^*(3) = \tbinom{2}{2}(0.6)^3(0.4)^0 = 0.216$$

Similarly, for $x = 4$

$$P^*(4) = \tbinom{3}{2}(0.6)^3(0.4)^1 = 0.259$$

and for $x = 5$

$$P^*(5) = \tbinom{4}{2}(0.6)^3(0.4)^2 = 0.207$$

---

[1] We use the symbol $P^*(x)$ to distinguish between the binomial and the negative binomial forms of the binomial distribution.

The probability that five, or fewer, orders are required to obtain three deliveries on time is

$$P(X \leqslant 5) = P*(3) + P*(4) + P*(5)$$
$$= 0.682.$$

The Hypergeometric Distribution

Consider again a population of M elements, of which M_1 have characteristic A, labelled 'success', and $M_2 = M - M_1$ have characteristic B, labelled 'failure'. Suppose that from this population we select a sample of N elements *without* replacement. What is the probability of observing exactly x successes in the sample?

Since the sampling is without replacement, the total number of different samples of size N that can be drawn from the population of M elements is $\binom{M}{N}$ (see section 4.7, p 108 above). If the sampling is random each of these occurs with probability $\frac{1}{\binom{M}{N}}$. Consider next how many of the $\binom{M}{N}$ samples contain exactly x successes and $(N - x)$ failures. As there are M_1 elements labelled 'success' in the population, there are $\binom{M_1}{x}$ ways of selecting x successes from the M_1 elements, and for each of these there are $\binom{M_2}{N - x}$ ways of selecting $(N - x)$ failures.

Hence the probability of observing x successes in a random sample of N items drawn *without replacement* from a population of M items, of which M_1 are 'successes' and $M_2 = M - M_1$ are 'failures', is given by the combinatorial formula

$$P(x) = \frac{\binom{M_1}{x}\binom{M_2}{N - x}}{\binom{M}{N}}, \qquad x = 0, 1, 2, \ldots, N \text{ (or } M_1 \text{ if } M_1 \leqslant N)$$

where
$$\binom{M_1}{x} = \frac{M_1!}{(x)!(M_1 - x)!}$$

and
$$\binom{M_2}{N - x} = \frac{M_2!}{(N - x)!(M_2 - N + x)!}$$

This probability distribution is known as the *hypergeometric distribution*.

As we have already remarked in our earlier discussion of the binomial distribution, when small samples are drawn without replacement from large populations, the non-replacement of items will have no appreciable effect on the probabilities of success and failure at each successive trial. In such cases, very little accuracy will be lost by setting the probability of success p equal to the proportion of 'successes' in the population, and approximating the hypergeometric distribution by the more easily computed binomial distribution.

Example 4.35

Consider again a box containing three white and seven black marbles. Let a sample of three marbles be selected from this box without replacement. If X is a random variable denoting the number of white marbles that may be observed in the sample, what is the probability distribution of X?

In this case, the successive drawings from the box cannot clearly be regarded as independent trials, and the appropriate probability model is the hypergeometric distribution with the parameters $M = 10$, $M_1 = 3$ and $N = 3$. We first find

$$\binom{M}{N} = \binom{10}{3} = 120$$

ie there are 120 possible samples of size 3, each containing different elements (numbered marbles). For $x = 0$, we have

$$\binom{M_1}{x} = \binom{3}{0} = 1 \text{ and } \binom{M_2}{N-x} = \frac{7!}{3!4!} = 35$$

Thus

$$P(0) = \frac{(1)(35)}{120} = \frac{35}{120}$$

Computing the probability values for the remaining values $x = 1, 2, 3$ in a similar manner, we obtain the probability table:

x	$P(x)$
0	35/120
1	63/120
2	21/120
3	1/120
	1

The Poisson Distribution

In certain classes of binomial experiments, the probability of success p at each trial is very small and the number of trials performed in the course of the experiment is rather large. It may then be shown that as n is increased without limit and p tends to zero, np remaining fixed, the binomial distribution approaches the limiting form

$$P(x;\mu) = \frac{e^{-\mu}\mu^x}{x!} \qquad x = 0, 1, 2 \ldots$$

where e is a mathematical constant (the base for natural logarithms) equal to approximately 2·71828, μ is the single parameter of the distribution, and x is the number of successes in an infinitely large sequence of trials. This limiting distribution is the *Poisson distribution*.

Because of this limiting property, the Poisson distribution is commonly used to approximate the binomial distribution when p is small and n is large. This is very convenient, for binomial probabilities based on small values of p and large values of n are cumbersome to calculate; also, such probabilities cannot be satisfactorily approximated by a smooth probability curve known as the normal curve.[1] As seen above, the Poisson distribution is characterised by a single parameter μ. In using the Poisson formula to approximate binomial probabilities, we generally know the values of p and n. Then $\mu = np$, and μ measures the mean number of occurrences of the event 'success' in the n trials.

Example 4.36

A machine is producing parts that contain, on the average, one per cent defectives. In a random sample of 150 parts taken from the production of the machine, what are the probabilities of observing 0, 1, 2, 3 defective items?

Assuming that large quantities are produced, we may regard the sample as being a binomial experiment with $p = 0·01$ and $N = 150$. Using the binomial formula

$$P(x) = \binom{150}{x}(0·01)^x(0·99)^{150-x} \qquad x = 0, 1, 2, 3$$

we find the required probability values as shown in the middle column of the accompanying table.

x	Probability $P(x)$ Binomial	Probability $P(x)$ Poisson
0	0·2215	0·2231
1	0·3355	0·3346
2	0·2525	0·2510
3	0·1258	0·1255

To show next how these probabilities can be approximated by the Poisson formula, for $x = 0$ and $\mu = np = (150)(0·01) = 1·5$ we have

$$P(0;1·5) = \frac{e^{-1·5}(1·5)^0}{0!} = e^{-1·5} = 0·2231$$

[1] See section 4.13 below.

where the value of 0.2231 for $e^{-1.5}$ can be found easily enough by looking up Table VII of Appendix A, which lists the values of the negative exponential function for various values of μ. Substituting next $X = 1$ in the Poisson formula, we obtain

$$P(1;1.5) = \frac{e^{-1.5}(1.5)}{1!} = 0.3346$$

and similarly for $X = 2$ and $X = 3$. As indicated by our table, the resulting Poisson probabilities are a very close approximation of the exact binomial probabilities.

As seen from the above example, the Poisson model provides a computationally convenient method for approximating binomial probabilities when p is small and n is large. In general, good results will be obtained when $p < 0.05$ and $n > 100$.

A second important application of the Poisson distribution arises when we are concerned with occurrences of random phenomena over specified intervals of time or space, eg the number of defects observed per unit of time, length, or area; the number of customers arriving at a petrol station during a fixed period of time; or the number of industrial accidents occurring at a given plant per month. To consider how the Poisson model may be applied in these and similar situations, let us suppose that an interval of time or space over which a random phenomenon occurs is divided into a very large number of small subintervals of uniform length. For instance, if the unit of time considered is one minute, the subdivisions may be seconds, tenths of seconds, etc. Then, if the subintervals chosen are sufficiently small, we would expect the probability of a random event occurring within each subinterval to be very small, and the probability of it occurring more than once within any given subinterval to be negligible. Furthermore, if the phenomenon being observed is distributed randomly over time or space, we would expect its occurrence within any arbitrarily chosen small interval to be independent of its occurrence or non-occurrence in any other such interval. Given these conditions, the process which generates occurrences of a random event over time or space is characterised by a single factor: the mean number of times the event can be expected to occur per unit of time or space. It is customary to indicate this number by the symbol λ (Greek lambda). Then, for any interval of length t, the expected number of occurrences of the random event will be approximately proportional to t; that is, if the event occurs per unit interval with an average frequency λ, it can be expected to occur in an interval of t such units with an average frequency (λt). It can then be shown by more advanced methods that the probability of observing exactly x occurrences of an event in a fixed interval t is given by the equation

$$P(x;\lambda t) = \frac{e^{-\lambda t}(\lambda t)^x}{x!} \qquad x = 0, 1, 2, \ldots$$

Evidently, this expression is algebraically equivalent to the equation defining the Poisson distribution with $\mu = \lambda t$. We conclude that the random variable X denoting the number of occurrences of an event per interval of time, length, etc has the Poisson distribution

$$P(x;\mu) = \frac{e^{-\mu}\mu^x}{x!} \qquad x = 0, 1, 2, \ldots$$

where μ is the average number of occurrences of the event within the specified interval. It is important to stress that in this equation μ is an empirical constant which must be determined by reference to past information or experimental data.

Example 4.37

Suppose that the records of a real-estate agency show that the agency sells, on the average, four houses per week. If the sales tend to conform to the Poisson model, what is the probability that the agency will sell fewer than four houses per week?

Setting $\mu = 4$ and finding $e^{-4} = 0 \cdot 0183$ from Table VII, Appendix A, we may compute the cumulative probability $P(X < 4; 4)$ by constructing the following table:

No. of houses sold x	$P(x;\mu)$	$P(X \leqslant x;\mu)$
0	$e^{-4}\dfrac{4^0}{0!} = 0 \cdot 0183$	$0 \cdot 0183$
1	$e^{-4}\dfrac{4^1}{1!} = 0 \cdot 0732$	$0 \cdot 0915$
2	$e^{-4}\dfrac{4^2}{2!} = 0 \cdot 1464$	$0 \cdot 2379$
3	$e^{-4}\dfrac{4^3}{3!} = 0 \cdot 1952$	$0 \cdot 4331$

The last entry in the third column gives the required probability as $0 \cdot 4331$.

Example 4.38

An engineering firm finds that breakdowns in one of its heavy presses occur at an average rate of one major breakdown per 800 hours of use. Assuming that the breakdowns follow a Poisson pattern, what is the probability that in any 500-hour run no major breakdown will occur? What is the probability that in an interval of 1500 working hours exactly two breakdowns will occur?

Let λ be the average number of major breakdowns per unit interval, ie per hour. We have

$$\lambda = \frac{1}{800}$$

Denote next by X the variable number of breakdowns that may occur during the specified interval of 500 hours; then $t = 500$, and

$$\mu = \lambda t = \left(\frac{1}{800}\right)(500) = 0.625$$

No serious loss of accuracy will result if μ is rounded to 0·6. From Table VII, Appendix A, we find

$$e^{-0.6} = 0.5488$$

Hence,

$$P(0;0.6) = \frac{e^{-0.6}}{0!} = 0.5488$$

ie the probability that no major breakdown occurs during an interval of 500 working hours is 0·5488.

Consider next the probability of experiencing two major breakdowns in an interval of length $t = 1500$ hours. Since for any given value of λ the expected value of a Poisson variable is proportional to the length of the interval t, we now have

$$\mu = \lambda t = \left(\frac{1}{800}\right)(1500) = 1.875$$

Rounding this figure to 1·9, we find $e^{-1.9} = 0.1496$. The probability of two major breakdowns occurring in 1500 working hours is

$$P(2;1.9) = e^{-1.9}\frac{(1.9)^2}{2!} = (0.1496)(1.8050)$$

$$= 0.27$$

4.12 Continuous Random Variables and Probability Distributions

Up until now we have been restricting our attention to random variables which can only take on isolated values, generally integer values such as 0, 1, 2, etc. As already remarked earlier, such variables are called discrete variables. Experience tells us, however, that not all variables associated with random experiments can be assumed to be discrete. Variables which are measured on a time scale, or measurements of ages, weights or rainfall, can take on a theoretically infinite number of values, even though in practice we can only approximate them with varying margins of error. A random variable which can assume any value in an interval of values, no matter how small the interval, is said to be *continuous* in that interval. Probability distributions associated with continuous random variables are called *continuous* probability distributions.

Suppose that X is a continuous random variable whose range consists of all real numbers lying within an interval of, say, 0 to 10. Since the sample space now consists of an unlimited number of possible values, ie real numbers with infinitely many decimal places, it is evidently impossible to attach a non-zero probability to any one of the possible sample points. Fortunately, this conceptual difficulty of measuring probabilities on a continuous scale turns out to be relatively unimportant, for we can rarely expect experimental results to be precise enough to give us measurements with extremely large numbers of decimal places. On conceptual, as well as on practical grounds, therefore, we shall need to measure probabilities associated with continuous variables not for individual *points*, as in the discrete case, but for *intervals* of values lying within the range of X. Thus, given that the range of X is 0 to 10, we may wish to know the probability that X falls within an interval of, say, 0 to 1, or 0 to 0·1, or, if our measurements are precise enough, within an interval as small as 0 to 0·000001. How are we to measure these probabilities? To answer this question we now introduce the fundamentally important notion that probabilities associated with continuous variables are measured as *areas* under smooth probability curves.

In section 4.8 we already noted that if we have a probability histogram for a discrete random variable we may represent probabilities graphically either by the height of each bar, or, since the total area of the histogram corresponds to unity, as proportionate areas under the histogram. Suppose now we have a large number of observations of a variable X which can be measured continuously. We could then arrange the data into a relative frequency distribution by the methods discussed in Chapter 3. Suppose next that the frequency of observation is increased, at the same time as the class interval of the distribution is narrowed until we have a very large number of classes, each of uniform width. If this process were continued long enough, the relative frequency in each class would increasingly approach the probability of obtaining a value within that class, and the resulting probability histogram would increasingly resemble a smooth curve. Let us suppose further that this curve can be defined by a mathematical relation which pairs each possible value x with one and only one point on the curve; as we have already noted, such a relation is said to be a function, which we now write as $f(x)$. Then, for any frequency block of infinitesimal width dx which is centred on x (in mathematics the symbol dx denotes an infinitesimally small increment of x) the height of the block is $f(x)$ and its area (width × height) is $f(x)dx$. Since in the limit the total area under the curve is equal to the area under the histogram, which equals 1, the proportional area given by $f(x)dx$ measures the probability of obtaining a value within any arbitrarily small interval

dx. Consider next the probability that X assumes a value within some larger interval, say, an interval $0 < x < a$. Intuitively we can see that this probability can be obtained as the sum of the infinitesimally small areas $f(x)dx$ between 0 and a. Mathematically, this is equivalent to finding the definite integral $\int_0^a f(x)dx$, given the function $f(x)$. For our purposes in this book, it suffices to note that definite integration serves as a technique for finding areas under continuous curves. Thus, in Fig 4.10, the shaded area under the curve $f(x)$ is given by the integral $\int_0^a f(x)dx$.

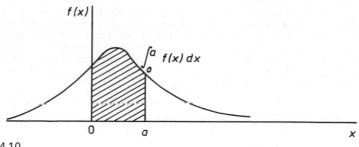

Fig 4.10

As with the discrete random variable, a function $f(x)$, such as that depicted in Fig 4.10, can only serve as a probability function if it has certain properties. Probability functions of continuous random variables are generally referred to as *probability density functions* or *probability densities*. A function $f(x)$ is said to be a probability density function if it satisfies the following two conditions:

$$f(x) \geqslant 0$$

and

$$\int_{-\infty}^{\infty} f(x)dx = 1$$

The first of these conditions states that for $f(x)$ to be a probability density it must have non-negative values throughout the range of X. The second condition requires that the sum of the probability elements $f(x)dx$ over the entire range of X is one. In practice, the symbols $-\infty$ and ∞ are a convenient way of writing that the summation performed by integrating $f(x)$ extends from the lowest to the highest value of X in the distribution.

If $f(x)$ can be shown to be a probability density function, then the probability of X falling within any two values x_1 and x_2 is

$$P(x_1 < X < x_2) = \int_{x_1}^{x_2} f(x)dx$$

As indicated above, this is shown as a proportional area under a smooth probability curve whose total area is equal to one.

Example 4.39

Consider the following example of a continuous probability distribution known as the *rectangular distribution*. At a certain crossing, the traffic light changes every 60 seconds. If a motorist arrives at the crossing at a random time when the light is red, what is the probability that he will have to wait no longer than 20 seconds?

Let X be the random variable 'waiting time'. Evidently, X may take on any value within the interval $0 < X \leqslant 60$ (seconds). Also, assuming randomness of arrival, we can expect X to be distributed uniformly over that interval. This means that over the range of X, $f(x)$ will be a horizontal line, ie a constant function $f(x) = k$. Because the distribution of X is a rectangle with base $x = 60$ whose total area must equal one, we have $k = \frac{1}{60}$. Thus, the probability density function of X is defined as

$$f(x) = \tfrac{1}{60} \quad \text{for } 0 < x \leqslant 60$$

Diagrammatically, this distribution appears as follows:

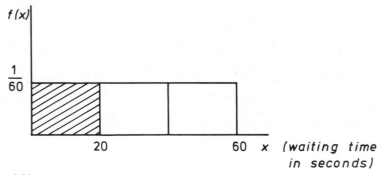

Fig 4.11

We note that in the special case where $f(x) = k$, the probability of obtaining a value within a particular interval will be proportional to the length of that interval. In the present case, we may therefore evaluate the required probability directly as

$$P(X \leqslant 20) = P(0 < X \leqslant 20) = 20/60 = 1/3$$

In the diagram, this probability is represented by the hatched area. To illustrate that this area corresponds to the value of a definite integral, we get

$$P(0 < X \leqslant 20) = \int_0^{20} f(x)dx = \int_0^{20} kdx = k \int_0^{20} dx$$

Evaluating, we find

$$k \int_0^{20} dx = kx \Big|_0^{20} = \tfrac{1}{60}(20 - 0) = \tfrac{1}{3}$$

4.13 The Normal Distribution

We now consider a continuous probability distribution which is the cornerstone of statistical and sampling theory: the *normal* or *Gaussian distribution*. To outline first the general characteristics of this distribution, let us consider again a binomial experiment involving n independent trials with a specified probability of success. Each of the trials represents an independent source of variation in the experiment, eg each of the coins in our earlier three-coin experiment contributes to the outcome of the experiment as a whole.

The question then arises, what probability distribution we can expect when n, ie the number of independent sources of variation, is increased indefinitely. By the reasoning outlined in the previous section we would expect the discrete binomial distribution to become more spread out as n increases, and also smoother. It can be shown with the use of more advanced techniques that as n becomes very large, the binomial distribution will approximate a curve whose general shape is shown in Fig 4.12.

x

Fig 4.12

We have already noted that when $p = \tfrac{1}{2}$ the binomial distribution will be symmetrical. The interesting fact is that even if p departs from $\tfrac{1}{2}$, the binomial distribution will closely approximate a symmetrical bell-shaped curve, provided that n is sufficiently large. This fact will be utilised in section 5.7 when we discuss sampling from dichotomous populations, ie populations classified according to only two attributes. The above curve, as illustrated in Fig 4.12, is known as the *normal curve*. The properties of the normal curve will be discussed below; here we comment on its general role in statistical applications.

The normal curve is sometimes referred to as the 'normal curve of errors'. This stems from the notion that observations involve errors which are caused by a multitude of small and independent chance factors. Whenever X is the sum of a true value plus a very large number of small independent errors each equally likely to be plus or minus, X will be distributed in the normal distribution.

Quite apart from the distribution of errors of measurement, the distributions of many variables are normal or approximately normal. Variables as diverse as men's heights and IQs, rents of dwellings, lengths of life of various types of equipment, growth of plants, and many others, tend to follow a pattern very similar to the normal curve. And more important, the distributions of various statistics, like the mean, are normal or nearly normal for large samples, even if the populations from which they have been drawn are not normal. Furthermore, for samples of sufficiently large size, the normal distribution serves as a very good approximation to a number of other distributions. We have already mentioned that the normal curve is the limiting form of the binomial distribution. Because binomial probabilities are quite laborious to calculate even for moderately large n, this property of the normal curve is frequently utilised in applied work.

In practice, one might seldom find an exactly normal distribution; thus economic variables are frequently positively skewed, but this does not detract from the importance of the normal distribution in sampling applications. Nor is the usefulness of the normal curve diminished by the fact that the variables with which we deal in practice are not strictly continuous because of inaccuracies of measurement, limitations of the data, etc. In fact, in many practical problems it is convenient to treat discrete variables as if they were distributed continuously according to the normal probability law. Because of the great importance of the normal distribution for our future work, we now consider its main characteristics in detail.

Properties of the Normal Distribution

If a variable X is normally distributed, the general shape of its distribution will be as in the diagram below.

This distribution is defined by the equation

$$f(x) = \frac{1}{\sqrt{2\pi}\,\sigma} e^{-\frac{1}{2}\left(\frac{x-\mu}{\sigma}\right)^2}$$

where μ is the expected value of the distribution and corresponds to the mean value of X in the population, σ is the standard deviation of X in the population, and $\pi = 3\cdot14159$ and $e = 2\cdot71828$ are mathematical constants. The normal distribution is bell-shaped, symmetrical and asymptotic in both directions to the X axis; thus, the normal density function $f(x)$ is everywhere positive. By more advanced calculus

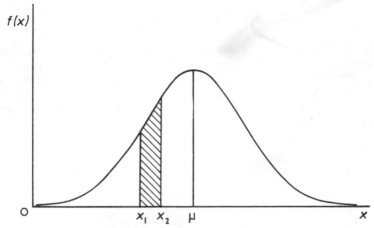

Fig 4.13 The normal distribution

methods it can be shown that the second requirement of a density function is also met and the normal distribution encloses unit area.

A second important property of the normal distribution is that it depends on the parameters μ and σ only, which are the mean and standard deviation of the distribution respectively. While the fact of normality dictates the general shape of the distribution, there will be a whole family of normal distributions, depending on the particular values which the parameters take. This is illustrated in Fig 4.14. As can be seen, the parameter μ indicates the central value of the distribution and σ the dispersion about it, so that μ fixes the general level of the distribution and σ the extent to which it is spread out. Diagrammatically, a change in μ shifts the curve along the X axis without changing its shape, and a change in σ changes its spread. Since the distribution is symmetrical, the mean μ is unambiguously the central value and coincides with the mode and median.

If a variable X has a normal distribution, we say that it is 'normally distributed about a mean μ, with a standard deviation σ'. We may write this symbolically as $N(\mu, \sigma)$; thus, for the two distributions depicted by Fig 4.14, we have $N(27, 8)$ and $N(32, 4)$ respectively. Suppose we have a particular normal distribution with given μ and σ and we wish to calculate the probability of X falling within certain values of the variable X, eg x_1 and x_2. As we saw in the previous section, this is equivalent to finding the corresponding area under the normal curve, as shown by the hatched area in Fig 4.13 above. We also saw that the numerical value of this area is the integral of $f(x)$ between x_1 and x_2, ie

$$P(x_1 < X < x_2) = \int_{x_1}^{x_2} \frac{1}{\sqrt{2\pi}\,\sigma}\, e^{-\frac{1}{2}\left(\frac{x-\mu}{\sigma}\right)^2}\, dx$$

This integration, however, cannot be performed analytically and must be done by numerical methods. To find the probability for a particular interval, therefore, it looks at first sight as if we should want a probability table for every particular combination of the parameters μ and σ. Fortunately, this is not the case, for the normal distribution can be transformed into a standard form.

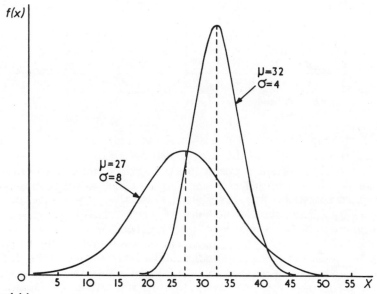

Fig 4.14

To do this, express the variable X as a deviation from its mean in terms of its standard deviation[1], thus:

$$Z = \frac{X - \mu}{\sigma}$$

For instance, if $\mu = 70$ and $\sigma = 5$, a particular value of X, say $X = 80$, is expressed as a deviation of two standard deviation units above the mean. For two given values x_1 and x_2, we may write

$$z_1 = \frac{x_1 - \mu}{\sigma} \quad \text{and} \quad z_2 = \frac{x_2 - \mu}{\sigma}$$

[1] In earlier editions of this book, the standardised normal variable was denoted by the symbol T, but here we shall follow the common usage and use the symbol Z.

If $x_1 < X < x_2$, we must have $z_1 < Z < z_2$
so that

$$P(x_1 < X < x_2) = P(z_1 < Z < z_2)$$

Thus, to find the probability that X falls within the required range x_1 and x_2, we need to find the probability that the standardised normal variable Z falls within the range z_1 and z_2. This latter probability can be shown to be[1]

$$P(z_1 < Z < z_2) = \int_{z_1}^{z_2} \frac{1}{\sqrt{2\pi}} e^{-\frac{1}{2}z^2} \, dz$$

It can be readily seen that the expression under the integral sign is in fact a normal distribution of Z with mean $\mu_Z = 0$ and standard deviation $\sigma_Z = 1$. Thus, we have the result that if X has a normal distribution $N(\mu, \sigma)$ then $Z = \dfrac{X - \mu}{\sigma}$ will have a normal distribution $N(0, 1)$. The probability density function

$$f(z) = \frac{1}{\sqrt{2\pi}} e^{-\frac{1}{2}z^2}$$

is known as the *standard normal distribution*. This distribution is unique in the sense that it does not depend on the values of the parameters μ and σ. Consequently it can be uniquely tabulated. Thus, in order to ascertain $P(x_1 < X < x_2)$ for given μ and σ, it is only necessary to transform the xs into zs and to evaluate $P(z_1 < Z < z_2)$.

The distribution of Z is tabulated in Table I of Appendix A. This table is known as a table of 'areas under the normal curve'. It gives, in the body of the table, the proportion of area under the normal curve lying between the central ordinate and any value $z = \dfrac{x - \mu}{\sigma}$ to the right

---

[1] This may be seen as follows:

We have $\qquad P(x_1 < X < x_2) = \displaystyle\int_{x_1}^{x_2} \frac{1}{\sqrt{2\pi}\,\sigma} e^{-\frac{1}{2}\left(\frac{x-\mu}{\sigma}\right)^2} \, dx$

Writing $\qquad\qquad\qquad z = \dfrac{x - \mu}{\sigma}$

we have $\qquad\qquad\qquad x = \mu + \sigma z$
and $\qquad\qquad\qquad dx = \sigma dz$

Changing the variable of integration from x to z, we shall obtain

$$P(z_1 < Z < z_2) = \int_{z_1}^{z_2} \frac{1}{\sqrt{2\pi}} e^{-\frac{1}{2}z^2} \, dz$$

of the central ordinate, such values being tabulated in steps of 0·01 in the margin of the table. Diagrammatically, the table gives proportions of area like the hatched segment in Fig 4.15. This area corresponds to the probability of Z lying between 0 and z_1, ie $P(0 < Z < z_1)$.

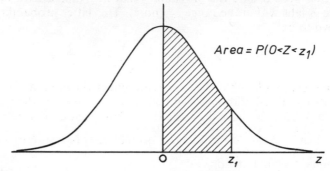

Area = $P(0 < Z < z_1)$

Fig 4.15

But $P(0 < Z < z_1)$ is the same thing as $P\left(0 < \dfrac{X - \mu}{\sigma} < \dfrac{x_1 - \mu}{\sigma}\right)$, so that the hatched area gives the probability that X will lie within z_1 standard deviations of its mean, or, given its standard deviation, that X will lie between x_1 and its mean. Given the table of areas, it is a straightforward matter to obtain the area between any two values of Z, and hence probabilities of the form $P(z_1 < Z < z_2)$, by adding or subtracting the areas given in the table. In doing this, it is helpful to sketch a small diagram, as in example 4.40 below. It should be remembered that since the distribution is symmetrical, each half of the curve covers 50 per cent of the total area. From the table we can always find out the probability that a variable will lie within a certain distance of its mean in terms of its standard deviation, for the area between the central ordinate and any given deviation of X from μ in terms of σ is always the same. Thus, if a variable has a mean of 100 and a standard deviation of 7, the probability that one observation of the variable will lie between 100 and 110 is the probability that an observation of a variable will lie within $\dfrac{110 - 100}{7} = 1\cdot43$ standard deviations from its mean. From the table this probability is found to be 0·4236. If we were to draw at random, say, 1000 observations of the variable under consideration from the population of the variable, we should expect on the average approximately 424 of the observations to have values between 100 and 110.

Example 4.40

From the table of areas under the normal curve we have

$$P(0 < Z < 1) = 0.3413$$

$$P(1 < Z < 2) = 0.4773 - 0.3413$$
$$= 0.1360$$

$$P(-1 < Z < 2) = 0.3413 + 0.4773$$
$$= 0.8186$$

$$P(Z > 1) = 0.5000 - 0.3413$$
$$= 0.1587$$

$$P(|Z| > 1) = 2 \times 0.1587$$
$$= 0.3174$$

$$P(|Z| < 1) = 2 \times 0.3413$$
$$= 0.6826$$

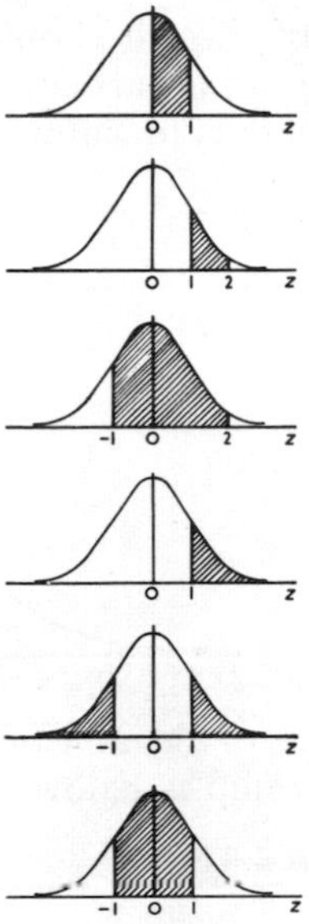

Fig 4.16

From the table of areas we see that the area between the central ordinate and one standard deviation to its right is 0·3413. Consequently, the range $\mu \pm \sigma$ will, in any normal distribution, contain 68·27 per cent of the population. Similarly, the range $\mu \pm 2\sigma$ will contain 95·45 per cent, and the range $\mu \pm 3\sigma$, 99·73 per cent. It is also useful to note at this stage that 95 per cent of the population will be contained in the range $\mu \pm 1.96\sigma$ and 99 per cent in the range $\mu \pm 2.58\sigma$. These facts about the normal distribution can be expressed in the following form and are illustrated in Fig 4.17.

$$P(|Z| < 1) = P(\mu - \sigma < X < \mu + \sigma)$$
$$= 0.6827$$
$$P(|Z| < 2) = P(\mu - 2\sigma < X < \mu + 2\sigma)$$
$$= 0.9545$$
$$P(|Z| < 3) = P(\mu - 3\sigma < X < \mu + 3\sigma)$$
$$= 0.9973$$
$$P(|Z| < 1.96) = P(\mu - 1.96\sigma < X < \mu + 1.96\sigma)$$
$$= 0.95$$

$$P(|Z| < 2 \cdot 58) = P(\mu - 2 \cdot 58\sigma < X < \mu + 2 \cdot 58\sigma)$$
$$= 0 \cdot 99$$

By this stage it should be clear that given the mean and standard deviation of a particular normal distribution, the table of areas tells us all there is to know about the distribution.

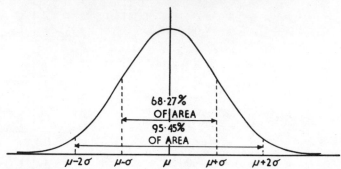

Fig 4.17

The use of the table of areas of the normal curve is further illustrated in the examples below.

Example 4.41

The weekly wages of tradesmen are normally distributed about a mean of $150 with a standard deviation of $12.
(a) Find the probability of a tradesman having a weekly wage lying
   (i)   between $150 and $156;
   (ii) between $144 and $150;
   (iii) between $147 and $156;
   (iv) over $165;
   (v)   under $132;
   (vi) more than $24 from the mean.
(b) What is the wage which 10 per cent of the tradesmen will exceed?
(c) Within what deviation on both sides of the mean will 95 per cent of the tradesmen's wages lie?

(a) (i) $P(150 < X < 156) = P(0 < Z < 0 \cdot 5)$
                        $= 0 \cdot 1915$

   (ii) $P(144 < X < 150) = P(-0 \cdot 5 < Z < 0)$
                        $= 0 \cdot 1915$

   (iii) $P(147 < X < 156) = P(-0 \cdot 25 < Z < 0 \cdot 5)$
                        $= P(-0 \cdot 25 < Z < 0) + P(0 < Z < 0 \cdot 5)$
                        $= 0 \cdot 0987 + 0 \cdot 1915$
                        $= 0 \cdot 2902$

   (iv) $P(X > 165) = P(Z > 1 \cdot 25)$
                   $= 0 \cdot 5000 - 0 \cdot 3944$
                   $= 0 \cdot 1056$

   (v) $P(X < 132) = P(Z < -1 \cdot 5)$
                   $= 0 \cdot 5000 - 0 \cdot 4332$
                   $= 0 \cdot 0668$

(vi) $P(|X - \mu| > 24) = P(|Z| > 2)$
$= 2[0.5000 - P(0 < Z < 2)]$
$= 2(0.5000 - 0.4773)$
$= 2 \times 0.0227$
$= 0.0454$

In ascertaining the above probabilities it is often helpful to use a diagram. Taking (iii) as an example, we should have

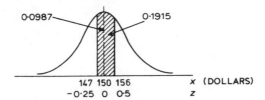

Fig 4.18

(b) We require x_1 such that

$$P(X > x_1) = 0.1$$

ie $\qquad P(Z > z_1) = 0.1, \quad \text{where } z_1 = \dfrac{x_1 - \mu}{\sigma}$

ie $\qquad P(0 < Z < z_1) = 0.4$

Referring to the table of areas we find that an area of 0.4 is included between the central ordinate and $Z = 1.28$ approximately. Hence $z_1 = 1.28$ and $x_1 = \$165.4$

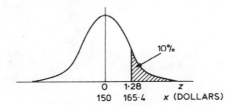

Fig 4.19

(c) We require D such that

$$P(\mu - D < X < \mu + D) = 0.95$$

ie $\qquad P\left(-\dfrac{D}{\sigma} < \dfrac{X - \mu}{\sigma} < \dfrac{D}{\sigma} \right) = 0.95$

ie $\qquad P\left(-\dfrac{D}{\sigma} < Z < \dfrac{D}{\sigma} \right) = 0.95$

ie $\qquad 2 \times P\left(0 < Z < \dfrac{D}{\sigma} \right) = 0.95$

ie $\qquad P\left(0 < Z < \dfrac{D}{\sigma} \right) = 0.475$

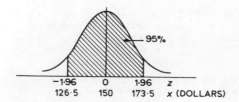

Fig 4.20

Referring to the table of areas we find that an area of 0·475 is included between the central ordinate and $Z = 1·96$. Hence

$$\frac{D}{\sigma} = 1·96$$

and

$$D = \$23·5$$

ie we can expect 95 per cent of tradesmen to have wages within the range $150 \pm \$23·5$.

Example 4.42

A random sample of 200 rents yields a mean of $23·82 and a standard deviation of $7·19. The rents of these houses are arranged into a frequency distribution with classes $2·5 and under $7·5, $7·5 and under $12·5, $12·5 and under $17·5, etc, as in Table 3.2 above. What frequency would we expect in each class if rents were distributed normally with the same mean and standard deviation as our data?

This problem can be dealt with most simply in tabular form:

Rent (dollars) (1)	Lower Class Limit x_1 (2)	$\dfrac{x_1 - \mu}{\sigma}$ (3)	Area between Lower Limit and Central Ordinate (4)	Area within Classes (5)	Expected Frequency (6)
	0	−3·31	0·5000	—	—
2·5 and under 7·5	2·5	−2·97	0·4985	0·0116	2.3
7·5 „ 12.5	7.5	−2.27	0·4884	0·0466	9.3
12·5 „ 17·5	12·5	−1·57	0·4418	0·1312	26·3
17.5 „ 22·5	17·5	−0·88	0·3106	0·2392	47·8
22·5 „ 27·5	22·5	−0·18	0·0714	0·2664	53·3
27·5 „ 32·5	27·5	0·51	0·1950	0·1919	38·4
32·5 „ 37·5	32·5	1·21	0·3869	0·0844	16·9
37·5 „ 42·5	37·5	1·90	0·4713	0·0240	4·8
42·5 „ 47·5	42·5	2·60	0·4953	0·0047	0·9
Total				1·0000	200·0

Column (3) expresses the lower class limits given in column (2) as deviations from the mean in standard deviation units. Column (4) is obtained directly from the table of areas. Column (5) is obtained from column (4) by successive subtraction of the areas except for that class in which the mean lies for which the two areas are added. Column (5) must add up to unity, since the probability of a variable falling anywhere must be unity. Any small fraction of area left over at either end of the scale should be included in the end classes. Column (6) is column (5) multiplied by 200. Since it contains the theoretically expected and not actually observed frequencies, the frequencies can be expressed with decimal places. Column (6) tells us how we can expect a sample of 200 houses drawn from a normally distributed population with a mean of $23·82 and a standard deviation of $7·19 to be distributed among the stated classes, ie we should expect repeated sampling of 200 to have these frequencies on the average.

The process outlined above is illustrated diagrammatically in Fig 4.21.

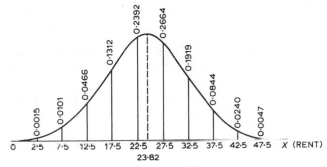

Fig 4.21

Approximation of the Binomial by the Normal Curve

As we already indicated earlier, the binomial distribution will approximate a normal curve for sufficiently large n. To illustrate how this approximation is made, let us assume a binomial experiment with $p = 0·4$ and $n = 20$ for which we wish to find the probability $P(10 \leqslant X \leqslant 12)$. Referring to the table of binomial probabilities given in Appendix A, we find $P(X = 10) = 0·1171$, $P(X = 11) = 0·0710$ and $P(X = 12) = 0·0355$. Thus, the exact binomial probability is

$$P(10 \leqslant X \leqslant 12) = 0·2236$$

Let us first consider the procedure for approximating the probability of obtaining exactly ten successes in the twenty trials, ie the probability $P(X = 10)$. We recall that if X is measured continuously, the probability associated with any single point is zero. To convert a discrete variable to a continuous one, therefore, we need to introduce a *continuity correction* of $\pm\frac{1}{2}$ unit for any single value of X whose probability we are seeking to approximate by the normal curve. Thus, in our case, the probability $P(X = 10)$ corresponds to the probability $P(9·5 < X$

< 10.5) on a continuous scale. Next, we set $\mu = np = (20)(0.4) = 8$ and $\sigma = \sqrt{npq} = \sqrt{(20)(0.4)(0.6)} = 2.19$. For the interval ($9.5 < X < 10.5$), the z values are computed as

$$z_1 = \frac{9.5 - 8}{2.19} = 0.685$$

and

$$z_2 = \frac{10.5 - 8}{2.19} = 1.142$$

Referring to the table of normal areas and interpolating the probability value corresponding to z_1, we obtain

$$P(0.685 < Z < 1.14) = 0.3729 - 0.2533$$

$$= 0.1196$$

Compared with the exact probability $P(X = 10) = 0.1171$, the normal approximation is quite close, resulting in a percentage error of about 2 per cent.

By a similar procedure, we may approximate the binomial probability $P(10 \leqslant X \leqslant 12)$ by finding the area under the normal curve corresponding to the interval ($9.5 < X < 12.5$). Here

$$P(0.685 < Z < 2.055) = 0.4800 - 0.2533$$

$$= 0.2267$$

and the percentage error is only 1.3 per cent. In general, more accurate approximations will be obtained for ranges of X than for its individual values.

For most practical purposes, normal approximations of binomial probabilities will have sufficient accuracy so long as $np > 5$ for $p < \frac{1}{2}$ (or $n(1 - p) > 5$ for $p > \frac{1}{2}$). Since for values of p very close to zero the binomial distribution would have a very high degree of positive skewness, whereas the standard normal curve is symmetrical, the method does not yield satisfactory results for extreme values of p. As we saw in example 4.36 above, in such cases the binomial distribution is well approximated by the Poisson distribution. One would also expect that as the number of repeated trials becomes larger, and the binomial distribution becomes smoother and more spread out, the need for introducing the correction of $\frac{1}{2}$ unit would diminish. In general, when several terms of the binomial distribution are approximated by the normal curve, one can dispense with the correction factor for $n > 50$. For n not greatly exceeding 50, however, such approximations will generally be more satisfactory for fairly wide ranges of values of X and for values in the proximity of the mean of the binomial distribution.

4.14 Joint Probability Distributions

We have until now been concerned with probability distributions involving one variable only. There are many types of experiments, however, in which we shall need to deal with more than one variable at a time. For instance, we might wish to select a sample of N individuals with a view to ascertaining the income, age, and educational background of each person in the sample. In this case, each of the three characteristics measured is a random variable. In our introductory discussion of probability, we already referred to probabilities assigned to the joint occurrence of two or more events as joint probabilities. When joint probabilities are assigned to two or more random variables, the resulting relationship is known as a joint probability distribution. Joint probability distributions of two random variables are referred to as *bivariate distributions*. When more than two random variables are being considered, the distribution is said to be *multivariate*. In this section, we shall extend some of the ideas presented earlier in this chapter to the concept of a joint probability distribution for two discrete random variables. The techniques of bivariate analysis will be further considered in Chapter 8 when we discuss regression and correlation.

As a simple illustration of a bivariate experiment, let us return to our earlier example of three successive tosses of a fair coin (see section 4.8 above). Let X denote again the number of heads occurring in the three trials; thus $x = 0, 1, 2, 3$. Let another random variable, Y, be defined as follows: if the first of the three tosses results in the occurrence of tails, $Y = 0$; if it results in the occurrence of heads, $Y = 1$. Thus, the range of Y is $y = 0, 1$. The possible values of X and Y, and their respective probabilities, are listed in the table below.

Table 4.5

RANDOM VARIABLES X AND Y FOR A COIN-TOSSING EXPERIMENT

Sample space	x	y	Probability
T T T	0	0	1/8
H T T	1	1	1/8
T H T	1	0	1/8
T T H	1	0	1/8
H H T	2	1	1/8
H T H	2	1	1/8
T H H	2	0	1/8
H H H	3	1	1/8

Consider now the probability that in a trial of the experiment X assumes the value x and Y assumes the value y. Symbolically, this may be written as $P(X = x, Y = y) = P(x, y)$. As can be seen from the above table, one of the possible joint events in the experiment is the event $(X = 0, Y = 0)$. This event corresponds to the single outcome TTT; hence the probability that X and Y both assume the value 0 is $P(X = 0, Y = 0) = P(0,0) = 1/8$. The joint event $(X = 1, Y = 0)$ occurs if the outcome is either THT or TTH, and so $P(X = 1, Y = 0) = P(1,0) = 2/8$. If we proceed in this manner, we can assign a probability value to each of the possible pairs of values of X and Y. The result gives the joint probability distribution of the random variables X and Y, which is shown in Table 4.6. The entries in the body of this table are the joint probabilities $P(x, y)$.

Table 4.6

BIVARIATE PROBABILITY DISTRIBUTION FOR A COIN-TOSSING EXPERIMENT

x	y		$P(x)$
	0	1	
0	1/8	0	1/8
1	2/8	1/8	3/8
2	1/8	2/8	3/8
3	0	1/8	1/8
$P(y)$	1/2	1/2	1

We observe that if two events $X = x$ and $Y = y$ cannot occur simultaneously, their intersection contains no elements, and is thus assigned the probability value of zero. We further note that the probabilities given in the body of our joint probability table sum to unity. In general, we may write this condition as

$$\sum_x \sum_y P(x, y) = 1$$

where the double summation sign $\sum_x \sum_y$ indicates that the entries in a joint probability table are added over all possible pairs of values of X and Y.

Marginal Probability Distributions

Suppose we are given the joint probability distribution of two random variables X and Y and we are interested in a problem involving only one of the variables, eg the variable X. From Table 4.6 it can be readily seen that the univariate distribution of X associated with the experiment can be found by adding the entries in the body of the table across each row, ie $P(X = 0) = P(0,0) + P(0,1) = 1/8$, $P(X = 1) = P(1,0) +$

$P(1,1) = 3/8$, etc. Since the univariate probability distribution $P(x)$ appears on the margin of the joint probability distribution from which it is derived, it is called the *marginal probability distribution* of the random variable X. The marginal probability distribution of Y, ie $P(y)$, is obtained similarly by summing the joint probabilities for each column, and is shown on the bottom margin of Table 4.6. Algebraically, the marginal distributions of X and Y are defined as

$$P(x) = \sum_y P(x, y)$$

and $$P(y) = \sum_x P(x, y)$$

Thus, to compute the marginal probability $P(Y = 0)$, we have

$$P(Y = 0) = \sum_x P(x, 0) = P(0, 0) + P(1, 0) + P(2, 0) + P(3, 0)$$

$$= \frac{1}{2}$$

Conditional Probability Distributions

Now suppose we are given the probability distribution of X and Y, and we also know that in a trial of the experiment X has assumed a particular value $X = x$. Given this condition, what is the probability that Y takes on a particular value y? From section 4.5 it will be recalled that the probability of an event E_2, given the occurrence of another event E_1, is the conditional probability

$$P(E_2|E_1) = \frac{P(E_1 E_2)}{P(E_1)} \qquad \text{for } P(E_1) > 0$$

Analogously, the conditional probability that Y takes on the value y, given that X has the value x, may be written as

$$P(Y = y|X = x) = P(y|x) = \frac{P(X = x, Y = y)}{P(X = x)} \qquad \text{for } P(X = x) > 0$$

In general, if x is fixed and y varies over all possible values within the range of Y, then

$$P(y|x) = \frac{P(x, y)}{P(x)} \qquad \text{for } P(x) > 0$$

is the *conditional probability distribution of the random variable* Y, ie the univariate distribution of Y given the condition that X has the value x.

Similarly, $$P(x|y) = \frac{P(x, y)}{P(y)} \qquad \text{for } P(y) > 0$$

is the conditional probability distribution of X, given $Y = y$. Thus, in our coin-tossing example, suppose that Y is known to have the value $Y = 0$. Then the conditional probability distribution of X, given $Y = 0$, is obtained by dividing each of the joint probabilities $P(x, 0)$ listed in the second column of Table 4.6 by the probability $P(Y = 0) = \frac{1}{2}$. The conditional probability distribution of X, given $Y = 1$, is computed similarly by dividing the entries in the third column of the joint probability table by $P(Y = 1) = \frac{1}{2}$. Thus, in the present case, we have *two* conditional distributions of X given Y, ie the distributions $P(x|Y = 0)$ and $P(x|Y = 1)$; these are tabulated in the middle columns of the table below. A similar conditional probability table may be constructed for the four separate conditional distributions of Y each corresponding to one of the possible values of X.

Table 4.7

CONDITIONAL PROBABILITY DISTRIBUTION OF X FOR A COIN TOSSING EXPERIMENT

x	$P(x|Y = 0)$	$P(x|Y = 1)$	$P(x)$
0	1/4	0	1/8
1	1/2	1/4	3/8
2	1/4	1/2	3/8
3	0	1/4	1/8

In our discussion in section 4.5 we further saw that if

$$P(E_1 E_2) = P(E_1)P(E_2)$$

then the events E_1 and E_2 are said to be statistically independent events. By similar argument, if for all possible values of two jointly distributed random variables X and Y

$$P(x, y) = P(x)P(y)$$

then X and Y are said to be *independent random variables*. Stated verbally, two random variables X and Y will be statistically independent if and only if each element in their joint probability distribution can be expressed as the product of the corresponding marginal probabilities. From the conditional probability formulae given above, it can be seen that this condition holds if $P(y|x) = P(y)$ or if $P(x|y) = P(x)$. Thus, for two random variables X and Y to be independent, the conditional probability distributions $P(y|x)$ and $P(x|y)$ must be the same as the respective unconditional, ie marginal distributions $P(y)$ and $P(x)$. To illustrate this, suppose a fair coin is tossed twice, and the random variable V is assigned the value of 0 or 1 if tails or heads occurs on the first toss, and the random variable W is assigned the value of 0 or 1 if tails or heads occurs on the second toss. The joint probability distribution for this experiment, together with the marginal probability distributions $P(v)$ and $P(w)$ and the conditional probability distributions $P(v|w)$ and $P(w|v)$, are shown in Table 4.8.

Table 4.8

JOINT PROBABILITY DISTRIBUTION OF (V, W) WITH MARGINAL AND CONDITIONAL PROBABILITIES

v	w 0	1	$P(v)$	Conditional probability $P(v|w)$ $P(v|W=0)$	$P(v|W=1)$
0	1/4	1/4	1/2	1/2	1/2
1	1/4	1/4	1/2	1/2	1/2
$P(w)$	1/2	1/2	1		

Conditional probability $P(w|v)$
$P(w|V=0)$ 1/2   1/2
$P(w|V=1)$ 1/2   1/2

As can be readily seen from the entries in this table, the conditional probability distributions $P(v|w)$ and $P(w|v)$ are the same as the marginal distributions $P(v)$ and $P(w)$ respectively, and the random variables V and W are thus shown to be statistically independent. This we would expect, since the outcome of the first toss can have no effect on the outcome of the second toss. From Table 4.7 on p 152 it is also apparent that the conditional distribution of X does not coincide with its marginal distribution $P(x)$, and we conclude that X (number of heads) and Y (outcome of the first toss) are not independent random variables.

The notion of independence can be extended to any number of random variables. Thus, the random variables $X_1, X_2, \ldots, X_n$ are statistically independent if the condition

$$P(x_1, x_2, \ldots, x_n) = P(x_1)P(x_2) \ldots P(x_n)$$

holds for all values of $X_1, X_2, \ldots, X_n$.

Covariance and Correlation

Given two jointly distributed random variables X and Y, we often wish to know if there exists a relationship between the values that the variables X and Y can assume in a random experiment. A measure of *linear* relationship between two random variables having the joint probability distribution $P(x, y)$ is called the *covariance* of the distribution, and is usually denoted by $\text{Cov}(X, Y)$ or σ_{XY}.

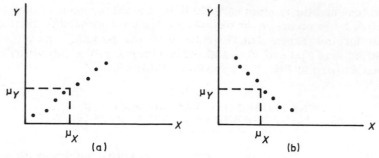

Fig 4.22 Covariance of X and Y (a) positive (b) negative

The covariance of two random variables X and Y is defined as the expectation

$$\text{Cov}(X, Y) = \sigma_{XY} = E[(X - \mu_X)(Y - \mu_Y)]$$
$$= \sum_x \sum_y (x - \mu_X)(y - \mu_Y)P(x, y)$$

It can be interpreted as a measure of the degree to which values drawn from the population of the Xs and of the Ys tend to move together in a long sequence of repetitions of a bivariate experiment. When large values of X tend to be paired with large values of Y, and small values of X to be paired with small values of Y, we should expect the mean product of deviations of X and Y from their respective means, and hence $\text{Cov}(X, Y)$, to be positive; this is illustrated diagrammatically in Fig 4.22(a). When small Xs tend to be associated with large Ys, and large Xs to be associated with small Ys, the linear relationship between X and Y, and hence $\text{Cov}(X, Y)$ will be negative, as illustrated in Fig 4.22(b).

Consider now the covariance of two random variables which are statistically independent. In this case, the event of obtaining a particular value of X will have no influence on the value of Y with which it is paired, and in a large number of cases we can expect the product of random deviations of X and Y from their means to average to zero. Diagrammatically, the scatter of points as in Fig 4.22 would display no discernible linear pattern. To show this important result more formally, by the definition of covariance we have

$$\sigma_{XY} = \sum_x \sum_y (x - \mu_X)(y - \mu_Y)P(x, y)$$

If X and Y are independent, then $P(x, y) = P(x)P(y)$, and hence

$$\sigma_{XY} = \sum_x \sum_y (x - \mu_X)(y - \mu_Y)P(x)P(y)$$

Rearranging the terms under their respective summation signs, we may write[1]

$$\sigma_{XY} = \left[\sum_x (x - \mu_X)P(x)\right]\left[\sum_y (y - \mu_Y)P(y)\right]$$

In this expression, since $\sum_x xP(x) = E(X) = \mu_X$ and $\sum_x P(x) = 1$,

$$\sum_x (x - \mu_X)P(x) = \sum_x xP(x) - \mu_X \sum_x P(x) = \mu_X - \mu_X = 0 \qquad \text{or} \quad \text{redifines} \quad P_K = \frac{t_i}{h}$$

Similarly,

$$\sum_y (y - \mu_Y)P(y) = 0$$

and hence $\qquad\qquad \sigma_{XY} = 0$

We have shown that, if two random variables X and Y are independent, their covariance σ_{XY} is zero. However, the converse of this theorem need not necessarily hold, ie it is possible for two variables to have a covariance of zero and yet be non-linearly related. Thus, it is important to note that a zero covariance only implies the absence of a *linear* relationship between two variables.

As can be seen from the definition of the covariance, its absolute size depends on the units in which X and Y are measured. For comparative purposes, therefore, it would be more useful to compute a measure of linear relationship between X and Y with the influence of the units of measurement eliminated. This can be accomplished by expressing the covariance in terms of standard deviation units. The ratio

$$\rho = \frac{\text{Cov}(X, Y)}{\sigma_X \sigma_Y}$$

where σ_X and σ_Y are the standard deviations of X and Y, is known as the *correlation coefficient* of the random variables X and Y. The correlation coefficient ρ (Greek rho) gives a measure of the extent to which X and Y are linearly associated. Because the absolute value of

---

[1] Consider, for example, the double summation

$$\sum_i \sum_j X_i Y_j \text{ for } i = 1, 2 \text{ and } j = 1, 2, 3$$

Multiplying and arranging the terms, we get

$$\sum_i \sum_j X_i X_j = X_1 Y_1 + X_1 Y_2 + X_1 Y_3 + X_2 Y_1 + X_2 Y_2 + X_2 Y_3$$

$$= (X_1 + X_2)(Y_1 + Y_2 + Y_3)$$

$$= (\sum_i X_i)(\sum_j Y_j)$$

the covariance of two random variables cannot exceed the product of their standard deviations, ie

$$|\sigma_{XY}| \leqslant \sigma_X \sigma_Y$$

we have

$$|\rho| = \frac{|\sigma_{XY}|}{\sigma_X \sigma_Y} \leqslant 1$$

ie the correlation coefficient must lie within the range ± 1. When $\rho = +1$, we have a case of perfect covariability between two variables, and one variable can be predicted from the other on the basis of a linear function with a positive slope. When $\rho = -1$, the relationship between X and Y is given by a straight line with a negative slope. In practice we shall very seldom find random variables that are perfectly correlated. In such cases, the closer the value of the correlation coefficient to $+1$ or -1, the stronger the degree of linear association between the variables. If X and Y are independent random variables, then $\rho = 0$, and we say that X and Y are uncorrelated. However, as with the covariance, if X and Y are uncorrelated, we cannot conclude that they are independent but only that there exists no linear relationship between them.

Our purpose in this section has been to introduce the covariance and the correlation coefficient as measures of covariability between two random variables X and Y having the joint probability distribution $P(x, y)$. Further applications of these concepts in bivariate analysis will be considered in more detail in Chapter 8 below.

Example 4.43

The employees of a firm are classified according to length of service with the firm (X) and salary grade (Y). There are three grades, 1, 2 and 3, grade 1 being the lowest and grade 3 the highest. The results for the firm's 200 employees are summarised by the following joint frequency table:

Length of service (years)	Salary grade (dollars) y			Total
x	1	2	3	
1	20	0	0	20
2	40	10	0	50
3	24	24	12	60
4	16	26	8	50
5	0	0	20	20
Total	100	60	40	200

From the data contained in this table:
(a) Construct a bivariate probability table, showing the marginal distributions of X and Y.

(b) Find the conditional probability distributions of Y for the given values of X. Are X and Y statistically independent?
(c) Find the covariance and the correlation coefficient of X and Y.
Do the results indicate the existence of a linear relationship between X and Y?

(a) To find the joint probability for each possible pair of values (x, y) we divide the number of elements in each cell by the total number of elements in the population. Thus, the probability of selecting an employee with one year's service and with a salary in the lowest grade is the joint probability $P(X = 1, Y = 1) = 20/200 = 0.10$, and similarly for the remaining cells. The result gives the joint probability distribution of X and Y, shown in the body of the table below.

x	y			$P(x)$
	1	2	3	
1	0·10	0	0	0·10
2	0·20	0·05	0	0·25
3	0·12	0·12	0·06	0·30
4	0·08	0·13	0·04	0·25
5	0	0	0·10	0·10
$P(y)$	0·50	0·30	0·20	

Summing the joint probabilities across each row, we obtain the marginal probability distribution of X, ie $P(x)$. Summing the entries for each column gives the marginal probability distribution of Y displayed in the lower margin of the table.
(b) The conditional probability distribution of Y given X is computed from the formula

$$P(y|x) = \frac{P(x, y)}{P(x)}$$

If $X = 1$, we have

$$P(1|X = 1) = \frac{P(1, 1)}{P(X = 1)} = \frac{0.10}{0.10} = 1$$

$$P(2|X = 1) = \frac{P(1, 2)}{P(X = 1)} = 0$$

$$P(3|X = 1) = \frac{P(1, 3)}{P(X = 1)} = 0$$

Similarly, for $X = 2$ we obtain

$$P(1|X = 2) = \frac{P(2, 1)}{P(X = 2)} = \frac{0.20}{0.25} = 0.80$$

$$P(2|X = 2) = \frac{P(2, 2)}{P(X = 2)} = \frac{0.05}{0.25} = 0.20$$

$$P(3|X = 2) = \frac{P(2, 3)}{P(X = 2)} = 0$$

There are five possible values within the range of X, and hence there are five conditional distributions of Y given X; these are set out in the table below.

Conditional probability $P(y\|x)$	y		
	1	2	3
$P(y\|X = 1)$	1	0	0
$P(y\|X = 2)$	0·80	0·20	0
$P(y\|X = 3)$	0·40	0·40	0·20
$P(y\|X = 4)$	0·32	0·52	0·16
$P(y\|X = 5)$	0	0	1

To check whether or not X and Y are statistically independent variables, we compare each of the five conditional probability distributions of Y with the unconditional or marginal distribution $P(y)$ tabulated in the lower margin of the joint probability table. Evidently, in each case the conditional and unconditional distributions are quite different, and we conclude that X and Y are not independent random variables.

(c) To compute the population covariance σ_{XY}, we make use of the formula[1]

$$\sigma_{XY} = \sum_x \sum_y (x - \mu_X)(y - \mu_Y) P(x, y)$$

From the marginal distributions $P(x)$ and $P(y)$ we find

$$\mu_X = E(X) = 3$$
$$\mu_Y = E(Y) = 1·7$$

(see section 4.9 above). The calculations needed to compute σ_{XY} are most conveniently carried out by setting up the table:

x	y	$x - \mu_X$	$y - \mu_Y$	$(x - \mu_X)(y - \mu_Y)$	$P(x,y)$	$(x - \mu_X)(y - \mu_Y)P(x,y)$
1	1	−2	−0·7	1·4	0·10	0·140
2	1	−1	−0·7	0·7	0·20	0·140
2	2	−1	0·3	−0·3	0·05	−0·015
3	1	0	−0·7	0	0·12	0
3	2	0	0·3	0	0·12	0
3	3	0	1·3	0	0·06	0
4	1	1	−0·7	−0·7	0·08	−0·056
4	2	1	0·3	0·3	0·13	0·039
4	3	1	1·3	1·3	0·04	0·052
5	3	2	1·3	2·6	0·10	0·260
						0·560

The first two columns of this table list all the possible pairs of values of X and Y for which the joint probability $P(x,y)$ has non-zero value. Adding the entries in the last column, we get

$$\sigma_{XY} = 0·56$$

[1] For a computationally simpler formula see p 161 and example 4.44 below.

The covariance being positive, the variables X and Y tend to vary together in the same direction, ie larger values of Y tend to be associated, on the average, with higher values of X.

To compute the correlation coefficient, we first need to know σ_X and σ_Y. Applying the variance formulae[1]

$$\sigma_X^2 = \sum_x (x - \mu_X)^2 P(x)$$

and $\quad \sigma_Y^2 = \sum_y (y - \mu_Y)^2 P(y)$

we find

$\sigma_X^2 = (-2)^2(0{\cdot}10) + (-1)^2(0{\cdot}25) + (1)^2(0{\cdot}25) + (2)^2(0{\cdot}10)$

$\quad = 1{\cdot}3$

and $\quad \sigma_Y^2 = (-0{\cdot}7)^2(0{\cdot}5) + (0{\cdot}3)^2(0{\cdot}3) + (1{\cdot}3)^2(0{\cdot}2)$

$\quad = 0{\cdot}61$

Hence, $\quad \sigma_X = 1{\cdot}14$ and $\sigma_Y = 0{\cdot}78$, and

$$\rho = \frac{\sigma_{XY}}{\sigma_X \sigma_Y} = \frac{0{\cdot}56}{(1{\cdot}14)(0{\cdot}78)}$$

$= 0{\cdot}63$

Thus, there is evidence of a positive linear relationship between X and Y. We would expect, on the average, employees with longer service to earn salaries in the higher salary grades.

4.15 Functions and Linear Combinations of Random Variables

In statistical analysis we often deal with random variables which are related to other random variables by some specified mathematical function. For instance, a random variable Y may be defined as a constant times another variable X, or a random variable Z may be defined as being equal to the sum of two random variables X and Y, etc. In this section, we shall develop some important theorems concerning the means and variances of random variables which are expressed as functions of other random variables.

Let X be a discrete random variable with probability distribution $P(x)$, and let $g(X)$ be any function of X. Then the expected value of $g(X)$, which we write as $E[g(X)]$ is

$$E[g(X)] = g(x_1)P(x_1) + g(x_2)P(x_2) + \ldots + g(x_n)P(x_n)$$

$$= \Sigma g(x_i)P(x_i)$$

To illustrate this important rule, let us consider some special forms of the function $g(x)$. Thus, suppose we have a variable X and we multiply every possible observation of X by a constant number a.

[1] See also p 161 and example 4.44 below.

Here

$$g(X) = aX$$

and we may write

$$E[g(X)] = E(aX) = \Sigma ax_i P(x_i) = a\Sigma x_i P(x_i)$$

Since $\Sigma x_i P(x_i) = E(X)$, we have

$$E(aX) = aE(X)$$

ie the expectation of (aX) is a times the expectation of X.

Let further

$$g(X) = c + bX$$

where c and b are constants. Then

$$E[g(X)] = E(c + bX) = \Sigma(c + bx_i)P(x_i) = \Sigma cP(x_i) + \Sigma bx_i P(x_i)$$
$$= c\Sigma P(x_i) + b\Sigma x_i P(x_i)$$

But $\Sigma P(x_i) = 1$ and $\Sigma x_i P(x_i) = E(X)$, and therefore

$$E(c + bX) = c + bE(X)$$

This result can be obtained more directly by using two important properties of expected values. The first of these is that the expected value of a constant is the constant itself, ie $E(c) = c$. This can be proved easily by noting that if $X = c$, then $P(X = c) = 1$, ie the probability that X assumes the value c is one, and hence

$$E(X) = E(c) = c \cdot P(X = c) = c$$

The second property of expectation is that the expected value of a sum of terms is the same as the sum of the expected values of the individual terms. Combining these two properties we may write

$$E(c + bX) = E(c) + E(bX)$$
$$= c + bE(X)$$

Suppose next that $g(X)$ is defined as $g(X) = X$, ie the function of X is X itself. Then

$$E(X) = \Sigma x_i P(x_i) = \mu_X$$

ie the expected value of $g(X) = X$ is the mean of the distribution of X. Let further $g(X) = (X - \mu_X)^2$. We then have

$$E[X - \mu_X]^2 = \Sigma(x_i - \mu_X)^2 P(x_i) = \sigma_X^2$$

Thus, the variance of X is defined as the expectation of the random variable $(X - \mu_X)^2$ which is itself a function of X. With the use of the two properties of expectation stated in the previous paragraph, we can now obtain a useful formula for computing the variance σ_X^2. Squaring the left-hand side of the expression for σ_X^2, we may write

$$\sigma_X^2 = E[X - \mu_X]^2 = E[X^2 - 2\mu_X X + \mu_X^2]$$
$$= E(X^2) - 2\mu_X E(X) + E(\mu_X^2)$$
$$= E(X^2) - 2\mu_X^2 + \mu_X^2$$
$$= E(X^2) - \mu_X^2$$

where

$$E(X^2) = \Sigma x_i^2 P(x_i)$$

A numerical illustration of this formula is given in example 4.44 below.

Consider next the case of two random variables X and Y with a joint probability distribution $P(x, y)$. If $g(X, Y)$ is defined as a function of X and Y, then the expected value of the new random variable $g(X, Y)$ is given by

$$E[g(X, Y)] = \sum_x \sum_y g(x, y) P(x, y)$$

As a special case, let $g(X, Y) = (X - \mu_X)(Y - \mu_Y)$. Then

$$E[(X - \mu_X)(Y - \mu_Y)] = \sum_x \sum_y (x - \mu_X)(y - \mu_Y) P(x, y) = \sigma_{XY}$$

Thus, the covariance σ_{XY}, introduced in the previous section as a measure of linear association between X and Y, is seen to be the expectation of a particular function of X and Y, ie the function $g(X, Y) = (X - \mu_X)(Y - \mu_Y)$. Expanding the term on the left-hand side of the covariance formula, we have

$$E[(X - \mu_X)(Y - \mu_Y)] = E[XY - X\mu_Y - \mu_X Y + \mu_X \mu_Y]$$
$$= E(XY) - \mu_Y E(X) - \mu_X E(Y) + E(\mu_X \mu_Y)$$

Since $E(X) = \mu_X$, $E(Y) = \mu_Y$ and $E(\mu_X \mu_Y) = \mu_X \mu_Y$, we have

$$\text{Cov}(X, Y) = \sigma_{XY} = E(XY) - \mu_X \mu_Y$$

where

$$E(XY) = \sum_x \sum_y xy P(x, y)$$

As already shown earlier, if X and Y are independent random variables, then $\sigma_{XY} = 0$ (see p 152 above). We then have

$$E(XY) - \mu_X \mu_Y = 0$$

and since by definition $\mu_X \mu_Y = E(X)E(Y)$,

$$E(XY) = E(X)E(Y)$$

ie the expected value of the product of two *independent* random variables is equal to the product of their expected values. This important result applies in the general case of n random variables. If X_1, $X_2, \ldots, X_n$ are n independent random variables with expected values $E(X_1), E(X_2), \ldots, E(X_n)$, then

$$E(X_1 X_2 \ldots X_n) = E(X_1)E(X_2) \ldots E(X_n).$$

Example 4.44

Applying the formulae derived in this section, calculate the variance of X and the covariance of X and Y for example 4.43 above.

We have $\qquad \sigma_X^2 = E(X^2) - \mu_X^2$

where $\qquad E(X^2) = \Sigma x_i^2 P(x_i)$

From the marginal distribution $P(x)$ given in example 4.43 on p 157 we find

$$E(X^2) = (1)^2(0\cdot10) + (2)^2(0\cdot25) + (3)^2(0\cdot30) + (4)^2(0\cdot25) + (5)^2(0\cdot10)$$
$$= 10\cdot3$$

From example 4.43 we also have $E(X) = \mu_X = 3$. Hence

$$\sigma_X^2 = 10\cdot3 - (3)^3$$
$$= 1\cdot3$$

For $\text{Cov}(X, Y)$ we write

$$\sigma_{XY} = E(XY) - \mu_X \mu_Y$$

where

$$E(XY) = \sum_x \sum_y xy P(x, y)$$

Setting out the calculation of $E(XY)$ in tabular form, we have:

x	y	xy	$P(x,y)$	$xyP(x,y)$
1	1	1	0·10	0·10
2	1	2	0·20	0·40
2	2	4	0·05	0·20
3	1	3	0·12	0·36
3	2	6	0·12	0·72
3	3	9	0·06	0·54
4	1	4	0·08	0·32
4	2	8	0·13	1·04
4	3	12	0·04	0·48
5	3	15	0·10	1·50
				5·66

The sum of entries in the last column gives

$$E(XY) = 5\cdot66$$

Also, $\mu_X = 3$, $\mu_Y = 1\cdot7$, and hence

$$\sigma_{XY} = 5\cdot66 - (3)(1\cdot7)$$
$$= 0\cdot56$$

Example 4.45

As a numerical illustration of the theorem that for two independent random variables $E(XY) = E(X)E(Y)$, consider again the experiment of two tosses of an unbiased coin in which the random variable V assumes the value 0 or 1 depending on whether tails or heads occurs on the first toss, and the random variable W assumes the value 0 or 1 depending on whether tails or heads occurs on the second toss. As can be seen from Table 4.8 on p 153, the joint probability distribution of V and W is given by the equation

$$P(v, w) = 1/4 \quad \text{for } v = 0, 1; w = 0, 1$$

Here

$$
\begin{aligned}
E(VW) &= \sum_v \sum_w vwP(v, w) \\
&= (0 + 0 + 0 + 1)(\tfrac{1}{4}) \\
&= \tfrac{1}{4}
\end{aligned}
$$

Also,

$$E(V) = \sum_v vP(v) = (0)(\tfrac{1}{2}) + (1)\tfrac{1}{2} = \tfrac{1}{2}$$

and

$$E(W) = \sum_w wP(w) = (0)\tfrac{1}{2} + (1)\tfrac{1}{2} = \tfrac{1}{2}$$

Hence

$$
\begin{aligned}
E(VW) &= \tfrac{1}{4} \\
&= E(V)E(W) = \tfrac{1}{4}
\end{aligned}
$$

Mean and Variance of a Linear Combination

We have already noted that if X is a random variable with expectation $E(X)$ and we form a new variable

$$W = aX$$

where a is a constant, then

$$E(W) = aE(X)$$

Writing $E(X)$ as the mean μ_X of the theoretical distribution of X, we may also state this result as

$$\mu_W = a\mu_X$$

where μ_W is the mean of W. In general, the mean of a constant times a variable is the constant times the mean of the variable.

Given that $W = aX$, what is now the variance of W? By definition, $\text{Var } W = E[W - \mu_W]^2$, and hence

$$
\begin{aligned}
\text{Var}(W) = E[aX - a\mu_X]^2 &= a^2 E[X - \mu_X]^2 \\
&= a^2 \text{Var}(X)
\end{aligned}
$$

or, in alternative notation,

$$\sigma_W^2 = a^2 \sigma_X^2$$

In general, the variance of a constant times a variable is the *constant squared* times the variance of the variable.

Suppose next that W is defined as $W = c + X$, where c is a constant and X is a random variable with variance $\text{Var}(X)$. Since $\mu_W = c + \mu_X$ (see p 160 above) we may write

$$\begin{aligned}
\text{Var}(W) &= E[(c + X) - (c + \mu_X)]^2 \\
&= E[X - \mu_X]^2 \\
&= \text{Var}(X)
\end{aligned}$$

ie adding a constant to every possible observation of a random variable leaves the variance unchanged.

Now, suppose we have a random variable Z which is related to two other random variables X and Y by the function $Z = g(X, Y) = aX + bY$, where a and b are fixed constants. Then Z is said to be a *linear combination* of the variables X and Y. We have already noted that the expected value of a sum of random variables is equal to the sum of their expected values. Hence, in the present case, we shall have

$$E(Z) = E(aX + bY) = E(aX) + E(bX) = aE(X) + bE(Y)$$

or, in alternative notation,

$$\mu_Z = a\mu_X + b\mu_Y$$

This result holds whether X and Y are statistically independent or not. Also, it applies generally in the case of n variables, ie the mean of a linear combination of the variables is the linear combination of their means.

To find next the variance of $Z = aX + bY$, we write

$$\begin{aligned}
\text{Var}(Z) &= E[Z - \mu_Z]^2 \\
&= E[(aX + bY) - (a\mu_X + b\mu_Y)]^2 \\
&= E[a(X - \mu_X) + b(Y - \mu_Y)]^2
\end{aligned}$$

Squaring this expression and making use of the properties of expectations and variances stated earlier, we obtain

$$\text{Var}(Z) = a^2 \text{Var}(X) + 2ab \text{Cov}(X, Y) + b^2 \text{Var}(Y)$$

From this theorem, an important result follows: if X and Y are independent random variables, then $\text{Cov}(X, Y) = \sigma_{XY} = 0$, and we may write

$$\sigma_Z^2 = a^2 \sigma_X^2 + b^2 \sigma_Y^2$$

Hence, the variance of a linear combination of two *independent* random variables is a linear combination of the variances of the variables having as their coefficients the squares of the coefficients of the original linear combination. It is worth noting that this result holds for any linear combination, ie irrespective of the sign which binds the variables together. For instance, if

$$Z = X - Y$$

then

$$\sigma_Z^2 = \sigma_X^2 - 2\sigma_{XY} + \sigma_Y^2$$

and the covariance term vanishes if X and Y are independent. Thus we have the simple but important case that if $Z = X \pm Y$, and X and Y are independent, $\sigma_Z^2 = \sigma_X^2 + \sigma_Y^2$. This result holds generally. If $X_1, X_2, \ldots, X_n$ are independent, and $Z = X_1 \pm X_2 \pm \ldots \pm X_n$, then the covariance between any pair of variables is zero, ie $\text{Cov}(X_i Y_j) = 0$ for all $i \neq j$, and we have

$$\text{Var}(Z) = \text{Var}(X_1) + \text{Var}(X_2) + \ldots + \text{Var}(X_n)$$

Another important result, which will not be proved here, is that if the independent variables are themselves normally distributed, a linear combination of them will be normally distributed, with mean and variance as above. In our subsequent discussion frequent use will be made of these results.

Example 4.46
The weekly wages of tradesmen (X) are normally distributed about a mean of $150 with a standard deviation of $12. If all tradesmen were awarded a wage increase of 12 per cent, what would be the mean and standard deviation of the new distribution of tradesmen's wages?

Let W denote the weekly wages earned by tradesmen after the rise. With $a = 1 \cdot 12$, $\mu_X = 150$, and $\sigma_X = 12$

$$\mu_W = a\mu_X$$
$$= (1 \cdot 12)(150)$$
$$= 168$$

and
$$\sigma_W^2 = a^2 \sigma_X^2$$
$$= (1 \cdot 12)^2 (12)^2$$

$$\therefore \quad \sigma_W = (1 \cdot 12)(12)$$
$$= 13 \cdot 4$$

The new variable W will also be distributed normally with a mean of $168 and a standard deviation of $13·4.

Suppose next that instead of being awarded a wage increase of 12 per cent all tradesmen receive a flat $15 increase per week. What is now the mean and standard deviation of W?

Here we write

$$W = c + X$$

where $c = 15$. Hence

$$\mu_W = c + \mu_X$$
$$= 15 + 150$$
$$= 165$$

Since

$$\text{Var}(W) = \text{Var}(c + X) = \text{Var}(X)$$

we have

$$\sigma_W = \sigma_X$$
$$= 12$$

ie granting a flat \$15 increase in wages increases the mean by the same amount but leaves the variance and standard deviation unchanged.

Example 4.47

A taxi service employs two drivers, one in the metropolitan area and one in a rural urban area. The weekly takings of the former are distributed with a mean of \$320 and a standard deviation of \$50, and those of the latter are distributed with a mean of \$240 and a standard deviation of \$60. What are the mean and standard deviation for the *total* weekly takings of the two drivers?

Let

$$Z = X + Y$$

where X and Y represent the weekly takings in the two areas, respectively. Then

$$\mu_Z = \mu_X + \mu_Y$$
$$= 320 + 240$$
$$= \$560$$

and, assuming independence of X and Y,

$$\sigma_Z^2 = \sigma_X^2 + \sigma_Y^2$$
$$\therefore \quad \sigma_Z = \sqrt{(50)^2 + (60)^2}$$
$$= \$78 \cdot 1$$

CHAPTER 5

SAMPLING AND SIGNIFICANCE

5.1 The General Problem of Statistical Inference

In discussing the concept of a probability distribution in the previous chapter we have already drawn attention to the need for distinguishing between the totality of observations of a variable, known as the population of the variable, and a sample of observations drawn from such a population. In terms of applications, this distinction is a familiar commonsense distinction. We are all accustomed to the idea of picking a sample as an indication of the larger totality from which the sample has come, eg a sample of suiting, a sample of wheat, a sample of political opinion. In some situations when analysing the characteristics of a variable, a sample of observations must be used because the population is infinite or so very large as to render an examination of the whole population impossible. This would be the case in the analysis of a particular variety of wheat. In other situations, although an examination of the whole population would be possible, the magnitude of the task may be so great as to render a sample the only practicable solution.

If we have a sample number of observations of a particular variable, we can describe the sample quite fully by the techniques which have been set out in Chapter 3. Thus, we can arrange the data into a frequency distribution, and compute measures such as the mean $\bar{X}$ and the standard deviation s; we have already referred to these measures as statistics. Corresponding to the parent population from which the sample has presumably come there will be another distribution of all the possible observations of X; this is the population distribution of X. Unfortunately, this distribution will only very rarely be exactly known. We may then wish to use the sample information either:

(i) to test hypotheses about the parameters of the underlying population, or

(ii) to make inferences about the likely values of these parameters.

These two uses, both part of the general problem of statistical inference, can be referred to as (i) testing hypotheses, and (ii) estimation. However, it is only possible to use samples for these purposes if the samples on which we base our judgment about the population are *random samples*. From section 4.7 it will be recalled that a random sample is a sample selected in such a way that every element in the population has a known probability of selection. For instance, if a sample of N items is selected at random and without replacement from a population of M items, each of the M elements has an equal chance of being selected on the first draw, each of the remaining $(M - 1)$ elements has an equal chance of being selected on the second draw, etc. As already explained in section 4.7, if we are only concerned with the composition of each sample and not with the order in which the elements appear, there will be altogether $\binom{M}{N}$ possible samples each occurring with probability $1/\binom{M}{N}$. We then define a *simple random sample* as any sample which occurs with probability $1/\binom{M}{N}$. Suppose, however, that the population in question is very large and the sample drawn from it without replacement is relatively small. Then, if the selection of elements from the population is governed entirely by chance, the outcome of any one drawing will have practically no effect on the outcome of any other drawing, ie the N sample drawings can be regarded as being statistically independent. We may therefore conclude that if the sampling is without replacement from very large or infinitely large populations, a simple random sample will be a sample consisting of N successive observations which are statistically independent.[1] In this chapter we discuss sampling procedures based on such simple random sampling. Furthermore, we restrict our attention to sampling problems involving only one variable.

Our general problem is, given the sample, to decide whether it could have come from a population of a certain kind with certain parameters, ie to test an hypothesis about the population from the sample information. Alternatively, given the sample, what are the values of the population parameters likely to be? This is the problem of estimation. As we shall see below, these two areas of statistical inference are closely related, but for expository purposes it will be more convenient if we discuss tests of hypotheses first.

Since a sample covers only a fraction of the population, it cannot be expected to be an exact replica of the population. Consequently, it will be a pure fluke if a sample mean coincides exactly with the corresponding population mean. The discrepancies between sample values (statistics) from random samples and population values (parameters) are known as *sampling errors*; thus, in the case of the sample mean, the difference $(\bar{X} - \mu)$ will be a measure of the sampling error for a particular sample. It is important to note that sampling errors are not in any sense due to faulty, ie non-random, sampling. Rather, they are the result of chance factors operating in the selection of each sample. Since all our sample statistics will be subject to sampling errors we shall never be quite certain about our results, for just due to chance

---

[1] See also section 4.10, pp 120–1 above.

alone a single random sample may yield a mean $\bar{X}$ which is very different from the true population mean μ. Suppose, however, that the process of drawing random samples of size N from a given population could be repeated indefinitely. We would then generate a distribution of all the possible values of the given statistic, that is, its probability distribution. This theoretical probability distribution is called a *sampling distribution*. Although the concept of a sampling distribution is new, we may note in passing that some of the distributions dealt with in the previous chapter are in fact sampling distributions. For instance, if we view a sequence of n independent trials as a sample of N observations of a binomial variable X, the binomial distribution can be regarded as the sampling distribution of the statistic 'sample number of successes'. Similarly, in sampling problems involving the sample mean we shall first want to derive its sampling distribution. Knowing the sampling distribution of the mean, we could compute the probability of $\bar{X}$ being different from μ by any given amount—or, in other words, we could decide whether a particular $\bar{X}$ could reasonably have come from a population with a particular μ.

To illustrate this type of problem, suppose a sample of 200 rents drawn at random from a given population of tenanted houses has a mean weekly rent of $25. It may be claimed, on the basis of evidence of one sort or another, that the mean rent of *all* tenanted houses is, say, $35 per week. This claim constitutes an hypothesis to be tested against the sample data. To be able to test this we would want to know the probability of drawing a sample of 200 rents with a mean as different from the population mean as $25 is from $35. To find this probability, we would want to know the way in which the means of samples of 200 drawn from the given population would be distributed, ie the sampling distribution of the mean. If we can show that the sample with the mean rent of $25 could not have reasonably come from a population with a mean rent of $35 because the probability of such a large discrepancy occurring is very small, then doubt is cast on the validity of the hypothesis about the nature of the parent population.

5.2 Sampling Distribution of the Mean

Suppose we have a variable X normally distributed about a mean μ with a standard deviation σ. We draw a random sample of N observations from the population of the Xs and calculate $\bar{X}$ for the sample. If we repeat the experiment, a whole series of $\bar{X}$s will be generated. These will evidently vary among themselves and from μ, just due to chance. In other words, sampling errors will arise. However, we should expect in the long run that the mean of the $\bar{X}$s would itself tend towards μ and that the variability of the $\bar{X}$s would be less than the variability of the Xs and would be smaller the greater N. Let us write $\mu_{\bar{X}}$ and $\sigma_{\bar{X}}$ for the mean and standard deviation of the infinite population of $\bar{X}$s which can be generated by repeated sampling, and μ and σ for the mean and standard deviation of the parent population of Xs.

The mean of a sample of size N is defined by

$$\bar{X} = \frac{\Sigma X}{N}$$

$$= \frac{X_1 + X_2 + \ldots + X_N}{N}$$

$$= \frac{X_1}{N} + \frac{X_2}{N} + \ldots + \frac{X_N}{N}$$

where $X_1, X_2, \ldots, X_N$ represent successive sample observations of the variable X. Since these observations are drawn at random from the same normal population, each will have the same normal distribution with mean μ and standard deviation σ (variance σ^2). Now it can be seen that $\bar{X}$ is a linear combination of N independent normal variables each having an equal weight $1/N$, and, by virtue of the theorems concerning means and variances of linear combinations (section 4.15, p 164) we shall have

$$\mu_{\bar{X}} = \frac{\mu}{N} + \frac{\mu}{N} + \ldots + \frac{\mu}{N}$$

$$= \mu$$

and

$$\sigma_{\bar{X}}^2 = \frac{\sigma^2}{N^2} + \frac{\sigma^2}{N^2} + \ldots + \frac{\sigma^2}{N^2}$$

$$= \frac{\sigma^2}{N}$$

ie

$$\sigma_{\bar{X}} = \frac{\sigma}{\sqrt{N}}$$

We may now use these results to state an important theorem: If X is a variable normally distributed about a mean μ with a standard deviation σ then $\bar{X}$, the mean of a sample of size N, will, with repeated sampling, be normally distributed about a mean μ with a standard deviation $\sigma_{\bar{X}} = \dfrac{\sigma}{\sqrt{N}}$. Diagrammatically, the sampling distribution of $\bar{X}$ will be a bell-shaped curve centred on μ, the mean of the parent population, and with dispersion measured by standard deviation $\sigma_{\bar{X}}$. This is illustrated in Fig 5.1.

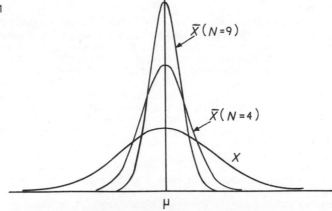

The standard deviation of a statistic is called the *standard error* of that statistic, eg $\sigma_{\bar{x}}$ is called the standard error of the mean. Since $\sigma_{\bar{x}} = \dfrac{\sigma}{\sqrt{N}}$, the standard error of the mean is smaller the larger the size of the sample, ie the variability of sample means is smaller the larger the size of the sample. Consequently, sampling errors will be smaller the larger is sample size. This is shown in Fig 5.1, where the distributions of means of samples of different sizes are compared with the distribution of the parent population. It can be seen that for larger samples the distribution is tighter. A few moments' thought will show that the standard error of a sample mean must always be less than the standard deviation of the population, since, for each sample, the sample mean averages out the variability of the observations within the sample.

We have seen that if the population distribution is normal, the sampling distribution of the mean will also be normal with mean and standard deviation as above. An important theorem, known as the *central limit theorem*, extends these results to the general case of non-normal populations: If $\bar{X}$ is the mean of a random sample of N independent observations drawn from a non-normal population with mean μ and standard deviation σ, the sampling distribution of $\bar{X}$ will be *approximately* normal with mean μ and standard error $\sigma_{\bar{x}} = \dfrac{\sigma}{\sqrt{N}}$, provided that N is sufficiently large. In practice, quite satisfactory approximations can be obtained for N as small as 30, but in general the sample will need to be larger the greater the departure of the parent population from normality. Because of the great significance of the central limit theorem in sampling applications, we now illustrate it with a numerical example.

Example 5.1

Suppose an experiment consists of repeated tosses of a fair six-sided die. As we saw in section 4.7 (see example 4.23) we may conceptualise this as a sampling experiment, with the number of dots on the die representing the six possible population values (X) and the number of repeated tosses representing a sample (with replacement) of N independent observations of the variable X. Now suppose $N = 30$, ie the die is rolled 30 times in succession and we average the observations obtained in the 30 rolls. This gives the mean $\bar{X}$ of a random sample of 30 observations drawn from a long sequence of repeated rolls of the die. Suppose further we repeat the experiment a large number of times, computing the mean for each sample of 30 observations. This process will generate a frequency distribution representing an empirical sampling distribution of $\bar{X}$. Although the population of the Xs has a uniform, ie non-normal, distribution, by the central limit theorem we should expect our empirical sampling distribution to have a shape resembling a normal distribution.

To test this empirically, the following simulation of a die experiment was performed. First, a 'sample' of 30 rolls of a balanced die was obtained by selecting 30 random numbers between 1 and 6 from a table of random digits (for the use of such tables see p 241 below). After averaging these numbers, another 30 digits were selected at random and averaged, and so on until a series of eighty values $\bar{X}_1, \bar{X}_2, \ldots, \bar{X}_{80}$ was obtained. The results are summarised by the following frequency table:

Class Interval	Class Mid-point $\bar{X}$	Frequency f	Relative Frequency (per cent)
2·75 and under 2·85	2·8	1	0·012
2·85 " 2·95	2·9	3	0·038
2·95 " 3·05	3·0	2	0·025
3·05 " 3·15	3·1	4	0·050
3·15 " 3·25	3·2	4	0·050
3·25 " 3·35	3·3	6	0·075
3·35 " 3·45	3·4	9	0·112
3·45 " 3·55	3·5	13	0·163
3·55 " 3·65	3·6	10	0·125
3·65 " 3·75	3·7	7	0·087
3·75 " 3·85	3·8	9	0·112
3·85 " 3·95	3·9	4	0·050
3·95 " 4·05	4·0	3	0·038
4·05 " 4·15	4·1	2	0·025
4·15 " 4·25	4·2	3	0·038
Total		80	1·000

When graphed, the relative frequency data appear as in Fig 5.2.

Since by assumption the die is a balanced die, the random variable X has the uniform distribution $P(x) = 1/6$, $x = 1, 2, 3, 4, 5, 6$. Computing next the mean and standard deviation of X, we have $\mu = 3·5$ and $\sigma = 1·708$. Consequently, the mean of the theoretical distribution of sample means of size 30 drawn from the population of the Xs is $\mu_{\bar{X}} = \mu = 3·5$ and the standard deviation is $\sigma_{\bar{X}} = \dfrac{\sigma}{\sqrt{N}} = \dfrac{1·708}{\sqrt{30}} = 0·312$. From the frequency data tabulated

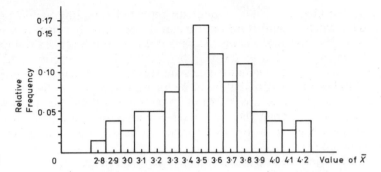

Fig 5.2

above the mean and standard deviation of the 80 sample means were found to be 3·538 and 0·320, respectively. Clearly, these values compare very closely with the values 3·5 and 0·312, which are the mean and standard deviation of the theoretical sampling distribution that would be generated by infinitely many repetitions of the same sampling experiment. We also note that the frequency distribution shown in the above diagram is similar in shape to the normal distribution even though the population on which this distribution is based is not normal and the sample size N is relatively small.

Given a sampling distribution of the mean which is normal or approximately normal, we may wish to ascertain the probability that an $\bar{X}$ will lie within a particular range. To do this, we transform $\bar{X}$ into the standard form

$$Z = \frac{\bar{X} - \mu}{\sigma_{\bar{X}}}$$

where $\sigma_{\bar{X}} = \dfrac{\sigma}{\sqrt{N}}$, and then refer to the table of normal areas in Appendix A. Thus, the probability that a sample mean will lie within the range $\mu \pm 1·96\sigma_{\bar{X}}$ is 0·95; in other words, in the long run we can expect 95 out of every 100 random samples of size N to have means within this range.

5.3 Tests of Significance

Having introduced the concept of a sampling distribution, we are now ready to consider its applications in testing hypotheses about population parameters from sample data. Such tests are referred to as tests of significance of statistical hypotheses. To illustrate the general nature of the problem, let us suppose we have a sample of a certain size drawn from a given population. Suppose the sample mean is $\bar{X}$ and we set up the hypothesis that it has come from a population with a mean of μ. This hypothesis implies that the discrepancy between $\bar{X}$ and μ is only due to chance, ie in the long run repeated sampling would produce data which would result in a mean discrepancy between $\bar{X}$ and μ of zero. We now ask what is the probability of our getting a discrepancy between $\bar{X}$ and μ as great as or greater than the actual one, *if the hypothesis were true*. We can answer this question from our knowledge of the sampling distribution of $\bar{X}$, for we can ascertain the probability of obtaining from a population, in which μ is the mean, an $\bar{X}$ further away from μ than the one under consideration. Suppose this probability turns out to be small ('small' to be defined later), we can then conclude

(i) hypothesis true and we have struck a fluke, or
(ii) hypothesis true but sampling has not been random, or
(iii) hypothesis false.

The choice lies between either (i) and (iii) if we can be certain that the sampling has been random, or between (i) and (ii) if we are certain that the hypothesis is true. In this latter case we are testing the randomness of the sampling. Let us assume, however, for the moment, that the sampling is random so that the choice is between (i) and (iii). By convention, we always conclude (iii), for a fluke is by its nature unlikely to occur. If the probability that a difference equal to or greater than the actual one between $\bar{X}$ and μ will occur just due to chance is small, we say that $\bar{X}$ is *significantly different* from μ, and we *reject* the hypothesis that $\bar{X}$ comes from a population with mean μ. Similarly, if the choice is between (i) and (ii), we conclude (ii).

The vital point is, of course, just how small the probability referred to above has to be, before it can be called 'small'. In general, our decision in this regard will be governed by the level of risk we are willing to take in either rejecting a true hypothesis or accepting a false hypothesis; we shall return to this question in section 5.10 below. In practice, however, statisticians conventionally take 5 per cent or 1 per cent as the critical levels at which hypotheses will be rejected. These are referred to as the *5 per cent level of significance* and the *1 per cent level of significance*.

The procedure for testing hypotheses is as follows:

1. *Set up an hypothesis* about the population from which the sample has been drawn. This is called the *null hypothesis*, because it asserts that there is no difference between the sample and the population in the particular matter under consideration. According to this hypothesis, the true population mean is some particular value, say, μ_o. But the null hypothesis can be either true or false, and if our test leads us to reject it, some other hypothesis, known as the alternative hypothesis, must be accepted. Thus we have

Null hypothesis: The population mean is μ_o
Alternative hypothesis: The population mean is not μ_o

For convenience and brevity, this may be written as

$$H_o : \mu = \mu_o$$

$$H_a : \mu \neq \mu_o$$

The alternative hypothesis is here stated in a general form which permits the testing of hypotheses about the true population mean lying in either direction of the assumed population mean μ_o. This type of testing procedure is known as a *two-tailed test*. In some circumstances, the appropriate alternative hypothesis may be in the form $\mu > \mu_o$ or in the form $\mu < \mu_o$. Tests of this latter type are called *one-tailed tests*. The procedure to be followed in such cases will be considered in section 5.9 below.

2. *Test the null hypothesis* by determining what is the probability of getting a discrepancy as great as or greater than the actual discrepancy between the sample and population just due to chance if the null hypothesis is true.

3. *Draw a conclusion* about the reasonableness of the null hypothesis. If the 5 per cent level of significance is used and the probability under (2) is greater than 5 per cent, do not reject the null hypothesis; if it is 5 per cent or less, reject it. Actually if the probability should turn out to be 5 per cent, the wisest course may be to reserve judgment and draw another sample if possible. We can never prove or disprove a statistical hypothesis. We can merely indicate that the sample is not inconsistent with it, or, on the other hand, we can cast doubt on its reasonableness. For when we reject an hypothesis there is always the possibility that the hypothesis is true and we have committed a statistical error. Thus, in rejecting an hypothesis, we can only conclude that it is very unlikely to be true. Similarly, when we accept one, we can never be quite certain that it holds, our data merely being not inconsistent with it.

5.4 Significance of the Difference Between $\bar{X}$ and μ, σ Known

We now illustrate the testing procedure outlined above with a simple case. We have a random sample of N items with mean $\bar{X}$. Could the sample have come from a normal population with mean $\mu = \mu_o$ and standard deviation σ? To test this, we set up the null and the alternative hypothesis

$$H_o : \mu = \mu_o$$

$$H_a : \mu \neq \mu_o$$

We know that if our hypothesis about the population is true the means of samples drawn from such a population will be normally distributed about μ_o with a standard error $\sigma_{\bar{X}} = \dfrac{\sigma}{\sqrt{N}}$. Consequently we can easily find the probability that $\bar{X}$ will differ from μ_o by an amount as great as or greater than any given amount. Thus we know that $\bar{X}$ will differ from μ_o by $1{\cdot}96\sigma_{\bar{X}}$ or more with a probability of 5 per cent. If, therefore, the sample mean $\bar{X}$ being tested falls outside the range $\mu_o \pm 1{\cdot}96\sigma_{\bar{X}}$, we conclude that the discrepancy between μ_o and $\bar{X}$ is too large to be attributed to chance. This being the case, we consider it unlikely that the sample has come from a population with the hypothesised value of μ, and we reject the null hypothesis at the 5 per cent level of significance. This is illustrated in Fig 5.3. In the diagram, the two tails each cover $2\frac{1}{2}$ per cent of the area, and constitute the *rejection* or *critical region* of a two-tailed test. The area corresponding to values of $\bar{X}$ lying within the range $\mu_o \pm 1{\cdot}96\sigma_{\bar{X}}$ is then the *acceptance region* for the test, ie if the observed value of $\bar{X}$ falls within this range, the null hypothesis is accepted.

Fig 5.3

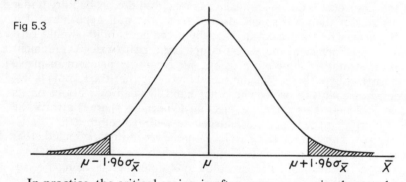

In practice, the critical region is often more conveniently stated not in terms of $\bar{X}$ but in terms of the standardised variable Z. From the previous section we recall that under the above conditions, $Z = \dfrac{\bar{X} - \mu}{\sigma_{\bar{X}}}$ will be normally distributed in the standard fashion about 0 with unit standard deviation. Consequently, Z will exceed $1{\cdot}96$ in magnitude with a probability of 5 per cent. Accordingly, if for given values of $\bar{X}$ and μ we calculate

$$|Z| = \frac{|\bar{X} - \mu_o|}{\sigma_{\bar{X}}}$$

where $|Z|$ means the magnitude of Z irrespective of sign, we shall obtain a measure of the discrepancy between the sample result and the null hypothesis. Now, if $|Z| > 1{\cdot}96$, the probability of obtaining such a discrepancy, or greater, is less than 5 per cent, if the null hypothesis is true. Consequently, if $|Z| > 1.96$, we reject the null hypothesis, and accept the alternative hypothesis. We say that $\bar{X}$ is significantly different from the hypothesised value of μ, ie μ_o. Conversely, if $|Z| <$ 1·96, then, if H_o is true, the probability of obtaining a discrepancy (as measured by $|Z|$) between the sample result and H_o as great as or greater than the one actually observed is more than 5 per cent. Such being the case, we conclude that the sample result could reasonably be attributed to chance, and we do not reject the null hypothesis. We then say that $\bar{X}$ is *not* significantly different from the hypothetical μ.

More generally, if we use the symbol α (Greek alpha) to indicate the level of significance and write $Z_{\alpha/2}$ for the critical value of Z which cuts off $\alpha/2$ per cent of the area in either tail of the standard normal curve, the decision rule for rejecting and accepting the null hypothesis may be stated as follows:

$$\text{If } |Z| > Z_{\alpha/2}, \text{ reject } H_o \text{ (accept } H_a)$$

$$\text{If } |Z| < Z_{\alpha/2}, \text{ accept } H_o \text{ (reject } H_a)$$

For example, in testing an hypothesis at the 1 per cent level of significance, ($\alpha = 0.01$), we shall reject H_o if $|Z| > Z_{.005} = 2.58$, and accept H_o if $|Z| < Z_{.005} = 2.58$.

Example 5.2

A random sample of 25 employees has a mean weekly wage of $130. Could this sample have been drawn from a population normally distributed about a mean of $120 with a standard deviation of $10?

Here we have

$$\bar{X} = 130 \qquad N = 25$$
$$\mu = 120 \qquad \sigma = 10$$

$$\sigma_{\bar{X}} = \frac{\sigma}{\sqrt{N}} = 2$$

Hypothesis: The sample is drawn from a normally distributed population with $\mu = 120$ and $\sigma = 10$, ie

$$H_o : \mu = 120$$
$$H_a : \mu \neq 120$$

Test:

$$|Z| = \frac{|\bar{X} - \mu_o|}{\sigma_{\bar{X}}}$$

$$= \frac{|130 - 120|}{2}$$

$$= 5$$

and

$$|Z| = 5 > Z_{.025} = 1.96$$

Conclusion: The value of the test statistic $|Z|$ being greater than the critical value of 1.96 at the 5 per cent level of significance, we reject the null hypothesis that $\mu = 120$. From the normal table it can be seen that if H_o were true, repeated sampling would yield a value of $|Z|$ equal to or greater than 5 with a probability of less than 0.001. We thus regard the null hypothesis as being inconsistent with the sample result, and accept the alternative hypothesis H_a. The sample could not have reasonably come from a hypothetical population with $\mu = 120$. We say that $\bar{X}$ differs significantly from μ.

In passing, we may note that, if we know that the sample has in fact been drawn from the specified population, the test in this instance would cast serious doubt on the randomness of the sample. For only very seldom would a random sample have a mean so different from the population mean. (See p 220 below).

The test outlined in this section can be used for samples of *any size*, provided that the underlying population is normal. When the parent population is not normal, the central limit theorem (see section 5.2) assures us that the sampling distribution of $\bar{X}$ will be *approximately* normal for sufficiently large N. In practical applications, for $N > 50$ the test can always be applied.

5.5 Significance of the Difference between $\bar{X}$ and μ, σ Not Known

Thus far we have considered tests of hypotheses about μ, where σ, the population standard deviation, is given. In practice we shall seldom know σ, for we shall have only sample results. Furthermore, the samples on which we must base our estimates of the unknown σ will often be quite small, say $N < 30$. In order to extend the hypothesis-testing procedure outlined above to the case of small samples drawn from normal populations with unknown parameters, we must introduce an important sampling distribution known as the *t-distribution*.

The t-Distribution

Previously we have stated that if $\bar{X}$ is normally distributed about μ with a standard error $\sigma_{\bar{X}} = \dfrac{\sigma}{\sqrt{N}}$, then $Z = \dfrac{\bar{X} - \mu}{\sigma_{\bar{X}}}$ will be distributed in the standard fashion about 0 with unit standard deviation. If σ is not known, it must be estimated from the sample. We can do this from the formula

$$s = \sqrt{\frac{\Sigma(X - \bar{X})^2}{N - 1}}$$

and we then write the sample estimate of $\sigma_{\bar{X}}$ as $s_{\bar{X}} = \dfrac{s}{\sqrt{N}}$. However, if we use $s_{\bar{X}}$ in place of $\sigma_{\bar{X}}$, the ratio $\dfrac{\bar{X} - \mu}{s_{\bar{X}}}$ is no longer the standard

normal variable $Z = \dfrac{\bar{X} - \mu}{\sigma_{\bar{X}}}$. This can be seen from the fact that whereas in the latter case $\bar{X}$ is the only source of variation from sample to sample ($\sigma_{\bar{X}}$ being constant for given σ and N), in the former case $s_{\bar{X}}$ is an additional source. The ratio

$$t = \frac{\bar{X} - \mu}{s_{\bar{X}}}$$

is thus seen to be a ratio of two random quantities, $(\bar{X} - \mu)$ and $s_{\bar{X}}$. Hence the t-ratio, commonly referred to as the t-statistic, is itself a random variable with its own probability distribution. This probability distribution is known as the t-distribution. The t-distribution plays a particularly significant role in sampling theory, since its applications enable us to make valid inferences about the parent population based entirely on sample data.[1]

First, an important assumption underlying the t-distribution must be stated. The distribution can be theoretically derived only if the sample statistics $\bar{X}$ and $s_{\bar{X}}$ are statistically independent, ie if with repeated sampling there is no association between the values of $\bar{X}$ and $s_{\bar{X}}$ obtained from particular samples. It can be shown that this requirement will be met only if the population of the variable X from which the sampling is made is normal. Thus, the t-distribution is only appropriate for samples drawn from a normally distributed population.

The t-distribution resembles the standard normal distribution in that it is a symmetrical, bell-shaped curve centred on $E(t) = 0$. But whereas the standard normal curve has unit variance, it can be shown that $\text{Var}(t)$ is greater than one in small samples and tends to unity as N is increased indefinitely. Hence, for small values of N, the t-distribution will be more dispersed than the standard normal curve. Intuitively, we can see that because t depends on two random quantities $\bar{X}$ and $s_{\bar{X}}$, in small samples extreme values of $\bar{X}$ may be paired with extreme values of s (and hence $s_{\bar{X}}$) just due to chance, and so t will tend to be more dispersed than Z. But because the variability of t diminishes as N is increased, there will in fact be a whole family of t-distributions, each member of the family being related to the sample size N. It can be shown that the t-distribution depends on a single parameter $v = N - 1$ (Greek nu). The parameter v is called the *number of degrees of freedom*.

[1] See footnote on p 212 below.

The term 'degrees of freedom' will recur in our subsequent discussion, and it may be useful to give a brief explanation of the concept here. As a general principle, if we want the sample variance s^2 to approximate the unknown population variance σ^2 as closely as possible, we must divide the sum of squares $\Sigma(X - \bar{X})^2$ by the number of values that can vary freely in each sample. If there are N observations, it might look at first sight as though this number must be N. From section 3.4 we recall, however, that the sum of deviations of sample values from their mean must always be zero, ie $\Sigma x = \Sigma X - N\bar{X} = 0$. Therefore, once a sample has been selected and the sample mean $\bar{X}$ computed, the number of independently chosen values in the sum of squares $\Sigma(X - \bar{X})^2$ is not N but $N - 1$, one degree of freedom being lost by virtue of the linear constraint $\Sigma X - N\bar{X} = 0$. It is also worth noting that if the population mean were known, this linear constraint would not apply, ie all the deviations in the sum of squares $\Sigma(X - \mu)^2$ would be independently determined. Ordinarily, we do not know μ, and so the divisor in the formula for s^2 (and hence s) is the number of degrees of freedom $N - 1$ and not the number of sample observations N. This principle is quite general: whenever we wish to estimate a population parameter (in our case σ^2) by using a sample statistic in place of another parameter (in our case $\bar{X}$ instead of μ) we lose one degree of freedom.[1]

In the t-distribution, the parameter 'degrees of freedom' reflects the fact that in computing values of t from sample data we have at our disposal only $v = N - 1$ independent sample values with which to compute an estimate of the unknown σ, and hence of $\sigma_{\bar{X}}$. The smaller v, ie the smaller N, the more dispersed is the t-distribution in relation to the normal curve. This is shown for $v = 4$ in Fig 5.4. As N gets larger, the distribution approaches the normal, and for $N > 30$ the two distributions are very nearly the same.

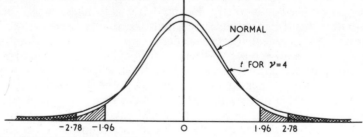

Fig 5.4 The normal and t-distributions

Practical work with the t-distribution is facilitated by the use of a special probability table known as the t-table (see Table II, Appendix

[1] See also pp 216–20 below.

A). In the table, the number of degrees of freedom v, ranging from 1 to 30, is shown in the left-hand margin. Thus, each row of the table corresponds to a different t-distribution, each with a particular value of the parameter v. For a specified value of v, the body of the table gives the value of t which cuts off tails covering certain proportions of area tabulated in the horizontal margin. Thus, for $v = 4$, $P(|t| > 2\cdot78) = 0\cdot05$, ie a distance equal to $2\cdot78$ from the centre of the distribution cuts off tails each equal to $2\frac{1}{2}$ per cent of the area, so that the probability of obtaining a value of t greater than $2\cdot78$ in magnitude is 5 per cent. This is shown in the diagram on p 180. The figure of $2\cdot78$ is obtained from the table by reading across from $v = 4$ and down the column headed $\alpha = 0\cdot05$. This example can be interpreted by saying that if random samples of size $N = 5$ were taken repeatedly from a normal population with mean μ, and if $\bar{X}$, s and $t = \dfrac{\bar{X} - \mu}{s_{\bar{X}}}$, where $s_{\bar{X}} = \dfrac{s}{\sqrt{N}}$, were calculated from them, t would exceed $2\cdot78$ in magnitude in 5 per cent of all such samples. For $N > 30$, the distribution of t would be approximately normal, and the corresponding figure would be $1\cdot96$. Thus, the smaller the size of the sample the greater is the value of t needed to cut off the two $2\frac{1}{2}$ per cent tails, ie the greater the critical value of t at the 5 per cent level of significance. Again, from the t-table we can ascertain that, say with $v = 10$ and $t = 1\cdot2$, $P(|t| > 1\cdot2)$ lies between $0\cdot3$ and $0\cdot2$, so that with repeated sampling a value of t larger than $1\cdot2$ would occur in from 20 per cent to 30 per cent of the cases.

Tests of Significance Involving the t-Distribution

If we have a small sample of 30 or fewer observations with mean $\bar{X}$ and standard deviation s, and the sample is known to have been drawn at random from a normally distributed population, we can test whether $\bar{X}$ differs significantly from an hypothetical μ by calculating

$$|t| = \frac{|\bar{X} - \mu_o|}{s_{\bar{X}}}, \text{ where } s_{\bar{X}} = \frac{s}{\sqrt{N}}$$

and referring it to the t-table with $v = N - 1$ degrees of freedom. We already know that for any predetermined level of significance, say $\alpha = 0\cdot05$, the critical value of t, ie the value of t which cuts off $2\frac{1}{2}$ per cent of area in either tail of the t-distribution, is no longer a constant number but depends on the value of $v = N - 1$. Let us denote this critical value symbolically by $t_{.025}$; thus, for $v = 4$, we write $t_{.025} = 2\cdot78$, etc. By analogy with the testing procedure outlined in the previous section, the decision rule for a two-tailed test now becomes:

If $|t| > t_{.025}$, reject H_o (accept H_a)

If $|t| < t_{.025}$, accept H_o (reject H_a)

As already mentioned, the t-distribution is satisfactorily approximated by the normal curve when N is large. Hence, for $N > 30$, the test statistic $|t|$ is replaced by

$$|Z| = \frac{|\bar{X} - \mu_o|}{s_{\bar{X}}}$$

where $s_{\bar{X}} = \dfrac{s}{\sqrt{N}}$ is a sample estimate of $\sigma_{\bar{X}}$.

Example 5.3

A census of retail establishments in a particular month revealed that the mean monthly turnover of suburban food stores was $2500. A random sample of 16 such stores taken in the following month had a mean monthly turnover of $2660 and a standard deviation of turnover of $480. Could you conclude that the mean monthly turnover had changed since the census?

Here

$$N = 16 \qquad \bar{X} = 2660$$

$$\mu = 2500 \qquad s = 480$$

$$s_{\bar{X}} = \frac{480}{\sqrt{16}} = 120$$

Hypothesis: The sample comes from a normal population with $\mu = 2500$

$$H_o : \mu = 2500$$

$$H_a : \mu \neq 2500$$

Test:

$$|t| = \frac{|\bar{X} - \mu_o|}{s_{\bar{X}}} = \frac{160}{120}$$

$$= 1{\cdot}33$$

From the t-table, the critical value of t for $\alpha = 0{\cdot}05$ and $\nu = 16 - 1 = 15$ is $2{\cdot}13$, and we have

$$|t| = 1{\cdot}33 < t_{.025} = 2{\cdot}13$$

Conclusion: The value of the test statistic $|t|$ being less than the critical value $t_{.025} = 2{\cdot}13$, we accept the null hypothesis that $\mu = 2500$. From the t-table it can be seen that if H_o were true, repeated sampling with 15 degrees of freedom would yield a value of $|t|$ as great as or greater than $1{\cdot}33$ with a probability of 20 per cent. Such being the case, the observed discrepancy (as measured by $|t|$) between the null hypothesis and the sample result could reasonably be attributed to chance, and we cannot conclude that there has been a statistically significant change in mean monthly turnover of suburban food stores since the census.

It is important to note that the above small sample test is only appropriate when the distribution of X (weekly turnover) is normal. If this assumption could not be justified, a larger sample would need to be selected. Given a large enough sample, the distribution of $\bar{X}$ would be approximately normal, and $s_{\bar{X}}$ would give a good approximation of the unknown $\sigma_{\bar{X}}$. The null hypothesis could then be tested by the standard Z-test, as if σ had been given.

5.6 Significance of the Difference between Two Sample Means $\bar{X}_1$ and $\bar{X}_2$

We may have two samples of size N_1 and N_2, giving means of $\bar{X}_1$ and $\bar{X}_2$, and we may wish to test statistically whether these two samples could reasonably have come from the same population or, what is the same thing, whether they could have come from two assumed populations with equal means μ_1 and μ_2 and with the same variance σ^2. In this case the hypotheses to be tested are

$$H_o : \mu_1 = \mu_2 \qquad (\text{or } H_o : \mu_1 - \mu_2 = 0)$$
and
$$H_a : \mu_1 \neq \mu_2 \qquad (\text{or } H_a : \mu_1 - \mu_2 \neq 0)$$

ie the null hypothesis that the true means of the two populations from which the samples have been drawn are equal against the alternative hypothesis that they are not.

First we shall need to know how the difference between two sample means, $\bar{X}_1 - \bar{X}_2$, will be distributed with repeated sampling. If the two samples have been selected independently, so that particular observations in the first sample are not associated with particular observations in the second sample, then the random variable $(\bar{X}_1 - \bar{X}_2)$ is a linear combination of two independent random variables $\bar{X}_1$ and $\bar{X}_2$. Hence, by virtue of the properties of means and variances of linear combinations of random variables (see section 4.15, pp 163 ff) the mean and variance of $(\bar{X}_1 - \bar{X}_2)$ may be written as

$$\mu_{\bar{X}_1 - \bar{X}_2} = \mu_{\bar{X}_1} - \mu_{\bar{X}_2}$$
and
$$\sigma^2_{\bar{X}_1 - \bar{X}_2} = \sigma^2_{\bar{X}_1} + \sigma^2_{\bar{X}_2}$$

But, by hypothesis, each pair of samples is drawn from the same population with standard deviation σ. Then

$$\mu_{\bar{X}_1 - \bar{X}_2} = \mu_1 - \mu_2$$
$$= 0$$

and

$$\sigma_{\bar{X}_1 - \bar{X}_2} = \sqrt{\sigma^2_{\bar{X}_1} + \sigma^2_{\bar{X}_2}}$$

$$= \sqrt{\frac{\sigma^2}{N_1} + \frac{\sigma^2}{N_2}}$$

$$= \sigma \sqrt{\frac{1}{N_1} + \frac{1}{N_2}}$$

ie with repeated sampling the difference between two sample means $(\bar{X}_1 - \bar{X}_2)$ is distributed with mean $(\mu_1 - \mu_2) = 0$ and standard error

$\sigma \sqrt{\dfrac{1}{N_1} + \dfrac{1}{N_2}}$. As in the case of a single sample mean the sampling distribution of $(\bar{X}_1 - \bar{X}_2)$ is normal for samples of any size drawn from normal populations, and it is *approximately* normal for samples drawn from non-normal populations, provided N_1 and N_2 are sufficiently large, say, each exceeding 30.

It now follows that, if we have two sample means $\bar{X}_1$ and $\bar{X}_2$ and we set up the null hypothesis that they come from the same population with a standard deviation σ, then we can test whether the difference between the means $(\bar{X}_1 - \bar{X}_2)$ differs significantly from zero, by writing

$$|Z| = \frac{|\bar{X}_1 - \bar{X}_2 - 0|}{\sigma_{\bar{X}_1 - \bar{X}_2}} = \frac{|\bar{X}_1 - \bar{X}_2|}{\sigma_{\bar{X}_1 - \bar{X}_2}}$$

where

$$\sigma_{\bar{X}_1 - \bar{X}_2} = \sigma \sqrt{\frac{1}{N_1} + \frac{1}{N_2}}$$

If $|Z| > 1{\cdot}96$, then it is unreasonable to suggest that the two samples come from the same population, because only rarely would two samples drawn from the same population have such different means. If $|Z| < 1{\cdot}96$, the difference between two sample means $\bar{X}_1$ and $\bar{X}_2$ could reasonably be attributed to chance, and the null hypothesis is accepted.

Example 5.4

A random sample of 40 male employees is taken at the end of a year and the mean number of hours of absenteeism for the year is found to be 63 hours. A similar sample of 50 female employees has a mean of 66 hours. Could these samples have been drawn from a population with the same mean and with $\sigma = 10$ hours?

Here we have
$$N_1 = 40 \qquad\qquad N_2 = 50$$
$$\bar{X}_1 = 63 \qquad\qquad \bar{X}_2 = 66$$
$$\sigma = 10$$
$$\sigma_{\bar{X}_1 - \bar{X}_2} = \sigma \sqrt{\frac{1}{N_1} + \frac{1}{N_2}}$$
$$= 10 \sqrt{\frac{1}{40} + \frac{1}{50}}$$
$$= 2{\cdot}12$$

Hypothesis: The samples were both drawn from the same population with $\sigma = 10$, ie

$$H_o : \mu_1 = \mu_2$$
$$H_a : \mu_1 \neq \mu_2$$

Test:

$$|Z| = \frac{|\bar{X}_1 - \bar{X}_2|}{\sigma_{\bar{X}_1 - \bar{X}_2}}$$

$$= \frac{|63 - 66|}{2 \cdot 12}$$

$$= 1 \cdot 42$$

and

$$|Z| = 1 \cdot 42 < 1 \cdot 96$$

Conclusion: The value of $|Z|$ obtained in the test being less than the critical value of $1 \cdot 96$, we retain the null hypothesis H_o. From the normal table, $P(|Z| > 1 \cdot 42) = 0 \cdot 16$, ie if the null hypothesis were true, repeated sampling would yield a value of $|Z|$ equal to or greater than $1 \cdot 42$ in about 16 cases in 100 due to chance. Such being the case, the two samples could reasonably have come from the same hypothetical population. We say that $\bar{X}_1$ and $\bar{X}_2$ do not differ significantly. There appears to be no difference in the incidence of absenteeism between the two groups of employees. We also note that since N_1 and N_2 are reasonably large (each exceeding 30) the test does not depend on the assumption that the underlying population is normally distributed.

The preceding test was based on the assumption that σ, the standard deviation of the hypothetical population from which the random samples with means $\bar{X}_1$ and $\bar{X}_2$ have supposedly come, is known. But generally we shall not know σ. However, we shall know s_1 and s_2 from the two samples. Accordingly, we must use this information to make an estimate s of the population σ. The best estimate is given by

$$s = \sqrt{\frac{(N_1 - 1)s_1^2 + (N_2 - 1)s_2^2}{N_1 + N_2 - 2}}$$

$$= \sqrt{\frac{\Sigma(X_1 - \bar{X}_1)^2 + \Sigma(X_2 - \bar{X}_2)^2}{N_1 + N_2 - 2}}$$

This estimate is a pooled or weighted estimate of the unknown σ.

Just as $t = \dfrac{\bar{X} - \mu}{s_{\bar{X}}}$ is distributed in the t-distribution with $N - 1$ degrees of freedom so $t = \dfrac{(\bar{X}_1 - \bar{X}_2) - 0}{s_{\bar{X}_1 - \bar{X}_2}}$ is distributed in the t-distribution with $N_1 + N_2 - 2$ degrees of freedom. The loss of two degrees of freedom reflects the fact that in computing a pooled estimate of σ the two sample variances are used with a loss of one degree of freedom each. Accordingly, by analogy with the preceding sections, to test the hypothesis of equality of two means, we compute

$$|t| = \frac{|\bar{X}_1 - \bar{X}_2|}{s_{\bar{X}_1 - \bar{X}_2}}$$

where

$$s_{\bar{X}_1 - \bar{X}_2} = s\sqrt{\frac{1}{N_1} + \frac{1}{N_2}}$$

and

$$s = \sqrt{\frac{(N_1 - 1)s_1^2 + (N_2 - 1)s_2^2}{N_1 + N_2 - 2}}$$

and refer it to the t-table with $N_1 + N_2 - 2$ degrees of freedom. If $N_1 + N_2 - 2 > 30$, the t-distribution can be taken as normal.

Example 5.5

Ten plots of land are treated with fertiliser A and twelve with fertiliser B. The mean yield of the first plots is 6·00 bushels with a standard deviation of 0·03 bushels. The yields of the second plots have a mean of 5·95 bushels with a standard deviation of 0·04 bushels. At a 1 per cent level of significance, is there a difference in the effects of the fertilisers?

Here

$$N_1 = 10 \qquad \bar{X}_1 = 6{\cdot}00 \qquad s_1 = 0{\cdot}03$$
$$N_2 = 12 \qquad \bar{X}_2 = 5{\cdot}95 \qquad s_2 = 0{\cdot}04$$

$$\begin{aligned}
s &= \sqrt{\frac{(N_1 - 1)s_1^2 + (N_2 - 1)s_2^2}{N_1 + N_2 - 2}} \\
&= \sqrt{\frac{9 \times 0{\cdot}0009 + 11 \times 0{\cdot}0016}{20}} \\
&= 0{\cdot}036
\end{aligned}$$

and

$$\begin{aligned}
s_{\bar{X}_1 - \bar{X}_2} &= s\sqrt{\frac{1}{N_1} + \frac{1}{N_2}} \\
&= 0{\cdot}036\sqrt{\frac{1}{10} + \frac{1}{12}} \\
&= 0{\cdot}015
\end{aligned}$$

Hypothesis: The two samples come from the same normal population, ie

$$H_o : \mu_1 = \mu_2$$
$$H_a : \mu_1 \neq \mu_2$$

Test:

$$\begin{aligned}
|t| &= \frac{|\bar{X}_1 - \bar{X}_2|}{s_{\bar{X}_1 - \bar{X}_2}} \\
&= \frac{0{\cdot}05}{0{\cdot}015} \\
&= 3{\cdot}3
\end{aligned}$$

From the t-table, the critical value of t at the 1 per cent level of significance and for $v = 10 + 12 - 2 = 20$ is 2.845, and hence

$$|t| = 3.3 > t_{.005} = 2.845$$

Conclusion: The value of the test statistic $|t|$ being greater than the critical value $t_{.005} = 2.845$, we reject the null hypothesis H_o and accept the alternative hypothesis H_a. If the null hypothesis were true, repeated sampling would yield a discrepancy (as measured by $|t|$) between $\bar{X}_1$ and $\bar{X}_2$ as great as or greater than the one actually obtained above with less than 1 per cent probability. Such being the case, the two samples are most unlikely to have come from the same population. We say that $\bar{X}_1$ and $\bar{X}_2$ differ significantly. The sample results are evidence of a difference in the effects of the two fertilisers.

In testing hypotheses involving the difference between two means we have so far assumed that the two samples have come from the same population, or what is an equivalent assumption, that they have been drawn from two hypothetical populations having the same means ($\mu_1 = \mu_2$) and the same standard deviations ($\sigma_1 = \sigma_2 = \sigma$). Suppose, however, that the standard deviations of the two populations are in fact different, ie $\sigma_1 \neq \sigma_2$. In this case, if $\bar{X}_1$ and $\bar{X}_2$ are the means of independent random samples drawn from the first and the second population, respectively, the random variable ($\bar{X}_1 - \bar{X}_2$) will again be distributed with a mean of $\mu_{\bar{X}_1} - \mu_{\bar{X}_2} = 0$ but with a standard error equal to

$$\sigma_{\bar{X}_1 - \bar{X}_2} = \sqrt{\frac{\sigma_1^2}{N_1} + \frac{\sigma_2^2}{N_2}}$$

and the test is precisely analogous to the case where $\sigma_1 = \sigma_2 = \sigma$. In practice, although we may have reasons to believe that the standard deviations of the two sampled populations are different, we shall very seldom know their values. We then have little choice but to resort to the approximate procedure of using the sample variances s_1^2 and s_2^2 as estimates of the unknown σ_1^2 and σ_2^2, and then obtaining an estimate of the standard error $\sigma_{\bar{X}_1 - \bar{X}_2}$ from the formula

$$s_{\bar{X}_1 - \bar{X}_2} = \sqrt{\frac{s_1^2}{N_1} + \frac{s_2^2}{N_2}}$$

As already remarked elsewhere, if N_1 and N_2 are large, the sample values of s_1^2 and s_2^2 will provide good estimates of the unknown population variances σ_1^2 and σ_2^2, and the t-distribution will be well approximated by the normal curve. To test then the hypothesis $H_o: \mu_1 = \mu_2$ against the alternative $H_a: \mu_1 \neq \mu_2$ we compute the test statistic

$$|Z| = \frac{|\bar{X}_1 - \bar{X}_2|}{s_{\bar{X}_1 - \bar{X}_2}}$$

and refer it to the normal table for a standard Z-test.

Example 5.6

A wholesaler of automobile tyres wishes to test the average wearing quality of a domestically produced tyre (X_1) and an imported tyre (X_2) under local conditions. Sixty tyres of each type were selected at random, and the length of life of each tyre was recorded. At the end of the experiment, the two sets of sample data yielded the following results:

$$\bar{X}_1 = 30\cdot9 \text{ ('000s km)} \qquad \bar{X}_2 = 28\cdot5 \text{ ('000s km)}$$
$$s_1 = 6\cdot0 \text{ ('000s km)} \qquad s_2 = 6\cdot3 \text{ ('000s km)}$$

Is there a significant difference between the two sample means at the 5 per cent level of significance?

Here

$$s_{\bar{X}_1 - \bar{X}_2} = \sqrt{\frac{s_1^2}{N_1} + \frac{s_2^2}{N_2}}$$
$$= \sqrt{\frac{36\cdot0}{60} + \frac{39\cdot7}{60}}$$
$$= 1\cdot123$$

Hypothesis: The samples have been drawn from two populations with the same mean, ie

$$H_o : \mu_1 = \mu_2$$
$$H_a : \mu_1 \neq \mu_2$$

Test:

$$|Z| = \frac{|\bar{X}_1 - \bar{X}_2|}{s_{\bar{X}_1 - \bar{X}_2}}$$
$$= \frac{|30\cdot9 - 28\cdot5|}{1\cdot123}$$
$$= 2\cdot14$$

and

$$|Z| = 2\cdot14 > 1\cdot96$$

Conclusion: The value of the test statistic $|Z|$ being greater than the critical value of $1\cdot96$, we reject the null hypothesis H_o and accept the alternative hypothesis H_a. Since N_1 and N_2 are reasonably large, we can expect the sampling distribution of $(\bar{X}_1 - \bar{X}_2)$ to be approximately normal, and from the normal table $P(|Z| > 2\cdot14) \simeq 0\cdot03$. We thus consider it very unlikely that the samples could have been drawn from two populations with the same mean. The two types of tyre appear to differ with respect to their average wearing quality.

5.7 Applications to Proportions

In sampling applications we frequently wish to make inferences about populations which can be divided into two categories each possessing a particular attribute, eg defective or non-defective production items, male or female employees, Labor or non-Labor voters etc. Populations which can thus be classified are called *dichotomous populations,* and they are completely specified by the proportion of the population falling into one of the categories; for convenience, these categories are labelled as 'successes' and 'failures'. We shall denote the population proportion of successes by π, and the population proportion of failures by $(1 - \pi)$.

If from such a population we draw a random sample of N observations, the sample may be regarded as a sequence of N independent trials with constant probabilities of success and failure π and $1 - \pi$, and the random variable X, the number of successes in the sample, will be distributed in the *binomial distribution* about a mean $N\pi$ and with a standard deviation $\sqrt{N\pi(1 - \pi)}$ (see section 4.10).

Now suppose we are interested in the proportion of successes obtained in a given sample of N items, eg the percentage of defectives in a production test-run, or the proportion of sample voting Labor, etc. Writing $p = \dfrac{X}{N}$, we can readily convert the number of successes into the proportion of successes obtained in the sample. If we repeat the sampling process, the statistic p will vary from sample to sample due to sampling errors. But it can be seen that the new random variable $p = \dfrac{X}{N}$ is in fact a simple transformation of the binomial variable X, ie the number of successes in N independent trials.[1] Hence, by virtue of section 4.15 above

$$E(p) = E\left(\frac{X}{N}\right) = \frac{1}{N} E(X)$$

But $E(X) = N\pi$, and hence

$$E(p) = \pi$$

and

$$\text{Var}(p) = \frac{1}{N^2} \text{Var}(X) = \frac{1}{N^2} [N\pi(1 - \pi)]$$

$$= \frac{\pi(1 - \pi)}{N}$$

We conclude that p, the sample proportion of successes, will in a large number of samples also be distributed in the binomial distribution with a mean π and a standard deviation $\sigma_p = \sqrt{\dfrac{\pi(1 - \pi)}{N}}$. This gives the

---

[1] A change of notation in this section should be noted. Whereas in section 4.10 on the binomial distribution the symbol p represented the probability of success on each trial, we now use p to indicate the proportion of successes found in samples of size N drawn from a dichotomous population. The proportion of successes in the population is indicated by π.

sampling distribution of a proportion in samples of size N drawn from a dichotomous population.

When the sample size N is small, the binomial distribution with parameters N and π must be used as the sampling distribution of the sample proportion of successes p. But, as we have shown in section 4.13 (pp 147–8) if the sample size is sufficiently large, the binomial distribution can be very closely approximated by the normal curve. Accordingly, for large N, p will be distributed nearly normally about a mean π and with a standard deviation $\sigma_p = \sqrt{\dfrac{\pi(1 - \pi)}{N}}$. For practical purposes the binomial distribution is near enough to normal for $N > 50$. Hence for large samples we can use the table of normal areas to calculate the probability that a sample of size N will have p lying within any specified range.

Example 5.7

Under the mortality conditions of a certain country the proportion of births which survive to age 70 years is 0·6. What is the probability that out of 1000 births taken at random, at least 630 will survive to age 70 years?

Here we have $\pi = 0·6$. In samples of 1000, p, the proportion of survivors, will be normally distributed about 0·6 with a standard deviation of

$$\sigma_p = \sqrt{\frac{\pi(1 - \pi)}{N}} = \sqrt{\frac{0·6 \times 0·4}{1000}} = 0·0155$$

We require $P(p > 0·63)$, ie $P\left(Z > \dfrac{0·63 - \pi}{\sigma_p}\right)$, ie $P(Z > 1·93)$. From the table of the normal distribution this probability is 0·0268. If, say, 1000 such samples were selected, in only about 27 of them would we expect more than 630 of the births to survive to age 70 years.

5.8 Tests of Significance Concerning Proportions

A random sample of N observations drawn from a dichotomous population has a proportion of successes of p. Could this sample have come from a population with a proportion of successes of π?

This problem is exactly analogous to the significance of the difference between $\bar{X}$ and μ, with σ known, described in section 5.4 above. The null hypothesis is that the sample does come from such a population, ie we test the null hypothesis

$$H_o : \pi = \pi_o$$

against the alternative that the true population proportion differs from the assumed value π_o

$$H_a : \pi \neq \pi_o$$

The test is

$$|Z| = \frac{|p - \pi|}{\sigma_p}$$

where

$$\sigma_p = \sqrt{\frac{\pi(1 - \pi)}{N}}$$

and is referred to the normal table.

Example 5.8

A sample of 400 electors selected at random gives a 51 per cent majority to the party in office and 49 per cent to the party in opposition. Could such a sample have been drawn from a population with a 50–50 division of political opinion?

Here $\qquad N = 400 \qquad\qquad p = 0.51 \qquad\qquad \pi = 0.50$

$$\sigma_p = \sqrt{\frac{\pi(1 - \pi)}{N}} = 0.025$$

Hypothesis: The sample has been drawn from a population in which $\pi = 0.50$, ie

$$H_o : \pi - 0.50$$
$$H_a : \pi \neq 0.50$$

Test:

$$|Z| = \frac{|p - \pi_o|}{\sigma_p}$$
$$= \frac{0.01}{0.025}$$
$$= 0.4$$

and

$$|Z| = 0.4 < 1.96$$

Conclusion: On the basis of the sample data, the null hypothesis cannot be rejected. From the normal table we find that, if the null hypothesis H_o were true, repeated sampling would yield a value of $|Z|$ as great as or greater than 0.4 in as many as 69 cases in 100 due to chance. We conclude that the sample could reasonably have come from a population with a 50–50 division of political opinion.

Significance of the Difference Between Two Sample Proportions, p_1 and p_2

Suppose we have two random samples of sizes N_1 and N_2 with proportions of successes p_1 and p_2, and we set up the null hypothesis that the two samples come from the same population (or from two hypothetical populations with the same proportion of successes π). If the null hypothesis is true, and the two samples are large and independent, then $p_1 - p_2$ will be normally distributed about a mean of 0 and with standard error $\sigma_{p_1-p_2}$. By analogy with the sampling distribution of the difference between two sample means (see section 5.6 above) the standard error of $p_1 - p_2$ is given by

$$\sigma_{p_1-p_2} = \sqrt{\sigma_{p_1}^2 + \sigma_{p_2}^2} = \sqrt{\frac{\pi(1-\pi)}{N_1} + \frac{\pi(1-\pi)}{N_2}}$$

$$= \sqrt{\pi(1-\pi)}\sqrt{\frac{1}{N_1} + \frac{1}{N_2}}$$

In practice we shall not know π. We must make an estimate of it, so that we can estimate $\sigma_{p_1-p_2}$. A good estimate of π is given by pooling the information from the two samples. We write

$$p = \frac{N_1 p_1 + N_2 p_2}{N_1 + N_2}$$

where p is an estimate of π. For large samples

$$s_{p_1-p_2} = \sqrt{p(1-p)}\sqrt{\frac{1}{N_1} + \frac{1}{N_2}}$$

may be used in conjunction with the normal distribution. The test is

$$|Z| = \frac{|p_1 - p_2|}{s_{p_1-p_2}}$$

referred to the normal table.

Example 5.9

A random sample of 100 business men in rural areas gives 54 per cent who expect business to improve next year, whereas one of 200 in city areas gives 48 per cent. Is this evidence of a difference in the expectations of business men in rural and city areas?

Here
$$N_1 = 100 \qquad p_1 = 0.54$$
$$N_2 = 200 \qquad p_2 = 0.48$$

$$p = \frac{54 + 96}{300} = 0.50$$

$$s_{p_1-p_2} = \sqrt{p(1-p)}\sqrt{\frac{1}{N_1} + \frac{1}{N_2}} = 0.061$$

Hypothesis: The two samples come from a population similar in respect of business expectations, ie

$$H_o : \pi_1 = \pi_2$$
$$H_a : \pi_1 \neq \pi_2$$

Test:

$$|Z| = \frac{|p_1 - p_2|}{s_{p_1 - p_2}}$$

$$= \frac{0 \cdot 06}{0 \cdot 061}$$

$$= 0 \cdot 98$$

and

$$|Z| = 0 \cdot 98 < 1 \cdot 96$$

Conclusion: Since the value of $|Z|$ lies within the acceptance region for the test, the two samples cannot be taken as evidence of a difference in business expectations in rural and city areas.

5.9 One-Tailed Tests of Statistical Hypotheses

Up until now we have considered procedures for testing hypotheses about a population parameter lying in either direction of its postulated value. As already mentioned earlier, such tests are referred to as two-tailed or two-sided tests. For generality, let us denote the parameter of interest in any given test by the symbol θ (Greek theta); thus, we may think of θ as being μ, π, $\mu_1 - \mu_2$, etc. Symbolically, a two-tailed test of a parameter θ is a test involving the hypotheses

$$H_o : \theta = \theta_o$$

$$H_a : \theta \neq \theta_o$$

The tests set out in sections 5.4 to 5.8 are all two-tailed tests. Two-tailed tests are appropriate when there is no particular reason to believe that, if the null hypothesis concerning a parameter θ, say μ, is false, the true hypothesis involves a mean lying above rather than below the hypothetical mean μ_o (or vice versa); or, when the action flowing from the rejection of a null hypothesis is the same whether the true hypothesis involves a mean lying above or below its postulated value μ_o. One-tailed tests are appropriate in cases where these conditions do not hold. In general, two-tailed tests test whether, for example, $\bar{X}$ *differs* significantly from μ_o; whereas one-tailed tests test whether $\bar{X}$ is significantly *greater* than or significantly *less* than μ_o (but not both).

To illustrate the procedure to be followed in one-tailed tests, suppose we are testing an hypothesis about μ with σ known at a 5 per cent level of significance, and are practically certain that if the mean is not μ_o it must lie above μ_o. Stated symbolically, we are considering the null hypothesis

$$H_o : \mu = \mu_o$$

against the alternative

$$H_a : \mu > \mu_o$$

As already explained in section 5.4, if the test were a two-tailed test, the acceptance region for the null hypothesis would be the range $\mu_o \pm 1.96\sigma_{\bar{X}}$ (see Fig 5.3, p 176). In the present one-tailed test this range is no longer appropriate, for if any $\bar{X}$ fell to the left of $\mu_o - 1.96\sigma_{\bar{X}}$ we should attribute this to chance and not to the true value of the mean being less than μ_o. Consequently, we should not want to reject the null hypothesis if $Z = \dfrac{\bar{X} - \mu_o}{\sigma_{\bar{X}}} < -1.96$. But, in order to maintain the level of significance at which the null hypothesis is rejected at 5 per cent[1], we must find the critical value of Z which cuts off 5 per cent of area only in the upper tail of the normal curve. From the normal table, this value is found to be 1.645. Therefore, if we have

$$H_o : \mu = \mu_o$$
$$H_a : \mu > \mu_o$$

the null hypothesis H_o is rejected if $Z > 1.645$, and it is accepted if $Z < 1.645$.

As a numerical illustration, suppose that a census of city-dwellers reveals an average family size of 4·2 with a standard deviation of 0·5. A random sample of 100 country families is taken and this reveals a family size of 4·29. We wish to test whether family size in the country is the same as in the city. The null hypothesis is that the sample comes from a population in which the mean is 4·2. If we were to apply a two-tailed test we should calculate

$$|Z| = \frac{|\bar{X} - \mu_o|}{\sigma_{\bar{X}}} = \frac{|4\cdot29 - 4\cdot20|}{0\cdot5/\sqrt{100}}$$
$$= 1\cdot8$$

Since $|Z| = 1\cdot8 < 1\cdot96$, we should retain the null hypothesis, and conclude that $\bar{X}$ is not significantly different from $\mu = 4\cdot2$. This would be quite appropriate if we had no reason to believe that, if the null hypothesis were wrong, the true hypothesis might as readily be that country families are smaller as that they are larger than city families. However, if we know, from other sources, that, whatever size country families are they are certainly no smaller than city families we should apply a one-tailed test. Comparing the computed Z value with the critical value of Z corresponding to a one-tailed test, we now have

---

[1] In doing so, we shall keep the size of the error of rejecting a null hypothesis when it is in fact true equal to 5 per cent; the nature of this error is explained in the following section.

$Z = +1\cdot8 > 1\cdot645$. We should then say that the null hypothesis $H_o:\mu = 4\cdot2$ should be rejected at the 5 per cent level of significance and the alternative hypothesis $H_a:\mu > 4\cdot2$ accepted. Thus our one-tailed test would lead us to conclude that $\bar{X}$ was significantly greater than the assumed μ.

More generally, let us write the critical one-tail value of Z at a level of significance α as Z_α. Then, if the null hypothesis concerning a parameter θ is $H_o:\theta = \theta_o$, and if the test statistic appropriate to the test is normally or approximately normally distributed, the decision rules for rejecting or accepting H_o against either $H_a:\theta > \theta_o$ or $H_a:\theta < \theta_o$ may be stated as follows:

$$H_a:\theta < \theta_o \qquad\qquad\qquad H_a:\theta > \theta_o$$

If $Z < -Z_\alpha$, reject H_o (accept H_a)   If $Z > +Z_\alpha$, reject H_o (accept H_a)

If $Z > -Z_\alpha$, accept H_o (reject H_a)   If $Z < +Z_\alpha$, accept H_o (reject H_a)

In section 5.5 we saw that when σ is not known, and N is small, the test statistic $t = \dfrac{\bar{X} - \mu_o}{s_{\bar{X}}}$ must be used instead of Z. It will be recalled that the t-table gives, for a given significance level α, the critical value of t that cuts off $\alpha/2$ in each tail of the t-distribution with ν degrees of freedom. Therefore, to find the critical value t_α for a one-tailed test, we need to look up twice the value of α corresponding to an equivalent two-tailed test. For instance, if $\alpha = 0\cdot05$ and $\nu = 4$, we read across from $\nu = 4$ and down from $\cdot1$ to find $t_{\cdot05} = 2\cdot132$; if $\alpha = 0\cdot01, t_{\cdot01} = 3\cdot747$, etc. In other respects the decision rules for small sample tests are quite analogous to those given for Z above.

In the tests of hypotheses we have considered so far the null hypothesis has always been stated in the form $H_o:\theta = \theta_o$. A null hypothesis which asserts that the true value of the population parameter is some *particular* value θ_o is referred to as an *exact* hypothesis. However, in one-tailed tests we shall sometimes want to consider null hypotheses of the form $H_o:\theta \leqslant \theta_o$ ie that the true value of θ is no greater than the postulated value θ_o, or of the form $H_o:\theta \geqslant \theta_o$, ie that θ is no smaller than θ_o. When a null hypothesis states that a population parameter lies within a range of values it is referred to as an *inexact* hypothesis.

To illustrate, let us consider the following simplified example. Suppose a large factory, producing a single product, has a normal output of 900 units per worker per day, with a standard deviation of 30 units. The management wishes to find out whether output will be affected by an alteration in the lay-out of the work benches. It modifies one small section of the factory and selects 25 workers at random to work under the new conditions. Let the mean output of these 25 workers be $\bar{X}$. There are now three possibilities: the new lay-out leaves output unchanged, it reduces output, it increases output. To test the hypothesis whether the mean output per worker is likely to be significantly greater with the new lay-out, the management may wish to test the null hypothesis

$$H_o : \mu \leqslant \mu_o$$

against the alternative hypothesis

$$H_a : \mu > \mu_o$$

Only in the event of $\bar{X}$ being significantly greater than 900 will the management wish to take action. If $\bar{X}$ should be smaller than 900, no action would be taken, just as if there were no significant difference between $\bar{X}$ and 900. Suppose that the experiment gives $\bar{X} = 915$. How should we test this result if H_o is an inexact hypothesis?

To consider this question, suppose first that we regard it as rather unlikely that the new lay-out in fact reduces output; in this case we should be justified to state the null hypothesis as $H_o : \mu = 900$, ie as an exact hypothesis. With this assumption, we can readily establish the 5 per cent (one-tail) critical value of $\bar{X}$ as $900 + 1 \cdot 645 \dfrac{30}{\sqrt{25}} = 910$.

Since $\bar{X} = 915 > 910$, we reject the null hypothesis $H_o : \mu = 900$ as being probably untrue. We can only say 'probably untrue', for it is conceivable that in finding $\bar{X} = 915$ we have struck a rare case and have thus rejected the hypothesis $H_o : \mu = 900$ when it is in fact true. Since the critical region chosen in our test is 5 per cent we can expect to make this type of error in 5 per cent of all samples taken under identical conditions. In other words, we have a 5 per cent risk of altering the lay-out when it is in fact ineffective.

Suppose next that the new arrangement can conceivably reduce output and we accept the figure of 895 as one of the possible hypothetical values of μ. Computing the critical value of $\bar{X}$ in this case gives $895 + 1 \cdot 645 \dfrac{30}{\sqrt{25}} = 905$. But $\bar{X} = 915$ lies further to the right from the critical value of 905 than it lies from the critical value of 910. Therefore, if we reject the hypothesis $H_o : \mu = 900$ with a tolerated error of 5 per cent we shall reject even with a smaller error the hypothesis $H_o : \mu = 895$, or, for that matter any other null hypothesis for which $\mu < 900$. Since the error involved in rejecting a true inexact null hypothesis is no larger than that of rejecting a corresponding exact hypothesis, we may treat inexact hypotheses as though they were exact ones, and apply the decision criteria outlined above. Thus, in our example, we would reject the null hypothesis $H_o : \mu \leqslant 900$, and accept the sample result as evidence of improved production. We now illustrate the use of one-sided tests with further examples.

Example 5.10

A soft-drink bottling company estimates that during the summer months of last year its home delivery sales averaged 18 bottles per household per month with a standard deviation of 5 bottles. Following a steep rise in the price of home-delivered bottles, a random sample of 40 households taken at the beginning of summer this year gives a mean of 16 bottles. Is this evidence of a significant reduction in the company's home-delivery sales? (Use $\alpha = 0.01$).

In this case, we base the alternative hypothesis on the economic hypothesis that if the price rise has had any significant effect it has been to reduce the volume of the company's sales.

We have

$$N = 40 \qquad \bar{X} = 16$$
$$\mu = 18 \qquad \sigma = 5$$
$$\sigma_{\bar{x}} = \frac{\sigma}{\sqrt{N}} = 0.79$$

Hypotheses:

$$H_o : \mu = 18$$
$$H_a : \mu < 18$$

Test:

$$Z = \frac{\bar{X} - \mu_o}{\sigma_{\bar{x}}} = \frac{16 - 18}{0.79}$$
$$= -2.53$$

and

$$Z = -2.53 < Z_{.01} = -2.33$$

Conclusion: Since the test statistic Z falls below the critical value of Z at the 1 per cent level of significance, we reject the null hypothesis H_o and accept the alternative H_a. If the null hypothesis were true, the probability of obtaining a sample mean equal to or smaller than 16 would be less than 1 per cent. Such being the case, it is very unlikely that the sample has come from a population with $\mu = 18$. We conclude that $\bar{X}$ is significantly less than the hypothetical μ.

Example 5.11

The management of a television plant wishes to test the effectiveness of a new technique in assembling a certain electronic device. Two randomly chosen groups of nine employees were selected, one group using the new technique and the other following the old method of assembly. At the end of the experiment, the mean length of time to assemble the device was found to be 52·8 minutes for the first group and 56·0 minutes for the latter group. From past experience, the variable 'assembly time' can be regarded as a normally distributed variable with a variance which is independent of the assembly technique being used. An estimate of this variance, obtained by pooling the sample results, was found to be $s^2 = 22.1$. What conclusions can be drawn from these results regarding the effectiveness of the two techniques? (Use $\alpha = 0.05$).

Here we have:

$$\text{Old technique:} \qquad\qquad \text{New technique:}$$

$$N_1 = 9 \qquad\qquad\qquad N_2 = 9$$

$$\bar{X}_1 = 56 \cdot 0 \qquad\qquad\qquad \bar{X}_2 = 52 \cdot 8$$

$$s \text{ (estimate of } \sigma) = \sqrt{22 \cdot 1} = 4 \cdot 7$$

$$s_{\bar{X}_1 - \bar{X}_2} = s\sqrt{\frac{1}{N_1} + \frac{1}{N_2}} = 4 \cdot 7 \sqrt{\frac{2}{9}}$$

$$= 2 \cdot 215$$

Let us write μ_1 and μ_2 as the means of the hypothetical populations from which the two samples have supposedly come. Since our purpose is to test the relative effectiveness of the two methods of assembly, we set up the alternative hypothesis as a one-sided hypothesis.

Hypotheses:

$$H_o : \mu_1 - \mu_2 = 0$$

$$H_a : \mu_1 - \mu_2 > 0$$

Test:

$$t = \frac{\bar{X}_1 - \bar{X}_2}{s_{\bar{X}_1 - \bar{X}_2}} = \frac{56 - 52 \cdot 8}{2 \cdot 215}$$

$$= 1 \cdot 44$$

From the t-table, the critical value of t which cuts off 5 per cent of area in the upper tail of the t-distribution with $v = 9 + 9 - 2 = 16$ degrees of freedom is $1 \cdot 746$ (reading down from $\cdot 1$, since this is a one-tailed test).

$$t = 1 \cdot 44 < t_{\cdot 05} = 1 \cdot 746$$

Conclusion: Since the t-value lies below the critical value of $+1 \cdot 746$ we do not reject the null hypothesis. The sample results do not provide sufficient evidence that the new assembly method is superior to the old method.

Example 5.12

A random sample of 1000 unemployed persons reveals that 12 per cent are tradesmen. Is this consistent with a claim put forward by an employment agency that of all unemployed persons at most 10 per cent are tradesmen?

Here

$$N = 1000 \qquad\qquad p = 0 \cdot 12 \qquad\qquad \pi = 0 \cdot 10$$

$$\sigma_p = \sqrt{\frac{\pi(1 - \pi)}{N}}$$

$$= 0 \cdot 0095$$

Hypotheses:

$$H_o : \pi \leqslant 0 \cdot 10$$

$$H_a : \pi > 0 \cdot 10$$

Test:

$$Z = \frac{p - \pi_o}{\sigma_p} = \frac{0\cdot12 - 0\cdot10}{0\cdot0095}$$

$$= 2\cdot11$$

and

$$Z = 2\cdot11 > Z_{\cdot05} = 1\cdot645$$

Conclusion: Because Z exceeds the critical value of Z at the 5 per cent level of significance, we reject the null hypothesis H_o and accept the alternative hypothesis that $\pi > 0\cdot10$. On the basis of the sample result, it is very unlikely that the agency's statement is correct.

5.10 Two Types of Error

In the preceding sections we have been concerned with procedures for testing hypotheses at the conventional levels of significance of 5 per cent and 1 per cent. We have seen that if the test statistic computed from a sample falls within the critical region corresponding to the chosen level of significance, the null hypothesis is rejected; otherwise it is accepted. However, we also mentioned that this two-choice decision procedure leads to statistical errors being made. Whenever we test a statistical hypothesis against sample data, we shall have one of the four possible results summarised by the following table:

	H_o true	H_o false
Accept H_o	Correct decision $(1 - \alpha)$	Type II error (β)
Reject H_o	Type I error (α)	Correct decision $(1 - \beta)$

When a null hypothesis is true but rejected, the resulting error is called *Type I error*. When it is false but accepted, the error is referred to as *Type II error*. In designing statistical tests it is important that we determine the probabilities associated with these two types of error. Let us consider first error Type I.

The probability that a true hypothesis will be rejected is given by the level of significance employed in the test. Thus, in the table above, the probability of committing error Type I is shown as α. At the 5 per cent level, for example, we know that we shall be rejecting on the average 5 per cent of all true hypotheses, because even if the null hypothesis were true the sample statistic being tested would fall within the rejection range with a probability of 5 per cent. This 5 per cent is called the *size* of the Type I error. Thus, suppose we are testing an hypothesis about a mean μ_o, with given standard deviation σ. By the decision rule for two-tailed tests we shall accept the null hypothesis when $\bar{X}$ lies within the range $\mu_o \pm 1.96\dfrac{\sigma}{\sqrt{N}}$, and we shall reject it when $\bar{X}$ lies outside this range. But if the null hypothesis is true (ie if the population really has a mean μ_o), 5 per cent of random samples drawn from this population will have $\bar{X}$s lying outside the acceptance range, so that with repeated sampling we shall reject 5 per cent of true hypotheses. This is illustrated in Fig 5.5. The two points, b and a,

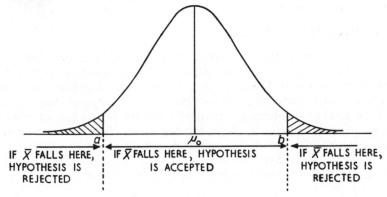

IF $\bar{X}$ FALLS HERE, HYPOTHESIS IS REJECTED   IF $\bar{X}$ FALLS HERE, HYPOTHESIS IS ACCEPTED   IF $\bar{X}$ FALLS HERE, HYPOTHESIS IS REJECTED

Fig 5.5

represent the values $\mu_o \pm 1.96\dfrac{\sigma}{\sqrt{N}}$ respectively, and the shaded area represents the size of Type I error, 5 per cent in this case. Evidently, by setting the level of significance at a certain level, we are also determining the margin of risk we are prepared to tolerate in rejecting a null hypothesis when it is true. To avoid this risk being too high, we conventionally set α at a small value, generally 5 per cent or less.

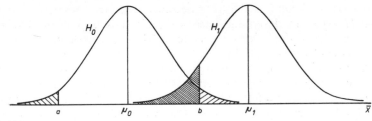

Fig 5.6

Now suppose that the hypothesis that the population mean is μ_o is in fact wrong, and that the correct population mean is some other value, say μ_1, the standard deviation σ being the same as before. In Fig 5.6 the probability distribution of the means of samples of size N

drawn from a population with mean μ_1 and standard deviation σ, ie the sampling distribution of $\bar{X}$ under the hypothesis $H_1 : \mu = \mu_1$, is superimposed on the distribution given in Fig 5.5 above.

If we are testing the hypothesis $H_o : \mu = \mu_o$, but the correct hypothesis is $H_1 : \mu = \mu_1$, whenever an $\bar{X}$ falls to the left of point b, the hypothesis H_o will be accepted, and a Type II error will be made. Thus, if the true population mean is μ_1, the probability of obtaining an $\bar{X}$ which is less than b will be given by the solidly shaded area, so that the probability of accepting the hypothesis $H_o : \mu = \mu_o$ when this is incorrect will be given by that area. Accordingly that area measures the size of the Type II error. It is customary to denote the size of the Type II error by β (Greek beta). If β measures the probability of committing an error Type II, ie of accepting a null hypothesis when it is false, then $(1 - \beta)$ gives the probability of correctly rejecting it. Graphically, this latter probability is shown in Fig 5.6 as that portion of area under the curve H_1 that lies to the right of point b.

To summarise, if the hypothesis is that the population mean is μ_o, we shall wrongly reject a true hypothesis whenever the mean really is μ_o but $\bar{X}$ lies *outside* the range a to b (ie make a Type I error) and we shall wrongly accept a false hypothesis whenever the mean really is μ_1 but $\bar{X}$ lies *inside* the range a to b (ie make a Type II error).

It should be plain from Fig 5.6 above that we can make the Type I error as small as we please by lowering the level of significance, ie by increasing the range a to b in which the hypothesis H_o is accepted. We have seen that if, for example, we work with a 1 per cent level of significance, the critical value of $|Z|$ is raised from 1·96 to 2·58. But by doing so we increase the risk of accepting a false null hypothesis. This can be seen from Fig 5.6, for as we widen the range a to b, we reduce the lightly shaded area, but increase the solidly shaded area. It follows that, for samples of a given size N, it is impossible to minimise both errors simultaneously.

It can be seen, however, that in practice the appropriate balance to be given to the two types of error in designing tests of significance will depend upon the relative consequences which flow from making errors of both kinds. Thus a factory making wire ropes may be contemplating introducing a new process which is expected to increase the strength of the ropes. A sample of ropes made under the new process is tested, the null hypothesis being that the process results in no improvement. A Type I error will occur if the process is really no improvement although the statistical test rejects the hypothesis, and a Type II error will occur if the process is really an improvement although the statistical test accepts the hypothesis. If the cost of making the innovation is small, whereas the possible improvements in strength are considerable, clearly a Type II error is more serious than a Type I error, whereas, if the cost is substantial and the possible improvements slight, the reverse is true.

The case of testing Salk anti-polio vaccine for viability provides a more graphic example. Suppose a sample is drawn from a large batch and tested. The hypothesis is that the vaccine is not viable. If a Type I error is made (vaccine not viable, but test rejects the batch) supplies of good vaccine will be discarded. People will go unvaccinated; and some may contract polio although had the vaccine been used they would have escaped it. If a Type II error is made (vaccine viable, but test accepts the batch) vaccination may itself produce polio. The relative importance of the two types of error is in practice seldom as clear-cut as these examples might suggest, but at least they indicate the significance of the two types of error in a practical setting.

Example 5.13

Suppose X is a normally distributed variable with assumed mean $\mu = 500$ and known standard deviation $\sigma = 42$. A random sample of $N = 49$ observations is selected, and the null hypothesis $H_o : \mu = 500$ is to be tested with significance level $\alpha = 0.05$. Suppose further that we know, from other sources, that if the population mean is not 500, then its true value is 505. What is the probability of accepting H_o when it is in fact false?

In this case, the null and the alternative hypothesis are

$$H_o : \mu = 500$$
$$H_1 : \mu = 505$$

ie the hypothetical μ is tested against the single alternative value $\mu = 505$. Also

$$\sigma_{\bar{X}} = \frac{\sigma}{\sqrt{N}} = \frac{42}{7}$$
$$= 6$$

Since $\alpha = 0.05$, we have P (error Type I) $= 0.05$; that is, the maximum tolerated error of rejecting H_o when it is true is 5 per cent. This implies that we shall reject H_o only when

$$\frac{\bar{X} - \mu_o}{\sigma_{\bar{X}}} > 1.645$$

ie when

$$\bar{X} > 500 + (1.645)(6) = 509.87$$

Therefore, if in a sample of 49 observations we obtain a sample mean exceeding the critical value of 509·87, we shall reject $H_o : \mu = 500$ in favour of $H_1 : \mu_1 = 505$ with a probability of 5 per cent that the hypothesis we are rejecting is in fact true.

Suppose next that H_o is false, ie H_1 is true. To find the probability that a Type II error will be committed, we first compute $P(\bar{X} < 509.87)$ when $\mu_1 = 505$. We have

$$P\left(Z < \frac{\bar{X} - \mu_1}{\sigma_{\bar{X}}}\right) = P\left(Z < \frac{509.87 - 505}{6}\right) = P(Z < 0.81)$$

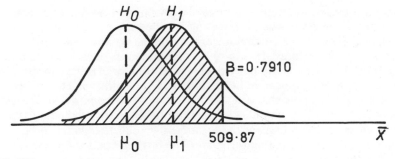

Fig 5.7

and from the normal table $P(Z < 0\cdot81) = 0\cdot5000 + 0\cdot2910 = 0\cdot7910$. Thus, the probability of an error Type II is $\beta = 0\cdot7910$. In the accompanying diagram, this probability is shown as the shaded area under the curve H_1 lying to the left of the point $\bar{X} = 509\cdot87$. The size of the Type II error is sometimes referred to as the *β-risk*. We conclude that if the competing hypotheses being tested are $H_o : \mu = 500$ and $H_1 : \mu = 505$, the β-risk is quite high, ie in four out of every five samples of size $N = 49$ drawn from the given population we would run the risk that the null hypothesis we are accepting is in fact false.

The Power of a Test

In the preceding example we found the size of the Type II error, or the β-risk, associated with a single alternative value of μ, ie $\mu_1 = 505$. In practice, however, the alternative hypothesis can very seldom be stated in this way. Thus, in our example, the alternative hypothesis for an upper-tail test will usually be of the form $H_a : \mu > 500$. How can we assess the β-risk for such a composite hypothesis? In general, we proceed in much the same way as in the case of a single alternative value of μ, except that β is now calculated for various feasible alternative values of μ, eg when $\mu_a = 510$, we shall have

$$P\left(Z < \frac{\bar{X} - \mu_a}{\sigma_{\bar{X}}} \right) = P\left(Z < \frac{509\cdot87 - 510}{6} \right)$$

$$= P(Z < -0\cdot02) = 0\cdot5000 - 0\cdot0080 = 0\cdot4920$$

and hence $\beta = 0\cdot4920$, etc. Table 5.1 gives values of β computed in a similar manner for several other alternative values of μ. As can be seen, the size of the Type II error diminishes rapidly as μ moves away from the value $\mu = 500$ postulated by the null hypothesis.

We have seen that whereas β gives the probability of making a wrong decision in a statistical test, ie accepting a false null hypothesis, the quantity $(1 - \beta)$ measures the probability of making the correct decision of rejecting a null hypothesis when it is false. The probability $(1 - \beta)$ is referred to as the *power* of the statistical test. A relationship which for each alternative μ gives the probability $1 - \beta$ of rejecting the null hypothesis when it is wrong is called a *power curve* or *power function*. The power function corresponding to the one-tailed test of $H_o:\mu = 500$ against $H_a:\mu > 500$ is tabulated in the second column of Table 5.2 below. When plotted for a large number of points, the power function would appear as a smooth curve, as illustrated by curve I in Fig 5.8. We note that if H_o is true, ie $\mu = 500$, the power of the test is equal to α, the probability of committing an error of the first type. For an exact hypothesis of the form $H_o:\mu = 500$ this will also be the minimum point on the power curve. The further apart the values of μ under the null and the alternative hypothesis, the greater the power of the test, ie the greater our ability to distinguish between true and false hypotheses. Thus, in our example, if the true value of μ were 505 and not 500, the power of the test would be low, for we would be correctly rejecting H_o in only about 20 per cent of all cases. If the true value of μ were 525, the corresponding probability would be 99·4 per cent, and in rejecting H_o we would be virtually certain of a correct decision.

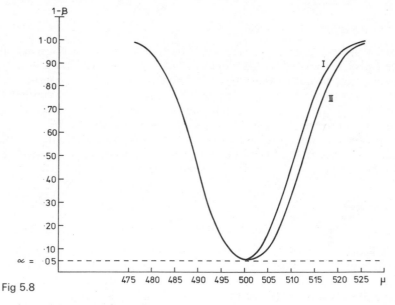

Fig 5.8

A power curve for a two-sided test of the hypothesis $H_o:\mu = 500$ against $H_a:\mu \neq 500$ may be constructed in a similar way as the power function for an upper-tail test. In this case, the critical values of $\bar{X}$ cutting off $2\frac{1}{2}$ per cent of area in either tail of the sampling distribution of $\bar{X}$ are

$$500 + (1 \cdot 96)(6) = 511 \cdot 76$$

and
$$500 - (1 \cdot 96)(6) = 488 \cdot 24$$

If H_o is true, it will be erroneously rejected if $\bar{X}$ falls outside these critical limits, ie if $\bar{X} > 511 \cdot 76$ or $\bar{X} < 488 \cdot 24$. If H_o is false, the prob-

Table 5.1

SIZE OF TYPE II ERROR FOR SPECIFIED VALUES OF μ

$H_o : \mu = 500, H_a : \mu > 500; \alpha = 0 \cdot 05, \sigma = 42, N = 49$

Alternative Values μ	Probability β
(500)	$(1 - \alpha = 0 \cdot 9500)$
505	$0 \cdot 7910$
510	$0 \cdot 4920$
515	$0 \cdot 1963$
520	$0 \cdot 0455$
525	$0 \cdot 0059$

Table 5.2

POWER FUNCTION FOR ONE-TAILED AND TWO-TAILED TEST

$H_o : \mu = 500; \alpha = 0 \cdot 05, \sigma = 42, N = 49$

Alternative Values μ	Probability of Rejecting False $H_o : 1 - \beta$	
	One-tailed Test $H_a : \mu > 500$	Two-tailed Test $H_a : \mu \neq 500$
485		$0 \cdot 7054$
490		$0 \cdot 3859$
495		$0 \cdot 1318$
(500)	$(\alpha = 0 \cdot 0500)$	$(\alpha = 0 \cdot 0500)$
505	$0 \cdot 2090$	$0 \cdot 1318$
510	$0 \cdot 5080$	$0 \cdot 3859$
515	$0 \cdot 8037$	$0 \cdot 7054$
520	$0 \cdot 9545$	$0 \cdot 9147$
525	$0 \cdot 9941$	$0 \cdot 9865$

ability that it will be rejected will depend on the particular alternative value of μ. Thus, suppose that if the mean μ is not 500 it is likely to be, say, 505. We then have

$$P(\bar{X} > 511 \cdot 76) = P\left(Z > \frac{511 \cdot 76 - 505}{6}\right) = P(Z > 1 \cdot 13)$$

and

$$P(\bar{X} < 488 \cdot 24) = P\left(Z < \frac{488 \cdot 24 - 505}{6}\right) = P(Z < -2 \cdot 79)$$

and from the table of normal areas

$$1 - \beta = P(Z > 1\cdot13) + P(Z < -2\cdot79)$$
$$= (0\cdot5000 - 0\cdot3708) + (0\cdot5000 - 0\cdot4974)$$
$$= 0\cdot1318$$

Other values of the power function resulting from the application of the two-tailed test are shown in the last column of Table 5.2, and a graph of this function appears as curve II in Fig 5.8. As can be seen, the curve is symmetrical about $\mu = 500$, the point for which the null hypothesis $H_o : \mu = 500$ is true. Comparing the two power curves in Fig 5.8 we can see that for all alternative values of μ above 500 the upper-tail test is more powerful than the corresponding two-tailed test; the same result holds, *mutatis mutandis*, for a power curve resulting from the application of a left-hand test where $\mu_a < \mu_o$. From this it may be concluded that whenever we have reason to believe that if the true population mean is not μ_o it must lie either to the right (or to the left) of μ_o we shall always prefer a one-sided to a two-sided test. We shall prefer the former since, for any given level of significance, it gives greater power to the decision rule to reject the null hypothesis when it is false.

We have already noted that for samples with a fixed number of observations the size of the Type II error (β) is inversely related to the size of the Type I error (α). It follows that one way of increasing the power of a statistical test is to raise the level of significance α, eg from 5 to 10 per cent. Diagrammatically, the power curve associated with the latter test would lie everywhere above the power curve corresponding to the former, and the 10 per cent test is said to be a uniformly more powerful test.

However, if we wish to make the test more powerful without at the same time incurring a higher risk of committing an error Type I,

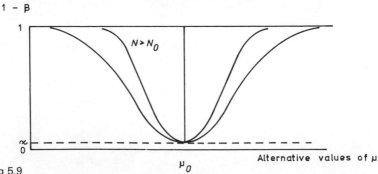

Fig 5.9

we can only do so by increasing the number of observations in the sample. Since the dispersion of the sampling distribution of $\bar{X}$ depends on the magnitude of the standard error $\sigma_{\bar{X}} = \dfrac{\sigma}{\sqrt{N}}$, it is clear that an increase in the sample size N will move the critical values of $\bar{X}$ closer to the centre of the distribution at an unchanged level of significance α. Consequently, by increasing N we shall also reduce the spread of the power curve around the value of μ postulated by the null hypothesis. As illustrated by Fig 5.9, a larger N increases the power of a two-sided test without affecting the size of the Type I error, and the same result holds for one-tailed tests.

We can conclude from the above that if we wish to design a test with sufficient power to discriminate between a false and a true hypothesis, we must consider the appropriate size of the sample to be selected. To illustrate, let us consider again the test of $H_o:\mu = 500$ against $H_a:\mu \neq 500$, with $\sigma = 42$. Suppose the risk of the Type I error has been set at 5 per cent, and suppose further that if the true value of μ should differ from $\mu = 500$ by ± 15 we should want to reject the null hypothesis with a probability of 90 per cent. Given $\alpha = 0.05$ and $1 - \beta = 0.90$, how shall we determine the required sample size N?

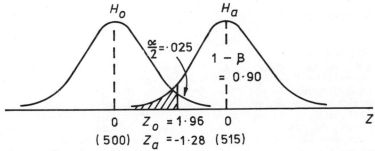

Fig 5.10

The sampling distributions corresponding to the hypotheses $H_o:\mu = 500$ and $H_a:\mu = 515$ are shown above in Fig 5.10. Since $\alpha = 0.05$, the critical region for the test is determined by $Z_o = +1.96$. But we also require that when $\mu = 515$ the null hypothesis is rejected with a probability of 90 per cent. From the table of normal areas, the value of Z for which 90 per cent of the area under curve H_a lies in the rejection region for the test is $Z_a = -1.28$. Since the critical region is determined by both $500 + 1.96\sigma_{\bar{X}}$ and $515 - 1.28\sigma_{\bar{X}}$, we may write

$$500 + 1.96\sigma_{\bar{X}} = 515 - 1.28\sigma_{\bar{X}}$$

from which we find

$$\sigma_{\bar{X}} = \frac{\sigma}{\sqrt{N}} = 4.63$$

Setting $\sigma = 42$ and solving for N, we obtain

$$N = \left(\frac{42}{4.63}\right)^2$$
$$= 82$$

In Table 5.2 on p 205 the probabilities $1 - \beta$ for the alternative values $\mu = 500 \pm 15$ were found to be 0·7054. However, these calculations were based on a sample of 49 observations. If we wish to raise the power of our test from 0·7054 to 0·90, we must increase the size of the sample from 49 to 82 observations.

In general, if μ_o and μ_a are the means stated by the null and the alternative hypothesis, and Z_o and Z_a are the values of the standard normal variable Z that correspond to the given significance level α and the desired power of the test $1 - \beta$, the required sample size is given by the formula

$$N = \frac{(|Z_o| + |Z_a|)^2 \sigma^2}{(\mu_a - \mu_o)^2}$$

Example 5.14

A manufacturer of jam wishes to keep a check on his production process by sample tests of the hypothesis that the average content of his jam jars is 460 grams against the hypothesis that it is less than 460 grams. From past data, the standard deviation of such jars is estimated to be 30 grams. It is decided that the tests should be at a 1 per cent level of significance and should have sufficient power to reject the null hypothesis with a probability of 95 per cent when the true average weight of the jars is as low as 440 grams. What size samples would be needed to satisfy these requirements?

Here we have

$$H_o : \mu = 460$$
$$H_a : \mu < 460$$

$$\alpha = 0.01 \qquad 1 - \beta = 0.95 \quad (\mu = 440) \qquad \sigma = 30$$

With $\alpha = 0.01$, the critical value for a lower-tail test is -2.33, ie $Z_o = -2.33$. If the true population mean is 440 grams, H_o will be rejected with probability 0·95 when $Z < Z_a = 1.645$. In the present case we therefore have

$$N = \frac{(2.33 + 1.645)^2 (30)^2}{(440 - 460)^2}$$
$$\simeq 36$$

5.11 χ^2 Tests of Statistical Hypotheses

In the tests of significance concerning means and proportions we have made use of two important sampling distributions, the normal distribution and the t-distribution. However, these distributions will no longer be appropriate when, for instance, we wish to draw inferences about the variance of a distribution. So that we may proceed with further tests commonly applied in practice it is necessary that we introduce another probability distribution known as the χ^2 *(chi-square) distribution.*

The χ^2-distribution

We have seen that if a variable X has a normal distribution $N(\mu, \sigma)$, then $Z = \dfrac{X - \mu}{\sigma}$ has the standard normal distribution $N(0,1)$. Suppose now that a sample of N independent observations is taken from a normal population with given μ and σ and we form a new variable

$$\sum Z_i^2 = \frac{(X_1 - \mu)^2}{\sigma^2} + \frac{(X_2 - \mu)^2}{\sigma^2} + \ldots + \frac{(X_N - \mu)^2}{\sigma^2}$$

$$= \sum \frac{(X_i - \mu)^2}{\sigma^2}$$

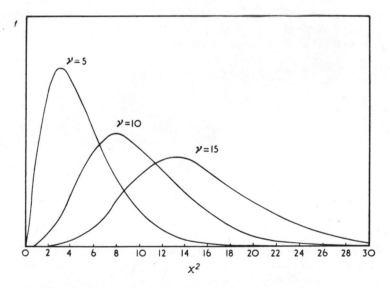

Fig 5.11 The χ^2-distribution

Like the t-ratio, the variable

$$\chi^2 = \sum \frac{(X_i - \mu)^2}{\sigma^2}$$

is not distributed normally but has its own distribution, the χ^2-distribution. This distribution depends on a single parameter v, the number of degrees of freedom. Three χ^2-distributions with different values of v are sketched in the diagram above.

Since χ^2 is a sum of squares, it must always be positive, and the probability curve of χ^2 starts at the origin. As can be seen from Fig 5.11, for small values of v, the χ^2-distribution is positively skewed. But as v increases the curve becomes more and more symmetrical, and for large values of v may be approximated by the normal curve.

The distribution of χ^2 is tabulated in Table III of Appendix A. It gives in the body of the table, for particular numbers of degrees of freedom tabulated in the vertical margin, the value of χ^2 which cuts off a tail at the right-hand side of the distribution covering certain proportions of area tabulated in the horizontal margin. Such a tail is shown in Fig 5.12. This tail measures $P(\chi^2 > \chi_\alpha^2)$. Thus, for $v = 9$, $\chi_{.05}^2 = 16·92$ and $P(\chi^2 > 16·92) = 0·05$ ie the probability of obtaining a value of the test statistic χ^2 as great as or greater than 16·92, with 9 degrees of freedom, is 5 per cent. Or if, with $v = 9$, on the basis of some hypothesis about the population, we obtained for a particular sample a value of $\chi^2 = 12$, we could ascertain from the table that $P(\chi^2 > 12)$ lies between 0·30 and 0·20, so that we could say that a value of χ^2 as great as or greater than 12 would crop up just due to chance in from 20 to 30 cases out of 100.

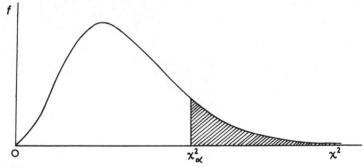

Fig 5.12

We now consider three important tests based on the χ^2-distribution:
(1) tests of variance,
(2) tests of goodness of fit, and
(3) tests of independence of classification.

Tests of Variance

Let us suppose we have a sample of N observations of a normally distributed variable X and we compute the sample variance by using the formula $s^2 = \dfrac{\Sigma(X - \bar{X})^2}{N - 1}$. Given the sample result, can it reasonably be concluded that the true population variance is some hypothesised value σ_o^2?

Before proceeding with the test, we must first establish the distribution of sample variances generated by repeated sampling. Consider again the random quantity $\Sigma\dfrac{(X - \mu)^2}{\sigma^2}$. Since in this case the deviations are computed from the population mean μ, the sum of squares $\Sigma(X - \mu)^2$ has a number of degrees of freedom equal to the number of independent sample observations N. Symbolically, we write

$$\sum\frac{(X - \mu)^2}{\sigma^2} = \chi_N^2$$

where χ_N^2 denotes a χ^2 variable with N *degrees of freedom*. In using sample data, however, $\bar{X}$ must be used in place of the unknown μ, and this results in the loss of one degree of freedom (see section 5.5, p 180 above). Therefore, $\Sigma\dfrac{(X - \bar{X})^2}{\sigma^2}$ will be distributed as χ^2 *with $N - 1$ degrees of freedom*,[1] ie

[1] To see this more formally, we recall from p 60 above that, for a sample of size N, the sample sum of squares may be written as

$$\Sigma(X - \bar{X})^2 = \Sigma(X - A)^2 - N(\bar{X} - A)^2$$

where A is an arbitrary origin. If we set $A = \mu$, and divide the resulting equation through by σ^2, we shall have

$$\sum\frac{(X - \bar{X})^2}{\sigma^2} = \sum\frac{(X - \mu)^2}{\sigma^2} - \frac{(\bar{X} - \mu)^2}{(\sigma/\sqrt{N})^2}$$

The first term on the right of this equation is a χ^2 variable with N degrees of freedom, ie χ_N^2. The second term, being the square of the standard normal variable Z, is likewise a χ^2 variable with 1 degree of freedom, that is

$$\frac{(\bar{X} - \mu)^2}{(\sigma/\sqrt{N})^2} = Z^2 = \chi_1^2$$

Now, it is an important property of the χ^2-distribution that if two independent χ^2 variables are distributed with v_1 and v_2 degrees of freedom respectively, then

$$\chi_{v_1}^2 \pm \chi_{v_2}^2 = \chi_{v_1 \pm v_2}^2$$

ie the sum (or difference) of two independent χ^2 variables is distributed with $v_1 + v_2$ (or $v_1 - v_2$) degrees of freedom. It can be shown that in the case we are considering the condition of independence is satisfied, and we therefore have

$$\sum\frac{(X - \bar{X})^2}{\sigma^2} = \chi_N^2 - \chi_1^2 = \chi_{N-1}^2$$

$$\sum \frac{(X - \bar{X})^2}{\sigma^2} = \chi^2_{N-1}$$

where

$$\sum \frac{(X - \bar{X})^2}{\sigma^2} = \frac{(N - 1)s^2}{\sigma^2}$$

Thus, we have the result that if samples of size N are drawn from a normal population with variance σ^2, the sample variance s^2, multiplied by the constant factor $\frac{N - 1}{\sigma^2}$, will have a χ^2-distribution with $v = N - 1$ degrees of freedom.[1]

With this result, we may now proceed with tests of hypotheses concerning a population variance σ^2. As an example, suppose that a normal variable X is known to have been distributed in the past about a mean μ and with variance $\sigma^2 = 48$. A random sample of 13 observations taken recently reveals a sample variance of 52. Can this result be attributed to chance or can it be taken as evidence that the variability of the population, as measured by σ^2, has increased?

The hypotheses to be tested in this case are:

$$H_o : \sigma^2 = 48 \qquad\qquad H_a : \sigma^2 > 48$$

[1] It may be useful to note here that the t-distribution introduced earlier and the χ^2-distribution are related. The t-distribution is defined as the probability distribution of the random variable

$$t = \frac{Z}{\sqrt{\dfrac{U}{v}}}$$

where Z and U are independently distributed random variables, Z having the standard normal distribution and U having the χ^2-distribution with v degrees of freedom. If samples of size N are drawn from a normal population we know that

$$Z = \frac{\bar{X} - \mu}{\sigma/\sqrt{N}}$$

has the standard normal distribution. We also know that

$$\frac{(N - 1)s^2}{\sigma^2} = \chi^2_{N-1}$$

so that

$$\frac{s}{\sigma} = \sqrt{\frac{\chi^2_{N-1}}{N - 1}} = \sqrt{\frac{U}{v}}$$

Therefore, if we write

$$t = \frac{\dfrac{\bar{X} - \mu}{\sigma/\sqrt{N}}}{\dfrac{s}{\sigma}} = \frac{\bar{X} - \mu}{s/\sqrt{N}} = \frac{\bar{X} - \mu}{s_{\bar{X}}}$$

the population standard deviation σ cancels out, and we can use the t-distribution to make inferences about the population μ even if we do not know σ.

Let the significance level be set at 5 per cent. With $\alpha = 0.05$ and $v = 13 - 1 = 12$, the critical value for the test is $\chi^2_{.05} = 21.026$. By analogy with previous tests, if $\chi^2 > \chi^2_{.05}$, we shall reject the null hypothesis H_o, and if $\chi^2 < \chi^2_{.05}$ we shall accept it. In the present case, the test statistic χ^2 is computed as

$$\chi^2 = \frac{(N-1)s^2}{\sigma_o^2} = \frac{(12)(52)}{48} = 13$$

Here $\chi^2 = 13 < \chi^2_{.05} = 21.026$, and we do not reject the null hypothesis that $\sigma^2 = 48$. For, if the null hypothesis were true, repeated sampling with 12 degrees of freedom would result in $\chi^2 > 13$ in about 40 per cent of all cases. This is very much greater than 5 per cent, and we conclude that the value of χ^2 obtained in the sample is not significant.

When we wish to test the null hypothesis $H_o : \sigma = \sigma_o$ either against $H_a : \sigma < \sigma_o$ or against $H_a : \sigma^2 \neq \sigma_o^2$ we shall also need to consider the rejection region lying in the lower tail of the χ^2-distribution. In the former case, the rejection region is determined by finding the value of χ^2 which cuts off the upper $1 - \alpha$ of the χ^2-distribution with $N - 1$ degrees of freedom. In our numerical example, this value is found to be $\chi^2_{.95} = 5.226$. Hence, in testing the hypothesis $H_o : \sigma = 48$ against the alternative $H_a : \sigma < 48$, we would reject H_o if $\chi^2 < \chi^2_{.95} = 5.226$ and we would accept H_o if $\chi^2 > \chi^2_{.95} = 5.226$. Similarly, in a two-tailed test of $H_o : \sigma^2 = \sigma_o^2$ against $H_a : \sigma^2 \neq \sigma_o^2$, the null hypothesis is rejected when $\chi^2 > \chi^2_{\alpha/2}$ (when the sample χ^2 lies in the upper rejection region) or when $\chi^2 < \chi^2_{1-\alpha/2}$ (when the sample χ^2 lies in the lower rejection region). Again, suppose that the hypothesis $H_o : \sigma^2 = 48$ is to be considered against the two-sided alternative $H_a : \sigma^2 \neq 48$ at a 10 per cent level of significance. Dividing $\alpha = 0.10$ equally between the two tails, we have $\chi^2_{.05} = 21.026$ and $\chi^2_{.95} = 5.226$ with $v = 12$ degrees of freedom. Hence, if in the test $\chi^2 > 21.026$ or $\chi^2 < 5.226$, we reject the null hypothesis and accept the alternative $H_a : \sigma^2 \neq 48$.

Example 5.15

The lengths of steel tubes produced by a machine are distributed normally with a standard deviation of 0.16 centimeters. After a certain mechanical adjustment to the machine has been made, a random sample of 25 tubes is selected and the sample standard deviation is found to be 0.125 centimeters. Test the hypothesis, at a 1 per cent level of significance, that the variability in the lengths of the steel tubes produced by the machine has been reduced. Here

$$\sigma^2 = (0.160)^2 = 0.0256$$
$$s^2 = (0.125)^2 = 0.0156$$
$$N = 25$$

Hypotheses:

$$H_o : \sigma^2 = 0.0256$$
$$H_a : \sigma^2 < 0.0256$$

Test:

$$\chi^2 = \frac{(N-1)s^2}{\sigma_o^2} = \frac{(24)(0.0156)}{0.0256}$$
$$= 14.62$$

With $\alpha = 0.01$ and $v = 25 - 1 = 24$ degrees of freedom the critical value of χ^2 for the left-hand side test is $\chi^2_{.99} = 10.856$, and we have

$$\chi^2 = 14.62 > \chi^2_{.99} = 10.856$$

Conclusion: The sample value of χ^2 lies within the acceptance range for the test, and we do not reject the null hypothesis that $\sigma = 0.16$. From the χ^2-table, for $v = 24$, $P(\chi^2 < 14.62) \simeq 0.07$, which is greater than 0.01. Thus, the sample result does not provide support for the hypothesis that the variability in the lengths of steel tubes is significantly less after the adjustment.

Tests of Goodness of Fit

Suppose we have a sample of size N of a variable X classified into various classes, and we set up an hypothesis that the population of the variable has a certain type of distribution, eg the normal, the uniform, or some other distribution. To test such an hypothesis, we should want to compare the frequencies observed in our sample, which we call the *observed frequencies*, with the frequencies which we should expect on the basis of the hypothesis, which we call the *expected frequencies*. This comparison involves what is known as a test of the *goodness of fit*, for we test how well the hypothesis fits the sample data. Naturally we should not expect our observed frequencies to equal exactly the expected ones even if the hypothesis were true, for just due to chance there will be discrepancies. The question is: Are the discrepancies too great to be attributed reasonably to chance? If so, doubt is cast on the hypothesis.

To take a simple example, suppose a coin is tossed 100 times and we observe 58 heads and 42 tails. Is this result consistent with the hypothesis that the coin is unbiased? If the hypothesis were true, we should expect heads and tails to occur with equal probability, and hence in 100 tosses, we should expect $(\frac{1}{2})(100) = 50$ heads and $(\frac{1}{2})(100) = 50$ tails. Writing E_i, $i = 1, 2$, for the possible outcomes of each trial of the experiment, f_{oi} for the observed frequency in each class, and f_{ei} for the corresponding frequency expected on the basis of the hypothesis, we obtain the following frequency table:

Event E_i	Observed Sample Frequency f_{oi}	Probability P_i	Expected Frequency (NP_i) f_{ei}
E_1 (heads) E_2 (tails)	$f_{o1} = 58$ $f_{o2} = 42$	$P_1 = \frac{1}{2}$ $P_2 = \frac{1}{2}$	$f_{e1} = 50$ $f_{e2} = 50$
Total	100	1	100

As the next step we require some summary measure of the overall discrepancy between the observed and expected frequencies. To derive such a measure, let us form the new variables

$$X_1 = \frac{f_{o1} - f_{e1}}{\sqrt{f_{e1}}}$$

and

$$X_2 = \frac{f_{o2} - f_{e2}}{\sqrt{f_{e2}}}$$

If we next write

$$X_1^2 + X_2^2 = \sum_{i=1}^{2} \frac{(f_{oi} - f_{ei})^2}{f_{ei}}$$

it can be shown that for sufficiently large N this quantity will be distributed approximately as a χ^2 variable with $v = 2 - 1 = 1$ degree of freedom. Thus, to test our hypothesis that the coin is unbiased, we first compute the value of the χ^2 statistic from the given data and then refer it to the table of the χ^2-distribution with 1 degree of freedom. This gives the probability of obtaining just due to chance a value of χ^2 as great as or greater than the one calculated, if the hypothesis were true. If this probability is small (ie less than 5 per cent), we can say that the hypothesis is a bad fit and we reject it, for the discrepancy between the f_os and the f_es could not then be reasonably attributed to chance; otherwise, the hypothesis is accepted. Here we have

$$\chi^2 = \sum \frac{(f_o - f_e)^2}{f_e} = \frac{(58 - 50)^2}{50} + \frac{(42 - 50)^2}{50} = 2 \cdot 56$$

and from the table of χ^2, with $v = 1$, $P(\chi^2 > 2 \cdot 56) = 0 \cdot 11$, which is greater than 0·05. Hence, the hypothesis that the coin is a fair coin is retained. We say that our measure of the relative discrepancy between the observed and expected frequencies indicates a good fit.

The above example provides an illustration of a goodness-of-fit test with only two classes. More generally, if we have a sample of N observations of a variable and the observations can be classified into k

mutually exclusive and exhaustive classes, the χ^2 statistic for measuring the overall discrepancy between the observed and expected frequencies becomes

$$\chi^2 = \sum_{i=1}^{k} \frac{(f_{oi} - f_{ei})^2}{f_{ei}} \qquad i = 1, 2, \ldots, k$$

and has $k - 1$ degrees of freedom provided that no parameters need to be estimated in computing the f_es; this is further explained below. Here it should be noted that tests of goodness of fit based on the χ^2-distribution should not be used when N, the total number of frequencies to be compared, is small (less than 50). Furthermore, the test should not be applied when any one f_e is very small, certainly not when an f_e is less than 5 and preferably not when one is less than 10. In such cases classes with few expected frequencies should be combined to produce higher f_es. This is also illustrated later.

As already explained earlier, the χ^2-distribution has a single parameter, the number of degrees of freedom v. In goodness-of-fit tests, the number of degrees of freedom is given by the number of independent comparisons between the f_os and the f_es, ie the number of comparisons less the number of constraints. Broadly, a constraint, in this connexion, can be defined as a relation between the f_os and the f_es. Since $\Sigma f_o = \Sigma f_e$, there must always be one constraint but, as will be illustrated in the case below, there may be more. Another way of looking at the number of degrees of freedom is to imagine that the f_es have been set down and to ask in how many of the classes we can freely set down f_os. Clearly, if there are k classes and $\Sigma f_o = \Sigma f_e$, we can freely fill in only $k - 1$ classes, since the kth class frequency will follow after the $k - 1$ classes have been set down; consequently there would be $k - 1$ degrees of freedom in this case. Whether additional degrees of freedom will be lost in computing χ^2 depends on whether or not sample estimates must be used to replace unknown parameters in deriving the theoretical frequencies f_e. By way of illustrating this, suppose we have a sample of size N of a variable X classified into a frequency distribution and we ask the question: is the distribution of the values of X in the sample such that the sample could have come from a normally distributed population? The question can be asked in two ways:

(a) Could the sample have come from a normally distributed population with given mean μ and given standard deviation σ; or

(b) Could it have come from any normal population? In this case μ and σ are unspecified, and the best we can do is to estimate them from the sample $\bar{X}$ and s.

In each of these two cases we shall want to compare the f_os of our sample frequency distribution with the class frequencies which we should expect to obtain on the average if we repeatedly sampled from the hypothetical normal population. These expected class frequencies can be obtained quite easily from the normal table (see example 4.42 in section 4.13 above). However, the number of degrees of freedom depends upon whether we are considering case (a) or (b) above. If, in the former case, the expected frequencies have been derived on the basis of a hypothetical μ and σ, there will be only one constraint, namely

$$\Sigma f_o = \Sigma f_e$$

so that if there are k classes there will be $k - 1$ degrees of freedom. On the other hand, if the expected frequencies have been derived on the basis of the sample $\bar{X}$ and s, there will be only $k - 3$ degrees of freedom, for there will be three constraints:

$\Sigma f_o = \Sigma f_e$ (observed and theoretical frequencies equal)

$$\frac{\Sigma X f_o}{\Sigma f_o} = \frac{\Sigma X f_e}{\Sigma f_e} \quad \text{(observed and theoretical means equal)}$$

$$\sqrt{\frac{\Sigma x^2 f_o}{\Sigma f_o}} = \sqrt{\frac{\Sigma x^2 f_e}{\Sigma f_e}} \quad \begin{array}{l}\text{(observed and theoretical standard} \\ \text{deviations equal)}\end{array}$$

Further examples illustrating the use of the χ^2-distribution in goodness-of-fit tests are given below.

Example 5.16

In a randomly selected week, the number of orders received by a manufacturer of a certain type of standard equipment was found to be distributed as follows: Monday 7; Tuesday 12; Wednesday 15; Thursday 11; Friday 15. Test the hypothesis ($\alpha = 0.05$) that the manufacturer's orders are distributed uniformly over the five days of the week.

Hypotheses: H_0: The orders are uniformly distributed

H_a: The orders are not uniformly distributed.

Test:

Day of Week	Observed Frequencies f_o	Expected Frequencies f_e	$(f_o - f_e)^2$	$\dfrac{(f_o - f_e)^2}{f_e}$
Monday	7	12	25	2·08
Tuesday	12	12	0	0
Wednesday	15	12	9	0·75
Thursday	11	12	1	0·08
Friday	15	12	9	0·75
	60	60		3·66

Since there are $k = 5$ cells and no further information is needed to compute the f_es, we have $5 - 1 = 4$ degrees of freedom. From the table of χ^2 we find $\chi^2_{.05} = 9.488$, and hence

$$\chi^2 = 3.66 < \chi^2_{.05} = 9.488$$

Conclusion: The computed value of χ^2 being less than the critical value of 9.488, we do not reject the null hypothesis. We say that the value of χ^2 obtained in the test is not significant and that the f_es are a good fit to the f_os. The sample of data could reasonably have come from a uniformly distributed population.

Example 5.17

The following table gives the number of industrial accidents per week recorded in a large industrial plant over a period of 50 weeks:

No. of accidents per week	No. of weeks (frequencies)
0	24
1	16
2	7
3	2
4	1

Can the hypothesis be substantiated that the number of industrial accidents in the plant is a variable with a Poisson distribution?

Hypotheses:
　　H_o : The accidents follow a Poisson distribution
　　H_a : The accidents do not follow a Poisson distribution

Test:
The Poisson distribution is given by the formula (see sect. 4.11, p 130)

$$P(x; \mu) = \frac{e^{-\mu}\mu^x}{x!} \qquad x = 0, 1, 2, 3, 4$$

where $\mu = \lambda t$ is the average number of occurrences of a random event (accident) per unit of time (week). In the present case μ is not known, and must be estimated from the sample data. The total number of accidents recorded over the 50-week period is

$$1 \times 16 + 2 \times 7 + 3 \times 2 + 4 \times 1$$
$$= 40$$

Dividing this number by the number of weeks, we find

$$\bar{X} = \frac{40}{50} = 0.8 \text{ accidents per week.}$$

The Poisson probabilities based on this estimate of μ, and the respective expected frequencies f_e, are tabulated below.

Number of Accidents per week x	Observed Frequencies f_o	Proba- bilities $P(x \cdot \mu)$	Expected Frequencies f_e	$(f_o - f_e)^2$	$\dfrac{(f_o - f_e)^2}{f_e}$
0	24	0·449	22.5	2·25	0·10
1	16	0·359	18·0	4·00	0·22
2	7 ⎫	0·144	7·2 ⎫		
3	2 ⎬ 10	0·038	1·9 ⎬ 9·5	0·25	0·03
4	1 ⎭	0·008	0·4 ⎭		
	50		50		0·35

It should be noted that the last three classes have been combined so that no class contains fewer than five expected frequencies. We also note that the use of the sample mean in place of the unknown μ entails the loss of an additional degree of freedom. Hence, the test statistic χ^2 is distributed with $k - 2$, ie $3 - 2 = 1$ degree of freedom. From the χ^2 table we have $\chi^2_{.05} = 3.841$.

Conclusion: The value of χ^2 obtained in the test is much less than the critical value of 3·841, and we do not reject the null hypothesis. We say that the Poisson distribution provides a very good fit to the sample data. It therefore appears very likely that the probability distribution of industrial accidents in the plant is the Poisson distribution with $\mu = 0.8$.

Example 5.18

A random sample of 200 rents is taken and their distribution is as below. Could this sample have come from a normal population?

Class (dollars)	Observed Frequencies f_o	Expected Frequencies f_e	$(f_o - f_e)^2$	$\dfrac{(f_o - f_e)^2}{f_e}$
2·5 and under 7·5	− ⎫ 12	2·3 ⎫ 11·6	0·16	0·014
7·5 ” 12·5	12 ⎭	9·3 ⎭		
12·5 ” 17·5	26	26·3	0·09	0·003
17·5 ” 22·5	45	47·8	7·84	0·164
22·5 ” 27·5	60	53·3	44·89	0·842
27·5 ” 32·5	37	38·4	1·96	0·051
32·5 ” 37·5	13	16·9	15·21	0·900
37·5 ” 42·5	5 ⎫ 7	4·8 ⎫ 5·7	1·69	0·296
42·5 ” 47·5	2 ⎭	0·9 ⎭		
All Rents	200	200·0		2·270

Since the mean and standard deviation of the hypothetical normal population are not specified, the sample mean and standard deviation must be used as estimates of the population parameters. These statistics can be calculated from the f_o column and are $\bar{X} = \$23.82$ and $\$7.19$ (see examples 3.3 and 3.12 on pp 46 and 61 above). From the table of areas for the normal curve we calculate the class frequencies which we should expect in the long run if the hypothesis that the sample has been drawn from a normal population were true. These expected frequencies are given in the f_e column of the table above (see example 4.42 on p 146 above).

Hypotheses:
   H_o: The population of rents is normally distributed
   H_a: The population of rents is not normally distributed
Test:

$$\chi^2 = \sum \frac{(f_o - f_e)^2}{f_e} = 2{\cdot}270$$

There are seven classes yielding seven comparisons, but there are three constraints—the total number of observations in the observed and expected frequency distributions are the same, as are their means and standard deviations. Hence there are 4 degrees of freedom. Referring to the table of χ^2, with $v = 4$, we find $\chi^2_{.05} = 9{\cdot}488$, and hence

$$\chi^2 = 2{\cdot}270 < 9{\cdot}488$$

Conclusion: The value of $\chi^2 = 2{\cdot}270$ is not significant, and we do not reject the null hypothesis. The sample could reasonably have come from a normal population. Incidentally, we should note that the χ^2-test as used here is only one way of testing normality. Other tests are available and some of them are more powerful.

Example 5.19

A sample of 500 factories was taken to investigate certain aspects of the working conditions obtaining in them. The method used was to select names at random from trade lists. The classification of the sample by size of factory in terms of number of employees is given in the first two columns of the table below. The classification of all factories by size is known, and the percentage distribution is shown in the third column. From this column the frequencies which we should expect to get in the long run with repeated random sampling of 500 factories from the population can be calculated, and these are shown in the fourth column. Can the contention that the sample is random be supported?

Size of Factory (persons employed)	Observed Sample Frequencies f_o	Distribution of All Factories (per cent)	Expected Sample Frequencies f_e
Under 5	180	39·3	197
5–10	123	27·0	135
11–20	92	14·6	73
21–50	51	11·5	57
51–100	29	4·0	20
101–200	14	2·0	10
over 200	11	1·6	8
Total	500	100·0	500

Hypotheses:

   H_o: The sample of 500 factories is random
   H_a: The sample is not random

Test:

$$\chi^2 = \sum \frac{(f_o - f_e)^2}{f_e} = 14\cdot89$$

There are seven comparisons, but the totals of expected and observed frequencies must agree; accordingly there are 6 degrees of freedom. With $v = 6$, $\chi^2_{.05} = 12\cdot592$, and thus $\chi^2 = 14\cdot89 > 12\cdot592$ ie $P(\chi^2 > 14\cdot89) < 0\cdot05$.
Conclusion: If the null hypothesis were true, we should expect to obtain a value of χ^2 as great as or greater than the one actually obtained in the test with less than 5 per cent probability. Such being the case, doubt is cast on the randomness of the sampling procedure, for only very rarely would a random sample of size 500 drawn from the given population yield observed frequencies so different from the expected frequencies.

Independence of Classification

An important application of the χ^2-test occurs when we test hypotheses about the relation between two attributes. Thus, we may have N observations classified according to two criteria and we may wish to know whether the criteria are related or independent. This problem can best be expressed by following through an example.

We have a random sample of 400 dwellings classified according to area and nature of occupancy, as shown in the table below. The question is, are the two classifications independent?

Table 5.3

Nature of Occupancy	Area			
	Metropolitan	Urban Provincial	Rural	Total
Owner-occupied	102	41	100	243
Tenanted	82	30	45	157
Total	184	71	145	400

This type of table is called a *contingency* table. The above one is a 3×2 contingency table, the horizontal classification containing three categories, the vertical one two categories, and the table six distinct cells. The frequencies belonging to each cell are called *cell frequencies*. The totals of the cell frequencies for each of the rows and columns are referred to as the *marginal frequencies*. Here we shall denote the marginal frequency for the ith row by R_i, and the marginal frequency for the jth column by C_j. Thus, in our example, we have $R_1 = 243$ as the marginal frequency for the first row, $C_1 = 184$ as the marginal frequency for the first column, etc.

Now suppose we wish to use the above data to test the hypothesis that the two classifications are independent against the alternative hypothesis that they are not. To conduct such a test, we first need to find the expected frequency for each of the six cells. In our previous discussion of joint probability distributions (section 4.14) we saw that the joint probability of two statistically independent variables is equal to the product of their marginal probabilities. Consequently, if the null hypothesis being considered is true, we should expect the joint probability $P(metropolitan$ and $owner\text{-}occupied)$ to be the product of the marginal probabilities $P(metropolitan)$ and $P(owner\text{-}occupied)$, and similarly for the other cells. These marginal probabilities are generally not known, and we must make use of the marginal frequencies obtained from the sample. Accordingly we estimate the probability of an observation falling in any given cell as

$$\left(\frac{R_i}{N}\right)\left(\frac{C_i}{N}\right) \qquad i = 1, 2; j = 1, 2, 3$$

where N is the total sample frequency, in our case 400. Multiplying these probabilities by $N = 400$ gives the expected frequency for each cell, which we write as

$$f_{ij} = \frac{R_i C_j}{N}$$

Applying this general formula to the data of Table 5.3, we find

$$f_{11} = \frac{R_1 C_1}{N} = \frac{(243)(184)}{400} = 111.8$$

$$f_{12} = \frac{R_1 C_2}{N} = \frac{(243)(71)}{400} = 43.1$$

and similarly for the remaining cells. The expected frequencies computed in this way are given in brackets in the table below.

Table 5.4

Nature of Occupancy	Area			
	Metropolitan	Urban Provincial	Rural	Total
Owner-occupied	102 (111·8)	41 (43·1)	100 (88·1)	243
Tenanted	82 (72·2)	30 (27·9)	45 (56·9)	157
Total	184	71	145	400

It is now a simple matter to compare observed with expected frequencies by means of the χ^2-test in the same way as in the preceding section. The simplest way of determining the number of degrees of freedom is to ask how many cells can be freely filled in, given that the expected frequencies for each of the columns and rows must add to the marginal frequencies in the contingency table. There are six cells, but, if two are filled in, the other four follow. Accordingly there are 2 degrees of freedom. In general, if we have a contingency table consisting of r rows and c columns, there will be $(r - 1)(c - 1)$ degrees of freedom.

Calculating χ^2 for the above table we have

$$\chi^2 = \sum \frac{(f_o - f_e)^2}{f_e}$$

$$= \frac{(9\cdot8)^2}{111\cdot8} + \frac{(2\cdot1)^2}{43\cdot1} + \frac{(11\cdot9)^2}{88\cdot1} + \frac{(9\cdot8)^2}{72\cdot2} + \frac{(2\cdot1)^2}{27\cdot9} + \frac{(11\cdot9)^2}{56\cdot9}$$

$$= 6\cdot55$$

From the table of χ^2 with $v = 2$ we find the critical value at the 5 per cent level of significance to be $5\cdot991$. If the null hypothesis that the two classifications are independent were true, repeated sampling with 2 degrees of freedom would yield a value of χ^2 as great as or greater than the one actually obtained above in less than 5 per cent of the cases due to chance. Thus, the value of χ^2 obtained in the test is significant, and we reject the null hypothesis. The sample suggests that area and nature of occupancy of dwellings are related in some way.

5.12 Estimation and Estimators

So far we have used sample data to test hypotheses about the population. The second important object of taking samples is to be able to make inferences about the population parameters. For instance, we may be interested to know the average rent of tenanted dwellings in a given area. To take a full count of such dwellings may be either impracticable or too costly, and we shall therefore need to pick a sample to obtain an estimate of the unknown population mean μ. Similarly, in making a prediction about the outcome of an election we shall have to estimate the proportions of voters likely to vote for the various political parties from a sample. Provided the sampling is properly random, statistical estimation procedures enable us to make inferences about population values from sample data.

Whenever a sample statistic is used to estimate a population parameter, the statistic is referred to as an *estimator*. Thus, the sample mean, defined by the formula

$$\bar{X} = \frac{\Sigma X}{N} = \frac{1}{N}(X_1 + X_2 + \ldots + X_N)$$

gives an estimator of the population mean μ. The actual value of $\bar{X}$ obtained from a sample, ie the value of the function $\frac{1}{N}(X_1 + X_2 + \ldots + X_N)$ for a particular set of observations of the variable X, is then called an *estimate* of the unknown μ. In inferential analysis, two types of estimates are distinguished: (i) *point estimates* and (ii) *interval estimates*. An estimate is a point estimate if a single number is used to represent the unknown parameter. For example, in tests of hypotheses with σ unknown (see section 5.5 above) we used the value of the sample standard deviation s as a point estimate of σ. In other instances it is more meaningful to establish a range within which we could be reasonably confident that the parameter would lie. For the present we shall be concerned with some important statistical properties of point estimators. The construction of interval estimates will be considered in section 5.13 below.

Suppose we have a sample of observations of a variable and we wish to find an estimate of some parameter θ; thus θ could be the mean, μ, or the variance, σ^2, etc. Let us further denote the statistic that serves as an estimator of θ by the symbol $\hat{\theta}$ (theta-hat). In many cases, however, there will be more than one way of estimating θ. For example, if the underlying population can be regarded as normal or very nearly normal, we can use the sample mean, median or mode as alternative estimators of the population mean μ. Or, to estimate σ^2, we use the estimator $\frac{\Sigma(X - \bar{X})^2}{N - 1}$, but another estimator could be $\frac{\Sigma(X - \bar{X})^2}{N}$. If there are several ways of estimating θ, how shall we choose an estimator which is in some sense best? To deal with this question, we need to consider what statistical properties characterise 'good' estimators.

Statistical Properties of Estimators

If we use a sample statistic $\hat{\theta}$ as an estimator of θ, the statistic will take on different values in repeated samples due to chance. Thus, each estimator $\hat{\theta}$ of θ will be a random variable characterised by its own probability distribution, the sampling distribution of $\hat{\theta}$. Generally speaking, we should expect an estimator to be a good estimator of an unknown population parameter if its sampling distribution is closely concentrated near the true value of the parameter being estimated. In practical work different estimators of a given parameter are commonly judged in terms of three properties that a good estimator should possess; these properties are known as *unbiasedness*, *efficiency* and *consistency*[1].

[1] See also footnote 2 on p 229 below.

Let $\hat{\theta}$ be an estimator of the parameter θ, and let $\hat{\theta}$ be distributed with mean $E(\hat{\theta})$ and variance $\text{Var}(\hat{\theta})$. The estimator $\hat{\theta}$ is said to be *unbiased* if its expected value is equal to the true value of θ, ie if

$$E(\hat{\theta}) = \theta$$

Graphically, an unbiased estimator may be represented as one whose distribution is centred on θ, as illustrated in Fig 5.13. Since the expected value of a statistic is its long-run average value, unbiasedness implies that in repeated samples of size N taken from a given population the average of values of $\hat{\theta}$ would tend to the true parameter value θ. Conversely, if the long-run average of $\hat{\theta}$ is not θ but some other value, the estimator $\hat{\theta}$ is said to be *biased*, the size of the bias being measured by the difference $E(\hat{\theta}) - \theta$.

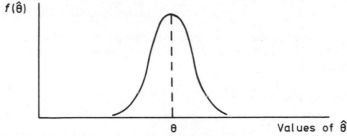

Fig 5.13

In section 5.2 above we have already shown that $E(\bar{X}) = \mu$. Thus, the mean of a random sample of N observations is an unbiased estimator of the population mean. It can further be shown that if the population distribution from which the sample has been drawn is symmetrical, the sample median Md is also an unbiased estimator of μ.

Before proceeding with the discussion of the other properties of estimators let us show why we defined the variance of a sample in section 3.5 above with $N - 1$ as the denominator rather than N. By the definition of unbiasedness, the sample variance s^2 will be an unbiased estimator of the population variance σ^2 if $E(s^2) = \sigma^2$. Making use of the relation (see footnote 1, p 211 above)

$$\Sigma(X_i - \bar{X})^2 = \Sigma(X_i - \mu)^2 - N(\bar{X} - \mu)^2 \qquad i = 1, 2, \ldots N$$

and taking the expectation of both sides, we obtain

$$E[\Sigma(X_i - \bar{X})^2] = \Sigma E[(X_i - \mu)^2] - NE[(\bar{X} - \mu)^2]$$

But by the definition of population variance $E[(X_i - \mu)^2] = \sigma^2$. Also, $E[(\bar{X} - \mu)^2] = \text{Var}(\bar{X}) = \dfrac{\sigma^2}{N}$ (see p 170 above). Hence, the above reduces to

$$E[\Sigma(X_i - \bar{X})^2] = N\sigma^2 - N\left(\frac{\sigma^2}{N}\right)$$

$$= (N - 1)\sigma^2$$

Writing next

$$E(s^2) = E\left[\frac{\Sigma(X_i - \bar{X})^2}{N - 1}\right]$$

we find

$$E(s^2) = \left(\frac{1}{N - 1}\right)(N - 1)\sigma^2 = \sigma^2$$

Thus, $s^2 = \dfrac{\Sigma(X - \bar{X})^2}{N - 1}$ will be an unbiased estimator of σ^2, in the sense that with repeated sampling the average of s^2 will tend towards σ^2. On the other hand, were we to define s^2 with N as the divisor, we would get

$$E\left[\frac{\Sigma(X_i - \bar{X})^2}{N}\right] = \frac{N - 1}{N}\sigma^2$$

so that $\dfrac{\Sigma(X - \bar{X})^2}{N}$ would be a downwardly biased estimator of the population variance σ^2. At this stage it is worth noting that although the sample variance s^2 is defined so as to avoid underestimation of the population variance σ^2, this definition does not imply that the square root of sample variance, ie the standard deviation s, is also an unbiased estimator of the population standard deviation σ. In fact, $s = \sqrt{\dfrac{\Sigma(X - \bar{X})^2}{N - 1}}$ is a biased estimator of σ for finite samples.[1]

As remarked earlier, a second desired property of a good estimator is that its values should be closely clustered around the true parameter

[1] From section 4.15 we recall that the variance of a random variable X may be written as

$$\sigma_X^2 = E(X^2) - \mu_X^2 = E(X^2) - [E(X)]^2$$

Substituting s for X, we may write

$$\sigma_s^2 = E(s^2) - [E(s)]^2$$

where σ_s^2 is the variance of the population of s's generated by repeated sampling. Since s^2 is an unbiased estimator of σ^2, $E(s^2) = \sigma^2$, and we may write

$$[E(s)]^2 = \sigma^2 - \sigma_s^2$$

and hence

$$E(s) = \sqrt{\sigma^2 - \sigma_s^2}$$

value θ, ie the variance of its sampling distribution should be small. Comparison of variances for different estimators of the same parameter gives a measure of their *efficiency*. Thus, suppose $\hat{\theta}_1$ and $\hat{\theta}_2$ are two unbiased estimators of θ with variances $\text{Var}(\hat{\theta}_1)$ and $\text{Var}(\hat{\theta}_2)$ respectively. If $\text{Var}(\hat{\theta}_1)$ is less than $\text{Var}(\hat{\theta}_2)$, estimator $\hat{\theta}_1$ is said to be *relatively more efficient* than estimator $\hat{\theta}_2$. Diagrammatically, the distribution of $\hat{\theta}_1$ will be less dispersed than the distribution of $\hat{\theta}_2$, as illustrated in Fig 5.14. The relative efficiency of two estimators can be measured by the ratio

$$\frac{\text{Var}(\hat{\theta}_2)}{\text{Var}(\hat{\theta}_1)}$$

As an illustration, suppose $\hat{\theta}_1$ and $\hat{\theta}_2$ are the mean $\bar{X}$ and median Md of a random sample of N observations drawn from a normal distribution. Here we have $\text{Var}(\bar{X}) = \sigma^2/N$ and $\text{Var}(Md) = \pi\sigma^2/2N$. Although both measures are unbiased estimators of the population mean, we have

$$\frac{\text{Var}(Md)}{\text{Var}(\bar{X})} = \frac{\pi}{2} = 1\cdot57$$

and hence $\bar{X}$ is the more efficient estimator of μ.

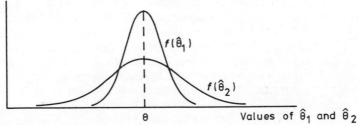

Fig 5.14

By now it should be evident that in choosing among alternative estimators of a parameter we shall always prefer an estimator that is both unbiased *and* efficient. If among all unbiased estimators of θ we can find one that has the smallest possible variance for all values of θ, we refer to it as the *best* estimator of θ (sometimes the terms

---

Evidently, so long as σ_s^2 is positive, $E(s)$ must be less than σ. But, for finite N, σ_s^2 is positive, since sample values of s will vary with repeated sampling. Thus, s is a biased estimator of σ, even though s^2 obtained from the same samples is an unbiased estimator of σ^2.

Suppose, however, that the sample size N is increased so that the variability of the s's between samples diminishes and σ_s^2 tends to zero as N becomes very large. Thus, in the limit, $E(s)$ tends to σ, and we say that s is an asymptotically unbiased estimator of σ (see also p 228 below).

'most efficient' or 'minimum variance' are also used). Suppose again that the parameter being estimated is the mean μ of a normal population. By analytical methods it can be shown that no estimator of μ can have a variance smaller than the quantity $\dfrac{\sigma^2}{N}$. But, as we already know, $\text{Var}(\bar{X}) = \dfrac{\sigma^2}{N}$, and hence the sample mean is the best or minimum-variance estimator of μ. Similarly, in the case of sampling from a normal population, the sample variance $s^2 = \dfrac{\Sigma(X - \bar{X})^2}{N - 1}$ is the best estimator of the population variance σ^2.

In the preceding discussion we have seen that, as a general principle, a good estimator should have a sampling distribution that is highly concentrated about the true parameter value θ. A difficulty sometimes arises that for samples of a given size the sampling distribution of the statistic that we wish to use as an estimator may not be known or cannot be easily derived. For this and other reasons it is often useful to investigate the properties of various estimators on the assumption that the sample size N can be increased without limit. The statistical properties of estimators based on samples of very large or infinite size are referred to as their *asymptotic* properties. We now comment on three desirable large-sample properties of estimators: *asymptotic unbiasedness, consistency*, and *asymptotic efficiency*.

An estimator $\hat{\theta}$ of a parameter θ is said to be *asymptotically unbiased* if its expected value $E(\hat{\theta})$ approaches the true value of θ as the sample size N goes to infinity. We have already noted that $\bar{X}$ is an unbiased estimator of μ for given N. Since with repeated sampling the mean of $\bar{X}$ tends to μ irrespective of sample size, it is also an asymptotically unbiased estimator of μ. If an estimator $\hat{\theta}$ is biased for finite N, asymptotic unbiasedness implies that the bias tends to zero as N is increased without limit. As an illustration, consider again the properties of the statistic $\dfrac{\Sigma(X - \bar{X})^2}{N}$ as an estimator of σ^2. As already seen above (p 226), this statistic has an expected value equal to $\dfrac{N - 1}{N}\sigma^2$, and therefore it is a biased estimator of σ^2 for small N. However, as N increases the bias diminishes, and becomes negligible for large N. We may conclude that as an estimator of σ^2 the uncorrected sample variance $\dfrac{\Sigma(X - \bar{X})^2}{N}$ is asymptotically unbiased.[1]

---

[1] By similar argument, the sample standard deviation s, although biased for finite N, is an asymptotically unbiased estimator of the population standard deviation σ (see p 226, footnote 1).

An important asymptotic property of estimators is *consistency*. An estimator is said to be consistent if it is asymptotically unbiased and if its variance tends to zero as N is increased indefinitely. Thus, as the sample size increases, the sampling distribution of a consistent estimator becomes progressively tighter and more closely concentrated around the true value of the estimated parameter.[1] This means that consistency increases the predictive accuracy of our results, albeit at a higher cost. Two important examples of consistent estimators are the sample mean $\bar{X}$ and the sample variance s^2. In the case of the mean, consistency can be easily verified by noting that, for every N, $\bar{X}$ is an unbiased estimator of μ and $\text{Var}(\bar{X}) = \dfrac{\sigma^2}{N}$ tends to zero as N tends to infinity.

Suppose we have two estimators $\hat{\theta}_1$ and $\hat{\theta}_2$ of a parameter θ that tend to be normally distributed as N becomes very large; an estimator whose sampling distribution tends to normality as N approaches infinity is said to be *asymptotically normal*. Given that $\hat{\theta}_1$ and $\hat{\theta}_2$ are asymptoticaly normal and asymptotically unbiased, the ratio of their variances for large but finite N gives a measure of their *asymptotic relative efficiency*. For example, in large samples the sample median can be shown to be approximately normally distributed with mean μ and variance $\pi\sigma^2/2N$, if the population distribution is symmetrical (if it is not, the sample median tends to the population median and not the population mean). The sample mean is likewise normal with mean μ and variance σ^2/N. It can thus be seen that no matter how large the sample size N, the ratio of the variances of these two estimators is constant and equal to $\dfrac{\pi}{2} = 1 \cdot 57$, ie in large samples the sample mean is again a more efficient estimator of the population mean. In general, if we have two asymptotically normal and unbiased estimators of a parameter θ, the estimator with the smaller asymptotic variance is said to be asymptotically more efficient.

We have now reviewed three important desirable properties of point estimators: unbiasedness, efficiency and consistency.[2] We

---

[1] Stated more formally, a consistent estimator satisfies the condition

$$\mathop{P\ lim}_{N \to \infty}(|\hat{\theta} - \theta| < d) = 1$$

This probability limit may be interpreted by saying that if N can be chosen large enough we shall be practically certain of obtaining an estimate of θ which will lie within an arbitrarily small distance d from the true value of θ.

[2] It should be mentioned that the fourth characteristic of good estimators is *sufficiency*. Generally speaking, an estimator is called sufficient if it makes use of all the available sample information about the parameter θ. For instance, the sample mean $\bar{X}$, or the sample proportion p, are sufficient estimators in the sense that no further sample information can make these statistics better estimators of the respective parameters, μ and π.

have noted that the sample mean and the sample variance satisfy all these criteria for choosing a good estimator; for this reason they play a central role in inferential statistics. In our discussion we have not considered the methods by which estimators possessing the above properties can be derived. However, we shall say more about this when in Chapter 8 we discuss the problem of fitting the linear model by an estimation technique known as the method of least squares.

5.13 Interval Estimation

As we have pointed out earlier, the main disadvantage of point estimators is that they provide us only with a single number as the estimate of the unknown population value. Depending on the sampling distribution and the sample size N, such an estimate may, or may not, be close to the true value of the parameter. Of course, in the case of a consistent estimator, we shall be able to improve the accuracy of our estimate by running a larger sample, but this may be undesirable because of cost. In many practical estimation problems, it would therefore seem more meaningful to establish an interval within which we can expect, with a given degree of confidence, that the unknown parameter would lie. This procedure is known as interval estimation.

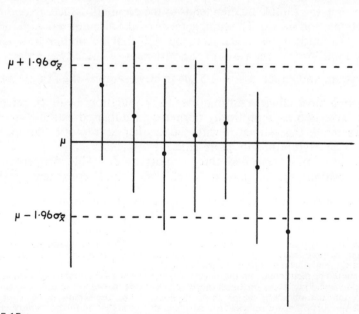

Fig 5.15

To illustrate the basic ideas of interval estimation, let us consider again the mean $\bar{X}$ of a sample of N items drawn from a normal population with mean μ and standard deviation σ. We know that $\bar{X}$ will be normally distributed about μ with a standard error of $\sigma_{\bar{X}} = \dfrac{\sigma}{\sqrt{N}}$. With repeated sampling, 95 per cent of sample means will lie within the range $\mu \pm 1{\cdot}96\sigma_{\bar{X}}$. Suppose now we do not know μ, but have calculated an $\bar{X}$, and further suppose we know σ. What can we say about the mean μ? If $\bar{X}$ happens to be in the range $\mu \pm 1{\cdot}96\sigma_{\bar{X}}$, then μ must be contained in the range $\bar{X} \pm 1{\cdot}96\sigma_{\bar{X}}$. The sample mean $\bar{X}$ will be in the range $\mu \pm 1{\cdot}96\sigma_{\bar{X}}$ for 95 per cent of samples, so that μ will lie in the range $\bar{X} \pm 1{\cdot}96\sigma_{\bar{X}}$ for 95 per cent of samples. The sample mean $\bar{X}$ varies, of course, from sample to sample, so that the range $\bar{X} \pm 1{\cdot}96\sigma_{\bar{X}}$ will also vary. This is illustrated diagrammatically in Fig 5.15. The population mean, μ, and the range $\mu \pm 1{\cdot}96\sigma_{\bar{X}}$ are scaled on the vertical axis. Each vertical line corresponds to a particular sample, is centred at $\bar{X}$ and ranges $\pm 1{\cdot}96\sigma_{\bar{X}}$.

It can be seen from the diagram that if $\bar{X}$ lies within $1{\cdot}96\sigma_{\bar{X}}$ of μ, then μ lies within $1{\cdot}96\sigma_{\bar{X}}$ of $\bar{X}$ also. This can easily be shown algebraically.

If

$$\mu - 1{\cdot}96\sigma_{\bar{X}} < \bar{X} < \mu + 1{\cdot}96\sigma_{\bar{X}}$$

then adding

$$-\bar{X} - \mu$$

we have

$$-\bar{X} - 1{\cdot}96\sigma_{\bar{X}} < -\mu < -\bar{X} + 1{\cdot}96\sigma_{\bar{X}}$$

and multiplying by -1

$$\bar{X} - 1{\cdot}96\sigma_{\bar{X}} < \mu < \bar{X} + 1{\cdot}96\sigma_{\bar{X}}$$

It follows that if we make the statement 'μ lies within $\bar{X} \pm 1{\cdot}96\sigma_{\bar{X}}$' we shall be right in 95 per cent of such statements. This is evidently true for estimates of μ for samples drawn from the same population but, since there is a 95 per cent chance of being right in stating 'μ lies within $\bar{X} \pm 1{\cdot}96\sigma_{\bar{X}}$' for any one population, it must also be true for all such statements taken together. If we make such statements, we shall be right 95 per cent of the time irrespective of what the statements refer to. Accordingly, the probability is 95 per cent that we shall be correct in stating that 'μ lies within $\bar{X} \pm 1{\cdot}96\sigma_{\bar{X}}$'; this may be written symbolically as $P(\bar{X} \pm 1{\cdot}96\sigma_{\bar{X}}) = 0{\cdot}95$. The range $\bar{X} \pm 1{\cdot}96\sigma_{\bar{X}}$ is called the 95 per cent *confidence interval*, and the limits of this range are referred to as the 95 per cent *confidence limits* for μ. In a particular case, where we have computed limits from the $\bar{X}$ of a given sample, we may say that we are 95 per cent confident that μ lies within the computed limits.

More generally, we may write the probability statement associated with an interval estimate of the population mean as

$$P(\bar{X} - Z_{\alpha/2}\sigma_{\bar{X}} < \mu < \bar{X} + Z_{\alpha/2}\sigma_{\bar{X}}) = 1 - \alpha$$

where the probability $1 - \alpha$ is referred to as the *level of confidence* in estimating μ. The level of confidence desired by the researcher determines the appropriate value of $Z_{\alpha/2}$. We have seen that if the confidence level chosen is 95 per cent, $Z_{\alpha/2} = 1.96$. If $1 - \alpha$ is 0.99, the value of Z which cuts off $\frac{1}{2}$ per cent in each tail of the sampling distribution of $\bar{X}$ is 2.58, and the 99 per cent confidence limits for μ are $\bar{X} \pm 2.58\sigma_{\bar{X}}$. Evidently, we can always increase our confidence by widening the limits. But in practice the limits are not much use unless they are fairly narrow. Since $\sigma_{\bar{X}} = \dfrac{\sigma}{\sqrt{N}}$, we can narrow them for a given degree of confidence by increasing the sample size. Confidence limits give an indication of the sampling error involved in making inferences about a population from sample data. Naturally, the larger the sample the less the sampling error and the narrower the confidence limits.

Confidence Limits for a Mean

We have shown that the 95 per cent confidence limits for a mean are $\bar{X} \pm 1.96\sigma_{\bar{X}}$. The difficulty in practice is that we do not know $\sigma_{\bar{X}}$, and we have to estimate it from the sample. If $\bar{X}$ and s are the mean and standard deviation from a sample of size N, we know that $t = \dfrac{\bar{X} - \mu}{s_{\bar{X}}}$, where $s_{\bar{X}} = \dfrac{s}{\sqrt{N}}$, is distributed in the t-distribution with $N - 1$ degrees of freedom. Hence we know that with repeated sampling 95 per cent of the ts will lie between $\pm t_{.025}$, where $t_{.025}$ is the value of t at the 5 per cent level of significance (ie cutting off $2\frac{1}{2}$ per cent in each tail of the t-distribution). Accordingly, there is a 95 per cent probability that

$$-t_{.025} < t < t_{.025}$$

ie

$$-t_{.025} < \frac{\bar{X} - \mu}{s_{\bar{X}}} < t_{.025}$$

Rearranging this inequality, we get

$$\bar{X} - t_{.025}s_{\bar{X}} < \mu < \bar{X} + t_{.025}s_{\bar{X}}$$

By the same argument as in the preceding section, the last statement gives the 95 per cent confidence limits for μ, ie $\bar{X} \pm t_{.025}s_{\bar{X}}$. In general, the confidence statement for μ, with σ not known, may be written as $P(\bar{X} \pm t_{\alpha/2}s_{\bar{X}}) = 1 - \alpha$. For large N this becomes $\bar{X} \pm Z_{\alpha/2}s_{\bar{X}}$, since $t_{\alpha/2} = Z_{\alpha/2}$ for large N.

Example 5.20

A random sample of 16 Australian men gives a mean height of 174 centimetres with a standard deviation of 5 centimetres. What are the (i) 95 per cent (ii) 99 per cent confidence limits for the mean height of Australian men?

Here

$$s_{\bar{X}} = \frac{s}{\sqrt{N}} = \frac{5}{4} = 1.25$$

(i) With $\alpha = 0.05$, we find $t_{.025} = 2.131$ with $N - 1 = 15$ degrees of freedom. Confidence limits are

$$\bar{X} \pm t_{.025}s_{\bar{X}} = 174 + (2.131)(1.25)$$
$$= 174 \pm 2.66$$

so that on the basis of the sample we can be 95 per cent confident that the mean height of Australian men lies between 171.3 and 176.7 centimetres.

(ii) With $\alpha = 0.01$, we find $t_{.005} = 2.947$, and the 99 per cent confidence limits are

$$\bar{X} \pm t_{.005}s_{\bar{X}} = 174 \pm (2.947)(1.25)$$
$$= 174 \pm 3.68 \text{ centimetres.}$$

Confidence Limits for a Proportion

If we have a sample of N from a dichotomous population with proportion of successes, p, within what range can we expect the proportion of successes in the population, π, to lie?

In large samples, these limits can be given by analogy with the mean, for p is then normally distributed about a mean π with standard deviation

$$\sigma_P = \sqrt{\frac{\pi(1 - \pi)}{N}}$$

Hence confidence limits to π will be $p \pm 1.96\sigma_p$. However, σ_p is itself dependent on π, and π is unknown. For the calculation of σ_p we can use p as an estimate of π, and we get as an approximate expression for the confidence limit for π

$$p \pm 1\cdot96 s_p$$

ie

$$p \pm 1\cdot96 \sqrt{\frac{p(1-p)}{N}}$$

Example 5.21
A random sample of 400 dwellings gives 30 per cent as being rented houses. Within what range can we be reasonably confident that the proportion for all dwellings lies?

Here

$$N = 400 \qquad p = 0\cdot3$$

and
$$s_p = \sqrt{\frac{p(1-p)}{N}} = \sqrt{\frac{(0\cdot3)(0\cdot7)}{400}}$$
$$= 0\cdot023$$

Confidence limits are

$$p \pm 1\cdot96 s_p$$

ie
$$0\cdot3 \pm 0\cdot045$$

so that on the basis of our sample we can be 95 per cent confident that the proportion of all dwellings which are rented houses lies between 25·5 and 34·5 per cent.

Confidence Limits for a Variance

In section 5.11 above we showed that the test statistic $\dfrac{(N-1)s^2}{\sigma^2}$, where s^2 is sample variance, has a χ^2-distribution with $N-1$ degrees of freedom. Given a level of confidence $1 - \alpha$, the confidence interval for the population variance σ^2 can be shown to be

$$\frac{(N-1)s^2}{\chi^2_{\alpha/2}} < \sigma^2 < \frac{(N-1)s^2}{\chi^2_{1-\alpha/2}}$$

where $\chi^2_{1-\alpha/2}$ and $\chi^2_{\alpha/2}$ are the lower and upper χ^2 values which cut off an area equal to $\alpha/2$ in each tail of the χ^2 distribution with $N-1$ degrees of freedom.

Example 5.22
In example 5.20, what would be the 98 per cent confidence limits for the variance and standard deviation of heights of Australian men?

Here we have

$$1 - \alpha = 0\cdot98 \qquad s^2 = 25 \qquad N = 16$$

From the table of χ^2 with $v = 15$ we find

$$\chi^2_{1-\alpha/2} = \chi^2_{\cdot99} = 5\cdot229$$
$$\chi^2_{\alpha/2} = \chi^2_{\cdot01} = 30\cdot578$$

Confidence limits for σ^2 are

$$\frac{(15)(25)}{30 \cdot 578} < \sigma^2 < \frac{(15)(25)}{5 \cdot 229}$$

ie

$$12 \cdot 26 < \sigma^2 < 71 \cdot 72$$

Taking the square root of these limits, we get

$$3 \cdot 50 < \sigma < 8 \cdot 47$$

so that, on the basis of our sample we can be 98 per cent confident that the standard deviation of heights of Australian men lies between 3·50 and 8·47 centimetres.

CHAPTER 6

SAMPLE SURVEYS

6.1 Advantages of Sample Surveys over Full Counts

In discussing the collection of data in Chapter 2 it was pointed out that in conducting a survey a decision would have to be made whether the survey should cover all units in the field of inquiry or whether only a sample of units should be examined.[1] In the present chapter this question is discussed. The use of sample surveys to elicit information about the populations from which the samples have been drawn is one of the most important applications of the theory of sampling and significance outlined in Chapter 5. The present chapter is intended to be an illustration of this application rather than a complete discussion of it, even at an elementary level. Indeed the subject of 'sample surveys' has a substantial and growing literature of its own, and reference should be made to this literature, some of which is listed in Appendix C, 4. It is hardly necessary to add that considerable practical experience as well as extensive knowledge of the theoretical principles is essential for those who engage in this highly specialised work. But against the few who are responsible for conducting sample surveys there are the many who use their results, and these should have at least some broad understanding of the principles involved. Some of the more important aspects of these principles are discussed in the following pages.

An inquiry like a census is said to be a full count. Every unit in which we are interested is included in the survey. However, in order to find out something about a certain characteristic of a population it is not necessary to make a full count of all the units in the population. In practice, we can get quite satisfactory results by taking a sample, eg a sample of wheat, a sample of rents, etc. In our previous work we have already drawn the distinction between the notions of a *sample* and a *population*.[2] We repeat that the term 'population' in statistics always means the totality or universe of units from which samples of various sizes may be drawn, eg the population of all the rents in some city, the population of wheat in a particular wheat-growing area, the population of family sizes, etc. When we take a full count we examine

---

[1] See p 18 above.
[2] See particularly sections 4.7, 4.9 and 5.1.

the entire population; when we take a sample we observe only a representative fraction of the whole field and use the sample results to calculate or infer something about the whole population.

Besides the fact that reliable results can be obtained from sound sampling procedures, there are several important advantages in taking samples rather than full counts, and these are listed below.

1. *Practicability*

A full count may be impracticable because the job is simply too big, eg quality of wheat, timber resources, frequent surveys of retail establishments.

2. *Speed*

The data may be collected and summarised much more quickly with a sample than with a full count. This may be a vital consideration when the information is urgently needed or when it is to be used as a basis for government policy.

3. *Accuracy*

More accurate results can often be obtained when questionnaires are filled in by skilled enumerators instead of by the respondents themselves. Personal interviews may elicit more accurate information than sending out questionnaires by post and requesting respondents to fill them in themselves, although some people may be reticent when interviewed personally and give less accurate answers than they would in a private signed questionnaire. In cases where the number of enumerators required varies directly with the number of questionnaires to be filled in, the personal interview is much more of a practical proposition with a sample than with a full count. Even if it is possible to employ enumerators in a full count, for a sample a smaller staff will be necessary and it may be possible to have more efficient and better trained enumerators. It may also be possible to allow the enumerators to spend more time and take greater care over each individual questionnaire and to ask a greater number of questions. Thus, although a sample does not give the coverage which a full count does, the accuracy of that part of the total information which is collected may be greater in certain cases.

4. *Cost*

If data are secured from only a fraction of the population, expenditures will be much smaller than if a full count is taken. The costs of an inquiry can be broken down into:
   (a) overhead cost of staff organisation
   (b) costs of collection of data

(c) costs of processing and tabulating data

(d) costs of publication.

Items (b) and (c) are in the nature of variable costs, (a) and (d) fixed costs. Items (b) and (c) will certainly be much smaller for a sample than a full count. On the other hand, the design of and the selection of the sample will involve expenditure. But in general a sample effects very considerable savings in cost.

Although the above considerations indicate that there are very real advantages in taking samples, this does not mean that full counts should never be taken. For some purposes it is not possible to select a satisfactory sample (eg to ascertain total population) and a full count must be taken. A sample if unreliable has no virtue simply because it is cheap. Apart from this, censuses are essential to provide certain information necessary for the selection of samples to give other information.

6.2 The Adequacy of a Sample

A sample is a substitute for a full count of the population from which it is drawn. We require the information derived from it not for its own sake, but to make inferences about certain characteristics of the parent population. For example, if we take a sample of rented dwellings we may want to use the sample mean as an estimate of the mean rent for the population of all dwellings. Naturally we should not expect the sample mean to coincide exactly with the population mean, for if we took repeated samples from the same population the sample means would differ amongst themselves due to chance, even though the population mean is always in any particular instance the same. In section 5.1 above we already referred to discrepancies between sample statistics and population parameters as *sampling errors*. These must be carefully distinguished from the inaccuracies which arise in collecting information (see section 2.2, p 14). Inaccuracies in collecting data arise both in full counts and sample surveys, and they may, for reasons outlined above, be reduced in sample surveys; but full counts do not by their nature contain sampling errors.

Discrepancies between sample statistics and population parameters arise for two reasons. First, the method of selection of the sample may lead to *bias* in the sample in the sense that with repeated sampling the mean of a sample statistic does not tend toward the true value of the corresponding parameter (see section 5.12, p 225). Secondly, even where bias is absent, discrepancies between sample values and population values occur as the result of the chance selection of sampling units. The first source of discrepancies can be eliminated by the use of proper sampling methods. Unless this is done, we can have no confidence in sample results as means of making inferences about the underlying population. With the elimination of bias the sampling errors which remain will be inevitable. They can be eliminated only by taking a full count, but they can of course be reduced by increasing the size of the sample.

It is not difficult to see how bias in the selection of a sample may arise. Thus, taking an extreme case, a sample survey inquiring into the general level of rents in a certain city would give biased results if the dwellings in the sample had all been taken from inner suburbs. Evidently, the mean rent of the sample could in no way be taken as an estimate of the mean rent of all dwellings in the city area. It follows that if we wish to select samples which are free of bias we must allow all items in the population an equal chance of selection. As already explained in section 5.1, a sample drawn in such a way that each element in the population has an equal probability of being included in the sample is called a *simple random sample*. In random sampling the selection is achieved by the operation of chance alone, so that neither the researcher nor the sampling units can have any influence in deciding which units should be included in the sample. Random selection occurs, for instance, when lottery marbles are drawn from a properly mixed barrel. In practice, however, the selection of random samples often has many technical difficulties, some of which will be discussed further below.

The sampling error between a sample statistic and the corresponding parameter for which the statistic is used as an estimate cannot, of course, be specified for any one particular sample, for if it could there would be no point in having the sample estimate. But the magnitude of the sampling error can be measured in the sense of the dispersion which sample values would have about the population value with repeated sampling. As will be recalled from the preceding chapter, a measure of the dispersion of a sample statistic is given by its *standard error*. The smaller the standard error, the smaller the dispersion of values of the statistic in repeated samples, and the greater the precision or reliability of the statistic as an estimator of the unknown population value. Hence, when we speak of the sampling error of a statistic as being smaller under one method of random sampling than another, we mean that the one method gives an estimator of the unknown population value with a smaller standard error than the other.

Whenever a sample value is used as an estimate of a population value, it is of the first importance to attach to the sample value an indication of the magnitude of the sampling error which may be involved. In practice, this may be done by constructing confidence limits within which we may be reasonably certain that the population parameter under consideration will lie (see section 5.13). It will be readily appreciated that a point estimate of a population parameter is of doubtful utility, for then no indication is given of how reliable the estimate is likely to be, and consequently our confidence in the estimate must be uncertain. Thus, if a random sample of rented dwellings reveals a mean weekly rent of $30, we should not state that 'our estimate of the mean weekly rent of all tenanted dwellings is $30', but rather that 'we can be 95 per cent confident that the mean weekly rent for all tenanted dwellings lies within the range $30 ± $3', say. We are 95 per cent confident of this latter statement in the sense that, if we make a large number of such statements, we shall be right in about 95 per cent of them. In this connexion it must be emphasised that confidence limits cannot be ascertained unless the sample under consideration is a properly random one. Indeed, all the methods of statistical analysis set out in Chapter 5 are valid only in reference to random samples.

6.3 Selecting a Random Sample

In principle the method of selecting a simple random sample is quite easy. We take all the units in the population, mix them up thoroughly, and draw out the sample quite at random. In practice we are not usually dealing with barrels of marbles, and the selection of a random sample is not quite so easy. However, it is possible to simulate very closely the random process. We can make a list of all the units in the population, and number each unit. Then, if we transfer the numbers on to marbles, we can select numbers as in a lottery and, by reference back to our original list, identify our sample.

Table 6.1

Random Numbers

03	47	43	73	86	36	96	47	36	61	46	98	63	71	62	33	26	16	80	45
97	74	24	67	62	42	81	14	57	20	42	53	32	37	32	27	07	36	07	51
16	76	62	27	66	56	50	26	71	07	32	90	79	78	53	13	55	38	58	59
12	56	85	99	26	96	96	68	27	31	05	03	72	93	15	57	12	10	14	21
55	59	56	35	64	38	54	82	46	22	31	62	43	09	90	06	18	44	32	53
16	22	77	94	39	49	54	43	54	82	17	37	93	23	78	87	35	20	96	43
84	42	17	53	31	57	24	55	06	88	77	04	74	47	67	21	76	33	50	25
63	01	63	78	59	16	95	55	67	19	98	10	50	71	75	12	86	73	58	07
33	21	12	34	29	78	64	56	07	82	52	42	07	44	38	15	51	00	13	42
57	60	86	32	44	09	47	27	96	54	49	17	46	09	62	90	52	84	77	27
18	18	07	92	46	44	17	16	58	09	79	83	86	19	62	06	76	50	03	10
26	62	38	97	75	84	16	07	44	99	83	11	46	32	24	20	14	85	88	45
23	42	40	64	74	82	97	77	77	81	07	45	32	14	08	32	98	94	07	72
52	36	28	19	95	50	92	26	11	97	00	56	76	31	38	80	22	02	53	53
37	85	94	35	12	83	39	50	08	30	42	34	07	96	88	54	42	06	87	98

To aid in this process there are available tables of *random numbers*. These tables simply list the digits 0 to 9 at random. Quite complicated methods have to be used to make sure the numbers are properly random. Such tables are to be found, among other places, in Fisher and Yates: *Statistical Tables for Biological, Agricultural and Medical Research* (Hafner Publishing Co, New York, 6th Edition, 1963) and a block of such numbers taken from page 134 of these tables is reproduced above by kind permission of the authors and publishers.

These tables are used as follows. Suppose we have a population containing 700 000 items, and we wish to draw a sample of 1000. We list the items in the population and number them 1 to 700 000. We then take any page of random numbers and, starting at any point, we write down the numbers in groups of six, eg 034743, 738636, 964736, 614698, 637162, 332616, etc. These will select the items in the population numbered 34 743; 614 698; 637 162; 332 616, etc. The second and third numbers do not correspond to any numbers on the list, and they are wasted. Methods are available to reduce this sort of wastage and hence to increase the speed of selecting the sample.

In order to draw a sample in this way, it is, of course, necessary to have a list of the units in the population to be sampled. Such a list is called the *frame*. Sometimes when the list is drawn up, the sample is drawn directly from the list, eg taking every 10th house on a list of houses to give a 1 in 10 sample. This is not strictly speaking random sampling. It is called *systematic sampling*, but, unless the list has periodic features (see below), it is usually quite satisfactory. It will be appreciated that in practice it may be very difficult to draw up a complete and accurate list of the population to be sampled. This applies particularly if the sampling is to be carried out periodically and the population is changing. For some purposes more or less satisfactory 'ready-made' frames are available, eg street directories, electoral rolls, etc.

If a sample is not properly random, no estimate of the likely sampling errors involved can be made; and use of the sample may lead to biased results. There are various ways of selecting samples which do not involve random processes and hence which lead to invalid samples.

The extent to which a particular sample is properly random depends not only on the determination of the investigator to make it random but also on the accuracy of the frame used to select the sample and the extent to which all the units selected for the sample can actually be incorporated into the sample. Some of the more common sources of bias are set out below.[1]

[1] This list is based on F Yates: *Sampling Methods for Censuses and Surveys* (Hafner Publishing Co, New York, 3rd Edition, 1963), sections 2.2 and 4.22, by permission of author and publishers.

1. *Deliberate Selection of a 'Representative' Sample*

This is a form of *purposive selection*. The investigator selects the units for the sample so that they will be what *he regards* as representative of the population. For example, an investigator wishes to sample 100 rents, and he walks round the streets and selects houses which he regards as representative. In practice, this means either trying to select 100 average houses or else trying to select different types of houses according to the proportions he believes them to be in the total population of houses. Clearly, in the first case the sample will not be representative since it will contain a much lower degree of variability than obtains in the population. But in both cases the investigator is really begging the question, ie he has some preconceived ideas about rents, and he picks his sample to be representative of them. It is clear that such selection must be unreliable. Similarly, interviews with representative people are almost certain to reveal incorrectly true average public opinion. What is a representative person? When the personality of the selector enters into selection, the sample cannot be unbiased. The selection should be governed only by the impersonal laws of chance.

2. *Conscious or Unconscious Bias in the Selection of a 'Random' Sample*

It may happen that, although the selection process is in the main random, there are points at which the personal judgment of the investigator is allowed to enter. For example, the investigator may reject certain units which have been sampled, on the grounds that they are extreme or atypical, or he may modify the frame before the sampling takes place.

3. *Selection Depending on Some Characteristic which Happens to be Related to the Properties of the Unit which are of Interest*

For example, an investigator wishes to sample coal and he decides to take ten shovelfuls from the edges of coal stacks; this is impersonal, but it so happens that the largest lumps tend to fall to the edge. Alternatively, to sample opinion about liquor laws, it would be unwise to stand outside an hotel near closing time and interview every man who passes. Again, a selection of 1000 names taken at random from the telephone book will not be a satisfactory method for obtaining information about people's spending habits, since people with telephones are probably of a different income and social status from those without.

4. *Systematic Selection*

Systematic selection occurs when a list of the population is compiled and every *n*th unit is selected. If there is any periodicity in the list, completely biased results may occur. For example, if a list of dwellings arranged in streets is sampled by taking every tenth dwelling, then if it happens that there are ten houses to a street block, the sample will contain either all corner houses or no corner houses. Most systematic selection, however, is equivalent to random selection.

5. *Substitution*

It sometimes happens that, given a properly selected sample, examination of all the units in the sample is not possible, and substitutions of other units are made. For example, in a budget inquiry certain households may have been selected. When the investigator calls, he may find no one at home in some houses, and he may substitute the house next door. This will necessarily lead to the over-representation in the sample of houses occupied all day, ie houses with families. To avoid this sort of bias, call-backs rather than substitutions are necessary.

6. *Failure to Cover the Whole Sample Chosen*

For example, investigators in a budget inquiry may not bother to visit the houses which are difficult to get to, and these houses may contain people who are significantly different from other people. Again, in a postal inquiry, only a proportion of the persons to whom the questionnaire has been posted generally replies. This may introduce bias, since the proportion which has answered may be of higher general intelligence than the average or may have an axe to grind. This is the problem of *non-response*, and, if possible, the non-respondents or a sub-sample of these should be interviewed personally.

7. *Quota Sampling*

This method is common in making surveys of public opinion. Interviewers are given definite quotas of persons in different social classes, different age groups, different regions, etc, and are then instructed to obtain the required number of interviews to fill each quota. The quotas ensure that the total sample includes approximately the right proportion of persons of the various categories which appear in the underlying population, but the actual persons sampled to fill each quota are not necessarily representative of the underlying population in that category. This is so because the quotas are not filled by a random selection, but by, for example, the first so many appropriate persons the interviewer strikes in a house-to-house survey or in a telephone survey. Quota sampling, however scientific it may be made to appear, is not equivalent to random sampling, unless the quotas are filled by proper random processes.

6.4 Sampling from a Finite Population

At this stage we should remind the reader that the sampling theory developed in Chapter 5 and referred to above was all based on the assumption that the populations from which samples are drawn are either very large in relation to the size of the sample or are infinitely large. The notion of an infinite population fits most easily with the notion of a random experiment which can be repeated, at least conceptually, an unlimited number of times, eg tossing a coin or a die. The populations with which we have to deal in economic and allied fields, however, are empirical populations which in most cases are in fact finite. In the remainder of this chapter we discuss sampling procedures by reference to populations consisting of a finite number of elements. Let us denote this number by the symbol P; we thus have P for the size of the population and N for the size of a random sample that may be drawn from it. For such a population, the mean and variance may be defined as

$$\mu = \frac{\Sigma X}{P}$$

and

$$\sigma^2 = \frac{\Sigma (X - \mu)^2}{P}$$

where the summation extends over the P elements in the population.

From our discussion in section 5.2 we also recall that when a population is infinite or when it is so large compared with samples drawn from it that it can be assumed so, we may regard a random sample of N observations from the population as a sequence of N independent random variables each having the same probability distribution, and the standard error of the sample mean $\bar{X}$ is then given by the well-known formula

$$\sigma_{\bar{X}} = \frac{\sigma}{\sqrt{N}}$$

Thus, given the population standard deviation σ, the sampling errors to which a sample mean is subject depend only on the absolute size of the sample and not on its size relative to the population. However, if the population is finite in size and the size of the sample is not very small compared with the size of the population, the relative coverage of the population by the sample must have some influence on the size of sampling errors. Thus a sample of 1000 from a population of 5000 must have greater reliability than the same-sized sample from a population of 5 000 000.

It can be shown that the standard error of a sample mean, when the sampling is without replacement from a finite population, is given by

$$\sigma_{\bar{X}} = \frac{\sigma}{\sqrt{N}} \sqrt{\frac{P - N}{P - 1}}$$

where P is the size of the population. Except for very small populations this can be written

$$\sigma_{\bar{X}} = \frac{\sigma}{\sqrt{N}} \sqrt{1 - F}$$

where F is the *sampling fraction*, ie the ratio of the sample size, N, to the population size, P. Hence the 95 per cent confidence limits for the population mean will, in this case, be given by

$$\bar{X} \pm 1.96 \frac{s}{\sqrt{N}} \sqrt{1 - F}$$

The influence of the factor $\sqrt{1 - F}$ in the above formula is to reduce the standard error of the mean and hence to narrow confidence limits based on this standard error. The higher the sampling fraction the lower the standard error, and, of course, when $F = 1$, the standard error is zero, since such a sampling fraction implies a full count and not a sample at all. A sampling fraction of 1 in 20 will give a standard error of the mean equal to $\sqrt{1 - \frac{1}{20}} = 97.5$ per cent of what it would have been if the sampling were from an infinite population; for a fraction of 1 in 10 the percentage is reduced to 94.9 per cent, for one of 1 in 5 to 89.4 per cent, and for one of 1 in 2 to 70.7 per cent. It is clear that so long as the sampling fraction is small, the refinement obtained by introducing the factor $\sqrt{1 - F}$ does not amount to much, and in what follows it will be ignored. However, when the sampling is from small populations, it may be of considerable importance. Thus, for example, if two populations of a variable X, sized 20 000 and 2000 respectively, have the same standard deviation, then it can easily be calculated that a sample of 690 from the smaller population will be as reliable as one of 1000 from the larger population.

6.5 Simple Random Sampling

In designing a sample survey the two major considerations are the selection of the sample and the estimation of population values from the results of the sample. These are now discussed in relation to simple random sampling.

In simple random sampling, apart from the technicalities of the actual selection of the sample, the main matter to be determined is the size of the sample. Since the size of the sample directly affects sampling error, it can be determined by specifying the degree of sampling error that will be tolerated. The degree of sampling error involved in making an estimate of a population parameter from sample data can be indicated by ascertaining the confidence limits for the population parameter in question. Thus we know that, if we have a sample of size N of a variable X with sample mean $\bar{X}$ and sample standard deviation s, the 95 per cent confidence limits for the population mean, μ, are given by

$$\bar{X} \pm t_{.025} \frac{s}{\sqrt{N}}$$

When N is large, the appropriate value for $t_{.025}$ is 1·96, and the confidence limits are

$$\bar{X} \pm 1·96 \frac{s}{\sqrt{N}}$$

In the remainder of this chapter we shall be concerned with large N, say $N > 30$. The confidence limits give us a range within which we can be reasonably certain the population mean lies. This range is based on the mean derived from the sample and takes into account the sampling error involved. It can, of course, be narrowed by reducing the desired level of confidence. For example, the 90 per cent confidence limits are given by

$$\bar{X} \pm 1·64 \frac{s}{\sqrt{N}}$$

Such a reduction in range, however, is obtained at the expense of the confidence which we place in our results. If we adhere to the conventional 95 per cent level of confidence, the size of the range will evidently depend on the size of the sample and, as will be shown in the following section, on the design of the sample.

Consequently the essence of sampling design is first to determine the margin of sampling error which we shall tolerate and then to design a sample which will meet the requirements. In the case of sampling with the object of estimating the population mean, we might specify that the sample must be such that the population mean lies within a range, say, $\pm\ d$ of the sample mean with 95 per cent confidence. With repeated samples of size N drawn from a population with known σ, in 95 per cent of the cases μ will be correctly located in the range $\bar{X} \pm 1·96 \dfrac{\sigma}{\sqrt{N}}$ Hence, given σ, we can ascertain the size of the sample which will make

$$1·96 \frac{\sigma}{\sqrt{N}} = d$$

$$N = \left(\frac{1·96\sigma}{d}\right)^2$$

Clearly, for given σ, N must be greater the greater the degree of accuracy required (ie the smaller d), and for given d, N must be greater the greater the variability in the underlying population (ie the greater σ). In practice, we shall seldom know σ—the standard deviation of the population from which we are sampling—but we may have an estimate of it from a previous census or survey, or we may be able to get an estimate of it from a pilot survey. This will enable us to estimate approximately the required size of N.

Example 6.1

Given that the standard deviation of metropolitan rents derived from a pilot survey is $9·5, what sized sample should be taken to ascertain the mean level of metropolitan rents, so that we shall be 95 per cent confident that the population mean rent lies within 50 cents either way of the sample mean rent?

Here we require $\quad 1·96\dfrac{\sigma}{\sqrt{N}} = 0·50, \quad$ where $\sigma = \$9·5$

ie $$\frac{1·96 \times 9·5}{0·50} = \sqrt{N}$$

ie $$N = 1387$$

Accordingly if we take a sample of about 1400 rents, we shall be able to be 95 per cent confident that the population mean rent lies within 50 cents of the resulting mean rent, provided, of course, that the standard deviation is about $9·5. We shall be 95 per cent confident, in the sense that in the long run of every 100 similar attempts at estimation we shall be right 95 times in locating the population value within the appropriate confidence limits.

This example is based on the assumption that the population of rents is sufficiently large for it to be treated as infinite. If, however, the population were relatively small, a smaller sample would suffice. Thus, if we were told that the population consisted of 10 000 rents, we should require

$$1·96\frac{\sigma}{\sqrt{N}}\sqrt{1 - \frac{N}{P}} = 0·50$$

ie $$\frac{1·96 \times 9·5}{0·50} = \frac{\sqrt{N}}{\sqrt{1 - \dfrac{N}{10\,000}}}$$

ie $$N = 1218$$

The above refers to sample size in relation to means, but a similar treatment can be used when other parameters are of interest. When more than one variable is to be investigated by the sample survey, the error requirements for one variable may conflict with those for others in the sense that the sample size to achieve the error requirement for one variable may differ from those necessary for another. In such cases either the sample size must be made large enough to meet all the requirements or some compromise in the various error requirements will be necessary.

As far as estimation from a simple random sample is concerned, the sample mean $\bar{X}$ provides an estimate of the population mean μ. Since with repeated random sampling the mean of $\bar{X}$s will tend to the population mean μ, $\bar{X}$ is an unbiased estimate of μ. However, no estimate is complete without attaching an indication of sampling errors. This is best done by determining confidence limits. In the case of a simple random sample the 95 per cent confidence limits are given by

$$\bar{X} \pm 1.96 \frac{s}{\sqrt{N}}$$

where s is the sample standard deviation. In this formula, s is used and not the estimate of σ which may have been used to determine N, for the latter would be only a rough estimate.

Frequently we are interested in totals rather than means, eg in total rent paid instead of mean rent paid. An estimate of the population total from a simple random sample is given by

$$P\bar{X}$$

where P is the number in the population. This can be written

$$\frac{P}{N}\Sigma X$$

where P/N is the reciprocal of the sampling fraction and ΣX the sample total. The ratio P/N is called the *raising factor*, and we sometimes speak of 'blowing up' sample totals to population totals. Since the variance of $P\bar{X}$ is P^2 times the variance of $\bar{X}$ (see section 4.15 above) the standard error of an estimate of a population total is

$$P\frac{\sigma}{\sqrt{N}}$$

so that the 95 per cent confidence limits for a population total calculated from a simple random sample are

$$P\bar{X} \pm 1.96\, P\frac{s}{\sqrt{N}}$$

ie

$$\left(\bar{X} \pm 1.96 \frac{s}{\sqrt{N}}\right) P$$

For proportions and numbers possessing a certain attribute (eg proportion of dwellings which are made of brick, total number of dwellings which are made of brick) analogous formulae apply. Thus a population proportion can be estimated from a simple random sample as the sample proportion p, and the 95 per cent confidence limits are

$$p \pm 1{\cdot}96 \sqrt{\frac{p(1-p)}{N}}$$

Similarly the number possessing a certain attribute in the population can be estimated from a simple random sample as Pp, with 95 per cent confidence limits

$$\left(p \pm 1{\cdot}96 \sqrt{\frac{p(1-p)}{N}}\right)P$$

The preceding estimation procedures are quite straightforward. Rather more complicated ones can be devised which make use of supplementary information and which are more efficient in the sense that they give rise to smaller standard errors. Such a method which is commonly used is that of *ratio estimation*. Suppose we know that the variable X, of which we wish to estimate the population mean, is related to another variable Z, of which we know the population mean. We can estimate the population mean of X by multiplying the population mean of Z by the ratio of the means of the values of X and Z in the sample, ie we write

$$\text{estimate of } \mu_X = \mu_Z \frac{\bar{X}}{\bar{Z}}$$

For example, suppose we take a sample of wage-earner households to ascertain mean annual expenditure on food. We find the sample mean to be $2268. We know from other sources that the annual mean earnings of all wage-earner households is in fact $5950. If the mean earnings of the sample is $5600, we can estimate the mean expenditure on food as $5950 \times \dfrac{2268}{5600} = \$2410$, instead of as $2268, which is the direct sample result.

Provided the relation between X and Z is close, the standard error of an estimate performed in this way is lower than that of a direct estimate from the sample mean $\bar{X}$. This means that in these circumstances estimates from repeated samples will fluctuate less if they are made by the ratio method. Hence the range of confidence limits will be narrower. The formula for the standard error of ratio estimates is rather complicated and will not be given here. Ratio estimates are not, in general, unbiased estimates, although for large samples ($N > 30$) the bias is negligible.

Ratio estimation is particularly useful when samples of the same data are taken periodically. For example, we may have a census which gives us the mean rent of tenanted dwellings accurately for the census year. In subsequent years sample surveys are taken. We can estimate post-censal mean rent either by the means of the samples or by marking up the census figure by the movements in the mean rent of sampled houses from the census period onwards. In this case the formula

$$\mu_Z \frac{\bar{X}}{\bar{Z}}$$

is interpreted as follows:

μ_Z is the mean rent in the census,

$\bar{X}$ is the mean rent of a sample taken subsequently,

$\bar{Z}$ is the mean rent of the houses in that sample at the time of the census.

The possible advantage of ratio estimation can be seen in the extreme case where all rents, say, doubled. In this case the ratio method would give the exact population mean, even though $\bar{X}$ differed from it because of the chances of sampling; for since the same houses are involved in $\bar{X}$ and $\bar{Z}$, we shall have $\bar{X} = 2\bar{Z}$.

6.6 Stratified Random Sampling

The simple random sample is the simplest type of sampling design, but when supplementary information about the population to be sampled (ie information other than the mere list of units to be sampled) is available, other designs can be used. When alternative sample designs for a particular survey are available, we need criteria for discriminating between different designs which conform to the same error requirements. Since one of the main reasons for using samples rather than full counts is the saving in cost, the most workable criterion is the one of cost. The cost of making a survey will be roughly proportional to the size of the sample. Thus we can determine the margin of sampling error which we will tolerate and design the survey to minimise its cost. Alternatively, we can determine the amount we are prepared to spend on the survey, and design the sample so that the margin of sampling error is a minimum, ie so that the range of the confidence limits is as narrow as possible. Obviously these two criteria amount to the same thing. It is important to appreciate that there can be no 'best' design in an absolute sense. There can only be a design which is 'best' in relation to a certain criterion—for example, one which minimises cost for a given error or minimises error for a given cost. No meaning can be attached to the absolute minimisation of sampling error for this can be achieved only by making the sample cover the whole population, ie by eliminating sampling altogether.

Of the more complicated designs the basic one is the *stratified random sample*. If the necessary information is available, the population can be divided into distinct *strata* and random samples taken from each stratum. The stratification is based upon some known characteristic of the population, eg rents may be stratified according to area, household budgets according to occupation of head of household, retail shops according to size of turnover, etc.

In certain circumstances a stratified random sample will give rise to smaller sampling errors than a simple random sample of the same size. This can best be seen by an example. Suppose our problem is to estimate the mean rent paid in South Australia. We divide the state into three areas—metropolitan, urban-provincial and rural. We may suppose that 50 per cent, 20 per cent and 30 per cent of houses are in these three strata respectively. We draw a simple random sample of 100 houses from the population. If rents vary within each stratum, but the distribution of rents is the same for the three strata, the way in which the three strata are represented in samples of 100 will not affect the pattern of variation of sample means resulting from repeated sampling. On the other hand, if rents are all the same within each stratum, but differ as between strata, the mean rent of a sample will depend entirely on the way in which the three strata are represented in the sample. Since with repeated random samples of 100 from the population the numbers of metropolitan, urban-provincial and rural houses in samples will fluctuate around 50, 20 and 30 respectively, the mean rent of samples will fluctuate although all rents within individual strata are the same. If, as will usually be the case in practice, rents vary within strata and the distributions of strata differ from each other, variations between mean rents of repeated simple random samples can be regarded as arising from two sources: first, from variations of rents within strata, and secondly, from variations in the proportions in which the strata are represented in different samples. By taking random samples from each stratum separately and combining the stratum sample means by the proportions in which the strata occur in the population, we can obtain a sample estimate for the population mean in which the second source of variation is controlled. This type of sample is a stratified random sample. With repeated sampling of this kind, the estimate of the population mean will vary only on account of the variation of rent within strata, and variations due to variations in the proportions in which the strata are represented in samples will be eliminated, ie the estimated mean rent from the sample will not differ from the population mean simply because the houses in the sample are distributed between strata differently from the way in which they are in the population. In the extreme case where the only variation in rents is between strata, all rents within a stratum being the same, all variation in the sample estimate of population mean rent will be eliminated by stratified sampling, and any one sample will correctly estimate the population mean. It follows that, with repeated sampling, the means of a stratified random sample will tend to vary less than those of a simple random sample of the same size (subject to certain restrictions about the allocation of the sample between the strata, to be discussed below) provided that stratum distributions differ. In these circumstances stratification reduces sampling error.

Suppose, we have a population of a variable X, which can be divided into various strata according to some characteristic, and we take a stratified random sample of size N. Let μ be the population mean, μ_s the mean of the sth stratum, P the number in the total population, P_s the number in the sth stratum, then

$$\mu = \frac{\Sigma P_s \mu_s}{P}$$

$$= \Sigma \alpha_s \mu_s$$

where $\alpha_s = P_s/P$ is the proportion of the population in the sth stratum, so that $\Sigma \alpha_s = 1$. Further, let N_s be the number in the sample drawn from the sth stratum, so that $\Sigma N_s = N$; and $\bar{X}_s$ be the mean of the sample drawn from the sth stratum. Then, by combining stratum sample means in the correct proportions, we shall have as an estimate of the population mean

$$\bar{X}^* = \alpha_1 \bar{X}_1 + \alpha_2 \bar{X}_2 + \alpha_3 \bar{X}_3 + \ldots$$

$$= \Sigma \alpha_s \bar{X}_s$$

where the star (*) indicates that $\bar{X}$ has been calculated from a stratified sample.

If we repeat the process of taking stratified random samples, then since $\bar{X}^*$ is a linear combination of the $\bar{X}_s$s, by virtue of section 4.15 above, we shall have for the mean of $\bar{X}^*$

$$\Sigma \alpha_s \mu_s$$

ie the population mean, and for the standard error of $\bar{X}^*$

$$\sigma_{\bar{X}^*} = \sqrt{\Sigma \alpha_s^2 \sigma_{\bar{X}_s}^2}$$

where

$$\sigma_{\bar{X}_s}^2 = \frac{\sigma_s^2}{N_s}$$

$\sigma_{\bar{X}_s}$ being the standard error of the mean of the sth stratum and σ_s being the standard deviation of the sth stratum.

Hence

$$\sigma_{\bar{X}^*} = \sqrt{\Sigma \left(\alpha_s^2 \frac{\sigma_s^2}{N_s} \right)}$$

The standard error of the mean computed from a simple random sample is

$$\sigma_{\bar{X}} = \frac{\sigma}{\sqrt{N}}$$

where σ is the standard deviation of the whole population, irrespective of stratification. The question arises: under what conditions will $\sigma_{\bar{x}*}$ be smaller than $\sigma_{\bar{x}}$? This is important, because it is only if $\sigma_{\bar{x}*}$ is appreciably smaller than $\sigma_{\bar{x}}$ that stratification is worth while.

Clearly the value of $\sigma_{\bar{x}*}$ will depend on how the sample size N is distributed between the different strata. One possibility immediately presents itself. The sample may be allocated as between strata in the same proportions as in the population. This is equivalent to having the same sampling fraction for each stratum and is called the method of a *constant sampling fraction*. We shall have

$$N_s = \alpha_s N$$

so that, in this case, $\bar{X}*$ can be calculated directly from the sample, without re-weighting, for

$$\bar{X}* = \Sigma\alpha_s\bar{X}_s$$

$$= \frac{\Sigma N_s\bar{X}_s}{N}$$

$$= \frac{\Sigma X}{N}$$

Here the sample is allocated to strata according to the importance of the strata in the population. In this case $\sigma_{\bar{x}*}$ reduces to

$$\sigma'_{\bar{x}*} = \sqrt{\frac{\Sigma\alpha_s\sigma_s^2}{N}}$$

where $\sigma'_{\bar{x}*}$ is the standard error of a sample mean calculated from a stratified random sample with a constant sampling fraction.

There are many ways in which the sample size might be allocated between the strata, of which the method of a constant sampling fraction is only one. Recalling that a criterion for sampling design is the minimisation of error for a given cost, it will be appreciated that the allocation ought to be made with some such end in mind. Indeed, when a series of alternative designs presents itself, a major task of the statistician is to select the *optimum* one according to some criterion. This general principle can be applied here. If we assume that the size of the sample is given, then the problem is to select an optimum allocation between strata which minimises sampling error. Accordingly we may fix the allocation of N between strata so as to minimise $\sigma_{\bar{x}*}$. This is called the method of *optimal allocation*.[1]

[1] This procedure and its results are exactly analogous to the problem in economic theory of allocating a given money income between alternative uses. The equal marginal utility principle is here paralleled by equal reductions of error, ie the numbers are allocated such that the reduction in the variance from adding an additional unit to a stratum is the same for all strata.

We require that $W = \Sigma\left(\alpha_s^2\dfrac{\sigma_s^2}{N_s}\right)$ be a minimum, subject to $\Sigma N_s = N$.

Bearing in mind that

$$N_1 = N - N_2 - N_3 \ldots,$$

we shall require $\dfrac{\partial W}{\partial N_s} = 0$ for all s, except $s = 1$,

ie we require $\dfrac{\alpha_1^2\sigma_1^2}{(N - N_2 - N_3 - \ldots)^2} - \dfrac{\alpha_s^2\sigma_s^2}{N_s^2} = 0$ for all s, except $s = 1$,

ie the expressions $\dfrac{\alpha_s^2\sigma_s^2}{N_s^2}$ are the same for all s. It follows that N_s must be proportional to $\alpha_s\sigma_s$,

ie $\qquad\qquad N_s = \lambda\alpha_s\sigma_s,$

where λ is a constant.

Hence $\qquad\qquad N = \lambda\Sigma\alpha_s\sigma_s$

so that $\qquad\qquad N_s = \dfrac{\alpha_s\sigma_s}{\Sigma\alpha_s\sigma_s}N.$

Here the sample is allocated to strata according not only to the importance of the strata in the population but also to the variability within strata, so that the more variable strata are allocated a relatively larger part of the sample. The formula for optimal allocation reduces to $N_s = \alpha_s N$ when σ_s is constant for all strata. From the above, it can be seen that, for optimal allocation, $\sigma_{\bar{x}^*}$ reduces to

$$\sigma''_{\bar{x}^*} = \dfrac{\Sigma\alpha_s\sigma_s}{\sqrt{N}}$$

where $\sigma''_{\bar{x}^*}$ is the standard error of a sample mean calculated from a stratified random sample with optimal allocation.

We now investigate the conditions under which $\sigma_{\bar{x}^*}$ is smaller than $\sigma_{\bar{x}}$. We must first express the population variance σ^2 in terms of the stratum variances σ_s^2. It will be recalled (section 3.5 above) that

$$\Sigma(X - \bar{X})^2 = \Sigma(X - A)^2 - N(\bar{X} - A)^2$$

ie $\qquad\Sigma(X - A)^2 = \Sigma(X - \bar{X})^2 + N(\bar{X} - A)^2$

where $\bar{X}$ is the mean of the Xs, N is the number of Xs and A is any arbitrary figure. Now consider the sth stratum. Writing X_s for the variable in this stratum, P_s for the number of the population in it, μ_s and σ_s for its population mean and standard deviation respectively, and μ for the mean of the population as a whole, we shall have

$$\Sigma(X_s - \mu)^2 = \Sigma(X_s - \mu_s)^2 + P_s(\mu_s - \mu)^2$$

ie $\qquad \Sigma(X_s - \mu)^2 = P_s[\sigma_s^2 + (\mu_s - \mu)^2]$

This holds for each stratum. Adding all strata and dividing by P, the total population, we get

$$\frac{\Sigma\Sigma(X_s - \mu)^2}{P} = \Sigma\alpha_s\sigma_s^2 + \Sigma\alpha_s(\mu_s - \mu)^2$$

since $\alpha_s = P_s/P$,

ie $\qquad \sigma^2 = \Sigma\alpha_s\sigma_s^2 + \Sigma\alpha_s(\mu_s - \mu)^2$

where σ^2 is the variance of the population as a whole. It can be seen that we have now split up the variability of X in the population into two components.[1] The first is a weighted average of stratum variances and measures variability within strata, and the second is a weighted variance of stratum means about the whole population mean and measures variability between strata. It follows from the above formula that we can write the standard error of the mean from a simple random sample of size N as

$$\sigma_{\bar{X}} = \frac{\sigma}{\sqrt{N}}$$

$$= \sqrt{\frac{\Sigma\alpha_s\sigma_s^2}{N} + \frac{\Sigma\alpha_s(\mu_s - \mu)^2}{N}}$$

Now if $\sigma'_{\bar{X}*}$ refers to the standard error of the mean from a stratified random sample of size N with a constant sampling fraction, we can write

$$\sigma_{\bar{X}} = \sqrt{\sigma'^2_{\bar{X}*} + \frac{\Sigma\alpha_s(\mu_s - \mu)^2}{N}}$$

It follows that

$$\sigma'_{\bar{X}*} < \sigma_{\bar{X}}$$

so long as all the μ_ss do not equal μ, ie so long as stratum means differ from each other.

Again, if $\sigma''_{\bar{X}*}$ refers to the standard error of the mean from a stratified random sample of size N with optimal allocation, we can write

---

[1] The breaking up of the variability of a variable, as measured by its variance, into components which can be attributed to different sources of variation is the central theme of a powerful tool of statistical analysis known as the *analysis of variance*. Although the notions of analysis of variance are of great generality, the application of its technique in the economic field is limited to more advanced problems than are covered by this text. The technique of analysis of variance is covered by most general texts on statistical methods (see Appendix C, 1).

$$\sigma_{\bar{X}} = \sqrt{\sigma_{\bar{X}^*}''^2 + \frac{1}{N}[\Sigma\alpha_s\sigma_s^2 - (\Sigma\alpha_s\sigma_s)^2] + \frac{\Sigma\alpha_s(\mu_s - \mu)^2}{N}}$$

$$= \sqrt{\sigma_{\bar{X}^*}''^2 + \frac{\Sigma\alpha_s(\sigma_s - \bar{\sigma}_s)^2}{N} + \frac{\Sigma\alpha_s(\mu_s - \mu)^2}{N}}$$

where $\bar{\sigma}_s = \Sigma\alpha_s\sigma_s$ is the mean of the σ_ss, weighted by the proportions α_s.[1] It follows that

$$\sigma''_{\bar{X}^*} < \sigma_{\bar{X}}$$

so long as either stratum means differ from each other or stratum standard deviations differ from each other or both.

We can conclude from the above that, if we are taking a sample of size N to estimate the population mean, μ, of a variable X, the reliability of the estimate can be increased by taking a stratified random sample with optimal allocation if the population can be stratified into categories which themselves have different mean values of X, and/or which themselves have different standard deviations of X. If the strata all have the same standard deviation, optimal allocation in fact involves a constant sampling fraction. In any event optimal allocation gives a minimum sampling error for a stratified random sample of a given size.

The reasons for the gain in reliability obtained through stratification should be fairly obvious. By stratifying we do not allow variations in the proportions of the sample lying in any stratum to affect the estimate of the population mean. This eliminates one source of variability. Furthermore, with optimal allocation we take a relatively larger sample from those strata with relatively greater variability. This averages out the variability within the different strata.

In order to determine whether or not a stratified sample is worth while in a particular case and, if so, what sized sample to take, and how to allocate it between strata, it is necessary to have estimates of the various σs in the above formulae. These may be available from a prior investigation, or it may be possible to make rough estimates of them. Once the sample is taken, confidence limits to $\bar{X}^*$ should be based on the sample standard deviations, since the estimates of the σs used in designing the sample will necessarily be fairly rough.

In general, a stratified random sample, appropriately allocated between strata, will enable a given margin of sampling error to be achieved with a smaller sample than a simple random sample. However, it does not follow that stratification is always worth while, for

---

[1] Note:

$$\Sigma\alpha_s(\sigma_s - \bar{\sigma}_s)^2 = \Sigma\alpha_s\sigma_s^2 - 2\bar{\sigma}_s\Sigma\alpha_s\sigma_s + \bar{\sigma}_s^2\Sigma\alpha_s$$

but $\Sigma\alpha_s\sigma_s = \bar{\sigma}_s$ and $\Sigma\alpha_s = 1$

Hence $\Sigma\alpha_s(\sigma_s - \bar{\sigma}_s)^2 = \Sigma\alpha_s\sigma_s^2 - (\Sigma\alpha_s\sigma_s)^2$

while stratification will reduce costs of collection and tabulation, the process of stratification may itself be costly, since the frame will have to be stratified and each stratum in the frame separately sampled. Furthermore stratification is impossible unless the proportions of the population falling into the different strata are known, ie unless we have supplementary information about the population. This can be seen by the fact that the α_ss occur in all the relevant formulae. Finally, the advantages of stratification are gained only when the sample is allocated between strata in one or another appropriate form. Any sort of allocation will not do. This becomes obvious when one considers what would happen if practically the whole sample were allocated to one stratum, the other strata being hardly sampled at all.

This section and the preceding one have dealt with the problem of sample design entirely in terms of means. Similar methods are available for handling proportions and totals. Strictly speaking, account should have been taken of the fact that a population which can be stratified is necessarily finite, although, if the population is large relatively to the sample to be drawn from it, this does not matter a great deal. In any case the basic principles of stratification have been dealt with. The example below illustrates these principles in numerical terms.

Example 6.2
A sample survey is to be undertaken to ascertain the mean annual income produced by farms in a certain area. The farms can be stratified according to their principal products. A census conducted several years earlier yielded the data set out in the table below.

Assuming that the proportions in the four strata have remained unchanged, and using the census standard deviations as approximations to the unknown current standard deviations, estimate:

(i) the margin of sampling error which can be expected to arise for a sample of 500 farms if it is (a) a simple random sample, (b) a stratified random sample with a constant sampling fraction, and (c) a stratified random sample with optimal allocation.

(ii) the size of (a) a simple random sample, (b) a stratified random sample with a constant sampling fraction, and (c) a stratified random sample with optimal allocation, in order to be reasonably confident that the population mean will lie within $100 of the sample estimate.

Type of Farm	Proportion of Farms in Stratum	Mean Annual Income $	Standard Deviation $
Wool	0·16	10946	2236
Wheat	0·19	6402	2644
Dairying	0·27	2228	606
Other	0·38	1458	230
All Farms*	1·00	4124	3788

*This line gives values for the population as a whole. The mean of the population as a whole is related to the stratum means by the identity

$$\mu = \Sigma \alpha_s \mu_s$$

and the population standard deviation is related to the stratum standard deviations by the identity

$$\sigma^2 = \Sigma \alpha_s \sigma_s^2 + \Sigma \alpha_s (\mu_s - \mu)^2$$

These relations necessarily hold. (See pp 252 and 255 above.)

The relation between the population variance and the stratum variances can, perhaps, be most readily understood by working in terms of an arbitrary origin of zero (see section 3.5, p 60). Thus we have, for the population variance

$$\sigma^2 = \frac{\Sigma (X - \mu)^2}{P} = \frac{\Sigma X^2 - P \mu^2}{P}$$

and for the variance of the sth stratum

$$\sigma_s^2 = \frac{\Sigma (X_s - \mu_s)^2}{P_s} = \frac{\Sigma X_s^2 - P_s \mu_s^2}{P_s}$$

Since ΣX^2 in the formula for σ^2 is simply the sum of the squares of the original observations, it can be obtained by adding the ΣX_s^2s for the individual strata. Thus we can derive ΣX^2 from a knowledge of the σ_s^2s. Thus, from the formula for σ_s^2

$$\Sigma X_s^2 = P_s (\sigma_s^2 + \mu_s^2)$$

and hence

$$\sigma^2 = \frac{\Sigma P_s (\sigma_s^2 + \mu_s^2) - P \mu^2}{P}$$

$$= \Sigma \alpha_s (\sigma_s^2 + \mu_s^2) - \mu^2$$

where the summation is a summation of stratum results. By rearrangement this latter formula becomes

$$\sigma^2 = \Sigma \alpha_s \sigma_s^2 + \Sigma \alpha_s \mu_s^2 - \mu^2$$

$$= \Sigma \alpha_s \sigma_s^2 + \Sigma \alpha_s (\mu_s - \mu)^2$$

since $\Sigma \alpha_s \mu_s = \mu$ and $\Sigma \alpha_s = 1$.

(i) (a) *Simple random sample*

Here $N = 500$, and we have $\sigma_{\bar{x}} = \dfrac{\sigma}{\sqrt{N}}$

$$= \$169 \cdot 4$$

(b) *Stratified random sample with constant sampling fraction*

Here $N_s = \alpha_s N$

and with $N = 500$

we have $N_1 = 80, N_2 = 95, N_3 = 135, N_4 = 190$

The sampling error will be reduced by this form of stratification since the data indicate that stratum means are likely to differ. We have

$$\sigma'_{\bar{x}\cdot} = \sqrt{\frac{\Sigma \alpha_s \sigma_s^2}{N}}$$

$$= \$67 \cdot 0$$

(c) *Stratified random sample with optimal allocation*

Here $N_s = \dfrac{\alpha_s \sigma_s}{\Sigma \alpha_s \sigma_s} N$

and with $$N = 500$$

we have $$N_1 = 161, N_2 = 226, N_3 = 74, N_4 = 39$$

The sampling error will be further reduced by this form of stratification since the data indicate that stratum standard deviations differ. Note that the wool and wheat strata which have relatively high standard deviations are relatively more heavily sampled in this design than in design (b). We have

$$\sigma''_{\bar{x}\cdot} = \frac{\Sigma \alpha_s \sigma_s}{\sqrt{N}}$$

$$= \$49\cdot6$$

This example shows how stratification can reduce sampling error. With repeated samples of 500, sample means from stratified samples, calculated by the formula $\bar{X}^* = \Sigma \alpha_s \bar{X}_s$, will show less variability than sample means from simple random samples, and design (c) will show less variability than design (b).

(ii) (a) *Simple random sample*
Using 95 per cent confidence limits we shall require

$$1\cdot96 \frac{\sigma}{\sqrt{N}} = 100$$

$$N = 5\,512$$

(b) *Stratified random sample with constant sampling fraction*

We shall require $$1\cdot96 \sqrt{\frac{\Sigma \alpha_s \sigma_s^2}{N}} = 100$$

ie $$N = 863, \text{ with } N_1 = 138, N_2 = 164, N_3 = 233, N_4 = 328$$

(c) *Stratified random sample with optimal allocation*

We shall require $$1\cdot96 \frac{\Sigma \alpha_s \sigma_s}{\sqrt{N}} = 100$$

ie $$N = 474, \text{ with } N_1 = 153, N_2 = 214, N_3 = 70, N_4 = 37$$

Provided the above σ_ss are close to the σ_ss currently obtaining in the population, we can be 95 per cent certain that the population mean lies within \$100 of the sample mean for the three sample designs set out above. Clearly stratification here involves appreciable savings in sample size. Design (c) gives the same accuracy as design (a) with a sample less than one-tenth the size.

As far as estimation from a stratified random sample is concerned, the estimate of the population mean is given by

$$\bar{X}^* = \Sigma \alpha_s \bar{X}_s$$

and the 95 per cent confidence limits by

$$\bar{X}^* \pm 1\cdot96 \sqrt{\Sigma \left(\alpha_s^2 \frac{s_s^2}{N_s} \right)}$$

Similarly the estimate of the population total is

$$P\bar{X}^*$$

and the 95 per cent confidence limits are

$$\left[\bar{X}^* \pm 1{\cdot}96 \sqrt{\Sigma\left(\alpha_s^2 \frac{s_s^2}{N_s}\right)} \right] P$$

where s_s is the sample standard deviation of the sth stratum.

For proportions and numbers possessing a certain attribute analogous formulae apply. Thus we have as an estimate of the population proportion

$$p^* = \Sigma\alpha_s p_s$$

where p_s is the proportion in the sth stratum in the sample, and the 95 per cent confidence limits are

$$p^* \pm 1{\cdot}96 \sqrt{\Sigma\left(\alpha_s^2 \frac{p_s(1 - p_s)}{N_s}\right)}$$

As an estimate of the number possessing a certain attribute we have

$$Pp^*$$

with 95 per cent confidence limits

$$\left[p^* \pm 1{\cdot}96 \sqrt{\Sigma\left(\alpha_s^2 \frac{p_s(1 - p_s)}{N_s}\right)} \right] P$$

Sometimes it is not possible to select a stratified random sample because the frame cannot be readily stratified, although it may be possible to *stratify after selection* if the distribution of the population between the various strata is known. Thus, if dwellings are known to be divided between metropolitan, urban-provincial and rural regions in the ratios 50:20:30, but the full list of dwellings is not so classified, a simple random sample can be stratified after selection by dividing the sample into the three strata. The above formulae can then be applied, and provided that a sufficient number of dwellings in the simple random sample fall into each of the strata, sampling error may be reduced. The advantage which stratification before selection holds over this method is that with such stratification we can ensure that adequate numbers of the sample are allocated to each stratum instead of relying on chance. But with stratification after selection, we shall control in the estimation process, at least, the distribution of the sample between strata.

Example 6.3

A simple random sample of 120 families taken at the beginning of a particular year yielded the following information about expenditure on entertainment in the previous three months:

Region	Number of Families	Mean Expenditure	Standard Deviation
		$	$
Metropolitan	52	61·23	9·99
Urban-Provincial	33	38·79	10·64
Rural	35	23·51	5·73
All Regions*	120	44·06	18·52

*The all regions values are related to the individual region values in an analogous manner to that set out in the example on pp 257–8 above. Here of course the values are sample values.

The population consisted of 10 000 families, and it was known to be distributed between the three strata in the proportions 5:3:2 respectively. Estimate 95 per cent confidence limits for the population mean expenditure and for the aggregate expenditure in the given quarter.

Treating the sample as a simple random sample of 120 families, the 95 per cent confidence limits for the mean will be

$$\bar{X} \pm 1·96 \frac{s}{\sqrt{N}}$$

ie $44·06 \pm 3·31

ie $40·75 to $47·37

and the 95 per cent confidence limits for the aggregate expenditure will be 10 000 times these,

ie $407 500 to $473 700

However, if we stratify the sample after selection on the basis of the given population distribution between strata, we get as an estimate of the population mean expenditure for the given quarter.

$$\bar{X}^* = \Sigma \alpha_s \bar{X}_s$$

$$= \$46·95$$

and the 95 per cent confidence limits will be

$$\bar{X}^* \pm 1·96 \sqrt{\Sigma \left(\alpha_s^2 \frac{s_s^2}{N_s} \right)}$$

ie $46·95 \pm 1·78

ie $45·17 to $48·73

The 95 per cent confidence limits for aggregate expenditure will be 10 000 times these,

ie $451 700 to $487 300

Here stratification after selection narrows the range of the confidence limits. It also raises the estimate of the mean expenditure, since the metropolitan stratum was under-represented in the simple random sample.

6.7 Other Designs for Sample Surveys

The simple random sample and the stratified random sample are the simplest of the various sample designs used in practice. More complicated techniques are available, and like the simpler ones they must be based on random selection to be satisfactory. Some designs involve *multi-stratification*, ie stratification by two or more characteristics, eg a stratification by size of income within each of the three regional strata in example 6.3 above. This increases the number of distinct strata, but does not affect the design in principle. Other designs involve *multi-stage sampling*.

In multi-stage sampling the population is first divided into first-stage sampling units. A random sample of these is taken. It is customary to select the first-stage sampling units with the probabilities of selection of units proportional to their size and not equal as in the case of simple random sampling. The first-stage sampling units which have been selected in this sample are then divided into smaller second-stage sampling units which are then sampled. This process can be continued for a number of stages until the final sampling units are selected. A simple example would be a survey of nutrition of school-children, where schools might be the first-stage sampling units. A sample of these would then be taken and from the selected ones individual children sampled. This would be a two-stage sample and the children would be the final sampling units. It should be plain that when the early-stage samples contain few units, the early-stage sampling units should be stratified before sampling to ensure adequate representation of the population, unless they are fairly similar in their characteristics. If, for example, different schools cater for different classes of children, a small sample of schools may miss out important categories of the population.

Multi-stage sampling is best exemplified in what is called *area sampling*. One of the difficulties in taking a sample of a human population for any purpose is that the population may extend over a very large area. This is certainly the case in Australia. Consequently a sample drawn from the whole area will be spread out and will be costly to contact. It will also be difficult to ensure adequate supervision of the field work. Not only this, but the listing of the whole population will be a long and costly procedure. The object of area sampling is to meet these difficulties. Area sampling involves dividing the area into small areas to provide first-stage sampling units. For example, in a particular country the first-stage units might be local government areas. A random sample of these would be taken. This is the first stage of the sampling. The second stage might be to take random samples of administrative districts from the already selected first-stage sampling units; the third might be to sample blocks of dwellings from the selected administrative districts; the fourth and final stage might be to sample dwellings from the selected blocks. This procedure has the effect of concentrating the final sample into a limited number of small areas with savings in costs of collection. At the same time listing is greatly reduced, since all that is required is a list of the first-stage sampling units, then a list of the second-stage units in the selected first-stage units and so on. Multi-stage area sampling is usually combined with stratification, the early-stage sampling units being stratified before they are sampled. Area sampling is also very useful when surveys are to be taken regularly, eg a monthly survey of employment. The earlier-stage sampling units once selected can be used permanently and permanent survey organisations can be established in them. Examples of this type of sampling—all more or less complex—abound in the literature.[1] Multi-stage samples will have greater sampling errors than single-stage samples of the same size, but it may be less costly to take a large multi-stage sample than a small single-stage one with the same error performance, so that a multi-stage sample may be the 'best' design to employ *in given circumstances*. This illustrates once again that there is no *absolute* 'best' sample design, but only one which is most efficient in terms of some criterion, like cost or speed.

In the past three decades sampling has become an established method for collecting economic and social data. In economic applications, sample survey methods have been widely used in two main ways: (i) to collect information for a special purpose, and (ii) to obtain continuous information of the behaviour of certain economic variables. Regular sample surveys conducted for the latter purpose are particularly useful for getting up-to-date information between censuses. The periodic full count can be used to check whether the sample surveys are showing any bias over time in one direction or another (due perhaps to changes in the composition of the frame, which cannot be adequately covered in selecting the sample). A brief account of two major surveys of this kind undertaken in Australia (the Population and Labour Force Survey and the Survey of Retail Establishments) is given in Appendix B, pp 588–91.

[1] cf Yates: *op cit.*

CHAPTER 7

QUALITY CONTROL

7.1 Statistical Control of Quality

An important application of the theory of sampling and significance in the industrial field is that of the statistical control of quality. It is discussed here very briefly to illustrate a different application of the principles set out in Chapter 5 from that considered in Chapter 6 above. Quality control is a specialised technique and, like sample surveys, has a literature of its own. This chapter attempts to do no more than to explain what it is and to indicate how it may be used to improve the technical efficiency of production processes.[1]

The quality of industrial products can be measured in various ways, but when we are concerned with mass-produced components, quality can generally be measured by a fairly simple characteristic of the component under consideration. Thus we may be interested in the width of a screw, the hardness of a bearing, the strength of a material, etc. If we think of quality in this way, it will be immediately evident that quality will never be absolutely constant. There will always be a certain amount of variation in quality, even if the production processes are themselves constant. Variation in quality can be attributed to two main types of cause:

1. *Chance causes.* These causes are very many in number, each one exercising only a trivial effect on the quality of the product. They are inherent in the production processes, in the sense that they will operate for any given set of processes. They can be modified only if the production processes are themselves modified. Small variations in the quality of raw materials or in the skill of manual operators are examples.

2. *Assignable causes.* These are causes which can be identified and will generally be related to variations in the productive processes themselves, eg mechanical faults in plant, faulty raw materials, etc. These causes interfere with the efficient working of the plant, and it is usually economically worth while to attempt to eliminate them.

---

[1] This chapter is largely based on Chapter 10 of O L Davies, (Ed): *Statistical Methods in Research and Production*, published in 1958 for the Imperial Chemical Industries, Ltd, by Oliver and Boyd, Ltd, by permission of the Imperial Chemical Industries, Ltd, and the Publishers.

If the variations in quality of a particular product are such that they can be attributed to chance causes solely, then we say that the process is under *statistical control*. This means that our observations of quality could all have come from the same homogeneous population, the variations in them being due to chance alone. This being so, valid predictions about the future behaviour of the data can be made, assuming that nothing affects the nature of the population from which the data are drawn. When a process is under statistical control, the variability of the quality of the product cannot be altered unless the production process is itself altered. However, if it can be shown that a process is out of statistical control, this means that certain assignable causes must be present affecting the variability of quality. These can be sought for and removed. The object of what is known as *quality control* is to detect assignable causes of variation in quality as soon as they occur in the production process.

7.2 Control Charts

If we have a certain measurable quality characteristic X (say, the width of a pipe) and we know that its mean value when the production process is in control is μ and its standard deviation is σ, then if we take samples of size N, we know that the sample mean $\bar{X}$ will be approximately normally distributed about a mean μ with a standard error $\frac{\sigma}{\sqrt{N}}$. Approximately 1 in 20 of samples drawn from the population will have means lying outside the limits $\mu \pm 1.96\frac{\sigma}{\sqrt{N}}$, and 1 in 500 will have them lying outside the limits $\mu \pm 3.09\frac{\sigma}{\sqrt{N}}$. As far as the latter set of limits are concerned, we can say that only very rarely will a mean $\bar{X}$ lie further away from μ than by about $3\frac{\sigma}{\sqrt{N}}$, just due to chance (in theory, about 27 times in 10 000). If we struck a particular $\bar{X}$ further from μ than $3\frac{\sigma}{\sqrt{N}}$, we should suspect that there was some assignable cause present which would account for it, eg something had gone wrong with the production process. This is the simple essence of quality control.

The application of quality control to a process of production can be divided into two stages:

1. The estimation of μ (known as the *process average*) and σ (the *process standard deviation*), and from μ and σ the estimation of the

control limits. In practice the limits $\mu \pm 3\dfrac{\sigma}{\sqrt{N}}$, where N is the size of samples to be tested, have been found satisfactory, in that it is usually economically worth while to check the production process when an observation lies outside these limits.

2. The selection of samples of the product of size N (in practice, a sample size of about 5 is satisfactory), such samples being taken from time to time as production proceeds, and the examination as to whether the means of the samples lie within the control limits. This is accomplished by means of a *control chart.*

To estimate μ and σ, it is usual to take about 100 observations. If the sample size is to be 5, these 100 observations are divided, in the order in which they were taken, into 20 samples of 5, and the 20 sample means are calculated, in order to see whether these twenty $\bar{X}$s are themselves within the control limits. For if they are not, the process cannot be initially under control and the estimation of μ and σ cannot be relied on. Once μ and σ have been satisfactorily estimated, the control limits can easily be ascertained and drawn on a chart. The μ and σ are, of course, only estimates of the underlying population values. The principles underlying quality control can, perhaps, best be appreciated by following through an example. Below are set out twenty samples of five observations each of the width of 10-centimetre steel pipes.

Table 7.1

MEASUREMENTS OF WIDTH OF STEEL PIPES
(to nearest one-hundredths cm)

(1)	(2)	(3)	(4)	(5)	(6)	(7)	(8)	(9)	(10)
9·81	10·05	10·29	9·79	10·12	9·89	9·87	9·75	9·91	10·00
9·93	10·13	9·94	9·96	10·11	9·72	9·99	10·05	9·94	10·07
9·97	9·97	9·96	9·98	9·82	10·05	10·01	9·95	10·00	9·84
9·99	10·03	10·03	9·98	9·93	9·95	10·13	9·95	10·20	9·88
10·04	9·87	10·10	10·04	10·00	10·00	10·11	9·91	10·02	10·07

(11)	(12)	(13)	(14)	(15)	(16)	(17)	(18)	(19)	(20)
9·84	10·01	10·03	10·05	9·90	9·86	10·06	9·96	9·93	9·93
10·23	10·07	10·03	9·96	9·99	10·03	9·97	10·14	10·09	10·06
9·96	10·06	9·85	9·97	10·04	10·09	9·94	10·15	9·94	9·94
9·96	9·89	10·08	10·01	10·17	9·91	10·19	9·86	10·10	10·02
10·04	9·97	10·12	10·00	10·15	9·90	10·00	9·92	10·13	9·99

The estimation of μ is straightforward. The mean of the above 100 observations is used as the estimate, or what amounts to the same thing, the mean of the sample means. The estimation of σ is usually carried out, not by computing it as the standard deviation of the 100 observations about their mean, but by computing the sums of squares of the deviations of the observations in each sample from the sample mean and pooling these sums. An estimate of σ^2 will then be given by the formula

$$\frac{\Sigma(X_1 - \bar{X}_1)^2 + \Sigma(X_2 - \bar{X}_2)^2 + \ldots \Sigma(X_k - \bar{X}_k)^2}{kN - k}$$

where the subscripts refer to the first, second sample, etc, and k is the number of samples. The advantage of this method of estimating σ is that it gives an estimate of variability based on variability within samples and hence eliminates any variability which might occur between samples due to other than chance causes. The presence of $kN - k$ in the denominator rather than kN is to avoid bias. In the following table are the necessary calculations using an arbitrary origin.

Table 7.2

COMPUTATION OF PROCESS AVERAGE AND STANDARD DEVIATION

Sample Number	Mean of Deviations from Arbitrary Origin of 10 cm		Sum of Squares of Deviations from Arbitrary Origin of 10 cm
	$\bar{x}'$	$\bar{x}'^2$	$\Sigma x'^2$
1	−0·052	0·002704	0·0436
2	0·010	0·000100	0·0381
3	0·064	0·004096	0·1002
4	−0·050	0·002500	0·0481
5	−0·004	0·000016	0·0638
6	−0·078	0·006084	0·0955
7	0·022	0·000484	0·0461
8	−0·078	0·006084	0·0781
9	0·014	0·000196	0·0521
10	−0·028	0·000784	0·0498
11	0·006	0·000036	0·0833
12	0·000	0·000000	0·0216
13	0·022	0·000484	0·0451
14	−0·002	0·000004	0·0051
15	0·050	0·002500	0·0631
16	−0·042	0·001764	0·0467
17	0·032	0·001024	0·0442
18	0·006	0·000036	0·0697
19	0·038	0·001444	0·0435
20	−0·012	0·000144	0·0126
Total	−0·082	0·030484	1·0503

$$\text{Estimate of } \mu = A + \frac{\bar{x}'_1 + \bar{x}'_2 + \ldots + \bar{x}'_k}{k}$$

$$= 10 - \frac{0 \cdot 082}{20} = 9 \cdot 996 \text{ centimetres}$$

Estimate of

$$\sigma = \sqrt{\frac{\Sigma x'_1{}^2 - N\bar{x}'_1{}^2 + \Sigma x'_2{}^2 - N\bar{x}'_2{}^2 + \ldots \Sigma x'_k{}^2 - N\bar{x}'_k{}^2}{kN - k}}$$

$$= \sqrt{\frac{1 \cdot 0503 - (5 \times 0 \cdot 030484)}{100 - 20}} = 0 \cdot 106 \text{ centimetres}$$

Having estimated μ and σ, the control limits are readily established at $\mu \pm 3\dfrac{\sigma}{\sqrt{N}}$, ie at $9 \cdot 996 \pm 0 \cdot 142$ for $N = 5$, ie the lower control limit will be $9 \cdot 854$ and the upper one $10 \cdot 138$. Fig 7.1 (opposite) shows these limits and also, to the left of the vertical line, the means of the 20 samples of 5 upon which the estimation of μ and σ is based.

It will be observed that the 20 sample means lie within the limits. This indicates that the process was under statistical control when these observations were made. Having established the control chart, samples of 5 are taken regularly, and their means are plotted. These are shown for samples number 21 to 23 to the right of the vertical line. It will be observed that sample 23 indicates that the process is out of control. Such a value for $\bar{X}$ would occur very rarely due to chance, and consequently there is a presumption that an assignable cause is present. It will be worth while looking for that cause immediately. However, in the case illustrated in Fig 7.1 the trouble probably started at about the 21st or 22nd sample. This is suggested by the trend of the points at the right-hand side of the diagram. Distinct trends are unlikely to be due to chance, and a trend in the points should be just as suggestive as a point lying outside the control limits. Likewise, a number of points hovering fairly close to a control limit would be suggestive. It will also be realised that occasionally a search for trouble may be undertaken when no trouble really exists, for points will occur outside the control limits very occasionally just due to chance. This corresponds to the Type I error discussed in section 5.10 above. As data are accumulated, μ and σ can be re-estimated from time to time, but only data obtained when the process is under control should be used. It will be appreciated by this stage that, in using a control chart, we are in fact testing the hypothesis that the samples come from a population with a mean and standard deviation as specified in the chart.

As well as watching the average level of quality, as in Fig 7.1, it is customary to watch the average variability of quality. This can be done by ascertaining control limits to the value of the standard devia-

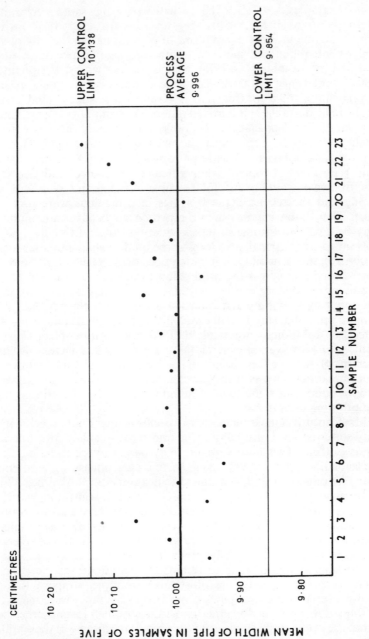

Fig 7.1 Control chart

tion of samples, s. Clearly the s's will vary from sample to sample. Methods are available for drawing up a control chart in terms of s, just as the one in Fig 7.1 is in terms of $\bar{X}$, although in the case of s the upper control limit will alone be of practical significance, since abnormal lack of variability will not be a cause for worry. Frequently in practice the range of the values in the samples is taken as a measure of variability, and a control chart in terms of the range is used, instead of one in terms of the standard deviation. This simplifies the arithmetic.

It should be clear that it is desirable that not only the mean level of quality should be kept constant but also its variability. Hence, a control chart for s is just as important as one for $\bar{X}$. It may happen that $\bar{X}$ goes out of control, while s remains in control and vice versa. The first case would occur, for example, if the setting of a tool were wrong and the second if the bearings in a machine were becoming worn. Hence, the way in which the two charts behave in conjunction may be a clue to trouble in the production process. Finally, it is important to emphasise that so long as the quality characteristics remain in control, the variability in it which does occur is inevitable and cannot be modified unless the production process is itself modified.

Sometimes quality can be judged, not by taking a direct measurement, but by setting up a standard and measuring the percentage not coming up to that standard in the samples. This is called the *percentage defective*, p. Methods are available for drawing up control charts in terms of p. However, in general, these are not as satisfactory as charts in terms of $\bar{X}$, since they do not make use of as much information. The percentage defective is utilised when Go—No Go gauges are used, and, of course, in some tests of quality it alone can be utilised, eg in the proofing of ammunition.

Most products must be made to specifications. These specifications may state the level of quality to be aimed at, together with tolerance limits outside of which the quality may be permitted to lie only very occasionally, say 1 in 500 times. In this case, unless these tolerance limits lie outside $\mu \pm 3.09\ \sigma$, the specifications cannot be met. This is so because, even if the process is under statistical control and working at the specified level of quality, 1 in 500 items will have a value outside the limits $\mu \pm 3.09\ \sigma$ just due to chance. If the tolerance limits lie within $\mu \pm 3.09\ \sigma$, it will be necessary either to widen the tolerance limits, ie to relax the specifications, or else to alter the process of production to reduce σ, ie to reduce the variability of the product. Thus, referring back to the illustrative example, suppose that the manufacturer of the steel pipes claimed that his pipes were made to a specification of 10 centimetres in width within 0.15 cm either way. From the calculations made above we have an estimate of the standard deviation of 0.106 centimetres. Consequently, even if the mean width of pipes were in the long run 10 centimetres exactly, we should expect about 15 per cent of all pipes to fail to meet the specifications. This is because a tolerance of $\pm\,0.15$ represents a distance of $\pm\,\dfrac{0.15}{0.106} = \pm\,1.42$ standard deviations away from the mean. Assuming that the distribution is normal, approximately 15 per cent of the population will lie further from the mean than this. The manufacturer must either relax his specifications or modify the production processes to reduce the variability of the product.

7.3 Advantages of Quality Control

The general objective of quality control is to maintain quality. The alternative and traditional technique is *100 per cent inspection* of the output of a product. Comparing quality control with 100 per cent inspection, quality control has outstanding advantages.

1. Since quality control involves inspecting only a fraction of the output of a product, costs of inspection are greatly reduced and efficiency of inspection increased.

2. With 100 per cent inspection, unwanted variations in quality may be detected later than with the continuous sampling technique of quality control. This means that a greater volume of faulty products will have been produced, and a greater delay in the rectification of faults in the production process will occur. Quality control ensures early detection of faults and, hence, a minimum waste of reject production. The control chart provides a graphic summary of how production is proceeding.

3. Quality control enables a process to be brought into and held in a state of statistical control, ie a state in which variability is the result of chance causes alone. When a process is under control, the quality of the product can be accurately specified, in that limits can be specified within which, say, 99 per cent of the product will lie. So long as statistical control continues, these specifications can be accurately predicted for the future, which even 100 per cent inspection cannot guarantee to do. Consequently it is possible to assess whether the production processes are capable of turning out products which will comply with any given set of specifications.

4. Whether or not a change in the production process results in a significant change in quality can be readily detected by quality control.

5. When the test of quality is destructive, eg proofing of ammunition, testing breaking strength in cables, etc, 100 per cent inspection is impossible. In such cases sampling must be resorted to, and the application of the proper sampling methods of quality control ensures not only that the quality is controlled, but also that valid inferences about the total output are drawn from the samples.

CHAPTER 8

REGRESSION AND CORRELATION

8.1 Relations between Variables

In the preceding chapters statistical description and statistical analysis have for the most part been treated in terms of one variable only. Thus, when we had a sample of houses, we considered only one variable at a time, eg rent. However, if we select a random sample of houses from a given population, we may take measurements of several characteristics associated with each unit in the sample, eg measurements relating to rent, age, size, location, etc. Given such information, we may wish to investigate whether a relationship exists among the variables, and if so, how such a relationship might be used to predict values of one variable, eg rent, from a knowledge of the values of the other variables. Our purpose in this chapter is to introduce the reader to the basic statistical methods for studying relationships between two or more variables.

It is well to emphasise from the outset that our concern in this chapter is with statistical as distinct from exact relationships. If we have an expression such as $V = h^3$, where V is the volume of a cube and h its dimension, the relationship between V and h is an exact relationship; that is, knowing, for instance, that $h = 4$, we can calculate *the* associated value of V as 64. In economics, and in the social sciences generally, we are seldom able to give exact predictions of the value of a variable from a knowledge of the values of other variables. Rather, if a relationship between two variables X and Y can be established, the relationship can tell us the value of Y which *on the average* we can expect to be associated with a given value of X. Relationships of this kind are also referred to as *stochastic* relationships in contrast with exact relationships.

If a stochastic relationship between two or more variables can be expressed by a mathematical equation, so that on the basis of this equation we can estimate the average values of Y associated with the given Xs, the method of analysis is known as *regression analysis*. In regression analysis, the variable whose average value is being estimated is called the *dependent* variable; it is generally denoted by the symbol Y. The variable, or variables, on which the estimate is to be based are referred to as the *independent* or *explanatory* variables. When a regression relationship contains only one independent variable, generally denoted by X, it is referred to as a *two-variable* or *simple* regression. When more independent variables are being used to explain the behaviour of the dependent variable Y, the analysis is known as *multiple regression*; often, the several explanatory variables are indicated by subscripts, eg X_1, X_2 etc. It should be stressed that the terms 'dependent' and 'independent' do not imply that the variables are necessarily related in a causal way. Rather, what is meant is that if we know the mathematical form of the relationship linking X and Y we can always compute values of Y corresponding to particular Xs. We also note that in regression analysis the independent variable X is a variable with values that can be preassigned or that can be predicted without error. The dependent variable, on the other hand, is a *random* variable with a known or assumed probability distribution.

Whereas regression analysis investigates the nature of the relationship between two variables X and Y, *correlation analysis* measures the strength of such relationship. The basic tool of correlation analysis is the correlation coefficient. As already explained in Chapter 4, section 4.14, the correlation coefficient measures the degree of linear association between two jointly distributed random variables. In most practical work, the variables being investigated are assumed to be distributed in a special joint probability distribution known as the normal bivariate distribution. As we shall explain further below, the regression and the correlation models are mathematically related, and the correlation coefficient also serves as a useful tool for measuring the goodness of fit of a regression relationship to the observed data.

In developing the basic ideas and techniques of regression and correlation analysis we shall first focus on the *description* of two-variable data; this discussion parallels Chapter 3 for one-variable data. The *analysis* of the data for purposes of statistical inference is found in sections 8.4 to 8.7. In section 8.8 the basic regression model is extended to more than two variables, and the last three sections consider some of the special problems arising from the application of regression and correlation analysis to economic data.

8.2 Descriptive Measures of Regression and Correlation for Ungrouped Data

Suppose we wish to investigate the relation between two variables X and Y. We have a group of N units, eg tenanted houses, and for each unit we have two measurements: the age of house in years (X) and the rent in dollars (Y). For illustration, suppose that our observations for 11 houses are as follows:

Table 8.1

House	Age (years)	Weekly Rent (dollars)
1st	3	50
2nd	12	32
3rd	5	40
4th	7	33
5th	8	45
6th	19	13
7th	10	30
8th	22	14
9th	15	28
10th	8	51
11th	25	26

The above data can be described with respect to the X- and Y- variable separately by the ordinary measures we have so far discussed, eg $\bar{X}$, $\bar{Y}$, s_X, s_Y, but we now need an additional measure (or measures) to describe the possible relationship between X and Y.

One can always get some idea whether there is any relationship present by plotting the values on a *scatter diagram*. We measure the X-variable on the horizontal and the Y-variable on the vertical axis and plot a point for each pair of X and Y values. This is done for the data of Table 8.1 in Fig 8.1.

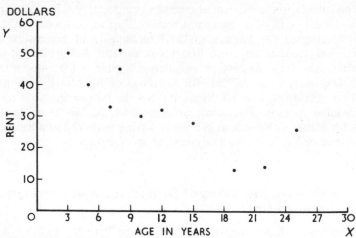

Fig 8.1 Rent and age of a group of eleven houses

It is evident that in this case there is some inverse relationship between rent and age, ie the greater the age the lower the rent.

If we had a large number of observations there would be a large number of points in the diagram. If there were no relationship we

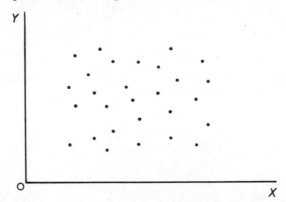

Fig 8.2

should expect the scatter to look as shown in Fig 8.2. Here there is no evidence of a tendency for the Y values to be related to the X values in any particular way. If there were a perfect relationship between X and Y, so that Y is determined when X is given, we might get

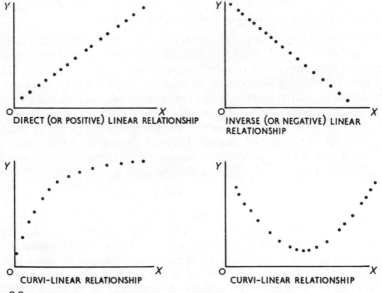

DIRECT (OR POSITIVE) LINEAR RELATIONSHIP

INVERSE (OR NEGATIVE) LINEAR RELATIONSHIP

CURVI-LINEAR RELATIONSHIP

CURVI-LINEAR RELATIONSHIP

Fig 8.3

In practice relationships are seldom perfect, and they tend to show up as in Fig 8.4.

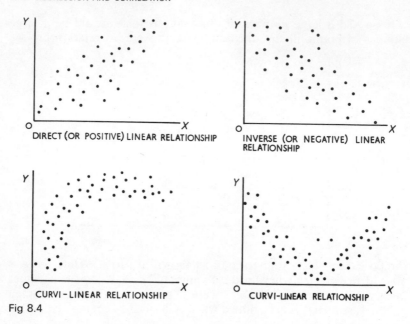

CURVI-LINEAR RELATIONSHIP

Fig 8.4

Fitting a Line by the Method of Least Squares

If we have a set of data for two variables X and Y, our first objective in regression analysis is to find a mathematical equation that would describe the average relationship between the values of X and Y. Of all possible equations that can be used to describe such relationship the simplest and the most commonly found is the equation of a straight line. Thus, suppose we have a set of N pairs of observations (X_1, Y_1), $(X_2, Y_2) \ldots (X_N, Y_N)$ which appear on the scatter diagram as shown in Fig 8.5. Although the relation between the values of X and Y is not an exact one, it would seem reasonable to approximate the relationship between X and Y by the linear equation

$$Y_c = a + bX$$

In this equation a and b are constants which determine the position of the line, a being the intercept of the straight line on the Y-axis and b its slope, ie the change in Y per unit change in X. The symbol Y_c stands for the value of Y *computed* from the relationship for a given X. Evidently, since the relationship is not perfect, observed values of Y will not necessarily be the same as Y_c, for given X. In Fig 8.5 below a straight line relationship has been drawn in. This line expresses the average relationship between Y and given Xs and is called the *linear regression of Y on X*. The constant b is known as the *regression co-*

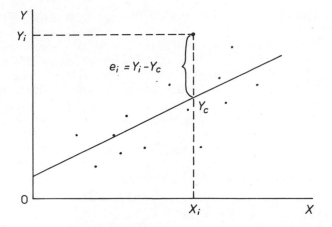

Fig 8.5

efficient of Y on X. The question is how shall we fit such a line to given plot points, ie how shall we determine the constants *a* and *b*.

Clearly we want to determine the values of *a* and *b* in such a way that the fitted line is as close as possible to the *N* plot points, ie we want to minimise the overall discrepancy between the plot points and the line. In Fig 8.5, consider the typical pair of observations, denoted by (X_i, Y_i). If the line fitted to the points has intercept *a* and slope *b*, then the value of *Y* computed from the relationship when *X* is X_i is $Y_c = a + bX_i$, and the deviation of the observed value Y_i from the computed value Y_c is measured by

$$e_i = Y_i - Y_c$$

The deviation e_i is called a *residual*. Evidently, the residuals can be positive or negative, depending on whether the observed value of *Y* lies above or below the fitted line. Now, it would seem that the sum of all the residuals would be a measure of the overall discrepancy of the points from the line, ie Σe_i, for $i = 1, 2, \ldots N$. However, since in this sum the positive residuals and the negative residuals will tend to cancel out, the sum Σe_i cannot be used as a measure of overall discrepancy, any more than the sum $\Sigma(X - \bar{X}) = \Sigma x$ could be used in Chapter 3 to measure overall dispersion of a variable *X* from its mean. However, if we square the residuals, and fix the line so that the sum of the squared residuals Σe_i^2 is made as small as possible, we shall obtain a line which will be representative of the relationship between *X* and *Y*. This is analogous to using $\bar{X}$ as representative of a set of values of the variable *X*, for it will be recalled (see section 3.4, p 44) that the sum of the squares of the deviations of a variable *X* from an origin is smallest when the origin is the mean, ie $\Sigma(X - A)^2$ is a minimum for $A = \bar{X}$.

Let us now recapitulate. We have N pairs of observations $(X_1, Y_1), (X_2, Y_2), \ldots, (X_N, Y_N)$. We wish to fit a line of relationship to these points. This line is to be $Y_c = a + bX$, and a and b are to be selected so that Σe_i^2 is a minimum, ie the sum of the squares of the vertical deviations of the observed points from the line is to be a minimum. This procedure is known as fitting a curve by the *method of least squares*. An important advantage of the method of least squares is that while being computationally simple, it also yields estimators with certain desirable statistical properties, as we shall explain further below.

To determine the values of a and b that satisfy the above requirements we now write[1]

$$W = \Sigma e^2$$
$$= \Sigma(Y - a - bX)^2$$

Differentiating W with respect to a and b, we have

$$\frac{\partial W}{\partial a} = -2\Sigma(Y - a - bX)$$

and

$$\frac{\partial W}{\partial b} = -2\Sigma X(Y - a - bX)$$

$$= -2\Sigma(XY - aX - bX^2)$$

For W to be a minimum $\dfrac{\partial W}{\partial a}$ and $\dfrac{\partial W}{\partial b}$ must both equal 0, which they will do when

$$\Sigma(Y - a - bX) = 0,$$

and

$$\Sigma(XY - aX - bX^2) = 0$$

ie when

$$\left. \begin{array}{l} \Sigma Y = Na + b\Sigma X \\ \Sigma XY = a\Sigma X + b\Sigma X^2 \end{array} \right\}$$

These two equations are known as the *normal equations* for determining a and b. If we determine the numerical values of a and b such that these equations hold, the least squares equation $Y_c = a + bX$ will satisfy two algebraic properties. First, the deviations of observations about the regression line sum to zero, ie $\Sigma e = 0$; secondly, the sum of squared deviations from the line, ie Σe^2 is a minimum.

Solving the normal equations for a and b, we have from the first

---

[1] For easier mathematical manipulation we omit the subscript i. Unless otherwise stated, the summation signs in this section refer to a set of N observations.

equation that

$$a = \bar{Y} - b\bar{X}$$

[handwritten: but $b = 0$ so $a = \bar{Y}$]

and from the second

$$\Sigma XY = \bar{Y}\Sigma X - b\bar{X}\Sigma X + b\Sigma X^2$$

ie
$$b = \frac{\Sigma XY - N\bar{X}\bar{Y}}{\Sigma X^2 - N\bar{X}^2}$$

[handwritten: $b\Sigma X^2 - b\bar{X}\Sigma X = \Sigma xy - \bar{Y}\Sigma x$]

The expression for b can be further simplified by putting $x = X - \bar{X}$ and $y = Y - \bar{Y}$, ie x and y are the deviations of X and Y from their respective means. Now

$$X = x + \bar{X}, \text{ and } Y = y + \bar{Y}$$

so that
$$\Sigma XY = \Sigma xy + \bar{X}\Sigma x + \bar{Y}\Sigma y + N\bar{X}\bar{Y}$$
$$= \Sigma xy + N\bar{X}\bar{Y} \quad (\text{since } \Sigma x \text{ and } \Sigma y = 0)$$

and similarly
$$\Sigma X^2 = \Sigma x^2 + N\bar{X}^2$$

Hence
$$b = \frac{\Sigma xy}{\Sigma x^2}$$

Accordingly we can write the regression of Y on X as

$$Y_c = \bar{Y} - b\bar{X} + bX \quad (\text{since } a = \bar{Y} - b\bar{X})$$

ie
$$(Y_c - \bar{Y} = b(X - \bar{X})$$

where
$$b = \frac{\Sigma xy}{\Sigma x^2}$$

Detailed consideration of the interpretation of the regression equation $Y_c = a + bX$ is reserved for sections 8.4 to 8.7 below. For the present it suffices to regard the equation as a measure of the average relationship between X and Y, such that for a given X, Y_c is the value of Y which we would on the average expect to be associated with that X. The regression coefficient b measures the change in Y which occurs on the average per unit change in X. Y_c is, of course, expressed in the same units as Y. It will be noted that when $X = \bar{X}$, $Y_c = \bar{Y}$, so that the regression line passes through the means of the Xs and Ys.

If there is no relationship between X and Y, the points on the scatter diagram will not show any particular pattern (see Fig 8.2 above). Consequently, values of X above their mean $\bar{X}$ will be paired with values of Y above their mean $\bar{Y}$ as often as they are paired with values below $\bar{Y}$, and similarly for values of X below $\bar{X}$, hence $\Sigma xy = \Sigma(X - \bar{X})$ $(Y - \bar{Y})$ will be approximately zero, since positive and negative xys will cancel out. In this case b will be zero, and the regression line will be the horizontal line $Y_c = \bar{Y}$. Such a line indicates that the value of Y does not depend on the associated value of X, ie that there is no relationship between X and Y.

The actual computation of $\dfrac{\Sigma xy}{\Sigma x^2}$ is rendered simple by working from arbitrary origins. In machine computations it is often simplest to choose arbitary origins of zero. In this case we can apply directly the results obtained from the normal equations, ie

$$b = \frac{\Sigma XY - N\bar{X}\bar{Y}}{\Sigma X^2 - N\bar{X}^2}$$

where ΣX^2, ΣXY, $\bar{X}$ and $\bar{Y}$ are readily obtainable from the observed data.[1] The fitting of a regression line to actual data is illustrated in the example below.

Example 8.1

The data in the table below refer to a sample of 11 tenanted houses.
(a) Plot the data on a scatter diagram.
(b) Calculate the linear regression equation of rent on age of houses.
(c) Draw in this equation on the scatter diagram.

Age (years) X	Rent (dollars) Y	XY	X^2	Y^2
3	50	150	9	2 500
12	32	384	144	1 024
5	40	200	25	1 600
7	33	231	49	1 089
8	45	360	64	2 025
19	13	247	361	169
10	30	300	100	900
22	14	308	484	196
15	28	420	225	784
8	51	408	64	2 601
25	26	650	625	676
		3658	2150	13 564

The last column in the above table and the sum Σy^2 computed below are required for subsequent examples. The primary calculations are as follows:

[1] For arbitrary origins other than zero, we write

$$x' = X - A, \text{ and } y' = Y - B$$

where A and B are arbitrary origins, so that

$$\bar{x}' = \bar{X} - A, \text{ and } \bar{y}' = \bar{Y} - B$$

Then

$$\Sigma xy = \Sigma x'y' - N\bar{x}'\bar{y}' - N\bar{x}'\bar{y}' + N\bar{x}'\bar{y}'$$
$$= \Sigma x'y' - N\bar{x}'\bar{y}'$$

$$\bar{X} = \frac{\Sigma X}{N} = 12 \cdot 18182 \qquad \bar{Y} = \frac{\Sigma Y}{N} = 32 \cdot 90909$$

$$\Sigma x^2 = \Sigma X^2 - N\bar{X}^2 = 2150 - 1632 \cdot 364 = 517 \cdot 636$$

$$\Sigma y^2 = \Sigma Y^2 - N\bar{Y}^2 = 13\,564 - 11\,913 \cdot 091 = 1650 \cdot 909$$

$$\Sigma xy = \Sigma X Y - N\bar{X}\bar{Y} = 3658 - 4409 \cdot 818 = -751 \cdot 818$$

We then have

$$b = \frac{\Sigma xy}{\Sigma x^2} = -\frac{751 \cdot 818}{517 \cdot 636} = -1 \cdot 4524$$

$$a = \bar{Y} - b\bar{X} = 32 \cdot 909 - (-1 \cdot 4524)(12 \cdot 182) = 50 \cdot 60$$

and the regression equation of rent on age of houses is

$$Y_c = 50 \cdot 60 - 1 \cdot 452X$$

This can be interpreted by saying that the data under consideration suggest that for an increase of one year in the age of a house we should expect rent on the average to fall by $1·45.

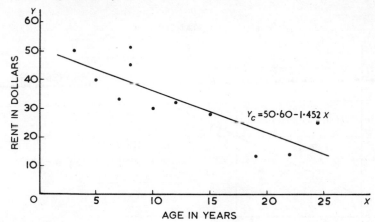

Fig 8.6

Measures of Closeness of Fit

The line $Y_c = a + bX$ gives a summary measure of the relationship between Y and given Xs. It does not measure the strength of the relationship. This depends on how well the line describes the relationship, ie how closely the points cluster about the line.

If we have N values of Y, they will vary amongst themselves, and a measure of this variation is $\Sigma(Y - \bar{Y})^2 = \Sigma y^2$. But some of this

and from section 3.5, p 60 above

$$\Sigma x^2 = \Sigma x'^2 - N\bar{x}'^2$$

These two results give Σxy and Σx^2 in terms of arbitrary deviations.

variation may be due to the fact that the Ys are associated with Xs, and the Xs are varying. If the relationship between the Xs and Ys were quite perfect so that a particular Y is always associated with a particular X, all the variability of the Ys would be explained by the relationship. On the other hand, if there were no relationship, none of the variability could thus be explained. In Fig 8.7 are plotted a number of observations and the regression line computed from them. A horizontal line at $\bar{Y}$ and a vertical line at $\bar{X}$ have been drawn in. As has been noted above, the regression line must pass through the intersection of these two lines. Let Y_i represent a particular observation of Y associated with a given value of X equal to X_i. As can be seen from the diagram, the distance representing the deviation of Y_i from the mean of the Ys, ie the deviation $(Y_i - \bar{Y})$, can be split into two parts—one, the deviation of the regression line from $\bar{Y}$, ie $(Y_c - \bar{Y})$, and the other, the deviation of Y_i from the regression line, ie $(Y_i - Y_c)$.

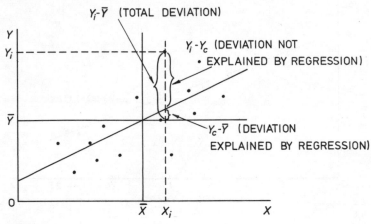

Fig 8.7

The first part arises because X_i lies to the right of $\bar{X}$, and hence the corresponding Y_c must be greater than $\bar{Y}$, since, as has been shown above, the regression line is $Y_c - \bar{Y} = b(X - \bar{X})$, and in this case b is positive. Consequently, this part of the total deviation can be regarded as being 'explained' by the regression. The other part of the deviation, the residual $e_i = Y_i - Y_c$, cannot thus be explained, as it results from the inherent variability of the Ys for a *given* X. For a particular observation Y_i we may therefore write

$$(Y_i - \bar{Y}) = (Y_c - \bar{Y}) + e_i$$

Table 8.2

COMPUTATION OF UNEXPLAINED, EXPLAINED AND TOTAL VARIATION:
REGRESSION OF RENT ON AGE OF HOUSES

| Rent | | Deviations | | | Variation | | |
Observed Y	Computed Y_c	$Y - Y_c$	$Y_c - \bar{Y}$	$Y - \bar{Y}$	Unexplained $(Y - Y_c)^2$	Explained $(Y_c - \bar{Y})^2$	Total $(Y - \bar{Y})^2$
50	46·2448	3·7552	13·3357	17·0909	14·1015	177·8409	292·0989
40	43·3400	−3·3400	10·4309	7·0909	11·1556	108·8037	50·2809
33	40·4352	−7·4352	7·5261	0·0909	55·2822	56·6422	0·0082
51	38·9828	12·0172	6·0737	18·0909	144·4131	36·8898	327·2807
45	38·9828	6·0172	6·0737	12·0909	36·2067	36·8898	146·1899
30	36·0780	−6·0780	3·1689	−2·9091	36·9421	10·0419	8·4629
32	33·1732	−1·1732	0·2641	−0·9091	1·3764	0·0697	0·8265
28	28·8160	−0·8160	−4·0931	−4·9091	0·6659	16·7535	24·0993
13	23·0064	−10·0064	−9·9027	−19·9091	100·1280	98·0635	396·3723
14	18·6492	−4·6492	−14·2599	−18·9091	21·6151	203·3447	357·5541
26	14·2920	11·7080	−18·6171	−6·9091	137·0773	346·5964	47·7357
		−0·0004	0·0003	−0·0001	558·9639	1091·9361	1650·9094
							(a)

(a) Because of rounding errors, there is a slight discrepancy between the sum of unexplained and explained variation and the amount of total variation recorded in the last column.

Squaring and summing over all N observations, we have

$$\Sigma(Y_i - \bar{Y})^2 = \Sigma(Y_c - \bar{Y})^2 + \Sigma e_i^2 + 2\Sigma(Y_c - \bar{Y})e_i$$

Since $Y_c - \bar{Y} = b(X - \bar{X})$, the last right-hand term becomes

$$2\Sigma(Y_c - \bar{Y})e_i = 2\Sigma b(X_i - \bar{X})e_i$$
$$= 2b[\Sigma X_i e_i - \bar{X}\Sigma e_i]$$

But, by the algebraic properties of the least-squares regression line, $\Sigma e_i = 0$, and it can be shown that $\Sigma X_i e_i = 0$ also.[1] Hence

$$2\Sigma(Y_c - \bar{Y})e_i = 0$$

We thus have the total variability of Y, as measured by the sum of squares $\Sigma(Y - \bar{Y})^2$, resolved into two components, ie

Total variation = Explained variation + Unexplained variation

$$\Sigma(Y - \bar{Y})^2 \quad = \quad \Sigma(Y_c - \bar{Y})^2 \quad + \quad \Sigma e^2$$

The first component measures the amount of variability of the Ys which is *explained* by the line of relationship in the sense that it is possible to attribute this amount to the effect of the relationship in translating variability in the Xs into variability in the Ys. The second component measures the amount of unexplained variability.[2] The stronger the relationship, ie the more closely the points are clustered about the line, the larger will be the first component relative to the second.

In Table 8.2, the partition of total variation of Y into these two components is verified arithmetically with reference to our example of 11 rents. The first column records the actual observations and the second the computed values obtained by substituting the given values of X, in ascending order, into the regression equation $Y_c = 50.60 - 1.452X$. From the table we can see that

Total variation = Explained variation + Unexplained variation

$$1650.90 \quad = \quad 1091.94 \quad + \quad 558.96$$

Dividing both sides of the equation derived in the preceding paragraphs by $\Sigma(Y - \bar{Y})^2$, we have

---

[1] This can be readily verified by substituting $Y_i = Y_c + e_i = a + bX_i + e_i$ into the second normal equation

$$\Sigma X_i Y_i = a\Sigma X_i + b\Sigma X_i^2$$

We then have

$$a\Sigma X_i + b\Sigma X_i^2 + \Sigma X_i e_i = a\Sigma X_i + b\Sigma X_i^2$$

and therefore

$$\Sigma X_i e_i = 0$$

[2] See footnote on p 255 above.

$$\frac{\Sigma(Y_c - \bar{Y})^2}{\Sigma(Y - \bar{Y})^2} + \frac{\Sigma e^2}{\Sigma(Y - \bar{Y})^2} = 1$$

We now define

$$r^2 = \frac{\text{Explained variation}}{\text{Total variation}}$$

ie

$$r^2 = \frac{\Sigma(Y_c - \bar{Y})^2}{\Sigma(Y - \bar{Y})^2}$$

$$= 1 - \frac{\Sigma e^2}{\Sigma(Y - \bar{Y})^2}$$

as the *coefficient of determination*, measuring the proportion of the total variation of Y that can be attributed to the relationship between X and Y. The coefficient of determination r^2 gives a measure of the closeness of fit of the regression line to the observed points. If all the observed values of Y lie on the line, the residual sum of squares Σe^2 is zero, and $r^2 = 1$. If X contributes nothing to the explanation of the variability in Y, then $\Sigma e^2 = \Sigma(Y - \bar{Y})^2$, and hence $r^2 = 0$.

A further measure of the goodness of fit of a regression line is the *coefficient of linear correlation*. The correlation coefficient r can be defined as the square root of the coefficient of determination, ie

$$r = \sqrt{\frac{\Sigma(Y_c - \bar{Y})^2}{\Sigma(Y - \bar{Y})^2}}$$

$$= \sqrt{\frac{\Sigma b^2 x^2}{\Sigma y^2}} \quad \text{(since } Y_c - \bar{Y} = b(X - \bar{X}))$$

$$r = \frac{\Sigma xy}{\sqrt{\Sigma x^2 \Sigma y^2}}$$

The sign of r is taken as the same as that of Σxy, (ie the same as that of b). We know that r^2 cannot exceed unity, and hence $-1 \leqslant r \leqslant +1$. Perfect negative relationship is indicated by $r = -1$ and perfect positive relationship by $r = 1$. For no relationship, the term Σxy in the above formula is zero, and hence r is also zero.

In interpreting the coefficients of determination and correlation in regression analysis it is important to bear in mind that both are measures of the goodness of fit of the least-squares regression line, but they give no indication of the *slope* of the relationship. It may happen that the fitted regression line is quite flat, and yet the numerical values of r and r^2 are relatively high. This would be the case if the observed points were closely concentrated about the regression line, so that the line provides a very good fit to the data. On the other hand, numerically low values of r and r^2, irrespective of the slope of the regression line, always indicate a poor fit.

Both the coefficient of correlation and determination can be obtained directly from the sums of squares $\Sigma(Y_c - \bar{Y})^2$ and $\Sigma(Y - \bar{Y})^2$, as given, for example, in Table 8.2 above. However, this method is computationally laborious, and in practice we make use of the previously computed quantities Σxy, Σx^2 and Σy^2.

Example 8.2

Find the coefficients of determination and linear correlation for the regression of rent on age of houses in Example 8.1 above.

We have $\quad \Sigma xy = -751{\cdot}818$, $\Sigma x^2 = 517{\cdot}636$, $\Sigma y^2 = 1650{\cdot}909$

so that
$$r^2 = \frac{(\Sigma xy)^2}{\Sigma x^2 \Sigma y^2} = 0{\cdot}6614$$

Verifying this result, from Table 8.2 we have

$$r^2 = \frac{\Sigma(Y_c - \bar{Y})^2}{\Sigma(Y - \bar{Y})^2} = \frac{1091{\cdot}9361}{1650{\cdot}9094} = 0{\cdot}6614$$

We can say that 66 per cent of the variability of rents in this case can be explained by the relation between rent and age; $r = -0{\cdot}81$ is the coefficient of linear correlation between rents and age.

Standard Error of Estimate

As well as having a line of regression of Y on X and the measures r and r^2 describing its goodness of fit, for certain purposes we want a measure of the *absolute* dispersion of the Y values about the line. Such a measure is analogous to the standard deviation calculated for a single variable measuring the dispersion of the Xs about $\bar{X}$. We have already used the sum of the squared residuals $\Sigma e^2 = \Sigma(Y - Y_c)^2$ as a measure of the variability of the Y values about the regression line. We now define

$$s_e^2 = \frac{\Sigma e^2}{N - 2}$$

as the *variance* of the values of the least-squares residuals e. The divisor $N - 2$ is to avoid bias, just as the divisor in the formula for the sample variance s^2 is $N - 1$. For practical purposes, however, variances are not so easily interpreted, and if we write

$$s_e = \sqrt{\frac{\Sigma e^2}{N - 2}} \quad .$$

we shall have a measure of dispersion about the line expressed in the same units as the variable Y. This is called the *standard error of estimate* of the least-squares regression of Y on X. If the sum of squares unexplained by the regression is known, s_e can be computed directly from the above formula. In machine computations, convenient formulae for finding s_e are[1]

$$s_e = \sqrt{\frac{\Sigma y^2 - b\Sigma xy}{N - 2}}$$

or

$$s_e = \sqrt{\frac{(1 - r^2)\Sigma y^2}{N - 2}}$$

Example 8.3

Calculate the standard error of estimate of the regression of rent on age of houses for example 8.1 above.

We have
$$s_e = \sqrt{\frac{\Sigma y^2 - b\Sigma xy}{N - 2}}$$
$$= \sqrt{\frac{1650\cdot909 - (-1\cdot452 \times -751\cdot818)}{9}}$$
$$= \$7\cdot88$$

Using the results of Table 8.2, it can be easily checked that
$$s_e = \sqrt{\frac{\Sigma(Y - Y_c)^2}{N - 2}} = \sqrt{\frac{558\cdot9639}{9}}$$
$$= \$7\cdot88$$

Linear Regression of X on Y

So far we have considered the regression of Y on X, ie we treated X as the independent variable and asked how Y is related to given Xs. However, in some situations we may equally well take Y as the independent variable and consider the linear equation $X_c = c + dY$

---

[1] These formulae may be derived as follows:
$$\Sigma e^2 = \Sigma(Y - Y_c)^2 = \Sigma[(Y - \bar{Y}) - b(X - \bar{X})]^2$$
$$= \Sigma(y - bx)^2$$
$$= \Sigma y^2 - b(2\Sigma xy - b\Sigma x^2)$$
$$= \Sigma y^2 - b(2\Sigma xy - \Sigma xy)$$
$$= \Sigma y^2 - b\Sigma xy$$

Dividing through by Σy^2, we also have
$$\Sigma e^2 = \left[1 - \frac{(\Sigma xy)^2}{\Sigma x^2 \Sigma y^2}\right]\Sigma y^2$$
$$= (1 - r^2)\Sigma y^2$$

as a measure of the average relationship between X and given Ys. The equation

$$X_c = c + dY$$

is known as the *linear regression of X on Y* and d is the *regression coefficient of X on Y*. Once again, we shall want the overall discrepancy between the observed values of X and the fitted line to be as small as possible. This can be accomplished by determining the constants c and d such that the sum of the squared deviations $\Sigma(X - X_c)^2$ is a minimum.

It can soon be appreciated that the two lines of regression will not coincide, unless there is a perfect fit. This can be seen from the following simple case in Fig 8.8, taking three points only. The regression of Y on X is found by minimising in the vertical direction and is given

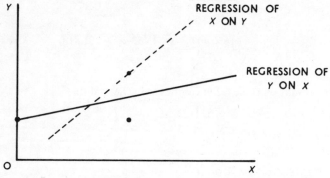

Fig 8.8

by the solid line, but the regression of X on Y is found by minimising in the horizontal direction and is given by the broken line. In the diagram the sum of the deviations $\Sigma(X - X_c)^2$ is obviously less from the broken than the solid line.

Using the least-squares criterion for determining c and d, we find

$$d = \frac{\Sigma xy}{\Sigma y^2} \qquad \text{and} \qquad c = \bar{X} - d\bar{Y}$$

The regression of X on Y will also pass through the two means, so that the two regression lines intersect at $(\bar{X}, \bar{Y})$. It can further be shown that

$$\Sigma(X - \bar{X})^2 = \Sigma(X - X_c)^2 + \Sigma(X_c - \bar{X})^2$$

and r can be defined as $r = \sqrt{\dfrac{\Sigma(X_c - \bar{X})^2}{\Sigma(X - \bar{X})^2}}$

This reduces to $\qquad r = \dfrac{\Sigma xy}{\sqrt{\Sigma x^2 \Sigma y^2}}$

as before. We note that the relative goodness of fit of the two lines of regression, as measured by r and r^2, is the same. If we next write $s_{e'}$ as the standard error of estimate of the regression of X on Y, we have

$$s_{e'} = \sqrt{\frac{\Sigma e'^2}{N-2}} \qquad \text{(where } \Sigma e'^2 = \Sigma(X - X_c)^2\text{)}$$

$$= \sqrt{\frac{\Sigma x^2 - d\Sigma xy}{N-2}}$$

or

$$s_{e'} = \sqrt{\frac{(1 - r^2)\Sigma x^2}{N-2}}$$

Further since $\qquad b = \dfrac{\Sigma xy}{\Sigma x^2} \quad \text{and} \quad d = \dfrac{\Sigma xy}{\Sigma y^2}$

then $\qquad r = \sqrt{bd}$

The two lines will coincide when $b = \dfrac{1}{d}$. In such a situation $r = 1$, and the relationship is perfect.

We may also note that

$$b = \frac{\Sigma xy}{\Sigma x^2}$$

$$= \frac{\Sigma xy}{\sqrt{\Sigma x^2 \Sigma y^2}} \frac{\sqrt{\dfrac{\Sigma y^2}{N-1}}}{\sqrt{\dfrac{\Sigma x^2}{N-1}}}$$

$$= r\frac{s_Y}{s_X}$$

and $\qquad d = r\dfrac{s_X}{s_Y}$

where s_X and s_Y are the standard deviations of the X and Y variables respectively. When $r = 0$, both b and d will be zero, so that the regression lines reduce to lines drawn at right angles through $\bar{X}$ and $\bar{Y}$.

Example 8.4

Calculate for example 8.1, p 280, the linear regression of age on rent of houses and the standard error of estimate of this regression. Draw in the regression lines of both rent on age and age on rent on the same scatter diagram.

The regression equation of X on Y is

$$X_c = c + dY$$

ie

$$(X_c - \bar{X}) = d(Y - \bar{Y})$$

where

$$\bar{X} = 12{\cdot}1818 \text{ years}, \quad \bar{Y} = \$32{\cdot}9091$$

and

$$d = \frac{\Sigma xy}{\Sigma y^2} = -\frac{751{\cdot}818}{1650{\cdot}909} = -0{\cdot}4554$$

ie

$$X_c - 12{\cdot}1818 = -0{\cdot}4554(Y - 32{\cdot}9091)$$

so that

$$X_c = 27{\cdot}17 - 0{\cdot}4554Y$$

is the required regression of age on rent.

This can be interpreted by saying that the data under consideration suggest that for an increase of one dollar in the rent of a house we should expect the house to be on the average 0·46 years younger.

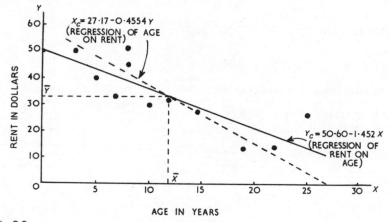

Fig 8.9

The standard error of estimate of the regression of age on rent of houses is given by

$$s_{e'} = \sqrt{\frac{\Sigma x^2 - d\Sigma xy}{N - 2}}$$

$$= \sqrt{\frac{517{\cdot}636 - (-0{\cdot}4554 \times -751{\cdot}818)}{9}}$$

$$= 4{\cdot}41 \text{ Years}$$

8.3 Descriptive Measures of Regression and Correlation for Grouped Data

In the one-variable case when we moved from ungrouped to grouped data, we introduced the frequency distribution. This frequency distribution involved a one-way classification, ie it consisted of items classified into groups according to one criterion of classification. In the two-variable case the frequency distribution will be a two-way classification as in the chart overleaf.

With grouped data, X and Y are class mid-points. We write f_{XY} for the frequency in the cell with X and Y as mid-points, f_X for the frequency in the class with X as mid-point irrespective of Y, and f_Y for the frequency in the class with Y as mid-point irrespective of X. It follows that the f_Xs and f_Ys are marginal totals and that $\Sigma f_X = \Sigma f_Y = N$, where N is the total number of observations. The effect on the formulae in section 8.2 above is slight. We merely replace Σxy with $\Sigma f_{XY}xy$, Σx^2 with $\Sigma f_X x^2$ and Σy^2 with $\Sigma f_Y y^2$, where x and y are the deviations of class mid-points from $\bar{X}$ and $\bar{Y}$ respectively.

Y

			Classes			All Classes
			f_{XY}			f_X
X / Classes						
All Classes			f_Y			N

It is usually convenient to work in class interval units. If h_X is the width of the X class interval and h_Y of the Y class interval, then we must multiply $\Sigma f_{XY}xy$ by $h_X h_Y$, $\Sigma f_X x^2$ by h_X^2 and $\Sigma f_Y y^2$ by h_Y^2 to obtain original units. This means that to obtain b we multiply the calculation in class interval units by $\dfrac{h_X h_Y}{h_X^2}$, ie by $\dfrac{h_Y}{h_X}$, and to obtain d we multiply by $\dfrac{h_X}{h_Y}$. The correlation coefficient is invariant with respect to the units in which X and Y are expressed and no adjustment is necessary.

Example 8.5

The following data refer to the weekly rents paid for and the ages of a group of 112 houses:

Rent in Dollars

Age in Years	10 and under 20	20 and under 30	30 and under 40	40 and under 50	50 and under 60	All Rents
0 and under 3	—	2	2	1	1	6
3 ,, 6	—	2	5	8	4	19
6 ,, 9	1	4	20	10	2	37
9 ,, 12	1	4	8	7	2	22
12 ,, 15	3	3	5	4	1	16
15 ,, 18	3	5	3	—	1	12
All Ages	8	20	43	30	11	112

Calculate:
  (a) the linear regression of rent on age
  (b) the linear regression of age on rent
  (c) the coefficient of linear correlation between rent and age
  (d) the standard error of estimate of the regression of rent on age
  (e) the standard error of estimate of the regression of age on rent.

We set out the table as shown on p 293.

In the table, f stands for f_Y (horizontally) and f_X (vertically), d stands for y' (horizontally) and x' (vertically) in class interval units, and the body of the table contains f_{XY}, in parentheses.

The sums $\Sigma f_X x'$, $\Sigma f_Y y'$, $\Sigma f_X x'^2$, $\Sigma f_Y y'^2$ are readily obtained by working in the margins of the table. To obtain $\Sigma f_{XY} x' y'$, first write the value of $x' y'$ in the top left-hand corner of each cell, and then the product $f_{XY} x' y'$ can be written in the bottom right-hand corner. Addition of these amounts for all cells gives $\Sigma f_{XY} x' y'$. The primary calculations are as follows:

Here
$$\bar{x}' = \frac{\Sigma f_X x'}{N} = 0.5268, \quad \bar{y}' = \frac{\Sigma f_Y y'}{N} = 0.1429$$

and
$$\bar{X} = A + (\bar{x}' \times h_X) = 9.08 \text{ years}$$

and
$$\bar{Y} = B + (\bar{y}' \times h_Y) = \$36.43$$

$$\Sigma f_X x^2 = [\Sigma f_X x'^2 - N\bar{x}'^2] \times h_X^2$$
$$= (237 - 31.0820) \times 9 = 205.9180 \times 9$$

$$\Sigma f_Y y^2 = [\Sigma f_Y y'^2 - N\bar{y}'^2] \times h_Y^2$$
$$= (126 - 2.2871) \times 100 = 123.7129 \times 100$$

$$\Sigma f_{XY} xy = [\Sigma f_{XY} x' y' - N\bar{x}'\bar{y}'] \times h_X h_Y$$
$$= (-44 - 8.4313) \times 30 = -52.4313 \times 30$$

(a) The linear regression of rent on age is given by
$$Y_c - \bar{Y} = b(X - \bar{X})$$

where

$$\bar{Y} = \$36.43, \ \bar{X} = 9.08 \text{ years}, \ b = \frac{\Sigma f_{XY} xy}{\Sigma f_X x^2} = \frac{-52.4313}{205.9180} \times \frac{30}{9} = -0.8487$$

RENT IN DOLLARS (Y)
(Arbitrary Origin B = 35)

AGE IN YEARS (X)
(Arbitrary Origin A = 7·5)

Each body cell shows: d'x·d'y (product) | (f) | f·d'x·d'y (contribution)

Class	Mid-point	f	d'	fd'	fd'²	10-	20-	30-	40-	50-	All Rents
0-	1·5	6	-2	-12	24	4	2 (2) 4	0 (2) 0	-2 (1) -2	-4 (1) -4	-2
3-	4·5	19	-1	-19	19	2	1 (2) 2	0 (5) 0	-1 (8) -8	-2 (4) -8	-14
6-	7·5	37	0	0	0	0 (1) 0	0 (4) 0	0 (20) 0	0 (10) 0	0 (2) 0	0
9-	10·5	22	1	22	22	-2 (1) -2	-1 (4) -4	0 (8) 0	1 (7) 7	2 (2) 4	5
12-	13·5	16	2	32	64	-4 (3) -12	-2 (3) -6	0 (5) 0	2 (4) 8	4 (1) 4	-6
15-	16·5	12	3	36	108	-6 (3) -18	-3 (5) -15	0 (3) 0	3	6 (1) 6	-27
All Ages		112		59	237	-32	-19	0	5	2	-44

Rent (Y) marginal distribution:

	10-	20-	30-	40-	50-	All Rents
Mid-point	15	25	35	45	55	
f	8	20	43	30	11	112
d'	-2	-1	0	1	2	
fd'	-16	-20	0	30	22	16
fd'²	32	20	0	30	44	126

ie $$Y_c = 44{\cdot}14 - 0{\cdot}8487X$$

(b) The linear regression of age on rent is given by
$$X_c - \bar{X} = d(Y - \bar{Y})$$
where

$\bar{X} = 9{\cdot}08$ years, $\bar{Y} = \$36{\cdot}43$, $d = \dfrac{\Sigma f_{XY}xy}{\Sigma f_Y y^2} = \dfrac{-52{\cdot}4313}{123{\cdot}7129} \times \dfrac{30}{100} = -0{\cdot}1271$

ie $$X_c = 13{\cdot}71 - 0{\cdot}1271Y$$

(c) The coefficient of linear correlation between rent and age is given by
$$r = \frac{\Sigma f_{XY}xy}{\sqrt{\Sigma f_X x^2 \Sigma f_Y y^2}} = -0{\cdot}33$$

(d) The standard error of estimate of the regression of rent on age is given by
$$s_e = \sqrt{\frac{\Sigma f_Y y^2 - b\Sigma f_{XY}xy}{N-2}} = \sqrt{100{\cdot}3304} = \$10{\cdot}02$$

(e) The standard error of estimate of the regression of age on rent is given by
$$s_{e'} = \sqrt{\frac{\Sigma f_X x^2 - d\Sigma f_{XY}xy}{N-2}} = \sqrt{15{\cdot}0304} = 3{\cdot}88 \text{ years}$$

8.4 Linear Regression Analysis

In the preceding two sections we considered the method of least squares as a technique for describing a set of given data. In most cases such data will be a sample of observations in the sense that the observations on Y represent but a fraction of all the possible values of Y that can be paired with the given Xs. Given a sample of bivariate data, we are generally not interested in the sample information for its own sake, but rather do we want to use it to make inferences about the possible relationship between X and Y in the larger totality of observations from which our sample has supposedly been drawn. Just as in the univariate case we cannot make inferences about population values unless we make assumptions about the distribution of the variable under consideration, so in the two-variable case we cannot proceed with statistical inference unless we specify the hypothesised relationship between the variables in terms of a probability model. While there are different sets of assumptions that could be made to formulate such a model, let us begin by supposing that for each possible value of the independent variable X there exists a probability distribution of the dependent variable Y with the following two characteristics: first, the mean of each distribution of Y is a linear function of X; and second, the variance of Y for each X is constant and equal to σ^2. Stating these assumptions symbolically, if we write $\mu_Y(X)$ as the mean and $\sigma_Y^2(X)$ as the variance of Y for each X, we have

$$\mu_Y(X) = \alpha + \beta X$$

and

$$\sigma_Y^2(X) = \sigma^2$$

The hypothesised relationship given by the linear equation $\mu_Y(X) = \alpha + \beta X$ is called the *population regression line*, and the constants α and β are the *population regression parameters*. The parameter α is the intercept of the line with the vertical axis; it is the expected value of Y when $X = 0$. The parameter β, the *population regression coefficient*, measures the amount of change in the mean value of Y as X changes by one unit. The assumption of constant variance implies that there is a uniform scatter of Y-values about the line, eg as in Fig 8.10.

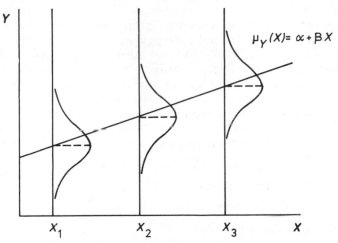

Fig 8.10

In practice, neither the line $\mu_Y(X) = \alpha + \beta X$ nor the variance σ^2 will be known, for we shall only have N pairs of observations (X_1, Y_1) $(X_2, Y_2), \ldots (X_N, Y_N)$. We must now add an important assumption concerning the manner in which these observations have been generated. We shall be assuming that for any given set of N values of X the observations $Y_1, Y_2, \ldots, Y_N$ are independent of each other, ie we shall be assuming that the Y_i, $i = 1, 2, \ldots, N$, are statistically independent random variables each distributed about mean $E(Y_i) = \mu_Y(X_i) = \alpha + \beta X_i$ and with variance $\text{Var}(Y_i) = \sigma_Y^2(X_i) = \sigma^2$.

Suppose (X_i, Y_i) represents any pair of observations of the two variables X and Y. By the very nature of the above assumptions, we cannot expect Y_i to coincide with the mean $\mu_Y(X_i)$. The difference

$$\varepsilon_i = Y_i - \mu_Y(X_i)$$

is called *random error*. If we next write

$$Y_i = \mu_Y(X_i) + \varepsilon_i = \alpha + \beta X_i + \varepsilon_i$$

it can be seen that any observation Y_i can be thought of as consisting of two parts: a *systematic* part due to the linear effect of X on the mean of Y_i, as measured by the regression $\alpha + \beta X_i$, and a *random* part contributed by the random or disturbance term ε_i. Random errors in statistical relationships arise in part from the presence of unpredictable chance factors and in part from errors of observation and from incomplete or incorrect specification of the factors influencing the relationship.

Before proceeding further it will be useful if we restate the regression model sketched out above in terms of the disturbance term ε instead of the variable Y. Since the observations Y_i are random variables, the ε_is are also random variables with properties that can be deduced from those of the Y_is. From the above, $\varepsilon_i = Y_i - \mu_Y(X_i) = Y_i - E(Y_i)$, and hence $E(\varepsilon_i) = E(Y_i) - E(Y_i) = 0$. Also, $\mathrm{Var}(\varepsilon_i) = E[\varepsilon_i - E(\varepsilon_i)]^2 = E(\varepsilon_i^2)$. But $E(\varepsilon_i^2) = E[Y_i - E(Y_i)]^2 = \mathrm{Var}(Y_i)$, and so, by assumption of constant variance, $\mathrm{Var}(\varepsilon_i) = \sigma_\varepsilon^2 = \sigma^2$. Finally, if the Y_i are statistically independent, the ε_i must also be statistically independent.

In summary form, the assumptions of the two-variable linear model may be stated as follows:

1. There is a 'true' relationship between X and Y given by the relation

$$Y_i = \alpha + \beta X_i + \varepsilon_i \qquad \text{for all } i$$

2. The ε_i have zero mean, ie

$$E(\varepsilon_i) = 0$$

3. The ε_i have the same variance, ie

$$\mathrm{Var}(\varepsilon_i) = \sigma_\varepsilon^2$$

4. The ε_i are statistically independent,[1] ie

$$\mathrm{Cov}(\varepsilon_i, \varepsilon_j) = 0 \qquad i \neq j; i, j = 1, 2, \ldots, N$$

5. The X_i in the above relation are non-random quantities, and remain fixed in successive samples, or experiments, involving measurement of the variable Y.

It is important to emphasise that the above assumptions concerning the nature of the random error ε and of the Xs need by no means hold in every practical situation. In economic applications, particularly those utilising time-series data, assumptions 3 and 4 (constancy of

---

[1] See pp 154 and 165 above.

variance and independence of successive observations) are frequently not justified, and need to be tested against the available data. Similarly, the assumption that the Xs are non-random quantities known in advance often cannot be sustained in practice. The consequences arising from the non-fulfilment of some of the assumptions will be considered in sections 8.10 and 8.11 below.

Let us now consider how the concepts introduced thus far can be related to our earlier work on regression. We have N pairs of sample values for the two variables X and Y, and we postulate that there exists a relationship between the variables which is of the form $Y_i = \alpha + \beta X_i + \varepsilon_i$. To estimate the values of the parameters α and β, which are not known, we use the method of least squares, obtaining values of a and b as point estimates of α and β. The sample regression relationship is then given by the relation $Y_i = a + bX_i + e_i$, where the e_i are the least-squares residuals of the actually observed Y-values from the fitted line. We are thus able to distinguish between the *population regression model*

$$Y_i = \alpha + \beta X_i + \varepsilon_i \qquad \text{(for all } i\text{)}$$

and the *sample regression model*

$$Y_i = a + bX_i + e_i \qquad \text{(for } i = 1, 2, \ldots, N)$$

Since the coefficients a and b are determined from sample data, every new sample of observations on Y, for the same values of X, can in general be expected to yield different values of a and b. In other words, the coefficients a and b calculated by the method of least squares are statistics subject to sampling errors. The question then arises: how good are the statistics a and b as estimators of the parameters α and β? As we saw in section 5.12 above, the general requirement of a good estimator is that it should have a sampling distribution which is closely concentrated around the true value of the parameter being estimated. Thus, to judge whether or not the method of least squares produces estimators with the desired properties we need to consider the mean and variance of the sampling distributions of the estimators a and b.

Consider first the least-squares estimator b of the unknown population regression coefficient β. From section 8.2, for a sample of size N we have

$$b = \frac{\Sigma x_i y_i}{\Sigma x_i^2} \qquad (i = 1, 2, \ldots N)$$

$$= \frac{\Sigma x_i (Y_i - \bar{Y})}{\Sigma x_i^2}$$

$$= \sum \left(\frac{x_i}{\Sigma x_i^2} \, Y_i \right) - \bar{Y} \sum \frac{x_i}{\Sigma x_i^2}$$

$$= \sum \left(\frac{x_i}{\Sigma x_i^2} \, Y_i \right)$$

since $\Sigma x_i = 0$. By assumption, the X_i are known values which remain fixed in repeated samples, and hence each $x_i/\Sigma x_i^2$ is a constant. If we let

$$c_i = \frac{x_i}{\Sigma x_i^2}$$

where $\Sigma c_i = 0$ (since $\Sigma x_i = 0$) we may write

$$b = \Sigma c_i Y_i \qquad (i = 1, 2, \ldots, N)$$

Thus, the estimator b of β can be seen as a linear combination of the sample observations Y_i, with the constants c_i serving as fixed weights. If we substitute $Y_i = \alpha + \beta X_i + \varepsilon_i$ into the expression for b, we shall have

$$b = \Sigma c_i \alpha + \beta \Sigma c_i X_i + \Sigma c_i \varepsilon_i$$

where

$$\Sigma c_i \alpha = \alpha \Sigma c_i = 0$$

and

$$\Sigma c_i X_i = \sum \left(\frac{x_i}{\Sigma x_i^2} \, X_i \right) = \sum \left(\frac{x_i}{\Sigma x_i^2} \, x_i \right) + \bar{X} \sum \frac{x_i}{\Sigma x_i^2} = 1$$

Therefore,

$$b = \beta + \Sigma c_i \varepsilon_i$$

and

$$E(b) = \mu_b$$

$$= \beta + \Sigma c_i E(\varepsilon_i)$$

$$= \beta \qquad \text{(since } E(\varepsilon_i) = 0\text{)}$$

Thus, b is an unbiased estimator of the population regression coefficient β, and by much the same argument it can be shown that the same holds for a as an estimator of α, ie $E(a) = \mu_a = \alpha$.

To consider next $\text{Var}(b)$, we have

$$\text{Var}(b) = \text{Var}(\beta + \Sigma c_i \varepsilon_i)$$

$$= \text{Var}(\Sigma c_i \varepsilon_i)$$

From section 4.15 we recall that when random variables are independent the variance of a weighted sum of the variables is equal to the sum of the variances of the variables having as their coefficients the squares of the weights. By assumption, the ε_i are independent and have equal variance σ_ε^2.

Hence

$$\text{Var}(b) = \Sigma c_i^2 \, \text{Var}(\varepsilon_i)$$
$$= \sigma_\varepsilon^2 \, \Sigma c_i^2$$

where

$$\Sigma c_i^2 = \sum \left(\frac{x_i}{\Sigma x_i^2}\right)^2 = \frac{\Sigma x_i^2}{(\Sigma x_i^2)^2} = \frac{1}{\Sigma x_i^2}$$

Therefore

$$\text{Var}(b) = \sigma_b^2$$
$$= \frac{\sigma_\varepsilon^2}{\Sigma x_i^2}$$

Similarly, if we write

$$a = \bar{Y} - b\bar{X} = \frac{\Sigma Y_i}{N} - \bar{X}\Sigma c_i Y_i$$
$$= \sum \left(\frac{1}{N} - \bar{X}c_i\right) Y_i$$

then by the same argument as above

$$\text{Var}(a) = \sum \left(\frac{1}{N} - \bar{X}c_i\right)^2 \sigma_\varepsilon^2$$

and upon expanding the term in the brackets, we find

$$\text{Var}(a) = \sigma_\varepsilon^2 \left(\frac{\Sigma x_i^2 + N\bar{X}^2}{N\Sigma x_i^2}\right)$$

where $\Sigma x_i^2 + N\bar{X}^2 = \Sigma X_i^2$ (see section 3.5, p 60). Omitting the subscripts, we have

$$\text{Var}(a) = \sigma_a^2$$
$$= \sigma_\varepsilon^2 \frac{\Sigma X^2}{N\Sigma x^2}$$

As can be seen from the above results, the variance of b depends on the scatter of Y-values about the population regression line, as measured by σ_ε^2, and on the amount of dispersion of the X-values from their mean, as measured by the term Σx^2. The larger the quantity Σx^2, the smaller the variance of the slope estimator b. Hence, in controlled experiments, it is always possible to increase the accuracy of estimating β by widening the range of the controlled variable X. From the formula for $\mathrm{Var}(a)$ it can be seen that the values of X enter the numerator of the formula as squared quantities (ΣX^2), and hence the precision with which a can be estimated diminishes rapidly the farther the values of X are from zero. Also, since $a = \bar{Y} - b\bar{X}$, the estimators a and b are not statistically independent, and can be shown to have a negative covariance (for positive $\bar{X}$). This means that overestimates of β, ie $b > \beta$, tend to be associated with underestimates of α, ie $a < \alpha$, and vice versa.

We have seen that if the assumption $E(\varepsilon_i) = 0$ holds true, then a and and b are unbiased estimators of the regression parameters α and β. We have also noted that each estimator a and b can be expressed as a linear combination of the sample observations Y_i. An estimator which is a linear combination of sample data is known as a *linear* estimator. Thus, we have the result that a and b are *linear unbiased* estimators of α and β respectively. However, as already mentioned earlier, among all unbiased estimators of α and β, good ones are those whose sampling distributions have a low variance. One may then ask: is it possible to derive some other estimator of β which is linear and unbiased but which has a smaller variance than the least-squares estimator b? As can be readily checked from p 298 above, if $E(\varepsilon_i) = 0$, the least-squares estimator $b = \Sigma c_i Y_i$ is an unbiased estimator of β by virtue of the fact that the constants c_i satisfy two algebraic properties: $\Sigma c_i = 0$ and $\Sigma c_i X_i = 1$. Now suppose that $b' = \Sigma d_i Y_i$ is any other linear estimator of β with the constants d_i chosen so that these two algebraic conditions hold, ie $\Sigma d_i = 0$ and $\Sigma d_i X_i = 1$. Then, since $Y_i = \alpha + \beta X_i + \varepsilon_i$ and $E(\varepsilon_i) = 0$, we shall have

$$E(b') = \beta + \Sigma d_i E(\varepsilon_i)$$
$$= \beta$$

and b' is also a linear unbiased estimator of β. However, it can be shown that the estimator b' cannot have a variance which is as small as $\mathrm{Var}(b) = \sigma_\varepsilon^2 / \Sigma x^2$. Similarly, there is no linear unbiased estimator of α which has variance as small as the least-squares estimator a. From section 5.12 we recall that an estimator which has the smallest variance among all unbiased estimators of its class is called 'best' estimator. We may therefore say that the least-squares estimators a and b are the *best linear unbiased estimators* (abbreviated as BLUE) of the regression parameters α and β. This means that, for given sample size and sampling cost, they yield more accurate point and interval estimates than any other estimators that are also linear and unbiased.

In deriving the mean and variance of the sampling distribution of a

and b it was not necessary to make assumptions about the form of the probability distribution of the error term ε. However, since ε is a composite of many unrelated chance factors, some of which tend to cancel out so that extreme values of ε_i are less likely to occur than small values of ε_i, in many practical situations we may reasonably expect that it will have a normal distribution. If the assumption of normality of the error term is added to the assumptions listed earlier in this section, then each of the least-squares estimators a and b will be a linear combination of independent normal variables and hence each will have a normal distribution with means α and β and variances as above; that is, if ε_i is $N(0, \sigma_\varepsilon^2)$, then a is $N\left(\alpha, \sigma_\varepsilon^2 \dfrac{\Sigma X^2}{N\Sigma x^2}\right)$ and b is $N\left(\beta, \dfrac{\sigma_\varepsilon^2}{\Sigma x^2}\right)$. In these circumstances the least-squares estimators a and b will each possess the optimal property of having the smallest variance among all unbiased estimators of α and β; ie in the case of normally distributed errors, a and b are the *best unbiased estimators* of α and β (BUE). If the assumption of normality of the error term holds, it is possible to test hypotheses and construct confidence intervals for the parameters α and β on the basis of quite small samples. When the assumption of normality of the ε_i cannot be justified, we can still proceed with statistical inference, provided the number of observations at our disposal is reasonably large, for then the sampling distributions of a and b will be approximately normal with means and variances as given above.

8.5 Tests of Significance in Regression Analysis

Suppose we have a sample of N pairs of observations of two variables X and Y and we have computed the sample regression coefficient b. Is the sample result evidence that a relationship between X and Y exists so that knowledge of values of the independent variable X is useful in making predictions about the variable Y? If there is no relationship between X and Y, then the population regression line is a horizontal line, and the population regression coefficient is zero. Consequently, to test the hypothesis of no relationship between the variables, we set up the null hypothesis $H_o : \beta = 0$ against the alternative hypothesis $H_a : \beta \neq 0$, and test H_o against the sample result. If the sample regression coefficient has been found to be significantly different from zero, we may wish to compute an interval estimate for β, usually at the 95 per cent level of confidence. The procedure is quite analogous to that described in Chapter 5 for a single variable.

From the preceding section we know that if each ε_i is normally distributed about mean 0 and with variance σ_ε^2, b is also normally distributed with mean β and standard error $\sigma_b = \sigma_\varepsilon / \sqrt{\Sigma x^2}$. Thus, if the null hypothesis is true, the test statistic $Z = \dfrac{b - \beta}{\sigma_b}$, where $\beta = 0$, is the standard normal variable with mean 0 and unit variance. In practice we should not know σ_ε, and we must estimate it from the sample. This estimate is the standard error of estimate s_e (see section 8.2, p 286 above). Accordingly the sample estimate of σ_b is

$$s_b = \frac{s_e}{\sqrt{\Sigma x^2}}$$

where s_e may be computed from the formula

$$s_e = \sqrt{\frac{\Sigma y^2 - b\Sigma xy}{N - 2}}$$

When we use s_b instead of σ_b, we must turn from the normal to the t-distribution and we have that

$$t = \frac{b - \beta}{s_b}$$

is distributed in the t-distribution with $N - 2$ degrees of freedom.

It follows that in testing whether or not b differs significantly from zero, ie whether or not the sample could have come from a population with $\beta = 0$, we compute $|t| = \dfrac{|b|}{s_b}$ and refer it to the t-table with $N - 2$ degrees of freedom. If $|t|$ is outside the critical limits $t_{\alpha/2}$, we reject the null hypothesis and conclude that $\beta \neq 0$.

Similarly, as in the case of a single variable, the 95 per cent confidence limits for β are given by

$$b \pm t_{.025} s_b$$

Since s_b varies inversely with Σx^2, in experimental work we can reduce the range of confidence limits based on a sample of a given size by making the range of the controlled variable as wide as possible. This procedure is quite legitimate provided the associated Ys are free to vary at random. Indeed, if there is too little variation in the Xs, the estimated variance of b is large and no reliable estimates of β can be made. Diagrammatically speaking, if all the Xs are closely bunched together, the slope of the fitted line is quite sensitive even to small variations in the observed values of Y, and individual estimates of β are therefore subject to large sampling errors.

By similar reasoning, to test an hypothesis $H_o : \alpha = \alpha_o$ against the alternative $H_a : \alpha \neq \alpha_o$, we estimate the standard error of a as

$$s_a = s_e \sqrt{\frac{\Sigma X^2}{N\Sigma x^2}}$$

and compute the test statistic

$$|t| = \frac{|a - \alpha_o|}{s_a}$$

which is then referred to the t-table with $N - 2$ degrees of freedom. A 95 per cent confidence interval for α is

$$a \pm t_{.025}s_a$$

Example 8.6

Suppose the data in example 8.1 (p 280) refer to a random sample of 11 tenanted houses.

(a) Test whether the sample regression coefficient b is significant. If it is significant calculate the 95 per cent confidence limits for the population regression coefficient.

(b) Compute a 95 per cent confidence interval for the population intercept coefficient α.

From previous results we have:

$$a = 50{\cdot}60 \qquad\qquad b = -1{\cdot}452$$
$$\Sigma x^2 = 517{\cdot}636 \qquad\qquad \Sigma X^2 = 2150$$
$$s_e = 7{\cdot}88$$

We next compute

$$s_a = s_e \sqrt{\frac{\Sigma X^2}{N\Sigma x^2}} = 4{\cdot}842$$

and

$$s_b = \frac{s_e}{\sqrt{\Sigma x^2}} = 0{\cdot}346$$

It is customary to show the estimated standard errors in brackets under the corresponding coefficients of the estimating equation, thus:

$$Y_c = 50{\cdot}60 - 1{\cdot}452X$$
$$(4{\cdot}842) \ (0{\cdot}346)$$

(a) *Hypothesis:* The sample comes from a population in which there is no linear relationship between rent and age, ie

$$H_o : \beta = 0$$
$$H_a : \beta \neq 0$$

Test:

$$|t| = \frac{|b|}{s_b} = \frac{1{\cdot}452}{0{\cdot}346}$$
$$= 4{\cdot}2$$

Conclusion: From the t-table with $v = 9$ degrees of freedom, the critical value of t for a two-tailed test is $t_{.025} = 2{\cdot}262$. Since the computed value of t exceeds the critical value at the 5 per cent level of significance we reject the null hypothesis H_o and accept H_a. We say that the sample regression coefficient is significant and conclude that the population β differs from zero. Accordingly, we are interested in determining confidence limits within which the population β can be expected to lie. These 95 per cent confidence limits are

$$b \pm t_{.025}s_b$$

ie
$$-1\cdot45 \pm 0\cdot78$$

Hence we can be 95 per cent confident that β lies between $-0\cdot67$ and $-2\cdot23$.

(b) Confidence limits are

$$a \pm t_{.025}s_a$$

where $a = 50\cdot60$, $t_{.025} = 2\cdot262$ for $v = 9$, and $s_a = 4\cdot842$

ie
$$50\cdot60 \pm 10\cdot95$$

so that on the basis of our sample we can state with 95 per cent confidence that the true value of α lies in the interval $39\cdot65$ to $61\cdot55$ dollars.

The F-Ratio Test

Another approach to testing the hypothesis of no relationship between two variables X and Y is based on an analysis of the variability of the Y values about their mean value $\bar{Y}$.[1] From section 8.2 it will be remembered that the total variation in Y can be split into two parts: variation 'explained' by the regression and 'residual' or 'unexplained' variation, ie

$$\Sigma(Y - \bar{Y})^2 = \Sigma(Y_c - \bar{Y})^2 + \Sigma e^2$$

Since
$$Y_c - \bar{Y} = b(X - \bar{X}) = bx$$

we have

$$\Sigma(Y_c - \bar{Y})^2 = b^2\Sigma x^2$$

and letting $\Sigma(Y - \bar{Y})^2 = \Sigma y^2$, we may write the above as

$$\Sigma y^2 = b^2\Sigma x^2 + \Sigma e^2$$

From this relation it can be seen that X has no explanatory value if $b = 0$.

Let us consider the two right-hand terms in the above expression. If the errors ε_i in the population regression model are normal each with mean 0 and variance σ_ε^2, then

$$Z = \frac{b - \beta}{\sigma_b} = \frac{b - \beta}{\sigma_\varepsilon/\sqrt{x^2}}$$

has the standard normal distribution $N(0, 1)$. But if Z is $N(0, 1)$, then

$$Z^2 = \frac{(b - \beta)^2}{\sigma_\varepsilon^2/\Sigma x^2}$$

[1] See also footnote on p 255.

has the χ^2 distribution with 1 degree of freedom (see footnote on p 211, section 5.11 above).

In that section we also explained that if s^2 is the variance of a random sample of size N drawn from a normal population, the test statistic $\dfrac{(N-1)s^2}{\sigma^2}$ for testing hypotheses about the population variance σ^2 is a χ^2 variable with $N-1$ degrees of freedom. Analogously, if we write s_e^2 as the variance of the residuals from the sample regression line $Y_c = a + bX$, the quantity $\dfrac{(N-2)s_e^2}{\sigma_\varepsilon^2}$ will have a χ^2 distribution with $N-2$ degrees of freedom, the loss of two degrees of freedom reflecting the fact that two parameters must be estimated before the residuals e_i can be computed. But $s_e^2 = \dfrac{\Sigma e^2}{N-2}$, and hence $\Sigma e^2/\sigma_\varepsilon^2$ is also a χ^2 variable with $N-2$ degrees of freedom. Now suppose a sample of N observations on X and Y has been drawn from a population in which $\beta = 0$. We then have

$$U_1 = \frac{(b-0)^2}{\sigma_\varepsilon^2/\Sigma x^2} = \frac{b^2 \Sigma x^2}{\sigma_\varepsilon^2}$$

and

$$U_2 = \frac{\Sigma e^2}{\sigma_\varepsilon^2}$$

as two independent χ^2 variables with $v_1 = 1$ and $v_2 = N-2$ degrees of freedom. The ratio of two independent χ^2 variables U_1 and U_2, each divided by its respective number of degrees of freedom, ie the ratio

$$F = \frac{U_1/v_1}{U_2/v_2}$$

has a probability distribution known as the F-distribution. In the present case we have

$$F = \frac{b^2 \Sigma x^2/1}{\Sigma e^2/N-2} = \frac{b^2 \Sigma x^2}{s_e^2}$$

As can be seen, the unknown variance σ_ε^2 cancels out, and the F-ratio is a test statistic based entirely on sample data.

The distribution of F is a theoretical distribution with two parameters v_1 and v_2 each representing the number of degrees of freedom associated with the numerator and the denominator of the test statistic F. In a table of areas for the F-distribution various values of v_1 and v_2 are entered in the upper margin and in the left-hand margin respectively;

in Table IV of Appendix A two such tables are given, one corresponding to 5 per cent level of significance and the other to 1 per cent level of significance. From the tables we can ascertain the values of F which cut off 5 per cent and 1 per cent of area in the right-hand tail of the

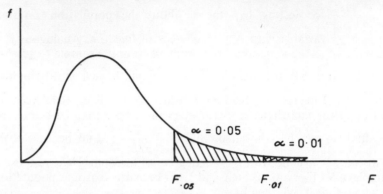

Fig 8.11 The F-distribution

distribution; this is illustrated in Fig 8.11. For example, if $v_1 = 1$ and $v_2 = 20$, then 5 per cent of the area under the curve lies to the right of 4·35, and 1 per cent lies to the right of 8·10. Therefore, with $v_1 = 1$ and $v_2 = 20$, the probability of a value of F being greater than 8·10 is less than 1 per cent.[1]

Let us now return to the matter of constructing an F-test for the hypothesis $H_o: \beta = 0$. As already mentioned, if $\beta = 0$, the ratio $\dfrac{b^2 \Sigma x^2}{s_e^2}$ is a ratio of two independent χ^2 variables, and has the F-distribution with $v_1 = 1$ and $v_2 = N - 2$ degrees of freedom. But if $\beta \neq 0$, we should expect the quantity $b^2 \Sigma x^2$ in the numerator of the F-ratio to be large relative to the residual variance s_e^2. Consequently, if we set up the null hypothesis that $\beta = 0$ and the value of the test statistic $F = b^2 \Sigma x^2/s_e^2$ is found to be greater than the critical value $F_{.05}$, the probability is less than 5 per cent that the observed F-ratio is a value drawn from an F-distribution, and we reject the hypothesis that $\beta = 0$; if $F < F_{.05}$, the hypothesis $H_o: \beta = 0$ is retained.

---

[1] We should point out that the F-distribution finds common use in tests of hypotheses of the equality of two population variances, ie of the hypothesis $\sigma_1^2 = \sigma_2^2$. Thus, if s_1^2 and s_2^2 are the variances of two random samples of size N_1 and N_2 drawn independently from two normal populations, the ratio $F = s_1^2/s_2^2$ is distributed in the F-distribution with $v_1 = N_1 - 1$ and $v_2 = N_2 - 1$ degrees of freedom. To test an hypothesis H_o: $\sigma_1^2 = \sigma_2^2$ against $H_a: \sigma_1^2 > \sigma_2^2$, we compute the value of the test statistic $F = s_1^2/s_2^2$, and refer it to the F-table with $N_1 - 1$ and $N_2 - 1$ degrees of freedom. If $F > F_{.05}$, we reject H_o and accept the alternative H_a.

We may further note that $s_b^2 = s_e^2/\Sigma x^2$, and hence the F-ratio may be written

$$F = \frac{b^2 \Sigma x^2}{s_b^2 \Sigma x^2}$$

$$= \left(\frac{b}{s_b}\right)^2$$

Recall, however, that in tests of the null hypothesis, $H_o : \beta = 0$, the test statistic b/s_b is a t-variable with $N - 2$ degrees of freedom. We thus have that $F = t^2$. This result shows that in the two-variable case the t-test and the F-test are equivalent tests, ie if the null hypothesis $H_o : \beta = 0$ is rejected (accepted) by the t-test, it is rejected (accepted) by the F-test also. However, this equivalence of the t- and the F-test ceases to hold when the analysis is extended to problems involving several explanatory variables. Then the t-test is the means for testing the significance of the individual coefficients in the regression, whereas the F-test enables us to test the significance of the regression relationship as a whole. For this reason we find both tests included in most standard computer regression programs.

In section 8.2 above we saw that a measure of the goodness of fit of the sample regression line is the coefficient of determination defined by

$$r^2 = 1 - \frac{\Sigma e^2}{\Sigma y^2}$$

This coefficient measures the proportion of the total variation in Y accounted for by the regression. Because in small samples r^2 tends to overstate the true proportion of the variability in Y explained by the regression, it is usual practice to correct for this possible bias by dividing the numerator and the denominator in the formula for r^2 by the appropriate number of degrees of freedom. The adjusted r^2 is then defined as

$$\bar{r}^2 = 1 - \frac{\Sigma e^2/N - 2}{\Sigma y^2/N - 1}$$

$$= 1 - \frac{s_e^2}{s_Y^2}$$

As shown in section 8.2, a convenient formula for computing r^2 is

$$r^2 = \frac{(\Sigma xy)^2}{\Sigma x^2 \Sigma y^2}$$

We may then compute $\bar{r}^2$ from r^2 by using the formula

$$\bar{r}^2 = 1 - \left[(1 - r^2)\left(\frac{N-1}{N-2}\right)\right]$$

Example 8.7

For the regression of rent on age of houses in example 8.1:
(a) Find the F-ratio, and use the result to test the hypothesis of no relationship between rent and age of houses.
(b) Calculate the adjusted coefficient of determination $\bar{r}^2$.

(a) *Hypotheses*:

$$H_o : \beta = 0$$
$$H_a : \beta \neq 0$$

Test: Using our previous results in Table 8.2 above, we may set out the data for the calculation of the F-ratio as follows:

Variation in Y due to:	Sum of Squares (SS)	Degrees of Freedom (d.f.)	(SS) ÷ (d.f.)
Regression	1 091·94	1	1 091·94 ÷ 1 = 1 091·94
Residual Error	558·96	9	558·96 ÷ 9 = 62·11

$$F = \frac{1091\cdot94}{62\cdot11} = 17\cdot58$$

Alternatively, using the results of examples 8.1 and 8.3, we find

$$b^2\Sigma x^2 = (-1\cdot4524)^2(517\cdot636)$$
$$= 1091\cdot94$$
$$s_e^2 = (7\cdot88)^2$$
$$= 62\cdot10$$

and hence

$$F = \frac{b^2\Sigma x^2/1}{s_e^2}$$
$$= 17\cdot58$$

as above.

Conclusion: From the table of F values in Appendix A, the 5 per cent critical value of F, with $v_1 = 1$ and $v_2 = 9$, is found to be 5·12. Since

$$F = 17\cdot58 > F_{.05} = 5\cdot12$$

we reject the hypothesis of no relationship between rent and age and accept the alternative hypothesis H_a. If the null hypothesis $\beta = 0$ were true, a value of F as great as or greater than the one actually observed would occur in much less than one per cent of all cases (since also $F = 17\cdot58 > F_{.01} = 10\cdot56$).

Thus, we may conclude that the observed relationship between rent and age of houses is significant. The sample is evidence that some of the variability in rents can be attributed to variability in the age of houses.

Comparing the results of this test with the previous t-test (see example 8.6) we have

$$|t| = \frac{|b|}{s_b} = \frac{1{\cdot}452}{0{\cdot}346} = 4{\cdot}196$$

$$\therefore \qquad t^2 = 17{\cdot}61$$

and t^2 differs from F only by a small rounding error. Also, $t_{.025} = 2{\cdot}262$ (with 9 degrees of freedom) and $(2{\cdot}262)^2 = 5{\cdot}12 = F_{.05}$ (with 1 and 9 degrees of freedom). Thus, the decision rules

$$|t| > t_{.025}$$

and

$$F > F_{.05}$$

for rejecting the hypothesis $H_o : \beta = 0$ are equivalent.

(b) The adjusted coefficient of determination is

$$\bar{r}^2 = 1 - \frac{s_e^2}{s_Y^2}$$

Here $s_e^2 = 62{\cdot}10$ and

$$s_Y^2 = \frac{\Sigma y^2}{N - 1} = \frac{1650{\cdot}909}{10}$$

$$= 165{\cdot}09$$

Thus

$$\bar{r}^2 = 1 - 0{\cdot}376$$

$$= 0{\cdot}624$$

Alternatively, we may use the formula

$$\bar{r}^2 = 1 - [(1 - r^2)(N - 1)/(N - 2)]$$

From example 8.2

$$r^2 = 0{\cdot}6614$$

and hence

$$\bar{r}^2 = 1 - [(0{\cdot}3386)(10)/9]$$

$$= 0{\cdot}624$$

8.6 Prediction from a Regression Equation

An important application of regression analysis arises when we wish to make predictions of values of the dependent variable Y on the basis of information relating to the independent variable X. Thus, suppose we wish to know what value of Y will result if X is set at a certain value, say X_o. As we already explained earlier in this chapter, we can never predict *the* value of Y associated with X_o exactly, for, even if the regression parameters α and β were known, errors of prediction would still arise because of the disturbance (or error) term ε. But if $E(\varepsilon_o) = 0$, we could find the *mean* value of Y associated with X_o by substituting X_o into the equation

$$\mu_Y(X_o) = \alpha + \beta X_o$$

In practice the parameters α and β will not be known, and to make a prediction about Y we shall need to use the observed relationship, as given by the sample regression $Y_c = a + bX$. We stress that we are using the term 'prediction' in the sense not of a forecast but of a conditional statement, ie if X has a certain value, then according to the regression, Y can be expected to have a certain value. To indicate that the observed relationship is being used for estimating the unknown $\mu_Y(X)$ we shall now write it as $\hat{Y} = a + bX$. Since $\hat{Y}$ is an estimator of the unknown population regression line, in much the same way as a and b are estimators of its parameters α and β, it is desirable that we determine the prediction limits to $\mu_Y(X)$, analogous to confidence limits for population parameters. To do this we must first derive the sampling distribution of $\hat{Y}$.
Since

$$\hat{Y} = a + bX$$

for $X = X_o$ we have

$$\hat{Y}_o = a + bX_o$$

and by the properties of the least-squares estimators a and b given in section 8.4

$$E(\hat{Y}_o) = E(a) + E(b)X_o$$
$$= \alpha + \beta X_o = \mu_Y(X_o)$$

ie $\hat{Y}_o$ is an unbiased estimator of the mean value of Y corresponding to the given X_o. To derive $\mathrm{Var}(\hat{Y}_o)$ we first write

$$\hat{Y}_o = a + bX_o$$
$$= \bar{Y} + b(X_o - \bar{X})$$

If the observations Y_i, for given Xs, are normally distributed and independent, $\bar{Y}$ and b will also be independent in repeated sampling, and $\hat{Y}_o$ is a linear combination of independent normal variables. Thus, by virtue of section 4.15, the variance of $\hat{Y}_o$ is

$$\mathrm{Var}(\hat{Y}_o) = \mathrm{Var}(\bar{Y}) + (X_o - \bar{X})^2 \mathrm{Var}(b)$$

Since the variance of the distribution of Y for each X is constant and equal to σ_ε^2, $\mathrm{Var}(\bar{Y}) = \dfrac{\sigma_\varepsilon^2}{N}$, and we have $\mathrm{Var}(b)$ from above.

Hence

$$\text{Var}(\hat{Y}_o) = \sigma_\varepsilon^2 \left[\frac{1}{N} + \frac{(X_o - \bar{X})^2}{\Sigma x^2} \right]$$

We may conclude that if the observations Y_i, and hence the error terms ε_i, are normally distributed, then $\hat{Y}_o$ will be normally distributed with mean $\mu_Y(X_o) = \alpha + \beta X_o$ and $\text{Var}(\hat{Y}_o)$ as above.

Generally, we shall not know σ_ε, and we must use s_e as an estimate of it. Accordingly,

$$t = \frac{\hat{Y}_o - \mu_Y(X_o)}{\sqrt{s_{\hat{Y}}^2}}$$

where

$$s_{\hat{Y}}^2 = s_e^2 \left[\frac{1}{N} + \frac{(X_o - \bar{X})^2}{\Sigma x^2} \right]$$

will be distributed in the t-distribution with $N - 2$ degrees of freedom. It follows that the 95 per cent prediction limits to $\mu_Y(X_o)$ can be written

$$\hat{Y}_o \pm t_{.025} s_e \sqrt{\frac{1}{N} + \frac{(X_o - \bar{X})^2}{\Sigma x^2}}$$

The width of the prediction limits is greater the further X_o is from $\bar{X}$. This is because sampling errors in b are multiplied as X_o moves away from $\bar{X}$. Consequently predictions of $\mu_Y(X_o)$ from a sample regression equation are subject to greater sampling errors the more extreme is the value of X under consideration. The above prediction limits mean that if we calculate $\hat{Y} = a + bX$ from repeated samples, we shall be right in 95 per cent of the cases in locating $\mu_Y(X_o)$ in the above range. It does not mean that 95 per cent of predictions based on *one* estimate $\hat{Y} = a + bX$ will rightly locate $\mu_Y(X_o)$ in the range, for in that case the same sampling errors in the estimates a and b will be exactly repeated each time.

The above prediction limits refer to the limits for the *mean* value of Y associated with a particular value of X. The range within which a *single* value of Y associated with a particular X is likely to lie will of course be much wider, because the variation of individual Ys about the mean of the Ys must also be taken into account. For a given X_o, we have

$$Y_o = \alpha + \beta X_o + \varepsilon_o$$

where ε_o is random error assumed to have a normal distribution with zero mean and variance σ_ε^2. However, the prediction of Y_o from the observed relationship between X and Y is

$$\hat{Y}_o = a + bX_o$$

and the difference $\qquad d = Y_o - \hat{Y}_o$

gives a measure of the prediction error which will arise if we estimate Y_o as $\hat{Y}_o = a + bX_o$. Since with repeated sampling both Y_o and $\hat{Y}_o$ are distributed about the same mean $\mu_Y(X_o) = \alpha + \beta X_o$, the mean of the prediction error is zero, ie

$$E(d) = \mu_Y(X_o) - \mu_Y(X_o) = 0.$$

For $\mathrm{Var}(d)$ we may write

$$\mathrm{Var}(d) = \mathrm{Var}(Y_o - \hat{Y}_o) = \mathrm{Var}(Y_o) + \mathrm{Var}(\hat{Y}_o)$$

But $\mathrm{Var}(Y_o) = \mathrm{Var}(\varepsilon_o^2) = \sigma_\varepsilon^2$, and $\mathrm{Var}(\hat{Y}_o)$ has been derived above. Hence the variance of the prediction error for a single value Y_o is

$$\mathrm{Var}(d) = \sigma_\varepsilon^2 \left[1 + \frac{1}{N} + \frac{(X_o - \bar{X})^2}{\Sigma x^2} \right]$$

Using s_e as an estimate of σ_ε, we shall have as 95 per cent prediction limits within which a single value of Y associated with a particular value of X is likely to fall:

$$\hat{Y}_0 \pm t_{.025} s_e \sqrt{1 + \frac{1}{N} + \frac{(X_o - \bar{X})^2}{\Sigma x^2}}$$

We now illustrate the methods of simple regression analysis discussed thus far with an example based on actual economic data.

Example 8.8

In the table below data are given for annual per capita consumption of lamb and the retail prices for lamb for Australia, 1964–65 to 1973–74. The price data are average retail prices deflated by the Australian Consumer Price Index, 1966–67 = 100.

Year	Consumption of Lamb (kg per Capita) Y	Retail Price of Lamb (cents per kg) X
1964–65	17·8	92·4
1965–66	16·7	100·5
1966–67	19·3	93·5
1967–68	19·6	94·1
1968–69	21·7	85·0
1969–70	21·5	85·5
1970–71	23·8	81·5
1971–72	24·4	75·6
1972–73	18·7	91·4
1973–74	16·0	114·0

Source: Bureau of Agricultural Economics, Australia: *Meat Situation and Outlook*, 1974, pp DA-65, D-36; 1975, pp D-116, D-39; and *National Agricultural Outlook Conference*, Canberra, 1973, p F-48; Australian Bureau of Statistics: *Monthly Review of Business Statistics*, June 1975, p 29.

When plotted on a scatter diagram, the data exhibited a strong linear pattern, suggesting a demand relationship of the form $Y_i = \alpha + \beta X_i + \varepsilon_i$, $\beta < 0$.

To estimate the parameters α and β and to investigate the plausibility of the postulated relationship we can work directly with the formulae developed in the preceding sections. However, such calculations tend to be laborious, and can be handled with very great speed and accuracy by modern electronic computers. In recent years the use of the computer in regression work has become widespread, and to help the reader make use of computer output in analysing regression results we now illustrate how the data tabulated above have been processed by an electronic computer using a fairly standard regression program. First, we reproduce the printed results for our problem as follows:

VARIABLE 1 IS CONSUMPTION OF LAMB PER CAPITA IN KG
VARIABLE 2 IS DEFLATED RETAIL PRICE OF LAMB PER KG

DATA

1	2
17.800	92.400
16.700	100.500
19.300	93.500
19.600	94.100
21.700	85.000
21.500	85.500
23.800	81.500
24.400	75.600
18.700	91.400
16.000	114.000

MOMENT MATRIX
0.7299E+01
−0.2521E+02   0.1030E+03

VARIABLE 1 MEAN= 19.95000   STANDR DEV= 2.84771
VARIABLE 2 MEAN= 91.35000   STANDR DEV= 10.69613

SIMPLE CORRELATION MATRIX

	1	2
1	1.00000	
2	−0.91953	1.00000

COMPUTATION OF REGRESSION EQUATION
    DEPENDENT VARIABLE IS 1
    INDEPENDENT VARIABLES ARE 2

INVERSE MATRIX   VECTOR OF DEPENDENT/INDEPENDENT MOMENTS
0.9712E−02   −0.2521E+02

B-COEFFICIENTS
−0.244813

STANDARD ERRORS
0.036995

T-TEST
−6.617487

RSQUARE= 0.84553342   VARESIDUALS= 0.14092188E+01
RSQUARE ADJUSTED FOR DF= 0.82622510

ANALYSIS OF VARIANCE

TSS = 72.985046   SSR = 61.711296   SSE = 11.273750
DF1 = 1.0   DF2 = 8.0   F-RATIO = 43.791139

CONSTANT TERM = 42.313672

STANDARD ERROR OF CONSTANT = 3.40026656

OBS	ACTUAL	PREDICTED	ERROR
1	17.800	19.693	−1.893
2	16.700	17.710	−1.010
3	19.300	19.424	−0.124
4	19.600	19.277	0.323
5	21.700	21.505	0.195
6	21.500	21.382	0.118
7	23.800	22.361	1.439
8	24.400	23.806	0.594
9	18.700	19.938	−1.238
10	16.000	14.405	1.595

DURBIN WATSON STATISTIC = 2.031740

Interpreting the above data, we note first that in printing some numbers the computer uses the so-called 'scientific' notation, eg the number $0.1030E + 03$. The symbol $E + 03$ following the decimal fraction 0.1030 indicates that the fraction is to be multiplied by 10 raised to the power of 3; thus $0.1030E + 03$ translates into $0.1030 \times 10^3 = 103.0$; similarly, $0.9712E − 02$ is 0.009712, etc.

As will be recalled from section 8.2, the primary calculations in simple regression involve finding the sums of squares Σx^2 and Σy^2, and the sum of cross-products Σxy. When the sum of squared deviations of values of a variable from their mean, eg the sum Σx^2, is divided by N, the number of sample observations, the result is called the second moment of the variable from its mean. Writing the second moment of X as m_{xx} and the second moment of Y as m_{yy}, we have

$$m_{xx} = \frac{\Sigma x^2}{N} \qquad m_{yy} = \frac{\Sigma y^2}{N}$$

Similarly, for the cross-product term we may write

$$m_{xy} = \frac{\Sigma(X - \bar{X})(X - \bar{X})}{N} = \frac{\Sigma xy}{N}$$

If the quantities ΣX^2, ΣY^2 and ΣXY have been calculated, the corresponding moments may be found from the formulae

$$m_{xx} = \frac{\Sigma X^2}{N} - (\bar{X})^2 \qquad m_{yy} = \frac{\Sigma Y^2}{N} - (\bar{Y})^2 \qquad m_{xy} = \frac{\Sigma XY}{N} - (\bar{X})(\bar{Y})$$

Some regression programs print the moments of the variables in the regression as an array of numbers labelled in our print-out as the 'moment matrix'. In tabular form:

	Y	X
Y	m_{yy}	
X	m_{xy}	m_{xx}

We note that the dependent variable Y is designated as 'variable 1' and is entered first; also, since $\Sigma xy = \Sigma yx$, the moment m_{xy} needs only be entered once. In our printed data, the element listed first is $0.7299E+01$; thus, $m_{yy} = 7.299$, and similarly $m_{xy} = -25.21$ and $m_{xx} = 103.0$.

Next, the computer prints the mean and standard deviation of the variables X and Y. The simple correlation matrix and the inverse matrix do not concern us in simple regression, and will be explained in section 8.8. Here we merely note that the regression coefficient b is computed as

$$b = \left(\frac{1}{m_{xx}}\right)\left(m_{xy}\right) = (0.009712)(-25.21)$$

$$= -0.244839$$

which differs slightly from the printed result of -0.244813 because of rounding. The estimated standard error of $b(s_b)$ is shown as 0.036995, and for the constant term we have $a = 42.313672$ and $s_a = 3.400267$.

A measure of the absolute fit of the observed data to the fitted line is given by the standard error of estimate s_e. This is not computed by our program, but we are given VARESIDUALS $= 0.14092188E+01$. Taking the square root, we find

$$s_e = \sqrt{1.40922} = 1.187105 \text{ (kg)}$$

The relative measures of goodness of fit are given by $r^2 = 0.84553$ and $r = -0.91953$.

We recall next that the variation of Y, as measured by the total sum of squares (TSS), can be partitioned into two components: the variation due to regression (SSR) and the variation due to error (SSE). From the analysis-of-variance data given in the print-out sheet we have

TSS	=	SSR	+	SSE
72.985046		61.711296		11.273750

Using this result and recalling that SSE $= \Sigma e^2$, we can readily check that

$$s_e^2 = \frac{\text{SSE}}{N-2} = \frac{11.273750}{8} = 1.40922$$

as above. Also since $s_b^2 = s_e^2/\Sigma x^2$, where $\Sigma x^2 = N m_{xx} = (10)(103.0)$,

$$s_b^2 = \frac{1.40922}{1030} = 0.0013682$$

and hence $s_b = 0.03699$, as above.

In the next three columns the actual values of Y are compared with the values 'predicted' by the regression, and the residuals e_i, $i = 1, 2, \ldots, 10$, are computed; these residuals may be regarded as observations of the unknown ε_i. Thus, for $X = 92.4$, we have

$$\hat{Y} = 42.3137 + (-0.244813)(92.4)$$

$$= 19.693$$

and $e_1 = 17.8 - 19.693 = -1.893$, etc. As can be easily verified, $e_1^2 + e_2^2 + \ldots + e_{10}^2 = \Sigma e_i^2 = $ SSE (with small rounding errors).

The last entry in the computer output sheet is the Durbin–Watson statistic; its meaning and use in regression analysis are discussed in section 8.11 below.

The computer output for the lamb consumption–price data provides us with all the information needed for analysis and prediction. We may now summarise and analyse the printed results by proceeding as follows:

Regression:

$$\hat{Y} = 42 \cdot 314 - 0 \cdot 245X$$

$$(3 \cdot 400) \quad (0 \cdot 037)$$

We interpret this result by saying that for a rise of one cent in the 'real' retail price of lamb, ie price corrected for increases in the general price level, we would expect annual per capita consumption of lamb to fall, on the average, by $0 \cdot 245$ kilograms.

Goodness of Fit:

The coefficient of determination r^2 is $0 \cdot 846$, and we may therefore say that nearly 85 per cent of the observed variation in lamb consumption can be accounted for by variations in price. However, because of the smallness of our sample, this may be an overestimate of the true proportion of the variation in Y explained by X. When corrected for this possible bias, the proportion of 'explained' variation is found to be $82 \cdot 6$ per cent ($\bar{r}^2 = 0 \cdot 8262$). These measures, together with the correlation coefficient of $-0 \cdot 9195$, indicate that the line of relationship is a good fit to the observed data.

Significance of b:

To assess whether or not a regression with slope $b = -0 \cdot 245$ could reasonably occur by chance if there were no relationship between lamb consumption and price we perform the standard two-sided test of the null hypothesis $H_o : \beta = 0$ against the alternative hypothesis $H_a : \beta \neq 0$. From the computer data, the value of $|t|$, computed for the null hypothesis $\beta = 0$, is $6 \cdot 617$, and from the t-table, with $v = 8$ degrees of freedom, we have $t_{.025} = 2 \cdot 306$ and $t_{.005} = 3 \cdot 355$. Since $|t| = 6 \cdot 617 > 3 \cdot 355$, we are able to reject the hypothesis of no relationship at the 1 per cent level of significance. If, however, on theoretical grounds we postulate that if a relationship between lamb consumption and price exists it is a linear function with a negative slope, then a more powerful test is the one-tailed test of $H_o : \beta = 0$ against $H_a : \beta < 0$. Referring to the t-table, we find $t = -6 \cdot 617 < t_{.01} = -2 \cdot 896$, and hence our test supports the economic hypothesis that in the true demand relationship lamb consumption and price are inversely related.

Confidence Limits for α and β:

To ascertain the range within which the true value of β can be expected to lie we compute the 95 per cent confidence limits

$$b \pm t_{.025} s_b$$

ie $\qquad -0 \cdot 245 \pm (2 \cdot 306)(0 \cdot 037)$

ie $\qquad -0 \cdot 160$ to $-0 \cdot 330$

Similarly, the confidence limits for α are

$$a \pm t_{.025} s_a$$

ie $\qquad 42 \cdot 314 \pm (2 \cdot 306)(3 \cdot 4)$

ie $\qquad 34 \cdot 47$ to $50 \cdot 15$

Thus, we can state with 95 per cent confidence that α lies within the range $34 \cdot 47$ to $50 \cdot 15$ and β lies within the range $-0 \cdot 16$ to $-0 \cdot 33$.

F-Ratio Test:

In simple regression, an equivalent test to the two-sided t-test is the F-test.

The value of the F-statistic, as calculated by the computer, is 43·791. Comparing this value with the critical value of $F_{.01}$, with $v_1 = 1$ and $v_2 = 8$ degrees of freedom, we find

$$F = 43·791 > 11·26$$

and the hypothesis of no relationship is again rejected at the 1 per cent level of significance.

Prediction:

Suppose we wish to use the regression equation $\hat{Y} = 42·314 - 0·245X$ to estimate the annual per capita consumption of lamb in a particular year for which the retail price of lamb is 90 cents/kg. Letting $X_o = 90$, from the regression equation we shall have

$$\hat{Y}_o = 42·314 + (-0·245)(90)$$
$$= 20·26 \text{ kilograms}$$

Let us use this result to find prediction limits for the mean value of Y associated with the given X, ie the value which we should expect to get if we averaged per capita lamb consumption over a number of periods for which the observed 'real' price of lamb was 90 cents/kg. We can ascertain 95 per cent prediction limits for the mean $\mu_Y(X = 90)$ as

$$\hat{Y}_o \pm t_{.025}s_e\sqrt{\frac{1}{N} + \frac{(X_o - \bar{X})^2}{\Sigma x^2}}$$

From the printed computer results we have $s_e = \sqrt{1·409} = 1·187$ and $\Sigma x^2 = Nm_{xx} = 1030$; also, with $v = 8$, $t_{.025} = 2·306$. We can be 95 per cent confident that $\mu_Y(X = 90)$ lies within the limits

$$20·26 \pm (2·306)(1·187)\sqrt{\frac{1}{10} + \frac{(90 - 91·35)^2}{1030}}$$

ie   19·39 to 21·13 kilograms

For practical purposes, we are more often interested in predicting an *individual* value of Y likely to be associated with a particular value of X. From our regression equation, for $X_o = 90$, the prediction limits for a single value Y_o are given by

$$\hat{Y}_o \pm t_{.025}s_e\sqrt{1 + \frac{1}{N} + \frac{(X_o - \bar{X})^2}{\Sigma x^2}}$$

ie $20·26 \pm 2·87$

ie   17·39 to 23·13 kilograms

A test of a prediction is, of course, how the prediction measures up against subsequently observed values of the predicted variable. From published sources, per capita consumption of lamb for the year 1974/75 was recorded as 18 kilograms, and the retail price of lamb deflated by the Consumer Price Index 1966–67 = 100 was calculated as 89.7 cents[1]; rounded to the nearest cent, this gives $X = 90$ as above. As can be seen, the actually observed value of 18 kilograms lies within the prediction range of 17·39 to 23·13 kilograms computed on the basis of our estimating equation.

[1] Bureau of Agricultural Economics: *Meat Situation and Outlook*, 1976, pp 32 and 88; and Australian Bureau of Statistics: *Monthly Review of Business Statistics*, June 1976, p 30.

8.7 Sampling from a Bivariate Normal Population

In the model of simple regression discussed thus far we have considered the dependent variable Y to be a random variable with a probability distribution, whereas the Xs were treated as known constants. Our next development is to consider a bivariate model in which the values of X, as well as those of Y, are assumed to be drawings from a probability distribution. In the most commonly applied model of this type, the sample values of X and Y are assumed to have been drawn from a joint probability distribution known as the bivariate normal distribution.[1] Thus, we may have N observations on X and Y and we may wish to know whether the sample data could reasonably have come from a bivariate normal population in which values of one variable tend to be associated with values of the other variable. As already remarked in section 8.1, a method of analysis which investigates the degree of association between two random variables is known as *correlation analysis*. Given that two jointly distributed normal variables are correlated, what is the form of the relationship between the variables likely to be? As we shall see below, this relationship will in fact be a linear one, and this provides a link between correlation analysis and the simple regression model discussed in the preceding sections.

The Bivariate Normal Distribution

Just as in Chapter 4 we represented the distribution of a single normal variable by a continuous probability curve in two dimensions, so we can represent one in two normal variables by a probability surface in three dimensions; this is illustrated in Fig 8.12. The volume under this surface is unity and the probability of selecting an element at random from the population with its X value between x_1 and x_2 *and* its Y value between y_1 and y_2 is measured by the fraction of total volume standing above the area shaded in the diagram.

The bivariate normal distribution is defined by a mathematical equation known as the bivariate normal density function of X and Y. The mathematical form of this function is quite complex, and will not be given here. It will suffice for our purposes to note that the bivariate normal distribution is defined by five parameters. These are μ_X, μ_Y, σ_X, σ_Y and ρ. The first two are the means and the second two the standard deviations of X and Y respectively. The parameter ρ, defined as

$$\rho = \frac{\sigma_{XY}}{\sigma_X \sigma_X}$$

[1] For the concept of a bivariate probability distribution, see section 4.14 above.

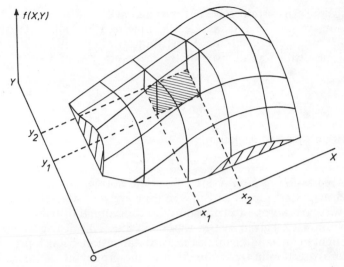

Fig 8.12 The normal probability surface

where σ_{XY} is the covariance between X and Y (see section 4.14, p 153), is the coefficient of linear correlation of the population distribution. It must lie within the range ± 1, and measures the degree to which values of X and Y tend to be associated in the population.

If we have two random variables X and Y, the probability distribution of Y, given some particular value of X, is a univariate probability distribution called the conditional probability distribution of Y (see section 4.14, p 151). From the mathematical formula for the bivariate normal distribution it can be shown that for any given X this conditional distribution is normal with mean $E(Y|X) = \mu_Y + \rho \dfrac{\sigma_Y}{\sigma_X}(X - \mu_X)$ and variance $\text{Var}(Y|X) = \sigma_Y^2(1 - \rho^2)$. Writing the conditional mean as $\mu_Y(X)$, we can see that $\mu_Y(X)$ is linearly related to X, ie it can be written

$$\mu_Y(X) = \alpha + \beta X$$

where $\qquad \beta = \rho \dfrac{\sigma_Y}{\sigma_X}$ and $\alpha = \mu_Y - \beta \mu_X$.

This is the regression of Y on X for a bivariate normal population with given parameters $\mu_X, \mu_Y, \sigma_X, \sigma_Y$ and ρ. Writing the standard deviation of the conditional distribution of Y as $\sigma_Y(X)$, we have

$$\sigma_Y(X) = \sigma_Y \sqrt{1 - \rho^2}$$

which is the same irrespective of the value of X.

By similar argument, if we select a value of Y and allow X to vary over its range, the conditional distribution of X will be a normal distribution with a mean given by the regression line of X on Y

$$\mu_X(Y) = \gamma + \delta Y$$

where $\qquad \gamma = \mu_X - \delta\mu_Y \quad \text{and} \quad \delta = \rho\dfrac{\sigma_X}{\sigma_Y}$

and with a standard deviation

$$\sigma_X(Y) = \sigma_X\sqrt{1 - \rho^2}$$

The regression of Y on X for a bivariate normal population is illustrated diagrammatically in Fig 8.13. For a given value of X, say X', there will be a normal distribution, the conditional distribution of Y, centred on $\mu_Y(X')$ given by the regression line. This distribution must be thought of as standing up in the third dimension, being a perpendicular cross-section in the Y-direction of the probability surface. Such cross-sections will, of course, be greater in size the nearer is X to its mean. The standard deviation of the distribution of Y for a given X in the normal bivariate distribution is always the same irrespective of

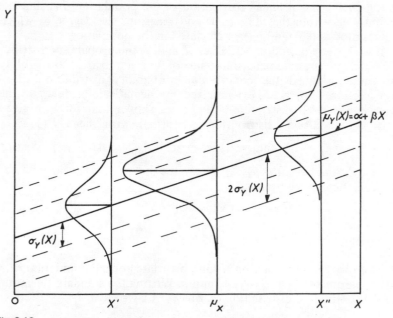

Fig 8.13

the particular value of the given X. This is illustrated in the diagram by the fact that the curves drawn there have identical absolute dispersion.

Since for a given X, Y is normally distributed about a mean $\mu_Y(X)$ = $\alpha + \beta X$ with a standard deviation $\sigma_Y(X) = \sigma_Y \sqrt{1 - \rho^2}$, the range $\mu_Y(X) \pm \sigma_Y(X)$ will contain about two-thirds of the Y values for the given X, and $\mu_Y(X) \pm 2\sigma_Y(X)$ will contain about 95 per cent of the values. It follows that bands running a distance $\sigma_Y(X)$ and $2\sigma_Y(X)$ from the regression of Y on X will contain approximately two-thirds and 95 per cent respectively of the population (in geometric terms two-thirds and 95 per cent of the volume) and similarly, *mutatis mutandis*, for the regression of X on Y. Such bands are shown in Fig 8.13 above. If we pick units at random from the population, as the sample gets larger approximately two-thirds of the plot points will lie in the narrower and 95 per cent in the wider bands.

If $\rho = 0$, ie if there is no correlation, then

$$\mu_Y(X) = \mu_Y \quad \text{and} \quad \mu_X(Y) = \mu_X$$

and

$$\sigma_Y(X) = \sigma_Y \quad \text{and} \quad \sigma_X(Y) = \sigma_X$$

In this case the value of X in no way affects the distribution of the Ys, the distributions of Y being identical for all given Xs and vice versa. This is the case of complete independence of X and Y.[1]

If two random variables X and Y are jointly normally distributed, the regression of Y on X gives the mean value of Y for a given X, and the regression of X on Y gives the mean value of X for a given Y. It is sometimes found rather puzzling to have two different regression lines associated with a bivariate normal population. These two lines are characteristics of the population and are not due to the chances of sampling. It will be recalled from section 8.2 that if we have N sample values of X and Y we may fit the two regression lines

$$Y_c = a + bX$$

and

$$X_c = c + dY$$

by the method of least squares. The first line is a 'best' fit in the sense that it minimises vertical deviations, whereas the second is a 'best' fit in the sense that it minimises horizontal deviations. Thus, the 'X' in the first equation, which denotes actual observations of the variable X, must be distinguished from the 'X_c' in the second equation, which is our estimate of the average value of X that we can expect to be

---

[1] See also footnote 2 on p 325 below.

associated with a particular Y. For the population, the corresponding lines of relationship are

$$\mu_Y(X) = \alpha + \beta X$$

and

$$\mu_X(Y) = \gamma + \delta Y$$

These two equations arise because in the present case both X and Y are random variables, and hence both are subject to random error. If we are conducting an experiment in which we control the values of X so that they do not vary due to chance, then only one of the two regression lines is relevant, namely the regression of Y on X. Similarly, if we have reason to believe that X in some sense 'determines' Y, eg the age of a house determines its rent rather than vice versa, we shall mainly be concerned with the Y on X regression. In general, however, if we have a sample of N observations drawn at random from a bivariate normal population we may wish to use the sample either to predict the expected value of Y for some given value of X or we may wish to use it to predict the expected value of X for some given value of Y. Thus, suppose the ages of husbands (X) and wives (Y) are jointly normally distributed, and we are interested in predicting the mean age of wives of men of a certain age. We have a random sample of N married couples, and from the sample data we compute a sample regression equation $\hat{Y} = a + bX$. Using $\hat{Y}$ as a point predictor of the unknown $\mu_Y(X)$, we may estimate the mean age of wives of thirty-year old husbands as, say, twenty-six years. However, since 'age of husband' in this instance is a given number whereas 'age of wife' is an expected value, it would be wrong to infer from our regression that the husbands of twenty-six-year-old women must on average be thirty years of age. To predict the *expected* or mean age of husbands of women who are twenty-six years of age we need to compute the regression of X on Y (see section 8.2, p 287 above) and then use the fitted line as an estimate of the population regression of age of husband on age of wife. When $\rho = \pm 1$, there is perfect covariability between two variables, and $\beta = \dfrac{1}{\delta}$. In this case we have only one value of Y associated with every X and vice versa, and only one line of relationship.

Testing the Significance of the Correlation Coefficient

If we have a random sample of N pairs of observations from a bivariate normal population, we may wish to estimate the regression lines and the coefficient of linear correlation. Since each point on the population regression line of Y on X is given by the mean of a normal conditional distribution of Y, and each of these conditional distributions has the same variance, the regression analysis outlined earlier in this chapter also applies to bivariate normal populations. Thus, the equation $Y_c = a + bX$ calculated from the sample by the method of least squares can be used as an estimate of the regression of Y on X in the population, and the same holds *mutatis mutandis* for the regression of X on Y.

In sampling from a bivariate normal population we are often not interested in estimating the population regression line but we merely wish to use the sample data to test whether the population relationship between the variables is likely to be weak or strong. An estimate of the unknown population correlation coefficient ρ is the sample correlation coefficient r calculated from the formula $r = \dfrac{\Sigma xy}{\sqrt{\Sigma x^2 \Sigma y^2}}$. Since r is computed from a sample, it is subject to sampling error. It follows that in correlation analysis it is always necessary to test whether a sample value of r could reasonably have come from a population in which there was no linear correlation, before concluding that the two variables are correlated. This can readily be handled by devising tests for the significance of r.

We have a sample of N pairs of observations with a correlation coefficient of r. Could such a value of r have come from a population in which there was no linear correlation, ie in which $\rho = 0$? In other words, is the correlation coefficient r statistically significant?

It will be readily appreciated that the distribution of sample values of r drawn from a population in which $\rho = 0$ cannot be normal, since the value of r is bounded by ± 1, and the normal distribution is asymptotic at both ends. However, since $\beta = \rho \dfrac{\sigma_Y}{\sigma_X}$, if $\rho = 0$, β must also $= 0$ (and $\delta = 0$ also). It follows that a test of the significance of b as against the hypothesis $\beta = 0$ is equivalent to a test of the significance of r against the hypothesis $\rho = 0$. This rather simplifies matters, for we already know that the test statistic for the hypothesis $H_o : \beta = 0$ is given by $t = \dfrac{b}{s_b}$, which has the t-distribution with $N - 2$ degrees of freedom.

The test $t = \dfrac{b}{s_b}$ can easily be put in terms of r, thus giving a direct test for r against the hypothesis that $\rho = 0$. Since

$$s_b = \frac{s_e}{\sqrt{\Sigma x^2}}$$

where

$$s_e = \sqrt{\frac{(1 - r^2)\Sigma y^2}{N - 2}}$$

we have

$$t = \frac{b}{s_b}$$

$$= \frac{\Sigma xy}{\sqrt{\Sigma x^2}} \frac{\sqrt{N - 2}}{\sqrt{(1 - r^2)\Sigma y^2}}$$

$$= \frac{r\sqrt{N - 2}}{\sqrt{1 - r^2}}$$

Hence $t = \dfrac{r\sqrt{N - 2}}{\sqrt{1 - r^2}}$ is distributed in the t-distribution with $N - 2$ degrees of freedom,[1] where r is the coefficient of linear correlation of a sample drawn from a population with $\rho = 0$. We may then test the null hypothesis $H_o: \rho = 0$ against the alternative hypothesis $H_a: \rho \neq 0$ by the procedure outlined in section 5.5 above.

Example 8.9

A random sample of 27 factories has a coefficient of linear correlation of $r = 0.60$ between the number of industrial accidents occurring over a year and the age of the factory. Is this evidence of a linear relationship between number of accidents and age?

Hypothesis: The sample comes from a normal bivariate population in which $\rho = 0$, ie

$$H_o: \rho = 0$$
$$H_a: \rho \neq 0$$

Test:
$$|t| = \frac{|r|\sqrt{N - 2}}{\sqrt{1 - r^2}}$$

$$= \frac{0.60 \times 5}{0.80}$$

$$= 3.75$$

Conclusion: From the t-table, with $v = 25$, the critical value of t at the 5 per cent level of significance is found to be 2.060, which is less than the t-value obtained in the test. Hence we reject the null hypothesis that $\rho = 0$ and accept the alternative hypothesis $H_a: \rho \neq 0$. We say that the sample correlation coefficient r is significant and its value is evidence of a linear relationship between number of accidents and age of factory.

---

[1] Tables giving the critical values of r direct for different levels of significance are available. See R A Fisher: *Statistical Methods for Research Workers* (Oliver and Boyd, 1958), pp 209–10.

Meaning of the Coefficient of Linear Correlation[1]

The interpretation of the sample correlation coefficient r depends upon whether we regard the regression model or the correlation model as being appropriate to our analysis. If we can regard the X values as non-random quantities and the Y values as drawings from the conditional distributions of Y for the given Xs, then r is interpreted as a measure of the closeness of fit of the regression line to the given data. If, on the other hand, we can regard the observations of both X and Y as random variables having as their joint probability distribution the bivariate normal distribution, we can use r as a sample estimate of the unknown population correlation coefficient ρ. In the remainder of this section we discuss the correlation coefficient as a measure of the covariability between two jointly distributed normal variables.

A positive relationship between X and Y will be indicated $(0 < \rho < 1)$ when large values of X tend to be associated with large values of Y, and conversely for small values of X. Similarly a negative relationship will be indicated $(-1 < \rho < 0)$ when large values of X tend to be associated with small values of Y, and conversely for small values of X. An absence of relationship will be indicated $(\rho = 0)$ when neither of the above tendencies is present. In this case X and Y are *independent*, for the particular value which Y assumes is quite unaffected by the value of X paired with it, and vice versa.[2]

The greater ρ the more reliance can we place on the line of regression as a predicting instrument. For example, suppose that X stands for age of houses and Y for rent. If we wish to predict the rent of a particular house and we have no information about the house, the best we can do is to use μ_Y—the mean rent of houses—as a prediction. This is the best we can do in the sense that the errors in making a series of such predictions will be smaller than if we were to use any figure other than μ_Y. Actual rents will be distributed about μ_Y with a dispersion measured by σ_Y, so that σ_Y will be an indication of the errors of prediction. In fact 95 per cent of houses will have rents within $\mu_Y \pm 1\cdot96\,\sigma_Y$. However, if we know the regression of rent on age of house

$$\mu_Y(X) = \alpha + \beta X$$

and we know the age of the particular house under consideration, we should do better by predicting the rent of the house as $\mu_Y(X)$. For actual rents of houses of the given age will be distributed about $\mu_Y(X)$

---

[1] See also sections 4.14 and 8.2.

[2] In section 4.14 we noted that if two random variables X and Y are independent, then they are also uncorrelated, ie $\rho = 0$. When X and Y have the bivariate normal distribution the converse of this theorem also holds: if $\rho = 0$, then X and Y are independent. Thus, for normally distributed random variables, zero correlation implies independence.

with a dispersion measured by $\sigma_Y(X) = \sigma_Y\sqrt{1 - \rho^2}$, so that $\sigma_Y(X)$ will be an indication of the errors of prediction. Again 95 per cent of houses of the given age will have rents within $\mu_Y(X) \pm 1.96\, \sigma_Y\sqrt{1 - \rho^2}$. It can be seen that the accuracy of a prediction of Y can be increased if we know X and the regression of Y on X, and the greater ρ for a given σ_Y the smaller the errors in using the regression for purposes of prediction. If $\rho = \pm 1$, the relationship between X and Y is exact, and no errors of prediction are incurred in estimating Y from a knowledge of X.

Just as the mean and standard deviation of a single variable are characteristics of the population, so in the case of a bivariate population is the coefficient of correlation (and the regression lines which are defined in terms of the parameters μ_X, μ_Y, σ_X, σ_Y and ρ). Thus, if the value of ρ between ages of husbands and wives were 0·9 in Australia and 0·7 in the United Kingdom, this would represent a real difference in the marriage habits of the two countries. These figures would indicate that the ages of husbands and wives were more closely associated in Australia than in the United Kingdom. A bivariate normal population cannot be fully specified without the correlation coefficient.

In section 8.2 above we saw that the sample correlation coefficient r can be defined as the square root of the coefficient of determination given by the ratio $\dfrac{\Sigma(Y_c - \bar{Y})^2}{\Sigma(Y - \bar{Y})^2}$. Although it can be shown that this ratio can be used as a measure of correlation where the regression is not linear, the sample correlation coefficient reduces to $r = \dfrac{\Sigma xy}{\sqrt{\Sigma x^2 \Sigma y^2}}$ only when $Y_c = a + bX$, ie when the regression is linear. Hence, the fact that for a particular sample of observations r is close to 0 (when calculated from the formula $r = \dfrac{\Sigma xy}{\sqrt{\Sigma x^2 \Sigma y^2}}$) does not neces-sarily indicate the absence of a relationship, sampling errors apart. It indicates only the absence of a linear relationship. This is illustrated in the following diagram:

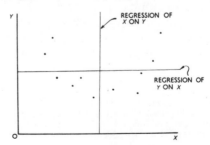

Fig 8.14

Here r would be very small, but there is clearly a relationship (curvilinear) between X and Y. Consequently, $r = \dfrac{\Sigma xy}{\sqrt{\Sigma x^2 \Sigma y^2}}$ can be used validly as a measure of correlation only if we can suppose that the sample has been drawn from a population in which the relationship is linear. As we have seen above, this will be the case when the sampling is made from a bivariate normal population.

Correlation and Causation

The existence of correlation does not necessarily imply causation. Correlation merely indicates association or, more strictly speaking, covariation. To infer a causal relationship between X and Y, just because a set of observations on X and Y yield a high value for r, is a very unsafe procedure. Often two variables are both related to a third one, with the result that they are highly correlated with each other, although they are not directly related in the sense that changes in the one would on the average produce changes in the other, other things being equal. This frequently happens when observations recorded over time are correlated.

As an illustration of this, Yule[1] correlated the proportion of Church of England marriages to all marriages in England and Wales for the years 1866–1911 with the standardised mortality rate for the same period and obtained a value of r of 0·95. To draw the conclusion that the greater the proportion of marriages solemnised by the Church of England the higher the death rate would be absurd. The fact is that both series of figures moved steadily downwards over the period for quite unconnected reasons, and consequently their values over the period varied together. It is easy to produce such nonsense correlations from observations recorded over time, and frequently they yield very high values for the correlation coefficient.[2] Accordingly, in such cases a high value for r, although it indicates strong covariation, has no significance whatever in indicating a *real* relationship.

Frequently correlations, while not of a nonsensical character, are brought about by the operation of a third factor. Thus we might find that fathers' IQs and the sizes of their families are negatively correlated. This suggests that the less intelligent tend to have larger families. It would be unwise to infer this, however, without further investigation. It may be, for example, that there is a positive correlation between

[1] G U Yule: 'Why do we sometimes get nonsense-correlations between time series?' *Journal of the Royal Statistical Society*, Vol. LXXXIX, January 1926, p 1.

[2] See section 9.7, p 375 below.

IQ and income and a negative one between income and family size. Consequently the relations between IQ and income, and family size and income would produce a negative correlation between observations on IQ and family size, even though for *given incomes* IQ and family size were quite unrelated. Such problems as these involve more than two variables and require *multivariate* analysis, an elementary introduction to which is given in the next section.[1]

A high value for *r* indicates a high degree of covariation between the two variables under consideration. This cannot be used as evidence for association or a causal relationship unless the possibility of the covariation being due to the operation of other related variables has been carefully investigated. In any event, the best procedure is usually to postulate an hypothetical causal relation which can be tested against observed date. If *r* turns out to be high, the hypothesis is supported as far as that piece of evidence is concerned. But a high value of *r* can never prove that a relationship between *X* and *Y* exists. It can only indicate that the data are not inconsistent with one. The reasonableness of the relationship on general theoretical grounds must always be carefully examined. It follows that a detailed knowledge of the data is necessary before general conclusions can be drawn from correlations.

8.8 Multiple Regression

Simple regression deals with the case of the relation between a dependent variable (*Y*) and one independent or explanatory variable (*X*). With the use of this model we were able to explain the basic principles of least-squares regression and to investigate its main statistical properties. The main limitation of the simple-regression model is that it enables us to judge accurately the relationship between two variables if all other variables that have an important effect on the relationship can be assumed to remain unchanged during the observation period, ie if the *ceteris paribus* condition can be assumed to hold. In investigations of economic phenomena this is seldom possible, and we therefore need a more general model in which the separate influences of two or more explanatory variables can be explicitly taken into account. Methods similar to those used for simple regression are available for fitting multiple-regression equations to observed data and for testing the significance of the regression coefficients. As in the simple-regression model, these methods require that the dependent variable *Y* is a random variable with certain statistical properties and the explanatory variables

[1] See also pp 348–50 below.

are either non-random variables or are statistically independent of the error term ε.

In this section we illustrate the technique of multiple regression by considering a three-variable case. In regression problems with several explanatory variables the computations become quite involved, and in practical work will usually be performed by an electronic computer using a library program. This section is intended purely as an introduction to multiple regression. For more advanced treatment of the subject reference should be made to the many available texts on multivariate methods and econometrics (see Appendix C, 1, 2 and 3).

In sections 8.2 and 8.4 we considered the linear model

$$Y_i = \alpha + \beta X_i + \varepsilon_i \qquad \text{(for all } i\text{)}$$

$$\mu_Y(X) = \alpha + \beta X$$

for the population, and the linear model

$$Y_i = a + bX_i + e_i \qquad \text{(for } i = 1, 2, \ldots, N)$$

$$Y_c = a + bX$$

for the sample. When there are k explanatory variables, the corresponding relations may be written

$$Y_i = \alpha + \beta_1 X_{1i} + \beta_2 X_{2i} + \ldots + \beta_k X_{ki} + \varepsilon_i$$

$$\mu_Y(X_1, X_2, \ldots, X_k) = \alpha + \beta_1 X_1 + \beta_2 X_2 + \ldots + \beta_k X_k$$

and

$$Y_i = a + b_1 X_{1i} + b_2 X_{2i} + \ldots + b_k X_{ki} + e_i$$

$$Y_c = a + b_1 X_1 + b_2 X_2 + \ldots + b_k X_k$$

Here we speak of the *multiple regression* of Y on $X_1, X_2, \ldots, X_k$, and $\beta_1, \beta_2, \ldots, \beta_k$ are known as the *partial regression coefficients*. The coefficient β_1 measures the amount of change in the mean value of Y that we can expect if X_1 changes by one unit, the values of the remaining explanatory variables remaining unchanged, and similarly for β_2, β_3, $\ldots, \beta_k$. As before, the relationship between Y and the explanatory variables involves random error ε, and the ε_i are assumed to be independently distributed random variables, each with mean zero and variance σ_ε^2. The Xs are considered to be given non-random numbers. Since the assumptions concerning the random term are identical with those made for simple regression, multiple-regression analysis is an extension of the two-variable analysis presented earlier in this chapter.

Suppose we have N observations of the three variables Y, X_1 and X_2 and we postulate that the true relationship between the variables is

$$Y_i = \alpha + \beta_1 X_{1i} + \beta_2 X_{2i} + \varepsilon_i$$

so that the mean value of Y for given X_1 and X_2 is given by

$$\mu_Y(X_1, X_2) = \alpha + \beta_1 X_1 + \beta_2 X_2$$

We wish to make an estimate of this relation from our sample data. This can be done by calculating the sample regression equation

$$Y_c = a + b_1 X_1 + b_2 X_2$$

Geometrically, this equation is an equation of a plane in three-dimensional space, with Y being measured on the vertical axis, and X_1 and X_2 being measured along the two horizontal axes forming the base of this space. As before, we wish to fit a regression plane to the values of Y, X_1 and X_2 in such a way that the sum of the squared vertical deviations of the Y values from the plane is a minimum. Writing again $\Sigma e^2 = \Sigma(Y - Y_c)^2$, where the summation is over the N sample values, we require

$$\Sigma e^2 = \Sigma(Y - a - b_1 X_1 - b_2 X_2)^2$$

to be a minimum. There are now three coefficients, a, b_1 and b_2, to be determined, and hence three normal equations. However, in working with more than one explanatory variable it is more convenient to reduce the number of normal equations by considering a separately. It will be recalled that in the two-variable case the fitted regression must pass through the mean of the Xs and of the Ys, ie when $X = \bar{X}$, $Y_c = \bar{Y} = a + b\bar{X}$. Similarly in the three variable case when $X_1 = \bar{X}$ and $X_2 = \bar{X}_2$ we have

$$Y_c = \bar{Y} = a + b_1 \bar{X}_1 + b_2 \bar{X}_2$$

and hence

$$a = \bar{Y} - b_1 \bar{X}_1 - b_2 \bar{X}_2$$

If we substitute for a in the above expression for Σe^2, we shall have

$$\Sigma e^2 = \Sigma[(Y - \bar{Y}) - b_1(X_1 - \bar{X}_1) - b_2(X_2 - \bar{X}_2)]^2$$
$$= \Sigma(y - b_1 x_1 - b_2 x_2)^2$$

Differentiating partially with respect to b_1 and b_2, and setting the derivatives to zero, we obtain the normal equations for determining b_1 and b_2. The normal equations are

$$\Sigma yx_1 = b_1 \Sigma x_1^2 + b_2 \Sigma x_1 x_2$$
$$\Sigma yx_2 = b_1 \Sigma x_1 x_2 + b_2 \Sigma x_2^2$$

Solving these equations simultaneously by substitution,[1] we get

[1] For another method of solution see example 8.12 below.

$$b_1 = \frac{\Sigma yx_1 \Sigma x_2^2 - \Sigma yx_2 \Sigma x_1 x_2}{D}$$

$$b_2 = \frac{\Sigma yx_2 \Sigma x_1^2 - \Sigma yx_1 \Sigma x_1 x_2}{D}$$

where $\qquad D = \Sigma x_1^2 \Sigma x_2^2 - (\Sigma x_1 x_2)^2$

Example 8.10

As a numerical illustration of the above formulae, suppose that for our earlier example of eleven tenanted houses (example 8.1, p 280) we have information about the size of each sampled house, as measured by the number of rooms. The hypothetical data appear as follows:

Weekly Rent (dollars) Y	Age (years) X_1	Size (no. of rooms) X_2
50	3	6
32	12	7
40	5	5
33	7	6
45	8	10
13	19	4
30	10	5
14	22	3
28	15	3
51	8	9
26	25	8

From example 8.1 we already have

$$\bar{Y} = 32.9091 \qquad \bar{X}_1 = 12.1818$$
$$\Sigma y^2 = 1650.909 \qquad \Sigma x_1^2 = 517.636 \qquad \Sigma yx_1 = -751.818$$

We now compute

$$\bar{X}_2 = 6$$
$$\Sigma X_2^2 = 450 \qquad \Sigma X_1 X_2 = 758 \qquad \Sigma YX_2 = 2367$$

and

$$\Sigma x_2^2 = \Sigma X_2^2 - N\bar{X}_2^2 = 54$$
$$\Sigma x_1 x_2 = \Sigma X_1 X_2 - N\bar{X}_1 \bar{X}_2 = -46$$
$$\Sigma yx_2 = \Sigma YX_2 - N\bar{Y}\bar{X}_2 = 195$$

Accordingly

$$b_1 = \frac{\Sigma yx_1 \Sigma x_2^2 - \Sigma yx_2 \Sigma x_1 x_2}{\Sigma x_1^2 \Sigma x_2^2 - (\Sigma x_1 x_2)^2}$$

$$= \frac{(-751.818)(54) - (195)(-46)}{(517.636)(54) - (-46)^2}$$

$$= -1.224$$

$$b_2 = \frac{\Sigma yx_2 \Sigma x_1^2 - \Sigma yx_1 \Sigma x_1 x_2}{\Sigma x_1^2 \Sigma x_2^2 - (\Sigma x_1 x_2)^2}$$

$$= \frac{(195)(517\cdot636) - (-751\cdot818)(-46)}{(517\cdot636)(54) - (-46)^2}$$

$$= 2\cdot568$$

and

$$a = \bar{Y} - b_1 \bar{X}_1 - b_2 \bar{X}_2$$

$$= 32\cdot91 - (-1\cdot224)(12\cdot18) - (2\cdot568)(6)$$

$$= 32\cdot41$$

The multiple regression equation is

$$Y_c = 32\cdot41 - 1\cdot224 X_1 + 2\cdot568 X_2$$

In a regression equation with two regressors, X_1 and X_2, the coefficient b_1 measures the amount of change in Y_c consequent upon a unit change in X_1 when X_2 is held constant. Thus, in comparing the rents of, say, twelve-year and thirteen-year old houses in the above example, we should expect the rents of the latter to be on average $1·22 lower than those of the former, given that the houses being compared are of the same size. Similarly, for houses of the same age, we should expect the rent to rise by an average amount of $2·57 for each additional room. The coefficients b_1 and b_2 are thus seen to measure the net separate effect on the estimated mean value of Y of a change in a single explanatory variable, the influence of the other variable remaining constant. Comparing the simple regression of rent on age calculated in example 8.1 on p 280 with our present result, we find the b value of $-1·452$ to be numerically larger than the value of the corresponding partial regression coefficient b_1. This is due to the fact that in the simple regression of rent on age the possible influence of size of house on rent had been left out of account, with the simple regression coefficient b 'picking up' some of the effect on rent of the omitted variable X_2. When X_2 is added as an explanatory variable, its net effect on the variable Y is measured by the partial regression coefficient b_2. The relation between simple and multiple regression is further discussed in the next section.

Corresponding to the coefficient of determination in the bivariate case is a measure called the *coefficient of multiple determination*. It likewise measures the proportion of variability in the dependent variable 'explained' by the regression relationship. As before, we split the variability of the Ys into the variability about the regression and the variability due to the regression, ie

$$(Y_i - \bar{Y}) = (Y_c - \bar{Y}) + e_i$$

where e_i are the deviations of the Y values from the fitted plane. Squaring and summing over N, we have

$$\Sigma(Y_i - \bar{Y})^2 = \Sigma(Y_c - \bar{Y})^2 + \Sigma e_i^2 + 2\Sigma(Y_c - \bar{Y})e_i$$

By analogy with the two-variable case (p 284) if we write

$$Y_c - \bar{Y} = b_1(X_1 - \bar{X}_1) + b_2(X_2 - \bar{X}_2)$$

then

$$\Sigma(Y_c - \bar{Y})e_i = b_1\Sigma X_{1i}e_i + b_2\Sigma X_{2i}e_i - b_1\bar{X}_1\Sigma e_i - b_2\bar{X}\Sigma e_i$$

$$= 0$$

since $\Sigma e_i = 0$, $\Sigma X_{1i}e_i = 0$ and $\Sigma X_{2i}e_i = 0$. Hence

$$\Sigma(Y_i - \bar{Y})^2 = \Sigma(Y_c - \bar{Y})^2 + \Sigma e_i^2$$

ie the total sum of squares (TSS) of the variable Y is equal to the sum of squares due to the regression (SSR) plus the sum of squares of the regression residuals or errors (SSE). We now define the coefficient of multiple determination as

$$R^2 = \frac{SSR}{TSS}$$

$$= 1 - \frac{SSE}{TSS} = 1 - \frac{\Sigma e_i^2}{\Sigma y^2}$$

Clearly R^2 measures the proportion of variability in Y accounted for by the explanatory variables in the regression. To derive a computational formula for R^2 we write

$$\Sigma e_i^2 = \Sigma(Y_i - Y_c)^2 = \Sigma(Y_i - Y_c)[(Y_i - \bar{Y}) - (Y_c - \bar{Y})]$$

$$= \Sigma(Y_i - Y_c)(Y_i - \bar{Y})$$

(since from above $\Sigma(Y_i - Y_c)(Y_c - \bar{Y}) = \Sigma e_i(Y_c - \bar{Y}) = 0$)

$$= \Sigma e_i y_i$$

For each e_i, $i = 1, 2, \ldots, N$, we also have $e_i = y_i - b_1 x_{1i} - b_2 x_{2i}$. Omitting the subscript i, we may therefore write

$$\Sigma e^2 = \Sigma(y - b_1 x_1 - b_2 x_2)(y)$$

$$= \Sigma y^2 - b_1 \Sigma y x_1 - b_2 \Sigma y x_2$$

and

$$R^2 = 1 - \frac{\Sigma e^2}{\Sigma y^2}$$

$$= \frac{b_1 \Sigma y x_1 + b_2 \Sigma y x_2}{\Sigma y^2}$$

The square root of R^2 gives the *coefficient of multiple correlation*. In three-variable regression this coefficient is interpreted as measuring the closeness of fit of the fitted regression plane to the given data.

As in the case of simple regression, the adjusted coefficient of multiple determination is obtained by dividing each of the quantities Σe^2 and Σy^2 in the formula for R^2 by their respective number of degrees of freedom. In computing Σe^2, three parameters are replaced by sample estimates, and in computing Σy^2 the sample mean of the Ys is used instead of the unknown μ_Y. Hence, in the three-variable case, the corrected R^2 is defined as

$$\bar{R}^2 = 1 - \frac{\Sigma e^2/N - 3}{\Sigma y^2/N - 1} = 1 - \left(\frac{\Sigma e^2}{\Sigma y^2}\right)\left(\frac{N - 1}{N - 3}\right)$$

In general, if there are k explanatory variables in the regression, then $k + 1$ parameters must be estimated, and the number of degrees of freedom associated with Σe^2 is $N - (k + 1) = N - k - 1$.

As a measure of absolute dispersion of the Y values about the fitted regression plane we have as before the standard error of estimate

$$s_e = \sqrt{\frac{\Sigma e^2}{N - 3}}$$

From the results just established, we may compute s_e from the formulae

$$s_e = \sqrt{\frac{\Sigma y^2 - b_1\Sigma yx_1 - b_2\Sigma yx_2}{N - 3}}$$

$$= \sqrt{\frac{(1 - R^2)\Sigma y^2}{N - 3}}$$

If we have computed a regression equation from a particular set of observations of the three variables Y, X_1 and X_2 we can measure the proportion of variability in Y explained by the regression by calculating the coefficient of multiple determination R^2. In practical work it will often be the case that the explanatory variables in the relationship are not statistically independent, and hence our sample observations of the X-variables will also tend to be intercorrelated. In the three-variable case the extent of such intercorrelation is measured by the simple correlation coefficient between X_1 and X_2 computed from the formula

$$r_{12} = \frac{\Sigma x_1 x_2}{\sqrt{\Sigma x_1^2 \Sigma x_2^2}}$$

In the analysis of multiple-regression results it is customary to compute coefficients of correlation (or determination) for each pair of variables entering the relationship. The results are usually displayed in the form of the following triangular table:

	Y	X_1	X_2
Y	1·00		
X_1	r_{Y1}	1·00	
X_2	r_{Y2}	r_{12}	1·00

The interpretation of each of these coefficients is quite analogous to the interpretation of the coefficient r in simple correlation: each measures the degree of pairwise linear dependence between the variables when the influence of the third variable is ignored. Evidently, there must be perfect correlation of each variable with itself, and hence the entries along the diagonal in the above table must all be 1s.

In addition to computing a table of simple correlation coefficients between each pair of variables it is often useful to calculate measures indicating the relative explanatory power of each of the independent variables in the regression. The measures computed for this purpose are called coefficients of *partial* determination. The coefficient of partial determination is analogous to the partial regression coefficient in that it measures the net explanatory effect of a single independent variable after the influence of the remaining independent variables has been allowed for. Thus, suppose we have a sample of N observations of the three variables Y, X_1 and X_2, and we first compute the simple regression of Y on X_1. The proportion of the observed variation in Y accounted for by X_1 is given by r_{Y1}^2 (the square of the correlation coefficient between Y and X_1) and the proportion left unexplained is given by $1 - r_{Y1}^2$. Next, we regress Y on both X_1 and X_2, and compute the coefficient of multiple determination R^2. The proportion of the variation in Y not explained previously by variable X_1 that is now explained by variable X_2 is given by the ratio

$$r_{Y2\cdot1}^2 = \frac{R^2 - r_{Y1}^2}{1 - r_{Y1}^2}$$

The ratio $r_{Y2\cdot1}^2$ is the coefficient of partial determination for measuring the net explanatory effect of X_2 while holding X_1 constant; this is denoted symbolically by placing '1' to the right of the dot in the subscript $Y2\cdot1$. By similar argument, the coefficient of partial determination for X_1, holding X_2 constant, is given by the formula

$$r_{Y1\cdot2}^2 = \frac{R^2 - r_{Y2}^2}{1 - r_{Y2}^2}$$

Example 8.11

For the data of example 8.10 (p 331) calculate:
(a) The standard error of estimate s_e of the regression of rent on age and size of houses.
(b) The coefficients of multiple determination R^2 and $\bar{R}^2$.
(c) A table of simple correlation coefficients.
(d) The coefficients of partial determination $r^2_{Y2 \cdot 1}$ and $r^2_{Y1 \cdot 2}$.

(a) Here

$$\Sigma e^2 = \Sigma y^2 - b_1 \Sigma y x_1 - b_2 \Sigma y x_2$$
$$= 1650 \cdot 909 - (-1 \cdot 224)(-751 \cdot 818) - (2 \cdot 568)(195)$$
$$= 229 \cdot 924$$

and

$$s_e = \sqrt{\frac{\Sigma e^2}{N - 3}} = \sqrt{\frac{229 \cdot 924}{8}}$$
$$= \$5 \cdot 36$$

(b)

$$R^2 = 1 - \frac{\Sigma e^2}{\Sigma y^2}$$
$$= 0 \cdot 861$$

or

$$R^2 = \frac{b_1 \Sigma y x + b_2 \Sigma y x_2}{\Sigma y^2}$$
$$= 0 \cdot 861$$

The coefficient of determination adjusted for degrees of freedom is

$$\bar{R}^2 = 1 - \left(\frac{\Sigma e^2}{\Sigma y^2}\right)\left(\frac{N - 1}{N - 3}\right)$$
$$= 0 \cdot 826$$

(c) From example 8.2 we already have

$$r_{Y1} = -0 \cdot 813$$

Similarly

$$r_{Y2} = \frac{\Sigma y x_2}{\sqrt{\Sigma y^2 \Sigma x_2^2}}$$
$$= 0 \cdot 653$$

and

$$r_{12} = \frac{\Sigma x_1 x_2}{\sqrt{\Sigma x_1^2 \Sigma x_2^2}}$$
$$= -0 \cdot 275$$

The result $r_{12} = -0 \cdot 275$ indicates a degree of negative correlation between the explanatory variables X_1 (age) and X_2 (size). In tabular form, we have:

$$\begin{array}{c|ccc} & Y & X_1 & X_2 \\ \hline Y & 1{\cdot}000 & & \\ X_1 & -0{\cdot}813 & 1{\cdot}000 & \\ X_2 & +0{\cdot}653 & -0{\cdot}275 & 1{\cdot}000 \end{array}$$

(d)
$$r^2_{Y2\cdot1} = \frac{R^2 - r^2_{Y1}}{1 - r^2_{Y1}} = \frac{0{\cdot}861 - 0{\cdot}661}{0{\cdot}339}$$
$$= 0{\cdot}590$$

ie 59 per cent of the variation in rents not explained by variable X_1 (age) is explained by variable X_2 (size).

$$r^2_{Y1\cdot2} = \frac{R^2 - r^2_{Y2}}{1 - r^2_{Y2}} = \frac{0{\cdot}861 - 0{\cdot}426}{0{\cdot}574}$$
$$= 0{\cdot}758$$

ie about 76 per cent of the variation in rents not explained by X_2 is explained by X_1.

Statistical Inference in Multiple Regression

To test whether the coefficients b_1 and b_2 are significantly different from zero we may proceed in a manner analogous to section 8.4 above. Given that the Xs have fixed values, the least-squares estimator b_1 obtained from the normal equations can be expressed as a linear combination of the observations Y_i, ie

$$b_1 = \Sigma c_{1i} Y_i \qquad (i = 1, 2, \ldots, N)$$

where

$$c_{1i} = \frac{x_{1i}\Sigma x^2_{2i} - x_{2i}\Sigma x_{1i} x_{2i}}{D} \quad .$$

Similarly as in the case of simple regression (see p 300 above), the constants c_{1i} are such that $\Sigma c_{1i} = 0$ (since $\Sigma x_{1i} = 0$ and $\Sigma x_{2i} = 0$), $\Sigma c_{1i} X_{1i} = 1$ and $\Sigma c_{1i} X_{2i} = 0$. Also

$$b_2 = \Sigma c_{2i} Y_i \qquad (i = 1, 2, \ldots, N)$$

where

$$c_{2i} = \frac{x_{2i}\Sigma x^2_{1i} - x_{1i}\Sigma x_{1i} x_{2i}}{D}$$

and $\Sigma c_{2i} = 0$, $\Sigma c_{2i} X_{2i} = 1$, and $\Sigma c_{2i} X_{1i} = 0$. Since the Y_i are assumed to have been generated by the model $Y_i = \alpha + \beta_1 X_{1i} + \beta_2 X_{2i} + \varepsilon_i$, for b_1 we have

$$b_1 = \Sigma c_{1i}(\alpha + \beta_1 X_{1i} + \beta_2 X_{2i} + \varepsilon_i)$$

$$= \alpha \Sigma c_{1i} + \beta_1 \Sigma c_{1i} X_{1i} + \beta_2 \Sigma c_{1i} X_{2i} + \Sigma c_{1i} \varepsilon_i$$
$$= \beta_1 + \Sigma c_{1i} \varepsilon_i$$

and similarly

$$b_2 = \beta_2 + \Sigma c_{2i} \varepsilon_i$$

By assumption, the ε_i are distributed with mean zero, ie $E(\varepsilon_i) = 0$. Hence

$$E(b_1) = \mu_{b_1}$$
$$= \beta_1 + \Sigma c_{1i} E(\varepsilon_i)$$
$$= \beta_1$$

and

$$E(b_2) = \mu_{b_2}$$
$$= \beta_2 + \Sigma c_{2i} E(\varepsilon_i)$$
$$= \beta_2$$

The derivation of the variances of b_1 and b_2 depends crucially on the assumptions that the ε_i are independent and have constant variance σ_ε^2. Then we may write

$$\text{Var}(b_1) = \text{Var}(\beta_1 + \Sigma c_{1i} \varepsilon_i)$$
$$= \Sigma c_{1i}^2 \text{Var}(\varepsilon_i)$$
$$= \sigma_\varepsilon^2 \Sigma c_{1i}^2$$

where Σc_{1i}^2 can be shown to reduce to $\dfrac{\Sigma x_{2i}^2}{D}$.[1] Thus, we have that

$$\text{Var}(b_1) = \sigma_{b_1}^2 = \sigma_\varepsilon^2 \frac{\Sigma x_2^2}{D}$$

where $D = \Sigma x_1^2 \Sigma x_2^2 - (\Sigma x_1 x_2)^2$, and similarly

$$\text{Var}(b_2) = \sigma_{b_2}^2 = \sigma_\varepsilon^2 \frac{\Sigma x_1^2}{D}$$

---

[1] Squaring the expression for c_{1i} given above and omitting the subscript i, we get

$$\sum \frac{x_1^2 (\Sigma x_2^2)^2 - 2x_1 x_2 \Sigma x_1 x_2 \Sigma x_2^2 + x_2^2 (\Sigma x_1 x_2)^2}{D^2}$$
$$= \frac{\Sigma x_2^2 [\Sigma x_1^2 \Sigma x_2^2 - (\Sigma x_1 x_2)^2]}{D^2}$$
$$= \frac{\Sigma x_2^2}{D}$$

From these results we may conclude that if the X_1s and the X_2s are given values, then b_1 and b_2 are linear unbiased estimators of the partial regression coefficients β_1 and β_2; they can also be shown to be estimators with the desired minimum variance properties. Furthermore, if the ε_i are normally distributed, the distributions of b_1 and b_2 will likewise be normal with means β_1 and β_2 and with variances $\sigma_{b_1}^2$ and $\sigma_{b_2}^2$ as above. Given the basic assumptions of least-squares regression analysis, these conclusions can be extended to the general case of k explanatory variables.

In practice, we do not know σ_ε and we must use s_e as an estimate. The estimated standard errors of b_1 and b_2 are then computed as

$$s_{b_1} = s_e \sqrt{\frac{\Sigma x_2^2}{D}}$$

$$s_{b_2} = s_e \sqrt{\frac{\Sigma x_1^2}{D}}$$

To test whether b_1 and/or b_2 differ significantly from zero, ie whether or not the sample results are consistent with the hypotheses $H_o : \beta_1 = 0$ and/or $H_o : \beta_2 = 0$, we use the t-test, referring

$$t = \frac{b_1}{s_{b_1}}$$

and

$$t = \frac{b_2}{s_{b_2}}$$

to the t-tables with $N - 3$ degrees of freedom. If b_1 is significantly different from zero, 95 per cent confidence limits for β_1 can be ascertained in the usual manner and will be

$$b_1 \pm t_{.025} s_{b_1}$$

and similarly for b_2.

In addition to testing the significance of the individual regression coefficients it is customary to test the significance of the multiple regression as a whole. The test appropriate for this purpose is the F-ratio test introduced earlier in this chapter. In the general case of k explanatory variables, the test is based on the ratio

$$F = \frac{(\text{Explained variation in } Y)/k}{(\text{Unexplained variation in } Y)/(N - k - 1)} = \frac{\text{SSR}/k}{\text{SSE}/(N - k - 1)}$$

which is the test statistic for the null hypothesis $\beta_1 = \beta_2 = \ldots = \beta_k = 0$. In tabular form the data for the F-ratio test may be presented as follows:

Variation in Y due to:	Sum of Squares (SS)	Degrees of Freedom (d.f.)	(SS) ÷ (d.f.)
$X_1, X_2, \ldots, X_k$	SSR = $b_1\Sigma yx_1 + b_2\Sigma yx_2 + \ldots + b_k\Sigma yx_k$	$v_1 = k$	SSR/k
Residual Error	SSE = $\Sigma y^2 - b_1\Sigma yx_1 - \ldots - b_k\Sigma yx_k$	$v_2 = N - k - 1$	SSE/$N - k - 1$
Total	$\Sigma(Y - \bar{Y})^2$	$N - 1$	

In the case of two explanatory variables X_1 and X_2, the null hypothesis to be tested is that neither variable has a statistically significant effect on Y, ie the hypothesis that $\beta_1 = \beta_2 = 0$. If the null hypothesis is true, the ratio

$$F = \frac{(b_1\Sigma yx_1 + b_2\Sigma yx_2)/2}{\Sigma e^2/N - 3}$$

has the F-distribution with $v_1 = 2$ and $v_2 = N - 3$ degrees of freedom. But if the sample value of the F-ratio is so large that it exceeds the critical value of $F_{.05}$, it is unlikely that it could have been drawn from an F-distribution. We then reject the null hypothesis $H_o : \beta_1 = \beta_2 = 0$ and conclude that Y is linearly related to X_1 and X_2. Alternatively, if we make use of the relations

$$\frac{b_1\Sigma yx_1 + b_2\Sigma yx_2}{\Sigma y^2} = R^2$$

and

$$\frac{\Sigma e^2}{\Sigma y^2} = 1 - R^2$$

the F-ratio may be written as

$$F = \frac{R^2/2}{(1 - R^2)/(N - 3)}$$

thus giving a direct test of the null hypothesis $H_o : R^2 = 0$ against the alternative hypothesis $H_a : R^2 \neq 0$.[1] If $F > F_{.05}$ we conclude that the coefficient of multiple determination is significant and that by regressing Y on X_1 and X_2 we can account for some of the variability of the Ys. Conversely, if $F < F_{.05}$, we cannot safely accept the sample

---

[1] Since R^2 cannot be negative, this is equivalent to a test of $H_o : R^2 = 0$ against $H_a : R^2 > 0$

value of R^2 as being statistically significant, and the null hypothesis $H_o : R^2 = 0$ is retained.

Finally, we may wish to use the equation

$$Y_c = a + b_1 X_1 + b_2 X_2$$

as an instrument of prediction. Putting again X_{1o} and X_{2o} for particular values of X_1 and X_2, the value of Y that the equation will predict will be

$$\hat{Y}_o = a + b_1 X_{1o} + b_2 X_{2o}$$

As before, we use the symbol $\hat{Y}_o$ to indicate that the sample regression equation is being used as an estimator of the mean value $\mu_Y(X_{1o}, X_{2o})$ associated with the values X_{1o} and X_{2o} of X_1 and X_2. Since the coefficients a, b_1 and b_2 in the estimating equation are unbiased estimators of the respective parameters, $\hat{Y}_o$ is an unbiased estimator of the mean $\mu_Y(X_{1o}, X_{2o})$, ie $E(\hat{Y}_o) = \mu_Y(X_{1o}, X_{2o})$. Writing

$$\hat{Y}_o = \bar{Y} + b_1(X_{1o} - \bar{X}_1) + b_2(X_{2o} - \bar{X}_2)$$

we have

$$\mathrm{Var}(\hat{Y}_o) = \mathrm{Var}(\bar{Y}) + (X_{1o} - \bar{X}_1)^2 \, \mathrm{Var}(b_1) + (X_{2o} - \bar{X}_2)^2 \, \mathrm{Var}(b_2)$$
$$+ 2(X_{1o} - \bar{X}_1)(X_{2o} - \bar{X}_2) \mathrm{Cov}(b_1, b_2)$$

The covariance term arises because b_1 and b_2 are not independent. $\mathrm{Var}(b_1)$ and $\mathrm{Var}(b_2)$ have been derived above, and for $\mathrm{Cov}(b_1, b_2)$ we have

$$\mathrm{Cov}(b_1, b_2) = -\sigma_\varepsilon^2 \frac{\Sigma x_1 x_2}{D}$$

where $D = \Sigma x_1^2 \Sigma x_2^2 - (\Sigma x_1 x_2)^2$. Hence, the variance of $\hat{Y}_o$ is given by

$$\mathrm{Var}(\hat{Y}_o) = \sigma_\varepsilon^2 \left[\frac{1}{N} + \frac{(X_{1o} - \bar{X}_1)^2 \Sigma x_2^2}{D} + \frac{(X_{2o} - \bar{X}_2)^2 \Sigma x_1^2}{D} \right.$$
$$\left. - 2 \frac{(X_{1o} - \bar{X}_1)(X_{2o} - \bar{X}_2)\Sigma x_1 x_2}{D} \right]$$

Using s_e as an estimate of σ_ε, and writing the expression in the square brackets in the above equation as C_o, we have as 95 per cent prediction limits for the mean $\mu_Y(X_{1o}, X_{2o})$

$$\hat{Y}_o \pm t_{.025} s_e \sqrt{C_o}$$

where $t_{.025}$ is obtained from the t-table with $N - 3$ degrees of freedom. Also, in accordance with the argument in section 8.6, we can express the 95 per cent limits for a *single* value of Y as

$$\hat{Y}_o \pm t_{.025} s_e \sqrt{1 + C_o}$$

The computation of prediction limits from the above formulae is illustrated in the example below.

Example 8.12

We may continue here example 8.8 on p 312 above. The explanatory variable, the retail price of lamb, accounted for nearly 85 per cent of the variation in annual per capita consumption of lamb, leaving 15 per cent unexplained. Some of this unexplained variation may be due to the influence of other relevant variables which have not been explicitly taken into account. On *a priori* grounds we should expect lamb consumption to be also influenced by the prices of close substitutes for lamb, and by consumers' income. Since our example is purely for illustrative purposes, we consider here only the latter variable and investigate the regression of lamb consumption on the retail price of lamb (X_1) and per capita income (X_2). The latter variable is represented by Gross Domestic Product per capita, valued at average 1966–67 prices.[1] As in example 8.8 above, the relevant computer output for the problem is reproduced here as follows:

VARIABLE 1 IS CONSUMPTION OF LAMB PER CAPITA IN KG
VARIABLE 2 IS DEFLATED RETAIL PRICE OF LAMB PER KG
VARIABLE 3 IS GDP AT 1966/67 PRICES PER CAPITA IN DOLLARS
DATA

1	2	3
17.800	92.400	1860.000
16.700	100.500	1850.000
19.300	93.500	1930.000
19.600	94.100	1960.000
21.700	85.000	2090.000
21.500	85.500	2160.000
23.800	81.500	2210.000
24.400	75.600	2260.000
18.700	91.400	2340.000
16.000	114.000	2430.000

MOMENT MATRIX
0.7299E+01
−0.2521E+02   0.1030E+03
0.1096E+03   0.3055E+02   0.3757E+05

VARIABLE 1 MEAN =   19.95000   STANDR DEV =   2.84771
VARIABLE 2 MEAN =   91.35000   STANDR DEV =   10.69613
VARIABLE 3 MEAN =   2109.00000   STANDR DEV =   204.31185

SIMPLE CORRELATION MATRIX

	1	2	3
1	1.00000		
2	−0.91953	1.00000	
3	0.20921	0.01553	1.00000

COMPUTATION OF REGRESSION EQUATION
DEPENDENT VARIABLE IS 1
INDEPENDENT VARIABLES ARE 2 3

[1] *Source*: Australian Bureau of Statistics: *Year Book*, 1970, pp 126, 470; 1973, pp 130, 484; 1974, p 136; and *Quarterly Estimates of National Income and Expenditure*, December Quarter 1974, p 2.

INVERSE MATRIX   VECTOR OF DEPENDENT/INDEPENDENT MOMENTS
   0.9714E−02   −0.7899E−05   −0.2521E+02
   −0.7899E−05   0.2662E−04   0.1096E+03

B-COEFFICIENTS
   −0.245737   0.003116

STANDARD ERRORS
   0.032535   0.001703

T-TEST
   −7.553131   1.829316

RSQUARE= 0.89549347   VARESIDUALS= 0.10896305E+01
RSQUARE ADJUSTED FOR DF= 0.86563446

ANALYSIS OF VARIANCE

TSS= 72.985046   SSR= 65.357633   SSE= 7.627414
DF1= 2.0   DF2= 7.0   F-RATIO= 29.990731

CONSTANT TERM= 35.826944

STANDARD ERROR OF CONSTANT= 4.63829607

OBS	ACTUAL	PREDICTED	ERROR
1	17.800	18.916	−1·116
2	16.700	16.895	−0.195
3	19.300	18.864	0.436
4	19.600	18.810	0.790
5	21.700	21.451	0.249
6	21.500	21.546	−0.046
7	23.800	22.685	1 115
8	24.400	24.291	0.109
9	18.700	20.657	−1.957
10	16.000	15.384	0.616

DURBIN WATSON STATISTIC= 2.351223

The interpretation of the 'moment matrix' is the same as in example 8.8, and the meaning of the simple correlation matrix was explained on p 335 above. We note that $r_{12} = 0·01553$ and hence the explanatory variables in the regression show only a very small degree of positive correlation. This is desirable, for, as we shall explain in section 8.10, a high degree of intercorrelation among the explanatory variables tends to make the estimates of the regression parameters unreliable.

Before proceeding with an analysis of the results, it may be useful to comment briefly on how the computer calculates the 'B-coefficients' b_1 and b_2. On p 331 above we solved for b_1 and b_2 directly from the normal equations

$$b_1 \Sigma x_1^2 + b_2 \Sigma x_1 x_2 = \Sigma y x_1$$

$$b_1 \Sigma x_1 x_2 + b_2 \Sigma x_2^2 = \Sigma y x_2$$

This method is entirely adequate when we are working with only two explanatory variables. If there are k explanatory variables, there are k normal equations, and some general method is clearly needed for solving the k normal equations simultaneously. This general method involves a sequence of numerical operations known as matrix inversion. Here we merely illustrate this method by reference to our printed data; for a better understanding of matrix operations the reader may wish to consult some of the available texts on elementary mathematics for economists.

Let us first write the above normal equations in moment form by dividing each equation by N, ie

$$b_1 m_{11} + b_2 m_{12} = m_{y1}$$

$$b_1 m_{12} + b_2 m_{22} = m_{y2}$$

As can be seen, the moments of the independent variables on the left-hand side of the above equations show a symmetrical pattern. Using this property, and the fact that $m_{12} = m_{21}$, we may write the normal equations in matrix form as follows

$$\begin{bmatrix} m_{11} & m_{12} \\ m_{12} & m_{22} \end{bmatrix} \begin{bmatrix} b_1 \\ b_2 \end{bmatrix} = \begin{bmatrix} m_{y1} \\ m_{y2} \end{bmatrix}$$

Written in this way, the normal equations can be seen to consist of the following three components: (i) a square matrix M whose elements are the moments of the independent variables in the regression (ii) the coefficients b_1 and b_2 appearing as what is known as a column vector, ie an ordered set of numbers arranged in a column; and (iii) another column vector whose elements are the moments m_{y1} and m_{y2}. If we write the latter two vectors as

$$\begin{bmatrix} b_1 \\ b_2 \end{bmatrix} = b^* \qquad \begin{bmatrix} m_{y1} \\ m_{y2} \end{bmatrix} = m^*$$

the normal equations can be written in matrix form as the single equation

$$Mb^* = m^*$$

Now, to solve for b^*, ie for b_1 and b_2 simultaneously, we require

$$b^* = M^{-1}m^*$$

where M^{-1} is a matrix whose elements are obtained by inverting the original matrix M. Let us denote the elements of the inverse matrix M^{-1} by the symbols c^{11}, c^{12}, c^{21} and c^{22}, ie

$$M^{-1} = \begin{bmatrix} c^{11} & c^{12} \\ c^{21} & c^{22} \end{bmatrix}$$

In machine calculations, to find the numerical values of the elements of the inverse matrix M^{-1} can be quite laborious even for a small number of explanatory variables, and it is precisely the advantage of the modern electronic computer that it can perform such calculations with great speed and accuracy. Once the inverse matrix M^{-1} has been found, the solutions for b_1 and b_2 are given by

$$b_1 = c^{11}m_{y1} + c^{12}m_{y2}$$

$$b_2 = c^{21}m_{y1} + c^{22}m_{y2}$$

In the computer print-out for our problem we are given the inverse matrix and the 'vector of dependent-independent moments' as follows:

$$M^{-1} = \begin{bmatrix} 0.009714 & -0.000007899 \\ -0.000007899 & 0.00002662 \end{bmatrix} \qquad m^* = \begin{bmatrix} -25.21 \\ 109.6 \end{bmatrix}$$

Computing the values of b_1 and b_2 from the elements of M^{-1} and m^*, we find

$$b_1 = (0.009714)(-25.21) + (-0.000007899)(109.6)$$

$$= -0.245756$$

and

$$b_2 = (-0.000007899)(-25.21) + (0.00002662)(109.6)$$

$$= 0.003117$$

As can be seen from the printed data, these values differ from those calculated by the computer only by very small rounding errors.
We may now proceed with an analysis of the computer output data.

Regression:

$$\hat{Y} = 35 \cdot 827 - 0 \cdot 246 X_1 + 0 \cdot 003 X_2$$
$$(4 \cdot 6383) \quad (0 \cdot 0325) \quad (0 \cdot 0017)$$

Since the value of b_1 of $-0 \cdot 246$ is very nearly the same as the value of the simple regression coefficient of $-0 \cdot 245$ calculated in example 8.8, our estimate of the effect of the retail price of lamb on lamb consumption is virtually unaffected by the inclusion of income as a second explanatory variable in the regression; we comment further on this result when we discuss the relation between simple regression estimates and multiple regression estimates in the following section. The value of b_2 of $0 \cdot 003$ indicates that for a rise of \$1 in real income, the retail price of lamb remaining unchanged, we would expect annual per capita consumption of lamb to rise, on the average, by 3 grams.

Goodness of Fit:

$$R^2 = 0 \cdot 895 \qquad \bar{R}^2 = 0 \cdot 866$$

Thus, nearly 90 per cent of the observed variation in lamb consumption is accounted for by variations in price and real income. When adjustment is made for the number of degrees of freedom, the estimated proportion of the variation in lamb consumption explained by these two variables is about 87 per cent.

Partial Correlation:

The coefficient of multiple determination R^2 is a measure of the joint contribution of X_1 and X_2 towards explaining the observed variability of the Ys. To measure the net relative contribution of the added income variable X_2 we compute the coefficient of partial determination

$$r_{Y2 \cdot 1}^2 = \frac{R^2 - r_{Y1}^2}{1 - r_{Y1}^2} = \frac{0 \cdot 895 - 0 \cdot 845}{0 \cdot 155}$$
$$= 0 \cdot 322$$

We may therefore conclude that about one-third of the variation in lamb consumption previously unexplained by the price variable X_1 is explained when the income variable X_2 is included in the analysis.

Significance of b_1 and b_2

Before proceeding with statistical inference we should make a rough check of the plausibility of the assumption that the error term in the hypothesised relationship has a normal distribution. It will be recalled from our previous discussion that the use of the t-distribution in small-sample tests is justified only if it can reasonably be assumed that the errors are normally distributed. Since these errors are not directly observable, we must regard the sample residuals as observations of the unknown ε_i and use $\bar{e}$ and s_e as estimates of $E(\varepsilon_i)$ and σ_ε. From our printed results we readily calculate $\bar{e} = \Sigma e_i / N = 0 \cdot 001$, which is approximately zero; we also have VARESIDUALS $= 1 \cdot 0896$, and hence $s_e = 1 \cdot 044$. Now, if the e_i were drawings from a normal distribution with $E(\varepsilon_i) = 0$ and $\sigma_\varepsilon = 1 \cdot 044$, we should expect about 68 per cent of the residuals to lie within ± 1 standard deviation (s_e) of the mean, and about 27 per cent of them to lie in the range of between 1 and $1 \cdot 96$ standard deviations on either side of the mean. As can be readily verified from our printed data, seven of the ten computed residuals lie in the former range and the remaining three all lie within the latter ranges. *Prima facie*, our data do not appear inconsistent with the assumption of normality of the error term, and we may reasonably apply the t-distribution to assess the significance of the partial regression coefficients b_1 and b_2.

On theoretical grounds we should expect the partial relationship between lamb consumption and price to be an inverse one, and the partial relationship between lamb consumption and real income to be a direct one. Accordingly, we have the hypotheses

$$H_o : \beta_1 = 0$$
$$H_a : \beta_1 < 0$$

and

$$H_o : \beta_2 = 0$$
$$H_a : \beta_2 > 0$$

From the printed results we have $t = b_1/s_{b_1} = -7.553$ and $t = b_2/s_{b_2} = 1.829$ and from the t-table, with $v = 10 - 3 = 7$ degrees of freedom, we find the critical value of t for a one-sided test to be 1.895 (at 5 per cent level of significance). Since

$$t = -7.553 < t_{.05} = -1.895$$

we reject the null hypothesis that $\beta_1 = 0$ and accept our sample result as evidence of a negative partial relationship between lamb consumption and the retail price of lamb. Testing the significance of b_2, we find

$$t = 1.829 < t_{.05} = 1.895$$

so that on the basis of a 5 per cent significance test our alternative hypothesis of a positive partial relationship between lamb consumption and real per capita income cannot be sustained. However, since the t-value in this instance lies just below the critical value for the test we may reasonably conclude the following: we have found evidence of a strong negative relationship between lamb consumption and the retail price of lamb; we have also found some evidence of a positive partial relationship between lamb consumption and real income, but because we are less certain about the significance of our result we should like to reserve our judgment until further sample evidence can be considered.

F-*Ratio Test:*

As well as testing the significance of the individual regression coefficients we ordinarily test the significance of the entire regression relationship by means of the F-ratio test. As explained on p 340 above, this test may be interpreted as a test of the coefficient of multiple determination R^2. Accordingly, we have the hypotheses

$$H_o : R^2 = 0$$
$$H_a : R^2 \neq 0$$

The value of the test statistic F calculated by the computer is 29.99. Checking this result against the values of $F_{.05}$ and $F_{.01}$, with $v = 2$ and $v_2 = 7$ degrees of freedom, we find $F > F_{.05} = 4.74$ and $F > F_{.01} = 9.55$. Thus, the hypothesis $H_o : R^2 = 0$, and the equivalent hypothesis $H_o : \beta_2 = \beta_2 = 0$, can be rejected, and we may conclude that the multiple regression of Y on X_1 and X_2 is statistically significant.

Prediction:

Since we have found R^2 to be significantly different from zero, we may consider using the multiple regression of Y on X_1 and X_2 for purposes of prediction. Thus, suppose we wish to construct a prediction interval for lamb consumption when the retail price of lamb (deflated) and the real gross domestic product per capita are 90 cents/kg and $2380 respectively. Setting $X_{1o} = 90$ and $X_{2o} = 2380 we calculate the value of Y predicted by our estimating equation as

$$\hat{Y}_o = 35{\cdot}827 - 0{\cdot}246(90) + (0{\cdot}003)(2380)$$

$$= 20{\cdot}82$$

To construct a prediction interval for $\hat{Y}_o$ we first need to evaluate the expression (see p 341 above)

$$C_o = \frac{1}{N} + \frac{(X_{1o} - \bar{X}_1)^2 \Sigma x_2^2}{D} + \frac{(X_{2o} - \bar{X}_2)^2 \Sigma x_1^2}{D}$$
$$- 2\frac{(X_{1o} - \bar{X}_1)(X_{2o} - \bar{X}_2)\Sigma x_1 x_2}{D}$$

where
$$N = 10 \qquad \bar{X}_1 = 91{\cdot}35 \qquad \bar{X}_2 = 2109$$

$$\Sigma x_1^2 = Nm_{11} = (10)(103{\cdot}0) = 1030 \qquad \Sigma x_2^2 = Nm_{22} = (10)(37\,570) = 375\,700$$

$$\Sigma x_1 x_2 = Nm_{12} = (10)(30{\cdot}55) = 305{\cdot}5$$

$$D = \Sigma x_1^2 \Sigma x_2^2 - (\Sigma x_1 x_2)^2 = 386\,877\,670$$

We have
$$C_o = 0{\cdot}10 + 0{\cdot}002 + 0{\cdot}196 - (2)(-0{\cdot}0003)$$

$$= 0{\cdot}299$$

The 95 per cent prediction limits within which individual values of per capita lamb consumption can be expected to lie are given by

$$\hat{Y}_o \pm t_{.025} s_e \sqrt{1 + C_o}$$

From the printed computer results we find $s_e = \sqrt{1{\cdot}08963} = 1{\cdot}044$ and the value of $t_{.025}$ with 7 degrees of freedom is $2{\cdot}365$. Hence, for $X_{1o} = 90$ and $X_{2o} = 2380$, the prediction limits are

$$20{\cdot}82 \pm (2{\cdot}365)(1{\cdot}044)(1{\cdot}140)$$

$$20{\cdot}82 \pm 2{\cdot}82$$

ie $\qquad\qquad$ 18·00 to 23·64 kilograms

From published sources, the per capita real gross domestic product for 1974–75 was calculated as $2380 (to the nearest $10)[1]; the deflated price of lamb for that year was 90 cents/kg, and the recorded lamb consumption was 18 kilograms per capita. As can be seen, the actual per capita lamb consumption for 1974–75 lies just within the 95 per cent prediction limits as computed above.

[1] Australian Bureau of Statistics, *Australian National Accounts*, 1974–75, p 26, and *Quarterly Summary of Australian Statistics*, No. 299, 1976, p 2.

8.9 Relation between Simple and Multiple Regression

Suppose we have a simple regression between two variables Y and X_1 estimated from sample data. The regression will be

$$Y_c = a + bX_1$$

If b is significantly different from zero, we can say that X_1 contributes to the explanation of the behaviour of Y. If we add another explanatory variable X_2, we shall have

$$Y_c = a' + b_1X_2 + b_2X_2$$

where the partial regression coefficient b_1 is a measure of the estimated average change in Y per unit change in X_1 when X_2 is held constant, and b_2 is a measure of the estimated average change in Y per unit change in X_2 when X_1 is held constant. Since the coefficient b in the first equation measures the amount of change in Y when the possible influence of X_2 on Y is disregarded, the coefficient b in the first equation and the coefficient b_1 in the second equation are evidently not the same thing. Let us suppose, however, that in investigating the behaviour of Y we have fitted the simple regression $Y_c = a + bX_1$, whereas the correct specification is $Y_c = a' + b_1X_1 + b_2X_2$. To illustrate further the relation between the two regressions, let us consider again the normal equations

$$\Sigma yx_1 = b_1\Sigma x_1^2 + b_2\Sigma x_1x_2$$

$$\Sigma yx_2 = b_1\Sigma x_1x_2 + b_2\Sigma x_2^2$$

If we divide the first normal equation through by Σx_1^2, we shall obtain

$$b = b_1 + b_2\frac{\Sigma x_1x_2}{\Sigma x_1^2}$$

where b gives the estimated effect of X_1 on Y computed from the simple regression of Y on X_1 alone $\left(\text{since } b = \frac{\Sigma yx_1}{\Sigma x_1^2}\right)$. The value of b will be the same as that of b_1 only if $b_2 = 0$ or $\frac{\Sigma x_1x_2}{\Sigma x_1^2} = 0$. Let us suppose, however, that there in fact exists a partial relationship between Y and X_2 so that a zero value of b_2 in a sample regression of Y on both X_1 and X_2 would be very unlikely to occur. Then $b = b_1$ if $\frac{\Sigma x_1x_2}{\Sigma x_1^2} = 0$.

This quantity can be readily identified as the regression coefficient in the simple regression of X_2 on X_1. Writing the regression coefficient between the explanatory variables as b_{12}, and making use of the algebraic property that $b_{12} = r_{12}\dfrac{s_{X_2}}{s_{X_1}}$ (see section 8.2, p 289 above)

where r_{12} is the simple correlation coefficient between X_1 and X_2 and s_{X_2} and s_{X_1} are the standard deviations of the X_1 and X_2 variables, we may write

$$b = b_1 + b_2\left(r_{12}\frac{s_{X_2}}{s_{X_1}}\right)$$

Thus, b will be equal to b_1 if $r_{12} = 0$, ie if there is no sample correlation between the explanatory variables X_1 and X_2. If X_1 and X_2 are correlated, then the simple regression coefficient b will measure not only the direct effect of X_1 on Y, as measured by b_1, but also the indirect effect of X_2 on Y contributed by the linear relationship between X_2 and X_1; that is, the simple regression coefficient picks up some of the effect of changes in X_2 that tend to be associated with changes in X_1.

The above discussion may be illustrated by reference to our previous examples. In example 8.1 the simple regression coefficient (b) of rent on age of houses was found to be $-1\cdot452$, and in example 8.10 the corresponding partial regression coefficient (b_1) in the regression of rent on age and size of houses was calculated as $-1\cdot224$. The matrix of simple correlation coefficients calculated in example 8.11 reveals that for the sample under consideration the variables X_2 (size) and X_1 (age) were negatively correlated ($r_{12} = -0\cdot275$), and the variables Y (rent) and X_2 (size) were positively correlated ($r_{Y2} = 0\cdot653$). Thus, some of the effect attributed to X_1 (age) in the simple regression of rent on age was in fact due to the influence of both age *and* size, ie b overstated the effect of age on rent since the older houses included in the sample were also on average smaller than the newer houses. On the other hand, if we consider the regression equations

$$Y_c = 42\cdot314 - 0\cdot245X_1$$

$$Y_c = 35\cdot827 - 0\cdot246X_1 + 0\cdot003X_2$$

fitted to the lamb-consumption data in examples 8.8 and 8.12, we find that although Y and X_2 are positively correlated, the correlation is not strong ($r_{Y2} = 0\cdot2092$), and the explanatory variables X_1 and X_2 are virtually uncorrelated ($r_{12} = 0\cdot0155$). Consequently, the simple regression estimate b differs from the multiple regression estimate b_1 only by a very small positive amount, ie

$$b - b_1 = b_2 r_{12}\frac{s_{X_2}}{s_{X_1}} = (0\cdot00312)(0\cdot0155)\left(\frac{204\cdot312}{10\cdot696}\right)$$
$$= 0\cdot000924$$
$$\simeq 0\cdot001$$

The above analysis also helps to explain why sometimes we find a simple regression coefficient b to be significant, although the corresponding partial regression coefficient b_1 is not significant. This may arise if the explanatory variable X_1 is strongly related to a third variable so that the indirect effect of the omitted variable in the simple regression of Y on X_1 results in b differing significantly from zero even though the direct relationship between Y and X_1 is quite weak. An example of this is provided by the case referred to on p 327 above, which was concerned with the behaviour of family size (Y). If we compute the simple regression of family size on father's IQ (X_1), we may find that b is significant, but if we introduce a second explanatory variable, say, family income (X_2), we may find that b_1 in the multiple regression of family size on father's IQ *and* family income is not significant. This may occur if there is a relationship between family size and family income, and one between family income and father's IQ. As a result of these relationships a simple regression of family size on father's IQ may give a significant result, although there is no direct relation between family size and father's IQ. For a given level of family income the two variables behave independently. Accordingly, if we have a simple regression of Y on X_1 which is significant, and we suspect that the apparent relationship may be due to the influence of a third variable (X_2), we should compute the multiple regression of Y on X_1 and X_2 and test the significance of the partial regression coefficient of Y on X_1. If this is not significant, then our suspicions are confirmed, and the data under consideration cannot be taken as evidence of a real relationship between Y and X_1.

8.10 Multicollinearity

The previous two sections have been concerned with the use of multiple regression in assessing the importance of each explanatory variable X in the overall regression equation. We must now draw attention to an important limitation of the analysis: multiple regression equations will enable us to make reliable estimates of the net effect of a unit change in each explanatory variable on the average value of Y only if the explanatory variables are not perfectly or highly correlated with each other. The presence of high intercorrelation among the explanatory variables gives rise to the problem of *multicollinearity*.

Let us first consider the case of exact collinearity in the three-variable regression of Y on X_1 and X_2. The variables X_1 and X_2 are exactly collinear if each can be expressed as a linear function of the other eg, $X_2 = BX_1$ or $X_2 = A + BX_1$. Knowing the values of the constants A and B, we can predict X_2 from X_1 without error, and hence

X_2 and X_1 are perfectly correlated. From the normal equations for b_1 and b_2, we have

$$b_1 = \frac{\Sigma yx_1 \Sigma x_2^2 - \Sigma yx_2 \Sigma x_1 x_2}{D}$$

$$b_2 = \frac{\Sigma yx_2 \Sigma x_1^2 - \Sigma yx_1 \Sigma x_1 x_2}{D}$$

where $D = \Sigma x_1^2 \Sigma x_2^2 - (\Sigma x_1 x_2)^2$. The strength of the linear relationship between X_1 and X_2 is measured by the simple correlation coefficient

$$r_{12} = \frac{\Sigma x_1 x_2}{\sqrt{\Sigma x_1^2 \Sigma x_2^2}}$$

Hence D may be written as

$$D = \Sigma x_1^2 \Sigma x_2^2 - r_{12}^2 \Sigma x_1^2 \Sigma x_2^2$$

$$= \Sigma x_1^2 \Sigma x_2^2 (1 - r_{12}^2)$$

It follows that if $r_{12} = \pm 1$, D will be zero, and the method of least squares will yield no determinate solutions for b_1 and b_2. The intuitive basis for this result is that if one explanatory variable stands in an exact linear relationship with another explanatory variable, the separate influence of the variables on the dependent variable Y cannot be distinguished, and the normal equations for determining b_1 and b_2 do not yield a unique solution.

When the explanatory variables X_1 and X_2 are highly, though not perfectly, correlated, we can expect the quantity D in the above equations to lie close to zero. Although the normal equations in this case yield determinate values of b_1 and b_2, the estimates so obtained will be subject to large estimation errors. This can be seen from inspection of the formulae for the estimated standard errors of b_1 and b_2

$$s_{b_1} = s_e \sqrt{\frac{\Sigma x_2^2}{D}} \qquad s_{b_2} = s_e \sqrt{\frac{\Sigma x_1^2}{D}}$$

Provided that the least-squares assumption that the errors ε_i are distributed with mean zero is fulfilled, we can still expect b_1 and b_2 to be unbiased estimators of the partial regression coefficients β_1 and β_2. But with D being close to zero, the standard errors of both b_1 and b_2 will be large. Hence, the efficiency of the estimates will be low, and this means that the true effects of X_1 on Y and of X_2 on Y cannot be reliably estimated. Thus, in extreme cases, we might find both coefficients b_1 and b_2 not to be significant, even though the value of R^2 is high and the F-test gives a significant result for the regression as a whole.

These considerations lead us to conclude that multicollinearity reduces the precision with which the *individual* regression parameters can be estimated from sample data. In a three-variable regression a measure of collinearity between X_1 and X_2 is given by the simple correlation coefficient r_{12}. In regression problems involving a number of variables multicollinearity is more difficult to assess because of the possible interactions among the several explanatory variables. However, if the explanatory variables are pairwise highly correlated, this suggests that multicollinearity is present even though its extent can only be assessed by more complex methods. One such method is to compute the multiple correlation coefficient for each independent variable regressed on the remaining independent variables; in this manner variables can be compared in terms of their linear dependence on the other explanatory variables in the regression equation.

In experimental situations the problem of multicollinearity can best be dealt with by proper experimental design which reduces the amount of interaction among the explanatory variables. In economic applications the experimental method is rarely applicable, and other ways must be found for overcoming multicollinearity in the available data. The problem is apt to arise in a serious form in regression models based on time-series data, since many of the important economic variables tend to exhibit strong correlations when recorded over time. One commonly used method in such cases is to redefine the estimating equation in such a way that extreme forms of collinearity among the explanatory variables are avoided. An illustration of this is provided by our example 8.12 above. Had we defined total apparent consumption of lamb in each year as a linear function of price, income and population, the regression coefficients for the latter two variables would not have been too reliable because of the high degree of collinearity exhibited by the two variables during the sample period. By expressing the consumption term and the income term in the estimating equation on a per capita basis we were still able to test a meaningful hypothesis without at the same time running into a serious collinearity problem.

In other instances, it may be possible to replace two or more inter-correlated variables by a single variable or by a suitably constructed index. The question then is whether such modifications will successfully remove multicollinearity without altering the basic hypothesis being tested. If multicollinearity causes us to exclude an important variable from the analysis, our estimates may be none the more reliable because of the resulting specification error.[1] In such circumstances it may not be possible to resolve the multicollinearity problem without additional sample information.

[1] See section 8.9 above.

In general, there are no firm rules to guide us in dealing with the problem of high collinearity in economic data. Even though multicollinearity tends to make the conventional t-tests of the individual regression coefficients unreliable, it is possible that the explanatory variables in the regression contribute jointly to a high value of R^2, and we may then use the estimated relationship for purposes of prediction. Used for such purposes, regression equations involving interdependent explanatory variables may yield quite satisfactory results, provided the interrelationships among the variables can be expected to hold during the period for which the prediction is made.

8.11 Autocorrelation

In specifying the theoretical regression model outlined in the previous sections it was necessary to make several assumptions about the distribution of the random error ε_i. Briefly, the assumptions were that the errors are independent, normally distributed random variables, each with mean zero and constant variance σ_ε^2. In some practical situations, these assumptions can be expected to hold, or at least can be expected to be reasonable approximations to reality. In other cases their validity needs to be tested against available data. Thus, it is sometimes found that the assumption of constant variance, or homoscedasticity, cannot be justified in practice. This is likely to occur when sampled units of different size are included in the regression. To the extent that larger variances tend to be associated with the larger units, the assumption of equal variance for all ε_i is likely to be violated. On the other hand, in fitting regression equations to time-series data it is almost always the case that the data show some degree of serial dependence, thus casting doubt on the reasonableness of the assumption that the ε_i are statistically independent. The most frequently investigated form of serial dependence in time-series data is the simple correlation between successive errors ε_i and ε_{i-1}. Such a correlation is commonly referred to as *first-order autocorrelation*. In concluding this chapter we discuss the problem of autocorrelation in least-squares regressions fitted to time-series data. Most computer programs for regression analysis include a standard test for first-order autocorrelation, and some familiarity with the testing procedure is therefore desirable. For treatment of heteroscedasticity, ie inequality of the variances of the ε_is, the reader may wish to consult some of the econometric texts listed in Appendix C.

Since the error term ε_i in the true regression relationship is not directly observable, one can only test for possible violations of the least-squares assumptions by examining the actual residuals from the fitted regression, ie the e_is. A first useful step in checking the results for symptoms of autocorrelation is to draw a scatter diagram of the residuals by plotting each e_i against the observation number i; for time-series data, this means that the residuals are plotted against time. Suppose that the plotted points display a pattern such as that illustrated

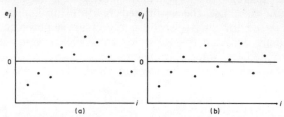

Fig 8.15 Autocorrelation of residuals (a) positive (b) negative

by Fig 8.15(a). We observe a tendency for positive residuals to be followed by positive residuals, and for negative residuals to be followed by negative residuals. When such a pattern occurs, the residuals are said to be *positively* autocorrelated. In time-series regressions, if autocorrelation occurs it is usually positive autocorrelation. This may result from the fact that many economic series follow trend and business-cycle patterns over time, or that the effects of economic changes are distributed over a number of observation periods. In other instances, positive correlation of the residuals may indicate the influence of an omitted cyclical variable. If the autocorrelation is negative, the values of e_i will show frequent changes of sign; this is illustrated diagrammatically in Fig 8.15 (b).

Now suppose that in the simple regression model

$$Y_i = \alpha + \beta X_i + \varepsilon_i$$

the random errors ε_i are positively autocorrelated, the other least-squares assumptions remaining the same as before. Then, by the same argument as in section 8.4 above, b remains an unbiased estimator of β, ie $E(b) = \beta$. Consider next $\text{Var}(b)$. This reduces to $\text{Var}(b) = \sigma_\varepsilon^2/\Sigma x^2$ only if the ε_i are independent, for then $\text{Cov}(\varepsilon_i \varepsilon_j) = 0$ for $i \neq j$. But if the ε_i are autocorrelated, they cannot be independent. Consequently, the covariance terms in the formula for $\text{Var}(b)$ no longer reduce to zero, and in the case of positive autocorrelation their sum will in fact tend to be positive. It follows that if there is positive autocorrelation between successive errors in the true relationship between X and Y, the statistic b will be distributed with a standard error which will tend to be larger than $\sigma_b = \dfrac{\sigma_\varepsilon}{\Sigma x^2}$. This means that if we estimate the standard error of b from the usual formula $s_b = \dfrac{s_e}{\Sigma x^2}$, the value of $t = b/s_b$

obtained in the standard t-test is likely to be too high, thus causing us to reject the null hypothesis $H_o : \beta = 0$ when there is in fact no linear relationship between X and Y. This conclusion holds generally for more than two explanatory variables.

Since the presence of autocorrelation may lead us into drawing wrong inferences about the statistical significance of our results, it is evidently desirable that we should check the sample residuals e_i for evidence of autocorrelation. The test statistic commonly used to test for the presence of first-order autocorrelation is the Durbin–Watson statistic defined as

$$
d = \frac{\sum_{i=2}^{N} (e_i - e_{i-1})^2}{\sum_{i=1}^{N} e_i^2}
$$

If most of the residuals e_i are followed by residuals with the same sign, as in the case of positive autocorrelation, the value of d will be small; if there is negative autocorrelation, the value of d will tend to be large. The question then is: how small (or large) must the value of d be before we can conclude that the observed data are likely to have been generated by a model in which there is positive (negative) autocorrelation? The critical values for two-tailed tests of the test statistic d at the 5 per cent level of significance are set out in Table V, Appendix A. The values of N tabulated in the vertical margin of this table refer to the number of observations in the sample and the values of k' tabulated in the horizontal margin refer to the number of explanatory variables in the regression. Unlike other tests we have encountered so far, the Durbin–Watson test for autocorrelation involves a comparison of the d value with two critical values in each tail of the sampling distribution of d. The two critical values in the left-hand tail of the distribution are denoted by d_L and d_U, and are tabulated in the body of the table for various values of N and k'. If $d < d_L$, the probability is less than $2\frac{1}{2}$ per cent that the observed residuals are drawings from a probability distribution in which successive errors are uncorrelated, and we accept the hypothesis of positive autocorrelation. However, if $d_L < d < d_U$ the result of the test is inconclusive, and we can neither accept nor reject the hypothesis that there is no autocorrelation. The critical values of d for the upper tail of the distribution are calculated as $(4 - d_L)$ and $(4 - d_U)$, respectively. If $d > 4 - d_L$, then by similar reasoning as above, we accept the hypothesis of negative autocorrelation, and if $4 - d_U < d < 4 - d_L$ the result of the test is again inconclusive. It now follows that if we set up a two-tailed test of the hypotheses

$$H_o : \text{the } \varepsilon_i \text{ are not autocorrelated}$$

$$H_a : \text{the } \varepsilon_i \text{ are autocorrelated}$$

the null hypothesis of no autocorrelation is accepted only if $d_U < d < 4 - d_U$; this is shown diagrammatically in Fig 8.16.

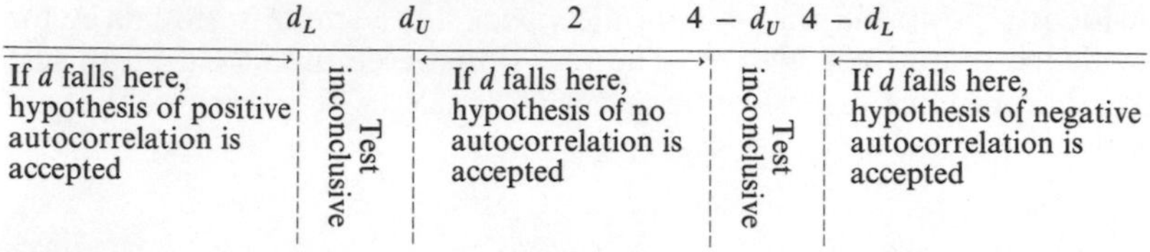

d_L	d_U	2	$4 - d_U$	$4 - d_L$
If d falls here, hypothesis of positive autocorrelation is accepted	Test inconclusive	If d falls here, hypothesis of no autocorrelation is accepted	Test inconclusive	If d falls here, hypothesis of negative autocorrelation is accepted

Fig 8.16

Example 8.13

Let us refer to example 8.12 to check the results for evidence of autocorrelation. Here

$$N = 10 \qquad k' = 2$$

and from the printed results the value of the Durbin-Watson statistic is

$$d = 2 \cdot 35$$

Referring to Table V, Appendix A, we find the critical values d_L and d_U not tabulated for $N < 15$. Extrapolating from $N = 15$ to $N = 10$, we get

$$d_L = 0 \cdot 83 - 5(0 \cdot 03) = 0 \cdot 68$$

$$d_U \simeq 1 \cdot 38$$

and

$$4 - d_L = 3 \cdot 32$$

$$4 - d_U = 2 \cdot 62$$

Diagrammatically, we have

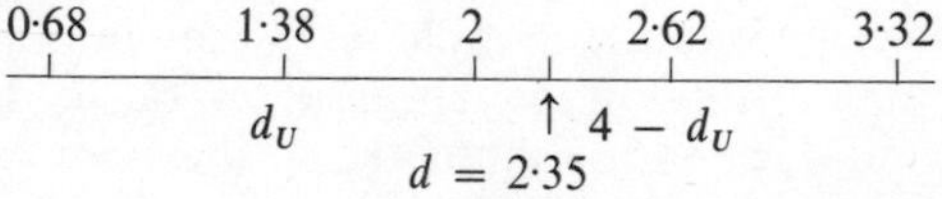

$$
\begin{array}{ccccc}
0 \cdot 68 & 1 \cdot 38 & 2 & 2 \cdot 62 & 3 \cdot 32 \\
& d_U & & \uparrow\ 4 - d_U & \\
& & d = 2 \cdot 35 & &
\end{array}
$$

Although our test is only an approximate one, the computed value of d can be seen to lie well within the limits d_U and $4 - d_U$, and we may therefore reasonably accept our result as being consistent with the hypothesis of no first-order autocorrelation.

CHAPTER 9

TIME SERIES

9.1 Objectives of the Analysis of Time Series

Most economic data are recorded over time. A series of observations recorded over time is called a *time* series, eg Australian National Income 1946–47 to 1974–75, coal production 1914–1975, etc. The objects of the analysis of time series are, first, to describe the past behaviour of time series, and, secondly, to analyse this behaviour.

The analysis of time series has developed in the main as a result of investigations into the nature and causes of those fluctuations in economic activity called *trade cycles*. Economic theory has suggested various explanations of trade cycles. Analysis of time series has attempted to test the plausibility or otherwise of these theories. At the same time, such analysis may suggest new hypotheses for economic theorists to work on. A large number of individual time series reveal cyclical fluctuations, and the relationship between these series can be investigated. Does one series lead another or lag behind it in its fluctuations? Are the movements of one series merely the reflection of the movements in another? These are the sorts of question which the analysis of time series attempts to answer.

Some economists believe that an analysis of time series may enable them to set up a model showing how the economy works and indicating the main forces which determine whether we have boom or depression. With such a model it might then be possible to forecast, at least for a short period ahead, what is likely to happen to the level of economic activity in the economy as a whole or even in some particular sector or industry. Thus one of the objects of the analysis of time series is to forecast how these series will behave in the future on the basis of how they have behaved in the past. This chapter is concerned with some of the main techniques used in the analysis of time series.

9.2 Characteristic Behaviour of Time Series

In examining any particular time series it is essential first to graph it in order to obtain a general picture of its behaviour. As an example of time series, the volume of Australian wool exports over a large number of years is shown in Fig 9.1.

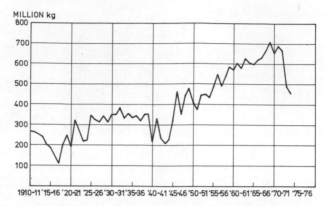

Fig 9.1 Exports of wool (greasy basis), Australia, 1910–11 to 1974–75

Source: Australian Bureau of Statistics: *Year Book*, No. 9, 1916, p 282; No. 12, 1919, p 295; No. 15, 1922, p 207; No. 18, 1925, p 662; No. 23, 1930, p 452; No. 28, 1935, p 671; No. 34, 1941, p 444; No. 36, 1944–45, p 749; No. 39, 1953, p 927; No. 42, 1956, p 921; *Quarterly Summary of Australian Statistics*, No. 228, 1958, p 48; No. 250, 1963, p 40; No. 268, 1968, p 79; No. 291, 1974, p 85; No. 299, 1976, p 82

If a large number of fairly long time series were examined, the following characteristics would be observed in many of them:

1. Secular trend.
2. Periodic movements.
3. Erratic movements.

The term *secular trend* is taken to mean the general long-term movement of the series. It need not have any particular shape, but the idea of trend implies a persistent movement in one direction or the other. The trend of a particular series may be due to, for example, the growth of population or a long-run increase in productivity or a steady change in economic habits. But the 'trend' itself is relative to the period to which the series refers, for an upward trend over a short period may only be an upward cyclical movement contained within a longer period.

Periodic movements may be of two kinds. There is first the strictly periodic movement which is associated with *seasonal variation*. Many economic time series are subject to this type of movement. Seasonal variation is evident when the data are recorded at weekly or monthly or quarterly intervals. Although the amplitude of seasonal variations may vary, their period is fixed—being one year. As a result, seasonal fluctuations do not appear in series of annual figures. Secondly, annual figures may themselves show more or less periodic movements about the trend. These movements are called *cyclical movements.* The amplitude and the period of the cycles may not be very regular, but in many series which reflect economic activity in one way or another, a cycle with a period of some eight or nine years is not uncommon. These cycles are what are usually called *trade cycles*, but minor cycles of about three years have been discerned in United States data, and there is some evidence that very long waves of about fifty years' period exist, although these are rather mixed up with secular trends.

Erratic movements may also be of two kinds. There is first the strictly random (chance) movements which turn the series first one way and then another in a purely chance manner. Secondly, certain isolated or irregular, but powerful, movements crop up from time to time—the influence of a strike or a political upheaval or a war. These may be called episodic movements. In a very long period these might be randomly distributed, but in the sorts of periods we have to analyse these movements may occur only once or twice, and they must be regarded as distinct from the more random movements which operate all the time.

9.3 Basic Assumptions in the Analysis of Time Series

The immediate objective of the analysis of time series is to break down the series into the main components which reflect the secular trend, the periodic movements and the erratic movements. In other words, the movement of the series is regarded as being compounded of these elements, and an attempt is made to reveal the magnitudes of each of these elements separately, showing how the movements of the separate components together account for the movement of the series.

The method of analysis depends very largely on the hypothesis as to how the components of the series are combined and interact. The simplest hypothesis is to assume that the separate influences have values which are additive and independent of each other. The latter assumption means that, for example, the seasonal influence will be the same irrespective of which phase of the cycle obtains. Thus we have

$$Y_t = T_t + C_t + S_t + E_t$$

where Y_t is the value of the variable at a particular time t, T_t is the trend value, C_t is the cyclical variation, S_t is the seasonal variation, E_t is the erratic variation. C_t will have positive or negative values according to whether we are in an 'above normal' or 'below normal' phase of the cycle; in other words, the cycle is conceived of as a fluctuation around a normal trend movement. The total positive and negative values for one cycle will be zero. Much the same considerations apply to the S_t term. S_t will be positive or negative according to the season of the year, and the total of S_t for a year will be zero. If the data are annual, the term S_t will disappear. E_t will also have positive or negative values, and in the long run ΣE_t will be zero. Occasionally E_t may take on an extreme value on account of some extraordinary occurrence, but such a movement should be regarded as an isolated occurrence.

In Fig 9.2 there are shown separately a trend, a cyclical variation and a random term over a number of years. These are then compounded to give a time series of the form

$$Y_t = T_t + C_t + E_t$$

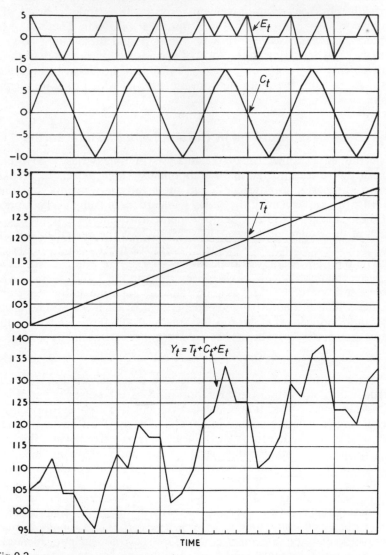

TIME

Fig 9.2

The data are supposed to be on an annual basis, so that no seasonal variation appears.

An alternative hypothesis to the above one is that

$$Y_t = T_t . C_t . S_t . E_t$$

where C, S and E, instead of being positive or negative values, are indexes fluctuating above or below unity. Since, by taking logarithms, we get

$$\log Y_t = \log T_t + \log C_t + \log S_t + \log E_t$$

it will be appreciated that there is no difference in principle between the two hypotheses. Both assume that the time series components are additive, but in the second case it is the logarithms which are added. If it is believed that the cyclical, seasonal and erratic forces operate with equal absolute effect irrespective of the trend value, then the first hypothesis is appropriate. If it is believed that they operate proportionately to the general level of the series, then the second is appropriate. The first regards the cyclical, seasonal and erratic variations as being plus or minus so many units, the second plus or minus such and such a percentage.

In practice a time series built up on either of the above hypotheses can be fairly readily decomposed into its elements. Fairly simple methods are available to ascertain the components T_t and S_t. If we subtract T_t and S_t from Y_t, we obtain a residual element which will be $C_t + E_t$. It may be quite difficult to separate off E_t from this, but generally one would suppose E_t to be small compared with C_t, so that this will not matter much. One of the objects of time-series analysis is to obtain the residual component, so that comparison of the cyclical patterns in various series can be made.

One could cast a good deal of doubt on the plausibility of the basic hypothesis outlined above. Is it reasonable to assume that the cyclical and trend components are determined by separate forces acting independently and then simply added together? In fact it is quite likely that this year's value of the variable will depend to some extent on last year's value, so that trend and cycle will get inextricably mixed and no meaningful separation of them will be possible. In such a situation a chance variation this year may affect the whole future course of the series, and it will not be possible to say how much of the value of the variable in any given year is 'due to' one or another of the components set out earlier. Thus an equation of the form

$$Y_t = [a(1 + g)^t] + [bY_{t-1} + c(Y_{t-1} - Y_{t-2})] + E_t$$

where a, g, b and c are constants and E_t is a random addition at time t, will for certain values of b and c generate a series with cycles about a trend. But, although the first square bracket contains the term which contributes the trend, being a straight-out growth function like compound interest, and E_t is the erratic component, no meaning can be attached to separating out the components, for the second square bracket which contains the mechanism which 'causes' the cycle cannot stand on its own, depending as it does on the value of the variable as a whole in preceding periods. A change in the trend or in E_t will change the whole nature of the cycle in subsequent periods.[1]

It should now be clear that the analysis of time series is a matter of great complexity, depending very much on the theory held regarding the generation of time series in general and of the given time series under consideration in particular. We shall now give methods for the analysis of trend and seasonal variation, strictly applicable only on the basis of the additive hypothesis, but nevertheless of a deal of general utility.

9.4 Measurement of Trend

Freehand Drawing

The immediate object of estimating the trend of a time series is to describe the general underlying movement of the series. Always the first thing to do is to graph the series. One simple way of obtaining the trend is then to draw a smooth freehand curve through the series. The main objection to this procedure is that it is necessarily rough and ready and the result will depend very much on the drawer of the trend himself, so that it is not an objective process.

Moving Averages

A second method for obtaining the trend is to attempt to smooth out the bumps in the series by a process of averaging. This can be done by what are called *moving averages*. Suppose we have annual data. Then, for example, a three-year moving average is obtained by averaging the values, first of periods 1 to 3, then of periods 2 to 4, etc. The averages are taken to represent the 'smoothed-out' values relating to the period in the middle of the span of the average. Thus the three-year average of periods 1 to 3 is centred at period 2, that of 2 to 4 at period 3, etc. This is illustrated as follows:

---

[1] See, for example, J Tinbergen, and J J Polak: *The Dynamics of Business Cycles* (Routledge and Kegan Paul, 1950), Chapter 16, p 252.

Period t	Value Y_t	Moving Average (3-year)
1	Y_1	
2	Y_2	$\frac{1}{3}(Y_1 + Y_2 + Y_3)$
3	Y_3	$\frac{1}{3}(Y_2 + Y_3 + Y_4)$
4	Y_4	$\frac{1}{3}(Y_3 + Y_4 + Y_5)$
5	Y_5	$\frac{1}{3}(Y_4 + Y_5 + Y_6)$
6	Y_6	.
.	.	.
.	.	.

If the moving average has an even number of terms, a second averaging process must be employed to centre the moving averages at periods rather than between periods:

Period t	Value Y_t	Moving Average (4-year)	Moving Average (2-year) of Moving Average (4-year)
1	Y_1		
2	Y_2		
3	Y_3	$\frac{1}{4}(Y_1 + Y_2 + Y_3 + Y_4)$	$\frac{1}{2}[\frac{1}{4}(Y_1 + Y_2 + Y_3 + Y_4) + \frac{1}{4}(Y_2 + Y_3 + Y_4 + Y_5)]$
4	Y_4	$\frac{1}{4}(Y_2 + Y_3 + Y_4 + Y_5)$	$\frac{1}{2}[\frac{1}{4}(Y_2 + Y_3 + Y_4 + Y_5) + \frac{1}{4}(Y_3 + Y_4 + Y_5 + Y_6)]$
5	Y_5	$\frac{1}{4}(Y_3 + Y_4 + Y_5 + Y_6)$	$\frac{1}{2}[\frac{1}{4}(Y_3 + Y_4 + Y_5 + Y_6) + \frac{1}{4}(Y_4 + Y_5 + Y_6 + Y_7)]$
6	Y_6	$\frac{1}{4}(Y_4 + Y_5 + Y_6 + Y_7)$	$\frac{1}{2}[\frac{1}{4}(Y_4 + Y_5 + Y_6 + Y_7) + \frac{1}{4}(Y_5 + Y_6 + Y_7 + Y_8)]$
7	Y_7	$\frac{1}{4}(Y_5 + Y_6 + Y_7 + Y_8)$	.
8	Y_8	$\frac{1}{4}(Y_6 + Y_7 + Y_8 + Y_9)$	.
9	Y_9	.	.
.	.	.	.

If the series consists of erratic fluctuations around a trend, a moving average will tend to reduce and smooth out these fluctuations. This must occur because the average of a number of terms must always lie between the smallest and largest of the terms. The larger the number of terms in the moving average, the smoother the resulting series; but the larger the number of terms the more information is lost at the end and the beginning of the series. A three-year moving average is often used for this kind of work.

On the other hand, if the series consists of periodic movements about a trend, a moving average with a span equal to the period of the cyclical movements will iron out these movements. This can be illustrated by the following example, in which an eight-year cycle has been artificially combined with a trend to produce the variable shown in the fourth column. An eight-year moving average appropriately centred eliminates the cyclical fluctuations and reduces the variable to the original trend.

Table 9.1

Period t	Trend T_t	Cycle C_t	Value $T_t + C_t$	Moving Average (8-year)	Moving Average (2-year) of Moving Average (8-year)
0	100	0	100		
1	101	6	107		
2	102	10	112		
3	103	6	109	103·5	104
4	104	0	104	104·5	105
5	105	−6	99	105·5	106
6	106	−10	96	106·5	107
7	107	−6	101	107·5	108
8	108	0	108	108·5	109
9	109	6	115	109·5	110
10	110	10	120	110·5	111
11	111	6	117	111·5	
12	112	0	112		
13	113	−6	107		
14	114	−10	104		
15	115	−6	109		

If the trend is not linear, moving averages will show a bias compared with the original trend so that the application of moving averages will not reveal the original trend. This can readily be seen by replacing the T_t column in the above table with a non-linear trend. Furthermore, if the period and/or the amplitude of the cycle is not constant, moving averages will not remove the whole of the cyclical element. Another difficulty in using moving averages is that, if they are calculated for a series of completely random fluctuations, they tend to produce a series with spurious periodic elements in it. Moving averages are useful in connexion with measuring seasonal variation, for the period of seasonal variation is always twelve months (see section 9.8), but we will not pursue the method in connexion with the estimation of trend.

Mathematical Curves

A third method for obtaining the trend, which we will now consider in some detail, is to fit a mathematical curve to the time series. This method has certain advantages. Once the form of the curve has been decided, the fitting of the curve, unlike the freehand drawing of one, is quite objective. Furthermore, the form of a mathematical curve can be interpreted in terms of the behaviour of the variable, so that a particular form of curve implies a certain type of trend. Thus, for example, a curve of the form $Y = a + bX$, where Y is the value of the variable and X measures time, means that the variable is changing by a constant amount per unit of time. This results in a convenient summarisation of the trend, and, perhaps, a logical description of it. This is an advantage not shared by moving averages.

The main method employed to fit mathematical curves to time-series data is that of least squares, which has already been discussed in section 8.2 above. We select the constants in our mathematical expression, whatever it is, such that $\Sigma(Y - Y_T)^2$ is a minimum, where the Ys are the observations over time and the Y_Ts the corresponding trend values as defined by the mathematical expression.[1]

9.5 Fitting a Mathematical Trend

Linear Trend

The simplest form of trend is a *linear trend*. It is defined by

$$Y_T = a + bX$$

where Y_T is the trend value of the variable under consideration, here assumed for convenience to be on an annual basis, and X is time. Such a trend is shown in Fig 9.3 on p 367.

The constant a is the trend value of Y at the origin of time (ie where $X = 0$) and the constant b is the increase in Y_T per unit of time (ie per unit change in X). We can place the origin of X at any place we please, provided we remember where we have placed it, eg if the series extends from 1955–1975, we can put 1955 = 0 and then 1965 = 10 and 1975 = 20 or we can put 1965 = 0 and then 1955 = −10 and 1975 = +10, etc. Since the curve $Y_T = a + bX$ is a continuous curve, the origin corresponds to a point of time. If the data refer to measurements over whole years, the origin should be at the middle of a year, whereas if they refer to measurements at a point of time, it should be at such a point of time. For example, coal production in calendar years should have its origin at 30 June of a year, population as at the end of calendar years should have its origin at 31 December of a year.

The normal equations to determine a and b by least squares (see section 8.2, p 278) are

$$\left. \begin{array}{l} \Sigma Y = Na + b\Sigma X \\ \Sigma XY = a\Sigma X + b\Sigma X^2 \end{array} \right\}$$

where N is the number of years covered by the time series. If the number of years covered is odd, we can place the origin at the middle

[1] The symbol Y_T used here is equivalent to the symbol T used on p 359 above.

year and then $\Sigma X = 0$. This is very convenient, for then the normal equations reduce to

$$\left.\begin{array}{l} \Sigma Y = Na \\ \Sigma XY = b\Sigma X^2 \end{array}\right\}$$

and

ie

$$a = \bar{Y} \text{ and } b = \frac{\Sigma XY}{\Sigma X^2}$$

When stating a trend, the units and the origin *must* be attached. An equation without them is quite meaningless. The origin should be expressed as a date, not as a year.

Example 9.1

Fit a linear trend to the annual values of Australian exports of merchandise over the years 1962–63 to 1974–75 given below, and compute the trend values of exports for the years under consideration.

Year	Exports of Merchandise (a) ($ '000 million) Y	X	XY	X^2	Y_T
1962–63	2·13	−6	−12·78	36	1·403
1963–64	2·73	−5	−13·65	25	1·855
1964–65	2·58	−4	−10·32	16	2·307
1965–66	2·63	−3	−7·89	9	2·759
1966–67	2·93	−2	−5·86	4	3·211
1967–68	2·94	−1	−2·94	1	3·663
1968–69	3·24	0	0	0	4·115
1969–70	3·99	1	3·99	1	4·567
1970–71	4·24	2	8·48	4	5·019
1971–72	4·77	3	14·31	9	5·471
1972–73	6·07	4	24·28	16	5·923
1973–74	6·76	5	33·80	25	6·375
1974–75	8·48	6	50·88	36	6·827
Total	53·49	0	82·30	182	

(a) Source: Australian Bureau of Statistics: *Quarterly Summary of Australian Statistics*, No. 269, 1968, p 62; No. 279, 1971, p 71; No. 299, 1976, p 67

Here we have $a = \dfrac{\Sigma Y}{N} = \dfrac{53\cdot49}{13} = 4\cdot115,$ $\quad b = \dfrac{\Sigma XY}{\Sigma X^2} = \dfrac{82\cdot30}{182} = 0\cdot452$

and the trend is

$$Y_T = 4\cdot115 + 0\cdot452X$$

where Y_T is the trend value of annual exports of merchandise in $ thousand million and X is financial years with origin at 31.12.68 (the middle of 1968–69).

This can be interpreted by saying that over the years under consideration the trend of Australian exports of merchandise has shown an increase, in value terms, of $0·452 thousand million per annum. The trend values corresponding to the observed data can easily be calculated by substitution in the trend equation and are given in the last column of the table.[1]

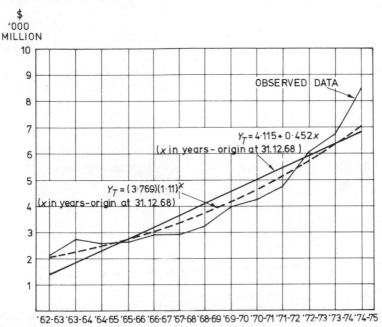

$
'000
MILLION

'62-63 '63-64 '64-65 '65-66 '66-67 '67-68 '68-69 '69-70 '70-71 '71-72 '72-73 '73-74 '74-75

Fig 9.3 Exports of merchandise, Australia, 1962–63 to 1974–75

Source: Australian Bureau of Statistics: *Quarterly Summary of Australian Statistics*, No. 269, 1968, p 62; No. 279, 1971, p 71; No. 299, 1976, p 67

Fig 9.3 shows for the preceding example the observed data together with the linear trend line. The broken line should for the present be ignored. Although the data reveal a distinct upward trend, it can be seen that it is not really linear in character.

If the number of years happens to be even, the origin can be put between the middle two years (ie at the end of the $\frac{N}{2}$th year), and time expressed in terms of half-years. In this case ΣX will again equal 0. In the equation $Y_T = a + bX$, the variable X will then be expressed

---

[1] For some purposes trend values for months (or quarters) are required. These can be obtained by substituting the appropriate value for X, expressed in years and fractions of years, in the trend equation. When the variable is such that the annual data, upon which the trend is based, are the sums of monthly (or quarterly) values, the trend value obtained upon substitution must be appropriately scaled down. For example, to obtain the trend value for September 1972, in example 9.1, we centre this at 15 September and substitute $X = 3\frac{17}{24}$ in the equation. This gives $Y_T = 5·791$. This is the trend value of *annual* exports centred at 15.9.72. The corresponding *monthly* trend value is $5·791 \div 12$ = $0·483 thousand million.

in half-years, and the origin will be at the end of the $\frac{N}{2}$th year. To convert the equation into one referring to full years, we shall have

$$Y_T = a + 2bX$$

where X is in full years and the origin is at the end of the $\frac{N}{2}$th year, since b measures the change per half-year and hence $2b$ measures it per full year. To shift the origin to the middle of a year we must add the change for a half-year to the constant a, since this constant represents the value of Y_T at the origin. We shall have

$$Y_T = a + b + 2bX$$

where X is in full years and the origin is in the middle of the $\left(\frac{N}{2} + 1\right)$th year. This is illustrated in the example below.

Example 9.2

Fit a linear trend to the annual values of Australian exports of merchandise over the years 1962–63 to 1973–74

Year	Exports of Merchandise ($ '000 million) Y	X	XY	X^2
1962–63	2·13	−11	−23·43	121
1963–64	2·73	−9	−24·57	81
1964–65	2·58	−7	−18·06	49
1965–66	2·63	−5	−13·15	25
1966–67	2·93	−3	−8·79	9
1967–68	2·94	−1	−2·94	1
1968–69	3·24	1	3·24	1
1969–70	3·99	3	11·97	9
1970–71	4·24	5	21·20	25
1971–72	4·77	7	33·39	49
1972–73	6·07	9	54·63	81
1973–74	6·76	11	74·36	121
Total	45·01	0	107·85	572

Here we have $a = \dfrac{\Sigma Y}{N} = 3\cdot751,$ $\qquad b = \dfrac{\Sigma XY}{\Sigma X^2} = 0\cdot189$

and the trend is

$$Y_T = 3\cdot751 + 0\cdot189X$$

where X is in half-years with origin at 30 June 1968. This can be readily converted to X in full years and origin at 31 December 1968, as in the other example. The coefficient of X is the increase in Y per unit increase in X. Hence, converting X into full years doubles the coefficient, ie

$$Y_T = 3{\cdot}751 + 0{\cdot}378X$$

where X is in years with origin at 30 June 1968. To shift the origin along half a year, we must add half a year's increment to the constant $3{\cdot}751$, in order to obtain the value of Y_T at the origin, ie

$$Y_T = 3{\cdot}751 + 0{\cdot}189 + 0{\cdot}378X$$

ie $\qquad\qquad Y_T = 3{\cdot}940 + 0{\cdot}378X$

where X is in financial years with origin at 31 December 1968.

The trends in the above example and the preceding one are different, since they are based on a different number of observations.

Exponential Trend

The linear trend

$$Y_T = a + bX$$

is one in which Y_T increases by a constant absolute amount per annum. This amount is given by the coefficient b. Many other types of trends are available. A commonly used one is where Y_T increases not by a constant absolute amount per annum, but by a constant percentage per annum. Such a trend is defined by

$$Y_T = AB^X$$

where A and B are constants. For example, if $B = 1{\cdot}01$, then Y_T increases by 1 per cent per annum. This type of trend is called an *exponential trend*.

It will be recalled from section 2.4 above that a function of this form when plotted on a semi-logarithmic scale gives a straight line. An exponential trend is shown on an arithmetic scale by the broken line in Fig 9.3 on p 367 and on a semi-logarithmic scale in Fig 9.4 on p 371.

An exponential trend is readily fitted by taking logarithms, for

$$\log Y_T = \log A + X \log B$$

This is now similar in form to

$$Y_T = a + bX$$

where Y_T is replaced by $\log Y_T$, a is replaced by $\log A$, and b is replaced by $\log B$.

To fit such a curve we write down the logarithms of the Ys and proceed as before. By suitable choice of the origin, we shall have

$$\log A = \frac{\Sigma \log Y}{N}$$

and
$$\log B = \frac{\Sigma X \log Y}{\Sigma X^2}$$

By looking up the anti-logarithms of log A and log B, we can readily ascertain A and B. As before, when the number of years is even, X can be expressed in half-years, and the conversion of the equation into full years and appropriate shift of origin can be performed by adjusting the logarithmic form of the equation.

Example 9.3

Fit an exponential trend to the annual values of Australian exports of merchandise over the years 1962–63 to 1974–75, and compute the trend values of exports for the years under consideration.

Year	Exports of Merchandise ($ '000 million)	log Y	X	$X \log Y$	X^2	log Y_T	Y_T
1962–63	2·13	0·3284	− 6	− 1·9704	36	0·3032	2·010
1963–64	2·73	0·4362	− 5	− 2·1810	25	0·3487	2·232
1964–65	2·58	0·4116	− 4	− 1·6464	16	0·3942	2·479
1965–66	2·63	0·4200	− 3	− 1·2600	9	0·4397	2·752
1966–67	2·93	0·4669	− 2	− 0·9338	4	0·4852	3·056
1967–68	2·94	0·4683	− 1	− 0·4683	1	0·5307	3.394
1968–69	3·24	0·5105	0	0	0	0·5762	3·769
1969–70	3·99	0·6010	1	0·6010	1	0·6217	4·185
1970–71	4·24	0·6274	2	1·2548	4	0·6672	4·647
1971–72	4·77	0·6785	3	2·0355	9	0·7127	5·161
1972–73	6·07	0·7832	4	3·1328	16	0·7582	5·731
1973–74	6·76	0·8299	5	4·1495	25	0·8037	6·364
1974–75	8·48	0·9284	6	5·5704	36	0·8492	7·066
Total	53·49	7·4903	0	8·2841	182		

Here we have
$$\log A = \frac{\Sigma \log Y}{N} = \frac{7·4903}{13} = 0·5762$$

$$\log B = \frac{\Sigma X \log Y}{\Sigma X^2} = \frac{8·2841}{182} = 0·0455$$

and the exponential trend is
$$\log Y_T = 0·5762 + 0·0455X$$
ie
$$Y_T = (3·769)(1·11)^X$$

with X in financial years with origin at 31 December 1968.

This can be interpreted by saying that over the years under consideration the trend of Australian exports of merchandise has shown an increase of 11 per cent per annum.

To obtain trend values for individual years it is easiest to work in logarithms from the equation

$$\log Y_T = 0·5762 + 0·0455X$$

and then look up the anti-logarithms. This has been done in the last two columns of the above table.

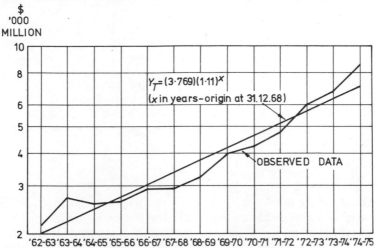

$\$$
'000
MILLION

Fig 9.4 Exports of merchandise, Australia, 1962–63 to 1974–75

Source: Australian Bureau of Statistics, *Quarterly Summary of Australian Statistics*, No. 269, 1968, p 62; No. 279, 1971, p 71; No. 299, 1976, p 67

Fig 9.4 shows for the preceding example the observed data, together with the exponential trend line, on a semi-logarithmic scale. In Fig 9.3 the exponential trend is also shown on an arithmetic scale alongside the linear trend for the same data. It can be seen that in this case the exponential trend gives a better description of the underlying movement of the series than the linear one.

Other Mathematical Trends

The linear and exponential are the simplest of trend types. Polynomials of the form

$$Y_T = a + bX + cX^2 + dX^3 + \ldots$$

may also be used, and these can be fitted by the method of least squares. For example, to fit the parabola

$$Y_T = a + bX + cX^2$$

the normal equations for determining a, b, c are derived as before from the conditions for minimising $\Sigma(Y - Y_T)^2$ and are

$$\left.\begin{array}{l}\Sigma Y = Na + b\Sigma X + c\Sigma X^2 \\ \Sigma XY = a\Sigma X + b\Sigma X^2 + c\Sigma X^3 \\ \Sigma X^2 Y = a\Sigma X^2 + b\Sigma X^3 + c\Sigma X^4\end{array}\right\}$$

By suitable choice of the origin ΣX and ΣX^3 can be made to vanish and we have

$$\left.\begin{array}{l} \Sigma Y = Na + c\Sigma X^2 \\ \Sigma XY = b\Sigma X^2 \\ \Sigma X^2 Y = a\Sigma X^2 + c\Sigma X^4 \end{array}\right\}$$

The second equation now gives b directly, and a and c can be obtained by solving simultaneously the first and third equations.

More complicated forms may be used, in which the fitting is rather more difficult. For example, a well-known curve is the *logistic* curve. Its equation is

$$Y_T = \frac{k}{1 + e^{a-bX}}$$

where k, a and b are constants (k and b positive) and $e = 2\cdot71828$. This curve is S-shaped and is asymptotic to the X-axis for large negative X and to the abscissa $Y = k$ for large positive X. It is useful for describing a series which starts growing slowly, then grows rapidly and finally reaches a saturation point, eg the sales of a new product, the population of insects reproducing in a confined space, etc. It is graphed in Fig 9.5.

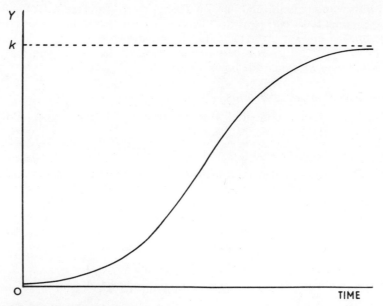

Fig 9.5 The logistic curve

In selecting a trend to fit to a given series, the choice of the curve is largely a matter of the subjective opinion of the fitter. But the idea is to use a trend which will describe the general underlying movement of the data. Furthermore, the movement in the trend should be one which is reasonable on *a priori* grounds. Thus a linear trend implies change by a constant amount per period, an exponential one change by a constant percentage, and a parabolic one implies that the amount of change per period itself changes by a constant amount per period (the first derivative of a parabola being linear), and so on. If the data when graphed on arithmetic paper give the impression of a straight line, then the linear trend $Y_T = a + bX$ should be used. If, when graphed on semi-logarithmic paper, they give one of a straight line, then the exponential trend $Y_T = AB^X$ should be used. For the use of more complicated trends a good deal of experience in the practice of fitting trends is required. However, higher degree polynomials should be used with caution for the very reason that the more constants in the equation the closer the fit. By selecting a function of sufficiently high degree it would always be possible to pass the curve through every point since a function with n disposable constants can be passed through n points. However, this would negate the whole idea of a trend. Moreover, it would be very difficult to justify the use of high-degree curves on theoretical grounds, since their rates of change cannot be interpreted in the simple ways in which they can for linear and exponential functions.

9.6 Interpretation of a Mathematical Trend

Mathematical curves are useful to *describe* the general movement of a time series, but it is doubtful whether any analytical significance should be attached to them, except in special cases. It is, of course, possible to interpret a mathematical trend analytically by regarding the trend value of the variable as dependent on time in some operative sense, eg the size of a population may be regarded as a function of the time which has elapsed since the beginning of the population. Thus we could say that a variable Y measured at any particular time is made up of a systematic component dependent on time and a random term

$$Y = [\alpha + \beta X] + \varepsilon$$

where X is time, α and β are parameters and ε is a random fluctuation. Here the term in the square brackets is the trend component of Y. If we have N observations of Y over time, we can fit by least squares

$$Y_T = a + bX$$

and having tested that *b* differs significantly from zero, use *a* and *b* as estimates of α and β respectively. This approach corresponds to that discussed in the preceding chapter, where it was shown how regression analysis can be used to test a theory about the way in which a dependent variable can be 'explained' by independent variables. However, it is seldom possible to justify on theoretical grounds any *real* dependence of a variable on the passage of time. Variables do change in a more or less systematic manner over time, but this can usually be attributed to the operation of other explanatory variables. Thus many economic time series show persistent upward trends over time due to a growth of population or to a general rise in prices, eg national income, and the trend element can to a considerable extent be eliminated by expressing these series *per capita* or in terms of constant purchasing power. For these reasons mathematical trends are generally best regarded as tools for describing movements in time series rather than as theories of the causes of such movements. It follows that it is extremely dangerous to use trends to forecast future movements of a time series. Such forecasting, involving as it does extrapolation, can be valid only if there is theoretical justification for the particular trend as an expression of a functional relationship between the variable under consideration and time. But if the trend is purely descriptive of past behaviour, it can give few clues about future behaviour. Often the extrapolation of a trend gives ridiculous results which themselves are *prima facie* evidence that the trend could not be maintained, eg if the world population continued to grow at the average rate of the past ten years, there would by the year AD 4000 be about $2\frac{1}{2}$ million million million million people on the globe.

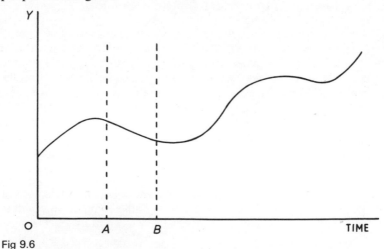

Fig 9.6

Moreover, the notion of trend is itself very elusive, because unless we can observe very long time series we can never be certain that what appears as a trend is not in fact the upward or downward phase of a cyclical movement and the trend is in fact quite different. Consequently, the concept of trend movements as distinct from cyclical movements is relative to the period of time observed. This does not prevent us from using mathematical curves to describe the movements of series, but it does make it difficult to sustain any contention that we have located *the* trend of a series. This point is illustrated in Fig 9.6 on the previous page. If the period *AB* is considered in isolation, a clear *downward* trend is apparent. However, if a larger period is considered, it is seen to be a cyclical phase in a long-period *upward* trend.

9.7 Use of Time Series in Correlation and Regression

It was shown in sections 8.5 and 8.7 above how correlation and regression analysis can be used to test hypotheses about economic relationships. Very often the only data available are in the form of time series, and special care is needed in correlating data which are in this form. It may well happen that two variables exhibit a high degree of correlation over time not because they are related in any way but because other factors have produced persistent trends causing both series to rise together or the one to rise and the other to fall steadily. Such circumstances as these may produce nonsense correlations. Consequently, in order to render a correlation between time series meaningful we must try to eliminate the influence of these other factors on the two series. But it may be very difficult to determine precisely what these factors are. One way out is to regard the trends in the series as measures of their influence. We then remove the trends from the series and correlate the *trend-free* series. The resulting correlation will indicate whether the position of the one variable relative to its trend is related to that of the other variable relative to *its* trend.

The removal of trend from a series is quite straightforward. If we regard the variable as being compounded as follows:

$$Y_t = T_t + C_t + E_t$$

the trend-free series is given by

$$Y_t - T_t$$

however T_t is arrived at. If T_t has been derived as a mathematical trend, it will correspond to Y_T in section 9.5 above. On the other hand, if we regard the variable as

$$Y_t = T_t . C_t . E_t$$

the trend-free series is given by

$$\frac{Y_t}{T_t}$$

Once the trends (if any) are removed, the two series can be correlated in the usual manner.

As an illustration of the need for using trend-free series in certain cases, we may quote an example given by Tippett.[1] Consider the annual marriage rate per 1000 of population and an index of real wages for England and Wales, 1850–90. The former shows a downward trend and the latter an upward one, both trends being approximately linear. Hence a correlation of the two original series will give substantial negative correlation, ie the higher the level of real wages the lower the marriage rate. But is this correlation of any value? We cannot conclude from it that higher real wages 'cause' a lower marriage rate, because the trends in the two series were caused by independent unrelated factors—the trend in the marriage rate being due to later marriage and an ageing population and that in real wages to increasing industrial efficiency. What we want to know is whether, when the index of real wages is above its trend, the marriage rate tends to be above or below its trend or whether the two variables are independent. By correlating trend-free series we may be able to throw some light on this, and in this particular case such a correlation gives an appreciable degree of positive correlation, ie the marriage rate and the level of real wages tend to move above or below their respective trends together. This result would support the hypothesis that economic conditions influence the marriage rate.

The above refers to the correlation of two variables the data for which are in the form of time series. Similarly, if we are interested in the regression of a dependent variable Z on an independent variable Y, where the data are in the form of time series, the regression should be performed in terms of trend-free data, so that it will be[2]

$$Z - Z_T = h(Y - Y_T)$$

where h is the regression coefficient of trend-free Z on trend-free Y. Moreover, if both the trends are linear, so that Z_T and Y_T can be written

$$Z_T = l + mX \text{ and } Y_T = p + qX$$

where l, m, p and q are constants and X is time, the above regression equation can be written

[1] L H C Tippett: *Statistics* (OUP, 1952), 1st edition, pp 37, 56.

[2] Since $\Sigma(Z - Z_T) = \Sigma(Y - Y_T) = 0$, there will be no constant term in the regression.

$$Z = (l - hp) + hY + (m - hq)X$$

This is an ordinary multiple regression equation of Z on Y and X. The regression coefficient of Y is h, as in the first formulation, so that h can be determined by the multiple regression methods of section 8.8 above. It measures the change in Z per unit change in Y, with the influence of time (ie the trends) eliminated.

9.8 Measurement of Seasonal Variation

When data are expressed annually there is no seasonal variation. But monthly or quarterly data frequently exhibit strong seasonal movements (see Fig 9.7, p 380) and considerable interest attaches to devising a pattern of average seasonal variation. It may be desired to compare the seasonal patterns of different series, but more often we may want to know the extent to which we should discount the most recently available statistics for seasonal factors. For example, average weekly earnings in Australia were $143·60 per week in the March quarter 1974–75 and then rose to $156·30 in the June quarter. Was this due to an underlying upward tendency or simply because the June quarter is usually seasonally higher than the March quarter? If we knew by how much the June quarter is usually above or below the March quarter for seasonal reasons, we could answer this question. In what follows we shall deal with quarterly movements, but monthly movements can be treated in identical fashion.

In order to analyse seasonal variation it is necessary to assume that the seasonal pattern is superimposed on a series of values and is independent of these in the sense that the same pattern is superimposed irrespective of the level of the series, eg the September quarter always contributes so much more or so much less to the series. For this purpose we can use the hypothesis about the composition of a time series set out in section 9.3 above

$$Y_{it} = T_{it} . C_{it} . S_i . E_{it}$$

where the subscripts refer to the ith quarter and the tth year. Here, however, it is only necessary to assume the independence of S_i and of E_{it} which is much more reasonable than assuming that all the terms are mutually independent. Consequently, the use of this hypothesis for the estimation of seasonal variation is of much greater generality than its use for analysing trend and cyclical movements. The component S_i will be above or below unity according to the quarter of the year, and is assumed to be the same from year to year. Its average value for the year will be unity,[1] eg S_i might have the values 1·00, 1·04, 0·95, 1·01,

---

[1] Strictly speaking, the average used here should be a geometric average, since the hypothesis is multiplicative, ie additive in the logarithms of the variables.

indicating that the March quarter has no seasonal influence, the June quarter adds 4 per cent for seasonal reasons, the September quarter subtracts 5 per cent and the December quarter adds 1 per cent. The component E_{it} is a random term with a mean value tending to unity for any given i.

The problem is: given a series of values for Y_{it}, to determine the unknown component S_i. There are several ways of doing this but the method of moving averages given below is perhaps the most satisfactory in practice and is relatively simple to apply. The *first step* is to take a four-quarter moving average of the series. This will give values centred between quarters, and a further two-quarter average of the four-quarter averages must be taken to centre the moving averages at quarters. Since the period of the average is the same as the period of the seasonal variations, such an average will tend to iron out the seasonal variations, and it will also smooth out the random fluctuations represented by the E_{it} term. As a result the moving averages will be an estimate of $(T_{it} . C_{it})$, ie of the trend-cyclical components. This is illustrated in Fig 9.7 below. If we now express the observed data (Y_{it}) as a ratio to the moving averages, we shall have a series consisting of seasonal and random components, ie

$$R_{it} = \frac{Y_{it}}{T_{it} . C_{it}} = S_i . E_{it}$$

where R_{it} is the ratio of the observed data to the moving average in the ith quarter of year t. Ratios such as these are illustrated in Fig 9.8 below. If we take a particular quarter and average the ratios for this quarter, we shall get for the ith quarter

$$\bar{R}_i = S_i . \bar{E}_{it} \cdot B$$

where the average is taken over the various years. But in the long run $\bar{E}_{it} = 1$, so this procedure will average out the random fluctuations, leaving us with the seasonal component $\bar{R}_i = S_i$. This is the *second step*. This would complete the process were it not for the fact that the moving averages are often biased estimates of $T_{it} . C_{it}$. As has been pointed out on p 364 above, a moving average may not only smooth out periodic and erratic fluctuations, but in doing so may produce a series which is biased with respect to the original series on which the periodic and erratic fluctuations have been superimposed. Consequently, $\bar{R}_i$, the mean of the ratios for a particular quarter, may not in fact give S_i, since R_{it} may not equal $(S_i . E_{it})$. In this case we can write

$$\bar{R}_i = S_i . B$$

where B stands for the bias resulting from the moving averages being biased estimates of $(T_{it} . C_{it})$, assumed here (not unreasonably) to be the

Table 9.2

Year and Quarter		Average Weekly Earnings. Observed Values (a) $	4-quarter Moving Totals $	Centred Moving Averages $	Ratios of Observed Values to Moving Averages
1965–66	S	57·60			
	D	59·60	231·40		
	M	55·50	234·90	58·29	0·952
	J	58·70	238·60	59·19	0·992
1966–67	S	61·10	242·60	60·15	1·016
	D	63·30	247·60	61·28	1·033
	M	59·50	250·90	62·31	0·955
	J	63·70	254·70	63·20	1·008
1967–68	S	64·40	258.40	64·14	1·004
	D	67·10	262·00	65·05	1·032
	M	63·20	265·40	65·92	0·958
	J	67·30	270·80	67·02	1·004
1968–69	S	67·80	276·10	68·36	0·992
	D	72·50	281·60	69·71	1·040
	M	68·50	287·90	71·19	0·962
	J	72·80	294·40	72·79	1·000
1969–70	S	74·10	298·60	74·13	1·000
	D	79·00	305·20	75·48	1·047
	M	72·70	312·00	77·15	0·942
	J	79·40	319·30	78·91	1·006
1970–71	S	80·90	328·60	80·99	0·999
	D	86·30	339·00	83·45	1·034
	M	82·00	348·10	85·89	0·955
	J	89·80	357·80	88·24	1·018
1971–72	S	90·00	365·00	90·35	0·996
	D	96·00	371·90	92·11	1·042
	M	89·20	378·70	93·83	0·951
	J	96·70	386·80	95·69	1·011
1972–73	S	96·80	394·80	97·70	0·991
	D	104·10	405·90	100·09	1·040
	M	97·20	419·30	103·15	0·942
	J	107·80	435·10	106·80	1·009
1973–74	S	110·20	451·20	110·79	0·995
	D	119·90	471·90	115·39	1·039
	M	113·30	499·60	121·44	0·933
	J	128·50	533·90	129·19	0·995
1974–75	S	137·90	564·20	137·26	1·005
	D	154·20	592·00	144·53	1·067
	M	143·60			
	J	156·30			

(a) Source: Australian Bureau of Statistics: *Average Weekly Earnings*, (Ref. 6.18), March quarter 1972, p 2; June quarter 1974, p 2; and March quarter 1976, p 3

same for all four quarters. This bias can be detected by averaging R_i for the four quarters. Since the average of S_i equals unity we shall have

$$\bar{R} = B$$

where $\bar{R}$ is the mean of the four $\bar{R}_i$. Where $\bar{R}$ differs from unity, bias exists. The *third step* is then to adjust S_i for bias by writing

$$S_i = \bar{R}_i / \bar{R}$$

so that the mean of S_i equals unity. The values of S_i are called an *index of seasonal variation*.

Since the pattern of seasonal variation is itself likely to change, it is usual to base an index of seasonal variation on a moderately short period. It must be emphasised that any seasonal pattern is valid only for the period on which it is based, and it can be used beyond that period only on the assumption that it remains unchanged. It is hardly necessary to point out that it is not worth while computing an index of seasonal variation unless there is clear evidence of a regular seasonal pattern. This evidence can best be obtained by graphing the data.

The above treatment is rather complicated, and perhaps the simplest way to explain the estimation of an index of seasonal variation is to do so by working through an example. We take as data the average weekly earnings of wage- and salary-earners in Australia 1965–66 to 1974–75. The observed values are given in Table 9.2 above and shown

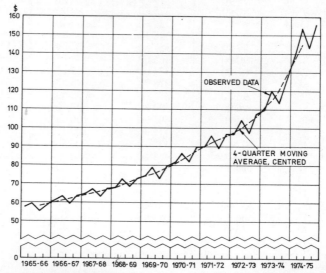

Fig 9.7 Average weekly earnings by quarters, Australia, 1965–66 to 1974–75
Source: Australian Bureau of Statistics: *Average Weekly Earnings* (Ref 6.18), March quarter 1972, p 2; June quarter 1974, p 2; and March quarter 1976, p 3

as the bold line in Fig 9.7. The presence of seasonal variation is evident from the diagram. The computation is carried through in three steps.

1. Calculating the Moving Averages and the Ratios of Observed Data to Moving Averages

First we calculate four-quarter moving averages of the data and then two-quarter moving averages of the four-quarter moving averages to centre them properly. This is best done by calculating four-quarter moving totals, adding adjacent totals and dividing by 8.[1] These moving averages will represent the series with the seasonal and random components largely smoothed out. They are graphed in Fig 9.7 as the broken line. Next we calculate the ratios of observed values to moving averages. These ratios will contain the seasonal and random components together with any bias resulting from the application of the moving average procedure. They are shown in Fig 9.8 and indicate a clear seasonal pattern, the December quarter being high and the March quarter low.

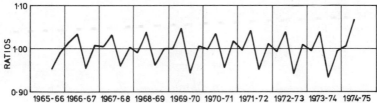

Fig 9.8 Average weekly earnings by quarters, Australia, 1965—66 to 1974—75
Ratio of observed data to moving averages

2. Averaging the Ratios

We arrange the ratios in columns for each quarter and average the values in each column. This will eliminate the random fluctuations in the ratios. In averaging these ratios the straight-out arithmetic mean is not always to be recommended. This is because occasionally

---

[1] Suppose that T_1 represents the total of the first four values of a series, T_2 represents the total of the next four values ($i = 2, 3, 4, 5$), etc. We then have as the four-quarter moving average centred at period 3

$$\tfrac{1}{2}[\tfrac{1}{4}(Y_1 + Y_2 + Y_3 + Y_4) + \tfrac{1}{4}(Y_2 + Y_3 + Y_4 + Y_5)] = \tfrac{1}{2}[\tfrac{1}{4}(T_1) + \tfrac{1}{4}(T_2)]$$
$$= \tfrac{1}{8}(T_1 + T_2).$$

Thus, for the first five values in Table 9.2 we have $T_1 = 231 \cdot 40$, $T_2 = 234 \cdot 90$, so that the four-quarter moving average value centred at 1965—66 M is $(231 \cdot 40 + 234 \cdot 90)/8 = 58 \cdot 29$, etc.

an irregular large fluctuation may occur, which must be regarded as of an *episodic* character and should be completely omitted from the calculations. Hence the median is often used or else a modified mean of the middle so-many items. When the number of observations per quarter is small, the latter is probably to be preferred. However, in this case there seems to be no reason for not taking an arithmetic mean of all the items. It is convenient at this stage to omit the decimal point, using 1000 as a base instead of unity.

Table 9.3

RATIOS OF OBSERVED VALUES TO MOVING AVERAGES

	September Quarter	December Quarter	March Quarter	June Quarter
1965–66			952	992
1966–67	1 016	1 033	955	1 008
1967–68	1 004	1 032	958	1 004
1968–69	992	1 040	962	1 000
1969–70	1 000	1 047	942	1 006
1970–71	999	1 034	955	1 018
1971–72	996	1 042	951	1 011
1972–73	991	1 040	942	1 009
1973–74	995	1 039	933	995
1974–75	1 005	1 067		
Average	1 000	1 042	950	1 005

3. Adjusting the Averages to Obtain the Index

As explained above, the average ratios just obtained may contain bias. With a base of 1000, these averages should average 1000, ie add to 4000. In this particular case they add to 3997, indicating negligible bias. Even so they should be adjusted to average 1000. This is done by multiplying each by the factor 4000/3997, so that we have the index, as in the following table:

Table 9.4

	Average Ratios	Index of Seasonal Variation
September Quarter	1 000	1 001
December Quarter	1 042	1 043
March Quarter	950	950
June Quarter	1 005	1 006
Mean	999·25	1 000

The index can be interpreted by saying that due to purely seasonal influences average weekly earnings in the December quarter, for example, tend to be about 4·3 per cent above what they otherwise would be. The seasonal pattern is shown diagrammatically in Fig 9.9. It must be thought of as being superimposed on what the series would be without seasonal influences.

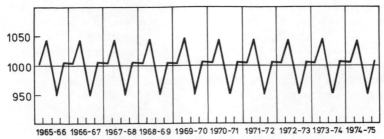

Fig 9.9 Average weekly earnings—Australia, 1965–66 to 1974–75
Index of seasonal variation

To *deseasonalise* a series, for which we have an index of seasonal variation, we divide the observed data by the index. The resulting figures then give a series indicating movements abstracted from seasonal influences. Consider, for example, the years 1973–74 and 1974–75 in Table 9.5. Although average earnings fell sharply in the March quarter of both years, it can be seen that this fall was entirely seasonal and that, for the eight quarters as a whole, average weekly earnings continued on a strongly upward trend.

Table 9.5
AVERAGE WEEKLY EARNINGS—AUSTRALIA 1973–74 AND 1974–75

Year and Quarter		Observed Data $	Seasonal Index	Deseasonalised Data $
1973–74	S	110·20	1 001	110·09
	D	119·90	1 043	114·96
	M	113·30	950	119·26
	J	128·50	1 006	127·73
1974–75	S	137·90	1 001	137·76
	D	154·20	1 043	147·84
	M	143·60	950	151·16
	J	156·30	1 006	155·37

Whenever up-to-date information on current economic trends is required, monthly or quarterly data are necessary. If these are subject to seasonal influences, they must be deseasonalised before they can be used as indicators of current trends. Nevertheless, unless the seasonal pattern is reasonably constant, little reliance can be placed on an index purporting to measure seasonal variation. If a seasonal index is to be applied continuously as fresh data become available, a careful watch should be kept for any changes in the seasonal pattern, and in any case the index should be kept up to date by frequent revisions. By a careful examination of the ratios of observed values to the corresponding moving averages, changes in seasonal pattern can be detected, and no index should be computed without such examination.

Reference is made to the official publication of deseasonalised economic time series in Australia in Appendix B.1, p 586 below. The method used, although sophisticated in its technique, is based on the principles set out above.

CHAPTER 10

SOCIAL ACCOUNTS AND THE MEASUREMENT OF NATIONAL INCOME

10.1 The Nature of Social Accounts

Businesses keep records of their transactions in the form of accounts. Amongst other things these accounts provide information upon which the business enterprises can base policy decisions. They provide a continuous commentary on the affairs of business concerns and are essential to management in controlling efficiency, in ensuring financial stability and a satisfactory rate of profit, and in facilitating balanced growth. The content of the accounts differs from business to business and is dictated, to a large extent, by the type of business and by the information which it is desired to extract from the accounts. In effect, the accounts may be regarded as a system through which the many individual transactions of the business are classified. In the course of a year a business enters into many transactions—it buys, it sells, it pays wages, it distributes profits, it borrows money—etc. A list of all these transactions, in chronological order, could be kept, but it would not be very useful. It would be very long and would present a mass of unorganised data. By entering the transactions into appropriate accounts, the transactions can be classified into like categories, can be aggregated and summarised, and presented in a form which leads to much more interesting and relevant information than can be obtained from the mass of unorganised transactions. Looked at from this point of view, the accounts of a business are essentially a system of classification.

Just as there are many reasons which make it necessary for individual businesses to keep records of their transactions, so it is most important to have records of the transactions which take place in the national economy as a whole. These records are called *social accounts*. If appropriate classifications are made, information can be derived about the annual income of the nation, how it is produced, distributed and spent, how the wealth of the nation is being built up, and so on. Such information provides a basis for national economic policy; it helps governments in their attempts to maintain economic stability and prosperity, and to ensure an efficient distribution of economic resources and a balanced growth of the economy. Moreover, empirical investigation of the working of an economy depends on the availability of data about aggregates of transactions of the kind recorded in the social accounts. In drawing up social accounts for an economy there are two main problems. First, the system of classification of transactions must be selected, ie criteria of classification must be set up; and secondly, the transactions (or their aggregates) must be measured. As far as the former is concerned, there is no unique system of classification. The system to be used will depend on the purposes for which the social accounts are intended and on certain postulated theoretical relationships between different classes of transaction. Generally speaking, social accounts are designed to reveal the significant interrelationships between those aggregates of transactions which play important roles in the theory of the determination of the level of economic activity,[1] eg consumption, investment, etc. Consequently, the criteria of classification are chosen so that the social accounting system will provide the desired information in a relevant form. These criteria are discussed in detail below. Moreover, given the criteria, there is no unique form of the resulting accounts. The system described in the following sections is one which is very useful for purposes of exposition, although it does not correspond exactly with the systems used by various countries in their official publications.[2]

10.2 Classification of Economic Transactions

We may start by defining an *economic transaction* as a transaction between two entities which can be measured in money, eg the sale of boots by a shop to an individual, the payment of wages by a firm to an employee, the payment of tax by an individual to the government, the loan of money by a bank to a firm, etc. Since two entities are involved in a transaction, it must have a two-sided character, for what one entity gives, the other must receive. Consequently, any individual transaction may be recorded from the point of view of the giver and from that of the receiver. When both the giving and receiving aspects are recorded in the one set of accounts, the system is described as *double-entry accounting*. The double-entry method is used both in ordinary commercial accounting and in the kind of social accounting system with which we are mainly concerned in this chapter, which we may describe more explicitly as national income accounting.

[1] See, for example, G C Harcourt, P H Karmel, and R H Wallace: *Economic Activity* (Cambridge University Press, 1967), Chapters 2, 3 and 4.

[2] These are influenced to a considerable extent by the availability of data. The Statistical Office of the United Nations has published a standard system of accounts in an attempt to standardise the practice of individual countries and organisations. (See United Nations, *Studies in Methods No. 2: A System of National Accounts and Supporting Tables.*) The accounts set out in this chapter differ in detail, although not generally in principle, from this standard form. It is believed that the system described here has certain advantages for purposes of exposition.

Economic transactions are measured in money terms. In some cases the *quid pro quo* for the money which passes is a good or service, eg the purchase of cigarettes or the employment of a tradesman. In these cases the money value of the transaction can be taken also as a measure of a 'real' transaction. In other cases the *quid pro quo* is a financial claim, eg borrowing by a business from a bank. Often there may be no *quid pro quo* at all, eg an allowance by a father to his son. Certain other events, which may not appear to come under the definition of economic transactions, nevertheless need to be recorded in the accounting system. Such events may be internal operations affecting only one entity, eg depreciation of fixed assets or produce consumed by a farmer himself. Although these events do not involve the passing of money, they may be valued in terms of money and can be included with the economic transactions already described.

Over a period, say a year, there are myriads of transactions in an economy. To obtain any useful information about the working of the economy, it is necessary to classify the transactions in some way so that like transactions can be aggregated and summarised. Each transaction can be classified in two basic respects:

(i) according to the entities affected, ie according to the types of transactors; and

(ii) according to the nature of the economic activity involved in the transaction.

1. *Types of Transactor*

Reduced to the simplest terms, the economic process consists of the production of goods and services. The rationale of this process is the use of these goods and services. Except in the simplest type of economy the producer of a good is not the consumer of the good, and the good must be transferred from producers to consumers. This is usually done through the market, although some services are not provided through the market, eg government services, the services of housewives, etc. Generally, goods are sold by producer to consumer for money, which the consumer has acquired by assisting in the production of other goods. We can, therefore, immediately distinguish those entities which are responsible for organising the production of goods and services. These we call *trading enterprises*, and we speak of the *trading-enterprises sector* of the economy. The term 'trading enterprise' is used in the widest sense. It includes all forms of productive activity—manufacturing businesses and trading organisations, as well as entities selling services to the community. It covers incorporated businesses such as public and private companies, state-owned business undertakings and unincorporated businesses such as partnerships and sole proprietorships. Under the latter would be such diverse enterprises as the master plumber and the lawyer, the landlord and the farmer. The distinguishing characteristic of the trading enterprise is that it organises the factors of production (labour, capital equipment, natural resources) and thereby produces goods or services for sale.

Just as the producing entities form a sector of the economy, so do the consuming entities. These are the individuals who enjoy the fruits of the production organised by the trading enterprises. These we call *persons* and the sector is called the *personal sector*. The trading enterprises produce goods and services. This production results in incomes being paid to the owners of the factors of production in the form of profits and wages, etc. For the most part, the owners of the factors of production are persons (exclusively so in the case of labour), and the incomes so earned enable the persons to consume or use up the production. The distinction between trading enterprises and persons is clear. The former organise production, usually with the object of making profits—the latter enjoy consumption with the object of satisfying their wants. Of course, a particular individual may be both a trading enterprise and a person, as is the case with the proprietor of an unincorporated business. This may seem confusing, but the individual's dual capacity is clear, for when he buys raw material for his business he is acting in a capacity different from that when he is buying chops for his dinner. The *personal sector* is sometimes called the *households sector*, and non-profit making institutions, which can be regarded as aggregations of persons, eg clubs and associations, are included in it.

The logical distinction between the trading-enterprises sector and the personal sector can be made in even the simplest type of economy, though the separation and measurement of transactions may be difficult in the case of an economy of subsistence farmers. However, in the modern complex economy other sectors must also be distinguished, for there are entities involved in economic transactions which do not fit into the mould of either of the two sectors already delineated. First are governments, so we must consider a third sector, namely the *public authority or government sector*. Included here are all public authorities, eg commonwealth, state and local authorities in Australia. The economic activities of governments are mainly concerned with the provision of *collective goods and services* for the collective consumption or use by the community. These are provided to the community as a whole—law and order, defence, health, education, roads, etc. They are financed by levying taxes or raising loans. In addition, by means of taxation and cash social-service payments, governments are able to effect a redistribution of income. However, government-owned business undertakings are separated off from the government sector and included in the trading-enterprises sector, because they, like private trading enterprises, produce goods and services for sale.

A fourth sector is the *financial-enterprises sector*. In this are included banks, life insurance and other insurance offices, health insurance funds, superannuation funds and various lending agencies. These institutions are not included with trading enterprises because their function is essentially different. Their activities lie mainly in borrowing and lending. They are concerned with the provision of financial facilities to the economy as a whole—they 'oil the wheels' of industry. They are thus more analogous to governments than to trading enterprises, although most of them do in fact operate in order to make profits. Their peculiarities make it desirable to treat them as a separate sector.

Since we are classifying the economic transactions of a particular economy, the four sectors already mentioned will cover the trading enterprises, persons, governments and financial enterprises of the particular economy under consideration only. However, there will be many transactions involving entities resident overseas. Consequently, we must have a fifth sector entitled *rest of world* to take care of those entities which are not resident in the economy, eg the entities to which we export and from which we import goods and services, the entities from which we raise overseas loans and so on.

We may now summarise the above by saying that we can classify the entities which undertake economic transactions into the following five sectors:

Trading Enterprises . . . . . . (T)

Personal . . . . (P)

Government . . . . (G)

Financial Enterprises . . . . . (F)

Rest of World . . . . (W)

We could make a more detailed classification—for example by classifying trading enterprises by type of industry (eg primary, secondary or tertiary), or persons by occupational status (employer, worker-on-own-account, employee). But the above is adequate for most purposes.

2. Nature of Transaction

Goods and services can be used to satisfy current wants or to add to the accumulated wealth of the economy. Thus we can distinguish between *current* and *capital* transactions. On the current side, further distinctions can be made. The production of goods and services can be termed the production of income—the 'income' being the money measure of the physical goods and services produced. Once income has been produced, it must be distributed (eg distributed from trading enterprises to persons) and once distributed, it must be disposed of (eg consumed). The three processes of *production, distribution* and *disposal* can be distinguished. Consequently, we can classify economic transactions according to whether they are concerned with

Production . . . . (1)

Distribution . . . . (2)

Disposal . . . . (3)

Accumulation . . . . (4)

It is customary to distinguish sub-categories of transactions within the above four categories, eg transactions concerned with distribution may be subdivided into dividends, wages, interest, etc.

We may now combine our classifications according to type of transactor and nature of transaction. If we take a transaction involving a trading enterprise, it can fall into any one of the four classes 1, 2, 3, 4. If it falls into class 1, we can call it a T1 transaction. But from T's point of view it may be either a payment or a receipt. Consequently, in any class of transactions (such as T1) we must distinguish between payments and receipts. Thus we can regard the class T1 as a pigeon-hole, subdivided into two compartments for the purpose of recording payments on the left-hand side and receipts on the right-hand side. For each sector we shall have four pigeon-holes subdivided in this way, so that altogether we shall have 20 pigeon-holes. Since economic transactions are necessarily two-sided,[1] any particular transaction can be recorded twice, once in the payments compartment of one pigeon-hole and once in the receipts compartment of another pigeon-hole. For example, if I buy cigarettes from a tobacconist, the transaction will be sorted into the payments compartment of P3 (because it is a disposal of income by a person) and the receipts compartment of T1 (because it is connected with the production of income by a trading enterprise). What we have done in effect is to establish a system of double-entry accounts. For each sector we have set up a production account, a distribution account, a disposal account and a capital account. These are the *national-income accounts*. An accounting form for the classification is convenient, but it is the system of classification rather than the form in which it is set down which is the important thing.

If we had a record of all transactions taking place in an economy over a year, we could sort them into their appropriate pigeon-holes and find out the total value of all the main types of transactions. We

---

[1] Some transactions take place between two accounts within the one entity, eg depreciation allowances. However, they should still be regarded as two-sided.

should then have a summary of the transactions for the economy. But before we proceed with this line of thought, it is necessary to consider just what sort of items we shall include in the four accounts of each sector.

10.3 Content of National-Income Accounts

A hypothetical set of national-income accounts drawn up along the lines of this section is given on pp 400–5. Reference to it may assist in the understanding of what follows. The production of goods and services is for the most part organised by the trading-enterprises sector, although the government sector organises the production of collective goods and services. The form of the production account (T1 Account) can best be understood by considering the contribution of an individual trading enterprise to the production of goods and services over a particular year. Clearly this contribution is not simply the value of the physical output of the enterprise because this includes the value of goods and services used in the production process which have been produced by other enterprises. The contribution to production of a particular enterprise is not great just because it uses expensive raw materials, the value of which is reflected in the value of its output. Rather, the productive contribution of an enterprise reflects *the work done within* the enterprise itself. Accordingly, we define the contribution to production of an enterprise as the value of its output over the course of the year under consideration, less the value of the inputs purchased from other enterprises and used up in the course of production. These latter are known as *intermediate* products, eg raw materials, legal advice, etc. They enter into the *final* products of the enterprise under consideration. Products which are intermediate to one enterprise are of course the final products of the enterprise producing them. The contribution to production as defined here is often referred to as the *value added*, for it is the value added to the raw materials, etc, by the process of production applied by the particular enterprise. It is also referred to as the *value of production* and should not be confused with the *value of output*, which is physical output valued at appropriate market prices.

The value of the annual output of the enterprise is made up of the value of its annual sales, plus (or minus) the value of any addition to (or subtraction from) its inventories of finished or semi-finished goods over the year. The value of its annual inputs purchased from other enterprises and used up in the course of production is its annual purchases from other enterprises for current productive activity (ie purchases of intermediate products), plus (or minus) the value of any net subtraction from (or addition to) inventories of inputs over the year. It follows that the contribution to production of an enterprise, which we now call its *gross product*, is

$\Big\{$ Sales of output during year
  + Additions to inventories of finished or semi-finished goods during year
                                   minus
$\Big\{$ Purchases of intermediate goods and services during year
  + Subtractions from inventories of intermediate goods during year.

Stated in summary form, *gross product* is

$\Big\{$ Sales of output during year
  + Net additions to inventories of all kinds during year
                                   minus
    Purchases of intermediate goods during year.

This can be set out in account form as follows:

Production Account of a Trading Enterprise

Purchases of intermediate goods and services . *x*	Sales of output . . *x*
Gross product . . *x*	Additions to inventories . *x*

So far we have ignored the capital equipment (eg buildings, machinery, etc) which the enterprise uses in conjunction with labour and intermediate goods to produce its final output. Purchases of such equipment are capital transactions and are not recorded in the production account. However, capital equipment is itself used up in the process of production (eg machinery wears out and becomes obsolete, etc). This using up is called *depreciation*. It is as much an input as are intermediate products. Consequently, to obtain the net contribution of an enterprise to production we must deduct from the gross product an allowance for depreciation, so that we shall have

Net product = Gross product − Depreciation allowances

However, it is convenient to leave the production account as above and charge depreciation to the distribution account. This is because the estimation of depreciation is, to a considerable extent, arbitrary, since there can be no exact measure of how much of the value of a piece of capital equipment has passed into the output of the enterprise in a particular period. Accordingly, it can be regarded as an appropriation from the gross product.

The quantities referred to above are all expressed in money terms, and should be valued at current market prices. As long as price levels are stable this presents no difficulties, but if price levels are changing the valuation of the items 'additions to inventories' and 'depreciation allowances' presents great problems. Additions to inventories are usually measured by subtracting the value of inventories at the beginning of the year from that at the end. Accordingly during a period of changing prices some of the difference in the values may be due to the price changes themselves—for example, physical stocks might remain unchanged, but the closing value might be higher than the opening one. Similarly, if depreciation allowances are calculated on the basis of the original cost of the equipment divided by its expected life (a customary procedure in accounting), they will not reflect the current value of the equipment used up if prices have been changing. Since gross and net product are intended to be measures of the contribution of an enterprise to the production of goods and services measured in current money values, the effect of changing price levels is distorting. For certain purposes, eg the measurement of production, the item 'additions to inventories' should be the value at current market prices of the physical additions to inventories (and not the additions to the value of inventories); and the item 'depreciation allowances' should be the value at current market prices of the estimated portion of capital equipment 'used up' over the course of the year. However, in general, the proper adjustments to make to 'additions to inventories' and 'depreciation allowances' depend on the purposes for which the social accounts are being used. The topic is extremely complicated, and it is not proposed to discuss it further.

We may now aggregate the production accounts of all trading enterprises to obtain the trading-enterprises production account. The sales of outputs of trading enterprises can be split up as follows:

sales to persons,
sales of intermediate goods[1] to other trading enterprises,
sales of capital equipment to other trading enterprises,
sales to financial enterprises,
sales to governments,
sales to rest of world,

and the purchases of intermediate products will be:

purchases from other trading enterprises,
purchases from rest of world.

Since sales by all enterprises of intermediate goods to other enterprises must equal purchases by all enterprises of intermediate goods from other enterprises, these two items will cancel out in the aggregation and we shall have:

---

[1] The goods are 'final' from the point of view of the seller.

Trading Enterprises—Production Account (T1 Account)

Purchases of intermediate goods and services from rest of world x	Sales to persons . . . x Sales of capital equipment to enterprises . . . x Sales to government . . x Sales to financial enterprises x Sales to rest of world . . x
Gross product x	Additions to inventories . x

This explains the content of the Trading-Enterprises Production Account (T1 Account). It will be appreciated that it is an account in a highly summarised form, involving the aggregation of myriads of individual transactions of a like nature. The balancing item in this account is the gross product of the trading-enterprises sector.

The Government Production Account (G1 Account) is more notional than real. Governments purchase certain goods and services from trading enterprises and the rest of world, employ public servants and, as a result, provide collective goods and services to the community. They do this without making direct charges (although the goods and services provided by governments are paid for indirectly through taxation). By analogy with the T1 Account we should define the 'gross product' of the government sector as the value of the collective goods and services provided, *minus* the value of the goods purchased from trading enterprises and rest of world which 'enter into' the collective goods and services. However, since these collective goods and services are not sold, they have no market price. We value them, conventionally, at cost, ie at the cost of the purchases entering into them, *plus* the wages of the public servants. We can call this amount the *value of government output*. Thus we have

Government—Production Account (G1 Account)

Purchases of goods and services from trading enterprises . x Purchases of goods and services from rest of world . . x Gross product . . . x	Value of government output . x

It should be evident that the gross product of the government sector is in fact equal to the wages paid to the public servants.

The financial-enterprises sector includes both private and public enterprises whose main concern is with the provision of financial services necessary for the functioning of the economy. It is the provision of these services which corresponds most closely to the outputs of the trading-enterprises and government sectors. However, the services provided by this sector are not fully charged for directly, and their cost is for the most part covered by the difference between interest receipts and interest payments. One method of valuing the gross output of the financial-enterprises sector is to value these services at cost, and to treat interest as a transfer payment passing through the distribution accounts of sectors. Looked at from this point of view, the financial-enterprises sector may be treated in precisely the same way as the government sector, so that its gross product is equal by definition to the wages the sector pays out; this is the method of treatment which we shall adopt here.[1]

The personal sector is by definition not concerned with production and hence has no production account.[2] The rest-of-world sector does not contribute to the production of the economy under consideration, although rest-of-world entities do, of course, contribute to the production of their own economies. Accordingly, there is no production account for the rest-of-world sector.

So much for the production accounts of the various sectors. The gross products recorded in these accounts are carried down to the distribution accounts, where they are distributed to the owners of factors of production in the form of factor payments (wages, profits, etc) in return for services rendered by the factors in the process of production. In addition, all current payments between sectors not in direct return for the rendering of services are recorded in the distribution accounts. Such payments are called *transfer payments*, eg personal taxes paid to the government, dividends paid by trading enterprises, etc.

The balance of the distribution account of a sector is called the *disposable income* of the sector and is carried down to the disposal account. The disposal of income takes the form of the purchase of current goods and services for *final use* by the sector under consideration, ie consumption by persons and expenditure on current goods and services by governments or financial enterprises. That part of the disposable income of a sector not expended for this purpose is called the *savings* of the sector, saving being interpreted simply as not spending

---

[1] Although this method is the most convenient one to adopt for purposes of exposition, we may note in passing that it is not in fact the method used in the Australian national accounts. This latter method follows the international practice of regarding a proportion of the interest received by financial enterprises as a service charge to customers and valuing the gross output of financial enterprises on a 'cost plus profit' basis, ie as the amount of wages paid to employees plus the gross operating surplus derived from their operations in providing financial facilities to the community. For a further discussion of this method of valuation, see, for example, Australian Bureau of Statistics: *Australian National Accounts; National Income and Expenditure, 1974–75* (Ref 7.1), Part I, pp 5–8.

[2] Sometimes a production account is set up for persons, to include the contribution to production of domestic servants. However, there is no reason why domestic servants should not be regarded as trading enterprises.

for current purposes. The savings item, which is carried down to the capital account of the sector, together with borrowing from other sectors (if any) finances the accumulation of fixed capital equipment and inventories and also any lending to other sectors. All these items are recorded in the capital accounts.[1]

Certain special features of the treatment of the accounts of the individual sectors should be noted.

1. Trading Enterprises

The gross product is carried down to the distribution account, where it is distributed to factors of production. Depreciation allowances are also charged to this account—their double-entry appears in the capital account, since they form part of the *gross savings* of enterprises from which the purchase of capital equipment is partly financed. Taxation is similarly charged to the distribution account. The profits of all unincorporated businesses (which include farms, professions, etc) are deemed to be wholly withdrawn to the persons' distribution account, because it is not usually possible to distinguish between the personal income of the proprietor and the income of the business. In so far as proprietorship funds in the businesses are increased, they are deemed to be increased by lending (ie by the provision of capital) from the proprietors as persons to the enterprises they control. This process involves entries in the capital accounts of the personal and trading-enterprises sectors. The surpluses of government business undertakings are transferred to the distribution account of the government sector. It follows that the balance of the distribution account, ie the disposable income of the trading-enterprises sector, must be the disposable income of companies,[2] since the remainder of the revenue recorded in the distribution account will be paid out in one form or another. Furthermore, since companies cannot by their nature indulge in the final use of current goods and services, their disposable income is wholly saved and is known as *undistributed company profits*. These undistributed company profits are in fact *enterprise savings*. This item, enterprise savings, is carried down to the right-hand side of the capital account which also includes depreciation allowances of private trading enterprises and net borrowing from other sectors. (Depreciation allowances

---

[1] In some systems of social accounts, for example, in Australia (see footnote 2 on p 386 above) the distribution and disposal accounts are combined to form one account, known as the *income and outlay* account. For purposes of exposition it is better to keep the two accounts separate as they refer to essentially different activities.

[2] In the Australian system of national accounts unincorporated businesses are included in the household sector, and hence the combined distribution and disposal account for the trading-enterprises sector (see footnote 1 above) refers only to the distribution and disposal of income by corporate non-financial enterprises and public trading enterprises.

of government trading enterprises are credited to the capital account of the government sector.) The left-hand side of the capital account records purchases of capital equipment by private trading enterprises from other enterprises and additions to inventories, the double entries for which items appear on the right-hand side of the production account. Purchases of capital equipment and additions to inventories constitute the bulk of *gross private investment*, sometimes called *gross private capital formation*.[1] Purchases of capital equipment by government business undertakings and additions to their inventories are recorded in the capital account of the government sector.

2. Government

The gross product is carried down to the distribution account where it is paid out as wages to public servants (the gross product and these wages being identically equal by definition). The revenue side of the distribution account records taxation receipts, and the expenditure side records subsidies, social service cash payments, interest, etc. The balance is government disposable income, which, in the disposal account, is available for expenditure on current collective goods and services (eg current expenditure on health and education services), known as *government expenditure on current goods and services*. The surplus of disposable income over current expenditure is *government savings*. These savings are carried down to the capital account, where they are available to finance *government expenditure on capital works* (eg roads and buildings). This capital expenditure includes the capital formation of government business undertakings, and is sometimes called *public capital formation*. To the extent to which these undertakings make provision for depreciation, the depreciation allowances are credited to the capital account. When capital expenditure exceeds savings, the government sector must borrow from other sectors. The amount of borrowing is the *net increase in indebtedness of the government sector*. This will be negative if the government is a net lender. The net increase in indebtedness, sometimes called the *government deficiency*, must not be confused with the *published budget deficit*, which usually refers to the overall cash deficit or to the deficit in the main current account of a single government, whereas the government deficiency in the social accounts embraces current and capital activities of all public authorities.

The sum of government expenditure on current goods and services and on capital works is known simply as *government expenditure on goods and services*. On the assumption that governments do not make

---

[1] The two other items usually included are capital formation by financial enterprises and by persons in the form of houses for owner-occupation.

direct charges for administrative services rendered, this sum is identically the same as the value of government output as defined on p 394 above. In so far as governments do make such charges (eg for scientific advice, etc) government expenditure on goods and services will be less than the value of government output by the amount of these fees, such fees being charged to the appropriate sector as expenditure items.

3. Financial Enterprises

The treatment of this sector is analogous to that of the government sector. Corresponding to government expenditure on current goods and services is an item *financial-enterprises expenditure on current goods and services*.[1] This is equal by definition to the value of financial-enterprises output *less* fees charged to other sectors; but, unlike governments, financial enterprises are deemed to purchase their capital equipment from trading enterprises rather than create it themselves, so that the double entry of the capital account item 'purchases of capital equipment' is to be found in the trading-enterprises production account and not the financial-enterprises production account.

The main items in the distribution account are interest receipts and payments for banks, and premiums and claims for life assurance companies. Because many of these enterprises are privately owned, dividends and taxes appear as debit items in the distribution account. Naturally the principal items in the capital account refer to borrowing and lending, since these are the main activities of financial enterprises. These items correspond to the changes which occur over the year in the liabilities (eg bank deposits) and assets (eg bank advances, bank holdings of government securities) of the enterprises.

4. Personal

Personal incomes are recorded in the distribution account and include not only incomes received for factor services rendered (eg wages and salaries) but also government social-services cash payments (eg old-age pensions). The main debit in the distribution account is personal income taxation. The balance of the account is *personal disposable income*, which is carried to the disposal account to be expended on goods and services or saved. The former item is called *consumers' expenditure* and the latter *personal savings*. Personal savings is carried down to the capital account. It is customary to exclude from consumers'

---

[1] This item does not appear in the Australian social accounts because of the different method used in valuing the gross output of financial enterprises (see footnote 1 on p 395 above). Under that system of valuation most of the current expenditures by the financial sector are treated as purchases of intermediate goods and services used up in the process of production, and as such they cancel out in the aggregation.

expenditure the purchase of houses for owner-occupation, since this expenditure is seldom financed from personal current disposable income. All other expenditure by persons is regarded as current consumers' expenditure, which therefore includes expenditure by consumers on durable goods such as cars, furniture, etc. Since houses are excluded from consumers' expenditure they must either be charged to persons capital account or house-ownership must be treated as a trading enterprise.[1] The balance of the personal capital account is lent to the sectors.

5. Rest of World

The accounts of this sector are drawn up to express the economic transactions of the home economy with the rest of the world, although the entries are made from the point of view of rest-of-world entities. Income received by rest-of-world entities from the home economy (eg dividends, interest, etc) are credited to the distribution account, whereas similar payments by rest-of-world entities to the home economy are debited to that account. The balance is the disposable income of the rest-of-world sector. It may be positive or negative. It is the difference between the income produced by rest-of-world factors in the home economy and payable to the rest of world, and the income produced in the rest of world by home factors and receivable from the rest of world. This balance is carried down to the disposal account where it can be regarded as available for financing the excess of the rest-of-world sector's purchases of goods and services from the home economy (the home economy's *exports*) over the rest-of-world sector's sales of goods and services to the home economy (the home economy's *imports*). The balance in this account is *rest-of-world savings*. It is savings from the point of view of the rest-of-world sector and may be positive or negative.

The item 'rest-of-world savings (or dissavings)' is carried down to the capital account, where it is balanced by lending by the rest-of-world sector (or borrowing by the rest-of-world sector). Lending by the rest-of-world sector is, of course, equivalent to *borrowing from the rest of world* by the home economy, sometimes called *net increase in indebtedness of the home economy to the rest of world*. This occurs when income receivable from abroad and the current export proceeds of the home economy are insufficient to cover income payable abroad and the cost of imports. Contrariwise, borrowing by the rest-of-world sector is equivalent to *lending to the rest of world* by the home economy, and is sometimes called *net increase in indebtedness of the rest of world to*

---

[1] The latter is the customary practice and is explained on pp 413–14 below. However, for the sake of simplicity the former is used in the hypothetical example in the next section.

the home economy. The distribution and disposal accounts, viewed from the point of view of the home country, make up what is generally called the *balance of international payments on current account,* and rest-of-world savings (dissavings) correspond to a deficiency (surplus) in that account. The capital account is the *balance of international payments on capital account.*

Below is set out a hypothetical set of social accounts constructed in accordance with the principles outlined above. For simplification, the financial-enterprises sector has been restricted to banks. Only major items have been included. More detail could be shown, if desired. Each entry contains a reference to the other account involved in the double entry. The entries are for the most part recorded on a net basis, eg some persons borrow from banks and some persons lend to banks, but if the amount lent exceeds that borrowed, the net amount is recorded as lending by persons to financial enterprises. These social accounts record the flows of money, goods and services between the different sectors of the economy classified according to the economic significance of the flows. They are a complete set of double-entry accounts and for this reason are said to be *articulated.* They give a record for the economy, just as the accounts of a private firm give a record for the firm. Basically they are a system of classification of economic transactions. As such they are not sacrosanct. Other systems are possible, but for many purposes the system given here is very useful.

TRADING ENTERPRISES
$million
Production Account (T1 Account)

9. Purchases of intermediate goods from rest of world (W3) 330	1. Sales to persons (P3) .	1 500
	2. Sales to persons (houses) (P4)	40
10. Gross product (T2) . . 2 255	3. Sales of capital equipment to trading enterprises (T4)	430
	4. Sales of capital equipment to financial enterprises (F4)	5
	5. Sales to governments (G1)	80
	6. Sales of current goods and services to financial enterprises (F1) . . .	5
	7. Sales to rest of world (W3)	500
	8. Additions to inventories (T4)	25

Distribution Account (T2 Account)

13. Depreciation allowances (T4)	100	11. Gross product (T1). .	2 255
14. Indirect taxes (G2) . .	230	12. Government subsidies	
15. Direct taxes (G2) . .	80	(G2)	50
16. Surplus of government business undertakings (G2) .	20		
17. Wages (P2) . . .	900		
18. Withdrawals, etc (P2) .	730		
19. Dividends payable to rest of world (W2) . . .	30		
20. Dividends payable at home (P2) . . .	40		
21. Interest (F2) . . .	100		
22. Disposable income (T3) .	75		

Disposal Account (T3 Account)

24. Savings (T4) . . .	75	23. Disposable income (T2) .	75

Capital Account (T4 Account)

30. Purchases of capital equipment from trading enterprises (T1) .	430	25. Savings (T3) . . .	75
31. Additions to inventories (T1)	25	26. Depreciation allowances (T2)	100
		27. Borrowing (F4) . .	130
		28. Borrowing (P4) .	120
		29. Borrowing (W4) . .	30

Notes
  1. Consumers' expenditure.
  7. Exports.
  9. Part of imports. Imports are purchased by trading enterprises and by governments. All imports for consumption (as well as for capital) purposes are the intermediate goods of importers, and enter into item 1 above.
  14. Taxes not levied on income or wealth.
  15. Income taxes on companies. All incomes of unincorporated businesses and persons are paid to P2 account and taxed there.
  16. Excess of revenue over working expenses of business undertakings owned by governments.
  18. Profits of unincorporated enterprises deemed to be wholly withdrawn by the proprietors.
  19. Dividends paid by domestic companies to rest-of-world shareholders.
  21. Interest on bank overdrafts, etc.
  22. In effect, undistributed company profits.
  27. Borrowing from banks, eg by overdrafts.
  28. Borrowing from persons, eg by share issues or loans, or, in the case of unincorporated businesses, by the provision of capital by the proprietors.
  29. Borrowing from rest of world by issue of shares and other securities to foreigners.
  30 and 31. These items, together with item 2 above debited to the P4 account and item 4 debited to the F4 account, make up gross private investment.

GOVERNMENT
$million
Production Account (G1 Account)

3. Purchases of goods and services from trading enterprises (T1) . . .	80	1. Value of government output (current items) (G3) .	175
4. Purchases of goods and services from rest of world (W3)	70	2. Value of government output (capital items) (G4) . .	125
5. Gross product (G2) . .	150		

Distribution Account (G2 Account)

12. Wages (P2) . . .	150	6. Gross product (G1) . .	150
13. Subsidies (T2) . . .	50	7. Direct taxes (P2) . .	250
14. Interest (F2) . . .	55	8. Direct taxes (T2) . .	80
15. Interest (P2) . . .	40	9. Direct taxes (F2) . .	5
16. Interest (W2) . . .	60	10. Indirect taxes (T2) . .	230
17. Cash benefits (P2) . .	100	11. Surplus of government business undertakings (T2) .	20
18. Disposable income (G3) .	280		

Disposal Account (G3 Account)

20. Government expenditure on current goods and services (G1)	175	19. Disposable income (G2) .	280
21. Savings (G4) . . .	105		

Capital Account (G4 Account)

25. Government expenditure on capital works (G1) .	125	22. Savings (G3) . . .	105
		23. Borrowing (P4) . .	10
		24. Borrowing (F4) . .	10

Notes

1 and 2. See items 20 and 25 below.

4. Part of imports.

7. Mainly personal income tax.

8 and 9. Company income tax.

12. Identically equal to gross product, by definition of gross product.

14 and 15. Interest on public debt domiciled at home.

16. Interest on public debt domiciled abroad.

17. Cash transfers not in return for goods or services rendered, eg old-age pensions, child endowment, etc.

20 and 25. These expenditures are deemed to be made from the disposal and capital accounts to the production account and constitute the value of government output, valued at cost.

21. Government surplus on current account.

23 and 24. These items represent the net increase in government indebtedness, financed by borrowing from persons and banks.

FINANCIAL ENTERPRISES
$million
Production Account (F1 Account)

2. Purchases of current goods and services from trading enterprises (T1) . . . 5	1. Value of financial-enterprise output (F3) . . . 40	
3. Gross product (F2) . . 35		

Distribution Account (F2 Account)

7. Wages (P2) . . . 35	4. Gross product (F1) . . 35	
8. Direct taxes (G2) . . . 5	5. Interest (T2) . . . 100	
9. Interest (P2) . . . 100	6. Interest (G2) . . . 55	
10. Dividends (P2) . . . 5		
11. Disposable income (F3) . 45		

Disposal Account (F3 Account)

13. Financial-enterprise expenditure on current goods and services (F1) . . 40	12. Disposable income (F2) . 45
14. Savings (F4) . . . 5	

Capital Account (F4 Account)

17. Purchases of capital equipment from trading enterprises (T1) . . . 5	15. Savings (F3) . . . 5
18. Lending (G4) . . . 10	16. Borrowing (P4) . . 185
19. Lending (T4) . . . 130	
20. Lending (W4) . . . 45	

Notes
1. See item 13 below.
5. Interests on overdrafts. It is assumed in this example that no overdrafts are granted to persons.
6. Interest on government securities held by banks.
7. Identically equal to gross product, by definition of gross product.
9. Interest on deposits.
13. This expenditure is deemed to be made from the disposal account to the production account and constitutes the value of financial-enterprise output, valued at cost.
16. Net increase in personal deposits over the year.
17. Mainly expenditure on buildings for office accommodation. Part of gross private investment.
18. Net increase in government securities held by banks.
19. Net increase in net debit balances (overdrafts) of trading enterprises over the year.
20. Net increase in loans to rest-of-world entities over the year.

PERSONAL
$million
Distribution Account (P2 Account)

11. Direct taxes (G2)	.	250	1. Wages (T2)	. .	900
12. Disposable income (P3)	.	1 855	2. Wages (F2)	. .	35
			3. Wages (G2)	. .	150
			4. Interest (F2)	. .	100
			5. Interest (G2)	. .	40
			6. Dividends (F2)	. .	5
			7. Dividends (W2)	. .	5
			8. Dividends (T2)	. .	40
			9. Withdrawals, etc (T2)	.	730
			10. Cash benefits (G2)	. .	100

Disposal Account (P3 Account)

14. Purchases of goods and services (T1)	. .	1 500	13. Disposable income (P2) .	1 855
15. Savings (P4)	. .	355		

Capital Account (P4 Account)

17. Lending (F4)	. .	185	16. Savings (P3) . .	355
18. Lending (G4)	. .	10		
19. Lending (T4)	. .	120		
20. Purchases of capital equipment from trading enterprises (T1)	. .	40		

Notes
14. Consumers' expenditure.
15. Personal savings.
17. Net increase in personal deposits in banks over the year.
18. Net increase in holdings of government securities.
19. Net increase in equity in and loans to trading enterprises.
20. Expenditure on houses for owner-occupation. Part of gross private investment.

REST OF WORLD
$million
Distribution Account (W2 Account)

3. Dividends (P2)	. .	5	1. Dividends (T2)	. .	30
4. Disposable income (W3)	.	85	2. Interest (G2)	. .	60

Disposal Account (W3 Account)

6. Purchases of goods and services (T1) . . .	500	5. Disposable income (W2) .	85
7. *less* Sales of intermediate goods and services to trading enterprises (T1)	−330		
8. *less* Sales of goods and services to government (G1)	− 70		
9. Savings (W4) . . .	− 15		

Capital Account (W4 Account)

12. Lending (T4) . . .	30	10. Savings (W3) . .	−15
		11. Borrowing (F4) . .	45

Notes

1 and 2. These items make up income received by rest of world from home country.

3. Dividends paid by rest-of-world companies to persons at home.

6. Exports of home country.

7 and 8. These items make up imports of home country.

9. In this case rest-of-world savings is negative. This deficiency of the rest of-world sector is financed by net borrowing from the home country (item 11 less item 12). This represents a net decrease in the indebtedness of the home country to the rest of the world.

10.4 Consolidation of Sector Accounts

Given a set of accounts such as that above, it is natural to go one step further by consolidating the accounts of the five sectors into one set of accounts for the whole economy. Indeed, this step is of the greatest importance and leads to fruitful results. The consolidation of the social accounts is effected by pooling the five sectors for each account, and cancelling out items which appear on both sides of the resulting national consolidated account. As far as the consolidated national production account is concerned, items 5 and 6 of the T1 Account cancel with item 3 of the G1 Account and item 2 of the F1 Account respectively. On the left-hand side this leaves, apart from the gross products, purchases of rest-of-world goods and services by trading enterprises and governments. These make up total imports. Hence the left-hand side can be cleared (except for the gross products) by subtracting imports from both sides. The final result is shown in the consolidated accounts below. The accounts are numbered 1, 2, 3 and 4, and, as before, the figures in brackets indicate the double entry.

CONSOLIDATED NATIONAL ACCOUNTS
$million

Production Account (1)

Gross product of T (2) .	. 2 255	Consumers' expenditure (3) .		1 500
Gross product of G (2) .	. 150	Gross private investment (4) .		500
Gross product of F (2) .	. 35	Government expenditure (current) (3) . . .		. 175
		Government expenditure (capital) (4) . . .		125
		Financial-enterprise expenditure (current) (3)		. 40
		Exports (3) . . .		. 500
		less Imports (3) . .		. −400
	2 440			2 440

Distribution Account (2)

Depreciation allowances (4) .	100	Gross product of T (1) .	. 2 255
Disposable income of T (3) .	75	Gross product of G (1) .	. 150
Disposable income of G (3) .	280	Gross product of F (1) .	. 35
Disposable income of F (3) .	45		
Disposable income of P (3) .	1 855		
Disposable income of W (3) .	85		
	2 440		2 440

Disposal Account (3)

Consumers' expenditure (1) .	1 500	Disposable income of T (2) .	75
Government expenditure (current) (1)	175	Disposable income of G (2) .	280
Financial-enterprises expenditure (current) (1) . .	40	Disposable income of F (2) .	45
Exports (1) . . .	500	Disposable income of P (2) .	1 855
less Imports (1) . .	−400	Disposable income of W (2) .	85
Enterprise savings (4) .	75		
Government savings (4) .	105		
Financial-enterprise savings (4)	5		
Personal savings (4) .	355		
Rest-of-world savings (4) .	−15		
	2 340		2 340

The consolidation of the production accounts records on the left-hand side the gross products of the trading enterprises, government and financial enterprises sectors. Since all production attributable to the factors of production located in the territory of the given economy takes place within these three sectors, and since it is all valued at market prices, the resulting gross product is termed *gross domestic*

Capital Account (4)

Gross private investment (1) .	500	Savings by T (3) . . . 75
Government expenditure on		Savings by G (3) . . . 105
capital works (1) . . .	125	Savings by F (3) . . . 5
		Savings by P (3) . . . 355
		Savings by W (3) . . . −15
		Depreciation allowances (2) . 100
	625	625

product at market prices.[1] The concept of gross domestic product at market prices is fundamental to any system of social accounting, in as much as it measures the total value of production of goods and services in the economy over the year, ie the total output of *all* goods and services, *less* that part of this total used up during the year in producing other parts of it. Gross domestic product at market prices is given by the total of the left-hand side of the consolidated domestic production account (in our example, $2440 million).[2]

In the process of producing the goods and services which make up the gross domestic product, trading enterprises, government and financial enterprises create incomes. These are distributed as factor incomes, which after transfers between sectors become the disposable incomes of the sectors. This is shown in the consolidated national distribution account. Not quite all of the gross domestic product represents disposable income, for some of it is set aside to make good the wear and tear on capital equipment. After deducting these depreciation allowances from the gross domestic product, we get the disposable income of the sectors which is either spent for current purposes or saved (see consolidated national disposal account). In so far as it is spent, it absorbs part of the gross domestic product. The savings, together with the depreciation allowances, are used to finance the absorption of the

[1] The standard international terminology distinguishes between the concepts of gross *domestic* product and gross *national* product. The latter aggregate may be defined as the gross domestic product at market prices, plus the excess of the income produced in the rest of world by factors of the home economy over the income produced by rest-of-world factors in the home economy. In terms of the social accounting framework set out on pp 400 ff above, this is equivalent to gross domestic product, minus the disposable income accruing to the rest-of-world sector.

[2] If we add imports of goods and services to gross domestic product, we have *gross market supplies*, or to use the terminology of the Australian social accounts, *national turnover of goods and services*. This measures the value of final goods and services available to the economy from domestic production and imports. If from these total available market supplies we subtract the home economy's exports, we shall obtain an aggregate known as *gross national expenditure* measuring the total expenditures by the domestic residents on all final goods of domestic as well as of foreign origin; thus, gross national expenditure is identically equal to gross domestic product *plus* imports *minus* exports.

other part, ie public and private capital formation, and this is shown in the consolidated national capital account.

Each of the four consolidated accounts results in an important economic identity. The production account shows how domestic production is absorbed by different forms of expenditure. We have

$$\text{Gross domestic product} = \begin{cases} \text{consumers' expenditure} \\ + \text{ gross private investment} \\ + \text{ government expenditure} \\ + \text{ financial-enterprise expenditure} \\ + \text{ exports} \\ - \text{ imports} \end{cases}$$

The total of the right-hand side of the consolidated domestic production account is known as *expenditure on gross domestic product*. It is, of course, identically equal to gross domestic product.

The distribution account shows how the domestic product net of depreciation allowances becomes the disposable income of one sector or another. The disposal account shows how disposable income is either spent or saved. The capital account shows the balance between investment and savings items. The identity relating these items can be written in various ways. One way in which it can be written is:

$$\left.\begin{array}{l} \text{Gross private investment} \\ + \text{ government expendi-} \\ \text{ture on capital works} \end{array}\right\} = \begin{cases} \text{personal savings} \\ + \text{ undistributed company profits} \\ + \text{ financial-enterprise savings} \\ + \text{ depreciation allowances} \\ + \text{ government savings} \\ + \text{ net increase in indebtedness to} \\ \quad \text{rest of world} \end{cases}$$

The above identities which emerge from the accounts do not represent anything more than *ex post* accounting identities. We have not 'proved' anything from the accounts. The identities emerge because the accounts have been designed so that they do emerge. They are the result of the structure of the accounts and the definitions of the items in the accounts. This structure and these definitions have been adopted because they are appropriate for modern use in a wide field of economic investigation. The identities are of the same character as the accounting identity:

$$\text{Revenue} = \text{Expenses} + \text{profit}$$

As long as profit is defined as the excess of revenue over expenses, this identity must always be true.

10.5 Gross Domestic Product and Allied Aggregates

The gross domestic product at market prices can be looked at from two distinct viewpoints.

1. *Production Viewpoint*

Gross domestic product represents a measure of the volume of goods and services produced over the year, valued at current market prices, such goods and services being in a *final* form as far as the year under consideration is concerned. Final goods and services are those which are produced during the year and are subject to no further productive processes during the year. It is necessary to include the phrase 'in a final form' for clearly we do not include separately any goods and services which during the year enter into other goods and services, eg wheat which has been used to produce bread is included within the bread, and only wheat which has been exported or which forms an addition to stocks is included separately. This can be seen by examining the right-hand side of the consolidated domestic production account, where only goods and services which enter into final expenditure are included. Similarly, the left-hand side of that account is the sum of values added, so that only the value added by the bread manufacturer is included, the value of the flour he uses being included in the values added by the flour-miller and the wheat-grower at previous stages of production.

Although the gross domestic product at market prices does measure the total production of goods and services, it makes no allowance for the depreciation of capital equipment which occurs during the year. Consequently, if the whole of gross domestic product were used up for current purposes (as it was more or less during the latter years of the Second World War), the nation would be impoverishing itself through not maintaining its capital intact. This could continue for only a few years without damage to the productive capacity of the economy. The allowance for depreciation is an estimate of fixed capital depletion over the year, and by deducting it from gross domestic production we get *net domestic product at market prices*. This measures the total *net* volume of goods and services produced whilst maintaining capital intact. It indicates the volume of production which can be used for current purposes without diminishing the economy's capital equipment and hence is the true figure for the annual income produced by an economy. However, it must be remembered that the depreciation allowances included in the social accounts are often based on estimates made by trading enterprises and accordingly may be in error. Moreover, they are no more than financial provisions for depreciation and do not correspond to expenditure on replacement of worn-out equipment. Parallel with net domestic product, we define *net private investment* as gross private investment, *less* depreciation allowances. Subject to the above qualifications net private investment measures the net increase in privately-owned real capital (equipment and inventories) over the year.

2. Income Viewpoint

The gross products of the government and financial-enterprises sectors are simply the wages paid to the employees of these sectors. Except for the items of depreciation allowances and net indirect taxes,[1] the gross product of the trading-enterprises sector is wholly made up of income earned by factors of production.[2] Consequently, if depreciation allowances and net indirect taxes are deducted from gross domestic product, we obtain a measure of the aggregate of money income earned by factors of production. This aggregate is sometimes called *net domestic product at factor cost*.[3] If from net domestic product at factor cost we deduct net income payable overseas, we have *national income*, which is the sum of the incomes earned by factors of production resident in the domestic economy. The relation between gross domestic product at market prices and net domestic product at factor cost can best be appreciated by considering in isolation a home-produced final good entering gross domestic product. If an individual good is considered, its whole market price, except for those elements in it representing depreciation and indirect taxes, can be seen to be distributed to the factors of production as income. Thus, suppose we exclude these two elements and consider a radio sold for $40. Of this, say $16 represents the wages paid by the retailer and his profit, and the other $24 is the cost of the radio paid to the manufacturer. Of this, say $14 represents profit and wages and $10 cost of raw materials, and so on. Ultimately, the whole $40 accrues as income to one entity or another. But if the $40 includes depreciation allowances and indirect taxes, these elements are paid into the capital account and to the government respectively, and only the remainder becomes incomes of factors of production.

The income of the personal sector, before the payment of direct taxes, is known as *personal income*. It is the disposable income of the personal sector, plus the direct taxes paid by persons, and is in fact the total of the right-hand side of the personal distribution account. It is the total income of all private individuals in the economy in the everyday sense of the word 'income'. But, because not all of net domestic product at factor cost is distributed to persons and because the

---

[1] The excess of indirect taxes over subsidies.

[2] See left-hand side of the distribution account, some of the components of which represent transfers of original factor earnings. Company income taxation, dividends and undistributed company profits make up company income, the income earned by factors of production owned by companies. Surplus of government business undertakings is income earned by factors owned by governments.

[3] This treatment differs slightly from that used in the Australian social accounts, where net indirect taxes are deducted first from gross domestic product to give *gross domestic product at factor cost*. Subtracting depreciation allowances from gross domestic product at factor cost gives what is known in the Australian terminology as *domestic factor incomes*; this is the same aggregate as net domestic product at factor cost referred to in the text.

incomes of some persons are derived as transfers of income from other sectors (eg pensions) or as incomes payable from overseas, personal income is not the same as net domestic product at factor cost.

The relationships between the various aggregates referred to above are illustrated below by using the figures from the hypothetical set of accounts.

		$m
Gross domestic product at market prices.	.	2 440
less depreciation allowances		− 100
Net domestic product at market prices .	.	2 340
less indirect taxes *minus* subsidies. . . .		− 180
Net domestic product at factor cost	.	2 160

less Income accruing to sectors other than persons:

company income excluding dividends to persons	185	
surplus of government business under-takings	20	
interest paid by trading enterprises to financial enterprises . . .	100	
		− 305

plus Income transferred from other sectors to persons:

dividends from rest of world . .	5	
dividends from financial enterprises .	5	
cash benefits from governments . .	100	
interest from governments . . .	40	
interest from financial enterprises .	100	
		+ 250

Personal income		2 105

The official published social accounts of an economy are usually not set out in the same systematic manner as has been employed above. This is largely due to the limitations of the statistics available to estimate the various items. But we should regard the systematic treatment as lying behind the published figures. As an illustration of the published presentation of social accounts (and this presentation differs considerably from economy to economy) the Australian national income accounts are set out in Appendix B.3, pp 591–7, with comments.

10.6 The Problem of Imputation

As a measure of the volume of goods and services produced over a year the concept of gross domestic product as developed above suffers from at least one important limitation. Included in it are only those goods and services which pass through or are valued in the market. In any year many goods and services are produced which do not pass through the market, but which belong to the total volume of production just as surely as those which do pass through the market. Many examples could be quoted but a few will suffice. If a man owns a dwelling and lets it, the provision of dwelling space is a service which is paid for by rent. This service can be measured by the net rent earned by the dwelling, ie the excess of the rent paid over costs of collection and maintenance expenditure, and net rent enters into gross domestic product as the value added by the enterprise of house-letting. On the other hand, if a man owns a dwelling and lives in it himself, no rent is paid, and the value of the service rendered to the man is not included. It follows that the greater the proportion of owner-occupied dwellings, other things being equal, the lower gross domestic product—clearly an anomalous situation. Again, a certain amount of farm produce is consumed on the farm. This does not pass through the market and does not directly enter into gross domestic product. The same holds for fruit and vegetables produced by the home-gardener. Similarly, the services of housewives are not counted in gross domestic product, whereas those of hired domestic servants are, so that when a man marries his housekeeper gross domestic product falls!

The question arises whether in drawing up the social accounts, and in estimating gross domestic product, we should include an estimate of the value which these items would have if they passed through the market, ie whether we should *impute* values to these items. It has been customary in national income computation to include the imputed value of the services of owner-occupied dwellings and of farm produce consumed on the farm, but of no other items. The reason for including these particular items is two-fold. In the first place, they are readily calculated, for data on the number of owner-occupied dwellings and on the volume of farm produce consumed on the farm are usually available; and since there are active markets in comparable dwelling accommodation and farm produce, an imputation of the value of these items can be made. In the second place, the proportion of owner-occupied dwellings and the proportion of farm produce consumed on the farm is likely to vary from period to period and from economy to economy. Since, for example, a significantly larger proportion of people own their own homes in Australia today than some years ago, a comparison of gross domestic product for Australia today with that for Australia some years ago would lead to a relative understatement of the current figure, unless the annual value of owner-occupied dwellings were included. Similarly, since in India a far greater proportion of farm produce is consumed on the farm than in Australia, a comparison of the gross domestic products of India and Australia would lead to a relative understatement of gross domestic product for India, unless the annual value of farm produce consumed on the farm were included. Other items, like housewives' services, which might be imputed, but which are not in fact so imputed, are either extremely difficult to estimate or else of no great significance from a comparative point of view.

The effect on the social accounts and gross domestic product of imputing values to items such as those mentioned above can be traced through by taking owner-occupied dwellings as an example. Owner-occupiers must now be treated as trading enterprises. Consequently, the purchase and financing of houses for owner-occupation will appear entirely in the T4 account. Any personal savings devoted to the finance of these houses must be conceived of as lent from the P4 to the T4 account. The effects on the hypothetical social accounts are shown below. All figures are changes to be applied to the accounts as set out on pp 400–405 above. We assume the imputed net rental value of owner-occupied dwellings (ie imputed gross rents *less* maintenance expenditure) to be $60 million, annual depreciation $10 million and new construction $40 million.

T1 Account
$million

4. Gross product (T2) .	. +60	1. Sales to persons (P3) .	+60
		2. *eliminate* Sales to persons (houses) (P4) .	−40
		3. Sales of capital equipment to trading enterprises (T4)	+40

T2 Account

6. Depreciation allowances (T4)	+10	5. Gross product (T1) .	. +60
7. Withdrawals, etc (P2) .	. +50		

T4 Account

10. Purchases of capital equipment from trading enterprises (T1) . . .	+40	8. Depreciation allowances (T2)	+10
		9. Borrowing (P4) . .	+30

P2 Account

12. Disposable income (P3) .	+50	11. Withdrawals, etc (T2) .	+50

P3 Account

14. Purchases of goods and services (T1) . . . +60		13. Disposable income (P2) . +50	
15. Savings (P4) . . . −10			

P4 Account

17. *eliminate* Purchases of capital equipment (T1) . −40		16. Savings (P3) . . . −10	
18. Lending (T4) . . . +30			

Notes

1. Imputed net rents paid by owner-occupiers as persons to themselves as trading enterprises for the use of house-room. This equals imputed gross rent *less* maintenance expenditure (already charged to consumers' expenditure) and becomes a part of consumers' expenditure (item 14).

2 and 3. Item 2 is eliminated, and item 3 replaces it. The double entry of item 2 is item 17, and of item 3 is item 10.

7. Imputed income earned by owner-occupiers through their renting house-room to themselves.

9 and 18. Imputed lending by owner-occupiers as persons to owner-occupiers as trading enterprises.

The effect on the consolidated national accounts will be as follows:

1 Account
$million

Gross product of T (2) . . +60	Consumers' expenditure (3) . +60	

2 Account

Depreciation allowances (4) . +10	Gross product of T (1) . . +60	
Disposable income of P (3) . +50		

3 Account

Consumers' expenditure (1) . +60	Disposable income of P (2) . +50	
Personal savings (4) . . −10		

4 Account

	Depreciation allowances (2) . +10	
	Personal savings (3) . . −10	

It can be seen from the above accounts that gross domestic product will be $60 million more, and net domestic product $50 million more, than without the imputation of rents for owner-occupied dwellings. The latter figure represents the net annual value of the dwellings to their occupiers. This increases personal disposable income. But owner-occupiers must now charge themselves rent, and personal savings in fact fall by the amount of depreciation on these dwellings. This occurs because previously no depreciation was specifically allowed on these dwellings. Total gross savings are, of course, unchanged, the fall in personal savings being offset by the rise in depreciation allowances. This process of imputation does not affect the *cash* position of any entity, it only affects the classification of certain items and the measures of *national* aggregates. The above discussion incidentally illustrates the usefulness of the social accounting framework for analysing the effects of alternative treatments for specific items.

10.7 Estimation of Items in Social Accounts

The compilation of the social accounts of an economy would be quite a simple matter if records were kept of every single economic transaction. These transactions could then be classified into the appropriate pigeon-holes of the social accounts and added through to yield the various national aggregates. Unfortunately, records of only a small portion of all the economic transactions are kept, and of these few are in a suitable form. In practice, it is necessary to make direct estimates of aggregates such as gross domestic product and consumers' expenditure, and to use the double-entry structure of the social accounts to fill in certain other items. The main sources for estimation of the items in the social accounts are statistical collections of data on income, production and expenditure, usually collected for purposes other than that of social accounting. Sometimes additional information is collected by sample surveys. The sampling of the accounts of individual businesses can also be used to provide detailed information. Reference is made to the sources used for the Australian social accounts in Appendix B.3.

Historically the estimation of value of production came well before the development of social accounting. We shall therefore first concern ourselves with the estimation of gross domestic product. In this matter an understanding of the structure of the social accounts is very useful. The consolidated national accounts show that gross domestic product can be regarded as the sum of one of the following:

1. Gross products of the trading enterprises, government and financial-enterprises sectors (left-hand side of production account),

2*a*. Consumers' expenditure, government expenditure, financial-enterprises expenditure, gross private investment and the excess of exports over imports (right-hand side of production account),

2b. Consumers' expenditure, government current expenditure, financial-enterprises current expenditure, the excess of exports over imports, depreciation allowances and savings of the five sectors (left-hand side of disposal account, together with depreciation allowances),

3a. Disposable incomes of the five sectors and depreciation allowances (left-hand side of distribution account),

3b. Incomes received by the five sectors and depreciation allowances.

Under number 3a, the disposable incomes are reckoned as the final incomes at the various sectors' disposal after the payment of taxes and after transfers between sectors, but these incomes could be readily reckoned before the payment of taxes and transfers between sectors. We designate incomes reckoned in this latter way as 'incomes received' because they represent the income received by the various sectors in return for services rendered by the sectors in the production process. Broadly speaking, the term 'income received' corresponds to what we ordinarily mean by income received before the payment of taxes. The totals of incomes received and of disposable incomes are the same, although for some sectors disposable income will be higher than income received at the expense of the other sectors, on account of transfer payments. Number 3b therefore also corresponds to gross domestic product. 'Incomes received' can be found among the items in the left-hand side of the distribution accounts of the three producing sectors.

It follows that we can estimate gross domestic product via any of the five sums enumerated above. In practice numbers 1, 2a and 3b have proved most tractable. These are termed respectively the *production*, the *expenditure* and the *incomes-received* methods of estimating national income.

Ideally, estimates should be made by the three methods, and they would provide checks on each other. In practice the availability of suitable data dictates the method. As far as the production method is concerned, it is necessary to estimate the gross products of trading enterprises and the wages paid to employees of governments and financial enterprises. If annual censuses of production are conducted, the gross products of primary and secondary industries can be fairly readily ascertained because they correspond to the values added by enterprises in the process of production. However, tertiary industries (distributive industries, service industries, professions, etc) usually present some difficulty, and it may be necessary to estimate their gross product as the incomes received in those industries, thus resorting to the incomes-received method.

The expenditure method can be applied only if data are available on the various items of final expenditure—consumers' expenditure, government and financial-enterprises expenditure, gross private investment, and exports and imports. Here, the items of consumers' expenditure and gross private investment usually present the greatest difficulty.

The incomes-received method naturally must place great reliance on statistics collected as a result of income taxation. The gross domestic product consists of the gross products of the trading-enterprises, government and financial-enterprises sectors. Referring back to our hypothetical set of accounts and having regard to the distribution account of trading enterprises, we shall have:

Gross domestic product =
 Depreciation allowances
+ Indirect taxes
− Subsidies
+ Direct company taxes
+ Dividends   (gross product of trading
+ Undistributed company profits   enterprises)
+ Surplus of government business undertakings
+ Withdrawals, etc
+ Interest paid by trading enterprises
+ Wages paid by trading enterprises
+ Wages paid by governments (gross product of governments)
+ Wages paid by financial enterprises (gross product of financial enterprises)

Bracketing certain items together and putting in the figures from our example this becomes:

Gross domestic product =

	$m
Depreciation allowances	100
+ Net indirect taxes	180
+ Company income	225
+ Surplus of government business undertakings . . .	20
+ Withdrawals, etc	730
+ Interest paid by trading enterprises	100
+ Wages	1 085
	2 440

This latter sum gives the gross domestic product broken up into the major components of incomes received, and indicates how gross domestic product may be estimated by the incomes-received method.

It is not proposed to discuss the estimation of the individual items which enter into the social accounts. This is a practical problem, usually fraught with great difficulty on account of gaps in the available data. However, some comment on the *balancing properties* of the accounts is desirable in this connexion.

If every economic transaction were recorded and classified into the appropriate accounts, the accounts would automatically balance (apart from clerical errors). This must be so on account of the formal definition of the accounts. However, in practice the various items are estimated from various statistical sources and not from complete records and are subject to quite wide margins of error. Since each account must balance, then provided that all the items are directly estimated a comparison of the sums of the items on the left-hand side and on the right-hand side will provide a very valuable check on accuracy. If these sums are not identical, then errors of estimation must have been made and the items must be adjusted to bring the two sides of the account into equality.

It frequently happens that one particular item in an account is extremely difficult to estimate. In that case, it can be estimated as a balancing item (ie the property of the account that the two sides must be equal is utilised), the item obtained as a difference being the amount necessary to ensure the balance. This method of estimation of a particular item is an indirect one and, although convenient, is inferior to direct estimation. In the first place, all errors in the other items of the account are absorbed into the balancing item. Consequently, small errors in a number of items directly estimated may result in a larger error in the balancing item, if they do not by chance cancel out. In the second place the use of a balancing item removes any possibility of utilising the balancing property of the account as a check. Nevertheless, when data are scarce, balancing items may have to be used.

The number of items which can be estimated in this way is, of course, limited. If there are N distinct accounts in a system of social accounts, at most only $N - 1$ items can be estimated as balancing items. For, given any $N - 1$ of the accounts, the other one can be immediately filled in by using the missing double entries of the items already included in the $N - 1$ accounts. Consequently, if $N - 1$ accounts are made to balance by estimating one item in each as a balancing item, the other account must necessarily balance, and no balancing item can be derived from it.

10.8 Uses of the Social Accounting Framework

Economists have always been interested in aggregates such as national income, but the systematic treatment of aggregated transactions in a social accounting framework dates only from about 1940. A social accounting system enables the structure of economic transactions to be set out in a consistent way and makes clear the dependence of the definition of any given aggregate on the particular system chosen. It helps to elucidate the relations between associated concepts, eg the distinction between gross domestic product at market prices and net domestic product at factor cost (see p 410 above). It readily reveals the effects of any change in the treatment of particular items on the various aggregates of transactions (see pp 413–14 above). An examination of the systems employed by various countries makes international comparisons possible, since the comparability or otherwise of concepts is made clear.

Social accounts provide a framework for the classification of transactions and hence suggest the form in which data should be collected. The aggregates recorded in the social accounts constitute a major source of data for empirical economic investigation. Research into the behaviour of the economy as a whole requires estimates of such aggregates as gross domestic product, consumers' expenditure, gross private investment, etc. In addition, movements in gross domestic product, valued at constant prices (see section 12.2, p 479 below) and expressed per head of the population, give an indication of movements in the standard of living. Similarly, movements in gross domestic product, valued at constant prices and expressed per head of the working population, give an indication of movements in the level of productivity. Changes in the components of national income throw light on questions of income distribution.

Social accounts also facilitate the actual estimation of the aggregates of transactions. They indicate alternative routes to the estimation of a given concept, eg the estimation of gross domestic product by the production, expenditure and incomes-received method (see pp 415–18 above); and make clear the precise nature of the routes necessary to obtain the same final result. Moreover, if all transactions can be measured directly, the classification of transactions into a social accounting framework reveals any discrepancies and errors and provides a basis for making adjustments of discrepancies. By the same token, if all transactions cannot be measured directly, the nature of the accounts permits some items to be estimated by double-entry or as balancing items (see p 418 above).

The social accounts are a meeting place for economic theory and practical measurement. The general structure of the accounts must be designed to encompass the categories of economic theory (eg income, consumption, investment) in such a way that these categories are capable of actual measurement. The accounts show the formal relationships between aggregates (eg personal disposable income = consumers' expenditure + personal savings). They form the basis for economic models for the purposes of analysing the behaviour of the economy as a whole, of economic forecasting and of illuminating problems of economic policy.

The social accounts give a picture *ex post* of the outcome of economic activity. They can also be used as a framework for drawing up an *ex ante* forecast of the likely outcome of the economy in the future.[1] In this connexion the social accounts ensure consistency of forecasts, both internally and in relation to other, external, known facts. Moreover they enable one to judge whether the expected outcome on the basis of known circumstances is likely to be consistent with over-riding policy objectives; and, if not, to formulate appropriate policy. An example from what is known as *national budgeting* will help to illustrate this important use of social accounts.

We assume a relatively simple closed economy, in which all firms are companies that distribute all profits after tax as dividends. We amalgamate the production, distribution and disposal accounts of the sectors to obtain the current accounts of the trading enterprises, persons and government sectors. From these we can obtain the national current account. We imagine that we are standing at 30 June 1975. The *ex post* accounts for the actual outcome of 1974–75 are set out below. No distinction is drawn between current and capital government expenditure. The national capital account is omitted. However, it can be used as a check on the other accounts, for investment must equal personal savings plus government surplus.

Trading Enterprises
$million

Wages.	.	.	. 6 100	Sales to consumers	.	.	6 400
Dividends	.	.	. 2 400	Investment (equipment)		.	1 500
Company tax	.	.	1 200	Investment (stocks)	.	.	500
				Sales to government	.	.	1 300

Government

Government expenditure*—			Company tax . . . 1 200	
Purchases from enterprises .	1 300		Personal income tax . . 2 000	
Wages	1 500			
Surplus	400			

*Both current and capital expenditure.

---

[1] The distinction between *ex post* and *ex ante* measurement is a common one in economic theory. *Ex post* measurements relate to events which have actually taken place. They are a record of what has happened. Ordinary commercial book-keeping is an *ex post* record. *Ex ante* measurements relate to expectations, intentions, plans, forecasts, etc. Budgets consist of essentially *ex ante* measurements.

Personal

Personal income tax	.	. 2 000	Wages—		
Consumers' expenditure		. 6 400	From government	.	. 1 500
Personal savings	.	. 1 600	From enterprises	.	. 6 100
			Dividends .	. .	. 2 400

National Current Account

Wages.	. .	. 7 600	Consumers' expenditure	. 6 400
Company profits	.	. 3 600	Investment .	. . . 2 000
			Government expenditure	. 2 800
Gross domestic product.		. 11 200		11 200

Now, suppose that we are attempting to make an estimate of what we expect to happen in 1975–76, on the following basis:
  (i) The plans of the government sector are known and are specified in the government current account as follows:

$million

Government expenditure—		Company tax	,	. 2 000
Purchases from enterprises	. 2 000	Personal income tax	.	. 3 200
Wages	. . . . 1 500			
Surplus	. . . 1 700			

(ii) We believe, on the basis of market forecasts, that consumers' expenditure and investment will be $7500 million and $1500 million respectively.

This information is sufficient to fill in the social accounts completely. This is done in the following tables. Unnumbered items are 'known' ones. Numbered items are derived as balancing items or by double entry, and the numbers indicate the order in which they can be derived.

Trading Enterprises
$million

				Sales to consumers	.	. 7 500
(1)	{Wages {Dividends}	.	. 9 000	Investment (equipment)} Investment (stocks) }	.	1 500
	Company tax.	.	. 2 000	Sales to government	.	. 2 000

Personal

Personal income tax.	. 3 200	Wages—	
Consumers' expenditure	. 7 500	From government	. 1 500
(3) Personal savings . .	−200	(2) { From enterprises } Dividends	. 9 000

National Current Account

Wages } Company profits	. . 12 500	Consumers' expenditure . Investment . . .	7 500 1 500
		Government expenditure	3 500
Gross domestic product . 12 500			12 500

From these tables, we see immediately that the 'known' factors imply negative personal savings of $200 million. We may ask: is this reasonable compared with the previous year's actual experience? Is it reasonable to suppose that consumers' expenditure will be $7500 million, when personal disposable income is only $7300 million? We also see that a gross domestic product of $12 500 million is implied in these forecasts. Again we may ask: is this possible with our given resources? If the answers to these questions are negative, the 'known' factors are not likely to eventuate as predicted.

This illustrates the inter-relatedness of the various aggregates. It also illustrates that the specification of some of the aggregates may imply nonsense values in others unless the functional dependence of some of the aggregates on others is taken into account. Aggregates must be estimated in a logical order. Thus consumers' expenditure clearly depends on personal disposable income and cannot be forecast prior to it or independently of it.

In order to make the social accounting framework an effective guide for economic policy, it is necessary to specify certain functional relationships between some of the aggregates, as distinct from the formal. relationships inherent in the system of accounting adopted. The distinction between functional and formal relationships can be seen by considering personal savings. Personal savings equals personal disposable income *minus* consumers' expenditure. This is a formal relationship; it always holds by definition. However, the manner in which personal savings varies with changes in personal disposable income is a functional relationship and can take many forms. The formal relationships are revealed by the social accounting framework; the functional relationships are not. They must be derived from theoretical reasoning and by empirical observation.

These points can be illustrated by extending the above analysis to investigate whether certain known plans about the future are consistent with some overall objective of economic policy. Continuing with our example, suppose:

(1) In 1974–75 the economy was operating at full employment. We believe that capacity will expand by about 7 per cent in 1975–76, so that gross domestic product at full employment will be about $12 000 million.

(2) We know the government intends to spend $3000 million on goods and services.

(3) From our knowledge of private investment plans we believe that investment in equipment will be $1300 million, and that this will take place independently of the level of activity actually achieved.

We now ask: is full employment likely to be achieved, or will there be a tendency towards unemployment or inflation? Before proceeding we must assume certain functional relationships. For simplicity we assume that the relationships between certain aggregates will be the same percentagewise in 1975–76 as in 1974–75, namely:

(a) 63 per cent of the gross product of trading enterprises is paid out in wages;

(b) the rate of company tax is $33\frac{1}{3}$ per cent;

(c) the rate of personal income tax is 20 per cent;

(d) 80 per cent of personal disposable income is devoted to consumers' expenditure;

(e) 54 per cent of government expenditure is spent on the wages of public servants.

Forecasts of the accounts for 1975–76 are given below. In these accounts we set out the magnitudes of the various items on the assumption that full employment is achieved and that the other assumptions listed above hold. As before, the numbers indicate the order in which the items are filled in. The letters indicate where use has been made of the functional relationships (a) to (e) above.

Trading Enterprises
$million

(a) (4)	Wages	.	.	6 540	(15) Sales to consumers	.	6 860
(b) (5)	Dividends .	.	.	2 560	Investment (equipment) .		1 300
	Company tax	.	.	1 280	(16) Investment (stocks)	.	840
					(2) Sales to government	.	1 380
(3)	Gross product* .		.	10 380			10 380

*$12 000 million *minus* government expenditure on wages.

Government

	Government expenditure—		(12) Company tax . . 1 280	
		Purchases from en-	(13) Personal income tax . 2 140	
(e) (1)		terprises . . 1 380		
		Wages . . 1 620		
	(14) Surplus . . . 420			

Personal

(c) (9) Personal income tax . 2 140		Wages—	
(d) (10) Consumers' expendi-		(6) From governments . 1 620	
	ture . . . 6 860	(7) From enterprises . . 6 540	
(11) Personal savings . 1 720		(8) Dividends . . . 2 560	

National Current Account

Wages 8 160		Consumers' expenditure . 6 860	
Company profits . . . 3 840		Investment 2 140	
		Government expenditure . 3 000	

It will be noted that the final item to be filled in, namely 'investment in stocks', is a balancing item. Since this item emerges as the difference between the components of expenditure and gross domestic product at full employment, it can be interpreted as indicating whether expenditures are likely to be too low to produce full employment or are likely to be so high that inflation will emerge. In this particular case, if it is judged that trading enterprises would not willingly accumulate stocks to the extent of $840 million, then it can be said that full employment is unlikely to emerge in 1975–76 unless there is some change in economic policy. Other things being equal, gross domestic product would be lower than $12 000 million, as enterprises would not in fact produce at a rate resulting in an unwanted accumulation of stocks. To avoid this situation, the government would have to modify its policy, for example by spending more itself or reducing taxes to induce consumers to spend more.

This analysis is known as *gap analysis*. The extent to which the implied changes in stocks are not planned by trading enterprises measures the gap between full employment supplies and planned expenditures. In the example the gap indicated a deficiency of expenditure (ie a *deflationary gap*). If the gap had been negative, it would have indicated an excess of expenditure (ie an *inflationary gap*).

There are many ways of using a social accounting system for the purposes of national budgeting. The preceding example is only one of these and is given here purely by way of illustration. No special significance should be attached to the detailed treatment in this example. Nor is it appropriate here to pursue further this analysis, which relates essentially to a branch of applied economics.

In the following two sections, two important extensions of social accounting methods are discussed in some detail.

10.9 Flow-of-Funds Accounting

Social accounts of the kind usually published are orientated to the analysis of the production, distribution and disposal of income and are mainly concerned with the recording of flows of goods and services. With the exception of certain borrowing and lending items, purely financial flows are ignored. This may be illustrated by referring back to the example (p 390 above) of my buying cigarettes from a tobacconist. Such a transaction is recorded twice in the social accounts—once as a sale of goods in the trading-enterprises production account and once as a purchase of goods in the persons disposal account. This concentrates on the movement of the goods. However, whereas the cigarettes will pass from the tobacconist to me, cash will pass from me to the tobacconist. If one takes into account the financial flows (including flows of financial claims as well as cash), it will be necessary to record each transaction four times. Such recording results in *flow-of-funds accounting*. In the case of the above example, we shall have:

	Trading Enterprises	*Personal*
Non-financial flow	Sale of goods	Purchase of goods
Financial flow	Receipt of cash	Payment of cash

Reading horizontally, the first line indicates a flow of goods, the second a flow of cash. Reading vertically, the columns indicate re-arrangements of assets.

Flow-of-funds accounting involves the quadruple recording of all transactions between separate economic entities (ie purely internal transactions, like depreciation, are not recorded) in which financial transfers occur. In particular it encompasses purely financial flows in which no real transaction is involved (eg the sale of securities), and the transfer of existing real assets through which no production takes place (eg the sale of second-hand equipment). The flow-of-funds accounts show, for sectors of the economy, how funds have been derived (through the earning of revenue or the incurring of financial obligations) and used (through the incurring of costs or the creation of assets). Such information is useful in analysing the financial structure of the economy and the impact of monetary and fiscal policy on that structure.

Flow-of-funds accounting can be used to analyse changes in the structure of financial assets and liabilities of each sector, reconciling these changes with the net increase in wealth (ie the savings) of the particular sector under consideration. Indeed the information to do this has already in principle been included in the capital accounts of the social accounting system set out above, although it is not usually included in published statements of social accounts. The capital accounts show on the right-hand side savings and on the left-hand side capital formation. The balances are shown as borrowing and lending items, with double-entries for the borrowers and lenders. If these items were aggregated to read simply 'net borrowing' or 'net lending' and these balances carried down to a fifth account, entitled 'changes in financial-claims account', these fifth accounts could be used to analyse the changes in the financial structure of each sector.[1]

This is illustrated for the hypothetical accounts on pp 400–5 above. The capital accounts would read:

T4 Account
$million

		Savings (T3) . . . 75
Purchases of capital equipment		Savings (T3) . . . 75
from trading enterprises (T1).	430	Depreciation allowances (T2) . 100
Additions to inventories (T1) .	25	Net borrowing (T5) . . 280

G4 Account

Government expenditure on cap-		Savings (G3) . . . 105
ital works (G1) . . .	125	Net borrowing (G5) . . 20

F4 Account

Purchases of capital equipment		Savings (F3) 5
from trading enterprises (T1).	5	
Net lending (F5) . . .	0	

P4 Account

Purchases of capital equipment		Savings (P3) 355
from trading enterprises (T1).	40	
Net lending (P5) . . .	315	

W4 Account

	Savings (W3) . . . −15
	Net borrowing (W5) . . 15

[1] The authors are indebted to Professor R L Mathews for this suggestion. See also, R L Mathews: *Accounting for Economists* (Cheshire, 1965) Ch 19.

All borrowing and lending transactions (ie all financial capital transactions) will now be recorded in the 'changes in financial-claims accounts'. These are set out below. They include rather greater detail than shown on pp 400–5 above, but are consistent with the accounts on those pages. It will be noted that changes in assets are shown on the left-hand side and changes in financial obligations on the right-hand side. In this particular example all changes happen to be increases. Decreases would be recorded as negative items.

T5 Account
$million

Net borrowing (T4)	.	. 280	*Changes in*—			
Changes in—			Bank advances (F5)	.	.	160
Bank balances (F5)	.	. 25	Equity capital held by persons			
Cash (F5)	.	. 5	(P5)	.	. . .	90
			Debentures held by persons			
			(P5)	.	. .	30
			Equity capital held by foreigners (W5)	.	. .	30

G5 Account

Net borrowing (G4)	.	. 20	*Changes in*—			
Changes in—			Government securities held			
Bank balances (F5)	.	. 5	by banks (F5)	.	. .	15
Cash (F5)	.	. 0	Government securities held			
			by persons (P5)	.	.	10

F5 Account

Changes in—			Net lending (F4)	. . .	0
Advances to trading enterprises (T5)	. .	160	*Changes in*—		
Advances to persons (P5)	.	20	Deposits of trading enterprises (T5)	. . .	25
Government securities (G5)	.	15	Deposits of governments (G5)		5
International reserves (W5)	.	45	Deposits of persons (P5)	.	200
			Cash*		
			trading enterprises (T5)	.	5
			governments (G5)	.	0
			persons (P5)	. . .	5

P5 Account

Changes in—			Net lending (P4)	. . .	315
Bank balances (F5)	.	. 200	*Changes in*—		
Cash (F5)	.	. 5	Bank advances (F5)	. .	20
Government securities (G5)	.	10			
Equity capital (T5)	.	90			
Debentures (T5)	.	. 30			

*Increased liabilities of central bank.

W5 Account

Net borrowing (W4) . . 15	Changes in—	
Changes in—	International reserves held by	
Equity capital in trading en-	banks (F5) . . . 45	
terprises (T5) . . . 30		

If the changes in financial-claims accounts are consolidated for the five sectors, the consolidated account will show the net borrowing and lending positions of the sectors, as follows:

Consolidated Changes in Financial-Claims Account
$million

Net borrowing of T . . 280	Net lending of F . . . 0
Net borrowing of G . . 20	Net lending of P . . . 315
Net borrowing of W . . 15	

If the capital and changes in financial-claims accounts are aggregated for each sector without further netting out, the resulting accounts will set out the uses (left-hand sides) and sources (right-hand sides) of capital funds for each sector.

The above example uses the same sector classification as for the national-income accounts. In practice a more detailed classification is employed, especially in respect of financial institutions.

10.10 Inter-Industry Analysis

In the preceding section we were concerned with an extension of social accounting, developed mainly through a more detailed recording of financial transactions. In this section we shall deal with an extension arising from a more detailed classification of production activities.

If the trading-enterprises sector is split up into a number of sub-sectors according to industries, the production accounts of the new sectors will have to record the sales and purchases of intermediate goods and services between sub-sectors as well as the sales of goods and services to final purchasers. These intermediate transactions are netted out in the aggregated trading-enterprises production account, but once the production accounts are shown on an industry basis *inter-industry* transactions become explicit. This is illustrated in the tables below. Three industrial sub-sectors are assumed—primary, secondary and tertiary—and production accounts for each sub-sector are set up. The transactions shown below are consistent with those in the tables on pp 400–5 above. However, to simplify the presentation private investment in equipment, houses, inventories and financial enterprises' equipment is amalgamated; and the current activities of financial enterprises have been amalgamated with those of governments.

The division of the trading-enterprises sector into three sub-sectors has greatly increased the detail and complexity of the accounts. If a fine industrial classification were used, the accounts would become very complicated indeed. One way of simplifying the presentation, whilst underlining the essential inter-dependence of the economic structure, is to present the data in the form of a *matrix*, that is, a table in which the entries run both horizontally and vertically, as, for example, in a contingency table (see p 221 above). This is done for the

Production Account—Primary Industries
$million

Purchases from secondary industries	130	Sales to secondary industries .	550
		Sales to tertiary industries .	30
Purchases from tertiary industries	80	Sales to government . .	10
		Sales to persons . . .	300
Purchases from rest of world .	30	Sales to enterprises (capital	
Gross product . . .	1 100	equipment and inventories)	50
		Sales to rest of world . .	400
Total purchases . . .	1 340	Total sales	1 340

Production Account—Secondary Industries

Purchases from primary industries	550	Sales to primary industries .	130
		Sales to tertiary industries .	40
Purchases from tertiary industries	80	Sales to government . .	50
		Sales to persons . . .	700
Purchases from rest of world .	300	Sales to enterprises (capital	
Gross product . . .	540	equipment and inventories)	450
		Sales to rest of world . .	100
Total purchases . . .	1 470	Total sales	1 470

Production Account—Tertiary Industries

Purchases from primary industries	30	Sales to primary industries .	80
		Sales to secondary industries .	80
Purchases from secondary industries	40	Sales to government . .	25
		Sales to persons . . .	500
Purchases from rest of world .	0	Sales to enterprises (capital	
Gross product . . .	615	equipment and inventories) .	0
		Sales to rest of world . .	0
Total purchases . . .	685	Total sales	685

Production Account—Government

Purchases from primary industries	10	Value of government output . 340
Purchases from secondary industries	50	
Purchases from tertiary industries	25	
Purchases from rest of world .	70	
Gross product . . .	185	
Total purchases . . . 340		Total value 340

above data in the table on p 431. Any system of inter-related accounts can be expressed in this form. A finer industrial classification would increase the numbers of columns and rows.

Reading horizontally, the table tells us, for example, how the *output* of primary industries valued at $1340 million was absorbed, partly as intermediate goods by other industries and partly as final goods by final purchasers. Reading vertically, the table tells us, for example, the *inputs* which were used up to produce the output of primary industries, including the inputs from other industries, from the rest of the world and from the factors of production who earned incomes ($1100 million in this case, including depreciation) in producing this output. Such a table is often called an *input–output table*. There are many forms in which these tables can be drawn up, but the table shown indicates the general pattern. It should be noted that the value of gross domestic product can be obtained from this table either by adding the 'factors of production' row, or by adding the 'aggregate final market expenditure' column and subtracting imports.

The input–output table reveals the inter-dependence of the various sectors of the economy. Thus, if an element in final market expenditure is changed, practically all other elements in the table must be affected. Suppose secondary exports are increased. Other things being equal, this will increase secondary output and hence inputs. Consequently primary and tertiary outputs and imports will increase. But the increases in primary and tertiary outputs will themselves involve further increases in the inputs from the three industrial sectors, and hence in their outputs, and so on. At each 'round' the adjustments become smaller, so that ultimately there will be a set of values for the various elements consistent with the increase in secondary exports.

The table itself will not enable us to work out the effects of changes in one element on the others. To do this one must know the technical input–output relationships. However, by making relatively simple assumptions, one can estimate these relationships from the table;

INTER-INDUSTRY TABLE
$million

Sold to: / Sold by:	Purchasing Industries			Purchases for Final Use					Total Sales
	Primary	Secondary	Tertiary	Consumers' Expenditure	Gross Private Investment	Government Expenditure	Exports	Aggregate Final Market Expenditure	
Primary Industries	—	550	30	300	50	10	400	760	1 340
Secondary Industries	130	—	40	700	450	50	100	1 300	1 470
Tertiary Industries	80	80	—	500	—	25	—	525	685
Rest of World	30	300	—	—	—	70	—	70	400
Factors of production	1 100	540	615	—	—	185	—	185	2 440
Total Purchases	1 340	1 470	685	1 500	500	340	500	2 840	6 335

for example, one could postulate that values of inputs are proportional to values of outputs. This assumption implies that relative prices and relative combinations of inputs do not vary with output. Accordingly it is somewhat unrealistic, although for small shifts in output it may do as a first approximation. The table below sets out for the previous table the input–output coefficients on the basis of this postulate.

Given the input–output coefficients, the determination of the effects of a change in a component of final market expenditure on the other aggregates in the economy requires mathematical manipulation. This is not the place for an exposition of what has become an important branch of economics in its own right,[1] but it is possible to indicate the line of argument in the case of a simple table such as the one below. Suppose we require an increase of $1 worth of output of secondary

Value of Inputs per Unit Value of Outputs
$

Inputs from:	Primary	Secondary	Tertiary
Primary . . .	—	0·38	0·04
Secondary . . .	0·10	—	0·06
Tertiary . . .	0·06	0·05	—
Imports . . .	0·02	0·20	—
Gross products . .	0·82	0·37	0·90
Total	1·00	1·00	1·00

industries for final expenditure, and we wish to ascertain the total increase in primary, secondary and tertiary output which this will imply. This can best be done in terms of a series of 'rounds'.

Round 1. An increase of $1 in secondary output will require increases of $0·38 and $0·05 in primary and tertiary inputs, respectively, and hence in outputs.

Round 2. The $0·38 increase in primary output will require increases of $0·38 × 0·10 = $0·04 and $0·38 × 0·06 = $0·02 in secondary and tertiary inputs, respectively, and hence in outputs.

The $0·05 increase in tertiary output will require negligible increases in primary and secondary inputs ($0·05 × 0·04 and $0·05 × 0·06).

Round 3. The $0·04 increase in secondary output will require $0·04 × 0·38 = $0·02 increase in primary input and a negligible increase in tertiary input ($0·04 × 0·05). The $0·02 increase in tertiary output will require negligible increases in primary and secondary inputs ($0·02 × 0·04 and $0·02 × 0·06).

[1] For a simple account, see H C Edey, and A T Peacock: *National Income and Social Accounting* (Hutchinson's University Library, 1963), Ch VIII. For further references see Appendix C.7.

To the order of accuracy here employed it is unnecessary to go further. We shall require for an increase of $1 of secondary output for final expenditure an increase in:

Primary output of:
        $0·38 (*Round 1*) + $0·02 (*Round 3*) = $0·40
Secondary output of:
        $1·00 (*Round 1*) + $0·04 (*Round 2*) = $1·04
Tertiary output of:
        $0·05 (*Round 1*) + $0·02 (*Round 2*) = $0·07

The application of inter-industry analysis to the problems of economic policy is limited by the difficulty of defining and deriving accurately the technical input–output coefficients and the need to assume their constancy at least in the short period. Nevertheless, inter-industry analysis is a more refined tool than analysis based on the simple national accounting aggregates. Thus, suppose a government decides, under conditions of full employment, to increase defence expenditure by $100 million. Simple aggregative analysis would indicate that, say, consumers' expenditure be cut by $100 million to release resources for defence. This is in the right direction; but resources are not homogeneous. The resources required for defence works and services will probably not coincide with resources released by cutting back consumers' expenditure, and some industries will have capacities which are not readily enlarged. Inter-industry analysis offers some hope of ascertaining what increased defence expenditure means in terms of increased outputs in different industries, and hence whether these outputs are physically possible, and how one should go about releasing resources to achieve the desired increase in defence expenditure. Again, suppose a country is committed to a programme of rapid economic growth, what industries should be expanded and in what order? And what are the likely changes in the demand for imports and in the balance of payments? Inter-industry analysis throws light on questions such as these.

CHAPTER 11

PRICE INDEX NUMBERS

11.1 The Concept of an Index Number

An *index number* is a device for comparing the general level of magnitude of a group of distinct, but related, variables in two or more situations. If we want to compare the output of, say, consumer-durable goods in Australia in 1975 with what it was in 1950, we shall have to consider a group of variables, such as the outputs of refrigerators, radios, carpets, etc, which have the common attribute of being consumer-durable goods. If all these variables change in exactly the same ratio, there will be no difficulty in speaking of the change in the output of consumer-durable goods as a whole. But in practice the outputs of individual items change in different ratios. Consequently, we shall have to examine the movements in a large number of distinct variables. The significance of such a host of diverse movements cannot be readily comprehended. What we want is one figure as an indicator or *index* of the change in the magnitude of the output of consumer-durable goods as a whole, so that we can say that the general level of output of these goods in 1975 is, say, 50 per cent or 100 per cent higher than in 1950. Thus, an index number performs a function similar to that of an average. An average is useful as a figure for representing the general level of magnitude of a particular variable. Similarly, an index number represents the general level of magnitude of the *changes* between two or more situations, of a number of variables taken as a whole.

Index numbers can be used for many different purposes. The example given in the preceding paragraph is one of an index of physical volume, the variables under consideration being the physical outputs of consumer-durable goods. A quite different type of index would be one of the relative wealth of the Australian states. This would have to combine those variables reflecting wealth. Or we might have one designed to reflect the relative social status of individuals, combining those variables reflecting social status. But the best-known index numbers are those of prices, and we shall be concerned for the rest of this chapter with price index numbers.

11.2 Price Index Numbers

A price index number is used for comparing changes in the general level of prices of a group of commodities. It may be an index of whole-sale prices, of retail prices, of the prices of building materials, of the prices of agricultural products, etc. Generally the index number refers to changes in the prices obtaining in a particular area over time, and it is expressed by putting a particular period (called the *base*) equal to 100 or 1000 and expressing the other periods under consideration relatively to 100 or 1000. The selection of a period for the base depends upon the purpose of the index number. For example, if we wished to compare current price levels with the pre-war price level, we should use, say, 1938 or 1939 as base, or if we wished to make the comparison with the immediate post-war period we should use 1946 or 1947. The base is quite flexible and generally can be easily shifted (see section 11.8, p 458). The table below gives an example of an Australian price index number. According to this index the level of wholesale prices of house-building materials in Australia was 59 per cent higher in 1974–75 than it had been in 1970–71.

Table 11.1

**WHOLESALE PRICE INDEX:
MATERIALS USED IN HOUSE BUILDING
AUSTRALIA, 1970–71 to 1974–75
(Base 1970–71 = 100)**

Period	Index
1970–71	100
1971–72	106
1972–73	113
1973–74	131
1974–75	159

Source: Derived from Australian Bureau of Statistics: *Quarterly Summary of Australian Statistics*, No. 299, 1976, p 148

Although price index numbers are most frequently used to make comparisons over time, they can also be used for making comparisons between the general level of prices obtaining in different areas at particular times.

If the prices of all the individual goods which constitute the group under consideration moved between two situations in exactly the same ratio, that ratio would measure the general movement in prices, and the construction of the required index number would be simple. How-ever, in practice the prices of individual goods move differently. This is tantamount to saying that *relative* prices change, ie the prices of goods relative to each other. Relative prices are affected by changes in both the supply of and the demand for particular goods. Changes in the technical conditions of production and changes in tastes can be cited as the most important factors. At the same time changes in the price of one particular commodity relative to other prices react back on the other prices. Thus the prices of competitive goods (substitutes) tend to move in the same direction (eg if the price of beef falls, the price of mutton will tend to fall), whereas the prices of complementary goods tend to move in opposite directions (eg if an excise duty on petrol raises its price, the number of cars demanded, and hence the price of cars, will tend to fall). Apart from these influences which operate on particular relative prices, there are the broader influences which operate on prices in general. In particular, there is the level of economic activity obtaining in the economy as a whole. All prices tend to rise in periods of increasing economic activity and tend to rise more slowly or move downwards in periods of declining economic activity. However, this influence itself affects different groups of prices differently, some being more sensitive to changes in the economic tempo than others. It will be readily appreciated that the movements of prices of individual goods will be diverse and that some device for measuring the general level of magnitude of changes in prices is necessary. Price index numbers furnish such a device.

11.3 Index-Number Formulae—Aggregative Type

In this and the following sections a number of price index-number formulae will be developed in terms of a comparison between two periods of time. These two periods will be designated 'period 0' and 'period 1'. The price of an individual good in period 0 will be written p_0 and its price in period 1 will be written p_1. The index number which is designed to measure the change in the general level of prices of a group of goods between periods 0 and 1 will be designated P_{01}. The figure P_{01} is a ratio between periods 0 and 1, such that if we take period 0 as a base and put its level of prices equal to 100, the index number for period 1 will be $100 \times P_{01}$.

The easiest way to outline the various index-formulae is to follow through a simple arithmetical example. In the first four columns of Table 11.2 are set out the necessary data concerning the prices of seven foodstuffs in two periods. Our task is to devise an index number for measuring the change in the general level of prices of this group of seven goods.

We have now to find a way of combining the movements in the prices of distinct commodities to form a single index number. One way of doing this is to ask the question: 'What would be the change from one period to another in the aggregate cost of purchasing a certain collection of the commodities under consideration?' This gives rise to index numbers of the *aggregative* type. We can imagine that we have a

Table 11.2

Commodity	Unit	Prices		Quantities		Aggregate Costs			
		Period 0 p_0	Period 1 p_1	q_0	q_1	p_0q_0	p_1q_0	p_0q_1	p_1q_1
(1)	(2)	(3)	(4)	(5)	(6)	(7)	(8)	(9)	(10)
		cents	cents			cents	cents	cents	cents
Bread	2 kg	18	21	100	90	1800	2100	1620	1890
Tea	kg	80	90	10	8	800	900	640	720
Potatoes	5 kg	49	35	20	30	980	700	1470	1050
Butter	kg	56	56	30	30	1680	1680	1680	1680
Milk	2 l	21	18	7	10	147	126	210	180
Beef	kg	42	63	80	60	3360	5040	2520	3780
Mutton	kg	30	40	70	60	2100	2800	1800	2400
		296	323			10867	13346	9940	11700

$$L: \frac{\Sigma p_1 q_0}{\Sigma p_0 q_0} = \frac{13346}{10867} \cdot 100 = 123$$

$$P: \frac{\Sigma p_1 q_1}{\Sigma p_0 q_1} = \frac{11700}{9940} \cdot 100 = 118$$

basket of goods and find the cost of the contents in the two periods. The relative movement in the cost will be our index number. Clearly, the main consideration will be the composition of the basket.

Simple Aggregate of Prices

A simple suggestion is to take the ratio of the total of the prices in the two periods. Such an index is called a *simple aggregate of prices*. The formula is

$$P_{01} = \frac{\Sigma p_1}{\Sigma p_0}$$

In our example, we shall have as our index number for period 1

$$(323 \div 296) \times 100 = 109$$

with base, period 0 = 100. This indicates a 9 per cent rise in the general level of prices of the group under consideration.

It is not difficult to see what this index measures. It measures the change in the aggregate cost of purchasing a collection of goods consisting of one unit each of the units in which the prices are quoted. In our example this collection is 2 kg bread, 1 kg tea, 5 kg potatoes, 1 kg butter, 2 litres milk, 1 kg beef and 1 kg mutton. Such a collection cost 296 cents in period 0 and 323 cents in period 1, an increase of 9 per cent.

Table 11.3

Commodity	Unit	Prices	
		Period 0 p_0	Period 1 p_1
		cents	cents
Bread	2 kg	18	21
Tea	kg	80	90
Potatoes	10 kg	98	70
Butter	kg	56	56
Milk	10 l	105	90
Beef	kg	42	63
Mutton	kg	30	40
		429	430

The simple aggregate of prices depends for its value very largely on the units on which the price quotations are based. If the units are changed, the collection being priced itself changes. Thus, if in our example the price quotations for potatoes and milk were in units of 10 kilograms and 10 litres respectively, our data would appear as in Table 11.3. Our index number would be

$$(430 \div 429) \times 100 = 100$$

showing no change in prices as against a rise in prices of 9 per cent when the original units were used. The second index is different from the first because the collection now contains more potatoes and milk— the two commodities whose prices have fallen.

Weighted Aggregate of Prices

The simple aggregate of prices is an unsatisfactory index because it covers a collection of goods determined arbitrarily by the units in which the prices happen to be quoted. What we must do is to pick a collection in which the various goods are given weight according to their importance in some sense or other. This leads to indexes known as *weighted aggregates of prices*. We write q for the quantity of an individual good to be included in the market basket to be priced. The qs are known as *quantity weights*. Our weighted aggregate index then measures the change in the cost of a collection consisting of q units of each item, q being different from item to item. The formula is

$$P_{01} = \frac{\Sigma p_1 q}{\Sigma p_0 q}$$

where $\Sigma p_0 q$ is the cost of the collection in period 0 and $\Sigma p_1 q$ the cost in period 1. Incidentally, the simple aggregate of prices is a special case of the above formula, where each q is one unit.

Clearly the qs ought to be fixed according to the relative importance of the commodities in question. The relative importance can be assessed on the basis of the quantities of the goods purchased relative to each other. If the quantities of the various goods purchased never changed or if they changed only in the same ratio, then the quantities purchased in any year could be used as weights, for the *relative* composition of the basket would always be the same, and hence the change in its cost would be the same irrespective of which period's purchases were used to determine the weights. However, quantities of various goods purchased do not all change in the same ratio, ie relative quantities purchased change from time to time. Consequently, there is no unique set of weights available. It was pointed out above that if prices all changed in the same proportion the construction of an index number would present no difficulties. We now see that the difficulties in index-number construction arise because both relative prices and relative quantities change. Indeed these changes are related because the quantities purchased of those goods whose prices have risen more than the average will, in general, tend to rise less (or fall more) than the average.

The question now is: 'How shall we determine the numerical values of the qs?' The most obvious suggestion is to use the quantities of the goods purchased in period 0, which we designate q_0, or to use the quantities purchased in period 1, which we designate q_1. The first alternative gives rise to what is known as Laspeyres's price index number (P_{01}^{La}) and the second to Paasche's (P_{01}^{Pa}). The formulae[1] are

$$P_{01}^{La} = \frac{\Sigma p_1 q_0}{\Sigma p_0 q_0} \text{ and } P_{01}^{Pa} = \frac{\Sigma p_1 q_1}{\Sigma p_0 q_1}$$

The precise meaning of the four money aggregates in the above formulae should be noted. $\Sigma p_0 q_0$ measures the cost of the base-year purchases at base-year prices, ie it is the value expended in the base year; $\Sigma p_1 q_1$ measures the cost of the given-year purchases at given-year prices, ie it is the value expended in the given year; $\Sigma p_1 q_0$ measures the cost of the base-year purchases at given-year prices, and $\Sigma p_0 q_1$ the cost of the given-year purchases at base-year prices. P_{01}^{La} is said to be a *weighted aggregate of prices with base-period weights* and P_{01}^{Pa} a *weighted aggregate of prices with given-period weights*. Both indexes measure the change in the cost of a certain collection of goods —in Laspeyres's the collection is the quantities purchased in period 0, while in Paasche's it is the quantities purchased in period 1. There is no reason why the change in the cost of two distinct collections should be the same, and P_{01}^{La} and P_{01}^{Pa} will in general be different.

In our example above (see Table 11.2), columns (5) and (6) give the q_0 and q_1 quantities expressed in the units in which the prices are quoted. The aggregate costs are computed in the final four columns. For Laspeyres's index we have

$$(13\,346 \div 10\,867) \times 100 = 123$$

and for Paasche's

$$(11\,700 \div 9940) \times 100 = 118$$

Both of these index numbers seem to be based on reasonable principles and *prima facie* there is no reason to prefer one formula to the other. Consequently, suggestions have been made for taking a

---

[1] These two formulae were named by C M Walsh in *The Measurement of Exchange Value* (Macmillan, 1901) after their originators—E Laspeyres (*Jahrbücher für Nationalökonomie und Statistik*, Vol III, 1864, p 81 and Vol XVI, 1871, p 296) and H Paasche (*ibid*, Vol XXIII, 1874, p 168).

mean between the two indexes. Thus Marshall and Edgeworth have suggested the formula[1]

$$P_{01}^{ME} = \frac{\Sigma p_1(q_0 + q_1)}{\Sigma p_0(q_0 + q_1)}$$

$$= \frac{\Sigma(p_1 q_0 + p_1 q_1)}{\Sigma(p_0 q_0 + p_0 q_1)}$$

This is equivalent to using the mean of the q_0s and q_1s as weights. Fisher has also suggested a formula, which he called the ideal index number[2]

$$P_{01}^{Id} = \sqrt{P_{01}^{La} \cdot P_{01}^{Pa}} = \sqrt{\frac{\Sigma p_1 q_0}{\Sigma p_0 q_0} \cdot \frac{\Sigma p_1 q_1}{\Sigma p_0 q_1}}$$

This is the geometric mean of Laspeyres's and Paasche's. In our example, for the Marshall–Edgeworth index we have

$$[(13\,346 + 11\,700) \div (10\,867 + 9940)] \times 100 = 120$$

and for Fisher's Ideal index

$$\sqrt{123 \times 118} = 120$$

If we had worked to another figure we should have found the former to be 120·4 and the latter 120·2. These two indexes are always very close.

The above formulae involve weights which change when the periods of comparison change. Thus the weights in Paasche's index change whenever the given period changes, and the weights in Laspeyres's whenever the base period changes. In contrast to these indexes with *changing weights* is the aggregative index with *fixed weights*, ie

$$P_{01} = \frac{\Sigma p_1 q}{\Sigma p_0 q}$$

where the qs are fixed weights irrespective of the periods of comparison. This type of index is the most commonly used form in practice (see sections 11.8 and 11.10).

11.4 Relation between Laspeyres's and Paasche's Index Numbers

Laspeyres's and Paasche's index numbers are probably the two most important index numbers in the statistical and economic theory

---

[1] See F Y Edgeworth, *Papers Relating to Political Economy* (Macmillan, 1925), Vol I, p 213.
[2] See I Fisher, *The Making of Index Numbers* (Houghton Mifflin, 1922), p 220.

of index numbers. As has been pointed out above, these two indexes will in general give different results when applied to the same data. However, if the prices of all the goods change in the same ratio, the two indexes will be equal, for then the weighting system is irrelevant; or, if the quantities of all the goods change in the same ratio, they will be equal, for then the two weighting systems are the same relatively. When, as occurs in practice, neither all prices nor all quantities move in the same ratio, the relation between the two indexes depends on the correlation between price and quantity movements. Normally, we shall expect negative correlation, ie people will buy relatively less of those commodities which have become relatively dearer.[1] In this case, those goods whose prices have risen more than the average when prices in general are rising (or whose prices have fallen less than the average when prices in general are falling) will tend to have q_1s relatively smaller than the corresponding q_0s, and consequently will have relatively less weight in Paasche's than in Laspeyres's index. Accordingly under these circumstances Paasche's index will tend to be less than Laspeyres's. This means that Paasche's index will show a smaller rise when prices are rising and a greater fall when prices are falling. It will be noted that in our examples Paasche's is less than Laspeyres's index (see also pp 453–5 below).

The relation between the two indexes can be derived analytically by means of the formula for the coefficient of linear correlation. If we have a series of pairs of observations of X and Y, each pair being weighted by a frequency f, the sum of the frequencies being N, the formula for the coefficient of linear correlation between X and Y will be

$$r_{XY} = \frac{\Sigma fxy}{\sqrt{\Sigma fx^2 \Sigma fy^2}}$$

$$= \frac{\dfrac{\Sigma fxy}{N}}{s_X s_Y}$$

$$= \frac{\dfrac{\Sigma fXY}{N} - \dfrac{\Sigma fX}{N}\dfrac{\Sigma fY}{N}}{s_X s_Y}$$

[1] This assumes that changes in prices and quantities over time are mainly the result of changes in supply conditions. In terms of the geometry of economic theory, it assumes that demand curves are stable while supply curves are shifted up and down, so that actual prices and quantities are located along the downward-sloping demand curves. If the reverse held and supply curves were upward-sloping (which they certainly are in the short period), the correlation between prices and quantities would be positive.

where s_X and s_Y are the standard deviations of the Xs and Ys respectively, with the fs included as weights.[1]

We now write p_1/p_0 for X, q_1/q_0 for Y and $p_0 q_0$ for f in the above formula; X then stands for relative price movements and Y for relative quantity movements of individual commodities. The statistics s_X and s_Y measure the dispersion of price and quantity movements respectively and r_{XY} measures the correlation between price and quantity movements. We shall have

$$r_{XY} s_X s_Y = \frac{\Sigma\left(\frac{p_1}{p_0}\cdot\frac{q_1}{q_0}\cdot p_0 q_0\right)}{\Sigma p_0 q_0} - \frac{\Sigma\left(\frac{p_1}{p_0}p_0 q_0\right)}{\Sigma p_0 q_0}\frac{\Sigma\left(\frac{q_1}{q_0}p_0 q_0\right)}{\Sigma p_0 q_0}$$

$$\frac{\Sigma p_1 q_0}{\Sigma p_0 q_0}\frac{\Sigma p_0 q_1}{\Sigma p_0 q_0} = \frac{\Sigma p_1 q_1}{\Sigma p_0 q_0} - r_{XY} s_X s_Y$$

and writing

$$V_{01} = \frac{\Sigma p_1 q_1}{\Sigma p_0 q_0}$$

this becomes

$$\frac{\Sigma p_1 q_0}{\Sigma p_0 q_0}\frac{\Sigma p_0 q_1}{\Sigma p_1 q_1} = 1 - \frac{r_{XY} s_X s_Y}{V_{01}} \qquad (*)$$

where V_{01} is an index of the values expended in the two periods.

It can be seen that the expression on the left-hand side of the relation (*) is the ratio P_{01}^{La}/P_{01}^{Pa}. This ratio will be equal to unity only if one of r_{XY}, s_X or s_Y is equal to zero, ie either if there is no correlation between price and quantity movements, or if all prices or all quantities move in the same ratio so that there is no dispersion in one or other of price or quantity movements. Normally we shall have $-1 < r_{XY} < 0$, $s_X \neq 0$ and $s_Y \neq 0$, so that the right-hand side of the relation will be greater than unity and we can conclude that normally

$$P_{01}^{La} > P_{01}^{Pa}$$

Furthermore the relative discrepancy between P_{01}^{La} and P_{01}^{Pa} will be greater the greater the degree of correlation between price and quantity movements and the greater the dispersion in these two sets of movements, relative to the overall movement in values expended. In practice, Laspeyres's and Paasche's indexes are usually fairly close so long as the periods being compared are not too far distant. But the further apart are the periods being compared the greater the opportunity for dispersion in price and quantity movements. Similarly, the force of

[1] See section 8.2, p 285 above. Here the standard deviations have N as their denominators.

habit in consumption patterns will tend to break down, and as a result the correlation between price and quantity movements is likely to be greater in the long period than in the short period.

11.5 Tests of Adequacy of Index-Number Formulae

In section 11.3 two important formulae (Laspeyres's and Paasche's) were presented together with two other formulae based on them. Are there any technical reasons why we should prefer one of these? Fisher has suggested two tests which he believes should be met by index-number formulae.[1] These tests are derived by analogy with the behaviour of individual prices. If we take a single commodity, using period 0 as the point of reference, its price movement between period 0 and period 1 is measured by the ratio p_1/p_0. On the other hand, using period 1 as the point of reference, its price movement between period 1 and period 0 is measured by p_0/p_1. Clearly

$$\frac{p_0}{p_1} = \frac{1}{\dfrac{p_1}{p_0}}$$

By analogy, the index number P_{01} measures price movements between period 0 and period 1, and the index number P_{10} measures price movements between period 1 and period 0. Accordingly we ought to have

$$P_{01} = \frac{1}{P_{10}}$$

ie

$$P_{01}P_{10} = 1$$

This is called the *time-reversal test*. In P_{10} the times are reversed. Thus, whereas

$$P_{01}^{\text{La}} = \frac{\Sigma p_1 q_0}{\Sigma p_0 q_0}$$

we have

$$P_{10}^{\text{La}} = \frac{\Sigma p_0 q_1}{\Sigma p_1 q_1}$$

This test is tantamount to saying that a formula which shows a rise in prices of, say, 25 per cent between period 0 and period 1, should show a fall in price of 20 per cent between period 1 and 0, $(1 \cdot 25 \times 0 \cdot 80 = 1)$, for this would certainly be true for one commodity.

Referring back to the relation (*) in the preceding section, it can be seen that the left-hand side can be expressed either as $P_{01}^{\text{La}} P_{10}^{\text{La}}$ or as

[1] I Fisher: *op. cit*, Chapter IV, p 62.

$\dfrac{1}{P_{01}^{\text{Pa}} P_{10}^{\text{Pa}}}$, so that neither Laspeyres's nor Paasche's formula will meet the time reversal test except in the unlikely circumstances of either r_{XY} or s_X or s_Y equalling zero. Furthermore, normally Laspeyres's will show an upward bias and Paasche's a downward one of the same relative magnitude *in relation to the test*.

In our example

$$P_{01}^{\text{La}} = 123 \text{ and } P_{10}^{\text{La}} = (9940 \div 11\,700) \times 100 = 85$$

Hence

$$P_{01}^{\text{La}} \times P_{10}^{\text{La}} = 1 \cdot 23 \times 0 \cdot 85 = 1 \cdot 045$$

which is greater than unity ($0 \cdot 85 \neq 1/1 \cdot 23$).

Similarly

$$P_{01}^{\text{Pa}} = 118 \text{ and } P_{10}^{\text{Pa}} = (10\,867 \div 13\,346) \times 100 = 81 \cdot 5$$

Hence

$$P_{01}^{\text{Pa}} \times P_{10}^{\text{Pa}} = 1 \cdot 18 \times 0 \cdot 815 = 0 \cdot 96,$$

which is less than unity ($0 \cdot 815 \neq 1/1 \cdot 18$).

The second test is known as the *factor-reversal test*. Again, for an individual good the price movement between periods 0 and 1 is measured by p_1/p_0. Similarly, the quantity movement is measured by q_1/q_0. Since value expended is the product of price and quantity, the movement in values is measured by $p_1 q_1/p_0 q_0$. Clearly

$$\frac{p_1 q_1}{p_0 q_0} = \frac{p_1}{p_0} \times \frac{q_1}{q_0}$$

By analogy, if P_{01} is an index number measuring price movements between periods 0 and 1 and Q_{01} is an index number measuring quantity movements, we ought to have

$$V_{01} = P_{01} \cdot Q_{01}$$

ie

$$\frac{P_{01} Q_{01}}{V_{01}} = 1$$

where

$$V_{01} = \frac{\Sigma p_1 q_1}{\Sigma p_0 q_0}$$

is an index measuring the movement in aggregate values expended. Thus, whereas the Laspeyres's price index number is defined by

$$P_{01}^{\text{La}} = \frac{\Sigma p_1 q_0}{\Sigma p_0 q_0}$$

ie the prices weighted by base-year quantities, the Laspeyres's quantity number will be defined by

$$Q_{01}^{La} = \frac{\Sigma q_1 p_0}{\Sigma q_0 p_0}$$

ie the quantities weighted by base-year prices.

This test is tantamount to saying that if values have increased by 80 per cent, then a formula which shows a price rise of 20 per cent ought, in its quantity form, to show a quantity rise of 50 per cent $(1.20 \times 1.50 = 1.80)$, for this would certainly be the case for one commodity.

Referring back to the relation (*) in the preceding section, it can be seen that the left-hand side can be expressed either as

$$\frac{P_{01}^{La} Q_{01}^{La}}{V_{01}}, \text{ or as } \frac{V_{01}}{P_{01}^{Pa} Q_{01}^{Pa}}$$

so that neither Laspeyres's nor Paasche's formula will meet the factor reversal test, except in the unlikely circumstances of either r_{XY} or s_X or s_Y equalling zero. Furthermore, normally Laspeyres's will show an upward bias and Paasche's a downward one of the same relative magnitude *in relation to the test*.

$$P_{01}^{La} = 123 \quad \text{and} \quad Q_{01}^{La} = (9940 \div 10\,867) \times 100 = 91.5$$

and $\qquad V_{01} = (11\,700 \div 10\,867) \times 100 = 107.7$

Hence,

$$(P_{01}^{La} \times Q_{01}^{La}) \div V_{01} = (1.23 \times 0.915) \div 1.077 = 1.045,$$

which is greater than unity $(1.23 \times 0.915 \neq 1.077)$.

Similarly

$$P_{01}^{Pa} = 118 \quad \text{and} \quad Q_{01}^{Pa} = (11\,700 \div 13\,346) \times 100 = 88$$

Hence

$$(P_{01}^{Pa} \times Q_{01}^{Pa}) \div V_{01} = (1.18 \times 0.88) \div 1.077 = 0.96,$$

which is less than unity $(1.18 \times 0.88 \neq 1.077)$.

Turning to the Marshall–Edgeworth and Fisher indexes, substitution of the formulae in the two tests reveals that the Marshall–Edgeworth index meets the time-reversal but not the factor-reversal test, whereas Fisher's meets both. It is largely for this reason that Fisher termed his formula the 'ideal' index.

However, it is not at all certain that there are good logical reasons for claiming that an index number ought to meet these tests. As far as the time-reversal test is concerned, one could hardly hope for consistent results. This test requires that $P_{01}^{La} P_{10}^{La} = 1$, but the collection of goods included in P_{01}^{La} is different from that included in P_{10}^{La} (q_0 as against q_1). As far as the factor-reversal test is concerned there may be a quantity index which in conjunction with the price index will satisfy the test. Thus, although

$$P_{01}^{La} Q_{01}^{La} \neq V_{01}$$

yet

$$P_{01}^{La} Q_{01}^{Pa} = V_{01}$$

and, although

$$P_{01}^{Pa} Q_{01}^{Pa} \neq V_{01}$$

yet

$$P_{01}^{Pa} Q_{01}^{La} = V_{01}$$

Furthermore, although the Ideal index does meet these tests, its meaning is not at all clear. Laspeyres's index measures the change in the cost of the collection being purchased in period 0 and Paasche's the change in the cost of that being purchased in period 1, but what does the geometric mean of the two measure? Clarity of meaning is always desirable in index-number construction.

The application of the above two tests gives rise to the notion of 'bias' in index-number formulae. Laspeyres's is sometimes spoken of as being upwardly biased and Paasche's as being downwardly biased. But to say a measure is biased implies that there is some 'true' value from which it is biased. No such 'true' value, however, can be postulated in this connexion, consequently talk of bias, except in relation to the two tests, is meaningless. The question of what it is we are 'ideally' trying to measure is discussed in section 11.9 below. But we can conclude at this stage that the fact that Laspeyres's and Paasche's formulae do not conform to the two tests is not very important. Nevertheless, a knowledge of how these two formulae fit in with the tests is important for a proper understanding of the mechanics of index-number construction.

11.6 Index-Number Formulae—Average Type

An alternative to constructing formulae in terms of aggregate costs, is to concentrate on the movements of the prices of individual commodities. If we take period 0 as base, the movement in the price of an individual commodity is given by p_1/p_0. Ratios such as this are known as *price relatives*. They refer to individual price movements. The price relatives for the seven commodities in our example are shown in column (5) of Table 11.4 below.

We now have a number of individual price movements, and a process of averaging will produce an index number which can be used to indicate the general movement in prices.

Table 11.4

Com- modity	Unit	Prices		Price Relatives p_1/p_0	$\log p_1/p_0$	Value Expended $v = p_0 q_0$	$\dfrac{p_1}{p_0} \times v$
		Period 0 p_0	Period 1 p_1				
(1)	(2)	(3)	(4)	(5)	(6)	(7)	(8)
		cents	cents			cents	cents
Bread	2 kg	18	21	1·167	0·06707	1 800	2 100
Tea	kg	80	90	1·125	0·05115	800	900
Potatoes	5 kg	49	35	0·714	$\bar{1}$·85370	980	700
Butter	kg	56	56	1·000	0·00000	1 680	1 680
Milk	2 *l*	21	18	0·857	$\bar{1}$·93298	147	126
Beef	kg	42	63	1·500	0·17609	3 360	5 040
Mutton	kg	30	40	1·333	0·12483	2 100	2 800
				7·696	0·20582	10 867	13 346

Simple Arithmetic Mean of Price Relatives

The simplest approach is to take a straight-out arithmetic mean of the price relatives. The formula will be

$$P_{01} = \frac{1}{N} \Sigma \frac{p_1}{p_0}$$

where N is the number of commodities. In our example this will be

$$(7·696 \div 7) \times 100 = 110$$

The arithmetic mean, however, is not a particularly suitable type of average for averaging ratios. It seems reasonable that if one ratio indicates a doubling and another a halving, the average of the two should indicate no change. But an arithmetic average will show a change in this situation of + 25 per cent, for $\frac{1}{2}(2·00 + 0·50) = 1·25$. A geometric mean does not suffer from this defect, for $\sqrt{2·00 \times 0·50} = 1·00$. For this reason, when a straight-out average of ratios is desired, the geometric mean is the appropriate average.

Simple Geometric Mean of Price Relatives

The formula for this index will be

$$P_{01} = \sqrt[N]{\Pi \left(\frac{p_1}{p_0} \right)}$$

where the symbol Π means 'the product of'. For purposes of calculation it is best to work in logarithms. We have

$$\log P_{01} = \frac{1}{N} \Sigma \log \frac{p_1}{p_0}$$

In our example the logarithms of the price relatives are given in column (6), and we have

$$\log P_{01} = 0{\cdot}20582 \div 7 = 0{\cdot}02940$$

The antilogarithm of $0{\cdot}02940$ is $1{\cdot}07$, so that our index number is 107. It should be noted that the geometric mean is always less than the arithmetic mean.

If we want an average of price relatives, in which we regard each commodity as of equal importance, then the simple geometric mean of price relatives is appropriate. However, generally we do not wish to regard each commodity as having equal importance—a large price change in an unimportant commodity may be of considerably less significance than a small change in an important one. This leads us to weighted averages of price relatives.

Weighted Arithmetic Mean of Price Relatives

In weighting price relatives the weights must be *values*. If we write v for value expended on a particular commodity, then the total value expended on all the commodities under consideration will be Σv. How will this sum change between periods 0 and 1 due to price changes? To obtain the same quantity of a particular commodity as we should have obtained by spending v in period 0, we must now spend $v \times p_1/p_0$ in period 1. Consequently, total value expended would have to change to $\Sigma \frac{p_1}{p_0} v$. Hence, our index number will be

$$P_{01} = \frac{\Sigma \frac{p_1}{p_0} v}{\Sigma v}$$

This is a weighted arithmetic mean of price relatives, where the vs are the weights.

How should we determine the numerical values of the vs? One suggestion would be to use the values expended in period 0, ie put $v = p_0 q_0$. We should then have

$$P_{01} = \frac{\Sigma \left(\frac{p_1}{p_0} p_0 q_0 \right)}{\Sigma p_0 q_0}$$

$$= P_{01}^{\text{La}}$$

Thus an arithmetic mean of price relatives weighted by base-year values is in fact Laspeyres's index number.

The calculation of a weighted arithmetic mean of price relatives of this type is shown in columns (5), (7) and (8) of Table 11.4. The index is

$$(13346 \div 10867) \times 100 = 123$$

and is, of course, identically equal to Laspeyres's.

Similarly, if we put $v = p_0 q_1$, we should get

$$P_{01} = \frac{\Sigma \left(\dfrac{p_1}{p_0} p_0 q_1 \right)}{\Sigma p_0 q_1}$$

$$= P_{01}^{\text{Pa}}$$

Alternatively, if we use given-year values and take an *harmonic* mean, we also get

$$P_{01} = \frac{1}{\dfrac{\Sigma \left(\dfrac{p_0}{p_1} p_1 q_1 \right)}{\Sigma p_1 q_1}}$$

$$= P_{01}^{\text{Pa}}$$

11.7 Relation between Aggregative and Average Types

It has been shown above that both Laspeyres's and Paasche's index numbers can be expressed as weighted arithmetic means of price relatives. In fact, any aggregative type can be expressed in average terms, and any arithmetic or harmonic average type can be expressed in aggregative terms.

Thus we can always express an aggregative type as follows:

$$P_{01} = \frac{\Sigma p_1 q}{\Sigma p_0 q} = \frac{\Sigma \left(\dfrac{p_1}{p_0} p_0 q \right)}{\Sigma p_0 q}$$

where $p_0 q$ is the value expended by pricing the qs at base-year prices. Conversely, we can always express a weighted arithmetic mean type as follows:

$$P_{01} = \frac{\Sigma \dfrac{p_1}{p_0} v}{\Sigma v} = \frac{\Sigma \left(p_1 \dfrac{v}{p_0} \right)}{\Sigma \left(p_0 \dfrac{v}{p_0} \right)}$$

where v/p_0 is the quantity which can be purchased by spending v at base-year prices. In interpreting these formulae it is important to remember that q is in physical units, and v is in money terms.

From the practical point of view the aggregative form is not only simpler to calculate but simpler to comprehend. The idea of a measure of the change in cost of a given collection of goods is straightforward. Consequently, the aggregative form is to be preferred when questions of interpretation are important. However, the average form has its uses. We may be interested in the price relatives themselves, for the purpose of analysing the presence or absence of homogeneity in price movements or for distinguishing between the characteristic behaviour of sub-groups of commodities within our group. Furthermore, if we wish to analyse the relative importance of the items in an index, it is essential to consider it in its price-relative form. An aggregative type index can be written

$$P_{01} = \frac{\Sigma p_1 q}{\Sigma p_0 q} = \frac{\Sigma \left(\dfrac{p_1}{p_0} p_0 q \right)}{\Sigma p_0 q} = \Sigma \left[\frac{p_1}{p_0} \cdot \frac{p_0 q}{\Sigma p_0 q} \right]$$

Since the sum of the fractions $\dfrac{p_0 q}{\Sigma p_0 q}$ equals unity, these fractions give the *relative* (or percentage) weights attaching to the price relative of each individual item. They are the relative expenditures in the index on individual items. Accordingly, the fraction $\dfrac{p_0 q}{\Sigma p_0 q}$ for an individual item gives its relative importance in the index in the sense that it is the weight attached to any change in the price of that item between periods 0 and 1. Some important applications of the price-relative form are given below.

Effect on an Index of a Change in the Price of One Item

The concept of relative weights can be used to ascertain the effect on the index, of the change in the price of one item, other things being equal. Suppose we have an index measuring price changes between periods 0 and t and we wish to consider the effect on the index of a given proportionate change in the price of one item. Let the index be

$$P_{0t} = \frac{\Sigma p_t q}{\Sigma p_0 q}$$

and the price of the particular item under consideration p_t' in period t and its weight q'. Let α be the assumed proportionate increase in price of that item, so that the assumed new price for the item is $p_t' + \alpha p_t'$. Then this increase in price will add $\alpha p_t' q'$ to the aggregate cost in period t, so that the index will become

$$\frac{\alpha p_t' q' + \Sigma p_t q}{\Sigma p_0 q}$$

which is a proportionate increase of

$$\left(\frac{\alpha p_t' q' + \Sigma p_t q}{\Sigma p_0 q} - \frac{\Sigma p_t q}{\Sigma p_0 q} \right) \Big/ \frac{\Sigma p_t q}{\Sigma p_0 q}$$

on the original index. This reduces to

$$\alpha \left(\frac{p_t' q'}{\Sigma p_t q} \right)$$

The term in brackets is the relative weight attached to the particular item in the index in period t, so that the proportionate change in the index is given by the product of the proportionate change in the price of the item and the relative expenditure in the index on the item in the period from which the change is measured. This should be self-evident, for if I spend 20 per cent of my income on food and the price of food goes up by 10 per cent, I shall have to increase my expenditure by 10 per cent of 20 per cent, ie by 2 per cent, to purchase the same collection as before. For example, Laspeyres's index gives an index number of 123 in the example set out in Table 11.2 on p 437. What would be the effect on the index of an increase in the price of beef from 63 cents to 70 cents? This is an increase of one-ninth. The relative importance of beef in period 1 is $\frac{5040}{13\,346}$, so that the rise in the price of beef will increase the index by $\frac{1}{9} \times \frac{5040}{13\,346}$, ie by 4 per cent. The index will increase from 123 to $123 \times 1 \cdot 04 = 128$.

The relative expenditure on a particular item in the index in period t $\left(\text{ie } \frac{p_t q}{\Sigma p_t q} \right)$ will in general vary from period to period as relative prices change, and consequently the effect of a given percentage change in the price of an item will vary according to the period from which the change is supposed to take place. It might be noted that in fixed-weight indexes the relative expenditure *in the index* of those items whose prices are rising consistently more than the average will increase over time (see section 11.11, p 469 below).

Combination of Indexes

Sometimes the items in an index are divided into groups for which separate indexes are given. The relation between these group indexes and the full index depends on the relative weights of the groups within the full index in the base period. This can be seen as follows. If C_t^G is the aggregate cost (ie $\Sigma p_t q$) for a particular group of the regimen in period t, a group index is given by

$$P_{0t}^G = \frac{C_t^G}{C_0^G}$$

The index for the whole regimen will be obtained by summing the numerators and denominators respectively of the group indexes to get

$$P_{0t} = \frac{\Sigma C_t^G}{\Sigma C_0^G}$$

where the summation is over the different groups. This is equivalent to

$$P_{0t} = \Sigma \left[P_{0t}^G \cdot \frac{C_0^G}{\Sigma C_0^G} \right]$$

ie the complete index is the weighted average of the group indexes, the weights being the relative aggregate costs in the base year. A shift in the base year will, of course, change the relative weights to be applied. For example, if the base is changed from period 0 to period 1, we shall have

$$P_{1t} = \Sigma \left[P_{1t}^G \cdot \frac{C_1^G}{\Sigma C_1^G} \right]$$

As an example we may take the Australian Consumer Price Index. This index was divided, until 1976, into five groups for which separate group indexes were published. The table on p 454 gives these indexes for December Quarter, 1975, based on December Quarter, 1974.

The index number for the whole group (1140) is in fact the average of the five group indexes weighted by the relative expenditure given in the right-hand column.

Comparison of Different Index-Number Formulae

The price relative form is also useful in analysing why two different aggregative type indexes give different results when applied to the same data. Suppose we have two such indexes, one with quantity weights q and the other with weights $\hat{q}$, namely

Table 11.5

	December Quarter, 1975 Base: December Quarter, 1974 = 1 000	Percentage of Aggregate Expenditure in Index December Quarter, 1974
Food	1 097	31·3
Clothing and drapery	1 158	14·1
Housing	1 186	14·2
Household supplies and equipment	1 135	12·5
Miscellaneous	1 155	27·9
Total	1 140	100·0

Source: Derived from Australian Bureau of Statistics: *Labour Report*, No. 58, 1973, p 8, and *Monthly Review of Business Statistics*, No. 452, 1976 p 30

$$\frac{\Sigma p_1 q}{\Sigma p_0 q} \text{ and } \frac{\Sigma p_1 \hat{q}}{\Sigma p_0 \hat{q}}$$

These can be rewritten

$$\Sigma \left[\frac{p_1}{p_0} \cdot \frac{p_0 q}{\Sigma p_0 q} \right] \text{ and } \Sigma \left[\frac{p_1}{p_0} \cdot \frac{p_0 \hat{q}}{\Sigma p_0 \hat{q}} \right]$$

The fractions $\dfrac{p_0 q}{\Sigma p_0 q}$ and $\dfrac{p_0 \hat{q}}{\Sigma p_0 \hat{q}}$ are the *relative* weights attaching to each individual price relative under the two systems of weighting. Consequently, by comparing these relative weights we can see whether the one system of weighting attaches more or less weight to particular price relatives than the other. To illustrate this we can consider the discrepancy between P_{01}^{La} and P_{01}^{Pa} in our example in section 11.3 above. In this example P_{01}^{La} was 123 and P_{01}^{Pa} was 118.

In Table 11.6 columns (3) and (4) are the relative distributions of columns (7) and (9) respectively in Table 11.2 above. The sum of the products of columns (2) and (3) will give Laspeyres's index and that of columns (2) and (4) Paasche's. It can be seen that less relative weight is given in Paasche's index to beef, which had the greatest price rise, and more to butter, which had no price rise, and potatoes, which fell in price. This helps to explain why Paasche's index was lower than Laspeyres's. Both indexes are weighted averages of the *same* price movements (the p_1/p_0s), but the relative weighting is different. The difference in relative weights in this example reflects normal negative correlation between prices and quantities. The order of magnitude of the price relatives is beef, mutton, bread, tea, butter, milk, potatoes, whereas that of the quantity relatives (see columns (5) and (6) of Table 11.2) is, with one exception, the reverse.

Table 11.6

Commodity	Price Relative	Relative Weights	
		Laspeyres's	Paasche's
	$\dfrac{p_1}{p_0}$	$\dfrac{p_0 q_0}{\Sigma p_0 q_0}$	$\dfrac{p_0 q_1}{\Sigma p_0 q_1}$
(1)	(2)	(3)	(4)
Bread	1·167	0·165	0·163
Tea	1·125	0·074	0·064
Potatoes	0·714	0·090	0·148
Butter	1·000	0·155	0·169
Milk	0·857	0·014	0·021
Beef	1·500	0·309	0·254
Mutton	1·333	0·193	0·181
		1·000	1·000

11.8 Comparisons between more than Two Points of Time

The above discussion has been exclusively concerned with making comparisons between two periods only. These are called *point-to-point* or *binary* comparisons. However, we are usually interested in making comparisons between a number of periods, say periods 0, 1, 2, 3, etc, and we will have a series of index numbers P_{01}, P_{02}, P_{03}, etc, each one expressing the level of prices relatively to the base period, in this case period 0. Each of the indexes P_{01}, P_{02}, P_{03}, etc, is itself a binary comparison between period 0 and the period under consideration.

However, if we wish to compare prices in period 2 relatively to period 1, we can make a direct binary comparison and calculate P_{12} or we can obtain a figure by dividing P_{02} by P_{01}. Thus, if prices rise to 120 in period 1 on base period $0 = 100$ and rise further to 180 in period 2 on the same base, period 2 prices based on period 1 should be $(180 \div 120) \times 100 = 150$. Thus it would appear that we could use either P_{12} or P_{02}/P_{01}.

Similarly, we could compare prices in period 2 with those in period 0 by a direct binary comparison P_{02} or by the product $P_{01} \times P_{12}$. Thus, if prices are up to 110 in period 1 on base period $0 = 100$ and are up to 120 in period 2 on base period $1 = 100$, period 2 prices based on period 0 should be $1·10 \times 1·20 \times 100 = 132$. It should be plain that these two cases are the same in principle.

Circular Test

At first sight it would appear desirable that

$$P_{02} = P_{01} \cdot P_{12}$$

ie

$$\frac{P_{01} P_{12}}{P_{02}} = 1$$

This requirement is called the *circular test*. This test is met by practically none of the index-number formulae outlined above (exceptions are the simple geometric mean of price relatives and the weighted aggregate with fixed weights). It is not met by Laspeyres's and Paasche's. Thus, for Laspeyres's, we have

$$P_{02}^{La} = \frac{\Sigma p_2 q_0}{\Sigma p_0 q_0}, \quad P_{01}^{La} = \frac{\Sigma p_1 q_0}{\Sigma p_0 q_0} \quad \text{and} \quad P_{12}^{La} = \frac{\Sigma p_2 q_1}{\Sigma p_1 q_1}$$

Consequently, we have

$$\frac{P_{01} P_{12}}{P_{02}} = \frac{\Sigma p_2 q_1}{\Sigma p_1 q_1} \div \frac{\Sigma p_2 q_0}{\Sigma p_1 q_0}$$

which is the quotient of two differently weighted aggregative indexes comparing periods 1 and 2 and hence not necessarily equal to unity.[1]

While it may seem reasonable to argue that if a price index between periods 0 and 1 has risen to M and between periods 1 and 2 to N, then between periods 0 and 2 it should have risen to MN, a moment's reflection will show that this requirement is not reasonable. An index number has meaning only in terms of the system of weighting adopted,

---

[1] The relation between P_{02} and $(P_{01} P_{12})$ can be developed by the method used in section 11.4 above. Writing $X = p_2/p_1$, $Y = q_1/q_0$ and $f = p_1 q_0$ in the formula on p 442, we get a formula equivalent to the starred one on p 443, namely

$$\frac{\Sigma p_2 q_0 \Sigma p_1 q_1}{\Sigma p_1 q_0 \Sigma p_2 q_1} = 1 - \frac{r_{XY} s_X s_Y}{\frac{\Sigma p_2 q_1}{\Sigma p_1 q_0}}$$

The left-hand side is the reciprocal of $\frac{P_{01} P_{12}}{P_{02}}$, and this will be equal to unity only if one of r_{XY}, s_X, s_Y equals zero. Here s_X and s_Y measure the dispersion in price movements between periods 1 and 2 and in quantity movements between periods 0 and 1 respectively, and they will not in general be zero. The statistic r_{XY} measures the correlation between quantity movements over periods 0 to 1 and price movements over periods 1 to 2. It is not possible to say anything very precise about this correlation other than there is no *a priori* reason for it to be zero. Indeed, since q_1/q_0 and p_1/p_0 are likely to be negatively correlated the correlation between q_1/q_0 and p_2/p_1 is likely to be considerably influenced by the correlation between p_1/p_0 and p_2/p_1, ie by the way in which the price movements of particular goods over one period are related to those in the subsequent period. The above result is for a comparison between three consecutive points, but it can easily be generalised for any kind of circular comparison.

and one may produce many numerically different but quite valid indexes for comparing two periods. The weighting system used in P_{02}^{La} is the same as that in P_{01}^{La}, but different from that in P_{12}^{La}; consequently the increase M is an increase in something different from that in which N is the increase. The product MN is therefore a mixture, the exact meaning of which is not clear and which could not be expected to equal a direct comparison between periods 0 and 2.

Chained Indexes

The argument in the preceding paragraph may be taken as suggesting that direct binary comparisons are to be preferred to roundabout ones, because the meaning which can be attached to the numerical results is clearer. Nevertheless, if we are making comparisons between two distant periods, another consideration enters. Suppose the periods are 0 and t. If we are using Laspeyres's index, our quantity weights will be q_0, if Paasche's, they will be q_t. If period t is distant from period 0, it is likely that the q_0s and the q_ts will be rather different. The q_0 weights are relevant to period 0 and the q_t ones to period t but neither set of weights is relevant to both periods. This is the problem of increasing out-of-dateness of weights as the periods being compared become further and further apart. For this reason it is sometimes considered desirable to make comparisons between closely situated periods in which the qs are not likely to have changed much and to obtain longer-term comparisons by a process of chaining binary comparisons. Such an index is called a *chained* index and the formula is

$$P_{0t}^{Ch} = P_{01} . P_{12} . P_{23} \ldots P_{t-1,t}$$

where the separate links in the chain are binary comparisons between adjacent periods made according to some index-number formula, eg Laspeyres's or Paasche's. For example, if we have $P_{01} = 110$, $P_{12} = 120$, $P_{23} = 90$, then the chained index

$$P_{03} = 100 \times 1 \cdot 10 \times 1 \cdot 20 \times 0 \cdot 90 = 119$$

Although the precise meaning of P_{0t}^{Ch} is not simple in character, because it is based on a changing collection of goods, nevertheless there is a sense in which the weights are kept up to date in the chained index, because the qs are unlikely to change radically as between adjacent periods. As explained above, the value of P_{0t}^{Ch} will not be the same as that of P_{0t} where a direct point-to-point comparison is involved. In any case, not a great deal of meaning can be attached to an index number which compares distant periods for which the relative quantities are very different.

The reason why Laspeyres's and Paasche's index numbers (and their derivatives, the Marshall–Edgeworth and the Ideal indexes) do not meet the circular test is because the weights in these index numbers depend on the periods between which comparisons are being made. If these periods change, the weights change; for example, if the base period is taken as period 2 rather than period 0, the weights in Laspeyres's index are no longer q_0 but q_2. However, an aggregative index with fixed weights of the form

$$P_{0t} = \frac{\Sigma p_t q}{\Sigma p_0 q}$$

does meet the circular test. Thus

$$P_{01} P_{12} = \frac{\Sigma p_1 q}{\Sigma p_0 q} \cdot \frac{\Sigma p_2 q}{\Sigma p_1 q} = \frac{\Sigma p_2 q}{\Sigma p_0 q} = P_{02}$$

A fixed-weight index is much simpler to calculate from period to period, since the weights do not have to be changed. Consequently, less information needs to be collected in order to calculate it. On the other hand, the weights being fixed, they become increasingly out of date as time passes. Sometimes it is convenient to use fixed weights for a number of periods and then revise the weights. The new series can then be chained to the old one, in a manner similar to that used in the chained index set out above.

Changing the Base

Sometimes we have an index for a number of periods with a certain base and wish to change the period used as a basis for comparison. Suppose the original base is period $0 = 100$ and we wish to change the base to period 2. The usual practice is to divide through the whole series by the original index number for the new base, eg, in our case, P_{02}. It can be seen that, in the case of a chained index or an aggregative index with fixed weights, this correctly accomplishes the change in base. In the case of the chained index we have, for example,

$$P_{2t}^{Ch} = \frac{P_{0t}^{Ch}}{P_{02}^{Ch}}$$

$$= \frac{P_{01} P_{12} P_{23} P_{34} \dots P_{t-1,t}}{P_{01} P_{12}}$$

$$= P_{23} P_{34} \dots P_{t-1,t}$$

and in the case of an aggregative index with fixed weights

$$P_{2t} = \frac{P_{0t}}{P_{02}}$$

$$= \frac{\Sigma p_t q}{\Sigma p_0 q} \div \frac{\Sigma p_2 q}{\Sigma p_0 q}$$

$$= \frac{\Sigma p_t q}{\Sigma p_2 q}$$

Strictly speaking, however, such a procedure is not valid where indexes with changing weights are being used, for a change in the period of reference then requires a change in weights. In practice, this is usually ignored. Thus, if we have index numbers 100, 170, 200, 230 for the years 1972, 1973, 1974 and 1975 respectively, with base 1972 = 100, to change the base to 1974 we simply divide through by 200 and multiply by 100, giving the index numbers 50, 85, 100, 115 for the four years respectively, with base 1974 = 100.

11.9 Choice of an Index Number—a Cost of Living Index

It is evident from the preceding sections that there are a large number of index-number formulae available. Applied to the same situation, these formulae generally give different results, although in practice weighted index numbers do not differ greatly unless the dispersion of individual price movements is substantial, a factor which is likely to be important only when the comparisons are over long periods of time. However, it should be plain that there is no a priori 'best' index-number formula. Each formula has a precise meaning—most of them measure the change in the aggregate cost of a certain collection of goods. The important question is: Does a particular formula measure what we want to measure? Each formula measures something, but is it the thing we want? This very important consideration is now illustrated by a discussion of the measurement of changes in the cost of living.

If we want to measure changes in the cost of living, we have first to determine what we mean by 'changes in the cost of living' and secondly to devise a formula to make the measurements. Various formulae for index numbers are available. These formulae all have precise and exact meanings. Consequently, if we have defined the concept to be measured and selected a formula, the following fundamental question arises. 'Is the precise thing which our formula measures, the thing which our concept requires us to measure?' The whole justification for the use of particular index numbers depends on the closeness of what we are in fact measuring to what we want to measure. Thus, we may have a concept for changes in the cost of living and an index number of retail prices. We know what we mean by the former, and we know what the latter means. Can the retail price index be used to measure changes in the cost of living?

Unfortunately, while we can usually understand the precise meaning of, say, a retail price index number, it is by no means easy to define what we mean by changes in the cost of living. It is plain that particular price changes will affect the cost of living of different individual persons in different ways, eg if the price of beer rises while the prices of other goods fall, the cost of living of the heavy beer drinker may rise while that of other people may fall. Consequently, we must consider the cost of living of an individual person as a starting point. It is reasonable to measure the change in the cost of living of an individual between two periods as the change in his money income which will be necessary for him to maintain his *original* standard of living—no more or no less. We now consider where this definition leads. First, it must be pointed out that, if all prices change in the same proportion, that proportion will measure the change in the cost of living and there will be no problem of measurement. However, all prices do not change in the same proportion. Suppose in period 0 an individual spends his income by purchasing q_0 of various commodities at prices p_0. Assuming he saves nothing, his total income equals his total expenditure, ie $\Sigma p_0 q_0$. In period 1 prices change to p_1. How much income does he need in period 1 to make him as well off as he was in period 0? If the quantities of goods which he would need to buy to leave him exactly as well off as he was in period 0 are $\bar{q}_1$, then with an income of $\Sigma p_1 \bar{q}_1$ he would be exactly as well off. It follows that the change in the cost of maintaining his original (period 0) standard of living will be given by

$$C_{01}^0 = \frac{\Sigma p_1 \bar{q}_1}{\Sigma p_0 q_0}$$

where the superscript (0) indicates that the change in his cost of living is being measured in terms of his period 0 standard of living.

Unfortunately we do not know the $\bar{q}_1$s because they are not the quantities he actually buys in period 1, but only what he would need to buy to be as well off as before. Consequently, we do not know the aggregate $\Sigma p_1 \bar{q}_1$. But we do know the aggregate $\Sigma p_1 q_0$. This is the amount of income he would require in period 1 to enable him to purchase in period 1 the *quantities* he purchased in period 0. It can be shown that $\Sigma p_1 q_0$ will be greater than $\Sigma p_1 \bar{q}_1$, provided his tastes have remained unchanged. If he did have the income $\Sigma p_1 q_0$ in period 1, he would not buy the same quantities as he bought in period 0 (the

q_0 quantities) because he would take advantage of the changes in relative prices and would alter his allocation of income, buying relatively more of those goods whose prices had fallen relatively more or risen relatively less. The fact that he would do this in preference to buying the q_0 quantities indicates that an income of $\Sigma p_1 q_0$ would make him better off than the original income of $\Sigma p_0 q_0$ and, hence, better off than an income of $\Sigma p_1 \bar{q}_1$ which is its equivalent. Accordingly we have

$$\Sigma p_1 q_0 > \Sigma p_1 \bar{q}_1$$

The proviso that his tastes must have remained unchanged is vital because, if they have changed, we cannot conclude that the quantities he would buy in period 1 with an income of $\Sigma p_1 q_0$ are preferred to those he actually did buy in period 0.

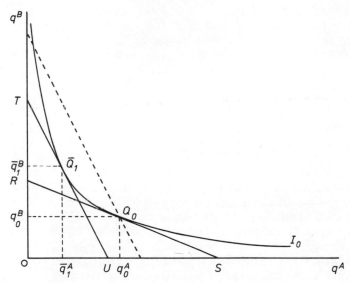

Fig 11.1

This can be illustrated, by means of indifference curves, in the case of an individual spending his income on two goods. We call the two goods A and B. Let the price of A in period 0 be p_0^A and of B be p_0^B. If the individual's money income in period 0 is M_0, we shall have

$$M_0 = p_0^A q^A + p_0^B q^B$$

where q^A and q^B are the quantities of A and B respectively which he can purchase under these circumstances (the greater q^A, the smaller q^B).

On the diagram above, q^A is measured on the X-axis and q^B on the Y-axis. The line RS corresponds to the equation

$$M_0 = p_0^A q^A + p_0^B q^B$$

$$q^B = \frac{M_0}{p_0^B} - \frac{p_0^A}{p_0^B} q^A$$

The individual can take up any position on the line, ie his income will buy him any combination of A and B which lies on the line. RS can be called the *budget line*. Its slope is given by the price of A relative to that of B, ie by p_0^A/p_0^B. Given this price ratio the budget line will be more to the right the greater M_0, ie the greater the money income.

In fact, the individual will move to the point Q_0 on the budget line, at which point he reaches his highest *indifference curve*.[1] This curve is labelled I_0 in the diagram. Consequently in period 0 the individual will purchase q_0^A of A and q_0^B of B. Suppose that in period 1 prices change to p_1^A and p_1^B. If relative prices change, the slope of RS will change. How much income will the individual now need to be as well off as he was before? He will need sufficient to enable him to take up a position just on the indifference curve I_0. We now draw the line TU with a slope given by p_1^A/p_1^B such that it just touches the indifference curve. With an income corresponding to this line, he would take up the position $\bar{Q}_1$, purchasing $\bar{q}_1^A$ of A and $\bar{q}_1^B$ of B. This would require an income of $\bar{M}_1 = p_1^A \bar{q}_1^A + p_1^B \bar{q}_1^B$ as against his old income $M_0 = p_0^A q_0^A + p_0^B q_0^B$. But he is indifferent between the positions Q_0 and $\bar{Q}_1$, so that the ratio $\bar{M}_1/M_0$ measures the change in his old income necessary to make him as well off in period 1 as he was in period 0.

Suppose that the individual is given income in period 1 sufficient to enable him to purchase the same quantities as he did in period 0. This income must be sufficient to make the budget line for the new prices pass through Q_0 and must be equal to $p_1^A q_0^A + p_1^B q_0^B$. This is shown as the broken line in the diagram, and it must lie parallel to but to the right of TU, indicating that it represents a larger income than TU, so that

$$p_1^A q_0^A + p_1^B q_0^B > p_1^A \bar{q}_1^A + p_1^B \bar{q}_1^B$$

This inequality can be extended to the case of more than two commodities, and summing for all the purchases of the individual, we have

---

[1] An indifference curve shows the combinations of A and B between which the individual is indifferent. The individual will prefer a point on a higher indifference curve to one on a lower curve, since more of a good is preferred to less. See G J Stigler: *The Theory of Price*, 3rd edn (Macmillan, 1966), Chap 4, p 48 ff, or the section on the theory of consumers' choice in any economics textbook.

$$\Sigma p_1 q_0 > \Sigma p_1 \bar{q}_1$$

as above. Clearly with the income represented by the broken line the individual will not purchase q_0^A of A and q_0^B of B, but will move along the broken line to the left until contact is reached with the highest indifference curve possible. Such a curve will be higher than I_0. He will purchase more of B which has become relatively cheaper.

From the inequality

$$\Sigma p_1 q_0 > \Sigma p_1 \bar{q}_1$$

we can write[1]

$$\frac{\Sigma p_1 q_0}{\Sigma p_0 q_0} > \frac{\Sigma p_1 \bar{q}_1}{\Sigma p_0 q_0}$$

ie

$$P_{01}^{\text{La}} > C_{01}^0$$

Thus, if we define the change in the cost of living as being the change in income necessary to make the individual as well off in period 1 as he was in period 0, Laspeyres's index number overstates rises and understates falls in the cost of living in this sense.

However, we might just as easily have defined the change in the cost of living as the ratio of the individual's income in period 1 to what he would have needed in period 0 (ie at period 0 prices) to have been as well off as he is in period 1. By analogy with the above this would give

$$C_{01}^1 = \frac{\Sigma p_1 q_1}{\Sigma p_0 \bar{q}_0}$$

where the superscript (1) indicates that the change in the individual's cost of living is being measured in terms of his period 1 standard of living, and we should have

$$\Sigma p_0 q_1 > \Sigma p_0 \bar{q}_0$$

The term on the left-hand side gives the income necessary to enable him to purchase the q_1 quantities at the original prices, and this will be greater than that necessary to make him just as well off. This is illustrated for the two goods case in Fig 11.2 overleaf.

The broken line lies to the right of the line passing through $\bar{Q}_0$, so that

$$p_0^A q_1^A + p_0^B q_1^B > p_0^A \bar{q}_0^A + p_0^B \bar{q}_0^B$$

---

[1] Strictly speaking, the inequality should read $P_{01}^{\text{La}} \geqslant C_{01}^0$. The equality occurs when all prices have changed in the same proportion.

It follows from the inequality[1]

$$\Sigma p_0 q_1 > \Sigma p_0 \bar{q}_0$$

that

$$\frac{\Sigma p_0 q_1}{\Sigma p_1 q_1} > \frac{\Sigma p_0 \bar{q}_0}{\Sigma p_1 q_1}$$

Inverting the inequality, this becomes

$$P_{01}^{\text{Pa}} < C_{01}^1$$

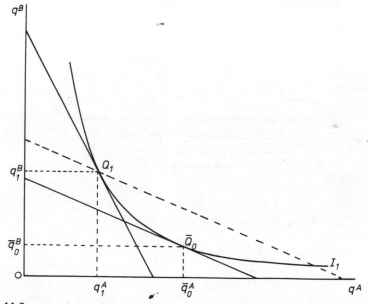

Fig 11.2

Thus Paasche's index understates rises and overstates falls in the cost of living, when the latter is defined in this sense.

It is important to realise that C_{01}^0 and C_{01}^1 are not the same thing.[2] Both measure changes in the cost of maintaining a given standard of living, but in C_{01}^0 the standard maintained is the period 0 standard and in C_{01}^1 it is the period 1 standard. Thus, for example, a particular individual may consume more whisky and less beer as his standard of living rises. If his period 1 standard is higher than his period 0 standard (because his money income has risen relatively to the price level), the

---

[1] See footnote on p 463.

[2] This is illustrated in Figs 11.1 and 11.2. The indifference curve in the former, labelled I_0 (representing the period 0 standard), is quite distinct from that in the latter, labelled I_1 (representing the period 1 standard).

change in the cost of maintaining his period 1 standard will be greater than that of maintaining his period 0 standard in a situation in which whisky prices rise more than beer prices. Clearly, in this case C_{01}^0 will differ from C_{01}^1. Consequently, we cannot use P_{01}^{La} and P_{01}^{Pa} as limits to changes in the cost of living. P_{01}^{La} is an upper limit when we are using C_{01}^0, and P_{01}^{Pa} a lower limit when we are using C_{01}^1, but they cannot be used in conjunction.

We may sum up the situation as follows. In the simplest possible case, when we are considering one individual with constant tastes in two different price situations, we can define two conceptually satisfactory measures for measuring the change in his cost of living, namely C_{01}^0 and C_{01}^1. However, in practice we should probably pay attention to C_{01}^0 only, for this measures the cost of maintaining a given base period standard of living, and that accords with our usual ideas about changes in the cost of living. This being so, we may take C_{01}^0 as our concept of an index number for measuring changes in the cost of living, ie the movement in money income necessary for an individual to maintain his original standard of living. But in practice, however clear C_{01}^0 may be conceptually, we cannot measure it precisely, because it contains hypothetical quantities of what would be necessary to make the individual as well off as he was originally. Nevertheless we can compute an index number P_{01}^{La}, which will overestimate increases and underestimate decreases in the cost of living, although by how much we do not know. But, if an individual starting off with a given income is compensated from time to time for changes in the cost of living by varying his income in accordance with P_{01}^{La}, he will never be worse off but will in general be better off, so long as his tastes do not change.

If we had a community of individuals, all with exactly the same tastes and exactly the same incomes, so that they each purchased the same collections of goods when faced with the same prices, and if their tastes remained constant, then C_{01}^0 would measure changes in the cost of living of each individual, and P_{01}^{La} could be used as an upwardly biased estimate of it, where

$$P_{01}^{La} = \frac{\Sigma p_1 q_0}{\Sigma p_0 q_0}$$

and the q_0s represent the total purchases of each commodity by the community in period 0. In these circumstances, if we were to measure changes in the cost of living by P_{01}^{La}, we should know precisely what P_{01}^{La} measured and its relation to C_{01}^0, which is what we want to measure. Such a state of affairs would not be as satisfactory as if we could measure C_{01}^0 itself, but it would be fairly satisfactory.

However, individuals have different incomes and different tastes, so that if we use P_{01}^{La} as an index of the change in the cost of living, it will only be relevant to those particular individuals who purchase the commodities in the same relative proportions as the community as a whole. Clearly the change in P_{01}^{La} will not be relevant to an individual with a markedly different consumption pattern from the average. Furthermore, if tastes change over time, it becomes impossible to define even the concept of a change in the cost of living.

Accordingly, if for a base period we ascertain the quantities of retail goods and services which a community purchases, q_0, at their then prices, p_0, and next calculate an index of the prices of the goods and services, $P_{01}^{La} = \dfrac{\Sigma p_1 q_0}{\Sigma p_0 q_0}$, this retail price index can be taken as an upwardly biased estimate of the change in the cost of living of those individuals in the community whose consumption patterns correspond to the consumption pattern of the community as a whole and whose tastes do not change. For other individuals, P_{01}^{La} bears no necessary relation to changes in their cost of living. This is all that can be said.

The above analysis illustrates a number of important points, namely:

1. The difficulty of defining changes in the cost of living as a concept.

2. The need to know (a) precisely what we want to measure, (b) what the index number measures, and (c) the relation between them.

3. The relation between the usual type of fixed-weight aggregative retail price index and the measure of changes in the cost of living which the former often purports to be but seldom is.

11.10 Constructing an Index Number

In constructing a price index number for any purpose, four questions immediately arise:

1. What formula is to be used?
2. What commodities are to be included?
3. What are the weights to be?
4. What price quotations are to be used?

The answers to these questions depend, of course, on the purpose for which the index is being constructed. However, attention may well be drawn to some general considerations.

1. Formula

No formula should be used which does not allow for a logical system of weights. This immediately rules out formulae like the simple aggregate of prices or the simple arithmetic mean of price relatives. Apart from these, formulae can be classified according to whether they involve changing or fixed weights. Formulae with changing weights involve a greater collection of data, since information on quantities must be obtained continuously as well as information on prices, and consequently, they are not always practicable. In addition, if the weights are fixed, the meaning of the index is clearer, since it will refer to changes in the cost of a *given* collection. Furthermore, comparisons between two periods will be the same whether made directly or by chaining. Consequently, the fixed-weight type of index is the most common found in practice, although it is customary to revise the fixed weights from time to time (see section 11.11). Nevertheless, occasionally one of the more complex formulae is used; for example, over the period 1928 to 1962 one of the Export Price Indexes published in Australia was a Fisher Ideal index. The Fisher index is practicable in this case because information on quantities of exports is collected continuously. However, in general the formulae used are of the form

$$P_{0t} = \frac{\Sigma p_t q}{\Sigma p_0 q}$$

where P_{0t} is the price index for the period t, with period 0 as base, and the qs are fixed-quantity weights. This formula can also be written as a weighted arithmetic mean of price relatives, and is sometimes found in this form:

$$P_{0t} = \frac{\Sigma \frac{p_t}{p_0} v}{\Sigma v}$$

where the vs are fixed-value weights.

2. *Regimen*

The list of commodities included in an index is sometimes called the *regimen*. It is clear that, if we are constructing, say, an index of retail prices, we shall not be able to include every commodity sold retail. To do so would be a task of gigantic proportions, not only from the point of view of computation but also from that of collection. However, we should include all the more important commodities, and we should try to make our regimen as representative as possible. This is a problem in sampling, but, because the regimen is usually largely governed by the practicability of getting the data, the ordinary procedure of statistical random sampling can seldom be applied. Nevertheless, it is most important to emphasise that if we are regarding our index of, say, retail prices as one of retail prices *generally* (and not simply as an index of the prices of those goods *included in the regimen*), we are making the tacit assumption that the prices of goods excluded from the regimen move on the average in the same way as the index calculated from those goods in the regimen.

3. Weights

Naturally the weights depend on the purpose of the index, but they ought to reflect the relative importance of the commodities in the regimen in the relevant sense. Thus the weight attached to a commodity in a retail price index should not be the total production of the commodity but rather its total consumption. Sometimes the prices of certain items omitted from the regimen are believed to move more in accordance with particular items in the regimen than with the regimen as a whole. In these cases, the weights of the omitted items are added to those of the particular 'representative' items.

In constructing an index number there is naturally a tendency to include all the major items and omit many of the less important ones. If the weights of the items are based on the actual consumption or production of the goods, the major items as a group will be relatively more important in the index number than they are in the whole field to which the index refers, due to the omission of many items which, although minor individually, are in total quite substantial. It is then said that the major items *dominate* the index.[1] Such dominance will not be of great moment if the price behaviour of the items in the dominant group is similar to that of other items, for then the dominant items may be as representative as other items. However, in practice the price behaviour of the dominant items may be quite atypical. This will especially be the case in economies in which government controls (eg price control) are customary, for it is the important items which are generally those subject to control.

4. Prices

In the first place we have to decide at what point in the production process we wish to ascertain our prices, eg whether retail, wholesale, factory, etc. This depends on the purpose of the index. Apart from this, we must decide how to get our price quotations. Here we have a straight-out problem in sampling. We cannot obtain all the prices charged for particular commodities by different selling agencies, so we must take a sample. But we must see that our sample is representative and that the price quotations we use closely correspond to the prices actually charged. Thus, in constructing an index of retail prices under conditions of price control, it would be wrong to include only price quotations from the more reputable firms which adhere to the control, if we knew that there existed a substantial black market. Furthermore,

---

[1] For example, the now discontinued Australian Wholesale Price (Basic Materials and Foodstuffs) Index contained 76 items, but was dominated by 14. These 14 accounted for 80 per cent of the aggregate expenditure in the regimen in 1960, and two of them accounted for 25 per cent.

when we are getting the prices for a particular commodity, we must be certain that the particular commodity is the same commodity for all the times at which we are taking the price quotations. That is, we must fix a standard of quality for each commodity and stick to it. For example, if we are pricing flour, we must not price sometimes loose flour and sometimes packaged flour. The problems associated with changes in the quality of goods are discussed in the section below.

11.11 Changes in the Regimen and Quality Changes

As has already been pointed out, the weights in the fixed-weight aggregative index will get out of date if comparisons are being made over long periods of time. This is due to three main factors. First, technical innovation alters the range of goods and services available, eg the replacement of kerosene by electricity as a form of lighting. Secondly, rising incomes bring a greater range of goods within the possibility of popular consumption, eg the growth of a mass market for consumer durables. Thirdly, whenever there is any substantial dispersion of movements in the prices of different goods, substitution takes place against those goods whose prices have risen relatively the most; as a result, a fixed-weight index inevitably overweights those items whose prices have risen more than the average.

This latter point can be illustrated by comparing, for the now obsolete Australian 'C' Series Retail Price Index, the weighting of the period, at about when the weights were formulated, with that of nearly thirty years later. Between 1923–27 and 1952 clothing prices rose much more than other prices in the 'C' Series and, consequently, the percentage of aggregate expenditure on clothing in the regimen rose considerably. In reality, people did not allocate their expenditure

Table 11.7

Group	Percentage of Aggregate Cost in 'C' Series Regimen	
	1923–27	December Quarter, 1952
I. Food and Groceries	38·7	40·8
II. Housing	21·3	11·3
III. Clothing	23·0	31·1
IV. Miscellaneous	17·0	16·8
	100·0	100·0

Source: Commonwealth Bureau of Census and Statistics, Australia: *Labour Report*, No. 41, 1952, p 16

as in the last column, but devoted less to clothing and more to housing. It is to a large extent *diverse* price changes themselves which make the weights of an index out of date.

If follows from the argument in the preceding two paragraphs that the regimen and weights of an index number must be revised from time to time. We might have, for example, an index for periods 0 to 5 on the basis of a certain regimen and a certain set of weights, q, with base period $0 = 100$, and then change the regimen and weights to $\hat{q}$, with base period $5 = 100$. In effect, we shall have two quite distinct indexes and, strictly speaking, no valid comparisons can be made between periods before period 5 and those after. In practice, however, the two indexes will often be chained together so that periods after period 5 can be compared with the original base. We might have, for example

$$P_{06} = P_{05} \times \hat{P}_{56}$$

where $\qquad P_{05} = \dfrac{\Sigma p_5 q}{\Sigma p_0 q}$ (the old regimen and weights)

and $\qquad \hat{P}_{56} = \dfrac{\Sigma p_6 \hat{q}}{\Sigma p_5 \hat{q}}$ (the new regimen and weights)

It is important to realise that the ratio $\Sigma p_6 \hat{q} / \Sigma p_0 q$, which measures the change in the aggregate cost of two different collections, is quite meaningless. It will be affected by the changes from q to $\hat{q}$ as well as by price changes.

Indeed, the periodic revision of regimen and weights is a customary practice in index-number construction although in many cases the revisions occur at rather lengthy intervals, perhaps every twenty years or so. In the case of the Australian Consumer Price Index, for example, the technique has been adopted of revising the regimen and weights at relatively short intervals (four or five years) and computing the index as a chain of short-term links.

In computing a price index it is essential that the price quotations for an item be for a standard quality of that item. If this is not so, some of the movement in the index will be due to changes in quality, whereas the index aims at measuring pure price changes. Consequently, the exact quality of each item in the index must be specified, and the specifications must be rigidly adhered to when securing price quotations. In practice, however, it is inevitable that the quality of items will change. Usually there is more than one quality of each item, and it frequently happens that over a period of time the quality originally in predominant use declines in popularity and is replaced by another one; the replacing of silk stockings by nylons is an example. When this happens, it would be preferable to measure the price changes of the item under consideration by the price movement of the new rather than the old quality, because the new quality is now more representative of the item. In fact, the old quality may sooner or later go right out of use, forcing a change in procedure.

The procedure for handling quality change is as follows. Suppose we have an item whose price is represented by that of variety A. There is also a variety B, which has been ousting A from its original popularity, and it is decided in, say, period 4 to base the variations in the price of the item in future on variety B rather than on A. The weight attached to this item is q. The contributions of this item to aggregate cost in the various periods up to and beyond period 4 are given by

$$p_0^A q, \ldots p_4^A q, p_5^B q, p_6^B q \ldots$$

Some of the change in this contribution between periods 4 and 5 may be due to the change in quality (eg if B is of a higher quality than A, p_5^B may be higher than p_4^A for this reason alone). Since we are interested in pure price changes this quality change must be eliminated. Assuming that variety A and B are both freely available in period 4, we can take the ratio p_4^A/p_4^B as an index of the relative valuation which consumers place on the two varieties. We can then argue[1] that the appropriate weight to be attached to the price of B is

$$\frac{q p_4^A}{p_4^B}$$

This is the quantity of B which can be purchased in period 4 by an expenditure equal to the expenditure involved in purchasing q units of A in the same period. We can use this weight from period 5 onwards, so that the contributions to aggregate cost will be

$$p_0^A q, \ldots p_4^A q, p_5^B \frac{q p_4^A}{p_4^B}, p_6^B \frac{q p_4^A}{p_4^B} \ldots$$

It will be observed that the new weight attached to the price of B in period 4 gives the same contribution as the old weight attached to the price of A in period 4. In effect, the weight has been modified so that the contribution to aggregate cost of the item in period 4 is the same irrespective of the variety priced.

---

[1] This argument is based on practical rather than theoretical considerations. If perfect competition obtains on the buying side of the market (as it usually does in markets for consumption goods) the ratio p_4^A/p_4^B equals the *marginal* relative valuation which consumers place on the two varieties. It does not follow that q of A will be valued as the equivalent of $\frac{q p_4^A}{p_4^B}$ of B.

The above contributions can be rewritten

$$p_0^A q, \ldots p_0^A q \cdot \frac{p_4^A}{p_0^A}, \, p_4^A q \cdot \frac{p_5^B}{p_4^B}, \, p_4^A q \cdot \frac{p_6^B}{p_4^B} \ldots$$

from which it can be seen that from periods 0 to 4 the expenditure on the particular item was being varied by the change in the price of variety A, but after that period it is being varied by the change in the price of variety B. The reason for the change is that the price movements of variety B are now regarded as more representative of the price movements of the item under consideration than those of variety A. If the prices of the two varieties moved in a similar fashion there would, of course, be no point in making the change.

This procedure which aims at eliminating price changes due to quality changes is called *splicing* and it is achieved in any period t by replacing the old weight q by a new weight $q \frac{p_t^A}{p_t^B}$. For example if, in an index of retail prices, it is decided in period 4 to replace variety of A of tea with variety B, the procedure would be as follows. The necessary data are given in the table below.

Table 11.8

Commodity	Unit	Period 0			Period 4			Period 5		
		Price	Quantity	Aggregate Cost	Price	Quantity	Aggregate Cost	Price	Quantity	Aggregate Cost
		cents		cents	cents		cents	cents		cents
Tea A . .	kg	36	10	360	48	10		54	10	
Tea B . .	kg				60	8*	480	72	8	576
Other items .				3 240			3 600			3 960
				3 600			4 080			4 536

*The new weight after splicing is given by $10 \times \frac{48}{60} = 8$. Note that in the period in which the splicing takes place, both variety A and variety B make the same contribution to aggregate cost, ie $48 \times 10 = 60 \times 8$.

With base period $0 = 100$,

$$P_{04} = (4080 \div 3600) \times 100 = 113$$

If variety A had been adhered to, P_{05} would have been

$$(4500 \div 3600) \times 100 = 125$$

but switching to B makes

$$P_{05} = (4536 \div 3600) \times 1000 = 126$$

This is a higher figure because the price of B has risen more than that of A between periods 4 and 5. Had variety B been introduced without splicing (a completely inadmissible procedure), P_{05} would have been (4680 ÷ 3600) × 100 = 130. This would have been quite wrong as it would include an increase of price due to a quality change (the price of variety B was 60 cents as against 48 cents for variety A in period 4).

11.12 Index Numbers in Practice

The statistical offices of most countries publish various price index numbers referring to the movements in the price levels of certain groups of commodities. These indexes are used by economists and others for many purposes. The greatest care should be exercised in their use to ensure that they are appropriate for the purpose in hand. Those who use index numbers can judge their appropriateness or otherwise only if they know the details of their regimens and understand the difficulties which must be overcome in their construction.

An understanding of the difficulties and intricacies of index-number construction can be appreciated by studying the anatomy of particular index numbers. Such a study is set out (although in limited detail) in reference to the Australian Consumer Price Index in Appendix B.4, p 599 ff below. This section is restricted to discussion of the interpretation of index numbers in practice, referring to a retail price index by way of illustration.

A retail price index, like the Australian one referred to above, is designed to measure variations in the retail prices of goods and services which enter into consumers' expenditure. This is done by selecting a regimen of goods and services which is believed to be representative (or as representative as is practicable, given the difficulties of collection, specifications, etc) and attaching to the goods and services weights reflecting the pattern of consumers' expenditure in some sense. At the very least, the index can then be said to measure changes in the prices of the collection of goods and services specified by quality and quantity in the regimen.

In practice retail price indexes are usually interpreted much more broadly than this. They are used both as measures of changes in retail prices *generally* and as measures of changes in the cost of living. In such uses they have their limitations. But they can hardly be criticised for not being entirely suitable for purposes for which they were not designed.

A consumer price index can be used as a measure of changes in retail prices generally only if the prices of items omitted from the regimen change in approximately the same way on the average as those in the regimen. The fact that a consumer price index *omits* certain items is itself unimportant unless the price behaviour of these items differs appreciably from the included items. But even if the coverage of a consumer price index is good, care must be taken not to strain its meaning, by, for example, treating it as if it measured changes in the price component of gross domestic product at current market prices; for, in this case, the price index could scarcely be relevant to the investment and government expenditure categories of gross domestic product unless the prices of those categories moved on the average in the same way as the index (see p 481 ff, below).

We have already adverted to the difficulties of measuring changes in the cost of living (see section 11.9 above) and pointed out the conditions under which a retail price index can be used as an approximate measure of such changes. A particular retail price index can in no way be a measure of changes in *the* cost of living. Indeed the concept of 'changes in the cost of living' is only fully meaningful in relation to a particular household. Households may range in type from the unmarried man to the married couple with children and elderly relatives. Their consumption patterns vary enormously. But in so far as given persons or groups of persons have consumption patterns approximating to that included in the particular index number's regimen and weights, that index number can be used to indicate changes in the cost of living of such persons or groups.[1]

When a retail price index is used as a measure of changes in the cost of living, misconceptions about the nature of index numbers often occur. These misconceptions are associated with the notion that, if the regimen omits certain items, changes in the cost of living will be understated. This is, of course, erroneous; but it is a common error and arises from a confusion about the function of price index numbers. It arises particularly in cases where wages are adjusted from time to time according to changes in a price index number. It is argued that the regimen of the index number in some way dictates the standard of living of the wage-earner whose wages are adjusted by it. If the index number omits fresh fruit and vegetables, for example, it is said that the

---

[1] Until 1953 the Australian 'C' Series Retail Price Index (see Appendix B.4, p 599 below) was for many years used by the Commonwealth Court of Conciliation and Arbitration to vary the basic wage. The Court periodically fixed the level of the basic wage and then varied it quarterly in accordance with movements in the 'C' Series. The 'C' series measured accurately the cost of a certain regimen, and that is all it was meant to do. The use of it by the Court as a measure of changes in the cost of living due to variations in prices was a matter for the Court's own judgment. Cost of living variations to the basic wage were abandoned in 1953 until 1975 when the Australian Conciliation and Arbitration Commission and the associated state tribunals resumed the indexation of award rates in accordance with variations in the Consumer Price Index. At the same time a standing tripartite commission comprised of union, employer and government representatives began meeting regularly to consider the representativeness of the index in measuring movements in the general level of retail prices. In 1975 the Commission granted full indexation of award wages for all the four quarters. However, award increases for the March and June quarters of 1976 were based only in part on the movements in the Consumer Price Index.

wage-earner's standard of living cannot be meant to include these items. This confuses the whole function of price index numbers, which is to measure *changes* in prices. A price index number measures *changes* in prices of a *given* regimen; or, when it is being used in relation to the cost of living, *changes* in the cost of a *given* standard of living. The adjustment of a wage by a price index number only attempts to preserve the real value of the wage in terms of purchasing power at the level *originally* determined. It is this level which determines the wage-earners' standard of living. If the index number does not contain certain items this can only affect the issue in so far as the prices of these items move differently from the index number. Indeed, if, when prices are rising generally, the prices of omitted items are rising less quickly than the average, the inclusion of such items would reduce the rate of increase of the index, and hence the measure of the change of the cost of living and any cost of living adjustment to wages. It does not matter how many or how few are the items in the regimen so long as they are properly representative of price changes generally. But, of course, if there is any considerable dispersion of price movements, a single index cannot be expected to measure changes in the cost of living of different households, which enjoy standards of living of markedly different quality and quantity.

CHAPTER 12

REAL DOMESTIC PRODUCT AND INDEXES OF PRODUCTION

12.1 Gross Domestic Product at Current and Constant Prices

The transactions which are recorded in the social accounts and the aggregates which make up gross domestic product, consumption, investment, etc are all expressed in money terms and reflect current prices and factor payments. A figure for gross domestic product at current prices for a single year is not very meaningful unless we have some idea of the value (ie the purchasing power) of money itself. A series of figures for money gross domestic product over a number of years has more meaning. It tells us how money national income and expenditure have changed. For some purposes money aggregates are all we want, eg for the estimation of tax yields, for assessing the extent to which the balance of payments is 'in balance', etc. However, the value of money will, in general, be changing from year to year as the general level of prices moves up and down, and this vitiates the use of money national income figures for examining trends in productivity or the standard of living or for examining changes in the allocation of resources between different sectors in the economy or between different purposes. Clearly, what we need is to go behind the façade of prices and to measure the various relevant aggregates in 'real' terms.

Consider gross domestic product. Gross domestic product can be regarded either as the value of goods and services produced for final purposes during the year or else as the sum of values added in the process of production. In the former sense, the 'real' element in gross domestic product can be clearly discerned, for gross domestic product consists of a great list of quantities of goods and services produced (the 'real' physical things) multiplied by the appropriate current market prices. Thus, in year 0, we can represent it by $\Sigma P_0 Q_0$, and in year 1 by $\Sigma P_1 Q_1$, and so on, where the Qs are quantities and the Ps the corresponding prices. The difference (if any) between the money aggregates $\Sigma P_1 Q_1$ and $\Sigma P_0 Q_0$ will be due to changes both in the Qs and in the Ps. If we are to measure real gross domestic product, we must eliminate the changes in the Ps, so that our measure refers only to quantity or 'real' changes, ie *quantum* changes. If all the Qs changed in exactly the same proportion, that proportion would represent the change in real gross domestic product, and our task would be simple. However, this is never the case. In practice we have to find ways of adding the Q_0s, and then the Q_1s, and comparing the totals. But the various Qs refer to different goods and services, and the question of how they can be added arises. How can we add metres of cloth and kilograms of butter? One way would be to work out a table of equivalences of the form: 1 metre of cloth $= 2$ kg of butter. These equivalences would have to be in terms of how the different goods and services are valued relatively to one another. Such a valuation is provided by the market. An equivalence between cloth and butter, for example, can be derived from their market prices. Thus if the price of one metre of cloth is $1·80 and the price of one kilogram of butter is 90 cents, these prices imply an equivalence between the two goods of 1 metre of cloth $= 2$ kg of butter.

It follows that to measure real gross domestic product, we must weight the quantities in some way so as to reflect their relative values before adding them. Thus, although real gross domestic product is a quantity measure, it measures quantity not simply in the physical sense, but rather in the economic sense of quantity of 'real value'. For example, if two grades of refrigerators are produced, an increase in the proportion of the more valuable grade, total numbers remaining constant, implies an increase in 'real' production in the economic sense. It will be readily appreciated that the main problem is in finding appropriate weights to reflect relative economic values. These weights can be derived from market prices, and if relative market prices never changed there would be no difficulty. In this case all prices would move up or down by the same proportion, and the real value of $\Sigma P_1 Q_1$ relative to $\Sigma P_0 Q_0$ would be given by dividing $\Sigma P_1 Q_1$ by the change in prices. In practice, all prices do not move up and down in the same ratio, and thus relative prices change.

The difficulty which arises as a result of this can be seen as follows. Suppose we wish to compare year 0 with year 1. We can use the prices of either year 0 or year 1 as weights. Thus we can compare

$$\Sigma P_0 Q_0 \text{ and } \Sigma P_0 Q_1$$

or

$$\Sigma P_1 Q_0 \text{ and } \Sigma P_1 Q_1$$

The first compares the gross domestic products of year 0 and year 1 valued at constant year 0 prices, and the second compares gross domestic product of year 0 and year 1 valued at constant year 1 prices. Both comparisons give us figures for real gross domestic product, valued at constant prices. Real gross domestic product, as here defined, is, of course, expressed in terms of money units, but it is 'real' in the sense that it is expressed in terms of money units of constant purchasing power. Both comparisons are equally valid but they will in general differ. The first comparison will generally show a greater rise or a smaller fall than the second, so long as the usual negative correlation between prices and quantities obtains. This can be proved in a manner analogous to that used in section 11.4 above. It is clear that there can be no single unambiguous measure of changes in real gross domestic product, just as there can be no single unambiguous measure of changes in the price level.

It would be possible to make the comparison between year 0 and year 1 with a set of prices other than those of year 0 or year 1—for example by comparing

$$\Sigma P_n Q_0 \text{ and } \Sigma P_n Q_1$$

This comparison, however, would rely on relative valuations which are relevant to neither year 0 nor year 1.

The statistical meaning of a series of figures for real gross domestic product valued at a set of constant prices is clear enough, but the greatest caution is needed in interpreting such a series in economic terms. In practice, such series expressed per head of population are frequently used to indicate movements in the standard of living of an economy. But we here come up against the type of problem discussed in section 11.9 above, namely the relation between a statistical measure and the theoretical concept we wish to measure. As yet no way of measuring the standard of living of even an individual has been satisfactorily defined, for a person's standard of living must be conceived of not in terms of the goods and services which are available to him but in terms of the satisfactions he derives from those goods and services, and these cannot be measured.[1] Moreover, if we are considering a group of individuals, we have no way of comparing the satisfactions of the individuals within the group. Thus, in two periods total production might be the same, but its distribution between the individuals might differ. Can we say that people are on the whole as well off as they were before?

In spite of these conceptual difficulties, however, we do frequently assume that changes in real domestic product per head can be taken to indicate changes in the standard of living of the economy, provided that there have been no substantial changes in income distribution. We should not, of course, attach any importance to a small change

---

[1] There is a substantial body of literature on this problem. See, for example, R G D Allen: 'The Economic Theory of Index Numbers', *Economica*, N.S., Vol XVI, August 1949, p 197; J R Hicks: 'The Measurement of Real Income', *Oxford Economic Papers*, Vol 10, June 1958, p 125.

in real product, but a large increase would suggest that the economy was, at least, in a position to enjoy a higher standard of living.

One serious difficulty in using real product figures is that there is no unique measure of real gross domestic product. Real gross domestic product is measured in terms of a set of constant prices and its movements over time depend on the set used. Thus gross domestic product for the years 1954–55 to 1974–75, valued at constant 1954–55 prices, will move differently and possibly very differently from the same gross domestic product valued at constant 1974–75 prices, since the weights attached to the various quantities will be different. There is no reason to prefer one set of constant prices to the other, so that if the results are very divergent their interpretation becomes virtually impossible. This difficulty increases the more distant are the periods of comparison.

12.2 Estimation of Real Gross Domestic Product

The two comparisons set out on p 477 can be put into index number form. Using year 0 as a base, we shall have:

$$Q_{01}^{La} = \frac{\Sigma P_0 Q_1}{\Sigma P_0 Q_0}$$

and

$$Q_{01}^{Pa} = \frac{\Sigma P_1 Q_1}{\Sigma P_1 Q_0}$$

The first of these indexes is Laspeyres's quantity index, and the second Paasche's. These indexes are indexes of quantity, sometimes called indexes of *quantum* or *physical volume*. They measure the change in the volume of a collection of goods and services valued at constant prices.

Although the exposition in this section is in terms of measuring the quantum of gross domestic product, these indexes of quantum can be applied quite generally, eg to measure changes in the volume of exports, the output of primary products, etc. Their central feature is that they involve the weighting of quantities of items by constant prices, which are taken to reflect the relative values of the items.

If we knew all the Ps and Qs it would be quite a simple matter to work out Q_{01}^{La} or Q_{01}^{Pa} for gross domestic product. In practice, of course, we do not have all this information, and we have to use the fact that

$$\text{value} = \text{quantity} \times \text{price}$$

Thus, for an individual good, we can write

$$\frac{V_1}{V_0} = \frac{P_1}{P_0} \times \frac{Q_1}{Q_0}$$

ie relative value change equals relative price change multiplied by relative quantity change. By analogy we can write, in index-number form, for an aggregate of goods and services

$$V_{01} = P_{01} \cdot Q_{01} \qquad (*)$$

where $V_{01} = \dfrac{\Sigma P_1 Q_1}{\Sigma P_0 Q_0}$ is an index of values, P_{01} is an index of prices, and Q_{01} is an index of quantum. If the relation (*) is true we can obtain Q_{01} from

$$Q_{01} = V_{01} \div P_{01}$$

As far as gross domestic product is concerned, we know V_{01} (ie the change in the money gross domestic product) and there are available various possible indexes of prices, calculated on a sample basis (ie on a sample of goods and services). The process of dividing value aggregates by price aggregates to obtain quantity aggregates is called the process of *deflation*, and the price index used is known as the *deflator*.

The relation (*) is only true when the indexes P_{01} and Q_{01} are correlative in a certain sense. Thus we know from the factor-reversal test (see section 11.5, p 447) that

$$V_{01} \neq P_{01}^{\text{La}} \cdot Q_{01}^{\text{La}}$$

and

$$V_{01} \neq P_{01}^{\text{Pa}} \cdot Q_{01}^{\text{Pa}}$$

However, we have

$$V_{01} = P_{01}^{\text{La}} \cdot Q_{01}^{\text{Pa}}$$

and

$$V_{01} = P_{01}^{\text{Pa}} \cdot Q_{01}^{\text{La}}$$

Consequently, if we desire to estimate Q_{01}^{La}, we must divide V_{01} by the appropriate Paasche price index. Then

$$Q_{01}^{\text{La}} = V_{01} \div P_{01}^{\text{Pa}}$$

and similarly,

$$Q_{01}^{\text{Pa}} = V_{01} \div P_{01}^{\text{La}}$$

On the other hand, if we use the quantities of some third year as weights in the price index, we get

$$Q_{01} = \frac{\Sigma P_1 Q_1}{\Sigma P_0 Q_0} \div \frac{\Sigma P_1 Q_n}{\Sigma P_0 Q_n}$$

$$= \frac{\Sigma P_0 Q_n}{\Sigma P_0 Q_0} \div \frac{\Sigma P_1 Q_n}{\Sigma P_1 Q_1}$$

$$= Q_{0n}^{\text{La}} \div Q_{1n}^{\text{La}}$$

and it is not clear what Q_{01} means. This is in contrast with Q_{01}^{La} and Q_{01}^{Pa} which have quite clear meanings.

The process of deflation can be accomplished either in the index-number form, as above, or by directly deflating gross domestic product itself. To obtain gross domestic product at constant period 0 prices, we have

period 0: $\Sigma P_0 Q_0$

period 1: $\Sigma P_1 Q_1 \div P_{01}^{Pa} = \Sigma P_0 Q_1$

To obtain gross domestic product at constant period 1 prices, we have

period 0: $\Sigma P_0 Q_0 \times P_{01}^{La} = \Sigma P_1 Q_0$

period 1: $\Sigma P_1 Q_1$

It is important to emphasise that the process of deflation gives a strictly valid result only if the correct formula for the price index is used and if the coverage of the price index is coextensive with the gross domestic product. In deflating an aggregate like gross domestic product, it is of fundamental importance to see that the deflator has a coverage coextensive with the quantity aggregate which is to be obtained from the process of deflation. In so far as the deflator does omit the prices of certain items, its use must imply the assumption that their prices have moved in the same degree as the movement of the deflator as a whole. Frequently this assumption is obviously invalid. In practice price indexes have to be used which are not of the correct form and are only partial in character. Thus, although we often divide $\Sigma P_1 Q_1$ by a price index P_{01} and designate the result as 'gross domestic product of year 1 valued at constant period 0 prices', this is seldom strictly correct.

Consider, as an example, a comparison of real gross domestic product for Australia for the two years 1971–72 and 1974–75. Valued at current market prices gross domestic product for the two years was $36 880 million and $58 456 million respectively. We wish to deflate the latter figure to obtain gross domestic product at constant 1971–72 prices. However, we must find a suitable price index number. Suppose, for argument's sake, we use the Consumer Price Index. On a base of 1966–67 = 100·0, this index rose from 122·4 to 171·1 over the period under consideration, ie from 1000 to 1398. Deflating by the Consumer Price Index we have 58 456 ÷ 1·398 = $41 814 million as an estimate of the gross domestic product valued at 1971–72 prices, giving a rise in real product of some 13 per cent over the three-year period. Apart from the fact that the price index is, strictly speaking, technically unsuitable, because its quantity weights should relate to production in 1974–75 (ie the deflator should be a Paasche type), this estimate of the movement in real gross domestic product is unreliable because of the inadequate coverage of the deflator. The gross domestic product

Table 12.1

ESTIMATION OF AUSTRALIAN GROSS DOMESTIC PRODUCT 1974–75 VALUED AT 1971–72 PRICES

Item and Deflator	Deflators as Published (a)		Deflators 1974–75 (Base 1971–72 = 1000) (b)	Gross Domestic Product at Current Prices		Gross Domestic Product at 1971–72 Prices
	1971–72	1974–75		1971–72 $m	1974–75 $m	1974–75 $m (c)
	(1)	(2)	(3)	(4)	(5)	(6)
Private Final Consumption Expenditures						
Food (Food Group, CPI (d))	116·8	164·0	1 404	4 144	6 053	4 311
Clothing, footwear, etc (Clothing and Drapery Group, CPI)	118·5	173·0	1 460	1 987	3 010	2 062
Rent of dwellings (Housing Group, CPI)	133·0	187·4	1 409	3 053	4 886	3 468
Household durables (Household Supplies and Equipment Group, CPI)	111·7	146·6	1 312	2 158	3 627	2 765
Other (Miscellaneous Group, CPI)	131·0	180·8	1 380	10 847	16 965	12 293
Gross Private Capital Expenditures						
Dwellings (Wholesale Price Index (e)) (Minimum Weekly Wage Rates—Adult Males)	122·7 218·0	183·4 373·5	1 604(g)	1 785	2 501	1 560
Other building and construction (Wholesale Price Index (f)) (Minimum Weekly Wage Rates—Adult Males)	123·0 218·0	179·2 373·5	1 585(g)	1 451	1 978	1 248

Other capital expenditures (Machinery Groups, Import Price Index (h))	120·8	143·5	1 190	3 075	4 309	3 621
Stocks (Wholesale Price Index (i))	102·6	145·1	1 414	–113	836	591
Government Expenditures						
Final Consumption (Minimum Weekly Wage Rates—Adult Males)	218·0	373·5	1 713	4 760	9 092	5 308
Building and construction (Wholesale Price Index (f)) (Minimum Weekly Wage Rates—Adult Males)	123·0 218·0	179·2 373·5	1 585(g)	2 278	3 845	2 425
All other (Machinery Groups, Import Price Index (h))	120·8	143·5	1 190	1 016	1 519	1 276
Exports (Export Price Index)	104·0	181·0	1 740	5 633	9 782	5 622
Less Imports (Import Price Index)	115·0	189·4	1 647	–5 194	–9 947	–6 040
Gross Domestic Product				36 880(j)	58 456(j)	40 510

(a) Base years:
  Consumer Price Index (CPI), 1966–67 = 100.
  Wholesale Price Indexes (see footnotes (e), (f) and (i).).
  Export Price Index, 1959–60 = 100.
  Import Price Index, 1966–67 = 100.
  Import Price Index—sectional indexes, 1970–71 = 100.
  Index of Minimum Weekly Wage Rates—Adult Males, 1954 = 100.
(b) (Col (2) ÷ col (1)) × 1000.
(c) (Col (5) ÷ col (3)) × 1000.
(d) Consumer Price Index.
(e) Price Index of Materials Used in House Building, 1966–67 = 100.
(f) Price Index of Materials Used in Building other than House Building, 1966–67 = 100.
(g) The index used here is a weighted average of the two indexes shown giving both indexes equal weight.
(h) The machinery, electrical machinery and transport equipment groups of the Import Price Index weighted by value of imports in 1970–71 in these groups. See Reserve Bank of Australia, *Statistical Bulletin*, Economic Supplement, July 1974, p 30.
(i) Price Index of Materials Used in Manufacturing Industry, 1968–69 = 100.
(j) Excluding statistical discrepancy as an element of expenditure; see Australian Bureau of Statistics, *Australian National Accounts*, 1974–75, p 26.

Source: For columns (1) and (2): Australian Bureau of Statistics: *Monthly Review of Business Statistics*, No. 452, 1976, pp 20, 21, 24, 26, 28, 30; *Quarterly Summary of Australian Statistics*, No. 299, 1976, p 138; and for the Import Price Index: Reserve Bank of Australia: *Statistical Bulletin*, April 1975, p 347 and September 1976, p 111.
For columns (4) and (5): Australian Bureau of Statistics: *Australian National Accounts*, 1974–75, pp 26, 49, 56 (these figures are subject to revision in subsequent publications).

is a collection of final goods and services of all kinds, but the Consumer Price Index represents price movements in a restricted sector. Thus:

1. The index does not include goods and services falling into the categories of gross private investment (other than private motor vehicles) and government expenditure.

2. Gross domestic product covers goods and services produced in Australia, whereas the Consumer Price Index represents consumption. . Thus gross domestic product includes exports but excludes imports. The Consumer Price Index includes some part of imports and covers export prices only to the extent that certain exportable goods enter home consumption. There is no weight attaching to exports as such in the Consumer Price Index.

3. At best the Consumer Price Index might be said to cover the elements of gross domestic product which enter into consumers' expenditure. But even here the coverage is not complete.

This inadequate coverage would not matter if the prices of items included in gross domestic product, but not represented in the Consumer Price Index regimen, moved on the average in a similar way to the prices of those items included in the regimen. In fact, this has not been the case, so that the Consumer Price Index is an unsuitable deflator.

The main trouble with using an index number like the Consumer Price Index as a deflator is that it is a sectional index and as such it covers only partially the content of gross domestic product. This consideration suggests that we should use other available index numbers in conjunction with the Consumer Price Index and deflate gross domestic product in sections, using appropriate sectional price indexes for the various sections. This is done by way of illustration in Table 12.1. The sectionalisation of gross domestic product has been to some extent dictated by considerations as to whether or not appropriate indexes are available, and could in fact be made more detailed. A more accurate and more detailed computation could be made if sufficient trouble were taken, and the table should be understood to be purely an example. It certainly does not contain an estimate of *the* gross domestic product of 1974–75 valued at 1971–72 prices, and no great reliance should be placed on the results of the table. Criticisms similar to those levelled above against the use of the Consumer Price Index could easily be levelled against some of the sectional deflators. According to the computation in the table, gross domestic product measured in constant 1971–72 prices rose by 10 per cent from $36 880 million to $40 510 million as between 1971–72 and 1974–75. This compares with an increase of nearly 59 per cent (from $36 880 million to $58 456 million) in gross domestic product at current prices, most of which was due to an inflationary rise in prices. A brief discussion of the estimation of Australian gross domestic product at constant prices is contained in Appendix B.5, pp 610–13 below.

The process of deflation has been illustrated above with reference to deflating gross domestic product to obtain an index of the movement in aggregate real production. Aggregate real production is a useful concept if one is interested in indicating movements in physical productivity. But frequently one is interested not so much in productivity as in the standard of living. These two concepts do not necessarily go hand in hand. One important reason for divergence lies in foreign trade. Gross domestic product consists of *home-produced goods and services for consumption*, investment, government purposes and exports. These are the goods and services actually produced in the economy, and consequently are relevant to a study of the quantum of production. But from the point of view of the standard of living, what is relevant is the aggregate of home-produced goods and services for consumption, investment and government purposes, together with the purchasing power over *imports* which the economy's exports give it. This means that instead of deflating exports by export prices and imports by import prices as was done in the example above, we should deflate them both by import prices, ie deflate net exports by import prices. If this is done for the data in Table 12.1 above, gross domestic product in 1974–75 valued at 1971–72 prices is $40 828 million, showing a rise not of 10 per cent but of 11 per cent over the 1971–72 gross domestic product. The larger increase in real gross domestic product measured in this way is due to the improved terms of trade in 1974–75. This improvement has increased the real value to Australians of export production in terms of its purchasing power over imports, quite apart from any change in the physical production of exports. Similarly, the question arises as to the extent to which current investment adds to the current standard of living. Its effect on productivity will be in the future, but it does add to the potential current standard of living in the sense that the economy could have devoted the resources bound up in the investment goods to current consumption. Consequently, if we are interested in the standard of living, the aggregate of investment in gross domestic product should perhaps be deflated by an index of consumer good prices.

The idea of deflating gross domestic product to obtain a measure of the quantum of production is relatively simple, for gross domestic product is an aggregate which has a price component and a quantity component. But frequently money aggregates are deflated which cannot conceptually be split into these two components. The question then is: What does the deflated aggregate measure? Consider the case of personal income. Personal income is not an aggregate of prices multiplied by quantities produced. A deflated personal income can only measure the purchasing power of the income over the regimen of the deflator. Thus the statistical interpretation of the aggregate of personal incomes divided by a consumer price index is clear, but its meaningfulness may be limited. If the consumer price index covered all items on which income is normally spent, then the meaningfulness of the deflated aggregate would undoubtedly be increased. The same considerations apply *a fortiori* to a deflation of, for example, bank clearings by a price index.

12.3 Measurement of Movements in the Quantum of Industrial Production

In the preceding section we discussed the measurement of movements in the quantum of national production in the aggregate. We now consider how to measure movements in the quantum of production of the individual firms and industries which contribute to the national aggregate. The indexes used in this connexion are usually called *indexes of industrial production*. Such indexes are generally limited to production taking place in secondary industries. Their compilation enables us to compare the rates of change of production in the various industries of an economy and to compare these rates with changes in employment, etc.

It is convenient to start by considering the measurement of movements in the quantum of production of an individual firm. For the sake of simplicity, we consider first a firm producing only one product (ie one output). Clearly we cannot measure the quantum of production of the firm by reference to the quantity of its output, for the output contains raw materials, etc (ie inputs) which have been produced by other firms. If, for example, output were to remain constant while inputs were reduced, the quantum of production of the firm should be regarded as having increased. It follows that the quantum of production of a firm should be defined as the quantity component of what we have previously called the gross product of or value added by the firm (see section 10.3, p 391). This is equivalent to relating the quantum of production to the amount of 'work done' by the firm. Thus, suppose that our firm in producing its one output uses only one input. Clearly, it is not possible to subtract the input from the output, for how can one subtract, for example, kilograms of flour from loaves of bread. In order to make the subtraction, it is necessary to express the units of output or input in terms of the other, and this can be done by using market prices as an indication of the equivalence between the output and the input. Thus, if we write P and Q for the price and quantity respectively of the output and p and q for the price and quantity of the input, the value of the production of the firm will be given by

$$PQ - pq$$

This is, in fact, the gross product of or value added by the firm. It is a money figure, and statistically it is impossible to resolve it into a price and a quantity component in the manner in which we can resolve the value of output (PQ) into a price component (P) and a quantity component (Q). However, as will be seen below, we can attempt to resolve changes in the value of production into price changes and quantity changes.

If we wish to measure the change in the value of production of the firm as between period 0 and period 1, we can do so by comparing $P_1 Q_1 - p_1 q_1$ with $P_0 Q_0 - p_0 q_0$. This comparison yields the ratio

$$\frac{P_1 Q_1 - p_1 q_1}{P_0 Q_0 - p_0 q_0}$$

as an index of the movement in the value of production. This ratio can be written

$$\frac{P_1 Q_1 - p_1 q_1}{P_0 Q_0 - p_0 q_0} = \frac{P_0 Q_1 - p_0 q_1}{P_0 Q_0 - p_0 q_0} \times \frac{P_1 Q_1 - p_1 q_1}{P_0 Q_1 - p_0 q_1}$$

The first term on the right-hand side measures the movement in value added when the quantities are valued at constant period 0 prices, and the second term the movement in prices when these are weighted by period 1 quantities. We can regard the former as a quantity and the latter as a price component of the movement in the value of production. The quantity component tells us how value added would have changed had prices remained constant at the period 0 level.

However, we can also write

$$\frac{P_1 Q_1 - p_1 q_1}{P_0 Q_0 - p_0 q_0} = \frac{P_1 Q_1 - p_1 q_1}{P_1 Q_0 - p_1 q_0} \times \frac{P_1 Q_0 - p_1 q_0}{P_0 Q_0 - p_0 q_0}$$

giving similar interpretations to the two terms on the right-hand side. Thus the first term tells us how value added would have changed had prices remained constant at the period 1 level, and can be regarded as a quantity component in the movement of the value of production.

It follows that, even under the highly simplified conditions assumed here, we shall have two measures of movement of the quantum of production:

$$\frac{P_0 Q_1 - p_0 q_1}{P_0 Q_0 - p_0 q_0} \quad \text{and} \quad \frac{P_1 Q_1 - p_1 q_1}{P_1 Q_0 - p_1 q_0}$$

each comparing values added in which outputs and inputs have been valued at constant prices and hence abstracting from the effects of price changes. These two measures are in fact quantity indexes with different price weights. They are the Laspeyres and Paasche types respectively and they will in general give different results unless either relative quantities (ie here the technical input-output ratio) or relative prices (ie here the price of input relative to that of output) remain the same for the two periods under comparison. It follows that the quantum of production of a firm producing only one output with one input cannot be unambiguously defined. This is in sharp contrast with the situation in which one is measuring the quantum of output. For, although we cannot unambiguously define changes in the quantum of output when it refers to more than one product (thus, we have the two measures $\Sigma P_0 Q_1 / \Sigma P_0 Q_0$ and $\Sigma P_1 Q_1 / \Sigma P_1 Q_0$), nevertheless we can unambiguously define changes in the quantum of one output as Q_1 / Q_0. However, there is no simple ratio corresponding to Q_1 / Q_0 in the elementary case, when one is measuring quantum of production instead of quantum of output. This emphasises the basic conceptual difficulty in trying to measure quantum of production. The reason for this basic difficulty is that in measuring the quantum of production at least two goods must always be involved—one output and one input —so that one is immediately faced with a problem of weighting.

In practice, an individual firm will have usually more than one output and always more than one input, and the same applies *a fortiori* to an industry. However, in measuring the quantum of production, the same principle which was used in the elementary case can be applied, namely the comparison of values added in which outputs and inputs have been valued at constant prices. This immediately leads us to two possible formulae:

$$N_{01}^{\text{La}} = \frac{\Sigma P_0 Q_1 - \Sigma p_0 q_1}{\Sigma P_0 Q_0 - \Sigma p_0 q_0}$$

and

$$N_{01}^{\text{Pa}} = \frac{\Sigma P_1 Q_1 - \Sigma p_1 q_1}{\Sigma P_1 Q_0 - \Sigma p_1 q_0}$$

where N_{01}^{La} and N_{01}^{Pa} are indexes of the quantum of production of the Laspeyres and Paasche type respectively and the summations extend over all outputs and inputs of the industrial sector under consideration.[1] Like the simpler Laspeyres's and Paasche's index numbers of

---

[1] This type of formula is known as Geary's formula, having been proposed by R C Geary in a paper 'The Concept of Net Volume of Output with Special Reference to Irish Data', *Journal of the Royal Statistical Society*, Vol CVII, Parts III, IV, 1944, p 251. However, it was suggested earlier by R Wilson in a paper 'Prices, Quantities and Values', read to the Victorian Branch of the Economic Society of Australia and New Zealand in September 1937, and published as a pamphlet.

prices and outputs they do not in general yield the same numerical results when applied to the same data. Their divergence will be greater, the greater the dispersion in the movements of prices of outputs, quantities of outputs, prices of inputs and quantities of inputs. However, in practice, the two formulae should lead to fairly close results, provided the periods of comparison are not too far apart. These formulae can be applied to the measurement of the quantum of production of a single firm, a single industry, a group of industries or industry as a whole.

Let us suppose we have computed N_{01}^{La} indexes for individual industries and we wish to combine them into an index of industrial production as a whole. This can be done by adding the numerators and the denominators and obtaining

$$\frac{\sum[\Sigma P_0 Q_1 - \Sigma p_0 q_1]}{\sum[\Sigma P_0 Q_0 - \Sigma p_0 q_0]}$$

where the small Σs are summations over outputs and inputs within the individual industries and the large $\sum$s are summations of industries. Precisely the same result can be achieved by taking the arithmetic mean of the individual N_{01}^{La} indexes weighting them by base-year values added,[1] ie

$$\frac{\sum[N_{01}^{La}(\Sigma P_0 Q_0 - \Sigma p_0 q_0)]}{\sum[\Sigma P_0 Q_0 - \Sigma p_0 q_0]}$$

This latter approach is useful in connexion with the method of indicators discussed below.

If we have the N_{01}^{La}'s computed for all industries in the economy (including primary and tertiary industries as well as secondary industries), their combination in the manner outlined in the preceding paragraph will lead to the Laspeyres's index of movements in real gross domestic product. The outputs of one industry which are inputs of another will subtract out when the denominators and numerators are summed, leaving only final outputs. This shows that indexes of the quantum of production for particular industries can be interpreted as indexes of the contributions of the particular industries to real gross domestic product. It also shows how real gross domestic product can be measured in terms of the gross products of individual enterprises

---

[1] Compare section 11.7, p 453 above, on the combination of group indexes.

rather than in terms of final expenditure, which was the approach used in section 12.2 above.

There are two important considerations to bear in mind in using the above formulae. First, account should be taken, as far as possible, of any changes in the quality of outputs and inputs, of any diversification of qualities of outputs and inputs, and of the introduction of new outputs and inputs. This can be done, in theory at least, by introducing new items into the index, ie by treating different qualities as different goods. However, if one is using the N_{01}^{La} index, there may be some difficulty in ascertaining appropriate prices of the new items in the base year, when perhaps the items were not being produced in any appreciable volume, although it would usually be possible to estimate notional prices based on the price movements of allied items. Secondly, the indexes must not be allowed to be distorted by changes in the volume of work in progress. Suppose the qs represent actual intake of raw materials, etc into the factory, then if the Qs represent actual deliveries of outputs from the factory, the expression $\Sigma PQ - \Sigma pq$ might bear little relation to the quantum of work done. The deliveries might have been made from stock, or the inputs might be going into work-in-progress without any immediate effect on outputs. It is conceivable that the expression might even become negative. This difficulty can be readily overcome, in principle, by including in the Qs not deliveries from the factory, but completed production together with any uncompleted intermediate products (valued at appropriate prices) held by the factory at the end of the period under consideration, and by including in the qs not only intake of inputs, but also intermediate products held at the beginning of the period under consideration. This is consistent with the original definition of the gross product of a firm or industry.[1]

In computing an index of industrial production as a whole the area which the index is to cover must first be defined. Generally indexes of this kind are limited to the fields of secondary production. Building and construction is sometimes regarded as a doubtful item for inclusion. A more difficult problem arises in the field of repair work. Some repair work is clearly not carried out under industrial conditions, eg repair work connected with a service trade such as boot and shoe repairs, automobile maintenance, etc whereas other repair work such as ship and locomotive repair is. It is clear that there will always be a certain amount of blurring around the edges of any definition of secondary production.

At this point it is well to emphasise the limitations of indexes of

---

[1] Compare p 391 above.

industrial production. Indexes of industrial production suffer from the usual limitations of index numbers in that different formulae give different numerical results and the results of any given formula depend on the weighting system adopted. Moreover, the statistical material upon which they are based is usually imperfect and incomplete. Furthermore, apart from these factors, the concept of 'production' is surrounded by the same complexities as those referred to in section 12.1 above in connexion with the measurement of real gross domestic product (see pp 477–8). 'Production' in the economic sense cannot be interpreted as merely physical output but rather it must be conceived in terms of the satisfactions which are produced by physical output. Accordingly, indexes of production should be interpreted with caution. This applies particularly to comparisons over long periods of time.

Having decided on the scope of the index, the main task is to find means of filling in the terms in the formula. Suppose we direct our attention to the formula

$$N_{01}^{La} = \frac{\Sigma P_0 Q_1 - \Sigma p_0 q_1}{\Sigma P_0 Q_0 - \Sigma p_0 q_0}$$

If we knew the individual Ps, ps, Qs and qs, our task would be simple and straightforward but in practice there is seldom such a wealth of statistical material available and we must use approximate methods. There are two broad types of methods available. They are known as the *method of deflation* and the *method of indicators*.

12.4 Computation of an Index of Industrial Production by the Method of Deflation

We may here restrict ourselves to the consideration of an index for a particular industry, since the extension to industrial production as a whole is straightforward. We consider the formula

$$N_{01}^{La} = \frac{\Sigma P_0 Q_1 - \Sigma p_0 q_1}{\Sigma P_0 Q_0 - \Sigma p_0 q_0}$$

The object of the method of deflation is to estimate the terms in the numerator by deflating the current value added ($\Sigma P_1 Q_1 - \Sigma p_1 q_1$) by appropriate price indexes. Thus we estimate $\Sigma P_0 Q_1$ by $\Sigma P_1 Q_1 \div P_{01}$, where $\Sigma P_1 Q_1$ is the current value of output and P_{01} is an index of the relevant output prices, and we estimate $\Sigma p_0 q_1$ by $\Sigma p_1 q_1 \div p_{01}$, where $\Sigma p_1 q_1$ is the current value of input and p_{01} is an index of the relevant input prices. If

$$P_{01} = \frac{\Sigma P_1 Q_1}{\Sigma P_0 Q_1} \text{ and } p_{01} = \frac{\Sigma p_1 q_1}{\Sigma p_0 q_1}$$

ie if the price indexes are of the Paasche type and if they are coextensive with the fields of production under consideration, the estimates will give the correct values. But if sufficient information were available to construct such indexes, $\Sigma P_0 Q_1 - \Sigma p_0 q_1$ could be computed directly and there would be no point in using the method of deflation. In practice, the price index numbers used will be based on only a portion of the field and will seldom be of the Paasche type, so that only an approximation to N_{01}^{La} can be obtained. Clearly, the method requires at least a knowledge of $\Sigma P_1 Q_1 - \Sigma p_1 q_1$ as well as of $\Sigma P_0 Q_0 - \Sigma p_0 q_0$ and will be feasible only if regular statistics of current value added are collected and if appropriate price indexes can be constructed. An example of an application of this method now follows.

Our object is to estimate the movement in the quantum of production of the Australian tobacco industry between 1969–70 and 1971–72.[1] We wish to obtain an estimate of

$$N_{01}^{La} = \frac{\Sigma P_0 Q_1 - \Sigma p_0 q_1}{\Sigma P_0 Q_0 - \Sigma p_0 q_0}$$

The data for the denominator are available and our task is to estimate the numerator. We do this by considering output and input separately. We have 1971–72 values and we must calculate a price index number with which to deflate these values, ie we must calculate P_{01}, so that we can use $\Sigma P_1 Q_1 \div P_{01}$ as an estimate of $\Sigma P_0 Q_1$.

We have quantity and value data of the two main items of output. We do not have price data but by dividing the value of output by the quantity, we get what are called *unit values*. If an item of output is homogeneous, its unit value and its price are the same thing, but if the item contains different qualities, then unit value is the price of a composite unit and movements in unit value may not correctly reflect price movements if the relative importance of the different qualities is changing. However, since we have no price data, we must make do with unit values. Since the index-number formula should be of the Paasche type, it is necessary to compare 1971–72 unit values weighted by 1971–72 quantities (ie 1971–72 total values) with 1969–70 unit values weighted by 1971–72 quantities. The calculations are performed in Table 12.2.

[1] The data for our example are from Australian Bureau of Statistics: *Manufacturing Commodities—Principal Articles Produced* (Ref 12.26), 1968–69 and 1969–70, p 25; 1971–72 and 1972–73, p 29; *Manufacturing Establishments—Details of Operations by Industry Class* (Ref 12.29), 1969–70, pp 8, 116, 132–133; 1971–72, pp 6, 97, 112–113; *Manufacturing Commodities—Principal Materials Used* (Ref 12.32), 1968–69 and 1969–70, p 13; 1971–72, p 23.

Table 12.2

COMPUTATION OF OUTPUT PRICE INDEX

Output	Unit	1969–70			1971–72		1969–70 Unit Values Weighted by 1971–72 Quantities (c)
		Quantity	Value	Unit Value (a)	Quantity	Value (b)	
		'000	$'000	$	'000	$'000	$'000
		(1)	(2)	(3)	(4)	(5)	(6)
Cigarettes and Cigars	kg	26 762	176 030	6·5776	29 312	212 520	192 803
Tobacco— Flake and Ready Rubbed	kg	3 119	13 329	4·2735	3 038	12 620	12 983
						225 140	205 786

(a) Col (3) = col (2) ÷ col (1).
(b) Col (5) is identically 1971–72 unit values weighted by 1971–72 quantities.
(c) Col (6) = col (3) × col (4).

From the above table we have as our index of output prices for 1971–72, with base 1969–70 = 100

$$(225\,140 \div 205\,786) \times 100 = 109{\cdot}40$$

The coverage of this index is good, for whereas the total value of output in 1969–70 was $192 061 000, the sum of column (2) indicates that the value of the principal items of output was $189 359 000. The method used assumes that the prices of items omitted from the index move in the same way as the average of the included items. To estimate the value of 1971–72 output valued at 1969–70 prices we divide the 1971–72 value by our index number. The latter value (see Table 12.5 below) is $228 529 000 so that the required figure is $228 529 000 ÷ 1·094 = $208 893 000. The ratio of this figure to the value of output in 1969–70 (ie the ratio $\Sigma P_0 Q_1 / \Sigma P_0 Q_0$) gives an index of quantum of output (sometimes called *gross output*). In this case we have

$$(208\,893\,000 \div 192\,061\,000) \times 100 = 108{\cdot}76$$

as the 1971–72 index for quantum of output, with base 1969–70 = 100.

On the input side, we require a price index number of inputs, p_{01}, so that we can use $\Sigma p_1 q_1 \div p_{01}$ as an estimate of $\Sigma p_0 q_1$. It is convenient to divide the inputs into three groups and deflate each separately. These groups are materials, fuels and containers. The first two groups are treated in a manner similar to that for output above. The quantum of containers is assumed to move in the same way as the index of gross output computed in the preceding paragraph. The calculation of the price indexes for materials and fuels are set out in the two tables below. The coverage of the materials-input price index is not as good as the coverage of the output and fuels indexes, for whereas the total value of materials and supplies used by the tobacco industry in 1969–70 was $89 923 000, the sum of column (2) in Table 12.3 indicates that the value of the principal materials included in the index is $70 159 000. However, as in the case of the output and fuels indexes we shall assume that the price movements of the omitted materials are not appreciably different from the average movement of the included items.

Table 12.3

COMPUTATION OF MATERIALS—INPUT PRICE INDEX

Materials Input	Unit	1969–70		1971–72			1969–70 Unit Values Weighted by 1971–72 Quantities
		Quantity	Value	Unit Value	Quantity	Value	
		'000	$'000	$	'000	$'000	$'000
		(1)	(2)	(3)	(4)	(5)	(6)
Tobacco— Australian Cured Leaf	kg	13 805	39 153	2·8361	14 065	39 000	39 890
Imported Cured Leaf	kg	11 780	31 006	2·6321	13 175	28 315	34 678
						67 315	74 568

The materials-input price index number is (67 315 ÷ 74 568) × 100 = 90·27.

Table 12.4

COMPUTATION OF FUELS—INPUT PRICE INDEX

Fuels Input	Unit	1969–70		1971–72			1969–70 Unit Values Weighted by 1971–72 Quantities
		Quantity	Value	Unit Value	Quantity	Value	
		tonnes	$'000	$	tonnes	$'000	$'000
		(1)	(2)	(3)	(4)	(5)	
Black coal	tonne	8 292	77	9·2861	9 382	95	87·1
Fuel Oil	tonne	4 066	79	19·4294	4 473	126	86·9
Electricity	—	—	527	—	—	636	623·5 (a)
						857	797·5

(a) This figure is obtained by deflating 1971–72 value by the electricity component of the Wholesale Price Index of Materials Used in Manufacturing Industry. In 1971–72 the value of this index stood at 102·00 (1969–70 = 100), and we have 636·0 ÷ 1·02 = 623·5.

The fuels-input price index number is (857 ÷ 797·5) × 100 = 107·46.

The calculation of the index of quantum of production (ie of quantum of value added, sometimes called *net output*) is given below.

Table 12.5

COMPUTATION OF INDEXES OF QUANTUM OF OUTPUT, INPUT AND PRODUCTION BY METHOD OF DEFLATION

	Values		Price Indexes (Base: 1969–70 = 100)	Estimate of 1971–72 Quantities Valued at 1969–70 Prices $'000 (a)	Indexes of Quantum (Base: 1969–70 = 100) (b)
	1969–70 $'000	1971–72 $'000			
	(1)	(2)	(3)	(4)	(5)
Output	192 061	228 529	109·40 (d)	208 893	108·76
Materials	89 923	84 615	90·27 (e)	93 735	
Fuels	714	871	107·46 (f)	811	
Containers	20 287	26 011	—	22 064 (c)	
Input	110 924 (g)	111 497 (g)		116 610 (g)	105·13
Value added	81 137	117 032		92 283	113·73

(a) Col (4) = (col (2) ÷ col (3)) × 100.
(b) Col (5) = (col (4) ÷ col (1)) × 100.
(c) Quantum of containers is assumed to move with gross output, so that we have 20 287 × 1·0876 = 22 064.
(d) from Table 12.2 above.
(e) from Table 12.3 above.
(f) from Table 12.4 above.
(g) The sum of the preceding three lines.

From the above table we see that the quantum of production (value added) in the tobacco industry rose by nearly 14 per cent between 1969–70 and 1971–72. This is against a rise of 44 per cent in current values added ($81 137 000 to $117 032 000), some of which was a price rise. Output rose in quantum by 9 per cent, but input rose by only 5 per cent; consequently value added or net output rose by appreciably more than the rise in gross output, and the different movements in quanta of output and production are thus explained. The relatively large difference between the indexes of quantum of gross output and value added in this example illustrates the danger of using an index of quantum of gross output as an approximation to one of quantum of value added.

12.5 Computation of an Index of Industrial Production by the Method of Indicators

The basis of the method of indicators is the breaking up of the industrial area under consideration into small sectors for which the values added in the base period are known and the estimation of what such values added would be in subsequent periods (if they were valued at constant base period prices) by marking them up by indicators of the movements in the quanta of production under consideration. The indicators may, for example, be movements in physical outputs, or in physical inputs or in employment. Thus, if V_0 is the value added in period 0 in a small sector (ie $V_0 = \Sigma P_0 Q_0 - \Sigma p_0 q_0$, where the summations are over the items contained in the small sector), and I_{01} is an indicator of the movement of the quantum of production from period 0 to period 1 in the small sector, we shall have $I_{01} V_0$ as an estimate of the value added in period 1 at constant period 0 prices (ie as an estimate of $\Sigma P_0 Q_1 - \Sigma p_0 q_1$). Aggregating small sectors, we obtain as an index of the quantum of production for the larger field

$$N_{01} = \frac{\Sigma I_{01} V_0}{\Sigma V_0}$$

This index, which is a weighted arithmetic mean of indicators, is an estimate of

$$\frac{\sum [\Sigma P_0 Q_1 - \Sigma p_0 q_1]}{\sum [\Sigma P_0 Q_0 - \Sigma p_0 q_0]}$$

$$= \frac{\sum \left[\dfrac{\Sigma P_0 Q_1 - \Sigma p_0 q_1}{\Sigma P_0 Q_0 - \Sigma p_0 q_0} (\Sigma P_0 Q_0 - \Sigma p_0 q_0) \right]}{\sum [\Sigma P_0 Q_0 - \Sigma p_0 q_0]}$$

where the small Σs are summations over outputs and inputs within small sectors and the large $\sum$s are summations of small sectors.[1] It will be appreciated that the I_{01}s are used as approximations to

$$\frac{\Sigma P_0 Q_1 - \Sigma p_0 q_1}{\Sigma P_0 Q_0 - \Sigma p_0 q_0}$$

for small sectors in the above formula.

Accordingly, the principal difference between the method of deflation and the method of indicators is that in the former method

$$\frac{\Sigma P_0 Q_1 - \Sigma p_0 q_1}{\Sigma P_0 Q_0 - \Sigma p_0 q_0}$$

is estimated directly in detail, whereas in the latter it is approximated by an indicator series. The method of indicators can be used when the values added in some base period are known and indicators of quanta of production in small sectors of industry can be constructed. It is,

[1] Compare p 489 above.

in general, a more approximate method than the method of deflation, but is usually more practicable and is the commonest method found in practice.

There are many possible indicators. Some will be more satisfactory than others but generally the actual choice of an indicator depends on the availability of suitable statistics. The main indicators are: output series, input series and employment series. These will be discussed in turn.

1. Output Indicators

If we are concerned with a small sector which produces only one product and we have data on the volume of output of that product, then clearly we can use this series as an indicator. Such an indicator has one big advantage—the series is itself in physical terms and there is no price problem involved. Here the indicator will be Q_1/Q_0, where the Qs refer to the volume of output of the commodity under consideration. However, even in this case there are two limitations to be noted. First, we are using the series as an indicator of work done or quantum of production and not as a measure of quantum of output, which is what the series really is. Any change in the technical relations between input and output will upset its validity. Moreover, if the indicator relates to deliveries or sales of output, any accumulation of work-in-progress will make it understate changes in the quantum of production. Finally, changes in quality will tend to be ignored.

Most small sectors will in fact be producing more than one product. Sometimes it will be possible to add these products directly. This will be the case where their unit of measurement is homogeneous. Thus we might have a series of 'square metres of wool textiles'. This area would consist of textiles of very different types. These different types may have very different value added contents. Clearly, an increase in area of 10 per cent will involve a quite different increase in quantum of production in the case where all types of textiles increase by 10 per cent from that case where the increase in area is mainly in the coarser forms of cloth. Strictly speaking, such an indicator series would be valid only if the average value added per square metre (measured in constant base-year prices) remained constant. Frequently, however, there will be many quite distinct products produced by a 'small sector', which cannot be added. Data may not be available for many of them and in that case we may be forced to assume that movements in the output of these items can be represented by movements in the output of items for which we have data. If we do have data for several items, the question of adding the quite distinct items arises. This can be done by using prices to determine the equivalences of different physical units and using an index of physical output, eg $\Sigma P_0 Q_1 / \Sigma P_0 Q_0$, as an indicator. The use of such an indicator will not be completely valid if the movements in the Qs do not properly reflect movements in the quantum of production because of changes in the technical relations between the various inputs and outputs.

2. Input Indicators

In some sectors movements in the quantum of production can be indicated by movements in inputs of materials, etc. The main advantage of input indicators, when available, is that for many industries the number of principal materials used is quite small. However, it can be readily appreciated that input indicators suffer from the same sort of limitations as do output indicators.

3. Employment Indicators

The relative movement in the number of persons employed in the small sector under consideration can be used as an indicator. Such employment indicators have the great advantage of being directly related to work done and hence avoid the problems associated with changes in work-in-progress. However, it is necessary to adjust employment series to take into account such factors as holidays and changes in the length of the working week. Even so, the possibility of overtime and slack time may upset an employment series as an indicator of the quantum of production. The principal disadvantage of using employment indicators is that they assume that labour productivity (ie value added measured in constant base-year prices per unit of employment[1]) is constant. For short-period comparisons this may be unimportant, but it becomes increasingly important in the long run.

An example of an application of the method of indicators now follows. This example makes use of a variety of types of indicators for illustrative purposes. Our object is to estimate the movement in the quantum of production of the Australian beverage industry as between 1969–70 and 1971–72[2]. The industry can be divided into four small sectors, namely soft drinks and cordials, malting, brewing, distilling and wine-making. The formula to be used is

$$N_{01} = \frac{\Sigma I_{01} V_0}{\Sigma V_0}$$

[1] See section 12.7, p 501 below.
[2] The data for Table 12.6 to 12.8 are from Australian Bureau of Statistics: *Manufacturing Commodities—Principal Articles Produced* (Ref 12.26), 1968–69 and 1969–70, p 24; 1971–72 and 1972–73, pp 28–29: *Manufacturing Establishments—Details of Operations by Industry Class* (Ref 12.29), 1969–70, p 8; 1971–72, p 6; and *Manufacturing Commodities—Principal Materials Used* (Ref 12.32), 1968–69 and 1969–70, p 7; 1971–72, p 6.

For indicator series we use employment for soft drinks and cordials; physical input of barley in tonnes for malting; physical output of ale, stout, and beer in litres for brewing. For distilling and wine-making we use an index of physical output obtained by combining the outputs of fortified wines, unfortified wines and potable spirits, using base-period unit values as weights. The calculation of the first three indicators is shown in Table 12.6 below, and that of the fourth in Table 12.7.

Table 12.6
COMPUTATION OF INDICATORS

Small Sector	Indicator Series	Units	Value of Indicator Series		Indicator for 1971–72 on 1969–70 base (a)
			1969–70	1971–72	
			(1)	(2)	(3)
Soft drinks, cordials, syrups, etc	Employment	persons	9 173	9 672	1·054
Malting	Input of barley	'000 tonnes	226·7	249·1	1·099
Brewing	Output of beer, stout and ale	mill. litres	1·555	1·665	1·071

(a) Col (3) = col (2) ÷ col (1).

We must now combine the four indicators by weighting them with 1969–70 values added. This is done in Table 12.8.

The index of the quantum of production for the beverage industry for 1971–72, with base 1969–70 = 100, is then

$$(202\,453 \div 194\,443) \times 100 = 104\cdot12$$

Table 12.7
COMPUTATION OF INDICATOR

Output	Unit	1969–70			1971–72	
		Quantity	Value	Unit Value (a)	Quantity	Quantity Valued at 1969–70 Unit Values (b)
		'000	$'000	$	'000	$'000
		(1)	(2)	(3)	(4)	(5)
Fortified wines	l	62 694	21 226	0·3386	58 237	19 720
Unfortified wines	l	89 312	32 932	0·3687	94 387	34 800
Potable spirits	l	27 996	15 247	0·5446	17 413	9 483
			69 405			64 003

(a) Col (3) = col (2) ÷ col (1).
(b) Col (5) = col (4) × col (3).

The distilling and wine-making indicator is 64 003 ÷ 69 405 = 0·922.

Table 12.8

COMPUTATION OF INDEX OF QUANTUM OF PRODUCTION
BY METHOD OF INDICATORS

Small Sector	Value Added in 1969–70 $'000	Indicator of Movement in Quantum of Production 1969–70 to 1971–72	Estimate of Value Added in 1971–72 at 1969–70 Prices (a) $'000
	(1)	(2)	(3)
Soft drinks, cordials, syrups, etc	66 382	1·054	69 967
Malting	8 362	1·099	9 190
Brewing	86 801	1·071	92 964
Distilling and wine-making	32 898	0·922	30 332
Beverage Industry	194 443		202 453

(a) Col (3) = col (1) × col (2).

Before concluding this section some comments are necessary on the treatment of small sectors within the industrial field for which no indicators or their equivalents exist. Three alternative treatments are:

1. The coverage of the index of industrial production under consideration can be defined to exclude these particular sectors. This is unsatisfactory, for although it results in a more accurate description of the index actually computed, it may mean that the field covered is ragged and does not cover industrial production in the usual sense.

2. The index can be calculated leaving the particular sectors right out of account but the coverage can be defined, formally, to include all industrial production. This is tantamount to assuming that the excluded sectors move in the same way as the average movement of the included sectors. Under (1) and (2) the index has precisely the same value but the interpretation of it differs.

3. The sectors for which data are lacking can be included both formally and statistically by assuming that their quanta of production behave in the same fashion as those of some other sector or sectors or part of a sector. This can be done by adding to the weight attached to the representing indicator an amount for the weight of the represented sector. This may be a much more reasonable procedure than that under (2), but it is necessary to make certain that there is some rational basis for selecting the representing indicator.

References to Australian indexes of quantum of production are contained in Appendix B.5, pp 610–13 below.

12.6 Comparisons over Short and Long Periods

Indexes of industrial production are usually required for the purpose of measuring both short-period and long-period movements in the quantum of production. As far as the former are concerned, monthly indexes are the ideal. The question then arises whether corrections ought to be made for the varying number of working days per month. This largely depends on the purpose of the index. If we wish to measure the actual course of production an unadjusted series will be required, but if we are trying to discern trends in the monthly figures, then it will be necessary to correct the series for the varying number of working days per month (and particularly for Easter, which comes in different months in different years). Further, it may be useful to calculate an index of seasonal variation on the basis of past experience and de-seasonalise the index of production. But the limitations of indexes of seasonal variation must be borne in mind (see p 384 above).

As far as long-period comparisons are concerned, the main difficulty is, as usual, one of weighting. If the index is calculated with fixed base-year weights, these weights will sooner or later get out of date, ie the base-year relative prices at which outputs and inputs are being valued will cease to be relevant. The influence of changes in relative prices can be seen by computing both the Laspeyres and Paasche forms of the index and comparing the results. The greater the changes in relative prices, the more likely that the two indexes will be far apart.

In practice, it is customary to compute indexes of industrial production by the method of indicators with fixed weights, the weights being base-year values added. Indicators can often be obtained in monthly series, in which cases a monthly index can be computed. For comparisons extending over a few years the use of fixed weights in this way may be quite satisfactory. But the weights should be revised from time to time as data on values added become available. Thus, if, for example, censuses of production are taken every five years, the weights can be revised every five years. This will mean a new index every five years, but quasi-continuity of the indexes can be achieved by a chaining process (see section 11.11, p 469 above). Not only should the weights be revised from time to time, but the possibility of using new and better indicators should always be borne in mind.

12.7 Measurement of Labour Productivity

Indexes of industrial production, whether of production as a whole or of particular industries, are often used in conjunction with employment series to measure labour productivity. According to the purpose for which the measurement of productivity is required, the employment figures used may refer to the available labour supply or the numbers actually in work or the number of man-hours worked per period under consideration.

We first consider productivity in reference to industrial production as a whole. If we write L_0 for the employment figure (however defined) in period 0, average value of production per employment unit in period 0 at period 0 prices will be

$$\frac{\sum[\Sigma P_0 Q_0 - \Sigma p_0 q_0]}{L_0}$$

where the small Σs are summations over outputs and inputs within individual industries and the large $\sum$s are summations of industries. Similarly average value of production per employment unit in period 1 at period 0 prices will be

$$\frac{\sum[\Sigma P_0 Q_1 - \Sigma p_0 q_1]}{L_1}$$

An index of productivity can be obtained by dividing the latter measure by the former. This reduces to

$$\frac{N_{01}}{L_{01}}$$

where N_{01} is an index of the quantum of production for industry as a whole and $L_{01} = \dfrac{L_1}{L_0}$ is an index of employment.

This index of productivity measures *overall productivity* and is affected both by changes in productivity in individual industries and by changes in the relative importance of industries. Thus, even though productivity in all individual industries rose, the index could fall if activity shifted from industries with higher than average to ones with lower than average productivity. Often, however, we may be concerned to see how productivity has moved quite apart from shifts in activity, ie we may wish to measure the first of the two factors mentioned above. For want of a better term we may call this *productivity proper*.

An index of productivity proper must be based on the movements in productivity of individual industries. For a single industry, productivity in periods 0 and 1 respectively, at period 0 prices, will be given by

$$\frac{\Sigma P_0 Q_0 - \Sigma p_0 q_0}{l_0} \quad \text{and} \quad \frac{\Sigma P_0 Q_1 - \Sigma p_0 q_1}{l_1}$$

where l_0 and l_1 are the employment figures for the industry in periods 0 and 1 respectively. If we combine these productivities for individual industries, weighting them by their base-period employments, ie by l_0, we shall obtain the index

$$\frac{\sum\left[\dfrac{\Sigma P_0 Q_1 - \Sigma p_0 q_1}{l_1} \times l_0\right]}{\sum[\Sigma P_0 Q_0 - \Sigma p_0 q_0]}$$

This is an index of productivity proper. The numerator is the value of production in period 1 valued at period 0 prices which the period 0 employment units would have produced if they had exhibited period 1 productivity in each industry. Consequently, this index eliminates the effects of changes in the distribution of employment.[1]

Table 12.9 gives hypothetical data to illustrate the points made above.

Table 12.9

Industry	Value Added in Period 0 at Period 0 Prices $'000	Employment in Period 0	Productivity in Period 0 (a) $'000	Value Added in Period 1 at Period 0 Prices $'000	Employment in Period 1	Productivity in Period 1 (b) $'000
	(1)	(2)	(3)	(4)	(5)	(6)
I	2 000	1 000	2·00	1 435	700	2·05
II	3 000	1 000	3·00	4 960	1 600	3·10
All	5 000	2 000	2·50	6 395	2 300	2·78

(a) Col (3) = col (1) ÷ col (2).
(b) Col (6) = col (4) ÷ col (5).

An index of overall productivity for period 1, with base-period 0 = 100 is given by

$$(2\cdot78 \div 2\cdot50) \times 100 = 111$$

This index contains not only the effect of changes in productivity in the two industries, but also the effect on overall productivity of the change in the distribution of employment. An index of productivity proper can be calculated by weighting the productivities for the two industries by their base-period employments. The resulting index is 103. Thus productivity proper has increased by 3 per cent, whereas overall productivity has increased by 11 per cent. The excess of the latter over the former is due to the shift in relative employment from

---

[1] The same index can be obtained by weighting the movements in productivity of individual industries (ie the ratios of the two expressions on the first half of this page) by their base-period values added (ie by $\Sigma P_0 Q_0 - \Sigma p_0 q_0$).

industry I to industry II, ie from an industry with lower than average to one with a higher than average productivity.

It should be emphasised that both changes in productivity proper and shifts in the distribution of employment are important in affecting the overall productivity of an economy. Indeed, the finer the classification of the industries of an economy, the greater will be the contribution of shifts in employment to any given change in overall productivity.

This section has been confined to a technical consideration of the formulae for measuring productivity. It should be hardly necessary to add that indexes of productivity, being based on indexes of quantum of production, are subject to the same limitations as those indexes (see pp 478–9 and 490 above) and should be interpreted with caution.

CHAPTER 13

DEMOGRAPHY

13.1 Demography and Demographic Data

Demography is the study of *the measurement of human populations*. It studies the size of a group of people, how the number in the group has changed in the past and how it is likely to change in the future. Demography is mainly concerned with the growth of populations, but it also covers the distribution of the population by industry, occupation, geographical area and so on. In fact the interests of demography are at least coextensive with the population census and in some respects go beyond it. This chapter is devoted to the techniques by which measurements of population and, in particular, measurements of population growth can be made.

It is hardly necessary to emphasise the important part which a study of population movements plays in the social sciences. The balance between population and resources is a problem which has been of great interest to economists since the days of Malthus, and interest in it has been revived today in the study of the economics of the so-called under-developed areas. This balance exerts a great influence on the standard of living enjoyed in any given area, and a knowledge of how population growth has behaved in the past and how it is likely to behave in the future is of the first importance. Populations in different parts of the world grow at different rates, and these differential rates determine very largely the distribution of world population, with its political and strategic implications. A knowledge of the statistical techniques of population measurements is basic to any general analysis of population questions.

Data on population are acquired periodically through censuses and continuously through birth and death registrations and marriage and migration records. These data enable records to be compiled of the numbers of population, births, deaths, marriages and migrants. In addition, censuses usually provide information on the distribution of the population by sex, age, marital status, duration of marriage and number of previous issue. Likewise, birth registration usually provides information on place of birth, sex, age of parents, legitimacy, number of previous issue and their sexes and ages, father's occupation and birthplace of parents; and death registration provides information on place of death, sex, age, marital status, number of previous issue, birthplace, occupation and cause of death. Similar information is also usually collected with respect to marriages and migrants.

As far as data on births are concerned, several points should be noted. Most published data on births refer to *live-births* only, *still-births* being shown separately, if at all. The ratio of still-births to live-births varies from country to country, but in the last ten years in Australia, the United Kingdom and the United States it has been from about 9 to 16 still-births per 1000 live-births. Births are usually classified by *date of registration* and not by *date of birth*. Thus in Australia in 1974 there were 245 177 births. This was the number of births registered in 1974 and not the number actually occurring. However, as long as the lag between birth and registration is small, the number registered in a year will be very close to the number actually taking place. The distinction between number of *confinements* and number of *births* should be noted, the difference being due to confinements resulting in *multiple live-births*. Likewise the division of births into *nuptial* and *ex-nuptial* (ie legitimate and illegitimate) should be noted.

The following table illustrates the relation between the numbers of confinements and births:

Table 13.1
CONFINEMENTS AND BIRTHS—AUSTRALIA, 1974 (a)

	Confinements	Births
Nuptial—		
Single	217 455	217 455
Multiple	2 174	4 314
Ex-nuptial—		
Single	22 982	22 982
Multiple	218	426
Total	242 829	245 177

(a) Excludes confinements where the births were of still-born children only.
Source: Australian Bureau of Statistics: *Births* 1974 (Ref. 4.4), p 15

Births are frequently classified by geographical area. Such a classification is one by *place of birth*. In border areas this may differ considerably from a classification by *usual residence of mother* and the latter is often the more relevant classification.[1]

[1] The case of the Australian Capital Territory provides an interesting illustration as shown by Table 13.2 (footnote continued next page):

As far as deaths are concerned, the terms *infant deaths* and *neo-natal deaths* should be noted. They refer respectively to deaths of children aged under one year and under one month. Neither includes still-births. The term *maternal deaths* refers to deaths of females from causes arising in childbirth.

13.2 Measurement of Total Population

Population at a Date

Total population is usually expressed as at a date, eg the Australian population as at the census taken on 30 June 1966, was 11 599 498. The total population measured at a census is usually very accurate in advanced countries. In any case, it is the most accurate information we can get, and we take it as being correct. However, censuses are taken only every so often—usually every five or ten years, and consequently it is necessary to make *inter-censal estimates* of the total population.

Since populations increase by:

(a) natural increase, ie the excess of births over deaths; and

(b) net migration, ie the excess of immigration over emigration, we need only add the figures of this year's natural increase and net migration to last year's total population to get an estimate of the total for this year. Table 13.3 on p 508 illustrates this.

How accurate are intercensal estimates? We have an opportunity of checking them whenever a census is taken. For example, censuses were taken in Australia at 30 June 1966 and 1971. At the 1966 Census

Table 13.2

BIRTHS PER 1000 PER ANNUM OF POPULATION IN THE AUSTRALIAN CAPITAL TERRITORY

	By Place of Birth	By Usual Residence of Mother
1931–35	15·8	19·5
1941–45	26·8	23·1
1946–50	37·9	29·1
1951–55	32·3	28·4
1956–60	30·3	30·3

Source: Australian Bureau of Statistics, *Year Book*, No. 47, 1961, p 339

Before there were extensive hospital facilities in the Australian Capital Territory, many Australian Capital Territory mothers had their confinements in Queanbeyan in New South Wales, just over the border. With improved hospitalisation in 1939 this practice was reversed, and many New South Wales mothers living near the border had their confinements in Canberra. The situation was again reversed in 1952, when improved maternity accommodation was provided in Queanbeyan. Clearly in this case, classification of births by place of birth is misleading.

the total population was 11 599 498. Casting this forward by adding natural increase and net migration year by year, the intercensal estimate at 30 June 1971 was 12 811 076.

Table 13.3
ESTIMATE OF TOTAL POPULATION OF AUSTRALIA AT 30 JUNE 1971

Population at 30/6/70 (Intercensal estimate)		12 551 700
Births registered 1/7/70–30/6/71	271 295	
Deaths registered 1/7/70–30/6/71	113 338	
Natural increase		157 957
Net recorded migration 1/7/70–30/6/71		101 419
Estimated population at 30/6/71		12 811 076

Source: Australian Bureau of Statistics: *Quarterly Summary of Australian Statistics*, No. 282, 1971, p 2

The 1971 Census revealed the true figure to be 12 755 638. The intercensal estimate was thus shown to be 55 438 too high—a surplus of about 0·4 per cent or an average of about 0·08 per cent per annum over the five years between the two censuses. This surplus can possibly be attributed to inaccuracies in migration records. Given the results of the 1971 Census, we know that our intercensal estimates between 1966 and 1971 were too high, so we must adjust them. This can be done by marking down the recorded annual increases in the intercensal years by the proportion in which the census total increase over the five years fell short of the recorded total increase.

Mean Population

In a census a population is counted on a particular day. Similarly, intercensal estimates are estimates of the population as at particular dates. If we have an annual figure (eg annual births or annual primary production) which we wish to relate to the population (eg to obtain annual births per 1000 of the population or annual primary production *per capita*), we must consider whether it is appropriate to relate an annual figure which has been built up over the course of a year to a population figure measured at a particular date. In fact, it is not appropriate to do this. We must always relate things to what is relevant. If we have an annual figure built up over the course of the year, we must relate it not to the population at a date but to the *mean population* existing over the course of the year.

The calculation of the mean population for a year is in principle quite simple. If we knew the population on each day of the year, we could add up all the figures and divide by 365 in order to get the mean population.[1] In practice, we do not have all this information. Usually the most we have are quarterly intercensal estimates as at the end of quarters. Suppose we know that

Date	Size of Population
31 December—	a
31 March—	b
30 June—	c
30 September—	d
31 December—	e

and we wish to estimate the mean population for the calendar year. Our data are illustrated graphically in Fig 13.1.

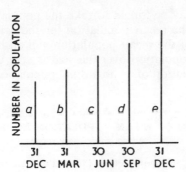

Fig 13.1

If we knew how the population had changed within quarters, so that we could draw a curve through the tops of the five ordinates in the diagram to represent its track, the mean population would be given by the average ordinate under the curve. We do not have this information, so we must make reasonable assumptions. If we assume that within each quarter the population has increased steadily, so that a straight line joining the tops of a and b would represent the track of population during the first quarter, etc, then the following formula will give an estimate of mean population:

$$\text{Mean population} = \frac{a + 2b + 2c + 2d + e}{8}$$

However, a further refinement leading to a smoother movement over the year is to assume that the tops of a, b and c are joined by a parabola

---

[1] In theory we should need to know the population continuously at every point of time within the year.

and the tops of *c*, *d* and *e* by another parabola, and these parabolas represent the track of population during the year. This gives the following formula:

$$\text{Mean population} = \frac{a + 4b + 2c + 4d + e}{12}$$

This formula is used by the Australian Statistician in calculating mean annual population for Australia. It is the most satisfactory of the formulae given here. Frequently, however, quarterly data are not available. If we know the population only at the end of years, we may have to take the simple arithmetic mean of end-of-year populations, ie

$$\text{Mean population} = \frac{a + e}{2}$$

Alternatively we may be forced to take the population as at 30 June as an estimate of the mean population for the calendar year. These various estimates of the mean population will all be close unless the rate of change of population over the year is very uneven. Table 13.4 illustrates the calculation of mean annual population.

Table 13.4

CALCULATION OF MEAN POPULATION AUSTRALIA, 1974

Date	Population P	Linear Method		Parabolic Method		End-of-year Data Only	
		W (a)	W × P	W (a)	W × P	W (a)	W × P
31/12/73	13 268 600	1	13 268 600	1	13 268 600	1	13 268 600
31/3/74	13 359 000	2	26 718 000	4	53 436 000		
30/6/74	13 338 300	2	26 676 600	2	26 676 600		
30/9/74	13 415 800	2	26 831 600	4	53 663 200		
31/12/74	13 485 000	1	13 485 000	1	13 485 000	1	13 485 000
		8	106 979 800	12	160 529 400	2	26 753 600

(*a*) Weights in formula.

Method	Mean Population
Linear	106 979 800 ÷ 8 = 13 372 475
Parabolic	160 529 400 ÷ 12 = 13 377 450
End-of-year	26 753 600 ÷ 2 = 13 376 800
Mid-year estimate	13 338 300

Source: Australian Bureau of Statistics: *Monthly Review of Business Statistics*, No. 452, 1976, p 2

It should be noted that semi-logarithmic charts are very useful for illustrating the movements of total population over time. Such a chart is shown in Fig 2.12 on p 28 above.

13.3 Sex and Age Distribution

Census Results

A classification of the population by sex and by age is usually obtained from censuses. Thus we have:

Table 13.5

**SEX AND AGE DISTRIBUTION OF AUSTRALIAN POPULATION
CENSUS 30th JUNE 1971**

Age Last Birthday	Males	Females	Persons
Under 1 year	130 673	125 501	256 174
1 year	125 251	119 433	244 684
2 years	126 524	121 533	248 057
3 years	121 907	116 106	238 013
4 years	121 647	114 867	236 514
5 years	118 854	113 601	232 455
6 years	121 214	114 945	236 159
.	.	.	.
.	.	.	.
.	.	.	.
.	.	.	.
All Ages	6 412 711	6 342 927	12 755 638

Source: Australian Bureau of Statistics: 1971 *Census Bulletin* (Ref 2.83.9), p 1

This is a frequency distribution of the population classified by sex and by single age groups. It tells us that at 30 June 1971, there were 130 673 males aged 0 and under 1; 125 251 aged 1 and under 2, etc.

The age distribution as it actually emerges from a census is called the *recorded* age distribution. It records the number of persons in each age group who stated themselves to be a certain age (or, in the case of children, whose parents stated them to be a certain age). But some people fail to state their ages in answering the census questionnaire. Thus the recorded age distribution would contain a group entitled 'age not stated'. In the Australian 1971 Census whenever a missing age was encountered on a census schedule the person was first allocated to a range of ages by using the other information on the schedule and was then allocated at random to a single age group within that range. Such a procedure gives what is called the *adjusted* age distribution. It contains no 'age not stated' group and is the one given in Tables 13.5 and 13.6.

The adjusted age distribution can be expected to portray more nearly the true age distribution of the population than the recorded distribution. However, it is by no means absolutely accurate because of misstatement of their ages by people at the census. These misstatements are of two kinds: there is a persistent bias on the part of some groups of people towards overstating or understating their ages; and second, there is a tendency to state ages to the nearest ten, and to a lesser extent to the nearest five or nearest even number. It is difficult to detect misstatements of the first kind, but those of the second kind are revealed by an examination of the adjusted age distribution. For example, at the 1971 Census, 74 925 females stated their age as 49, 78 065 stated their age as 50, 65 413 stated their age as 51, and a similar concentration occurred at age 60. Such concentrations may be smoothed out by allocating the excess numbers to the age groups on both sides. Various methods are available—some mathematical ones being quite complicated. The resulting age distribution is called the *graduated age distribution*. The graduated distribution attempts to smooth out the artificial bumps and to present more accurately the true age distri-

Table 13.6

ADJUSTED SEX AND AGE DISTRIBUTION OF AUSTRALIA CENSUS 30th JUNE 1971

Age Last Birthday (Years)	Males	Females	Persons
0–4	626 002	597 440	1 223 442
5–9	625 955	594 300	1 220 255
10–14	628 600	597 755	1 226 355
15–19	567 960	542 236	1 110 196
20–24	558 166	538 779	1 096 945
25–29	480 748	452 779	933 527
30–34	412 476	388 657	801 133
35–39	380 948	358 888	739 836
40–44	407 539	379 976	787 515
45–49	399 611	381 913	781 524
50–54	332 641	330 295	662 936
55–59	301 464	303 971	605 435
60–64	243 740	257 804	501 544
65–69	183 270	203 493	386 763
70–74	123 915	168 735	292 650
75–79	76 080	123 687	199 767
80–84	42 926	76 940	119 866
85 and over	20 670	45 279	65 949
All ages	6 412 711	6 342 927	12 755 638

Source: Australian Bureau of Statistics: *Year Book*, No. 60, 1974, p 148

bution. The smoothing process is very arbitrary, however, and there is a danger that genuine bumps due to fluctuations in past births will be smoothed out. It is doubtful whether in fact a graduated distribution is much superior to an unadjusted one.

Table 13.6 sets out the adjusted age distribution for Australia at the 1971 Census, in *quinquennial* age groups. The age group 0–4 means aged 0 and under 5 years, the age group 5–9 means aged 5 and under 10 years and so on.

Intercensal Estimates

We obtain direct information about the sex and age distribution only at censuses. These have to be kept up to date by making intercensal estimates. The techniques for making intercensal estimates vary according to the data available; but they are all based on the obvious proposition that the people in a particular age group this year must be those who were a year younger last year, depleted by death and augmented by net migration.

Suppose we wish to estimate the male age distribution at 30 June 1974, given

The age distribution at 30 June 1973.
Births over the year 1 July 1973 to 30 June 1974.
Deaths by age at death over the year 1 July 1973 to 30 June 1974.
Migration by age at entry or exit over the year 1 July 1973 to 30 June 1974.

Let us ignore migration for the time being and consider as an example the age group 15 years and under 16. Clearly, we shall have

Number aged 15 years and under 16 at 30 June 1974
equals
(a) Number aged 14 years and under 15 at 30 June 1973
minus
(b) Number who were aged 14 years and under 15 at 30 June 1973, but who died during 1973–74

We know (a), but we do not know (b). Instead, we know the number of those who died when aged 14 years and under 15 years in 1973–74, which is not the same thing. Of those who were aged 14 years and under 15 at 30 June 1973, but who died during 1973–74, some will have died in the age group 14 years and under 15 and some in the age group 15 years and under 16. But we know only the total deaths in the age groups 14 years and under 15, and 15 years and under 16, and we do not know how many of these would have been aged 14 years and under 15 at 30 June 1973. This latter group of deaths, however, will consist of a fraction of those who died in 1973–74 aged 14 years and under 15 at death and a fraction of those who died in 1973–74 aged 15 years and under 16 at death. How can we estimate these fractions?[1]

These fractions will be evidently close to one-half. If deaths occur evenly through the year and if the ages of those who die are evenly distributed within each age group, exactly one-half of those aged 14 years and under 15 who die in 1973–74 will have had their fourteenth birthday prior to 1 July 1973, and hence will have been aged 14 years and under 15 at 30 June 1973. Similarly, exactly one-half of those who die aged 15 years and under 16 years in 1973–74 will have had their fifteenth birthday on 1 July 1973, or after, and hence will have been aged 14 years and under 15 at 30 June, 1973. This can be illustrated diagrammatically. The square in Fig 13.2 represents the number of deaths aged 14 and under 15 during 1973–74. The date of death is shown along the horizontal axis and the age at death along the vertical axis. We assume that the number of deaths are distributed evenly over the year, and that the ages of those who die at any date are distributed evenly over the year of age.

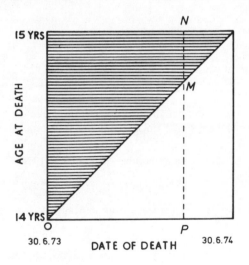

Fig 13.2

Draw in the ascending diagonal. Consider the date shown by point P, ie OP days from 30 June 1973. Then NP is the number of deaths

---

[1] This problem would not arise if deaths were classified by date of birth. In such a case the formula in the preceding paragraph in the text could be applied directly.

occurring at that date. Since the angle MOP is 45°, $MP = OP$, and persons dying at an age less than (14 years $+$ MP days) must have had their fourteenth birthday subsequently to 30 June 1973. Thus, of the NP deaths occurring at date P, MP will have had their fourteenth birthday after 30 June 1973, and NM before 30 June 1973. It follows that, if we let P move along over the whole year, the hatched area will represent the deaths of those persons who were in the age group 14 and under 15 at 30 June 1973. This area is evidently half of the whole.

Similarly, if we consider the number of deaths aged 15 and under 16 during 1973–74, we obtain Fig 13.3 below, and the hatched area (again half of the whole) represents the deaths of those persons who were in age group 14 and under 15 at 30 June 1973, but who died aged 15 and under 16 during 1973–74.

In fact, deaths and ages are very nearly evenly distributed within single years, so that

Number aged 15 years and under 16 at 30 June 1974
equals
Number aged 14 years and under 15 at 30 June 1973
minus
$\left\{ \begin{array}{l} \text{One-half of deaths during 1973–74 aged 14 years and under 15} \\ \text{One-half of deaths during 1973–74 aged 15 years and under 16} \end{array} \right\}$

This method can be used for all age groups except the first two. To obtain those aged 0 and under 1 at 30 June 1974, we must take all the births over the year 1973–74 and subtract the deaths of those babies born during that year. We know how many infants under the age of 1 year died in 1973–74, but some of these will have been born in 1972–73.

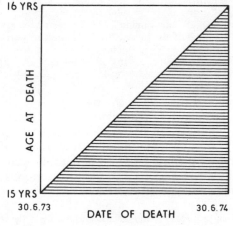

Fig 13.3

Deaths are not distributed evenly over the first year of life. In Australia, for example, the mean age at which infants die is about two months. In such a case[1] we can attribute about 85 per cent of infant deaths in 1973–74 to births of 1973–74 and the other 15 per cent to births of 1972–73. Thus 15 per cent of infant deaths in 1973–74 will already have been aged 0 years and under 1 at 30 June 1973. Hence we have

> Number aged 0 years and under 1 at 30 June 1974
> *equals*
> Births during 1973–74
> *minus*
> 85 per cent of deaths during 1973–74 aged 0 years and under 1

and

> Number aged 1 year and under 2 at 30 June 1974
> *equals*
> Number aged 0 years and under 1 at 30 June 1973
> *minus*
> { 15 per cent of deaths during 1973–74 aged 0 years and under 1
> One-half of deaths during 1973–74 aged 1 year and under 2 }

To take net migration into account, we use the same reasoning and we shall have

> Number aged 15 years and under 16 at 30 June 1974
> *equals*
> Number aged 14 years and under 15 at 30 June 1973
> *minus*
> { One-half of deaths during 1973–74 aged 14 years and under 15
> One-half of deaths during 1973–74 aged 15 years and under 16 }
> *plus*
> { One-half of overseas arrivals during 1973–74 aged 14 years and under 15
> One-half of overseas arrivals during 1973–74 aged 15 years and under 16 }
> *minus*
> { One-half of overseas departures during 1973–74 aged 14 years and under 15
> One-half of overseas departures during 1973–74 aged 15 years and under 16 }

It will be observed that when the numbers in each age group are added through to give total population at 30 June 1974, this will agree with the total obtained by adding natural increase and net migration for 1973–74 to the population at 30 June 1973, as illustrated in Table 13.3 above. It should be also noted that while it is necessary to work here in single age groups, age distributions are frequently quoted in quinquennial age groups.

---

[1] The method given here requires modification according to the conditions of infant mortality in the country under consideration.

As an example of the above method, we estimate the age distribution of a population at 31 December 1974, given the following data

Age Last Birthday	Population 31/12/73	Deaths in 1974	Overseas Arrivals in 1974	Overseas Departures in 1974	Net Migration in 1974 (a)
Under 1 year	90 000	2 600	1 000	300	700
1 year	89 000	250	1 100	300	800
2 years	93 000	160	1 300	450	850
3 years	77 000	120	1 500	300	1 200
4 years	79 000	80	1 600	200	1 400
5 years	75 000	70	1 800	350	1 450
etc	etc	etc	etc	etc	etc

Births in 1974 = 95 000

(a) Overseas arrivals *less* overseas departures.

We shall have

Table 13.7

Intercensal Estimate of Age Distribution of a Population

Population 31/12/73		Half Deaths in Given Age Group	Half Deaths in Next Age Group	Half Net Migrants in Given Age Group	Half Net Migrants in Next Age Group	Population 31/12/74	
Age last Birthday	Numbers (1)	(2)	(3)	(4)	(5)	Age last Birthday	Numbers (a) (6)
Births 1974	95 000		2 210 (b)		350	Under 1 year	93 140
Under 1 year .	90 000	390 (c)	125	350	400	1 year	90 235
1 year .	89 000	125	80	400	425	2 years	89 620
2 years .	93 000	80	60	425	600	3 years	93 885
3 years .	77 000	60	40	600	700	4 years	78 200
4 years .	79 000	40	35	700	725	5 years	80 350
5 years .	75 000	etc	etc	etc	etc	etc	etc
etc	etc						

(a) Col (6) = col (1) − col (2) − col (3) + col (4) + col (5).
(b) 85 per cent of infant deaths.
(c) 15 per cent of infant deaths.

Factors Determining the Age Distribution

The births, deaths and migrations of the past determine the current age distribution. It is important to realise that current age distributions are related in a quasi-mathematical fashion to past distributions and that future age distributions are related to current ones. We can

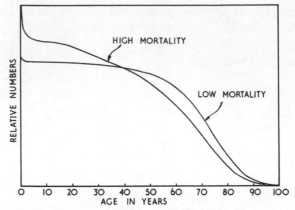

Fig 13.4 Age distribution for a constant stream of births

High mortality based on mortality of Australian males, 1881–90. Low mortality based on mortality of Australian males, 1970–72.

illustrate the way in which age distributions are built up by considering some hypothetical examples. These are illustrated in Figs 13.4 to 13.6 which indicate the general shapes of the relative age distributions.

If the number of births per annum has been constant for a long time, in the absence of migration, the age distribution will depend on the incidence of mortality. The numbers in age groups will become progressively smaller the older the age group, as mortality takes its toll. The higher the rate of mortality the more rapidly will the numbers in the upper age groups tail off, and hence the younger the population on the average. This is pictured in Fig 13.4.

If the annual number of births has been steadily increasing over the past, the younger age groups will contain a relatively greater proportion of the population, since they will be the survivors of relatively greater numbers of births. The more rapid the rate of growth, the younger will be the population on the average. This is shown in Fig 13.5.

If the annual number of births has been steadily decreasing over the past, the older age groups will be the survivors of relatively greater numbers of births. This will result in a tendency for the numbers in age groups to increase with age, but mortality will sooner or later reduce the older age groups, so that the age distribution will become humped, as in Fig 13.6.

Wars and migrations introduce elements of irregularity into age distributions. The immediate effect of a war is to 'bite' into the numbers of males in the ages of from about 20 to 30 years. This bite will then move forward in the age distribution as time passes and the original 20–30 year age group grows older. The same holds for emigration,

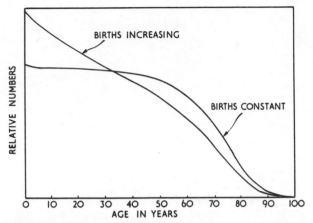

Fig 13.5 Age distribution for given mortality conditions
Mortality based on mortality of Australian males, 1970–72. Increasing births are increasing at 10 per 1000 per annum.

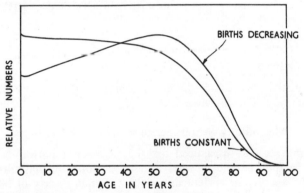

Fig 13.6 Age distribution for given mortality conditions
Mortality based on mortality of Australian males, 1970–72. Decreasing births are decreasing at 10 per 1000 per annum.

which usually is concentrated in the age groups of young active people. Immigration has the converse effect of adding a 'lump' to the age distribution.

The customary diagrammatic method of illustrating sex and age distribution is shown in Fig 13.7. The diagram is called a *population silhouette*. It is a histogram with the axes reversed.

The relatively small numbers in the age groups 30–34 years and 35–39 years reflect the substantial drop in the number of births which took place in the 1930s.

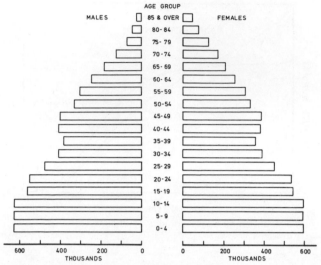

Fig 13.7 Age distribution of males and females, Australia, 30 June 1971
Source: Australian Bureau of Statistics, *Year Book*, No. 60, 1974, p 148

Factors Determining the Sex Distribution

The sex distribution of a population is measured by the *masculinity* of the population. This is defined as

Masculinity = number of males per 100 females

Masculinity can be measured for the whole population or for age groups. In the absence of wars and migration, the masculinity of a particular age group is determined by the masculinity of births and deaths. Masculinity of births is measured by the number of male births per 100 female births, and is usually about 105. But male mortality is heavier than female mortality, so that as age rises the males gradually lose their preponderance. In Australia, for example, other things being equal, the sexes would break even at about age 50 to 55, and thereafter the females would be preponderant. For the whole population, therefore, masculinity depends on the age distribution and hence on the rate of growth of the population. Normally the sexes are fairly evenly balanced. The immediate effect of wars is to reduce masculinity mainly in the 20–30 age group. As the years go by, this deficiency works its way up the age distribution. The immediate effect of immigration is to increase masculinity in the 20–50 age group, since migrants tend to be predominantly male. These considerations are illustrated in Table 13.8.

Table 13.8

MASCULINITY OF THE AUSTRALIAN POPULATION
CENSUS 30th JUNE 1971

Age	Males per 100 Females	Comment
0–4	105	Masculinity at birth = 105
5–9	105	
10–14	105	
15–19	105	
20–24	104	
25–29	106	
30–34	106	
35–39	106	1948–1971 Migration
40–44	107	
45–49	105	
50–54	101	1939–1945 War
55–59	99	
60–64	95	
65–69	90	
70–74	73	Heavier male mortality
75 and over	57	
All ages	101	

Source: *Table* 13.6, p 512

Significance of Sex and Age Distribution

The sex and age distribution of a population is of considerable importance from both social and economic points of view, and it is subject to quite substantial changes with the passage of time. The significance of sex and age distribution is illustrated in Tables 13.9 to 13.11 below which refer to Australian experience. The first shows the highly abnormal sex distribution of Australia in the days of its early development and the continuous drop in masculinity which has been taking place from pioneering days onwards. This has had a profound influence on society. The second shows how the ratio of active males to all males has changed over the past years, due to improvements in longevity and to the fall and partial recovery in the birth rate. This ratio has an important effect on the standard of living of the country, since it influences the volume of production relative to the number of consumers in the economy. The third table shows how the ratio of reproductive females to all females has changed. The substantial change in the proportion of immature females has important implications for the reproductive capacity of the population in the future.

Table 13.9

MASCULINITY OF THE AUSTRALIAN POPULATION
1820–1974

Year	Males per 100 Females
1820	244
1840	202
1860	140
1880	117
1900	111
1920	103
1940	102
1960	102
1974	101

Source: Australian Bureau of Statistics: *Demography Bulletin*, No. 67, 1949 pp 150–153; No. 78, 1960, pp 170–171; and *Estimated Age Distribution of the Population: States and Territories of Australia*, 30 June 1974 (Ref 4.15), pp 2–3.

Table 13.10

AGE DISTRIBUTION OF MALES AT AUSTRALIAN CENSUSES

Age Group (years)	1891	1933	1971
	per cent	per cent	per cent
0–14: Young dependants	34·8	27·5	29·3
15–64: Active producers	62·0	66·1	63·7
65 and over: Old dependants	3·2	6·4	7·0
All Ages	100·0	100·0	100·0

Source: Australian Bureau of Statistics: *Census of the Commonwealth of Australia*, 30 June 1933, *Statistician's Report*, p 69, and Vol I, p 717; *Year Book*, No. 60, 1974, pp 147–148

Table 13.11

AGE DISTRIBUTION OF FEMALES AT AUSTRALIAN CENSUSES

Age Group (years)	1891	1933	1971
	per cent	per cent	per cent
0–14: Immature	39·4	27·4	28·2
15–44: Reproductive	47·1	47·5	42·0
45 and over: Sterile	13·5	25·1	29·8
All Ages	100·0	100·0	100·0

Source: Australian Bureau of Statistics: *Census of the Commonwealth of Australia*, 30 June 1933, *Statistician's Report*, p 70 and Vol I, p 717; *Year Book*, No. 60, 1974, p 148.

13.4 Birth and Death Rates and Rates of Increase

Crude Birth Rate

The annual *crude birth rate* is defined:

$$\text{Crude birth rate} = \frac{\text{annual births}}{\text{annual mean population}} \times 1000$$

In this measure the births are related to the *mean* population and not to the population at a particular date. The crude birth rate of a given year tells us at what rate births have augmented the population over the course of the year. For 1974 for Australia we have

$$\text{Crude birth rate} = \frac{245\,177}{13\,377\,450} \times 1000 = 18\cdot33 \text{ per 1000 per annum}$$

The crude birth rate usually lies between 10 and 55 per 1000. In Western European type countries the crude birth rate has shown a general downward trend over the past 100 years. It rose during the post-war years, but has again fallen quite appreciably in the past decade. For crude birth rates of various countries, see Table 13.12, p 532.

The level of the crude birth rate is determined by

 (i) the sex and age distribution of the population; and

 (ii) the fertility of the population, ie the average rate of childbearing of females.

A relatively high crude birth rate can be recorded if the sex and age distribution is favourable even though fertility is low, eg countries with a relatively large proportion of population in the 15–50 years age groups will have a relatively high crude birth rate, other things being equal. We consider how to measure fertility in section 13.7 below.

Crude Death Rate

The annual *crude death rate* is defined:

$$\text{Crude death rate} = \frac{\text{annual deaths}}{\text{annual mean population}} \times 1000$$

The crude death rate for a given year tells us at what rate deaths have depleted the population over the course of the year. We can calculate the crude death rate for males and females separately. For 1974 for Australia we have

$$\text{Crude death rate (males)} = \frac{64\,299}{6\,714\,350} \times 1000$$

$$= 9\cdot58 \text{ per 1000 per annum}$$

$$\text{Crude death rate (females)} = \frac{51\,534}{6\,663\,100} \times 1000$$

$$= 7 \cdot 73 \text{ per 1000 per annum}$$

$$\text{Crude death rate (persons)} = \frac{115\,833}{13\,377\,450} \times 1000$$

$$= 8 \cdot 66 \text{ per 1000 per annum}$$

The crude death rate usually lies between 8 and 30 per 1000. The female rate is generally lower than the male rate. In most countries crude death rates have fallen substantially over the past half-century or so. For crude death rates of various countries, see Table 13.12, p 532.

The level of the crude death rate is determined by

(i) the sex and age distribution of the population; and

(ii) the mortality of the population, ie the average longevity of the population.

An old population can exhibit a relatively high crude death rate even if longevity is high (ie mortality is low). We consider how to measure mortality in section 13.5 below.

Crude Rate of Natural Increase

The annual *crude rate of natural increase* is defined:

Crude rate of natural increase

$$= \frac{\text{annual natural increase}}{\text{annual mean population}} \times 1000$$

$$= \frac{\text{annual births} - \text{annual deaths}}{\text{annual mean population}} \times 1000$$

$$= \text{crude birth rate} - \text{crude death rate}$$

The crude rate of natural increase for a given year tells us at what rate natural increase has augmented the population over the course of the year. For 1974 for Australia we have:

$$\text{Crude rate of natural increase} = 18 \cdot 33 - 8 \cdot 66$$

$$= 9 \cdot 67 \text{ per 1000 per annum}$$

The crude rate of natural increase varies considerably from country to country. It can be negative (natural decrease, ie excess of deaths over births), but it is unlikely to be much higher than about 30 per 1000. For crude rates of natural increase of various countries, see Table 13.12, p 532. The level of the crude rate of natural increase is dependent on those factors determining the crude birth and death rates. A population with a relatively large proportion in the age group 15–50 years is likely to have a comparatively high crude rate of natural increase, other things being equal, for its crude birth rate will tend to be high and its crude death rate low.

Rate of Net Migration

The annual *rate of net migration* is defined:
Rate of net migration

$$= \frac{\text{overseas arrivals} - \text{overseas departures}}{\text{annual mean population}} \times 1000$$

$$= \frac{\text{annual net migration}}{\text{annual mean population}} \times 1000$$

The rate of net migration for a given year tells us at what rate net migration has augmented the population over the course of the year. For 1974 for Australia we have:

$$\text{Rate of net migration} = \frac{1\,496\,529 - 1\,409\,408}{13\,377\,450} \times 1000$$

$$= 6\cdot51 \text{ per 1000 per annum}$$

This rate varies a great deal according to world economic and political conditions and government policy. It can, of course, be negative.

Rate of Total Increase

The annual *rate of total increase* is defined:
Rate of total increase

$$= \frac{\text{annual total increase}}{\text{annual mean population}} \times 1000$$

$$= \frac{\text{annual natural increase} + \text{annual net migration}}{\text{annual mean population}} \times 1000$$

$$= \text{crude rate of natural increase} + \text{rate of net migration}$$

The rate of total increase for a given year tells us at what rate the population has increased over the year. For 1974 for Australia we have

$$\text{Rate of total increase} = 9\cdot67 + 6\cdot51$$
$$= 16\cdot18 \text{ per 1000 per annum}$$

Rate of Population Growth

The annual *rate of population growth* is defined:
Rate of population growth

$$= \frac{\text{annual total increase}}{\text{population at beginning of year}} \times 1000$$

$$= \frac{\text{population at end of year} - \text{population at beginning of year}}{\text{population at beginning of year}}$$
$$\times 1000$$

The rate of population growth for a given year tells us by what proportion the population has increased over the year. Whereas the rate of total increase measures the *average rate* at which the population has been increasing over the year, the annual rate of population growth measures the *proportion* by which the population has grown over the year. Numerically the difference between the two rates is always small and the rate of population growth is always a little greater than the rate of total increase. Mathematically speaking, the rate of population growth is the rate of total increase compounded continuously over a year. For 1974 for Australia we have:

$$\text{Rate of population growth} = \frac{13\,485\,000 - 13\,268\,600}{13\,268\,600} \times 1000$$

$$= 16\cdot31 \text{ per 1000 per annum}$$

$$\text{or } 1\cdot631 \text{ per cent}$$

Sometimes we want to ascertain the average annual rate of population growth which has obtained over a period of years. Suppose we know that the population at the end of the year 0 is P_0 and the population at the end of year t (ie t years later) is P_t, and ask what the average annual rate of growth has been. The question is: At what annual rate of growth will P_0 accumulate to P_t after t years? This is simply a problem in compound interest. If t is the rate of growth in decimals then we have:

$$P_t = P_0(1 + i)^t$$

Taking logarithms,

$$\log P_t = \log P_0 + t \log(1 + i)$$

ie $$\log(1 + i) = \frac{\log P_t - \log P_0}{t}$$

and i can be obtained from the anti-logarithm.

For example:
The population of Australia at 30 June 1954 was 8 986 530. By 30 June 1974, it had grown to 13 338 300. What was the average annual rate of population growth over this period?

We have $\qquad 13\,338\,300 = 8\,986\,530(1 + i)^{20}$

hence $\qquad \log 13\,338\,300 = \log 8\,986\,530 + 20\log(1 + i)$

ie $\qquad \log(1 + i) = \dfrac{7{\cdot}12510 - 6{\cdot}95359}{20}$

$$= 0{\cdot}008576$$

and $\qquad 1 + i = 1{\cdot}0199$

The required average rate is 19·9 per 1000 per annum

Infant Mortality Rate

The *infant mortality rate* is defined:

$$\text{Infant mortality rate} = \frac{\text{annual infant deaths}}{\text{annual births}} \times 1000$$

The rate approximately measures for a given year the chances of a birth failing to survive one year of life. Still-births are not included in the infant deaths. The rate can be calculated for males and females separately. For 1974 for Australia we have:

$$\text{Infant mortality rate (males)} \quad = \frac{2325}{126\,295} \times 1000$$

$$= 18{\cdot}41 \text{ per 1000 per annum}$$

$$\text{Infant mortality rate (females)} \quad = \frac{1633}{118\,882} \times 1000$$

$$= 13{\cdot}74 \text{ per 1000 per annum}$$

$$\text{Infant mortality rate (all births)} = \frac{3958}{245\,177} \times 1000$$

$$= 16{\cdot}14 \text{ per 1000 per annum}$$

The infant mortality rate varies considerably according to time and place. In countries with high standards of maternal and infant welfare it is as low as 10 to 18 per 1000, but in some developing countries it is still well over 100 per 1000. In many countries it has fallen spectacularly over the past 60 years or so. The male rate is appreciably higher than the female rate. For infant mortality rates of various countries, see Table 13.12, p 532.

Ideally we wish to measure by the infant mortality rate the probability[1] at birth of a child dying before attaining the age of one year,

[1] See section 4.3, p 74ff.

according to the mortality conditions of a given year. The deaths of infants in any one year can be of children born in the given year or in the preceding year and are influenced by the trend of births between the two years. For example, if last year's births were much lower than this year's, this year's infant deaths will be lower than otherwise, and if we relate this year's infant deaths to this year's births, we shall understate the true infant mortality position for this year. One way of handling this problem[1] is to regard the probability at birth of a child surviving to the age of one year as being compounded of the probability of a child surviving to the end of the calendar year in which it was born and the probability of a child who has survived to the end of the calendar year in which it was born surviving to the age of one. When both these component probabilities are based on the mortality conditions of a given year we have:

$$p_0 = \frac{B^t - D^{t(t)}}{B^t} \times \frac{B^{t-1} - D^{t-1(t-1)} - D^{t(t-1)}}{B^{t-1} - D^{t-1(t-1)}}$$

where p_0 is the probability at birth of surviving to the age of one year according to the mortality conditions of year t,

B^t is the number of births in year t,

$D^{t(t)}$ is the number of infant deaths in year t of children born in year (t).

The numerator of the first term in the above formula is the number of births in year t surviving to the end of year t, and that of the second term is the number of births surviving from the previous calendar year who survive to the age of one in year t.

Since p_0 is the probability at birth of surviving to the age of one, we can write

$$q_0 = 1 - p_0$$

where q_0 is the probability at birth of a child dying before attaining the age of one year.

In order to compute q_0 as defined above, it is necessary to have the infant deaths of a particular year classified according to the calendar year of birth of the infants. Frequently this information is not available. In such a situation, it is often possible to estimate a *separation factor* by which the infant deaths in any one year can be separated into those of children born in the current and those of children born in the preceding year. Evidently the proportion of infant deaths of a particular year which is due to births of the current year will be higher the lower the mean age at death of infants. This mean age is generally lower the

[1] See V G Valaoras: 'Refined Rates for Infant and Childhood Mortality', *Population Studies*, Vol IV, No. 3, 1950, p 253.

lower the rate of infant mortality, since low rates of infant mortality are due more to low rates of mortality after the first month of life than within the first month. For Australia the separation factor is at present about 0·85. In 1973 and 1974 male births were 126 969 and 126 295 respectively, and male infant deaths were 2356 and 2325. Accordingly, the refined infant mortality rate for 1974 is:

$$q_0 = 1 - \left[\frac{126\,295 - (0·85)2325}{126\,295} \times \frac{126\,969 - (0·85)2356 - (0·15)2325}{126\,969 - (0·85)2356} \right]$$

$$= 0·018396, \text{ or } 18·4 \text{ per 1000 per annum}$$

The use of a separation factor is not entirely satisfactory, since the factor itself ought to be adjusted for changes in the rate of births. In principle, refined rates of infant mortality are to be preferred to crude rates, but, in practice, such procedures are most important for countries in which the mean age of infants at death is appreciably higher than in Australia. Furthermore, one would not place a great deal of reliance on the infant mortality rate for one year, but would prefer to calculate the rate for, say, three years combined, by relating three years' deaths to three years' births. In this case, in countries like Australia, about 95 per cent of the infant deaths taking place in the three year period will be deaths of children born in the same period, and the crude measure can be regarded as fairly satisfactory. For example, for males for Australia 1970–72 we have

$$\text{Infant mortality rate} = \frac{\text{infant deaths during 1970, 1, 2}}{\text{births during 1970, 1, 2}} \times 1000$$

$$= \frac{2718 + 2684 + 2577}{131\,972 + 141\,114 + 136\,009} \times 1000$$

$$= 19·50 \text{ per 1000 per annum}$$

This will closely approximate[1] the probability at birth of a child dying within the first year of life according to the mortality conditions of 1970–72, ie on the average out of every 1000 male births subjected to the mortality conditions of Australia, 1970–72, 19 will not survive to the end of their first year of life.

Neo-natal Mortality Rate

The *neo-natal mortality rate* is defined:

[1] Using a more complicated procedure, the Australian Government Actuary has estimated this probability at 19·49 per 1000. See Australian Bureau of Statistics: *Australian Life Tables 1970–72* (Ref 4.31), pp 7, 16.

Neo-natal mortality rate

$$= \frac{\text{annual deaths of infants under the age of 1 month}}{\text{annual births}} \times 1000$$

The rate measures for a given year the chance of a birth failing to survive one month of life. For 1974 for Australia we have:

Neo-natal mortality rate (males) $\quad = \dfrac{1670}{126\,295} \times 1000$

$$= 13 \cdot 22 \text{ per } 1000 \text{ per annum}$$

Neo-natal mortality rate (females) $\quad = \dfrac{1184}{118\,882} \times 1000$

$$= 9 \cdot 96 \text{ per } 1000 \text{ per annum}$$

Neo-natal mortality rate (all births) $= \dfrac{2854}{245\,177} \times 1000$

$$= 11 \cdot 64 \text{ per } 1000 \text{ per annum}$$

The neo-natal mortality rate is a component of the infant mortality rate. For Australia, for example, it covers about 70 per cent of it—in other words, most infant deaths occur within the first month of life. In fact, the neo-natal mortality rate represents to a very large extent the hard core of infant mortality. Thus, over the past 60 years in Australia, the infant mortality rate has fallen from above 80 to about 16 per 1000, whereas the neo-natal mortality rate has fallen from above 30 to about 12 per 1000—the greatest part of this latter fall occurring in the past 20 years. Of the neo-natal deaths most occur within the first week of life, and the mean age of neo-natal deaths is only 4 or 5 days, hence almost all neo-natal deaths are derived from births occurring in the same year, and the neo-natal mortality rate is not subject to the same limitations as the uncorrected infant mortality rate.

Maternal Mortality Rate

The *maternal mortality rate* is defined:

$$\text{Maternal mortality rate} = \frac{\text{annual maternal deaths}}{\text{confinements}} \times 1000$$

The rate measures the probability of a woman dying from childbirth. For 1974 for Australia we have:

$$\text{Maternal mortality rate} = \frac{28}{242\,829} \times 1000$$

$$= 0 \cdot 12 \text{ per } 1000 \text{ per annum}$$

Like the infant mortality rate this rate depends largely on the standard of maternal welfare in the country under consideration.

Crude Marriage Rate

The *crude marriage rate* is defined:

$$\text{Crude marriage rate} = \frac{\text{annual marriages}}{\text{annual mean population}} \times 1000$$

The crude marriage rate for a given year tells us at what rate marriages have been taking place over the year. For 1974 for Australia we have:

$$\text{Crude marriage rate} = \frac{110\,673}{13\,377\,450} \times 1000$$

$$= 8\text{·}27 \text{ per 1000 per annum}$$

The level of the crude marriage rate is determined by
 (i) the sex and age distribution of the population; and
 (ii) the nuptiality of the population, ie the propensities of people to marry.

Hence a population which has an evenly-balanced sex distribution and which has a relatively high proportion of unmarried persons in the younger age groups will exhibit a high crude marriage rate, other things being equal. Techniques for measuring nuptiality are beyond the scope of this chapter, but they are analogous to those for measuring mortality.[1] It should be noted, however, that nuptiality varies according to economic conditions, and hence the crude marriage rate tends to be high in booms and low in slumps. In addition the crude marriage rate tends to increase in times of war.

Table 13.12 sets out some of the rates referred to above for selected countries. Table 13.13 shows more detail for Australia.

13.5 Measurement of Mortality

Our object is to find a method of expressing the level of mortality in a particular area during a given year or period of years. Suppose, for example, we wish to examine the mortality conditions to which Australian males were subject in the year 1974. The simplest way to

[1] See, for example, D V Glass: *Population Policies and Movements in Europe* (Cass and Co Ltd, 1967), Appendix, pp 399–405.

Table 13.12

BIRTH AND DEATH RATES FOR SELECTED COUNTRIES
1920–24, 1935–39, 1958, 1966 and 1974

Country and Period	Crude Birth Rate per 1000 pa	Crude Death Rate per 1000 pa	Crude Rate of Natural Increase per 1000 pa	Infant Mortality Rate per 1000 pa
Australia—				
1920–24	24·4	9·8	14·6	61·0
1935–39	17·2	9·6	7·6	39·1
1958	22·6	8·5	14·1	20·5
1966	19·3	9·0	10·3	18·2
1974	18·3	8·7	9·6	16·1
India—				
1920–24	33·0	26·8	6·2	184·2
1935–39	33·8	22·6	11·2	161·6
1951–61	41·7	22·8	18·9	139·0
1965–70	42·8	16·7	26·1	(a)
Italy—				
1920–24	30·1	17·5	12·6	128·8
1935–39	23·2	13·9	9·3	102·7
1958	17·9	9·4	8·5	48·2
1966	18·9	9·5	9·4	34·3
1974	15·7	9·6	6·1	22·6
Japan—				
1920–24	35·0	23·0	12·0	164·7
1935–39	29·2	17·4	11·8	110·4
1958	18·0	7·5	10·5	34·6
1966	13·7	6·8	6·9	19·3
1973	19·4	6·6	12·8	11·3
Netherlands—				
1920–24	26·7	11·0	15·7	74·4
1935–39	20·3	8·7	11·6	37·4
1958	21·1	7·5	13·6	17·2
1966	19·2	8·1	11·1	14·7
1974	13·8	8·0	5·8	11·0
Sweden—				
1920–24	20·3	12·4	7·9	61·4
1935–39	14·5	11·7	2·8	43·2
1958	14·2	9·6	4·6	15·8
1966	15·8	10·0	5·8	12·6
1974	13·4	10·6	2·8	9·2
United Kingdom—				
1920–24	21·7	12·5	9·2	79·2
1935–39	15·3	12·2	3·1	58·5
1958	16·8	11·7	5·1	23·5
1966	17·9	11·8	6·1	19·6
1974	13·1	12·1	1·0	17·2
United States—				
1920–24	22·8	12·0	10·8	76·7
1935–39	17·1	11·0	6·1	53·2
1958	24·3	9·5	14·8	26·9
1966	18·5	9·5	9·0	23·4
1974	15·0	9·1	5·9	16·5

(a) Not available

Source: United Nations: *Demographic Year Book*, 1954, pp 252, 516, 588; 1959, pp 209–17, 547–53, 599–605; 1966, pp 116–19; *Population and Vital Statistics Report*, 1968, pp 17, 22–24; *Demographic Year Book*, 1974, pp 122–24.

summarise these mortality conditions is to calculate the age to which Australian males can, on the average, expect to live if they are subjected to 1974 mortality conditions. We can start with a hypothetical group of 1000 male births (known as a *cohort* of births) and estimate the numbers which will survive to every age, if they are subjected to the mortality conditions under consideration. Then we can say, for example, that out of our initial 1000, 976 will reach the age of 10, 966 the age of 20 and so on, and that the mean age at which they will die is 68·0 years. This is a simple and concise way of expressing the conditions of mortality (or, in other words, of longevity) under which Australian males lived in 1974. The technique suggested above gives rise to what is known as a *life table*.

Table 13.13

POPULATION, AND BIRTH, DEATH AND MARRIAGE RATES
AUSTRALIA, 1861–1974

Period	Population at Middle of Period '000	Crude Birth Rate per 1000 pa	Crude Death Rate per 1000 pa	Crude Rate of Natural Increase per 1000 pa	Rate of Net Migration per 1000 pa	Rate of Population Growth per 1000 pa (b)	Infant Mortality Rate per 1000 pa	Crude Marriage Rate per 1000 pa
1861–70	1 390	41·0	16·6	24·3	12·1	37·0	(c)	8·0
1871–80	1 898	36·2	15·7	20·5	10·0	30·8	120·8	7·2
1881–90	2 695	35·2	15·3	19·9	14·2	35·1	122·2	7·9
1891–1900	3 492	30·0	13·0	17·0	0·7	18·0	110·4	6·7
1901–10	4 033	26·5	11·3	15·3	1·0	16·3	87·3	7·5
1911–20	4 969	26·6	10·8	15·8	4·2	20·4	67·5	8·3
1921–30	6 003	22·4	9·4	13·0	5·2	18·5	54·9	7·8
1931–40	6 756	17·2	9·3 (a)	7·9	0·5	8·6	40·0	8·3
1941–50	7 430	21·8	9·9 (a)	12·0	4·8	16·5	31·1	9·9
1951–60	9 313	22·7	9·0	13·7	8·8	22·7	22·2	7·9
1961–70	11 505	20·7	8·8	11·9	8·1	19·1	18·8	8·2
1974	13 338	18·3	8·7	9·6	6·5	16·3	16·1	8·3

(a) Exclusive of deaths of defence personnel, September 1939 to 30 June 1947.
(b) This column is not the sum of the two preceding columns. It expresses the rate of growth per annum over the period in relation to the population at the beginning of the period (see p 525 above). Moreover, it is based on census figures, while the two preceding columns are based on annual registrations.
(c) Not available.
Source: Australian Bureau of Statistics: *Demography Bulletin.* No. 67, 1949, pp 154–5; No. 78, 1960, pp 12, 32, 51, 69, 152, 172; No. 86, 1969 and 1970, pp 6, 7, 9, 19, 91, 140, 233

Construction of a Life Table

The data required for the construction of a life table are the age distribution of the population during the period under consideration and
the number of deaths occurring during that period, distributed according to age. We start with a hypothetical cohort of births. These births
are, of course, exactly aged 0. We wish to trace through the number
of these births which will survive to the various ages. We write l_x for
the number of the initial cohort of births which will survive to the
exact age of x. For short we call l_x *survivors at age x*. If we start
with 1000 births, then clearly $l_0 = 1000$. As x gets larger, l_x gets
smaller, until finally, when $x = 100$ years or so, $l_x = 0$. We also write
p_x for the *probability at age x of surviving one year to reach age* $(x + 1)$.
By this we mean that if we have, say, 1000 males aged x exactly, we
should expect, on the average, $1000 \times p_x$ of them to reach their next
birthday, if they were subject to the mortality conditions under consideration. All the p_xs are fractions less than unity. If we start with l_0
new-born babies, the number which will survive to the exact age of
1 year will be $l_1 = l_0 \times p_0$, the number which will survive to the exact
age of 2 years will be $l_2 = l_1 \times p_1$, and so on. In general then, we have:

$$l_{x+1} = l_x \times p_x$$

It follows that in order to calculate the l_xs we must calculate the
p_xs.

We have already touched on p_0 in discussing the infant mortality
rate. It was pointed out that this rate was an approximation to the
probability at birth of dying within one year. Since one must either
die or survive we must have:

$$p_0 = 1 - \text{infant mortality rate}$$

where the infant mortality rate is expressed in decimals.

The subsequent p_xs can be computed as follows. For any age group x years and under $(x + 1)$, we know for the actual population the mean number of males for the year under consideration. Let this number be designated P_x. Similarly, we know the actual number of deaths in the various age groups which took place during the year under consideration. For the age group x years and under $(x + 1)$, let this be designated D_x. With these data we define *specific mortality rates*. The specific mortality rate for the age group x years and under $(x + 1)$ is the ratio of the annual number of deaths in that age group to the mean population in that age group, that is

$$m_x = \frac{D_x}{P_x}$$

where m_x is the specific mortality rate for the age group x years and under $(x + 1)$. This rate represents that rate at which persons of a particular age group are dying, throughout the year under consideration. The specific mortality rates represent the basic conditions of mortality and are readily calculable.

If from our initial hypothetical group of births l_0, there were l_x survivors at age x and l_{x+1} at age $(x + 1)$, the mean number of survivors in the age group x years and under $(x + 1)$ will be $\frac{1}{2}(l_x + l_{x+1})$, provided that the deaths take place evenly over the year. The number of deaths in this age group will be given by $(l_x - l_{x+1})$. If the l_x values are to reflect the mortality conditions of the population, this number of deaths must be equal to the number which would take place by applying to the mean number in the age group the relevant specific mortality rate. Hence we must have

$$l_x - l_{x+1} = \tfrac{1}{2}(l_x + l_{x+1}) \times m_x$$

but
$$l_{x+1} = l_x \times p_x$$

hence
$$1 - p_x = \tfrac{1}{2}(1 + p_x) \times m_x$$

ie
$$p_x = \frac{1 - \tfrac{1}{2}m_x}{1 + \tfrac{1}{2}m_x}$$

Consequently, given the m_xs we can readily calculate the p_xs and hence the l_xs. Actually we can calculate the p_xs direct from the raw data, for

$$p_x = \frac{1 - \tfrac{1}{2}\dfrac{D_x}{P_x}}{1 + \tfrac{1}{2}\dfrac{D_x}{P_x}} = \frac{P_x - \tfrac{1}{2}D_x}{P_x + \tfrac{1}{2}D_x}$$

It is possible to interpret the above formula for p_x in a fairly simple way by assuming as an approximation that all those in the age group x and under $(x + 1)$ years in the actual population are exactly aged $(x + \frac{1}{2})$ years at the middle of the year under consideration. Then P_x would represent the number aged $(x + \frac{1}{2})$ years at the middle of the year. Since D_x is the number of those aged x and under $(x + 1)$ who die over the course of the year, then, provided that the deaths take place evenly over the year, half the deaths will occur between the beginning and the middle of the year and half will occur between the middle and the end of the year. Consequently, $P_x + \frac{1}{2}D_x$ will be the number of males aged exactly x at the beginning of the year, and $P_x - \frac{1}{2}D_x$ will be the number of them who have survived to the end of the year to attain the exact age of $(x + 1)$. It follows that the probability at age x of surviving one year will be given, as above, by

$$p_x = \frac{P_x - \frac{1}{2}D_x}{P_x + \frac{1}{2}D_x}$$

In practice the calculation of the l_xs will be rather tedious, for the p_xs will have to be calculated for about 100 ages and then successively multiplied. A great simplification can be achieved (without much loss in accuracy) by working in quinquennial age groups, ie by using population and deaths classified into five-year groups and calculating every fifth l_x only. We write $_5p_x$ for the probability at age x of surviving five years to age $(x + 5)$, so that

$$l_{x+5} = l_x \times {}_5p_x$$

The specific mortality rates are calculated for quinquennial age groups, so that m_x now stands for the rate at which persons aged x and under $(x + 5)$ die in any given year. Following the preceding argument we must have

$$l_x - l_{x+5} = \frac{1}{2}(l_x + l_{x+5}) \times 5m_x$$

The multiplier is $5m_x$, because m_x is an annual rate, and in surviving from age x to $(x + 5)$, five years must be lived through. Accordingly,

$$_5p_x = \frac{1 - 2\frac{1}{2}m_x}{1 + 2\frac{1}{2}m_x} = \frac{P_x - 2\frac{1}{2}D_x}{P_x + 2\frac{1}{2}D_x}$$

where P_x and D_x here refer to the population and deaths respectively in the age group x years and under $(x + 5)$. The abridged quinquennial method is satisfactory so long as deaths are fairly evenly distributed over the quinquennial age groups. This condition holds sufficiently well except for the first few years of life.[1] Accordingly, we calculate l_1, as before, from

$$l_1 = l_0 \times p_0$$

and l_5 from

$$l_5 = l_1 \times {}_4p_1$$

where

$${}_4p_1 = \frac{1 - 2m_1}{1 + 2m_1} = \frac{P_1 - 2D_1}{P_1 + 2D_1}$$

and P_1 and D_1 here refer to population and deaths respectively in the age group 1 year and under 5.

Table 13.14

CONSTRUCTION OF ABRIDGED LIFE TABLE—AUSTRALIAN MALES, 1974: CALCULATION OF PROBABILITIES OF SURVIVING

Age Group (years) x	Population at 30/6/74 P_x	Deaths During 1974 D_x	$P_x - 2\frac{1}{2}D_x$	$P_x + 2\frac{1}{2}D_x$	$\dfrac{{}_5p_x}{} = \dfrac{P_x - 2\frac{1}{2}D_x}{P_x + 2\frac{1}{2}D_x}$
Births	126 295	2 325 (a)			0·98159 (b)
1–4	527 510	500	526 510 (c)	528 510 (d)	0·99622
5–9	613 907	268	613 237	614 577	0·99782
10–14	647 988	257	647 345	648 630	0·99802
15–19	609 976	987	607 508	612 443	0·99194
20–24	576 145	1 013	573 612	578 677	0·99125
25–29	558 610	774	556 675	560 545	0·99310
30–34	453 212	685	451 499	454 924	0·99247
35–39	395 985	862	393 830	398 140	0·98917
40–44	386 371	1 329	383 048	389 693	0·98295
45–49	404 067	2 509	397 794	410 339	0·96943
50–54	369 882	3 746	360 517	379 247	0·95061
55–59	294 371	4 917	282 078	306 663	0·91983
60–64	264 168	7 093	246 435	281 900	0·87419
65–69	196 079	8 152	175 699	216 459	0·81170
70–74	136 267	8 841	114 164	158 369	0·72087
75–79	75 882	7 795	56 394	95 370	0·59132
80–84	41 595	6 515	25 307	57 882	0·43722
85–89	17 022 (f)	4 044	6 912	27 132	0·25475
90–94	4 150 (f)	1 377	707	7 592	0·09312
95–99	650 (f)	310	−125 (e)	1 425	0·00000

(a) Infant deaths

(b) $1 - \dfrac{\text{infant deaths}}{\text{births}}$

(c) $P_1 - 2D_1$

(d) $P_1 + 2D_1$

(e) The negative value occurs because deaths in this age group are not spread evenly over the five-year range but are concentrated near the lower end. This value is treated as if it were zero, giving a probability of surviving from 95 to 100 years of zero.

(f) Estimated

Source: Australian Bureau of Statistics: Deaths 1974 (Ref 4.8), pp 8, 9, 30

[1] Also except for the last few years of life, but the tail end of the life table is relatively unimportant.

Table 13.15

CONSTRUCTION OF ABRIDGED LIFE TABLE—AUSTRALIAN MALES, 1974: CALCULATION OF SURVIVORS

Exact Age (years) x	Survivors (a) l_x
0	(b) 1 000
1	1 000 × 0·98159 = 982
5	981·59 × 0·99622 = 978
10	977·88 × 0·99782 = 976
15	975·75 × 0·99802 = 974
20	973·82 × 0·99194 = 966
25	965·97 × 0·99125 = 958
30	957·52 × 0·99310 = 951
35	950·91 × 0·99247 = 944
40	943·75 × 0·98917 = 934
45	933·53 × 0·98295 = 918
50	917·61 × 0·96943 = 890
55	889·56 × 0·95061 = 846
60	845·62 × 0·91983 = 778
65	777·83 × 0·87419 = 680
70	679·97 × 0·81170 = 552
75	551·93 × 0·72087 = 398
80	397·87 × 0·59132 = 235
85	235·27 × 0·43722 = 103
90	102·86 × 0·25475 = 26
95	26·20 × 0·09312 = 2
100	2·44 × 0·00000 = 0

(a) $l_{x+5} = l_x \times {}_5p_x$
(b) Figures hereunder are taken from last column in Table 13.14

The survivor values, l_x, constitute the principal element of the life table. As an example, an abridged life table for Australian males for 1974 is constructed in Tables 13.14 and 13.15.

The interpretation of the l_x column is as follows. Starting with 1000 male births subject to the conditions of mortality affecting males in Australia, 1974, as expressed in the specific mortality rates, we trace through their survivorship. Eighteen die before reaching age 1, and 982 survive; of these 4 die before reaching age 5, and 978 survive, and so on. From the l_x column we can readily derive the probability at birth of surviving to an exact age, by dividing l_x by l_0 eg the probability at birth of surviving to age 25 is 958 ÷ 1000 = 0·958. On the other hand, the ${}_5p_x$ column tells us the proportion of males aged x which we can expect to reach age $(x + 5)$, if they are subject to the given mortality conditions. The l_x column gives a picture of the mortality conditions under consideration, but it would be useful to have a summary measure. Our original aim was to calculate the age to which

Australian males, on the average, can expect to live if they are subject to the mortality conditions of 1974. This calculation can now be made.

Mean Expectation of Life at Birth

The mean age to which, on the average, the 1000 male births can expect to live is called the *mean expectation of life at birth* and is, of course, the same thing as the mean age at death of these 1000 births. This can be calculated by computing the mean age at which the deaths in the life table occur. If we write d_x for the deaths occurring in the life table between the age of x and $x + 5$ we shall have

$$d_x = l_x - l_{x+5}$$

Thus, 18 will die between age 0 and 1; 4 between ages 1 and 5; 2 between ages 5 and 10, and so on. As has already been pointed out (p 516), deaths in the first year of life have a mean age at death of about 0·15 years, but for subsequent years deaths may be assumed to be evenly distributed. Hence we shall have 18 deaths centred at 0·15 years, 4 at 3 years, 2 at $7\frac{1}{2}$ years, etc. The mean age at death of the whole original 1000 births can thus be readily calculated from this frequency distribution of age at death. In our example it comes to 68·0 years.

However, it is preferable to proceed in another way, which leads ultimately to more information. We may ask: How many years on the average will the original 1000 births live? As has been pointed out above, this is precisely the same as the mean age at which they will die. How many years will the original 1000 births live between them? First, how many years will they live in their first year of life? The mean age of those who die in that year is approximately 0·15, so that the whole l_0 will live on the average for 0·15 years and l_1 of them will live a further 0·85 years. Hence

$$L_0 = 0·15 \, l_0 + 0·85 \, l_1$$

where L_0 is the number of years lived by the original l_0 births between the ages of 0 and 1. The mean age at death between the ages of 1 and 5 can be taken as 3 years; hence all the l_1 will live on the average for 2 years between the ages of 1 and 5, and l_5 of them will live another 2 years. Hence

$$L_1 = 2l_1 + 2l_5$$

where L_1 is the number of years lived by the original l_0 births between the ages of 1 and 5. Similarly

$$L_5 = 2\frac{1}{2} \, l_5 + 2\frac{1}{2} \, l_{10}$$

and, in general

$$L_x = 2\tfrac{1}{2}(l_x + l_{x+5})$$

where L_x is the number of years lived by the original l_0 births between the ages of x and $(x + 5)$. The total number of years lived by the original births will then be given by $L_0 + L_1 + L_5 + \ldots = \Sigma L_x$, and the number per birth by $\dfrac{\Sigma L_x}{l_0}$. This is the mean expectation of life at birth and is written

$$e_0^0 = \frac{\Sigma L_x}{l_0}$$

The mean expectation of life at birth is the best overall measure of the mortality of a population at a given time. For Australian males in 1974 the mean expectation of life at birth was 68·0 years. This means that on the average, new-born male babies can expect to live 68 years, if throughout their lifetime they are subject to the same mortality conditions as operated in Australia in 1974.

We can calculate the mean expectation of life at ages other than at birth. Thus the mean expectation of life at age 25 is the number of years which the original births will live after attaining the age of 25 divided by the number who survive to 25. In general, we can write the mean expectation of life at age x

$$e_x^0 = \frac{L_x + L_{x+5} + \ldots}{l_x} = \frac{\displaystyle\sum_{i=x} L_i}{l_x}$$

This mean expectation tells us the number of years a person can expect to live after attaining the age of x. For example, for Australian males in 1974 the mean expectation of life at age 25 was 45·6 years, so that having attained age 25 a man can expect to live to 70·6 years if he is subjected for the remainder of his life to the 1974 conditions. Thus if persons attain the age x, they can expect, on the average, to live to $(x + e_x^0)$ years. Clearly $(x + e_x^0)$ will be greater than e_0^0, for once people survive x years they will have overcome the hazards of life in those x years and can expect to live to a riper age than those just starting out on life. Table 13.16 sets out the calculation of e_0^0 and e_x^0.

Table 13.16

CONSTRUCTION OF ABRIDGED LIFE TABLE—AUSTRALIAN MALES, 1974: CALCULATION OF MEAN EXPECTATION OF LIFE

Exact Age (years) x	Survivors l_x	L_x	$\sum_{i=x} L_i$	$e_x^0 = \dfrac{\sum\limits_{i=x} L_i}{l_x}$
	(a)	(b)	(c)	(d)
0	1 000	985	68 005	68·0
1	982	3 920	67 020	68·2
5	978	4 885	63 100	64·5
10	976	4 875	58 215	59·6
15	974	4 850	53 340	54·8
20	966	4 810	48 490	50·2
25	958	4 772·5	43 680	45·6
30	951	4 737·5	38 907·5	40·9
35	944	4 695	34 170	36·2
40	934	4 630	29 475	31·6
45	918	4 520	24 845	27·1
50	890	4 340	20 325	22·8
55	846	4 060	15 985	18·9
60	778	3 645	11 925	15·3
65	680	3 080	8 280	12·2
70	552	2 375	5 200	9·4
75	398	1 582·5	2 825	7·1
80	235	845	1 242·5	5·3
85	103	322·5	397·5	3·9
90	26	70	75	2·9
95	2	5	5	2·5
100	0		0	

(a) Taken from last column in Table 13.15
(b) The number of years lived by the original 1000 births between the stated age and the next higher age.
(c) The number of years lived by the original 1000 births after attaining the stated age. It is the L_x column accumulated upwards.
(d) The quotient of the $\sum L_i$ and l_x columns.

We may now set out our abridged life table in detail:

Table 13.17

ABRIDGED LIFE TABLE—AUSTRALIAN MALES, 1974

Exact Age (years) x	l_x (a)	d_x (b)	p_x (c)	q_x (d)	e_x^0 (e)
0	1 000	18	0·982	0·018	68·0
1	982	4	0·996	0·004	68·2
5	978	2	0·998	0·002	64·5
10	976	2	0·998	0·002	59·6
15	974	8	0·992	0·008	54·8
20	966	8	0·991	0·009	50·2
25	958	7	0·993	0·007	45·6
30	951	7	0·992	0·008	40·9
35	944	10	0·989	0·011	36·2
40	934	16	0·983	0·017	31·6
45	918	28	0·969	0·031	27·1
50	890	44	0·951	0·049	22·8
55	846	68	0·920	0·080	18·9
60	778	98	0·874	0·126	15·3
65	680	128	0·812	0·188	12·2
70	552	154	0·721	0·279	9·4
75	398	163	0·591	0·409	7·1
80	235	132	0·437	0·563	5·3
85	103	77	0·255	0·745	3·9
90	26	24	0·093	0·907	2·9
95	2	2	0·000	1·000	2·5
100	0				0

(a) Taken from last column in Table 13.15. The l_x column gives the number of survivors of the original l_0 births. The ratios l_x/l_0 (ie $l_x \div 1000$) give the probabilities at birth of surviving to the exact age of x.

(b) By definition $d_x = l_x - l_{x+5}$. The d_x column gives the number of deaths of the original l_0 births between the age of x and the next highest age shown. The ratios d_x/l_0 (ie $d_x \div 1000$) give the probabilities at birth of dying between the age of x and the next highest age shown.

(c) Taken from last column in Table 13.14. The p_x column gives the probabilities at age x of surviving to the next highest age shown. By definition $l_{x+5} = l_x \times {}_5p_x$.

(d) By definition $q_x = 1 - p_x = d_x/l_x$. The q_x column gives the probabilities at age x of dying between the age of x and the next highest age shown.

(e) Taken from last column in Table 13.16. The e_x^0 column gives the mean expectation of life at age x when that age has been exactly attained.

For most demographic purposes an abridged life table is sufficiently accurate. It loses some accuracy in the later years of survivorship, since the assumption that deaths are spread out evenly over the quinquennial age groups becomes less valid. Complete life tables which are necessary for actuarial purposes are calculated in single age groups and involve complicated techniques for smoothing out errors in the basic data.

In most countries complete life tables are calculated whenever there is a census. Abridged life tables can be quite rapidly calculated and are particularly useful for intercensal years for which complete tables do not exist. Generally, however, it is unwise to base a life table on one year's data. The Australian Government Actuary, for example, has been in the habit of using three years' data, eg the latest Official Life Table is for 1970–72. Mortality experience of one year alone may be rather unreliable. The year 1970 for Australia is a good example. In that year, mortality in Australia was, in fact, somewhat higher than in either 1971 or 1972. This can be seen by examining the crude death rate which for males was 9·97, 9·51, 9·36 per 1000 for the years 1970, 1971 and 1972 respectively.

Life tables are drawn up for given areas at certain times. They are based on the mortality conditions existing in the given area at the time under consideration. These mortality conditions are expressed in detail in the specific mortality rates. Given these rates, which can readily be computed for the population with which we are concerned, we can calculate the life table.

13.6 Applications of the Life Table

Computation of Probabilities of Surviving and Dying

It is possible to derive from the life table the probabilities of more or less complex events happening. Thus the probability at birth of dying between the ages of 20 and 30 years will be given by the number of the original births dying between the ages of 20 and 30, divided by the number of original births, ie in our example by $15 \div 1000 = 0·015$. This probability tells us that on the average out of every 1000 male births subject to the Australian mortality of 1974, 15 will die between the ages of 20 and 30 years. Similarly, if we wish to estimate the probability at birth of dying between the ages of 25 and 33 years, we shall have to estimate the number of the original births dying between these ages. We know that 7 die between 25 and 30 and to ascertain those dying between 30 and 33 we must interpolate within the age group 30 to 35, ie the required number will be estimated as $3/5 \times 7 = 4$. The required probability will then be $(7 + 4) \div 1000 = 0·011$. Again, if we want the probability at age 20 of dying before reaching 30, we shall calculate the ratio of deaths between 20 and 30 to survivors at age 20, ie $15 \div 966 = 0·016$. This means that out of every 1000 males who reach 20, on the average 16 will die before reaching 30 years. Finally, we may consider a case involving two lives. What is the probability that a man aged 30 and a man aged 50 will both survive 10 years? The answer for our example is $\frac{934}{951} \times \frac{778}{890} = 0.859$. This holds, of course, only if the probabilities of surviving of the two men are independent.

Life Assurance

The life table was developed primarily to meet the needs of life assurance offices. It forms the basis for calculations of the premiums necessary to purchase various amounts of life assurance. Actually these calculations are very complex, but the underlying principles are simple. For example, according to 1974 mortality, what annual premium would an Australian have to pay on a full-life policy worth $1000 if his life was assured at birth, assuming that the assurance office earns no income on its funds? Let the premium be $x per annum. Since a male on the average can be expected to live 68·0 years, over his lifetime a man will have paid $x × 68·0 in premiums. This will have to equal the value of the policy, $1000, so that the annual premium must be $1000 ÷ 68 = $14·70. If the policy was taken out at age 20, then total premiums paid will be $x × 50·2, for 50·2 years is the expectation of life at 20, and the annual premium must be $19·92. If the policy were an endowment policy, taken out at, say, 20 and payable at 30 or prior death, we should proceed in a somewhat different fashion. From Table 13.16, we know that the 966 survivors at age 20 live 4810 + 4772·5 years between them between the ages of 20 and 30. Consequently, on the average a total of $x × (9582·5 ÷ 966) premiums will be collected and hence the annual premium must be $1000 ÷ 9·920 = $100·80.

Mortality Due to Specific Causes[1]

It is of interest to know the relative importance of various causes of death. Data are usually available showing deaths distributed according to specific causes, and a percentage distribution can be readily calculated. Such a distribution is not, however, very satisfactory, since causes differ in their age-incidence. For example, the younger groups are susceptible to transport accidents, whereas heart disease attacks the old age groups. Consequently a young population will have a relatively high proportion of accidental deaths and a relatively low one of deaths from heart disease. What we really want to ascertain are the probabilities at given ages of dying from a specific cause. With the help of a life table these can be calculated.

[1] See R R Kuczynski: *The Measurement of Population Growth* (Gordon and Breach, 1969), pp 194–5.

As an illustration there are worked out below the probabilities at birth of dying from motor vehicle accidents and heart disease for Australian males in 1974. First, it is necessary to calculate the ratios which deaths from these causes bear to total deaths in the various age groups. Decennial groups will suffice for this purpose.

Table 13.18

DEATHS FROM MOTOR VEHICLE ACCIDENTS AND HEART DISEASE AUSTRALIAN MALES, 1974

Age Group (years)	All Causes	Motor Vehicle Accidents		Heart Disease	
		Numbers (a)	Proportion of Deaths from All Causes	Numbers (a)	Proportion of Deaths from All Causes
0–5	2 825	72	0·02549	8	0·00283
5–14	525	133	0·25333	9	0·01714
15–24	2 000	1 159	0·57950	31	0·01550
25–34	1 459	421	0·28855	110	0·07539
35–44	2 191	233	0·10634	593	0·27065
45–54	6 255	255	0·04077	2 457	0·39281
55–64	12 010	234	0·01948	5 300	0·44130
65–74	16 993	174	0·01024	7 142	0·42029
75 and over	20 041	121	0·00604	8 028	0·40058
All Ages	64 299	2 802	0·04358	23 678	0·36825

(a) Four deaths from heart disease and one from motor vehicle accidents, age not stated, have been allocated proportionately.
Source: Australian Bureau of Statistics: *Deaths 1974* (Ref 4.8), p 16

From the life table we know that out of the 1000 original births 22 will die between ages 0 and 5. From the above we can estimate that of these deaths 22 × 0·02549 = 0·56 will be due to motor vehicle accidents and 22 × 0·00283 = 0·06 to heart disease. If we do this for all age groups, we can readily calculate the numbers of the original 1000 births which will die due to these specific causes. This is done in Table 13.19.

From the table we see that, according to the Australian mortality conditions of 1974, out of the 1000 original births 29 will ultimately die from motor vehicle accidents. Accordingly, the probability at birth of a male dying from a motor vehicle accident is 0·029. Likewise, the probability at birth of dying from heart disease is 0·388. These compare with the actual proportions of deaths from these causes in 1974, shown in Table 13.18 as 0·044 and 0·368 respectively. If we look at these latter figures only, we might be inclined to say that the incidence of heart disease was 8 times that of motor vehicle accidents, whereas in fact a man is about 13 times more likely to die from the former than from the latter cause over his lifetime. This apparent discrepancy is due to the relatively high percentage of the Australian population in the younger age groups. This conflict occurs because the two sets of figures measure different things, the one measures the actual incidence of the causes in 1974, the other the probability at birth of a man dying from the causes throughout his lifetime.

Table 13.19
CALCULATION OF PROBABILITIES AT BIRTH OF DYING FROM MOTOR VEHICLE ACCIDENTS AND HEART DISEASE, AUSTRALIAN MALES, 1974

Age Group (years)	Deaths of Original 1 000 Births in Life Table (1)	Proportion due to Motor Vehicle Accidents (2)	Number of Deaths in Life Table due to Motor Vehicle Accidents (3)	Proportion due to Heart Disease (4)	Number of Deaths in Life Table due to Heart Disease (5)
0–5	22	0·02549	0·56	0·00283	0·06
5–14	4	0·25333	1·01	0·01714	0·07
15–24	16	0·57950	9·27	0·01550	0·25
25–34	14	0·28855	4·04	0·07539	1·06
35–44	26	0·10634	2·76	0·27065	7·04
45–54	72	0·04077	2·94	0·39281	28·28
55–64	166	0·01948	3·23	0·44130	73·26
65–74	282	0·01024	2·89	0·42029	118·52
75 and over	398	0·00604	2·40	0·40058	159·43
All Ages	1 000		29·10		387·97

Col (1): From third column of Table 13.17 above.
Cols (2) and (4): From Table 13.18 above.
Col (3) = col (1) × col (2).
Col (5) = col (1) × col (4).

It is important to realise that a rise, say, in the probability at birth of a male dying from heart disease over his lifetime does not necessarily indicate that males are becoming more susceptible to death from that cause. Since people must die from one cause or another sooner or later, a fall in the rates at which males of given ages die from certain diseases must, through increasing the number surviving those diseases, result in an increase in the proportion dying from other diseases, even though the rates, at which males of given ages die from those other diseases, remain constant. It is the complex of such age-specific rates (ie number of deaths of males aged x from a certain cause per 1000 of the population of males aged x) to which we must look if we wish to examine the susceptibility of people to death from certain causes.

Stationary Population

So far we have viewed the life table as the life history of an initial group of births subject to given mortality conditions. We have taken 1000 births and traced out how many of these will survive to various ages. Now, suppose that 1000 births take place every year, spread out evenly over the year, and that these births are subject to the mortality conditions under consideration. These births will result in the building up of a population. We could take a count of that population at the end of any year, say. If we do so, how many people shall we find in the age group x years and under $(x + 5)$? Take a particular age group, say 50 years and under 55 in the year 2000. Those in that age group at 31 December 2000 must have been born during 1950, 1949, 1948, 1947 or 1946. Of the 5000 births during these years, $5l_{50}$ will survive to attain the exact age of 50 during the years 1996–2000, and $5(l_{50} - l_{55})$ will die between the exact ages of 50 and 55 during the years 1996–2005. By the end of the year 2000, half of these latter deaths will have taken place, so that the number in the age group as at 31 December 2000 will be $5l_{50} - 2\frac{1}{2}(l_{50} - l_{55}) = 2\frac{1}{2}(l_{50} + l_{55})$. This number will be the same whether or not the count is made at 31 December 2000, or any other year, provided only that there have been 1000 births per annum in the past and they have been subject to the given mortality conditions.

We can generalise the above argument by saying that a population built up from a constant stream of births per annum subject to given mortality conditions will have $2\frac{1}{2}(l_x + l_{x+5})$ persons in the age group x years and under $(x + 5)$, whenever a count of the population is made. Since the population will have the same number in each age group whenever measured, it must contain the same total number of persons, ie it must be *stationary* in numbers. Consequently, if there are 1000 births per annum there will also be 1000 deaths per annum.

The *stationary population* of a particular life table is the population which would be built up if there were 1000 births per annum continuously subject to the mortality conditions of which the life table is an expression. The age distribution of the stationary population for the age group x years and under $(x + 5)$ is given by $2\frac{1}{2}(l_x + l_{x+5})$, which is in fact the L_x which we have already calculated and which represents the number of years lived by an original 1000 births between the ages of x years and $(x + 5)$. Consequently, the age distribution of the stationary population in quinquennial age groups is defined by:

$$L_x = 2\tfrac{1}{2}(l_x + l_{x+5})$$

Thus we can use a life table to indicate either the life history of a group of births or the age distribution of the population which would be built up from a constant stream of births, provided the births (in both cases) are subject to the given mortality conditions.

The concept of a stationary population can perhaps best be appreciated by considering a hypothetical single-age life table:

Age Group (years)	Population as at End of			
	Year 0	Year 1	Year 2	Year 3
0 and under 1	973	973	973	973
1 ,, ,, 2	966	966	966	966
2 ,, ,, 3	964	964	964	964
3 ,, ,, 4	962	962	962	962
4 ,, ,, 5	961	961	961	961
.	.	.	.	.
.	.	.	.	.
.	.	.	.	.
All Ages	66 070	66 070	66 070	66 070

During year 3, for example, there are 1000 births; of these 973 are surviving in the age group 0 and under 1 at the end of the year. In the age group 1 and under 2 there are 966 persons being survivors of the 973 in the preceding age group in the previous year, and so on. Furthermore, in year 3 total deaths are given by infant deaths (1000 − 973) plus the depletions of the age groups from the preceding year (973 − 966 and 966 − 964, etc). Clearly, total deaths must add to 1000.

Referring back to Table 13.16 containing the L_x values, we see that 1000 male births per annum would ultimately result in a total stationary population of 68 005, if they were subject to 1974 mortality. Moreover, the numbers in each group would be stationary; for example, there would always be 4340 males in the age group 50 and under 55, whenever a count was made.

Comparisons of Mortality Conditions

The mean expectation of life at birth is the best general overall index of mortality. It varies considerably according to place and time, ranging between about 25 and 75 years. In most countries it has risen steadily over the past half-century or so, largely due to the decline in infantile mortality. The female expectation of life is usually higher than the male, except where maternal mortality is high. The tables below set out the mean expectation of life at birth for various countries.

Table 13.20

MEAN EXPECTATION OF LIFE AT BIRTH FOR SELECTED COUNTRIES

Country and Period	Males	Females
	(years)	(years)
India—		
1921–31 . . .	26·91	26·56
1941–50 . . .	32·45	31·66
1951–60 . . .	41·89	40·55
Italy—		
1921–22 . . .	49·27	50·75
1930–32 . . .	53·76	56·00
1954–57 . . .	65·75	70·02
1960–62 . . .	67·24	72·27
1970–72 . . .	68·97	74·88
Japan—		
1921–25 . . .	42·06	43·20
1935–36 . . .	46·92	49·63
1958 . . .	64·98	69·58
1965 . . .	67·73	72·95
1972 . . .	70·49	75·92
Netherlands—		
1921–30 . . .	61·9	63·5
1931–40 . . .	65·7	67·2
1953–55 . . .	71·0	73·9
1961–65 . . .	71·1	75·9
1973 . . .	71·2	77·2
Sweden—		
1921–30 . . .	60·97	63·16
1931–40 . . .	63·76	66·13
1956 . . .	70·92	74·35
1961–65 . . .	71·60	75·70
1973 . . .	72·12	77·66
United Kingdom (a)—		
1920–22 . . .	55·62	59·58
1930–32 . . .	58·74	62·88
1958 . . .	67·95	73·69
1963–65 . . .	68·10	74·20
1968–70 . . .	67·81	73·81
United States—		
1919–21 . . .	55·50	57·40
1939–41 . . .	61·60	65·89
1958 . . .	66·40	72·70
1965 . . .	66·80	73·70
1972 . . .	67·4	75·2

(a) England and Wales

Source: United Nations: *Demographic Year Book*, 1959, pp 640–4 and 1966, pp 116–19; 1974, pp 120–4

Table 13.21
MEAN EXPECTATION OF LIFE AT BIRTH—AUSTRALIA, 1881–1972

Period	Males	Females
	(years)	(years)
1881–90	47·20	50·84
1891–1900	51·06	54·76
1901–10	55·20	58·84
1920–22	59·15	63·31
1932–34	63·48	67·14
1946–48	66·07	70·63
1953–55	67·14	72·75
1960–62	67·92	74·18
1970–72	67·81	74·49

Source: Australian Bureau of Statistics: *Year Book*, No. 46, 1960, p 352, No. 53, 1967, p 234; *Australian Life Tables 1970–72*, (Ref 4.31), pp 7, 8

When a more detailed comparison of mortality is required, comparison of the probabilities of dying within, say, 5 or 10 years at different ages, or of the mean expectation of life at different ages, or of the number of survivors at different ages is useful. Direct comparison can also be made of specific mortality rates for different age groups. Tables 13.22 to 13.25 give examples.

Table 13.22
PROBABILITY OF DYING WITHIN 10 YEARS AT STATED AGES ($_{10}q_x$)—AUSTRALIAN MALES

Exact Age (years)	1881–90	1901–10	1920–22	1932–34	1946–48	1970–72	1970–72 as Ratio to 1881–90
0	0·203	0·134	0·106	0·068	0·044	0·026	0·13
10	0·039	0·025	0·019	0·015	0·011	0·010	0·26
20	0·080	0·043	0·034	0·024	0·017	0·016	0·20
30	0·091	0·061	0·046	0·034	0·023	0·019	0·21
40	0·133	0·101	0·080	0·063	0·054	0·047	0·35
50	0·218	0·168	0·147	0·137	0·136	0·126	0·58
60	0·372	0·326	0·301	0·284	0·297	0·296	0·80
70	0·618	0·626	0·580	0·556	0·564	0·572	0·93
80	0·873	0·885	0·885	0·868	0·862	0·849	0·97

Source: Derived from Australian Bureau of Statistics: *Demography Bulletin*, No. 64, 1946, p 180, No. 74, 1956, p 204; No. 77, 1959, p 193; *Australian Life Tables 1970–72* (Ref 4.31), p 7

Table 13.23
EXPECTATION OF LIFE AT STATED AGES (e_x^0)
AUSTRALIAN MALES

Exact Age (years)	1881–90	1901–10	1920–22	1932–34	1946–48	1970–72	1970–72 as Ratio to 1881–90
0	47·2	55·2	59·1	63·5	66·1	67·8	1·44
10	48·9	53·5	56·0	58·0	59·0	59·7	1·22
20	40·6	44·7	47·0	48·8	49·6	50·2	1·24
30	33·6	36·5	38·4	39·9	40·4	40·9	1·22
40	26·5	28·6	30·1	31·1	31·2	31·6	1·19
50	19·7	21·2	22·2	22·8	22·7	22·9	1·16
60	13·8	14·3	15·1	15·6	15·4	15·3	1·11
70	8·8	8·7	9·3	9·6	9·6	9·5	1·08
80	5·1	5·0	5·0	5·2	5·4	5·5	1·08

Source: Australian Bureau of Statistics: *Demography Bulletin*, No. 64, 1946, p 180; No. 77, 1959, p 196; *Australian Life Tables* 1970–72 (Ref 4.31), p 7

Table 13.24
NUMBER OF 1000 BIRTHS SURVIVING AT STATED AGES (l_x)
AUSTRALIAN MALES

Exact Age (years)	1881–90	1901–10	1920–22	1932–34	1946–48	1970–72	1970–72 as Ratio to 1881–90
0	1000	1000	1000	1000	1000	1000	1·00
10	797	866	894	932	956	974	1·22
20	766	845	877	918	946	965	1·26
30	705	808	847	896	930	949	1·35
40	641	759	808	865	908	931	1·45
50	556	682	743	811	859	888	1·60
60	435	568	634	700	743	776	1·78
70	273	383	443	501	522	546	2·00
80	104	143	186	222	228	234	2·25
90	13	17	21	29	31	35	2·69

Source: Australian Bureau of Statistics: *Demography Bulletin*, No. 64, 1946, p 179; No. 74, 1956, p 203; No. 77, 1959, p 193; *Australian Life Tables* 1970–72 (Ref 4.31), p 13

Table 13.25

MALE SPECIFIC MORTALITY RATES
NEW SOUTH WALES AND SOUTH AUSTRALIA, 1972

Age Group (years)	Specific Mortality Rates per 1000 per annum		Ratio of SA to NSW
	New South Wales	South Australia	
Under 1	20·10	18·72	0·93
1–4	0·94	1·07	1·14
5–9	0·46	0·44	0·96
10–14	0·37	0·45	1·22
15–19	1·37	1·34	0·98
20–24	1·65	1·43	0·87
25–29	1·34	1·17	0·87
30–34	1·41	1·26	0·89
35–39	2·23	1·77	0·79
40–44	3·47	3·34	0·96
45–49	6·69	5·63	0·84
50–54	10·06	9·47	0·94
55–59	17·01	15·65	0·92
60–64	29·06	25·22	0·87
65–69	41·91	42·03	1·00
70–74	67·98	59·91	0·88
75–79	105·69	97·90	0·93
80–84	150·97	141·03	0·93
85 and over	246·26	238·34	0·97

Source: Australian Bureau of Statistics: *Year Book*, No. 60, 1974, p 193

The crude death rate is sometimes used as an index of mortality. As such it can be extremely misleading. As has already been pointed out, it depends not only on mortality conditions but also on the age distribution of the population. In particular, a population with a preponderance in the ages 15 to 50 will tend to have a lower crude death rate than otherwise, and a growing population will tend to have a lower one than a declining population. The age distribution of a population depends on its past history of births, deaths and migrations. Hence, the particular value which the crude death rate takes is largely fortuitous. However, the mean expectation of life at birth is clear of such a charge. For example, the crude death rate in Australia, 1901–10, was 11·3 per 1000 per annum, and in France for 1928–33 it was 16·3 per 1000, but in both countries at those periods the mean expectation of life was approximately 57 years. The higher crude death rate for France was only a reflection of an older population, and no indication that one's chances of longevity were less in France.[1]

[1] A similar example is given in section 1.3, p 5 above.

There is also a measure closely connected with e_0^0, which is sometimes used. If given mortality conditions are applied to a constant stream of births, they give rise to a stationary population uniquely determined by these mortality conditions themselves (see p 546 above). The death rate of such a population is known as the *true death rate*, and it can be used as an index of mortality. The total stationary population is given by ΣL_x. If it has been built up from 1000 births per annum, there will be 1000 deaths per annum. Accordingly,

$$\text{True death rate} = \frac{1000}{\Sigma L_x} \times 1000$$

Since $e_0^0 = \frac{\Sigma L_x}{1000}$, the true death rate is simply the reciprocal of the mean expectation of life. It is the crude death rate of the stationary population and is unaffected by the age distribution of the actual population. For 1974 for Australian males we have:

$$\text{True death rate} = \frac{1000}{68\,005} \times 1000 = 14\cdot70 \text{ per 1000 per annum}$$

The true death rate is sometimes used instead of the mean expectation of life when comparing mortality conditions. But the concept behind e_0^0 would seem to be simpler, and for that reason e_0^0 should be preferred. However, the true death rate can be very useful in interpreting the crude death rate. For example, in 1974 Australian males had a crude death rate of 9·58 per 1000 per annum, whereas the true death rate was 14·70. Past growth of and past higher mortality in the Australian population had produced by 1974 an age distribution younger than that of the stationary population implied in the mortality conditions of which the true death rate of 14·70 is an expression. This accounts for the difference in the two death rates. How can we expect the crude death rate to move in the future? If mortality remains at about the 1974 level, and if the population ultimately becomes stationary, the actual age distribution will become older. Consequently the crude death rate must rise ultimately to 14·70 per 1000. Such a rise would not indicate any increase in mortality. The crude death rate will, however, remain lower than the true death rate if the population is increasing, for then the actual population will be younger than the stationary one implied in the 1974 mortality conditions, and the more rapidly the population is increasing the lower will be the crude death rate relatively to the true rate. On the other hand, it is unlikely that the Australian population will increase rapidly for ever. This implies that the crude death rate will rise in the future unless mortality falls substantially. Such a rise should not cause concern, for it does not in itself mean any deterioration in mortality conditions. In fact, if the Australian population did become stationary, mortality would have to fall beyond all reasonable hopes to maintain the crude death rate at 9·58 per 1000. For such a death rate in a stationary population implies a mean expectation of life at birth of $1000 \div 9·58 = 104·4$ years.

Table 13.26
PROJECTING AGE GROUPS

At 30 June 1974		Survivorship Ratio (b)	At 30 June 1984	
Age Group (years)	Number (a)		Age Group (years)	Number (c)
50 and under 55	369 882	$\dfrac{3645}{4340} = 0·8399$	60 and under 65	310 700
55 and under 60	294 371	$\dfrac{3080}{4060} = 0·7586$	65 and under 70	223 300
60 and under 65	264 168	$\dfrac{2375}{3645} = 0·6516$	70 and under 75	172 100
Total	928 421		Total	706 100

(a) Source: Australian Bureau of Statistics: *Estimated Age Distribution of the Population, 30 June 1974* (Ref 4.15), p 3.
(b) From L_x column of Table 13.16 above.
(c) The number at 30 June 1974, multiplied by the appropriate survivorship ratio.

Population Projections

Since the persons in the age group x and under $(x + 5)$ at a particular date are the survivors of those aged $(x - 5)$ and under x five years earlier, it is possible to project forward age groups by applying to existing age groups appropriate *survivorship ratios*. Thus, suppose in 1974 it is required to estimate the number of males aged 60 and under 75 at 30 June 1984, in Australia. These males will be the survivors of those aged 50 and under 65 at 30 June 1974. From the 1974 life table (Table 13.16) we know that the number of males aged 50 and under 55 in the stationary population which would result from a constant stream of 1000 births per annum is 4340. In ten years' time these will be aged 60 and under 65, and will have been reduced in number to 3645. Hence $3645 \div 4340$ of the 50–54 age group will survive ten years to become the 60–64 group, provided they are subject to 1974 mortality conditions. Accordingly we proceed as given in Table 13.26.

Such a population projection will be accurate provided that there are no radical changes in mortality conditions and that migration is negligible. Of course, we might guess at probable migration and add it in. The example illustrates the projection into the future only of already existing age groups. Projection of the whole age distribution is much more difficult, and much less reliable, since some of the future age groups will not yet be in existence and future births must be estimated. It is possible to make such estimates and also to allow for changes in mortality, but these questions will not be dealt with here.[1]

Limitations of the Life Table

The life table suffers from one important limitation. Whilst it reflects the actual mortality experience of a given year or period of years, it does not reflect the actual mortality experience of any group of births. Thus the births of 1900 are subject in their first year to the mortality conditions of 1900–1, in their second year to those of 1901–2, in their third year to those of 1902–3, and so on. Since mortality is selective in the biological sense, relatively low rates for the higher age groups in, say, 1974 may be due to the selective force of higher than current mortality rates in the earlier ages of those higher age groups. Consequently it is by no means certain that the current mortality rates of 1974 could apply throughout to a generation born in 1974. Although we say that the mean expectation of life at birth for Australian males is now about 68·0 years, this does not mean that persons born now will, on the average, actually live to that age; it only means that if persons born now were subject to existing mortality conditions *throughout their whole lives*, that is the age to which they could expect to live on the average. Consequently, the life table and all the measures associated with it are strictly *hypothetical*. This does not prevent the life table being very useful, nor does it prevent the mean expectation of life at birth being the best available index of overall mortality, but it is a limitation which should always be borne in mind.

13.7 Measurement of Fertility

In demography the term *fertility* refers to the actual production of children. Fertility must be distinguished from *fecundity* which refers to the capacity to bear children. Fecundity sets an upper limit to fertility. The simplest way to summarise the fertility conditions of a particular area during a given period is to calculate the mean number of children

[1] See P R Cox: *Demography*, 4th edition (Cambridge University Press, 1970) Chapters 14 and 15, pp 234–72; United Nations: *Methods for Population Projections by Sex and Age* (New York, 1956).

which females living right through their child-bearing period will (on the average) bear, if they are subject to the fertility conditions holding in the particular area during the given period. Such a measure is known as the *total fertility rate*. The full child-bearing period of a female is usually taken to be the span from 15 years of age to 50.

Total Fertility Rate

The data required for the calculation of the total fertility rate are the female age distribution and the number of births classified by the age of mother. Suppose, for example, that at 30 June of the year under consideration there were 122 000 females aged 15 and under 16 years, 118 000 females aged 16 and under 17 years, 115 000 females aged 17 and under 18 years, and so on. Suppose further that during that year there were 480, 1880 and 4600 births respectively to females in the above three age groups. If we start with 1000 females exactly aged 15 and subject them to the fertility conditions of the year under consideration, we shall expect them to have $480/122\,000 \times 1000 = 4$ births during the year in which they pass from 15 to 16 years old, $1880/118\,000 \times 1000 = 16$ births during the year in which they pass from 16 to 17 years old, $4600/115\,000 \times 1000 = 40$ births during the year in which they pass from 17 to 18 years old, and so on. At the exact age of 15 they will have borne 0 children, by the age of 16 they will have borne 4 children, by the age of 17 they will have borne $4 + 16 = 20$ children, by the age of 18 they will have borne $4 + 16 + 40 = 60$ children, and so on. If we continue this process, we can readily ascertain the total number of children which the 1000 females will bear over their whole child-bearing period.

We now define the *specific fertility rate* for the age group x years and under $(x + 1)$:
Specific fertility rate

$$= \frac{\text{annual births to females aged } x \text{ and under } (x + 1)}{\text{mean number of females aged } x \text{ and under } (x + 1)} \times 1000$$

The specific fertility rate for a particular age group is the rate per 1000 per annum at which the females in that age group produce offspring. It follows that the sum of the specific fertility rates for the age groups between 15 and 50 will give the total number of children born to 1000 females living right through their child-bearing period and subject to the given fertility conditions as expressed in the specific fertility rates. The mean number of children born per female will be given by dividing this total by 1000, and this is the total fertility rate. Accordingly the total fertility rate is the mean number of children which a female aged 15 can expect to bear if she lives until at least the age of 50, provided that she is subject to the given fertility conditions over the whole of her child-bearing period. The total fertility rate for a particular area during a given period is a summary measure of the fertility conditions operating in that area during that period.

In order to calculate the total fertility rate we shall have to calculate 35 specific fertility rates and then add them. In practice, we can shorten this procedure by working in quinquennial age groups. We define the specific fertility rate for group x years and under $(x + 5)$:

Specific fertility rate

$$= \frac{\text{annual births to females aged } x \text{ and under } (x + 5)}{\text{mean number of females aged } x \text{ and under } (x + 5)} \times 1000$$

Such a specific fertility rate is the rate per 1000 per annum at which the females in the particular age group produce offspring. Thus, for Australia in 1974, there were 581 314 females aged 15–19 at 30 June 1974. This figure must be used as an estimate of the mean number in

Table 13.27

CALCULATION OF TOTAL FERTILITY RATE—AUSTRALIA, 1974

Age Group (years)	Female Population at 30 June 1974 (1)	Births by Age of Mother (2)	Specific Fertility Rates per 1000 per annum (d) (3)
15–19	581 314	26 301 (*a*)	45·24
20–24	552 009	82 862	150·11
25–29	530 444	87 266	164·52
30–34	424 141	34 556	81·47
35–39	378 135	11 350	30·02
40–44	362 125	2 667	7·36
45–49	382 585	175 (*b*)	0·46
Total		245 177 (*c*)	479·18

(*a*) Includes births to females under 15 years.
(*b*) Includes births to females over 50 years.
(*c*) Forty-six births, age of mother not stated, have been allocated proportionately.
(*d*) Col (3) = (col (2) ÷ col (1)) × 1000
Source: Australian Bureau of Statistics: *Births 1974* (Ref 4.4), p 7 and Appendix.

Total fertility rate = (479·18 × 5) ÷ 1000 = 2·396

the age group. These females gave birth to 26 301 children. Hence the specific fertility rate for the age group 15–19 was 26 301/581 314 × 1000 = 45·24 per 1000 per annum. Accordingly, 1000 females exactly aged 15 would by the time they reached 20 have borne 45·24 × 5 = 226·20 children. It is necessary to multiply by 5 since the specific fertility rate is a rate per annum and by the time the females reach the age of 20 they will have spent 5 years in the age group 15–19. It follows that, if we add the quinquennial specific fertility rates and multiply by 5, we shall have the total number of children which 1000 females aged 15 will bear over their lifetimes. A calculation based on quinquennial age groups involves only one-fifth of the arithmetic of one based on single age groups and is very nearly as accurate. The calculation of the total fertility rate for Australia, 1974, is shown in Table 13.27.

In the table below is shown the number of births which 1000 females will have borne by the time they reach certain ages. The table is in a sense analogous to a life table.

Table 13.28

Exact Age (years)	Total Births Produced per 1 000 Females Aged 15 by Stated Ages (a)
15	0
20	226
25	977
30	1 800
35	2 207
40	2 357
45	2 394
50	2 396

(a) Last column of Table 13.27 multiplied by 5 and accumulated downwards.

A total fertility rate of 2·396 for Australia in 1974 means that on the average a female aged 15 could expect to produce 2·396 births over the course of her lifetime if she were subject to 1974 Australian fertility conditions, but *not* subject to mortality over her child-bearing period.

Gross Reproduction Rate

The total fertility rate refers to the number of children which a female can expect to produce. A more significant figure is the number of *female* children. For this will give an indication of the number of females which a female will produce over her lifetime to replace herself. The total fertility rate can be calculated in terms of female births only, by restricting the births in the specific fertility rates to female births. Such a calculation leads to a measure called the *gross reproduction rate*. The gross reproduction rate measures the mean number of female children which a female aged 15 can expect to bear if she lives right through the child-bearing period and is subject to the given fertility conditions. It follows that the gross reproduction rate measures the mean number of female children which will be born to a newly-born female who is subject to the given fertility conditions throughout her lifetime, but is *not* subject to mortality.

The gross reproduction rate can be calculated directly by the method referred to above, or very nearly as accurately by multiplying the total fertility rate by the proportion of all births which are female births. Thus

Gross reproduction rate

$$= \text{total fertility rate} \times \frac{\text{number of female births}}{\text{number of births}}$$

For Australia, for 1974, we have:

$$\text{Gross reproduction rate} = 2 \cdot 396 \times \frac{118\,882}{245\,177}$$

$$= 1 \cdot 162$$

The gross reproduction rate is used as a measure of the fertility of a population. As such it has certain limitations which are discussed later (see pp 572–4 below). However, it is superior to the crude birth rate as such a measure, because, as has already been pointed out, the latter rate depends to some extent on the sex and age distribution of the population and this distribution may be favourable to a high or low number of births irrespective of current fertility conditions. On the other hand, the gross reproduction rate depends only on the fertility conditions current to the period under consideration. Furthermore, the gross reproduction rate corresponds more closely to what we mean by 'fertility' than the crude birth rate, which is simply the rate at which the population is augmenting its numbers through births.

The gross reproduction rate is useful for comparing fertility in different areas or in the same area at different times. In the latter case, if the periods to be compared are close to one another (eg adjacent years), movements in the gross reproduction rates and the crude birth rate usually closely correspond, for the sex and age distribution cannot undergo very substantial changes over very short periods. However, for comparisons over longer periods the two measures can give different impressions, and the crude birth rate can be misleading. For example, in Australia in 1881 the crude birth rate was 35·26 per 1000. In 1891 it was 34·47 per 1000, a fall of only 2 per cent. However, over this period the proportion of females aged between 20 and 45 years in the total population rose appreciably from $14\frac{1}{2}$ per cent to 16 per cent. Consequently for this reason alone the crude birth rate in 1891 would overstate the level of fertility relatively to that in 1881.

In fact, the gross reproduction rates for the two years were 2·65 and 2·30 respectively, a fall of 13 per cent. The fall in fertility was very much greater than that revealed by the fall in the crude birth rate. The gross reproduction rate could, in theory, range from 0 to about 5. Values of gross reproduction rates actually recorded range from 0·80 in Austria for 1933 to 3·65 in the Ukraine, 1896–7.[1] The corresponding total fertility rates were approximately 1·64 and 7·48. The gross reproduction rate in England and Wales, for example, was 1·31 in 1921, 0·92 in 1931, 1·39 in 1963 and 1·16 in 1971. The course of the gross reproduction rate in Australia is given in Table 13·29. As can be seen from this table, fertility declined from the latter part of the nineteenth century until the Second World War, rose during the post-war period, and has fallen again quite substantially over the past decade. This movement is characteristic of most Western European type countries. Recent gross reproduction rates for a number of countries are given in Table 13.33 on p 563 below.

Table 13.29

**GROSS REPRODUCTION RATES
AUSTRALIA, 1881–1974**

1881	. . . .	2·65 (a)
1891	. . . .	2·30 (a)
1901	. . . .	1·74 (a)
1911	. . . .	1·71
1921	. . . .	1·51
1931	. . . .	1·14
1941	. . . .	1·15
1951	. . . .	1·49
1961	. . . .	1·73
1971	. . . .	1·44
1974	. . . .	1·16

(a) Approximate only

Source: Australian Bureau of Statistics: *Year Book*, No. 40, 1954, p 390; No. 60, 1974, p 182

13.8 Measurement of Population Replacement

We have discussed the measurement of mortality and fertility separately. We now combine the, two and discuss the measurement of population replacement and population growth. Apart from migration, population growth depends on the balance between mortality and fertility. The central questions in demography are: Would a given population replace itself if the fertility and mortality conditions currently holding continued to hold indefinitely? Would it grow or

[1] See Kuczynski: *op cit*, p 126.

decline? At what rate? In answering such questions we leave aside migration, since we are interested in whether or not the population will grow from its own resources.

The gross reproduction rate measures the mean number of female children which will be born to a newly-born female who is subject to the given fertility conditions throughout her lifetime but is *not* subject to mortality. If the rate is exactly unity, this means that, on the average, each female will produce sufficient female offspring to replace herself *only* if she is not subject to mortality. Since, in fact, some females die before they reach the end of their child-bearing period and therefore before they will have produced the mean number of *one* female replacement, a gross reproduction rate of unity will not ensure population replacement. It follows from this that in order to measure population replacement we must calculate the mean number of female children which will be born to a newly-born female who is subject to the given fertility *and* mortality conditions throughout her lifetime. Such a measure is known as the *net reproduction rate*. The fertility conditions are expressed by the specific fertility rates and the mortality conditions by the specific mortality rates as combined into a life table.

Net Reproduction Rate

Consider the calculation of the net reproduction rate for Australia, 1974. We start with 1000 female births. The relevant portion of the life table is given below.

Table 13.30

LIFE TABLE—AUSTRALIAN FEMALES, 1974

Exact Age (years) x	l_x	L_x
0	1 000	
15	980	
20	978	4 895
25	975	4 882·5
30	972	4 867·5
35	969	4 852·5
40	962	4 827·5
45	952	4 785
50	935	4 717·5

Source: Computed by the authors using same method as in Tables 13.14–13.16 above

Of the initial 1000 female births, 980 will reach the age of 15. These 980 will live 4895 years between them between the ages of 15 and 20.

But we know from the specific fertility rates (see Table 13.27, p 550) that females between the ages of 15 and 20 have children at the rate of 45·24 per 1000 per annum. Consequently, in the five years between 15 and 20 we can expect our initial 1000 births to produce 4895 × 45·24/1000 = 221·45 offspring. Again, between the ages of 20 and 25 our initial 1000 births will live 4882·5 years between them and can be expected to produce a further 4882·5 × 150·11/1000 = 732·91 offspring. Proceeding in this way, we can readily calculate the total number of offspring which will be produced. If we multiply this figure by the ratio of female births to all births, we get the total number of female off-spring born to the initial 1000 female births over their lifetimes. By dividing by 1000, we get the mean number per female birth, and this is the net reproduction rate. The calculations are shown below.

Table 13.31

CALCULATION OF NET REPRODUCTION RATE—AUSTRALIA, 1974

Age Group (years)	Specific Fertility Rate per 1 000 per annum (1)	Years Lived by 1 000 Female Births (2)	Births per 1 000 Female Births (3)
15–19	45·24	4 895	221·45
20–24	150·11	4 882·5	732·91
25–29	164·52	4 867·5	800·80
30–34	81·47	4 852·5	395·33
35–39	30·02	4 827·5	144·92
40–44	7·36	4 785	35·22
45–49	0·46	4 717·5	2·17
Total			2 332·80

Col (1): From Table 13.27 above.
Col (2): From Table 13.30 above.
Col (3) = (Col (1) × Col (2)) ÷ 1000

$$\text{Net reproduction rate} = \left(2332{\cdot}80 \times \frac{118\,882}{245\,177}\right) \div 1000 = 1{\cdot}131$$

In Table 13.32 on p 562 is shown the number of births which 1000 females will have borne by the time they reach certain ages.

The net reproduction rate measures the mean number of female children which will be born to a newly-born female who is subject to the given fertility and mortality conditions throughout her lifetime. If the net reproduction rate equals unity, then throughout her lifetime each female will, on the average, produce one female to replace herself. Under such conditions the population will *ultimately* become stationary. We emphasise *ultimately* because the age distribution of the population may be such as to ensure a current excess of births over deaths (see p 564 below), but ultimately, if the given fertility and mortality conditions continue, each female will just replace herself and the population must become stationary, for each female on her death will have left only one female to take her place. If the net reproduction rate is greater than unity, the population will ultimately increase if the given conditions continue, because each female on her death will have left more than one female to take her place. If the net reproduction rate is less than unity, the population will ultimately decrease.

Table 13.32

Exact Age (years)	Total Births Produced per 1 000 Female Births at Stated Ages (a)
15	0
20	221
25	954
30	1 755
35	2 151
40	2 296
45	2 331
50	2 333

(a) Last column of Table 13.31 accumulated downwards

The net reproduction rate is a measure of the *replacement potential* of the population. It tells us what will happen to the population ultimately if the given conditions upon which it has been based continue to hold. It is thus a measure which is both *potential* and *hypothetical*—potential, because it does not tell us whether the population is currently increasing or decreasing but whether the population will ultimately increase or decrease; and hypothetical, because it does not tell us what will actually happen but only what will happen if certain conditions continue to hold. It is in no sense a forecast of what can be anticipated, only a projection of what will happen if certain conditions continue to hold. Only in so far as it is likely that these conditions will continue to hold has it any value for prognostication.

The net reproduction rate could, in theory, range from 0 to about 5. Values of net reproduction rates as low as 0·67 (for Austria, 1933) and as high as 2·25 (for Panama, 1970) have been recorded. The net reproduction rates of most Western European type countries had fallen from about 1·5 in the latter part of the nineteenth century to rather less than unity in the 1930s. After the Second World War the rates rose above their pre-war level, but there has been a downturn in most countries since about the mid 1960s. Thus, the rate for England and Wales was 1·12 in 1921, 0·77 in 1933, 1·34 in 1963 and 1·13 in 1971. Table 13.33 gives recent gross and net reproduction rates for a cross-section of countries. Table 13.34 sets out the course of the rates for Australia over a long period.

Table 13.33

GROSS AND NET REPRODUCTION RATES OF SELECTED COUNTRIES

Country	Period	Reproduction Rates	
		Gross	Net
Australia	1971 (*a*)	1·44	1·40
Canada	1971	1·05	1·03
Czechoslovakia	1970	1·01	0·97
England and Wales	1971	1·16	1·13
Finland	1969	0·90	0·86
France	1969	1·23	1·20
Ireland	1969	1·93	1·85
New Zealand	1970	1·49	1·45
Panama	1970	2·49	2·25
Scotland	1968	1·35	1·30
Sweden	1970	0·94	0·92
United States	1968	1·20	1·16
Taiwan	1970	1·94	1·84

(*a*) Based on 1970–72 mortality experience.

Source: Australian Bureau of Statistics: *Year Book*, No. 60, 1974, p 182

Table 13.34

NET REPRODUCTION RATES AUSTRALIA, 1881–1974

1881	1·88 (*a*)
1891	1·73 (*a*)
1901	1·39 (*a*)
1911	1·42
1921	1·31
1931	1·04
1941	1·05
1951	1·41
1961	1·67
1971	1·40
1974	1·13

(*a*) Approximate only.

Note that the above figures are based on the fertility *and* mortality of the year under consideration.

Source: Australian Bureau of Statistics: *Year Book*, No. 40, 1954, p 390; No. 60, 1974, p 182

If the net reproduction rate of a country is below unity, the population will ultimately decrease and die out unless fertility is raised and/or mortality lowered. The fact that the population is currently increasing is irrelevant. For example, in Australia in 1934 the net reproduction rate was 0·939, although there was an excess of births over deaths in that year at the rate of 7·07 per 1000 of the population. But in 1934 there was a relatively high proportion of females in the child-bearing ages and a relatively low proportion of the population in the ages of high mortality. This state of affairs can be accounted for by the relatively high fertility and mortality of former years. With 1934 mortality and fertility conditions obtaining, this situation could not continue and the age distribution of the population would change, thus converting the current excess of births into an excess of deaths. This would happen inevitably, provided the 1934 conditions of mortality and fertility persisted into the future (see p 568).

The margin between the gross and net reproduction rate indicates the extent to which mortality offsets fertility in population replacement. The higher the mortality in the ages below 50 the greater the margin. This can be seen in Table 13.33 above. The gross reproduction rate shows what the net reproduction rate would be if there were no female mortality up to the age of 50. If the gross reproduction rate is below unity, then no improvement in mortality can raise the net reproduction rate to replacement level. If the population is not to die out ultimately, fertility must be raised. The margin between the gross and net reproduction rate has narrowed greatly over the past 100 years with the great reductions in mortality. This is shown for Australia in Table 13.35.

Table 13.35
**TOTAL FERTILITY, GROSS REPRODUCTION AND
NET REPRODUCTION RATES—AUSTRALIA, 1881 AND 1974**

	Total Fertility Rate	Gross Reproduction Rate	Net Reproduction Rate	Ratio of Net to Gross Reproduction Rate
1881	5·43	2·65	1·88	0·71
1974	2·40	1·16	1·13	0·97

If 1881 conditions of mortality had held in 1974, the net reproduction rate would have been only approximately 0·82.

True Rate of Natural Increase

The net reproduction rate can be interpreted as the ratio between two successive generations. For example, in Australia in 1974 the net reproduction rate was 1·131. If 1000 female births will produce 1131 female births over their lifetimes, then 1131:1000 represents the ratio of the second generation to the first. Consequently, the net reproduction rate tells us the rate at which the population will ultimately turn over per generation. Hence, ultimately each generation will see the Australian population multiplied by 1·131, or, in other words, ultimately the population will increase by 131 per 1000 per generation.

Since the net reproduction rate gives a per-generation rate of growth, if the length of a generation is known, a per-annum rate can be obtained. If we write R for the net reproduction rate, T for the length of a generation in years, and r for the per-annum rate of growth, we shall have:

$$(1 + r)^T = R$$

If we know T and R, we can readily find r (see section 13.4, p 526).

The precise definition of the length of a generation is rather complex, but it can be interpreted approximately as the mean interval between the birth of a female and the birth of her children. Given an initial 1000 female births this latter is the mean age at which these births are themselves confined. This mean age can be readily calculated. For Australia 1974 we have:

Table 13.36

CALCULATION OF APPROXIMATE LENGTH OF A GENERATION

Age Group (years)	Mid-point of Class Interval Deviated from Arbitrary Origin of 27·5, in Class Interval Units x'	Births per 1 000 Female Births (a) f	fx'
15–19	−2	221	−442
20–24	−1	733	−733
25–29	0	801	0
30–34	1	396	396
35–39	2	145	290
40–44	3	35	105
45–49	4	2	8
Total		2 333	−376

(a) From Table 13.31

Mean age at confinement $= 27·5 + \left(\dfrac{-376}{2333} \times 5 \right)$

$= 26·7$ years

It follows that we can now compute r approximately from the above formula. For 1974 for Australia, we have:

$$(1 + r)^{26\cdot7} \approx 1\cdot131$$

$$\log(1 + r) \approx \frac{\log 1\cdot131}{26\cdot7}$$

$$\approx \frac{0\cdot05346}{26\cdot7}$$

$$\approx 0\cdot00200$$

$$1 + r \approx 1\cdot00462$$

$$r \approx 0\cdot00462 \text{ or } 4\cdot6 \text{ per } 1000 \text{ per annum}$$

It can be demonstrated mathematically that any population irrespective of its age distribution will, if subjected constantly to given fertility and mortality conditions, as expressed by the specific fertility and mortality rates, ultimately (in practice after about 60 to 70 years) produce a flow of births increasing (or decreasing) at a constant rate per annum.[1] It follows that, with given probabilities of surviving, the number in any age group will increase at the same constant rate per annum, and hence the total population will similarly increase.

---

[1] Consider a population of any given age distribution at a particular time, provided only that it contains some individuals in the reproductive age groups. We limit our attention to females only. Assume that there is no migration and that the given fertility and mortality conditions obtain indefinitely into the future. We treat these conditions as continuous functions of age, representing them by $b(x)$ and $l(x)$, where $b(x)$ is the rate at which females produce female offspring at age x (specific fertility rates) and $l(x)$ is the probability at birth of a female surviving to the exact age of x (survivor column of the life table).

After the passage of about 50 years all females of reproductive age in the population will be the offspring of the original population. The number of such females of age x at time t will be given by $B(t - x)l(x)$, where $B(t - x)$ is the number of female births which took place at time $(t - x)$, ie x years ago. The number of female births to females of age x at time t will consequently be $B(t - x)l(x)b(x)$. It follows that the total number of female births taking place at time t will be given by:

$$B(t) = \int_0^\infty B(t - x)l(x)b(x)dx$$

This integral equation will be satisfied by a function of the form:

$$B(t) = \sum_{i=0}^\infty Q_i e^{r_i t}$$

where $e = 2\cdot71828$, the Qs are constants determined by the initial age distribution and the r_is are the roots of the characteristic equation:

$$1 = \int_0^\infty e^{-rx}l(x)b(x)dx \qquad (*)$$

But since $l(x)b(x) \geqslant 0$ for all x, the right-hand side of (*) is monotonic decreasing in r, so that (*) has only one real root, say r_0. If $r = u + iv$ be a complex root, then by taking real parts of both sides of (*) we have:

$$1 = \int_0^\infty e^{-ux} \cos vx \, l(x)b(x)dx$$

This rate of increase is known as the *true rate of natural increase* and corresponds to the *r* we have defined above. The true rate of natural increase is the rate at which a population subjected to given fertility and mortality conditions will ultimately grow. Furthermore, since the numbers in all age groups will ultimately increase at the same rate, the relative age distribution of the population will ultimately become stable, ie there will be the same proportion of persons in each age group year in and year out. Such a population is called a *stable population*. A stationary population is a particular type of stable population, namely one in which the rate of increase is zero.

The interpretations of the true rate of natural increase and the net reproduction rate are the same, because the true rate of natural increase is simply the per-annum rate corresponding to the net reproduction rate, which is a per-generation rate. The true rate of natural increase is, like the net reproduction rate, a potential and hypothetical measure. It tells us at what rate per annum the population will *ultimately* grow, *if* the given fertility and mortality conditions continue to hold. Thus the fertility and mortality conditions of Australia in 1974 were such that if they continued to operate, ultimately (perhaps by about the

---

and since cos $vx < 1$, then $u < r_0$. Hence r_0 is greater than the real parts of any of the complex roots. It follows that

$$B(t) = \sum_{i=0}^{\infty} Q_i e^{r_i t}$$

is made up of one aperiodic term (corresponding to the one real root) and a number of periodic terms (corresponding to the complex roots), but the aperiodic term is dominant, so that, for large t, $B(t)$ will tend asymptotically towards

$$B(t) = Q_0 e^{r_0 t}$$

where r_0 is the one real root of (*), and corresponds to 'r' in the text, and Q_0 is a constant.

This demonstrates that any given population, if subjected continuously to given fertility and mortality conditions, will ultimately give rise to a stream of births increasing or decreasing at a constant rate.

The equation (*) cannot be solved exactly for its real root, and r can be obtained by approximation only. The formula given in the text is such an approximation, based on an approximation to the length of a generation. A more accurate approximation can be obtained by solving

$$\log_e R - r k_1 + \frac{r^2}{2} k_2 = 0$$

where k_1 is the mean age of mothers at confinement as defined in the text and k_2 is the corresponding variance of age of mothers at confinement. (See P H Karmel,: 'The Relations Between Male and Female Nuptiality in a Stable Population', *Population Studies*, Vol I, 1947–48, p 359, footnote.)

The above theory is due to A J Lotka. For an early formulation, see A J Lotka, and F R Sharpe: 'A Problem in Age Distribution,' *Philosophical Magazine*, Vol 21, 1911, p 435. The complete theory of the stable population is set out in A J Lotka, *Analyse démographique avec application particulière à l'espèce humaine*, Actualités scientifiques et industrielles 780 (Hermann, Paris, 1939).

year 2030) the Australian population would grow, migration apart, at 4·6 per 1000 per annum.

The true rate of natural increase can differ quite considerably from the crude rate of natural increase defined in section 13.4, p 524 above. This is because the crude rate depends not only on fertility and mortality conditions, but also on the sex and age distribution inherited from the past. A good example of contrasts in crude and true rates is provided by Australia in 1934. The net reproduction rate was 0·939, and the corresponding true rate of natural increase was −2·2 per 1000 per annum, ie a rate of decrease. On the other hand, the crude rate was 7·07 per 1000. The Australian population was actually increasing, but the underlying fertility and mortality conditions were such that ultimately the population would decrease unless these conditions changed (see p 564 above). In fact, to provide an ultimate rate of increase of 7·07 per 1000, fertility would have had to be raised by some 25–30 per cent. This underlines the fact that statistics cannot always be taken at their face value and that it is frequently necessary to go further than the more obvious data and measures. In considering population replacement the net reproduction rate or the true rate of natural increase must be examined. For some purposes the one is more convenient, for other purposes the other. They both lead to identical conclusions.

The table below sets out the crude rate of natural increase and an approximation to the value of the true rate for Australia, 1881–1974.

Table 13.37
**CRUDE AND TRUE RATES OF NATURAL INCREASE
AUSTRALIA, 1881–1974**

	Crude Rate per 1000 per annum	True Rate per 1000 per annum
1881	20·6	23·4
1891	19·6	20·0
1901	14·9	11·6
1911	16·5	12·4
1921	15·0	9·4
1931	9·5	1·4
1941	8·9	2·4
1951	13·2	12·3
1961	14·4	18·6
1971	13·0	12·5
1974	9·6	4·6

Source: Crude rates: Australian Bureau of Statistics: *Demography Bulletin*, No. 78, 1960, p 179; *Year Book*, No. 60, 1974, pp 179, 190. True rates: computed by the authors

Table 13.38

AGE DISTRIBUTION, BIRTHS AND DEATHS OF HYPOTHETICAL POPULATION

Age (years)	Year							
	0	1	2	3	4	5	6	7
1	1 000	1 350	1 200	1 155	1 065	1 112	1 026	1 000
2	1 500	1 000	1 350	1 200	1 155	1 065	1 112	1 026
3	1 500	1 500	1 000	1 350	1 200	1 155	1 065	1 112
4	1 500	1 500	1 500	1 000	1 350	1 200	1 155	1 065
5	1 000	1 500	1 500	1 500	1 000	1 350	1 200	1 155
Total Population	6 500	6 850	6 550	6 205	5 770	5 882	5 558	5 358
Births	1 350	1 200	1 155	1 065	1 112	1 026	1 000	961
Deaths	1 000	1 500	1 500	1 500	1 000	1 350	1 200	1 155

Age (years)	Year							
	8	9	10	11	12	13	14	15
1	961	941	896	871	839	812	782	757
2	1 000	961	941	896	871	839	812	782
3	1 026	1 000	961	941	896	871	839	812
4	1 112	1 026	1 000	961	941	896	871	839
5	1 065	1 112	1 026	1 000	961	941	896	871
Total Population	5 164	5 040	4 824	4 669	4 508	4 359	4 200	4 061
Births	941	896	871	839	812	782	757	730
Deaths	1 065	1 112	1 026	1 000	961	941	896	871

Age (years)	Year							
	16	17	18	19	20	21	22	23
1	730	705	681	658	635	613	592	572
2	757	730	705	681	658	635	613	592
3	782	757	730	705	681	658	635	613
4	812	782	757	730	705	681	658	635
5	839	812	782	757	730	705	681	658
Total Population	3 920	3 786	3 655	3 531	3 409	3 292	3 179	3 070
Births	705	681	658	635	613	592	572	552
Deaths	839	812	782	757	730	705	681	658

Stable Population

In order to illustrate the arguments of the preceding paragraphs a hypothetical (and highly imaginative) example is worked below. We suppose that we have a population of one sex, with an upper limit to life of 5 years. All births take place on 31 December, so that at the end of any year the population is aged exactly 1, 2, 3, 4 or 5 years. At the end of year 0, the numbers at these five ages are assumed to be 1000, 1500, 1500, 1500, 1000 respectively. The mortality conditions are defined by supposing that no deaths occur before the age of 5, and when persons turn 5 they die immediately. Consequently, the mean expectation of life is 5 years. The fertility conditions are defined as follows: no births to persons aged 1 and 5, and births at the rate of 300 per 1000 per annum to those aged 2, 3 and 4. It follows that the gross reproduction rate is $(300 + 300 + 300) \div 1000 = 0.9$ and, since no deaths occur before the end of the child-bearing period, the

Table 13.39

BIRTH AND DEATH RATES FOR HYPOTHETICAL POPULATION

Year	Crude Birth Rate per 1 000 pa	Crude Death Rate per 1 000 pa	Crude Rate of Natural Increase per 1 000 pa (a)
0	208	154	53·9
1	175	219	−43·8
2	176	229	−52·7
3	172	242	−70·1
4	193	173	19·4
5	174	230	−55·1
6	180	216	−36·0
7	179	216	−36·2
8	182	206	−24·0
9	178	221	−42·8
10	181	213	−32·1
11	180	214	−34·5
12	180	213	−33·1
13	179	216	−36·5
14	180	213	−33·1
15	180	214	−34·7
16	180	214	−34·2
17	180	214	−34·6
18	180	214	−34·0
19	180	214	−34·6
20	180	214	−34·3
21	180	214	−34·4
22	180	214	−34·3
23	180	214	−34·5

(a) Crude rate of natural increase = crude birth rate − crude death rate, but the crude rates of natural increase are taken to an additional decimal place.

net reproduction rate is also 0·9. The approximate length of a generation will be 3 years (3 years being the mean age at confinement) and hence the true rate of natural increase will be given approximately by $(1 + r)^3 \approx 0·9$, ie $r \approx - 34·5$ per 1000 per annum. The number of births occurring at 31 December year 0, will be $(1500 + 1500 + 1500) \times 0·3 = 1350$, and the number of deaths will be the 1000 exactly aged 5. At the end of year 1, there will be 1350 aged 1, and the number aged 2 will be the 1000 aged 1 in the previous year, and so on. In year 0, the crude birth rate will be $1350/6500 \times 1000 = 207$ per 1000, the crude death rate will be $1000/6500 \times 1000 = 154$ per 1000 and the crude rate of natural increase will be $350/6500 \times 1000 = 54$ per 1000. In Table 13.38 the age distribution and the numbers of births and deaths occurring as at the ends of year 0 to year 23 inclusive are set out.

In Table 13.39 the crude birth rate, crude death rate and crude rate of natural increase are set out, all measured as at the end of years.

There are a number of interesting features about Table 13.39. Although the fertility and mortality conditions remain constant over the whole period, the crude birth and crude death rates fluctuate a great deal until about year 10. In general, the crude birth rate falls, and the crude death rate rises over the whole period. The high crude birth rate and low crude death rate in year 0 is due to a particularly favourable age distribution with a preponderance of persons in the child-bearing ages. Furthermore, although the crude rate of natural increase is +53·9 per 1000 in year 0, the population will ultimately decline. By about the year 20 a steady rate of decline of 34·4 per 1000 sets in. This is close to the approximate value for the true rate of natural increase of −34·5 per 1000 computed above. The misleading character of the crude rates is clearly illustrated. By about the year 20, not only have the various crude rates stabilised, but the population has achieved a stable age distribution, as can be seen in the table below.

Table 13.40

PERCENTAGE AGE DISTRIBUTION OF HYPOTHETICAL POPULATION

Age (years)	Year 0	Year 10	Year 20	Year 21	Year 22	Year 23
1	15·4	18·6	18·6	18·6	18·6	18·6
2	23·1	19·5	19·3	19·3	19·3	19·3
3	23·1	19·9	20·0	20·0	20·0	20·0
4	23·1	20·7	20·7	20·7	20·7	20·7
5	15·4	21·3	21·4	21·4	21·4	21·4
Total	100·0	100·0	100·0	100·0	100·0	100·0

This example illustrates the proposition that a population, irrespective of its initial age distribution, subjected constantly to given fertility and mortality conditions, will ultimately attain a stable age distribution and will increase or decrease at a constant rate per annum. A fair degree of stability is reached after about three generations. It can now be seen why the population in year 0 shows a substantial increase, whereas in fact it will ultimately decrease if the given fertility and mortality conditions continue to hold. In year 0 some 69 per cent of the population is in the child-bearing ages, whereas ultimately only 60 per cent will be in those ages. This favours a high number of births. On the other hand only 15 per cent are of the age subject to mortality, whereas ultimately some 21 per cent will be of that age. This favours a low number of deaths.

Limitations of the Gross and Net Reproduction Rates

Finally attention must be drawn to certain limitations of the gross and net reproduction rates and the true rate of natural increase. These three measures are based on fertility conditions as expressed by the specific fertility rates. In so far as these rates do not properly represent the underlying fertility conditions of the population at the time under consideration, the gross and net reproduction rates and the true rate of natural increase will be defective. The underlying fertility conditions depend basically on two factors. The first may be called the *propensity to marry* and the second the *propensity to have families of various sizes*.

It may be the case, for example, that 90 per cent of all males will marry at some time or another during their lifetimes and that on the average married couples plan to have familities of three children. If for any reason marriages are abnormally high in any particular year (eg due to high prosperity causing people to marry earlier than usual), then there will be an abnormal proportion of newly-weds among the females. This will lead to relatively high specific fertility rates, and these rates cannot be said to reflect fertility conditions truly. For if an abnormally high number of marriages occurs for a few years, it is inevitable that an abnormally low number must occur in the near future, since the pool of marriageable people will have been reduced. Consequently an abnormally high marriage rate will inflate specific fertility rates now and will inevitably exercise a depressing effect on them in the future, even though the propensity to marry and the propensity to have children in the broader sense have remained unchanged.

Similarly, if the sex distribution is unbalanced, this will lead to abnormal behaviour in the marriage rate. Thus, a substantial excess of males (due, say, to migration) will lead to a greater proportion of married females than normal and will inflate specific fertility rates. For these rates are the rates at which *all* females produce children, and the greater the proportion of females married the higher they will be. But with the passage of time, other things being equal, the excess of males will disappear and the specific fertility rates will inevitably fall.[1] Furthermore, married couples will be influenced by a variety of factors in determining the spacing of their families. Thus in times of economic depression couples may postpone having their children and in times of prosperity have them earlier than they would otherwise do. Consequently, an economic boom may lead to a rise in specific fertility rates even though the propensity to have families of various sizes remains unchanged, the rise in specific fertility rates later being followed by a fall.

From this discussion it can be seen that short-term fluctuations in specific fertility rates, and hence in the gross and net reproduction rates and the true rate of natural increase which are based on them, may occur even though the underlying propensities to marry and to have children remain unchanged. Consequently, great care must be taken in interpreting fluctuations in these rates.

Two examples may be taken to illustrate this. From about 1880 to 1930 there was a steady downward trend in the net reproduction rate in Australia, a rate of 1·88 in 1881 falling to 1·04 in 1931. By 1934 the net reproduction rate was as low as 0·94. From that year onwards it rose, until in 1947 it reached 1·42. Was this rise a reversal of the previous trend? There are reasons for doubting that it was wholly this. During the depression of the early '30s, marriages were postponed and additions to families delayed. These abnormally depressed the net reproduction rate. With economic recovery between 1935 and 1939 these marriages and births took place, thus raising the net reproduction rate. Then came the Second World War and a boom in marriages. The war and post-war expansion brought full employment and economic prosperity. These factors led to the bringing forward of marriages and births and hence raised the net reproduction rate further. Consequently, the upward movement in the rate between 1934 and 1947 could possibly be explained in these terms and could have occurred without any fundamental change in the underlying fertility conditions. In fact, research, which makes due allowance for the factors referred to above, suggests that between 1934 and 1942, fertility, if anything, fell a little

---

[1] See P H Karmel: 'The Relations between Male and Female Net Reproduction Rates', *Population Studies*, Vol I, 1947–48, p 249, 'The Relations between Male and Female Nuptiality in a Stable Population', *Population Studies*, Vol I, 1947–48, p 353, and 'An Analysis of the Sources and Magnitudes of Inconsistencies between Male and Female Net Reproduction Rates in Actual Populations', *Population Studies*, Vol II, 1948–49, p 240.

but that between 1943 and 1947 it rose somewhat, although by no means by as much as the net reproduction rate suggests.[1] Since 1947 fertility had been increasing to reach a peak in 1961, after which it began declining again towards replacement level.

A second example compares the net reproduction rate in Australia in 1881 with that in 1921. In 1881 the rate was 1·88, and in 1921, 1·31, but in 1881 the masculinity of the Australian population was 118 males per 100 females, whereas in 1921 it was 103. It follows that the proportion of females married in 1881 was abnormally high and that the net reproduction rate for that year was rather too high to be a correct reflection of the underlying conditions. Consequently the decline in the rate between 1881 and 1921 exaggerates the fall in fertility.

One way of partially overcoming the difficulties illustrated above is to pay attention not so much to the current specific fertility rates obtaining in a particular year, but rather to the reproductive behaviour of a particular generation of females over their lifetime. Thus we may trace out the actual marriage and child-bearing experience of females born in a particular year.[2] The main limitation in such a study of *generation fertility* is that it is never possible to be up to date, since, at any particular time, the more recent generations of females will not have completed their reproductive span. Nevertheless, this sort of analysis enables short-term fluctuations in current fertility rates to be placed in their proper perspective.

[1] See P H Karmel: 'Fertility and Marriages—Australia, 1933–42', *Economic Record*, Vol XX, 1944, p 74, and 'Population Replacement—Australia, 1947', *Economic Record*, Vol XXV, 1949, p 83.
[2] See, for example, P K Whelpton: *Cohort Fertility—Native White Women in the United States* (Princeton University Press, 1954).

APPENDIXES

APPENDIX A
STATISTICAL TABLES

Table I[1]

AREAS UNDER THE NORMAL
PROBABILITY CURVE

$\dfrac{Z =}{X - \mu}{\sigma}$	·00	·01	·02	·03	·04	·05	·06	·07	·08	·09
0·0	·0000	·0040	·0080	·0120	·0159	·0199	·0239	·0279	·0319	·0359
0·1	·0398	·0438	·0478	·0517	·0557	·0596	·0636	·0675	·0714	·0753
0·2	·0793	·0832	·0871	·0910	·0948	·0987	·1026	·1064	·1103	·1141
0·3	·1179	·1217	·1255	·1293	·1331	·1368	·1406	·1443	·1480	·1517
0·4	·1554	·1591	·1628	·1664	·1700	·1736	·1772	·1808	·1844	·1879
0·5	·1915	·1950	·1985	·2019	·2054	·2088	·2123	·2157	·2190	·2224
0·6	·2257	·2291	·2324	·2357	·2389	·2422	·2454	·2486	·2518	·2549
0·7	·2580	·2612	·2642	·2673	·2704	·2734	·2764	·2794	·2823	·2852
0·8	·2881	·2910	·2939	·2967	·2995	·3023	·3051	·3078	·3106	·3133
0·9	·3159	·3186	·3212	·3238	·3264	·3289	·3315	·3340	·3365	·3389
1·0	·3413	·3438	·3461	·3485	·3508	·3531	·3554	·3577	·3599	·3621
1·1	·3643	·3665	·3686	·3708	·3729	·3749	·3770	·3790	·3810	·3830
1·2	·3849	·3869	·3888	·3907	·3925	·3944	·3962	·3980	·3997	·4015
1·3	·4032	·4049	·4066	·4083	·4099	·4115	·4131	·4147	·4162	·4177
1·4	·4192	·4207	·4222	·4236	·4251	·4265	·4279	·4292	·4306	·4319
1·5	·4332	·4345	·4357	·4370	·4382	·4394	·4406	·4418	·4430	·4441
1·6	·4452	·4463	·4474	·4485	·4495	·4505	·4515	·4525	·4535	·4545
1·7	·4554	·4564	·4573	·4582	·4591	·4599	·4608	·4616	·4625	·4633
1·8	·4641	·4649	·4656	·4664	·4671	·4678	·4686	·4693	·4699	·4706
1·9	·4713	·4719	·4726	·4732	·4738	·4744	·4750	·4758	·4762	·4767
2·0	·4773	·4778	·4783	·4788	·4793	·4798	·4803	·4808	·4812	·4817
2·1	·4821	·4826	·4830	·4834	·4838	·4842	·4846	·4850	·4854	·4857
2·2	·4861	·4865	·4868	·4871	·4875	·4878	·4881	·4884	·4887	·4890
2·3	·4893	·4896	·4898	·4901	·4904	·4906	·4909	·4911	·4913	·4916
2·4	·4918	·4920	·4922	·4925	·4927	·4929	·4931	·4932	·4934	·4936
2·5	·4938	·4940	·4941	·4943	·4945	·4946	·4948	·4949	·4951	·4952
2·6	·4953	·4955	·4956	·4957	·4959	·4960	·4961	·4962	·4963	·4964
2·7	·4965	·4966	·4967	·4968	·4969	·4970	·4971	·4972	·4973	·4974
2·8	·4974	·4975	·4976	·4977	·4977	·4978	·4979	·4980	·4980	·4981
2·9	·4981	·4982	·4983	·4984	·4984	·4984	·4985	·4985	·4986	·4986
3·0	·4987	·4987	·4987	·4988	·4988	·4988	·4989	·4989	·4989	·4990
3·1	·4990	·4991	·4991	·4991	·4992	·4992	·4992	·4992	·4993	·4993

[1] This table is reproduced from H O Rugg: *Statistical Methods Applied to Education*, published by Houghton Mifflin Company, Boston, USA., by permission of the publishers.

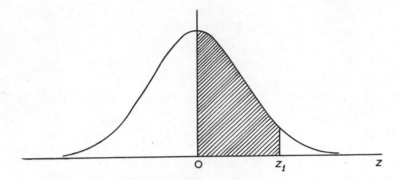

Note. The figures in the body of the table opposite give proportions of total area under the curve lying between the central ordinate and the value of $Z = \dfrac{X - \mu}{\sigma}$ under consideration. These correspond in the diagram above to the ratio of the hatched area to the total area. They give the probability that Z will lie between 0 and Z_1, ie the probability that X will lie between μ and X_1.

Table II[1]

VALUES OF t

	Level of Significance (α)											
ν	·9	·8	·7	·6	·5	·4	·3	·2	·1	·05	·02	·01
1	·158	·325	·510	·727	1·000	1·376	1·963	3·078	6·314	12·706	31·821	63·657
2	·142	·289	·445	·617	·816	1·061	1·386	1·886	2·920	4·303	6·965	9·925
3	·137	·277	·424	·584	·765	·978	1·250	1·638	2·353	3·182	4·541	5·841
4	·134	·271	·414	·569	·741	·941	1·190	1·533	2·132	2·776	3·747	4·604
5	·132	·267	·408	·559	·727	·920	1·156	1·476	2·015	2·571	3·365	4·032
6	·131	·265	·404	·553	·718	·906	1·134	1·440	1·943	2·447	3·143	3·707
7	·130	·263	·402	·549	·711	·896	1·119	1·415	1·895	2·365	2·998	3·499
8	·130	·262	·399	·546	·706	·889	1·108	1·397	1·860	2·306	2·896	3·355
9	·129	·261	·398	·543	·703	·883	1·100	1·383	1·833	2·262	2·821	3·250
10	·129	·260	·397	·542	·700	·879	1·093	1·372	1·812	2·228	2·764	3·169
11	·129	·260	·396	·540	·697	·876	1·088	1·363	1·796	2·201	2·718	3·106
12	128	·259	·395	·539	·695	·873	1·083	1·356	1·782	2·179	2·681	3·055
13	·128	·259	·394	·538	·694	·870	1·079	1·350	1·771	2·160	2·650	3·012
14	·128	·258	·393	·537	·692	·868	1·076	1·345	1·761	2·145	2·624	2·977
15	·128	·258	·393	·536	·691	·866	1·074	1·341	1·753	2·131	2·602	2·947
16	·128	·258	392	·535	·690	·865	1·071	1·337	1·746	2·120	2·583	2·921
17	·128	·257	·392	·534	·689	·863	1·069	1·333	1·740	2·110	2·567	2·898
18	·127	·257	·392	·534	·688	·862	1·067	1·330	1·734	2·101	2·552	2·878
19	·127	·257	·391	·533	·688	·861	1·066	1·328	1·729	2·093	2·539	2·861
20	·127	·257	·391	·533	·687	·860	1·064	1·325	1·725	2·086	2·528	2·845
21	·127	·257	·391	·532	·686	·859	1·063	1·323	1·721	2·080	2·518	2·831
22	·127	·256	·390	·532	·686	·858	1·061	1·321	1·717	2·074	2·508	2·819
23	·127	·256	·390	·532	·685	·858	1·060	1·319	1·714	2·069	2·500	2·807
24	·127	·256	·390	·531	·685	·857	1·059	1·318	1·711	2·064	2·492	2·797
25	·127	·256	·390	·531	·684	·856	1·058	1·316	1·708	2·060	2·485	2·787
26	·127	·256	·390	·531	·684	·856	1·058	1·315	1·706	2·056	2·479	2·779
27	·127	·256	·389	·531	·684	·855	1·057	1·314	1·703	2·052	2·473	2·771
28	·127	·256	·389	·530	·683	·855	1·056	1·313	1·701	2·048	2·467	2·763
29	·127	·256	·389	·530	·683	·854	1·055	1·311	1·699	2·045	2·462	2·756
30	·127	·256	·389	·530	·683	·854	1·055	1·310	1·697	2·042	2·457	2·750
∞	·126	·253	·385	·524	·674	·842	1·036	1·282	1·645	1·960	2·326	2·576

[1] This table is reproduced from R A Fisher, and F Yates: *Statistical Tables for Biological, Agricultural and Medical Research*, published by Hafner Publishing Co, New York, by permission of the authors and publishers.

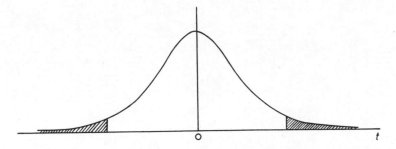

Note. The body of the table gives, for particular numbers of degrees of freedom (v), the value of t which cuts off tails together covering a proportion of area equal to the required level of significance (α). The last row of the table for $v = \infty$, shows values of t corresponding to the normal distribution, which the t-distribution approximates for large v.

Table III [1]
VALUES OF χ^2

Level of Significance (α)

ν	·99	·98	·95	·90	·80	·70	·50	·30	·20	·10	·05	·02	·01
1	·0002	·0006	·0039	·0158	·0642	·148	·455	1·074	1·642	2·706	3·841	5·412	6·635
2	·0201	·0404	·103	·211	·446	·713	1·386	2·408	3·219	4·605	5·991	7·824	9·210
3	·115	·185	·352	·584	1·005	1·424	2·366	3·665	4·642	6·251	7·815	9·837	11·341
4	·297	·429	·711	1·064	1·649	2·195	3·357	4·878	5·989	7·779	9·488	11·668	13·277
5	·554	·752	1·145	1·610	2·343	3·000	4·351	6·064	7·289	9·236	11·070	13·388	15·086
6	·872	1·134	1·635	2·204	3·070	3·828	5·348	7·231	8·558	10·645	12·592	15·033	16·812
7	1·239	1·564	2·167	2·833	3·822	4·671	6·346	8·383	9·803	12·017	14·067	16·622	18·475
8	1·646	2·032	2·733	3·490	4·594	5·527	7·344	9·524	11·030	13·362	15·507	18·168	20·090
9	2·088	2·532	3·325	4·168	5·380	6·393	8·343	10·656	12·242	14·684	16·919	19·679	21·666
10	2·558	3·059	3·940	4·865	6·179	7·267	9·342	11·781	13·442	15·987	18·307	21·161	23·209
11	3·053	3·609	4·575	5·578	6·989	8·148	10·341	12·899	14·631	17·275	19·675	22·618	24·725
12	3·571	4·178	5·226	6·304	7·807	9·034	11·340	14·011	15·812	18·549	21·026	24·054	26·217
13	4·107	4·765	5·892	7·042	8·634	9·926	12·340	15·119	16·985	19·812	22·362	25·472	27·688
14	4·660	5·368	6·571	7·790	9·467	10·821	13·339	16·222	18·151	21·064	23·685	26·873	29·141
15	5·229	5·985	7·261	8·547	10·307	11·721	14·339	17·322	19·311	22·307	24·996	28·259	30·578
16	5·812	6·614	7·962	9·312	11·152	12·624	15·338	18·418	20·465	23·542	26·296	29·633	32·000
17	6·408	7·255	8·672	10·085	12·002	13·531	16·338	19·511	21·615	24·769	27·587	30·995	33·409
18	7·015	7·906	9·390	10·865	12·857	14·440	17·338	20·601	22·760	25·989	28·869	32·346	34·805
19	7·633	8·567	10·117	11·651	13·716	15·352	18·338	21·689	23·900	27·204	30·144	33·687	36·191
20	8·260	9·237	10·851	12·443	14·578	16·266	19·337	22·775	25·038	28·412	31·410	35·020	37·566
21	8·897	9·915	11·591	13·240	15·445	17·182	20·337	23·858	26·171	29·615	32·671	36·343	38·932
22	9·542	10·600	12·338	14·041	16·314	18·101	21·337	24·939	27·301	30·813	33·924	37·659	40·289
23	10·196	11·293	13·091	14·848	17·187	19·021	22·337	26·018	28·429	32·007	35·172	37·968	41·638
24	10·856	11·992	13·848	15·659	18·062	19·943	23·337	27·096	29·553	33·196	36·415	40·270	42·980
25	11·524	12·697	14·611	16·473	18·940	20·867	24·337	28·172	30·675	34·382	37·652	41·566	44·314
26	12·198	13·409	15·379	17·292	19·820	21·792	25·336	29·246	31·795	35·563	38·885	42·856	45·642
27	12·879	14·125	16·151	18·114	20·703	22·719	26·336	30·319	32·912	36·741	40·113	44·140	46·963
28	13·565	14·847	16·928	18·939	21·588	23·647	27·336	31·391	34·027	37·916	41·337	45·419	48·278
29	14·256	15·574	17·708	19·768	22·475	24·577	28·336	32·461	35·139	39·087	42·557	46·693	49·588
30	14·953	16·306	18·493	20·599	23·364	25·508	29·336	33·530	36·250	40·256	43·773	47·962	50·892

[1] This table is reproduced from R A Fisher, and F Yates: *Statistical Tables for Biological, Agricultural and Medical Research*, published by Hafner Publishing Co, New York, by permission of the authors and publishers.

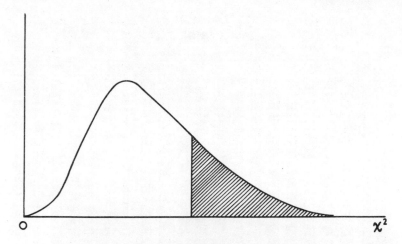

Note. The body of the table gives, for particular numbers of degrees of freedom (v), the value of χ^2 which cuts off a tail covering a proportion of area equal to the required level of significance (α). For large values of v, the statistic $\sqrt{2\chi^2}$ is approximately normally distributed about a mean $\sqrt{2v - 1}$ with a standard deviation of unity.

Table IV A [1]

VALUES OF $F_{.05}$

v_2	\ v_1				Degrees of freedom for numerator														
	1	2	3	4	5	6	7	8	9	10	12	15	20	24	30	40	60	120	∞
1	161·4	199·5	215·7	224·6	230·2	234·0	236·8	238·9	240·5	241·9	243·9	245·9	248·0	249·1	250·1	251·1	252·2	253·3	254·3
2	18·51	19·00	19·16	19·25	19·30	19·33	19·35	19·37	19·38	19·40	19·41	19·43	19·45	19·45	19·46	19·47	19·48	19·49	19·50
3	10·13	9·55	9·28	9·12	9·01	8·94	8·89	8·85	8·81	8·79	8·74	8·70	8·66	8·64	8·62	8·59	8·57	8·55	8·53
4	7·71	6·94	6·59	6·39	6·26	6·16	6·09	6·04	6·00	5·96	5·91	5·86	5·80	5·77	5·75	5·72	5·69	5·66	5·63
5	6·61	5·79	5·41	5·19	5·05	4·95	4·88	4·82	4·77	4·74	4·68	4·62	4·56	4·53	4·50	4·46	4·43	4·40	4·36
6	5·99	5·14	4·76	4·53	4·39	4·28	4·21	4·15	4·10	4·06	4·00	3·94	3·87	3·84	3·81	3·77	3·74	3·70	3·67
7	5·59	4·74	4·35	4·12	3·97	3·87	3·79	3·73	3·68	3·64	3·57	3·51	3·44	3·41	3·38	3·34	3·30	3·27	3·23
8	5·32	4·46	4·07	3·84	3·69	3·58	3·50	3·44	3·39	3·35	3·28	3·22	3·15	3·12	3·08	3·04	3·01	2·97	2·93
9	5·12	4·26	3·86	3·63	3·48	3·37	3·29	3·23	3·18	3·14	3·07	3·01	2·94	2·90	2·86	2·83	2·79	2·75	2·71
10	4·96	4·10	3·71	3·48	3·33	3·22	3·14	3·07	3·02	2·98	2·91	2·85	2·77	2·74	2·70	2·66	2·62	2·58	2·54
11	4·84	3·98	3·59	3·36	3·20	3·09	3·01	2·95	2·90	2·85	2·79	2·72	2·65	2·61	2·57	2·53	2·49	2·45	2·40
12	4·75	3·89	3·49	3·26	3·11	3·00	2·91	2·85	2·80	2·75	2·69	2·62	2·54	2·51	2·47	2·43	2·38	2·34	2·30
13	4·67	3·81	3·41	3·18	3·03	2·92	2·83	2·77	2·71	2·67	2·60	2·53	2·46	2·42	2·38	2·34	2·30	2·25	2·21
14	4·60	3·74	3·34	3·11	2·96	2·85	2·76	2·70	2·65	2·60	2·53	2·46	2·39	2·35	2·31	2·27	2·22	2·18	2·13
15	4·54	3·68	3·29	3·06	2·90	2·79	2·71	2·64	2·59	2·54	2·48	2·40	2·33	2·29	2·25	2·20	2·16	2·11	2·07
16	4·49	3·63	3·24	3·01	2·85	2·74	2·66	2·59	2·54	2·49	2·42	2·35	2·28	2·24	2·19	2·15	2·11	2·06	2·01
17	4·45	3·59	3·20	2·96	2·81	2·70	2·61	2·55	2·49	2·45	2·38	2·31	2·23	2·19	2·15	2·10	2·06	2·01	1·96
18	4·41	3·55	3·16	2·93	2·77	2·66	2·58	2·51	2·46	2·41	2·34	2·27	2·19	2·15	2·11	2·06	2·02	1·97	1·92
19	4·38	3·52	3·13	2·90	2·74	2·63	2·54	2·48	2·42	2·38	2·31	2·23	2·16	2·11	2·07	2·03	1·98	1·93	1·88
20	4·35	3·49	3·10	2·87	2·71	2·60	2·51	2·45	2·39	2·35	2·28	2·20	2·12	2·08	2·04	1·99	1·95	1·90	1·84
21	4·32	3·47	3·07	2·84	2·68	2·57	2·49	2·42	2·37	2·32	2·25	2·18	2·10	2·05	2·01	1·96	1·92	1·87	1·81
22	4·30	3·44	3·05	2·82	2·66	2·55	2·46	2·40	2·34	2·30	2·23	2·15	2·07	2·03	1·98	1·94	1·89	1·84	1·78
23	4·28	3·42	3·03	2·80	2·64	2·53	2·44	2·37	2·32	2·27	2·20	2·13	2·05	2·01	1·96	1·91	1·86	1·81	1·76
24	4·26	3·40	3·01	2·78	2·62	2·51	2·42	2·36	2·30	2·25	2·18	2·11	2·03	1·98	1·94	1·89	1·84	1·79	1·73
25	4·24	3·39	2·99	2·76	2·60	2·49	2·40	2·34	2·28	2·24	2·16	2·09	2·01	1·96	1·92	1·87	1·82	1·77	1·71
26	4·23	3·37	2·98	2·74	2·59	2·47	2·39	2·32	2·27	2·22	2·15	2·07	1·99	1·95	1·90	1·85	1·80	1·75	1·69
27	4·21	3·35	2·96	2·73	2·57	2·46	2·37	2·31	2·25	2·20	2·13	2·06	1·97	1·93	1·88	1·84	1·79	1·73	1·67
28	4·20	3·34	2·95	2·71	2·56	2·45	2·36	2·29	2·24	2·19	2·12	2·04	1·96	1·91	1·87	1·82	1·77	1·71	1·65
29	4·18	3·33	2·93	2·70	2·55	2·43	2·35	2·28	2·22	2·18	2·10	2·03	1·94	1·90	1·85	1·81	1·75	1·70	1·64
30	4·17	3·32	2·92	2·69	2·53	2·42	2·33	2·27	2·21	2·16	2·09	2·01	1·93	1·89	1·84	1·79	1·74	1·68	1·62
40	4·08	3·23	2·84	2·61	2·45	2·34	2·25	2·18	2·12	2·08	2·00	1·92	1·84	1·79	1·74	1·69	1·64	1·58	1·51
60	4·00	3·15	2·76	2·53	2·37	2·25	2·17	2·10	2·04	1·99	1·92	1·84	1·75	1·70	1·65	1·59	1·53	1·47	1·39
120	3·92	3·07	2·68	2·45	2·29	2·17	2·09	2·02	1·96	1·91	1·83	1·75	1·66	1·61	1·55	1·50	1·43	1·35	1·25
∞	3·84	3·00	2·60	2·37	2·21	2·10	2·01	1·94	1·88	1·83	1·75	1·67	1·57	1·52	1·46	1·39	1·32	1·22	1·00

[1] This table is reproduced from *Biometrika Tables for Statisticians*, Vol I, 1962, Table 18, by permission of the *Biometrika* Trustees.

Table IV B [1]

VALUES OF $F_{.01}$

v_2	\ v_1				Degrees of freedom for numerator														
	1	2	3	4	5	6	7	8	9	10	12	15	20	24	30	40	60	120	∞
1	4052	5000	5403	5625	5764	5859	5928	5982	6022	6056	6106	6157	6209	6235	6261	6287	6313	6339	6366
2	98·50	99·00	99·17	99·25	99·30	99·33	99·36	99·37	99·39	99·40	99·42	99·43	99·45	99·46	99·47	99·47	99·48	99·49	99·50
3	34·12	30·82	29·46	28·71	28·24	27·91	27·67	27·49	27·35	27·23	27·05	26·87	26·69	26·60	26·50	26·41	26·32	26·22	26·13
4	21·20	18·00	16·69	15·98	15·52	15·21	14·98	14·80	14·66	14·55	14·37	14·20	14·02	13·93	13·84	13·75	13·65	13·56	13·46
5	16·26	13·27	12·06	11·39	10·97	10·67	10·46	10·29	10·16	10·05	9·89	9·72	9·55	9·47	9·38	9·29	9·20	9·11	9·02
6	13·75	10·92	9·78	9·15	8·75	8·47	8·26	8·10	7·98	7·87	7·72	7·56	7·40	7·31	7·23	7·14	7·06	6·97	6·88
7	12·25	9·55	8·45	7·85	7·46	7·19	6·99	6·84	6·72	6·62	6·47	6·31	6·16	6·07	5·99	5·91	5·82	5·74	5·65
8	11·26	8·65	7·59	7·01	6·63	6·37	6·18	6·03	5·91	5·81	5·67	5·52	5·36	5·28	5·20	5·12	5·03	4·95	4·86
9	10·56	8·02	6·99	6·42	6·06	5·80	5·61	5·47	5·35	5·26	5·11	4·96	4·81	4·73	4·65	4·57	4·48	4·40	4·31
10	10·04	7·56	6·55	5·99	5·64	5·39	5·20	5·06	4·94	4·85	4·71	4·56	4·41	4·33	4·25	4·17	4·08	4·00	3·91
11	9·65	7·21	6·22	5·67	5·32	5·07	4·89	4·74	4·63	4·54	4·40	4·25	4·10	4·02	3·94	3·86	3·78	3·69	3·60
12	9·33	6·93	5·95	5·41	5·06	4·82	4·64	4·50	4·39	4·30	4·16	4·01	3·86	3·78	3·70	3·62	3·54	3·45	3·36
13	9·07	6·70	5·74	5·21	4·86	4·62	4·44	4·30	4·19	4·10	3·96	3·82	3·66	3·59	3·51	3·43	3·34	3·25	3·17
14	8·86	6·51	5·56	5·04	4·69	4·46	4·28	4·14	4·03	3·94	3·80	3·66	3·51	3·43	3·35	3·27	3·18	3·09	3·00
15	8·68	6·36	5·42	4·89	4·56	4·32	4·14	4·00	3·89	3·80	3·67	3·52	3·37	3·29	3·21	3·13	3·05	2·96	2·87
16	8·53	6·23	5·29	4·77	4·44	4·20	4·03	3·89	3·78	3·69	3·55	3·41	3·26	3·18	3·10	3·02	2·93	2·84	2·75
17	8·40	6·11	5·18	4·67	4·34	4·10	3·93	3·79	3·68	3·59	3·46	3·31	3·16	3·08	3·00	2·92	2·83	2·75	2·65
18	8·29	6·01	5·09	4·58	4·25	4·01	3·84	3·71	3·60	3·51	3·37	3·23	3·08	3·00	2·92	2·84	2·75	2·66	2·57
19	8·18	5·93	5·01	4·50	4·17	3·94	3·77	3·63	3·52	3·43	3·30	3·15	3·00	2·92	2·84	2·76	2·67	2·58	2·49
20	8·10	5·85	4·94	4·43	4·10	3·87	3·70	3·56	3·46	3·37	3·23	3·09	2·94	2·86	2·78	2·69	2·61	2·52	2·42
21	8·02	5·78	4·87	4·37	4·04	3·81	3·64	3·51	3·40	3·31	3·17	3·03	2·88	2·80	2·72	2·64	2·55	2·46	2·36
22	7·95	5·72	4·82	4·31	3·99	3·76	3·59	3·45	3·35	3·26	3·12	2·98	2·83	2·75	2·67	2·58	2·50	2·40	2·31
23	7·88	5·66	4·76	4·26	3·94	3·71	3·54	3·41	3·30	3·21	3·07	2·93	2·78	2·70	2·62	2·54	2·45	2·35	2·26
24	7·82	5·61	4·72	4·22	3·90	3·67	3·50	3·36	3·26	3·17	3·03	2·89	2·74	2·66	2·58	2·49	2·40	2·31	2·21
25	7·77	5·57	4·68	4·18	3·85	3·63	3·46	3·32	3·22	3·13	2·99	2·85	2·70	2·62	2·54	2·45	2·36	2·27	2·17
26	7·72	5·53	4·64	4·14	3·82	3·59	3·42	3·29	3·18	3·09	2·96	2·81	2·66	2·58	2·50	2·42	2·33	2·23	2·13
27	7·68	5·49	4·60	4·11	3·78	3·56	3·39	3·26	3·15	3·06	2·93	2·78	2·63	2·55	2·47	2·38	2·29	2·20	2·10
28	7·64	5·45	4·57	4·07	3·75	3·53	3·36	3·23	3·12	3·03	2·90	2·75	2·60	2·52	2·44	2·35	2·26	2·17	2·06
29	7·60	5·42	4·54	4·04	3·73	3·50	3·33	3·20	3·09	3·00	2·87	2·73	2·57	2·49	2·41	2·33	2·23	2·14	2·03
30	7·56	5·39	4·51	4·02	3·70	3·47	3·30	3·17	3·07	2·98	2·84	2·70	2·55	2·47	2·39	2·30	2·21	2·11	2·01
40	7·31	5·18	4·31	3·83	3·51	3·29	3·12	2·99	2·89	2·80	2·66	2·52	2·37	2·29	2·20	2·11	2·02	1·92	1·80
60	7·08	4·98	4·13	3·65	3·34	3·12	2·95	2·82	2·72	2·63	2·50	2·35	2·20	2·12	2·03	1·94	1·84	1·73	1·60
120	6·85	4·79	3·95	3·48	3·17	2·96	2·79	2·66	2·56	2·47	2·34	2·19	2·03	1·95	1·86	1·76	1·66	1·53	1·38
∞	6·63	4·61	3·78	3·32	3·02	2·80	2·64	2·51	2·41	2·32	2·18	2·04	1·88	1·79	1·70	1·59	1·47	1·32	1·00

[1] This table is reproduced from *Biometrika Tables for Statisticians*, Vol I, 1962, Table 18, by permission of the *Biometrika* Trustees.

Table V[1]

DURBIN–WATSON STATISTIC
SIGNIFICANCE POINTS OF d_L AND d_U: 2.5%

n	$k' = 1$		$k' = 2$		$k' = 3$		$k' = 4$		$k' = 5$	
	d_L	d_U	d_L	d_U	d_L	d_U	d_L	d_U	d_L	d_U
15	0·95	1·23	0·83	1·40	0·71	1·61	0·59	1·84	0·48	2·09
16	0·98	1·24	0·86	1·40	0·75	1·59	0·64	1·80	0·53	2·03
17	1·01	1·25	0·90	1·40	0·79	1·58	0·68	1·77	0·57	1·98
18	1·03	1·26	0·93	1·40	0·82	1·56	0·72	1·74	0·62	1·93
19	1·06	1·28	0·96	1·41	0·86	1·55	0·76	1·72	0·66	1·90
20	1·08	1·28	0·99	1·41	0·89	1·55	0·79	1·70	0·70	1·87
21	1·10	1·30	1·01	1·41	0·92	1·54	0·83	1·69	0·73	1·84
22	1·12	1·31	1·04	1·42	0·95	1·54	0·86	1·68	0·77	1·82
23	1·14	1·32	1·06	1·42	0·97	1·54	0·89	1·67	0·80	1·80
24	1·16	1·33	1·08	1·43	1·00	1·54	0·91	1·66	0·83	1·79
25	1·18	1·34	1·10	1·43	1·02	1·54	0·94	1·65	0·86	1·77
26	1·19	1·35	1·12	1·44	1·04	1·54	0·96	1·65	0·88	1·76
27	1·21	1·36	1·13	1·44	1·06	1·54	0·99	1·64	0·91	1·75
28	1·22	1·37	1·15	1·45	1·08	1·54	1·01	1·64	0·93	1·74
29	1·24	1·38	1·17	1·45	1·10	1·54	1·03	1·63	0·96	1·73
30	1·25	1·38	1·18	1·46	1·12	1·54	1·05	1·63	0·98	1·73
31	1·26	1·39	1·20	1·47	1·13	1·55	1·07	1·63	1·00	1·72
32	1·27	1·40	1·21	1·47	1·15	1·55	1·08	1·63	1·02	1·71
33	1·28	1·41	1·22	1·48	1·16	1·55	1·10	1·63	1·04	1·71
34	1·29	1·41	1·24	1·48	1·17	1·55	1·12	1·63	1·06	1·70
35	1·30	1·42	1·25	1·48	1·19	1·55	1·13	1·63	1·07	1·70
36	1·31	1·43	1·26	1·49	1·20	1·56	1·15	1·63	1·09	1·70
37	1·32	1·43	1·27	1·49	1·21	1·56	1·16	1·62	1·10	1·70
38	1·33	1·44	1·28	1·50	1·23	1·56	1·17	1·62	1·12	1·70
39	1·34	1·44	1·29	1·50	1·24	1·56	1·19	1·63	1·13	1·69
40	1·35	1·45	1·30	1·51	1·25	1·57	1·20	1·63	1·15	1·69
45	1·39	1·48	1·34	1·53	1·30	1·58	1·25	1·63	1·21	1·69
50	1·42	1·50	1·38	1·54	1·34	1·59	1·30	1·64	1·26	1·69
55	1·45	1·52	1·41	1·56	1·37	1·60	1·33	1·64	1·30	1·69
60	1·47	1·54	1·44	1·57	1·40	1·61	1·37	1·65	1·33	1·69
65	1·49	1·55	1·46	1·59	1·43	1·62	1·40	1·66	1·36	1·69
70	1·51	1·57	1·48	1·60	1·45	1·63	1·42	1·66	1·39	1·70
75	1·53	1·58	1·50	1·61	1·47	1·64	1·45	1·67	1·42	1·70
80	1·54	1·59	1·52	1·62	1·49	1·65	1·47	1·67	1·44	1·70
85	1·56	1·60	1·53	1·63	1·51	1·65	1·49	1·68	1·46	1·71
90	1·57	1·61	1·55	1·64	1·53	1·66	1·50	1·69	1·48	1·71
95	1·58	1·62	1·56	1·65	1·54	1·67	1·52	1·69	1·50	1·71
100	1·59	1·63	1·57	1·65	1·55	1·67	1·53	1·70	1·51	1·72

[1] This table is reproduced from J Durbin and G S Watson, 'Testing for Serial Correlation in Least Squares Regression', *Biometrika*, Vol 38, 1951, pp 159–177, Table 5, by permission of the *Biometrika* Trustees.

Table VI

BINOMIAL PROBABILITIES FOR SELECTED VALUES OF *n* AND *p*

x	·05	·10	·15	·20	·25	·30	·35	·40	·45	·50
					$n = 5$					
0	·7738	·5905	·4437	·3277	·2373	·1681	·1160	·0778	·0503	·0312
1	·2036	·3280	·3915	·4096	·3955	·3602	·3124	·2592	·2059	·1562
2	·0214	·0729	·1382	·2048	·2637	·3087	·3364	·3456	·3369	·3125
3	·0011	·0081	·0244	·0512	·0879	·1323	·1811	·2304	·2757	·3125
4	·0000	·0004	·0022	·0064	·0146	·0284	·0488	·0768	·1128	·1562
5	·0000	·0000	·0001	·0003	·0010	·0024	·0053	·0102	·0185	·0312
					$n = 10$					
0	·5987	·3487	·1969	·1074	·0563	·0282	·0135	·0060	·0025	·0010
1	·3151	·3874	·3474	·2684	·1877	·1211	·0725	·0403	·0207	·0098
2	·0746	·1937	·2759	·3020	·2816	·2335	·1757	·1209	·0763	·0439
3	·0105	·0574	·1298	·2013	·2503	·2668	·2522	·2150	·1665	·1172
4	·0010	·0112	·0401	·0881	·1460	·2001	·2377	·2508	·2384	·2051
5	·0001	·0015	·0085	·0264	·0584	·1029	·1536	·2007	·2340	·2461
6	·0000	·0001	·0012	·0055	·0162	·0368	·0689	·1115	·1596	·2051
7	·0000	·0000	·0001	·0008	·0031	·0090	·0212	·0425	·0746	·1172
8	·0000	·0000	·0000	·0001	·0004	·0014	·0043	·0106	·0229	·0439
9	·0000	·0000	·0000	·0000	·0000	·0001	·0005	·0016	·0042	·0098
10	·0000	·0000	·0000	·0000	·0000	·0000	·0000	·0001	·0003	·0010
					$n = 15$					
0	·4633	·2059	·0874	·0352	·0134	·0047	·0016	·0005	·0001	·0000
1	·3658	·3432	·2312	·1319	·0668	·0305	·0126	·0047	·0016	·0005
2	·1348	·2669	·2856	·2309	·1559	·0916	·0476	·0219	·0090	·0032
3	·0307	·1285	·2184	·2501	·2252	·1700	·1110	·0634	·0318	·0139
4	·0049	·0428	·1156	·1876	·2252	·2186	·1792	·1268	·0780	·0417
5	·0006	·0105	·0449	·1032	·1651	·2061	·2123	·1859	·1404	·0916
6	·0000	·0019	·0132	·0430	·0917	·1472	·1906	·2066	·1914	·1527
7	·0000	·0003	·0030	·0138	·0393	·0811	·1319	·1771	·2013	·1964
8	·0000	·0000	·0005	·0035	·0131	·0348	·0710	·1181	·1647	·1964
9	·0000	·0000	·0001	·0007	·0034	·0116	·0298	·0612	·1048	·1527
10	·0000	·0000	·0000	·0001	·0007	·0030	·0096	·0245	·0515	·0916
11	·0000	·0000	·0000	·0000	·0001	·0006	·0024	·0074	·0191	·0417
12	·0000	·0000	·0000	·0000	·0000	·0001	·0004	·0016	·0052	·0139
13	·0000	·0000	·0000	·0000	·0000	·0000	·0001	·0003	·0010	·0032
14	·0000	·0000	·0000	·0000	·0000	·0000	·0000	·0000	·0001	·0005
15	·0000	·0000	·0000	·0000	·0000	·0000	·0000	·0000	·0000	·0000

$$n = 20$$

0	·3585	·1216	·0388	·0115	·0032	·0008	·0002	·0000	·0000	·0000
1	·3774	·2702	·1368	·0576	·0211	·0068	·0020	·0005	·0001	·0000
2	·1887	·2852	·2293	·1369	·0669	·0278	·0100	·0031	·0008	·0002
3	·0596	·1901	·2428	·2054	·1339	·0716	·0323	·0123	·0040	·0011
4	·0133	·0898	·1821	·2182	·1897	·1304	·0738	·0350	·0139	·0046
5	·0022	·0319	·1028	·1746	·2023	·1789	·1272	·0746	·0365	·0148
6	·0003	·0089	·0454	·1091	·1686	·1916	·1712	·1244	·0746	·0370
7	·0000	·0020	·0160	·0545	·1124	·1643	·1844	·1659	·1221	·0739
8	·0000	·0004	·0046	·0222	·0609	·1144	·1614	·1797	·1623	·1201
9	·0000	·0001	·0011	·0074	·0271	·0654	·1158	·1597	·1771	·1602
10	·0000	·0000	·0002	·0020	·0099	·0308	·0686	·1171	·1593	·1762
11	·0000	·0000	·0000	·0005	·0030	·0120	·0336	·0710	·1185	·1602
12	·0000	·0000	·0000	·0001	·0008	·0039	·0136	·0355	·0727	·1201
13	·0000	·0000	·0000	·0000	·0002	·0010	·0045	·0146	·0366	·0739
14	·0000	·0000	·0000	·0000	·0000	·0002	·0012	·0049	·0150	·0370
15	·0000	·0000	·0000	·0000	·0000	·0000	·0003	·0013	·0049	·0148
16	·0000	·0000	·0000	·0000	·0000	·0000	·0000	·0003	·0013	·0046
17	·0000	·0000	·0000	·0000	·0000	·0000	·0000	·0000	·0002	·0011
18	·0000	·0000	·0000	·0000	·0000	·0000	·0000	·0000	·0000	·0002
19	·0000	·0000	·0000	·0000	·0000	·0000	·0000	·0000	·0000	·0000
20	·0000	·0000	·0000	·0000	·0000	·0000	·0000	·0000	·0000	·0000

Table VII

VALUES OF $e^{-\mu}$

μ	$e^{-\mu}$	μ	$e^{-\mu}$
0·0	1·0000	3·0	0·0498
0·1	0·9048	3·1	0·0450
0·2	0·8187	3·2	0·0408
0·3	0·7408	3·3	0·0369
0·4	0·6703	3·4	0·0334
0·5	0·6065	3·5	0·0302
0·6	0·5488	3·6	0·0273
0·7	0·4966	3·7	0·0247
0·8	0·4493	3·8	0·0224
0·9	0·4066	3·9	0·0202
1·0	0·3679	4·0	0·0183
1·1	0·3329	4·1	0·0166
1·2	0·3012	4·2	0·0150
1·3	0·2725	4·3	0·0136
1·4	0·2466	4·4	0·0123
1·5	0·2231	4·5	0·0111
1·6	0·2019	4·6	0·0101
1·7	0·1827	4·7	0·0091
1·8	0·1653	4·8	0·0082
1·9	0·1496	4·9	0·0074
2·0	0·1353	5·0	0·0067
2·1	0·1225	5·5	0·0041
2·2	0·1108	6·0	0·0025
2·3	0·1003	6·5	0·0015
2·4	0·0907	7·0	0·0009
2·5	0·0821	7·5	0·0006
2·6	0·0743	8·0	0·0003
2·7	0·0672	8·5	0·0002
2·8	0·0608	9·0	0·0001
2·9	0·0550	9·5	0·0001

APPENDIX B

SOURCES OF AUSTRALIAN STATISTICS

1 General

In Australia most governmentally collected statistics are published by the Central Office of the Australian Bureau of Statistics on a commonwealth and state basis. In addition, each state office of the bureau publishes in respect of its own state a series of publications similar to that of the Central Office, eg the *Quarterly Abstract of South Australian Statistics*, but which contain greater detail for the state, and in some instances information for subdivisions of the state. Other governmentally collected statistics can also be found in such publication as the *Report of the Commissioner of Taxation*, the *Budget Papers*, other financial statements of the Commonwealth and State governments, the reports of government business undertakings, the publications of the Australian Bureau of Agricultural Economics and of the Industries Division of the Department of Trade, etc. There are few private statistical publications, but mention should be made of the *Reserve Bank of Australia Statistical Bulletin*, and of the company statistics included in the *Australian Stock Exchange Journal* and in Jobson's *Year Book*.

The following are the principal general publications of the Central Office of the Australian Bureau of Statistics:

Official Yearbook of Australia (Ref No 1.1, annual)
Pocket Compendium of Australian Statistics (Ref No 1.2, annual)
Monthly Review of Business Statistics (Ref No 1.4, monthly)
Digest of Current Economic Statistics (Ref No 1.5, monthly)
Seasonally Adjusted Indicators (Ref No 1.10, annual)

The *Official Yearbook of Australia* provides the most comprehensive statistical survey of economic and social conditions in Australia, and is a very useful reference work although inevitably published with some time-lag. Similar information, but with less detail, is contained in the *Pocket Compendium of Australian Statistics*. The most generally useful of the bureau's monthly publications are the *Monthly Review of Business Statistics* and the *Digest of Current Economic Statistics*, the former containing a comprehensive range of monthly and quarterly economic series and the latter summarising the main quarterly and monthly statistical indicators of Australian economic activity. Long-term series of both original and seasonally adjusted indicators are published annually in *Seasonally Adjusted Indicators*, together with explanatory matter on 'seasonal adjustment'.

A major recent addition to the publications of the Australian Bureau of Statistics is *Social Indicators* (Ref No 13.16, annual). First issued in 1976, this publication is intended to bring together a selection of statistics relevant to social questions in Australia, and includes information on population, health, education, working life, income, social security, crime, housing, and the Aborigines.

In addition to the general publications listed above the bureau provides more specialised statistical information in a wide variety of regular bulletins and occasional publications covering the following major fields: building and construction, demography, finance, foreign ownership, health, wages and employment, national accounts, overseas trade and balance of payments, prices and price indexes, primary and secondary industries, retail trade, tourist accommodation, transport and communication, and wholesale trade. The scope and nature of Australian official statistics are being continuously reviewed and expanded, and for up-to-date catalogue and brief descriptions of the main publications issued by the Central Office and the state branches of the bureau reference should be made to *Catalogue of Publications* (Ref No 1.8, annual). Supplementary information relating to current releases may be found in issues of *Publications Issued During the Month* (Ref No 1.9, monthly).

Population census results are published as they become available, and the full results for the 1954, 1961, 1966 and 1971 censuses have been published for each state, Australia and the territories. The 1976 census results are at present being issued in preliminary releases. Since Federation, censuses have been conducted in 1911, 1921, 1933, 1947, 1954, 1961, 1966, 1971 and 1976. Life tables, calculated on the basis of census results, are published separately, the latest being for the period 1970–72 (Ref No 4.31). With the exception of the *Year Book*, the *Labour Report*, the *Australian National Accounts*, the *Balance of Payments* and the budget paper on *National Income and Expenditure*, the printed publications provide little textual comment on the statistics. It is most important, however, that anyone using the publications should be aware of the precise meaning of the various series contained in them. Definitions and other explanatory matter are contained in most of the publications, and can be further clarified by the bureau upon request. As part of its expanding technical services, the bureau is developing a comprehensive computer-based file system of standard terms and definitions which can be readily referred to through visual-display computer terminals; such a facility is presently available for its *Integrated Economic Censuses and Surveys*.

In addition to its publishing activities, the Australian Bureau of

Statistics maintains large computer files of many types of statistical information. Such information can be made available for analysis, within the constraints of confidentiality, safeguards and cost, to users whose requests for statistical information cannot be met from the published sources or from other existing tabulations.

2 Sample Surveys

The Australian Bureau of Statistics undertakes some of its statistical collections on a sample basis. Apart from *ad hoc* surveys organised to obtain special information, the bureau conducts regular sample surveys to provide continuing information in a number of fields. Regular sample surveys are as follows:
Surveys of Retail Establishments:
    Quarterly Sales Sample
    Monthly Sales Sub-Sample
Survey of International Trade Credit (quarterly)
Import Orders Survey (monthly)
Survey of Stocks and Sales (quarterly)
Survey of Capital Expenditure (quarterly)
Survey of Earnings and Hours (May and October)
Job Vacancies (annual)
Population Survey (quarterly)
Sheep and Wool Survey (three times a year)
Combined Cereal Survey (annual)
Agricultural Finance Survey (annual)
These surveys involve sampling designs of varying degrees of complexity. In order to illustrate some of the aspects of sample design, a brief discussion of the Population Survey and of the Survey of Retail Establishments is set out below.

The Population Survey is the general title given to the household sample survey carried out quarterly throughout Australia to collect data on demographic and labour force characteristics of the population. Designed as a multi-stage sample, the Population Survey Sample covers approximately 32 000 dwellings in the six Australian states and the two internal territories. The fieldwork for the survey is carried out by specially trained interviewers. The proportion of households included in the surveys varies from state to state, but in the aggregate about two-thirds of one per cent of all households in Australia are represented. Since 1964, the principal purpose of the regular surveys based on the Population Survey Sample has been to provide comprehensive quarterly estimates of the civilian labour force in Australia. Statistics obtained from the quarterly Labour Force Survey include numbers employed and unemployed, labour force participation and unemployment rates, duration of unemployment, as well as age, sex, occupation and industry characteristics. In addition to providing regular information on the labour force, the Population Survey Sample also serves as a vehicle for a number of supplementary studies which are generally conducted in conjunction with the labour force survey, but may involve separate field inquiries. These have recently included: incomes of individuals and families in 1973–74; the incidence of chronic illness, injuries and impairments (1974); journey to work and school (1974); duration of employment (1975); job tenure (1976); and the distribution of weekly earnings in August 1975.[1] Other *ad hoc* surveys based on the Population Survey Sample have included: Survey of Migrants (1973); Household Expenditure Survey (1974–76); and General Social Survey (1975).

The purpose of the quarterly Survey of Retail Establishments is to provide estimates of quarterly retail sales in Australia and for each state by type of commodity sold. Censuses of retail establishments are taken at five-yearly intervals, the Census of Retail Establishments conducted for the year ended 30 June 1974 being the basis for the current survey. This census gives for states and areas within states a classification of aggregate retail sales by description of store, by commodity group and by size of turnover. This enables a detailed stratification of the population to be made. The population of stores is stratified by states (six strata), by area (metropolitan and country— two strata), by description of store (thirteen strata) and by size of annual turnover (six strata), making a total of 936 distinct strata or cells. One such cell would be, for example, New South Wales, metropolitan, non-chain grocers, of size $20 000–$59 999.

All told there are approximately 123 000 retail stores (excluding motor establishments). The sample now in use consists of 7100 stores. In addition to these, there are 531 chain retail organisations which are completely enumerated. The sample is optimally allocated between cells with the object of producing estimates of comparable precision for each commodity within each state. The population variances used in the optimum allocations are those appropriate to ratio estimates. In accordance with the optimum design all chain stores and the cells containing the largest firms, ie those with a turnover in 1973–74 of $325 000 or more in Tasmania and of $1 000 000 or more in the other states, are fully enumerated on account of their importance and small numbers. A simple random sample is selected from each of the remaining cells.

---

[1] For a full list of supplementary population survey studies, see Australian Bureau of Statistics, *The Labour Force* (Ref No 6.22).

The survey is made quarterly, and stores once selected remain in the sample until the sample is re-designed following the next census. This simplifies administration and increases the co-operation of the stores. In any particular quarter non-response to questionnaires is somewhat less than 2 per cent in all states, and this is due mainly to unavoidable circumstances. The ratio method of estimation is used to estimate the value of retail sales. This method is used in several ways in this survey, but the general principle involved is illustrated as follows. For an individual cell, we put Z_i for the total value of sales recorded in the 1973–74 census for cell i, z_i for the value of sales recorded in the census for stores now in the sample, x_i for the value of sales reported currently by stores in the sample, and X_i for the estimated current total value of sales for cell i. Then we have

$$X_i = Z_i \frac{x_i}{z_i}$$

This method of estimation is equivalent to assuming that for an individual cell the value of retail sales of non-sample stores moves in the same ratio as those of sample stores. Since the sampling in each cell is random, this assumption is reasonable, subject, of course, to the usual errors of sampling. The above formula gives an estimate for an individual cell. Estimates of broader classifications are made by aggregating individual cell estimates or by aggregating cells before estimation.

The accuracy of the estimates derived from the sample can be judged by obtaining the 95 per cent confidence limits for the population values being estimated. Thus, for total turnover for Australia, the range of these limits is of the order of ± 0.6 per cent of total turnover, and for the turnover in each commodity group for Australia between ± 1.2 per cent and ± 3.6 per cent of turnover in the group. For state estimates these limits range between ± 1.2 per cent and ± 2.0 per cent, and between ± 2.0 per cent and ± 10.8 per cent respectively. (The more detailed estimates naturally have wider confidence limits because they are based on a smaller number of stores.) For example, sales of groceries in Australia for the March quarter, 1975, were estimated at \$656.1 million. This is a sample estimate, and with 95 per cent confidence limits of ± 1.2 per cent the population value is estimated to lie within the range \$656.1 million ± 1.2 per cent, ie \$648.2 million to \$664.0 million.

There are certain difficult problems in a survey of this kind, connected with the passage of time. As time moves on from the benchmark of the census the relationship between current sales and census sales becomes less and less precise. One consequence of this is that the size stratification becomes less exact. This does not of itself introduce bias, but it does increase the sampling error. This can be allowed for by increasing the size of sample over time.

Another serious problem is that some stores go out of business and new stores are created. If the number of stores as a whole is increasing over time, estimates of retail trade based on the above methods will tend to be downwardly biased, unless some account is taken of the increase in the population relative to the sample. Furthermore, if new stores are not introduced into the sample, the sample will become smaller as sample stores go out of business from time to time. Allowance for the births and deaths of stores is made by taking a census of new stores each September and grafting these onto the frame, and by removing defunct stores from the frame. Apart from these difficulties which are associated with the sampling procedure, there are, of course, all the census problems of definition and classification of retail stores, eg whether a bootmaker is a retail store, how a departmental store is to be classified, etc.

3 National Income Statistics

For Australia, unofficial estimates of national income date back to 1887. The most recent and most comprehensive of these unofficial estimates were made in 1938 by Colin Clark and J G Crawford in *The National Income of Australia* (Angus and Robertson, Sydney, 1938). During the Second World War, however, more detailed estimates of the items entering into the social accounts were found necessary for the formulation of wartime economic policy, and in 1945 detailed official estimates of national income and allied aggregates were published in a paper accompanying the Commonwealth Budget. These estimates referred to the financial years 1938–39 to 1944–45 inclusive. Since 1945 the paper on *National Income and Expenditure* has been an annual accompaniment to the Budget. In 1963, *Australian National Accounts, National Income and Expenditure 1948–49 to 1961–62* introduced a number of changes in the structure and presentation of the national accounts. Further major changes in the conceptual basis of the accounts and definitions of the principal aggregates were made in 1971–72, and a new series of estimates, revised from 1962–63 onwards, was published in the 1972–73 issue of *Australian National Accounts*. Although the detailed estimates of items of national income and expenditure in the current and in the previous series are not fully consistent, some major series for the years 1948–49 to 1961–62 which are comparable with the present estimates have been compiled by the bureau and have been published in Appendix C of successive issues of *Australian National Accounts*. Further details relating to the balance of payments are given in the yearly bulletin *Balance of Payments*.

Clark and Crawford's estimates of national income were made primarily by the production method. They also made some estimates by the income-received method, the two sets of estimates being about 6 per cent apart. In all, perhaps about two-thirds of the content of their estimates derived by the production method and only about one-third of those derived by the income-received method were based on reliable data. Since the early 1940s, due to the introduction of payroll tax resulting in a substantially comprehensive collection of statistics on wages and salaries paid, to the lowering of the exemption limit for payment of income tax resulting in a greater cover of incomes, and to improved tabulation methods, the data available for estimating national income by the incomes-received method have vastly improved. Official estimates of national income are in the main derived by the incomes-received method. These estimates are based mainly on payroll tax tabulations, personal and company income tax statistics and annual collections of statistics of the value of farm production.

Estimates of gross domestic product by the expenditure method are also made. These are adjusted to equality with those made by the incomes-received method by means of an item entitled 'statistical discrepancy,' which is, in practice, shown on the expenditure side of the account. These estimates are derived mainly from censuses and sample surveys of retail trade establishments and from statistics of motor vehicle registrations (for private final consumption expenditure); the accounts of public authorities (for government expenditure); sample surveys of businesses, statistics of dwelling construction, taxation statistics, and manufacturing census statistics (for gross private investment); and oversea trade statistics (for exports and imports).

Estimates of the many detailed items published in the social accounts are based on a wide variety of sources as well as on those referred to in the preceding two paragraphs.

The main tables of the Australian social accounts for 1974–75 are reproduced below. These tables are not set out in the highly systematised form of Chapter 10, above. This is in part due to the limitations of the statistics available to estimate the various items. But the form of accounts of Chapter 10 can be conceived as lying behind the published figures. Table 1 is the consolidated domestic production account, although the left-hand side is in terms of factor payments instead of values added, and so includes some items which are shown in Chapter 10 in the distribution accounts. Gross domestic product is estimated by the incomes-received method in the left-hand side of the account and by the expenditure method in the right-hand side. Balance is achieved

THE AUSTRALIAN NATIONAL ACCOUNTS
1974–75[1]

Table 1

DOMESTIC PRODUCTION ACCOUNT

	$m		$m
Wages, salaries and supplements	35 190	Final consumption expenditure—Private	34 541
Gross operating surplus—		Government	9 092
Trading enterprises—		Gross fixed capital expenditure—Private	8 788
Companies	6 201	Public enterprises	2 654
Unincorporated enterprises	7 005	General government	2 710
Dwellings owned by		Increase in stocks	836
persons	3 478	Statistical discrepancy	547
Public enterprises	1 146		
Financial enterprises	937		
Less Imputed bank service		Gross national expenditure	59 168
charge	1 625	Exports of goods and services	9 782
Gross domestic product at		National turnover of goods	
factor cost[2]	52 332	and services[3]	68 950
Indirect taxes less subsidies	6 671	Less Imports of goods and	
		services	9 947
		Expenditure on gross	
Gross domestic product	59 003	domestic product	59 003

[1] Source: Australian Bureau of Statistics: *Australian National Accounts: National Income and Expenditure 1974–75* (Ref 7.1), pp 23–25 (figures in Tables 1 to 8 are subject to revision in subsequent publications).
[2] For definition of this aggregate see footnote 3 on p 410 above.
[3] See footnote 2 on p 407 above.

by including the balancing item 'statistical discrepancy'. Tables 2, 3, 4, 5 and 8 are the current accounts of the five sectors. Table 6 consolidates these accounts into a single national account. Table 7 is the consolidated national capital account.

In 1960, quarterly publication of the social accounts commenced under the title of *Quarterly Estimates of National Income and Expenditure*. These estimates cover most of the items in the annual publication and include more details for some items. Naturally, they are not as reliable as the annual figures, as they must in many cases be based on less complete information. However, they are of crucial importance for the analysis of short-term fluctuations in economic activity. They are being produced with a relatively short lag (about eight weeks after the end of the quarter).

REFERENCES

Australian National Accounts, National Income and Expenditure (Australian Bureau of Statistics, Ref No 7.1)

National Income and Expenditure, latest issue (Government Printer, Canberra)

Quarterly Estimates of National Income and Expenditure (Australian Bureau of Statistics, Ref Nos 7.5 and 7.10)

Balance of Payments (Australian Bureau of Statistics, Ref No 8.1)

Haig, B D: *Quarterly Estimates of National Income and Expenditure* (Paper read to Section G of the Australian and New Zealand Association for the Advancement of Science, Brisbane, 1960) (Mimeographed)

Haig, B D and McBurney, S S: *The Interpretation of National Income Estimates* (ANU Press, 1968)

Table 2

INCOME AND OUTLAY ACCOUNT
CORPORATE TRADING ENTERPRISES
(Including Public Trading Enterprises)

	$m		$m
Interest, etc paid	1 683	Net operating surplus	
Third party insurance		Trading enterprise	
transfers to persons	83	companies	4 218
Public enterprise income	555	Public trading enterprises	555
		Interest, etc received	496
Company income—		Dividends received	133
Income tax payable ⎫			
Dividends paid ⎬	3 081		
Undistributed income ⎭			
Disbursements	5 402	Receipts	5 402

Table 3
INCOME AND OUTLAY ACCOUNT
FINANCIAL ENTERPRISES

	$m		$m
Interest on life and superannunation funds imputed to households	877	Net operating surplus	775
		Less Imputed bank service	
Other interest, etc paid	2 417	charge	1 625
Income tax on life and		Interest, etc received	4 820
superannuation funds	62	Dividends received	148
Extraordinary insurance		Extraordinary insurance	
claims paid	218	claims from overseas	75
Public enterprise income—			
Paid to general government	12		
Retained income	209		
Company income—			
Income tax payable ⎫			
Dividends paid ⎬	398		
Undistributed income ⎭			
Disbursements	4 193	Receipts	4 193

Table 4
INCOME AND OUTLAY ACCOUNT
HOUSEHOLDS
(Including Unincorporated Enterprises)

	$m.		$m.
Private final consumption expenditure	34 541	Net operating surplus— Dwellings owned by	
Consumer debt interest	538	persons	3 069
Income tax payable	7 144	Unincorporated enterprises	6 159
Other direct taxes, fees,		Less Interest, etc paid	
fines, etc	580	relating thereto	2 169
Transfers overseas	235	Less Third party insurance	
Saving	7 728	transfers to persons	65
		Wages, salaries and supplements	35 190
		Interest on life and superannuation funds (imputed)	877
		Other interest, etc received	2 098
		Dividends received	595
		Transfers from general government	4 619
		Third party insurance transfers	148
		Transfers from overseas	245
Disbursements	50 766	Receipts	50 766

Table 5
INCOME AND OUTLAY ACCOUNT
GENERAL GOVERNMENT

	$m		$m
Final consumption		Income from public	
expenditure	9 092	enterprises	567
Subsidies	328	Interest, etc received	524
Interest etc paid	1 288	Indirect taxes	6 999
Transfers to persons	4 619	Direct taxes on income—	
Grants for private capital		Companies, etc	2 431
purposes	133	Households	7 709
Transfers overseas	350	Other direct taxes,	
Surplus on current		fees, fines, etc	580
transactions	3 000		
Disbursements	18 810	Receipts	18 810

Table 6
NATIONAL INCOME AND OUTLAY ACCOUNT

	$m		$m
Final consumption		Wages, salaries and	
expenditure—		supplements	35 190
Private	34 541	Net operating surplus	13 151
Government	9 092		
Saving	10 657	Domestic factor incomes	48 341
		Less Net income paid	
		overseas	457
		Indirect taxes	6 999
		Less subsidies	328
		National income	54 555
		Less Net transfers to	
		overseas	265
Disposal of income	54 290	National disposable income	54 290

Table 7
NATIONAL CAPITAL ACCOUNT

	$m		$m
Gross fixed capital expenditure—		Depreciation allowances	3 991
Private—		Saving	
Dwellings	2 501	Increase in income tax provisions	−452
Other building and construction	1 978	Undistributed (company) income	−179
All other	4 309	Retained income of	
Public enterprises	2 654	public financial	
General government	2 710	enterprises	209
Increases in stocks—		Household saving	7 728
Farm and miscellaneous	359	General government	
Private non-farm	477	surplus on current	
Statistical discrepancy	547	transactions	3 000
Net lending to overseas	−887	General government grants for private capital purposes	133
		Extraordinary insurance claims paid	218
Gross accumulation	14 648	Finance of gross accumulation	14 648

Table 8
OVERSEAS TRANSACTIONS ACCOUNT

	$m		$m
Exports of goods and services	9 782	Imports of goods and services	9 947
Property income from overseas	370	Property income to overseas	827
Transfers from overseas—		Transfers to overseas—	
Personal	245	Personal	235
Extraordinary insurance claims	75	General government	350
		Net lending to overseas	−887
Current receipts from overseas	10 472	Use of current receipts	10 472

In 1961 the Reserve Bank of Australia published flow-of-funds statements for Australia 1953–54 to 1957–58. These estimates were revised and extended in 1965 to cover the period 1953–54 to 1961–62. Subsequently, estimates have been prepared annually and published in the *Flow of Funds Supplement* to the *Statistical Bulletin* of the Reserve Bank of Australia, the most recent issue covering the period 1963–64 to 1972–73. These statements concentrate on transactions in financial claims. They show sources and uses of funds classified into some twenty types of financial transactions for twelve sectors of the economy (mainly financial sectors), some of which are further divided into sub-sectors.

REFERENCES
Staff Paper: Flow-of-Funds, Australia, 1953–54 to 1961–62 (by A S Holmes), (Reserve Bank of Australia, Sydney, 1965)
Statistical Bulletin: Flow of Funds Supplement, June 1975 (Reserve Bank of Australia)
Mathews, R L: 'The Australian Flow-of-Funds Accounts', *Economic Record*, Vol 38, No 81, 1962, p 94.

The first major work in the field of input-output data in Australia was done by Professor Burgess Cameron of the Australian National University. Transaction tables for 1946–47, 1953–54 and 1955–56 for an eighty, forty and twenty sector classification respectively were published in the *Economic Record* with explanation, comment and extension of the analysis. The first semi-official input-output tables for Australia were published in 1964. These tables were compiled for the year 1958–59. They were the result of a preliminary examination of the relevance of existing statistical information for the purpose of compiling more detailed input-output tables in future years, and included transactions tables for thirty-four producing sectors. Input-output tables have since been completed for two more recent years, 1962–63 and 1968–69.

REFERENCES
Input-Output Tables, 1958–59 (Australian Bureau of Statistics)
Input-Output Tables, 1962–63 (Australian Bureau of Statistics)
Input-Output Tables, 1968–69 (Australian Bureau of Statistics, Ref No 7.11).
Cameron, Burgess: 'The 1946–47 Transaction Table,' *Economic Record*, Vol 33, No 66, 1957, p 353; 'New Aspects of Australia's Industrial Structure,' *Economic Record*, Vol 34, No 69, 1958, p 362; 'Inter-Sector Accounts, 1955–56' *Economic Record*, Vol 36, No 74, 1960, p 269.
Haig, B D: 'Input-Output Relationships, 1958–59,' *Economic Record*, Vol 41, No 93, 1965, p 118.

4 Index Numbers of Prices

Descriptions of the main Australian price indexes are set out below. With the exception of the Import Price Index they are all prepared by the Australian Bureau of Statistics.

Consumer Price Index

The Consumer Price Index was first published in 1960. It extends back to the September quarter, 1948, and is published quarterly in special releases of the bureau and in the *Monthly Review of Business Statistics*, the *Digest of Current Economic Statistics* and the *Labour Report*. It is computed for the six state capital cities separately and in combination, and for Canberra. Indexes for the major commodity groups within the complete index are also computed. The Consumer Price Index was preceded by the 'C' Series Retail Price Index and the Interim Retail Price Index. The 'C' Series was, until 1954, the principal Australian retail price index, being a continuous series extending back to 1914.[1] In its last years its regimen and weighting became increasingly out of date,[2] and it was supplemented in 1954 by the computation of the Interim Retail Price Index, which was extended back to 1950–51.[3]

The Consumer Price Index, like its predecessors, is designed, in the words of the Australian Statistician, 'to measure quarterly variations in retail prices of goods and services representing a high proportion of the expenditure of wage earner households'. With the frequent and marked changes which occurred in the quality and pattern of expenditure since the end of the Second World War, the determination of a fixed regimen, which would have remained representative for any length of time, was found to be virtually impossible. Consequently the Consumer Price Index was designed as a series of short-term indexes linked together to form a continuous chain (see p 470 above). Since 1948 nine separate linked series have been employed (1948–52, 1952–56, 1956–60, 1960–63, 1963–68, 1968–73, 1973–74,[4] 1974–76 and 1976 onwards). Further revisions in the content of the index involving additional short-term indexes will be made as occasion demands.

Each short-term index is a fixed-weight aggregative type, namely

$$P_{0t} = \frac{\Sigma p_t q}{\Sigma p_0 q}$$

[1] See *Labour Report*, No 40, 1951 (Australian Bureau of Statistics) Appendix Section V, p 160, and *Labour Report*, No 41, 1952 (Australian Bureau of Statistics) Chapter I, p 1 and Appendix Section V, p 164.
[2] See Karmel, P H: *Applied Statistics for Economists* (Pitman, Melbourne, 1957) (1st edition), pp 317–20 and 431–3.
[3] See *Labour Report*, No 46, 1958 (Australian Bureau of Statistics), Chapter I, p 1.
[4] The change in the composition of the index introduced in September quarter of 1974 was a minor one involving the deletion of the item 'radio and television licences'.

However, it is probably more convenient to think of this formula as a weighted arithmetic mean of price relatives

$$P_{0t} = \sum \left[\frac{p_t}{p_0} \left(\frac{p_0 q}{\Sigma p_0 q} \right) \right]$$

in order to examine the relative weighting of the items covered by the index.

The *regimen* of the index is divided into eight major groups: food, clothing, housing, household equipment and operation, transportation, health and personal care, recreation, tobacco and alcohol. These major groups are themselves broken up into sections. Within sections there are about 300 distinct items and a much greater number of grades, types, brands, etc, for which prices are obtained. The next table illustrates the composition and the relative weighting of the Consumer Price Index as at the beginning of the ninth linked series (September quarter, 1976).

The *prices* for the groups other than housing are the averages of prices obtained from representative and reputable retailers and service establishments in each city, for each class of commodity and each service covered by the index. Prices are collected from vendors and are those actually being charged for normal cash purchases of new articles. 'Bargain' or 'sale' prices of imperfect goods or discontinued lines are not used. Otherwise actual transaction prices (eg those reflecting grocery 'specials') are used in all cases. Prices are collected for specified standards of goods and services. When qualities change, adjustments are made (by splicing, where appropriate, see p 472 above) to ensure that changes in prices are alone reflected in the index. The actual collection of prices is carried out by qualified field officers, who check the returns and make certain that the price quotations are for items of the type and standard required for the index.

The main price elements in the housing group are rents of privately-owned houses, rents of privately-owned flats, rents of government-owned houses and flats, house prices and rates, repairs and maintenance. The first of these are obtained from returns furnished by house agents in each city, relating to weekly rents for four-, five- and six-roomed houses classified according to whether constructed of wood or brick. These returns cover an extensive sample of houses (currently numbering about 2900 for all cities) selected by field officers as being of appropriate standards. Flat rentals, based on a sample of about 2000 flats in all cities, are collected in a similar manner, but are not classified according to size. The rents of government-owned houses are obtained from housing authorities. The prices of houses are collected from private and governmental bodies engaged in constructing houses for home ownership. The prices are for new houses and exclude the value of land. They comprise contract prices, sale prices and estimated building costs per square metre. They are obtained for houses in selected representative categories classified by size, type of construction and material of walls. To smooth out random fluctuations in price data, four quarter moving averages are used, so that the house prices used currently in the index relate to prices over the preceding year.

CONSUMER PRICE INDEX—SIX STATE CAPITAL CITIES COMBINED COMPOSITION AS AT SEPTEMBER QUARTER 1976

Group, sub-group, etc	Percentage contribution to total index aggregate (a)	
	Sub-group etc	Group
FOOD		21·026
Dairy produce	2·138	
Cereal products	2·384	
Meat and seafoods—	4·957	
Beef and veal	2·028	
Lamb and mutton	0·908	
Pork	0·252	
Poultry	0·514	
Other meat	0·835	
Fish	0·420	
Fruit and vegetables—	2·906	
Fresh fruit and vegetables	2·017	
Processed fruit and vegetables	0·889	
Soft drinks, ice-cream and confectionery	2·080	
Meals out, takeaway food	4·403	
Other food	2·158	
CLOTHING		10·141
Men's and boys'	2·928	
Women's and girls'	4·489	
Piecegoods and other clothing	0·538	
Footwear	1·651	
Clothing and footwear services	0·535	
HOUSING		13·544
Rent—	5·247	
Privately-owned dwellings	4·779	
Government-owned dwellings	0·468	
Home ownership—	8·297	
Local government rates and charges	1·759	
House price, repairs and maintenance	6·538	

HOUSEHOLD EQUIPMENT AND OPERATION   14·761

Fuel and light	2·235
Furniture and floorcoverings	3·222
Appliances	1·909
Drapery	1·077
Household utensils and tools	1·507
Household supplies and services	3·319
Postal and telephone services	1·492

TRANSPORTATION   18·453

Private transport—	16·311
Motor vehicle purchase	5·523
Motor vehicle operation	10·788
Public transport fares	2·142

HEALTH AND PERSONAL CARE   3·950

Health services	1·484
Personal care products	1·799
Personal care services	0·667

RECREATION   7·878

Books, newspapers, magazines	1·428
Other recreation goods	3·215
Holiday accommodation	0·921
Other recreation services	2·314

TOBACCO AND ALCOHOL   10·247

Alcoholic beverages	7·001
Cigarettes and tobacco	3·246

ALL GROUPS   100·000   100·000

(*a*) Percentage contributions shown are in proportion to expenditure in 1974–75 valued at relevant prices of September quarter 1976.

Note. Similar information showing data for the series which commenced at December quarter 1973 is shown on pages 354 to 359 of Labour Report No 58. However, the changes in composition have been significant and the two sets of data cannot be compared directly.

Source: Australian Bureau of Statistics.

As has been pointed out above, the regimen and weights of the index have been revised several times in the series extending back to 1948. The weights used from the beginning of the ninth linked series (ie from September quarter 1976) have been largely based on data from the first Household Expenditure Survey (*HES*) conducted by the Australian Bureau of Statistics in respect of the year 1974–75. The *HES* data used refer to a defined 'target group' of the population comprising metropolitan wage- and salary-earner households with total income of more than the minimum weekly wage but excluding the top ten per cent of such households. The use of *HES* as the primary data source has enabled separate weighting patterns to be compiled for each of the six state capital cities and for Canberra. The indexes for the individual cities are then combined to produce the Six Capital Cities index by weighting by the number of 'target group' households in each of the cities as at 1974–75.

The *computation* of the index follows the formula, and is relatively straightforward, except for the Housing Group. Households fall into five main groups: those renting a house from a private owner, those renting a flat from a private owner, those renting a house from a government authority, those renting a flat from a government authority, and those who own or are purchasing their own houses. These five groups are represented in the index. For the first four groups the weighting is simply the reported expenditure on rent for each group in the base period relative to total household expenditure on items included in the index. For the fifth group items covering house price, municipal, water and sewerage rates, and repairs are included. The weighting for the house price is obtained by estimating a normal rate of purchase of new houses per household over the intercensal period 1947 to 1971, and multiplying this by a basic average price to obtain a basic average expenditure. This is then expressed relative to total household expenditure on items included in the index. The normal rate of purchase is estimated as what the ratio of the number of new houses acquired per annum to the stock of houses would have been if the population had been stationary. To the extent to which new houses in a stationary population are purely for replacement purposes, the ratio of new houses to the stock of houses is, in fact, the reciprocal of the average life of the houses,[1] so that this ratio is a measure of the average rate of depreciation per annum. To this extent, then, the weighting method adopted for owner-occupied houses implies that each owner 'consumes' a certain fraction of a house per year, and this fraction is priced in the index at current prices. (However, no doubt some new houses in the intercensal period were second houses (eg holiday homes), and, thus, some allowance for these is included). This is consistent with the treatment of other items in the regimen, which essentially relates to households' expenditure. No weight is included in the owner-occupied houses section for interest charges on moneys borrowed in connexion with house-purchase. In the same way, hire-purchase charges on motor vehicles and consumer durable goods are omitted.

The measurement of the price changes relevant to the Housing Group is somewhat complicated. A basic requirement in the com-

[1] ie the true death rate of the population of houses. See p 552 above.

pilation of any index number is that the quality of all items must be kept constant over periods for which price comparisons are made; otherwise the index will cease to measure price changes only and will include changes due to quality changes (see p 471 above). In the case of houses, this requirement is especially difficult to achieve. Houses by their nature change in quality. Existing houses age as time passes. They are reconstructed and extended. New houses differ in style and amenities. Consequently, a comparison of the average rent or price paid for houses in two periods will inevitably contain elements of a comparison of quality as well as of price. But it is only the price element which should be included in the index.

The following are the methods used in the Consumer Price Index in an attempt to overcome this difficulty. For privately-rented houses, as has been pointed out above, the rents used are ones collected from house agents. The average rise in rent from quarter to quarter is calculated for those houses which are on the agents' books for *both* quarters, for each of the six classes of four-, five- and six-roomed, wood or brick houses. For example, suppose that between March quarter, 1976, and June quarter, 1976, the average rent of the sample of four-roomed brick houses (privately rented) of the appropriate quality which were on the agents' books in both quarters rose by 3 per cent; and suppose that between June quarter, 1976, and September quarter, 1976, the average rent of similar (but not necessarily identical) houses which were on the agents' books in both these quarters rose by 4 per cent; then we should argue that, compared with the base, March quarter, 1976 = 100, average rents of this type of house for the September quarter, 1976, stood at $100 \times 1.03 \times 1.04 = 107.12$. Moreover this represents a pure price change, since all comparisons have been made between identical houses.[1] The sample of houses used for these computations is carefully watched by field officers to keep its quality as constant as possible and revised from time to time.

As far as the rents charged by government authorities are concerned, the above method would hardly be suitable, since these rents are only infrequently varied after the houses are initially occupied. Under a

---

[1] This contention is not strictly valid. If rent tends to vary inversely with age of house, other things being equal, this method inevitably introduces a cumulative bias in rent variation due to the ageing of houses. Thus, if over a period of years the rent of no house changed except by reason of its increasing age, this method would produce an index showing a continuous decline in rents, in spite of the fact that there were no 'price' variations in the rents of houses. Moreover this would be so, even if the sample of houses used were kept constant in respect of age distribution, since the comparisons are between the *same* houses in two consecutive quarters and hence some ageing is unavoidable. On the other hand, improvements are made to many houses from time to time, so that perhaps these can be assumed to offset the ageing.

regime of rising building costs, measurement of rent changes by this method would lead to a serious understatement of rent changes. Thus, if the rents of these houses were rigidly fixed at levels based on building costs, the rent of no single house would change, although the average level of rent actually paid would rise more and more as new houses were built at higher costs. The method used for this section of the Housing Group is to average all rents actually paid in appropriate categories and to weight these categories to provide a measure of average changes in these rents. Since the newly built houses are of much the same quality as the old ones, the quality of the houses is fairly constant. However, some quality changes are certainly taking place and these are inevitably included. Thus the measure of changes in the rents of government-owned houses relates to a changing stock of houses.

Reference has already been made to the collection of data for measuring changes in house prices. An attempt is made to keep quality reasonably constant by classifying houses into certain quality categories, measuring price changes within those categories, and combining these price changes in fixed proportions reflecting the relative importance of the categories. This achieves reasonable constancy of quality for short-period comparisons. For long-period comparisons it may be impossible to hold quality constant in the face of trends in house design.

Finally, two comments on the Consumer Price Index. First, since the index consists of a chain of relatively short links, one cannot strictly speaking describe it as measuring the changes in the cost of a given basket of goods and services. Unavoidably, precision in interpretation has had to be sacrificed for up-to-dateness in weighting (see p 457 above). Secondly, as regards composition and weighting, the index is much superior to the various retail price indexes compiled by the Australian Statistician prior to 1960. Compared with the 'C' Series Retail Price Index, for example, the index currently (1976) in use contains nearly twice as many distinct items.[1] While the Housing Group has been periodically revised in the light of changing conditions, there are still some outstanding questions, the answers to which must depend on the purpose of the index being constructed. In particular what should be done with interest payable on houses being purchased by instalments? It would seem that if the Consumer Price Index is to be conceived in terms of a measure of the price component of households' expenditure, some account should be taken of such interest

---

[1] For a comparison of the relative weighting of broad groups of items in the 'C' Series and the Consumer Price Index, see Karmel, P H, and Polasek, M: *Applied Statistics for Economists* (Pitman, Melbourne, 1970) (3rd edition), pp 494–5.

payments and possibly also of the cost of land. Their omission results in an underweighting of the Housing Group. On the other hand, variations in interest rates would have to be suitably averaged since many interest payments are not adjusted with changes in current interest rates and the measurement of variation in the price of land could present considerable difficulties.

REFERENCE
Labour Report, No 58, 1973 (Australian Bureau of Statistics, Ref No 6.7), Chapter I, pp 1–42

Wholesale Price Indexes

In 1969 the Australian Statistician began publishing a new series of wholesale price index numbers designed to measure price movements of materials used and articles produced by sectors of industry. The first of the new series was the *Price Index of Materials Used in Building other than House Building* (1969), followed by the *Price Index of Materials Used in House Building* (1970) and the *Price Index of Metallic Materials Used in the Manufacture of Fabricated Metal Products* (1972). To these were later added the *Price Index of Materials Used in Manufacturing Industry* (1975) and the *Price Index of Articles Produced by Manufacturing Industry* (1976). The bureau also prepares two special-purpose indexes: the *Price Index of Electrical Installation Materials* and *Price Indexes of Copper Materials Used in the Manufacture of Electrical Equipment*.

The Price Index of Materials used in Building other than House Building is an index of wholesale prices of selected materials used in the construction of the following building 'use-types': high-rise flats (ie flats of more than three storeys), offices, factories, health buildings (ie hospitals, etc) education buildings (ie schools, etc) and commercial premises (ie shops, hotels, etc.) Its regimen contains seventy-two items combined into eleven groups. The weighting pattern is designed to reflect average materials usage over the stated range of building use-types. The index is computed monthly for the six state capital cities separately and in combination, as well as for each of the eleven groups and for all groups combined.

The Price Index of Materials used in House Building is also compiled monthly, with separate indexes being available for each state capital city and for each of eleven groups of building materials, in addition to an 'all groups' index. Its object is to measure movements in wholesale prices of basic materials entering into residential construction (including low-rise flats). This index, like the previous one, is of the fixed-weight average type (weighted arithmetic mean of price relatives), with reference base 1966–67 = 100.

The Price Index of Metallic Materials used in the Manufacture of Fabricated Metal Products relates to wholesale prices of basic metallic materials selected and combined in accordance with a weighting pattern reflecting value of usage as reported at the 1968–69 Census of Manufacturing Establishments. There are four groups of metallic materials represented in the index, with index numbers being published monthly for the four groups and for all groups combined. The formula used is of the fixed-weight average type, with reference base 1968–69 = 100.

The Price Index of Materials used in Manufacturing Industry is designed to measure price changes of materials entering manufacturing establishments (Division C of the Australian Standard Industrial Classification) from other sectors of the Australian economy or from overseas. In addition to an 'all groups' index, index numbers are published for ten groupings on an industry-of-origin basis and for seven groupings on a commodity basis. The index has a regimen of some ninety items, each with a fixed weight, and is calculated monthly with reference base 1968–69 = 100.

The object of the Price Index of Articles Produced by Manufacturing Industry is to measure price changes in articles produced by establishments in the Manufacturing Division (Division C of the Australian Standard Industrial Classification) for sale or transfer to other sectors of the Australian economy, for export overseas or for use as capital equipment. Separate indexes are also computed for seven selected subdivisions within the Manufacturing Division. The index is published monthly, and its regimen contains about seven-hundred individual commodities, each with a fixed weight relating to its production in 1971–72.

REFERENCE
Labour Report, No 58, 1973 (Australian Bureau of Statistics, Ref No 6.7) Chapter II, pp 43–71

Export Price Index
The current export price index uses a fixed-weight aggregative formula, with reference base 1959–60. Over the period 1959 to 1969 there were twenty-nine items in the regimen, covering about 83 per cent of the value of exports. Index numbers from July 1969 have been compiled on an interim basis which incorporates a re-weighting of the items originally included in the index, and the four additional items: iron ore, bauxite, alumina and mineral sands. The weights in the interim series are based on export values for the year 1969–70. The prices used relate to specified standards for each commodity and in most cases are combinations of prices for a number of representative grades, types, etc.

The indexes are published for individual commodities (wool, sugar, gold) and groups of commodities (meats, dairy produce, cereals, dried and canned fruits, hides and tallow, metals and coal) as well as for the regimen as a whole.

REFERENCES

Official Yearbook of Australia, No 60, 1974 (Australian Bureau of Statistics), Chapter X, pp 248–60

Export Price Index (Australian Bureau of Statistics, Ref No 9.2)

Import Price Index

This index, which is prepared in the Research Department of the Reserve Bank of Australia and published in the *Reserve Bank of Australia Statistical Bulletin*, is a fixed-weight aggregative type. The index is available from 1928 onwards. It is at present calculated monthly but quarterly figures only are available prior to July 1955.

The weighting system has been revised periodically. The latest revision, using 1966–67 as a base, was calculated back to 1965–66, and linked with earlier data compiled using different weights. In addition to the change in base some revisions were made in the classification of imports by commodity groups, which now corresponds closely to the Australian Import Commodity Classification.

The index attempts to measure prices f.o.b. at the time of entry into Australia. The effects of changes in freight and insurance charges are excluded from the index. Imports of live animals, aircraft and parts, ships, passengers' effects, military equipment and imports due for re-export are not covered. The import index is calculated as a weighted average of 50 group indexes (10 commodity groups × 5 sources-of-origin groups), with import values in 1966–67 serving as weights. The regimen covers about 90 percent of the value of imports in that year.

A classification of the total index by commodity groups is also available monthly. The following categories are distinguished: food, beverages and tobacco; crude materials (inedible); mineral fuels and lubricants; chemicals; manufactured goods classified chiefly by material; textiles; machinery (except electrical); electrical machinery, apparatus and appliances; transport equipment; and miscellaneous manufactured articles. Details of a classification of the total index by source of origin are also published monthly. This classification distinguishes: United Kingdom; USA and Canada; European Economic Community; Japan; and Other Countries.

In principle, the index is a fixed-weight aggregative type, but because of the difficulty in obtaining figures of actual prices paid by importers, the index is based largely on overseas price indicators, most of which are in fact index numbers themselves. Thus, the price index for goods imported from the United Kingdom is based almost entirely on unit value indexes for exports. The index for imports from Japan is compiled entirely from export price indexes, while that for imports from the USA and Canada is mainly based on indexes of wholesale prices.

REFERENCE
Statistical Bulletin, Economic Supplement, January 1971 (Reserve Bank of Australia) pp 37–39

Wage Rates Indexes
These indexes are calculated monthly and date back to 1939 for adult males and 1951 for adult females (although a now obsolete index carries back to 1891 for males and 1914 for females). The indexes are of the fixed-weight aggregative type and their object is to measure movements in minimum weekly and hourly wages as prescribed in the awards and determinations of industrial tribunals or as specified in formal agreements. The regimen consists of specified representative occupations in fifteen distinct industry groups, covering all industries except rural. The weights for the industries are based on the number of employees covered by awards, determinations and agreements in 1954. Within industry groups, the weights for occupations are based on the number of employees within selected awards.

The minimum wage rates used in the indexes are derived from awards, determinations and agreements in force at the end of each month. For adult males 3415 award designations, covering 2313 distinct award occupations are included. For females the figures are 1100 and 515 respectively. The regimen is kept up to date by including representative occupations from awards in new industries, where these are important in particular industry groups.

The indexes are derived from the averages of awards, weighted in the way indicated above, and are published both as weighted average minimum weekly wage rates (in dollars and cents) and as index numbers with base 1954 = 100·0. The aggregate weighted averages and indexes (for adult males and adult females separately) are published for Australia and the six states separately. Weighted averages and indexes are also published for the fifteen industry groups separately.

The Australian Statistician also publishes weighted average weekly wage rates, split into commonwealth and state awards separately for Australia and for each state, in the monthly bulletin, *Wage Rates and Earnings*.

These indexes relate to prescribed *minimum* wage rates for a full week's work, for a given structure of occupations, and they must not be used as indicators of changes in average earnings. Movements in average earnings can diverge from movements in minimum adult wage rates by reason of changes in industrial structure, in age structure, in amount of overtime worked, in amount of bonuses or over-award payments made, and in occupational grading. A series of average weekly wage and salary earnings per employed male unit, based on payroll tax and other statistics, is published in the *Monthly Review of Business Statistics* and the monthly bulletin, *Wage Rates and Earnings*.

REFERENCES
Labour Report, No 58, 1973 (Australian Bureau of Statistics), Chapter III, pp 73–105
Wage Rates Indexes (Australian Bureau of Statistics, Ref Nos 6.21 and 6.33)
Wage Rates and Earnings (Australian Bureau of Statistics, Ref No 6.16)

5 Measures of Quantum

Until comparatively recently there were no official measures of quantum of gross domestic product or industrial production in Australia. However, in the early 1950s, several private research workers produced indexes of quantum of industrial production of varying degrees of quality, and in 1954 the Australia and New Zealand Bank began publishing an index of factory production.

This index was originally based on 1948–49 and carried back to that year. However, in 1958, 1960, 1964 and 1967, it was revised substantially by extending its coverage and bringing its weighting up to date. The method of construction of the index is that of indicators with fixed weights given by 1963–64 values added (see section 12.5, p 495 above). There are 448 series included in the index and its coverage is stated to be 73 per cent of the value added in all factory industry, including fuel and power. Movements in actual production serve as indicators in the case of about 90 per cent of the items, while material inputs and hours worked are used as indicators for the majority of the other items. The index is calculated monthly and published in the *Quarterly Survey* of the Australia and New Zealand Bank and in special monthly releases. The index is corrected for variations in the length of the working month and for public holidays, and is seasonally adjusted. Broadly speaking, the index corresponds to the usual concept of an index of industrial production. It is published for total factory production, including and excluding power, and for nine major industrial groupings and for a number of sub-groupings. The major groupings are: metals, machinery and apparatus; transport equipment; building and construction materials; furniture and household goods; textiles, clothing and footwear;

food, drink and tobacco; chemicals and allied industries; miscellaneous industries; fuel and power.

Since 1963, annual estimates of gross domestic product at constant prices have been published in *Australian National Accounts—National Income and Expenditure* and in the budget paper *National Income and Expenditure*. These are derived by revaluing the components of expenditure on gross domestic product (see section 12.2 p 479 above). The period 1948–49 to 1974–75 has been covered by three overlapping series, the first (1948–49 to 1959–60) at average 1953–54 prices, the second (1953–54 to 1967–68) at average 1959–60 prices, and the third (1963–64 to 1974–75) at average 1966–67 prices.

A number of methods are used in preparing these estimates. For some components (eg for a considerable part of personal consumption expenditure) the method adopted is to revalue directly quantities at base-year prices. For other components it is often not possible to express the values in successive years as the product of prices and homogeneous units of quantity. These components are revalued by means of price or volume indexes for final use goods, or where this is impracticable (eg for current expenditure by public authorities and for parts of gross fixed capital expenditure) values are divided by indexes of input costs (ie prices of labour and materials). The table below illustrates the revaluation of Australian gross domestic product at constant prices.

The Australian Statistician also publishes Indexes of the Value of Exports and Imports of Merchandise at Constant Prices and Indexes of Quantum of Farm Production. The former have been compiled from 1947–48 onwards, the period 1947–48 to 1966–67 being covered by two series, one at constant 1955–56 prices (1947–48 to 1959–60) and one at constant 1959–60 prices (1959–60 to 1966–67). From 1966–67 onwards, a new series of indexes has been published at average 1966–67 prices, and a detailed description of the series is contained in the initial bulletin *Exports and Imports of Merchandise at Constant Prices*. The indexes are now published quarterly in a bulletin of this title, as well as in the *Monthly Review of Business Statistics* and in the annual bulletin *Balance of Payments*. Broadly, the indexes are derived by expressing the value of exports (or imports) at the prices of the base year, either by direct revaluation of quantities at base-year prices or by division of values by price indexes.

Indexes of Quantum of Farm Production are published each year in the statistical bulletin *Value of Primary Commodities Produced and Indexes of Quantum and Average Unit Gross Values of Agricultural Commodities Produced*, and are available back to 1911–12. The indexes are of the fixed-weight aggregative type with reference base 1968–69 = 100, the weights currently in use being average unit gross values of the three years ended 1970–71. Separate indexes are published for three broad commodity groups (crops, livestock slaughterings and livestock products) and the main items in each group (eg wool, sugar, etc), as well as an index for all farm production.

EXPENDITURE ON GROSS DOMESTIC PRODUCT
AT CURRENT AND AVERAGE 1966–67 PRICES
($ million)

	1970–71	1971–72	1972–73	1973–74	1974–75
AT CURRENT PRICES					
Final consumption expenditure—					
Private	19 991	22 189	24 836	29 072	34 541
Government	4 198	4 760	5 441	6 756	9 092
Gross fixed capital expenditure—					
Private	5 851	6 311	6 586	7 956	8 788
Public enterprises	1 550	1 774	1 777	2 013	2 654
General government	1 377	1 520	1 692	1 951	2 710
Increase in stocks	327	−113	−340	1 602	836
Statistical discrepancy	−318	−151	216	1 195	547
Gross national expenditure	32 976	36 290	40 208	50 545	59 168
Exports of goods and services	5 070	5 633	6 949	7 774	9 782
National turnover of goods and services	38 046	41 923	47 157	58 319	68 950
Less Imports of goods and services	5 118	5 194	5 327	7 650	9 947
Expenditure on gross domestic product	32 928	36 729	41 830	50 669	59 003
AT AVERAGE 1966–67 PRICES					
Final consumption expenditure—					
Private	17 140	17 911	18 997	20 008	20 348
Government	3 229	3 272	3 439	3 668	3 886
Gross fixed capital expenditure—					
Private	4 983	5 020	4 964	5 353	4 842
Public	2 455	2 600	2 534	2 571	2 823
Increase in stocks	313	−95	−184	1 004	562
Statistical discrepancy	−259	−110	172	815	321
Gross national expenditure	27 861	28 598	29 922	33 419	32 782
Exports of goods and services	5 165	5 501	5 715	5 501	5 845
Less Imports of goods and services	4 866	4 715	4 906	6 438	6 462
Expenditure on gross domestic product	28 160	29 384	30 731	32 482	32 165

Source: Australian Bureau of Statistics: *Australian National Accounts: National Income and Expenditure 1974–75*, (Ref 7.1), pp 26, 27 (these figures are subject to revision in subsequent publications).

Estimates of gross product at current and constant prices, classified by industry, are available for the years 1962–63 to 1973–74 in *Gross Product by Industry at Current and Constant Prices*. This bulletin updates *Estimates of Gross Product by Industry at Current and Constant Prices, 1959–60 to 1965–66* (Ref No 7.7) which was published as a supplement to *Australian National Accounts, National Income and Expenditure, 1953–54 to 1966–67* (Ref No 7.1). It contains, for the first time, information on gross product at constant prices per person employed classified by industry.

REFERENCES

Australian National Accounts, National Income and Expenditure (Australian Bureau of Statistics, Ref No 7.1)

Australian National Accounts, Gross Product by Industry at Current and Constant Prices 1962–63 to 1973–74 (Australian Bureau of Statistics, Ref No 7.12)

Exports and Imports of Merchandise at Constant Prices (Australian Bureau of Statistics, Ref No 8.22)

Value of Primary Commodities Produced and Indexes of Quantum and Average Unit Gross Values of Agricultural Commodities Produced (Australian Bureau of Statistics, Ref No 10.27)
Quarterly Survey, Vol 4, October 1954, p 14; Vol 7, July 1958, p 18; Vol 10, January 1961, p 5; Vol 13, April 1964, p 4; Vol 17, October 1967, p 5; and following issues (Australia and New Zealand Bank, Melbourne)
Horner, F B: 'The Meaning of Production Indexes', *Economic Record*, Vol 37, No 77, 1961, p 82
Haig, B D: 'Indexes of Australian Factory Production, 1949–50 to 1962–63', *Economic Record*, Vol 41, No 95, 1966, p 451
Report of the Working Party on the Measurement of Labour Productivity (Department of Employment and Industrial Relations, November 1975)

6 Demography

Data on population are published in detail in census volumes and annually in the bulletins *Overseas Arrivals and Departures* (Ref No 4.23), *Births* (Ref No 4.4), *Causes of Death* (Ref No 4.7), *Deaths* (Ref No 4.8), *Perinatal Deaths* (Ref No 4.29), *Marriages* (Ref No 4.10), and *Divorce* (Ref No 13.1). Summary information is published in the *Official Yearbook of Australia*, *Social Indicators*, and the *Monthly Review of Business Statistics*. For textual comment on Australian demographic statistics reference should be made to:
Official Yearbook of Australia (Australian Bureau of Statistics)
Census of Australia, 30th June 1976 (Australian Bureau of Statistics)
Australian Life Tables, latest issue (Australian Bureau of Statistics)

APPENDIX C

A SHORT LIST OF REFERENCES

The following is a small selection from the very extensive literature which exists on statistical methods and theory and on the various specialised fields covered in the test. The books listed represent convenient avenues for further study and some also contain reading lists.

1 Statistical Methods

F E Croxton, D J Cowden and S Klein: *Applied General Statistics*, Prentice-Hall, 1967.
R A Fisher: *Statistical Methods for Research Workers*, Oliver and Boyd, 1958.
E J Kane: *Economic Statistics and Econometrics*, Harper and Row, 1969.
W C Merrill and K A Fox: *Introduction to Economic Statistics*, Wiley, 1970.
T H Wonnacott and R J Wonnacott: *Introductory Statistics for Business and Economics*, Wiley, 1972.
T Yamane: *Statistics: An Introductory Analysis*, Harper and Row, 1973.
G U Yule and M G Kendall: *An Introduction to the Theory of Statistics*, Griffin, 1958.

2 Mathematical Statistics and Probability

J E Freund: *Mathematical Statistics*, Prentice-Hall, 1971.
P G Hoel: *Introduction to Mathematical Statistics*, Wiley, 1971.
R V Hogg and A T Craig: *Introduction to Mathematical Statistics*, Macmillan, 1970.
M G Kendall and A Stuart: *The Advanced Theory of Statistics*, Vols I, II and III, Griffin, 1969–1973.
B W Lindgren and G W McElrath: *Introduction to Probability and Statistics*, Macmillan, 1966.
A M Mood, F A Graybill and D C Boes: *Introduction to the Theory of Statistics*, McGraw-Hill, 1974.
E Parzen: *Modern Probability Theory and its Applications*, Wiley, 1963.

C E Weatherburn: *A First Course in Mathematical Statistics*, Cambridge University Press, 1962.

3 Econometrics

D J Aigner: *Basic Econometrics*, Prentice-Hall, 1971.
A S Goldberger: *Econometric Theory*, Wiley, 1964.
J Johnston: *Econometric Methods*, McGraw-Hill, 1972.
J Kmenta: *Elements of Econometrics*, Macmillan, 1971.
H Theil: *Principles of Econometrics*, North Holland, 1971.
A A Walters: *An Introduction to Econometrics*, Macmillan, 1970.
R J Wonnacott and T H Wonnacott: *Econometrics*, Wiley, 1970.

4 Sample Surveys

W G Cochran: *Sampling Techniques*, Wiley, 1963.
W E Deming: *Sampling Design in Business Research*, Wiley, 1960.
M H Hansen, W N Hurwitz and W G Madow: *Sample Survey Methods and Theory*, Vols I and II, Wiley, 1964.
L Kish: *Survey Sampling*, Wiley, 1965.
J B Lansing and J N Morgan: *Economic Survey Methods*, Survey Research Center of the Institute for Social Research, The University of Michigan, 1974.
C A Moser: *Survey Methods in Social Investigation*, Heinemann, 1963.
United Nations: *A Short Manual on Sampling*, Vols I and II, (Studies in Methods) Series F, No. 9, New York, 1972.
F Yates: *Sampling Methods for Censuses and Surveys*, Hafner Pub Co, 1963.

5 Quality Control

O L Davies (ed): *Statistical Methods in Research and Production*, 3rd edition, Oliver and Boyd, 1961, Chapters 10 and 11.
E L Grant and R S Leavenworth: *Statistical Quality Control*, McGraw-Hill, 1972.
A Huitson and J Keen: *Essentials of Quality Control*, Heinemann, 1965.

6 Time Series

F E Croxton, D J Cowden and S Klein: *Applied General Statistics*, Prentice-Hall, 1967, Chapters 11–16 and 22.
M G Kendall and A Stuart: *The Advanced Theory of Statistics*, Griffin, 1969–73, Chapters 45–47.

W Mendenhall and J E Reinmuth: *Statistics for Management and Economics*, Duxbury Press, 1974, Chapters 14 and 15.

7 National Income and Social Accounts

M A Copeland: *A Study of Moneyflows in the United States*, National Bureau of Economic Research, 1952.

R I Downing: *National Income and Social Accounts*, Melbourne University Press, 1970.

H L Edey and A T Peacock: *National Income and Social Accounting*, Hutchinson's University Library, 1963.

W W Leontieff: *Input-Output Economics*, Oxford University Press, 1966.

Russell Mathews: *Accounting for Economists*, Cheshire, 1965, Chapters 18 and 19.

Organization for European Economic Co-operation: *A Standardized System of National Accounts*, Paris, 1958.

Reserve Bank of Australia Staff Paper (A S Homes): *Flow-of-Funds, Australia, 1953–54 to 1961–62*, Sydney, 1965.

United Nations: *Methods of National Income Estimation*, (Studies in Methods) Series F, No. 8, New York, 1955.

United Nations: *A System of National Accounts and Supporting Tables* (Studies in Methods) Series F, No. 2, Rev 3, New York, 1968.

8 Price Index Numbers

I Fisher: *The Making of Index Numbers*, 3rd edition, Kelley, 1967.

E v Hofsten: *Price Indexes and Quality Changes*, George Allen and Unwin, 1952.

International Labour Office: *Computation of Consumer Price Indices (Special Problems)* Geneva, 1962.

Joint Economic Committee, 87th Congress, 1st Session, *Government Price Statistics*, US Government Printing Office, Washington, 1961.

Ministry of Labour: *Method of Construction and Calculation of the Index of Retail Prices*, Studies in Official Statistics, No. 6, HMSO, 1964.

W C Mitchell: *The Making and Using of Index Numbers*, Kelley, 1965.

9 Quantum Index Numbers

C F Carter, W B Reddaway and R Stone: *The Measurement of Production Movements*, Cambridge University Press, 1965.

Central Statistical Office: *The Index of Industrial Production*, Studies in Official Statistics, No. 2, HMSO, 1952.

R Stone: *Quantity and Price Indexes in National Accounts*, OEEC, Paris, 1956 and HMSO, 1957.

United Nations: *Index Numbers of Industrial Production* (Studies in Methods) Series F, No. 1, New York, 1961.

10 Demography

P R Cox: *Demography*, 4th edition, Cambridge University Press, 1970.

L I Dublin, A J Lotka and M Spiegelman: *Length of Life*, Ronald Press, 1949.

D V Glass: *Population Policies and Movements in Europe*, Cass and Co Ltd, 1967.

P R Kuczynski: *The Measurement of Population Growth*, Sidgwick and Jackson, 1935, and Gordon and Breach, 1969.

National Population Inquiry: *Population and Australia: A Demographic Analysis and Projection*, Vols I and II, Australian Government Publishing Service, 1975.

United Nations: *The Determinants and Consequences of Population Trends*, New York, 1974.

INDEX